ROGER EBERT'S MOVIE HOME COMPANION 1987 EDITION

by Roger Ebert

Andrews, McMeel & Parker
A Universal Press Syndicate Affiliate
Kansas City • New York

Library of Congress Cataloging in Publication Data.

Ebert, Roger.
    Roger Ebert's movie home companion.

    Reviews originally appeared in the Chicago Sun-Times.

    Includes index.
    1. Moving-pictures—Reviews.   2. Video
recordings—Reviews.   I. Title.   II. Title:
Movie home companion
PN1995.E318   1986   791.43'75   86-22283
ISBN 0-8362-6211-5

All the reviews in this book originally appeared
in the *Chicago Sun-Times*.

This book is dedicated to
Robert Zonka, 1928–1985,
editor and friend

Acknowledgments

Donna Martin, editor and friend, was instrumental in the conception of this book. The design is by Cameron Poulter and the cover photographs by Jack Lane, fellow Chicagoans. Patty Dingus typed the reviews and she and Dorothy O'Brien prepared the manuscript. Without them, the *Movie Home Companion* would still be trapped somewhere inside the yellowing pile of tearsheets pictured on the cover of my last book.

ROGER EBERT

Contents

Key to Symbols

★ ★ ★ ★   A great film
★ ★ ★   A good film
★ ★   Fair
★   Poor

G, PG, PG-13, R   Ratings of the Motion Picture Association of America
    G   indicates that the movie is suitable for general audiences
    PG   suitable for general audiences but parental guidance is suggested
    PG-13   recommended for viewers 13 years or above; may contain material
        inappropriate for younger children
    R   recommended for viewers 17 or older

141 m.   Running time

1983   Year of theatrical release

✓   Indicates movie for which videocassette was not yet available at time of publication

Introduction

In the introduction to my last book, I wrote, "television is just not a first-class way to watch movies." Now here I am with a companion for owners of videocassette players. Have I changed my mind? Not at all. I still believe that the best way to see a movie is in a large, darkened room, with a giant screen at one end of it, and strangers all around. The strangers are especially important, because they set up a democracy in the dark; their massed response to the movie makes it easier for us to join the communal experience, to enter into the film-going reverie and shut down our awareness of self.

And yet I own a VCR, and I use it. Recently I was watching the documentary *George Stevens: A Filmmaker's Journey*, and as I saw the famous scenes once again (Astaire courting Rogers on the dance floor, James Dean joyfully climbing to the top of a windmill), I was reminded of the first times I'd seen the original movies. I saw *Swing Time* in 1961 on a sixteen-millimeter print in an auditorium at the University of Illinois, where, watching Astaire and Rogers for literally the first time, I was so moved by the grace and beauty of their movement that I made a basic discovery: The greatness of a film has nothing to do with the importance of its message. All that really matters is exactly what's there on the screen.

If I had seen *Swing Time* for the first time on a videocassette, would my experience have been as intense? I doubt it. The spontaneous applause in the audience that night gave me confidence in my own reaction, and, since I never took a film class, it might have been the lessons from all the audiences I was a member of that started me along the path to film criticism.

I still believe that nothing can replace the experience of seeing a movie with an audience in a theater, and although the logistics would be easier on my syndicated television show if we could occasionally review a film after seeing it only on cassette, we insist on big-screen viewings and have reviewed cassette versions of films less than half a dozen times in ten years. Frequently I hear that today's audiences "talk too much" during the movie, destroying the experience, but I have rarely heard an audience talking during a movie that really worked. Audience noise is often a response to the lack of anything interesting to see on the screen.

Now. Having got that off my chest, here we are with a guide to recent movies available on cassette. The obvious reason to own and use videocassette players is, of course, that they exist, and that unless we happen to be Hollywood moguls or American presidents with our private screening rooms, there is no other way to see the movie of our choice, at the time of our choice. In all but the largest cities, there is also the problem that many good films simply never open locally. *Porky's II* or the unrelenting *Friday the 13th* series will inevitably play every fair-sized town in America, but many of the best films in this book have played only thirty or forty American cities. Renting cassettes is the only way most people have of seeing the offbeat, innovative, noncommercial film, and I have included a lot of sleepers, documentaries, and smaller independent productions in this book with the thought that you might be intrigued by the descriptions and track them down.[1]

Seeing otherwise unseeable films is the best reason to own a VCR. The next best reason is the opportunity to see your favorite films over again, and even to own cassettes. Most cassettes are overpriced in the $70 range, however, and I agree with the market researchers who have found that $19.95 seems to be the price threshold at which many people might choose to buy instead of rent. I've personally bought very few cassettes: *Citizen Kane, The Third Man,* Keaton's *The General, Casablanca, Say Amen, Somebody.* At $19.95, or twice the price of an LP album, I might buy more freely.

As I write, there are about twenty million VCR owners in America. Cassette machines are no longer a luxury item. Good cassette *players* (not recorders) are in the pipeline from Korea, and the Japanese will no doubt match the lower prices. Within a year there should be forty million of them in use in this country. Eventually they will be as common as stereo sets and audiocassette decks.[2]

When there are forty, or sixty, or eighty million cassette machines in use, a revolution will take place in the way Hollywood makes movies, and the kinds of movies it makes. It will have to. The demographics of moviegoers and VCR owners split the population in two; the majority of frequent moviegoers are under twenty-five, and the majority of VCR owners are over twenty-five. The two population groups have distinctively different tastes. Theatrical movies are increasingly aimed at teen-agers, and in the first half of 1985 there were more than thirty movies with specifically teen-age themes. The older VCR owners are not as interested in teen-age movies, except for the exceptional hit like *Flashdance* or *Risky Business,* or the crossover hit that breaks through all demographic groups, like *E. T.,* or *Raiders of the Lost Ark.* Viewers over twenty-five want to see films made more or less for them, and so there's the case of a movie like *The Right Stuff,* which got great reviews, failed to interest teen-agers, flopped at the box office, and then went right ahead to become one of the best-

---

[1]Many video stores, alas, seem to have shelves lined with *Porky's II, Friday the 13th,* nasties, pornos, and of course the usual mainstream hits. That's why a mail-order video rental organization like Home Film Festival is invaluable. After you sign up and provide credit card information, you call a toll-free number (1-800-258-3456) to order from their catalog of art, foreign, classic, underground, documentary, sleeper, and cult films. When the cassette arrives, you have three days to watch it before returning it in a handy mailer, which is provided. This is a plug.

[2]The Koreans are on the right track by selling machines that play but do not record. Industry surveys show, incredibly, that two-thirds of VCR owners are not quite sure how to use the record function on their machines, and use them only for playing cassettes.

selling and renting videos of 1984. There was an audience for *The Right Stuff*, all right—but it was at home, not in theater lines.

As the after-market for theatrical movies becomes more and more important, it will influence many production decisions. The day is not more than three years away when cassette rentals and sales will represent more income, for all but the biggest hits, than the traditional theatrical box office. Will this create a crisis for movie theaters? Apparently not: Industry statistics have come up with the surprising discovery that VCR owners attend theatrical movies *more* often than they did before they bought their VCRs—apparently because cassette viewing has made them more interested in new movies in general. What will happen, when the financial balance shifts to the older population group, is that Hollywood will have compelling reasons to make movies for viewers over twenty-five. More movies like *Terms of Endearment, Gandhi, On Golden Pond,* and *The Big Chill*, to go with food-fight epics.

So far, there is no evidence that people will buy or rent cassette versions of movies that have not played theatrically. Some sort of voodoo seems to be at work: Unless somebody, somewhere, sometime, has paid to walk into a theater and see a movie, VCR owners have a reluctance to buy it or rent it and bring it home.[3] If more films for adults are made, more of them will have a chance to succeed, in an industry where teen-age films have recently had a green light. (For example: Albert Brooks' *Lost in America,* about a couple in their thirties, was postponed by one studio so it could use the same money to budget *National Lampoon's Class Reunion.*) If these trends hold up, we may see a different mix at the American box office: Teen-age films, yes, but better ones (*The Breakfast Club* instead of *Fraternity Reunion*), and more films aimed at audiences over twenty-five. Some of those films may be using theaters as a way-station on the road to video stores, but at least they will be made, and they will have a chance.

* * *

In this book, I have not concentrated only on box office hits. I've been able to include a good number of sleepers (*Repo Man, The Long Good Friday*), cult films (*This Is Spinal Tap, Choose Me*), great documentaries (*Say Amen, Somebody, Streetwise*), independent American productions (*El Norte, Testament*) and unclassifiable but indispensable films (*My Dinner with André, Secret Honor*). I have also included a few older films that became available recently in restored versions, like *A Star Is Born.* Foreign films are a problem, because subtitles are notoriously hard to read on TV screens, and dubbing usually sounds false, but I have included some of the best recent releases, like *Fanny and Alexander* and *Kagemusha.* I have also been careful to include films that I despise, like *I Spit on Your Grave* and *Caligula.* You will also find virtually every film from these years that has made a substantial impact at the box office. In an Afterword, I look back into film history with the benefit of the unique poll which *Sight & Sound,* the British film magazine, conducts every ten years among the world's film

---

[3]The exception is pornography; 70 percent of porno film income now comes from cassettes, and adult theaters are closing all over the country.

critics. Using their forty years of lists of the "greatest films of all time" as a guideline, you could, I imagine, construct a cinematic version of the Great Books program on your TV.

* * *

Someday, I know, they will perfect TV screens the size of walls. You will be able to order the film of your choice, and it will arrive in your home via cable. The sound will be in perfect stereo. Even the subtitles will be readable. When that day comes, I know I'll want the miraculous new equipment, so I can summon up *Casablanca* and hear Sam claim yet once again that he doesn't remember how to play that song. But when that day comes, I know I will still want to see new movies in real movie theaters, with real audiences, whenever I can. Who says you can't have it both ways?

ROGER EBERT

Introduction to the 1987 Edition

This edition has been expanded by about 50 percent, to include some one hundred movies released since the previous Companion was published in October 1985, as well as another two hundred or so titles from the 1970s. The start date for the first edition of the Companion was 1980, based on my observation that many video stores seem to stock only the most recent titles. But competition between stores has caused the better ones to expand their stocks, and this edition reflects that commendable development.

Once again, I've included movies so new that they were not available on videocassette as of publication date; they are marked with a ✔. I have also included many interesting titles that may not be easily available; documentaries like *Harlan County, U.S.A.*, or the haunting *28 Up;* animated films like *Allegro, non Tropo;* features like *Stay Hungry* and *The Late Show;* foreign films like *Cries and Whispers* and *Amarcord;* oddities like *Nosferatu* and *Mishima*. These titles are stocked in the larger, more ambitious video stores, and are also available for rental by mail. As in the first edition, I recommend Home Film Festival, a mail-order operation that specializes in offbeat, cult, and art films. Their telephone is 1-800-258-3456, or, in Pennsylvania, 1-800-633-3456.

Many of you wrote me after the first edition. I welcomed the feedback, and answered as many letters as I could. Many of your observations touched on what might be called the Hindsight Syndrome. In the review of the original *Rocky,* for example, you will find me referring to "a relatively unknown actor" named Sylvester Stallone, and being reminded of the young Marlon Brando. Should this review have been rewritten in light of what we now know about Stallone, who (a) is no longer unknown, and (b) has, at least for the moment, more in common with Schwarzenegger than Brando? I've decided to retain the original wording in these reviews, instead of rewriting them with the benefit of hindsight. It would be easy to revise an early opinion of Stallone, now that he has made a career choice for high-tech action, but more valuable, I think, to recall what an extraordinary impression he made in 1976, and how good the original *Rocky* was—no matter how *Rocky IV* abandoned the legacy. By and large, except for a little tightening and some factual corrections, these are my original reviews.

Some reviewers complained that I awarded too many four-star ratings, and one even counted them. But a book like this contains a statistical bias, since in choosing from some two hundred reviews a year, I am more likely to include the four-star movies than the dreck. The bias is even more exaggerated in this edition, since I have eliminated forty-four reviews of less interesting movies to include more good films from 1970 to 1980. Perhaps, all the same, I am too easy, or too hard; my taste is not your taste, and this book is a companion, not a tribunal.

For those who found errors, my thanks. I would particularly urge owners of the first edition to turn to page 77 and, in the review of *Conan the Barbarian,* change *Dumbo* to *Bambi.* That's the sort of mistake that could only be made by someone whose favorite Disney character is Monstro.

ROGER EBERT

About Last Night . . . ★ ★ ★ ★
R, 116 m., 1986 ✓

Rob Lowe (Danny), Demi Moore (Debbie), James Belushi (Bernie), Elizabeth Perkins (Joan), George DiCenzo (Mr. Favio), Michael Alldredge (Mother Malone), Robin Thomas (Steve), Joe Greco (Gus). Directed by Edward Zwick and produced by Jason Brett and Stuart Oken. Screenplay by Tim Kazurinsky and Denise DeClue.

If one of the pleasures of moviegoing is seeing strange new things on the screen, another pleasure, and probably a deeper one, is experiencing moments of recognition—times when we can say, yes, that's exactly right, that's exactly the way it would have happened. *About Last Night . . .* is a movie filled with moments like that. It has an eye and an ear for the way we live now, and it has a heart, too, and a sense of humor.

It is a love story. A young man and a young woman meet, and fall in love, and over the course of a year they try to work out what that means to them. It sounds like a simple story, and yet *About Last Night . . .* is one of the rarest of recent American movies, because it deals fearlessly with real people, instead of with special effects.

If there's anyone more afraid of a serious relationship than your average customer in a singles bar, it's a Hollywood producer. American movies will cheerfully spend millions of dollars on explosions and chases to avoid those moments when people are talking seriously and honestly to one another. After all, writing good dialogue takes some intelligence.

And intelligence is what sparkles all through *About Last Night . . .*—intelligence and a good, bawdy comic sensibility. The movie stars Rob Lowe as a salesman for a Chicago grocery wholesaler, and Demi Moore as an art director for a Michigan Avenue advertising agency. They meet at a softball game in Grant Park. Their romance blossoms in the singles bars of Rush Street, with a kindly bartender as father figure. At first they are attracted mostly by biological reasons (they belong to a generation that believes it's kind of embarrassing to sleep with someone for the first time after you know them too well). Then they get to like each other. Then it is maybe even love,

although everyone tap-dances around that word. Commitment, in their world, is the moment when Lowe offers Moore the use of a drawer in his apartment. Her response to that offer is one of the movie's high points.

Meanwhile, there is counterpoint, too. Lowe's best friend is his partner at work, played by James Belushi. Moore's best friend is Elizabeth Perkins, her roommate and fellow warrior on the singles scene. While Lowe and Moore start getting really serious about each other, Belushi and Perkins grow possessive—and also develop a spontaneous dislike for one another.

The story is kind of predictable in *About Last Night . . .*, if you have ever been young and kept your eyes open. There are only a limited number of basic romantic scenarios for young people in the city, and this movie sees through all of them. What's important is the way the characters look and sound, the way they talk, the way they reveal themselves, the way they grow by taking chances. Time after time, there are shocks of recognition, as the movie shows how well it understands what's going on.

Lowe and Moore, members of Hollywood's "Brat Pack," are survivors of 1985's awful movie about yuppie singles, *St. Elmo's Fire.* This is the movie *St. Elmo's Fire* should have been. The 1985 movie made them look stupid and shallow. *About Last Night . . .* gives them the best acting opportunities either one has ever had, and they make the most of them. Moore is especially impressive. There isn't a romantic note she isn't required to play in this movie, and she plays them all flawlessly.

Belushi and Perkins are good, too, making us realize how often the movies pretend that lovers live in a vacuum. When a big new relationship comes into your life, it requires an adjustment of all the other relationships, and a certain amount of discomfort and pain. Belushi and Perkins provide those levels for the story, and a lot of its loudest laughs, too.

The movie is based on *Sexual Perversity in Chicago*, a play by David Mamet. The screenplay by Tim Kazurinsky and Denise DeClue smooths out Mamet's more episodic structure, and adds three-dimensional realism. It's a wonderful writing job, and Edward Zwick, directing a feature for the first time, shows a sure touch. His narrative spans an entire year, and the interest never lags.

Why is it that love stories are so rare from Hollywood these days? Have we lost faith in romance? Is love possible only with robots and cute little furry things from the special-effects department? Have people stopped talking? *Top Gun* was so afraid of a real relationship that its real love affair was with airplanes. *About Last Night . . .* is a warm-hearted and intelligent love story, and one of 1986's best movies.

Absence of Malice ★ ★ ★
PG, 116 m., 1981

Paul Newman (Michael Gallagher), Sally Field (Megan Carter), Bob Balaban (Rosen), Melinda Dillon (Teresa), Wilford Brimley (D.A.), John Harkins (Libel Lawyer). Directed and produced by Sydney Pollack. Screenplay by Kurt Luedtke.

There are at least two ways to approach *Absence of Malice,* and I propose to take the second. The first approach, no doubt, would be to criticize this film's portrait of an investigative newspaper reporter—to say that no respectable journalist would ever do the things that Sally Field does about, to, and with Paul Newman in this movie. She is a disgrace to her profession. What journalistic sins does she commit in this film? She allows the facts of a secret investigation to be leaked to her. She prints an unattributed story about the investigation. Then she becomes "personally involved with the subject of the investigation," as they say. In other words, she falls in love with Paul Newman. Then she prints another story she should never have printed, and as a result an innocent bystander commits suicide. Then . . .

But you get the idea. Would real investigative reporters actually commit Field's mistakes, improprieties, misjudgments, indiscretions, and ethical lapses? Generally speaking, no, they wouldn't. And if they did, they shouldn't have. And furthermore, their editors would never let them get away with it. (The unbelievable laxity of the editors in *Absence of Malice* creates the movie's greatest credibility gap.) But let's face it: Sometimes reporters *do* commit acts such as Sally Field allows herself in this movie. Sometimes news of an investigation is printed without official attribution. And so on.

One of my colleagues cornered me at the water fountain to say indignantly that, whatever else you might think about this movie, you'd have to admit that no reporter would *ever* sleep with a news source.

"Oh yeah?" asked a woman who was standing by. "Who was the news source?"

"Paul Newman," I said.

"I'd sleep with that news source in a second," she said.

And that leads us out of the first, or socially responsible, approach to *Absence of Malice,* and into the second, or romantic, approach. I not only liked this movie despite its factual and ethical problems—I'm not even so sure they matter so much to most viewers. In the newspaper business we're quick to spot the errors of movies about newspaper reporters, but where were we when the archaeologists squirmed over Harrison Ford's barbaric conduct in *Raiders of the Lost Ark?* The fact is, this movie is *really* about a woman's spunk and a common man's sneaky revenge. And on that level it's absorbing and entertaining. Sally Field's newspaper reporter is created through a quietly original performance that is *not* Norma Rae with a pencil behind her ear, but is an earnest, nervous, likable young woman who makes mistakes when she listens too closely to her heart, her ambition, or her editor (which of us cannot admit the same?).

Paul Newman's character is a liquor distributor who is (presumably) totally innocent of the murder for which he is being investigated. But because his father was a Mafioso, he finds his name being dragged through the press, and he achieves a vengeance that is smart, wicked, appropriate, and completely satisfying to the audience. Besides these two performances, there are some other good ones, most notably one by Wilford Brimley, as a district attorney who takes brusque command of an informal hearing and reduces everyone but Newman to quivering surrender, and another by John Harkins, as a newspaper libel lawyer who is able to make the restraints (and freedoms) of libel law clear not only to Sally Field but even to us.

There's a story about a legendary Chicago editor who was presented with a major scoop obtained by dubious means. First he convinced himself the story was factually sound. Then he issued the classic instruction: "Print it tonight, and call the lawyers in the morning." Now there's an editor who might have enjoyed *Absence of Malice*. He would not have approved of what Sally Field does in this movie. But he would have understood it.

After Hours ★ ★ ★ ★
R, 96 m., 1985

Griffin Dunne (Paul Hackett), Rosanna Arquette (Marcy), Linda Fiorentino (Kiki), Verna Bloom (June), Thomas Chong (Pepe), Teri Garr (Julie), John Heard (Bartender), Catherine O'Hara (Gail). Directed by Martin Scorsese and produced by Amy Robinson, Griffin Dunne, and Robert F. Colesberry. Screenplay by Joseph Minion.

Martin Scorsese's *After Hours* is a comedy, according to the strict definition of that word: It ends happily, and there are indications along the way that we're not supposed to take it seriously. It is, however, the tensest comedy I can remember, building its nightmare situation step by insidious step until our laughter is hollow, or defensive. This is the work of a master filmmaker who controls his effects so skillfully that I was drained by this film—so emotionally depleted that there was a moment, two-thirds of the way through, when I wondered if maybe I should pause and gather my thoughts and come back later for the rest of the "comedy."

The movie tells the story of a night in the life of Paul Hackett (Griffin Dunne), a midtown Manhattan word processing specialist who hates his job and his lonely private life. One night in a restaurant he strikes up a conversation with a winsome young woman (Rosanna Arquette). They seem to share some of the same interests. He gets her telephone number. He calls her, she suggests he come downtown to her apartment in Soho, and that is the beginning of his Kafkaesque adventure.

The streets of Soho are dark and deserted. Clouds of steam escape from the pavement, as they did in Scorsese's *Taxi Driver*, suggesting that Hades lurks just below the field of vision. The young woman is staying for a few days in the apartment of a friend (Linda Fiorentino), who makes bizarre sculptures, has kinky sexual tastes, and talks in a strange, veiled way about being burned. In Arquette's bedroom, Dunne makes the usual small talk of a first date, and she gushes that she's sure they'll have a great time, but then everything begins to fall apart.

At first, we think perhaps Dunne is the victim of random bad luck, as he is confronted with nightmares both tragic and trivial: Ominous strangers, escalating subway fares, a shocking suicide, sadomasochistic sexual practices, a punk nightclub where he almost has his head shaved, a street mob that thinks he is a thief. Only later, much later, on this seemingly endless night, do we find how everything is connected—and even then, it doesn't make any logical sense. For Paul Hackett, as for the Job of the Old Testament, the plague of bad luck seems generated by some unexplained divine wrath.

And yet Scorsese does not simply make a horror movie, or some kind of allegory of doom. Each of his characters is drawn sharply, given quirky dialogue, allowed to be offbeat and funny. Teri Garr has a scene as a waitress who has tried to make sense of New York for so long that it has driven her around the bend. Fiorentino has a dry, sardonic angle on things. Arquette speaks wonderingly of a lover who was so obsessed by *The Wizard of Oz* that he always called her Dorothy in bed. John Heard is a bartender who has seen everything walk in through the doors of his all-night saloon and has lost the capacity for astonishment.

After Hours is another chapter in Scorsese's continuing examination of Manhattan as a state of mind; if he hadn't already used the title *New York, New York*, he could have used it this time. The movie earns its place on the list with his great films *Mean Streets*, *Taxi Driver*, and *Raging Bull*. For New Yorkers, parts of the film will no doubt play as a documentary. In what other city is everyday life such an unremitting challenge?

After Hours is a brilliant film, one of the year's best. It is also a most curious film. It comes after Scorsese's *The King of Comedy*, a film I thought was fascinating but unsuccessful, and continues Scorsese's attempt to combine comedy and satire with unrelenting pressure and a sense of all-pervading paranoia. This time he succeeds. The result is a film that is so original, so particular, that we are uncertain from moment to moment exactly how to respond to it. The style of the film creates, in us, the same feeling that the events in the film create in the hero. Interesting.

After the Rehearsal ★ ★ ★ ★
R, 72 m., 1984

Erland Josephson (Henrik Vogler), Ingrid Thulin (Rakel), Lena Olin (Anna Egerman), Nadja Palmstjerna-Weiss (Anna at Twelve). Directed by Ingmar Bergman and produced by Jorn Donner. Screenplay by Bergman.

Ingmar Bergman's *After the Rehearsal* seems to be as simple and direct as a tape recording of actual conversations, and yet look at the thickets of interpretation it has inspired in its critics. After seeing it, I thought I understood the film entirely. Now I am not so sure. Like so many of Bergman's films, and especially the spare "chamber films" it joins *(Winter Light, Persona)*, it consists of unadorned surfaces concealing fathomless depths.

It is safest to begin with the surfaces. All of the action takes place on a stage prepared for a production of Strindberg's *A Dream Play.* An aging director sits among the props, and every chair and table reminds him of an earlier production. The rehearsal has ended some time ago, and now the director simply sits, as if the stage were his room. A young actress returns to the stage for a missing bracelet. But of course the bracelet is an excuse, and she wants to talk to the great man, and perhaps to begin a relationship with him (as, perhaps, she has heard that many other actresses have done over the years). The old director was once the lover of the girl's mother. It is even possible that this girl is his daughter. They talk. Then an older actress enters. She has a few lines in the play, and wants to know—frankly, brutally—if her career as a leading actress is really over because she is known as a drunk. She cries, she rants, she bares her breasts to show the old man that her body is still sound, if sodden. The director is tempted: He was once this woman's lover, and perhaps her daughter is his.

The young girl stays on stage during the extraordinary display of the older actress. When the older woman leaves, the director and ingenue talk again, and this time the old man, who has been through the turmoil of love too many times, talks her through their probable future: We could make love, we could have an affair, we would call it part of our art, you would be the student, I would be the teacher, I would grow tired, you would feel trapped, all our idealism would turn into ashes. Since the relationship is foredoomed, why bother with it?

Just in terms of these spare passages of dialogue and passion, *After the Rehearsal* is an important and painful confessional, for the old director, of course, bears many points of resemblance to Bergman, whose lovers have included his actresses Harriet Andersson, Bibi Anderson, and Liv Ullmann, among others, and whose daughter by Ullmann appeared in *Face to Face.* But the film is not a scandalous revelation: It is actually more of a sacramental confession, as if Bergman, the son of a Lutheran bishop, now sees the stage as his confessional and is asking the audience to bless and forgive him. (His gravest sin, as I read the film, is not lust or adultery, but the sin of taking advantage of others—of manipulating them with his power and intellect.)

If that were the extent of *After the Rehearsal*, it would be deep enough. But Bergman has surrounded the bare bones of his story with mystifying problems of interpretation. Just as in *Persona* he included scenes in which his characters exchanged personalities and engaged in scenes that might have or might not have been fantasies and dreams, so here, too, he gives us things to puzzle over. Reading the earlier reviews of the film, I discover that one critic realized only belatedly that the younger actress, Anna, was onstage the whole time the older actress, Rakel, poured out her heart. Strange, and yet another critic thought the whole scene with Rakel was the director's own dream. Yet another suggested that Anna represents not only herself but also Rakel's absent daughter. And another theory is that Anna is the daughter of the director and Rakel, and is brought into being by the residual love between them, as a sort of theatrical Holy Spirit. The age of Anna has been variously reported as ranging from twelve to twenty, with one critic reporting that both ages of the character are represented.

Which is the correct interpretation? They are all correct. Each and every one is equally correct; otherwise what is the use of a dream play? The point is not to find the literal meaning, anyway, but to touch the soul of the director, and find out what still hurts him after all these years. After all the sex and all the promises, all the lies and truths and messy affairs, there is still one critical area where he is filled with guilt and passion. It is revealed when Anna tells him she is pregnant. He is enraged. How could she, a young actress given the role of a lifetime, jeopardize her career and his play by getting pregnant? Then she tells him she has had an abortion, for the sake of the play. And then he really is torn in two, for he does not believe, after all, that a play—not even his play—is worth the sacrifice of a life. What we are left with at the end of *After the Rehearsal*, however, is the very strong sense of an artist who has sacrificed many lives for the sake of his art, and now wonders if perhaps one of those lives was his own.

Against All Odds ★ ★ ★
R, 128 m., 1984

Rachel Ward (Jessie Wyler), Jeff Bridges (Terry Brogan), James Woods (Jake Wise), Alex Karras (Hank Sully), Jane Greer (Mrs. Wyler), Richard Widmark (Ben Caxton). Directed by Taylor Hackford and produced by Hackford and William S. Gilmore. Screenplay by Eric Hughes.

There have been too many sweet girls in thrillers. What we need are more no-good, double-dealing broads who can cross their legs and break your heart. *Against All Odds* has a woman like that, and it makes for one of the most intriguing movie relationships in a long time; in thirty-five years, to be exact, which is when they told this story for the first time. You may remember the original movie. It was called *Out of the Past*. It starred Robert Mitchum and Kirk Douglas, and it was the greatest cigarette-smoking movie of all time. Mitchum and Douglas smoked all the way through every scene, and they were always blowing sinister, aggressive clouds of smoke at each other. The movie was shot so there was always a lot of light on the place in

midair where their smoke was aimed. The only drawback to the fact that smoking is no longer fashionable in movies is that we don't get any great smoking scenes anymore. Anyway, if you remember that movie, you remember that Kirk Douglas was a hoodlum and Robert Mitchum was a guy who would take a job for a buck, and Douglas hired Mitchum to track down his missing girlfriend, who was played by Jane Greer. After Mitchum found Greer, they had a big love affair—or so Mitchum thought. But Greer, that no-good, two-timing, double-crossing broad, liked security more than passion.

Against All Odds is not really a remake of *Out of the Past*. The only similarity between the two movies is in the cynical love triangle. And it was a real inspiration to tell that story again, since it makes for an intriguing, complicated, interesting romance. This time, the bad guy is a gambler, played by James Woods. His girlfriend (Rachel Ward) is the daughter of the owner of a pro-football team (played by Jane Greer, of all people). And the guy who tracks her down (Jeff Bridges), is a team player who's just been fired after a knee injury.

There is a lot of plot in this movie—probably too much. The best thing to do is to accept the plot, and then disregard it, and pay attention to the scenes of passion. They really work. Bridges and Ward have an interesting sexual tension in *Against All Odds*, since their relationship is not simply sweetness and light, but depends upon suspicion, dislike, and foul betrayal. That's ever so much more interesting than just falling in love. And the situation liberates Ward from the trap she'd been in; the trap of playing attractive, sexy, strong heroines. This time, as a complicated schemer, she's fascinating.

The movie has a lot of muted social criticism in it, involving professional sports and ecology. The Jane Greer character has a plan to destroy several beautiful canyons to build houses. The Bridges character is a victim of unfair labor practices. And so on. Sometimes we get the idea we're watching a clone of *Chinatown*—but not with that jealous triangle. Woods is the villain, so he does smoke, of course. But Bridges and Ward are so consumed with passion, they don't even need to.

Agnes of God ★
PG-13, 99 m., 1985

Jane Fonda (Dr. Livingston), Anne Bancroft (Mother Miriam), Meg Tilly (Sister Agnes), Anne Pitoniak (Dr. Livingston's Mother), Winston Rekert (Detective Langevin), Gratien Gelinas (Father Martineau). Directed by Norman Jewison and produced by Patrick Palmer and Jewison. Screenplay by John Pielmeier.

It might have been impossible to convert *Agnes of God* from a play into a movie under any circumstances, since the intrinsic reality of film throws the play's conceits and contrivances into sharp relief. Speeches that seemed stylishly theatrical onstage seem, in screen close-ups, to be . . . merely theatrical. But that's just the beginning of this film's problems. It considers, or pretends to consider, some of the most basic questions of human morality and treats them on the level of *Nancy Drew and the Secret of the Old Convent.*

The story: A dead baby is found in a lonely convent, where the nuns lead a sequestered life and there are no men who could possibly have been the father—unless you count poor old Father Martineau, the nuns' spiritual adviser, who has a drinking problem.

The police investigation indicates that the baby's mother, and possibly its murderer, was Sister Agnes (Meg Tilly), a young, simple-minded girl of total naiveté. It is never made quite clear what specific problem Sister Agnes suffers from, but she clearly has parts on order.

A psychiatrist (Jane Fonda) is assigned to the case, and it quickly becomes clear that she will learn little from Sister Agnes, who has total amnesia regarding the entire incident. The convent's mother superior (Anne Bancroft) at first seems more helpful—she is a "modern" woman who was married before she entered the convent and who shares a forbidden cigarette with Fonda—but she turns hostile as the investigation continues.

I will be giving away no essential secrets if I reveal that the precise details of the conception, birth, and murder of the child are never cleared up to anybody's satisfaction. More to the point: The solution to the crime hardly seems to be the point of the movie. It reaches for a far loftier philosophical subject, which is, I think, the possibility of miracles.

Although the movie deals in the basic materials of a criminal investigation (cynical cops, forensic details, courtroom testimony), it has a seriously clouded agenda. The mechanism of the crime story whirls busily and goes nowhere, and meanwhile, we learn that Fonda has a personal hatred of the Catholic church, that Mother Miriam seems overly concerned with protecting Sister Agnes, that Sister Agnes herself has made the sort of ecstatic world-vision usually reserved for saints, and that we should not overlook the possibility that the baby, in fact, had no father. In other words, Sister Agnes had a virgin birth. Or, in case the point still seems obscure, the murdered infant was a child of God.

There is a certain amount of pressure on the Fonda character, an agnostic, to accept the possibility that a miracle has occurred. She resists it, quite sensibly, since the implications of the miracle are horrifying: If God indeed conceived the child in Sister Agnes's womb, then why did he in his omnipotence allow her to kill it? But of course (you argue), God also gave Sister Agnes free will, so she was free to kill the child no matter what the details of its conception. True, and yet then, we must ask, why did God create a baby to be killed?

Here we enter, of course, into the still larger question of why God has created all of us and placed us in this life where we will most assuredly all die. Religion centers on the answers to that question. The infuriating thing about *Agnes of God* is that it tells a story that makes such questions essential and then ignores them.

This is a very badly confused movie. It takes the form of a murder investigation and then uses hints of the supernatural to avoid all the hard-edged questions raised by the murder. Then—just when it seems to be edging close to the fundamental supernatural questions it contains—it's back to the courtroom. The movie uses each half of its story to avoid dealing with the other.

Under the circumstances, the performances are as good as can be expected. Given dialogue that sounds as if it were written to be read, given characters who consistently avoid asking the obvious questions, given a story that refuses to declare what it is about, Bancroft, Fonda, and Tilly use their craft to give the illusion that they know where they stand. It is service in a lost cause.

Airplane! ★ ★ ★
PG, 88 m., 1980

Lloyd Bridges (McCroskey), Peter Graves (Captain Oveur), Kareem Abdul-Jabbar (Murdock), Julie Hagerty (Elaine), Robert Hays (Ted Striker), Leslie Nielsen (Dr. Rumack), Howard Jarvis (Man in Taxi), Ethel Merman (Lieutenant Hurwitz). Directed and written by Jim Abrahams, David Zucker, and Jerry Zucker and produced by Howard W. Koch.

Airplane! is a comedy in the great tradition of high school skits, the Sid Caesar TV show, *Mad* magazine, and the dog-eared screenplays people's nephews write in lieu of earning their college diplomas. It is sophomoric, obvious, predictable, corny, and quite often very funny. And the reason it's funny is frequently *because* it's sophomoric, predictable, corny, etc. Example:

Airplane Captain (Peter Graves): Surely you can't be serious!

Doctor (Leslie Nielsen): Of course I am! And stop calling me Shirley!

This sort of humor went out with Milton Berle, Jerry Lewis, and knock-knock jokes. That's why it's so funny. Movie comedies these days are so hung up on being contemporary, radical, outspoken, and cynically satirical that they sometimes forget to be funny. And they've lost the nerve to be as corny as *Airplane!*—to actually invite loud groans from the audience. The flop *Wholly Moses*, for example, is no doubt an infinitely more intelligent comedy—but the problem was, we didn't laugh.

Airplane! has a couple of sources for its inspiration. One of them is obviously *Airport* (1970) and all of its sequels and rip-offs. The other might not come immediately to mind unless you're a fan of the late show. It's *Zero Hour!* (1957), which starred the quintessential 1950s B-movie cast of Dana Andrews, Linda Darnell, and Sterling Hayden. *Airplane!* comes from the same studio (Paramount) and therefore is able to cheerfully borrow the same plot (airliner is imperiled after the crew and most of the passengers are stricken with food poisoning). The *Zero Hour!* crisis situation (how to get the airplane down) was also borrowed for the terrible *Airport 1975*, in which Karen Black played a stewardess who tried to follow instructions radioed from the ground.

Airplane! has two desperate people in the cockpit: Julie Hagerty, as the stewardess, and Robert Hays, as a former Air Force pilot whose traumatic war experiences have made him terrified of flying. (The cockpit also contains a very kinky automatic pilot . . . but never mind.)

The movie exploits the previous films for all they're worth. The passenger list includes a little old lady (like Helen Hayes in *Airport*), a guitar-playing nun (like Helen Reddy in *Airport 1975*), and even a critically ill little girl who's being flown to an emergency operation (Linda Blair played the role in *Airport 1975*). Predictable results occur, as when the nun's guitar knocks loose the little girl's intravenous tubes, and she nearly dies while all the passengers sing along inspirationally.

The movie's funniest scene, however, occurs in a flashback explaining how the stewardess and the Air Force pilot first met and fell in love years ago. The scene takes place in an exotic Casablanca-style bar, which is miraculously transformed when somebody's hurled at the jukebox and it starts playing "Stayin' Alive" by the Bee Gees. The scene becomes a hilarious send-up of the disco scenes in *Saturday Night Fever*, with the young pilot defying gravity to impress the girl.

Airplane! is practically a satirical anthology of classic movie clichés. Lloyd Bridges, as the ground-control officer, seems to be satirizing half of his straight roles. The opening titles get an enormous laugh with an unexpected reference to *Jaws*. The neurotic young pilot is talked back into the cockpit in a scene from *Knute Rockne, All American*. And the romantic scenes are played as a soap opera. None of this really adds up to great comic artistry, but *Airplane!* compensates for its lack of original comic invention by its utter willingness to steal, beg, borrow, and rewrite from anywhere.

Airport ★ ★
G, 137 m., 1970

Burt Lancaster (Mel Bakersfield), Dean Martin (Vernon Demerest), Jean Seberg (Tanya), Jacqueline Bisset (Gwen Meighen), George Kennedy (Patroni), Helen Hayes (Ada Quonsett), Van Heflin (D.O. Guerrero). Directed by George Seaton and produced by Ross Hunter. Screenplay by Seaton.

On some dumb fundamental level, *Airport* kept me interested for a couple of hours. I can't quite remember why. The plot has few surprises (you know and I know that no airplane piloted by Dean Martin ever crashed). The gags are painfully simpleminded (a priest, pretending to cross himself, whacks a wise guy across the face). And the characters talk in regulation B-movie clichés like no B-movie you've seen in ten years. Example: A bomb blows a hole in the airplane and weakens the tail structure. Martin's co-pilot says: "Listen, Vern, I want you to know that if there's anything I can do. . . ." What's he talking about? Martin's girl.

The movie has a lot of expensive stars, but only two (Helen Hayes and Van Heflin) have wit enough to abandon all pretense of seriousness. Even Martin, who can be charming in a movie when he relaxes, plays a straight hero-type this time. Burt Lancaster is even straighter and more heroic, as needs be, since he has to run the airport, supervise George Kennedy in pulling out a stuck Boeing 707, and decide to divorce his wife, all at the same time.

But Miss Hayes and Heflin apparently realized early on that *Airport* was going to be a deadly dull affair, and they went about salvaging their own roles, at least. Miss Hayes milks her role of a little-old-lady stowaway for all it's conceivably worth, and I have a suspicion she wrote some of her own dialogue. It's warmer and more humorous than the stiff lines everyone else has to recite, and she won an Oscar for the role.

Heflin, as the guy with the bomb in his briefcase, is perhaps the only person in the cast to realize how metaphysically absurd *Airport* basically is. The airplane already has a priest, two nuns, three doctors, a stowaway, a customs officer's niece, a pregnant stewardess, two black GIs, a loudmouthed kid, a henpecked husband, and Dean Martin aboard, right? So obviously the bomber has to be typecast, too. Heflin sweats, shakes, peers around nervously, clutches his briefcase to his chest, refuses to talk to anybody, and swallows a lot. The customs officer sees him going on the plane and notices "something in his eyes." Also in his ears, nose, and throat. What Heflin does is undermine the structure of the whole movie with a sort of subversive overacting. Once the bomber becomes ridiculous, the movie does, too. That's good, because it never had a chance at being anything else.

Airport 1975 ★ ★ ½
PG, 106 m., 1974

Charlton Heston (Murdock), Karen Black (Nancy), George Kennedy (Patroni), Efrem Zimbalist, Jr. (Stacy), Susan Clark (Mrs. Patroni), Helen Reddy (Sister Ruth). Directed by Jack Smight and produced by William Frye. Screenplay by Don Ingalls.

The original *Airport* was never one of my favorite movies, but I had to admire the slick, competent way it worked us over for two hours. Its clichés were ancient and its typecasting was relentless, but it didn't bore us. *Airport 1975*, a reworking of the same good old ingredients happens, by some happy chance, to be better than the original.

The story is familiar to anyone. A private plane crashes into the flight deck of a 747, killing or disabling its crew. A stewardess pilots the plane by following radioed instructions, and then a rescue pilot (Charlton Heston, inevitably) is lowered from an Air Force helicopter into the gaping hole in the plane. Meanwhile, a young kidney patient grows weaker, a drunk accosts the pilot, and Gloria Swanson dictates the finishing touches on her autobiography ("I never did want the damn thing published while I was alive, anyway").

What makes this work so well is that the screenplay and direction concentrate on the action, instead of getting bogged down in so many subplots, as *Airport* did. It can't be helped, I suppose, that Heston and the brave stewardess (Karen Black) have been having an affair for six years, or that the airline vice president (George Kennedy, promoted from his operations command in *Airport*) has a wife and daughter on the crippled plane, or that we have the usual ecumenical mixture of stereotypes, racial groups, ages, sexes, and occupants on board. That's all part of the formula.

But at least *Airport 1975* introduces its characters quickly and without fuss, and then gets on with the business at hand. And after the midair collision (which has been telegraphed for at least twenty minutes), the movie's excellent special effects become really gripping. With *Airport*, you never quite felt those people were on a real plane. The exterior shots looked faked. *Airport 1975* has a much more plausible look and a lot of effective aerial photography.

It also gives us a compelling performance by Karen Black, the stewardess. She's probably too good an actress for a role like this, but she makes it real. (And who could ever quite believe Dean Martin as the pilot in *Airport?*) The only quarrel I have with the role is that it falls into the trap of assuming she's incompetent because she's a woman. Her lip quivers, her eyes well up with tears, she's indecisive at key moments. The men on the ground decide they have to get a real pilot on board. My notion is that a real stewardess, faced with such an unlikely situation, would respond professionally and coolly.

No matter. While the wind rips into the plane and the passengers bundle up with blankets and the mountains loom up ahead and the first rescue pilot falls to his death and Gloria Swanson remembers her first flight ("It was in 1917, Cecil B. DeMille was the pilot, and we flew nonstop from Los Angeles to Pasadena"). *Airport 1975* is good, exciting, corny escapism and the kind of movie you would *not* want to watch as an in-flight film.

Alex in Wonderland ★ ★ ★ ★
R, 109 m., 1971

Donald Sutherland (Alex), Ellen Burstyn (Beth), Meg Mazursky (Amy), Glenna Sergent (Nancy), Viola Spolin (Mother), Paul Mazursky (Hal Stern). Directed by Paul Mazursky and produced by Larry Tucker. Screenplay by Mazursky and Tucker.

"Who are you," said the Caterpillar.
This was not an encouraging opening for a conversation. Alice replied rather shyly. "I—hardly know, Sir, just at present—at least I know who I was when I got up this morning, but I think I must have changed several times since then."

That was exactly the case in Hollywood in the early seventies. Works of genius were showered on us by bright, radical, young, etc., filmmakers who announced their intention to overturn the Hollywood establishment. Occasionally one of their films did make it very big, as *Easy Rider* did. Within weeks, the Hollywood hills were jammed with other would-be geniuses, shooting nihilistic cycle flicks with pseudo-Dylan lyrics. Meanwhile, the original boy wonders . . . Have got to make themselves another film. That was the situation for Paul Mazursky and Larry Tucker, who wrote, produced, and directed *Bob & Carol & Ted & Alice*. That movie was an artistic and financial success. It was chosen to open the New York Film Festival. It was argued about in all the best publications. Elliott Gould became a star. Natalie Wood made her comeback. Tucker and Mazursky got rich. The whole enchilada, baby.

Alex in Wonderland was their response to that situation; it's a movie about a director whose first movie is a success and who's at a loss for another project. In this sense, it's autobiographical; not in the details of life, but in the crises. Mazursky himself even appears, as Hal Stern, the doggedly mod movie producer who hopes to interest Donald Sutherland in *Don Quixote* as a Western? Or maybe . . . ?

If the director's dilemma sounds familiar, perhaps you're reminded of Fellini's *8½*. Mazursky and Tucker were. The blocked director's daughter even asks why he doesn't do a movie about not knowing what to do next, and he says, no, Fellini already did that. *Alex in Wonderland* is a deliberately Felliniesque movie, all the same, and all the more fun for that. Fellini himself appears briefly, to no special purpose, and Fellini trademarks like parades, circuses, and clowns keep turning up in the hero's daydreams.

If *Alex* had been left just on this level, however, it would have been of little interest. What makes it so good is the gift Mazursky, Tucker, and their actors have of fleshing out the small scenes of human contact that give the movie its almost frightening resonance.

Sutherland, as the director, has trouble

handling his success. His uncertainty about what to do next spills over into aloofness, even cruelty, toward his wife (Ellen Burstyn) and mother (Viola Spolin). A short scene in a car with his mother, and a long scene in a kitchen with his wife, actually make the rest of the movie work, because they give the character a depth that sticks even through the superficial dream sequences.

And beyond these intimate scenes, there are icily observant portraits of the "new Hollywood." Of aimless "idealistic" arguments on the beach, of luncheon meetings, of idle people trying somehow to be idly committed. These scenes are the 1970 equivalent of Fitzgerald's *The Last Tycoon* or Nathanael West's *The Day of the Locust*: Unforgivingly accurate studies of the distance between America and the filmmakers who would be "relevant" about it.

The Fellini elements are laid onto the film and don't quite sink in (although buffs will enjoy them just as parody). But the human story does work, remarkably well, and if the movie doesn't hold together we're not disposed to hold that against it. Half an enchilada is better than none.

Alice Doesn't Live Here Anymore
★ ★ ★ ★
PG, 113 m., 1975

Ellen Burstyn (Alice Hyatt), Kris Kristofferson (David), Billy Green Bush (Donald), Diane Ladd (Flo), Alfred Lutter (Tommy), Harvey Keitel (Ben). Directed by Martin Scorsese and produced by David Susskind and Audrey Maas. Screenplay by Robert Getchell.

Martin Scorsese's *Alice Doesn't Live Here Anymore* opens with a parody of the Hollywood dream world little girls were expected to carry around in their intellectual baggage a generation ago. The screen is awash with a fake sunset, and a sweet little thing comes strolling along home past sets that seem rescued from *The Wizard of Oz*. But her dreams and dialogue are decidedly not made of sugar, spice, or anything nice: This little girl is going to do things her way.

That was her defiant childhood notion, anyway. But by the time she's thirty-five, Alice Hyatt has more or less fallen into society's rhythms. She's married to an incommunicative truck driver, she has a precocious twelve-year-old son, she kills time chatting with the neighbors. And then her husband is unexpectedly killed in a traffic accident and she's left widowed and—almost worse than that—independent. After all those years of having someone there, can she cope by herself?

She can, she says. When she was a little girl, she idolized Alice Faye and determined to be a singer when she grew up. Well, she's thirty-five, and that's grown-up. She has a garage sale, sells the house, and sets off on an odyssey through the Southwest with her son and her dreams. What happens to her along the way provides one of the most perceptive, funny, occasionally painful portraits of an American woman I've seen.

The movie has been both attacked and defended on feminist grounds, but I think it belongs somewhere outside ideology, maybe in the area of contemporary myth and romance. There are scenes in which we take Alice and her journey perfectly seriously, there are scenes of harrowing reality and then there are other scenes (including some hilarious passages in a restaurant where she waits on tables) where Scorsese edges into slight, cheerful exaggeration. There are times, indeed, when the movie seems less about Alice than it does about the speculations and daydreams of a lot of women about her age, who identify with the liberation of other women, but are unsure on the subject of themselves.

A movie like this depends as much on performances as on direction, and there's a fine performance by Ellen Burstyn (who won an Oscar for this role) as Alice. She looks more real this time than she did as Cybill Shepherd's available mother in *The Last Picture Show* or as Linda Blair's tormented mother in *The Exorcist*. It's the kind of role she can relax in, be honest with, allow to develop naturally (although those are often the hardest roles of all). She's determined to find work as a singer, to "resume" a career that was mostly dreams to begin with, and she's pretty enough (although not good enough) to almost pull it off. She meets some generally good people along the way, and they help her when they can. But she also meets some creeps, especially a deceptively nice guy named Ben (played by Harvey Keitel, the autobiographical hero of Scorsese's two films set in Little Italy). The singing jobs don't materialize much, and it's while she's waitressing that she runs into a divorced young farmer (Kris Kristofferson).

They fall warily in love, and there's an interesting relationship between Kristofferson and Alfred Lutter, who does a very good job of playing a certain kind of twelve-year-old kid. Most women in Alice's position probably wouldn't run into a convenient, understanding, and eligible young farmer, but then a lot of the things in the film don't work as pure logic. There's a little myth to them, while Scorsese sneaks up on his main theme.

The movie's filled with brilliantly done individual scenes. Alice, for example, has a run-in with a fellow waitress with an inspired vocabulary (Diane Ladd, an Oscar nominee for this role). They fall into a friendship and have a frank and honest conversation one day while sunbathing. The scene works perfectly. There's also the specific way her first employer backs into offering her a singing job, and the way Alice takes leave from her old neighbors, and the way her son persists in explaining a joke that could only be understood by a twelve-year-old. These are great moments in a film that gives us Alice Hyatt: female, thirty-five, undefeated.

Aliens ★ ★ ★ ½
R, 135 m., 1986 ✔

Sigourney Weaver (Ripley), Carrie Henn (Newt), Michael Biehn (Corporal Hicks), Paul Reiser (Burke), Lance Henriksen (Bishop), Jenette Goldstein (Private Vasquez). Directed by James Cameron and produced by Gale Anne Hurd. Screenplay by Cameron.

This movie is so intense that it creates a problem for me as a reviewer: Do I praise its craftsmanship, or do I tell you it left me feeling wrung out and unhappy? When I walked out of the theater, there were knots in my stomach from the film's roller-coaster ride of violence. This is not the kind of movie where it means anything to say you "enjoyed" it.

Aliens is a sequel to the very effective 1979 film, *Alien*, but it tells a self-contained story that begins fifty-seven years after the previous story ended. The first time around, you may recall, Sigourney Weaver and a

shipload of her fellow space voyagers were exploring a newly discovered planet when they found an abandoned spaceship. Surviving in the ship was an alien life-form that seemed to consist primarily of teeth. The aliens were pure malevolence; their only function was to attack and eat anything that was warm and moved. And they incubated their young inside the bodies of their victims.

Weaver was the only survivor of that first expedition, and after saving her ship by expelling an alien through the air lock into deep space, she put herself into hibernation. She is found fifty-seven years later by a salvage ship, and when she awakes she is still tormented by nightmares. (The script does not provide her, however, with even a single line of regret after she learns that fifty-seven years have passed and everyone she knew is dead.)

A new expedition is sent back to the mystery planet. Weaver is on board. She knows what the aliens are like and thinks the only sane solution is to nuke them from outer space. But in the meantime, she learns to her horror that a human colony has been established on the planet and billions of dollars have been invested in it. Now Earth has lost contact with the colony. Has it been attacked by aliens? Are there stars in the sky?

The crew is made up of an interesting mixed bag of technicians and military personnel. My favorites were Lance Henriksen as a loyal android, Jenette Goldstein as a muscular marine private, and Michael Biehn as the uncertain Corporal Hicks. Also on board is the slimy Burke (Paul Reiser), who represents the owners of the planet's expensive colony and dreams of making millions by using the aliens as a secret weapon.

The movie gives us just enough set-up to establish the characters and explain the situation. Then the action starts. The colony has, of course, been overrun by the aliens, all except for one plucky little girl (Carrie Henn) who has somehow survived by hiding in the air ducts. The marines explore the base on foot, which seems a little silly in view of the great speed with which the aliens attack. Nobody seems very interested in listening to Weaver's warnings. After all, she's only the one person who has seen an alien, so what does she know? And then the movie escalates into a nonstop war between human and alien.

It's here that my nerves started to fail. *Aliens* is absolutely, painfully, and unremittingly intense for at least its last hour. Weaver goes into battle to save her colleagues, herself, and the little girl, and the aliens drop from the ceiling, pop up out of the floor, and crawl out of the ventilation shafts. (In one of the movie's less plausible moments, one alien even seems to know how to work the elevator buttons.) I have never seen a movie that maintains such a pitch of intensity for so long; it's like being on some kind of hair-raising carnival ride that never stops.

I don't know how else to describe this: The movie made me feel bad. It filled me with feelings of unease and disquiet and anxiety. I didn't want to talk to anyone. I was drained. I'm not sure *Aliens* is what we mean by entertainment. Yet I have to be accurate about this movie: It is a superb example of filmmaking craft.

The director, James *(The Terminator)* Cameron, has been assigned to make an intense and horrifying thriller, and he has delivered. Weaver, who is onscreen almost all the time, comes through with a very strong, sympathetic performance: She's the thread that holds everything together.

The supporting players are sharply drawn. The special effects are professional. I'm giving the movie a high rating for its skill and professionalism and because it does the job it says it will do. I am also advising you not to eat before you see it.

All of Me ★ ★ ★ ½
PG, 93 m., 1984

Steve Martin (Roger Cobb), Lily Tomlin (Edwina Cutwater), Victoria Tennant (Terry Hoskins), Madolyn Smith (Peggy), Richard Libertini (Prahka Lasa), Jason Bernard (Tyrone Wattel). Directed by Carl Reiner. Screenplay by Phil Alden Robinson.

All of Me shares with a lot of great screwball comedies a very simple approach: Use absolute logic in dealing with the absurd. Begin with a nutty situation, establish the rules, and follow them. The laughs happen when ordinary human nature comes into conflict with ridiculous developments.

We can identify with almost all of the motives of the characters in *All of Me*. There is, for example, the millionaire spinster Edwina Cutwater (Lily Tomlin), who wants to live forever and thinks she has found a way to do that. There is the unhappy lawyer Roger Cobb (Steve Martin), who is desperately unhappy with his work and will do anything to get a promotion—even cater to nutcase clients like Edwina. There is the evil Terry Hoskins (Victoria Tennant), who plans to cruelly deceive Edwina, and there is the beatific Prahka Lasa (Richard Libertini), who hopes to transfer Edwina's soul into a brass pot, and then insert it in Miss Hoskins's body. There is, however, a terrible psychic miscalculation, and when Edwina dies, she transmigrates instead into Cobb's body. When I heard *All of Me* described, I couldn't think of any way this plot could possibly work. To begin with, why put one of my favorite comedians, Tomlin, inside Martin, a man whose movies I have not admired? And yet it does work. The moment it starts to work is the first time Martin has to deal with this alien female entity inside his brain. He retains control of the left side of his body. She controls the right. They are trying to cross the sidewalk together, each in their own way, and this sets up a manic tug-of-war that is one of the funniest scenes I've seen in a long time.

There are other great scenes, some of them probably obligatory, as when Martin has to go to the bathroom. The movie doesn't just go for obvious physical jokes, however; it scores a lot of points by speculating on the ways in which a man and a woman could learn to coexist in such close quarters. Against all the odds, a certain tenderness and sweetness develops by the end of the film. Although it is Tomlin who disappears into Martin's body, she does not disappear from the movie. For one thing, her reflection can be seen in mirrors, and there is some exquisite timing involved in the way they play scenes with each other's mirror images. For another thing (and this is really curious), there is a real sense of her presence even when Martin is alone on the screen: The film's premise, which seems so unlikely, begins to work.

The movie is filled with good supporting performances. My favorites are Richard Libertini, as the guru of transmigration, who speaks incomprehensible words in a tone of complete agreement, and Jason Bernard, as a black musician who is Martin's friend and partner during several tricky scenes of body-snatching and brain-grabbing. *All of Me* is in a class with *Ghostbusters*, and for some of the same reasons.

All the President's Men ★ ★ ★ ½
PG, 135 m., 1976

Robert Redford (Bob Woodward), Dustin Hoffman (Carl Bernstein), Jack Warden (Harry Rosenfeld), Martin Balsam (Howard Simons), Hal Holbrook (Deep Throat), Jason Robards (Ben Bradlee), Jane Alexander (Bookkeeper), Stephen Collins (Hugh Sloan), Robert Walden (Donald Segretti), Frank Wills (Frank Wills). Directed by Alan J. Pakula and produced by Walter Coblenz. Screenplay by William Goldman.

All the President's Men is truer to the craft of journalism than to the art of storytelling, and that's its problem. The movie is as accurate about the processes used by investigative reporters as we have any right to expect, and yet process finally overwhelms narrative—we're adrift in a sea of names, dates, telephone numbers, coincidences, lucky breaks, false leads, dogged footwork, denials, evasions, and sometimes even the truth. Just such thousands of details led up to Watergate and the Nixon resignation, yes, but the movie's more about the details than about their results. That's not to say the movie isn't good at accomplishing what it sets out to do. It provides the most observant study of working journalists we're ever likely to see in a feature film (Bob Woodward and Carl Bernstein may at last, merciful God, replace Hildy Johnson and Walter Burns as career models). And it succeeds brilliantly in suggesting the mixture of exhilaration, paranoia, self-doubt, and courage that permeated the *Washington Post* as its two young reporters went after a presidency.

Newspaper movies always used to play up the excitement and ignore the boredom and the waiting. This one is all about the boredom and the waiting and the tireless digging; it depends on what we already know about Watergate to provide a level of excitement. And yet, given the fact that William Goldman's screenplay is almost all dialogue,

almost exclusively a series of scenes of people talking (or not talking) to each other, director Alan J. Pakula has done a remarkable job of keeping the pace taut. Who'd have thought you could build tension with scenes where Bernstein walks over to Woodward's desk and listens in on the extension phone? But you can. And the movie's so well paced, acted, and edited that it develops the illusion of momentum even in the scenes where Woodward and Bernstein are getting doors slammed in their faces.

When Robert Redford announced that he'd bought the rights to *All the President's Men*, the joke in the newsroom was about reporters becoming movie stars. What in fact has happened is that the stars, Redford as Woodward and Dustin Hoffman as Bernstein, became reporters: They sink into their characters and become wholly credible. There's not a false or "Hollywood" note in the whole movie, and that's commendable—but how much authenticity will viewers settle for? To what secret and sneaky degree do they really want Redford and Hoffman to come on like stars?

There must have been a temptation to flesh out the Woodward and Bernstein characters, to change the pace with subplots about their private lives, but the film sticks resolutely to its subject. This is the story of a story: of two reporters starting with an apparently minor break-in and following it, almost incredulously at times, as it finally leads all the way to the White House. At times the momentum of Watergate seems to propel Woodward and Bernstein, instead of the other way around. It must have occasionally been like that at the time, and it's to the movie's credit that it doesn't force its characters into the center of every scene.

All the President's Men doesn't dwell on the private lives of its characters, but it does have a nice touch with their professional lives, and especially with their relationships with editors. The Watergate story started as a local story, not a national one, and it was a continuing thorn in the side of the *Post*'s prestigious national staff as Woodward and Bernstein kept it as their own. We meet the *Post* metro editor, Harry Rosenfeld (Jack Warden), defending and badgering "Woodstein" as the team came to be known. Martin Balsam plays Howard Simons, the managing editor, and Jason Robards is Benjamin Bradlee, the executive editor. All three are well cast; they may never have been in a newspaper office before, but they've learned the correct tone, they carry on a news conference as if they've held one before, and they even exhibit typical shadings of office fashion—the closer in time you are to having once covered a daily beat, the more you're permitted to loosen your tie and have baggy pants.

The movie has dozens of smaller character roles, for all the people who talked to Woodstein, or who refused to, and there's one cameo from real life: Frank Wills, the Watergate guard who found the fateful tape on the lock, plays himself. Some of the other roles tend to blend into one faceless Source, but Robert Walden makes a memorable Donald Segretti, playing the "dirty tricks" expert with bravado shading into despair. And two of the key informants are portrayed in interestingly different ways. Jane Alexander is a bookkeeper who gives the team some of their best leads, and is plain, honest, and scared; Hal Holbrook, as the mysterious "Deep Throat," the source inside the administration, is disturbingly detached, almost as if he's observing the events with a hollow laugh.

All of these elements in *All the President's Men* are to be praised, and yet they don't quite add up to a satisfying movie experience. Once we've seen one cycle of investigative reporting, once Woodward and Bernstein have cracked the first wall separating the break-in from the White House, we understand the movie's method. We don't need to see the reporting cycle repeated several more times just because the story grows longer and the sources more important. For all of its technical skill, the movie essentially shows us the same journalistic process several times as it leads closer and closer to an end we already know. The film is long, and would be dull if it weren't for the wizardry of Pakula, his actors, and technicians. What saves it isn't the power of narrative, but the success of technique. Still, considering the compromises that could have been made, considering the phony "newspaper movie" this could have been, maybe that's almost enough.

All the Right Moves ★ ★ ★
R, 91 m., 1983

Tom Cruise (Stef), Craig T. Nelson (Nickerson), Lea Thompson (Lisa). Directed by Michael Chapman and produced by Stephen Deutsch. Screenplay by Michael Kane.

I started on newspapers as a sportswriter, covering local high school teams. That was a long time ago, and I had almost forgotten, until I saw *All the Right Moves*, how desperately important every game seemed at the time. When the team members and the fans are all teen-agers, and when a school victory reflects in a significant way upon your own feelings of worth, when "We won!" means that we won, a football game can take on aspects of Greek tragedy.

All the Right Moves remembers the strength of those feelings, but does not sentimentalize them. The movie stars Tom Cruise (from *Risky Business*) as a high school football player in a small Pennsylvania mill town where unemployment is a way of life. His ticket out of town is a football scholarship to a good engineering school. The high school football coach (Craig T. Nelson) also is looking for a ticket, to an assistant coaching job in a college. On the night of the big game, these two people get into a position where each one seems to have destroyed the hopes of the other.

The movie plays this conflict against an interesting background. This isn't another high school movie with pompom girls and funny principals and weirdo chem teachers. The movie gets into the dynamics of the high school student body and into the tender, complicated relationship between the Cruise character and his girlfriend (Lea Thompson).

After all the junk high school movies in which kids chop each other up, seduce the French teacher, and visit whorehouses in Mexico, it is so wonderful to see a movie that remembers that most teen-agers are vulnerable, unsure, sincere, and fundamentally decent. The kid, his girlfriend, and all of their friends have feelings we can recognize as real. The plot feels real, too, because it centers around those kinds of horrible misunderstandings and mistakes that we all remember from high school. A lot of teen-agers walk around all day feeling guilty, even if they're totally innocent. Get them into a situation that gives them the appearance of guilt and they're in trouble. And it is so easy to get into trouble when you are old enough to do wrong but too young to move independently to avoid it. A lot of kids who say they were only along for the ride are telling the simple truth.

The movie frames the Cruise character in a situation like that, one we can identify with. And then it does an interesting thing. Instead of solving the problem with a plot twist, it solves it through the exercise of genuine human honesty: Two people finally tell each other the truth. This is, of course, an astonishing breakthrough in movies about teen-agers, and *All the Right Moves* deserves credit for that achievement.

Allegro non Tropo ★ ★ ★ ½
NO MPAA RATING, 75 m., 1977

An animated feature by Bruno Bozzetto.

Classical music illustrated with animated fantasies! What an inspiration! The impresario in the vast old Italian opera house can hardly contain himself. He bustles about the stage, confiding his plans: He'll have an animator as his chief soloist. A full orchestra of little old ladies. A selection from the greatest symphonic works of all time . . .

The telephone rings. It's Hollywood calling. The impresario can't believe his ears. It's been done already! Somebody had the same idea years ago—somebody named, ah, Prisney. Something like that. No matter. He'll do it anyway! His little old ladies arrive in a horse-drawn wagon guided by the impresario himself. Did that Prisney, or whatever his name is, give you stuff like this?

And so Bruno Bozzetto introduces his *Allegro non Tropo*, a tribute to Walt Disney's *Fantasia* and at the same time a delightfully original animated feature itself. The two movies show how limitless the possibilities are: Animation, which has few boundaries, reveals none here.

Bozzetto's animated fantasies are funny and sad, erotic and the opposite, pessimistic and visionary. He selects such familiar symphonic works as Stravinsky's *Firebird*, Sibelius's *Valse Triste*, Vivaldi's *Concerto in C*, Debussy's *Prelude to the Afternoon of a Faun*, and Ravel's *Bolero*, and then he finds ways of illustrating them that are inspired, and amusing, and somehow just right.

Take *Bolero*, for example, that majestic progression to larger and larger statements. How would you visualize it? Bozzetto begins with an empty Coke bottle, tossed from a spaceship visiting a barren planet. The bottle comes to rest just as the spaceship departs. There's a little Coke left in the bottom of it. And as Ravel's music relentlessly builds, the stuff in the bottle ferments. Simple forms of life become more complex. Weird and wonderful shapes form, and try to crawl up the side of the bottle, and fail. And then finally one succeeds. And Bozzetto marches through the stages of a strange evolution, as bizarre monsters struggle across the barren landscape, learning very suddenly to fly, and swim, and do the other things to keep from becoming meals.

The Sibelius is illustrated with an affecting idea: A scrawny house cat wanders forlorn through the streets of a city destroyed by war. No people live there anymore, but some ancient racial cat memory inhabits the ruins with dream-images of people: with quiet domestic scenes that evaporate, one after another, leaving the cat alone, lonely and afraid. An idea like this is in Loren Eiseley's biography, *All the Strange Hours*. He wonders if the dogs and cats that cast their lot with us so many tens of thousands of years ago will remember us uneasily for a few generations after we've annihilated ourselves; Bozzetto illustrates the idea beautifully.

And then there's his version of Stravinsky's *Firebird*, in which the serpent in the Garden of Eden eats the apple himself and has a very hard time of it as a result. And the aging, self-deluded rake in *Prelude to the Afternoon of a Faun*, trying to make himself look younger in his doomed pursuit of a nymph. And the busy little bee in Vivaldi's *Concerto in C*, who sets her table at one promising flower after another, only to be disturbed by two vulgar, gigantic humans who insist on making love in her meadow.

Bozzetto, one of the best animators now at work, has been making shorts for years. *Allegro non Tropo*, his first feature, is a treasure. It deserves its place beside *Fantasia*, is as delightful and inspired, and will no doubt be around as long. Even what's-his-name, Prisney, would agree.

Altered States ★ ★ ★ ½
R, 103 m., 1980

William Hurt (Eddie Jessup), Blair Brown (Emily Jessup), Bob Balaban (Arthur Rosenberg), Charles Haid (Mason Parrish), Thaao Penghlis (Eccheverria), Miguel Godreau (Primal Man). Directed by Ken Russell and produced by Howard Gottfried. Screenplay by Sidney Aaron.

Altered States is one hell of a movie—literally. It hurls its characters headlong back through billions of years to the moment of creation and finds nothing there except an anguished scream of "No!" as the life force protests its moment of birth. And then, through the power of the human ego to insist on its own will even in the face of the implacable indifference of the universe, it turns "No!" into "Yes!" and ends with the basic scene in all drama, the man and the woman falling into each other's arms.

But hold on just a second here: I'm beginning to sound like the movie's characters, a band of overwrought pseudo-intellectuals who talk like a cross between Werner Erhard, Freud, and Tarzan. Some of the movie's best dialogue passages are deliberately staged with everybody talking at once: It doesn't matter what they're saying, only that they're incredibly serious about it. I can tell myself intellectually that this movie is a fiendishly constructed visual and verbal roller coaster, a movie deliberately intended to overwhelm its audiences with sensual excess. I know all that, and yet I *was* overwhelmed, I *was* caught up in its headlong energy.

Is that a worthy accomplishment for a movie? Yes, I suppose it is, if the movie earns it by working as hard as *Altered States* does. This is, at last, the movie that Ken Russell was born to direct—the same Ken Russell whose wretched excesses in the past include *The Music Lovers, The Devils,* and *Lisztomania.* The formula is now clear. Take Russell's flair for visual pyrotechnics and apocalyptic sexuality, and channel it through just enough scientific mumbo jumbo to give it form. The result may be totally meaningless, but while you're watching it you are not concerned.

The movie is based on a Paddy Chayevsky novel, which was, in turn, inspired by the experiments of Dr. John Lilly, the man who placed his human subjects in total immersion tanks—floating them in total darkness so that their minds, cut off from all external reality, could play along the frontiers of sanity. In *Altered States,* William Hurt plays a Harvard scientist named Jessup who takes such an experiment one step further, by ingesting a drug made from the sacred hallucinatory mushrooms of a primitive tribe. The strange thing about these mushrooms, Hurt observes in an easily missed line of dialogue in the movie, is that they give everyone who takes them the same hallucinatory vision. Perhaps it is our cellular memory of creation: There is chaos, and then a ball of light, and then the light turns into a crack, and the crack opens onto Nothing, and that is all there was and all there will be, except for life, which has its only existence in the mind.

Got that? It hardly matters. It is a breathtaking concept, but *Altered States* hardly slows down for it. This is the damnedest movie to categorize. Just when it begins to sound like a 1960s psychedelic fantasy, a head trip—it turns into a farce. The scientist immerses himself in his tank for too long, he regresses to a simian state, physically turns into some kind of ape, attacks the campus security guards, is chased by a pack of wild dogs into the local zoo, and kills and eats a sheep for his supper before turning *back* into the kindly Professor Jessup, the Intellectual Hulk.

The movie splits up into three basic ingredients: The science, the special effects, and the love relationship between the professor and his wife. The science is handled deliciously well. We learn as much as we need to (that is, next to nothing) about total immersion, genetics, and the racial memory. Then come the special effects, in four long passages and a few short bursts. They're good. They may remind you at times of the sound-and-light extravaganza toward the end of 2001, but they are also supposed to evoke the birth of the universe in a pulsating celestial ovum. In the center of this vision is Dr. Jessup, his body pulsing in and out of an ape-shape, his mouth pulled into an anguished "O" as he protests the hell of being born. These scenes are reinforced by the music and are obviously intended to fuel the chemically altered consciousness of the next generation of movie cultists.

But then there is the matter of the love relationship between the professor and his wife (Blair Brown), and it is here that we discover how powerful the attraction of love really is. During the professor's last experiment, when he is disappearing into a violent whirlpool of light and screams on the laboratory floor, it is his wife who wades into the celestial mists, gets up to her knees in eternity, reaches in, and pulls him out. And this is despite the fact that he has filed for divorce. The last scene is a killer, with the professor turning into the protoplasm of life itself, and his wife turning into a glowing shell of rock-like flesh, with her inner fires glowing through the crevices (the effect is something like an overheated Spiderman). They're going through the unspeakable hell of reliving the First Moment, and yet as the professor, as Man, bangs on the walls and crawls toward her, and she reaches out, and the universe rocks, the Man within him bursts out of the ape-protoplasm, and the Woman within her explodes back into flesh, and they collapse into each other's arms, and all the scene really needs at that point is for him to ask, "Was it as good for you as it was for me?"

Altered States is a superbly silly movie, a magnificent entertainment, and a clever and brilliant machine for making us feel awe, fear, and humor. That is enough. It's pure movie and very little meaning. Did I like it? Yeah, I guess I did, but I wouldn't advise trying to think about it very deeply.

Amadeus ★ ★ ★ ★
PG, 158 m., 1984

F. Murray Abraham (Salieri), Tom Hulce (Mozart), Elizabeth Berridge (Constanze), Simon Callow (Emanuel Schikaneder), Roy Dotrice (Leopold Mozart), Christine Ebersole (Katerina Cavalieri), Jeffrey Jones (Joseph II). Directed by Milos Forman and produced by Saul Zaentz. Screenplay by Peter Shaffer.

Milos Forman's *Amadeus* is one of the riskiest gambles a filmmaker has taken in a long time—a lavish movie about Mozart that dares to be anarchic and saucy, and yet still earns the importance of tragedy. This movie is nothing like the dreary educational portraits we're used to seeing about the Great Composers, who come across as cobwebbed profundities weighed down with the burden of genius. This is Mozart as an eighteenth-century Bruce Springsteen, and yet (here is the genius of the movie) there is nothing cheap or unworthy about the approach. *Amadeus* is not only about as much fun as you're likely to have with a movie, it also is disturbingly true. The truth enters in the character of Salieri, who tells the story. He is not a great composer, but he is a good enough composer to know greatness when he hears it, and that is why the music of Mozart breaks his heart. He knows how good it is, he sees how easily Mozart seems to compose it, and he knows that his own work looks pale and silly beside it.

The movie begins with the suggestion that Salieri might have murdered Mozart. The movie examines the ways in which this possibility might be true, and by the end of the film we feel a certain kinship with the weak and jealous Salieri—for few of us can identify with divine genius, but many of us probably have had dark moments of urgent self-contempt in the face of those whose effortless existence illustrates our own inadequacies. Salieri, played with burning intensity by F. Murray Abraham, sits hunched in a madhouse confessing to a priest. The movie flashes back to his memories of Wolfgang Amadeus Mozart, the child genius who composed melodies of startling originality and who grew up to become a prolific, driven artist.

One of the movie's wisest decisions is to cast Mozart not as a charismatic demigod, not as a tortured superman, but as a goofy, immature, likable kid with a ridiculous laugh. The character is played by Tom Hulce, and if you saw *Animal House*, you may remember him as the fraternity brother who tried to seduce the mayor's daughter, while an angel and a devil whispered in his ears. Hulce would seem all wrong for Mozart, but he is absolutely right, as an unaffected young man filled with delight at his own gifts, unaware of how easily he wounds Salieri and others, tortured only by the guilt of having offended his religious and domineering father.

The film is constructed in wonderfully well-written and acted scenes—scenes so carefully constructed, unfolding with such delight, that they play as perfect compositions of words. Most of them will be unfamiliar to those who have seen Peter Shaffer's brooding play, on which this film is based; Shaffer and Forman have brought light, life, and laughter to the material, and it plays with grace and ease. It's more human than the play; the characters are people, not throbbing packages of meaning. It centers on the relationships in Mozart's life: with his father, his wife, and Salieri. The father never can be pleased, and that creates an undercurrent affecting all of Mozart's success. The wife, played by delightful, buxom Elizabeth Berridge, contains in one person the qualities of a jolly wench and a loving partner: She likes to loll in bed all day, but also gives Mozart good, sound advice and is a forceful person in her own right. The patrons, especially Joseph II, the Austro-Hungarian emperor, are connoisseurs and dilettantes, slow to take to Mozart's new music but enchanted by the audacity with which he defends it. And then there is Salieri (F. Murray Abraham), the gaunt court composer whose special torture is to understand better than anybody else how inadequate he is, and how great Mozart is.

The movie was shot on location in Forman's native Czechoslovakia, and it looks exactly right; it fits its period comfortably, perhaps because Prague still contains so many streets and squares and buildings that could be directly from the Vienna of Mozart's day. Perhaps his confidence in his locations gave Forman the freedom to make Mozart slightly *out* of period. Forman directed the film version of *Hair*, and Mozart in this movie seems to share a spirit with some of the characters from *Hair*. Mozart's wigs do not look like everybody else's. They have just the slightest suggestion of punk, just the smallest shading of pink. Mozart seems more a child of the 1960's than of any other age, and this interpretation of his personality—he was an irreverent proto-hippie who trusted, if you will, his own vibes— sounds risky, but works.

I have not mentioned the music. There's probably no need to. The music provides the understructure of the film, strong, confident, above all, *clear* in a way that Salieri's simple muddles only serve to illustrate. There are times when Mozart speaks the words of a child, but then the music says the same things in the language of the gods, and all is clear.

Amadeus is a magnificent film, full and tender and funny and charming—and, at the end, sad and angry, too, because in the character of Salieri it has given us a way to understand not only greatness, but our own lack of it. This movie's fundamental question, I think, is whether we can learn to be grateful for the happiness of others, and that, of course, is a test for sainthood. How many movies ask such questions and succeed in being fun, as well?

Amarcord ★ ★ ★ ★
R, 127 m., 1974

Magali Noel (Gradisca), Bruno Zamin (Titta), Pupella Maggio (His Mother), Armando Drancia (His Father), Giuseppe Lanigro (His Grandfather), Nando Orfei (Pataca), Chiccio Ingrassia (Uncle Teo), Luigi Rossi (Lawyer). Directed by Federico Fellini and produced by Iranco Cristaldi. Screenplay by Fellini.

Federico Fellini's *Amarcord* takes us back to the small Italian town of his birth and young manhood, and gives us a joyful, bawdy, virtuoso portrait of the people he remembers there. He includes a character undoubtedly meant to be young Federico—earnest, awkward, yearning with all the poignancy of adolescent lust after the town beauties. But the movie's not an autobiography of a character. It's the story of the town itself.

We see it first when the dandelion seeds blow in from the fields, signaling the arrival of spring. The townspeople gather in the piazza to build a ceremonial bonfire and burn the witch of winter, and as they dance around the flames in one of Fellini's beloved processions, we get to know them.

They're of all sizes, sexes, and ages, but they're bound together by their transparent simplicity and a strain of cheerful vulgarity. Fellini likes their weaknesses as much as their virtues, and gives us the pompous lawyer, the egotistical theater owner (who cultivates a resemblance to Ronald Coleman), the buxom beautician Gradisca flaunting her delightful derriere and especially the lustful adolescents and their tormenting fantasies.

Fellini also gives us, in a much more subtle way, some notion of the way fascist Italy of the early 1930s helped to shape these people. In an authoritarian system, the individual has fewer choices to make, and there's a temptation to surrender the responsibilities of freedom. The townspeople are almost children in their behavior, taking delight in the simple joys of eating and making love and parading around the square and gossiping about each other and about the hypnotic Gradisca. Fellini implies that this simple behavior is nourished by a system that encourages a mindless going along—but *Amarcord* isn't a political movie. It is a memory, fond but merciless, of how it was in Italy at a certain time.

It's also absolutely breathtaking filmmaking. Fellini has ranked for a long time among the five or six greatest directors in the world, and of them all, he's the natural. Bergman achieves his greatness through thought and soul-searching, Hitchcock built with meticulous craftsmanship, and Bunuel used his fetishes and fantasies to construct barbed jokes about humanity. But Fellini . . . well, moviemaking for him seems almost effortless, like breathing, and he can orchestrate the most complicated scenes with purity and ease. He's the Willie Mays of movies.

He did hit upon hard critical times, though. After the towering success of *La Dolce Vita* and *8½*, and such 1950s landmarks as *La Strada* and *I Vitelloni*, he began to indulge himself (his critics said). *Juliet of the Spirits* was too fantastical and structureless, and *Satyricon* was an exercise in excess, and *The Clowns* was really only a TV show, and *Fellini Roma* was episodic—a great director spinning out sequences that contained brilliance, yes, but no purpose or direction.

I couldn't agree with those criticisms. I find Fellini's magic spellbinding even when he's only marking time, as he was to some extent in *Roma*. But now, with *Amarcord*, Fellini returns to the very top of his form. And he has the last laugh on the critics of his "structureless" films. Because *Amarcord* seems at first to be a series of self-contained episodes and then reveals a structure so organic and yet so effortless that at its end, we can only marvel at this triumph over ordinary movie forms.

And we can marvel, too, at how universal *Amarcord* is. This is a movie for everybody, even those who hardly ever see foreign or "art" films. Fellini's greatest achievement, in my opinion, was *8½*. But that was a difficult film that revealed its meaning only after a good deal of thought and repeated viewings.

Amarcord, on the other hand, is a totally accessible film. It deals directly, hilariously, and sometimes poignantly with the good people of this small town (actually Fellini's birthplace, Rimini). It's no more complicated than they are, it understands them inside-out, and the audiences I've seen it with (three times) have been moved to horse-laughs, stilled by moments of beauty, and then brought back almost to tears. It's not only a great movie, it's a great joy to see.

Someone once remarked that Fellini's movies are filled with symbols, but they're all obvious symbols. At the beginning of *La Dolce Vita*, for example, he wanted to symbolize the gulf between modern, decadent Rome and its history as the center of the Church, so he gave a statue of Christ being helicoptered by pilots who wave and whistle at girls sunning themselves in bikinis. The scene says everything it needs to say, openly and with great economy.

Amarcord is obvious in that way, with a showman's flair for the right effect. There is a night, for example, when all the people of the town get into their boats and sail out to wait for the great new Italian liner to pass by. And when it comes, it towers hundreds of feet above the waves and has thousands of portholes—and is, of course, only a prop built by the special-effects men. It drifts away into invisibility like a candle dying out. The image is of Italy itself in the 1930s: all grandeur and pomp and nationalism, but with an insubstantial soul.

The movie is filled with moments like that, and they're just right. But then there are moments of inexplicable, almost mystical beauty, as when the dandelion seeds drift in on the wind, or when an old lady sweeps up the ashes of the bonfire, or when a peacock spreads its tail feathers in the snow.

At moments like that we're almost blinded with delight. Hitchcock once said he wanted to play his audiences like a piano. Fellini requires the entire orchestra.

American Flyers ★ ★ ½
PG-13, 113 m., 1985

Kevin Costner (Marcus), David Grant (David), Rae Dawn Chong (Sarah), Alexandra Paul (Becky), Janice Rule (Mrs. Sommers), John Amos (Dr. Conrad), Doi Johnson (Randolph), Luca Bercovici (Muzzin). Directed by John Badham and produced by Gareth Wigan and Paula Weinstein. Screenplay by Steve Tesich.

American Flyers tells the story of a grueling bicycle race named "The Hell of the West" and of the grueling relationships within a sick family. That is apparently too much for the movie to deal with, and so we get a bike race surrounded by giant unanswered questions. This is one of those stories timed so that all of the personal crises come to a climax at the finish line, and maybe the approach would work if there weren't so many enormous inconsistencies and loose ends and puzzlements.

The movie stars Kevin Costner as an eighteen-year-old in St. Louis who trains on his bicycle every day, hoping someday to be as good a racer as his older brother. David Grant is the big brother, a doctor in Madison, and Janice Rule is their mother. A painful dinner scene at the beginning of the movie sets up the conflict in the family, caused because the father died painfully and the mother apparently did nothing during his last two weeks on earth to make his passing less painful. The movie never spells out what she didn't do, but that's only the first of many mysteries.

The father died of a stroke from a weakened blood vessel in the brain. Now Grant fears that Costner may have the same condition. He takes him to Madison and runs him through a series of tests, which do indeed indicate the family condition. Then he decides not to tell him, and the two brothers set out by van to compete in the Hell of the West race, in Colorado. Meanwhile, we meet Grant's girlfriend (Rae Dawn Chong), and

along the way they pick up a hitchhiker (Alexandra Paul) who pairs off with Costner.

The race then becomes several showdowns. The brothers must compete against the other racers, and also against the shadow of death. Their main competition comes from a mean SOB named Muzzin (Luca Bercovici), who used to be married to Rae Dawn Chong. The race is run in three stages, and in the second stage, the older brother begins to bleed from the nose and lose his orientation. So then it's up to the kid brother to win the race.

That leaves us with certain problems.

1. Does the older brother have the family condition, or only a nosebleed? I ask because after the frightening scene where he loses control and almost dies, he is taken, not to a hospital, but to his hotel room.

2. Is Muzzin as mean as he seems? I ask because he is cruel to Chong early in the movie and threatens to make her boyfriend "bleed." Then, after Grant's illness, he is tender toward Chong and she is sweet toward him. Then he tries to kill Costner.

3. What's with the mother? Since we never know what she did, or didn't, do during her husband's last weeks, we don't know how to read her. But she turns up for the finish of the race, and there is a reconciliation which is happy or not, depending on issues we don't understand.

Against these large and troubling matters, which probably indicate that many key scenes were cut from the movie, there are several good things to consider. The bicycle race is brilliantly photographed, and very exciting, despite the fact that we can easily guess who will win. The performances are all interesting, especially Rae Dawn Chong's sweet patience as the girlfriend. There are some great supporting characters, including John Amos as Grant's trainer and Doi Johnson as his chubby teen-age son who hates to exercise and dreams of being the first black bowling star. But the movie is shaky at the core, because it tries to tap-dance around its own central issues.

American Gigolo ★ ★ ★ ½
R, 117 m., 1980

Richard Gere (Julian), Lauren Hutton (Michelle), Hector Elizondo (Sunday), Nina Van Pallandt (Anne), Bill Duke (Leon Jaimes), Brian Davies (Stratton). Directed by Paul Schrader and produced by Jerry Bruckheimer. Screenplay by Schrader.

The bare outline of its plot makes *American Gigolo* sound like a fairly sleazy package: A Hollywood male prostitute is framed in a kinky murder case, tracks down the pimp who's responsible for the framing, watches in horror as the pimp himself is killed, and then finds himself faced with prison unless the wife of a senator provides him with an alibi. This is strong stuff—almost sensational enough for daytime soap opera.

But the film *American Gigolo* is a stylish and surprisingly poignant handling of this material. The experiences in the film may be alien to us, but the emotions of the characters are not: Julian Kay, the gigolo of the title, is played by Richard Gere as tender, vulnerable, and a little dumb. We care about him. His business—making love to rich women of a certain age—allows him to buy the baubles by which Beverly Hills measures success, and he has his Mercedes, his expensive wardrobe, his antique vases, his entrée to country clubs.

But he says he's in business for reasons other than money, and we believe him, if only because he hardly seems to value his possessions as anything other than props. He feels a sense of satisfaction when he makes a middle-aged woman happy, he says. He seems to see himself as a cross between a sexual surrogate and a therapist, and the movie does, too: Why, he's hardly a whore at all, not even counting his heart of gold.

The movie sentimentalizes on this point, setting up the character of Julian Kay as so sympathetic that we forgive him his profession. That's a tactic that *American Gigolo*'s writer and director, Paul Schrader, is borrowing from one of his own heroes, the French director Robert Bresson, whose *Pickpocket* make a criminal into an antihero. Schrader is setting the stage for the key relationship in the film, between Julian and the senator's wife (Lauren Hutton).

He tries to pick her up in an exclusive restaurant, but breaks off their conversation when he decides she's not a likely client. But she is all *too* likely, and tracks him down to his apartment. They fall in love, at about the time he's being framed for the murder of a Palm Springs socialite, and the movie wants us to believe in the power of love to redeem both characters: Julian learns to love unselfishly, without money, and the woman learns to love honestly, without regard for her husband's position.

This business of redemption would work better if *American Gigolo* had at least a few more scenes developing the relationship between Gere and Hutton: Her character, so central to the movie's upbeat conclusion, isn't seen clearly enough. We aren't shown the steps by which she moves from sex to love with him (unless she's simply been won over by the old earth-shaking orgasm ploy). We aren't given enough detail about their feelings.

That's a weakness, but not a fatal one, because when Schrader cuts away from their relationship, it's to develop a very involving story about the murder, the framing, and the police investigation. The movie has an especially effective performance by Hector Elizondo as a cigar-chomping vice detective who cheerfully admits he thinks Gere is guilty as sin.

Gere tries to find out who's framing him by descending into the Los Angeles sexual underground. Schrader explored this same universe in his previous film, *Hardcore*, but this time he seems more restrained: The sexual netherlands seem less lurid, more commonplace and sad.

The whole movie has a winning sadness about it; take away the story's sensational aspects and what you have is a study in loneliness. Richard Gere's performance is central to that effect, and some of his scenes—reading the morning paper, rearranging some paintings, selecting a wardrobe—underline the emptiness of his life. We leave *American Gigolo* with the curious feeling that if women weren't paying this man to sleep with them, he'd be paying them: He needs the human connection and he has a certain shyness, a loner quality, that makes it easier for him when love seems to be just another deal.

An American Werewolf in London ★ ★
R, 95 m., 1981

David Naughton (David), Griffin Dunne (Jack), Jenny Agutter (Alex), John Woodvine (Dr. Hirsch). Directed by John Landis and produced by George Folsey, Jr. Screenplay by Landis.

An American Werewolf in London seems curiously unfinished, as if director John Landis spent all his energy on spectacular set-pieces and then didn't want to bother with things like transitions, character development, or an ending. The movie has sequences that are spellbinding, and then long stretches when nobody seem sure what's going on. There are times when the special effects almost wipe the characters off the screen. It's weird. It's not a very good film, and it falls well below Landis's work in the anarchic *National Lampoon's Animal House* and the rambunctious *Blues Brothers*. Landis never seems very sure whether he's making a comedy or a horror film, so he winds up with genuinely funny moments acting as counterpoint to the gruesome undead. Combining horror and comedy is an old tradition (my favorite example is *The Bride of Frankenstein*), but the laughs and the blood co-exist very uneasily in this film.

One of the offscreen stars of the film is Rick Baker, the young makeup genius who created the movie's wounds, gore, and werewolves. His work is impressive, yes, but unless you're single-mindedly interested in special effects, *American Werewolf* is a disappointment. And even the special effects, good as they are, come as an anticlimax if you're a *really* dedicated horror fan, because if you are, you've already seen this movie's high point before: the onscreen transformation of a man into a werewolf was anticipated in *The Howling*, in which the special effects were done by a Baker protegé named Rob Bottin.

The movie's plot involves two young American students (David Naughton and Griffin Dunne), who are backpacking across the English moors. They stumble into a country pub where everyone is ominously silent, and then one guy warns them to beware the full moon and stick to the road. They don't, and are attacked by werewolves.

Dunne is killed, Naughton is severely wounded, and a few days later in the hospital Naughton is visited by the decaying cadaver of Dunne—who warns him that he'll turn into a werewolf at the full moon. Naughton ignores the warning, falls in love with his nurse (Jenny Agutter), and moves in with her when he's discharged from the hospital. Then follows a series of increasingly gruesome walk-ons by Dunne, who begs Naughton to kill himself before the full moon. Naughton doesn't, turns into a werewolf, and runs amok through London. That gives director Landis his chance to stage a spectacular multi-car traffic accident in Piccadilly Circus; crashes have been his specialty since the homecoming parade in *Animal House* and the nonstop carnage in *Blues Brothers*.

The best moments in *American Werewolf* probably belong to Dunne, who may be a decaying cadaver but keeps right on talking like a college student: "Believe me," he says at Naughton's bedside, "this isn't a whole lot of fun." The scene in which Naughton turns into a werewolf is well done, with his hands elongating and growing claws, and his face twisting into a snout and fangs. But it's as if John Landis thought the technology would be enough. We never get a real feeling for the characters, we never really believe the places (especially that awkwardly phony pub and its stagy customers), and we are particularly disappointed by the ending. I won't reveal the ending, such as it is, except to say it's so sudden, arbitrary, and anticlimactic that, although we are willing for the movie to be over, we still can't quite believe it.

Amityville II: The Possession ★ ★
R, 110 m., 1982

Burt Young (Father), James Olson (Priest), Jack Magner (Son), Diane Franklin (Daughter). Directed by Damiano Damiani and produced by Dino De Laurentiis. Screenplay by Tommy Lee Wallace.

This movie is actually slightly better than *The Amityville Horror* (1979), maybe because it rips off superior source material. It starts with the most notorious piece of real estate in North America. Then it lifts ingredients from *The Exorcist*, *Poltergeist*, and *Murder in Amityville*, which was the book about the *original* Amityville horror. Perhaps a bit of history is called for. Although there is great doubt about whether the best-selling *The Amityville Horror* was fact or fiction, there seems to be no doubt that a terrible mass murder did occur in the infamous Amityville house, some years prior to the events in *Horror*. A young man living in the house went berserk and killed his parents, two sisters, and a brother. After he was institutionalized, the house stood empty for a while before being sold to the Bill Lutz family. As all Amityville fans already know, the Lutzes soon began to wonder if they'd made a good buy after the house filled up with green slime, swarms of flies, and pigs with glowing red eyes. They eventually fled the house. (These days, of course, a lot of people would be happy to live with the slime and the flies if they could assume the Lutzes' 8½ percent mortgage.)

Amityville II is actually a prequel, then, instead of a sequel, since it tells what happened in the house before the Lutzes entered the picture. The movie itself is vague about exactly when it's set, however, and although *Amityville Horror* came out in 1979, this prequel contains 1982 automobiles.

The movie opens with a foggy shot of the house, with those eerie attic windows gleaming like diabolical eyes. There is a "For Sale" sign in the front yard—which inspired me, I fear, to laugh out loud. Before long, though, a family moves in. The father is Burt Young (Rocky's brother-in-law). He beats his wife and kids. The wife weeps and refuses to sleep with him. Meanwhile, the older brother (Jack Magner) successfully seduces his sister (Diane Franklin), who confesses to the local priest (James Olson). The house is already acting up. It was, we learn, built over an ancient Indian burial ground (cf. *Poltergeist*) and contains a secret room leading to a crypt (this room is different in *Amityville Horror*, but never mind). After the incestuous son begins hearing voices, he shoots everyone in his family, and is jailed. Then the priest realizes the lad has been possessed by an evil spirit, and the last act of the movie turns into a rehash of *The Exorcist*.

For a movie that's filled with crucifixes, monsignors, confessionals, and Bibles, *Amityville II* is curiously inattentive to such theological questions as (a) Why would the desecration of a pagan burial ground be offensive to evil spirits, as opposed to benevolent ones? and (b) Why does this case call for a Catholic priest instead of a Mohawk medicine man? But never mind. There are some good performances here, by Jack Magner and Olson in particular, and some good technical credits, especially Sam O'Steen's editing. It's just that this whole Amityville saga is such absolute horse manure.

Angelo My Love ★ ★ ★ ½
R, 91 m., 1983

Angelo Evans, Michael Evans, Steve Tsigonoff, Millie Tsigonoff. Written and directed by Robert Duvall. Associate producer, Gail Youngs.

The late Italian director Vittoria De Sica once said that anyone can play at least one role—himself—better than anybody else possibly could. De Sica illustrated that belief in his late-1940s neo-realist films like *Bicycle Thief*, and now the American actor Robert Duvall proves it again, in a wonderful and unique movie he has written and directed, named *Angelo My Love*. Here is a movie that could not exist without the people who are in it—and of how many movies is that true? The film is about the lives, feuds, rivalries, and dreams of a group of New York Gypsies, and Duvall has recruited real Gypsies to play themselves. His inspiration for the movie came when he saw a young Gypsy boy named Angelo Evans conning a much older woman during an argument on a Manhattan sidewalk.

Duvall thought Angelo belonged in the movies. Having seen the movie, I agree. Here is a street-smart, inventive kid of about eleven or twelve who has some of the moves and some of the cynicism of an experienced con man. ("He's got his tiny macho moves down so pat," David Anson wrote in *Newsweek*, "he's like a child impersonator.") Angelo is the product of a culture that has taught him that the world owes him a living, and he cheerfully agrees. What we sometimes almost forget is that Angelo is also a child, vulnerable and easily wounded, and that a lot of his act is a veneer.

Duvall weaves his story around Angelo. We meet his mother, father, sister, and girlfriend, and a couple of villainous Gypsies who steal a ring that Angelo had intended to present to his future bride. All of these people play themselves, more or less. Angelo's family really is his family; the villains are played by a brother and sister, Steve and Millie Tsigonoff, whom Duvall met in Los Angeles. Although the movie's plot is basically a device for letting us watch the lives of the characters, it's the kind of plot, I suspect, that Gypsies might be able to identify with—involving theft, pride, thwarted justice, and revenge. After the Tsigonoffs steal the ring, there's an ill-advised chase to Canada to get it back (and a wonderful set-piece in a Gypsy camp supposedly under attack by ghosts). Then there's a trial scene in the backroom of an Irish-American bar in Brooklyn. It's all done with great energy and seriousness, even though by the movie's end the ring hardly seems to matter.

Angelo also stars in several fairly self-contained scenes that abundantly illustrate why Duvall found him so fascinating. He makes a defiant mess of his one day in school. He attempts to pick up a pretty country singer who is at least ten years older than he is. He and his sister engage in a long, ingratiating conversation with an old lady in a cafeteria; they want to inveigle her into their mother's fortune-telling parlor, but the lady is a New Yorker and wasn't born yesterday.

All of these scenes have a special magic because we sense that they're real, that they come out of people's lives. Angelo My Love is technically a fictional film, but Duvall has worked so close to his sources that it has the conviction of a documentary. Maybe because he's such a good actor, Duvall has been able to listen to his characters, to really see *them* rather than his own notion of how they should move and behave. There are moments in this movie when the camera lingers for an extra moment, and scenes that do not quite dovetail into everything else, and we sense that Duvall left them in because they revealed something about his Gypsies that he had observed and wanted to share.

At the end of the movie we ask ourselves a question the movie does not attempt to answer: What will become of Angelo in the years to come? It's one thing to be a cute, street-wise kid. It's another thing to try to carry that role on through life with you. Angelo might be able to pull it off, but the movie doesn't try to sell us that romanticized hope. Instead, Duvall seems to be suggesting that Angelo is more than a colorful Gypsy kid; that he has real potential as a person, if he can grow out of the trap of his glib mannerisms and is not too badly scarred by his upside-down childhood. Who knows? One day ten years from now, there might be a movie named *Angelo My Friend*.

Annie ★ ★ ★
PG, 128 m., 1982

Aileen Quinn (Annie), Albert Finney (Daddy Warbucks), Carol Burnett (Miss Hannigan), Bernadette Peters (Lily), Ann Reinking (Grace Farrell), Tim Curry (Rooster), Geoffrey Holder (Punjab), Edward Herrmann (F.D.R.). Directed by John Huston and produced by Ray Stark. Screenplay by Carol Sobieski.

In the abstract, *Annie* is fun. It has lots of movement and color, dance and music, sound and fury. In the particular, it has all sorts of problems, and I guess the only way to really enjoy the movie is to just ignore the particulars. I will nevertheless mention a few particulars. One is the story itself, about how Little Orphan Annie is rescued from a cruel orphanage by a billionaire who wants a Rent-An-Orphan for Christmas. This is said to be a universal story. Critics have written that you just can't help cheering for Annie as she faces the cold world with pluck and courage. I didn't find myself cheering much, though, since Annie didn't seem to need the encouragement; as played by the feisty young Aileen Quinn, she is the sort of child who makes adults run for the hills.

The adventures she gets herself into are likewise questionable. I've never thought of *Oliver!* as a particularly realistic musical, but at least when its little hero said "Please, sir, more food?" there was a hint of truth. *Annie* has been plunged into pure fantasy, into the mindless sort of musical boosterism that plays big for Broadway theater parties but almost always translates to the movie screen as sheer contrivance. *Annie* is not *about* anything. It *contains* lots of subjects (such as cruel orphanages, the Great Depression, scheming conmen, heartless billionaires, and President Franklin Delano Roosevelt) but it isn't *about* them. It's not even really about whether Annie will survive her encounters with them, since the book of this musical is so rigorously machine-made, so relentlessly formula, it's one of those movies where you can amaze your friends by leaving the auditorium, standing blindfolded in the lobby and correctly predicting the outcome.

And yet I sort of enjoyed the movie. I enjoyed the energy that was visible on the screen, and the sumptuousness of the production numbers, and the good humor of several of the performances—especially those by Albert Finney, as Daddy Warbucks, and Carol Burnett, as the wicked orphanage supervisor, Miss Hannigan. Aileen Quinn sort of grew on me, too. She cannot be said to really play a child—at least not the sort of plausible flesh-and-blood child that Henry Thomas creates in *E.T.* But Quinn is talented, can dance well and sing passably, and does not seem to be an overtrained puppet like, say, Ricky Schroeder. She seems more like the kind of kid who will get this acting out of her system and go on to be student body president.

If there is a center to the film, it belongs to Albert Finney. He has a thankless task: He must portray Daddy Warbucks as a self-centered, smug rich man who has everything in the world, except love, and who learns to love through the example of a little girl. This is the sort of role actors kill over—to avoid playing. Albert Finney has the true grit. He's gone through this personality transformation twice; he starred in *Scrooge* in 1970. This time, he even pulls it off, by underplaying. He isn't too aloof at the beginning, and he's not too softhearted at the end. He has a certain detachment. Annie may win his heart, but she'll still have to phone for an appointment.

Will kids like the movie? I honestly don't know. When I was a kid, I didn't much like movies about other kids, maybe because I was jealous (why does *that* kid get to ride a horse in the Derby?). The movie was promoted as a family entertainment, but was it really a family musical, even on the stage? I dunno. I think it was more of a product, a clever concoction of nostalgia, hard-sell sentiment, small children, and cute dogs. The movie is the same mixture as before. It's like some kind of dumb toy that doesn't do anything or go anywhere, but it is fun to watch as it spins mindlessly around and around.

Annie Hall ★ ★ ★ ½
PG, 95 m., 1977

Woody Allen (Alvy Singer), Diane Keaton (Annie Hall), Tony Roberts (Rob), Carol Kane (Allison), Paul Simon (Tony Lacey), Shelley Duvall (Pam), Janet Margolin (Robin), Colleen Dewhurst (Mom Hall). Directed by Woody Allen and produced by Charles H. Joffe. Screenplay by Allen and Marshall Brickman.

Woody Allen's *Annie Hall* explores new dimensions of the persona Allen has constructed in movies, on the stage, and even in a comic strip. We're all familiar by now with "Woody," the overanxious, underachieving intellectual with the inept social life. We've watched him develop from bits in a stand-up comedy routine to a fully developed comic character in the tradition of Chaplin's tramp or Fields's drunk. We know how "Woody" will act in so many situations that we're already laughing before the punch line. Maybe nobody since Jack Benny has been so hilariously predictable.

And yet there's always the realization that "Woody" is a projection of a real Woody Allen. That beneath the comic character is a certain amount of painful truth. That just as W.C. Fields really *was* a drunk, so Woody Allen perhaps really is insecure about his height, shy around girls, routinely incompetent in the daily joust with life.

It's not that the "real" Woody Allen is as hapless as his fictional creation, but that the character draws from life by exaggerating it. *Annie Hall* is the closest Allen has come to dealing with that real material. It's not an autobiography, but we get the notion at times that scenes in the movie have been played before, slightly differently, for real.

Allen plays Alvy Singer, stand-up comic and incurable combination of neurotic and romantic. He's self-consciously a New Yorker, a liberal, a Jew, an intellectual, a seeker after the unattainable, and an expert at *making* it unattainable. One of Alvy Singer's problems is that he understands this all so well. He's not a victim of forces beyond his control, but their author.

And one of the problems he keeps providing for himself is the problem of love. He falls in love too easily, to girls who are right for him in all the little ways and incompatible in all the big ones. His girls tend to reflect the stages he's going through. When he's an Adlai Stevenson liberal in the late 1950s, he marries another one. When he's a romantic ten or fifteen years later, he finds another one, a kookier one. His only trouble is that women are people, not stages.

The movie dares to go into this material a little more seriously and cohesively than is usually the case in an Allen film. *Annie Hall* is a comedy, yes, and there are moments in it as funny as anything Woody has done, but the movie represents a growth on Allen's part. From a filmmaker who would do anything for a laugh, whose primary mission seemed to be to get through the next five minutes, Allen has developed in *Sleeper*, *Love and Death*, and this film into a much more thoughtful and (is it possible?) more mature director.

Maybe that's why *Annie Hall* is called a "nervous romance": because Allen himself is a little nervous about this frankly nostalgic, romantic, and sentimental material. He throws in a few gags (like the hilarious walk-on by Marshall McLuhan) almost to reassure his old fans that all's well at the laugh works. But he wants to do a lot more this time than just keep us laughing. By looking into some of his own relationships, some of his own patterns, he wants to examine how a personality works.

And so there are two Woody Allens here: Our old pal the original Woody, who's given to making asides directly into the camera, and a new Allen who creates Alvy Singer in his own image and then allows him to behave consistently, even sometimes at the cost of laughs. It's this new Woody who has the nervous romance, the complicated relationship with the would-be nightclub singer Annie Hall (played by Diane Keaton with an interesting mixture of maternal care, genuine love, and absolute craziness).

At the end of the affair, we've learned only two things for certain: That enduring relationships are very likely impossible in this time and place (i.e., New York City during Woody Allen's lifetime), and that life without the search for relationships is unthinkable. In the movie, Woody quotes Groucho Marx's statement that he'd never belong to any club that would accept someone like him as a member. Then Allen muses that maybe

he should never get into a relationship in which one of the partners is himself. Tricky, isn't it? And in *Annie Hall* he makes it very funny, and sad, and tricky indeed.

Any Which Way You Can ★ ★
PG, 116 m., 1980

Clint Eastwood (Philo Beddoe), Sondra Locke (Lynne), Geoffrey Lewis (Orville), William Smith (Jack Wilson), Harry Guardino (James Beekman), Ruth Gordon (Ma). Directed by Buddy Van Horn and produced by Fritz Manes. Screenplay by Stanford Sherman.

Clint Eastwood's *Any Which Way You Can* is not a very good movie, but it's hard not to feel a grudging affection for it. Where else, in the space of 116 minutes, can you find a country and western road picture with two fights, a bald motorcycle gang, the Mafia, a love story, a pickup truck, a tow truck, Fats Domino, a foul-mouthed octogenarian, an oversexed orangutan, and a contest for the bare-knuckle championship of the world?

The movie seems designed as a free-association exercise involving all of the above elements, in no particular order. That gives it a certain clarity of form. It opens, for example, with a bare-knuckle fight between Eastwood and someone else. (Who else? Doesn't matter). While Eastwood is slugging it out, his highly intelligent orangutan, Clyde, is relieving himself in the front seat of a state police car. And somehow we know—never mind how, we just *know*—that one of the recurring subjects of this movie is going to be orangutan crap in squad cars. We are correct. It's that kind of movie.

After seeing the big fight, Eastwood returns to his home, which seems to be an Okie hovel somewhere in a large Western state. He still lives with Ma, played by Ruth Gordon as a cross between Ma Kettle and Ma Barker. Clint and his partner, Orville Boggs, spend all day hard at work banging on things with wrenches. Occasionally Clyde amuses himself by ripping apart old Mercurys with his bare hands. Then the Mafia decides to set up a bare-knuckle fight between Eastwood and the defending Eastern champion, a guy named Jack Wilson.

It was to my immense delight that I immediately recognized the actor playing Jack

Wilson. He is William (Big Bill) Smith, who played a lot of motorcycle gang leaders in films of the late 1960s, and still looks as fearsome as ever. He and Eastwood meet while out jogging one morning, and then he falls off a cliff and is rescued by Eastwood, after which he beats up a lot of guys who insult Eastwood's girlfriend in a bar. All in a day's work.

The girlfriend is played by Sondra Locke, who was also in *Every Which Way But Loose*, the prequel to the present film. You gotta give Eastwood and Locke credit. Unlike Burt Reynolds and Sally Field, who spent the first half of *Smokey and the Bandit II* holding a deep, interpersonal philosophical argument about the issues raised by their relationship in *Smokey and the Bandit*, Eastwood and Locke don't agonize over their reunion. Two minutes after their meeting in a country and western bar, Locke is being consoled by Eastwood's orangutan. Ten minutes later, they're starting a riot at the YWCA. It's that kind of movie.

Anyway, the Mafia kidnaps Sondra Locke in order to force Eastwood to fight. Then Big Bill Smith and Eastwood wipe out the Mafia, but decide to fight anyway. It is some fight. It's one of those brawls where everytime somebody gets hit on the chin, it sounds like they're beating the hell out of a Naugahyde sofa with a Ping-Pong paddle. If we had any slight lingering doubts that this was a Clint Eastwood movie, they are dispelled when Eastwood breaks his right arm during the fight, gets up off the floor and growls, "It's not over yet."

Apocalypse Now ★ ★ ★ ★
R, 139 m., 1979

Marlon Brando (Colonel Kurtz), Robert Duvall (Lieutenant Colonel Kilgore), Martin Sheen (Captain Willard), Frederic Forrest (Chef), Albert Hall (Chief), Sam Bottoms (Lance), Larry Fishburne (Clean), Dennis Hopper (Photographer). Directed and produced by Francis Ford Coppola. Screenplay by John Milius and Coppola.

In his book *The Films of My Life*, the French director François Truffaut makes a curious statement. He used to believe, he says, that a successful film had to simultaneously express "an idea of the world and an idea of cinema." But now, he writes: "I demand that a film express either the joy of making cinema or the agony of making cinema. I am not at all interested in anything in between; I am not interested in all those films that do not pulse."

It may seem strange to begin a review of Francis Coppola's *Apocalypse Now* with those words, but consider them for a moment and they apply perfectly to this sprawling film. The critics who have rejected Coppola's film have mostly done so on Truffaut's earlier grounds: They have arguments with the ideas about the world and the war in *Apocalypse Now*, or they disagree with the very idea of a film that cost $31 million to make and was then carted all over the world by a filmmaker *still* uncertain whether he had the right ending.

That "other" film on the screen—the one we debate because of its ideas, not its images—is the one that caused so much controversy about *Apocalypse Now*. We have all read that Coppola took as his inspiration the Joseph Conrad novel *Heart of Darkness*, and that he turned Conrad's journey up the Congo into a metaphor for another journey up a jungle river, into the heart of the Vietnam War. We've all read Coppola's grandiose statements (the most memorable: "This isn't a film about Vietnam. This film *is* Vietnam."). We've heard that Marlon Brando was paid $1 million for his closing scenes, and that Coppola gambled his personal fortune to finish the film, and, heaven help us, we've even read a journal by the director's wife in which she discloses her husband's ravings and infidelities.

But all such considerations are far from the reasons why *Apocalypse Now* is a good and important film—a masterpiece, I believe. Now, when Coppola's budget and his problems have long been forgotten, *Apocalypse* stands, I think, as a grand and grave and insanely inspired gesture of filmmaking—of moments that are operatic in their style and scope, and of other moments so silent we can almost hear the director thinking to himself.

I should at this moment make a confession: I am not particularly interested in the "ideas" in Coppola's film. Critics of *Apocalypse* have said that Coppola was foolish to translate *Heart of Darkness*, that Conrad's vision had nothing to do with Vietnam, and that Coppola was simply borrowing Conrad's cultural respectability to give a gloss to his own disorganized ideas. The same objection was made to the hiring of Brando: Coppola was hoping, according to this version, that the presence of Brando as an icon would distract us from the emptiness of what he's given to say.

Such criticisms are made by people who indeed are plumbing *Apocalypse Now* for its ideas, and who are as misguided as the veteran Vietnam correspondents who breathlessly reported that *The Deer Hunter* was not "accurate." What idea or philosophy could we expect to find in *Apocalypse Now*—and what good would it really do, at this point after the Vietnam tragedy, if Brando's closing speeches *did* have the "answers"? Like all great works of art about war, *Apocalypse Now* essentially contains only one idea or message, the not-especially-enlightening observation that war is hell. We do not see Coppola's movie for that insight—something Coppola, but not some of his critics, knows well.

Coppola also well knows (and demonstrated in the *Godfather* films) that movies aren't especially good at dealing with abstract ideas—for those you'd be better off turning to the written word—but they *are* superb for presenting moods and feelings, the look of a battle, the expression on a face, the mood of a country. *Apocalypse Now* achieves greatness not by analyzing our "experience in Vietnam," but by re-creating, in characters and images, something of that experience.

An example: The scene in which Robert Duvall, as a crazed lieutenant colonel, leads his troops in a helicopter assault on a village is, quite simply, the best movie battle scene ever filmed. It's simultaneously numbing, depressing, and exhilarating: As the rockets jar from the helicopters and spring through the air, we're elated like kids for a half-second, until the reality of the consequences sinks in. Another wrenching scene—in which the crew of Martin Sheen's U.S. Army gunboat massacres the Vietnamese peasants in a small boat—happens with such sudden, fierce, senseless violence that it forces us to understand for the first time how such things could happen.

Coppola's *Apocalypse Now* is filled with moments like that, and the narrative device of the journey upriver is as convenient for him as it was for Conrad. That's really why he uses it, and not because of literary cross-references for graduate students to catalog. He takes the journey, strings episodes along it, leads us at last to Brando's awesome, stinking hideaway . . . and then finds, so we've all heard, that he doesn't have an ending. Well, Coppola *doesn't* have an ending, if we or he expected the closing scenes to pull everything together and make sense of it. Nobody should have been surprised. *Apocalypse Now* doesn't tell any kind of a conventional story, doesn't have a thought-out message for us about Vietnam, has no answers, and thus needs no ending. The way the film ends now, with Brando's fuzzy, brooding monologues and the final violence, feels much more satisfactory than any conventional ending possibly could.

What's great in the film, and what will make it live for many years and speak to many audiences, is what Coppola achieves on the levels Truffaut was discussing: the moments of agony and joy in making cinema. Some of those moments come at the same time; remember again the helicopter assault and its unsettlng juxtaposition of horror and exhilaration. Remember the weird beauty of the massed helicopters lifting over the trees in the long shot, and the insane power of Wagner's music, played loudly during the attack, and you feel what Coppola was getting at: Those moments as common in life as art, when the whole huge grand mystery of the world, so terrible, so beautiful, seems to hang in the balance.

The Apprenticeship of Duddy Kravitz
★ ★ ★
PG, 121 m., 1974

Richard Dreyfuss (Duddy), Micheline Lanctot (Yvette), Jack Warden (Max), Randy Quaid (Virgil), Joseph Wiseman (Uncle Benjy), Denholm Elliott (Friar), Henry Ramar (Dingleman), Joe Silver (Farber). Directed by Ted Kotcheff and produced by John Kemeny. Screenplay by Mordecai Richler.

Duddy Kravitz has grown up hearing about the Boy Wonder. The Wonder, real name Dingleman, started out in life picking up bus transfers from the street and selling them for three cents. When he had a quarter, he got into a gin game and ran it up to ten dollars. With that as a nest egg, the Wonder parlayed a string of poker games and fly-by-night investments into a fortune, and returned home (according to legend) in a chauffeured limousine and with his own string of racehorses. And all from a handful of lousy three-cent bus transfers!

Duddy thinks he can do better than that. When we meet him, he's a sixteen-year-old Jewish kid from Montreal whose mother is dead and whose father drives a cab and does a little part-time pimping to send the older son through medical school. The Boy Wonder was a boyhood friend of Duddy's father; the story, whether true or not, has been told so many times that Duddy naturally assumes he will be a millionaire, or something, by the time he's twenty. And he's right. By the time he's twenty, he's something.

The Apprenticeship of Duddy Kravitz is a movie that somehow manages to be breakneck and curiously touching at the same time. It's a story of ambition and greed, with a hero that will stop at almost nothing (by the movie's end, Duddy has succeeded in alienating the girl who loves him, has lost all his friends, has brought his grandfather to despair, and has paralyzed his most loyal employee). And yet we like Duddy, with a kind of exasperation, because we get some notion of the hungers that drive him, and because nobody suffers at his hands more than he does himself.

The movie's a sort of Canadian *What Makes Sammy Run?* Duddy Kravitz even gets into the movie business, as Budd Schulberg's hero did. But Duddy doesn't exactly get to Hollywood. He runs across a blacklisted, alcoholic American director, in exile from Hollywood during the dark days of McCarthyism (the film is set somewhere in the late 1940s and early 1950s).

Duddy forms a movie production company (Dudley Kane Productions, inevitably), hires the director, and produces films of bar mitzvahs. Their first production, shown in its entirety, is a lunatic montage of off-the-wall images that have no perceptible relevance to the bar mitzvah itself; the director arguably got himself drunk and spliced together stock footage (after the opening temple scenes played over Beethoven's

Fifth). But Duddy's client is (somewhat dazedly) pleased by the film, and Duddy is off and running.

His ambition is to own land. "A man without land is a nobody," his grandfather has told him. During a summer spent as a waiter at a resort, he finds a beautiful, half-hidden lake. He determines to buy it and develop it, and his dream is shared by a plain-pretty French Canadian girl who is a maid at the resort. They fall into love. Or, more precisely, she loves him and Duddy loves a prospect of his future life which includes her, slightly to one side of center. The ways in which he finally succeeds in driving her away, the ways in which he makes himself miserable before he is even twenty-one, are played against his own series of get-rich-fast schemes (during which he not only succeeds in meeting the real Boy Wonder but even unknowingly smuggles heroin over the border for him).

The movie is based on a Mordecai Richler novel and was the most popular film to have come out of Canada through the early seventies (that country which, in cinema as in other things, remains more foreign for many Americans than any place in Europe). It was filmed on location with a great sense of life and energy and with details seen as Duddy sees them. It's populated with an incredible gallery of character roles (I've only suggested a few of them). It's a little too sloppy, and occasionally too obvious, to qualify as a great film, but it's a good and entertaining one, and it leaves us thinking that Duddy Kravitz might amount to something after all, should he ever grow up.

Arthur ★ ★ ★ ½
PG, 97 m., 1981

Dudley Moore (Arthur Bach), Liza Minelli (Linda Marolla), John Gielgud (Hobson), Geraldine Fitzgerald (Martha Bach), Jill Eikenberry (Susan), Stephen Elliott (Burt), Tod Ross (Bitterman), Barney Martin (Linda's Father). Directed and written by Steve Gordon. Produced by Robert Greenhut.

Only someone with a heart of stone could fail to love a drunk like Arthur Bach, who spends his wasted days in a poignant search for someone who will love him, will care for him, will inflame his passions, and soothe his pain, and who, most of all, will laugh at his one-liners. Arthur is such a servant of humanity that he even dedicates himself to thinking up new one-liners and holding them in reserve, lest he be unprepared if someone walks into his life and needs a laugh, quick.

Arthur, played by Dudley Moore, is the alcoholic hero of *Arthur*, a comedy about a man who is worth $750 million and who would never think of trying to buy anyone's love with his money. Arthur is like the woman in the poem by Yeats, who spent her days in innocent good will, and her nights in argument, till her voice grew shrill. Arthur, God love him, is a drunk. He slips into his bath of a morning, and his butler brings him a martini. After he completes his bath, Arthur sets about the day's business, which consists of staying drunk, and being driven about Manhattan in a limousine in his endless quest for love.

Now the problems with searching for love while you are drunk are many. They include (a) no one will want to love you while you are drunk, (b) you are not at your best while you are drunk, so they won't know what they're missing, (c) you may be too drunk to notice it if someone does finally fall in love with you, and (d) if you survive all of these pitfalls, you will nevertheless wake up hung over, and scientific studies prove that hangovers dissolve love. All of these things having been said, Arthur, against all odds, does find love. He finds it in the person of Linda (Liza Minelli), a smart cookie who doesn't care about his money but is overwhelmed by the dimensions of his needs. Arthur would like to marry Linda. But his billionaire father insists that he marry a perfectly boring WASP (Jill Eikenberry) whose idea of a good holiday is probably the January white sales.

Arthur turns for help to his loyal butler, Hobson, who is played by John Gielgud with an understated elegance and a naughty tongue. Hobson is dying. But Hobson wishes to see Arthur prevail, for once, against Arthur's father, a sadistic puppet-master. So Hobson subtly manipulates the situation so that the lovers are thrown together at the party announcing Arthur's engagement to the WASP. That inspires a rupture within the family, and a very drunken odyssey by Arthur, who wants to press $100,000 upon Linda, and visits her at home. When Linda turns him down, her father (Barney Martin) becomes a grown man who sheds tears, creating perhaps the funniest moment in the movie.

Dudley Moore became a star, of course, with *10*, playing a man who became obsessed with Bo Derek, and who could blame him? In *Arthur*, he makes his bid for world-class status as a comic character actor. He brings a wonderful intensity to scenes like the one near the beginning of the film where he has invited a hooker to dinner at the Plaza and then forgotten who she is, and what she is, or why he is with her. It is marvelous to see him try to focus his attention, which he seems to believe is all concentrated in his eyebrow muscles.

Apart from Moore, the treasure of *Arthur* is in its many supporting performances, especially Gielgud's, although everyone in this movie has great moments. You might be tempted to think that *Arthur* would be a bore, because it is about a drunk who is always trying to tell you stories. You would be right if *Arthur* were a party and you were attending it. But *Arthur* is a movie. And so its drunk, unlike real drunks, is more entertaining, more witty, more human, and more poignant than you are. He embodies, in fact, all the wonderful human qualities that drunks fondly, mistakenly believe the booze brings out in them.

At Close Range ★ ★ ★ ½
R, 115 m., 1986 ✔

Sean Penn (Brad, Jr.), Christopher Walken (Brad, Sr.), Mary Stuart Masterson (Terry), Christopher Penn (Tommy), Millie Perkins (Julie), Eileen Ryan (Grandma). Directed by James Foley and produced by Elliott Lewitt and Don Guest. Screenplay by Nicholas Kazan.

Here is a spare, violent, unforgiving story of a boy's need for a father who does not love him and who would, if necessary, murder him. It is also a story with passages of love and adventure and cheerfulness, as a teenager grows up in the hills of rural Pennsylvania. The way that the two sides of the story grow together creates a tragedy that reminds me of myth, of the ancient stories of children betrayed by their parents, and yet *At Close*

Range is based on a true story. It happened in 1978.

The movie stars Sean Penn, probably the best of the younger actors, as Bradford Whitewood, Jr. He lives with his divorced mother and grandmother and half-brother in a setting of shabby poverty, nonstop TV watching, and boredom. Once in a while, his father, Brad Senior, appears out of nowhere and throws money on the table. Then Brad Senior drives away in a fast car with a pretty girl. The kid would like a taste of his father's life. It looks a lot better than what he has.

The father is played by Christopher Walken, in one of the great hateful performances of recent years. Walken is a strange actor, hard to pin down, but when he is given the right role (as he is here, and in *Dead Zone* and *The Deer Hunter*), there is nobody to touch him for his chilling ability to move between easy charm and vile evil. In the movie, he's the leader of a gang of professional thieves who have recently been specializing in stealing tractors. He likes to play the big shot, and in a way he enjoys the fact that his young son has started to idolize him.

Penn, as Brad Junior, isn't really criminal material, but he's a misfit and an outcast and absolutely nothing is happening for him in his own life. He drifts into the orbit of his father, looking for love but also looking for action. He's the leader of a young gang of his own, and his father assigns the kids to a couple of easy jobs—getting them ready for the big time. But when the big time turns dangerous, and it looks as if the gang might be busted, the Walken character is absolutely prepared to save his own skin, even at the cost of betraying his own child.

At Close Range is not a pleasant movie. Few recent films have painted such a bleak picture of human nature. The Walken character is pure evil, wrapped in easy charm, and most of the other characters in the film are weak, or deprived, or lacking in the ability to see beyond their own immediate situation. That's especially true of Brad Junior's mother (Millie Perkins) and grandmother (Eileen Ryan), who sit endlessly around the house, their eyes straying away from every conversation, toward the TV set. Only Brad Junior and his local girlfriend (Mary Stuart Masterson) have a chance of breaking free,

and their love affair is on a collision course with Brad Senior.

Because this film is violent and cruel and very sad, why would you want to see it? For a couple of reasons, perhaps. One might be to watch two great actors, Penn and Walken, at the top of their forms, in roles that give them a lot to work with. Another might be to witness some of the dynamics of a criminal society, some of the forces that push criminals farther than they intend to go. It's the same dynamic you could see in the great crime film *In Cold Blood* (1967)—seemingly ordinary people whose moral sense is missing, and who drift into actions so evil that perhaps even they are appalled.

Autumn Sonata ★ ★ ★ ★
PG, 97 m., 1978

Ingrid Bergman (Charlotte), Liv Ullmann (Eva), Lena Nyman (Helena), Halvor Bjork (Viktor), Georg Lokkeberg (Leonardo), Knut Wigert (The Professor). Directed by Ingmar Bergman. Screenplay by Bergman.

Ingrid Bergman was certainly one of the most beautiful women to ever appear in a film, but that is not the source of her mysterious appeal. There is something there, in that voice and those eyes and in the way her mouth thinks words before she says them, that is, quite simply, unduplicated in the movies. It took Ingmar Bergman thirty-five years to finally cast her in one of his films, and then, in her fortieth year as an actress, Ingrid Bergman called *Autumn Sonata* her last film. Sweden's two most important film artists finally worked together.

The movie is a historic event, taking us back to so many different areas of our memories. We remember Ingrid Bergman from some of the basic cinematic artifacts of all time, movies like *Casablanca* and *Notorious*. But we've never seen her really pushed, really tested, by a director whose commitment to honesty is nothing short of merciless.

Ingmar Bergman didn't cast her for reasons of nostalgia, or sentiment: He cast her because he had an idea for a role she could brilliantly contain and that would contain her, and in *Autumn Sonata* she gives nothing less than the performance of her lifetime. We can only be quietly grateful that she performs opposite Liv Ullmann, who is herself good enough to meet her on the same very high level.

They play mother and daughter. The mother is an internationally famous pianist (and we remember Ingrid Bergman's first great success, as the pianist in *Intermezzo*). She has not seen her daughter for seven years. She's too busy and always traveling and booked up almost every night of the week . . . and, not incidentally, terrified of confronting her daughter.

There are, in fact, two daughters: The one played by Ullmann, who is serious and introspective and filled with guilt and blame and love, and then the other daughter (Lena Nyman), who lives with her, and who suffers from a degenerative nerve disease. The mother's solution to this daughter's illness was to place her in a "home;" Ullmann has taken her out of the institution and brought her home to live with her.

On the morning when the mother arrives for her long-delayed visit, she has no idea that the sick daughter will be there. Her response, on learning that her other daughter is upstairs, is dismay. She's never been able to deal with the illness—but, then, she's never been able to deal at all with the fact of being a mother. She doesn't merely reject the responsibility; she flees from it.

Autumn Sonata then gives us a sort of long day's journey into night in which the pleasantries of the opening hours give way to deeper and deeper terrors and guilts, accusations and renunciations, cries and whispers. And Ingmar Bergman, standing apart from this material and regarding it with clarity and detachment, refuses to find any solutions. There are none, I suppose. A lesser filmmaker would have resolved everything at the end in some sort of neat Freudian bookkeeping, but Bergman finds in his story only two people, each demanding love from the other, each doomed by the past to fall just short of the ability to love.

This is excruciatingly difficult material. Ingrid Bergman and Liv Ullmann confront it with a courage and skill that is astonishing. We've always known that Liv Ullmann was a great actress (that is one of the givens of film in the past two decades), and we've known, too, that Ingrid Bergman was a great movie star. But how important that in her sixties,

acting in her native language for the first time in four decades, working with one of the supreme film directors, Bergman was able to use not only her star qualities but also every last measure of her artistry and her humanity. It is not just that *Autumn Sonata* was Ingrid Bergman's last film. It's that she knew she had to make it before she died.

Baby . . . The Secret of the Lost Legend ★
PG, 95 m., 1985

William Katt (George), Sean Young (Susan), Patrick McGoohan (Dr. Kiviat), Julian Fellowes (Nigel), Kyalo Mativo (Caphu), Olu Jacobs (The Colonel). Directed by B.W.L. Norton and produced by Jonathan T. Taplin. Screenplay by Clifford and Ellen Green.

The death of Sinbad, the elderly gorilla at the Lincoln Park Zoo, was a reminder of how we like to sentimentalize animals, turning them into images of cute, incomplete human beings, instead of loving them for their differences from us. *Baby*, a comedy about an infant brontosaurus, is another example, a dreary one, of the glory of nature being turned into a cliché of man. Imagine that somewhere in the heart of Africa, a colony of dinosaurs still survives. Wouldn't it be a great wonder to actually see one of them, living evidence of the world of one hundred million years ago? I'd think I'd rather see a brontosaurus than see a man walk on the moon, because I am less amazed by technology than by the wonders that life has provided on its own.

If *Baby* has shared that sense of wonder, it might have been a really special movie. The raw materials were in place: the special effects in this movie provide surprisingly believable dinosaurs, and if the screenplay had been equally believable, they might have had something here. Instead, *Baby* turns out to be a real no-brainer. The movie even blows the one moment you'd assume couldn't fail—the first sighting of a brontosaurus. Instead of a moment of quiet awe, the movie gives us the gee-whiz approach of a *Godzilla* remake. But then maybe that's not surprising: This movie has no serious ambition at all, and is content to surround its wonderful creatures with a plot that even the kids have seen too many times before.

Here you have a family of dinosaurs, and the filmmakers use it as a prop in a movie about good guys and bad guys. The good guys are a couple of Peace Corps volunteers (William Katt and Sean Young), who trek off into the wilderness to find and protect the creatures. The bad guys include a greedy scientist (Patrick McGoohan), his bitchy sidekick (Julian Fellowes), and a trigger-happy African mercenary (Olu Jacobs). The bad guys actually drug the female brontosaurus, and fly around in a helicopter firing machine guns at the male. Why? To rid the jungle of all those bothersome brontosauri?

Meanwhile, the husband-and-wife team finds a baby brontosaurus and tries to drag the cute little thing back to civilization and safety. Their mission is accompanied by a great many manufactured discussions; the wife is a feminist, and we learn in the movie that feminists feel strongly on the issue of Brontosaurus Rights. The whole story is trivial. The scenes that work best are the ones where the little dinosaur acts like a baby, and playfully nuzzles the people or carelessly uproots their tent. But is this why we need a brontosaurus? So it can do its clever puppy imitation? Wasn't there anybody who saw this story idea as more than a cheap gimmick? The movie is subtitled *The Secret of the Lost Legend,* and that sounds like an exciting movie they might want to make sometime.

Baby, It's You ★ ★ ★
R, 105 m., 1983 ✓

Rosanna Arquette (Jill), Vincent Spano (Sheik), Joanna Merlin (Mrs. Rosen), Jack Davidson (Dr. Rosen). Directed by John Sayles and produced by Griffin Dunne and Amy Robinson. Screenplay by Sayles.

Rosanna Arquette has a way about her. She's a natural actress, and by that I don't mean she was born talented (although perhaps she was), but that she is able to appear onscreen with such an unaffected natural quality that I feel as if I'm looking past the script and direction and actually experiencing the life of her character. That's the feeling I got during *Baby, It's You,* a sometimes very good, sometimes disappointingly uneven movie that she carries from beginning to end. Even when her scenes aren't working, her char-

acter is, and we're getting to know this young woman she plays, this Jill Rosen, who turns from an uncommonly engaging high school student to a scared-stiff college freshman.

The movie is by John Sayles, who has built a career for himself out of the carefully observed events that make up ordinary lives. His first film was *Return of the Secaucus Seven,* about some thirty-fiveish survivors of the 1960s. Then he made *Lianna,* about a thirty-fiveish faculty wife who discovers, with fear and some anticipation, that she is a lesbian. Now here is Jill Rosen, a high school student from the 1960s who could, we suspect, easily grow up to be any of the women in Sayles's first two films.

Jill is smart and pretty, especially when she smiles. Her brains and her smile are only the half of it. She's also got a personal style. She has this way of letting you know she's listening, even when she seems to be ignoring you. A way of caring for you, even when she's mad at you. You get the feeling this is a woman whose love would be a very important thing for you to count on. And that's certainly the opinion of the Sheik (Vincent Spano), a semi-greaser who is consumed by his desire to be exactly like Frank Sinatra. The Sheik and (actually) a lot of this movie seem to belong more to the fifties than the sixties—but never mind. Here is a kid who's a sharp dresser, has a lot of apparent self-confidence, and doesn't mind that he stands out like a sore thumb with his brazen ways and his Sinatra wardrobe. He's a rebel with ambitions. Jill loves him, but when she leaves Trenton, New Jersey, and enters the uncertain world of Sarah Lawrence College, the Sheik doesn't fit in.

Baby, It's You does two things with this material. First, it remembers it accurately, right down to the irritating mannerisms of preppy college boys with too much unearned self-confidence. Then, it uses it as a meditation on growing up—which means learning to listen to your heart as well as to your ambitions. The movie works best in its high school segments, and the opening hour is wonderful. Then the infuriating stuff begins, when this movie that has been so surefooted loses its way in the college scenes, and allows us to wonder at times what we're supposed to be thinking. Rosanna Arquette is equally good, however, in the good parts and the disappointing ones.

Bachelor Party ★ ★ ★
R, 100 m., 1984

Tom Hanks (Rick), Tawny Kitaen (Debbie), Adrian Zmed (Jay), George Grizzard (Mr. Thompson), Robert Prescott (Cole). Directed by Neal Israel and produced by Ron Moler and Bob Israel. Screenplay by Neal Israel and Pat Proft.

Bachelor Party is 1984's version of the Annual Summer Food Fight Movie. With a movie like this, it doesn't really matter whether anyone actually throws mashed potatoes across the room; what matters is whether the movie is faithful to the spirit of Blotto Bluto in *Animal House* when he yelled "Food fight!" and the madness began. The story this time is about this guy who decides to get married, and his friends decide to throw him a bachelor party. That's about it. The first half of the movie sets up the party and the second half of the movie is the party. Both halves of the movie are raunchy, chaotic, and quite shameless in aiming at the lowest possible level of taste, of course.

The bachelor in the movie is played by Tom Hanks. He was the guy from *Splash* who the mermaid fell in love with. I didn't think he was all that terrific in *Splash*—I thought he was miscast, and they should have gone for somebody who was less of a conventional leading man—but in *Bachelor Party* he's a lot more funny and I enjoyed the performance. He plays the kind of guy who goes over to his fiancée's house for dinner and drops table scraps onto the floor in *case* they have a dog. He has a great one-liner when he has to introduce himself to his fiancée's nerdy ex-boyfriend: "The name is Bond. James Bond." During the chaos of the party itself, one of his primary roles is simply to direct traffic.

The idea during the party, I think, is to approximate the spirit of one of those Jack Davis drawings in *Mad* magazine, where dozens of people are running around like crazy, and down in the corners you can see strange little figures doing inexplicable things. Most of the gags depend on varieties of public embarrassment and some of them are pretty funny, especially when the women

decide to have their revenge by visiting a male go-go bar.

Is *Bachelor Party* a great movie? No. Why do I give it three stars? Because it honors the tradition of a reliable movie genre, because it tries hard, and because when it is funny, it is very funny. It is relatively easy to make a comedy that is totally devoid of humor (cf. my review of *Cannonball Run II*), but not all that easy to make a movie containing some genuine laughs. *Bachelor Party* has some great moments and qualifies as a raunchy, scummy, grungy Blotto Bluto memorial.

Back Roads ★ ★
R, 94 m., 1981

Sally Field (Amy Post), Tommy Lee Jones (Elmore Pratt), David Keith (Mason), Miriam Colon (Angel). Directed by Martin Ritt and produced by Ronald Shedlo. Screenplay by Gary Devore.

What we have here is a movie about a Good Ol' Girl, made with the Good Ol' Boy formula. The Good Ol' Person gets in trouble with the law, hitches up with another drifter of the opposite sex, and hits the road for California. After a series of adventures involving weird people and tight scrapes, the two persons learn to trust each other and have more confidence in themselves. The movie ends on a note of moral triumph: In this case, for example, the heroes find the courage to keep *on* heading for California.

If I'm somewhat muted in my enthusiasm for *Back Roads*, it's because the movie is so relentlessly willing to follow the Road Movie formula. One of the most predictable things about movies such as this is that the filmmakers remain under the delusion that *this* time, they can find an original approach by populating their formula screenplay with bizarre, eccentric, colorful characters. This approach might work, if they didn't always discover the same colorful characters that a dozen other movies have already discovered. In *Back Roads*, for example, we are expected to be newly astonished by a tough-talking Latino madam, a hard-drinking fight promoter, a bullet-headed evil bruiser, and a homesick sailor. The movie's two leads also are less than amazingly original: Sally Field plays a hooker with a heart of gold, and

Tommy Lee Jones is a corrupt ex-prize-fighter with one good fight left in him.

How could they take this material and make it *really* original? Maybe by refusing to be seduced by the screenwriter's stock Hollywood "originality" and probing more deeply into the real human lives of the characters. The people in *Back Roads* are so heavily laden with schtick that they never have a chance to develop personalities. Take, for example, the hooker. Field plays the part with enormous appeal and gives a performance that cannot be faulted. But the character she's been given to play is a complete fiction. We are expected to believe the usual clichés about how she got to be a hooker: She was taken advantage of by a sailor; she had to give her little boy up for adoption; she weeps every time she sees the little tyke walking into school; she has to prostitute herself in order to eat. She meets another street person (Jones); he sleeps with her and doesn't pay her; they team up together and hitch to the coast.

This is all out of the Damon Runyon school of romantic realism. Think how much more interesting this movie would have been if the screenplay had played tough and uncompromising with the characters. Let's face it: The Field character is a low-life street hooker who's over the hill. In real life, she would undoubtedly be a drug addict or alcoholic. She'd hustle because she couldn't get her act together for two consecutive hours of straight work. She would not trust anybody and possibly would be so emotionally and physically crippled by her habit that a trip to California would kill her.

Instead, the movie's lovebirds hitchhike for days on end. They sleep in the open, they get soaked in ditches, they rob cops and customers, and all the time we're expected to believe that it is an act of growth and courage for them to keep heading west. Actually, it's just another self-deceiving escape, and if the movie had been willing to deal honestly with the plight of its characters, it wouldn't need to be cluttered up with eccentrics and hearts of gold.

Back to School ★ ★ ★
PG-13, 94 m., 1986 ✔

Rodney Dangerfield (Thornton Melon), Sally Kellerman (Diane), Burt Young (Lou), Keith Gordon (Jason Melon), Robert Downey, Jr. (Derek), Paxton Whitehead (Philip Barbay), M. Emmet Walsh (Coach Turnbull), Ned Beatty (Dean Martin). Directed by Alan Metter and produced by Chuck Russell. Screenplay by Steven Kampmann, Will Porter, Peter Torokvei, and Harold Ramis.

Rodney Dangerfield has been giving interviews lately on the subject of his loneliness. Why, he asks, should a guy like him, who is able to fill up giant concert halls and pull down millions of dollars a year, be condemned to go through life without the love of a woman? This is not the sort of thing you want to hear from a comedian. You want him to be zany and madcap, to stand astride the problems of the mundane world and laugh at them.

Yet in Dangerfield, there has always been something else in addition to the comedian. This is a man who has failed at everything, even comedy. Rodney Dangerfield is his third name in show business; he flopped under two earlier names as well as his real name. Who is really at home inside that red, sweating face and that knowing leer?

The most interesting thing about *Back to School*, which is otherwise a pleasant but routine comedy, is the puzzle of Rodney Dangerfield. Here is a man who reminds us of some of the great comedians of the early days of the talkies—of Groucho Marx and W.C. Fields—because, like them, he projects a certain mystery. Marx and Fields were never just being funny. There was the sense that they were getting even for hurts so deep that all they could do was laugh about them. It's the same with Dangerfield.

He plays Thornton Melon, a millionaire clothing manufacturer who owns a chain of Tall & Fat Shops. His father was a penniless Italian immigrant who took him into the family business as a child. He never had the opportunity to get an education. Now he is rich, his second wife is an obnoxious bauble, and all he cares about is his son, Jason, who is a college student.

Dangerfield fondly believes Jason is a fraternity member and a star of the diving team. But actually Jason is the campus wimp, the team's towel boy, and, naturally, he gets no respect. When Dangerfield discovers the truth, he decides to enroll in the university as a freshman so he can teach his son the ropes. Of course, there's resistance to this plan, but not after Dangerfield endows the Melon School of Business Administration.

The campus characters are predictable, but well-cast. Sally Kellerman is the sexy English teacher, Paxton Whitehead is the Anglophile business teacher, and Ned Beatty is the venal administrator, always referred to as Dean Martin. Dangerfield takes the "drinks for everybody" approach, throwing his money around and hiring expensive coaches to help him pass his classes. Kurt Vonnegut, Jr., turns up as a paid expert on his own work. Meanwhile, young Jason learns how to be a big man on campus.

This is exactly the sort of plot Marx or Fields could have appeared in. Dangerfield brings it something they might also have brought along: a certain pathos. Beneath his loud manner, under his studied obnoxiousness, there is a real need. He laughs that he may not cry.

Dangerfield has been looking for a movie style for a couple of years now. The problem with his last movie, *Easy Money*, was that he wanted to seem like a basically nice guy. He isn't a nice guy. Or at least, when he is nice, there is nothing simple about his niceness. The interesting achievement of *Back to School* is its ability to make contradictions part of the character.

Back to the Future ★ ★ ★ ½
PG, 116 m., 1985

Michael J. Fox (Marty McFly), Christopher Lloyd (Dr. Brown), Lea Thompson (Lorraine Baines), Crispin Glover (George McFly), Thomas F. Wilson (Biff Tannen), Claudia Wells (Jennifer Parker). Directed by Robert Zemeckis and produced by Bob Gale and Neil Canton. Screenplay by Zemeckis and Gale.

One of the things all teen-agers believe is that their parents were never teen-agers. Their parents were, perhaps, children once. They are undeniably adults now. But how could they have ever been teen-agers, and yet not understand their own children? This view is actually rather optimistic, since it assumes that you can learn something about teen-agers by being one. But *Back to the Future* is even more hopeful: It argues that you can travel back in time to the years when your parents were teen-agers and straighten them out right at the moment when they need help the most.

The movie begins in the present, with a teen-ager named Marty (Michael J. Fox). His parents (let's face it) are hopeless nerds. Dad tells corny jokes and Mom guzzles vodka in the kitchen and the evening meal is like feeding time at the fun house. All that keeps Marty sane is his friendship with the nutty Dr. Brown (Christopher Lloyd), an inventor with glowing eyes and hair like a fright wig.

Brown believes he has discovered the secret of time travel, and one night in the deserted parking lot of the local shopping mall, he demonstrates his invention. In the long history of time travel movies, there has never been a time machine quite like Brown's, which resembles nothing so much as a customized DeLorean.

The gadget works, and then, after a series of surprises, Marty finds himself transported back thirty years in time, to the days when the shopping mall was a farmer's field (there's a nice gag when the farmer thinks the DeLorean, with its gull-wing doors, is a flying saucer). Marty wanders into town, still wearing his 1985 clothing, and the townsfolk look at his goose down jacket and ask him why he's wearing a life preserver.

One of the running gags in *Back to the Future* is the way the town has changed in thirty years (for example, the porno house of 1985 was playing a Ronald Reagan movie in 1955). But a lot of the differences run more deeply than that, as Marty discovers when he sits down at a lunch counter next to his dad— who is, of course, a teen-ager himself. Because the movie has so much fun with the paradoxes and predicaments of a kid meeting his own parents, I won't discuss the plot in any detail. I won't even get into the horrifying moment when Marty discovers his mother "has the hots" for him. The movie's surprises are one of its great pleasures.

Back to the Future was directed by Robert (*Romancing the Stone*) Zemeckis, who shows not only a fine comic touch but also some of the lighthearted humanism of a Frank Capra. The movie, in fact, resembles Capra's *It's a Wonderful Life* more than other, conventional time-travel movies. It's about a character who begins with one view of his life and reality, and is allowed, through magical intervention, to discover another. Steven Spielberg was the executive producer, and the movie's world view (smart kid in Yuppie suburb redefines reality for his parents) is part of the basic Spielberg approach. This time it comes with charm, brains, and a lot of laughter.

Bad Boys ★ ★ ★ ½
R, 123 m., 1983

Sean Penn (Mick O'Brien), Reni Santoni (Ramon Herrera), Esai Morales (Paco Moreno), Jim Moody (Gene Daniels), Eric Gurry (Horowitz), Clancy Brown (Viking Lofgren). Directed by Richard Rosenthal and produced by Robert Solo. Screenplay by Richard Di Lello.

Bad Boys tells the story of some tough Chicago street-gang kids who get in a lot of trouble, get sent to a juvenile correctional institution, and get in a lot more trouble once they're inside. Following the tradition governing such movies, the story eventually comes to a moral crossroad at which a bad boy has to decide whether to become a good man—and that's too bad, because until the movie turns predictable it is very, very good. The acting, the direction, and the sense of place in *Bad Boys* is so strong that the movie deserves more than an obligatory fight scene for its conclusion.

The movie stars Sean Penn as Mick O'Brien, a teen-age Irish-American hood and Esai Morales as Paco, a Latino hood. They are both tough, mean, anti-social kids; this movie doesn't sentimentalize street gangs. Their paths cross in connection with a drug deal that Paco is doing with a black gang. There's a misunderstanding, a sudden, shocking exchange of gunfire, and Paco's kid brother is dead. Mick killed him. Mick is sent to prison, and then Paco has his revenge by raping Mick's girlfriend (Ally Sheedy). Paco is caught and sent to the same prison where Mick is being held. Mick already has learned the ropes, and Paco learns them quickly: The prison guards preside sincerely but ineffectually over a reign of terror enforced by the toughest kids in the prison. Violence and sexual crimes are commonplace. The strongest survive. This situation is complicated, of course, by the fact that everyone in the prison immediately knows that Mick and Paco will have to fight to the death over the feud of honor.

And it's at precisely that moment, when the two kids are being set up for an eventual showdown, that *Bad Boys* begins to unwind. The first hour of this movie is so good it's scary; Penn and Morales and the supporting actors are completely convincing, and *Bad Boys* is the first movie I've seen in which the street gangs are not glamorized *(West Side Story)*, stylized *(The Warriors)*, or romanticized *(The Wanderers)*. We believe, watching *Bad Boys*, that we are observing an approximation of the real thing. The direction, by Richard Rosenthal, is sure-footed, confident, and fluid; we are in the hands of a fine director, even if he *did* make *Halloween II*. Sean Penn is mean and defiant in a real star performance, and the other kids in the prison include such inimitable characters as Horowitz (Eric Gurry), a bright kid who invents things and talks casually of his arson conviction; Viking (Clancy Brown), the hard but vulnerable boss of the prisoners; and Tweety (Robert Lee Rush), who rules at Viking's side.

These performances are good. That's why it's such a disappointment when the movie allows itself to become just another prison picture. Although the second half of the movie continues its close, convincing observations of everyday life in the youth prison, the story structure begins to feel programmed: We know we're heading for a big fight, we think we know who'll win—and what is this, anyway? They've *already* made *Rocky* three times. *Bad Boys* misses its chance at greatness, but it's saying something that this movie *had* a chance. It stands as one of those benchmark movies that we'll look back at for the talent it introduced. On the basis of their work here, Penn, Morales, and Rosenthal prove they have important careers ahead of them, and some of the supporting actors do, too. This movie's not a complete success, but it's a damned good try.

Badlands ★ ★ ★ ★
PG, 94 m., 1974

Martin Sheen (Kit), Sissy Spacek (Holly), Warren Oates (Holly's Father), Ramon Bieri (Cato), Ramon Vint (Deputy). Directed, produced, and written by Terence Malick.

They meet for the first time when she is in her front yard practicing baton-twirling. He has just walked off his job on a garbage truck. She thinks he is the handsomest man she's ever seen—he looks just like James Dean. He likes her because he never knew a fifteen-year-old who knowed so much: "She could talk like a grown-up woman, without a lot of giggles." Within a few weeks, they will be the targets of a manhunt after he has shot down half a dozen victims.

Terence Malick's *Badlands* calls them Kit and Holly, but his characters are inspired, of course, by Charles Starkweather and Caril Ann Fugate. They went on a wild ride in 1958 that ended with eleven people shot dead. The press named him the Mad Dog Killer, and Sunday supplement psychoanalysts said he killed because the kids at school kidded him about his bowlegs. Starkweather got the electric chair on June 25, 1959. From time to time a story appears about Caril Fugate's appeals to her parole board. She was sentenced to life.

She claimed she was kidnapped and forced to go along with Starkweather. When they first were captured, he asked the deputies to leave her alone: "She didn't do nothing." Later, at his trial, he claimed she was the most trigger-happy person he ever knew, and was responsible for some of the killings. It is a case that is still not closed, although *Badlands* sees her as a child of vast simplicity who went along at first because she was flattered that he liked her: "I wasn't popular at school on account of having no personality and not being pretty."

The film is tied together with her narration, written like an account of summer vacation crossed with the breathless prose style of a movie magazine. Some of the dialogue is loosely inspired by a book written by James Reinhardt, a criminologist who interviewed Starkweather on death row. Starkweather was offended by his death sentence. He viewed his crimes with total uninvolvement and asked how it was fair for him to die before he'd even been to a big city, or eaten in a fine restaurant, or seen a major-league game. That's what the movie captures, too: The detachment with which Kit views his killings, as Holly eventually draws away from him. He gets no pleasure from killing. He sees it only as necessary. He offers explanations which satisfy her for a while: "I killed them because they was bounty hunters who wanted the reward money. If they was policemen, just being paid for doing their job, that would have been different."

The movie makes no attempt to psychoanalyze its Kit Carruthers, and there are no symbols to note or lessons to learn. What comes through more than anything is the enormous loneliness of the lives these two characters lived, together and apart. He is ten years older than she is, but they're both caught up in the same adolescent love fantasy at first, as if Nat King Cole would always be there to sing "A Blossom Fell" on the portable radio while they held their sweaty embrace. He would not. To discourage his daughter from seeing "the kind of a man who collects garbage," her father punishes her by shooting her dog. She is "greatly distressed."

Kit is played by Martin Sheen, in one of the great modern film performances. He looks like James Dean, does not have bowlegs, and plays the killer as a plain and simple soul who has somehow been terribly damaged by life (the real Starkweather, his father explained at the time, was never quite right after being hit between the eyes with a two-by-four). Holly is played by the freckle-faced redhead Sissy Spacek. She takes her schoolbooks along on the murder spree so as not to get behind. She is in love with Kit at first, but there is a stubborn logic in her makeup and she eventually realizes that Kit means trouble. "I made a resolution never again to take up with any hell-bent types," she confides.

After the first murder and their flight, they never have any extended conversations about anything, nor are they seen to make love, nor is their journey given any symbolic meaning. They hope to reach refuge in the "Far North," where Kit might find employment as a mounted policeman. They follow their case in the newspapers, become aware of themselves as celebrities, and, in a brilliant scene at the end, the captured Kit hands out his comb, his lighter, and his ballpoint pen as souvenirs to the National Guardsmen who had been chasing him.

The movie is very reserved in its attitude toward the characters. It observes them, most of the time, dispassionately. They are strange people, as were their real-life models; they had no rationalizations like Dillinger's regard for the poor or Bonnie and Clyde's ability to idealize themselves romantically. They were just two dumb kids who got into a thing and didn't have the sense to stop. They're something like the kids in Robert Altman's *Thieves Like Us* and the married couple in *The Sugarland Express*. They are in over their heads, incapable of understanding murder as a crime rather than a convenience, inhabitants of lives so empty that even their sins cannot fill them.

Bang the Drum Slowly ★ ★ ★ ★
PG, 98 m., 1973

Michael Moriarty (Henry Wiggen), Robert De Niro (Bruce Pearson), Vincent Gardenia (Dutch Schnell), Phil Foster (Joe), Ann Wedgeworth (Katie), Patrick McVey (Mr. Pearson). Directed by John Hancock and produced by Maurice and Lois Rosenfield. Screenplay by Mark Harris.

Bang the Drum Slowly is the ultimate baseball movie—and, despite what a plot summary might suggest, I think it's more about baseball than death. It takes place during the last season on this Earth of one Bruce Pearson, an earnest but dumb catcher from Georgia who learns, in the movie's first scene, that he is suffering from an incurable disease. The movie is about that season and about his friendship with Henry Wiggen, a pitcher, who undertakes to see that Bruce at least lives his last months with some dignity, some joy, and a few good games.

On the surface, then, the movie seems a little like *Brian's Song*. But it's not: It's mostly about baseball and the daily life of a major league club on the road. The fact of Bruce's approaching death adds a poignancy to the season, but *Bang the Drum Slowly* doesn't brood about death and it isn't morbid. In its mixture of fatalism, roughness,

tenderness, and bleak humor, indeed, it seems to know more about the ways we handle death than a movie like *Love Story* ever guessed. The movie begins at the Mayo Clinic, follows the team through spring training, and then carries it through a season that feels remarkably like a Chicago Cubs year: a strong start, problems during the hot weather, dissension on the team, and then a pennant drive that (in the movie, anyway) is successful. There isn't a lot of play-by-play action, only enough to establish the games and make the character points. So when the team manager and the pitcher conspire to let Bruce finish his last game, despite his illness, the action footage is relevant and moving.

Bang the Drum Slowly was adapted for the screen by Mark Harris, from his observant 1955 novel. He seems to understand baseball players, or at least he can create convincing ones; if real baseball players aren't like the ones in this movie, somehow they should be. The director, John Hancock, is good with his actors and very good at establishing a lot of supporting characters without making a point of it (in this area he reminds me of Robert Altman's shorthand typecasting in *M*A*S*H* and *McCabe and Mrs. Miller*). Some of the best scenes are in the clubhouse, an arena of hope, despair, anger, practical jokes, and impassioned speeches by the manager.

He's played by Vincent Gardenia as a crafty, tough tactician with a heart of gold he tries to conceal. ("When I die," he says during one pre-game pep talk, "in the newspapers they'll write that the sons of bitches of this world have lost their leader.") He knows Bruce and Henry are concealing something, but he doesn't know what, and his efforts to find out are hilariously frustrated. At various times, the midwinter visit to the Mayo Clinic is explained as a fishing trip, a hunting trip, a wenching trip, and a secret mission to rid Bruce of the clap.

Gardenia, as the manager, is the third angle of a triangle that includes very good acting by Michael Moriarty, as Henry, and Robert De Niro, as Bruce. Henry is the All Star with the $70,000 contract and Bruce is a mediocre catcher who is constantly being ragged by his teammates. Henry's his only friend, until somehow when the team comes together for the pennant stretch, Bruce starts playing the best ball in his life, and the club (somewhat predictably) accepts him.

Hancock and Harris avoid any temptation to structure *Bang the Drum Slowly* as a typical sports movie. Although the team does win the pennant, not much of a point is made of that. There are no telegraphed big moments on the field, when everything depends on a strikeout or a home run or something. Even Bruce's last big hit in his last time at bat is limited, tactfully, to a triple.

Instead of going for a lot of high points, the movie paints characters in their everyday personalities. We get some feeling of life on the road as Henry talks with a hotel telephone operator who's a baseball fanatic, and Bruce moons over the prostitute he's in love with. Phil Foster has a great cameo role as a first-base coach with a genius for luring suckers into card games with remarkably elastic rules. Occupying the background in a lot of shots is the team's Cuban third baseman, who has it written into his contract that he be provided with a translator. And then, as the movie's shape begins to be visible, we realize it's not so much a sports movie as a movie about those elusive subjects, male bonding and work in America. That the males play baseball and that sport is their work is what makes this the ultimate baseball movie; never before has a movie considered the game from the inside out.

Being There ★ ★ ★ ★
PG, 130 m., 1980

Peter Sellers (Chance), Shirley MacLaine (Eve Rand), Melvyn Douglas (Ben Rand), Jack Warden (President), Richard Dysart (Dr. Allenby), Richard Basehart (Skrapinov). Directed by Hal Ashby and produced by Andrew Braunsberg. Screenplay by Jerzy Kosinski.

There's an exhilaration in seeing artists at the very top of their form: It almost doesn't matter what the form is, if they're pushing their limits and going for broke and it's working. We can sense their joy of achievement—and even more so if the project in question is a risky, off-the-wall idea that could just as easily have ended disastrously.

Hal Ashby's *Being There* is a movie that inspires those feelings. It begins with a cockamamie notion, it's basically one joke told for two hours, and it requires Peter Sellers to maintain an excruciatingly narrow tone of behavior in a role that has him onscreen almost constantly. It's a movie based on an idea, and all the conventional wisdom agrees that emotions, not ideas, are the best to make movies from. But *Being There* pulls off its long shot and is a confoundingly provocative movie.

Sellers plays a mentally retarded gardener who has lived and worked all of his life inside the walls of an elegant Washington town house. The house and its garden are in a decaying inner-city neighborhood, but what goes on outside is of no concern to Sellers: He tends his garden, he watches television, he is fed on schedule by the domestic staff, he is content.

Then one day the master of the house dies. The household is disbanded. Sellers, impeccably dressed in his employer's privately tailored wardrobe, wanders out into the city. He takes along the one possession he'll probably need: His remote-control TV channel switcher. He uses it almost immediately; surrounded by hostile street kids, he imperturbably tries to switch channels to make them go away. He hasn't figured out that, outside his garden, life isn't television.

And that is the movie's basic premise, lifted intact from a Jerzy Kosinski novel. The Sellers character knows almost nothing about real life, but he has watched countless hours of television and he can be pleasant, smile, shake hands, and comport himself; he learned from watching all those guests on talk shows. He knows nothing about *anything*, indeed, except gardening. But when he stumbles into Washington's political and social upper crust, his simple truisms from the garden ("Spring is a time for planting") are taken as audaciously simple metaphors. This guy's a Thoreau! In no time at all, he's the closest confidant of a dying billionaire industrialist (Melvyn Douglas)—and the industrialist is the closest confidant of the president.

This is, you can see, a one-joke premise. It has to be if the Sellers performance is to work. The whole movie has to be tailored to the narrow range within which Sellers's gardener can think, behave, speak, and make choices. The ways in which this movie could have gone out of control, could have been relentlessly boring on the one hand, or manic with its own audacity on the other, are endless. But the tone holds. That's one of the most exhilarating aspects of the joy you can sense, as Ashby pulls this off: Every scene needs the confidence to play the idea completely straight.

There are wonderful comic moments, but they're never pushed so far that they strain the story's premise. Some of them involve: a battle between the CIA and the FBI as to which agency destroyed the gardener's files; Shirley MacLaine unsuccessfully attempts to introduce Sellers to the concept of romance; Sellers as a talk-show guest himself (at last!), and Sellers as the hit of a Washington cocktail party. The movie also has an audacious closing shot that moves the film's whole metaphor into a brand-new philosophical arena.

What is *Being There* about? I've read reviews calling it an indictment of television. But that doesn't fit; Sellers wasn't warped by television, he was retarded to begin with, and has TV to thank for what abilities he *has* to move in society. Is it an indictment of society, for being so dumb as to accept the Sellers character as a great philosophical sage? Maybe, but that's not so fascinating either. I'm not really inclined to plumb this movie for its message, although I'm sure that'll be a favorite audience sport. I just admire it for having the guts to take this weird conceit and push it to its ultimate comic conclusion.

Best Boy ★ ★ ★
NO MPAA RATING, 111 m., 1980

A documentary produced, directed, and edited by Ira Wohl.

Sometimes there are movies that absorb you so completely that you forget you're watching them: They're simply happening to you. Ira Wohl's *Best Boy* is a movie like that. To see it is to participate in the lives of other people and to learn just a little more about being human. *Best Boy*, which won the 1980 Academy Award as best documentary, is the story of an only son named Philly, whose parents have always been too protective of him. But as the movie opens, it is time for Philly to go out a little more on his own—to go down

to the corner for an ice cream cone, for example, or to look forward to his first day of school. Philly is fifty-two years old. He is mentally retarded, but otherwise, as a psychiatrist explains in the film, "quite normal." He is also warm and lovable, and when Wordsworth wrote that heaven was all about us when we were children, did he guess that would also be true for someone like Philly, who will never really leave childhood?

Best Boy deals intelligently with real people and their problems. It is not simply a documentary; it contains the surprises of true drama, and it is put together so thoughtfully that it takes what could have been a case study and turns it into a cliffhanger. That is largely due to the complete access that the filmmaker, Ira Wohl, had to his subject. Philly is Wohl's cousin, and Philly's parents are Wohl's aunt and uncle. All the time he was growing up, Ira knew Philly—he played with him, presumably, when he was four or five and Philly seemed to be about the same age. Philly stayed four or five. As Wohl grew older, he realized that sooner or later Philly's parents would die, and that Philly's total dependence on them would leave him defenseless.

Philly had been at home almost all his life. The movie begins as his parents make the first reluctant, tentative steps to allow him a little more independence—to set him free. *Best Boy* moves very delicately around this subject, and with good reason: As we watch it, we realize that the parents have come to depend on Philly, too. He provided them with a rationale for their own lives and choices. He is their crutch as well as their burden. And there is yet another drama that unfolds within the film—unfolds so subtly we barely realize it is there, and yet concludes so inevitably that it casts a light back on all the scenes that went before. Philly's father is dying. There is a time in the film when the father clearly knows that and no one else in the film does, but we, strangers, share his secret with him.

You see what I mean when I say *Best Boy* isn't a case study. It's not about what should be done with Philly, and it has little to do with the "problem" of mental retardation. It is so specifically about Philly and his family and their daily choices in life that we almost feel adopted into the family. And we get to like Philly so much! He is sweet and cheerful, patient and good-humored, with a child's logic that cuts right through so much of the confusion adults surround him with. There is a wonderful scene with a psychiatrist, who is trying to administer a series of questions Philly obviously feels are silly. There is a visit to the theater, where Philly is allowed backstage to meet Zero Mostel, and they sing "If I Were a Rich Man" together. Why is it, the movie asks but never answers, that Philly can remember songs better than speech?

Best Boy suffers, I suppose, from being labeled a documentary: Some small-minded people make it a policy never to watch one. But at the Toronto Festival of Festivals, where the patrons are asked to vote for their favorite film, it astonished everyone by defeating all the features in the festival and placing first. It's a wonderfully positive experience.

The Best Little Whorehouse in Texas ★ ★
R, 114 m., 1982

Burt Reynolds (Ed Earl), Dolly Parton (Miss Mona), Charles Durning (Governor), Dom DeLuise (Melvin Thorpe), Jim Nabors (Deputy), Lois Nettleton (Dulcie Mae), Theresa Merritt (Jewel). Directed by Colin Higgins and produced by Thomas L. Miller, Edward K. Milkis, and Robert L. Boyett. Screenplay by Larry L. King, Peter Masterson, and Higgins.

If I were asked what image dominates *The Best Little Whorehouse in Texas*, the honest answer would have to be: Dolly Parton's plunging neckline. I am not trying to be cute. The awesome swell of her wondrous bosom dominates every scene Dolly appears in, and that includes just about every scene in the movie. W.C. Fields, the old scene-stealer, rebelled against appearing on screen with an animal, a child, or a plunging neckline, on the not unreasonable grounds that audiences would not be looking at him. Fields could have appeared incognito in *Whorehouse*, as, indeed, Burt Reynolds occasionally does.

The puzzling thing about the Parton décolletage is that so little is made of so much. You'd think there would be sizzling chemistry between Parton and Reynolds, who are two of my favorite movie sex symbols simply because they always seem so full of good cheer. But that isn't the case here. They're great looking, they smile a lot, they've been provided with good dialogue, but somehow they seem a little bored with each other, as if their affair has been going on a little too long; they're a happy old cheatin' couple. There is some passion in the movie, but it's concentrated in two scenes where Dolly is absent. In both of them, Reynolds lets loose with a non-stop cussing barrage, chewing out a foppish TV interviewer (Dom DeLuise) and a slippery governor (Charles Durning). Dolly never *really* gets to let go, and the limitless exuberance she displayed in *9 to 5* seems as tightly corseted here as her costumes are.

What's the problem? I think maybe the movie's story got misplaced somewhere in the middle of the movie's legend. The best little whorehouse of the movie's title was a legendary Texas brothel named the Chicken Ranch, which was immortalized first by generations of young Texans and later in a Broadway play by Larry King and Peter Masterson. Whorehouses, Texas ones included, are not exactly very nice places, but the whorehouse in this movie almost seems like a refuge for wayward girls. The story has been cleaned up so carefully to showcase Parton and Reynolds that the scandal has been lost; the movie has been turned into a defense of free enterprise and a hymn to romance.

That's too bad. I kept waiting for Dolly Parton to be sexy in this movie, and she never was. She was cheerful, spunky, energetic, angry, sad, and loyal, but she was never sexy—not even in bed. Her feelings for Reynolds seemed to be largely therapeutic, and I believe there were even times when they discussed the nature of their relationship. Since just the mere word "relationship" is profoundly subversive to eroticism and sexuality, we're a little baffled to see the madam and the sheriff turned into the sort of couple that discusses itself in first-person articles for *Cosmo*. This is carried so far that Parton's only reference to her bosom (indeed, the only moment in the movie when anyone deigns to even *notice* it) is about her problems "luggin' these around." It's all so matter-of-fact, it's asexual.

Parton and Reynolds are pleasant enough in *Whorehouse*, and we expect that from two such likable actors. Dom DeLuise is wildly improbable and distractingly bizarre as the TV investigative reporter who wants to shut down the Chicken Ranch. Charles Durning has a lot of fun with a sly song-and-dance routine. Lois Nettleton has a thankless role as Reynold's "other" mistress (we never do know what to make of *their* relationship, which must have been mangled in the editing). There are a few funny jokes, some raunchy one-liners, some mostly forgettable songs set to completely forgettable choreography, and then there is Dolly Parton. If they ever give Dolly her freedom and stop packaging her so antiseptically, she could be terrific. But Dolly and Burt and *Whorehouse* never get beyond the concept stage in this movie.

Betrayal ★ ★ ★ ★
R, 95 m., 1983

Jeremy Irons (Jerry), Ben Kingsley (Robert), Patricia Hodge (Emma). Directed by David Jones and produced by Sam Spiegel. Screenplay by Harold Pinter.

Love stories have beginnings, but affairs . . . affairs have endings, too. Even sad love stories begin in gladness, when the world is young and the future reaches out cheerfully forever. Then, of course, eventually you get Romeo and Juliet dead in the tomb, but that's the price you have to pay. Life isn't a free ride. Think how much *more* tragic a sad love story would be, however, if you could see into the future, so that even *this* moment, *this* kiss, is in the shadow of eventual despair.

The absolutely brilliant thing about *Betrayal* is that it is a love story told backward. There is a lot in this movie that is wonderful—the performances, the screenplay by Harold Pinter—but what makes it all work is the structure. When Pinter's stage version of *Betrayal* first appeared, back in the late 1970s, there was a tendency to dismiss his reverse chronology as a gimmick. Not so. It is the very heart and soul of this story. It

means that we in the audience know more about the unhappy romantic fortunes of Jerry and Robert and Emma at *every moment* than they know about themselves. Even their joy is painful to see.

Jerry is a youngish London literary agent, clever, good-looking, confused about his feelings. Robert, his best friend, is a publisher. Robert is older, stronger, smarter, and more bitter. Emma is Robert's wife and becomes Jerry's lover. But that is telling the story chronologically. And the story begins at the end, with Robert and Emma fighting, and with Robert slapping her, and with Emma and Jerry meeting in a pub for a painful reunion two years after their affair is over. Each additional scene takes place further back in time, and the sections have uncanny titles: Two years earlier. Three years earlier. We aren't used to this. At a public preview of the film, some people in the audience actually *resisted* the backward timeframe, as if the purpose of the playwright was just to get on with the story, damn it all, and stop this confounded fooling around.

The *Betrayal* structure strips away all artifice. It shows, heartlessly, that the very capacity for love itself is sometimes based on betraying not only other loved ones, but even ourselves. The movie is told mostly in encounters between two of the characters; all three are not often on screen together, and we never meet Jerry's wife. These people are smart and they talk a lot—too much, maybe, because there is a peculiarly British reserve about them that sometimes prevents them from quite saying what they mean. They lie and they half-lie. There are universes left unspoken in their unfinished sentences. They are all a little embarrassed that the messy urges of sex are pumping away down there beneath their civilized deceptions.

The performances are perfectly matched. Ben Kingsley (of *Gandhi*) plays Robert, the publisher, with such painfully controlled fury that there are times when he actually is frightening. Jeremy Irons, as Jerry, creates a man whose desires are stronger than his convictions, even though he spends a lot of time talking about his convictions, and almost none acknowledging his desires. Patricia Hodge, as Emma, loves them both and hates them both and would have led a much happier life if they had not been her two choices.

But how could she know that when, in life, you're required by the rules to start at the beginning?

Beverly Hills Cop ★ ★ ½
R, 105 m., 1984

Eddie Murphy (Axel Foley), Judge Reinhold (Detective Billy Rosewood), John Ashton (Sergeant Taggart), Lisa Eilbacher (Jenny), Ronny Cox (Lieutenant Bogomil). Directed by Martin Brest and produced by Don Simpson and Jerry Bruckheimer. Screenplay by Daniel Petrie.

Eddie Murphy looks like the latest victim of the Star Magic Syndrome, in which it is assumed that a movie will be a hit simply because it stars an enormously talented person. Thus it is not necessary to give much thought to what he does or says, or to the story he finds himself occupying. *Beverly Hills Cop* is a movie with an enormously appealing idea—a tough black detective from Detroit goes to Beverly Hills to avenge the murder of a friend—but the filmmakers apparently expected Murphy to carry this idea entirely by himself.

Murphy plays a street-wise rebel who is always getting in trouble with his commanding officer because he does things his own way. The movie opens with an example of that: Murphy is single-handedly running a sting operation when the cops arrive unexpectedly, setting off a wild car-truck chase through the city streets. Even while we're watching the thrilling chase, however, stirrings of unease are beginning to be felt: Any movie that *begins* with a chase is not going to be heavy on originality and inspiration. Then Murphy's old friend comes to town, fresh from a prison term and six months of soaking up the rays in California. The friend has some negotiable bonds with him, and then some friends of the guy who owns the bonds turn up and murder Murphy's friend. That makes Eddie mad, and he drives his ancient beater out to Beverly Hills, where it sort of stands out among the Porsches and Mercedes. He also meets a childhood friend (Lisa Eilbacher) who now works for an art dealer.

At this point, the movie can go in one of two directions. It can become a perceptive and pointed satire about American attitudes, showing how the ultrachic denizens of Beverly Hills react to this black cop from Detroit. Or it can go for broad, cheap laughs, and plug into a standard plot borrowed from countless TV crime shows. *Beverly Hills Cop* doesn't pause a moment before taking the low road. We figure that out right away, when Murphy tries to register in a hotel and is told there isn't any room. He loudly pulls both ranks and race, claiming to be a correspondent from *Rolling Stone* and accusing the desk clerk of racism. This is (a) not funny, and (b) not convincing, because Beverly Hills desk clerks were not born yesterday. If the people who made this movie had been willing to listen to the ways that real people really talk, they could have made the scene into a jewel instead of an embarrassment.

Meanwhile, the plot thickens. It turns out that the killers of Eddie's friend were employees of the evil Victor Maitland (Steven Berkoff), a Beverly Hills criminal whose art gallery—where Eilbacher works—is a front for cocaine smuggling. When Murphy tries to move against Maitland, he comes up against the Beverly Hills Cops, including an Abbott and Costello team that supplies unnecessary pratfalls, successfully undermining the credibility of any police scene that threatens to work. But wait a minute. What's this movie about, anyway? Is it a comedy or an action picture? Audiences may expect a comedy, but the closing shootout seems inspired by the machine gun massacre at the end of Brian De Palma's *Scarface*, and the whole business with the cocaine is so very, very tired that when we see the boss and his henchmen in the warehouse, we feel like we've switched to another movie—maybe a dozen other movies. Murphy is one of the smartest and quickest young comic actors in the movies. But he is not an action hero, despite his success in *48 Hours*, and by plugging him into an action movie, the producers of *Beverly Hills Cop* reveal a lack of confidence in their original story inspiration. It's like they had a story conference that boiled down to: "Hey gang! Here's a great idea! Let's turn it into a standard idea and fill it with clichés, and take out the satire and put in a lot of machine guns!"

Beyond the Limit ★ ★ ½
R, 103 m., 1983

Michael Caine (Charlie Fortnum), Richard Gere (Eduardo Plan), Bob Hoskins (Colonel Perez), Joaquim De Alameia (Leon), Elpidia Carrilo (Clara). Directed by John Mackenzie and produced by Norma Heyman. Screenplay by Christopher Hampton.

There are times when this movie is a mess. There are other times when it becomes quietly moving. *Beyond the Limit* has one of the best endings I can remember in a mediocre film, an ending that goes a long way toward redeeming some of the sloppiness that went before. And all through the film, there is a remarkable performance by Michael Caine, who has been around for so long, in so many movies, that it's easy to forget what a fine actor he is.

The film is based on *The Honorary Consul*, Graham Greene's novel about a bungled South American terrorist kidnapping. The movie tells most of the same story, involving the alcoholic British honorary consul (Caine), the young half-British doctor (Richard Gere), the priest turned revolutionary (Joaquim De Alameia), and the beautiful Indian prostitute (Elpidia Carrilo) who becomes Caine's wife and Gere's lover. The film is also fairly faithful to Greene's ending, a study in conflicting morality, where the priest kidnaps the worthless British consul under the impression he is the American ambassador—and then the doctor's loyalties are torn between his friend the consul, his lover the consul's wife, and his old friend the priest.

What is not faithful to the novel is the casting of Gere as the doctor. Gere is so wrong for the role that he undermines every scene he's in, distracting attention from Caine's understated, quietly poignant performance. Halfway through the movie, as I was witnessing the obligatory Gere sex scene, I began to grow angry. Not at Gere, who can be effective in the right role, but at the producers, who chose his popular appeal over the obvious demands of the material. The doctor in the Greene novel is not a swaggering bodybuilder with a smoldering sexuality, but a troubled, worried, overworked young man with a conscience. The amoral way in which

Gere possesses his friend's wife is totally false to the spirit of the book.

What is true, though, is the Michael Caine performance. The character he plays is Charlie Fortnum, a pathetic drunk holding onto the honorary consulship as a last vestige of dignity, investing all of his higher feelings into love for his wife. Caine gives a great performance, sweaty, exhausted, red-eyed, filled with false bonhomie, always with his eye on the level in the whiskey bottle. There is a kind of nobility in the way he accepts his fate, after the terrorists kidnap him and nobody, frankly, cares enough to ransom him. There is also a real person here, in a performance that suggests Fortnum's life up until this point, his history of failure, his essential good nature. The movie's final scene, between Caine and Carrillo, is one of the best scenes Caine has ever played.

Unhappily, it comes in a movie that never comes together, and that lingers too long on a Richard Gere who seems to have wandered in from another movie, would-be British accent and all. The casting is one of the movie's mysteries; another one is the change to a meaningless and forgettable title; a third is how Michael Caine succeeded in delivering an intact performance right there in the middle of all the lost dreams.

The Big Chill ★ ★ ½
R, 108 m., 1983

Tom Berenger (Sam), Glenn Close (Sarah), William Hurt (Nick), Jeff Goldblum (Michael), Meg Tilly (Chloe), Kevin Kline (Harold), Mary Kay Place (Meg), JoBeth Williams (Karen). Directed by Lawrence Kasdan. Screenplay by Kasdan and Barbara Benedek.

I was going through some old papers the other night, from cardboard boxes that were packed at the end of college and have followed me around ever since. To open them up was like walking into a time capsule. There they were, the little campus literary magazines and the yellowing issues of the University of Illinois' *Daily Illini*, and a photo of a political demonstration on the steps of the student union.

On the other hand, I was going through my mail today and I got a letter from a teenager who wanted to know why they were making so many movies about the 1960s.

"These are the 1980s," he informed me. "Who cares what happened in the olden days?" I think "olden days" was an attempt at humor.

In any event, I wrote back that the 1960s were big in the movies right now because the people who make the movies were students in the 1960s, and that the teen-agers of 2001 would no doubt be sick and tired of the olden days of the 1980s. And then I thought about *The Big Chill*, a movie in which survivors of the 1960s ask themselves how they could possibly be in their thirties. This is the second movie on almost exactly the same theme—a weekend reunion among college friends from the sixties, during which they relive the past, fear the present, and regret the interim. They could have called it *Son of the Return of the Secaucus Seven*.

It's a good movie. It's well acted, the dialogue is accurately heard, and the camera is extremely attentive to details of body language. It observes wonderfully well how its veterans of the 1960s have grown up into adulthood, consumerhood, parenthood, drunkenhood, adulteryhood, and regrethood. These people could all be wearing warm-up jackets with *poignancy* stenciled on the backs.

The movie begins at a funeral. One of the old college friends has killed himself, for reasons that never become clear. The others gather for his funeral and stay for a weekend in a big old summer house. We get to meet them: the intellectual, the failed writer, the confused TV star, the woman who wants to have a baby and can't tear her eyes away from the biological clock. They eat, they drink, they pair up in various combinations, and they ask themselves questions like, Who were we? Who are we now? What happened to us? What will happen to us?

Because they are all graduates of the University of Michigan at Ann Arbor, they phrase these questions with style, of course. The dialogue sounds like a series of bittersweet captions from *New Yorker* cartoons. And at the end, of course, nothing is really discovered, nothing is really settled, and they go back into holding patterns until the next funeral.

The Big Chill is a splendid technical exercise. It has all the right moves. It knows all the right words. Its characters have all the right clothes, expressions, fears, lusts, and ambitions. But there's no payoff and it doesn't lead anywhere. I thought at first that was a weakness of the movie. There also is the possibility that it's the movie's message.

Big Foot ½★
PG, 76 m., 1971

John Carradine (Trader), Joi Lansing (Girl Pilot), Chris Mitchum (Second Cyclist), Ken Maynard (Shopkeeper), Lindsay Crosby (Motorcyclist). Directed by Robert F. Slater and produced by Tony Cardoza. Screenplay by Slater and James Gordon White.

Why, you are asking, did I decide to see *Big Foot*? Why am I taking your time—time you could spend trimming your toenails and talking to your indoor plants, telling them what nice plants they are—to review *Big Foot*? What strange light in the sky, what weird whistling in my ear, what blood-soaked note tied to a rock and thrown through my window, sent me to see *Big Foot*? These are good questions. The cast alone convinced me. Let me put it as simply as I can. If you have ever wanted to see a movie starring John Carradine, Joi Lansing, Lindsay Crosby, Chris Mitchum, and Ken Maynard, then *Big Foot* is almost certainly going to be your only chance. Not since Joan Crawford starred in *Trog* has there been such an opportunity.

Joi Lansing began her career as a model in a provocative magazine. Lansing is still startling, especially with a jumpsuit. She parachutes in it. It conceals a minidress slit to the waist, and a top that is slashed to the belt, and she runs away from Big Foot for about five minutes in this costume, bouncing through the woods but not (for some mysterious reason) from her blouse.

No matter. There is always John Carradine. He plays a backwoods trader with a line of goods packed into the rear of his 1958 Ford station wagon. He stops at a general store run by Ken Maynard (yes, Ken Maynard) and Ken makes a phone call while standing in front of a poster from one of his old movies (*Texas Gunfighter*, if I remember correctly) wearing the same ten-gallon hat that's on the poster. "There have been a lot of strange things going on up in those hills," he informs the sheriff, after Chris Mitchum's girlfriend has been carried away by a half-human, half-animal creature with big feet. But the sheriff refuses to go up on the mountain after dark, and so Chris enlists his buddies in a motorcycle gang led by Lindsay Crosby (yes, Lindsay Crosby).

This is no ordinary motorcycle gang. All of its members ride identical brand-new medium-sized Yamahas, which are credited in the titles to a Hollywood Yamaha agency. The gang members also wear bright-colored nylon Windbreakers with pull-strings at the bottom, and they wear new knit shirts and dress loafers. The girls wear bikinis. The gang's hairstyle is set by Lindsay Crosby's receding ducktail.

Meanwhile, Lansing and another girl are tied to trees (saplings would be a better word) by the creatures, and then Lansing is carried off and given to Big Foot. Big Foot is usually shot from a camera angle between his toes, making him loom over the camera like King Kong, but when we see him straight-on he looks about five feet ten inches or eleven inches tall. He wears a shaggy costume stitched together out of old, dirty brown shag rugs.

Anyway, there is an exciting chase through the woods, which is only slowed down a little bit by the fact that the movie has nine unidentified extras who have to file past the camera. Then Big Foot runs into a cave. This has us hoping that Joan Crawford will appear and explain that the creature has been misunderstood (in *Trog*, she went into the cave with a twenty-nine-cent bunch of carrots, calling "Here, Trog?").

But, no, a motorcyclist pulls a bundle of dynamite from his belt and throws it into the cave. No fuse, just the dynamite. Then we cut to footage apparently taken from another film, showing towers of flame. The mountain shakes. Yards below, an old Indian woman cocks her head and nods wisely at the sky. Mountain speak with big voice. Then we cut to a sound stage set decorated with trees, bushes, and a steaming pile of rocks in one corner—the remains of the cave and the mountain, too, for that matter. "Do you . . . think it's dead?" Joi Lansing asks. "Nothing could live through that," Lindsay Crosby assures her. I certainly hope he is right.

The Big Red One ★ ★ ★
PG, 113 m., 1980

Lee Marvin (Sergeant), Mark Hamill (Griff), Robert Carradine (Zab), Bobby Di Cicco (Vinci), Kelly Ward (Johnson), Siegfried Rauch (Schroeder), Stephanie Audran (Walloon). Directed and written by Samuel Fuller and produced by Gene Corman.

Sam Fuller's *The Big Red One* is a lot of war stories strung together in a row, almost as if the director filmed it for the thirty-fifth reunion of his old Army outfit, and didn't want to leave anybody out. That's one of the most interesting things about it—the feeling that the movie's events are included, not because they help the plot or make a point, but just because they happened.

Some of them happened to Fuller himself, he tells us, and there's a kid in the movie who's obviously supposed to be young Sam. Other scenes are based on things Fuller heard about. Some of them are brutal and painful, some of them are romantic, a lot of them are corny. The movie takes no position on any of them: This movie is resolutely nonpolitical, is neither pro- nor anti-war, is deliberately just a record of five dogfaces who found themselves in the middle of the action.

The movie's title refers to the U.S. Army's First Infantry Division, and the action follows one rifle squad through the entire war. The squad leader is a hard-bitten sergeant, played by Lee Marvin with the kind of gravel-voiced, squint-eyed authority he had more than a decade before in *The Dirty Dozen*. His four squad members are kids in their teens, and his job is to whip them into shape. He does. The squad is so efficient, or competent, or just plain lucky, that it survives to see action in half the major theaters of the war in Europe. At a rough count, they fight in North Africa, Tunis, Sicily, Normandy, Omaha Beach, rural France, Belgium, Czechoslovakia, and Germany. Halfway through this litany, we begin to suspect that *The Big Red One* is supposed to be something more than plausible.

The squad fights in so many places, stays together in one piece for so long, experiences so many of the key events of World War II (from the invasion of Europe to the liberation of the Nazi death camps) that of course these characters are meant to be symbols of all the infantrymen in all the battles. But Fuller, who fought in the First Division, seems determined to keep his symbols from illustrating a message. They fight. They are frightened. Men kill, other men are killed. What matters is if you're still alive. "I don't cry because that guy over there got hit," Fuller said in an interview, "I cry because I'm gonna get hit next."

This leads to a deliberately anecdotal structure for the film. One battle ends, another begins. A little orphan kid appears out of the smoke, is befriended, braids flowers into the netting of a helmet, is forgotten for the rest of the film. What we have is a series of experiences so overwhelming that the characters can't find sense or pattern in them, and so simply try to survive them through craft and experience.

Is this all Fuller got out of the war? He seems to believe it's all anybody really gets, that the vast patterns of war's meaning are really just the creations of novelists, film-makers, generals, and politicians, and that for the guy under fire there is no pattern, just the desperately sincere desire to get out in one piece.

The Big Red One is Sam Fuller's first film in more than a decade, and by far the most expensive and ambitious film he's ever made. It's like a dream come true, the capstone of a long career. Fuller began as a newspaperman in New York, he fought in the war, he went to Hollywood and he directed a lot of B-action pictures that are considered by connoisseurs to be pulp landmarks: *I Shot Jesse James, Pickup on South Street, Hell and High Water, Shock Corridor.* His previous film, hardly seen in this country, was a 1972 West German production with the marvelous title *Dead Pigeon on Beethoven Street.*

While this is an expensive epic, he hasn't fallen to the temptations of the epic form. He doesn't give us a lot of phony meaning, as if to justify the scope of the production. There aren't a lot of deep, significant speeches. In the ways that count, *The Big Red One* is still a B-movie—hard-boiled, filled with action, held together by male camaraderie, directed with a lean economy of action. It's one of the most expensive B-pictures ever made, and I think that helps it fit the subject. "A" war

movies are about War, but "B" war movies are about soldiers.

Billy Jack ★ ★ ½
PG, 112 m., 1971

Tom Laughlin (Billy Jack), Delores Taylor (Jean), Clark Howat (Sheriff), Julie Webb (Barbara). Directed and produced by T.C. Frank (Tom Laughlin). Screenplay by Frank and Teresa Christina.

Billy Jack was not only the first film by Tom Laughlin and Delores Taylor since *Born Losers* (1967), but in many respects the same film, with the same hero and the same theme. Both films were directed by Laughlin himself, using the pseudonym of T.C. Frank, and they represent a passionate obsession with the role of violence in society. Laughlin and Taylor surface so rarely because their movies are personal ventures, financed in unorthodox ways and employing the kind of communal chance-taking that Hollywood finds terrifying. The chances they take sometimes create flaws in their films, but flaws that suggest they were trying to do too much, never too little.

What I find interesting is that they decided, in effect, to remake their earlier film: not to copy it, but to grapple again with the same identities and ideas. Both films are about a character named Billy Jack (Laughlin), who is a returned Vietnam hero, half-Indian, a master of karate, who takes the law into his own hands because he believes that's the only way to obtain justice.

In *Born Losers* an outlaw motorcycle gang terrorizes a community and its sheriff's office. When they brutally beat a teen-ager, Billy Jack steps in and shoots one of them. He gets ninety days. The gang members get a slap on the wrist for assault. But when he gets out of jail he finds the police powerless and the community terrified. So, because he feels he must, he fights them again, using karate, gasoline, Indian tricks, and his rifle.

In *Billy Jack*, the same character has become more mythic and supernatural. "We don't know how to contact Billy Jack," one of his friends says. "We communicate with him Indian-style; when we need him, somehow he's there." And indeed he is, riding his horse or motorcycle out of the woods, an almost supernatural presence. This time the town is terrorized, not by a bike gang, but by a brutal local businessman and his half-crazy sadomasochistic son. With the exception of the sheriff himself, who has good intentions but is ineffectual, the local law officers are on the side of evil against good.

"Good" is represented by a freedom school run by Delores Taylor, "where children can come when they have no place else to go." The townspeople (who are conveniently represented as hateful, violent, and prejudiced) resent the "hippie school," but it's on an Indian reservation and thus accountable only to federal law.

The daughter of a deputy sheriff runs away after a beating and is hidden at the school, and this provides the food for the plot: The deputy and the other bad guys go after Billy Jack, who single-handedly cuts them down with karate blows, etc. The kids and staff at the school are all pacifists, but Billy Jack can't buy that. His morality is a simple Old Testament one, an eye for an eye.

There are a lot of things in *Billy Jack* that are seriously conceived and very well-handled. Some of the scenes at the school, for example, with real kids experimenting with psychodrama, are interesting. Some of the action scenes are first-rate. There's a lot of dialogue, mostly involving putdown of the older generation.

But the movie has as many causes in it as a year's run of the *New Republic*. There's not a single contemporary issue, from ecology to gun control, that's not covered, and toward the movie's end you're wondering how these characters—who are just ordinary folks in a small Southwestern town—managed to confront every single ethical hurdle in a few weeks of living. It's possible, I guess, but it would keep you awfully busy, and then there are always the Jews in the Soviet Union to think about, and the Pakistan refugees.

I'm also somewhat disturbed by the central theme of the movie. *Billy Jack* seems to be saying the same thing as *Born Losers*, that a gun is better than a constitution in the enforcement of justice. Is democracy totally obsolete, then? Is our only hope that the good fascists defeat the bad fascists? Laughlin and Taylor are still asking themselves these questions, and *Billy Jack* arrives at a conclusion that is only slightly more encouraging.

Birdy ★ ★ ★ ★
R, 120 m., 1985

Nicolas Cage (Al), Matthew Modine (Birdy). Directed by Alan Parker and produced by Alan Marshall. Screenplay by Sandy Kroopf and Jack Behr.

The strangest thing about *Birdy*, which is a very strange and beautiful movie indeed, is that it seems to work best at its looniest level, and is least at ease with the things it takes most seriously. You will not discover anything new about war in this movie, but you will find out a whole lot about how it feels to be in love with a canary.

The movie is about two friends from South Philadelphia. One of them, Al, played by Nicolas Cage, is a slick romeo with a lot of self-confidence and a way with the women. The other, nicknamed Birdy (Matthew Modine), is goofy, withdrawn, and absolutely fascinated with birds. As kids, they are inseparable friends. In high school, they begin to grow apart, separated by their individual quests for two different kinds of birds. But they still share adventures, as Birdy hangs upside-down from elevated tracks to capture pigeons, or constructs homemade wings that he hopes will let him fly. Then the war comes. Both boys serve in Vietnam and both are wounded. Cage's face is disfigured, and he wears a bandage to cover the scars. Modine's wounds are internal: He withdraws entirely into himself and stops talking. He spends long, uneventful days perched in his room at a mental hospital, head cocked to one side, looking up longingly at a window, like nothing so much as a caged bird.

Because *Birdy* is not told in chronological order, the story takes a time to sort itself out. We begin with an agonizing visit by Cage to his friend Birdy. He hopes to draw him out of his shell. But Birdy makes no sign of recognition. Then, in flashbacks, we see the two lives that led up to this moment. We see the adventures they shared, the secrets, the dreams. Most importantly, we go inside Birdy's life and begin to glimpse the depth of his obsession with birds. His room turns into a birdcage. His special pets—including a cocky little yellow canary—take on individual characteristics for us. We can begin to understand that his love for birds is sensual, romantic, passionate. There is a wonderful scene where he brushes his fingers against a feather, showing how marvelously it is constructed, and how beautifully.

Most descriptions of *Birdy* tend to dwell on what seems to be the central plot, the story of the two buddies who go to Vietnam and are wounded, and about how one tries to help the other return to the real world. I felt that the war footage in the movie was fairly routine, and that the challenge of dragging Birdy back to reality was a good deal less interesting than the story of how he arrived at the strange, secret place in his mind. I have seen other, better, movies about war, but I have never before seen a character quite like Birdy.

As you may have already guessed, *Birdy* doesn't sound like a commercial blockbuster. More important are the love and care for detail that have gone into it from all hands, especially from Cage and Modine. They have two immensely difficult roles, and both are handicapped in the later scenes by being denied access to some of an actor's usual tools; for Cage, his face; for Modine, his whole human persona. They overcome those limitations to give us characters even more touching than the ones they started with.

The movie was directed by Alan Parker. Consider this list of his earlier films: *Bugsy Malone, Fame, Midnight Express, Shoot the Moon, Pink Floyd: The Wall.* Each one coming out of an unexpected place, and avoiding conventional movie genres. He was the man to direct *Birdy*, which tells a story so unlikely that perhaps even my description of it has discouraged you—and yet a story so interesting it is impossible to put this movie out of my mind.

The Black Cauldron ★ ★ ★ ½
PG. 80 m., 1985 ✓

With the voices of Grant Bardsley (Taran), Susan Sheridan (Eilonwy), Freddie Jones (Dallben), Nigel Hawthorne (Fflewddur), Arthur Malet (King Eidilleg), John Byner (Gurgi and Doli), Lindsay Rich (Fairfolk), Eda Reiss Merin (Orddu), John Hurt (Horned King). Directed by Ted Berman and Richard Rich and produced by Joe Hale.

The best of the Disney animated features were not innocent children's entertainments, but bloodcurdling stories of doom and obsession (with a few smiles along the way, of course). They only looked innocent because they were cartoons. Reflect for a moment on the Island of Lost Boys in *Pinocchio* or what happened to Bambi's mother. The great Disney cartoons contained all of the fearsome possibilities of the Grimm fairy tales—or, for that matter, of life itself. Only in recent years have the Disney feature cartoons grown pale and innocuous, as part of the general delusion that harmless means colorless.

This Disney animated film is in the old tradition. *The Black Cauldron* is a rip-roaring tale of swords and sorcery, evil and revenge, magic and pluck and luck. It tells the story of a search for a magic cauldron that can, if it falls into the hands of the evil Horned King, be used as a bottomless source of evil. And it takes us on a journey through a kingdom of some of the more memorable characters in any recent Disney film.

There is, for example, Hen Wen, the psychic pig. She can look into a pot of water and picture there the current location of the black cauldron. That makes her invaluable to the Horned King—and also to Taran, the young man who dreams of someday becoming a great warrior.

The Black Cauldron is a quest movie, telling the story of Taran's progress toward manhood, his journey through the kingdom, and his race against the Horned King for possession of the cauldron. All of this could, of course, look very silly. Stories like this have to be told with complete conviction or they lose their passion. What surprised me, as I sat through *The Black Cauldron*, was how quickly the story did absorb me. Instead of thinking deep thoughts about the past and future of Disney animation, I was caught up in the movie, amused by some of the characters, and sort of excited by the sky-splitting conclusion.

The story was so involving, indeed, that at one moment an allegedly mature adult in the audience leaned over to me and whispered, "But Rog . . . if the pig is really psychic, how come they can't just find out where the cauldron is, and get there before the king?"

A good point, but a better point is this one: How long has it been since anyone took a Disney cartoon that seriously?

The key to the movie is in the richness of the characterizations, and the two best characters, I think, are the Horned King (with voice by John Hurt), and a fuzzy little creature named Gurgi (voice by John Byner). Gurgi is a slavishly devoted little yes-man who gurgles with appreciation for everything done by anyone within earshot who is stronger than he is. The main character, the young knight Taran, is not one of the stronger characters in the movie, but maybe that's to be expected. His thankless task is to be brave and noble, and those are not fascinating aspects of character—particularly not when contrasted to all the other weird characters in the movie.

The story is based on material I'm not familiar with, *The Chronicles of Prydain* series by Lloyd Alexander. But some of the visuals do look rather familiar, particularly Taran's magic sword, which seemed to be borrowed from the laser swords in *Star Wars*, and the final apocalyptic conclusion, where the special effects fireworks look like the end of *Raiders of the Lost Ark*. The movie uses this borrowed material with such energy, however, that it earns its right to it. By the end of *The Black Cauldron* I was remembering, with something of a shock of nostalgia, the strength and utter storytelling conviction of the early Disney animators. *The Black Cauldron* is a return to the tradition.

The Black Marble ★ ★ ★ ½
PG, 110 m., 1980

Robert Foxworth (Sergeant Valnikov), Paula Prentiss (Sergeant Zimmerman), Harry Dean Stanton (Philo Skinner), Barbara Babcock (Madeline Whitfield), John Hancock (Clarence Cromwell), Raleigh Bond (Captain Hooker), Judy Landers (Pattie Mae), Pat Corley (Itchy Mitch). Directed by Harold Becker and produced by Frank Capra, Jr. Screenplay by Joseph Wambaugh.

The Black Marble is a delightfully twisted comedy, backing into itself, starting out in one direction, ending up somewhere else, constantly surprising us with its offbeat characters. It's so many things at once it's a juggling act: It's a police movie with lots of authentic details; it's a bizarre comedy about a kidnapped prize dog; it's a shaggy romance; it's got the most excruciating chase sequence I can remember; it's goofy, but it moves us.

The movie centers around several days in the life of a Los Angeles police sergeant named Valnikov (Robert Foxworth), an incurably romantic Russian who has been drinking too much since his partner's suicide. He gets a new partner, Sgt. Natalie Zimmerman, played by Paula Prentiss as a combination of Sally Kellerman and Lucille Ball. His new partner thinks Valnikov is insane. Maybe she's right.

The case they begin working on together involves a prize bitch that has been kidnapped and is being held for $85,000 ransom. Valnikov goes to interview kidnapped dog's grieving owner, an attractive woman of a certain age. And, in a delightful scene that illustrates the movie's gift of being able to slide ever so lightly from drama into cheerful comedy, he winds up on the sofa with the woman, drying her tears and vowing, "Don't worry; I promise I'll get your doggie back."

The dry tone Foxworth brings to the pronunciation of such lines is one of the movie's charms. He is mustachioed, mournful-eyed, usually hung over, and filled with ancient Russian dreams and curses. It is inevitable, of course, that he and the sexy Zimmerman fall in love, and they have a wonderful seduction scene in his apartment. He puts sweepingly romantic Russian folk music on his stereo. They dance. "Translate the lyrics for me!" she whispers into his ear. He does. It does not bother either of them that there *are* no lyrics since the song is instrumental.

Meanwhile, a parallel plot involves the evil dog kidnapper, played by that uniquely malevolent character actor Harry Dean Stanton, who looks and talks like Robert Mitchum's mean kid brother. Stanton is a veterinarian who has never hurt a dog in his life. But he needs the ransom to pay a gambling debt before he is killed. Coughing, wheezing, and spitting through an endless chain of cigarettes, he makes telephone threats to the dog's owner, who counters with descriptions of her own financial plight, unpaid bills, and tax problems.

When Valnikov and the kidnapper finally

meet face to face, they get into what is undoubtedly the most painful chase sequence I can remember, a chase that requires them to climb mesh fences separating a series of savage and terrified dogs that snap maniacally at their legs. The chase is another scene illustrating the curious way in which *The Black Marble* succeeds in being funny, painful, and romantic, sometimes simultaneously. The movie's not altogether a comedy, although we laugh; it's a love story that kids itself and ends up seriously; it contains violence but is not really violent. What it always does is keep us off balance. Because we can't anticipate what's going to happen next, the movie has a persistent interior life; there's never the sense that a scene is included because it's expected.

The performances go to show you that a good actor in a bad film can have a very hard time appearing to be any good. Foxworth's previous screen credits include *The Omen, Part II* and *Prophecy.* Neither film gave me the slightest reason to look forward to him in *The Black Marble,* but he's wonderful here. He gives his character weariness and craziness and then covers them both with warmth. He and Prentiss have so much fun with the long seduction scene that we can sense the joy of acting craftsmanship going into it.

The movie's the second production by Joseph Wambaugh, the L.A. cop who became a best-selling novelist only to see Hollywood doing terrible things to his novels. Wambaugh vowed to produce his own books. The industry had its doubts, especially when Wambaugh hired a little-known British director, Harold Becker, to direct his first project, *The Onion Field.* But that was a strong, edgy, effective movie, and now Wambaugh and Becker are back with this unusual and distinctive comedy. Because it is uneven and moves so easily among its various tones and moods, it's possible, I suppose, to fault it on form: This isn't a seamless piece of work, but it's infectious and charming.

The Black Stallion ★ ★ ★ ★
G, 120 m., 1980

Kelly Reno (Alec Ramsey), Mickey Rooney (Henry Dailey), Teri Garr (Alec's Mother), Clarence Muse (Snoe), Hoyt Axton (Alec's Father), Michael Higgins (Neville). The black stallion is portrayed by Cass-ole, owned by San Antonio Arabians. Directed by Carroll Ballard and produced by Francis Ford Coppola, Fred Roos, and Tom Sternberg. Screenplay by Melissa Mathison, Jeanne Rosenberg and William D. Wittliff.

The first half of *The Black Stallion* is so gloriously breathtaking that the second half, the half with all the conventional excitement, seems merely routine. We've seen the second half before—the story of the kid, the horse, the veteran trainer, and the big race. But the first hour of this movie belongs among the great filmgoing experiences. It is described as an epic, and earns the description.

The film opens at sea, somewhere in the Mediterranean, forty or so years ago, on board a ship inhabited by passengers who seem foreign and fearsome to a small boy. They drink, they gamble, they speak in foreign tongues, they wear caftans and beards and glare ferociously at anyone who comes close to their prize possession, a magnificent black stallion.

The boy and his father are on board this ship for reasons never explained. The father gambles with the foreigners and the boy roams the ship and establishes a shy rapport with the black stallion, and then a great storm sweeps over the ocean and the ship catches fire and is lost. The boy and the stallion are thrown free, into the boiling sea. The horse somehow saves the boy, and in the calm of the next morning they both find themselves thrown onto a deserted island.

This sequence—the storm, the ship's sinking, the ordeal at sea—is a triumphant use of special effects, miniature models, back projection, editing, and all the tricks of craft that go into the filming of a fantasy. The director, Carroll Ballard, used the big water tank at Cinecitta Studios in Rome for the storm sequences; a model ship, looking totally real, burns and sinks headfirst, its propellers churning slowly in the air, while the horse and boy struggle in the foreground.

The horse in this film (its name is Cass-ole) is required to perform as few movie horses ever have. But its finest scene is the quietest one, and takes place on the island a few days after the shipwreck. Ballard and his cinematographer, Caleb Deschanel, have already established the mood of the place, with gigantic, quiet, natural panoramas. The boy spears a fish. The horse roams rest-lessly from the beaches to the cliffs. And then, in a single shot that is held for a long time, Ballard shows us the boy inviting the horse to eat out of his hand.

It is crucial here that this action be seen in a *single* shot; lots of short cuts, edited together, would simply be the filmmakers at work. But the one uninterrupted shot, with the horse at one edge of the screen and the boy at the other, and the boy's slow approach, and the horse's skittish advances and retreats, shows us a rapport between the human and the animal that's strangely moving.

All these scenes of the boy and horse on the island are to be treasured, especially a montage photographed underwater and showing the legs of the two as they splash in the surf. There are also wonderfully scary sequences, such as one in which the boy awakens to find a poisonous snake a few feet away from him on the sand. This scene exploits the hatred and fear horses have for snakes, and is cut together into a terrifically exciting climax.

But then, as all good things must, the idyll on the island comes to an end. The boy and the horse are rescued. And it's here that the film, while still keeping our interest, becomes more routine. The earlier passages of the film were amazing to look at (they were shot, with great difficulty and beauty, on Sardinia). Now we're back to earth again, with scenes shot around an old racetrack in Toronto.

And we've seen the melodramatic mate-rials of the movie's second half many times before. The boy is reunited with his mother, the horse returns home with him, and the boy meets a wise old horse trainer who admits that, yes, that Arabian *can* run like the wind—but the fool thing doesn't have any papers. The presence of Mickey Rooney, who plays the trainer, is welcome but per-haps too familiar. Rooney has played this

sort of role so often before (most unforgetta-bly in *National Velvet*) that he almost seems to be visiting from another movie. His Acad-emy Award nomination for the performance is probably a recognition of that.

Still, the melodrama is effective. Every-thing depends on the outcome of the big race at the film's end. The young boy, of course, is the jockey (the Elizabeth Taylor role, so to speak). Ballard and Deschanel are still gifted at finding a special, epic look for the movie; one especially good scene has the stallion racing against time, in the dark before dawn, in the rain.

The Black Stallion is a wonderful experi-ence at the movies. The possibility remains, though, that in these cynical times it may be avoided by some viewers because it has a G rating—and G movies are sometimes dis-missed as being too innocuous. That's sure not the case with this film, which is rated G simply because it has no nudity, profanity, or violence—but it does have terrific energy, beauty, and excitement. It's not a children's movie; it's for adults *and* for kids.

Blade Runner ★ ★ ★
R, 114 m., 1982

Harrison Ford (Deckard), Rutger Hauer (Batty), Sean Young (Rachel), Edward James Olmos (Gaff), M. Emmet Walsh (Bryant), Daryl Hannah (Pris). Directed by Ridley Scott and produced by Michael Deeley. Screenplay by Hampton Fancher and David Peoples.

The strangest thing about the future is that *this* is now the future that was once foretold. Twenty years ago, we thought of "now" as "the year 1985," and we wondered what life would be like. Little could we have guessed that there would be no world government, that the cars would look like boxes instead of rocket ships, and that there would still be rock 'n' roll on the radio. *Blade Runner* asks us to imagine its own future, in "the year 2020." The movie takes place in a Los Angeles that looks like a futuristic Tokyo, with gigantic billboards showing smiling Japanese girls drinking Coca-Cola. I would have predicted L.A. would be Hispanic, but never mind, it looks sensational. The city is dominated by almost inconceivably huge skyscrapers. People get around in compact vehicles that fly, hover, climb, and swoop.

(In a lot of fictional futures, people seem to zip around the city in private aircraft; can you imagine the traffic problems?) At ground level, however, the L.A. of the future is an urban jungle.

The movie stars Harrison Ford as a cop who moves confidently through the city's mean streets. He is laconic, cynical, competent. He has a difficult assignment. A group of "replicants," artificial people who seem amazingly human, have escaped from "offworld," and are trying to inflict themselves on Earth. Ford's job is to track them down and eliminate them. Anyone who has read this far can predict what happens next: He falls in love with one of the replicants. She may not be quite human, but, oh, you kid.

This basic story comes from a Philip K. Dick novel with the intriguing title, *Do Androids Dream of Electric Sheep?* The book examined the differences between humans and thinking machines, and circled warily around the question of memory: Does it make an android's personal memories less valid if they are inspired by someone else's experiences—especially if the android does not know that? Ford says he originally signed on for *Blade Runner* because he found such questions intriguing. For director Ridley Scott, however, the greater challenge seemed to be creating that future world. Scott is a master of production design, of imagining other worlds of the future *(Alien)* and the past *(The Duellists).* He seems more concerned with creating his film worlds than populating them with plausible characters, and that's the trouble this time. *Blade Runner* is a stunningly interesting visual achievement, but a failure as a story.

The special effects were supervised by Douglas Trumbull, whose credits include *2001* and *Silent Running,* and who is about as good as anyone in the world at using miniatures, animation, drawings, optical effects, and other ways of tricking the eye. The visual environments he creates for this film are wonderful to behold, and there's a sense of detail, too; we don't just get the skyways and the monolithic skyscrapers and the sky-taxis, we also get notions about how restaurants, clothes, and home furnishings will look in 2020 (not too different). *Blade Runner* is worth seeing just to witness this artistry. The movie's weakness, however, is

that it allows the special effects technology to overwhelm its story. Ford is tough and low-key in the central role, and Rutger Hauer and Sean Young are effective as two of the replicants, but the movie isn't really interested in these people—or creatures. The obligatory love affair is pro forma, the villains are standard issue, and the climax is yet one more of those cliffhangers, with Ford dangling over an abyss by his fingertips. The movie has the opposite trouble as the replicants: Instead of flesh and blood, its dreams are of mechanical men.

Blame It on Rio ★
R, 101 m., 1984

Michael Caine (Matthew), Michelle Johnson (Jennifer), Joseph Bologna (Victor). Directed and produced by Stanley Donen. Screenplay by Charlie Peters and Larry Gelbart.

As a general rule, I think it's wrong for a married man of forty-seven years to have an affair with his best friend's seventeen-year-old daughter. Don't you? And especially if the girl has emotional problems. I can imagine a movie being made about the situation, and indeed the right movie might even be sensitive and poignant. But to make a cynical sitcom out of it is questionable. That's what they've done with *Blame It on Rio.* This movie is clearly intended to appeal to the prurient interests of dirty old men of all ages. It starts with the basic idea of *10* (an unhappy man flees to a beach and discovers an agreeable nymphet of startling sexuality). But in *10* Bo Derek was old enough to take care of herself, God knows, and her affair with Dudley Moore was handled with at least some wit and sophistication.

Blame It on Rio, however, has the mind of a 1940s bongo comedy and the heart of a porno film. It's really unsettling to see how casually this movie takes a serious situation. A disturbed girl is using sex to play mind games with a middle-aged man, and the movie get its yuks with slapstick scenes where one guy goes out the window when the other guy comes in the door. What's shocking is how many first-rate talents are associated with this sleaze. The director is Stanley Donen, of *Singin' in the Rain.* The man having the affair is Michael Caine, one of my favorite actors. His friend (the father of the girl) is Joseph Bologna. The girl is played by a *zaftig* model named Michelle Johnson, who is set up as the new Bo Derek.

The plot is the usual silliness: Two families are planning a vacation in Rio, but then Caine has a disagreement with his wife, who decides to go to Club Med instead. What finally happens is that the two fathers and their teen-age daughters go to Rio, where Johnson shamelessly seduces Caine with techniques that seem more appropriate to a brazen hussy than to a seventeen-year-old kid. The rest of the movie alternates uneasily between the girl's neurotic attempts to manipulate Caine with sex, Caine's real qualms, and wildly inappropriate screwball scenes. Sample: Caine thinks Bologna has found out the secret. He has to listen as Bologna reads from his daughter's diary. The daughter mentions her new lover's great teeth. Caine tries to hide his teeth with his lips while he talks. Funny, sure, but not in a movie where the underlying subject is so potentially serious.

Does the movie have redeeming qualities? Quite frankly, yes, it does, but not the kind it makes you proud to enjoy. Johnson *could* indeed be the next Bo Derek: She has a winning way, a cheerful personality, and a body that the camera never tires of exploring. Caine does as well with the material as we could possibly hope; in the hands of a lesser actor, we wouldn't be uneasy over the material, we'd be appalled. A lot of skill has gone into the awkward subject matter of this movie, and it's thought-provoking that *Blame It on Rio* sometimes almost works.

Blood Simple ★ ★ ★ ★
R, 96 m., 1985

John Getz (Ray), Frances McDormand (Abby), Dan Hedaya (Julian Marty), M. Emmet Walsh (Detective), Samm-Art Williams (Meurice). Directed by Joel Coen and produced by Ethan Coen. Screenplay by Coen and Coen.

A lot has been written about the visual style of *Blood Simple*, but I think the appeal of the movie is more elementary: It keys into three common nightmares: (1) You clean and clean, but there's still blood all over the place; (2) You know you have committed a murder, but you are not sure quite how or why; (3) You know you have forgotten a small detail that will eventually get you into a lot of trouble. *Blood Simple* mixes those fears and guilts into an incredibly complicated plot, with amazingly gory consequences. It tells a story in which every individual detail seems to make sense, and every individual choice seems logical, but the choices and details form a bewildering labyrinth in which there are times when even the murderers themselves don't know who they are.

Because following the plot is one of this movie's most basic pleasures, I will not reveal too much. The movie begins with a sleazy backwoods bar owner's attempt to hire a scummy private detective to murder his wife. The private eye takes the money and then pulls a neat double-cross, hoping to keep the money and eliminate the only witness who could implicate him. Neat. And then it *really* gets complicated.

The movie has been shot with a lot of style, some of it self-conscious, but deliberately so. One of the pleasures in a movie like this is enjoying the low-angle and tilt shots that draw attention to themselves, that declare themselves as being part of a movie. The movie does something interesting with its timing, too. It begins to feel inexorable. Characters think they know what has happened; they turn out to be wrong; they pay the consequences, and it all happens while the movie is marching from scene to scene like an implacable professor of logic, demonstrating one fatal error after another.

Blood Simple was directed by Joel Coen, produced by his brother, Ethan, and written by the two of them. It's their first film, and has the high energy and intensity we associate with young filmmakers who are determined to make an impression. Some of the scenes are virtuoso, including a sequence in which a dead body becomes extraordinarily hard to dispose of, and another one in which two people in adjacent rooms are trapped in the same violent showdown. The central performance in the movie is by the veteran character actor M. Emmet Walsh, who plays the private eye like a man for whom idealism is a dirty word. The other actors in the movie are all effective, but they are obscured, in a way, by what happens to them: This movie weaves such a bloody web that the characters are upstaged by their dilemmas.

Is the movie fun? Well, that depends on you. It is violent, unrelenting, absurd, and fiendishly clever. There is a cliché I never use: "Not for the squeamish." But let me put it this way. *Blood Simple* may make you squeam.

Blow Out ★ ★ ★ ★
R, 107 m., 1981

John Travolta (Jack), Nancy Allen (Sally), John Lithgow (Burke), Dennis Franz (Manny Karp), Peter Boydon (Sam), Curt May (Donohue). Directed by Brian De Palma and produced by George Litto. Screenplay by De Palma.

There are times when *Blow Out* resembles recent American history trapped in the "Twilight Zone." Episodes are hauntingly familiar, and yet seem slightly askew. What if the "grassy knoll" recordings from the police radio in Dallas had been crossed with Chappaquiddick and linked to Watergate? What if Jack Ruby had been a private eye specializing in divorce cases? What if Abraham Zapruder—the man who took the home movies of President John F. Kennedy's death—had been a sound effects man? And what if Judith Exner—remember her?—had been working with Ruby? These are some of the inspirations out of which Brian De Palma constructs *Blow Out*, a movie which continues his practice of making cross-references to other movies, other directors, and actual historical events, and which nevertheless is his best and most original work.

The title itself, of course, reminds us of *Blow Up*, the 1966 film by Michelangelo Antonioni in which a photographer saw, or thought he saw, a murder—and went mad while obsessively analyzing his photographs of the "crime." *Was* there a dead body to be found on that fuzzy negative? Was there even such a thing as reality? In *Blow Out*, John Travolta plays the character who confronts these questions. He's a sound man for a sleazy Philadelphia B-movie factory. He works on cheap, cynical exploitation films. Late one night, while he's standing on a bridge recording owls and other night sounds, he becomes a witness to an accident. A car has a blow out, swerves off a bridge, and plunges into a river. Travolta plunges in after it, rescues a girl inside (Nancy Allen),

and later discovers that the car's drowned driver was a potential presidential candidate. Still later, reviewing his sound recording of the event, Travolta becomes convinced that he can hear a gunshot just before the blow out. Was the accident actually murder? He traces down Nancy Allen, discovers that she was part of a blackmail plot against the candidate, and then comes across the trail of a slimy private eye (Dennis Franz) who wanted to cause a blow out, all right, but didn't figure on anybody getting killed.

The plot thickens beautifully. De Palma doesn't have just a handful of ideas to spin out to feature length. He has an abundance. We meet a gallery of violent characters, including Burke (John Lithgow), a dirty-tricks specialist who seems inspired by G. Gordon Liddy. The original crime is complicated by a series of other murders, designed to lay a false trail and throw the police off the scent of political conspiracy.

Meanwhile, the Travolta character digs deeper. For him, it's a matter of competence, of personal pride. Arguing with a cop about his tapes, Travolta denies that he's just imagining things: "I'm a *sound* man!" He stumbles across a series of photos of the fatal accident. In a brilliantly crafted sequence, we follow every step as he assembles the film and his recording into a movie of the event, doggedly extracting what seem to be facts from what looks like chaos.

De Palma's visual images in *Blow Out* invite comparison to many Alfred Hitchcock films, and indeed De Palma invited such comparisons when the posters for *Dressed to Kill*, described him as "Master of the Macabre." In *Blow Out* there are such Hitchcock hallmarks as a shower scene (played this time for laughs rather than for the chills of *Dressed to Kill*), several grisly murders in unexpected surroundings, violence in public places, and a chase through Philadelphia on the anniversary of the ringing of the Liberty Bell. This last extended chase sequence reminds us of two Hitchcock strategies: His juxtaposition of patriotic images and espionage, as in *North by Northwest* and *Saboteur*, and his desperate chases through uncaring crowds, reminders of *Foreign Correspondent* and *Strangers on a Train*.

But *Blow Out* stands by itself. It reminds us of the violence of *Dressed to Kill*, the startling images of *The Fury*, the clouded identities of *Sisters*, the uncertainty of historical "facts" from *Obsession*, and it ends with the bleak nihilism of *Carrie*. But it moves beyond those films, because this time De Palma is more successful than ever before at populating his plot with three-dimensional characters. We believe in the reality of the people played by John Travolta, Nancy Allen, John Lithgow, and Dennis Franz. They have all the little tics and eccentricities of life. And although they're caught in the mesh of a labyrinthine conspiracy, they behave as people probably would behave in such circumstances—they're not pawns of the plot.

Best of all, this movie is inhabited by a real cinematic intelligence. The audience isn't condescended to. In sequences like the one in which Travolta reconstructs a film and sound record of the accident, we're challenged and stimulated: We share the excitement of figuring out how things develop and unfold, when so often the movies only need us as passive witnesses.

Blue Collar ★ ★ ★ ★
R, 114 m., 1978

Richard Pryor (Zeke), Harvey Keitel (Jerry), Yaphet Kotto (Smokey), Ed Begley, Jr. (Bobby Joe), Harry Bellaver (Eddie Johnson), George Memmoli (Jenkins). Directed by Paul Schrader and produced by Don Guest. Screenplay by Paul and Leonard Schrader.

Detroit. Dawn. The next shift arrives for work. On the sound track, music of pounding urgency, suggesting the power of the machines that stamp out car doors from sheets of sheel. The camera takes us into the insides of an automobile factory, takes us close enough to almost smell the sweat and shield our eyes against the sparks thrown off by welding torches.

Blue Collar is about life on the Detroit assembly lines, and about how it wears men down and chains them to a lifetime installment plan. It is an angry, radical movie about the vise that traps workers between big industry and big labor. It's also an enormously entertaining movie; it earns its comparison with *On the Waterfront*. And it's an extraordinary directing debut for Paul Schrader, whose credits include *Taxi Driver* and *Rolling Thunder*.

Schrader tells the story of three workers, buddies on and off the job, who are all more or less in the same boat. They work, they drink after work in the bar across the street, they go home to mortgages or bills or kids who need braces on their teeth. One day they get fed up enough to decide to rob the safe in the office of their own union. What they find there is only a few hundred bucks—and a ledger that seems to contain the details of illegal loans of union funds.

The three guys are played by Richard Pryor, Harvey Keitel, and Yaphet Kotto, and they're all three at the top of their forms. Pryor, in particular, is a revelation: He's been good in a lot of movies, but almost always as himself, fast-talking, wise-cracking, running comic variations on the themes suggested by his dialogue. This time, held in rein by Schrader, he provides a tight, convincing performance as a family man.

Yaphet Kotto plays his opposite, an ex-con who likes to throw all-night parties with lots of sex, booze, and grass. And Harvey Keitel is their white friend, always behind on his loan company payments, who comes home one day to discover that his daughter has tried to bend paper clips over her teeth to convince her friends at school that she's got the braces she should have.

Schrader goes for a nice, raunchy humor in the scenes involving the three guys: The movie is relaxed and comfortable with itself, and we get the precise textures and tones of the society they live in. We understand their friendship, too, because it defies one of the things the movie passionately charges: That unions and management tacitly collaborate on trying to set the rich against the poor, the black against the white, the old against the young, to divide and conquer.

The burglary caper begins innocently enough with Pryor's demand, at a union meeting, that the company repair his locker: He's cut his hand trying to get the damn thing open. But the union representatives seem indifferent to Pryor and just about everyone else, and so Pryor marches into the office of the shaggy, white-maned union leader who was a radical himself, once, back in the 1930s. And while the great statesman is feeding him several varieties of lies, Pryor sees the office safe and gets his idea.

The burglary itself finds the right line between humor and suspense, and then the movie's anger begins to burn. Because when the three men discover that the ledger may be more important than any money in the safe, they're torn between using it for blackmail, or using it to expose the corruption of their own union. Schrader gradually reveals his total vision in the film's second hour: A friendship that was sound and healthy suddenly goes sour. The system drives a wedge between them, as Pryor is offered a union job, Keitel becomes an FBI informer, and Kotto is killed in a scene of great and gruesome power.

It took a measure of courage to make *Blue Collar,* and especially to follow its events through to their inevitable conclusion. The movie could have copped out in its last thirty minutes, and given us a nice, safe Hollywood ending. Instead, it makes criticisms of mass production that social critics like Harvey Swados and Paul Goodman might have agreed with. This isn't a liberal movie but a radical one, and one I suspect a lot of assembly-line workers might see with a shock of recognition.

It took courage to make the movie that honest. But it also took a special filmmaking gift to make it burst with humor, humanity, and suspense as well. Like *On the Waterfront,* it's both an indictment and an entertainment, working just as well on its human levels as with its theoretical concerns. Paul Schrader has been a Hollywood wonder kid ever since negotiating a $450,000 deal for his first screenplay, *The Yakuza.* After *Taxi Driver* and *Obsession,* he was able to demand that he direct his own work, and *Blue Collar* is a stunning debut, taking chances and winning at them.

The Blue Lagoon ½★
R, 102 m., 1980

Brooke Shields (Emmeline), Christopher Atkins (Richard), Leo McKern (Paddy Button), William Daniels (Arthur Lestrange). Directed and produced by Randal Kleiser. Screenplay by Douglas Day Stewart.

This movie made me itch. It's about a young girl and a young boy who are shipwrecked on a beautiful Pacific island. It shows how they grow up, mostly at sunset. It follows their progress as they discover sex and smile sweetly at each other, in that order. It concludes with a series of scenes designed to inspire the question: If these two young people had grown up in civilized surroundings, wouldn't they have had to repeat the fourth grade?

The Blue Lagoon was the dumbest movie of the year. It could conceivably have been made interesting, if any serious attempt had been made to explore what might really happen if two seven-year-old kids were shipwrecked on an island. But this movie isn't a realistic movie. It's a wildly idealized romance, in which the kids live in a hut that looks like a Club Med honeymoon cottage, while restless natives commit human sacrifice on the other side of the island. (It is a measure of the filmmakers' desperation that the kids and natives never meet one another and the kids leave the island without even one obligatory scene of being tied to a stake.)

Why was this movie made? Presumably because Randal Kleiser, the director and producer, read the 1903 novel it's based on and vowed that this story had to be brought to the screen. It had been filmed previously, as Jean Simmons's 1949 movie debut, but no matter. Kleiser had another go.

It's intriguing to try to guess, on the basis of the film he made, what he thought the original story had to tell us. This movie could have been made as a tale of wilderness survival: *The Swiss Family Robinson Meets Lord of the Flies.* But Kleiser's details about daily life are wildly unconvincing. This movie could have been made as an adventure epic, but, as I've already mentioned, the threat of the natives on the other side of the island is introduced only to be dropped. This movie could have been made as a softcore sex film, but it's too restrained: There are so many palms carefully arranged in front of genital areas, and Brooke Shields's long hair is so carefully draped to conceal her breasts, that there must have been a whole squad of costumers and set decorations on permanent Erogenous Zone Alert.

Let's face it. Going to this film knowing what we've heard about it, we're anticipating the scenes in which the two kids discover the joys of sex. This is a prurient motive on our part, and we're maybe a little ashamed of it, but our shame turns to impatience as Kleiser intercuts countless shots of the birds and the bees (every third shot in this movie seems to be showing a parrot's reaction to something). And there is no way to quite describe my feelings about the scene that takes place the morning after the young couple have finally made love. They go swimming, see two gigantic *turtles* copulating, and smile sweetly at each other. Based on the available evidence in the movie, they know more at this point about the sex lives of turtles than about their own.

But wait, these kids aren't finished. They have a baby, after long, puzzled months of trying to figure out those stirring feelings in the girl's stomach. "Why did you have a baby?" the boy asks. "I don't know," the girl says. They try to feed the kid fresh fruit, and then they look on in wonder as the baby demonstrates the theory and practice of breastfeeding (so *that's* what they're for!).

The movie's ending is enraging. It turns out the boy's father has been sailing the South Seas for years, looking for the castaways, who meanwhile manage to set themselves adrift at open sea again (they lose their oars . . . but never mind). Despairing of being rescued, the kids have just eaten berries that are supposed to put them permanently asleep. Then their unconscious bodies are rescued. Will they live? Die? What were those berries, anyway? The movie cops out: The burden of contriving an ending was apparently too much for such a feeble movie to support.

The Blues Brothers ★ ★ ★
R, 133 m., 1980

John Belushi (Jake Blues), Dan Aykroyd (Elwood Blues), Ray Charles (Ray), Aretha Franklin (Waitress), James Brown (Rev. James), Cab Calloway (Curtis), Charles Napier (Good Ol' Boy), Henry Gibson (Nazi), John Candy (Burton Mercer), Murphy Dunne (Piano Player), Carrie Fisher (Mystery Lady). Directed by John Landis and produced by Robert K. Weiss. Screenplay by Dan Aykroyd and Landis.

The Blues Brothers is the Sherman tank of musicals. When it was being filmed in Chicago in 1979—with dozens of cars piling up in intersections, caroming down Lake Shore Drive and crashing through the Daley Center—it seemed less like a film than a war. The movie feels the same way. It's a big, raucous powerhouse that proves against all the odds that if you're loud enough, vulgar enough, and have enough raw energy, you can make a steamroller into a musical, and vise versa.

This is some weird movie. There's never been anything that looked quite like it; was it dreamed up in a junkyard? It stars John Belushi and Dan Aykroyd as the Blues Brothers, Jake and Elwood, characters who were created on "Saturday Night Live" and took on a fearsome life of their own. The movie tells us something of their backgrounds: They were reared in a sadistic West Side orphanage, learned the blues by osmosis, and, as the movie opens, have teamed up again after Jake's release from the Joliet pen.

The movie's plot is a simple one, to put it mildly. The brothers visit their old orphanage, learn that its future is in jeopardy because of five thousand dollars due in back taxes, and determine to raise the money by getting their old band together and putting on a show. Their odyssey takes them to several sleazy Chicago locations, including a Van Buren flophouse, Maxwell Street, and lower Wacker Drive. They find their old friends in unlikely places, like a restaurant run by Aretha Franklin, a music shop run by Ray Charles, and a gospel church run by James Brown.

Their adventures include run-ins with suburban cops, good ol' boys, and Nazis who are trying to stage a demonstration. One of the intriguing things about this movie is the way it borrows so freely and literally from news events. The plot develops into a sort of musical *Mad Mad Mad Mad World*, with the Blues Brothers being pursued at the same time by avenging cops, Nazis, and an enraged country and western band led by Charles Napier, that character actor with the smile like Jaws. The chase is interrupted from time to time for musical numbers, which are mostly very good and filled with high-powered energy.

Aretha Franklin occupies one of the movie's best scenes, in her South Side soul food restaurant. Cab Calloway, as a sort of road manager for the Blues Brothers, struts through a wonderful old-style production of *Minnie the Moocher*. The Brothers themselves star in several improbable numbers; the funniest has the band playing in a country and western bar where wire mesh has been installed to protect the band from beer bottles thrown by the customers.

I was saying the musical numbers interrupt the chases. The fact is, the whole movie is a chase, with Jake and Elwood piloting a used police car that seems, as it hurdles across suspension bridges from one side to the other, to have a life of its own. There can rarely have been a movie that made so free with its locations as this one. There are incredible, sensational chase sequences under the elevated train tracks, on overpasses, in subway tunnels under the Loop, and literally through Daley Center. One crash in particular, a pileup involving maybe a dozen police cars, has to be seen to be believed: I've never seen stunt coordination like this before.

What's a little startling about this movie is that all of this works. *The Blues Brothers* cost untold millions of dollars and kept threatening to grow completely out of control. But director John Landis (of *Animal House*) has somehow pulled it together, with a good deal of help from the strongly defined personalities of the title characters. Belushi and Aykroyd come over as hard-boiled city guys, total cynics with a world-view of sublime simplicity, and that all fits perfectly with the movie's other parts. There's even room, in the midst of the carnage and mayhem, for a surprising amount of grace, humor, and whimsy.

Blume in Love ★ ★ ★ ★
R, 116 m., 1973

George Segal (Blume), Susan Anspach (Nina), Kris Kristofferson (Elmo), Marsha Mason (Arlene), Shelley Winters (Mrs. Cramer), Donald F. Muhich (Analyst), Paul Mazursky (Hellman). Directed, produced, and written by Paul Mazursky.

Paul Mazursky's *Blume in Love* begins with a busted-up Southern California marriage.

The marriage belonged to Blume, divorce lawyer, and his wife Nina, a social worker. It busted up all of a sudden one weekday after-

noon when Nina came home with a cold and found Blume in bed with his secretary. Why, you may ask (Blume certainly does), could his wife not forgive this indiscretion—especially as Blume is madly in love with Nina and must have her back or die? ("And I don't want to die," he reasons, "so I have to get her back.")

Well, maybe Nina was sort of halfway ready for the marriage to end. She's into her own brand of self-improvement and women's lib, and isn't sure she approves of marriage anymore. She takes up with an out-of-work (for twelve years) musician who lives in a VW truck with his dreams. She gets into yoga and learns to play the guitar and to rely on herself instead of men.

Little good that does Blume, whose love for her becomes a consuming passion. It is complicated by the fact that he gets to like the musician, too: thinks, in fact, that the bearded Elmo is the nicest man he has ever met. Blume even goes so far as to start a beard himself. But nothing will work for him, because of the fact he refuses to accept: Nina simply does not love him anymore. Does not. Period. Blume is driven into a frenzy of love, desire, frustration.

This material, so far, doesn't exactly sound like the stuff of a great film. It sounds more like the brainy, funny dissections of California dreamin' that Mazursky carried out in three previous films, *I Love You, Alice B. Toklas, Bob & Carol & Ted & Alice,* and *Alex in Wonderland.* Those were all fine films—Mazursky is one of the best directors of comedy in Hollywood—but they were all more concerned with the laugh than with reality.

With *Blume in Love,* however, he seems to have pulled off what everybody is always hoping for from Neil Simon: a comedy that transcends its funny moments, that realizes we laugh so we may not cry, and that finally is about real people with real desperations. He's done that in a number of scenes, and yet somehow even during the movie's gloomiest moments he keeps some sort of hope alive. That's probably because Blume is played by the charming George Segal, who seems intrinsically optimistic. No matter what Nina says, he cannot quite give up on her, because he knows she must eventually love him again—because he loves her.

He carries this hope with him on a trip to Venice, which is where the film opens; she's asked him to go away somewhere for a couple of weeks, while she thinks. They had their first and second honeymoons in Venice, but now Blume wanders through Piazza San Marco in the autumn, stranded with a few other lonely tourists looking for love. The story is told in flashbacks from Venice, and it ends there. It ends with a note so unashamedly romantic that Mazursky gets away with "Tristan and Isolde" as his sound track music. He's right. The ending would not be believable at all, except as hyperbole.

Nina—thin, earnest, determined to do the right thing and no longer be mastered by mere emotion—is played with a very complex charm by Susan Anspach. We have to like her even though she doesn't like Blume, whom we're cheering for. We do, and we like her boyfriend as much as Blume does. The itinerant musician is played by Kris Kristofferson, who gives evidence once again that he has a real acting talent—particularly in the scene where he hits Segal and then bursts into tears, and in the scene where he tells Segal he's hitting the road again.

Blume in Love has a quality that's hard to analyze but impossible to miss: It sets up an intimate rapport with its audiences.

Body Double ★ ★ ★ ½
R, 110 m., 1984

Craig Wasson (Jake), Melanie Griffith (Holly), Gregg Henry (Sam), Deborah Shelton (Gloria). Directed and produced by Brian De Palma. Screenplay by Robert H. Averch and De Palma.

Body Double is an exhilarating exercise in pure filmmaking, a thriller in the Hitchcock tradition in which there's no particular point except that the hero is flawed, weak, and in terrible danger—and we identify with him completely. The movie is so cleverly constructed, with the emphasis on visual storytelling rather than dialogue, that we are neither faster nor slower than the hero as he gradually figures out the scheme that has entrapped him. And the casting of a Hitchcockian average guy also helps.

The movie stars Craig Wasson, an open-faced actor with an engaging smile, as its hero, an unemployed actor named Jake. He isn't smart, he isn't dumb, he isn't perfect, he isn't bad. He is an ideal choice to set up as a witness to a murder. Jake needs a place to stay, and another actor (Gregg Henry) offers him a job house-sitting in a weird, modernistic home on stilts up in the hills above Los Angeles. The other actor also points out all the sights—including a shapely neighbor who does a nightly striptease dance in front of her open window. Jake is only human. For two nights, he uses a telescope to watch the striptease. He also begins to suspect that the woman may be in danger. In sequences inspired by *Rear Window,* he begins to follow the woman (Deborah Shelton), but he keeps his distance because he's caught in the same dilemma as Jimmy Stewart was in the Hitchcock picture: He is, after all, technically a Peeping Tom, and he wouldn't know the woman was in danger if he hadn't been breaking the law.

Since the plot is so important in *Body Double,* and because the movie contains so many nice surprises, I won't reveal very much more of the story. Let me describe in a carefully vague way, however, some of the pleasures of the movie. After a murder does indeed seem to have been committed, Jake's path leads him into the world of pornographic filmmaking. He wants to meet and hire a porno superstar (Melanie Griffith) who he thinks can help him figure out the mystery. His attempts lead to a series of very funny conversations, as the blonde porno actress talks to him with a Runyonesque mixture of jaded sophistication and startling ignorance. The speech in which she explains exactly what she will, and will not, do in a movie is shocking, sad, and curiously moving. *Body Double*'s excursion into the world of pornography (we see some fairly mild porno scenes, shot by De Palma himself) is part of a veritable anthology of styles in this movie. The film opens with a satire on vampire movies, includes a Hitchcockian cat-and-mouse sequence, and even borrows some of the clichés of 1940s thrillers, including a detailed recapitulation at the end, complete with flashbacks. There is also a sharp 1940s look to the cinematography, which uses dramatic lighting, tilted cameras, and carefully constructed shots to make the style part of the story.

But the movie is not just an exercise in style. It is also a genuinely terrifying thriller, in which an almost clockwork plot brings the hero and the killer together without a single logical glitch. De Palma is at home in this genre. Although his *Scarface* was more of a serious social commentary, thrilling suspense movies are his specialty, and his credits include *Carrie, Obsession,* and *Dressed to Kill.* With *Body Double,* he has his most airtight plot. He also has, once again, his almost unique courage to go over the top—to push scenes beyond the edge of common sense and into cheerfully heightened and impassioned overkill. The graveyard sequence next to the Hollywood reservoir, for example, or the photography in the tunnel during one of the Jake's attacks of claustrophobia, are so uninhibited that they skirt the dangerous edge of being ridiculous. But because the story's so strong, they're not. They work.

Bolero ½★
NO MPAA RATING, 105 m., 1984

Bo Derek, George Kennedy, Andrea Occhipinti. Directed by Gordon Douglas.

Bolero is a film starring Bo Derek as a woman who believes that the cure for a man's impotence is for his woman to train as a bullfighter. "Bolero" is also the name of the composition by Ravel which Dudley Moore played in *10* while making love with Derek. So much we already know. Also, let's see here, paging through the old dictionary . . . a bolero is a Spanish dance, characterized by sharp turns and revolutions of the body and stamping of the feet, and it also is a jacket of waist-length or shorter, usually worn open. So *that* explains the jacket of waist-length or shorter, usually worn open, which is Bo Derek's only item of clothing during one scene in the movie! It also explains the sharp turns and revolutions of her body during the same scene, although there is no stamping of the feet, except in the audience.

But I am still a little confused by the relationship between Derek and the bullfighter who is her lover. If you have not seen the movie, let me explain. Derek has graduated from a fancy women's boarding school, and after mooning her professors she departs in search of a tall, dark, and handsome lover. First she meets a sheik, but he turns out to be a dud, maybe because he spends too much time inhaling the magic fumes of his hookah.

So Bo goes to Spain, where she meets this all-around guy who herds cattle on a mountaintop, owns a winery, and is a bullfighter. If he also was an investment banker whose last book read was *The Prophet,* he could be a Dewar's Profile. Bo and the guy make love at sunrise. Unfortunately, the sun rises directly into the camera at crucial moments. Then her lover goes into the ring to fight with the bull, and is gored in that portion of his anatomy he could least afford to spare in any continuing relationship with Derek. He is brave. While doctors fight to save his life, his only thought is for his dog. He asks Bo to be sure that the dog gets home safely.

Before long, Bo is observing that her lover is acting depressed and distant. Could this possibly be because of his horrible injuries? You would think so, and I would think so, but Bo tells him it doesn't matter, and then she vows that he will live to fight again another day, so to speak. Then she starts taking bullfighting lessons. Oh, but I almost forgot. The Arab sheik tears himself away from his hookah long enough to fly to Spain and kidnap her. She is tied up in his open biplane, but manages to untie herself and jump over the edge. Then Bo is immediately back in her lover's hacienda again. How did she get to the ground? For anyone with Bo's faith, all is possible, and I think this is a real good omen for the lover. If she can get down in one piece, think what he might be able to do.

Let's face it. Nobody is going to *Bolero* for the plot anyway. They're going for the Good Parts. There are two Good Parts, not counting her naked ride on horseback, which was the only scene in the movie that had me wondering how she did it. The real future of Bolero is in home cassette rentals, where your fast forward and instant replay controls will supply the editing job the movie so desperately needs.

The Bostonians ★ ★ ★
PG, 120 m., 1984

Basil Ransom (Christopher Reeve), Olive Chancellor (Vanessa Redgrave), Verena Tarrant (Madeleine Potter), Miss Birdseye (Jessica Tandy), Mrs. Burrage (Nancy Marchand). Directed and produced by Ismail Merchant, James Ivory, and Ruth Prawer Jhabvala. Screenplay by Merchant, Ivory, and Jhabvala.

One of the qualities I like best in the novels of Henry James is the way his characters talk and talk about matters of passion and the heart, and never quite seem to act. One of his favorite words, in many of his books, is "intercourse," by which, significantly, he seems to mean conversation, although you can never quite be sure. James's novels run long and deep, and because he was writing for a 19th century that was not always open to the kinds of passions felt by his characters, he beat a lot, if you will, around the bush, so to speak, with lots of commas and asides and subtle hints of unspeakable practices. *The Bostonians* is a novel with a lot of asides, and hundreds of pages of hints. We can summarize it boldly: It is about a sweet and somewhat inconsequential young woman who has inspired crushes in two of her admirers. One of her would-be lovers is a straight-spoken lawyer from the South, who wants to sweep her off her feet and make her his wife. The other is a woman, who does not seem quite in touch with the true nature of her feelings; today she would know she was a lesbian, but in the world of James it is necessary for her to displace her feelings—to convince herself that she is in love with the young woman's politics. Those politics are mostly secondhand, made up of things the young woman has been told by others. The story is set at the birth of the suffragette movement, and women meet in each others homes to talk about the right to vote and, by extension, the right to lead full lives. *The Bostonians* shows us several of those women, including the veteran leader Mrs. Birdseye (wonderfully played by Jessica Tandy) and the younger firebrand Olive Chancellor (Vanessa Redgrave).

Chancellor is in love with Verena Tarrant (Madeleine Potter). That is clear to us, but not as clear to Chancellor. She promotes the young woman as a lecturer and campaigner, filled with visions of her role in social reform—a role that will necessarily require her to become Chancellor's associate, and have little to do with men. Then the tall Southern lawyer (Christopher Reeve) arrives on the scene, and the movie turns into a tug-of-war in which nobody is quite frank about the real nature of the battle.

The Bostonians is by the veteran producer-director-writer team of Ismail Merchant, James Ivory and Ruth Prawer Jhabvala, who collaborated on a 1979 film version of Henry James's *The Europeans*. This is a much better film, intelligent and subtle and open to the underlying tragedy of a woman who does not know what she wants, a man who does not care what he wants, and a girl who does not need what she wants.

The Bounty ★ ★ ★ ★
PG, 130 m., 1984

Anthony Hopkins (Lieutenant William Bligh), Mel Gibson (Fletcher Christian), Tevaite Vernette (Mauatua), Laurence Olivier (Admiral Hood), Edward Fox (Captain Greetham), Daniel Day-Lewis (Fryer). Directed by Roger Donaldson and produced by Bernard Williams. Screenplay by Robert Bolt.

The relationship between Fletcher Christian and Captain William Bligh is one of the most familiar in the movies: We've seen it acted between Clark Gable and Charles Laughton, and between Marlon Brando and Trevor Howard, but it's never before been quite as intriguing as in *The Bounty*, the third movie based on the most famous mutiny in the history of the sea. The movie suggests that Bligh and Christian were friends, of all things, and that Bligh—far from being the histrionic martinet of earlier movies—was an intelligent, contemplative man of great complications. The story is well-known, and simple: *HMS Bounty* sets sail for the South seas, has a difficult voyage that frays everyone's tempers, and then anchors at a Polynesian island. During the trip, the original first mate has been replaced by the young Fletcher Christian, whom Bligh decides to trust. But Christian tires of the voyage and of the dangers and probable death that lie ahead. He falls in love with a native girl and leads a mutiny of sailors who choose to stay on their island paradise. Bligh is played by Anthony Hopkins in one of the most interesting performances of 1984: He is unyielding, but not mindlessly rigid; certain he is right, but not egotistical; able to be realistic about his fate and his chances, and yet completely loyal to his ideas of a British naval officer's proper duties. When Fletcher Christian leads a mutiny against his command, it is not seen simply as a revolt against cruel authority (as in the earlier movies) but as a choice between a freer life-style, and Bligh's placing of duty above ordinary human nature.

Every *Bounty* movie seems to shape its Fletcher Christian somewhat to reflect the actor who plays him. Gable's Christian was a man of action, filled with physical strength and high spirits. Brando's was introverted and tortured. Mel Gibson's is maybe the hardest to figure of the three. He is a man of very few words (the screenplay gives him little to say, and almost no philosophizing), quiet, observant, an enigma. Only in the arms of the woman he comes to love, the Tahitian girl Mauatua, does he find the utter simplicity that perhaps he was looking for when he went to sea. It is a decision of some daring to give Gibson so noticeably little dialogue in this movie, but it works.

This *Bounty* is not only a wonderful movie, high-spirited and intelligent, but something of a production triumph as well. Although this third *Bounty* film was originally conceived as a big-budget, two-part epic to be directed by David *(Dr. Zhivago)* Lean, the current version was prepared and directed after only a few months' notice by a talented young New Zealander named Roger Donaldson, whose previous credits included the brilliant *Smash Palace*, a critical hit and commercial failure. What's interesting is that Donaldson's film doesn't feel like a secondhand treatment; he directs with flair and wit, and the spectacular scenes (like a stormy crossing of the Cape) never allow the special effects to steal the film away from the actors.

The sea voyage is done with the sort of macho confidence that a good sea movie needs, and the land portions to do an interesting job of contrasting the proper, civilized British (represented by Laurence Olivier, as an admiral) with the cheerful absolute freedom of Polynesia. The romance between Gibson and the beautiful Tevaite Vernette, as his island lover, is given time to develop instead of just being thrown in as a plot point. And the Polynesians, for once, are all allowed to go topless all the time (the movie nevertheless gets the PG rating, qualifying under the *National Geographic* loophole in which nudity doesn't count south of the equator). *The Bounty* is a great adventure, a lush romance, and a good movie.

Brazil ★ ★
R, 130 m., 1985

Jonathan Pryce (Sam Lowry), Robert De Niro (Tuttle), Katherine Helmond (Ida Lowry), Ian Holm (Kurtzmann), Bob Hoskins (Spoor), Michael Palin (Jack Lint). Directed by Terry Gilliam and produced by Arnon Milchan. Screenplay by Tom Stoppard, Charles McKeown, and Gilliam.

Just as Orwell's *1984* is an alternative vision of our times, so *Brazil* is an alternative to Orwell. The movie happens in a time and place that seem vaguely like our own, but with different graphics, hardware, and politics. Society is controlled by a monolithic organization, and citizens lead lives of paranoia and control. Thought police are likely to come crashing through the ceiling and start bashing at dissenters. Life is mean and grim.

The hero of *Brazil* is Sam Lowry (Jonathan Pryce), a meek, desperate little man who works at a computer terminal all day. Occasionally he cheats; when the boss isn't looking, he and his fellows switch the screens of their computers to reruns of exciting old TV programs. Sam knows his life is drab and lockstep, but he sees no way out of it, and his only escape is into his fantasies—into glorious dreams of flying high above all the petty cares of the world, urged on by the vision of a beautiful woman.

His everyday life offers no such possibilities. Even the basic mechanisms of life support seem to be failing, and one scene early in the movie has Robert De Niro, in a walk-on, as an illegal free-lance repairman who defies the state by fixing things. De Niro makes his escapes by sliding down long cables to freedom, like Spider-Man. For Sam, there seems to be no escape.

But then he gets involved in an intrigue that involves the girl of his dreams, the chief executive of the state, and a shadowy band of dissenters. All of this is strangely familiar; the outlines of *Brazil* are much the same as those of *1984*, but the approach is different. While Orwell's lean prose was translated, last year, into an equally lean and dour film, *Brazil* seems almost like a throwback to the psychedelic 1960s, to an anarchic vision in which the best way to improve things is to blow them up.

The other difference between the two worlds—Orwell's, and the one created here by director and co-writer Terry Gilliam—is that Gilliam has apparently had no financial restraints. Although *Brazil* has had a checkered history since it was made (for a long time, Universal Pictures seemed unwilling to release it), there was a lot of money available to make it, and the movie is awash in elaborate special effects, sensational sets, apocalyptic scenes of destruction, and a general lack of discipline. It's as if Gilliam sat down and wrote out all of his fantasies, heedless of production difficulties, and then they were filmed—this time, heedless of sense.

The movie is very hard to follow. I have seen it twice, and am still not sure exactly who all the characters are, or how they fit. Perhaps I am not supposed to be clear; perhaps the movie's air of confusion is part of its paranoid vision. There are individual moments that create sharp images (shock troops drilling through a ceiling, De Niro wrestling with the almost obscene wiring and tubing inside a wall, the movie's obsession with bizarre ductwork), but there seems to be no sure hand at the controls.

The best scene in the movie is one of the simplest, as Sam moves into half an office and finds himself engaged in a tug-of-war over his desk with the man through the wall. I was reminded of a Chaplin film like *Modern Times*, and reminded, too, that in Chaplin economy and simplicity were virtues, not the enemy.

The Breakfast Club ★ ★ ★
R, 95 m., 1985

Emilio Estevez (Andrew Clark), Anthony Michael Hall (Brian Johnson), Judd Nelson (Carl), Molly Ringwald (Claire Standish), Ally Sheedy (Allison Reynolds), Paul Gleason (Teacher), John Kapelos (Janitor). Directed by John Hughes and produced by Ned Tanen and Hughes. Screenplay by Hughes.

The Breakfast Club begins with an old dramatic standby. You isolate a group of people in a room, you have them talk, and eventually they exchange truths about themselves and come to new understandings. William Saroyan and Eugene O'Neill have been here before, but they used saloons and drunks. *The Breakfast Club* uses a high school library and five teen-age kids.

The movie takes place on a Saturday. The five kids have all violated high school rules in one way or another, and they've qualified for a special version of detention, all day long, from eight to four, in the school library. They arrive at the school one at a time. There's the arrogant, swaggering tough guy (Judd Nelson). The insecure neurotic (Ally Sheedy) who hides behind her hair and her clothes. The jock from the wrestling team (Emilio Estevez). The prom queen (Molly Ringwald). And the class brain (Anthony Michael Hall). These kids have nothing in common, and they have an aggressive desire *not* to have anything in common. In ways peculiar to teen-agers, who sometimes have a studious disinterest in anything that contradicts their self-image, these kids aren't even curious about each other. Not at first, anyway. But then the day grows longer and the library grows more oppressive, and finally the tough kid can't resist picking on the prom queen, and then there is a series of exchanges.

Nothing that happens in *The Breakfast Club* is all that surprising. The truths that are exchanged are more or less predictable, and the kids have fairly standard hang-ups. It comes as no surprise, for example, to learn that the jock's father is a perfectionist, or that the prom queen's parents give her material rewards but withhold their love. But *The Breakfast Club* doesn't need earthshaking revelations; it's about kids who grow willing to talk to one another, and it has a surprisingly good ear for the way they speak. (Ever notice the way lots of teen-age girls, repeating a conversation, say "she goes . . ." rather than "she says . . ."?)

The movie was written and directed by John Hughes, who also made 1984's *Sixteen Candles*. Two of the stars of that movie (Ringwald and Hall) are back again, and there's another similarity: Both movies make an honest attempt to create teen-agers who might seem plausible to other teen-agers. Most Hollywood teen-age movies give us underage nymphos or nostalgia-drenched memories of the 1950s. The performances are wonderful, but then this is an all-star cast, as younger actors go; in addition to Hall and Ringwald from *Sixteen Candles*, there's Sheedy from *WarGames* and Estevez from *Repo Man*. Judd Nelson is not yet as well known, but his character creates the strong center of the film; his aggression is what breaks the silence and knocks over the walls. The only weaknesses in Hughes's writing are in the adult characters: The teacher is one-dimensional and one-note, and the janitor is brought onstage with a potted philosophical talk that isn't really necessary. Typically, the kids don't pay much attention.

Note: The "R" rating on this film refers to language; I think a PG-13 rating would have been more reasonable. The film is certainly appropriate for thoughtful teen-agers.

Breakin' 2—Electric Boogaloo ★ ★ ★
PG, 94 m., 1984

Adolfo "Shabba-Doo" Quinones (Ozone), Michael "Boogaloo Shrimp" Chambers (Turbo), Lucinda Dickey (Kelly). Directed by Sam Firstenberg and produced by Menachem Golan and Yoram Globus. Written by Jan Ventura and Julie Reichert.

Movie musicals used to be allowed to be goofy and lightweight, but in recent years they've turned into ponderous, over-budgeted artifacts that take themselves so seriously you feel guilty if you're having a good time. Remember all the self-importance of *Annie?* That's why a modest, cheerful little movie like *Breakin' 2—Electric Boogaloo* is so refreshing. Here is a movie that wants nothing more than to allow some high-spirited kids to sing and dance their

way through a silly plot just long enough to make us grin.

The movie is a sequel to 1983's very successful *Breakin'*. I guess that explains the ungainly title. It involves the same actors, including a team of street-dance artists named Shabba-Doo Quinones and Boogaloo Shrimp Chambers, who more or less seem to be playing themselves. The plot is so familiar that if you're a fan of Mickey Rooney musicals or even the Beach Party movies, you may start rubbing your eyes. But the movie is a lot of fun.

Familiar? Try this plot out on your nearest trivia expert. A bunch of kids get together to turn a run-down old theater into a community center. The center is run by a nice old guy (who is not, for some reason, called "Pops"), and the ringleaders are Shabba-Doo and Boogaloo. In the last movie, they formed a dance team with a rich girl (Lucinda Dickey), and as this movie opens she visits their center and decides to stay and pitch in, despite the opposition of her WASP parents, who want her to enroll in an Ivy League university. Then the plot thickens, when an evil real estate developer wants to tear down the center and put up a big retail development. With just a few minor modifications, this story could be about Mickey and Judy, or Frankie and Annette. But what does it matter, when the whole point of the enterprise is to provide an excuse for song and dance? Quinones, Chambers, and Dickey can indeed dance, very well, and there are a lot of other street dancers in the movie, but what's interesting is the way the traditions of street dancing are combined in this movie with the older traditions of stage dancing and chorus lines. The big extravaganza at the end (a benefit to save the center, needless to say) is a unique hybrid of old and new dance styles.

Electric Boogaloo is not a great movie, but it's inexhaustible, entertaining, and may turn out to be influential. It could inspire a boomlet of low-priced movie musicals—movies not saddled with multimillion dollar budgets, Broadway connections, and stars who are not necessarily able to sing and dance. And at a time when movie musicals (as opposed to movie sound tracks) are seriously out of touch with the music that is really being played and listened to by teen-agers, that could be a revolutionary development.

Breaking Away ★ ★ ★ ★
PG, 100 m., 1979

Dennis Christopher (Dave), Dennis Quaid (Mike), Daniel Stern (Cyril), Jackie Earle Haley (Moocher), Paul Dooley (Dad), Barbara Barrie (Mom), Robyn Douglass (Katherine). Directed and produced by Peter Yates. Screenplay by Steve Tesich.

Here's a sunny, goofy, intelligent little film about coming of age in Bloomington, Indiana. It's about four local kids, just out of high school, who mess around for one final summer before facing the inexorable choices of jobs or college or the Army. One of the kids, Dave (Dennis Christopher), has it in his head that he wants to be a champion Italian bicycle racer, and he drives his father crazy with opera records and ersatz Italian.

His friends have more reasonable ambitions: One (Dennis Quaid) was a high school football star who pretends he doesn't want to play college ball, but he does; another (Jackie Earle Haley) is a short kid who pretends he doesn't want to be taller, but he does; and another (Daniel Stern) is one of those kids like we all knew, who learned how to talk by crossing Eric Sevareid with Woody Allen.

There's the usual town-and-gown tension in Bloomington, between the jocks and the townies (who are known, in Bloomington, as "cutters"—so called after the workers in the area's limestone quarries). There's also a poignant kind of tension between local guys and college girls: Will a sorority girl be seen with a cutter? Dave finds out by falling hopelessly in love with a college girl named Kathy (Robyn Douglass), and somehow, insanely, convincing her he's actually an Italian exchange student.

The whole business of Dave's Italomania provides the movie's funniest running joke: Dave's father (Paul Dooley) rants and raves that he didn't raise his boy to be an Eye-talian, and that he's sick and tired of all the eenees in the house: linguini, fettucini . . . even Jake, the dog, which Dave has renamed Fellini. The performances by Dooley and Barbara Barrie as Dave's parents are so loving and funny at the same time that we remember, almost with a shock, that *every* movie doesn't have to have parents and kids who don't get along.

The movie was directed as a work of love by Peter Yates, whose big commercial hits have included *Bullitt* and *The Deep*. The Oscar-winning original screenplay was written by Steve Tesich, who was born in Yugoslavia, was moved to Bloomington at the age of thirteen, won the Little 500 bicycle race there in 1962, and uses it for the film's climax. Yates has gone for the human elements in *Breaking Away*, but he hasn't forgotten how to direct action, and there's a bravura sequence in which Dave, on a racing bicycle, engages in a high-speed highway duel with a semitrailer truck.

In this scene, and in scenes involving swimming in an abandoned quarry, Yates does a tricky and intriguing thing: He suggests the constant possibility of sudden tragedy. We wait for a terrible accident to happen, and none does, but the hints of one make the characters seem curiously vulnerable, and their lives more precious.

The whole movie, indeed, is a delicate balancing act of its various tones: This movie could have been impossible to direct, but Yates has us on his side almost immediately. Some scenes edge into fantasy, others are straightforward character development, some (like the high school quarterback's monologue about his probable future) are heartbreakingly true. But the movie always returns to light comedy, to romance, to a wonderfully evocative instant nostalgia. *Breaking Away* is a movie to embrace. It's about people who are complicated but decent, who are optimists but see things realistically, who are fundamentally comic characters but have three full dimensions. It's about a Middle America we rarely see in the movies, yes, but it's not corny and it doesn't condescend. Movies like this are hardly ever made at all; when they're made this well, they're precious cinematic miracles.

Breathless ★ ★ ½
R, 100 m., 1983

Richard Gere (Jesse Lujack), Valerie Kaprisky (Monica Poiccard). Directed by Jim McBride and produced by Martin Erlichman. Screenplay by McBride and L.M. (Kit) Carson.

There are several levels of cinematic incest at work in *Breathless*, an American film inspired by a 1959 French film that was itself inspired by countless even earlier Hollywood crime films, including *Gun Crazy*—a movie that turns up in this movie. This is the kind of movie for which you need your *Filmgoer's Companion*. Or maybe not; for its announced purpose, as a lurid melodrama about sex and death, it works well enough even without the cross-references. The movie stars Richard Gere, Hollywood's ranking male sex symbol, and Valerie Kaprisky, an unknown French actress, in a story of doom and obsession adapted from Jean-Luc Godard's *Breathless*.

The 1959 *Breathless* starred Jean-Paul Belmondo as a loutish young Frenchman who modeled his behavior on Bogart and Cagney, and bluffed his way into a fatal confrontation with the cops. Jean Seberg played a young American girl who came to Paris to study, met Belmondo, and found herself sharing his bed and his fate. Godard's *Breathless* superimposed Hollywood images on French life-styles. Jim McBride's 1983 *Breathless*, from a script by L.M. (Kit) Carson, does a reverse on the same theme. This time the student (Kaprisky) is French; she's studying in Los Angeles. The lout (Gere) is an American hustler who has to get out of Las Vegas in a hurry, is chased by a highway patrolman, and kills him in a confrontation that is deliberately ambiguous: Did he mean to shoot him or not?

On the run, Gere moves in with Kaprisky, whom he knows only from a weekend fling in Vegas. They make passionate love. The girl gradually becomes aware that her lover is the subject of a statewide manhunt, and the chase leads from punk discos to the Hollywood hills. McBride and Carson position their film somewhere between plausibility (in scenes on a campus, in a grocery store, and in a Mexican restaurant) and stylized fantasy (in the garish red tones of the open-ing scenes and in Gere's deliberate overacting).

Although movie buffs will probably enjoy this movie's cross-references, this *Breathless* is going to depend on its appeal to ordinary audiences. I imagine they'll be attracted by the notion of Gere as an erotic outlaw on the run, but how will they like him in this role? I thought Gere was deliberately repugnant, but in an interesting way. He plays a character so conceited, so self-absorbed and, I'm afraid, so dim-witted, that there's no opportunity to ever really care for or about him. Kaprisky, as the young French student, is an unknown in a role too large and complex for her, and there are times when she seems lost in a scene, looking to Gere for guidance. The result is a stylistic exercise without any genuine human concerns we can identify with—and yet, an exercise that does have a command of its style, is good looking, fun to watch, and develops a certain morbid humor.

Brewster's Millions ★
PG, 101 m., 1985

Richard Pryor (Brewster), John Candy (Spike Nolan), Lonette McKee (Angela Drake), Hume Cronyn (Great-uncle), Jerry Orbach (Baseball Manager). Directed by Walter Hill and produced by Lawrence Bordon and Joel Silver. Screenplay by Jerschel Weingrod and Timothy Harris.

Here's the deal. Richard Pryor's millionaire great-uncle, a relative he never knew he had, has died and left him $300 million. There is a catch. The uncle wants Pryor to grow so thoroughly sick of money that he never wants to see another dollar bill. Therefore, the fortune comes with a condition attached: To qualify for the $300 million, Pryor has to spend the first $30 million in thirty days—and have absolutely no assets to show at the end of the month.

Brewster's Millions is the story of how Pryor spends the month, and the money. As a story, it may sound slightly familiar to you from the "Late Show." The original novel by George Barr McCutcheon has been filmed six times before, including once by Fatty Arbuckle and by the British under the title *Three on a Spree*. The story may be old, but I walked in figuring Pryor might have been able to do something new with it—especially with the goofy John Candy as co-star, and Walter (*Trading Places*) Hill as director. I was wrong.

Brewster's Millions is a one-note story. The movie begins with the challenge to Pryor, it observes Pryor as he tries to spend the money, and that's about it. There are three subplots (Pryor's relationship with a bush-league baseball team, his courtship of a beautiful accountant, and the efforts of some lawyers to bilk him out of his inheritance). All three are predictable from beginning to end. Even John Candy can't cheer things up; he waves his hands a lot and gets manic, but he isn't given a character to play and a lot of the time he just seems to be standing there.

The problem, I think, is that the movie has only been given one level. Pryor is supposed to spend the money, and he spends the money. Maybe he should have gotten trapped in some weird situation along the way—a situation he couldn't buy his way out of. Or maybe the romance (with Lonette McKee, from *The Cotton Club*) could have presented some special problems, instead of the same old misunderstandings that seem phoned in from another movie.

Pryor, as Brewster, has one real passion in the movie, and that's for baseball. He and Candy are veterans of the Hackensack Bulls, a third-rate team with a railroad track running through its outfield. One of the ways Brewster thinks up to spend money is to realize his lifelong dream and play the Yankees. But after he finances a special exhibition game between the two teams, there's no comic climax, just a sort of bittersweet fizzle.

I think maybe the basic problem with *Brewster's Millions* is that it's too nice. Richard Pryor is best when he's got an edge to him, as he does in his concert films. This time, as a sweet, naive innocent, he drifts through the plot without really colliding with anybody. Maybe what I'm saying is that the story itself is too innocent for these cynical times.

Bring Me the Head of Alfredo Garcia
★ ★ ★ ★
R, 112 m., 1974

Warren Oates (Bennie), Isela Vega (Elita), Kris Kristofferson (Paco), Gig Young (Killer). Directed by Sam Peckinpah and produced by Martin Baum. Screenplay by Gordon T. Dawson and Peckinpah.

Sam Peckinpah's *Bring Me the Head of Alfredo Garcia* is a weird, horrifying film that somehow transcends its unlikely material. It's the story of a drunken and violent odyssey across Mexico by a dropout bartender who, if he returns Alfredo Garcia's head, stands to be paid a million dollars. The head accompanies him in a burlap bag, tossed into the front seat of a beat-up old Ford convertible, and it gathers flies and symbolic meaning at about the same pace.

The movie is some kind of bizarre masterpiece. It's probably not a movie that most people would like, but violence, with Peckinpah, sometimes becomes a psychic ballet. His characters don't look for it, they don't like it, and they negotiate it with weariness and resignation. They're too beat up by life to get any kind of exhilaration from a fight. They've been in far too many fights already, and lost most of them, and the violence they encounter is just another cross to bear.

That's the case with Bennie, the antihero of *Bring Me the Head of Alfredo Garcia.* He's played by Warren Oates, one of that breed of movie actors who attract us, somehow, through their negative qualities. He's like some of the characters played by Jack Nicholson or Bruce Dern; we like him because he's suffered so much more than we ever will (we hope) that no matter what horrors he goes through, or inflicts, we still care about him.

Bennie is a bartender and plays a little piano, and he hears about the head of Alfredo Garcia from a couple of bounty hunters who pass through his saloon. They're played, by the way, by the unlikely team of Gig Young and Robert Webber, who between them define dissipation. Garcia's head is worth a million bucks because Garcia, it turns out, has impregnated the daughter of a rich Mexican industrialist. The millionaire is almost a caricature of macho compulsiveness; he simultaneously puts a price on the head of the culprit, and looks forward with pride to the birth of a grandson.

Bennie sees the million dollars as his ticket out of hell, and on the way to finding it he runs across Alfredo Garcia's former lover, Elita (Isela Vega, looking as moistly erotic as anyone since young Anna Magnani). They fall in love, or something; their relationship is complicated by Bennie's crude shyness and her own custom of being abused by men. The most perversely interesting relationship in the movie, however, is the friendship that grows between Bennie and Alfredo's head, once Bennie has gotten possession of it. That's made somewhat easier by the fact that Alfredo, it turns out, is already dead. But there is a gruesome struggle over his grave, and once Bennie finally gets the head he has to kill to protect his prize. His drive across Mexico is fueled by blood and tequila, and about halfway through it we realize why Peckinpah set his movie in the present, instead of in the past; this same material wouldn't have worked as a historical Western. The conventions of the genre would have insulted us from the impact of what happens. There would have been horses and watering holes and clichés. Instead, we get unforgettable scenes of Warren Oates with that grisly burlap bag and the bottle next to him in the front seat, and the nakedness of his greed is inescapable.

Somewhere along the way Oates, as Bennie, makes a compact with the prize he begins to call "Al." They both loved the same woman, they are both being destroyed by the same member of an upper class, they're both poor bastards who never asked for their grief in life. And slowly, out of the haze of the booze and the depths of his suffering, Bennie allies himself with Al and against the slob with the money. *Bring Me the Head of Alfredo Garcia* is Sam Peckinpah making movies flat out, giving us a desperate character he clearly loves, and asking us to somehow see past the horror and the blood to the sad poem he's trying to write about the human condition.

Broadway Danny Rose ★ ★ ★ ½
PG, 86 m., 1984

Woody Allen (Danny Rose), Mia Farrow (Tina Vitale), Nick Apollo Forte (Lou Canova). Directed by Woody Allen and produced by Robert Greenhut and Charles H. Joffe. Screenplay by Allen.

The first time we see him, he's talking fast, and his arms are working like a guy doing an imitation of an air traffic controller. His hands keep coming in for landings. This is Broadway Danny Rose, the most legendary talent agent in New York, the guy who will represent you after you've been laughed off every stage in the Catskills. He represents blind xylophonists, piano-playing birds, and has-been crooners with drinking problems. He's the kind of guy that comics sitting around on their day off tell stories about. He also is Woody Allen, but he is less like Woody Allen than some of the other characters Allen has played. After the autobiography of *Stardust Memories*, after the whimsy of *A Midsummer Night's Sex Comedy*, and the antiseptic experimentation of *Zelig*, this movie has Allen creating a character and following him all the way through a crazy story. After a period when Allen seemed stuck in self-doubt and introspection, he loosens up and has a good time.

Broadway Danny Rose, like all of Allen's best movies, is a New York movie. It starts at the Carnegie Deli, with comedians sitting around a table trading Danny Rose stories, and then it flashes back to the best Danny Rose story of them all, about how Danny signed up this has-been alcoholic tenor and carefully nurtured his career back to the brink of stardom. Riding the nostalgia boom, Danny takes the guy and books him into Top Forty concerts, until finally he gets him a date at the Waldorf—and Milton Berle is in the audience, looking for guests for his TV special. Except the crooner has a complicated love life. He has a wife, and he also has a girlfriend. He wants Danny Rose to be the "beard" and take the girlfriend to the concert. Otherwise he won't feel right. But then the crooner and the girl have a fight, and the girl goes back to her Mafioso boyfriend, and Danny Rose winds up at a mob wedding with a gun in his face.

All of this is accomplished with wonderfully off-the-wall characterizations. Allen makes Danny Rose into a caricature, and then, working from that base, turns him back into a human being: By the end of the film, we see the person beneath the mannerisms. Nick Apollo Forte, an actor I've never seen before, plays the has-been crooner with a soft touch: he's childish, he's a bear, he's loyal, he has a monstrous ego. The real treasure among the performances, however, is Mia Farrow's work as Tina Vitale, the crooner's girlfriend. You would think that Mia Farrow would be one of the most instantly recognizable actresses in the movies with those finely chiseled features and that little-girl voice. But here she is a chain-smoking, brassy blonde with her hair piled up on top of her head, and a pair of fashionable sunglasses, and dresses that look like they came from the boutique in a Mafia resort hotel.

Broadway Danny Rose uses all of the basic ingredients of Damon Runyon's Broadway: the pathetic acts looking for a job, the guys who get a break and forget their old friends, the agents with hearts of gold, the beautiful showgirls who fall for Woody Allen types, the dumb gangsters, big shots at the ringside tables (Howard Cosell plays himself). It all works.

The Brother from Another Planet
★ ★ ★ ½
PG, 110 m., 1984

Joe Morton (The Brother), Maggie Renzi (Noreen), Fisher Stevens (Card Trickster), John Sayles (Man in Black). Directed by John Sayles and produced by Sayles and Maggie Renzi. Screenplay by Sayles.

When the movies started to talk, they began to lose the open-eyed simplicity with which they saw the world. *The Brother from Another Planet* tells the story of a man who cannot talk, but who can read minds, listen carefully, look deep into eyes, and provide a sort of mirror for our society. That makes it sound serious, but like all the most serious movies, it's a comedy.

The film stars Joe Morton as a visitor from outer space, who looks like a black human being, unless you look carefully at the three funny toes on his feet. He arrives on Earth in a spaceship that looks borrowed from the cheapest B space operas from the 1950s, swims ashore, and finds himself on Manhattan Island. At first he is completely baffled. Before long, everyone he meets is just as baffled. It is strange to deal with people who confound all your expectations: It might even force you to reevaluate yourself.

The brother is not looking for trouble, is not controversial, wants only to make sense of this weird new world. Because his instinctive response to most situations is a sort of blank reserve, people project their own feelings and expectations upon him. They tell him what he must be thinking, and behave as if they are right. He goes along.

The movie finds countless opportunities for humorous scenes, most of them with a quiet little bite, a way of causing us to look at our society. The brother runs into hookers and connivers, tourists from Indiana, immigrant shopkeepers, and a New York weirdo who, in one of the movie's best scenes, shows him a baffling card trick, and then demonstrates another trick that contains a cynical grain of big-city truth. The brother walks through this menagerie with a sometimes bemused, sometimes puzzled look on his face. People seem to have a lot of problems on this planet. He is glad to help out when he can; for example, curing video games by a laying on of hands. His right hand contains the power to heal machines, and it is amazing how quickly people accept that, if it is useful to them.

The Brother from Another Planet was written and directed by John Sayles, who is a one-man industry in the world of the American independent film. His credits include *Return of the Secaucus Seven*, *Lianna*, and *Baby, It's You*, and in this film—by using a central character who cannot talk—he is sometimes able to explore the kinds of scenes that haven't been possible since the death of silent film. There are individual moments here worthy of a Keaton, and there are times when Joe Morton's unblinking passivity in the midst of chaos really does remind us of Buster.

There is also a curious way in which the film functions as more subtle social satire than might seem possible in a low-budget, good-natured comedy. Because the hero, the brother, has literally dropped out of the skies, he doesn't have an opinion on anything. He only gradually begins to realize that on this world he is "black," and that his color makes a difference in some situations. He tries to accept that. When he is hurt or wronged, his reaction is not so much anger as surprise: It seems to him so unnecessary that people behave unkindly toward one another. He is a little surprised they would go to such an effort. His surprise, in its own sweet and uncomplicated way, is one of the most effective elements in the whole movie.

Brubaker ★ ★ ½
R, 131 m., 1980

Robert Redford (Brubaker), Yaphet Kotto (Dickie Coombes), Jane Alexander (Lillian), Murray Hamilton (Deach), David Keith (Larry Lee Bullen), Morgan Freeman (Walter), M. Emmet Walsh (C.P. Woodward), Matt Clark (Purcell), Richard Ward (Abraham). Directed by Stuart Rosenberg and produced by Ron Silverman. Screenplay by W.D. Richter.

Brubaker is a grim and depressing drama about prison outrages—a movie that should, given its absolutely realistic vision, have kept us involved from beginning to end. That it doesn't is the result, I think, of a deliberate but unwise decision to focus on the issues involved in the story, instead of on the characters.

All the people in this movie have roles that represent something; there's the Idealistic Reformer, the Pragmatic Politician, the Corrupt Administrator, the Noble Prisoner, the Tough Guard. The problem is that once they're assigned an ideological niche at the beginning of the movie, they behave with absolute consistency. There's no room for the spontaneity of real human personalities caught in real situations.

That's especially annoying with the character of Brubaker himself, played well but within a frustratingly narrow range by Robert Redford. Brubaker is the reform warden assigned to clean up the violence and corruption of Wakefield Prison Farm, a hellhole of sadism where no guards are needed because the prisoner trusties are armed and get time off their sentences for shooting escapees. The movie's first twenty or thirty minutes, which are sickeningly

effective, document conditions in the prison, where the commonplaces include beatings, bribery, rape, and slum living conditions.

Brubaker finds out about these outrages firsthand. He has himself been brought into the prison anonymously, as a prisoner. This is supposed to provide the movie's biggest surprise, when he finally steps forward and identifies himself, but the ads for the movie spoiled the surprise by identifying Redford as the warden. What seems a little unlikely in these opening scenes is that Redford, as a new prisoner, would emerge unscathed: He observes, he listens, and he's mostly left alone by the other prisoners, even though his fellow new recruits are being raped, beaten, and forced into the prison's system of corruption.

After Redford takes charge, the movie disintegrates into predictability. He takes a position in favor of progressive reforms, and the state board of corrections takes a position in favor of corrupt business as usual. Some interesting characters are introduced, especially Yaphet Kotto as a hard-boiled trusty who can't make up his mind about the warden, and Jane Alexander, as a pragmatic aide to the state governor. Murray Hamilton, as a corrupt member of the state prison board, does his usual venal capitalist and does it well, but he has played this role so frequently (in the first two *Jaws* movies, for example), that he must know it by heart.

In the meantime, we're growing a little restless because of the movie's refusal to permit its characters more human dimensions. We want to know these people better, but the screenplay throws up a wall; they act according to the ideological positions assigned to them in the screenplay, and that's that. Half of Redford's speeches could have come out of newspaper editorials, but we never find out much about him. What's his background? Was he ever married? Is this his first prison job? What's his relationship with the Jane Alexander character, who seems to have gotten him this job? (Alexander has one almost subliminal moment when she fans her neck and looks at Redford and seems to be thinking unpolitical thoughts, but the movie hurries on.) *Brubaker* is a well-crafted film that does a harrowingly effective job of portraying the details of its prison, but it populates it with positions rather than people.

The Buddy Holly Story ★ ★ ★ ½
PG, 113 m., 1978

Bill Jordan (Riley Randolph), Maria Richwine (Maria Elena Holly), Conrad Janis (Ross Turner), Dick O'Neil (Sol Zuckerman), Gary Busey (Buddy Holly), Don Stroud (Jesse), Charles Martin Smith (Ray Bob). Directed by Steve Rash and produced by Fred Bauer. Screenplay by Robert Gittler.

On February 3, 1959, a small plane crashed outside Mason City, Iowa, killing Buddy Holly, Richie Valens, and J.P. (The Big Bopper) Richardson. Don McLean sang about that day in "American Pie." He called it the day the music died.

Walking out of *The Buddy Holly Story*, you wonder if maybe he wasn't right. It's no use trying to guess how things might have turned out if Holly hadn't been on that flight. He might have continued to develop as the most original rock and roll artist of his generation. He might, on the other hand, have gradually become a Paul Anka or a Barry Manilow, a polished performer of comfortably mainstream pop. The movie makes a pretty good case for the first possibility.

It also involves us as show biz biographies rarely do. This is one rock and roll movie with a chance of being remembered, one with something to say and the style and energy to say it well. That's partly because it had good material to start with; Holly's life provides a microcosm of rock and roll's transformation into the dominant music of the last decades. But it's also because of Gary Busey's remarkable performance as Buddy Holly. If you're a fan of Holly and his music, you'll be quietly amazed at how completely Busey gets into the character. His performance isn't an imitation, a series of "impressions." It's a distillation of how Holly *seemed*, and how he sounded. That's all the more impressive because the movie doesn't use dubbing from the original records: Busey himself sings Holly's arrangements. And the movie's many concert scenes don't use post-dubbing, which almost always result in a flat and unconvincing sound (see *Sgt. Pepper*). Busey did the material live.

That's crucial, in a way, because if *The Buddy Holly Story* doesn't convince (or remind) us that Holly's music was good, and

important, the movie itself fails. Busey and the filmmakers do convince us, without even seeming to try. Walking out of the theater, I overheard a teen-age couple expressing surprise that Holly had composed "It's So Easy to Fall in Love." They thought it was a Linda Ronstadt original.

More performers than Ronstadt learned from Holly. All the important rockers of the last thirty years, and particularly the Beatles, benefited from Holly's fusion of basic rock and roll, deeper musical sophistication, and lyrics that came with a sincere intensity ("I *was* Buddy Holly," John Lennon once said.) Most albums cut in 1958 or 1959 sound dated today, even the good ones. Holly's old albums still sound fresh.

The movie follows the events of Holly's life, more or less, from his beginnings in Lubbock, Texas, through his early hit records, his quick national fame, his performances on "The Ed Sullivan Show," his marriage, his death. Rock historians have pointed out the ways in which the screenplay alters the facts (Holly's parents were not opposed to his musical career; his romance with his wife, Maria, was whirlwind, not the stubborn courtship in the movie; the decision to take a plane that last night was made, not because the bus broke down, but because Holly and the others wanted to get their laundry done).

Details like that don't matter much. The movie gets the feel right, and there's real energy in the concert scenes, especially the tricky debut of Buddy Holly and the Crickets as the first white act in Harlem's famous Apollo Theater. And the supporting performances are convincing; they're not walk-ons, as they tend to be in show biz movies. Don Stroud and Charles Martin Smith are just right as the down-home Crickets. Maria Richwine brings a sweetness, an understanding to the role of Holly's wife, and Gloria Irricari, as her aunt, steals a wonderful scene. And Dick O'Neil, as the white booker who thought Holly was black when he booked him into the Apollo, does an inspired double-take.

When all of this has been said, there are still the songs to be considered. "That'll Be the Day." "Peggy Sue." "Oh, Boy!" "Words of Love." "True Love Ways." "It's So Easy." "It Doesn't Matter Anymore."

Gary Busey sings them with a style that does Holly justice. And that's saying something. They live, and the movie's concert sequences have the immediacy and energy of documentary footage—which is essentially what they are.

Bugsy Malone ★ ★ ★ ½
G, 94 m., 1976

Jodie Foster (Nightclub Singer), Scott Baio (Bugsy Malone), John Cassisi (Boss), Paul Murphy (Hit Man). Directed by Alan Parker and produced by Alan Marshall. Screenplay by Parker.

At first the notion seems alarming: a gangster movie cast entirely with kids. Especially when we learn that *Bugsy Malone* isn't intended as a kid's movie so much as a cheerful comment on the childlike values and behavior in classic Hollywood crime films. What are kids doing in something like this? But then we see the movie and we relax. *Bugsy Malone* is like nothing else. It's an original, a charming one, and it has yet another special performance by Jodie Foster, who at thirteen was already getting the roles that grown-up actresses complained weren't being written for women anymore. She plays a hard-bitten nightclub singer and vamps her way through a torch song by Paul Williams with approximately as much style as Rita Hayworth brought to *Gilda*. She starts on stage, drifts down into the audience, arches her eyebrows at the fat cats (all about junior high school age), and, in general, earns herself an Oscar nomination. And her performance seems just right in the film; *Bugsy Malone* depends almost totally on tone, put kids in these situations and direct them just a little wrongly and the movie would be offensive. But it's not, and it's especially right with Foster.

It tells a gangster story we know almost by heart, about the tough new gang that wants to take over the territory. Da Boss (a kid named John Cassisi who looks like he was born wearing a carnation in the lapel of his pinstripe) recruits hired guns to help protect his turf. Bugsy Malone (Scott Baio in training for John Garfield) is the guy he's gotta have. But maybe even Bugsy can't help, because the other gang has a dreaded new weapon. In Al Capone's day, it was machine

guns. In Bugsy's movie, it's marshmallow guns. They open up on you with one of these, and you got more than egg on your face. Old-fashioned weapons like custard pies are useless in a one-on-one situation.

Halfway through *Bugsy Malone*, I started wondering how anyone ever came up with this idea for a movie. Alan Parker, who wrote and directed it, claims his inspiration came while he was watching *The Godfather*. I dunno, I think the movie has more insights into kids than into gangsters.

When kids play, it's real. That's one of the things we lose when we grow up: the ability to turn the backyard into the OK Corral. The kids in *Bugsy Malone* don't behave as if the material is camp or a put-on. For them, it's real—especially the indignity of catching a marshmallow in your ear. And so in an uncanny way the movie works as a gangster movie and we remember that the old Bogart and Cagney classics had a childlike innocence, too. The world was simpler then. Now it's so complicated maybe only a kid can still understand the Bogart role.

Burden of Dreams ★ ★ ★
NO MPAA RATING, 94 m., 1982

Featuring Werner Herzog, Klaus Kinski, Claudia Cardinale, Jason Robards, Jr., and Mick Jagger. Directed and produced by Les Blank, with Maureen Gosling.

Les Blank's *Burden of Dreams* is one of the most remarkable documentaries ever made about the making of a movie. There are at least two reasons for that. One is that the movie being made, Werner Herzog's *Fitzcarraldo*, involved some of the most torturous and dangerous on-location shooting experiences in film history. The other is that the documentary is by Les Blank, himself a brilliant filmmaker, who is unafraid to ask difficult questions and portray Herzog, warts and all.

The story of Herzog's *Fitzcarraldo* is already the stuff of movie legend. The movie was shot on location deep within the rain forests of South America, one thousand miles from civilization. When the first version of the film was half-finished, its star, Jason Robards, was rushed back to New York with amoebic dysentery and forbidden by his doctors to return to the location. Herzog replaced Robards with Klaus Kinski (star of his *Aguirre, the Wrath of God*), but meanwhile, co-star Mick Jagger left the production because of a commitment to a concert tour. Then the Kinski version of *Fitzcarraldo* was caught in the middle of a border war between tribes of Indians. The whole production was moved twelve hundred miles, to a new location where the mishaps included plane crashes, disease, and attacks by unfriendly Indians. And all of those hardships were on top of the incredible task Herzog set himself to film: He wanted to show his obsessed hero using teams of Indians to pull an entire steamship up a hillside using only block and tackle!

Blank and his associate, Maureen Gosling, visited both locations of Herzog's film. Their documentary includes the only available record of some of the earlier scenes with Robards and Jagger. It also includes scenes in which Herzog seems to be going slowly mad, blaming the evil of the jungle and the depth of his own compulsions. In *Fitzcarraldo*, you can see the incredible strain as men try to pull a steamship up a sharp incline, using only muscle power and a few elementary principles of mechanics. In *Burden of Dreams*, Blank's camera moves back one more step, to show the actual mechanisms by which Herzog hoped to move his ship. A giant bulldozer is used to augment the block-and-pulley, but it proves barely equal to the task, and at one point the Brazilian engineer in charge of the project walks off, warning that lives will be lost.

What drives Herzog to make films that test his sanity and risk his life and those of his associates? Stanley Kauffmann, in the *New Republic*, argued that, for Herzog, the purpose of film is to risk death, and each of his films is in some way a challenge hurled at the odds. Herzog has made films on the slopes of active volcanoes, has filmed in the jungle and in the middle of the Sahara, and has made films about characters who live at the edges of human achievement. *Burden of Dreams* gives us an extraordinary portrait of Herzog trapped in the middle of one of his wildest dreams.

Buster and Billie ★ ★ ★
R, 100 m., 1974

Jan-Michael Vincent (Buster), Joan Goodfellow (Billie), Pamela Sue Martin (First Girlfriend). Directed by Dan Petrie and produced by Ron Silverman. Screenplay by Ron Turbeville.

The problem with a lot of nostalgia is that it captures the surface sound and style of a decade with an appreciation that works only with hindsight. People didn't spend all their time listening to Elvis, lowering their Chevys, and scuffing their white bucks in the fifties. Adolescence then, as now, was a time of uncertainty and confusion, and the surface stuff often only concealed the kids inside. *The Lords of Flatbush* did a good job of seeing past its black leather jackets and into the hearts of the essentially immature and unsure people who wore them, as does *Buster and Billie* with a memory of what it might have been like to go to high school in the South, circa 1948.

The movie's no masterpiece, but it's an affecting story well told, it observes its teenage characters with a fine insight, and it almost earns its tragic ending. Happy endings used to be Hollywood clichés; now, if we ever got one, it would almost feel original.

The story gives us some ordinary high school kids growing up in a pleasant semirural section of Georgia. They drive around in cars and pickup trucks, they go to dances, they study, and when the guys hang around with the guys and the girls hang around with the girls, the subject of conversation is, always and eternally, the mysteries of the opposite sex. Nobody knows much about sex, period, much less the opposite one, but there's a lot of big talk and an insatiable curiosity.

Curiosity is satisfied, however, for some of the guys through the friendliness of Billie, a shy, pretty girl who lives with subliterate parents and who is so lacking in self-confidence that she seeks to find acceptance by, as the fine old phrase has it, putting out. Several guys in the school have been with Billie, or say they have, or mean to, or in any event may.

But not Buster, who is your typical high school jock and a little something more. He knows his own mind, is independent, is admired, and has a much larger measure of compassion than his friends. He's engaged to marry an insipid girl, the kind who wins the Homecoming Queen title and believes the momentum will carry her straight through life. But Buster becomes intrigued with Billie. He senses something about her that has value; he seems to instinctively understand why she behaves as she does, and (more importantly) why she doesn't have to.

Most of the movie is about the love that slowly grows up between them as Buster wins Billie's trust and helps her to develop self-confidence. The fact that Buster would be seen publicly with Billie (would, indeed, take her to Sunday church) causes indignation within the cliquish high school crowd he runs with, and especially among Billie's numerous former boyfriends.

What's good about the movie—what you'll remember—are the tender and rather lovely scenes between Buster and Billie, and the strength with which Buster faces down the disapproval of his friends. What doesn't work, for me, anyway, is the violent and tragic ending. It's not that the ending isn't plausible; indeed, as it's presented, it seems inevitable enough. It's just that somehow the human values in the film should have been developed more fully, so that at the end we could have some sort of resolution based on changes in the characters, rather than on their violent acts.

Much of the movie's affecting quality comes from fine performances by Jan-Michael Vincent and Joan Goodfellow, as the young lovers. There's a scene showing their first date, with the girl too shy, almost, to talk, and it's so quiet and warm we can really understand how these two kids feel. There's a scene where Buster defends Billie to his parents, and another one in a pool room where he faces his friends. This kind of movie, honestly examining the bonds of both friendship and cruelty that hold together adolescent peer groups, is a lot more accurate about the old days than any number of golden-oldie sound tracks and gee-whiz sock hops.

Butley ★ ★ ★ ★
NO MPAA RATING, 127 m., 1974 ✔

Alan Bates (Ben Butley), Richard O'Callaghan (Joey), Jessica Tandy (Edna Shaft), Susan Engel (Ann Butley), Michael Byrne (Reg), Georgina Hale (Miss Heasman). Directed by Harold Pinter and produced by Ely A. Landau. Screenplay by Simon Gray.

Once, in the dim recesses of his alcoholic past, Ben Butley was an authority on T.S. Eliot. But now his photograph of Eliot is peeling from the wall, and Butley is peeling, too. During the course of Simon Gray's *Butley*, which was brilliantly directed for the American Film Theater by Harold Pinter, Butley peels off one layer, and then another, and finally comes down to his self-hating, desperately lonely core.

Butley is one of the most affecting characters of modern theater. He tries to bind people to himself with sarcasm, insult, and a merciless eye for their vulnerabilities. Eventually, it seems, he always fails. But the way Alan Bates plays him (and Bates, who created the role on the London stage, knows him as well as anybody), his mind is still resilient and panther-quick, with a streak of saving humor. So we don't pity him, even though we should. He somehow doggedly weathers each crisis, and we even feel a sneaky affection for him. Maybe that's the way the role is written, or maybe it's because of the double-reverse charm Bates brings to it; I couldn't quite tell.

The film takes place during a day in an office shared by two English instructors at Queen Mary's College, London. One is Butley, who, as he approaches middle age, has abandoned the difficulties of Eliot and taken up nursery rhymes. The other is Joey, who began as Butley's protégé, then became his roommate, and then (after Butley's marriage and separation) became his roommate again. Joey is as meticulous as Butley is a shambles. Butley spends his day in psychological warfare against the truths that would batter him down. His wife tells him she intends to marry another man. Bad enough. But then Joey acknowledges that he's leaving, too—also for another man. Butley faces being left totally alone, and he fights back with wit, with obscenity, with insult, with booze.

Butley was born lonely, I'd say. He needs to have somebody there. After his marriage fails, he needs Joey again, because Joey had at least admired him at one time. It doesn't really seem to be relevant that Joey is a homosexual; Butley's needs are not sexual but psychological. Butley doesn't have much affection for women: He has some feeling left for his wife, but conceals it well, and he has contempt for the other women in his day—the spinster Byron scholar (played by Jessica Tandy) and the would-be tutorial student (Georgina Hale). True, but he doesn't succeed in acting much better with the men. His loneliness seems to be asexual, if anything. And his tragedy is that he can't admit his hungers and needs—not until the play's end, anyway, when he makes an oblique but honest assessment of his current situation. Butley attempts to keep Joey by attacking his weaknesses, and he taunts Reg, Joey's new friend, in a futile attempt to drive him away. He's a dazzler with words, and even during the most pathetic scenes, he still somehow doesn't lose the poetry.

The Alan Bates performance reminded me of how good he was in a movie that never got a proper American playoff, *A Day in the Death of Joe Egg*. He gives the character so much spirit that the material never feels as depressing as it sounds. We get the feeling that here's one old campaigner who will stay on his feet no matter what, and give the bastards as good as he gets. The supporting cast (especially Richard O'Callaghan as Joey) is also good, and Pinter's direction moves with such awareness of what the play is about that we're hardly conscious of any sense of filmed theater. The play hasn't been opened up so much as opened in: The camera gets closer to the characters and sees more. What it sees in *Butley* is a man with a desperate problem. He needs other people, and his only strategy for attracting them is to drive them away.

Cabaret ★ ★ ★ ½
PG, 119 m., 1972

Liza Minnelli (Sally Bowles), Michael York (Brian Roberts), Joel Grey (Master of Ceremonies), Helmut Griem (Fritz Wendel), Fritz Wepper (Fraulein Schneider). Directed by Bob Fosse and produced by Cy Feuer. Screenplay by Jay Allen.

Cabaret explores some of the same kinky territory celebrated in Visconti's *The Damned*. Both movies share the general idea that the rise of the Nazi party in Germany was accompanied by a rise in bisexuality, homosexuality, sadomasochism, and assorted other activities. Taken as a generalization about a national movement, this is certainly extreme oversimplification. But taken as one approach to the darker recesses of Nazism, it may come pretty close to the mark. The Nazi gimmicks like boots and leather and muscles and racial superiority and outdoor rallies and Aryan comradeship offered an array of machismo-for-rent that had (and has) a special appeal to some kinds of impotent people.

Cabaret is about people like that, and it takes place largely in a specific Berlin cabaret, circa 1930, in which decadence and sexual ambiguity were just part of the ambience (like the women mud-wrestlers who appeared between acts). This is no ordinary musical. Part of its success comes because it doesn't fall for the old cliché that musicals have to make you happy. Instead of cheapening the movie version by lightening its load of despair, director Bob Fosse has gone right to the bleak heart of the material and stayed there well enough to win an Academy Award for Best Director.

The story concerns one of the more famous literary inventions of the century, Sally Bowles, who first came to life in the late Christopher Isherwood's *Berlin Stories*, and then appeared in the play and movie *I Am a Camera* before returning to the stage in this musical, and then making it into the movies a second time—a modern record, I'd say.

Sally is brought magnificently to the screen in an Oscar-winning performance by Liza Minnelli, who plays her as a girl who's bought what the cabaret is selling. To her, the point is to laugh and sing and live forever in the moment; to refuse to take things seriously—even Nazism—and to relate with people only up to a certain point. She is capable of warmth and emotion, but a lot of it is theatrical, and when the chips are down she's as decadent as the "daringly decadent" dark fingernail polish she flaunts.

Liza Minnelli plays Sally Bowles so well and fully that it doesn't matter how well she sings and dances, if you see what I mean. In several musical numbers (including the stunning finale *Cabaret* number), Liza demonstrates unmistakably that she's one of the great musical performers of our time. But the heartlessness and nihilism of the character is still there, all the time, even while we're being supremely entertained.

Sally gets involved in a triangular relationship with a young English language teacher (Michael York) and a young baron (Helmut Griem), and if this particular triangle didn't exist in the stage version, that doesn't matter. It helps define the movie's whole feel of moral anarchy, and it is underlined by the sheer desperation in the cabaret itself.

Here the festivities are overseen by a master of ceremonies (Joel Grey, whose performance received an Oscar for best supporting actor) whose determination to keep the merriment going, at whatever psychic cost, has a poignant compulsiveness. When the song *Cabaret* comes at the end, you realize for the first time that it isn't a song of happiness, but of desperation. The context makes the difference. In the same way, the context of Germany on the eve of the Nazi ascent to power makes the entire musical into an unforgettable cry of despair.

Caddyshack ★ ★ ½
R, 99 m., 1980

Chevy Chase (Ty Webb), Rodney Dangerfield (Al Czervik), Ted Knight (Judge Smails), Michael O'Keefe (Danny), Bill Murray (Carl), Sarah Holcomb (Maggie). Directed by Harold Ramis and produced by Douglas Kenney. Screenplay by Brian Doyle-Murray, Ramis, and Kenney.

Caddyshack never finds a consistent comic note of its own, but it plays host to all sorts of approaches from its stars, who sometimes hardly seem to be occupying the same movie. There's Bill Murray's self-absorbed craziness, Chevy Chase's laid-back bemusement, and Ted Knight's apoplectic overplaying. And then there is Rodney Dangerfield, who wades into the movie and cleans up.

To the degree that this is anybody's movie, it's Dangerfield's—and he mostly seems to be using his own material. He plays a loud, vulgar, twitching condo developer who is thinking of buying a country club and using

the land for housing. The country club is one of those exclusive WASP enclaves, a haven for such types as the judge who founded it (Knight), the ne'er-do-well club champion (Chase), and the manic assistant grounds keeper (Murray).

The movie never really develops a plot, but maybe it doesn't want to. Director Harold Ramis brings on his cast of characters and lets them loose at one another. There's a vague subplot about a college scholarship for the caddies, and another one about the judge's nubile niece, and continuing warfare waged by Murray against the gophers who are devastating the club. But Ramis is cheerfully prepared to interrupt everything for moments of comic inspiration, and there are three especially good ones: The caddies in the swimming pool doing a Busby Berkeley number, another pool scene that's a scatalogical satire of *Jaws*, and a sequence in which Dangerfield's gigantic speedboat devastates a yacht club.

Dangerfield is funniest, though, when the movie just lets him talk. He's a Henny Youngman clone, filled with one-liners and insults, and he's great at the country club's dinner dance, abusing everyone and making rude noises. Surveying the crowd from the bar, he uses lines that he has, in fact, stolen directly from his nightclub routine ("This steak still has the mark of the jockey's whip on it"). With his bizarre wardrobe and trick golf bag, he's a throwback to the Groucho Marx and W.C. Fields school of insult comedy; he has a vitality that the movie's younger comedians can't match, and they suffer in comparison.

Chevy Chase, for example, has some wonderful moments in this movie, as a studiously absent-minded hedonist who doesn't even bother to keep score when he plays golf. He's good, but somehow he's in the wrong movie: His whimsy doesn't fit with Dangerfield's blatant scenery-chewing or with the Bill Murray character. Murray, as a slob who goes after gophers with explosives and entertains sexual fantasies about the women golfers, could be a refugee from *Animal House*.

Maybe one of the movie's problems is that the central characters are never really involved in the same action. Murray's off on his own, fighting gophers. Dangerfield arrives, devastates, exits. Knight is busy impressing the caddies, making vague promises about scholarships, and launching boats. If they were somehow all drawn together into the same story, maybe we'd be carried along more confidently. But *Caddyshack* feels more like a movie that was written rather loosely, so that when shooting began there was freedom—too much freedom—for it to wander off in all directions in search of comic inspiration.

California Split ★ ★ ★ ★
R, 109 m., 1974

George Segal (Bill Denny), Elliott Gould (Charlie Waters), Ann Prentiss (Barbara Miller), Gwen Welles (Susan Peters), Edward Walsh (Lew), Joseph Walsh (Sparkle), Bert Remsen ("Helen Brown"). Directed by Robert Altman and produced by Altman and Joseph Walsh, based on a screenplay by Walsh.

They meet in a California poker parlor. One wins, despite a heated discussion with a loser over whether or not a dealt card hit the floor. They drink. They become friends after they are jointly mugged in the parking lot by the sore loser.

They did not know each other before, and they don't know much about each other now, but they know all they need to know: They're both compulsive gamblers, and the dimensions of the world of gambling equal the dimensions of the world they care anything about. It is a small world and a flat one, like one of those maps of the world before Columbus, and they are constantly threatened with falling over the edge.

They're the heroes (or at least the subjects) of *California Split*, the magnificently funny, cynical film by Robert Altman. Their names are Bill and Charlie, and they're played by George Segal and Elliott Gould with a combination of unaffected naturalism and sheer raw nervous exhaustion. We don't need to know anything about gambling to understand the odyssey they undertake to the tracks, to the private poker parties, to the bars, to Vegas, to the edge of defeat, and to the scene of victory. Their compulsion is so strong that it carries us along. The movie will be compared with *M*A*S*H*, the first big hit by Altman (who is possibly our best

and certainly our most diverting American director). It deserves that comparison, because it resembles *M*A*S*H* in several big ways: It's funny, it's hard-boiled, it gives us a bond between two frazzled heroes trying to win the rules in a game where the rules require defeat. But it's a better movie than *M*A*S*H* because here Altman gets it all together. Ever since *M*A*S*H*, he's been trying to make a kind of movie that would function like a comedy but allow its laughs to dig us deeper and deeper into the despair underneath.

Bill and Charlie are driven. We laugh at their hangovers, their bruises (treated with hot shaving cream), the kooky part-time prostitutes who serve them breakfasts of Froot Loops and beer. We move easily through the underworld of their friends, casually introduced through Altman's gift of overlapping dialogue and understated visual introductions, so that we're not so much shown a new character as encouraged to assume we knew him all along. And because Joseph Walsh's screenplay is funny and Segal and Gould are naturally engaging, we have a good time.

But then there are moments that take on bleaker meanings. At one point, for example, at the ragged edge of sleep, boozed out, defeated, Bill and Charlie cling desperately to a bar and very seriously bet with each other on the names of the Seven Dwarfs (There was Droopy . . . Sleepy . . . Dumbo?). And at another time, cornered with their winnings in still another parking lot by still another mugger, this one armed, they hand over half their winnings and bet him that's all they have.

He takes it and runs; they win; they could have been killed but their gambler's instinct forced them to make the try. At the end of *California Split* we realize that Altman has made a lot more than a comedy about gambling; he's taken us into an American nightmare, and all the people we met along the way felt genuine and looked real. This movie has a taste in its mouth like stale air-conditioning, and no matter what time it seems to be, it's always five in the morning in a second-rate casino.

As always, Altman fills his movie with quirky supporting roles—people who have somehow become caricatures of themselves.

At the private poker game, Segal stands at the bar, surveys the table, and quietly describes every player. He's right about them, although he (and we) have never seen them before. We know he's right because these people wear their styles and destinies on their faces.

So do the hookers (played with a kind of tart-next-door wholesomeness by Ann Prentiss and Gwenn Welles). So does "Helen Brown," one of their customers who's a middle-aged man who likes drag as much as he's terrified of the cops (inspiring a scene of true tragicomedy). Altman's movies always seem full, somehow; we don't have the feeling of an empty screen into which carefully drawn characters are introduced, but of a camera plunging into a boiling sea of frenzied human activity.

What Altman comes up with is sometimes almost a documentary feel; at the end of *California Split* we know something about organized gambling in this country we didn't know before. His movies always seem perfectly at home wherever they are, but this time there's an almost palpable sense of place. And Altman has never been more firmly in control of his style. He has one of the few really individual visual styles among contemporary American directors; we can always see it's an Altman film. He bases his visual strategies on an incredibly attentive sound track, using background noises with particular care so that our ears tell us we're moving through these people—instead of that they're lined up talking to us. *California Split* is a great movie and it's a great experience, too; we've been there with Bill and Charlie.

Caligula   no stars
NO MPAA RATING, 143 m., 1980

Malcolm McDowell (Caligula), Teresa Ann Savoy (Drusilla), John Gielgud (Nerva), Peter O'Toole (Tiberius). Produced by Bob Guccione and Franco Rossellini.

Caligula is sickening, utterly worthless, shameful trash. If it is not the worst film I have ever seen, that makes it all the more shameful: People with talent allowed themselves to participate in this travesty. Disgusted and unspeakably depressed, I walked out of the film after two hours. This film is not only garbage on an artistic level, but it is also garbage on the crude and base level where it no doubt hopes to find its audience. *Caligula* is not good art, it is not good cinema, and it is not good porn.

I've never had anything against eroticism in movies. There are X-rated films I've enjoyed, from the sensuous fantasies of *Emmanuelle* to the pop-comic absurdities of Russ Meyer. All I can say is that the makers of *Caligula* have long since lost touch with any possible common erotic denominator, and that they suggest by the contents of this film that they are jaded, perverse, and cruel human beings. There are no scenes of joy, natural pleasure, or good sensual cheer. There is, instead, a nauseating excursion into base and sad fantasies.

This is a violent film. There are scenes depicting a man whose urinary tract is closed, and who has gallons of wine poured down his throat. His bursting stomach is punctured with a sword. There is a scene in which a man is emasculated, and his genitals thrown to dogs, who eagerly eat them on the screen. There are scenes of decapitation, evisceration, rape, bestiality, sadomasochism, necrophilia.

These scenes—indeed, the movie itself—reflect a curiously distanced sensibility. Nobody in this film really seems to be there. Not the famous actors like Malcolm McDowell and (very briefly) Peter O'Toole and John Gielgud, whose scenes have been augmented by additional porn shot later with other people inserted to spice things up. Not the director (who removed his credit from the film). Not the writer (what can it mean that this movie is "*Adapted* from an Original Screenplay by Gore Vidal"?). Not even the sound track. The actors never quite seem to be speaking their own words, which are so badly dubbed that the dialogue never seems to be emerging from the drama itself.

The film even fails to involve itself in the action. *Caligula* has been photographed and directed with such clumsiness and inelegance that pieces of action do not seem to flow together, the plot is incomprehensible, the events are frequently framed as if the camera was not sure where it was, and everything is shot in muddy, ugly, underlit dungeon tones. The music is also execrable. So what are we left with? A movie, I am afraid, that may be invulnerable to a review like this one. There are no doubt people who believe that if this movie is as bad as I say it is, it must be worth seeing. People who simply cannot believe any film could be this vile. But people learn fast. "This movie," said the lady in front of me at the drinking fountain, "is the worst piece of shit I have ever seen."

Cannery Row ★ ★ ½
PG, 120 m., 1982

Nick Nolte (Doc), Debra Winger (Suzy), Audra Lindley (Fauna), Frank McRae (Hazel), M. Emmet Walsh (Mack), Sunshine Parker (The Seer). Directed by David S. Ward and produced by Michael Phillips. Screenplay by Ward.

Old skid-row drunks are a lot of things. They are sick, they are lice-ridden, they are often prematurely senile and sometimes they are so far gone they're not even tragic anymore, just wasted. Two things they are not is colorful and romantic, and when the Greek chorus of winos and bums marches onscreen in *Cannery Row*, we know the movie is in trouble. Dressed in colorful rags, each one an unforgettable character, they think they're Mr. Doolittle and his pals in *My Fair Lady*. They sleep in drain pipes at night because it's colorful. I mention the bums first, not because I think *Cannery Row* has any obligation to provide us with an accurate portrait of skid row, but because they are symptomatic of what is wrong with this movie.

It was made, I suppose, out of a desire to find some larger truth by taking reality and stylizing it into colorful romanticism: To take a bunch of down-and-outers and find the essential humanity in them. Writers were always dredging the essential humanity out of the proletariat in the thirties and forties, and John Steinbeck, who wrote *Cannery Row* and *Sweet Thursday*, the novels that inspired this movie, was no exception. I doubt, though, that even Steinbeck would be able to believe the extremes to which this movie goes. It populates its gigantic and impressive set (an indoor and outdoor replica of the Monterey docks) not only with lovable bums, but also with the requisite hookers with hearts of gold and with a guy named Doc, who dreams of making a breakthrough in marine biology. If life were like this, Norman Rockwell would have eclipsed Edward Hopper.

Doc is played by Nick Nolte, and he is the best thing in the movie. He provides a sound, solid, dignified performance, and there are times when we even believe he's a real human being who just accidentally wandered into this fantasy. Doc was once a big-league pitcher, and he had twenty-one wins and ten losses when he suddenly quit pitching and moved to Cannery Row. There is a guilty secret in his past, and it has something to do with The Seer, a loony, saintly bum who wanders the beach and serenades the dawn. Doc stares at octopuses all day, as if he could make a great discovery about them just by *looking* hard enough. One day he meets Suzy (Debra Winger), a young girl with ambitions of becoming a floozy. Doc loves her, I guess. She loves him, I suppose. She goes to work in the local cathouse, where the madam is named Fauna, maybe because Flora was already taken. But the hookers and the bums all catch on about Doc and Suzy, and the middle of the movie is devoted to their ill-conceived schemes to get the two lovers together. All of this is photographed and written in such a mixture of the wistful, the whimsical, the eccentric, and the romantic that the characters don't even seem to be living; they seem to be auditioning. Occasionally scenes come to life; there's a real sweetness in a passage where Nolte and Winger boogie with one another.

The movie is almost always good to look at, thanks to Richard MacDonald's sets (he linked together two giant sound stages) and Sven Nykvist's photography. And Nolte and Winger are almost able to make their relationship work, if only it didn't seem scripted out of old country songs and lonely hearts columns. It's tough to pull off a movie like this, in the semi-cynical 1980s (it would have been impossible in the truly cynical seventies). I guess we no longer believe in the essential heroism of the little guy, and in the proposition that anyone can succeed with a little luck. In the movie, Doc dreams of making a big discovery and impressing those eggheads at the annual biology convention. Does he succeed? Well, I understand that the original Doc, a man named Ed Ricketts who was a drinking buddy of Steinbeck's, never did make that breakthrough and died in 1953 when his car stalled on the skid-row railroad tracks and he didn't think to get out in time. Now that would have made an ending for the eighties.

The Cannonball Run ½★
PG, 95 m., 1981

Burt Reynolds (J.J. McClure), Roger Moore (Seymour), Farrah Fawcett (Pamela), Dom DeLuise (Victor), Dean Martin (Jamie Blake), Sammy Davis, Jr. (Fenderbaum). Directed by Hal Needham and produced by Albert S. Ruddy. Screenplay by Brock Yates.

The Cannonball Run is an abdication of artistic responsibility at the lowest possible level of ambition. In other words, they didn't even care enough to make a good lousy movie. *Cannonball* was probably always intended as junk, as an easy exploitation picture. But it's possible to bring some sense of style and humor even to grade-zilch material. This movie doesn't even seem to be trying.

Burt Reynolds sleepwalks through a role he's played several times before, but never so indifferently. He's a hotshot driver in a big, illegal cross-country road race; first one to California wins. That means Reynolds gets to drink a lot of beer, talk like a good ol' boy, and get in the middle of a lot of crashes and other stunts. The movie was directed by Hal Needham, a onetime stuntman who graduated to directing with *Smokey and the Bandit* (1977), the first and still the best of the Burt Reynolds car-chase movies. After that, each Needham movie has been worse than the one preceding it. His downward spiral has included *Hooper, The Villain,* and *Smokey and the Bandit II.* Movie buffs will note that three of Needham's four movies have starred Burt Reynolds, one of the most important properties in Hollywood. Reynolds is so popular he can make money in almost anything—a maxim that *Cannonball Run* puts to the extreme test. Reynolds and Needham are friends, and indeed the whole cast of *Cannonball* seems to consider the movie a reunion. The film ends with outtakes—spoiled shots during which somebody breaks up or says the wrong line or otherwise goofs. It's supposed to show us how much fun everybody had. Alas, the outtakes don't look much more goofy than the takes they intended to put in the movie; *Cannonball* assembles a giant cast around an absolutely minimal amount of screenplay, and allows them to kill time expensively. There's not much plot and no suspense. The filmmakers' excuse, no doubt, is that they were really making a comedy, not a road-race picture. That would work if there were any laughs in the movie.

But just look at the cast. It's like a cattle call. It's like an Actor's Guild picket line. It's like Hollywood Squares on Wheels. Some of the actors are talented, some are not, but they look equally awful in this movie. At one time or another during this unspeakable experience, you can share it with not only Burt Reynolds but also Roger Moore, Farrah Fawcett, Dom DeLuise, Dean Martin (looking as if a big-a pizza pie hit him straight in the eye), Sammy Davis, Jr. (looking like a severe case of vitamin deficiency), Jack Elam, Adrienne Barbeau (whose role consists of unzipping her jump suit), Terry Bradshaw, Jackie Chan, Bert Convy, Jamie Farr, Peter Fonda (as an aging Hells Angel), Michael Hui, Bianca Jagger, Molly Picon, Jimmy "the Greek" Snyder, and Mel Tillis. This isn't a cast, it's the answer to a double acrostic.

Cannonball Run II ½★
PG, 108 m., 1984

Burt Reynolds (J.J.), Dom DeLuise (Victor), Dean Martin (Blake), Sammy Davis, Jr. (Fenderbaum), Marilu Henner (Betty), Shirley MacLaine (Veronica). Directed by Hal Needham and produced by Albert S. Ruddy. Screenplay by Needham, Ruddy, and Harvey Miller.

The clue to *Cannonball Run II* is in Frank Sinatra's first scene, but you have to look carefully. The scene starts in Sinatra's office, and we're looking over Sinatra's head at Burt Reynolds and some other people. At least, it *looks* like Sinatra's head, except there's something a little funny about the ears. Then we see Sinatra. He talks. We see Reynolds. He talks. And so on, until, if we know something about movie editing techniques, we realize *there isn't a single shot showing Sinatra and Reynolds at the same time.* Also, there's something funny about Sinatra's voice: He doesn't seem to be quite matching the tone of the things said to him. That's the final tip-off: Sinatra did his entire scene by sitting down at a desk and reading his lines into the camera, and then, on another day, Reynolds and the others looked into the camera and pretended to be looking at him. The over-the-shoulder shots are of a double.

This is the movie equivalent to phoning it in. You can't blame Sinatra. Everybody else is walking through this movie, so why shouldn't he? Refusing to appear in a scene with your fellow actors is no worse than agreeing to appear in a scene that nobody has bothered to write. *Cannonball Run II* is one of the laziest insults to the intelligence of moviegoers that I can remember. Sheer arrogance made this picture.

The movie stars Burt Reynolds as J.J. McClure, cross-country racer. Dom DeLuise is back as his sidekick. Some of the other familiar faces from the first awful *Cannonball* movie include Dean Martin and Sammy Davis, Jr., and they are joined here by Shirley MacLaine, Jamie Farr, Susan Anton, Marilu Henner, Telly Savalas, Catherine Bach, Foster Brooks, Sid Caesar, Jackie Chan, Tim Conway, Richard ("Jaws") Kiel, Don Knotts, Ricardo Montalban, Jim Nabors, Louis Nye, Molly Picon, and the pathetic Charles Nelson Reilly. It's a roll call of shame. Some of these actors are, of course, talented. Shirley MacLaine won an Academy Award the same year she made this. Burt Reynolds can be good, but you can't tell that from this movie. *Cannonball Run II* is a day off for most of these performers, who are not given characters to play, readable dialogue to recite, or anything to do other than to make fools of themselves.

The name of the director is Hal Needham. He is a crony of Reynolds's, a former stunt driver who has brilliantly demonstrated the Peter Principle by becoming a director, thus rising far above his level of competence. This is the sixth time Needham has directed Reynolds. Greater love hath no actor, than that he sacrifice his career on the altar of friendship. When Reynolds appeared in Needham's awful *Stroker Ace* in 1983, he excused himself by saying the role had been intended for Steve McQueen; he stepped in after McQueen's death as a favor to his friend Needham. What's his excuse this time?

Cannonball Run II was made for one reason: The original picture made money. There may be a sucker born every minute, but so many of them fell for *Cannonball Run* that there may not be many left who are willing to fall twice for the same scam.

Car Wash ★ ★ ★ ½
PG, 97 m., 1976

Franklin Ajaye (T.C.), Sully Boyer (Mrs. B.), Richard Brestoff (Irwin), George Carlin (Taxi Driver), Prof. Irwin Corey (Mad Bomber), Ivan Dixon (Lonnie), Richard Pryor (Daddy Rich). Directed by Michael Schultz and produced by Art Linson and Gary Stein. Screenplay by Joel Schumacher.

The boss is named Mr. B. and he walks around with a dead cigar stuck in his face, pleading "Wash the cars! Wash the cars!" But that's the last thing they get around to in *Car Wash*, a sunny, lively comedy. The movie covers a day in the life of the DeLuxe Car Wash, down from the Strip in Los Angeles, and by actual count only three totally sane people stop by all day. We meet the rest in a dizzying, nonstop kaleidoscope of cars, soul music, characters, crises, crazy kids on skateboards, hookers, television preachers, and lots of suds and hot wax—not to mention the Mad Pop Bottle Bomber, whose bottle turns out to be a cruel disappointment. The movie's put together with a manic energy, we never even quite get introduced to half the people in the cast, but by the movie's end we know them, and what they're up to, and we like them.

We meet the employees of the car wash in the locker room, as they're putting on their work clothes. Floyd and Lloyd enter doing their James Brown imitation. T.C. is convinced he'll be the lucky caller to win the free concert tickets in a radio station give-away. Lindy, probably the first drag queen employed full-time by a car wash, corrects his makeup. Lonnie, the straw boss, provides an element of sanity, but he's outnumbered.

Sooner or later during the day, everyone seems to come through the car wash. While Floyd and Lloyd, as the steam men, practice their stage act on astonished customers, we watch the parade go by. George Carlin plays a bewildered taxi driver. Professor Irwin

Corey is briefly mistaken for the Mad Pop Bottle Bomber. A limousine a yard long wheels up and discharges Richard Pryor, as Daddy Rich, the famous television evangelist. He has his backup singers with him: the Pointer Sisters, who do a number right in front of the gas pumps.

The movie looks like joyful chaos on the surface, but there are several stories running through it. One involves Bill Duke as a young Black Muslim with fierce resentments. Another—delicately handled—involves a young black hooker who changes clothes in the rest room and then hangs around the corner all day lonely and lost. Another is the relationship between Mr. B. and Lonnie—Mr. B. tense and worried, Lonnie filled with ideas he can't get an audience for.

The car wash seems almost a natural gathering place. The kid on the skateboard whizzes past on a regular schedule. Wives and girlfriends of the workers stop by for brief sessions of fighting and making up. A guy named Kenny, who looks like he stepped out of the fashion ads, stops in and gets a date with the office girl. A man in a head-to-toe cast goes through the wash, considerably shaken. So does a little boy who first throws up on his mother's Mercedes and, when it's been washed, throws up on her.

All of this is held together by the music, which is nearly wall-to-wall, and by the picture's tremendous sense of life. It's one thing to have an idea like this—a zany, sometimes serious day in the life of a car wash—and another thing to make it work. But the screenplay and the direction juggle the characters so adroitly, this is almost a wash-and-wax *M*A*S*H*.

Carmen ★ ★ ★ ★
R, 95 m., 1983

Antonio Gades (Antonio), Laura Del Sol (Carmen), Paco De Lucia (Paco), Cristina Hoyos (Cristina). Sung by Regina Resnik and Maria Del Monaco. Directed by Carlos Saura and produced by Emiliano Piedra. Screenplay by Saura and Antonio Gades.

Carlos Saura's *Carmen* is an erotic roller coaster of a movie, incorporating dance into its story more effectively than any other movie I can remember. It isn't a "ballet movie," and it's not like one of those musicals where everybody is occasionally taken with the need to dance. It's a story of passion and jealousy—the story of Bizet's *Carmen*—with dance as part and parcel of its flesh and blood. The movie is based on the opera by Bizet, keeping the music and the broad outlines of the story of a poor girl whose fierce romantic independence maddens the men who become obsessed with her. Everything else is new. Saura, the greatest living Spanish film director, has collaborated with Antonio Gades, the Spanish dancer and choreographer, to make this *Carmen* into a muscular, contemporary story. Their strategy is to make a story within a story. The film begins with Gades as a dance teacher who is looking for the "perfect" Carmen. He finds one in a flamenco dancing school, and as he attempts to mold her into Carmen, their relationship begins to resemble the story of the opera.

Given this approach, *Carmen* could easily have turned into an academic exercise, one of those clever movies in which all the pieces fit but none of them matter. That doesn't happen, and one of the reasons it doesn't is the casting of a young woman named Laura Del Sol as Carmen. She is a twenty-one-year-old dancer who combines convincing technique with a healthy, athletic sexiness, and her dance duets (and duels) with Gades are bold, erotic, and uninhibited. What's fascinating is the way Saura is able to blend the dance, the opera, and the "modern" story. For example, Del Sol and Gades use dance to create a scene that begins as an argument, develops into fierce declarations of independence, and then climaxes in passionate romance. In another scene, a routine day in a dance studio becomes charged by the unexpected appearance of Carmen's other lover, an ex-convict.

I have an ambivalence about dance on film. I begin with the assumption that the ideal way to see dance is live, on a stage. Everything in dance begins with the fact that the dancers are physically present and are using their bodies to turn movement into art. Movies, with their complete freedom over time and space, break that contract between real time and the dancer. Dances can be constructed out of many different shots and even out of the work of more than one dancer (see *Flashdance*). If I can't see dancing on a stage, then, my preference is for classical movie dancing, by which I mean frankly artificial constructions of the Astaire and Rogers variety. Serious dance on film usually feels like a documentary. The great achievement of *Carmen* is that it takes serious dance and music, combines them with a plausible story, suspends our disbelief, and gives us a mesmerizing, electric experience.

Carmen ★ ★ ★ ★
PG, 152 m., 1984

Julia Migenes-Johnson (Carmen), Placido Domingo (Don Jose), Ruggero Raimondi (Escamillo), Faith Esham (Micaela), Jean-Philippe Lafont (Dancairo). Directed by Francesco Rosi and produced by Patrice Ledoux.

Bizet's *Carmen* is what movies are all about. It's one of the few modern movies that requires one of those legendary Hollywood advertising men who'd cook up copy like, for example . . .
Cheer! As Bizet's towering masterpiece blazes across the screen! Cry bravo! To passion, romance, adventure! From the bullrings of Spain to the innermost recesses of her gypsy heart, Carmen drives men mad and immortalizes herself as a romantic legend! Thrill! To the golden voice of Placido Domingo, and the tempestuous screen debut of the smouldering Julia Migenes-Johnson!
The temptation, of course, is to approach, a film like this with hushed voice and bended knee, uttering reverent phrases about art and music. But to hell with it: This movie is the *Indiana Jones* of opera films, and we might as well not beat around the bush. *Carmen* is a Latin soap opera if ever there was one, and the sheer passionate joy of Bizet's music is as vulgar as it is sublime, as popular as it is classical. *Carmen* is one of those operas ideally suited to the movies, and this version by Francesco Rosi is exciting, involving, and entertaining.
You are doubtless already familiar with the music. The sound track was recorded in Paris with Lorin Maazel conducting the National Orchestra of France. Placido Domingo is in great voice, and a relatively unknown American soprano named Julia Migenes-Johnson not only can sing the title

role but, perhaps just as importantly, can look it and act it. There is chemistry here, and without the chemistry—without the audience's belief that the scornful gypsy Carmen could enslave the soldier Don Jose—there would only be an illustrated sound track. After the recording was completed, the movie was shot on locations in Spain by Francesco Rosi, the Italian director of *Three Brothers* and *Christ Stopped at Eboli*. He has discovered lush, sun-drenched villages on hillsides, and a bullring of such stark Spanish simplicity that the ballet within the ring for once seems as elegant as the emotions it is reflecting. He also has found moonlight, rich firelight, deep reds and yellows—colors so glowing that the characters seem to warm themselves at his palette.
Opera films are traditionally not successful. They play in festivals, they find a small audience of music lovers, maybe they make some money in Italy. Domingo broke that pattern with his *La Traviata* (1983), directed by Franco Zeffirelli. It had good long runs around the United States, and even broke through to audiences beyond the core of opera lovers. But we Americans are so wary of "culture." Opera for many of us still consists of the fat lady on "The Ed Sullivan Show." And for many of the rest, it is something that inhabits a cultural shrine and must be approached with reverence. Maybe it takes the movies, that most popular of art forms, to break that pattern. Rosi, Domingo, and Migenes-Johnson have filmed a labor of love.

Carrie ★ ★ ★ ½
R, 98 m., 1976

Sissy Spacek (Carrie), John Travolta (Her Prom Date), Piper Laurie (Her Mother). Directed by Brian De Palma and produced by Paul Monash. Screenplay by Lawrence D. Cohen.

Brian De Palma's *Carrie* is an absolutely spellbinding horror movie, with a shock at the end that's the best thing along those lines since the shark leaped aboard in *Jaws*. It's also (and this is what makes it so good) an observant human portrait. This girl Carrie isn't another stereotyped product of the horror production line; she's a shy, pretty, and complicated high school senior who's a lot like kids we once knew. There is a difference, though. She has telekenesis, the ability to manipulate things without touching them. It's a power that came upon her gradually, and was released in response to the shrill religious fanaticism of her mother. It manifests itself in small ways. She looks in a mirror, and it breaks. Then it mends itself. Her mother tries to touch her and is hurled back against a couch. But then, on prom night . . .

Well, what makes the movie's last twenty minutes so riveting is that they grow so relentlessly, so inevitably, out of what's gone before. This isn't a science-fiction movie with a tacked-on crisis, but the study of a character we know and understand. When she fully uses (or is used by) her strange power, we know why. This sort of narrative development hasn't exactly been De Palma's strong point, but here he exhibits a gift for painting personalities; we didn't know De Palma, ordinarily so flashy on the surface, could go so deep. Part of his success is a result of the very good performances by Sissy Spacek, as Carrie, and by Piper Laurie, as Carrie's mother. They form a closed-off, claustrophobic household, the mother has translated her own psychotic fear of sexuality into a twisted personal religion. She punishes the girl constantly, locks her in closets with statues of a horribly bleeding Christ, and refuses to let her develop normal friendships.

At school, then, it's no wonder Carrie is so quiet. She has long blonde hair but wears it straight and uses it mostly to hide her face. She sits in the back of the room, doesn't speak up much, and is the easy butt of jokes by her classmates. Meanwhile, the most popular girl in the class devises a truly cruel trick to play on Carrie. It depends on Carrie being asked to the senior prom by the popular girl's equally popular boyfriend—he's one of your average Adonises with letters in every sport. He's not in on the joke, though, and asks Carrie in all seriousness.

And then De Palma gives us a marvelously realized scene at the prom—where Carrie does, indeed, turn out to be beautiful. There's a little something wrong, though, and De Palma has an effective way to convey it: As Carrie and her date dance, the camera moves around them, romantically at first, but then too fast, as if they're spinning out of control.

I wouldn't want to spoil the movie's climax for you by even hinting at what happens next. Just let me say that *Carrie* is a true horror story. Not a manufactured one, made up of spare parts from old Vincent Price classics, but a real one, in which the horror grows out of the characters themselves. The scariest horror stories—the ones by M.R. James, Edgar Allan Poe, and Oliver Onions—are like this. They develop their horrors out of the people they observe. That happens here, too. Does it ever.

Cat People ★ ★ ★ ½
R, 118 m., 1982

Nastassja Kinski (Irena Gallier), Malcolm McDowell (Paul Gallier), John Heard (Oliver Yates), Annette O'Toole (Alice Perrin), Ruby Dee (Female), Ed Begley, Jr. (Joe Creigh). Directed by Paul Schrader and produced by Charles Fries. Screenplay by Alan Ormsby.

It is a preposterous idea. Untold centuries ago, when all the world was a desert of wind-whipped, blood-orange sand, and leopards lounged lazily in barren trees and arrogantly ruled all they could see, a few members of the puny race of human beings made their own accommodation with the fearsome beasts. They sacrificed their women to them. And the leopards did not kill the women, but mated with them. From those mists of prehistory, the race they created lives even today: The Cat People.

These people have had a hard time of it. They have the physical appearance of ordinary humans, except for something feline around the eyes and a certain spring in their step. They have all the mortal appetites, too, but there are complications when they make love, because in the heat of orgasm they are transformed into savage black leopards and kill their human lovers. They should mate only with their own kind. But as our story opens, there are only two Cat People—and, like their parents before them, are brother and sister.

This is the stuff of audacious myth, combining the perverse, the glorious, and the ridiculous. The movies were invented to tell such stories. Paul Schrader's *Cat People* moves boldly between a slice-of-life in present-day New Orleans and the wind-swept deserts where the Cat People were engendered, and his movie creates a mood of doom, predestination, forbidden passion, and, to be sure, a certain silliness. It's fun in the way horror movies should be fun; it's totally unbelievable in between the times it's scaring the popcorn out of you.

Nastassja Kinski stars as the young sister, Irena. She is an orphan, reunited in New Orleans with her long-lost brother, Paul (Malcolm McDowell). She also is a virgin, afraid of sex and liquor because they might unleash the animal inside of her. (Little does she suspect that is literally what would happen.) She is tall, with a sensual mouth, wide-set green eyes, and a catlike walk. She catches the attention of the curator at the New Orleans zoo (John Heard). He senses danger in her. He also senses that this is the creature he has been waiting for all his life—waiting for her as the leopards in their cells wait, expecting nothing, ready for anything.

We have here, then, a most complex love triangle. Kinski fears her brother because she fears incest. She fears the curator but loves him. To love him is, eventually, to kill him. The curator is in love with the idea of her threat, but does not realize she *really* will turn into a leopard and rend his flesh. There are some supporting characters: Annette O'Toole is the sensible friend who senses danger, and Ed Begley, Jr. is the lackadaisical custodian whose arm is ripped from its socket. You shouldn't mess with leopards.

Schrader tells his story in two parallel narratives. One involves the deepening relationships among the sister, the brother, and the curator. The other, stunningly photographed, takes place in an unearthly terrain straight from Frank Herbert's Dune books. The designer, Ferdinando Scarfiotti, and the veteran special effects artist, Albert Whitlock, have created a world that looks completely artificial, with its drifting red sands and its ritualistic tableau of humans and leopards—and yet looks realistic in its fantasy. In other words, you know this world is made up, but you can't see the seams; it's like the snow planet in *The Empire Strikes Back*.

Cat People moves back and forth between its mythic and realistic levels, held together primarily by the strength of Kinski's per-formance and John Heard's obsession. Kinski is something. She never overacts in this movie, never steps wrong, never seems ridiculous; she just steps onscreen and convincingly underplays a leopard. Heard also is good. He never seems in the grip of an ordinary sexual passion, but possesses one of those obsessions men are willing (and often are called upon) to die for. *Cat People* is a good movie in an old tradition, a fantasy-horror film that takes itself just seriously enough to work, has just enough fun to be entertaining, contains elements of intrinsic fascination in its magnificent black leopards, and ends in one way just when we were afraid it was going to end in another.

Chapter Two ★ ★
PG, 124 m., 1980

James Caan (George), Marsha Mason (Jennie), Joseph Bologna (Leo), Valerie Harper (Faye), Alan Fudge (Lee), Judy Farrell (Gwen). Directed by Robert Moore and produced by Ray Stark. Screenplay by Neil Simon.

After the early loss of his first wife, playwright Neil Simon married again soon afterwards. Six months after the death, he fell in love at first sight with actress Marsha Mason, and they were married after a romance of only twenty-two days. Simon transformed those events of 1973 into an autobiographical play that opened in 1977, and now this film stars Mason in a role that is based, we guess, more or less upon herself.

Simon says the story isn't an actual record of what happened, but was just loosely inspired by his remarriage. There is no way for us to know. What we can say, on the basis of *Chapter Two*, is that if the key dialogue between husband and new wife wasn't taken from life, it is possibly taken from that wonderful category of what they *should* have said. And there is a great deal that they should have said. Simon is usually the most quick-footed and -witted of dialogue writers, but this time he gives us more than two hours of discussions, arguments, debates, reconciliations, and accusations that quickly become tedious.

The conversations in his screenplay are too long and too literal to begin with, but they suffer from two additional handicaps:

(a) They do not take place between two characters whose motives have been well established, and (b) they have the misfortune to involve James Caan, who is so tense, uptight, and verbally constipated that it's a trial to wait out his speeches.

Caan plays the Simon-like character, a writer and new widower who is inconsolable in his grief until Mason happens along. Caan has previously survived a series of blind dates with the usual assortment of hopeless choices, and so Mason enchants him: She's outspoken, direct, spunky. Their first "trial date" lasts five minutes (one of those standard Hollywood "meet cutes"), and in no time at all they're in Bermuda on their honeymoon.

So far, not so bad. This is all the stuff of dependable romantic comedy, and we know where we stand. But we are about to find ourselves at sea for the rest of the movie, because the Caan character suddenly has agonizing second thoughts . . . his new bride gets on his nerves . . . he doesn't know what's bugging him . . . he's hurtful . . . he splits. The movie never really bothers itself with *why* he behaves this way, unless we're supposed to supply our own instant Freudian analysis. Caan is awkward all through this movie (he never seems happy playing this part), but he's never more lost than when he undergoes this dramatic character transformation. And you can't really blame him: Simon just hasn't given him the words or actions to make himself clear.

After the split, the rest of the movie is devoted to attempts by first one and then the other of the newlyweds to figure out what went wrong. Their scenes are so tediously top-heavy with dialogue that we can barely stand to listen. And then there's the added distraction of a parallel plot involving an affair between their best friends (Valerie Harper and Joe Bologna).

There is absolutely no rational reason why this subplot is in the movie. Maybe it made sense in the mechanics of the stage play, but it doesn't belong here. And it's all the more distracting because, whatdaya know, Bologna and Harper are much better than Caan and Mason at conjuring up the romantic and comic juices of a love affair. Their scenes are meaningless and unnecessary, but at least they're alive, and just when they get

their emotional rhythm flowing, the movie cuts back to the nonstop marriage counseling session that occupies the main plot.

Chapter Two is called a comedy, maybe because that's what we expect from Neil Simon. It's not, although it has that comic subplot. It's a middlebrow, painfully earnest, overwritten exercise in pop sociology. I'm not exactly happy describing Neil Simon's semi-real-life in those terms, but then those are the terms in which he's chosen to present it. My notion is that Simon would have been wiser to imagine himself writing about another couple, and writing for another actress than his own wife; that way maybe he wouldn't have felt it so necessary to let both sides have the last word.

Chariots of Fire ★ ★ ★ ★
PG, 123 m., 1981

Ben Cross (Harold Abrahams), Ian Charleson (Eric Liddell), Nigel Havers (Lord Andrew Lindsay), Ian Holm (Coach Mussabini), Sir John Gielgud (Master of Trinity), Lindsay Anderson (Master of Caius), David Yelland (Prince of Wales), Nicholas Farrell (Aubrey Montague). Directed by Hugh Hudson and produced by David Puttnam. Screenplay by Colin Welland.

This is strange. I have no interest in running and am not a partisan in the British class system. Then why should I have been so deeply moved by *Chariots of Fire*, a British film that has running and class as its subjects? I've toyed with that question since I first saw this remarkable film in May 1981 at the Cannes Film Festival, and I believe the answer is rather simple: Like many great films, *Chariots of Fire* takes its nominal subjects as occasions for much larger statements about human nature.

This is a movie that has a great many running scenes. It is also a movie about British class distinctions in the years after World War I, years in which the establishment was trying to piece itself back together after the carnage in France. It is about two outsiders—a Scot who is the son of missionaries in China, and a Jew whose father is an immigrant from Lithuania. And it is about how both of them use running as a means of asserting their dignity. But it is about more than them, and a lot of this film's greatness is hard to put into words. *Chariots of Fire* creates deep feelings among many members of its audiences, and it does that not so much with its story or even its characters as with particular moments that are very sharply seen and heard.

Seen, in photography that pays grave attention to the precise look of a human face during stress, pain, defeat, victory, and joy. Heard, in one of the most remarkable sound tracks of any film in a long time, with music by the Greek composer Vangelis Papathanassiou. His compositions for *Chariots of Fire* are as evocative, and as suited to the material, as the different but also perfectly matched scores of such films as *The Third Man* and *Zorba the Greek*. The music establishes the tone for the movie, which is one of nostalgia for a time when two young and naturally gifted British athletes ran fast enough to bring home medals from the 1924 Paris Olympics.

The nostalgia is an important aspect of the film, which opens with a 1979 memorial service for one of the men, Harold Abrahams, and then flashes back sixty years to his first day at Cambridge University. We are soon introduced to the film's other central character, the Scotsman Eric Liddell. The film's underlying point of view is a poignant one: These men were once young and fast and strong, and they won glory on the sports field, but now they are dead and we see them as figures from long ago.

The film is unabashedly and patriotically British in its regard for these two characters, but it also contains sharp jabs at the British class system, which made the Jewish Abrahams feel like an outsider who could sometimes feel the lack of sincerity in a handshake, and placed the Protestant Liddell in the position of having to explain to the peeved Prince of Wales why he could not, in conscience, run on the Sabbath. Both men are essentially proving themselves, their worth, their beliefs, on the track. But *Chariots of Fire* takes an unexpected approach to many of its running scenes. It does not, until near the film's end, stage them as contests to wring cheers from the audience. Instead, it sees them as *efforts*, as endeavors by individual runners—it tries to capture the exhilaration of running as a celebration of the spirit.

Two of the best moments in the movie: A moment in which Liddell defeats Abrahams, who agonizingly replays the defeat over and over in his memory. And a moment in which Abrahams' old Italian-Arabic track coach, banned from the Olympic stadium, learns who won his man's race. First he bangs his fist through his straw boater, then he sits on his bed and whispers, "My son!"

All of the contributions to the film are distinguished. Neither Ben Cross, as Abrahams, nor Ian Charleson, as Liddell, are accomplished runners but they are accomplished actors, and they *act* the running scenes convincingly. Ian Holm, as Abrahams' coach, quietly dominates every scene he is in. There are perfectly observed cameos by John Gielgud and Lindsay Anderson, as masters of Cambridge colleges, and by David Yelland, as a foppish, foolish young Prince of Wales. These parts and others make up a greater whole.

Chariots of Fire is one of the best films of recent years, a memory of a time when men still believed you could win a race if only you wanted to badly enough.

Cheech and Chong's Next Movie ★
R, 99 m., 1980

Richard Marin (Cheech), Thomas Chong (Chong), Evelyn Guerrero (Donna), Betty Kennedy (Candy), Sy Kramer (Mr. Neatnik), Rikki (Gloria). Directed by Thomas Chong and produced by Howard Brown. Screenplay by Chong and Marin.

The problem with your average dope movie is that you have to be stoned to get the jokes. That's because there aren't any jokes. The movie has the giggles, and if the audience is in the same chemical euphoria it gets the giggles, too. Sitting there straight and just watching the movie is kind of a sad experience, because the movie's not intrinsically funny. It's one of those things where you hadda be there.

Cheech and Chong's Next Movie is an experience like that, a movie that's not particularly funny unless you happen to be laughing anyway—in which case, you don't need the movie. It's a formless, shapeless, thoughtless mess of a comedy that tries to sneak through by flattering its audience that everybody's in on the same joke.

There's a subtle blackmail at work here: If you're not laughing, does that mean you missed the point? The movie's invitation is clear. It stars Cheech and Chong, two cult comedians, one Mexican-American, one Chinese-Canadian, whose anti-establishment, pothead credentials are impeccable. Since what they're doing is funny (by their own definition), if we don't laugh that makes us part of the problem instead of part of their solution. Half the people in the basic Cheech and Chong audience are stoned (kids stoke up for this one), and they laugh, so the movie's funny, right?

Well, no. You might get a contact high from the Cheech and Chong fans, but you won't get one from the screen. This movie is embarrassing. There's no invention in it, no imagination, no new comic vision, no ideas about what might be *really* funny—instead of just dope-funny, something to laugh at if you're in the bag anyway. I didn't see *Up in Smoke*, Cheech and Chong's first movie, which grossed something like $60 million. But could it have been this bad?

Cheech and Chong's Next Movie is directed by Chong himself; he no doubt got the job, without any previous directing experience, because of the Hollywood wisdom that says if you gross $60 million you're obviously a genius in all fields. Chong isn't a genius as a director. The movie's jokes aren't funny anyway, but he sabotages them with inept camera placement: There's a gag involving a magic trick with a handkerchief, and Chong mangles the punch line by cutting to a long shot so far away from the action we almost miss it. There's no rhythm in the movie, no sense of an overall idea about the material, and when the movie ends abruptly and unexpectedly, the audience is a little surprised: Is that all?

Now, I have to report that the audience did laugh a lot at the performance I attended. Why? Maybe because Cheech and Chong portray complete, stoned irresponsibility as a life-style, and borderline idiocy as a behavioral style. I was reminded of my own childhood slapstick comedy heroes, Huntz Hall and the Bowery Boys, who also spent whole movies acting dumb and getting into trouble.

But there's a difference between Cheech and Chong and the Bowery Boys. The Boys acted silly and goofy because they were supposed to *be* silly and goofy—it was an end in itself. The gag with Cheech and Chong is that they're drug addicts. As a guy I know once said, it's not nice to laugh at dopeheads if you're not one, and not funny to laugh at them if you are one.

The China Syndrome ★ ★ ★ ★
PG, 122 m., 1979

Jane Fonda (Kimberly Wells), Jack Lemmon (Jack Godell), Michael Douglas (Richard Adams), Scott Brady (Herman DeYoung), James Hampton (Bill Gibson), Peter Donat (Don Jacovich), Wilford Brimley (Ted Spindler). Directed by James Bridges and produced by Michael Douglas. Screenplay by Mike Gray, T.S. Cook, and Bridges.

The China Syndrome is a terrific thriller that incidentally raises the most unsettling questions about how safe nuclear power plants really are. It was received in some quarters as a political film, and the people connected with it make no secret of their doubts about nuclear power. But the movie is, above all, entertainment: well-acted, well-crafted, scary as hell.

The events leading up to the "accident" in *The China Syndrome* are indeed based on actual occurrences at nuclear plants. Even the most unlikely mishap (a stuck needle on a graph causing engineers to misread a crucial water level) really happened at the Dresden plant outside Chicago. And yet the movie works so well not because of its factual basis, but because of its human content. The performances are so good, so consistently, that *The China Syndrome* becomes a thriller dealing in personal values. The suspense is generated not only by our fears about what might happen, but by our curiosity about how, in the final showdown, the characters will react.

The key character is Godell (Jack Lemmon), a shift supervisor at a big nuclear power plant in Southern California. He lives alone, quietly, and can say without any self-consciousness that the plant is his life. He believes in nuclear power. But when an earthquake shakes his plant, he becomes convinced that he felt an aftershock—caused not by an earthquake but by rumblings deep within the plant.

The quake itself leads to the first "accident." Because a two-bit needle gets stuck on a roll of graph paper, the engineers think they need to lower the level of the water shield over the nuclear pile. Actually, the level is already dangerously low. And if the pile were ever uncovered, the result could be the "China syndrome," so named because the superheated nuclear materials would melt directly through the floor of the plant and, theoretically, keep on going until they hit China. In practice, there'd be an explosion and a release of radioactive materials sufficient to poison an enormous area.

The accident takes place while a TV news team is filming a routine feature about the plant. The cameraman (Michael Douglas) secretly films events in the panicked control room. And the reporter (Jane Fonda) tries to get the story on the air. Her superiors refuse, influenced by the power industry's smoothly efficient public relations people. But the more Fonda and Douglas dig into the accident, the less they like it.

Meanwhile, obsessed by that second tremor, Lemmon has been conducting his own investigation. He discovers that the X-rays used to check key welds at the plant have been falsified. And then the movie takes off in classic thriller style: The director, James Bridges, uses an exquisite sense of timing and character development to bring us to the cliffhanger conclusion.

The performances are crucial to the movie's success, and they're all the more interesting because the characters aren't painted as anti-nuclear crusaders, but as people who get trapped in a situation while just trying to do their jobs. Fonda is simply superb as the TV reporter; the range and excellence of her performance are a wonder. Douglas is exactly right as the bearded, casually anti-establishment cameraman. And Jack Lemmon, reluctant to rock the boat, compelled to follow his conscience, creates a character as complex as his Oscar-winning businessman in *Save the Tiger*.

Chinatown ★ ★ ★ ★
R, 131 m., 1974

Jack Nicholson (J.J. Gittes), Faye Dunaway (Evelyn Mulwray), John Huston (Noah Cross), Perry Lopez (Escobar), John Hillerman (Yelburton), Darrell Zwerling (Hollis Mulwray), Diane Ladd (Ida Sessions), Roman Polanski (Man with Knife). Directed by Roman Polanski and produced by Robert Evans. Screenplay by Robert Towne.

Roman Polanski's *Chinatown* is not only a great entertainment, but something more, something I would have thought almost impossible: It's a 1930s private-eye movie that doesn't depend on nostalgia or camp for its effect, but works because of the enduring strength of the genre itself. In some respects, this movie actually could have been made forty-five years ago. It accepts its conventions and categories at face value and doesn't make them the object of satire or filter them through a modern sensibility, as Robert Altman did with *The Long Goodbye*. Here's a private-eye movie in which all the traditions, romantic as they may seem, are left intact.

At its center, of course, is the eye himself: J.J. Gittes, moderately prosperous as a result of adultery investigations. He isn't the perenially broke loner like Philip Marlowe, inhabiting a shabby office and buying himself a drink out of the office bottle. He's a successful investigator with a two-man staff, and he dresses well and is civilized and intelligent. He does, however, possess the two indispensable qualities necessary for any traditional private eye. He is deeply cynical about human nature, and he has a personal code and sticks to it.

There is also, of course, the woman, who comes to the private eye for help but does not quite reveal to him the full dimensions of her trouble. And there are the other inevitable ingredients of the well-crafted private-eye plot, as perfected by Raymond Chandler and Dashiell Hammett and practiced by Ross Macdonald. There's the woman's father, and the skeletons in their family closet, and the way that a crime taking place now has a way of leading back to a crime in the past.

These plots work best when they start out seeming impossibly complicated and then end up with watertight logic, and Robert Towne's screenplay for *Chinatown* does that with consummate skill. But the whole movie is a tour de force; it's a period movie, with all the right cars and clothes and props, but we forget that after the first ten minutes. We've become involved in the movie's web of mystery, as we always were with the best private-eye stories, whether written or filmed. We care about these people and want to see what happens to them.

And yet, at the same time, Polanski is so sensitive to the ways in which 1930s' movies in this genre were made that we're almost watching a critical essay. Godard once said that the only way to review a movie is to make another movie, and maybe that's what Polanski has done here. He's made a perceptive, loving comment on a kind of movie and a time in the nation's history that are both long past. *Chinatown* is almost a lesson on how to experience this kind of movie.

It's also a triumph of acting, particularly by Jack Nicholson, who is one of the most interesting actors now working and who contributes one of his best performances. He inhabits the character of J. J. Gittes like a second skin; the possession is so total that there are scenes in the movie where we almost have telepathy; we *know* what he's thinking, so he doesn't have to tell us. His loyalty is to the woman, but on several occasions, evidence turns up that seems to incriminate her. And then he must pull back, because his code will not admit clients who lie to him. Why he's this way (indeed, even the fact that he's this way) is communicated by Nicholson almost solely in the way he plays the character; dialogue isn't necessary to make the point.

The woman is Faye Dunaway, looking pale and neurotic and beautiful, and justifying for us (if not always for him) J. J.'s trust in her. And then there are all the other characters, who revolve around a complicated scheme to float a bond issue and build a dam to steal water from Los Angeles, in a time of drought. Because the film depends so much on the exquisite unraveling of its plot, it would be unfair to describe much more; one of its delights is in the way that dropped remarks and chance clues gradually build up the portrait of a crime.

And always at the center, there's the Nicholson performance, given an eerie edge by the bandage he wears on his nose after it's slit by a particularly slimy character played by Polanski himself. The bandage looks incongruous, we don't often see a bandaged nose on a movie private eye, but it's the kind of incongruity that's creepy and not funny. The film works similar ground: Drifting within sight of parody every so often, it saves itself by the seriousness of its character.

Choose Me ★ ★ ★ ½
R, 106 m., 1984

Genevieve Bujold (Dr. Love), Keith Carradine (Mickey), Lesley Ann Warren (Eve), Patrick Bauchau (Zack), Rae Dawn Chong (Pearl). Directed by Alan Rudolph and produced by Carolyn Pfeiffer and David Blocker. Screenplay by Rudolph.

Apart from its other qualities, which are many, Alan Rudolph's *Choose Me* is an audaciously intriguing movie. Its main purpose, indeed, may be to intrigue us—as other films aim to thrill or arouse or mystify. There is hardly a moment in the whole film when I knew for sure what was going to happen next, yet I didn't feel manipulated; I felt as if the movie were giving itself the freedom to be completely spontaneous.

The movie begins with strangers talking to each other. One of the strangers is a radio talk show host. Her name is Dr. Love, and she gives advice to the lovelorn over the radio (most of her advice seems to be variations on "That's not my problem"). One of her regular callers, we learn, is a woman named Eve who owns a bar. One day a mental patient named Mickey, a guy whose past seems filled with mysterious connections to the CIA, the space program, and the Russians, walks out of a closed ward and into the bar and meets Eve. A few days later, Dr. Love, hoping to do some research into the ways that we ordinary folk live, adopts an assumed name and goes looking for a roommate. She finds Eve and moves in with her, and neither woman knows who the other woman really is. They also don't make the connection that Eve is a regular caller to the radio program (highly unlikely, since she speaks with an accent). None of this is really as hard to follow as it sounds. And since one of the pleasures of this movie is the leisurely and logical way it explores the implications of mistaken identity, I'm not going to write another word about the confusions the characters get involved in.

Choose Me is a deliberate throwback to the *film noir* of the 1940s—to those movies made up of dark streets and wet pavements, hookers under streetlamps, pimps in shiny postwar Studebakers, and people who smoke a lot. It's also about lonely people, but it's not one of those half-witted TV movies about singles bars and single women. It's about smart, complicated people who are trying to clear a space for themselves and using romance as an excavating tool. The performances are key to this strategy. The best thing in the movie is Genevieve Bujold's performance as Dr. Love. She is interesting, if detached, as the radio personality, but when love finally does touch her life, she is so unabashedly open and confessional and redfaced and sincere that we want to hug her. Bujold just gets better and better; coming so soon after her good work in *Tightrope*, this is a reminder of how many different kinds of roles she can play so well.

Keith Carradine is the drifter with the dangerous past. We are never quite sure how seriously to take him, and that's the idea behind his performance, I think: He is able to quite sincerely tell two different women he loves them and wants to marry them, and the funny thing is, we believe him, both times. Eve, the former hooker who owns a bar, is played by Lesley Ann Warren. It's another good performance, nervous and on-edge; she's the kind of woman who seeks a different man every night as a protection against winding up with the same guy for a whole lifetime in a row. There are other intriguing characters in this story, most notably Rae Dawn Chong as a cute young alcoholic with a weird marriage, a naive way of trusting strangers, and dreamy plans of becoming a poet someday. Her husband (Patrick Bauchau) begins to get real tired of seeing the Carradine character, who through a series of misunderstandings seems to specialize in robbing him of poker pots, dates, and the attentions of his wife.

All of these people interact throughout the whole movie without *Choose Me* ever settling into familiar patterns. It's as if Rudolph wanted to tell a story as it might actually have happened, with coincidental meetings, dumb misunderstandings, random chance, and the endless surprises of human nature. At the end of the movie we haven't learned anything in particular, but we have met these people and their loneliness and punch-drunk optimism, and we have followed them a little time through the night.

A Chorus Line ★ ★ ★ ½
PG-13, 117 m., 1985

Michael Blevins (Mark), Yamil Borges (Morales), Sharon Brown (Kim), Gregg Burge (Richie), Michael Douglas (Zach), Cameron English (Paul), Tony Fields (Al), Nicole Fosse (Kristine), Vicki Frederick (Sheila), Jan Gan Boyd (Connie), Michelle Johnston (Bebe), Janet Jones (Judy), Pam Klinger (Maggie), Audrey Landers (Val), Terrence Mann (Larry), Charles McGowan (Mike), Alyson Reed (Cassie), Justin Ross (Greg), Blane Savage (Don), Matt West (Bobby). Directed by Richard Attenborough and produced by Cy Feuer and Ernest Martin. Screenplay by Arnold Schulman.

Show business is the only business that reminds us there is no business like it. And it never tires of that message. If there were as many books about books as there are musicals about musicals, there wouldn't be room on the shelf for books about anything else. *A Chorus Line* is the quintessential backstage musical, a celebration of the lives and hard times of the gypsy dancers who turn up by the hundreds to audition for a handful of jobs on Broadway. It takes years of brutal hard work to become a good enough dancer to dare go to an audition, and then the reward is usually a brusque "thank you" and a sweaty ride home on the subway. In order to succeed as a Broadway dancer, applicants need a limitless capacity to absorb rejection, and *A Chorus Line* celebrates that masochism in song and dance.

A Chorus Line has spent more than a decade on stages all over the world; its story is by now well known. A choreographer is casting eight dancers for a new musical he hopes to stage, and during one long and truthful day he auditions dozens of dancers before he makes his final selection. Richard Attenborough's film treatment of this story sticks to the outlines of the stage version, by and large, although he leaves the stage to fill in the details of the choreographer's old romance, and he leaves out some of the original songs to make room for some new ones.

The result may not please purists who want a film record of what they saw on stage, but this is one of the most intelligent and compelling movie musicals in a long time— and the most grown-up, since it isn't limited, as so many contemporary musicals are, to the celebration of the survival qualities of geriatric actresses.

Most of the scenes take place inside a theater. Zack (Michael Douglas), the choreographer, sits behind a writing platform somewhere out there in the darkness. Occasionally he lights a cigarette, and the ash glows as he takes the measure of the dancers on the stage. He can see them. They can't see him. He communicates by microphone. They step hesitantly to the edge of the stage, blinded by the spotlight, and talk into the void. Well, if that isn't the life they wanted, why did they volunteer for it?

Platoons of dancers are brought on stage, winnowed, dismissed. Finally there are sixteen left, and Zack asks each one of them to talk on a personal level—talk about when they were born, and where, and what their lives have been like, and what their dreams are. Many of the dancers have the most extraordinary difficulties in doing this, and one of them is frank: "Give me the lines, and I can play anybody. Just don't ask me to talk about myself."

Meanwhile, backstage drama is taking shape. An unexpected dancer has appeared for the auditions—Cassie (Alyson Reed), Zack's former girlfriend. They met in the theater, courted in the theater, broke up because Zack's job left no time for a personal life. Cassie was a star, but now she simply needs a job.

The movie opens up the play by going offstage for flashbacks to their affair, but the flashbacks are notable mostly for the way they focus on the theatrical lives of this couple—the way their private lives seem valid only to the degree that they reflect acceptance from the audience. The underlying tension in the movie circles around Zack's eventual decision: Will his heart or his profession make the eventual decision about Cassie? Douglas plays Zack on a staccato, harsh note; this is a workaholic who walks around with a lot of anger. That makes it all

the more effective when he occasionally relents and gives one of the dancers a break; softening momentarily before putting his mask on again.

I thought Zack's most revealing moment came when he made the cut from sixteen dancers to eight, reading out eight names and then, when the eight were assembled downstage with smiles on their faces, thanking them and dismissing them; he had chosen the eight he did not name. Was this a misguided attempt to tell the rejected eight that they were also winners? Or was it simply cruelty? We are left to answer for ourselves.

Such questions are intercut with song and dance, with virtuoso solo numbers (my favorite was Charles McGowan's "I Can Do That!") and ensemble production numbers, leading up to a big and splashy finale, in which all of the dancers who originally auditioned are back on stage, together once again.

That leads to my one major difference with Attenborough's approach. Since *A Chorus Line* is a musical about itself, and since the whole hard, bitter, romantic truth of the story is that many are called but few are chosen, the roll call at the end strikes a false note of triumph. Better, perhaps, to have eight dancers on stage, and then cut to the others putting on their street clothes, waiting at bus stops, explaining to friends how they didn't get the job, or going to their dance classes yet again. I think the message of the play is that you don't get called back for a grand finale; you simply go to another audition.

Christiane F. ★ ★ ★ ½
R, 124 m., 1982

Natja Brunkhorst (Christiane), Thomas Haustein (Detlev), Jens Kuphal (Axel), Reiner Wolk (Leiche). Directed by Ulrich Edel and produced by Bernd Eichinger and Hans Weth.

This is one of the most horrifying movies I have ever seen. The fact that it's based on actual events makes it heartbreaking. *Christiane F.* is the portrait of a young girl who between her thirteenth and fifteenth years went from a fairly average childhood into the horrors of drug addiction, prostitution, and life on the brink of death.

The movie has become notorious in Europe, where both the film and book versions of Christiane's adventures have been bestsellers. The real Christiane first came to light as a witness in the trial of a man accused of having sex with minors. A reporter at the trial was intrigued by her appearance on the witness stand and tracked her down. His tape-recorded interviews with her became the basis for a twelve-part series in *Stern*, the German news magazine, which inspired the movie.

It is one of the most unremittingly grim portraits of drug addiction ever filmed. The only American equivalent that comes to mind is Shirley Clarke's *The Connection* (1961), but in that film the hell of heroin addiction was tempered by the story construction of the film, which evolved as a well-told play. *Christiane F.* simply evolves as one lower plateau of suffering after another, until Christiane hits a low bottom.

The movie opens with Christiane as an unexceptional young teen-ager, given to such minor vices as playing rock records too loud and staying out too late. She lives in an apartment with her mother and resents the regular presence of her mother's boyfriend. With friends, she experiments with alcohol and pot, and them, after a rock concert (David Bowie, playing himself), she sniffs some heroin, "just out of curiosity." She likes the feeling it gives her. She tries to get it again. She has young friends who are already junkies, but she disregards their warnings that she'll get hooked. She mindlessly repeats the addict's ageless claim: "I can't get hooked if I just use a little, only once in a while. I can control my using." She cannot. Before long, she's shooting heroin, and not much longer after that she is selling her body to buy it.

This is a common story in the big cities of the world. It is relatively unusual among girls as young as Christiane (I hope), but even more unusual is the fact that she finds her own way into the heroin-and-hooker underground, without being enslaved by a pimp. The movie is relentless in depicting the drug culture of West Berlin. We see unspeakable sights: a junkie leaping over a toilet stall to yank the needle from Christiane's arm and plunge it into his own, stealing her fix; Christiane and her boyfriend trying to withdraw cold turkey and vomiting all over one another; the discovery of dead overdose victims, and, unforgettably, the pale, sad faces of the junkies lined up in a subway station, all hope gone from their once-young eyes.

Christiane F. made lots of the "best ten" lists of European critics in 1982, but I found it hard to judge its artistic quality because of the shockingly bad dubbing job. The film has been dubbed into mid-Atlantic British, by voices that are often clearly too old and in slang that is ten to fifteen years out of date. New World should ask for its money back from the dubbers. And yet—the movie still works. After a time we forget the bad dubbing, because the images are so powerful, the horrors so strong and the performances (by a cast of young unknowns) so utterly, bleakly, realistic. This is a movie of hell.

Christine ★ ★ ★
R, 110 m., 1983

Keith Gordon (Arnie), John Stockwell (Dennis), Alexandra Paul (Leigh), Robert Prosky (Garage owner), Harry Dean Stanton (Junkins). Directed by John Carpenter and produced by Richard Kobritz. Screenplay by Bill Phillips.

I've seen a lot of movies where the teen-age guy parks in a car with the girl he loves. This is the first one where he parks with a girl in the car he loves. I knew guys like this in high school. They spent their lives customizing their cars. Their girlfriends were accessories who ranked higher, say, than foam-rubber dice, but lower than dual carbs.

The car is named *Christine*. It's a bright red 1958 Plymouth Fury, one of those cars that used to sponsor the "Lawrence Welk Show," with tail fins that were ripped off for the *Jaws* ad campaign. This car should have been recalled, all right—to hell. It kills one guy and maims another before it's off the assembly line. Its original owner comes to a sad end in the front seat. And later, when Christine is twenty-one years old and rusting away, Arnie buys her. Arnie is a wimp. He's the kind of guy you'd play jokes on during lunch period, telling him the class slut wanted to talk to him, and then hiding his lunch tray while she was telling him to get lost. The kind of guy who was always whining, "Come on, guys—the joke's over!" But after Arnie buys Christine, he undergoes a strange metamorphosis. He becomes cool. He starts looking better. He stops with the greasy kid stuff. He starts going out with the prettiest girl in the school. That's where he makes his mistake. Christine gets jealous.

The entire movie depends on our willingness to believe that a car can have a mind of its own. I have believed in stranger things in the movies. Christine can drive around without a driver, play appropriate 1950s rock songs, lock people inside, and repair its own crushed fenders. The car is another inspiration from Stephen King, the horror novelist who specializes in thrillers about everyday objects. We saw his *Cujo*, about a rabid St. Bernard, and any day now I expect him to announce *Amityville IV: The Garage Door-Opener.*

Christine is, of course, utterly ridiculous. But I enjoyed it anyway. The movies have a love affair with cars, and at some dumb elemental level we enjoy seeing chases and crashes. In fact, under the right circumstances there is nothing quite so exhilarating as seeing a car crushed, and one of the best scenes in *Christine* is the one where the car forces itself into an alley that's too narrow for it.

Christine was directed by John Carpenter, who made *Halloween*, and his method is to take the story more or less seriously. One grin and the mood would be broken. But by the end of the movie, Christine has developed such a formidable personality that we are actually taking sides during its duel with a bulldozer. This is the kind of movie where you walk out with a silly grin, get in your car, and lay rubber halfway down the freeway.

A Christmas Story ★ ★ ★
PG, 94 m., 1983

Melinda Dillon (Mrs. Parker), Darren McGavin (The Old Man), Peter Billingsley (Ralphie). Directed by Bob Clark and produced by Rene Dupont and Clark. Screenplay by Jean Shepherd, Leigh Brown, and Clark.

Of course. That's what I kept saying during *A Christmas Story*, every time the movie came up with another one of its memories about growing up in the 1940s. Of course, any nine-year-old kid in the '40s would passionately want, for Christmas, a Daisy Brand Red Ryder repeating BB carbine with a compass mounted in the stock. Of course. And of course, his mother would say, "You'll shoot your eye out." That's what mothers always said about BB-guns. I grew up in downstate Illinois. The hero of this film, Ralphie, grew up in Gary, Ind. Looking back over a distance of more than thirty years, the two places seem almost identical—Middle American outposts where you weren't trying to keep up with the neighbors, you were trying to keep up with Norman Rockwell.

The movie is based on a nostalgic comic novel named *In God We Trust, All Others Pay Cash,* by Jean Shepherd, the radio humorist, who also narrates it. He remembers the obvious things, like fights with the bullies at school, and getting into impenetrable discussions with younger kids who do not quite know what all the words mean. He remembers legendary schoolteachers and hiding in the cupboard under the sink and having fantasies of defending the family home with a BB-gun.

But he also remembers, warmly and with love, the foibles of parents. The Old Man in *A Christmas Story* is played by Darren McGavin as an enthusiast. Not an enthusiast of anything, just simply an enthusiast. When he wins a prize in a contest, and it turns out to be a table lamp in the shape of a female leg in a garter, he puts it in the window, because it is the most amazing lamp he has ever seen. Of course. I can understand that feeling. I can also understand the feeling of the mother (Melinda Dillon), who is mortified beyond words.

The movie's high point comes at Christmastime, when Ralphie (Peter Billingsley) goes to visit Santa Claus. Visits to Santa Claus are more or less standard in works of this genre, but this movie has the best visit to Santa I've ever seen. Santa is a workaholic, processing kids relentlessly. He has one helper to spin the kid and deposit him on Santa's lap, and another one to grab the kid when the visit is over, and hurl him down a chute to his parents below. If the kid doesn't want to go, he gets Santa's boot in his face. Of course.

City Heat ¹/₂ ★
PG, 94 m., 1984

Clint Eastwood (Lieutenant Speer), Burt
Reynolds (Mike Murphy), Jane Alexander
(Addy), Madeline Kahn (Caroline Howley),
Rip Torn (Prime Pitt), Irene Cara (Ginny Lee).
Directed by Richard Benjamin and produced
by Fritz Maners. Screenplay by Sam O.
Brown and Joseph C. Stinson.

Sometimes you get the idea that the deal behind a movie was so complicated and exhausting that they just didn't have the strength left to make the movie itself. *City Heat*, for example, stars two of the top box-office attractions in the recent history of Hollywood: Clint Eastwood and Burt Reynolds. It was originally going to be directed by Blake Edwards, but he was fired after "creative differences" with the two stars, and then several other directors were approached before Richard Benjamin agreed to pick up the reins. The depth of Edwards's feelings about the whole episode can be guessed from the *nom de plume* he used for his original screenplay credit, "Sam O. Brown." Check the initials.

We will never know what Edwards might have made of *City Heat*. That's bad enough. What's worse is that we can barely tell what Benjamin made of it. This movie is a confusing mess with a plot so pointless that there's a fight scene every ten minutes, just to distract us. The movie's so bewildered it doesn't even seem sure about the relationship between Eastwood and Reynolds: Are they really enemies, or just friends who talk tough to one another, or are they former friends who became enemies and are now becoming friends again? And does it matter?

The movie's a period gangster picture, with lots of antique cars and mustaches and snap-brim fedora hats. Eastwood plays a police detective who is mild-mannered, and somebody crosses him, and then he turns into a ferocious fighting machine. Reynolds is a former cop who is now a private eye. Early in the film, he goes to his office for consultations with Richard Roundtree and Jane Alexander, and it is a measure of the film's confusion that when he mentions his partner, we are not quite sure which one he means. There are other loose ends. For example, Reynolds kisses Alexander tend-

erly, but then she goes on a date with Eastwood. The guys go to a boxing match that has no logical purpose other than to serve as a setup for a meeting *after* the match. A criminal gang, headed by Rip Torn, will kill to get its hands on a box that contains . . . what? Ledger records, I think. Of illegal gambling debts, I think. You know a movie is desperately in trouble when the audience isn't even sure what the bad guys are after.

There are a lot of talented people in this movie, including Irene Cara in a throwaway role as a nightclub singer, and Madeline Kahn in her basic performance as a Dietrich-esque vamp. There are also incessant fight scenes and shoot-outs, in which the bad guys are consistently unable to hit the side of a barn, and Eastwood is incapable of missing. All of this is maybe supposed to be an ironic commentary on Eastwood's Dirty Harry character, but so what? Almost every scene in the movie seems to have been a separate inspiration, thrown in with no thought for the movie as a whole.

How do travesties like this get made? I have a feeling the problem starts at the level of negotiations, in which everybody protects his own turf, and the movie suffers. There are moments here when you want to squirm, especially when Clint Eastwood allows his incomparable screen persona to be parodied. The Dirty Harry movies themselves border on parody—that's part of their charm—but they know what they're doing. *City Heat* is a movie in which people almost obviously don't have a clue.

City of Women ★ ★ ¹/₂
R, 140 m., 1981

Marcello Mastroianni (Snaporaz), Ettor
Manni (Dr. Zberkock), Anna Prucnal (Elena),
Bernice Stegers (Woman on Train), Donatella
Damiani (Feminist on Skates). Directed by
Federico Fellini. Screenplay by Fellini and
Bernardino Zapponi.

If there is one central image in the work of Federico Fellini, it's of Fellini's autobiographical hero being smothered by women. They come in all shapes and ages, from old crones to young innocents, from heavy-breasted mother figures to seductive nymphs. One of Fellini's favorite strategies is to gather all the women into one fantasy and place his hero at the center of it. That's what he did in the celebrated harem sequence in *8½*, and that's what he does throughout *City of Women*.

There is, however, an additional twist this time. Since the basic Fellini universe was created in *La Strada, La Dolce Vita, 8½,* and *Juliet of the Spirits*, beliefs about the role of women have undergone a revolution, even in Italy. It is no longer enough that Fellini deal with the ways women tantalize, dominate, and possess his male heroes. Now he must also deal with the women themselves. For Fellini, this is probably not nearly so much fun. His idea of a liberated woman is fairly clear from the wife-character in *8½* (1963). She is severe, wears tailored suits and horn-rim glasses, and wants to spoil all the fun. Fellini's hero, in that film and in *City of Women*, is named Guido, is played by Marcello Mastroianni, and wants to escape from the horn-rim types and lose himself in the capacious bosom of a thoroughly undemanding sex object.

At the beginning of *City of Women*, however, Guido finds himself riding on a train across from a severe-looking woman in a tailored suit. He tries to seduce her. She sentences him to an imaginary odyssey through a series of sexual fantasies, most of them devoted to the unpleasant fates of men who do not have the correct attitude about women. Most of these fantasies, and indeed many of the specific images, are familiar to anyone who has seen several Fellini films. There is a long circus chute for Mastroianni to tumble down (*Juliet*), and a group of circus scenes (from half his other films), and a wall covered with portraits (remember *Fellini Roma?*), and an insatiable satyr, and, of course, the full-lipped, full-bosomed, smiling and inexhaustible temptress who turns up, in one manifestation or another, throughout Fellini.

City of Women does nothing original or very challenging with this material. Although it pretends to be Fellini's film about feminism, it reveals no great understanding of the subject; Fellini basically sees feminists as shrill harems of whip-wielding harridans, forever dangling the carrot of sex just out of reach of his suffering hero. Fellini has rarely been able to discover human beings hidden inside his female characters,

and it's a little late for him to start blaming that on the women's liberation movement.

Is *City of Women* worth seeing? Yes, probably, even though it is not a successful movie and certainly not up to Fellini's best work. It's worth seeing because it's a bedazzling collection of images, because at times it's a graceful and fluid celebration of pure film-making skill, and because Fellini can certainly make a bad film but cannot quite make a boring one.

Claire's Knee ★ ★ ★ ★
PG, 103 m., 1971

Jean-Claude Brialy (Jerome), Aurora Cornu (Aurora), Beatrice Romand (Laura), Laurence de Monaghan (Claire). Directed by Eric Rohmer and produced by Pierre Cottrell. Screenplay by Eric Rohmer.

Now if I were to say, for example, that *Claire's Knee* is about Jerome's desire to caress the knee of Claire, you would be about a million miles from the heart of this extraordinary film. And yet, in a way, *Claire's Knee* is indeed about Jerome's feelings for Claire's knee, which is a splendid knee.

Jerome encounters Claire and the other characters in the film during a month's holiday he takes on a lake between France and Switzerland. He has gone there to rest and reflect before he marries Lucinda, a woman he has loved for five years. And who should he run into but Aurora, a novelist who he's also been a little in love with for a long time.

Aurora is staying with a summer family that has two daughters: Laura, who is sixteen and very wise and falls in love with Jerome, and Claire, who is beautiful and blonde and full of figure and spirit. Jerome and Aurora enter into a teasing intellectual game, which requires Jerome to describe to Aurora whatever happens to him during his holiday. When they all become aware that Laura has fallen in love with the older man, Jerome encourages her in a friendly, platonic way. They have talks about love and the nature of life, and they grow very fond of each other, although of course the man does not take advantage of the young girl.

But then Claire joins the group, and one day while they are picking cherries, Jerome turns his head and finds that Claire has climbed a ladder and he is looking directly at her knee. Claire herself, observed playing volleyball or running, hand-in-hand, with her boyfriend, is a sleek animal, and Jerome finds himself stirring with desire.

He doesn't want to run away with Claire, or seduce her, or anything like that; he plans to marry Lucinda. But he tells his friend Aurora that he has become fascinated by Claire's knee; that it might be the point through which she could be approached, just as another girl might respond to a caress on the neck, or the cheek, or the arm. He becomes obsessed with desire to test this theory, and one day has an opportunity to touch the knee at last.

As with all the films of Eric Rohmer, *Claire's Knee* exists at levels far removed from plot (as you might have guessed while I was describing the plot). What is really happening in this movie happens on the level of character, of thought, of the way people approach each other and then shy away. In some movies, people murder each other and the contact is casual; in a work by Eric Rohmer, small attitudes and gestures can summon up a university of humanity.

Rohmer has an uncanny ability to make his actors seem as if they were going through the experiences they portray. The acting of Beatrice Romand, as sixteen-year-old Laura, is especially good in this respect; she isn't as pretty as her sister, but we feel somehow she'll find more enjoyment in life because she is a . . . well, a better person underneath. Jean-Claude Brialy is excellent in a difficult role. He has to relate with three women in the movie, and yet remain implicitly faithful to the unseen Lucinda. He does, and since the sexuality in his performance is suppressed, it is, of course, all the more sensuous. *Claire's Knee* is a movie for people who still read good novels, care about good films, and think occasionally.

Clan of the Cave Bear ★ ½
R, 120 m., 1985

Darryl Hannah (Ayla), Pamela Reed (Iza), James Remar (Creb), Thomas G. Waites (Broud), John Doolittle (Brun), Curtis Armstrong (Goov). Directed by Michael Chapman and produced by Gerald I. Isenberg. Screenplay by John Sayles.

What was it like, back there at the dawn of time? What was it like to be a human being, and yet have none of the things we take for granted, like houses, feminism, and shoes? How did we take that first great leap, out of the caves and into the Iron Age? Or, if you really want to get idealistic about it, that leap out of the rain and into the caves?

Clan of the Cave Bear attempts to answer those questions by making a great leap backward in the imagination, to that precise moment when the first Cro-Magnons were moving in and the last Neanderthals were becoming obsolete. Unfortunately, the movie never really does reconcile itself to the prehistoric past. It approaches those times with a modern sensibility. It shows us a woman winning respect from a patriarchal tribe, when in reality the men would have just banged her over the head real good. It isn't grim enough about what things were probably like back then.

It tells a nice little modern parable about a distant past that is hardly less idealistic than the Garden of Eden. Instead of people who are scarred, wind-burned, thin, and toothless, it gives us graduates of the Los Angeles health club scene, and a heroine who looks as if she just walked over from make-up.

It also packs a lot of things into a short span of that long-ago time. Although whole eons were available to it, the movie covers just a few short seasons, as a wandering tribe of primitive Neanderthals encounters an amazing sight: A Cro-Magnon woman (Darryl Hannah), tall and blonde and smarter than they are.

The girl is adopted into the tribe, and right away she causes trouble. She can't understand why the men get to have all the fun, and use all of the weapons, and make all of the decisions. One day she sneaks out and practices on the slingshot. On another day, she challenges the tribe's attitude about sex, seniority, and even about self-defense. In her spare time, she invents arithmetic and becomes chief adviser to the medicine man. This isn't the first Cro-Magnon, it's the first Rhodes scholar.

The movie dresses its actors in furs and skins, and has them walk around barefoot and talk in monosyllables. But it never quite makes them seem frightened and ignorant and vulnerable and bewildered. To capture the sense of wonder of those days when the human race reached its turning point, *Clan of the Cave Bear* needs great images, not tidy little dramatic scenes with predictable conclusions. It needs sights like the opening of *2001*, when the bone went flying into the air. Or it needs the muddy, exhausted desperation of the characters in *Quest for Fire*, a movie that *did* feel as if it took place in prehistory. *Clan of the Cave Bear* is about the first generation of designer cavemen.

The performances are doomed from the start, because the actors are asked to play characters who are modern in everything but dress and language. Every one of these people has motives that are instantly recognizable and predictable. There is no sense of the alien and the unknown, no sense that these people have ideas and feelings that would be strange to us. Even their quasi-religion is familiar: They believe each person has an animal spirit which is its partner or symbol, and that if a person's spirit is strong, it gives them strength. This is pseudo-anthropology crossed with Indian folklore and the Boy Scouts.

The ending of *Clan of the Cave Bear* betrays its bankruptcy, because there isn't really an ending, just a conclusion—a romantic shot of the woman continuing on her lonely quest. The great failure of the movie is a failure of imagination. The filmmakers made no effort to empathize with their prehistoric characters, to imagine what it might really have been like back then. They are content to assemble the usual narrative clichés and standard storylines, and apply them to some actors in costume. If modern men came from beginnings like this, why did they even bother to develop civilization, since they already possess its most wretched excesses?

Clash of the Titans ★ ★ ★ ½
PG, 118 m., 1981

Harry Hamlin (Perseus), Judi Bowker (Andromeda), Burgess Meredith (Ammen), Laurence Olivier (Zeus), Maggie Smith (Thetis), Neil McCarthy (Calibos). Directed by Desmond Davis and produced by Charles H. Schneer and Ray Harryhausen, with special effects created by Harryhausen.

Clash of the Titans is a grand and glorious romantic adventure, filled with grave heroes, beautiful heroines, fearsome monsters, and awe-inspiring duels to the death. It is a lot of fun. It was quite possibly intended as a sort of Greek mythological retread of *Star Wars* (it has a wise little mechanical owl in it who's a third cousin of R2-D2), but it's also part of an older Hollywood tradition of special-effects fantasies, and its visual wonderments are astonishing.

The story, on the other hand, is robust and straightforward. Perseus (Harry Hamlin) is locked into a coffin with his mother and cast into the sea, after she has angered the gods. But Zeus (Laurence Olivier) takes pity and sees that the coffin washes ashore on a deserted island, where Perseus grows to manhood and learns of his mission in life. The mission, in a nutshell, is to return to Joppa and rescue Andromeda (Judi Bowker) from a fate worse than death: marriage to the hideously ugly Calibos, who was promised her hand in marriage before he was turned into a monster by the wrath of the gods. Calibos lives in a swamp and dispatches a gigantic, scrawny bird every night to fetch him the spirit of the sleeping Andromeda in a gilded cage. If Perseus is to marry Andromeda, he must defeat Calibos in combat and also answer a riddle posed by Cassiopeia, Andromeda's mother. Those who answer the riddle incorrectly are condemned to die. Love was more complicated in the old days.

There are, of course, other tests. To follow the bird back to the lair of Calibos, the resourceful Perseus must capture and tame Pegasus, the last of the great winged horses. He must also enter the lair of Medusa, who turns men to stone with one glance, and behead her so that he can use her dead eyes to petrify the gargantuan monster Kraken, who is unchained from his cage on the ocean floor so that he can ravish Joppa in general and Andromeda in particular.

All of this is gloriously silly. But because the movie respects its material, it even succeeds in halfway selling us this story; movies that look like *Clash of the Titans* have a tendency to seem ridiculous, but this film has the courage of its convictions. It is also blessed with a cast that somehow finds its way past all the monsters and through all the heroic dialogue and gets us involved in the characters. Harry Hamlin is a completely satisfactory Perseus, handsome and solemn and charged with his own mission. Judi Bowker is a beautiful princess and a great screamer, especially in the scene where she's chained to the rock and Kraken is slobbering all over her. Burgess Meredith has a nice little supporting role as Ammon, an old playwright who thinks he may be able to turn all of this into a quick epic. And Laurence Olivier is just as I have always imagined Zeus: petulant, but a pushover for a pretty face.

The real star of the movie, however, is Ray Harryhausen, who has worked more than forty years as a creator of special effects. He uses combinations of animation, miniatures, optical tricks, and multiple images to put humans into the same movie frames as the most fantastical creatures of legend, and more often than not, they look pretty convincing: when Perseus tames Pegasus, it sure looks like he's dealing with a real horse (except for the wings, of course).

Harryhausen's credits include *Mighty Joe Young, Jason and the Argonauts,* and *The Golden Voyage of Sinbad,* but *Clash of the Titans* is his masterwork. Among his inspired set-pieces: the battle in the Medusa's lair, with her hair writhing with snakes; the flying horse scenes; the gigantic prehistoric bird; the two-headed wolf-dog, Dioskilos; the Stygian witches; and, of course, Kraken, who rears up from the sea and causes tidal waves that do a lot of very convincing damage to a Greek city that exists only in Harryhausen's art. The most lovable special-effects creation in the movie is little Bubo, a golden owl sent by the gods to help Perseus in his trials. Bubo whistles and rotates his head something like R2-D2 in *Star Wars,* and he has a similar personality, too, especially at the hilarious moment when he enters the film for the first time.

Clash of the Titans is a family film (there's nothing in it that would disturb any but the most impressionable children), and yet it's not by any means innocuous: It's got blood and thunder and lots of gory details, all presented with enormous gusto and style. It has faith in a story-telling tradition that sometimes seems almost forgotten, a tradition depending upon legends and myths, magical swords, enchanted shields, invisibility helmets, and the overwhelming power of a kiss.

The Class of 1984 ★ ★ ★ ½
R, 93 m., 1982

Perry King (Andy Norris), Timothy Van Patten (Stegman), Roddy McDowell (Terry Corrigan). Directed by Mark Lester and produced by Lester and Merrie Lynn Ross. Screenplay by Lester, John Saxton, and Tom Holland.

Movies like this either grab you, or they don't. *The Class of 1984* grabbed me. I saw it for the first time at the 1982 Cannes Film Festival, where I wandered into the theater expecting to find the dog of the week and wandered out two hours later, a little dazed and sort of overwhelmed. *The Class of 1984* is not a great movie but it works with quiet, strong efficiency to achieve more or less what we expect from a movie with such a title. It is violent, funny, scary, contains boldly outlined characters, and gets us involved. It also has a lot of style. One of the reasons for the film's style may be that it was made by people who knew what they were doing. The whole Dead Teen-ager genre has been seriously weakened in the last several years by wave upon wave of cheap, idiotic tax shelter films from Canada and elsewhere: films in which a Mad Slasher and a lot of screaming adolescents have been substituted for talent, skill, and craft—movies such as *Prom Night* and *Terror Train* and *The Burning.*

Mark Lester's *The Class of 1984* stands head and shoulders above movies like that. It tells a strong, simple story. It is acted well. It is not afraid to be comic at times and, even better, it's not afraid at the end to pull out all the stops and give us the sort of Grand Guignol conclusion that the slasher movies always botch. You may or may not think it's any good, but you'll have to admit that it works.

The movie stars Perry King, a skilled actor who has survived a lot of junk, as a music teacher who takes a job at a big city high school. The first day he walks into class, he faces trouble, and trouble is personified by Stegman (Timothy Van Patten), the brilliant but crazed leader of the high school gang. Stegman dresses as a cross between a punk rocker and a Hell's Angel. He terrorizes half the school with his violence and mesmerizes the other half with his charisma. He also happens to be a brilliant musician. King tries to deal with him, reason with him, outthink him, and even outmuscle him, but the kid is strong, smart, and mean. The other teachers and the school officials have mostly surrendered to the reign of terror. A few put up a fight, most memorably the biology teacher, played by Roddy McDowell. He has one of the great scenes in the movie as he pulls a gun on his class and invites them to share with him the joys of education, or else.

The movie builds toward one of those nightmarish conclusions where everything's happening at once. While the teacher prepares to lead his school orchestra in a concert, the thugs terrorize his helpless wife at home. The teacher turns the baton over to his best student, a shy young girl, and goes off to do battle with the punks. After a great deal of blood has been shed, the teacher and the gang leader are finally face to face, high in the wings over the high school auditorium stage, and the climax is a cross between *The Hunchback of Notre Dame* and *Beyond the Valley of the Dolls.*

The Class of 1984 has received some really savage criticism. Newsweek called it *"The Class of 1982* with herpes." What does that mean? I dunno. I guess it means the critic found the movie so hateful that it wasn't worth anything more than cheap wisecracks. But unless we can accept talent wherever we find it in the movies, and especially in smaller genre movies without big stars, we're going to be left with nothing but overpriced lead balloons and delicate little exercises in sensibility. *The Class of 1984* is raw, offensive, vulgar, and violent, but it contains the sparks of talent and wit, and it is acted and directed by people who cared to make it special.

Close Encounters of the Third Kind: The Special Edition ★ ★ ★ ★
PG, 152 m., 1980

Richard Dreyfuss (Roy Neary), Francois Truffaut (Claude Lacombe), Teri Garr (Ronnie Neary), Melinda Dillon (Jillian Guiler).
Directed and written by Steven Spielberg and produced by Julia Phillips and Michael Phillips.

Close Encounters of the Third Kind: The Special Edition is the movie Steven Spielberg wanted to make in the first place. The changes Spielberg has made in his original 1978 film are basic and extensive, adding up to essentially a new moviegoing experience. Spielberg's changes fall into four categories:

• He's provided an entirely new conclusion, taking us inside the alien spaceship that visits at the end of the film.

• He's provided more motivation for the strange behavior of the Richard Dreyfuss character—who is compelled by "psychic implanting" to visit the Nevada mountain where the spaceship plans to land.

• He's added additional manifestations of UFO intervention in earthly affairs—including an ocean-going freighter deposited in the middle of the Gobi Desert.

• In addition to the sensational ending, he's added more special effects throughout the film. One shot seems like a light-hearted quote from Spielberg's own *Jaws.* In that film, a high-angle shot showed the shadow of the giant shark passing under a boat. In this one, a high-angle shot shows the shadow of a giant UFO passing over a pickup truck.

Spielberg's decision to revise the original version of *Close Encounters* is all but unprecedented. Some directors have remade their earlier films (Hitchcock did British and American versions of *The Man Who Knew Too Much*), and others have thought out loud about changes they'd like to make (Robert Altman wanted to edit a nine-hour version of *Nashville* for TV). And countless directors, of course, have given us sequels—"part two" of their original hits.

Spielberg's *Special Edition* is sort of a *Close Encounters: Part 1½.* It is also a very good film. I thought the original film was an astonishing achievement, capturing the feeling of awe and wonder we have when considering the likelihood of life beyond the Earth. I gave that first version a four-star rating. This new version gets another four stars: It is, quite simply, a better film—so much better that it might inspire the uncharitable question, "Why didn't Spielberg make it this good the *first* time?"

His changes fall into three categories. He has (1) thrown away scenes that didn't work, like the silly sequence in which Dreyfuss dug up half of his yard in an attempt to build a model of the mountain in his vision; (2) put in scenes he shot three years ago but did not use, such as the Gobi sequence and Dreyfuss flipping out over the strange compulsion that has overtaken him, and (3) shot some entirely new scenes.

The most spectacular of these is the new ending, which shows us what Dreyfuss sees when he enters the spacecraft. He sees a sort of extraterrestrial cathedral, a limitless interior space filled with columns of light, countless sources of brilliance, and the machinery of an unimaginable alien technology. (The new special effects were designed by the underground artist R. Cobb, I understand; no credit is given.) This new conclusion gives the movie the kind of overwhelming final emotional impact it needed; it adds another dimension to the already impressive ending of the first version.

The movie gains impact in another way. Spielberg has tightened up the whole film. Dead ends and pointless scenes have been dropped. New scenes do a better job of establishing the characters—not only of Dreyfuss, but also of Francois Truffaut, as the French scientist. The new editing moves the film along at a faster, more absorbing pace to the mind-stretching conclusion. *Close Encounters*, which was already a wonderful film, now transcends itself; it's one of the great moviegoing experiences. If you've seen it before, I'm afraid that now you'll have to see it again.

Coal Miner's Daughter ★ ★ ★
PG, 125 m., 1980

Sissy Spacek (Loretta Lynn), Tommy Lee Jones (Mooney Lynn), Beverly D'Angelo (Patsy Cline), Levon Helm (Ted Webb), Phyllis Boyens (Clara Webb). Directed by Michael Arted and produced by Bernard Schwarts. Screenplay by Tom Rickman.

What improbable lives so many Americans lead, compared to the more orderly and predictable careers of the Swedes, say, or the French. It's not just that we're the most upwardly mobile society in history, we're the most mobile, period: We go to ruin as swiftly and and dramatically as we hit the jackpot. No wonder one of our favorite myths involves a rags to riches story in which success then destroys the hero.

Look at country music star Loretta Lynn. If we can believe *Coal Miner's Daughter* (and I gather that, by and large, we can), here's a life which began in the poverty of the coalfields of Kentucky and led almost overnight to show-business stardom. And what's astonishing is that it wasn't even really planned that way: Loretta learned to play on a pawnshop guitar, her husband thought she could sing, and one day she just sorta found herself on stage. The movie's about Loretta Lynn's childhood, her very early marriage, her quick four kids, her husband's move to Washington State looking for a job, her humble start in show business, her apparently quick rise to stardom, and then the usual Catch-22 of self-destructivenss.

We're not surprised, somehow, that right after the scenes where she becomes a superstar, there are scenes where she starts using pills, getting headaches, and complaining that everybody's on her case all the time. We fiercely want to believe in success in this country, but for some reason we also want to believe that it takes a terrible human toll. Sometimes it does—and that always makes for a better story. Straightforward success sagas, in which the heroes just keep on getting richer, are boring. We want our heroes to suffer. We like to identify—it makes stars more human, somehow, if they get screwed by Valium, too.

What's refreshing about *Coal Miner's Daughter* is that it takes the basic material (rags to riches, overnight success, the onstage breakdown, and, of course, the big comeback) and relates them in wonderfully human terms. It's fresh and immediate. That is due most of all to the performance by Sissy Spacek as Loretta Lynn. With the same sort of magical chemistry she's shown before, when she played the high school kid in *Carrie*, Spacek at twenty-nine has the ability to appear to be almost any age onscreen. Here she ages from about fourteen to somewhere in her thirties, always looks the age, and never seems to be wearing makeup. I wonder if she does it with her posture; early in the film, as a poor coal miner's kid, she slouches and slinks around, and then later she puts on dignity with the flashy dresses she wears onstage.

The movie is mostly about Lynn's relationships with her husband, Mooney (played by Tommy Lee Jones), and her first close show-business friend and mentor, Patsy Cline (Beverly D'Angelo). Both of these relationships are developed in direct, understated, intelligent ways; we are spared, for example, a routine portrait of Mooney Lynn as Official Show Biz Husband, and given instead a portrait of a recognizable human being who is aggressive, confident, loving, and fallable. The fact that this movie felt free to portray Mooney as hard-nosed is one of the most interesting things about it: Loretta Lynn, who had a certain amount of control over the project, obviously still has her feet on the ground and didn't insist that this movie be some kind of idealized fantasy.

We are left to speculate, of course, on whether Lynn's rise to stardom was really as picaresque as *Coal Miner's Daughter* suggests. She seems to get on the Grand Ole Opry mighty fast, and Patsy Cline seems to adopt her almost before she knows her. But then the amazing thing about Loretta Lynn's life seems to be how fast everything happened, and how wide open the avenues to success are in this country—if you're talented and, of course, lucky.

The most entertaining scenes in the movie are in the middle, after the coal mines and before the Top 40, when Loretta and Mooney are tooling around the back roads trying to convince country disc jockeys to play her records. The scene with Mooney taking a publicity photo of Loretta is a little gem illustrating the press agent that resides within us all.

So, anyway . . . how good *is* this movie? I think it's one of those films people like so much while they're watching it that they're inclined to think it's better than it is. It's warm, entertaining, funny, and centered around that great Sissy Spacek performance, but it's essentially pretty familiar material (not that Loretta Lynn can be blamed that Horatio Alger wrote her life before she lived it). The movie isn't great art, but it has been made with great taste and style; it's more intelligent and observant than movie biographies of singing stars used to be. That makes it a treasure to watch, even if we sometimes have the feeling we've seen it before.

The Coca-Cola Kid ★ ★ ★
NO MPAA RATING; 94 m., 1985

Eric Roberts (Becker), Greta Scacchi (Terri), Bill Kerr (T. George), Chris Haywood (Kim), Kris McQuade (Juliana). Directed by Dusan Makavejev and produced by David Roe. Screenplay by Frank Moorhouse.

"Give me churches," the man from Atlanta says. Little symbols appear on the computer screen. "Schools." More symbols. "Taverns." Lots more symbols. "You see," the man said, "I *knew* there had to be people there."

The reason for his confusion is very simple. He is a troubleshooter from Coca-Cola headquarters in Atlanta, and he is looking at the statistics for a district in Australia where absolutely no Coca-Cola is consumed. Not one drop. He has been sent all the way from America to find out why. That's the opening dilemma of Dusan Makavejev's *The Coca-Cola Kid*, an oddball comedy that was particuarly well-timed to coincide with the 1985 "New Coke" marketing circus.

The movie stars Eric Roberts, the demented killer from *Star 80*, as the American Coke expert, and one of the movie's incidental oddities is that Roberts seems just as obsessed in this role as he did as a killer. He brings such a murderous intensity to marketing that he seems a lot like the marketing people I know.

It doesn't take him long to discover the reason for Coke's problems in Australia. The folks in that isolated district don't drink Coke because they prefer a local soda pop manufactured in a steam-powered plant by an eccentric named T. George McDowell (Bill Kerr). Roberts spies on T. George, and maps a giant public relations campaign that includes an appearance at the local Rotary Club. Meanwhile, at regional Coke headquarters, he is pursued by a weird and beautiful young girl (Greta Scacchi), who has a secret: She is T. George's daughter.

The movie unwinds in an unpredictable fashion, which is Makavejev's trademark. From his early films like *Innocence Unprotected* through such controversial episodes as *Sweet Movie* and *W.R.: Mysteries of the Organism* to his 1983 hit *Montenegro*, Makavejev always has used a cheerful juxtaposition of sex, violence, and politics.

The Coca-Cola Kid is light on violence and the politics are implied rather than stated (Coke represents American imperialism, I think). But the sex is accompanied by the usual Makavejev trademark, an interest in textures. In *Sweet Movie*, sex took place on giant mountains of sugar. This time, Scacchi dresses in a red-and-white Santa suit, and tries to seduce Roberts in a flurry of feathers.

The movie is filled with moments of inspiration, of which the most unforgettable include an Aborigine Coke commercial; Scacchi creeping about the office and hiding in a Coke cooler; and T. George's final solution for his steam-powered soda factory.

The last half of the film, alas, does not quite deliver on the promises of the first half, perhaps because Eric Roberts's performance is so intense and mannered that he eventually seems to be sliding off into another level of existence. He never really connects with Scacchi, so we don't know how they feel about each other, and therefore we can't track the progress of their relationship. The movie has so many other delights, though, that it's fun anyway. Maybe it wasn't exactly intended to be a love story.

Cocoon ★ ★ ★
PG-13. 115 m., 1985

Wilford Brimley (Ben), Steve Guttenberg (Jack), Brian Dennehy (Walter), Hume Cronyn (Joe), Don Ameche (Art), Maureen Stapleton (Mary), Jessica Tandy (Alma), Jack Gilford (Bernie), Tahnee Welch (Kitty). Directed by Ron Howard and produced by Richard D. Zanuck, David Brown, and Lili Fini Zanuck. Screenplay by Tom Benedek.

Cocoon is one of the sweetest, gentlest science-fiction movies I've seen, a hymn to the notion that aliens might come from outer space and yet still be almost as corny and impulsive as we are. It is also the first film since *On Golden Pond* to deal at length with old people, and you can tell by their performances that these older actors have been waiting a long time to get something nice and meaty and silly to sink their choppers into.

The movie opens with the suggestion that aliens have landed on Earth. Then we see apparently normal human beings renting a boat and a beachfront estate. Meanwhile, in a nearby retirement home, three of the old guys have started sneaking onto the estate to take illegal swims in a big enclosed pool. One day, they discover some large, mossy rocks on the bottom of the pool. That doesn't stop them. They dive in, and before long they feel terrific—and curiously youthful.

The rocks are actually cocoons collected from the bottom of the sea by aliens, who left them behind 10,000 years ago when they were forced to evacuate Atlantis in a hurry. The pool has been charged with a life force to reawaken the cocoons, and the force works on elderly humans, too. When the leader of the aliens (Brian Dennehy) finds the old guys in the pool, he doesn't zap them with extraterrestrial weaponry. He smiles and tells them to go ahead and keep using the pool—but not to tell anyone else.

That's impossible. The old guys can't keep a secret long in a retirement home, and before long this literal fountain of youth has totally changed the lifestyles of the senior citizens. The old guys are played by three wonderful actors: Hume Cronyn, Don Ameche, and, best of all, Wilford Brimley, who has a way of investing each word with such simple truth that his dialogue seems more weighted, more real, than the other dialogue in the movie.

Brimley is sort of a ringleader. He is also a homespun philosopher, who goes fishing with his grandson and talks about the meaning of life and death. Others in the retirement home are not so serene, especially the stubborn Jack Gilford, who does not want to feel young and does not want to go swimming and thinks we should all be satisfied with the time allotted us on this planet. The introduction of the mysterious pool and its life force tests Gilford's friendships with the others, and it also puts strains on the marriage between Cronyn and Jessica Tandy. The scenes involving these characters are the best scenes in the movie.

But I also liked the treatment of the aliens, especially the Dennehy character, who observes that every 10,000 years he's entitled to do something silly. Dennehy eventuallly offers the old folks eternal life, under certain rather difficult conditions, and the way they consider his offer is rather thought-provoking—especially in the scenes between Brimley and his grandson. That's really the payoff of the movie, right there, but the ending is too drawn-out. We could also do without the romance between the boat's human captain (Steve Guttenberg) and the beautiful alien (Tahnee Welch). But the good parts in *Cocoon* are warm and sort of tender.

Code of Silence ★ ★ ★ ½
R, 102 m., 1985

Chuck Norris (Eddie Cusack), Henry Silva (Luis Comacho), Bert Remsen (Commander Kates), Mike Genovese (Tony Luna), Molly Hagan (Diana Luna), Nathan Davis (Felix Scalese), Ralph Roody (Cragie). Directed by Andy Davis and produced by Raymond Wagner. Screenplay by Michael Butler, Dennis Shryack, and Mike Gray.

Chuck Norris is still identified with a series of grade-zilch karate epics, but *Code of Silence* is a heavy-duty thriller—a slick, energetic movie with good performances and a lot of genuine human interest. It grabs you right at the start with a complicated triple-cross, and then it develops into a stylish urban action picture with sensational stunts. How sensational? How about an unfaked fight on top of a speeding elevated train, ending when both fighters dive off the train into the Chicago River? The stunts are great, but not surprising; Chuck Norris is famous for the stunts he features in all of his movies. What is surprising is the number of interesting characters in *Code of Silence*. The screenplay doesn't give us the usual cardboard clichés; there's a lot of human life here, in a series of carefully crafted performances. For once, here's a thriller that realizes we have to care about the characters before we care about their adventures.

Norris stars as a veteran Chicago vice cop named Cusack. He's a straight arrow, an honest cop that his partners call a "one-man army." As the film opens, he's setting up a drug bust, but a Latino gang beats him to it, stealing the money and the drugs and leaving a roomful of dead gangsters. That sets off a Chicago mob war between the Italian and Latino factions, and as bodies pile up in the streets, Cusack begins to worry about the daughter of a Mafia chieftain—a young artist named Diana (Molly Hagan) who wants nothing to do with her father's business, but finds she can't be a bystander. After an elaborate cat-and-mouse chase through the Loop, she's kidnapped and Cusack wants to save her.

Meanwhile, the movie has an interesting subplot about a tired veteran cop (Ralph Roody) who has mistakenly shot and killed a Latino kid while chasing some mobsters through a tenement. The veteran's young partner (Joseph Guzaldo) watches him plant a gun on the dead kid and claim that the shooting was in self-defense. It's up to the rookie, backed up by Cusack, to decide what he'll say at the departmental hearing.

The movie has a knack for taking obligatory scenes and making them more than routine. Among the small acting gems in the movie is the performance of Chicago actor Nathan Davis as Felix Scalese, a wrinkled, wise old Mafia godfather who sits on his yacht and counsels against a mob war—to no avail. Mike Genovese plays the mob chief whose daughter is kidnapped, and his first scene, as he wishes his wife a happy birthday while hurrying out the door to do battle, is wonderfully timed. Roody has some nice scenes as the tired old cop, hanging around a bar talking big and looking scared.

Holding all of the performances together is Norris's work as Cusack. Bearded, dressed in jeans for undercover street duty, and driving a battered old beater, Norris seems convincing as a cop—with, of course, the degree of heroic exaggeration you need in a role like this. By the end of the film, when he is reduced to functioning as a one-man army, we can't really believe the armored robot tank that he brings into action, but, what the hell, we accept it. Norris resembles Clint Eastwood in his insistence on the barest minimum of dialogue; there's a scene where he quietly, awkwardly tries to comfort the mobster's daughter, and it rings completely true. He also seems to be doing a lot of his own stunts, and although the credits list a lot of stuntmen and they were all obviously kept busy, it looks to me like that's really Norris on top of that elevated train.

The movie was directed by Andy Davis, who was a cinematographer on Haskell Wexler's 1968 Chicago film *Medium Cool*, and returned to some of the same locations to film this picture. Davis's directorial debut was the low-budget *Stony Island* (1977), which had moments of truth and insight but nothing like the assurance he shows this time; *Code of Silence* is a thriller so professional that it has the confidence to go for drama and humor as well as thrills. It may be the movie that moves Norris out of the ranks of dependable action heroes and makes him a major star.

The Color Purple ★ ★ ★ ★
PG-13, 155 m., 1985 ✔

Danny Glover (Mister), Whoopi Goldberg (Celie), Margaret Avery (Shug Avery), Oprah Winfrey (Sofia), Willard Pugh (Harpo), Akosua Busia (Nettie), Adolph Caesar (Old Mister), Rae Dawn Chong (Squeak), Dana Ivey (Miss Millie). Directed by Steven Spielberg and produced by Kathleen Kennedy, Frank Marshall, Quincy Jones, and Spielberg. Screenplay by Menno Meyjes.

There is a moment in Steven Spielberg's *The Color Purple* when a woman named Celie smiles and smiles and smiles. That was the moment when I knew this movie was going to be as good as it seemed, was going to keep the promise it made by daring to tell Celie's story. It is not a story that would seem easily suited to the movies.

Celie is a black woman who grows up in the rural South in the early decades of this century, in a world that surrounds her with cruelty. When we first see her, she is a child, running through fields of purple flowers with her sister. But then she comes into clear view, and we see that she is pregnant, and we learn that her father has made her pregnant, and will give away the child as he has done with a previous baby.

By the time Celie is married—to a cruel, distant charmer she calls only "Mister"—she will have lost both her children and the ability to bear children, will have been separated from the sister who is the only person on Earth who loves her, and will be living in servitude to a man who flaunts his love for another woman.

And yet this woman will endure, and in the end she will prevail. *The Color Purple* is not the story of her suffering but of her victory, and by the end of her story this film had moved me and lifted me up as few films have. It is a great, warm, hard, unforgiving, triumphant movie, and there is not a scene that

does not shine with the love of the people who made it.

The film is based on the novel by Alice Walker, who told Celie's story through a series of letters, some never sent, many never received, most addressed to God. The letters are her way of maintaining sanity in a world where few others ever cared to listen to her. The turning point in the book, and in the movie, comes after Celie's husband brings home the fancy woman he has been crazy about for years—a pathetic, alcoholic juke-joint singer named Shug Avery, who has been ravaged by life yet still has an indestructible beauty.

Shug's first words to Celie are: "You are as ugly as sin." But as Shug moves into the house, and Celie obediently caters to her husband's lover, Shug begins to see the beauty in Celie, and there is a scene where they kiss, and Celie learns for the first time that sex can include tenderness, that she can dare to love herself. A little later, Celie looks in Shug's eyes and allows herself to smile, and we know that Celie didn't think she had a pretty smile until Shug told her so. That is the central moment in the movie.

The relationship between Shug and Celie is a good deal toned down from the book, which deals in greater detail with sexual matters. Steven Spielberg, who made the movie, is more concerned with the whole world of Celie's life than he is with her erotic education. We meet many members of the rural black community that surrounds Celie. We meet a few of the local whites, too, but they are bit players in this drama.

Much more important are people like Sofia (Oprah Winfrey), an indomitable force of nature who is determined to marry Harpo, Mister's son by a first marriage. When we first see Sofia, hurrying down the road with everyone trying to keep up, she looks like someone who could never be stopped. But she is stopped, after she tells the local white mayor to go to hell, and the saddest story in the movie is the way her spirit is forever dampened by the beating and jailing she receives. Sofia is counterpoint to Celie: She is wounded by life, Celie is healed.

Shug Avery is another fascinating character, played by Margaret Avery as a sweet-faced, weary woman who sings a little bit like Billie Holiday and has long since lost all of her illusions about men and everything else. Her contact with Celie redeems her; by giving her somebody to be nice to, it allows her to get in touch with what is still nice inside herself.

Mister, whose real name is Albert, is played by Danny Glover, who was the field hand in *Places in the Heart*. He is an evil man, his evil tempered to some extent by his ignorance; perhaps he does not fully understand how cruel he is to Celie. Certainly he seems outwardly pleasant. He smiles and jokes and sings, and then hurts Celie to the quick—not so much with his physical blows as when he refuses to let her see the letters she hopes are coming from her long-lost sister.

And then, at the center of the movie, Celie is played by Whoopi Goldberg in one of the most amazing debut performances in movie history. Goldberg has a fearsomely difficult job to do, enlisting our sympathy for a woman who is rarely allowed to speak, to dream, to interact with the lives around her. Spielberg breaks down the wall of silence around her, however, by giving her narrative monologues in which she talks about her life and reads the words in the letters she composes.

The wonderful performances in this movie are contained in a screenplay that may take some of the smoking edges off Walker's novel, but keeps all the depth and dimension. The world of Celie and the others is created so forcibly in this movie that their corner of the South becomes one of those movie places—like Oz, like Tara, like Casablanca—that lay claim to their own geography in our imaginations. The affirmation at the end of the film is so joyous that this is one of the few movies in a long time that inspires tears of happiness, and earns them.

Come Back to the 5 & Dime, Jimmy Dean, Jimmy Dean ★ ★ ★
PG, 109 m., 1982

Sandy Dennis (Mona), Cher (Sissy), Karen Black (Joanne), Sudie Bond (Juanita), Kathy Bates (Stella Mae), Marta Heflin (Edna). Directed by Robert Altman and produced by Scott Bushnell. Screenplay by Ed Graczyk.

If Robert Altman hadn't directed this movie, the reviews would have described it as Altmanesque. It's a mixture of the bizarre and the banal, a slice of lives that could never have been led, a richly textured mixture of confessions, obsessions, and surprises.

The movie takes place in a worn-out Woolworth's in a small Texas town not far from the locations where James Dean shot *Giant* in 1955. The story begins twenty years later, at a reunion of the local James Dean fan club; the members swore a solemn vow to get together after two decades, and they drift in one by one, greeted by the tired waitress who's still on duty. There's Sandy Dennis, the flaky, visionary local woman who's convinced that she bore a son by James Dean. Then Cher walks in—looking not like the glamorous Cher of television, but like a small-town sexpot unsure of her appeal. The last arrival is Karen Black, who drove in all the way from California, and is not surprised when nobody recognizes her at first.

The fan club members and a few local good ol' girls join in a long afternoon of memories, nostalgia, self-analysis, accusation, shocking revelations, and anger, while heat-lightning flickers offscreen. And their memories trigger flashbacks to the time twenty years earlier when the proximity of James Dean served as a catalyst in all of their lives, giving some the courage to realize their dreams and others, the timid ones, the courage at least to dream them.

Jimmy Dean was a Broadway play before it was a movie, and Altman, who directed it first on stage, stays pretty close here to Ed Graczyk's script. He works just as closely with David Gropman's extraordinary stage set, on which the movie was shot. Gropman has actually created two dime stores, one a mirror-image of the other. They're separated by a two-way mirror, so that at times we're looking at the reflection of the "front" store, and at other times, the glass is transparent and we see the second store. Altman uses the front as the present and the back as the past, and there are times when a foreground image will dissolve into a background flashback. In an age of sophisticated optical effects, this sort of dissolve looks routine—until you learn that Altman isn't using optics, he's actually shooting through the two-way mirror. His visual effects sometimes require fancy offscreen footwork for his actors to be in two places during the same shot.

Jimmy Dean's script also requires some

fancy footwork, as we reel beneath a series of predictable revelations in the last twenty minutes. This is not a great drama, but two things make the movie worth seeing: Altman's visual inventiveness and the interesting performances given by everyone in the cast. Although Sandy Dennis and Karen Black in many ways have more difficult roles, Cher is the one I watched the most because her performance here is a revelation. After years and years of giving us "Cher," she gives us a new character here, in a fine performance that creates sympathy for a sexpot who doubts her own sensuality.

Coming Home ★ ★ ★ ★
R, 127 m., 1978

Jane Fonda (Sally Hyde), Jon Voight (Luke Martin), Bruce Dern (Bob Hyde), Robert Carradine (Bill Munson), Penelope Milford (Vi Munson), Robert Ginty (Sergeant Mobley). Directed by Hal Ashby and produced by Jerome Hellman. Screenplay by Waldo Salt and Robert C. Jones.

Sally Hyde makes an ideal wife for a Marine: She is faithful, friendly, sexy in a quiet way, and totally in agreement with her husband's loyalties. Since his basic loyalty is to the Marine Corps, that presents difficulties at times. ("You know what they tell them," a girl friend says. " 'If the Marine Corps had wanted you to have a wife, they would have issued you one.' ") Still, she's reasonably happy in the spring of 1968, as her husband prepares to ship out for a tour of duty in Vietnam. There's every chance he'll get a promotion over there. And the war, of course, is for a just cause, isn't it? It has to be, or we wouldn't be fighting it.

That is the Sally Hyde at the beginning of Hal Ashby's *Coming Home*, an extraordinarily moving film. The Sally Hyde at the end of the film—about a year later—is a different person, confused in her loyalties, not sure of her beliefs, awakened to new feelings within her. She hasn't turned into a political activist or a hippie or any of those other radical creatures of the late 1960s. But she is no longer going to be able to accept anything simply because her husband, or anybody else, says it's true.

Coming Home considers a great many subjects, but its heart lies with that fundamental change within Sally Hyde. She is played by Jane Fonda as the kind of character you somehow wouldn't expect the outspoken, intelligent Fonda to play. She's reserved, maybe a little shy, of average intelligence and tastes. She was, almost inevitably, a cheerleader in high school. She doesn't seem to have a lot of ideas or opinions. Perhaps she even doubts that it's necessary for her to have opinions—her husband can have them for her.

When her husband (Bruce Dern) goes off to fight the war, though, she finds herself on her own for the first time in her life. There's no home, no high school, no marriage, no Officers' Club to monitor her behavior. And she finds herself stepping outside the role of a wife and doing . . . well, not strange things, but things that are a little unusual for her. Like buying a used sports car. Like renting a house at the beach. Like volunteering to work in the local Veterans' Administration hospital. That's where she meets Luke (Jon Voight), so filled with his pain, anger, and frustration. She knew him vaguely before; he was the captain of the football team at her high school. He went off to fight the war, came home paralyzed from the waist down, and now, strapped on his stomach to a table with wheels, uses canes to propel himself furiously down hospital corridors. In time, he will graduate to a wheelchair. He has ideas about Vietnam that are a little different from her husband's.

Coming Home is uncompromising in its treatment of Luke and his fellow paraplegics, and if that weren't so the opening sequences of the film wouldn't affect us so deeply. Luke literally runs into Sally on their first meeting, and his urine bag spills on the floor between them. That's the sort of embarrassment he has to learn to live with—and she too, if she is serious about being a volunteer.

She is, she finds. Luke in the early days is a raging troublemaker, and the hospital staff often finds it simpler just to tranquilize him with medication. Zombies are hardly any bother at all. Sally tries to talk to Luke, gets to know him, invites him for dinner. He begins to focus his anger away from himself and toward the war; he grows calmer, regains maturity. One day, softly, he tells her: "You know there's not an hour goes by that I don't think of making love with you."

They do eventually make love, confronting his handicap in a scene of great tenderness, beauty, and tact. It is the first time Sally has been unfaithful. But it isn't really an affair; she remains loyal to her husband, and both she and Luke know their relationship will have to end when her husband returns home. He does, too soon, having accidentally wounded himself, and discovers from Army Intelligence what his wife has been up to. The closing scenes show the film at its most uncertain, as if Ashby and his writers weren't sure in their minds how the Dern character should react. And so Dern is forced into scenes of unfocused, confused anger before the film's not very satisfying ending. It's too bad the last twenty minutes don't really work, though, because for most of its length *Coming Home* is great filmmaking and great acting.

And it is also greatly daring, since it confronts the relationship between Fonda and Voight with unusual frankness—and with emotional tenderness and subtlety that is, if anything, even harder to portray.

Consider. The film has three difficulties to confront in this relationship, and it handles all three honestly. The first is Voight's paralysis: "You aren't one of these women that gets turned on by gimps?" he asks. She is not. The second is the sexual and emotional nature of their affair, an area of enormous dramatic danger, which the movie handles in such a straightforward way, and with such an obvious display of affection between the characters, that we accept and understand.

The third is the nature of the *friendship* between Voight and Fonda, and here *Coming Home* works on a level that doesn't depend on such plot elements as the war, the husband, the paralysis, the time and place, or anything else. Thinking about the movie, we realize that men and women have been so polarized in so many films, have been made into so many varieties of sexual antagonists or lovers or rivals or other couples, that the mutual human friendship of these two characters comes as something of a revelation.

The Company of Wolves ★ ★ ★
R, 95 m., 1985

Angela Lansbury (Granny), David Warner (Father), Graham Crowden (Old Priest), Brian Glover (Amorous Boy's Father), Catherine Pogson (Young Bride), Stephen Rea (Young Groom). Directed by Neil Jordan and produced by Chris Brown and Stephan Woolley. Screenplay by Angela Carter and Jordan.

A wolf is sometimes much more than he seems.—Granny

The key word there is "he." There are no female wolves in this film, or at least not in the leading roles. The wolves are all male, and the males are almost all wolves. Granny warns her young granddaughter to beware of men whose eyebrows meet, for in the full of the moon their hidden natures are likely to emerge, and they will have fangs, and sharp claws, and eyes that glow in the dark. The girl believes her, but she still puts on her red hood and walks through the woods to grandmother's house, and is surprised by what big teeth Granny has.

The Company of Wolves is a dream about werewolves and little girls and deep, dark forests. It is not a children's film and it is not an exploitation film; it is a disturbing and stylish attempt to collect some of the nightmares that lie beneath the surface of "Little Red Riding Hood." The movie begins in the present, but quickly enters the dreams of an adolescent girl. She dreams many variations on the same theme: That men may turn out to be wolves, and that little girls should never, ever, stray from the path through the woods. The movie creates its dream world on British sound stages, which have been used to make a gloomy, fantastical universe filled with gnarled trees, wicked thorn bushes, clammy mists, tortuous paths, and birds' nests filled with mirrors and lipsticks, and eggs that don't have chicks inside of them. In this world, the characters tell each other stories. All of the stories begin with those delicious words, "Once upon a time." Granny (Angela Lansbury) tells most of the stories to her granddaughter, but the girl tells stories too, and after one of them her mother says, "Granny knows a great deal, but she doesn't know everything. And if there is a beast inside every man, he meets his match in the beast inside of every woman."

Most of the stories seem to take place in the nineteenth century, in a dark forest that encircles frightened and ignorant peasants. In the night, they light great torches and go out into the woods to trap the wolves, but when they cut off a giant paw as a trophy and bring it home and look at it, they are holding a severed human hand. Wolves are men, and men are wolves, and the message that repeats itself over and over in *The Company of Wolves* is that the bridegroom may be loving and handsome on his wedding night, but should he step into the light of the moon, he may turn into a hairy demon with glowing eyes.

The movie is based on a novel and a screenplay by Angela Carter, who has taken Red Riding Hood as a starting-place for the stories, which are secretly about the fearsomeness of sexuality. She has shown us what those scary fairy tales are really telling us; she has filled in the lines and visualized the parts that the Brothers Grimm left out (and they did not leave out all that many parts). The movie has an uncanny, hypnotic force; we always know what is happening, but we rarely know why, or how it connects with anything else, or how we can escape from it, or why it seems to correspond so deeply with our guilts and fears. That is, of course, almost a definition of a nightmare.

The Competition ★ ★ ★
PG, 125 m., 1981

Richard Dreyfuss (Paul Dietrich), Amy Irving (Heidi Schoonover), Lee Remick (Greta Vandemann), Sam Wanamaker (Erskine). Directed and written by Joel Oliansky and produced by William Sackheim.

The Competition is a cornball, romantic, old-fashioned, utterly predictable movie—and enormously entertaining. It's the kind of movie where you speculate on what's going to happen next, and usually you're right. When you're wrong, somehow *that's* predictable, too, as in the big international piano competition that ends the movie. We think we know who's going to win, but the surprise ending is a built-in convention of this kind of movie.

The movie's about a big international competition in San Francisco among six world-class pianists who are fighting for a $20,000 first prize and a two-year concert contract. The movie has two counterpoints to its main theme. One involves a love affair between two of the finalists, Richard Dreyfuss and Amy Irving. The other one, ridiculous but forgivable, involves a Russian piano teacher who defects to the United States, creating an international incident that causes the competition to be postponed a week.

Both of these story lines are somehow time-honored, once we realize that *The Competition* is not intended as a deadly serious treatise on big-league pianists, but as an offbeat love story. Dreyfuss and Amy Irving have a real charm and rapport as the two lovers, especially in the scenes where they argue that love has absolutely no place in a piano competition—not if it's being used as a psychological weapon to undermine one of the competitors. That's exactly what Amy Irving's piano coach (Lee Remick) thinks the dastardly Dreyfuss is trying to do.

There are three areas that the movie gets into, superficially but earnestly. One has to do with the competition itself—with the idea of artists competing with one another. Another has to do with relationships between men and women: Will the love affair between Amy and Richard be destroyed if she should win? How will his fragile male ego be able to take that? The third has to do with the idea of the artist's career, and here Remick has several good scenes and intelligently written speeches, as she tries to explain the realities of a concert career to Irving.

There is, of course, a lot of music in this movie, in addition to all the scenes of romance, backstage butterflies, international intrigue, and self-examination. And *The Competition* does an extraordinary job of persuading us that the actors are really playing their own pianos. They're not. Stay for the credits if you want the names of the real pianists on the sound track. But Dreyfuss, Irving, and the rest really *look* as if they're playing, and it took them four months of daily rehearsal to learn to fake it so well.

The Competition isn't a great movie, but it's a warm, entertaining one. It has the nerve to tell a story about serious, interesting, complicated people, who are full of surprises, because Joel Oliansky, the writer-director, has thought about them and cared enough about them to let their personalities lead him down unexpected avenues. There's only one major lapse: the inclusion, after two hours of great piano compositions, of Lalo Schifrin's dreadful song, "People Alone," sung by Randy Crawford over the end titles as if none of those great composers should be allowed to rest in peace.

Compromising Positions ★ ★
R, 98 m., 1985

Susan Sarandon (Judith Singer), Raul Julia (David Suarez), Judith Ivey (Nancy Miller), Edward Herrmann (Bob Singer), Mary Beth Hurt (Peg Tuccio), Joe Mantegna (Dr. Fleckstein), Josh Mostel (Dicky Dunck), Deborah Rush (Brenda Dunck). Directed and produced by Frank Perry. Screenplay by Susan Isaacs.

If I were simply to describe the story of *Compromising Positions*, it might sound like lighthearted, slightly kinky fun. But the movie has such a bitter core, such a distaste for its characters, that I ended up feeling uncomfortable in its company. I think it's supposed to be a comedy, but I felt depressed by its world of rich, neurotic, bitchy suburbanites.

The movie takes place in those regions of Long Island where there aren't any sidewalks, the sculptors change their designer outfits three times a day, and it always seems like the first, brisk week of autumn. A dentist is found murdered in his office. He was a society dentist, dripping with gold chains, a ladies' man who had regular rendezvous with his patients in the local motels. A lot of people may have had reason to murder him, especially because of the Polaroids he took during his private sessions.

One of the last people to have seen him alive is a housewife (Susan Sarandon), who used to be a reporter for *Newsday* but has lately turned into a bored, resentful wife of a workaholic executive (Edward Herrmann). Sarandon is intrigued by the case, and begins to act like a private eye, interviewing suspects and searching for evidence. Her dream is to sell the story to *Newsday* and regain her newspaper career. But her old editor isn't much interested, and the only person she intrigues is the local police detective (Raul Julia), who considers her a suspect.

One of the pleasures of most whodunits is the introduction of the characters, who are supposed to be suitably bizarre specimens. *Compromising Positions* outdoes itself by introducing a group of suspects who come across like fingernails on a blackboard. Since they are played by actors who are usually likable, I assume it's the decision of the director, Frank Perry, to make them so unpleasant.

We meet the catty local sculptress (Judith Ivey), who likes to sweep in through the door with cynical generalizations about sex; the neurotic neighbor (Mary Beth Hurt), who seems to harbor unsavory secrets; the in-laws of the murdered dentist (Josh Mostel and Deborah Rush), who are drawn as such caricatures that we can never believe them, and the dentist's widow (Ann DeSalvo), a basket case. The remaining characters include Herrmann, who plays Sarandon's husband as such a cold-hearted career man that we almost wish he'd been murdered, too, and the dentist himself (Joe Mantegna), who of course disappears early but emerges in the later testimony as a man without a shred of redeeming humanity.

Don't get me wrong. I don't require that murder stories be about nice people. I like it when the characters are mean and crabby and eccentric, because that shows invention on the part of the authors and gives the actors room to have fun. What I object to in *Compromising Positions* is the streak of misanthropic cruelty that seems to run through the film; it's one thing when we hate a movie's characters, and another thing when the movie hates them.

Susan Sarandon is fairly lost in this situation. On paper, her role may have looked great. She gets to play a smart, plucky, rebellious housewife whose curiosity results in a triple play: She solves a murder, attracts the romantic attentions of a macho cop, and starts a new career. The movie is so top-heavy with plot and other characters, alas, that she ends up as more of a traffic cop, racing from one scene to another, tying the threads together. At the end, she isn't victorious, she's exhausted.

Conan the Barbarian ★ ★ ★
R, 129 m., 1982

Arnold Schwarzenegger (Conan), James Earl Jones (Thulsa Doom), Max von Sydow (King Osric), Sandahl Bergman (Valeria), Ben Davidson (Rexor). Directed by John Milius and produced by Buzz Feitshans and Rafella de Laurentiis. Screenplay by Milius and Oliver Stone.

Not since Bambi's mother was killed has there been a cannier movie for kids than *Conan the Barbarian*. It's not supposed to be just a kids' movie, of course, and I imagine a lot of other moviegoers will like it—I liked a lot of it myself, and with me, a few broadswords and leather jerkins go a long way. But *Conan* is a perfect fantasy for the alienated preadolescent. Consider: Conan's parents are brutally murdered by the evil Thulsa Doom, which gets *them* neatly out of the way. The child is chained to the Wheel of Pain, where he goes around in circles for years, a metaphor for grade school. The kid builds muscles so terrific he could be a pro football player. One day he is set free. He teams up with Subotai the Mongol, who is an example of the classic literary type—the Best Pal—and with Valeria, Queen of Thieves, who is a *real* best pal.

Valeria is everything you could ever hope for in a woman, if you are a muscle-bound preadolescent, of course. She is lanky and muscular and a great sport, and she can ride, throw, stab, fence, and climb ropes as good as a boy. Sometimes she engages in sloppy talk about love, but you can tell she's only kidding, and she quickly recovers herself with coverup talk about loyalty and betrayal—emotions more central to Conan's experience and maturity.

With the Mongol and the Queen at his side, Conan ventures forth to seek the evil Thulsa Doom and gain revenge for the death of his parents. This requires him to journey to the mysterious East, where he learns a little quick kung-fu, and then to the mountainside where Doom rules his slave-priests from the top of his Mountain of Power. There are a lot of battles and a few interesting nights at crude wayside inns and, in general, nothing to tax the unsophisticated. *Conan the Barbarian* is, in fact, a very nearly perfect visualization of the Conan legend, of Robert E.

Howard's tale of a superman who lived beyond the mists of time, when people were so pure, straightforward, and simple that a 1930s pulp magazine writer could write about them at one cent a word and not have to pause to puzzle out their motivations.

The movie's casting is ideal. Arnold Schwarzenegger is inevitably cast as Conan, and Sandahl Bergman as Valeria. Physically, they look like artist's conceptions of themselves. What's nice is that they also create entertaining versions of their characters; they, and the movie, are not without humor and a certain quiet slyness that is never allowed to get out of hand. Schwarzenegger's slight Teutonic accent is actually even an advantage, since Conan lived, of course, in the eons before American accents.

The movie is a triumph of production design, set decoration, special effects and makeup. At a time when most of the big box-office winners display state-of-the-art technology, *Conan* ranks right up there with the best. Ron Cobb, the sometime underground cartoonist who did the production design on this film (and on *Alien*) supervises an effort in which the individual frames actually do look like blowups of panels from the Marvel Comics "Conan" books. Since this Conan could have so easily looked ridiculous, that's an accomplishment.

But there is one aspect of the film I'm disturbed by. It involves the handling of Thulsa Doom, the villain. He is played here by the fine black actor James Earl Jones, who brings power and conviction to a role that seems inspired in equal parts by Hitler, Jim Jones, and Goldfinger. But when Conan and Doom meet at the top of the Mountain of Power, it was, for me, a rather unsettling image to see this Nordic superman confronting a black, and when Doom's head was sliced off and contemptuously thrown down the flight of stairs by the muscular blonde Conan, I found myself thinking that Leni Reifenstahl could have directed the scene, and that Goebbels might have applauded it.

Am I being too sensitive? Perhaps. But when Conan appeared in the pulps of the 1930s, the character suggested in certain unstated ways the same sort of Nordic super-race myths that were being peddled in Germany. These days we are more innocent again, and Conan is seen as a pure fantasy, like his British cousin, Tarzan, or his contemporary, Flash Gordon. My only reflection is that, at a time when there are *no* roles for blacks in Hollywood if they are not named Richard Pryor, it is a little unsettling to see a great black actor assigned to a role in which he is beheaded by a proto-Nordic avenger.

That complaint aside, I enjoyed *Conan.* Faithful readers will know I'm not a fan of Sword & Sorcery movies, despite such adornments as Sandahl Bergman—having discovered some time ago that heaving bosoms may be great, but a woman with a lively intelligence and a sly wit is even greater.

The problem with *Conan* is the problem with all S & S movies. After the initial premise (which usually involves revenge) is established, we suspect there's little to look forward to *except* the sets, special effects, costumes, makeup, locations, action, and surprise entrances. Almost by definition, these movies exclude the possibility of interesting, complex characters. I'd love to see them set loose an intelligent, questing, humorous hero in one of these prehistoric sword-swingers. Someone at least as smart as, say, Alley Oop.

Conan the Destroyer ★ ★ ★
PG, 103 m., 1984

Arnold Schwarzenegger (Conan), Grace Jones (Zula), Wilt Chamberlain (Bombaata), Mako (The Wizard), Tracey Walter (Malak), Sarah Douglas (Queen). Directed by Richard Fleischer and produced by Raffaella de Laurentiis. Screenplay by Stanley Mann.

What you can see in *Conan the Destroyer,* if you look closely, is the beginning of a movie dynasty. This is the film that points the way to an indefinite series of Conan adventures—one that could even replace Tarzan in supplying our need for a noble savage in the movies. Tarzan was more or less stuck in Africa; Conan can venture wherever his sword and sorcery can take him. The first Conan movie, *Conan the Barbarian,* was a dark and gloomy fantasy about the shadows of prehistory. This second film is sillier, funnier, and more entertaining. It doesn't take place

before the dawn of time, but instead in that shadowy period of movie history occupied by queens and monsters, swords and castles, warriors and fools. There's more Prince Valiant and King Arthur than *Quest for Fire.*

And Conan is defined a little differently, too. He doesn't take himself as seriously. He's not just a muscle-bound superman, but a superstitious half-savage who gets very nervous in the presence of magic. Arnold Schwarzenegger, who plays Conan again, does an interesting job of defining his pop hero: Like James Bond, Conan now stands a little aside from the incessant action around him, and observes it with a bit of relish. The story this time involves the usual nonsense. Conan is recruited by an imperious queen (Sarah Douglas, looking vampirish) to take a virgin princess (Olivia D'Abo) on a mission to an enchanted crystal palace guarded by a monster, etc. He will be joined on his quest by the head of the queen's palace guard (Wilt Chamberlain). And along the way he rescues a savage woman warrior (Grace Jones) and earns her undying gratitude.

Let's face it. The Conan series does not require extraordinary acting ability, although Schwarzenegger provides a sound professional center to the story, and the film would be impossible if he couldn't carry off Conan. The characters around him, however, are basically atmosphere, and that frees the filmmakers to abandon the usual overexposed Hollywood character actors and go for really interesting types like Chamberlain and Jones. And Grace Jones is really sensational. She has all the flash and fire of a great rock stage star, and it fits perfectly into her role as Zula, the fierce fighter. Sarah Douglas provides the necessary haughty iciness as the queen, Chamberlain gives a good try at the thankless role of the turncoat guard, and only D'Abo is a disappointment: Her princess seems to have drifted in from a teen-age sitcom.

Conan the Destroyer is more entertaining than the first Conan movie, more cheerful, and it probably has more sustained action, including a good sequence in the glass palace. Compared to the first Conan movie, which was rated R for some pretty gruesome violence, this one is milder. That's part of the idea, I think: They're repackaging Conan as your friendly family barbarian.

Continental Divide ★ ★ ★
PG, 103 m., 1981

John Belushi (Souchak), Blair Brown (Nell), Allen Goorwitz (Howard), Carlin Glynn (Sylvia), Tony Ganios (Possum), Val Avery (Yablonowitz). Directed by Michael Apted and produced by Bob Larson. Written by Lawrence Kasdan.

Here is a movie that is supposed to be about a newspaperman—a columnist for the *Chicago Sun-Times*, in fact—who is like no newspaperman I know, but exactly like every newspaperman would like to be. In my opinion, that makes it accurate. *Continental Divide* stars John Belushi as the journalist, obviously inspired by Mike Royko. He likes to walk along the lakeshore with the towers of the city outlined behind him against the lonely sky at dusk, a notebook stuck in his pocket and a cigarette stuck in his mug, on his way to rendezvous with stoolie aldermen and beautiful women.

The movie takes this character, played by Belushi with a surprising tenderness and charm, and engages him in an absolute minimum of newspaper work before spiriting him off to the Rocky Mountains for what the movie is *really* about, a romance with an eagle expert. The movie opens as if it's going to be a tough Chicago slice-of-life, with Belushi getting tips from an insider about city graft and payola, but then the columnist is beaten up by a couple of cops on an alderman's payroll. The managing editor suggests this might be a good time for Belushi to spend a few weeks out of town, and so the columnist heads for the Rockies to get an interview with a mysterious and beautiful woman (Blair Brown) who has generated worldwide curiosity by becoming a hermit to spy on the habits of bald eagles.

The whole center section of the movie takes place in the mountains, and if nothing very original happens there, we are at least reminded of several beloved movie clichés that seemed, until this film, to belong exclusively in the comedies that Katharine Hepburn and Spencer Tracy used to make together. After the city slicker Belushi crawls wearily up a mountainside (losing his booze and cigarette supply in the process), he meets the beautiful birdwatcher and falls instantly in love. She's having none of it.

She's one of those independent women who marches from crag to aerie in her L.L. Bean boots and designer wardrobe.

Because Belushi's grizzled mountain guide already has disappeared down the mountain, the two of them are destined to spend the next two weeks together in a cabin. This sets up a classic situation in which the girl talks tough but starts to fall for the big lunkhead. And there are the obligatory switches on male-female roles as Brown climbs mountains and Belushi stays home and makes goulash. Occasionally, a mountain lion attacks.

This all sounds predictable, of course, and yet this movie's predictability is one of its charms. It's rare these days to find a film that is basically content to be about a colorful man and an eccentric woman who are opposites and yet fall madly in love. It is even rarer to find a movie cast with performers who are offbeat and appealing and do not have obvious matinee-idol appeal. Belushi's character in this movie is quite unlike his self-destructive slob in *National Lampoon's Animal House;* it shows the gentleness and vulnerability that made him so appealing in some of Second City's quieter skits. Brown is also a revelation. She has been in several other movies without attracting a great deal of attention, but here she is unmistakably and wonderfully a star, a tousled-haired, big-eyed warm person who does not project sex appeal so much as warmth and humor. In other words, she has terrific sex appeal.

One of Belushi's special qualities was always an underlying innocence. Maybe he created his Blues Brothers persona in reaction to it. He's an innocent in this movie, an idealist who's a little kid at heart and who wins the love of Brown not by seducing her but by appealing to her protective qualities. That's the secret of the character's appeal. We're cheering for the romance because Belushi makes us protective, too, and we want him to have a woman who'd be good for him.

What about the movie's view of journalism? It's really just a romanticized backdrop, *The Front Page* crossed with "Lou Grant" and modernized with a computerized newsroom. The newspaper scenes in the movie were shot on location in the *Sun-Times* features department, and one of the quietly amusing things about *Continental Divide*'s view of newspaper life is that in the movie it's more sedate and disciplined than the real thing. In the "real" *Sun-Times* features department, there's a lot of informality and chaos and good-natured confusion and people shouting at one another and eating lunch at their desks. In the movie, the extras (recruited from the *Sun-Times* staff) forget about real life and sit dutifully at their video display terminals, grinding out the news.

The newspaper's managing editor is played by Allen Goorwitz, a gifted character actor who usually plays manic overcompensators, but who this time is reasonable, calm, civilized, compassionate, and understanding, just like my boss. The movie's city of Chicago is populated by colorful old newsstand operators, muggers who apologize before taking your watch, and city council bosses who make sure their shady deals don't get into the official transcript. The newsies and muggers are fiction. The movie itself is fun: goofy, softhearted, fussy, sometimes funny, and with the sort of happy ending that columnists like to find for their stories and hardly ever find themselves.

The Conversation ★ ★ ★ ★
PG, 113 m., 1974

Gene Hackman (Harry Caul), John Cazale (Stan), Allen Garfield (Bernie Moran), Frederic Forrest (Mark), Cindy Williams (Ann), Michael Higgins (Paul). Directed by Francis Ford Coppola and produced by Fred Roos. Screenplay by Coppola.

As he is played by Gene Hackman in *The Conversation*, an expert wiretapper named Harry Caul is one of the most affecting and tragic characters in the movies; he ranks with someone like Willy Loman in *Death of a Salesman* or the pathetic captives of the middle class in John Cassavetes's *Faces*. Hackman is such a fine actor in so many different roles, from his action roles like *The French Connection* to this introverted, frightened, paranoid who is "the best bugger on the West Coast." He is, indeed, maybe the best wiretapper in the country, but he hasn't gone back to the East Coast since a bugging assignment there led to the deaths of three people. He tries to force himself not to care. He goes to confession and begs forgiveness for not paying for some newspapers, but not for bringing about a murder—because the murder, you see, was none of his business. He is only a professional. He does his job and asks no questions: doesn't *want* to know the answers.

His latest job has been a tactical masterpiece. The assignment: Bug a noon-hour conversation between two young people as they walk in a crowded plaza. He does it by tailing them with a guy who's wired for sound, and also by aiming parabolic microphones at them from buildings overlooking the plaza. This gives him three imperfect recordings of their conversation, which he can electronically marry into one fairly good tape. He is a good craftsman, and, although the film doesn't belabor his techniques, it does show us enough of how bugging is done to give us a cynical education.

It's a movie not so much about bugging as about the man who does it, and Gene Hackman's performance is a great one. He does not want to get involved (whenever he says anything like that, it sounds in italics)—but he does. After he has recorded the conversation, he plays it again and again and becomes convinced that a death may result from it, if he turns the tape in. The ways in which he interprets the tape, and the different nuances of meaning it seems to contain at different moments, remind us of Antonioni's *Blow Up.* Both movies are about the unreality of what seems real: We have here in our hands a document that is maddeningly concrete and yet refuses to reveal its meaning. And the meaning seems to be a matter of life and death.

The movie is a thriller with a shocking twist at the end, but it is also a character study. Hackman plays a craftsman who has perfected his skill at the expense of all other human qualities; he lives in paranoia in a triple-locked apartment, and is terrified when it turns out his landlady has a key. She explains she might have to get in in case of some emergency—his furniture might burn up or something. He explains that none of his possessions is important to him—except his keys.

He has no friends, but he does have acquaintances in the bugging industry, and they're in town for a convention. One of them (played by Allen Garfield) is a truly frightening character. He's the one who talks about the three murders, and he's the one whose hateful envy reveals to us how good Harry Caul really is. A boozy scene in Harry's workshop, with some colleagues and their random dates, provides a perfect illustration of the ways in which even Harry's pathetically constrained social life is expressed through his work.

The Conversation is about paranoia, invasion of privacy, bugging—and also about the bothersome problem of conscience. The Watergate crew seems, for the most part, to have had no notion that what they were doing was objectively wrong. Harry wants to have no notion. But he does, and it destroys him.

The Cotton Club ★ ★ ★ ★
R, 121 m., 1984

Richard Gere (Dixie Dwyer), Gregory Hines (Sandman Williams), Diane Lane (Vera Cicero), Lonette McKee (Lila Rose Oliver), Bob Hoskins (Owney Madden), James Remar (Dutch Schultz), Fred Gwynne (Frenchy). Directed by Francis Ford Coppola and produced by Robert Evans. Screenplay by William Kennedy and Coppola.

After all the rumors, all the negative publicity, all the stories of fights on the set and backstage intrigue and imminent bankruptcy, Francis Ford Coppola's *The Cotton Club* is, quite simply, a wonderful movie. It has the confidence and momentum of a movie where every shot was premeditated—and even if we know that wasn't the case, and this was one of the most troubled productions in recent movie history, what difference does that make when the result is so entertaining?

The movie takes place in New York in the 1920s and 1930s, where Irish and Jewish gangsters battled the Italians for the rackets. Most of their intrigues were played out in public, in flashy settings like the Cotton Club, a Harlem nightclub that featured the nation's most talented black entertainers on stage—playing before an all-white audience. By telling us two love stories, Coppola shows us both sides of that racial divide. He begins by introducing Dixie Dwyer (Richard Gere), a good-looking young musician who saves the life of a gangster and is immediately recruited into the hood's inner circle. There

he meets the gangster's teen-age girlfriend (Diane Lane), and they immediatley fall in love—but secretly, because they'll live longer that way. Then we meet Sandman Williams (Gregory Hines), a black tap dancer who dreams of appearing at the Cotton Club, and falls in love with a member of the chorus line (Lonette McKee), a mulatto who talks about her secret life among people who think she is white.

The two love stories are developed against a background of a lot of very good jazz, some great dancing, sharply etched character studies of the gang bosses, and a couple of unexpected bursts of violence that remind us, in their sudden explosion, of moments in Coppola's *Godfather* films. Indeed, there's a lot of *The Godfather* in *The Cotton Club*, especially in the movie's almost elegiac sadness: We get the feeling of time passing, and personal histories being written, and some people breaking free and other people dying or surrendering to hopelessness.

There's another reminder of *The Godfather* movies, and that's in the brilliant, in-depth casting. There's not an uninteresting face or a boring performance in this movie, but two supporting characters really stand out: Bob Hoskins, as a crooked club owner named Madden, and Fred Gwynne, as a towering hulk named Frenchy. They are friends. They also are criminal associates. Hoskins is a bantamweight filled with hostility; Gwynne is a giant with a deep voice and glowering eyes. After Gwynne is kidnapped and Hoskins pays the ransom, the scene between the two of them begins as a routine confrontation and unfolds into something surprisingly funny and touching.

Coppola has a way, in this film, of telling all the different stories without giving us the impression he's jumping around a lot. Maybe the music helps. It gives the movie a continuity and an underlying rhythm that makes all of the characters' lives into steps in a sad ballet. We like some of the characters, but we don't have much respect for them, and the movie doesn't bother with clear distinctions between good and evil. *The Cotton Club* is a somewhat cynical movie about a very cynical time, and along with the music and the romance there is racism, cruelty, betrayal, and stunning violence. Romance with a cutting edge.

The performances are well-suited to the material. Richard Gere is especially good as Dixie Dwyer, maybe because the camera has a way of seeing him off-balance, so that he doesn't dominate the center of each shot like a handsome icon; Coppola stirs him into the action. Diane Lane, herself still a teen-ager, is astonishing as the party girl who wants to own her own club. Gregory Hines and his brother, Maurice, create a wonderful moment of reconciliation when they begin to tap dance and end by forgiving each other for a lifetime's hurts. And Hoskins, the British actor who played the unforgettable mob chief in *The Long Good Friday*, is so wound-up and fierce and funny as the mobster that he takes a cliché and turns it into an original.

The Cotton Club took months to shoot, and they claim they have another 200,000 feet of footage as good as this movie. I doubt it. Whatever it took to do it, Coppola has extracted a very special film out of the checkered history of this project.

Country ★ ★ ★ ½
PG, 108 m., 1984

Jessica Lange (Jewell Ivy), Sam Shepard (Gil Ivy), Wilford Brimley (Otis Stewart), Matt Clark (Tom McMullen), Therese Graham (Marlene Ivy), Levi L. Knebel (Carlisle Ivy). Directed by Richard Pearce and produced by William D. Wittliff and Jessica Lange. Screenplay by Wittliff.

The opening moments of *Country* show a woman frying hamburgers and wrapping them up and sending them out to her men, working in the fields. The movie is using visuals to announce its intentions: It wants to observe the lives of its characters at the level of daily detail and routine, and to avoid pulling back into "Big Country" cliché shots. It succeeds. This movie observes ordinary American lives carefully, and passionately. The family lives on a farm in Iowa. Times are hard, and times are now. This isn't a movie about symbolic farmers living in some colorful American past. It is about the farm policies of the Carter and Reagan administrations, and how the movie believes that those policies are resulting in the destruction of family farms. It has been so long since I've seen a Hollywood film with specific political beliefs that a funny thing

happened: The movie's anger moved me as much as its story.

The story is pretty moving, too. We meet the members of the Ivy family: Jewell Ivy (Jessica Lange), the farm wife; her husband, Gil (Sam Shepard); her father, Otis (Wilford Brimley), and the three children, especially Carlisle (Levi L. Knebel), the son who knows enough about farming to know when his father has given up. The movie begins at the time of last year's harvest. Some nasty weather has destroyed part of the yield. The Ivys are behind on their FHA loan. Ordinarily, that would be no tragedy; farming is cyclical and there are good years and bad years, and eventually they'll catch up with the loan. But this year is different. An FHA regional administrator, acting on orders from Washington, instructs his people to enforce all loans strictly, and to foreclose when necessary. He uses red ink to write his recommendation on the Ivy's loan file: *Move toward voluntary liquidation*. Since there is no way the loan can be paid off, the Ivys will lose the land that Jewell's family has farmed for one hundred years. The farm agent helpfully supplies the name of an auctioneer.

All of this sounds just a little like the dire opening chapters of a story by Horatio Alger, but the movie never feels dogmatic or forced because *Country* is so clearly the particular story of these people and the way they respond. Old Otis is angry at his son-in-law for losing the farm. Jewell defends her husband, but he goes into town to drink away his impotent rage. There are loud fights far into the night in a house that had been peaceful. The boy asks, "Would somebody mind telling me what's going on around here?"

The movie's strongest passages deal with Jewell's attempts to enlist her neighbors in a stand against the government. The most touching scenes, though, are the ones showing how abstract economic policies cause specific human suffering, cause lives to be interrupted, and families to be torn apart, all in the name of the balance sheet. *Country* is as political, as unforgiving, as *The Grapes of Wrath*.

The movie has, unfortunately, one important area of weakness, in the way it handles the character of Gil (Shepard). At the beginning we have no reason to doubt that he is a good farmer. Later, the movie raises questions about that assumption, and never clearly answers them. Gil starts drinking heavily, and lays a hand on his son, and leaves the farm altogether for several days. The local farm agent tells him, point blank, that he's a drunk and a bad farmer. Well, is he? In an affecting scene where Gil returns and asks for the understanding of his family, his drinking is not mentioned. It's good that the movie tries to make the character more complex and interesting—not such a noble hero—but if he really is a drunk and a bad farmer, then maybe that's why he's behind on the loan. The movie shouldn't raise the possibility without dealing with it.

In a movie with the power of *Country*, I can live with a problem like that because there are so many other good things. The performances are so true you feel this really is a family; we expect the quality of the acting by Lange, Shepard, and gruff old Brimley, but the surprise is Levi L. Knebel, as the son. He is so stubborn and so vulnerable, so filled with his sense of right when he tells his father what's being done wrong, that he brings the movie an almost documentary quality; this isn't acting, we feel, but eavesdropping.

Creator ★ ★ ½
R, 108 m., 1985

Peter O'Toole (Harry), Mariel Hemingway (Meli), Vincent Spano (Boris), Virginia Madsen (Barbara), David Ogden Stiers (Kuhlenbeck). Directed by Ivan Passer and produced by Stephen Friedman. Screenplay by Jeremy Leven.

A London critic once described a stage performance by Peter O'Toole as his "Douglas Bader imitation," a reference to the Battle of Britain hero who walked on two artificial legs. O'Toole gives another Bader performance in *Creator*, lurching perilously through a chemistry laboratory and bludgeoning everyone around him with his lethal charm. It is the same sort of performance he gave in *My Favorite Year* and *The Stunt Man*— indeed, it is the basic performance he seems to be giving this decade—and, as usual, it works.

O'Toole plays a Nobel Prize-winning scientist who lives in the grip of an overwhelming obsession. He believes that he will someday learn how to clone the genes of his wife, Lucy, who died thirty years ago—and then he will have a new Lucy, or someone very like her, as the companion of his old age. To further his secret plan, O'Toole steals equipment, funds, and laboratory assistants from his university, although not without the bitter opposition of his lifelong enemy, Prof. Kuhlenbeck (David Ogden Stiers).

Soon after the movie opens, O'Toole gathers two new recruits to his side: a young lab assistant (Vincent Spano) and a nutty undergraduate (Mariel Hemingway) who has a giant crush on O'Toole. Spano really wants nothing to do with this distinguished nut who insists that everyone call him Harry. He only wants to get his degree and to win the love of the gorgeous coed (Virginia Madsen) who wanders across the campus like a dream.

In the middle passages of the movie, O'Toole pursues his goal of resurrecting Lucy, Hemingway pursues O'Toole, Spano pursues Madsen, and the jealous and vindictive Stiers pursues evidence that O'Toole is robbing the university blind. O'Toole develops a great deal of charm during these scenes; he has a warmth and gentleness that seems born of great weariness, and a desire to forgive others now that he has forgiven himself for almost everything.

Meanwhile, the love affair between Spano and Madsen develops its own touching qualities. Here are two of the most interesting newcomers in Hollywood—Spano, the charming greaser in *Baby, It's You*, and Madsen, the cellist who lived upstairs from the computer expert in *Electric Dreams*. The movie gives them one of those simple, cleareyed, glowing romances that we used to go to the movies to see.

Then tragedy strikes. Madsen suddenly goes into a coma and is pronounced braindead. Stiers heads the committee that decides to unplug her life-support systems. But Spano and O'Toole can tell that she is really only suffering from Ali McGraw's Disease, that dependable movie ailment in which illness consists of growing more and more beautiful. So now *Creator* arrives at its crisis: Can O'Toole, who dreams of creating life, really deliver when the chips are down?

The movie was directed by Ivan Passer (*Cutter's Way*), with his usual attention to personal quirks that preserve his characters from becoming trapped in the plot. I liked all of the casting, and I liked the fact that it found new combinations of familiar faces; who would expect to find O'Toole, Stiers, Hemingway, Spano, and Madsen in the same movie, and yet who familiar with their work would not enjoy seeing them together?

And yet the movie doesn't quite work. It tries to do too many things. It gives us two love affairs, a professional rivalry, a goofy campus, a mad scientist's obsession, *and* a deathbed soap opera. By the end of the film, there are so many problems to resolve that the characters are reduced to running from one to another. We could, I think, have probably done without the Hemingway character—who is fun, but an unnecessary complication. And maybe we could have done without some of the all-too-heartwarming bedside scenes. *Creator* is ambitious and tries to do a lot of things and does most of them well, but it's a close miss.

Creepshow ★ ★ ★
R, 129 m., 1982

Hal Holbrook (Henry Northrup), Adrienne Barbeau (Wilma Northrup), Fritz Weaver (Dexter Stanley), Leslie Nielsen (Richard Vickers), Carrie Nye (Sylvia Graham), E.G. Marshall (Upson Pratt), Viveca Lindfors (Aunt Bedelia). Directed by George A. Romero and produced by Richard P. Rubinstein. Screenplay by Stephen King.

Creepshow plays like an anthology of human phobias. What could be more horrifying that sticking your hand into a long-forgotten packing crate and suddenly feeling teeth sink into you? Unless it would be finding yourself buried up to the neck on the beach, with the tide coming in? Or trapped in an old grave, with the tombstone toppling down on top of you? Or having green stuff grow all over you? Or how about being smothered by cockroaches?

The horrors in *Creepshow* are universal enough, and so is the approach. These stories have been inspired, right down to the very camera angles, by the classic EC Comics of the early 1950s—titles like "Tales from the Crypt," which curdled the blood of Eisenhower-era kids raised on such innocent stuff as Captain Marvel, and appalled their elders. (EC Comics almost single-handedly inspired the creation of the Comics Code Authority.) The filmmakers of *Creepshow* say they were raised on those old comics, and it would appear that their subsequent careers were guided by the Ol' Crypt-Keeper's bag of tales. The movie's director is George A. Romero, whose most famous credit is *Night of the Living Dead*, and the original screenplay is by Stephen King, who wrote *Carrie* and *The Shining*. What they've done here is to recapture not only the look and the storylines of old horror comics, but also the peculiar feeling of poetic justice that permeated their pages. In an EC horror story, unspeakable things happened to people—but, for the most part, they deserved them.

The five stories told in this film often center around a fatal flaw. Upson Pratt, for example, the hero of the fifth story, is a compulsively neat and tidy man who lives in a hermetically sealed command center, much like Howard Hughes. What could be more suitable than an invasion of his stronghold by cockroaches? The professors in the story about the thing in the box have spent their lives collecting old facts: how perfect that one long-collected piece of evidence should still bite back!

Romero and King have approached this movie with humor and affection, as well as with an appreciation of the macabre. They create visual links to comic books by beginning each segment with several panels of a comic artist's version of the story, and then dissolving from the final drawn panel to a reality that exactly mirrors it. The acting also finds the right note. Such veterans of horror as Hal Holbrook, E.G. Marshall, and Adrienne Barbeau know how to paint their personalities broadly, edging up to caricature. Nobody in this movie is a three-dimensional person, or is meant to be. They are all types. And their lives are all object lessons.

The original full name of EC Comics was "Educational Comics," and you got an education, all right. You learned it was unwise to stick your hand into a box labeled "Danger—Do Not Open." It was unwise to speak ill of the dead. And it was quite unwise to assume that cockroaches would never decide to gang up and fight back.

Cries and Whispers ★ ★ ★ ★
R, 106 m., 1973

Harriet Andersson (Agnes), Kari Sylwan
(Anna), Ingrid Thulin (Karin), Liv Ullmann
(Maria), Erland Josephson (Lakaren),
Henning Moritzen (Joakim). Directed,
produced, and written by Ingmar Bergman.

Cries and Whispers is like few movies we'll
ever see. It is hypnotic, disturbing, frightening. It envelops us in a red membrane of passion and fear, and in some way that I do not
fully understand, it employs taboos and
ancient superstitions to make its effect. We
slip lower in our seats, feeling claustrophobia
and sexual disquiet, realizing that we have
been surrounded by the vision of a filmmaker who has absolute mastery of his art.
Cries and Whispers is about dying, love,
sexual passion, hatred, and death—in that
order.

The film inhabits a manor house set on a
vast country estate. The rooms of the house
open out from each other like passages in the
human body; with the exception of one
moment when Agnes, the dying woman,
opens her window and looks at the dawn, the
house offers no views. It looks in upon itself.

Three woman stay in the house with
Agnes (Harriet Andersson), waiting for her
to die. She is in the final stages of cancer and
in great pain. The women are Karin and
Maria, her sisters, and Anna, the stout,
round-cheeked servant. In elliptical flashbacks (intended to give us emotional information, not to tell a story), we learn that the
three sisters have made little of their lives.
Karin (Ingrid Thulin) is married to a diplomat she despises. Maria (Liv Ullmann) is
married to a cuckold, and so she cuckolds
him (what is one to do?). Agnes, who never
married, gave birth to a few third-rate water-
colors. Now, in dying, she discovers at last
some of the sweetness of life.

The sisters remember that they were close
in childhood, but somehow in growing up
they lost the ability to love, to touch. Only
Anna, the servant, remembers how. When
Agnes cries out in the night, in fear and
agony, it is Anna who cradles her to her
bosom, whispering soft endearments. The
others cannot stand to be touched. In a
moment of conjured nostalgia, Maria and
Karin remember their closeness as children.

Now, faced with the fact of their sister's
death, they deliberately try to synthesize
feeling and love. Quickly, almost frantically,
they touch and caress each other's faces, but
their touching is a parody and by the next
day they have closed themselves off again.

These two scenes—of Anna embracing
Agnes, and of Karin and Maria touching like
frightened kittens—are two of the greatest
Bergman has ever created. The feeling in
these scenes—I should say, the way they
force us to feel—constitutes the meaning of
this film. It has no abstract message; it communicates with us on a level of human feeling
so deep that we are afraid to invent words for
the things found there.

The camera is as uneasy as we are. It stays
at rest mostly, but when it moves it doesn't
always follow smooth, symmetrical progressions. It darts, it falls back, is stunned. It
lingers on close-ups of faces with the
impassivity of God. It continues to look
when we want to turn away; it is not moved.
Agnes lies thrown on her deathbed, her body
shuddered by horrible, deep gasping
breaths, as she fights for air, for life. The sisters turn away, and we want to, too. We know
things are this bad—but we don't want to
know. Bergman's camera stays and watches.

The movie is drenched in red. Bergman
has written in his screenplay what he thinks
of the inside of the human soul as a mem-
branous red. Color can be so important; in
Two English Girls, a movie about the absence
of passion, Francois Truffaut kept red out of
his compositions until the movie's one
moment of unfeigned feeling, and then he
filled his screen with red.

All of *Cries and Whispers* is occupied with
passion—but the passion is inside, the characters can't get it out of themselves. None of
them can, except Anna (Kari Sylwan). The
film descends into a netherworld of the
supernatural; the dead woman speaks (or is
it only that they think they hear her?). She
reaches out and grasps for Karin (or does
Karin move the dead arms?—Bergman's
camera doesn't let us see).

The movie, like all supernatural myths,
like all legends and fables (and like all
jokes—which are talismans to take the pain
from truth) ends in a series of threes. The
dead woman asks the living women to stay
with her, to comfort her while she pauses

within her dead body before moving into the great terrifying void. Karin will not. Maria will not. But Anna will, and makes pillows of her breasts for Agnes. Anna is the only one of them who remembers how to touch and love. And she is the only one who believes in God.

We saw her in the morning, praying. We learned that she had lost her little daughter, but is resigned to God's will. Is there a God in Bergman's film, or is there only Anna's faith? The film ends with a scene of astonishing, jarring affirmation: We see the four women some months earlier, drenched with the golden sun, and we hear Anna reading from Agnes's diary: "I feel a great gratitude to my life, which gives me so much." And takes it away.

Crimes of Passion ★ ½
R, 102 m., 1984

Kathleen Turner (Joanna/China Blue), Anthony Perkins (Shayne), John Laughlin (Grady), Annie Potts (Amy). Directed by Ken Russell and produced by Barry Sandler. Screenplay by Sandler.

I like what George Burns said about his sex life: "I got more laughs in bed than I ever got in vaudeville." Sex is an activity of great and serious importance to its participants, but as a spectator sport it has a strange way of turning into comedy. Look, for example, at Ken Russell's overwrought film *Crimes of Passion*, in which good performances and an interesting idea are metamorphosed into one of the silliest movies in a long time.

Part of the fault for that lies with Russell. A great deal of the fault no doubt lies with the movie rating system, which required massive cuts in the movie before it could qualify for an R rating, and with New World Pictures, which was too chicken to release the movie with an X.* But some of the fault also lies with the subject of sex itself, because there is nothing quite so ridiculous as someone else's sexual fantasies, and nothing as fascinating as our own.

The movie stars Kathleen Turner in a performance which must have taken a great deal of nerve and curiosity. She plays a woman with a dual identity: by day, she's a sophisticated fashion designer named Joanne, and by night she's a kinky hooker named China Blue. The psychological reasons behind this double existence are dished up out of the usual Freudian stew. Turner's day work is photographed in a matter-of-fact way. The nighttime street scene is seen by Russell, however, as a lurid *film noir* world of flashing red neon signs, garter belts, squirming sadomasochists, and perverts like the one played by Anthony Perkins, who proves in this movie that there is probably no role he would turn down because it would be bad for his image. Perkins plays a demented street preacher who sniffs uppers, hangs out in peep shows, and brandishes a murder weapon that looks like *Jaws* crossed with the latest electronic sex toy.

Perkins is just one of the clients who enlivens Turner's evenings. Others are more poignant as when Turner is hired by the wife of a dying man, who wants her husband to feel like a man for one last time. She enters the man's room, and as they begin to talk, a touchingly authentic atmosphere is established.

The purpose of *Crimes of Passion* was apparently to explore the further shores of sexual behavior. Because of the double standard of the movie ratings system, which prizes violence more highly than sex, a great deal of the behavior is missing from the movie, and what is left is a steamy, bloody thriller. I'm not sure that's what Russell had in mind. Anthony Perkins distorts most of the scenes he's in, with overacting so blatant that the plausibility of the whole movie is undermined. Turner tries. So does John Laughlin, as a square young husband who learns a lot from her about sex and love. but when *Crimes of Passion* is over, what's left? Not much. You know you're in trouble in a sex movie when you spend more time thinking about the parts they left out than the parts they put in.

*The videocassette version restores some of the excised footage.

Critters ★ ★ ★
PG-13, 97 m., 1986 ✓

Dee Wallace Stone (Helen), M. Emmet Walsh (Harv), Billy Green Bush (Jay Brown), Scott Grimes (Brad Brown), Nadine Van Der Velde (April Brown), Don Opper (Charlie McFadden), Terrence Mann (Johnny Steele).

Directed by Stephen Herek and produced by Rupert Harvey. Screenplay by Herek and Domonic Muir.

If perfect fools can hold drivers' licenses, why can't creatures from outer space be just as dumb? And if they *are* bounty hunters, why shouldn't they be trigger-happy—firing at everything that moves, like a television set, for example? We always assume that visitors from other worlds will be far more intelligent than we are, but maybe they'll just turn out to have faster means of intergalactic travel.

In the opening scenes of *Critters,* a spaceship is approaching a barren asteroid which has been converted into a prison. It carries on board several of the dreaded Cripes, who are furry little bowling balls with dozens of rows of sharp teeth. The Cripes escape, take over the ship, and land on earth. And bounty hunters follow them here, while the nasty little critters are terrorizing the countryside.

What this gives us is a truly ambitious rip-off of not one but four recent science-fiction movies: *Gremlins, E.T., The Terminator,* and *Starman.* We get the critters from the first and the hunters from the second, and from *Starman* the notion that an alien can assume the outward appearance of a human being. (That is a particularly attractive quality for an alien to have, especially in a low-budget picture, because then you can hire an actor and claim he is inhabited by an alien, and you can save a lot of money on special effects.) From *E.T.,* there is Dee Wallace Stone, who played Henry Thomas's mother in that film and is now the equally dubious and harried mother of young Scott Grimes, a plucky kid who goes into battle against the invaders.

The movie takes place in a small town and the surrounding countryside, where the vicious little furballs start attacking everything that moves. They have a lot of tricks at their command: They can eat you like a piranha, shoot darts at you from their foreheads, and curl up into a ball and roll away. That leads up to the big scene in the bowling alley, where we expect that someone's going to reach down and pick up a critter instead of a ball, but as it turns out, that scene contains other surprises.

We meet the folks in the area. There's the friendly farmer (Billy Green Bush), his wife (Stone), son (Grimes), and daughter (Nadine Van Der Veldt). They live on a farm that gives the critters their first haven, and there's the obligatory scary scene where the father goes down in the basement with his flashlight to see what's making the noise.

Meanwhile, the local lawman (that dependably slimy character actor M. Emmet Walsh) notices that strange things are happening in his territory. Two strangers from out of town have turned up and started to blast everybody away, and dang if one of them doesn't look exactly like the local minister! The other one soon assumes the outward appearance of the village idiot.

All of these plot threads move inexorably toward the final showdown, but what's interesting is the way the movie refuses to be just a thriller. The director, Stephen Herek, likes to break the mood occasionally with a one-liner out of left field, and he gives the critters some of the funniest lines. What makes *Critters* more than a rip-off are its humor and its sense of style. This is a movie made by people who must have had fun making it.

Crossover Dreams ★ ★ ★
PG-13, 85 m., 1985

Ruben Blades (Rudy Veloz), Shawn Elliott (Orlando), Tom Signorelli (Lou Rose), Elizabeth Pena (Liz Garcia), Frank Robles (Ray Solo), Joel Diamond (Neil Silver). Directed by Leon Ichaso and produced by Manuel Arce. Screenplay by Ichaso and Manuel Arce.

Crossover Dreams does not begin with an original idea. It shows the rise and fall of a musician whose talent takes him to the top, and whose ego and weaknesses pull him back to the bottom again. The first time I saw this story, it was about Gene Kruppa, and in his big comeback concert in Carnegie Hall, he dropped his drumsticks and had to find the courage to start again. I've seen the same story countless times again, translated into the idioms of jazz, country, rock, and classical, and now here is the salsa version, starring Ruben Blades.

The story isn't new, but it sure does wear well. Maybe that's because Blades is such an engaging performer, playing a character who is earnest and sincere when he needs to be, but who always maintains a veil over his deepest secrets. The story is formula, but the film's treatment of it is fresh and perceptive, and there's an exhilarating energy level. The opening shots, in fact, reminded me of the extraordinary opening of Martin Scorsese's first film, *Who's That Knocking at My Door?* Music pounds on the sound track, as young men race around the streets of New York, filled with their own life and importance.

The movie takes place largely in Spanish Harlem, where the Blades character, Rudy Veloz, makes the rounds of Latino nightclubs, working with a band of old friends and mentors. He dreams of "crossing over," of breaking out of the Latino circuit and making it downtown, to the world of national TV, music videos, and record contracts. And for a moment it looks as if he might.

He meets a shabby Broadway talent agent, who fails to impress him (but who gives him some of the most realistic advice he'll receive in this movie). Then he's "discovered" by a record producer, who picks him up out of his life, briefly shines the spotlight on him, and then throws him back into obscurity again. The movie's most convincing and painful scenes come after Veloz's brief moment of fame, when he has to return to his friends and try to conceal the extent of his failure.

Against this serious undertone, the movie hurls a lot of good music. Blades, the Panamanian salsa star who has crossed over, is not only a good singer but a surprisingly versatile actor who never seems to be straining for an effect, never seems to stray outside his character, and will probably get some more serious acting jobs after this debut.

Crossroads ★ ★ ★ ½
R, 98 m., 1985

Ralph Macchio (Eugene Martone), Joe Seneca (Willie Brown), Jami Gertz (Frances), Joe Morton (Scratch's Assistant), Robert Judd (Scratch), Harry Carey, Jr. (Bartender). Directed by Walter Hill and produced by Mark Carliner. Screenplay by John Fusco.

Crossroads borrows so freely and is a reminder of so many other movies that it's a little startling, at the end, to realize how effective the movie is and how original it manages to feel despite all the plunderings.

The movie stars Ralph Macchio as a bright teen-ager who studied classical guitar at Juilliard and worships as his heroes the great old blues musicians of the 1930s and 1940s. One day he tracks down a survivor of that era, a harmonica player named Willie Brown (Joe Seneca) in a nursing home. Macchio helps him escape, and they hit the road, hoboing their way down South to a crossroads where Seneca once made a deal with the devil.

With the devil? You bet. *Crossroads* is a cheerful cross between a slice of life and a supernatural fable. And at the end, it's up to the kid to pick up his guitar and outplay the devil's man, to save Seneca's soul. This story is a combination of no less than two reliable genres. It borrows, obviously, from Macchio's 1984 *The Karate Kid*, which was also the story of a young man's apprenticeship with an older master. It also borrows from the countless movies in which everything depends on who wins the big fight, match, game, or duel in the last scene. The notion of the showdown with the devil may have been suggested by the country song "Devil Went Down to Georgia."

And yet the remarkable thing is how fresh all this material seems, and how entertaining it is. Just when I'm ready to despair of a movie coming up with a fresh plot, a movie like *Crossroads* comes along to remind me that acting, writing, and direction can redeem any plot, and make any story new. The foundation for *Crossroads* is the relationship between the boy and the old man, and here we have two performances that are well suited to one another. Macchio, once again, as in *The Karate Kid*, has an unstudied, natural charm. A lot of young actors seem to take themselves seriously, but not many have Macchio's gift of seeming to take other things seriously. We really believe, in this movie, that he is a fanatic about the blues, and has read all the books and listened to all the records.

Seneca does a terrific job as a rock-solid, conniving, no-nonsense old man who doesn't take this kid seriously at first, and uses him as a way to get out of the nursing home and back down South to the crossroads, where he has a longstanding rendezvous. The kid knows that Willie was a partner of the legendary blues musician

Robert Johnson and he makes a deal with the old man. He'll help him return to that crossroads if the old man will teach him a lost Johnson song.

Along the way, the two men pick up a third partner, a tough young runaway named Frances (Jami Gertz), and there is a brief, sweet romance between the two young people before she leaves one morning, perhaps because it is better for the old man and the young one to move on toward their mutual destiny.

Gertz is a newcomer: this was her second major movie in 1985, after a somewhat thankless role in *Quicksilver*, in which she worked for a bicycle messenger service. She's just right for this movie, with the toughness required by the character, and yet with the tenderness and the romantic notes that remind us that this is really a myth. Another good performance in the movie is by Joe Morton, who played *The Brother from Another Planet* and this time is the devil's assistant, sinister and ingratiating.

The film was directed by Walter Hill, who specializes in myths, in movie characters who seem to represent something greater than themselves. Detailed character studies are not his strong point; he makes movies like *The Warriors*, *48 Hours*, and *Streets of Fire*, in which the characters seem made out of the stuff of legend. In *48 Hours*, though, he also found the human qualities in the Nick Nolte and Eddie Murphy characters, and he does that again this time, making Seneca and Macchio so individual, so particular, that we aren't always thinking that this movie is really about an old man and a boy and the devil.

A word about the music. Ry Cooder did most of the sound track, drawing from many blues scores, and the movie is wonderful to listen to: confident and sly and not all tricked up for Hollywood. The closing scene, the dueling guitars, presents a challenge that perhaps no film composer could quite solve (what's the right approach to music as a weapon?), but somehow Cooder actually does pull off the final showdown.

D.A.R.Y.L. ★ ★ ★
PG, 99 m., 1985

Barret Oliver (Daryl), Mary Beth Hurt (Joyce Richardson), Michael McKean (Andy Robinson), Daniel Bryan Corkill (Turtle), Josef Sommer (Dr. Stewart), Kathryn Walker (Ellen Lamb). Directed by Simon Wincer and produced by John Heyman and Burtt Harris. Screenplay by David Ambrose.

They know there is something odd about the kid when he starts doing his own laundry. That's not natural for a grade-schooler. Daryl has some other strange attributes. He is unfailingly polite, obsessively honest, and bats 1.000 in Little League. Finally his friend, Turtle, pulls him aside and explains that adults don't like it when a kid is too perfect. It makes them nervous. They need to connect with him so they can relax around him. Daryl nods gravely, and his next time at bat, he strikes out.

Daryl's history is strange. He was discovered by the side of the road, a neatly dressed little boy with amnesia. He didn't know who his parents were, or what his last name was, or where he lived. He is placed with a foster family, and by halfway through the movie *D.A.R.Y.L.* he is beginning to develop into a more typical kid, with real human emotions. That is against the game plan, unfortunately, because Daryl is both more and less than human. He is a prototype of a secret government attempt to combine a computer brain with a genetically cloned body, creating a humanoid who can use his five senses as input for his silicon mind.

D.A.R.Y.L. is sort of *Charly* in reverse. Instead of a retarded man who is allowed, through science, to have a brief glimpse of what it would be like to be normal, what we have here is a super-intelligent thinking machine who gets a taste of being a real little boy. It's an intriguing premise, and the movie handles it with skill. The boy is played by Barret Oliver with an earnest, touching solemnity. The people around him (including his foster parents, Mary Beth Hurt and Michael McKean) are out of a Norman Rockwell drawing: loving, generous, loyal. His best friend Turtle (Daniel Bryan Corkill) is tactful in trying to get this odd kid to act normal.

Tacked onto this small-town story, the

details of the intrigue seem almost unnecessary. The movie contains the usual hard-nosed military men, visionary scientists, and officious cops. They've lost track of their expensive *D.A.R.Y.L.*, and want to find him and deprogram him. Daryl fights back by borrowing a supersecret fighter plane (as the movie is borrowing its ending from Clint Eastwood's *Firefox*), and the ending is really sort of neat; it's high-tech and heartwarming at the same time.

D.A.R.Y.L. is a good movie that could have been better. Maybe they should have screened *Charly* before making it. That would have reminded them that the scientific parts of their story are more or less predictable, and that the human elements are what keep us involved.

Dance With a Stranger ★ ★ ★ ★
R, 102 m., 1985

Miranda Richardson (Ruth Ellis), Rupert Everett (David Blakely), Ian Holm (Desmond Cussen), Matthew Carroll (Andy), Tom Chadbon (Anthony Findlater), Jane Bertish (Carole Findlater). Directed by Mike Newell and produced by Roger Randall Cutler. Screenplay by Shelagh Delaney.

Ruth Ellis and David Blakely were a tragedy waiting to happen. She was a B-girl, pouring drinks and massaging men's egos in a sleazy little 1950s London nightclub. He was a rich young brat, whose life centered around his career as a race driver. They met one boozy night in the club, and there was an instant spark of lust between them—Ruth, whose profession was to keep her distance from men, and David, who had never felt love in his life.

Dance With a Stranger is the story of their affair, which led to one of the most famous British murder trials of the decade. After Ellis shot Blakely dead in the street outside a pub, she was brought to trial, convicted, and executed with heartless speed; her trial began on June 20, 1955, and she was hanged on July 19—the last woman to receive the death penalty in England.

In the thirty years since Blakely and Ellis died, the case has fascinated the British, perhaps because it combines sexuality and the class system, two of their greatest interests. Blakely was upper-class, polished, affected,

superior. Ellis was a working-class girl who made herself up to look like Marilyn Monroe and used the business of bar hostess as a way to support her young son and maintain her independence from men. Ironically, she was finally undone by her emotional dependence on Blakely, who gave and then withdrew his affection in a way that pushed her over the edge.

Their story is told by Mike Newell in a film of astonishing performances and moody, atmospheric visuals. Ruth Ellis is the emotional center of the film, and she is played by a newcomer, Miranda Richardson, as a woman who prides herself on not allowing men to hurt her, and who almost to the end cannot believe that the one man she loves would hurt her the most.

We see her first in the nightclub, where her blonde Monroe looks supply the only style in the whole shabby room. We meet her regular "friends," including Desmond Cussen (Ian Holm), a quiet, loyal bachelor who adores her in an unpossessive way. Then Blakely (played by Rupert Everett) walks into her life, and in an instant there is erotically charged tension between them; the way they both flaunt their indifference is a clue. Their relationship falls into a pattern: lust, sex, tears, quarrels, absences, and then lust and sex again. Newell tells the story only in terms of the events and characters themselves. There are no detours into shallow psychology; just the patterns of attraction and repulsion.

For Ruth Ellis, a woman living at a time when women's options were cruelly limited, the obsession with Blakely becomes totally destructive. She loses her job. She grows more dependent as he grows more cold and unpredictable, and everything is complicated by their mutual alcoholism. Cussen, the inoffensive, long-suffering admirer, takes her in, and she makes an effort to shape up, but Blakely sounds chords in her that she cannot ignore.

By the end of the movie, Blakely has done things to her that she cannot forgive. And they are not the big, melodramatic things like the violence that breaks out between them. They are little unforgivable things, as when he raises her hopes and then disappoints her. By the end, he is hardly even hurting her intentionally. He drinks in the company of fawning friends, he ignores responsibilities, he disappears into his own drunken absent-mindedness, and forgets her. And then one night outside a pub, she reminds him, once and for all.

Daniel ★ ★ ½
R, 130 m., 1983

Timothy Hutton (Daniel Isaacson), Ed Asner (Jacob Ascher), Mandy Patinkin (Paul Isaacson), Lindsay Crouse (Rochelle Isaacson), Joseph Leon (Selig Mindish), Amanda Plummer (Susan Isaacson). Directed by Sidney Lumet and produced by Burtt Harris. Screenplay by E.L. Doctorow.

I can just vaguely remember the Rosenberg case from the early 1950s; long-ago adult voices echo in my memory, saying "they gave away the secret of the atomic bomb to the Russians." It is a large exaggeration to suggest that the Rosenbergs literally gave the Russians the bomb, but they were found guilty of giving them classified information and for that they were executed, in one of the most famous and painful cases in American legal history. Thirty years have passed, many books have been written on the Rosenbergs, and a controversy raged over a book published in 1982 that concluded that Julius Rosenberg was probably guilty of spying—although his wife's involvement is less clear.

The controversy has spilled over into considerations of *Daniel*, a movie that would seem to be about the Rosenbergs and their children (what other historical figures could possibly have inspired it?), although the filmmakers claim it is not. Sidney Lumet, who directed the movie, and E.L. Doctorow, who based the screenplay on his own novel, *The Story of Daniel*, are at pains to separate themselves from the Rosenbergs—who are renamed the Isaacsons. Beyond the usual disclaimers, they say that their movie isn't really about the parents, but about the legacy of the children.

As a viewer, I don't really care. I don't expect *Daniel* to be historically accurate about the original court case, nor do I want the story of the children to follow the real lives of the Rosenberg children. What I do want, though, is for the movie to make it clear where it stands on the Isaacsons. I don't mean I want the movie to declare whether

they were innocent or guilty—but whether they were good or bad. And there the movie holds back. The parents in this film are seen through such a series of filters—political, emotional, historical—that they are finally not seen at all.

The movie begins with a close-up of Daniel's eyes. He is dispassionately reciting a dictionary entry about electrocution. These stark words summarize what happened to his parents and they are about the only knowable facts about the case. Then we meet other characters—Daniel's sister, Susan, and the adoptive parents who took in the Isaacson children. Susan seems terribly scarred by her childhood; she is hysterical, angry, suicidal. Daniel is less visibly scarred, but he is brutally cruel to his young wife and we wonder if she represents, for him, the mother who left—who chose death over her children.

The movie then begins to move back and forth through time. There are warm sepia-toned flashbacks to left-wing days in the 1930s, when the Isaacsons are swept up in the euphoria of the American Communist Party. The present-day scenes, usually shot with lots of blues and greens, follow Daniel's quest for friends of his parents who might share their secrets. The frustrating thing about this approach is that the flashbacks—which presumably could contain the information Daniel desires—are noncommittal. They show how the Isaacsons behaved, but are never clear about exactly what it was they did, or didn't do. It's easy to assume that's because the flashbacks are limited to what the children themselves witnessed. But, no, there are scenes in which the only people present are the parents (for example, a scene on a subway train where Jacob lectures Rochelle about Marx). Once the movie uses a single scene with an omniscient point of view, it becomes guilty of withholding additional information; if the film can see into the Isaacson's private moments when no children were present, then it can show us whether they passed secrets to the Russians. But the film doesn't want to. Its real subjects are the euphoric moments of left-wing idealism in the 1930s and how the passions of those moments are being paid for to this day by the children. Because the Isaacsons were swept up in a movement which gave them identity, support, and a sense of participating in history, these poor, miserable kids have to pay the dues.

Now *that* would be a subject, if the kids were dealt with in-depth. But the movie tries to encompass too much. It devotes so much time to the past, to the children's childhoods, that the present-day scenes are slighted. Susan is clearly so disturbed that she's of little help as a witness, but Daniel, the character the movie *could* have examined in three dimensions, is so manipulated by the plot that he remains a mystery. He's always the detective, seeking out his parents' friends, asking impassioned questions, functioning as the story device instead of as the subject. At the end of *Daniel* we know that some emotionally careless parents left behind some emotionally crippled children. We suspect, oddly, that spy secrets and charges of subversion were not really relevant to the damage done to the children. I don't think that was the movie's intention.

The Dark Crystal ★ ★ ½
PG, 94 m., 1982

Performed by Jim Henson, Kathryn Mullen, Frank Oz, Dave Goelz, Brian Muehl, Jean Pierre Amiel, Kiran Shah. Directed by Jim Henson and Frank Oz and produced by Henson and Gary Kurtz.

You've got to hand it to Jim Henson and Frank Oz. First they enchanted a generation of kids with the Muppets. Now they're ready to scare the pants off them with the Skeksis, the Mystics and, not least, the Garthim. Those are three new races of ugly beasties invented by the Muppeteers for *The Dark Crystal*, an otherworldly fantasy. There are others. Watching this movie, I wondered at times whether Henson and Oz, who are longtime partners in the Muppet saga, made it in violent reaction to the charm of Miss Piggy, Kermit, and the other Muppets. There is nothing charming about most of the characters in this movie. They are hairy, smelly, cadaverous, loathsome, evil, cannibalistic, vindictive, slimy, mean-spirited, dripping, scaling, unkempt, and hateful, but charming they're not.

The movie *does* have a couple of heroes, who belong to the race of Gelflings, and who look related to those solemn children with gigantic, tearful eyes that you find on paintings in re-sale shops. There are two Gelflings, a boy and a girl, and they follow in a time-hallowed tradition of monster fantasies, which says that the villains can be interesting, but the good guys have to be squeaky-voiced and innocuous.

The story takes place on a faraway planet that circles three suns. A thousand years ago, so the legend goes, the planet was prosperous and peaceful. But then there was a struggle over the Dark Crystal, a shard of it was lost and the ruling race on the planet split into two kinds of creatures: the Skeksis, who are reprehensible, and the Mystics, who are merely reptilian. (The Garthim are sort of a combination of crabs and armored beetles, and do the Skeksis's dirty work.) As the movie opens, the three suns are about to get back together again, and a little Gelfling gets a mission: Find the missing shard and repair the damage of the past millennium. *The Dark Crystal* is the story of his quest. And it *is* quite a quest, since the quest was designed and executed by some of the best special-effects people in the business, led by producer Gary *(Star Wars)* Kurtz, George Lucas's Industrial Light and Magic Co., and, of course, the Muppeteers themselves.

There are all sorts of amazing sights in this movie. An otherworldly rain forest is populated with weird plants that have lives of their own. A cliffside is the home of a race of beings who look like sponge-rubber sink scrubbers. The high point in animation is probably reached during a banquet scene—a slurpfest at which the slovenly Skeksis smear food all over their faces before bringing in the dessert, which is alive, and looks like what you fear may be lurking at the bottom of Love Canal.

The Dark Crystal is a labor of love, and on that basis, I salute it. A great deal of creativity and ingenious thinking went into the creation of these strange beings and their planet. But as a work of fiction, and more specifically as entertainment, I think it has two problems: (1) Many of the scenes last too long, because the special effects are lingered over, and (2) any kid younger than ten is probably going to lose some sleep after seeing the horrendous creatures in this movie. Sure, the Gelflings are cute, but the Garthim are unforgettable.

Dawn of the Dead ★ ★ ★ ★
R, 126 m., 1979

With David Emge, Ken Foree, Scott H.
Reiniger, and Gaylen Ross. Directed by
George A. Romero and produced by Richard
P. Rubenstein. Screenplay by Romero.

Dawn of the Dead is one of the best horror
films ever made—and, as an inescapable
result, one of the most horrifying. It is
gruesome, sickening, disgusting, violent,
brutal, and appalling. It is also (excuse me
for a second while I find my other list) brilliantly crafted, funny, droll, and savagely
merciless in its satiric view of the American
consumer society. Nobody ever said art had
to be in good taste.

It's about a mysterious plague that sweeps
the nation, causing the recently dead to rise
from their graves and roam the land, driven
by an insatiable hunger for living flesh. No
explanation is offered for this behavior—
indeed, what explanation would suffice?—
but there is a moment at which a survivor solemnly intones: "When there is no more
room in hell, the dead will walk the Earth."

Who's that a quotation from? From
George A. Romero, who wrote and directed
Dawn of the Dead as a sequel to his *Night of
the Living Dead*, which came out in 1968 and
now qualifies as a cult classic. If you have
seen *Night*, you will recall it as a terrifying
horror film punctuated by such shocking
images as zombies tearing human flesh from
limbs. *Dawn* includes many more scenes
like that, more graphic, more shocking, and
in color. I am being rather blunt about this
because there are many people who will *not*
want to see this film. You know who you are.
Why are you still reading?

Well . . . maybe because there's a little of
the ghoulish voyeur in all of us. We like to be
frightened. We like a good creepy thrill. It's
just, we say, that we don't want a movie to go
too far. What's too far? *The Exorcist? The
Omen?* George Romero deliberately intends
to go too far in *Dawn of the Dead.* He's dealing very consciously with the ways in which
images can affect us, and if we sit through
the film (many people cannot) we make some
curious discoveries.

One is that the fates of the zombies, who
are destroyed wholesale in all sorts of terrible

ways, don't affect us so much after awhile.
They aren't being killed, after all: They're
already dead. They're even a little comic,
lurching about a shopping center and trying
to plod up the down escalator. Romero teases
us with these passages of humor. We relax,
we laugh, we see the satire in it all, and
then—*pow!* Another disembowelment, just
when we were off guard.

His story opens in a chaotic television studio, where idiotic broadcasters are desperately transmitting inaccurate information
(one hopes the Emergency Broadcast System will do a whole lot better). National
Guard troops storm public housing, where
zombies have been reported. There are ten
minutes of unrelieved violence, and then the
story settles down into the saga of four survivors who hijack a helicopter, land on the
roof of a suburban shopping center, and
barricade themselves inside against the
zombies.

Their eventual fates are not as interesting
as their behavior in the meantime; there is
nothing quite like a plague of zombies to
wonderfully focus your attention on what
really matters to you. Romero has his own
ideas, too, and the shopping center becomes
a brilliant setting for a series of comic and
satiric situations: Some low humor, some
exquisitely sly.

But, even so, you may be asking, how can
I defend this depraved trash? I do not defend
it. I praise it. And it is not depraved,
although some reviews have seen it that way.
It is *about* depravity. If you can see beyond
the immediate impact of Romero's imagery,
if you can experience the film as being more
than just its violent extremes, a most unsettling thought may occur to you: The zombies
in *Dawn of the Dead* are not the ones who are
depraved. They are only acting according to
their natures, and, gore dripping from their
jaws, are blameless.

The depravity is in the behavior of the
healthy survivors, and the true immorality
comes as two bands of human survivors fight
each other for the shopping center: *Now*
look who's fighting over the bones! But
Dawn is even more complicated than that,
because the survivors have courage, too, and
a certain nobility at times, and a sense of
humor, and loneliness and dread, and are not
altogether unlike ourselves. A-ha.

Day for Night ★ ★ ★ ★
PG, 116 m., 1974

Francois Truffaut (Ferrand), Jean-Pierre
Aumont (Alexandre), Jacqueline Bisset
(Julie), Jean-Pierre Leaud (Alphonse),
Valentina Cortese (Séverine). Directed by
Francois Truffaut and produced by Marcel
Bébert. Screenplay by Truffaut, Jean-Louis
Richard, and Suzanne Shiffman.

Movies about movies usually don't quite get
things right. The film business comes out
looking more romantic and glamorous (or
more corrupt and decadent) than it really is,
and none of the human feeling of a movie set
is communicated. That is not the case with
Francois Truffaut's funny and touching
film, *Day for Night*, which is not only the
best movie ever made about the movies but is
also a great entertainment.

A movie company, especially if it's away
from home on a location somewhere, is a
family that's been thrown into close and
sometimes desperate contact; strangers
become friends and even intimates in a few
weeks, and in a few more weeks they're scattered to the winds. The family is complicated by the insecurities and egos of the
actors, and by the moviemaking process
itself: We see the result, but we don't see the
hours and days spent on special effects, on
stunts, on making it snow or making it rain
or making an allegedly trained cat walk from
A to B. *Day for Night* is about all of these
aspects of moviemaking; about the technical
problems, the boredom between takes (a
movie set is one of the most boring places on
earth most of the time), and about the
romances and intrigues. It's real; this is how
a movie set really looks, feels, and smells.
Truffaut's story involves a movie company on
location in Nice. They're making a melodrama called *Meet Pamela*, of which we see
enough to know it's doomed at the box
office. But good or bad, the movie must be
made; Truffaut, who plays the director in his
own film, says at one point: "When I begin a
film, I want to make a great film. Halfway
through, I just hope to finish the film."

His cast includes a beautiful American
actress (Jacqueline Bisset); an aging matinee
idol (Jean-Pierre Aumont), and his former
mistress, also past her prime (Valentina Cor-

tese); the young, lovestruck male lead (Jean-
Pierre Leaud), and the entire crew of script
girls, camera operators, stunt men, and a
henpecked production manager. (And if you
have ever wondered what the key grip does in
a movie, here's your chance to find out.)
Truffaut sets half a dozen stories in motion,
and follows them all so effortlessly it's almost
as if we're gossiping with him about his colleagues. The movie set is a microcosm: there
is a pregnancy and a death; a love affair
ended, another begun, and a third almost
but not quite destroyed; and new careers to
be nourished and old careers to be preserved.

Truffaut was always a master of quiet comedy, and there are fine touches like the aging
actress fortifying herself with booze and
blaming her lack of memory on her makeup
girl. Then there's the young male lead's ill-
fated love for Jacqueline Bisset; she is happily married to a doctor, but unwisely
extends her sympathy to the youth, who
repays her by very nearly destroying her
marriage as well as himself. And all the time
there is the movie to be made: Truffaut gives
us a hilarious session with the "trained" cat,
and shows us without making a point of it
how snow is produced on a set, how stunt
drivers survive car crashes, and how third-
floor balconies can exist without buildings
below them.

What we see on the screen is nothing at all
like what happens on the set—a truth the
movie's title reflects. ("Day for night" is the
technical term for "night" scenes shot in
daylight with a special filter. The movie's
original French title, *La Nuit Americaine*, is
the French term for the same process—
acknowledging their debt to Hollywood.)

The movie is just plain fun. Movie buffs
will enjoy it like *Singin' in the Rain* (that perfect musical about the birth of talkies), but
you don't have to be a movie buff to like it.
Truffaut knows and loves the movies so
much he's infectious; one of *Day for Night*'s
best scenes is a dream in which the adult
director remembers himself, as a little boy,
slinking down a darkened street to steal a
still from *Citizen Kane* from in front of a theater. We know who the little boy grew up to
be, and that explains everything to us about
how he feels now.

Day of the Dead ★ ½
R, 91 m., 1985

Lori Cardille (Sarah), Terry Alexander (John, the Pilot), Joseph Pilato (Rhodes), Richard Liberty (Dr. Logan), Howard Sherman (Bub, the Zombie). Directed by George A. Romero and produced by Richard P. Rubinstein. Screenplay by Romero.

The ghouls in *Day of the Dead* are marvels of special effects, with festoons of rotting flesh hanging from their purple limbs as they slouch toward the camera, moaning their sad songs. Truth to tell, they look a lot better than the ghouls in *Night of the Living Dead*, which was director George Romero's original ghoul film. His technology is improving; perhaps the recent emphasis on well-developed bodies (in *Perfect*, *Rambo*, etc.) has inspired a parallel improvement in dead bodies.

But the ghouls have another problem in *Day of the Living Dead:* They're upstaged by the characters who are supposed to be real human beings. You might assume that it would be impossible to steal a scene from a ghoul, especially one with blood dripping from his orifices, but you haven't seen the overacting in this movie. The characters shout their lines from beginning to end, their temples pound with anger, and they use distracting Jamaican and Irish accents, until we are so busy listening to their endless dialogue that we lose interest in the movie they occupy.

Maybe there's a reason for that. Maybe Romero, whose original movie was a genuine inspiration, hasn't figured out anything new to do with his ghouls. In his second ghoul film, the brilliant *Dawn of the Dead* (1980), he had them shuffling and moaning their way through a modern shopping mall, as Muzak droned in the background and terrified survivors took refuge in the Sears store. The effect was both frightening and satirical. The everyday location made the ghouls seem all the more horrible, and the shopping mall provided lots of comic props (as when several ghouls tried to crawl up the down escalator).

This time, though, Romero has centered the action in a visually dreary location—an underground storage cavern, one of those abandoned salt mines where they store

financial records and the master prints of old movies. The ghouls have more or less overrun the surface of America, we gather, and down in the darkness a small team of scientists and military men are conducting experiments on a few captive ghoul guinea-pigs.

It's an interesting idea, especially if they had kept the semiseriousness of the earlier films. Instead, the chief researcher is a demented butcher with blood-stained clothes, whose idea of science is to teach a ghoul named Bub to operate a Sony Walkman. Meanwhile, the head of the military contingent (Joseph Pilato) turns into a violent little dictator who establishes martial law and threatens to end the experiments. His opponent is a spunky woman scientist (Lori Cardille), and as they shout angry accusations at each other, the real drama in the film gets lost.

In the earlier films, we really identified with the small cadre of surviving humans. They were seen as positive characters and we cared about them. This time, the humans are mostly unpleasant, violent, insane, or so noble that we can predict with utter certainty that they will survive. According to the mad scientist in *Day of the Dead*, the ghouls keep moving because of primitive impulses buried deep within their spinal columns—impulses that create the appearance of life long after consciousness and intelligence have departed. I hope the same fate doesn't befall Romero's ghoul movies. He should quit while he's ahead.

The Day of the Jackal ★ ★ ★ ★
PG, 150 m., 1973

Edward Fox (The Jackal), Terence Alexander (Lloyd), Michel Auclair (Colonel Rolland), Alan Badel (The Minister), Tony Britton (Inspector Thomas), Denis Carey (Casson), Olga Georges-Picot (Denise), Cyril Cusack (The Gunsmith). Directed by Fred Zinnemann and produced by John Woolf. Screenplay by Kenneth Ross.

Fred Zinnemann's *The Day of the Jackal* is one hell of an exciting movie. I wasn't prepared for how good it really is: it's not just a suspense classic, but a beautifully executed example of filmmaking. It's put together like a fine watch. The screenplay meticulously assembles an incredible array of material, and then Zinnemann choreographs it so that the story—complicated as it is—unfolds in almost documentary starkness.

The "jackal" of the title is the code name for a man who may (or may not) be a British citizen specializing in professional assassinations. He allegedly killed Trujillo of the Dominican Republic in 1961 and, now, two years later, he has been hired by a group of Frenchmen who want de Gaulle assassinated. His price is $500,000; he says, "and considering that I'm handing you France, I wouldn't call that expensive."

Zinnemann, working from Frederick Forsyth's bestseller, tells both sides of the story that unfolds during the summer of 1963. The jackal prepares two disguises and three identities, gets a legal passport by applying in the name of a child who died in 1931, and calls on European experts for his materials. An old gunsmith hand-makes a weird-looking lightweight rifle with silencer, sniper scope, and explosive bullets. A forger provides French identity papers and a driver's license (and comes to an unexpected end). And then the jackal enters France.

Meanwhile, the government has received information that an attempt will be made on de Gaulle's life. The general absolutely insists that he will make no changes in his public schedule, and that any attempt to prevent an assassination must be made in secret. The French police cooperate "unofficially" with the top police forces of other nations in attempting an apprehension. But they don't even know who the jackal is.

How can they stop him? The movie provides a fascinating record of police investigative work, which combines exhaustive checking with intuition. But the jackal is clever, too, particularly when he's cornered. Some of the movie's finest moments come after the jackal's false identity is discovered and his license plates and description are distributed. He keeps running—and always convincingly; this isn't a movie about a killer with luck, but about one of uncommon intelligence and nerve.

Playing the jackal, Edward Fox is excellent. The movie doesn't provide much chance for a deep characterization, but he projects a most convincing persona. He's boyishly charming, impeccably groomed, possessed of an easy laugh, and casually ruthless. He will kill if there's the slightest need to. Fox's performance is crucial to the film, of course, and the way he carries it off is impressive.

The others on the case are uniformly excellent, especially Tony Britton as a harried police inspector and Cyril Cusack, in a nicely crafted little vignette, as the gunsmith. The movie's technical values (as is always the case with a Zinnemann film) are impeccable. The movie was filmed at great cost all over Europe, mostly on location, and it looks it. A production of this scope needs to appear absolutely convincing, and Zinnemann has mastered every detail—including the casting of a perfect de Gaulle look-alike.

The Day of the Jackal is two and a half hours long and seems over in about fifteen minutes. There are some words you hesitate to use in a review, because they sound so much like advertising copy, but in this case I can truthfully say that the movie is spellbinding.

Days of Heaven ★ ★ ★ ★
PG, 95 m., 1978

Richard Gere (Bill), Brooke Adams (Abby), Sam Shepard (The Farmer), Linda Manz (Linda), Robert Wilke (Foreman), Jackie Shultis (Linda's Friend), Stuart Margolin (Mill Foreman). Directed by Terence Malick and produced by Bert and Harold Schneider. Screenplay by Malick.

Can any description of Terence Malick's *Days of Heaven* quite evoke the sense of wonder this film inspires? It's about a handful of people who find themselves shipwrecked in the middle of the Texas Panhandle—grain country—sometime before World War I. They involve themselves in a tragic love triangle, but their secrets seem insignificant, almost pathetic, seen against the awesome size of their world. Our wonder is that they endure at all in the face of the implacable land.

The land is farmed by a sick young man (Sam Shepard) who is widely believed to be on the edge of death. In the autumn, he and his foreman hire crews of itinerant laborers who ride out from the big cities on the tops of boxcars: swaggering, anonymous men who will follow the harvest north from Texas to Canada. Others pass through to entertain them and live off their brief periods of wage earning: aerial barnstormers, circus troupes, all specks on the great landscape.

We meet three people who set out together from the grime of Chicago, looking for harvest work: A strong young man (Richard Gere), his kid sister (Linda Manz), and the woman he lives with and also claims, for convenience, as his sister (Brooke Adams). They arrive at the farm of the sick young man, who falls in love with the older "sister."

Because they are so poor, because the farmer has a house, land, and money, the three keep quiet about his mistake and eventually the farmer and the "sister" marry. Her "brother"—her man—works on the farm and observes the marriage from a resentful, festering distance. The younger girl also observes, and the film's narration comes from her comments, deeply cynical, pathetically understated.

So goes the story of *Days of Heaven,* except that Malick's film doesn't really tell a story at all. It is an evocation of emptiness, loneliness, desolation, the slow accumulation of despair in a land too large for its inhabitants and blind to their dreams. Willa Cather wrote novels about such feelings—*The Lost Lady, Death Comes for the Archbishop,* the middle section of *The Professor's House*—and now Malick joins her company. This is a huge land we occupy. The first people to settle it must have wondered if they could ever really possess it.

Malick's vision of the land, indeed, is so sweeping that an ordinary, human-scale "story" in the foreground would be a distraction. We get a series of scenes, like tableaux, as the characters involve themselves in their mutual tragedy. The visual compositions often place them against vast backdrops (this is one of the most beautifully photographed films ever made), but Malick finds terror, too, in extreme close-ups of grasshoppers, of a germinating seed, of the little secrets with which nature ultimately builds her infinite secret.

When it develops that the girl has really fallen in love with her new husband, that she is not a con artist but just another victim, we might expect, in another movie, all sorts of blame and analysis. A director not sure of this material could have talked it away. But

Malick brings a solemnity to his revelations, as the farmer gradually discovers the deception, as the laborer discovers his loss, as the little sister loses what little childhood she had.

Days of Heaven is a unique achievement—I can't think of another film anything like it. It's serious, yes, very solemn, but not depressing. More than anything else, it wants to re-create its time and place, as if Malick believes the decisions of his characters (and maybe his very characters themselves) come out of the time and place, and are caused by them.

So many movies are jammed with people talking to each other all the time, people obsessed with the conviction they're saying something. The people of *Days of Heaven* are so overwhelmed by the sheer force of nature, by the weight of the land, the bounty of the harvest, the casual distraction of fire and plague, the sharp, involuntary impulses of their passions, that they hardly know what to say. When you look at it that way, who does?

The Dead Zone ★ ★ ★ ½
R, 103 m., 1983

Christopher Walken (Johnny), Brooke Adams (Sarah), Herbert Lom (Dr. Weizak), Tom Skerritt (Sheriff), Martin Sheen (Candidate). Directed by David Cronenberg and produced by Debra Hill. Screenplay by Jeffrey Boam.

The Dead Zone does what only a good supernatural thriller can do: It makes us forget it is supernatural. Like *Rosemary's Baby* and *The Exorcist,* it tells its story so strongly through the lives of sympathetic, believable people that we not only forgive the gimmicks, we accept them. There is pathos in what happens to the Christopher Walken character in this movie and that pathos would never be felt if we didn't buy the movie's premise.

Walken plays a high school teacher whose life is happy (he's in love with Brooke Adams), until the night an accident puts him into a coma for five years. When he "returns," he has an extrasensory gift. He can touch people's hands and "know" what will happen to them. His first discovery is that he can foresee the future. His second is that he can change it. By seeing what "will" happen and trying to prevent it, he can bring about a different future. Of course, then he's left with the problem of explaining how he knew something "would have" happened, to people who can clearly see that it did not. Instead of ignoring that problem as a lesser movie might have, *The Dead Zone* builds its whole premise on it.

The movie is based on a novel by Stephen King and was directed by David Cronenberg, the Canadian who started with low-budget shockers *(The Brood, It Came From Within)* and worked up to big budgets *(Scanners)*. It's a happy collaboration. No other King novel has been better filmed (certainly not the dreadful *Cujo*), and Cronenberg, who knows how to handle terror, also knows how to create three-dimensional, fascinating characters.

In that he gets a lot of help from Walken, whose performance in this movie in a semi-reputable genre is the equal of his work in *The Deer Hunter*. Walken does such a good job of portraying Johnny Smith, the man with the strange gift, that we forget this is science fiction or fantasy or whatever, and just accept it as this guy's story.

The movie is filled with good performances: Adams, as the woman who marries someone else during Johnny's coma, but has a clear-eyed, unsentimental love for him at a crucial moment; Tom Skeritt, as the local sheriff who wants to enlist this psychic to solve a chain of murders; Herbert Lom as a sympathetic doctor; and Martin Sheen as a conniving populist politician. They all work together to make a movie that could have been just another scary thriller, and turn it into a believable thriller—which, of course, is even scarier.

Death in Venice ★ ★ ½
PG, 127 m., 1971

Dirk Bogarde (Aschenbach), Bjorn Andresen (Tadzio), Silvana Mangano (The Mother), Romolo Valli (Hotel Manager). Directed and produced by Luchino Visconti. Screenplay by Visconti and Nicola Badalucco.

I think the thing that disappoints me most about Luchino Visconti's *Death in Venice* is its lack of ambiguity. Visconti has chosen to abandon the subtleties of the Thomas Mann novel and present us with a straightforward story of homosexual love, and although

that's his privilege, I think he has missed the greatness of Mann's work somewhere along the way. In the novel, Count Aschenbach goes to Venice at a certain season in his life, driven by a compulsion he does not fully understand and confronted by strange presences who somehow seem to be mocking or tempting him. Once settled in his grand hotel on the Lido, he becomes aware of a beautiful boy who is also visiting there with his family from Poland. His feelings toward this boy are terribly complicated, and to interpret them as a simple homosexual attraction is vulgar and simplistic. The boy represents, above all, an ideal of perfect physical beauty apart from sexuality; the irony is that this beauty stirs emotions in a man who (in the novel) has insisted on occupying the world of the intellect. The boy's youth and naturalness become a reproach to the older man's vanity and creative sterility.

Visconti undermines this contrast between beauty and the intellect by changing the Aschenbach character from a writer to a composer. He made the change, reportedly, because he decided that Mann had "really" based his character on Gustav Mahler, but so what? There are flashbacks where Aschenbach argues that beauty resides in the intellect, and a friend declares that beauty is a quality naturally possessed by beautiful things. Aschenbach's position could be held by a philosopher and scholar, but not (I imagine) by the composer of the romantic Mahler symphonies that are constantly present on the sound track.

Visconti also misses, or avoids, the subtlety of the novel's development of the relationship between the two characters. In the Mann version, the man can never really know what the boy thinks of him; they do not speak, and if the boy favors him sometimes with a look or a smile, he favors many others as well, because that is his nature. It is entirely possible, the way Mann tells the story, that the boy is totally unaware of any homosexual implication—and the man, indeed, may also be in love with an ideal rather than a person. No such possibility exists in the heavy-handed Visconti retelling. The boy's function in the film, which he performs at least two dozen times, is to self-consciously pose in front of the man, turn slowly, smile sweetly, and turn languorously away. This is almost literally the only physical characteristic the boy has in the movie; and Visconti lays on the turns, looks, and smiles with such a heavy hand that the boy could almost be accused of hustling.

By choosing to limit his story to this level, Visconti loses the philosophical content of the Thomas Mann work, and no amount of heavy-handed flashbacks can restore it. We see Aschenbach in discussions with colleagues, with his wife and child, and then at the child's funeral; we see him seemingly impotent in a bordello, and, unforgivably, Visconti even throws in a concert at which Aschenbach is booed, then comforted by his wife. Scenes in which the genius is assured that (someday!) his genius will be recognized went out, I thought, with *The Eddy Duchin Story.*

Visconti fails, then, to develop characters and relationships that matter. The failure is fatal to the movie's success; but the physical beauty of the film itself is overwhelming. The world of the Lido of sixty years ago has been re-created in painstaking detail. The fashions, the entertainments, the table settings reveal Visconti's compulsion for accuracy. The photography is almost the first I have seen that is fully worthy of the beauty of Venice; the pink-and-gray city rises from waters of a glasslike smoothness, so that the water and the quality of light itself seem to suggest the presence of the plague-bearing sirocco wind. The wind brings both plague and beauty, which is its function in the Mann novel, and Visconti's mastery of visual style almost succeeds in creating the very ideas and feelings that his heavy-handed narrative entirely misses.

Death Wish ★ ★ ★
R, 94 m., 1974

Charles Bronson (Paul Kersey), Hope Lange (Joanna Kersey), Vincent Gardenia (Frank Ochoa), Steve Keats (Jack Toby), William Redfield (Sam Kreutzer), Stuart Margolin (Ames), Jack Wallace (Policeman). Directed by Michael Winner and produced by Dino de Laurentis. Screenplay by Wendell Mayes.

Death Wish is a quasifascist advertisement for urban vigilantes, done up as a slick and exciting action movie; we like it even while we're turned off by the message. It gives us Charles Bronson in a role that starts out by being somewhat out of character: He plays a liberal, an architect, a former conscientious objector. But he turns into the familiar Bronson man of action after his wife is murdered and his daughter reduced to catatonia by muggers.

His immediate reaction is one of simple grief. But then, seeking a change of scenery, he visits his firm's Arizona office. And there he meets an architect with two deep convictions: a love for the land and a love of guns. He takes Bronson to his gun club, watches him squeeze off a few perfect practice rounds and slips a present into his suitcase when he heads back to New York. It's a .32-caliber revolver.

Alone in his apartment, Bronson examines snapshots from his recent Hawaiian vacation with his wife. Then he examines the gun. He goes out into the night, is attacked by a mugger and shoots him dead. Then he goes home and throws up. But the taste for vengeance, once acquired, has a fascination of its own. And the last half of *Death Wish* is essentially a series of cat-and-mouse games, in which Bronson poses as a middle-aged citizen with a bag of groceries and then murders his attackers.

They are, by the way, everywhere. Director Michael Winner gives us a New York in the grip of a reign of terror; this doesn't look like 1974, but like one of those bloody future cities in science fiction novels about anarchy in the twenty-first century. Literally every shadow holds a mugger; every subway train harbors a killer; the park is a breeding ground for crime. Urban paranoia is one thing, but *Death Wish* is another. If there were really that many muggers in New York, Bronson could hardly have survived long enough to father a daughter, let alone grieve her.

The movie has an eerie kind of fascination, even though its message is scary. Bronson and Winner have worked together on several films, and they've perfected the Bronson persona. He's a steely instrument of violence, with few words and fewer emotions. In *Death Wish* we get just about the definitive Bronson; rarely has a leading role contained fewer words or more violence.

And Winner directs with a cool precision.

He's one of the most efficient directors of action and violence. His muggings and their surprise endings have a sort of inevitable rhythm to them; we're set up for each one almost like the gunfights in Westerns. There's never any question of injustice, because the crimes are attempted right there before our eyes. And then Bronson becomes judge and jury—and executioner.

That's what's scary about the film. It's propaganda for private gun ownership and a call to vigilante justice. Even the cops seem to see it that way; Bronson becomes a folk hero as the New York Vigilante, and the mugging rate drops fifty percent. So the police want to catch Bronson, not to prosecute him for murder, but to offer him a deal: Get out of town, stay out of town, and we'll forget this. Bronson accepts the deal, and in the movie's last scene we see him taking an imaginary bead on a couple of goons in Chicago.

Death Wish II   no stars
R, 89 m., 1982

Charles Bronson (Paul Kersey), Jill Ireland (Geri Nichols), Vincent Gardenia (Frank Ochoa), Anthony Frannciosa (Commissioner), Robert F. Lyons (Fred). Directed by Michael Winner and produced by Menachem Golan and Yoram Globus. Screenplay by David Engleback.

You will have noticed that I've given a "no stars" rating for *Death Wish II*, starring Charles Bronson as an urban vigilante. A word of explanation. In my movie rating system, the most a movie can get is four stars *(My Dinner With André)* and the least is ordinarily half a star (even *The Beast Within* got a whole star). I award "no stars" only to movies that are artistically inept and morally repugnant. So *Death Wish II* joins such unsavory company as *Penitentiary II* and *I Spit on Your Grave*. And that, in a way, is a shame. I have a certain admiration for the screen presence of Charles Bronson. In his good roles, he can be lean, quiet, and efficient. He often co-stars with his wife, Jill Ireland, as he does in this movie, and she is a pleasant and capable actress. They were charming together in a little-seen movie named *From Noon to Three*.

This time, however, Bronson and Ireland

and everyone else involved with *Death Wish II* create a great disappointment. Although the original *Death Wish* (1974) had its detractors, it was an effective movie that spoke directly to the law-and-order mentality of the Nixon-Ford era. It was directed with a nice slick polish by Michael Winner, and, on its own terms, it worked. *Death Wish II* is a disaster by comparison. It has the same director, Winner, but he directs the dialogue scenes as if the actors' shoes were nailed to the floor. It has two of the same stars—Bronson and New York cop Vincent Gardenia—but they seem shell-shocked by weariness in this film. It has the same plot (Bronson's loved ones are attacked, and he goes out into the streets to murder muggers). But while the first film convinced me of Bronson's need for vengeance, this one is just a series of dumb killings.

You will remember that *Death Wish* opened with home invaders killing Bronson's wife and raping his daughter. After Bronson used himself as bait to trap and kill nine New York City muggers, he became a folk hero. Gardenia, the cop, found out who he was, but decided not to arrest him. Bronson left town, and in this film, he's in Los Angeles. The film opens with his daughter being killed, and then Bronson hits the streets again. Ireland plays the woman he loves, and who suspects his guilty secret.

What's most shocking about *Death Wish II* is the lack of artistry and skill in the filmmaking. The movie is underwritten and desperately underplotted, so that its witless action scenes alternate with lobotomized dialogue passages. The movie doesn't contain an ounce of life. It slinks onto the screen and squirms for a while, and is over.

Death Wish 3 ★
R, 100 m., 1985

Charles Bronson (Paul Kersey), Ed Lauter (Captain Striker), Gavan O'Herlihy (Fraker), Martin Balsam (Bennett), Kirk Taylor (Giggler), Deborah Raffin (Kathryn). Directed by Michael Winner and produced by Menahem Golan and Yoram Globus. Screenplay by Michael Edmonds.

Death Wish 3 is a marginally better movie than the second part of this series; enough better to earn a one-star rating, instead of none. The action, direction, and special effects are all better than the last time around, which isn't saying much, since *Death Wish II* was so ineptly directed and edited that it was an insult even to audiences that were *looking* for a bad movie.

The plot is as before. Charles Bronson plays Paul Kersey, who was an architect in the original 1974 film, but has now apparently moved into a new career, as a professional vigilante. After knocking off several muggers in Kansas City and a few thieves in Chicago, he is back in New York at the beginning of this film, just in time to find an old friend dying after a vicious beating.

Kersey is arrested for the crime, but allowed back on the streets by the police captain (Ed Lauter), who offers a deal: Kersey can murder all the creeps he wants, if he keeps the cops informed. Kersey does not agree to this deal, but Lauter does not seem to notice. Indeed, by the end of the film, the two of them are stalking the mean streets side-by-side, like killers in the old West.

Bronson moves into a tenement building which seems to be in the middle of a vast burned-out wasteland, but which is still occupied by terrified old people. Among the tenants are an old watch repairman (Martin Balsam), who keeps a couple of machine guns in his closet, and an elderly Jewish couple who live on the first floor and make stuffed cabbage rolls while the creeps jump in through the window and toss their TV set outside. It is a little amazing that they still have a TV set when this movie opens, since the neighborhood has been under siege for weeks.

The neighborhood is ruled by a gang headed by Fraker (Gavan O'Herlihy), who wears a reverse Mohawk: He keeps his hair on the sides, but shaves down the middle, to make room for a gang symbol in warpaint. O'Herlihy looks a little like Richard Widmark, and is quite satisfactory as a snarling, sadistic creep. He is also, of course, white. One of the hypocrisies practiced by the *Death Wish* movies is that they pretend to ignore racial tension in big cities. In their horrible new world, all of the gangs are integrated, so that the movies can't be called racist. I guess it's supposed to be heartwarming to see whites, blacks, and Latinos work-

ing side-by-side to rape, pillage, and murder.

Not quite so much equality applies to the victims, however. All of the good speaking roles go to white victims (especially Balsam). Two Latinos get to be minor supporting players (the wife is raped and murdered, the husband gets to sob and pound his fist on the table). The black victims are represented by an old lady who gets her purse snatched.

If it seems strange for me to be making a racial head-count like this, reflect that the filmmakers no doubt assigned races to their characters with equal cynicism. Since there is not a single character in this movie who *has* to belong to any particular race, *Death Wish 3* could have had Bronson protecting black citizens against black gang violence. That would reflect the reality of most big cities, but it would not, of course, have been as commercial as the integrated violence we get instead.

My only other observation has to be about Bronson himself. He looks very tired in this movie. In interviews, he has expressed his unhappiness with it. Despite the fact that he's the central character, he doesn't seem eager to leap in and take charge. And he probably says fewer words in *Death Wish 3* than any other major leading character since the introduction of sound. My guess is that he utters less than one hundred words in the whole movie. My hunch is he would have liked that number to be closer to zero.

Deathtrap ★ ★ ★
R, 116 m., 1982

Michael Caine (Sidney Bruhl), Christopher Reeve (Clifford Anderson), Dyan Cannon (Myra Bruhl), Irene Worth (Psychic). Directed by Sidney Lumet, produced by Burtt Harrisand. Screenplay by Jay Presson Allen.

Deathtrap is a wonderful windup fiction machine with a few modest ambitions: It wants to mislead us at every turn, confound all our expectations, and provide at least one moment when we levitate from our seats and come down screaming. It succeeds, more or less. It's a thriller that depends on all sorts of surprises for its effects, and you may continue reading in the confidence that I'll reveal none of them.

That doesn't leave me much to write about, however. Let's see. I can tell you something about how the movie begins. Michael Caine plays a very successful Broadway playwright whose latest mystery is a total flop. We see him at the outset, standing at the back of the house, a gloomy witness to a disastrous opening night. (It's a Broadway in-joke that the play he's watching is being performed on the stage set of *Deathtrap*.) Caine gets drunk and goes home to his farmhouse in Connecticut and sinks into despair. There is perhaps, however, some small shred of hope. In the mail the next day Caine receives a manuscript from a former student (Christopher Reeve). It is a new thriller, and Caine sees at once that it's a masterpiece. It could run for years and earn millions of dollars. As he talks with his wife (Dyan Cannon) about it, he slowly develops the idea that he could *steal* the play, kill Reeve, and produce the hit himself.

A plausible plan? Perhaps. Caine and Cannon invite Reeve to come for a visit to the country. They grill him, subtly, and discover that absolutely no one else knows he has written the play. The stage is set for murder, betrayal, and at least an hour and a half of surprises. The tables are turned so many times in this movie that you would think they were on wheels.

Anyway, that's all I'll say about the plot. It is fair to observe, however, that *Deathtrap* is a comic study of ancient and honorable human defects, including greed, envy, lust, pride, avarice, sloth, and falsehood. Interest in the movie depends on its surprises, but its delight grows basically out of the human characteristics of its performers. They do a very good job. Thrillers like this don't always bother to pay attention to the human nature of their characters (for example, the Agatha Christie omnibus whodunits, with their cardboard suspects). *Deathtrap*, however, provides a fascinating, quirky character in Sydney Bruhl, played by Caine, and two strong supporting performances in his goofy, screaming wife (Cannon, looking great) and his talented, devious student (Reeve, who has a light, handsome comic touch not a million miles removed from Cary Grant's). The dialogue is witty without being Neil Simonized. The sets are so good they're almost distracting (a windmill appears to operate in close association with the Bruhls' bed). The only distraction is a strange character played by Irene Worth—a next-door neighbor who's a busybody, snooping psychic who sniffs down false leads. We don't know why she's even in the play, until it's much too late.

Deathtrap is not a great film and will not live forever, but if you're an aficionado of whodunits and haven't seen this one, it'll be a treat. It's more fiendishly complicated than, for example, Caine's similar outing in *Sleuth*. It plays absolutely fair, more or less, and yet fools us every time, more or less. And perhaps its greatest gift is the sight of three lighthearted comic actors having a good time chewing on the dialogue, the scenery, and each other.

The Deer Hunter ★ ★ ★ ★
R, 183 m., 1979

Robert De Niro (Michael), John Cazale (Stan), John Savage (Steven), Christopher Walken (Nick), Meryl Streep (Linda), George Dzundza (John), Chuck Aspegren (Axel). Directed by Michael Cimino and produced by Barry Spikings, Michael Deeley, Cimino, and John Peverall. Screenplay by Deric Washburn.

Michael Cimino's *The Deer Hunter* is a three-hour movie in three major movements. It is a progression from a wedding to a funeral. It is the story of a group of friends. It is the record of how the war in Vietnam entered several lives and altered them terribly forever. It is not an anti-war film. It is not a pro-war film. It is one of the most emotionally shattering films ever made.

It begins with men at work, at the furnaces of the steel mills in a town somewhere in Ohio or Pennsylvania. The klaxon sounds, the shift is over, the men go down the road to a saloon for a beer. They sing "I Love You Bay-bee" along with the jukebox. It is still morning on the last day of their lives that will belong to them before Vietnam.

The movie takes its time with these opening scenes, with the steel mill and the saloon and especially with the wedding and the party in the American Legion Hall. It's important not simply that we come to know the characters, but that we feel absorbed into their lives, that the wedding rituals and rhythms feel like more than just ethnic details. They do.

The opening moment is lingered over; it's like the wedding celebration in *The Godfather*, but celebrated by hard-working people who have come to eat, dance, and drink a lot and wish luck to the newlyweds and to say good-bye to the three young men who have enlisted in the army. The party goes on long enough for everyone to get drunk who is ever going to, and then the newlyweds drive off and the rest of the friends go up into the mountains to shoot some deer. There is some Hemingwayesque talk about what it means to shoot deer: We are still at a point where shooting something is supposed to mean something.

Then Vietnam occupies the screen, suddenly, with a wall of noise, and the second movement of the film is about the experiences that three of the friends (Robert De Niro, John Savage, and Christopher Walken) have there. At the film's center comes one of the most horrifying sequences ever created in fiction, as the three are taken prisoner and forced to play Russian roulette while their captors gamble on who will, or will not, blow out his brains.

The game of Russian roulette becomes the organizing symbol of the film: Anything you can believe about the game, about its deliberately random violence, about how it touches the sanity of men forced to play it, will apply to the war as a whole. It is a brilliant symbol because, in the context of this story, it makes any ideological statement about the war superfluous.

The De Niro character is the one who somehow finds the strength to keep going and to keep Savage and Walken going. He survives the prison camp and helps the others. Then, finally home from Vietnam, he is surrounded by a silence we can never quite penetrate. He is touched vaguely by desire for the girl that more than one of them left behind, but does not act decisively. He is a "hero," greeted shyly, awkwardly, by the hometown people.

He delays for a long time going to the VA hospital to visit Savage, who has lost his legs. While he is there he learns that Walken is still in Vietnam. He had promised Walken—on a drunken moonlit night under a basketball hoop on a playlot, the night of the wedding—

that he would never leave him in Vietnam. They were both thinking, romantically and naively, of the deaths of heroes, but now De Niro goes back in an altogether different context to retrieve the living Walken. The promise was adolescent stuff, but there is no adolescence left when De Niro finds Walken still in Saigon, playing Russian roulette professionally.

At about this point in a review it is customary to praise or criticize those parts of a film that seem deserving: the actors, the photography, the director's handling of the material. It should be said, I suppose, that *The Deer Hunter* is far from flawless, that there are moments when its characters do not behave convincingly, such as implausible details involving Walken's stay and fate in Vietnam, and unnecessary ambiguities in the De Niro character. It can also be said that the film contains greatly moving performances, and that it is the most impressing blending of "box office" and "art" in American movies since *Bonnie and Clyde*, *The Godfather*, and *Nashville*. All of those kinds of observations will become irrelevant as you experience the film: It gathers you up, it takes you along, it doesn't let up.

The Deer Hunter is said to be about many subjects: About male bonding, about mindless patriotism, about the dehumanizing effects of war, about Nixon's "silent majority." It is about any of those things that you choose, if you choose, but more than anything else it is a heartbreakingly effective fictional machine that evokes the agony of the Vietnam time.

If it is not overtly "anti-war," why should it be? What *The Deer Hunter* insists is that we not *forget* the war. It ends on a curious note: The singing of "God Bless America." I won't tell you how it arrives at that particular moment (the unfolding of the final passages should occur to you as events in life) but I do want to observe that the lyrics of "God Bless America" have never before seemed to me to contain such an infinity of possible meanings, some tragic, some unspeakably sad, some few still defiantly hopeful.

The Delta Force ★ ★ ★
R, 129 m., 1985

Chuck Norris (Major McCoy), Lee Marvin (Colonel Alexander), Robert Forster (Abdul), Martin Balsam (Ben Kaplan), Joey Bishop (Harry Goldman), Lainie Kazan (Sylvia Goldman), George Kennedy (Father O'Malley) Hanna Schygulla (Ingrid), Bo Svenson (Captain). Directed by Menahem Golan and produced by Golan and Yoram Globus. Screenplay by James Bruner and Golan.

Some of the opening moments of *The Delta Force* had me ready to laugh. Here was a movie about an airplane hijacking, and who was on the passenger list? Why, George Kennedy, of course—fresh from four *Airport* movies and *Earthquake*—and Shelley Winters, going on her first vacation since the *Poseidon* sank. I thought this was going to be another hilarious disaster movie, but I was wrong. *The Delta Force* settles down into a well-made action film that tantalizes us with its parallels to real life.

The movie was inspired by the June 1985 hijacking of the TWA airplane and the hostage crisis after the passengers were held captive in Beirut. (In the movie, the airline is renamed ATW—real subtle.) Many of the moments in the film are drawn directly from life, as when an American serviceman is beaten to death by terrorists, and his body is dumped on the runway, or when a terrorist holds a gun to the head of the pilot during a press conference.

The docudrama approach gives an eerie conviction to the movie, although later, after Chuck Norris and Lee Marvin arrive on the scene, there's not much we would mistake for reality. The movie caters directly to our national revenge fantasies; in *The Delta Force*, the hijacking ends the way we might have wanted it to.

The story establishes the plane and its passengers, and then intercuts the hijacking with the movements of the Delta Force, a crack U.S. commando unit that specializes in antiterrorist missions. Delta is led by grizzled old Lee Marvin, and its best fighter is a hot dog played by Chuck Norris, who once again this time is depicted as a man who yearns only for retirement, but cannot resist the call to action, and arrives at the last moment in his trusty pickup truck. (If I were Chuck Norris's agent, I'd insist that his next movie include a new way of introducing him into the plot.)

There are a couple of hazards here that the movie has to face. The action inside the airplane has a tendency to degenerate into a retread of the old *Airport* movies, but director Menahem Golan wisely has his cast keep their acting fairly low-key. And the action involving Norris has a tendency to resemble his activities in *Missing in Action* and *Invasion USA*. Golan does nothing to fight this tendency—indeed, he relishes it, in scenes like the one where Norris drives his rocket-firing motorcycle right through the window of a terrorist hideout, and socks the bad guy on the jaw. This is the second movie in a row where Norris has possessed X-ray vision; in *Invasion USA* he drove his pickup into a department store to stop a terrorist attack. How does he know what's on the other side of the barriers he crashes through?

It's a funny thing about action movies. When they don't work, we have a lot of fun picking holes in them, like the fallacy of the hero's X-ray vision. When they do work, though, we forgive them their inconsistencies. *The Delta Force* works. It is taut and exciting and well-tuned to the personalities of Marvin and Norris, who work together here like a couple of laconic veterans of lots of tough jobs.

The movie also has the one other attribute that any good thriller needs: A first-rate performance by the actor playing the villain. As Abdul, the chief terrorist, an American actor named Robert Forster gives a frightening, good performance, intense and uncompromising. He makes the threat real, and keeps *The Delta Force* from becoming just an action comic book.

Desperately Seeking Susan ★ ★ ★
PG-13, 103 m., 1985

Rosanna Arquette (Roberta), Madonna (Susan), Aidan Quinn (Dez), Mark Blum (Gary), Robert Joy (Jim), Laurie Metcalf (Leslie). Directed by Susan Seidelman and produced by Sarah Pillsbury and Midge Sanford. Screenplay by Leora Barish.

Desperately Seeking Susan is a movie that begins with those three words, in a classified ad. A time and place are suggested where Susan can rendezvous with the person who is desperately seeking her. A bored housewife (Rosanna Arquette) sees the ad and becomes consumed with curiosity. Who is Susan and who is seeking her, and why? So Arquette turns up at the rendezvous, sees Susan (Madonna), and inadvertently becomes so involved in her world that for a while she even *becomes* Susan.

This sounds complicated, but, believe me, it's nothing compared to the complexities of this movie. *Desperately Seeking Susan* is a screwball comedy based on several cases of mistaken identity. Susan, for example, is a punk drifter who is in a hotel room with a mobster the first time we see her. Shortly after, the mobster is killed and the mob hit man comes back looking for Susan, who may have been a witness. But meanwhile, Susan has sold the jacket that is her trademark, and the housewife has bought it, and then the housewife has banged her head and become a temporary amnesia victim, and there are people who see her jacket and think she's Susan.

But enough of the plot. I wouldn't even dream of trying to explain how Arquette ends up being sawed in half by a nightclub magician. The plot isn't the point, anyway; once you realize the movie is going to be a series of double-reverses, you relax and let them happen. The plot is so unpredictable that, in a way, it's predictable; that makes it the weakest part of the movie.

What I liked in *Desperately Seeking Susan* was the cheerful way it hopped around New York, introducing us to unforgettable characters, played by good actors. For example, Aidan Quinn plays a guy who thinks Arquette is Susan, his best friend's girl. He lets her spend the night, and inadvertently feeds her amnesia by suggesting that she *is* Susan. Laurie Metcalf plays Arquette's yuppie sister-in-law. Robert Joy plays Susan's desperately seeking lover. Peter Maloney is the broken-down magician. New York underground characters such as Richard Hell, Anne Carlisle, and Rockets Red Glare also surface briefly. The director is Susan Seidelman, whose previous film, *Smithereens*, was a similar excursion through the uncharted depths of New York.

Desperately Seeking Susan does not move

with the self-confidence that its complicated plot requires. But it has its moments, and many of them involve the different kinds of special appeal that Arquette and Madonna are able to generate. They are very particular individuals, and in a dizzying plot they somehow succeed in creating specific, interesting characters.

Diamonds Are Forever ★ ★ ★
PG, 119 m., 1971

Sean Connery (James Bond), Jill St. John (Tiffany Case), Charles Gray (Blofeld), Lana Wood (Plenty O'Toole), Jimmy Dean (Willard Whyte), Bruce Cabot (Saxby), Bernard Lee (M), Desmond Llewelyn (Q). Directed by Guy Hamilton and produced by Albert R. Broccoli and Harry Saltzman.

The cultists like the early James Bond movies best, but I dunno. They may have been more tightly directed films, but they didn't understand the Bond mythos as fully as *Goldfinger* and *Diamonds Are Forever*. We see different movies for different reasons, and *Diamonds Are Forever* is great at doing the things we see a James Bond movie for.

Not the least of these is the presence of Sean Connery, who was born to the role: dry, unflappable (even while trapped in a coffin at a crematorium), with a mouth that does as many kinds of sly grins as there are lascivious possibilities in the universe. There's something about his detachment from danger that props up the whole Bond apparatus, insulating it from the total ridiculousness only an inch away.

In *Diamonds Are Forever*, for example, Bond finds himself driving a moon buggy (antennae wildly revolving and robot arms flapping) while being chased across a desert—never mind why. The buggy looks comical, but Connery does not; he is completely at home, as we know by now, with every form of transportation. Later, after outsmarting five Las Vegas squad cars in a lovely chase scene, he nonchalantly flips his Mustang up on two wheels to elude the sixth. But not a sign of a smile. There is an exhiliration in the way he does it, even more than in the stunt itself.

The plot of *Diamonds Are Forever* is as complicated as possible. That's necessary in order to have somebody left after nine dozen bad guys have been killed. It has been claimed that the plot is too complicated to describe, but I think I could if I wanted to. I can't imagine why anyone would want to, though. The point in a Bond adventure is the moment, the surface, what's happening now. The less time wasted on plot, the better.

Diary of a Mad Housewife ★ ★ ★
R, 95 m., 1970

Carrie Snodgress (Tina Balser), Richard Benjamin (Jonathan Balser), Frank Langella (George). Directed and produced by Frank Perry. Screenplay by Eleanor Perry.

Frank Perry's *Diary of a Mad Housewife* is about a long-suffering young woman who has somehow gotten herself married to the most supercilious dope in Manhattan. He's egotistical, cruel, insecure, immature, and bitchy. He sides with "his" children against his wife. He considers her a household drudge, good for housework during the day, and, maybe, a "little roll in de hay" at night. He humiliates her in public, and humiliates himself, too, by his shameless social-climbing. Does she hate him? Not exactly.

She's a masochistic type who sees her husband as, somehow, her fate in life. She enjoys martyrdom, I guess; I can't imagine any other reason why she'd put up with this monster she's married to. And that's at the base of our initial irritation with the film; she stays with this guy we can't stand, and so we have trouble admiring her. We even begin to doubt her sanity, until she falls into a love affair with a writer. And then *he* turns out to be such an egotistical, selfish, cruel type that we just about give up on her. She has what's known, I believe, as self-destructive tendencies. Not that she'd ever try suicide; that'd be too easy, and end the delight of suffering. What makes the movie work, however, is that it's played entirely from the housewife's point of view, and that the housewife is played brilliantly by Carrie Snodgress. We're irritated by the things the character puts up with, but Miss Snodgress is beautifully good at putting up with them.

Still, when you've finished watching this movie you start getting mad at Richard Benjamin. He overplays his character so much that he nearly destroys the role; nobody, but nobody, is that supercilious. Near the begin-

ning of the movie there's a scene when the whole family is in an elevator, and Benjamin gives instructions to his wife about packing a suitcase. He describes everything in highly specific brand names, and with such precision that the dialogue passes beyond reality and becomes satire. You can see it as a caption under a *New Yorker* cartoon.

But then, then . . . you start thinking about the title and the point of view of the movie, and you realize this is indeed a diary; that we're getting the housewife's version of the story. So of course she seems noble and long-suffering, and of course he's a witless bastard—because that's the way she sees it. And of course his dialogue is extreme and hers isn't, because in her version of the story, she's sane, and he's not.

Dim Sum ★ ★ ★
PG, 88 m., 1985 ✔

Laureen Chew (Geraldine Tam), Kim Chew (Mrs. Tam), Victor Wong (Uncle Tam), Ida F.O. Chung (Auntie Mary), Cora Miao (Julia), John Nishio (Richard). Directed by Wayne Wang and produced by Tom Sternberg, Wang, and Danny Yung. Screenplay by Terrel Seltzer.

Director Wayne Wang says his favorite image in *Dim Sum* is the sight of the shoes left outside the living room door in the Tam household in San Francisco's Chinatown. They are Western shoes, taken off as the characters enter a home that is still run according to Chinese values by old Mrs. Tam, a sweet widow with a strong but quietly concealed will. After the success of *Chan Is Missing*, his first slice-of-life about Chinese-Americans, Wang was looking for another story, and when he saw some shoes left outside a Chinese home, he knew he had his viewpoint, and only had to create his characters.

He has created some unforgettable ones, including Mrs. Tam (Kim Chew), a sixtyish woman whose husband is dead and whose children have left home, all except for the youngest daughter; Geraldine Tam (Laureen Chew), the daughter, who says she wants to get married but feels she should stay with her mother, and Uncle Tam (Victor Wong), a jolly, worldly bartender who would marry Mrs. Tam if Geraldine would only get out of the way.

These three characters dance a subtle little emotional ballet during the film, as we gradually become aware of their true motives. Mrs. Tam is given to sadly shaking her head and bemoaning the fact that her daughter is thirty and still single, but there are clues that she enjoys the fact that Geraldine has stayed at home with her. That way, she will not have to deal with Uncle Tam, who, for that matter, may only be paying lip service to his desire to marry her. Meanwhile, Geraldine has a boyfriend in Los Angeles who has been waiting patiently to marry her, and perhaps Geraldine uses her mother as an excuse to avoid the idea of marriage.

What is remarkable is the way Wang deals with this complex set of emotions, in a movie that is essentially a comedy. Some of the scenes in *Dim Sum* are as quietly funny as anything I've seen, especially Mrs. Tam's birthday party, a long conversation she has over the back fence with a neighbor, and the way Uncle Tam effortlessly mixes his Chinese wisdom with the lessons he has learned as a bartender.

The movie is not heavily plotted, and that's good; a heavy hand would spoil this fragile material. Wang's camera enters quietly and observes as his characters lead their lives, trying to find a compromise between too much loneliness and too much risk. At the end, everyone is more or less happy, and more or less sad, and in this movie that is satisfactory.

Note: Although this is no doubt not what Wang had in mind, I couldn't help thinking, as I watched Dim Sum, *that the movie's characters and situations could be effortlessly spun off into a wonderful TV sitcom.*

Diner ★ ★ ★ ½
R, 110 m., 1982

Steve Guttenberg (Eddie), Daniel Stern (Shrevie), Mickey Rourke (Boogie), Kevin Bacon (Fenwick), Timothy Daly (Billy), Ellen Barkin (Beth). Directed by Barry Levinson and produced by Jerry Weintraub. Screenplay by Levinson.

Women are not strange, not threatening, not mysterious, unless you happen to be a man. Young men in particular seem to regard women with a combination of admiration, desire, and dread that is quite out of their control. This was especially true in the late 1950s, a decade during which the Playmate of the Month was more alien than E.T. is today. Women were such a puzzling phenomenon to 1950s young men that, after a date, the best way for males to restore their equilibrium was to regroup with the guys for the therapeutic consumption of cheeseburgers, greasy fries, black coffee, chocolate malteds, Lucky Strikes, and loud arguments about football teams and pop singers. *Diner* is a story about several such young men, who live in Baltimore. They share one awkward problem: They are growing up, painfully and awkwardly, at an age when they are supposed to have already grown up. Adolescence lasts longer for some people than society quite imagines. These guys are best friends for this summer, although in the fall they will go separate ways, to schools and jobs and even marriage, and it's possible they will never be this close again. They cling to one another for security, because out there in the real world, responsibility lurks, and responsibility is spelled *woman*. They have plans, but their plans are not as real as their dreams.

Diner is structured a lot like *American Graffiti* and Fellini's *I Vitelloni*. It's episodic, as the young men venture out for romantic and sexual adventures, practical jokes, drunken Friday evenings, and long mornings of hangovers and doubt. Some of the movie's situations seem quite implausible, but they all fit within the overall theme of fear of women. One bizarre sequence, for example, involves a young man who insists that his fiancée pass a tough quiz about pro football before he'll agree to marry her. He's serious: If she flunks, the wedding is off. This situation doesn't seem possible to me, but it's right symbolically, since what the man is really looking for in a wife is one of the guys—a woman who will agree to become an imitation man.

Another character, already married, is much more realistic. He has absolutely no communication with his wife and no way to develop any, since he sees her only as a "wife" and not as a friend, a companion, or even a fellow human being. Her great failure is an inability to regard his life with the proper reverence; when she gets his record collection out of alphabetical order, it's grounds for a fight. He's flabbergasted that she hasn't memorized the flip sides of all the Top 40 hits of 1958, but he never even suspects that he doesn't know what's inside her mind.

Diner is often a very funny movie, although I laughed most freely not at the sexual pranks but at the movie's accurate ear, as it reproduced dialogue with great comic accuracy. If the movie has a weakness, however, it's that it limits itself to the faithful reproduction of the speech, clothing, cars, and mores of the late 1950s, and never quite stretches to include the humanity of the characters. For all that I recognized and sympathized with these young men and their martyred wives, girlfriends, and sex symbols, I never quite believed that they were three-dimensional. It is, of course, a disturbing possibly that, to the degree these young men denied full personhood to women, they didn't *have* three-dimensional personalities.

Dirty Harry ★ ★ ★
R, 103 m., 1971

Clint Eastwood (Harry), Harry Guardino (Bressler), Reni Santoni (Chico), Andy Robinson (Killer), John Vernon (Mayor). Directed and produced by Don Siegel. Screenplay by Harry Julian Fink.

There is a book named *From Caligari to Hitler* that tries to penetrate the German national subconscious by analyzing German films between 1919 and the rise of the Nazis. I have my doubts about the critical approach (it gets cause and effect backwards), but if anybody is writing a book about the rise of fascism in America, they ought to have a look at *Dirty Harry.* The film is directed by Don Siegel, and like *Coogan's Bluff* it considers the role of a cop in society with lots of dynamite action and enough wry cynicism to keep the blood from getting too thick. It is photographed all over San Francisco, and is filled with good character actors.

The presence of Eastwood in an action role is enough to explain the movie's popularity, but when you see it you discover that the movie has a message with a vengeance. It is loosely based on 1970's headlines, and makes Eastwood a cop who is assigned to find a mysterious killer named Scorpio. The killer has kidnapped and killed various girls, he

has tried to extract $200,000 ransom from the city, and in the film's climax he hijacks a school bus. The gimmick is that Eastwood is so filled with hatred for Scorpio that he violates the poor fiend's civil rights. While attempting to find out where a kidnapped girl is, for example, Eastwood gets no less than four amendments wrong. And so the city has to set Scorpio free—even though they have a murder weapon and a confession.

Eastwood doesn't care; he says to hell with the Bill of Rights and stalks out of the district attorney's office. But when Scorpio hijacks the school bus, it is Eastwood again, who is asked to be bag man and carry the ransom. This time he refuses. He wants Scorpio on his own. We've already seen him twisting Scorpio's broken arm ("I have a right to a lawyer!" Scorpio shouts), and soon we will see him kill Scorpio in cold blood. Then, in a thoughtful final scene, Eastwood takes his police badge and throws it into a gravel pit.

It is possible to see the movie as just another extension of Eastwood's basic screen character: He is always the quiet one with the painfully bottled-up capacity for violence, the savage forced to follow the rules of society. This time, by breaking loose, he did what he was always about to do in his earlier films. If that is all, then *Dirty Harry* is a very good example of the cops-and-killers genre, and Siegel proves once again that he understands the Eastwood mystique.

But wait a minute. The movie clearly and unmistakably gives us a character who understands the Bill of Rights, understands his legal responsibility as a police officer, and nevertheless takes retribution into his own hands. Sure, Scorpio is portrayed as the most vicious, perverted, warped monster we can imagine—but that's part of the same stacked deck. The movie's moral position is fascist. No doubt about it.

I think films are more often a mirror of society than an agent of change, and that when we blame the movies for the evils around us we are getting things backward. *Dirty Harry* is very effective at the level of a thriller. At another level, it uses the most potent star presence in American movies—Clint Eastwood—to lay things on the line. If there aren't mentalities like Dirty Harry's at loose in the land, then the movie is irrelevant. If there are, we should not blame the bearer of the bad news.

Diva ★ ★ ★ ★
R, 123 m., 1981

Wilhelmenia Wiggins Fernandez (Cynthia,) Frédéric Andrei (Jules), Richard Bohringer (Gordorish), Thay An Luu (Alba), Jacques Fabbri (Saporta), Chantal Deruaz (Nadia). Directed by Jean-Jacques Beineix and produced by Irene Silberman. Screenplay by Beineix and Jean Van Hamme.

The opening shots inform us with authority that *Diva* is the work of a director with an enormous gift for creating visual images. We meet a young Parisian mailman. His job is to deliver special delivery letters on his motor scooter. His passion is opera, and, as *Diva* opens, he is secretly tape-recording a live performance by an American soprano. The camera sees this action in two ways. First, with camera movements that seem as lyrical as the operatic performance. Second, with almost surreptitious observations of the electronic eavesdropper at work. His face shows the intensity of a fanatic: He does not simply admire this woman, he adores her. There is a tear in his eye. The operatic performance takes on a greatness, in this scene, that is absolutely necessary if we're to share his passion. We do. And, doing so, we start to like this kid.

His name is Frédéric Andrei, an actor I do not remember having seen before. But he could be Antoine Doinel, the subject of *The 400 Blows* and several other autobiographical films by Francois Truffaut. He has the same loony idealism, coexisting with a certain hard-headed realism about Paris. He lives and works there, he knows the streets, and yet he never quite believes he could get into trouble. *Diva* is the story of the trouble he gets into. It is one of the best thrillers of recent years but, more than that, it is a brilliant film, a visual extravaganza that announces the considerable gifts of its young director, Jean-Jacques Beineix. He has made a film that is about many things, but I think the real subject of *Diva* is the director's joy in making it. The movie is filled with so many small character touches, so many perfectly observed intimacies, so many visual inventions—from the sly to the grand—that

the thriller plot is just a bonus. In a way, it doesn't really matter what this movie is about; Pauline Kael has compared Beineix to Orson Welles and, as Welles so often did, he has made a movie that is a feast to look at, regardless of its subject.

But to give the plot its due: *Diva* really gets under way when the young postman slips his tape into the saddlebag of his motor scooter. Two tape pirates from Hong Kong know that the tape is in his possession, and, since the American soprano has refused to ever allow any of her performances to be recorded, they want to steal the tape and use it to make a bootleg record. Meanwhile, in a totally unrelated development, a young prostitute tape-records accusations that the Paris chief of police is involved in an international white-slavery ring. The two cassette tapes get exchanged, and *Diva* is off to the races.

One of the movie's delights is the cast of characters it introduces. Andrei, who plays the hero, is a serious, plucky kid who's made his own accommodation with Paris. The diva herself, played by Wilhelmenia Wiggins Fernandez, comes into the postman's life after a most unexpected event (which I deliberately will not reveal, because the way in which it happens, and *what* happens, are enormously surprising). We meet others: A young Vietnamese girl who seems so blasé in the face of Paris that we wonder if anything truly excites her; a wealthy man-about-town who specializes in manipulating people for his own amusement; and a grab bag of criminals.

Most thrillers have a chase scene, and mostly they're predictable and boring. *Diva's* chase scene deserves ranking with the all-time classics, *Raiders of the Lost Ark, The French Connection,* and *Bullitt.* The kid rides his motorcycle down into the Paris Metro system, and the chase leads on and off trains and up and down escalators. It's pure exhilaration, and Beineix almost seems to be doing it just to show he knows how. A lot of the movie strikes that note: Here is a director taking audacious chances, doing wild and unpredictable things with his camera and actors, just to celebrate moviemaking.

There is a story behind his ecstasy. Jean-Jacques Beineix has been an assistant director for ten years. He has worked for directors ranging from Claude Berri to Jerry Lewis. But the job of an assistant director is not always romantic and challenging. Many days, he's a glorified traffic cop, shouting through a bullhorn for quiet on the set, and knocking on dressing room doors to tell the actors they're wanted. Day after day, year after year, the assistant director helps set up situations before the director takes control of them. The director gives the instructions, the assistant passes them on. Perhaps some assistants are always thinking of how *they* would do the shot. Here's one who finally got his chance.

Divine Madness ★ ★ ★ ½
R, 94 m., 1980

Bette Midler, with the Harlettes (Jocelyn Brown, Ula Hedwig, Diva Gray) and Irving Sudrow as the Head Usher. Directed and produced by Michael Ritchie. Written by Jerry Blatt, Bette Midler, and Bruce Vilanch.

Think of a concert film and you think of a camera bolted to the floor in front of the stage and shooting straight up into the singer's nostrils, which are half-concealed by the microphone. Those films are all right as recordings of song performances, but as cinema they stink. Some directors have broken out of the mold by making documentaries about the event of a concert; the best of those films is still Michael Wadleigh's *Woodstock* (1970).

Here Michael Ritchie, whose background is almost entirely in dramatic features *(Downhill Racer, The Candidate, The Bad News Bears)*, tries a new approach. There are times in Ritchie's *Divine Madness* when he seems to be trying to turn a live Bette Midler stage concert into a Hollywood genre musical. He opens as if *Divine Madness* is going to be a traditional concert film—Bette charges on stage, the audience cheers, there's an electric performance feel. But from that beginning, Ritchie subtly moves into the material until there are times when we almost forget we're watching an actual concert performance.

Ritchie's first decision was to declare an absolute ban on visible cameras. At no moment during *Divine Madness* do we see any cameras or any members of Ritchie's crew onstage, even though twenty cameras were used to shoot the performance. Ritchie

and Midler used a week of rehearsal to choreograph the camera moves and time them to Midler's own abundant energy. So instead of looking beyond the performer and being distracted by cinematographers carrying handheld cameras and sneaking around in their Adidas, we see only the stage, Midler, and her backup singers, the Harlettes. Ritchie also uses camera techniques that are rarely seen in concert films. There are, for example, crane shots in this movie—shots where the camera swoops up to look down on Midler or to circle down and toward her. That's especially effective during the Magic Lady sequence, in which Bette portrays a sort of dreamy bag lady on a park bench. This sequence comes closest to capturing the feel of a studio musical. That's not to say that *Divine Madness* loses the impact of a live concert performance. This movie is amazingly alive and involving, and Midler, who has become one of the great live performers, has an energy that steamrollers through an incredible variety of material.

When you think about *Divine Madness* after it's over, you realize what a wide range of material Midler covers. She does rock 'n' roll, she sings blues, she does a hilarious stand-up comedy routine, she plays characters (including a tacky show-lounge performer who enters in a motorized wheelchair outfitted with a palm tree), she stars in bizarre pageantry, and she wears costumes that Busby Berkeley would have found excessive. That's one reason *Divine Madness* doesn't drag: Midler changes pace so often that there's never too much of the same thing.

Is there a weakness in the film? I think there's one—a curious one. I don't think Ritchie intercuts enough close-up shots of the audience. That may seem like a curious objection, since I've already praised *Divine Madness* for sometimes feeling more like a movie musical than a concert documentary. But you can use people in an audience as characters. Richard Lester did in the original Beatles film, *A Hard Day's Night* (and who can ever forget that blonde girl weeping and screaming?).

With a Midler concert, the audience is part of the show. Intercutting selected audience shots with the stage material could have set up a nice byplay in some of the numbers. But

Ritchie keeps the audience mostly in long shot; it looks like a vast, amorphous mass out there in the dark. Since the film was actually edited together from three different concert performances, maybe he was concerned about matching audiences. But close-ups would have eliminated that problem.

No matter, though, really. Bette Midler is a wonderful performer with a high and infectious energy level and a split-second timing instinct that allows her to play with raunchy material instead of getting mired in it. She sings well, but she performs even better than she sings: She's giving a dramatic performance in music, and *Divine Madness* does a good job of communicating that performance without obscuring it in the distractions of most concert documentaries.

Dog Day Afternoon ★ ★ ★ ½
R, 120 m., 1975

Al Pacino (Sonny), Charles Durning (Moretti), James Broderick (FBI Man), John Cazale (Sal), Chris Sarandon (Leon), Judith Malina (Sonny's Mother). Directed by Sidney Lumet and produced by Martin Bregman and Martin Elfand. Screenplay by Frank Pierson.

There's a point midway in *Dog Day Afternoon* when a bank's head teller, held hostage by two very nervous stick-up men, is out in the street with a chance to escape. The cops tell her to run. But, no, she goes back inside the bank with the other tellers, proudly explaining, "My place is with my girls." What she means is that her place is at the center of live TV coverage inspired by the robbery. She's enjoying it.

Criminals become celebrities because their crimes provide fodder for the media. Many of the fashionable new crimes—hijacking, taking hostages—are committed primarily as publicity stunts. And a complex relationship grows up among the criminals, their victims, the police, and the press. Knowing they're on TV, hostages comb their hair and killers say the things they've learned on the evening news. That's the subject, in a way, of Sidney Lumet's pointed film. It's based on an actual bank robbery that took place in New York in the 1970s. And it seems to borrow, too, from that curious episode in Stockholm when hostages, barricaded in a bank vault with would-be robbers, began to identify with their captors. The presence of reporters and live TV cameras changed the nature of those events, helped to dictate them, made them into happenings with their own internal logic.

But Lumet's film is also a study of a fascinating character: Sonny, the bank robber who takes charge, played by Al Pacino as a compulsive and most complex man. He's street-smart, he fought in Vietnam, he's running the stick-up in order to get money for his homosexual lover to have a sex-change operation. He's also married to a chubby and shrill woman with three kids, and he has a terrifically possessive mother (the Freudianism gets a little thick at times). Sonny isn't explained or analyzed—just presented. He becomes one of the most interesting modern movie characters, ranking with Gene Hackman's eavesdropper in *The Conversation* and Jack Nicholson's Bobby Dupre in *Five Easy Pieces*.

Sonny and his zombie-like partner, Sal, hit the bank at closing time (a third confederate gets cold feet and leaves early). The stick-up is discovered, the bank is surrounded, the live TV mini-cams line up across the street, and Sonny is in the position, inadvertently, of having taken hostages. Sal (John Cazale) is very willing to shoot them, a factor in all that follows.

There are moments when *Dog Day Afternoon* comes dangerously close to the clichés of old Pat O'Brien gangster movies and the great Lenny Bruce routine inspired by them (the Irish cop shouts into his bullhorn "Come on out, Sonny, and nobody's gonna get hurt," and Sonny's mother pleads with him from the middle of the street). But Lumet is exploring the clichés, not just using them. And he has a good feel for the big-city crowd that's quickly drawn to the action. At first, Sonny is their hero, and he does a defiant dance in front of the bank, looking like a rock star playing to his fans. When it becomes known that Sonny's bisexual, the crowd turns against him. But within a short time (New York being New York), gay libbers turn up to cheer him on.

The movie has an irreverent, quirky sense of humor, and we get some notion of the times we live in when the bank starts getting obscene phone calls—and the giggling tellers breathe heavily into the receiver. There's also, in a film that's probably about fifteen minutes too long, an attempt to take a documentary look at the ways police and banks try to handle situations like this. And through it all there's that tantalizing attraction of instant celebrityhood, caught for an instant when a pizza deliveryman waves at the cameras and shouts, "Hey, I'm a star!"

The Dogs of War ★ ★ ★
R, 102 m., 1981

Christopher Walken (Shannon), Tom Berenger (Drew), Colin Blakely (North), Hugh Millais (Endean), Maggie Scott (Gabrielle), Olu Jacobs (Customs Man), George W. Harris (Colonel Bobi), Winston Ntshona (Dr. Okoye). Directed by John Irvin and produced by Larry DeWaay. Screenplay by Gary DeVore and George Malko.

The Dogs of War seems to know a great deal about the lives and minds of mercenary soldiers—more than it's willing to share with us. Based on the bestseller by sometime mercenary Frederick Forsyth, it centers on the exploits of Shannon (Christopher Walken), a young American who stages military escapades in Central American and Africa. Early in the film we see him as a mercenary-on-leave, going to his doctor for a depressing checkup not much different from the ones James Bond and Modesty Blaise used to go through. He's falling apart. His body can't take much more torture. So he agrees to a mission in Africa.

Walken is an interesting actor to watch: His face, not unlike a young Robert Mitchum, keeps its own counsel and yet suggests that there is a lot going on underneath. We wait through this whole movie to find out what is going on in there, but we never find out. This movie is ambitious—but not, apparently, so ambitious that it's willing to sacrifice an action-packed payoff for scenes exploring the psyche of its hero. *The Day of the Jackal*, Fred Zinnemann's 1973 film based on an earlier novel by Forsyth, had a similar reticence. The plots move like clockwork, but the characters keep their secrets to themselves.

In compensation, however, the plot of *The Dogs of War* is fascinating. In the movie's best sustained sequence, Shannon goes alone to an African nation to scout the terrain for a large mining company that wants to move in. Is the government secure? Could it be toppled? How strong is the opposition? Shannon tries to pass himself off as a photographer for a nature magazine. He meets an assortment of locals and visitors who seem to have wandered in from the novels of Graham Greene or V.S. Naipaul. They have fascinating dimensions. There's Gabrielle (Maggie Scott), the beautiful black woman who gives him a guided tour; Dr. Okoye (Winston Ntshona), the progressive leader who was thrown in jail; Dexter (Thomas Baptiste), the hotelman and entrepreneur, and North (Colin Blakely), the alcoholic TV reporter doing a documentary on the country for the BBC. These characters all have their quirks and ambitions, and flesh out the world around the enigmatic Shannon.

This section of the film is so good that it sets us up for an extraordinary payoff. Alas, we get only an ordinary one, a routine action sequence with lots of fancy machine guns and exploding fortress walls. The last twenty-five minutes of *The Dogs of War* are essentially the same as the last twenty-five minutes of countless other movies—action that's so routine we're hardly even stirred by the violence.

What were we expecting? Well, maybe that the human involvements established in the film's middle would be continued and that the contradictions in the lives of Gabrielle and Dexter, in particular, would be developed. Instead, when Shannon returns with his fellow mercenaries to overthrow the country's government, he's an avenging angel who settles scores, distributes death, and presides over a very routine climax. There is, of course, a twist at the end, designed I suppose to show that Shannon was more complicated all along than we thought. Well, of course he was. That's why we wanted to know more about him.

Down and Out in Beverly Hills
★ ★ ★ ★
R, 103 m., 1986 ✓

Nick Nolte (Jerry Baskin), Richard Dreyfuss (Dave Whiteman), Bette Midler (Barbara Whiteman), Little Richard (Orvis Goodnight), Tracy Nelson (Jenny Whiteman), Elizabeth

Pena (Carmen). Directed and produced by Paul Marzursky. Screenplay by Marzursky and Leon Capetanos.

Buddy Hackett once said that the problem with Beverly Hills is, you go to sleep beside your pool one day and when you wake up you're seventy-five years old. *Down and Out in Beverly Hills* understands that statement inside-out.

It tells the story of a rich family that lives in the timeless comfort of a Beverly Hills mansion—in the kind of house where they use *Architectural Digest* for pornography. One day a bum wanders down the alley and into their backyard and tries to drown himself in their swimming pool. After he is saved, he changes their lives forever.

In its broad outlines, this story is borrowed from Jean Renoir's classic film *Boudo Saved from Drowning.* But this isn't just a remake. The director, Paul Mazursky, makes his whole film depend on the very close observation of his characters. Mazursky knows Beverly Hills (he lives there, on the quiet cloistered flatlands below Sunset Boulevard), and he knows the deceptions and compromises of upper-middle-class life (his credits include *An Unmarried Woman* and *Bob & Carol & Ted & Alice*). With great attention and affection, he shows us the lives that are disrupted by the arrival of the derelict—this seedy failure whose whole life is an affront to the consumer society.

The film's heroes are the Whitemans, Dave and Barbara (Richard Dreyfuss and Bette Midler), and the bum, Jerry Baskin. He is played by Nick Nolte as the kind of guy who didn't set out in life to be a failure, but just sort of drifted from one plateau down to the next one, until finally he was spending most of his time talking to his dog.

It is, indeed, the dog's disappearance that inspires Nolte's suicide attempt, and it will be the Whitemans' own amazing dog, named Matisse, that gets some of the loudest laughs in the movie. Maybe Mazursky is trying to tell us something about the quality of human relationships in Beverly Hills.

The Dreyfuss character is a coat-hanger manufacturer. He didn't set out in life to be rich (one of his favorite conversational gambits involves his own good luck and

assurances that it could have happened to you as easily as to him—nice if you are him, but not if you are you). Here he is, living in a manicured mansion, exploiting wetback labor, sleeping with the Mexican maid, driving a Rolls convertible, selling 900 million coat hangers to the Chinese, and yet, somehow, something is missing. And almost from the first moment he sets eyes on the Nolte character, he realizes what it is: the authenticity of poverty.

The movie has a quiet, offhand way of introducing us to the the rich man's milieu. We meet his wife, whose life involves long sessions with masseurs, yogis, and shrinks (even her dog has a doggie psychiatrist). We meet his daughter (Tracy Nelson), a sunny-faced, milk-fed child of prosperity. We meet the Whitemans' neighbor, played by Little Richard with an incongruous mixture of anger and affluence (he complains that he doesn't get full service from the police; when he reports prowlers, they don't send helicopters and attack dogs).

We meet Carmen (Elizabeth Pena), the maid, who greets her employer lustily in her servant's quarters, but who grows, during the movie, from a soap opera addict into a political radical. We also meet the extended family and friends of the Whitemans, each one a perfectly written vignette, right down to the dog's analyst.

Down and Out in Beverly Hills revolves around the fascination that Dreyfuss feels for Nolte's life of dissipation and idleness. He is drawn to the shiftless sloth like a moth to a flame. A bum's life seems to have more authenticity than his own pampered existence. And, indeed, perhaps the last unreachable frontier of the very rich, the one thing they cannot buy, is poverty. Dreyfuss spends a night down on the beach with Nolte and his bum friends, and there is a breathtaking moment at sundown when Nolte (who claims to be a failed actor) recites Shakespeare's lines beginning "What a piece of work is a man!"

Certain predictable things happen. Nolte not only becomes Dreyfuss's good buddy, but is enlisted by all of the women in the household—the wife, the daughter, and the maid—as a sex therapist. Dreyfuss will put up with almost anything, because he really likes this guy, and Nolte's best hold on them is the threat to leave. Mazursky makes the most of that paradox, and gradually we see the buried theme of the movie emerging, and it is the power of friendship. What these people all really lacked, rich and poor, sane and crazy alike, was the power to really like other people.

The movie should get some kind of award for its casting. Dreyfuss, who has been so good in the past as a hyperactive over-achiever, succeeds here in slightly deflecting that energy. He has the success, but is be-dazzled by it, as if not quite trusting why great wealth should come to him for doing so little. He channels his energy, not into work, but into enthusiasms—and Nolte becomes his greatest enthusiasm.

For Bette Midler, Barbara Whiteman is the perfect character, all filled with the dis-tractions of living up to her level of consump-tion. Nolte in some ways has the subtlest role to play, although when we first see it, it seems the broadest. His shiftless drifter has to metamorphose into a man who under-stands his hosts so deeply that he can play them like a piano.

The supporting roles are so well filled, one after another, that we almost feel we recog-nize the characters before they're intro-duced. And Mike, the dog, should get an honorary walk-on at the Oscars.

Perhaps I have made the movie sound too serious. Mazursky has a way of making com-edies that are more intelligent and relevant than most of the serious films around; his last credit, for example, was the challenging *Moscow on the Hudson.* So let me just say that *Down and Out in Beverly Hills* made me laugh longer and louder than any film I've seen in a long time.

Dragonslayer ★ ★ ★
PG, 108 m., 1981

Peter MacNicol (Galen), Caitlin Clarke (Valerian), Ralph Richardson (Ulrich), John Haliam (Tyrian), Peter Eyre (Casidorus Rex), Albert Saimi (Grell). Directed by Matthew Robbins and produced by Hal Barwood. Screenplay by Barwood and Robbins.

I'd like to think the Dark Ages looked some-thing like *Dragonslayer,* all fearsome and muddy and overcast most of the time, and that their inhabitants walked around in a constant state of fear that something unspeakably evil was just about to eat off their ear. *Dragonslayer*'s vision is more con-vincing than the Dark Ages created by John Boormann in *Excalibur,* with everybody rid-ing around in suits of armor that wouldn't be invented for another seven hundred years.

The real Dark Ages must have been a time of ignorance, tyranny, and superstition. And its heroes must have been something like the two young heroes of *Dragonslayer,* Peter MacNicol and Caitlin Clarke, both looking about fifteen years old. In a time of disease, plague, and epidemic, fifteen was old.

Here is a movie with the courage to be grungy. Dragons live in smelly lairs deep beneath crumbling mountains, and to reach them you have to cross lakes of fire and somehow avoid being eaten alive by little baby dragons. The mission in this movie is a simple one, as all fairy-tale missions must be: Galen, a young sorcerer's apprentice (Mac-Nicol) must travel to a faraway kingdom and kill a fearsome dragon who holds the coun-tryside under its fiery scorn. The ruler of the kingdom has meanwhile instituted some stopgap measures. He holds a lottery every year involving all the virgins in his kingdom, and the unlucky virgin who loses the lottery is sacrificed to the dragon. Galen, the drag-onslayer, vows to save the virgins by killing the dragon. (There are easier ways of saving a girl from being sacrificed as a virgin, but they didn't call these the Dark Ages for nothing.) Before he leaves on his mission, Galen is inspired by the grave words and magical death of his teacher, Ulrich the Sor-cerer (Ralph Richardson, in an absolutely wonderful performance). On his way to the far-off kingdom, he meets a youth named Valerian (Caitlin Clarke), who turns out to be a girl disguised as a boy so that she can avoid being drafted in the lottery.

The scenes involving the dragon are first-rate. The beast is one of the meanest, ugliest, most reprehensible creatures I've ever seen in a film, and when it breathes flames it looks like it's *really* breathing flames. Its lair, its flaming lake, and its monstrous attacks on the population are also well handled. The real star of the movie, indeed, is the produc-tion designer, Elliott Scott, who created the look of this world. (The special effects were produced at Industrial Light and Magic

Inc., which is George Lucas's shop in Marin County, Calif.)

If the movie has a flaw, it is in MacNicol's performance, which is so feckless, cheerfully adolescent, and untextured that he could almost be a surfer caught in a time warp. MacNicol isn't bad in the role, mind you— just awfully cheeky. But then maybe dragonslaying is a young man's trade, and when you grow old and wise and have a long beard and are the sorcerer, you've learned enough to send your apprentice to kill the dragon.

The Draughtsman's Contract
★ ★ ★ ★
R, 103 m., 1983

Anthony Higgins (Mr. Neville), Janet Suzman (Mrs. Herbert), Anne Louise Lambert (Mrs. Talmann). Directed by Peter Greenaway and produced by David Payne.

What we have here is a tantalizing puzzle, wrapped in eroticism and presented with the utmost elegance. I have never seen a film quite like it. *The Draughtsman's Contract* seems to be telling us a very simple story in a very straightforward way, but after it's over you may need hours of discussion with your friends before you can be sure (if even then) exactly what happened.

The film takes place in 1694, in the English countryside. A rich lady (Janet Suzman) hires an itinerant artist to make twelve detailed drawings of her house. The artist (Anthony Higgins) strikes a hard bargain. In addition to his modest payment, he demands "the unrestricted freedom of her most intimate hospitality." Since the gentleman of the house is away on business, the lady agrees, and thus begins a pleasant regime divided between the easel and the boudoir.

All of this is told in the most precise way. All of the characters speak in complete, elegant, literary sentences. All of the camera strategies are formal and mannered. The movie advances with the grace and precision of a well-behaved novel. There is even a moment, perhaps, when we grow restless at the film's deliberate pace. But then, if we are sharp, we begin to realize that strange things are happening under our very noses.

The draughtsman demands perfection. There must be no change, from day to day, in the view he paints. He aims for complete realism. But little changes do creep in. A window is left open. A ladder is found standing against a wall. There are things on the lawn that should not be on the lawn. The lady's daughter calls on the artist and suggests that a plot may be under way and that her father, the lord of the manor, may have been murdered. Furthermore, the artist may be about to be framed for the crime. As a payment for her friendship, the daughter demands the same payment in "intimate hospitality" as her mother. Now the artist is not only draughtsman but lover to mother and daughter *and* the possible object of a plot to frame him with murder.

There is more. There is a lot more, all allowed to unfold at the same deliberate pace. There is a mysterious statue in the garden. An eavesdropper. Misbehaved sheep. The raw materials of this story could have been fashioned into a bawdy romp like *Tom Jones*. But the director, Peter Greenaway, has made a canny choice. Instead of showing us everything, and explaining everything, he gives us the clues and allows us to draw our own conclusions. His movie is like a crossword puzzle for the senses.

Dreamchild ★ ★ ★
PG, 94 m., 1985

Coral Browne (Mrs. Hargreaves), Ian Holm (Reverend Dodgson), Peter Gallagher (Jack Dolan), Caris Cofman (Sally Mackeson), Nicola Cowper (Lucy), Jane Asher (Mrs. Liddell). Directed by Gavin Miller and produced by Rick McCallum and Kenith Trodd. Screenplay by Dennis Potter.

It probably comes as no surprise that the man who wrote *Alice's Adventures in Wonderland* was not an absolute paragon of normality. His biographers have recently revealed that the Rev. Charles Dodgson (who wrote under the pen name Lewis Carroll) had an obsession with young girls, which he satisfied through hundreds of photographic studies and through lots of chummy friendships and correspondence. *Dreamchild* deals with his obsession as a problem that he tried to resolve in basically healthy ways, but it does argue that the writing of *Alice* created lifelong problems for the girl who inspired it.

According to this movie, which is fiction

inspired by fact, the original Alice was a girl named Alice Liddell. She suffered Dodgson's attentions for a time and allowed herself to be rowed up and down a river by him one sunny afternoon, but she was more interested in playing with her friends than in having the original manuscript of *Alice* read to her. "But I wrote this just for you!" protests the anguished clergyman (played with a nice quiet intensity by Ian Holm).

Dreamchild is not, in any event, a psychological case study. It's too much fun for that. The movie begins some seventy years after the book was published. The young girl, now eighty years old, is known as Mrs. Alice Hargreaves (Coral Browne) and is sailing for America to receive an honorary degree on the centennial of Dodgson's birth. She is accompanied by a young traveling companion named Lucy (Nicola Cowper), and on arrival in New York in 1932 she is surrounded by a mob of aggressive newspaper reporters. One of them (Peter Gallagher) succeeds in pushing his way into Mrs. Hargreaves's life and Lucy's heart.

What happens next is sort of sweet. As the reporter and Lucy gradually fall in love, Hargreaves at first is violently opposed to their relationship. She is, indeed, a rather unpleasant old lady—inflexible and dogmatic, with definite ideas about the proper conduct of young people.

But she is much more complex than we think, as we learn by sharing her private nightmares and fantasies. In her mind, the world of Alice's Wonderland still has a scary reality, and we see the original fantasy figures (the king and queen, the Cheshire cat, and so on) as grotesque caricatures designed not to delight a little girl, but to frighten her. The movie uses these fantasy sequences as counterpoint for more realistic flashbacks in which we meet Dodgson, see Alice as a young girl, and begin to sense some of the pathetic extremes to which Dodgson went to satisfy his passion for her, which was platonic but nonetheless bothering. We begin to realize, as old Mrs. Hargreaves herself begins to realize, that her whole life has been shaped by things that happened seventy years before.

Dreamchild is a remarkable film in many ways, not least because it gives itself such freedom of style and subject matter. For example, all the creatures in Alice's fantasies appear as muppetlike creations done by Jim Henson and his Creature Shop, but they are not Muppets. The movie has some subtle points to make with them.

At the same time, *Dreamchild* is not unremittingly grim, and it is not just a case study. The newspaper world of New York in the 1930s is re-created with style and humor, and the love story between the two young people is handled with a lot of cheerful energy. *Dreamchild* is an ambitious movie that tries to do a lot of things, and does most of them surprisingly well.

Dreamscape ★ ★ ★
PG-13, 99 m., 1984

Dennis Quaid (Alex), Max von Sydow (Dr. Novotny), Kate Capshaw (Jane DeVries), Christopher Plummer (Bob Blair), Eddie Albert (President), David Patrick Kelly (Tommy Ray). Directed by Joseph Ruben and produced by Bruce Cohn Curtis. Screenplay by David Loughery, Chuck Russell, and Ruben.

Dreamscape is three different movies, all fighting to get inside one another. It's a political conspiracy thriller, a science fiction adventure, and sort of a love story. Most movies that try to crowd so much into an hour and a half end up looking like a shopping list, but *Dreamscape* works, maybe because it has a sense of humor.

The movie stars Dennis Quaid, that open-faced specialist in crafty sincerity, as the possessor of rare psychic powers. Once, years before, he had been the best ESP subject in the laboratory of a kindly old parapsychologist (Max von Sydow), but then he disappeared. Now he is wanted again. The government is sponsoring explosive secret research in a brand new field: It believes there is a way for people to enter other people's dreams. The possibilities are limitless. For example, a therapist could enter the nightmares of his clients and become an eyewitness to buried phobias. Jungians could rub shoulders with subconscious archetypes. Lovers could visit each other's erotic dreams. And, of course, evil dreamers could drive their victims mad, or kill them with fright.

Quaid reluctantly agrees to become a subject for dream research, and almost immediately falls in love with von Sydow's assistant, the healthy and cheerful Kate Capshaw, of *Indiana Jones*. Then the plot thickens. Christopher Plummer turns up as the head of U.S. "covert intelligence." He is best friends with the president (Eddie Albert), who is, needless to say, having trouble sleeping these days. Albert has nightmares about starting World War III, and Plummer has nightmares that Albert will turn into a pacifist. He wants to use the dreamscape program to control the presidency. All of this plot stuff alternates with visits to people's dreams, and it's here that the movie gets interesting; movie dreams are usually clichés, and *Dreamscape* remains within the tradition, but comes up with some nice touches, including a crazy staircase that zigzags into darkness and looks precarious and surreal. There is also a funny sequence in which Quaid discovers Capshaw taking a nap, and impudently enters her dream with lust on his mind.

The whole business about the plot against the president is recycled from countless other thrillers. Two things redeem it: The gimmick of the dream invasions and the quality of the acting. Science fiction movies routinely run the risk of seeming ridiculous, and with bad performances they can inspire unwanted laughs. *Dreamscape* places its characters in a fantastical situation, and then lets them behave naturally, and with a certain wit. Dennis Quaid is especially good at that; his face lends itself to a grin, and he is a hero without ever being self-consciously heroic.

As for the dreams themselves, as I watched the movie I found myself trying to remember some of my own dreams. The movie's dreams include rooms with lots of windows and doors at crazy angles, railway coaches that are twice as wide as train tracks, and other visual distortions. I usually have more realistic dreams. Rooms and spaces have realistic proportions, and the distortions of reality come, not in the set decorating, but in the editing; flashbacks and intercutting points of view are not uncommon in my dreams, maybe because I see so many films. But movies can't use flashbacks and viewpoint tricks to manufacture dreams—because then the movie would look like a movie and not like a dream. So the movies

have created a conventional dream language. What *Dreamscape* does is enlarge it with brief, sometimes funny little asides that do feel like dreams, as when Quaid is inside the nightmare of a little boy, and they're running from a Snake Man, and they see an adult seated at the end of a long table, and the kid says, "That's my dad. He won't be any help."

Dressed to Kill ★ ★ ★
R, 105 m., 1980

Michael Caine (Dr. Elliott), Angie Dickinson (Kate Miller), Nancy Allen (Liz Blake), Keith Gordon (Peter Miller), Dennis Franz (Detective Marino), David Margulies (Dr. Levy). Directed by Brian De Palma and produced by George Litto. Screenplay by De Palma.

When Alfred Hitchcock died, the obituaries puzzled over the fact that Hitchcock had created the most distinctive and easily recognizable visual style of his generation—but hadn't had a great influence on younger filmmakers. The obvious exception is Brian De Palma, who deliberately set out to work in the Hitchcock tradition, and directed this Hitchcockian thriller that's stylish, intriguing, and very violent.

The ads for De Palma's *Dressed to Kill* describe him as "the master of the macabre," which is no more immodest, I suppose, than the ads that described Hitchcock as "the master of suspense." De Palma is not yet an artist of Hitchcock's stature, but he does earn the right to a comparison, especially after his deliberately Hitchcockian films *Sisters* and *Obsession*. He places his emphasis on the same things that obsessed Hitchcock: precise camera movements, meticulously selected visual details, characters seen as types rather than personalities, and violence as a sudden interruption of the most mundane situations.

He also has Hitchcock's delight in bizarre and unexpected plot twists, and the chief delight of the first and best hour of *Dressed to Kill* comes from the series of surprises he springs on us. Although other key characters are introduced, the central character in these early scenes is Kate Miller (Angie Dickinson), an attractive forty-fiveish Manhattan woman who has a severe case of unsatiated lust. De Palma opens with a deliberately shocking shower scene (homage to Hitch), and then follows the woman as her sexual fantasies become unexpectedly real during a lunchtime trip to the museum.

The museum sequence is absolutely brilliant, tracking Dickinson as she notices a tall, dark, and handsome stranger. She makes eye contact, breaks it, tries to attract the stranger's attention by dropping her glove, and then is tracked *by* the stranger. To her, and our, astonishment, this virtuoso scene (played entirely without dialogue) ends in a passionate sexual encounter in the back of a taxicab.

Later, she wakes up in the stranger's apartment, and De Palma shamelessly manipulates her, and us, by springing a series of plot surprises involving embarrassment and guilt: What would *you* do if you were a cheating wife and had just forgotten your wedding ring in a stranger's apartment? The plot now takes several totally unanticipated turns, and I, of course, would not dream of revealing them. Indeed, I'll be vague about the plot from now on, because De Palma's surprises are crucial to his effect.

The movie's other characters include Michael Caine, who's the psychiatrist of two of the characters in the film. Then there's Nancy Allen, who's wonderfully off-beat as a sweet Manhattan hooker who discovers a body and gets trapped in the investigation. And there's Keith Gordon: He's one of those teen-age scientific geniuses, and he invents brilliant gimmicks to investigate the crime.

Some people are going to object to certain plot details in *Dressed to Kill*, particularly the cavalier way it explains a homocidal maniac's behavior by lumping together transsexuality and schizophrenia. But I doubt that De Palma wants us to take his explanations very seriously; the pseudoscientific jargon used to "explain" the case reminds me of that terrible psychiatric explanation at the end of *Psycho*—a movie De Palma has been quoting from all along.

Dressed to Kill is an exercise in style, not narrative; it would rather look and feel like a thriller than make sense. Its plot has moments of ludicrous implausibility, it nearly bogs down at one point near the end and it cheats on us with the old "it was only a dream!" gimmick. But De Palma has so much fun with the conventions of the thriller that we forgive him and go along. And there are really nice touches in the performances: Dickinson's guilt-laden lust, Caine's analytical detachment, Allen's street-wise cool in life and death situations, Gordon's wiseguy kid. De Palma earns the title of master, all right . . . but Hitch remains the grand master.

The Dresser ★ ★ ★ ★
PG, 118 m., 1984

Albert Finney (Sir), Tom Courtenay (Norman), Edward Fox (Oxenby), Zena Walker (Her Ladyship). Directed and produced by Peter Yates. Screenplay by Ronald Harwood.

Much of mankind is divided into two categories, the enablers and the enabled. Both groups accept the same mythology, in which the enablers are self-sacrificing martyrs and the enabled are egomaniacs. But the roles are sometimes reversed; the stars are shaken by insecurities that are subtly encouraged by enablers who, in their heart of hearts, see themselves as the real stars. It's human nature. Ever hear the one about the guy who played the gravedigger in *Hamlet*? He was asked what the play was about, and he answered, "It's about this gravedigger. . . ."

The Dresser is about a guy like that, named Norman. He has devoted the best years of his life to the service of an egomaniacal actor, who is called Sir even though there is some doubt he has ever been knighted. Sir is an actor-manager who runs his own traveling theatrical troupe, touring the provinces to offer a season of Shakespeare. One night he plays King Lear. The next night, Othello. The next, Richard III. Most nights he has to ask his dresser what role he is playing. Dressers in the British theater do a great deal more than dress their employers. In *The Dresser*, Norman is also Sir's confidant, morale booster, masseur, alter ego, and physician, nursing him through hangovers with medicinal amounts of brandy. Norman has been doing this job for years, and Sir is at the center of his life. Sir, however, takes Norman very much for granted, and it is this difference between them that provides the emotional tension.

The Dresser is a backstage movie, based on a backstage play, but the movie leaves the theater for a few wonderful additions to the play, as when Sir commands a train to stop, and the train does. Mostly, though, the action is in a little provincial theater, where tonight's play is *King Lear*, and Sir looks as if he had spent the last week rehearsing the storm scene. It is Norman's job to whip him into shape. Sir is seriously disoriented. He is so hung over, shaky, and confused that he can't even remember how the play begins—indeed, he starts putting on the makeup for *Othello*. There are other problems for Norman to handle, such as Sir's relationships with his wife, his adoring stage manageress, and a young actress he is considering for Cordelia (she is slim, and would be easier to carry onstage). There are also an angry supporting player and a quaking old trouper who is being pressed into service as the Fool.

The minor characters are all well-drawn, but *The Dresser* is essentially the story of two people, and the movie has been well-cast to make the most of both of them; no wonder both actors won Oscar nominations. Norman is played by Tom Courtenay, who had the role on stage in London and New York and will also be remembered from all those British Angry Young Men films like *Billy Liar* and *Loneliness of the Long Distance Runner*. He is perfect for playing proud, resentful, self-doubting outsiders. Sir is played by Albert Finney, who manages to look far older than his forty-seven years and yet to create a physical bravura that's ideal for the role. When he shouts "Stop . . . that . . . train!" we are not too surprised when the train stops.

On the surface, the movie is a wonderful collection of theatrical lore, detail, and superstition (such as the belief that it is bad luck to say the name "Macbeth" aloud—safer to refer always to "the Scottish tragedy"). The physical details of makeup and costuming are dwelled on, and there is a great backstage moment when the primitive thunder machine is rattled to make a storm. Beneath those details, though, a human relationship arrives at a crisis point and is resolved, in a way. Sir and Norman come to the end of their long road together, and, as is

the way with enablers and enabled, Norman finally understands the real nature of their relationship, while Sir, of course, can hardly be bothered. This is the best sort of drama, fascinating us on the surface with color and humor and esoteric detail, and then revealing the truth underneath.

Drive, He Said ★ ★ ★
R, 90 m.,1971

William Tepper (Hector), Karen Black (Olive), Michael Margotta (Gabriel), Bruce Dern (Coach Builion), Robert Towne (Richard), Harry Jaglom (Conrad). Directed by Jack Nicholson and produced by Steve Blauner and Nicholson. Screenplay by Jeremy Larner and Nicholson.

Jack Nicholson's *Drive, He Said* is a disorganized but occasionally brilliant movie about two college students and the world they, and we, inhabit. Their campus is a microcosm of the least reassuring aspects of contemporary America; the two overwhelming mental states are paranoia and compulsive competitiveness. Sufferers from both conditions are obsessed by the fear that something might be gaining on them. In *Drive, He Said*, the paranoic student is afraid of the draft, the System, and They, whoever They are. The other student is a star basketball player, or, as his friends tell him, "You stay after school to run around in your underwear." His fears are more general and vague and, therefore, more frightening.

The movie has a sort of jumpy, nervous rhythm, as if it were on speed, and sometimes that works but it's finally just distracting. The problem is that the stories of the two main characters don't mesh. They're roommates, to be sure, but that's a tenuous connection. And when the paranoid (Michael Margotta) has his three big adventures—freaking out at the draft physical, attacking a faculty wife, and freeing all the animals in a biology lab—the scenes feel like set-pieces, unrelated to the movie.

The movie that surrounds them involves Hector (played with laconic charm by William Tepper), who plays basketball not because he's a jock but because he enjoys the self-testing that the game involves. By the time we meet him, he has become a star and a prime choice for the pro draft, but, well, somehow the whole thing is falling apart on him.

One of his problems is the faculty wife, played by Karen Black. He has been having an affair with her, but she breaks it off just as he discovers, uncomfortably, that he might be in love. And then it turns out she's pregnant. This is a real-life experience of the most unsettling sort, and makes it difficult for him to take basketball as seriously as his coach thinks he should.

The coach is an intense competitor who positively believes in all the values, moral and physical, that have been preached by all coaches since the dawn of time-outs. Bruce Dern's performance as the coach, by the way, is a small masterpiece of accurate observation.

The performances, indeed, are the best thing in the movie. Nicholson himself is a tremendously interesting screen actor, and he directs his actors to achieve a kind of intimacy and intensity that is genuinely rare. But if Nicholson is good on the nuances, he's weak on the overall direction of his film. It doesn't hang together for us as a unified piece of work.

I have a notion he may have been trying for an effect similar to that in his three previous films as an actor (*Easy Rider, Five Easy Pieces,* and *Carnal Knowledge*), which were deliberately episodic and depended on the cumulative effect of the episodes for a structure that occurred to us only gradually. But the episodes refuse to come together in *Drive, He Said,* and what we're left with are some very good scenes in search of a home.

Dune ★
PG-13, 145 m., 1984

Kyle MacLachlan (Paul), José Ferrer (Emperor), Brad Dourif (De Vries), Kenneth McMillan (Baron), Sting (Feyd-Rautha). Directed by David Lynch and produced by Raffaella DeLaurentiis. Screenplay by Lynch.

"It's like a dream," my friend from Hollywood was explaining. "It doesn't make any sense, and the special effects are straight from the dime store but if you give up trying to understand it, and just sit back and let it wash around in your mind, it's not bad." That was not exactly a rave review for a movie that someone paid $40 million to

make, but it put me into a receptive frame of mind for *Dune,* the epic based on the novels by Frank Herbert. I was even willing to forgive the special effects for not being great; after all, in an era when George Lucas's *Star Wars* has turned movies into high tech, why not a film that looks like a throwback to *Flash Gordon.* It might be kind of fun.

It took *Dune* about nine minutes to completely strip me of my anticipation. This movie is a real mess, an incomprehensible, ugly, unstructured, pointless excursion into the murkier realms of one of the most confusing screenplays of all time. Even the color is no good; everything is seen through a sort of dusty yellow filter, as if the film was left out in the sun too long. Yes, you might say, but the action is, after all, on a desert planet where there isn't a drop of water, and there's sand everywhere. David Lean solved that problem in *Lawrence of Arabia,* where he made the desert look beautiful and mysterious, not shabby and drab.

The movie's plot will no doubt mean more to people who've read Herbert than to those who are walking in cold. It has to do with a young hero's personal quest. He leads his people against an evil baron and tries to destroy a galaxy-wide trade in "spice," a drug produced on the desert planet. Spice allows you to live indefinitely while you discover you have less and less to think about. There are various theological overtones, which are best left unexplored.

The movie has so many characters, so many unexplained or incomplete relationships, and so many parallel courses of action that it's sometimes a toss-up whether we're watching a story, or just an assembly of meditations on themes introduced by the novels (the movie is like a dream). Occasionally a striking image will swim into view: The alien brain floating in brine, for example, or our first glimpse of the giant sand worms plowing through the desert. If the first look is striking, however, the movie's special effects don't stand up to scrutiny. The heads of the sand worms begin to look more and more as if they came out of the same factory that produced Kermit the Frog (they have the same mouths). An evil baron floats through the air on trajectories all too obviously controlled by wires. The spaceships in the movie are so shabby, so lacking in detail or dimension, that they look almost like those student films where plastic models are shot against a tablecloth.

Nobody looks very happy in this movie. Actors stand around in ridiculous costumes, mouthing dialogue that has little or no context. They're not even given scenes that work on a self-contained basis; portentious lines of pop profundity are allowed to hang in the air unanswered, while additional characters arrive or leave on unexplained errands. *Dune* looks like a project that was seriously out of control from the start. Sets were constructed, actors were hired; no usable screenplay was ever written; everybody faked it as long as they could. Some shabby special effects were thrown into the pot, and the producers crossed their fingers and hoped that everybody who has read the books will want to see the movie. Not if the word gets out, they won't.

E.T.—The Extra-Terrestrial ★ ★ ★ ★
PG, 115 m., 1982* ✔

Henry Thomas (Elliott), Dee Wallace (Mary), Peter Coyote (Keys), Robert MacNaughton (Michael), Drew Barrymore (Gertie). Directed by Steven Spielberg and produced by Spielberg and Kathleen Kennedy. Screenplay by Melissa Mathison.

This movie made my heart glad. It is filled with innocence, hope, and good cheer. It is also wickedly funny and exciting as hell. *E.T.—The Extra-Terrestrial* is a movie like *The Wizard of Oz*, that you can grow up with and grow old with, and it won't let you down. It tells a story about friendship and love. Some people are a little baffled when they hear it described: It's about a relationship between a little boy and a creature from outer space that becomes his best friend. That makes it sound like a cross between *The Thing* and *National Velvet*. It works as science fiction, it's sometimes as scary as a monster movie, and at the end, when the lights go up, there's not a dry eye in the house.

E.T. is a movie of surprises, and I will not spoil any of them for you. But I can suggest some of the film's wonders. The movie takes place in and around a big American suburban development. The split-level houses march up and down the curved drives, carved out of hills that turn into forest a few blocks beyond the backyard. In this forest one night, a spaceship lands, and queer-looking little creatures hobble out of it and go snuffling through the night, looking for plant specimens, I guess. Humans arrive—authorities with flashlights and big stomping boots. They close in on the spaceship, and it is forced to take off and abandon one of its crew members. This forlorn little creature, the *E.T.* of the title, is left behind on Earth—abandoned to a horrendous world of dogs, raccoons, automobile exhausts, and curious little boys.

The movie's hero is one particular little boy named Elliott. He is played by Henry Thomas in what has to be the best little boy performance I've ever seen in an American film. He doesn't come across as an over-coached professional kid; he's natural, defiant, easily touched, conniving, brave, and childlike. He just *knows* there's something living out there in the backyard, and he sits up all night with his flashlight, trying to coax the creature out of hiding with a nearly irresistible bait: Reese's Pieces. The creature, which looks a little like Snoopy but is very, very wise, approaches the boy. They become friends. The E.T. moves into the house, and the center section of the film is an endless invention on the theme of an extra-terrestrial's introduction to bedrooms, televisions, telephones, refrigerators, and six-packs of beer. The creature has the powers of telepathy and telekinesis, and one of the ways it communicates is to share its emotions with Elliott. That's how Elliott knows that the E.T. wants to go home.

And from here on out, I'd better not describe what happens. Let me just say that the movie has moments of sheer ingenuity, moments of high comedy, some scary moments, and a very sad sequence that has everybody blowing their noses.

What is especially wonderful about all of those moments is that Steven Spielberg, who made this film, creates them out of legitimate and fascinating plot developments. At every moment from its beginning to its end, *E.T.* is really *about* something. The story is quite a narrative accomplishment. It reveals facts about the E.T.'s nature; it develops the personalities of Elliott, his mother, brother, and sister; it involves the federal space agencies; it touches on extra-terrestrial medicine, biology, and communication, and *still* it inspires genuine laughter and tears.

A lot of those achievements rest on the very peculiar shoulders of the E.T. itself. With its odd little walk, its high-pitched squeals of surprise, its tentative imitations of human speech, and its catlike but definitely alien purring, E.T. becomes one of the most intriguing fictional creatures I've ever seen on a screen. The E.T. is a triumph of special effects, certainly; the craftsmen who made this little being have extended the boundaries of their art. But it's also a triumph of imagination, because the filmmakers had to imagine E.T., had to see through its eyes, hear with its ears, and experience this world of ours through its utterly alien experience in order to make a creature so absolutely convincing. The word for what they exercised is empathy. *E.T.—The Extra-Terrestrial* is a reminder of what movies are for. Most movies are not for any one thing, of course. Some are to make us think, some to make us feel, some to take us away from our problems, some to help us examine them. What is enchanting about *E.T.* is that, in some measure, it does all of those things.

E.T. was held off the cassette market until after its 1985 re-release.

Easy Money ★ ★ ½
R, 95 m., 1983

Rodney Dangerfield (Monty Capuletti), Joe Pesci (Nicky Cerone), Geraldine Fitzgerald (Mrs. Monahan), Candy Azzara (Rose), Taylor Negron (Julio), Jennifer Jason Leigh (Allison). Directed by James Signorelli and produced by John Nicoletta. Screenplay by Dangerfield, Michael Enderl, P.J. O'Rourke, and Dennis Blair.

Easy Money is an off-balance and disjointed movie, but that's sort of okay, since it's about an off-balance and disjointed kinda guy. The credits call him Monty Capuletti, but he is clearly Rodney Dangerfield, gloriously playing himself as the nearest thing we are likely to get to W.C. Fields in this lifetime.

The movie's plot is simply a line to hang

gags on. It stars Rodney as a baby photographer whose rich mother-in-law leaves him an inheritance of a $10 million department store. He can collect—but only if he stops drinking, gambling, smoking dope, running around late, and betting on the horses. This is a very tall order, but Rodney tries to fill it. The movie surrounds Dangerfield with a lot of good New York character actors, who populate the endless poker games and saloon scenes his life revolves around. There's also a very funny sequence involving his daughter's wedding to a Puerto Rican, an alliance that inspires a great backyard wedding party scene.

Because Rodney is Rodney, I laughed a lot during this movie. But I left it feeling curiously unsatisfied. I think maybe that was for two reasons: Because the movie introduces too many subplots that it never really deals with, and because Rodney isn't allowed to be hateful enough. First, the plot. I have the strangest feeling that *Easy Money* once had a much longer script than it has now. There are big scenes (like one where the Puerto Rican groom is sneaking into the bathroom) that end abruptly without a payoff or follow-through. There are whole sequences (like the department store's fashion show, based on Rodney's wardrobe) that seem to coexist uneasily with the rest of the movie. And the movie doesn't get enough comic mileage out of Rodney's attempt to quit drinking, smoking, and gambling (think of the fun you could have with Dangerfield attending an A.A. meeting).

Second, Rodney. I like him best when he's cynical and hard-edged. The Dangerfield of his concerts and records has been smoothed out for this movie, into a slightly more lovable guy. It looks like a masterstroke to make Rodney a baby photographer (think of W.C. Fields in that role), but not enough is done with it. He occasionally loses his temper at the little monsters, but he never seems to detest and despise them enough to be really funny. That's a problem. If you are a Rodney Dangerfield fan, it will not be insurmountable. If you are not a Dangerfield fan, of course, probably nothing on earth could induce you to go to this movie. The great Dangerfield movie, however, has still to be made. This one doesn't get quite enough respect.

Eating Raoul ★ ★
R, 87 m., 1983

Paul Bartel (Paul Bland), Mary Woronov (Mary Bland), Robert Beltran (Raoul). Directed by Paul Bartel. Screenplay by Bartel and Richard Blackburn.

Eating Raoul is one of the more deadpan black comedies I've seen: It tries to position itself somewhere between the bizarre and the banal, and most of the time, it succeeds. This has got to be the first low-key, laid-back comedy about murder, swingers' ads, and dominating women. Problem is, it's so laid-back it eventually gets monotonous. If the style and pacing had been as outrageous as the subject matter, we might have had something really amazing here.

The movie's about a happily married couple, Paul and Mary Bland, who are victims of bad times. Paul gets fired from his job in the liquor store, and there's just not much work around for a dilettante with no skills. He's spent his last rent money when providence suggests a way for the Blands to support themselves. A lecherous swinger from the upstairs apartment tries to assault Mary, and Paul bops him over the head with the frying pan. The swinger dies, and the Blands overcome their horror long enough to check out his wallet. He's loaded.

What the movie does next is to present the most outrageous events in the most matter-of-fact manner. The Blands hit upon a scheme to take ads in swingers' tabloids, lure victims to their apartment, tap them over the head with the trusty skillet, and rob them. The only problem is disposing of their victims' bodies. That's where Raoul comes in. He's a locksmith who discovers the Blands' dirty little secret and offers to sell the bodies to a dog-food factory. All's well until Raoul becomes smitten with Mary. Then Paul grows jealous, especially when he discovers that Raoul has been stealing from them. The next step is perhaps suggested by the title of the movie, or perhaps not—I wouldn't want to give anything away.

The plot of *Eating Raoul* reminds me a little of *Motel Hell*, that truly ghastly movie about a farmer who kidnapped his motel customers, buried them in the garden up to their necks, force-fed them until they were plump, and then turned them into sausages.

(His motto: "It takes lots of critters to make Farmer Vincent's fritters.") I liked *Motel Hell* more than *Eating Raoul*, however, because it had the courage of its execrable taste. *Eating Raoul*, on the other hand, wants to be an almost whimsical black comedy. It's got its tongue so firmly in cheek there's no room for Raoul. The movie's got some really funny stuff in it, and I liked a lot of it, and I wouldn't exactly advise not seeing it, but it doesn't quite go that last mile. It doesn't reach for the truly unacceptable excesses, the transcendent breaches of taste, that might have made it inspired instead of merely clever.

Eddie and the Cruisers ★ ★
PG, 92 m., 1983

Tom Berenger (Frank), Michael Pare (Eddie Wilson), Joe Pantoliano (Doc Robbins), Matthew Laurence (Sal Amato), Helen Schneider (Joann Carlino), Michael 'Tunes' Antunes (Wendell Newton). Directed by Martin Davidson and produced by Joseph Brooks. Written by Martin and Arlene Davidson.

Eddie and the Cruisers is all buildup and no payoff. It tells us about this unsung rock 'n' roll genius named Eddie Wilson, whose Chevy crashed off a bridge back in 1963, and then it suggests that Eddie might still be alive. Now, leaving aside the possibility that Eddie might, in fact, have gone down with his Chevy, this premise has all sorts of possibilities. I will name some of them:

1. Eddie could have surfaced as another rock 'n' roller.

2. Eddie could have been a Buddy Holly who never died, and he disappeared to escape discovery.

3. Eddie could have been horribly disfigured and decided to spend the rest of his life in a recording studio, masterminding other people's music.

4. Eddie could have dropped out, in a grand existential gesture.

Now, I will *not* give away the ending to this movie. But I will make the following complaint: Even though one of the above possibilities does, indeed, turn out to be true—*it is still not the ending of the movie!* The movie makes the fatal flaw of arriving at a dramatic conclusion that does not settle the Eddie

Wilson mystery. Instead, all we get is a big buildup to a dumb revelation. What a disappointment.

The movie makes another mistake. It never really explores Eddie Wilson as a human being. He's played in the movie by Michael Pare, a good-looking hunk. Pare does a good job of seeming to be a charismatic rock star, a sort of Bruce Springsteen crossed with Richard Gere. But Pare has hardly any real dramatic scenes; instead, he postures a lot, makes speeches, takes stands, and is idolized onstage.

After he disappears with the Chevy, twenty years go by, and the members of the old Cruisers all make their separate peace with the Wilson legend. The key figure in the movie is Tom Berenger, playing one of the Cruisers. These days he's a high school teacher, but he still remembers his rock 'n' roll past; so do Eddie's old girlfriend (Helen Schneider) and the group's manager (Joe Pantoliano), who is now a broken-down DJ. Suddenly, there's renewed interest in the tapes of Eddie's last session. A TV investigative reporter wants to learn the real Eddie Wilson story. And then messages are received from . . . Eddie? We learn that the original tapes *were* saved; they were hidden years ago in Eddie's favorite place, a sculptor's combination of a junkyard and the Watts Towers. (Of course, the tapes have survived twenty years of rain, ice, snow, and sun.) And then . . .

You know, they could have had a good movie here. They had the cast for one and they even had the music (the sound track is terrific). If they'd just gone ahead and *dealt* with Eddie's disappearance, even in melodramatic terms, the movie would have paid off. But the ending is so frustrating, so dumb, so unsatisfactory, that it gives a bad reputation to the whole movie.

Educating Rita ★ ★
PG, 110 m., 1983

Michael Caine (Dr. Frank Bryant), Julie Walters (Rita). Directed and produced by Lewis Gilbert. Screenplay by Willy Russell.

If only I'd been able to believe they were actually reading the books, then everything else would have fallen into place. But I didn't believe it. And so *Educating Rita*, which

might have been a charming human comedy, disintegrated into a forced march through a formula relationship. The movie stars Michael Caine as a British professor of literature and Julie Walters as the simple cockney girl who comes to him for night-school lessons. She has problems: She is a working-class punk with an unimaginative husband. He has problems: He is a drunk whose only friends are cheating on him with each other. They have problems: Walters begins to idealize Caine, who then falls in love with her.

Perhaps it would be more accurate to say they both fall into love with the remake job they'd like to do on each other. Caine sees Walters as a fresh, honest, unspoiled intelligence. She sees him as a man who ought to sober up and return to his first love, writing poems. The idea of the curmudgeon and the cockney was not new when Bernard Shaw wrote *Pygmalion*, and it is not any newer in *Educating Rita*. But it could have been entertaining, if only I'd believed they were reading those books. They pass the books back and forth a lot. They sometimes read a line or two. There is a lot of talk about Blake this and Wordsworth that. But it's all magic. The books are like incantations that, used properly, will exorcise cockney accents and alcoholism. But the movie doesn't really believe that, so it departs from the stage play to bring in a lot of phony distractions.

The original *Educating Rita*, a long-running London stage hit by Willy Russell, had only the two characters. They were on the stage together for a long time, and by the end of the play we had shared in their developing relationship. Russell's movie rewrite has added mistresses, colleagues, husbands, in-laws, students, and a faculty committee, all unnecessary.

To the degree that *Educating Rita* does work, the credit goes to Michael Caine, who plays a man weary and kind, funny and self-hating. There is a real character there, just as there was in Caine's boozy diplomat in *Beyond the Limit*. In both movies, though, the characters are not well-served by the story. They're made to deliver speeches, take positions, and make decisions that are required by the plot, not by their own inner promptings. When Caine's professor, at the end of this movie, flies off to Australia to maybe sober up and maybe make a fresh start, it's a total cop-out—not by him, but by the screenplay. Maybe that's what happens when you start with an idealistic, challenging idea, and then cynically try to broaden its appeal.

El Norte ★ ★ ★ ★
R, 141 m., 1983

Zaide Sylvia Gutierrez (Rosa), David Villalpando (Enrique), Ernesto Gomez Cruz (Father), Alicia del Lago (Mother), Trinidad Silva (Monty). Directed by Gregory Nava and produced by Anna Thomas. Screenplay by Nava and Thomas.

From the very first moments of *El Norte*, we know that we are in the hands of a great movie. It tells a simple story in such a romantic and poetic way that we are touched, deeply and honestly, and we know we will remember the film for a long time. The movie tells the story of two young Guatemalans, a brother and sister named Rosa and Enrique, and of their long trek up through Mexico to *el Norte*—the United States. Their journey begins in a small village and ends in Los Angeles, and their dream is the American Dream.

But *El Norte* takes place in the present, when we who are already Americans are not so eager for others to share our dream. Enrique and Rosa are not brave immigrants who could have been our forefathers, but two young people alive now, who look through the tattered pages of an old *Good Housekeeping* for their images of America. One of the most interesting things about the film is the way it acknowledges all of the political realities of Latin America and yet resists being a "political" film. It tells its story through the eyes of its heroes, and it is one of the rare films that grants Latin Americans full humanity. They are not condescended to, they are not made to symbolize something, they are not glorified, they are simply themselves.

The movie begins in the fields where Arturo, their father, is a *bracero*—a pair of arms. He goes to a meeting to protest working conditions and is killed. Their mother disappears. Enrique and Rosa, who are in their late teens, decide to leave their village and go to America. The first part of the film shows their life in Guatemala with some of the same beauty and magical imagery of Gabriel Garcia Marquez's *One Hundred Years of Solitude*. The middle section shows them going by bus and foot up through Mexico, which is as harsh on immigrants from the South as America is. At the border they try to hire a "coyote" to guide them across, and they finally end up crawling to the promised land through a rat-infested drainage tunnel.

The final section of the film takes place in Los Angeles, which they first see as a glittering carpet of lights, but which quickly becomes a cheap motel for day laborers, and a series of jobs in the illegal, shadow job market. Enrique becomes a waiter. Rosa becomes a maid. Because they are attractive, intelligent, and have a certain naive nerve, they succeed for a time, before the film's sad, poetic ending.

El Norte is a great film, one of 1983's best, for two different kinds of reasons. One is its stunning visual and musical power; the approach of the film is not quasidocumentary, but poetic, with fantastical images that show us the joyous hearts of these two people.

The second reason is that this is the first film to approach the subject of "undocumented workers" solely through *their* eyes. This is not one of those docudramas where we half-expect a test at the end, but a film like *The Grapes of Wrath* that gets inside the hearts of its characters and lives with them.

The movie was directed by Gregory Nava and produced by Anna Thomas, who wrote it together. It's been described by *Variety* as the "first American independent epic," and it is indeed an epic film made entirely outside the studio system by two gifted filmmakers (their credits include *The Confessions of Amans*, which won a Gold Hugo at the Chicago Film Festival, and *The Haunting of M*, one of my favorite films from 1979). This time, with a larger budget and a first-rate cast, they have made their breakthrough into the first ranks of young directors.

Electric Dreams ★ ★ ★ ½
PG, 96 m., 1984

Lenny Von Dohlen (Miles), Virginia Madsen (Madeline), Maxwell Caulfield (Bill), Bud Cort (Computer). Directed by Steve Barron and produced by Rusty Lemorande and Larry DeWaay. Screenplay by Lemorande.

In a way, it's one of the oldest stories in the movies. You start with a sweet guy who's kind of a wimp. You have him rent an apartment downstairs from a good-looking blonde girl who's really classy—maybe she even plays cello in a symphony orchestra. Then you supply the wimp with a know-it-all roommate who can do anything. Then the wimp has the roommate compose a love song for the girl upstairs. The girl falls for it, there's love at first sight, but then the wimp feels that he is living a lie. He must tell the girl the truth or he will not truly deserve her. (This begs the question, of course, of whether he should make an ethical investment in a girl who can be swayed by a single love song.)

In *Electric Dreams*, they've made one slight change in this age-old scenario, to bring it up to date. The roommate is a computer. In the old movies, there was usually a touchy moment or two when it looked like the roommate was going to fall for the girl upstairs. They even have a version of that here: The computer gets wildly jealous and possessive about its owner, and begins to inquire winsomely about the meanings of all those nice words in the love songs: How, exactly, *does* one touch? The guy in the movie is one of those cases of chronic disorganization: He's right on time but this is yesterday's training session. Somebody tells him he ought to get a computer to help him keep track of things. He buys a computer and, predictably, drops it while he is taking it out of the box. Apparently that was just what the computer needed to upgrade itself to a level of sophistication far above anything ever dreamed of by the folks at the computer store.

If *Electric Dreams* were only about this ancient old plot, it would have been a fairly routine movie. Several things make it more than that, and, in order of importance, they are: (1) the ingenious way the movie creates a personality for the computer, with the help of Bud Cort as the computer's voice; (2) the perfect casting of Lenny Von Dohlen as the wimp, and Virginia Madsen, an engaging newcomer, as the girl upstairs; (3) the graphics, and particularly the way the movie pictures the computer's wilder flights of fancy, and (4) the music by Giorgio Moroder, who seems to compose the scores for half the films in Hollywood these days, but who has certainly found the right tone for this one.

One of the nicest things about the movie is the way it maintains its note of slightly bewildered innocence. When Van Dohlen unpacks his computer and starts to assemble it, he reminds us a little of somebody like Harold Lloyd, determined to lick this thing. It's not often that a modern movie has the courage to give us a hero who doesn't seem to be a cross between a disco god and an aerobics instructor, but the Von Dohlen character is a nice change. He's likable, incompetent, and slightly dense. Virginia Madsen makes it clear right from the start that she loves her cello more than almost anything else in the world, and the movie's best single scene is the one where the computer, eavesdropping through a ventilation duct as she rehearses, joins in and plays a duet with her.

That scene, and a lot of other virtuoso moments in the movie, are photographed by Alex Thompson with a kind of fluid, poetic visual abandon that makes the movie a lot of fun to watch. The camera sweeps low over a keyboard, taking a flight that's almost as exhilarating as one of those swoops in *Star Wars*. During the songs, the screen fills with a kind of orgasmic computer screen display. They didn't stop after they figured out the story of this movie; it's obvious that the director, Steve Barron, spent a lot of time with his collaborators talking about how they could elevate their simple little story into something approaching a romantic flight of fancy. They were successful.

The Electric Horseman ★ ★ ★
PG, 120 m., 1979

Robert Redford (Sonny), Jane Fonda
(Hallie), Valerie Perrine (Charlotta), Willie
Nelson (Wendell), John Saxon (Hunt Sears),
Nicholas Coster (Fitzgerald). Directed by
Sydney Pollack and produced by Ray Stark.
Screenplay by Robert Garland.

The Electric Horseman is the kind of movie
they used to make. It's an oddball love story
about a guy and a girl and a prize racehorse,
and it has a chase scene and some smooching
and a happy ending. It could have starred
Tracy and Hepburn, or Gable and Colbert,
but it doesn't need to because this time it
stars Robert Redford and Jane Fonda.

The movie almost willfully wants to be
old-fashioned. It's got bad guys from a big
corporation, and big kisses seen in silhouette
in the sunset, and it works Fonda and Redford for all the star quality they've got. But
Electric Horseman doesn't try to be completely guileless. It has a bunch of contemporary themes and causes to dress up its basic
situation—which is, let's face it, Girl meets
Boy (and Horse). And although we are never
for a moment in doubt about the happy ending, there *is* a certain basic suspense as Redford and Fonda head for the hills and the evil
corporation follows by helicopter.

The movie begins with Redford in the process of downfall. He plays a former five-time
national champion rodeo cowboy named
Sonny, who has retired from competition and
signed on as the spokesman for a cereal
named "Ranch Breakfast." This is some
cereal. It is fortified, we gather, not only with
vitamins, minerals, and bran, but also with
leather, nails, and sagebrush. Redford
makes personal appearances on behalf of the
cereal, wearing a garish electrified cowboy
suit that plugs into the saddle of his horse.
The cowboy outfit isn't the only thing that's
lit up: Redford's drunk most of the time, and
ignominiously falls off his horse during a
half-time show.

Things come to a climax during a big Las
Vegas convention sponsored by the conglomerate that owns Ranch Breakfast. Redford's supposed to ride onstage on a
multimillion-dollar champion racehorse.
But he has a run-in with the president of the
conglomerate, discovers that the horse is

drugged and on steroids, and decides to
make his own personal gesture of defiance.
He rides onstage, all right—and right offstage, too, and down the Vegas strip, and out
into the desert.

Jane Fonda plays a TV newswoman who's
covering the convention, and she does some
clever detective work to figure out where
Redford might be headed. And then the
movie's more or less predictable: Fonda
finds Redford, grows to share his indignation at how the horse has been treated, and
trades her loyalty for exclusive rights to the
story. It turns out to be a really big story, of
course, as the conglomerate tries to track
down its racehorse and the TV networks get
in a race to find Redford.

If you spend much time scrutinizing the
late show on television, some of this material
might not sound dazzlingly original. The
device of the famous runaway with a journalist in hot pursuit, for example, is straight
out of *It Happened One Night*—and as Fonda
calls her office from remote pay phones,
we're reminded of Clark Gable in exactly the
same situations. The notion of the last of the
cowboys heading for the hills and being
tracked by helicopters is also familiar; it's
from *Lonely Are the Brave*, with Kirk Douglas, and some of the shots look hauntingly
familiar.

The relationship between Fonda and Redford is also pretty basic stuff, in which the
gruff outdoorsman and the perfect lady grow
to respect each other while sharing the rigors
of life on the run. Bogart and Hepburn made
that relationship a classic in *The African
Queen*, but Redford and Fonda have much
the same chemistry. Remember that scene on
the boat with Hepburn putting her chin in
her hand and giving Bogart the old once-
over? Fonda does that to Redford, and it's
about as erotic as six of your average love
scenes.

Both Redford and Fonda have identified
themselves with a lot of the issues in this
movie (which are—I have a list right here—
the evils of corporate conglomeratism, the
preservation of our wild lands, respect for
animals, the phoniness of commercialism,
the pack instinct of TV journalism, and
nutritious breakfasts). But although this is a
movie filled with messages, it's not a message movie. The characters and plot seem to

tap-dance past the serious stuff and concentrate on the human relationships.

If *Electric Horseman* has a flaw, it's that the movie's so warm and cozy it can hardly be electrifying. The director, Sydney Pollack, gives us solid entertainment, but he doesn't take chances and he probably didn't intend to. He's an ideal choice for orchestrating Redford and Fonda; he directed Fonda in *They Shoot Horses, Don't They?* and has made a subsidiary career out of directing Redford (in *This Property is Condemned, Jeremiah Johnson, The Way We Were,* and *Three Days of the Condor*). He has grown up with them, he respects the solidity of their screen personas, and he seems to understand (as the directors of Bogart, Hepburn, Gable, et al., did in the forties) that if you have the right Boy and the right Girl and the right story, about all you have to do is stay out of the way of the Horse.

Eleni ★ ★ ★
PG, 116 m., 1985

Kate Nelligan (Eleni), John Malkovich (Nick), Linda Hunt (Katina), Ronald Pickup (Spiro), Oliver Cotton (Katis), Alfred Molina (Young Christus), Steve Plytas (Old Christus). Directed by Peter Yates and produced by Nick Vanuff and Mark Pick. Screenplay by Steve Tesich.

Eleni is based on the true story of a *New York Times* reporter who went searching for his past in Greece. The reporter's name is Nicholas Gage. As a very young boy, he was sent to America to join relatives at the end of World War II. He has a sharp memory of his mother promising to join him as soon as possible, but his mother never arrived, and word finally came that she had been killed—shot by a firing squad in the confused days of the Greek civil war.

As the movie opens, years have passed, but the agony of that loss has not faded for Nick Gage. He feels he cannot rest until he finds the answers to the questions that haunt him: Why was his mother killed? Who killed her? He arranges to be sent to Greece on assignment for his newspaper, and his wife, who has had to live with his agony, realizes how special this trip is when she discovers him packing a gun to take along.

Eleni tells Gage's story in the present day,

and then uses flashbacks to tell his mother's story. The adult Nick is played by John Malkovich as an introspective, wryly intelligent man who harbors deep hurts and angers. The flashbacks center around the last days of his mother, played by Kate Nelligan as a remarkably strong, courageous, clearheaded peasant woman.

Both performances are good, but the second one is not necessary. In a curious way that has to be seen to be understood, the flashbacks weaken the story. The movie has started by looking through the eyes of an adult American who seeks answers from his childhood and his past. By allowing us to see the events of forty years ago, the screenplay makes a tactical error: It shows us things that Nick Gage himself never saw, and could never have known. The importance of his mystery is lessened. And the movie dissipates tension by providing us with information Gage is still searching for.

That said, there are still many fine qualities in *Eleni*. Some of them are not quite apparent until near the end of the movie, when the climactic scenes help us appreciate what went before. In particular, there is a moment when Nicholas Gage actually sits down at a table across from the man who killed his mother, and looks into that man's eyes, and tries to decide what to do next. It provides the emotional payoff for all of the groundwork in the Malkovich performance: We see the decision of a man we have grown to know.

Malkovich is developing into one of the great strong quiet zones of contemporary film acting. His characters internalize their feelings. Anger causes his voice to drop, or, when it rises, to seem as if feelings are being forced out of him. The result is more effective than if he pounded on tables and waved his arms—choices some other actors might have made, given a volatile Greek-American to play. This is a character who has been hurt very deeply inside, and has spent years brooding on that hurt.

Kate Nelligan, on the other hand, provides a more demonstrative performance as Eleni. Her eyes flash, her temper flares, she is passionate in her care for her children. She is among my very favorite movie actresses (remember her performance in *Eye of the Needle*). But she is probably not quite right for this role, because she seems too finished, too sophisticated, for this woman who lives in a house with earth floors and goes to the well for her water in the morning. She tries, but she is too polished.

The movie's fatal flaw, however, is to even show us Eleni in the first place. What happened in 1947 is one thing. What Nicholas Gage does about it thirty years later is very much another thing, and has to do with memory and revenge, not with the literal rediscovery of the past that we get from flashbacks.

The Elephant Man ★ ★
PG, 123 m., 1980

Anthony Hopkins (Frederick Treves), John Hurt (John Merrick), Anne Bancroft (Mrs. Kendal), John Gielgud (Carr Gomm). Directed by David Lynch and produced by Jonathan Sanger. Screenplay by Christopher DeVore, Eric Bergren, and David Lynch.

The film of *The Elephant Man* is not based on the successful stage play of the same name, but they both draw their sources from the life of John Merrick, the original "elephant man," whose rare disease imprisoned him in a cruelly misformed body. Both the play and the movie adopt essentially the same point of view, that we are to honor Merrick because of the courage with which he faced his existence.

The Elephant Man forces me to question this position on two grounds: first, on the meaning of Merrick's life, and second, on the ways in which the film employs it. It is conventional to say that Merrick, so hideously misformed that he was exhibited as a sideshow attraction, was courageous. No doubt he was. But there is a distinction here that needs to be drawn, between the courage of a man who chooses to face hardship for a good purpose, and the courage of a man who is simply doing the best he can, under the circumstances.

Wilfrid Sheed, an American novelist who is crippled by polio, once discussed this distinction in a *Newsweek* essay. He is sick and tired, he wrote, of being praised for his "courage," when he did not choose to contract polio and has little choice but to deal with his handicaps as well as he can. True

courage, he suggests, requires a degree of choice. Yet the whole structure of *The Elephant Man* is based on a life that is said to be courageous, not because of his hero's achievements, but simply because of the bad trick played on him by fate. In the film and the play (which are similar in many details), John Merrick learns to move in society, to have ladies in to tea, to attend the theater, and to build a scale model of a cathedral. Merrick may have had greater achievements in real life, but the film glosses them over. How, for example, did he learn to speak so well and eloquently? History tells us that the real Merrick's jaw was so misshapen that an operation was necessary just to allow him to talk. In the film, however, after a few snuffles to warm up, he quotes the Twenty-Third Psalm and *Romeo and Juliet*. This is pure sentimentalism.

The film could have chosen to develop the relationship between Merrick and his medical sponsor, Dr. Frederick Treves, along the lines of the bond between doctor and child in Truffaut's *The Wild Child*. It could have bluntly dealt with the degree of Merrick's inability to relate to ordinary society, as in Werner Herzog's *Kaspar Hauser*. Instead, it makes him noble and celebrates his nobility.

I kept asking myself what the film was *really* trying to say about the human condition as reflected by John Merrick, and I kept drawing blanks. The film's philosophy is this shallow: (1) Wow, the Elephant Man sure looked hideous, and (2) gosh, isn't it wonderful how he kept on in spite of everything? This last is in spite of a real possibility that John Merrick's death at twenty-seven might have been suicide.

The film's technical credits are adequate. John Hurt is very good as Merrick, somehow projecting a humanity past the disfiguring makeup, and Anthony Hopkins is correctly aloof and yet venal as the doctor. The direction, by David *(Eraserhead)* Lynch, is competent, although he gives us an inexcusable opening scene in which Merrick's mother is trampled or scared by elephants or raped—who knows?—and an equally idiotic closing scene in which Merrick becomes the Star Child from *2001*, or something.

The Emerald Forest ★ ★
R, 115 m., 1985

Powers Boothe (Bill Markham), Charley Boorman (Tommy Markham), Meg Foster (Jean Markham), Dira Paes (Kachiri), Rui Polonah (Wanadi). Directed and produced by John Boorman. Screenplay by Rospo Pallenberg.

The Emerald Forest begins as a breathtaking fable and ends as a routine action movie. Somewhere along the way, there was a failure of the imagination. Or was it just cynicism that made the filmmakers abandon their daring subject matter to give us one more movie where people jump out of trees and shoot machine guns at each other? The first half of this movie seems inspired by such great, visionary jungle films as *Aguirre, the Wrath of God*. The second half is lacking only Rambo to make it complete.

The film is based on a true story, we are told, about the young son of an American construction engineer. While his father was surveying at the edge of the rain forest, the little boy wandered off among the trees and disappeared. He was captured by a native tribe. In the years to come, he was raised to manhood in the tribe, learning its ways, and eventually becoming a full-fledged member. In real life, I am told, the young man still is living with the tribe in the jungle. In *The Emerald Forest*, he is kidnapped a second time—this time, by Hollywood clichés.

Director John Boorman shot the movie on location in the jungles of the Amazon, and it looks absolutely wonderful. The jungle is like a living, breathing participant in every scene. The little boy is taken off by the tribe, and in a series of brief scenes we see him growing toward manhood. He is taught by Wanadi, a tribal elder. He falls in love with Kachiri, a girl with a smiling face. Their love resembles one of those South Sea idylls like *The Blue Lagoon*, but no matter; it is sweet and innocent. Wanadi resembles every tribal elder in movie history, but, again, we don't mind because his role is simple and necessary. Meanwhile, the boy's father (Powers Boothe) makes yearly expeditions into the jungle, and on one of them, he astonishingly comes face-to-face with his son, who recognizes him from dreams. And it is precisely at this moment that the film takes its wrong turn, with a preposterous adventure involving an enemy tribe that kidnaps young maidens and sells them as prostitutes to white traders. One moment we're looking at the mysteries of the jungle, and the next minute we get one of those machine-made scenes where the good guys hunker down in the jungle and watch while the evil guards make their rounds.

There are moments in the film that are very effective. In one of them, the young man (Charley Boorman) climbs the side of a modern skyscraper. In another, he enters into courtship in a series of interesting rituals and dances. Some of the ideas in the movie are provoking, especially the way the tribe refers to the jungle as "The World," and to whites as "termites," because they eat away at the trees.

The Amazonian rain forest is a precarious ecology, being stripped away by greed and turned into desert at an alarming rate. A film that teaches the beauty of the jungle is a great treasure. Why did this one have to turn into a retread of those weary old pulp jungle tales?

Emmanuelle ★ ★ ★
X, 92 m., 1975

Sylvia Kristel (Emmanuelle), Alain Cuny (Mario), Marika Green (Bee), Daniel Sarky (Jean), Jeanne Colletin (Ariane), Christine Boisson (Marie-Ange). Directed by Just Jaeckin and produced by Yves Rousset-Rouard. Screenplay by Jean-Louis Richard.

Emmanuelle is a silly, classy, enjoyable erotic film that became an all-time box office success in France. It's not remotely significant enough to deserve that honor, but in terms of its genre (soft-core skin flick) it's very well done: lushly photographed on location in Thailand, filled with attractive and intriguing people, and scored with brittle, teasing music. Now that hard-core porno has become passé, it's a relief to see a movie that drops the gynecology and returns to a certain amount of sexy sophistication.

There have been movies influenced by other movies, and directors influenced by other directors, but *Emmanuelle* may be the first movie influenced by magazine centerfolds. Its style of color photography seems directly ripped off from the centerfolds in *Penthouse*, including even the props and decor. Its characters (French diplomats and—especially—their women in Thailand) inhabit a world of wicker furniture, soft pastels, vaguely Victorian lingerie, backlighting, forests of potted plants, and lots of diaphanous draperies shifting in the breeze. It's a world totally devoid of any real content, of course, and Emmanuelle is right at home in it. She's the young, virginal wife of a diplomat, and has just flown out from Paris to rejoin him. Her husband refuses to be possessive, and indeed almost propels her into a dizzying series of sexual encounters that range from the merely kinky to the truly bizarre. In the midst of this erotic maelstrom, Emmanuelle somehow retains her innocence.

The director, Just Jaeckin, correctly understands that gymnastics and heavy breathing do not an erotic movie make, nor does excessive attention to gynecological detail. Carefully deployed clothing can, indeed, be more erotic than plain nudity, and the decor in *Emmanuelle* also tends to get into the act. Jaeckin is a master of establishing situations; the seduction of Emmanuelle on the airplane, for example, is all the more effective because of its forbidden nature. And the encounter after the boxing match (Emmanuelle is the prize for the winning fighter and tenderly licks the sweat from his eyebrow) is given a rather startling voyeuristic touch (the spectators don't leave after the fight).

The movie's first hour or so is largely given over to lesbian situations, but then Emmanuelle comes under the influence of the wise old Mario (played by Alain Cuny, the French actor immortalized as Steiner, the intellectual who committed suicide in Fellini's *La Dolce Vita*). She is turned off at first by his age, but with age, she is assured, comes experience, and does it ever. Mario delivers himself of several profoundly meaningless generalizations about finding oneself through others and attaining true freedom, and then he introduces her to a series of photogenic situations. Mario's philosophy is frankly foolish, but Cuny delivers it with such solemn, obsessed conviction that the scenes become a parody, and *Emmanuelle*'s comic undertones are preserved.

What also makes the film work is the performance of Sylvia Kristel as Emmanuelle.

She's a slender actress who isn't even the prettiest woman in the film, but she projects a certain vulnerability that makes several of the scenes work. The performers in most skin flicks seem so impervious to ordinary mortal failings, so blasé in the face of the most outrageous sexual invention, that finally they just become cartoon characters. Kristel actually seems to be present in the film, and as absorbed in its revelations as we are. It's a relief, during a time of cynicism in which sex is supposed to sell anything, to find a skin flick that's a lot better than it probably had to be.

Endless Love ★ ★
R, 115 m., 1981

Brooke Shields (Jade), Martin Hewitt (David), Shirley Knight (Anne), Don Murray (Hugh), Richard Kiley (Arthur), Beatrice Straight (Rose), Penelope Milford (Ingrid). Directed by Franco Zeffirelli and produced by Dyson Lovell. Screenplay by Judith Rascoe.

The novel *Endless Love* is about a teen-age boy who remembers, with full ferocity and grief and yearning, the great love of his life, after it has been ended by fate and the adult world. The movie *Endless Love* is about a teen-age boy and girl who are in love, until fate and adults end their relationship. There is all the difference in the world between these two story sequences, and although there are a great many things wrong with the movie, this blunder on the narrative level is the worst.

Didn't the makers of this movie understand the poignancy at the very heart of the novel? The book begins with its hero, David, committing an act that will end all of his happiness for years. Forbidden to see his girl, Jade, for thirty days, he sets a fire of newspapers on the porch of her house—hoping to win a reprieve by being the hero who "discovers" the fire. The house burns down, and David is sent into a long exile in a mental institution. The novel's point of view is of a boy who has lost everything he values and remembers it with undying passion. But the movie rearranges the events of the book into chronological order. That means that the love affair between Jade and David, instead of being remembered as a painful loss, is seen in the "now" as . . . well, as a teen-age romance. Its additional level of meaning is lost.

A story that began as a poem to the fierce pride of adolescent passion gets transmuted into a sociological case study. This movie contains some of the same characters and events as Scott Spencer's wonderful novel (indeed, at times it is unnecessarily faithful to situations and dialogue from the book), but it does not contain the book's reason for being. It is about events and it should be about passion.

There are many other problems in the film. One crucial mistake is in casting: Martin Hewitt, as David, the seventeen-year-old boy, is a capable actor but is too handsome, too heavily bearded, too old in appearance to suggest an adolescent bundle of vulnerability and sensitivity. Another mistake is in narrative: The sequence of events involving David's release from the institution, his trip to New York, and exactly what happens there, is so badly jumbled that some audience members will not know how and why he went to New York, and hardly anyone will be able to follow the circumstances that reunite him with Jade.

A third mistake is in this movie's ending, or rather, its lack of one: The final three minutes in this movie are enraging to anyone who has made an emotional investment in it, because they are a cop-out, a refusal to deal with the material and bring it to a conclusion. The fourth mistake is the one that made me most angry, because it deals with the central act of the narrative, with the disaster around which the story revolves. In the book, David sets fire to the newspaper as an act of passion, confusion, and grief—sure it's dumb, but he's confused and in turmoil. The movie, with offensive heavy-handedness, has another youth *suggest* the fire to David as a strategy. Apparently the filmmakers thought the fire had to be "explained." The result is to take a reckless act and turn it into a stupid one, diminishing both David's intelligence and the power of his passion.

The movie's central relationship, between Jade (Brooke Shields) and David, comes out as a disappointment, because their scenes are not allowed to develop human resonances. We never really feel and understand the bond between these two people. That's partly because of Hewitt's inability to project uncertainty and adolescent awkwardness; he comes on so strong and self-confident that David seems like a young man making a bold bid for a good-looking girl, rather than as one-half of a pair of star-crossed adolescent lovers.

Is there anything good in the movie? Yes. Brooke Shields is good. She is a great natural beauty, and she demonstrates, in a scene of tenderness and concern for Jewitt and in a scene of rage with her father, that she has a strong, unaffected screen acting manner. But the movie as a whole does not understand the particular strengths of the novel that inspired it, does not convince us it understands adolescent love, does not seem to know its characters very well, and is a narrative and logical mess.

Enemy Mine ★ ★ ½
PG-13, 109 m., 1985

Dennis Quaid (Davidge), Louis Gossett, Jr. (Shigan), Brian James (Stubbs), Richard Marcus (Arnold). Directed by Wolfgang Petersen and produced by Stephen Friedman. Screenplay by Edward Kharma.

Enemy Mine is *Robinson Crusoe* set under the two suns and six moons of the volcanic planet Fyrine IV, a grim red landscape lashed by meteors and savage cold. One day a century in the future, the spaceships of two warring pilots crash-land not far from each other. One of the pilots is a gee-whiz earthling, and the other one is a reptilian humanoid from the planet Dracon. Although they are natural enemies, they learn to live together, to help each other, and eventually even to love each other.

The look of the planet in *Enemy Mine* is so convincing, the special effects are so elaborate, and the performances are so good that I only gradually became aware of what a clinker the story is. The movie has the potential to be a truly great story about communication between alien species; it could have been a space thriller with a mind and a heart. Instead, it gives us an alien that is too human, too familiar. It takes that amazing planet and gives it food, water, gravity, and atmosphere that are suitable for both humans and Dracs. It depends on plot gimmicks like the convenient arrival of enemies and the equally convenient arrival of friends to the rescue. It doesn't dare enough.

How should it dare? The world of science fiction is filled with fascinating aliens—intelligent creatures who are infinitely more than lovable characters in reptile skins. Why couldn't the Drac be truly alien in this film? There are occasional moments of inspiration, such as the fact that Dracs are male and female rolled into one, but *Enemy Mine* simply uses that as an excuse for a couple of weepy scenes and the creation of a Drac child that seems destined for the Little League.

The idea of aliens with combined sexes has been handled much more interestingly in books like Isaac Asimov's *The Gods Themselves,* in which there were three sexes, not two. And even the most rudimentary science fiction aliens usually manage to seem truly different from humans; once the Drac in *Enemy Mine* learns English, he seems scarcely less human than the human.

The earthman in the movie is played by Dennis Quaid, and the Drac by Louis Gossett, Jr. They are both very good, but saddled with a predictable and sentimental script. If they had been left all alone on their barren planet, they might just possibly have arrived at some interesting story possibilities. Instead, *Enemy Mine* descends to the level of 1930s space opera with the arrival of evil human slave-traders who kidnap Dracs and force them to work in mines. As the slavers stood over their captives with whips, I found myself wondering how cost-effective it would be to transport manual laborers millions of light years. Surely a technology capable of arriving at the planet Fyrine IV would have figured out a better way to mine its ores?

Then there are the truly unbelievable moments, as when Quaid's apparently lifeless body is found by a human spaceship that is never seen; the cornball moment when he comes back to life; the human spaceships returning to Fyrine like the Cavalry to the rescue, and the final idiotic shoot-out. Were they so bankrupt of ideas, in a movie rich with them, that they had to resolve the plot with yet another fistfight and gunfight? By the time the noble, uplifting ending arrived, I'd given up. Here is a movie that made no compromises in its art direction, its special effects, and its performances—and then compromised everything else in sight.

Escape from New York ★ ★ ½
R, 99 m., 1981

Kurt Russell (Snake Plissken), Lee Van Cleef (Bob Hauk), Ernest Borgnine (Cabbie) Donald Pleasence (President), Harry Dean Stanton (Brain), Isaac Hayes (Duke), Season Hubley (Girl in Store), Adrienne Barbeau (Maggie). Directed by John Carpenter and produced by Larry France and Debra Hill. Screenplay by Carpenter and Nick Castle.

John Carpenter's *Escape from New York* is a cross between three of the most reliable ingredients in pulp fantasy: (1) the President Is Missing, (2) New York Is a Jungle, and (3) the Antihero as Time Bomb. Carpenter has gone after an original angle on each of the ingredients, with disappointing results. The president, for example, would be much more convincing if he were not played as a sniveling wimp by Donald Pleasance. The movie's New York of 1997 would have been more interesting if it were seen as a genuinely different prison society, rather than as a recycled version of *The Warriors.* And the antihero needs more human qualities and quirks; he seems lifted from old spaghetti Westerns.

These basic problems prevent the movie from becoming more than it is, a competent job of craftsmanship. And yet it's fun to see old standby science-fiction ingredients rehashed for our cynical times.

At the beginning of *Escape from New York,* we learn that the city was turned into a federal maximum security prison in 1987, and that several years later the island is ruled by prowling gangs who have their own sources of power, food, and clout. When we see New York, however, it is essentially just a garbage-strewn junkyard roamed by wild-eyed crazies. How *do* people survive there? If the movie had provided specific details, it could have been fascinating. Instead, we get tantalizing hints of how things work; for example, a gang leader (Isaac Hayes) has a small oil well pumping inside his headquarters.

The resident has been missing, endangered, kidnapped, blackmailed, or otherwise inconvenienced in countless other movies and novels. This time, after terrorists hijack Air Force One and crash it into Manhattan Island, the president escapes inside an ingenious armored crash pod that is never explained. He is then held hostage, along with a cassette tape that contains the means of preventing World War III. Carpenter's decision to cast Donald Pleasance in the role reminds us that Pleasance added great credibility and psychic weight to *Halloween,* in the role as the psychiatrist. But he never makes a convincing president.

The movie's plot revolves around the decision of the police commissioner (Lee Van Cleef) to send a convicted criminal into New York to bring the president back alive. The criminal is a Special Forces veteran (he fought, we learn, at Leningrad and in Siberia). If he gets the president out within twenty-four hours, he gets a pardon. If he doesn't, tiny time bombs rupture his major arteries. The criminal is played by Kurt Russell, a talented veteran of several Disney movies. Russell is so determined to shake his Disney image that he goes whole hog, with an eye patch, a three-day beard, and a growl so hoarse he seems to be moaning most of the time. It's an interesting idea for a performance, maybe, but nothing is done to give the character human qualities, and so we're allowed to remain detached about his plight.

A bunch of familiar faces turn up in supporting roles. Ernest Borgnine is the last of the wise-guy New York cabbies, *still* looking for fares in the jungle. Isaac Hayes is the gang leader, the inimitable Harry Dean Stanton is his personal advisor, and Adrienne Barbeau is his "squeeze." Making this list, I keep being reminded of the word I started out with: Ingredients. Everything is here, and it all works fairly well, but it never quite comes together into an involving story or an overpowering adventure.

Eureka ★ ★ ★
R, 130 m., 1984

Gene Hackman (Jack McCann), Theresa Russell (Tracy), Rutger Hauer (Claude), Jane Lapotaire (Helen McCann), Helena Kallianiotis (Frieda), Ed Lauter (Perkins), Mickey Rourke (D'Amato), Joe Pesci

(Mayakofsky). Directed by Nicolas Roeg and produced by Jeremy Thomas. Screenplay by Paul Mayersberg.

Eureka is a strange, perverse film about passion and greed, and it leads us through a labyrinthine story to a simple message: Money can't buy you love. It stars Gene Hackman as an obsessed gold prospector in the Yukon, who screams into the wind that he will "never make a nickel off another man's sweat." He stalks out into a blizzard, almost freezes to death, and then is saved through the supernatural intervention of a fortune-teller (Helena Kallianiotis). She arranges for him to find the mother lode and become the richest man in the world.

We then flash foward to the 1930s, when he lives on his own Caribbean island. He should be a man without worries, but he is desperately unhappy because his beloved daughter (Theresa Russell) has married a scheming playboy (Rutger Hauer). While monsoons blow and parrots squawk, he bans Hauer from his table and vows to see him dead. "At first I thought you wanted my daughter. Then I thought you wanted my gold," Hackman screams at him. "Now I think you want my soul." He is right, but there is a battle over that soul, and the other contestant is the daughter herself. The film's director, Nicholas Roeg, says he has friends who seem to be the soul-clones of their parents, and apparently the closing passages of *Eureka* are meant to be seen with that notion in mind. Meanwhile, there are so many other notions to keep in mind that the film all but sinks under the weight of its inspiration.

Roeg is a fascinating director. Remember some of his films: *Walkabout, Don't Look Now, Performance, The Man Who Fell to Earth, Bad Timing.* They almost all seem to deal with supernatural intervention in the affairs of man, and with the way those mysteries get tangled up with the bedsheets. His films are also a visual feast; Roeg, a former editor, loves to construct complicated fantasies out of images and memories, shocks and beautiful meditations.

Straightforward storytelling is not his strong point. But so what? The basic facts of *Eureka* (man strikes gold, becomes rich, grows old and jealous, suffers for greed) are familiar from Jack London, Edgar Allan

Poe, and von Stroheim's *Greed*. What Roeg brings to the party is a flair for the sensational, for characters who are larger than their weaknesses, who are connected to great archetypal forces. Hackman is wonderful here, with the intensity of his obsessions, and once again Russell (*still* only in her mid-twenties) is brilliant; in some ways this is her movie, and she steals scenes from everybody except, sometimes, Hackman. If *Eureka* is not completely successful—if, indeed, it is sometimes merely silly and often confusing—maybe that's the price we pay for Roeg's intensity. At least it is never boring.

Evil Under the Sun ★ ★ ★
PG, 102 m., 1982

Peter Ustinov (Hercule Poirot), Colin Blakely (Sir Horace Blatt), Jane Birkin (Christine Redfern), Nicholas Clay (Patrick Redfern), Maggie Smith (Daphne Castle), Roddy McDowall (Rex Brewster), Sylvia Miles (Myra Gardener), James Mason (Odell Gardener). Directed by Guy Hamilton and produced by John Brabourne and Richard Goodwin. Screenplay by Anthony Shaffer.

The delicious moments in an Agatha Christie film are supposed to come at the end, when the detective (in this case, the redoubtable Hercule Poirot) gathers everyone in the sitting room and toys with their guilt complexes before finally fingering the murderer. Well, there are delicious moments in the final fifteen minutes of *Evil Under the Sun*, but what I especially liked about this Christie were the opening scenes—the setup. They had a style and irreverence that reminded me curiously of *Beat the Devil*, with Bogart and Robert Morley chewing up the scenery. *Evil Under the Sun* is not, alas, as good as *Beat the Devil*, but it is the best of the recent group of Christie retreads (which include *Murder on the Orient Express, Death on the Nile*, and *The Mirror Crack'd*).

It begins in the usual way, with a corpse. It continues in obligatory fashion with the gathering of a large number of colorful and eccentric suspects in an out-of-the-way spot, which just happens to also be the destination of Hercule Poirot. It continues with the discovery of another corpse, with the liberal distribution of gigantic clues and with Poirot's lip-smacking summary of the evidence. It's the cast that makes *Evil* more fun than the previous manifestations of this identical plot. As Poirot, Peter Ustinov creates a wonderful mixture of the mentally polished and physically maladroit. He has a bit of business involving a dip in the sea that is so perfectly timed and acted it tells us everything we ever wanted to know about Poirot's appetite for exercise. He is so expansive, so beaming, so superior, in the opening scenes that he remains spiritually present throughout the film, even when he's not on screen.

All of the rest of the cast are suspects. They include Maggie Smith, a former actress who now runs an elegant spa in the Adriatic Sea; Diana Rigg, as her jealous contemporary; Sylvia Miles and James Mason, as a rich couple who produce shows on Broadway; Jane Birkin and Nicholas Clay as a young couple constantly arguing over his roving eye; Colin Blakely as a rich knight who's been taken by a gold digger; Emily Hone as the young new wife, and Roddy McDowell as a bitchy gossip columnist who knows the dirt about everybody. The newly discovered corpse belongs to one of the above. The murderer is one (or more) of the above. Nothing else I could say about the crime would be fair.

I can observe, however, that one of the delights of the movies made from Agatha Christie novels is their almost complete lack of passion: They substitute wit and style. Nobody really cares who gets bumped off, and nobody really misses the departed. What's important is that all the right clues be distributed, so that Poirot and the audience can pick them up, mull them over, and discover the culprit. Perhaps, then, one of the reasons I liked *Evil Under the Sun* was that this time, when Ustinov paused in his summation (after verbally convicting everyone in the room), and it was clear he was about to finger the real killer, I guessed the killer's identity, and I was right. Well, half right. That's better than I usually do.

Excalibur ★ ★ ½
R, 140 m., 1981

Nigel Terry (Arthur), Helen Mirren (Morgana),
Nicholas Clay (Lancelot), Nicol Williamson
(Merlin), Cherie Lunghi (Guenevere), Paul
Geoffrey (Perceval). Directed by John
Boorman and produced by Edgar F. Gross
and Robert A. Eisenstein. Screenplay by
Rospo Pallenberg and Boorman.

What a wondrous vision *Excalibur* is! And
what a mess. This wildly ambitious retelling
of the legend of King Arthur is a haunting
and violent version of the Dark Ages and the
heroic figures who (we dream) populated
them. But it's rough going for anyone determined to be sure what is happening from
scene to scene. Great armored figures clank
through the forest and bury broadaxes in
each other's bodies. Young Arthur frees the
magic sword Excalibur from the granite
boulder where it was embedded. Castles are
stormed. Arthur marries Guenevere and the
kingdom rejoices. Camelot reigns. Merlin
the Magician enters into a doomed pact with
Morgana, Arthur's half-sister, and Morgana
assumes the appearance of Guenevere to
seduce Arthur. She plans for their son born
of incest, Mordred, to take his place as
king . . .

And all of this is buried in such a wealth of
detail, such an impenetrable atmosphere,
such tumultuous alarms and excursions, that
the audience is quite likely to lose its place.
John Boorman, the director of *Excalibur,* is
brilliant at staging the life and times of
Arthur—the film is a triumph of production
design, costumes, and special effects. But he
hasn't hammered out a clear story line. His
male characters, bearded and hiding within
medieval helmets, sometimes look and
sound like one another. If Robert Bresson's
Lancelot of the Lake (1973) deliberately made
all the knights into interchangeable, clank-
ing clones, Boorman seems to have arrived at
the same place inadvertently. This is a film
we almost have to squint to see and to
understand.

As a panorama of sword and sorcery, however, it is very beautiful to watch. And as a
showcase for Nicol Williamson's Merlin, it is
sometimes a lot of fun; Williamson plays the
magician as a medieval Noel Coward, always
armed with the wry witticism. His relationship with Morgana (the lovely Helen
Mirren) is actually the most interesting thing
in the film. Morgana borrows Merlin's
magic to deceive Arthur and to stay young.
Inhabiting a dragon's cave that is apparently
somewhere beneath Camelot, she wears
brass brassieres and other obligatory props,
but she's intriguing.

It's curious how our tastes in myth
change; heroes seem to be devalued and our
fascination is with villains. Arthur almost
recedes into the scenery toward the end of
Excalibur, upstaged by the sins of Lancelot,
the schemes of Morgana, the arch amusement of Merlin and, finally, by the astonishing appearance of Mordred—who wears a
golden helmet that makes him into a muscular Cupid. *Excalibur* is a revisionist view
of what Arthur's people and times looked
like. But the film has a tendency to drift into
soft focus and impenetrable fogs. Many
scenes are shot through filters that soften
and dissipate their effect. The movie's very
last shot, of a ship plunging out to sea,
should have been hard-edged and forlorn,
but it's all misty and evanescent.

There is another problem, too: one common not only to many movie versions of
Arthurian legends, but epidemic in the modern sword-and-sorcery genre. The people in
this film seem doomed to their behavior.
They have no choice. Arthur is courageous
as a youth, but then presides over the disintegration of the Round Table, for no apparent reason. The brave and pure Lancelot,
accused of being Guenevere's lover, engages
in a deadly joust to defend her honor. Not
much later, however, they make love. Merlin
is a great and powerful magician, but allows
Morgana to outwit him; he seems to decide
from moment to moment whether to possess
vast powers or none.

Since there is no consistency in the behavior of the characters, *Excalibur* is maddeningly arbitrary. Anyone is likely to do
anything—and when they do, Boorman
springs another battle scene on us, with
horses whinnying and swords thumping into
flesh until the novelty wears thin. One of the
joys of *Star Wars,* which is really a sword-
and-sorcery fantasy of the future, is that
everyone plays by the rules, lives by the
Force, and is true to himself. Boorman's
Excalibur is a record of the comings and

goings of arbitrary, inconsistent, shadowy figures who are not heroes but simply giants run amok. Still, it's wonderful to look at.

The Exorcist ★ ★ ★ ★
R, 121 m., 1973

Ellen Burstyn (Chris), Linda Blair (Regan), Jason Miller (Father Karras), Max von Sydow (Father Merrin), Kitty Winn (Sharon), Lee J. Cobb (Kinderman). Directed by William Friedkin and produced by William Peter Blatty. Screenplay by Blatty.

1973 began and ended with cries of pain. It began with Ingmar Bergman's *Cries and Whispers*, and it closed with William Friedkin's *The Exorcist*. Both films are about the weather of the human soul, and no two films could be more different. Yet each in its own way forces us to look inside, to experience horror, to confront the reality of human suffering. The Bergman film is a humanist classic. The Friedkin film is an exploitation of the most fearsome resources of the cinema. That does not make it evil, but it does not make it noble, either.

The difference, maybe, is between great art and great craftsmanship. Bergman's exploration of the lines of love and conflict within the family of a woman dying of cancer was a film that asked important questions about faith and death, and was not afraid to admit there might not be any answers. Friedkin's film is about a twelve-year-old girl who either is suffering from a severe neurological disorder or—perhaps has been possessed by an evil spirit. Friedkin has the answers; the problem is that we doubt he believes them.

We don't necessarily believe them ourselves, but that hardly matters during the film's two hours. If movies are, among other things, opportunities for escapism, then *The Exorcist* is one of the most powerful ever made. Our objections, our questions, occur in an intellectual context after the movie has ended. During the movie there are no reservations, but only experiences. We feel shock, horror, nausea, fear, and some small measure of dogged hope.

Rarely do movies affect us so deeply. The first time I saw *Cries and Whispers*, I found myself shrinking down in my seat, somehow trying to escape from the implications of

Bergman's story. *The Exorcist* also has that effect—but we're not escaping from Friedkin's implications, we're shrinking back from the direct emotional experience he's attacking us with. This movie doesn't rest on the screen; it's a frontal assault.

The story is well-known; it's adapted, more or less faithfully, by William Peter Blatty from his own bestseller. Many of the technical and theological details in his book are accurate. Most accurate of all is the reluctance of his Jesuit hero, Father Karras, to encourage the ritual of exorcism: "To do that," he says, "I'd have to send the girl back to the sixteenth century." Modern medicine has replaced devils with paranoia and schizophrenia, he explains. Medicine may have, but the movie hasn't. The last chapter of the novel never totally explained in detail the final events in the tortured girl's bedroom, but the movie's special effects in the closing scenes leave little doubt that an actual evil spirit was in that room, and that it transferred bodies. Is this fair? I guess so; in fiction the artist has poetic license.

It may be that the times we live in have prepared us for this movie. And Friedkin has admittedly given us a good one. I've always preferred a generic approach to film criticism; I ask myself how good a movie is of its type. *The Exorcist* is one of the best movies of its type ever made; it not only transcends the genre of terror, horror, and the supernatural, but it transcends such serious, ambitious efforts in the same direction as Roman Polanski's *Rosemary's Baby*. Carl Dreyer's *The Passion of Joan of Arc* is a greater film—but, of course, not nearly so willing to exploit the ways film can manipulate feeling.

The Exorcist does that with a vengeance. The film is a triumph of special effects. Never for a moment—not when the little girl is possessed by the most disgusting of spirits, not when the bed is banging and the furniture flying and the vomit is welling out—are we less than convinced. The film contains brutal shocks, almost indescribable obscenities. That it received an R rating and not the X is stupefying.

The performances are in every way appropriate to this movie made this way. Ellen Burstyn, as the possessed girl's mother, rings especially true; we feel her frustration when doctors and psychiatrists talk about lesions on the brain and she *knows* there's something deeper, more terrible, going on. Linda Blair, as the little girl, has obviously been put through an ordeal in this role, and puts us through one. Jason Miller, as the young Jesuit, is tortured, doubting, intelligent.

And the casting of Max von Sydow as the older Jesuit exorcist was inevitable; he has been through so many religious and metaphysical crises in Bergman's films that he almost seems to belong on a theological battlefield the way John Wayne belonged on a horse. There's a striking image early in the film that has the craggy von Sydow facing an ancient, evil statue; the image doesn't so much borrow from Bergman's famous chess game between von Sydow and Death (in *The Seventh Seal*) as extend the conflict and raise the odds.

I am not sure exactly what reasons people will have for seeing this movie; surely enjoyment won't be one, because what we get here aren't the delicious chills of a Vincent Price thriller, but raw and painful experience. Are people so numb they need movies of this intensity in order to feel anything at all? It's hard to say.

Even in the extremes of Friedkin's vision there is still a feeling that this is, after all, cinematic escapism and not a confrontation with real life. There is a fine line to be drawn there, and *The Exorcist* finds it and stays a millimeter on this side.

**Experience Preferred . . .
But Not Essential** ★ ★ ★
PG, 77 m., 1983

Elizabeth Edmonds (Annie), Sue Wallace (Mavis), Geraldine Griffith (Doreen), Karen Meagher (Paula), Ron Bain (Mike), Alun Lewis (Hywel). Directed by Peter Duffell and produced by David Puttnam and Chris Griffin. Screenplay by June Roberts.

This movie is so slight and charming you're almost afraid to breathe during it, for fear of disturbing the spell. It's about ordinary people in an ordinary setting, but because the setting is a small resort hotel in Wales, and the time is the summer of 1962, there's also the strange feeling that we've entered another time and place, where some of the same rules apply, but by no means all of them.

The movie tells the story of a young woman named Annie (Elizabeth Edmonds) who comes to work for the summer in a hotel, and finds that she's entered a cozy little backstairs world with its own sets of loyalties and jealousies. All of the other waitresses at the hotel have their own stories, some funny, some sad, and Annie feels a little left out. "I'm the only one here without a past," she complains, but of course one of the reasons for spending your summer working in a hotel is to accumulate a past. The other women are suspicious of her because she's a student, but as the waitresses cram into the servants' quarters, three to a room and sometimes two to a bed, a sort of democracy sets in, and Annie is accepted.

The movie uses a wonderfully offhand style for filling us in on the characters. There's the gallant cook, who immediately takes a liking to Annie. And the redheaded bartender, who makes it a nightly habit to sleepwalk in the nude. And the conceited young waiter whose idea of a courtship is to belt his girl in the eye every once in a while. And the pretty hostess of the dining room, who owes her position and her private boudoir to the favors she supplies the hotel's owner. ("How did you get such a nice room?" Annie asks her, innocently.)

There's not much of a plot. Things just sort of happen. Young men and women work from dawn to dusk and then collapse into each other's arms, almost but not quite too exhausted for sex. And the sexual customs of the pre-Pill era take on a certain quaintness, and a certain desperation, as couples grimly try to walk the line between lust and prudence. *Experience Preferred* is charming precisely because of its inconsequential air. It's funny because it goes for whimsical little insights into human nature rather than for big, obvious jokes. It's charming because it doesn't force the charm.

Explorers ★ ★
PG, 109 m., 1985

Ethan Hawke (Ben Crandall), River Phoenix (Wolfgang Muller), Jason Presson (Darren Woods), Amanda Peterson (Lori Swenson), Dick Miller (Charlie Drake). Directed by Joe Dante and produced by Edward S. Feldman and David Bombyk. Screenplay by Eric Luke.

This movie takes a deep breath and plunges headlong into the unknown, and belly-flops into a universe full of Jell-O. What an anticlimax. It begins with three brainy kids figuring out a way to conquer gravity and fly to the stars, and it ends with a bunch of sideshow aliens who repeat material they've learned by watching television. This is the cinematic equivalent of the chimp that learned to play chess and won a gumball.

The opening scenes of *Explorers* promise so much that maybe they heightened my eventual disappointment. We meet three smart junior high school students who shrug off attacks by the local bullies and spend their evenings down in a basement, fiddling with a computer. At night, they communicate by walkie-talkie. And one night, one of the kids calls up with some astonishing news: he has dreamed up a way to program the computer to generate some weird kind of anti-gravity force-field.

In one of the movie's best scenes, the kids feed a program into their computer, and it takes over and starts to program itself, generating a transparent ball of green glowing energy that floats in midair, right there in the basement, before suddenly zapping its way straight through a whole shelf of old sci-fi magazines. This is big stuff. The kids take their computer outdoors and try the experiment again, and this time the green glob encompasses one of the boys and takes him on a trip through the sky. The kids don't know how their invention works, or why, but it looks like they've solved the problem of space travel.

They seem strangely blasé in the face of this development. In fact, they are probably the coolest kids in their town and maybe their state. They're thrilled, all right, but they're not gaga. They steal some parts from a junkyard, create a makeshift space capsule, enclose it in the computer-generated energy field, and start flying around. And all of

these scenes have a sort of magic to them; the movie generates a sort of innocent wonderment, an aura of awesome discovery that allows us to go along with the spirit of their quest.

That's before the scenes set in outer space. They should be the emotional payoff of the movie, but instead they're a disappointing comedown. The three kids fly into space, their little bubble is captured by an alien spacecraft and after a funny encounter with an inquisitive mechanical spider, they meet their hosts. The aliens look like comic monsters from Saturday morning TV cartoons. They're pot-bellied, bug-eyed caricatures (one looks like an extraterrestrial Miss Piggy), and they've spent the last thirty years watching television. That's why they speak like Ed Sullivan, game show hosts, and Mr. Ed.

A very, very little of this inspiration would have been enough. (Indeed, the first three words spoken by an alien get a big laugh, and the movie should have stopped while it was ahead.) The TV amateur hour goes on much too long, all sense of suspense and involvement is lost, and the movie becomes a showcase for special effects. What *E.T.* knew and *Explorers* doesn't know is that a special effect becomes magical only when it is used for a genuine narrative purpose. By the time the kids ended their adventure, I was disappointed. They'd started out on a journey to the stars, but they got only as far as the "Amateur Hour."

Exposed ★ ★ ★ ½
R, 100 m., 1983

Nastassja Kinski (Elizabeth), Rudolph Nureyev (Daniel), Harvey Keitel (Rivas), Ian McShane (Miller), Bibi Andersson (Margaret), Pierre Clementi (Vic). Directed and produced by James Toback. Screenplay by Toback.

This movie contains moments so exhilarating they reawakened me to the infinite possibilities of movies. Yet this movie loses itself in its closing sequences and meanders through the details of a routine terrorist plot. Somewhere between its greatness and its wandering there must be a compromise, and I would strike it this way: *Exposed* contains the most exciting evidence I have seen so far that Nastassja Kinski is the next great female superstar. I do not say that she is a great actress; not yet, and perhaps not ever. I do not compare her with Meryl Streep or Kate Nelligan, Jill Clayburgh or Jessica Lange. I am not talking in those terms of professional accomplishment. I am talking about the mysterious, innate quality that some performers have to cast a special spell, to develop a relationship with the camera that you can call stardom or voodoo or magic, because its name doesn't really matter.

Kinski has it. There are moments in this film (two virtuoso scenes, in particular, and then many other small moments and parts of scenes) when she affects me in the same way that Marilyn Monroe must have affected her first viewers, in movies like *The Asphalt Jungle* or *All About Eve*. She was not yet a star and audiences did not even know her name, but there was a quality about her that could not be dismissed. Kinski has that quality. She has exhibited it before in better films, such as *Tess*, and in ambitious, imperfect films such as *Cat People* and *One from the Heart*. Now here is *Exposed*, written and directed by James Toback, who in screenplays such as *The Gambler* and his brilliant, little-seen directing debut *Fingers*, has specialized in characters who live on the edge.

There are two sequences in *Exposed* where he pulls out all the stops. In one of them, Kinski (who plays a college dropout, lonely and sexually frustrated) dances all by herself in a nearly empty apartment. In another one, she meets a violinist (Rudolph Nureyev), they fall instantly into a consuming passion, and after he has tantalized her with a violin bow they make sudden, passionate love. The sheer quality of Kinski's abandon in these two scenes made me realize how many barriers can sometimes exist between a performance and an audience: Here there are none.

The movie is wonderful for its first hour or more. It follows Kinski through a brief, unhappy love affair with her professor (played by Toback), shows her moving to New York, has her discovered by a photographer and becoming a world-famous model (because she is Kinski, this is believable), and brings her up through the love affair with Nureyev. At this moment, *Exposed* seems poised on the brink of declar-ing itself one of the most riveting character portraits ever made.

And that is the moment where it falters, and loses itself in the details of a plot involving Harvey Keitel, as the leader of an underground terrorist cell in Paris. It's as if Toback didn't trust the strength of this character he had created (or, more likely, didn't know when he wrote his thriller that Kinski would bring the character so completely to life). The rest of the movie is okay, I suppose, in a somewhat familiar way. But its special quality is lost in plot details. Too bad. But if a movie can electrify me the way this one did, not once but twice and then some, I'm prepared to forgive it almost anything.

The Exterminator   no stars
R, 101 m., 1980

Christopher George (Detective Dalton), Samantha Eggar (Dr. Stewart), Robert Ginty (John Eastland), Steve James (Michael Jefferson). Directed and written by James Glickenhaus and produced by Mark Buntzman.

The Exterminator is a sick example of the almost unbelievable descent into gruesome savagery in American movies. It's a direct rip-off of *Death Wish*, a 1974 Charles Bronson hit about a man who kills muggers to avenge the death of his wife. *Death Wish* was violent, yes, but it remained within certain boundaries. It established a three-dimensional character, it gave him reasons for his actions, it allowed us to sympathize with those reasons and yet still disapprove of the murders he was committing. *The Exterminator* does none of those things. It is essentially just a sadistic exercise in moronic violence, supported by a laughable plot. The "exterminator" of the movie's title (Robert Ginty) has his life saved in Vietnam by a black man (Steve James), who becomes his closest friend. Back home in Brooklyn, they break up a gang in the process of stealing beer from a loading dock. The gang gets revenge by attacking and permanently paralyzing the black man. The hero vows revenge.

So far, so good. What's profoundly disturbing about the film is that it uses this "justification" in the plot as an excuse for revenge scenes of the sickest possible perver-

sion. The motive is obviously to shock or tit-
illate the audience, not to show plausible
actions by the character. For example: Ginty
gets one gang member to talk by tying him to
a wall and threatening him with an acetylene
torch. Then he machine-guns the men who
attacked his buddy.

They get off easy. Determined to get
money to support the family of his paralyzed
friend, Ginty kidnaps a Mafia boss. He
hangs him by chains over a huge meat
grinder, goes to rob his house and then
lowers the man into the grinder, converting
him to ground meat. He justifies this crime
in a letter to anchorman Roger Grimsby
(who plays himself—to his horror, no doubt,
when he saw this film). And then he goes on a
one-man vigilante campaign to clean up New
York.

To help him in his campaign, the movie
shows the audience evil situations and then
lets the "exterminator" remedy them. For
example, a hooker is lured to a house of male
prostitution, where a sadistic client disfigures her with a soldering iron. Some
weeks later, the "exterminator" picks up the
hooker, sees the burn scars when she
undresses and decides to avenge her. He goes
to the male brothel, sets the owner on fire
and shoots a customer dead.

There's more, involving an insipid policeman (Christopher George) and his girlfriend
(Samantha Eggar), who turns out to be the
paralyzed man's doctor. This is the kind of
movie that establishes their relationship by
sending them to a concert and then focusing
on the concert because they have no
dialogue. The CIA also gets involved, but
who cares? *The Exterminator* exists primarily
to show burnings, shootings, gougings,
grindings, and beheadings. It is a small,
unclean exercise in shame.

Eye of the Needle ★ ★ ★
R, 118 m., 1981

Donald Sutherland (Faber), Kate Nelligan
(Lucy), Christopher Cazenova (David), Ian
Bannon (Canter). Directed by Richard
Marquand and produced by Stephen
Friedman. Screenplay by Stanley Mann.

Eye of the Needle resembles nothing so much
as one of those downbeat, plodding, quietly
horrifying, and sometimes grimly funny war

movies that used to be made by the British
film industry, back when there was a British
film industry. They used to star Stanley
Baker or Trevor Howard. This one stars
Donald Sutherland, as the kind of introverted psychopath who should inhabit only
black-and-white movies, although the color
here is sometimes gloomy enough to suffice.
I admired the movie. It is made with quiet
competence, and will remind some viewers
of the Alfred Hitchcock who made *The 39
Steps* and *Foreign Correspondent*. It is about a
German spy, the "Needle," who dropped
out of sight in Germany in 1938 and now
inhabits a series of drab bed-sitting-rooms in
England while he spies on the British war
effort. He is known as the Needle because of
his trademarked way of killing people by
jabbing a stiletto into their rib cages. He kills
with a singular lack of passion; this is Jack
the Ripper crossed with J. Alfred Prufrock.
As played by Sutherland, the Needle is a
very lonely man. We are given hints to
explain his isolation: He was raised by parents who did not love him, he was shipped
off to boarding schools, he spent parts of his
childhood in America, where he learned
English. None of these experiences fully
explains his ruthlessness, but then perhaps it
is just a spy's job to be ruthless.

The plot is part espionage, part cliffhanger. The Needle discovers phony
plywood "airplanes" intended to look, from
the air, like Patton's invasion force—a ruse to
throw off the Germans. His assignment is to
personally deliver news of the actual Allied
invasion plans to Hitler. This he intends to
do with every fiber of his being, and yet we
never get the feeling that the this man is a
patriotic Nazi. He is more of a dogged func-
tionary. In his attempts to rendezvous with a
Nazi submarine, he's shipwrecked on an isolated island occupied only by a lighthouse-
keeper and by a young married couple—a
woman (Kate Nelligan), her legless husband
(Christopher Cazenove), and their son. The
last third of the movie turns into a bloody
melodrama, as the Needle kills the husband
and the lighthouse-keeper and threatens the
woman, first in a psychological way and then
with violence. But before the final standoff,
he pretends to be merely a lost sailor. And
the woman, frustrated by her husband's
drunkenness and refusal to love, becomes

attracted to the stranger. They make love. She grows fond of him. Does he grow fond of her? We can never be sure, but he tells her things he has told to no one else.

Some people will find the movie slow going. I preferred to think of it as deliberate. It is effective, I think, to develop a plot like this at a deliberate pace, instead of rushing headlong through it. That gives us time to meditate on the character of the Needle, and to ponder his very few, enigmatic references to his own behavior. We learn things about him that he may not even know about himself, and that is why the film's final scene is so much more complex than it seems. "The war has come down to the two of us," Sutherland tells Nelligan, and in the final exchange of desperate looks between the man and the woman there is a whole universe left unspoken. The movie ends with Nelligan regarding a man who is either a treacherous spy or an unloved child, take your choice.

Eyewitness ★ ★ ★
R, 102 m., 1981

William Hurt (Daryll Deever), Sigourney Weaver (Tony Sokolow), Christopher Plummer (Joseph), James Woods (Aldo), Irene Worth (Mrs. Sokolow), Pamela Reed (Linda). Directed and produced by Peter Yates. Screenplay by Steve Tesich.

Somebody was explaining the difference between European and American movies to me the other day: European movies are about people, but American movies are about stories. It's an interesting idea, especially when it's applied to a thriller like *Eyewitness*, which is good precisely because it pays more attention to its people than its story. Does that make it European? Well, it was directed by Peter Yates, who is British but has directed some of the most "American" movies of the past decade, from *Bullitt* to *Breaking Away*. It is definitely set in America—from the bowels of a Manhattan boiler room to the newsroom of a TV station. But it's about such interesting, complicated, quirky, and sometimes funny people that it must at the least be mid-Atlantic.

The movie stars William Hurt as a janitor who stumbles across evidence that could lead to the solution of a murder investiga-

tion. But he doesn't go to the police with it because he's too complicated, too introspective, too distrustful of his own discovery . . . and, mostly, he's too much in love from afar with a TV news reporter (Sigourney Weaver). Maybe he can win her attention by giving her the scoop?

There are other complications. Sigourney Weaver is engaged to an Israeli agent (Christopher Plummer) who is involved in secret international negotiations to smuggle Jews out of the Soviet Union. His plan involves clandestine payments to a Vietnamese agent who got rich on the black market in Saigon and has now moved to Manhattan. The other characters include James Woods, as Hurt's eccentric and unpredictable fellow janitor, and Steven Hill and Morgan Freeman as a couple of cops who wearily track down leads in the case (their best line: "When Aldo was a little boy, he must have wanted to grow up to be a suspect").

The development and solution of the murder mystery are handled with professional dispatch by Yates and his writer, Steve Tesich (who also wrote *Breaking Away*). A final shoot-out in a midtown riding stable has a touch of Hitchcock to it; the old master always loved to mix violence with absolutely inappropriate settings. But what makes this movie so entertaining is the way Yates and Tesich and their characters play against our expectations.

Examples. Weaver is not only a TV newswoman, but also a part-time serious pianist and the unhappy daughter of her domineering parents. Hurt is not only a janitor but also a sensitive soul who can talk his way into Weaver's heart. Woods is not only a creepy janitor but also the enthusiastic promoter of a marriage between his sister and Hurt. Hurt and the sister (Pamela Reed) carry on the courtship because they are both too embarrassed to tell the other one they're not in love. Plummer is the most complicated character of all, and it's a very good question whether he's a villain. It all depends on how you view his own personal morality.

I've seen so many thrillers that, frankly, I don't always care how they turn out—unless they're really well-crafted. What I like about *Eyewitness* is that, although it *does* care how it turns out, it cares even more about the tex-

ture of the scenes leading to the denouement. There's not a scene in this movie that
exists only to provide us with plot information. Every scene develops characters. And
they're developed in such offbeat fidelity to
the way people do behave that we get all the
more involved in the mystery, just because,
for once, we halfway believe it could really be
happening.

F/X ★ ★ ★ ½
R, 108 m., 1985

Bryan Brown (Rollie Tyler), Cliff DeYoung
(Lipton), Brian Dennehy (Lieutenant Leo
McCarthy), Trey Wilson (Lieutenant
Murdoch), Mason Adams (Mason), Martha
Gehman (Andy), Diane Venora (Ellen), Jerry
Orbach (DeFranco), Tim Gallin (Adams).
Directed by Robert Mandel and produced by
Dodi Fayed and Jack Wiener. Screenplay by
Robert T. Megginson and Gregory Fleeman.

F/X is Hollywood shorthand for "effects,"
or special effects, the art form that creates
bullet holes and gaping wounds, fake shotgun blasts, and severed limbs.

In the movie, Bryan Brown plays a special
effects man whose customized truck is a
mobile effects lab. He can create his illusions
almost anywhere, and is in big demand from
the Hollywood studios. Then one day he gets
an unusual request from the federal government. As part of their witness relocation and
protection program, they want to fake the
murder of an organized crime leader. Their
reasoning: If everybody thinks DeFranco is
dead, nobody will try to kill him, and he will
survive and be able to testify in court.

This premise is only the beginning of the
movie's ingenuity. Like *Jagged Edge,* this is
one of those tightly constructed plots in
which the hero is almost the last person to
find out anything. Who can he trust? Who is
really on his side, who is lying to him, who is
trying to kill him? One of the pleasures of
Jagged Edge was that we could watch the central character, the lawyer played by Glenn
Close, use all of her intelligence and intuition and still walk right into danger, because
she could not believe that people could be
such deceptive swine.

The same thing happens in *F/X,* and I will

have to tread carefully to avoid giving away
too much of the plot. Briefly, there are large,
basic questions about who wants DeFranco,
the underworld leader, killed, and who
wants him alive. There are other fundamental questions about whether special effects
have indeed been used, or whether he actually was killed. And there are great ominous
possibilities that the special effects man himself might be next on the hit list.

The movie moves quickly through a large
gallery of players. At the center of everything is Rollie Tyler, the effects man, given a
nice, laconic professionalism by Bryan
Brown, whose Australian accent reminds us
that he was not brought up to automatically
trust the U.S. government in all matters.

The Broadway veteran Jerry Orbach plays
DeFranco as an expensively barbered creep.
Halfway through the movie, the dependable
character actor Brian Dennehy turns up as a
city cop not in on the scam. Cliff DeYoung is
the slippery Lipton, mastermind of the
federal scheme. Martha Gehman is Andy,
the loyal assistant of the effects man, and
Diane Venora is his doomed girlfriend.

I mention so many of these actors because,
more than most thrillers that depend on
tightly constructed plots, *F/X* also depends
on good, well-observed performances. This
movie takes a lot of delight in being more
psychologically complex than it has to be. It
contains fights and shoot-outs and big chase
scenes, but they're all firmly centered on
who the characters are and what they mean
to one another. And by the end of the film
when everything comes down to the events
in a large, scary, and isolated mansion, the
movie is able to use the personalities of the
characters as part of the payoff.

Every year should bring a few good
thrillers, to balance out all the failed and
shallow attempts. The irony of *F/X,* which
is a very good thriller indeed, is that it avoids
the pitfall of so many thrillers; it doesn't
degenerate into a mindless display of special
effects. The effects in this film just happen to
be the ways the hero has of expressing
himself.

Fade to Black ★ ★ ½
R, 100 m., 1980

Dennis Christopher (Eric Binford), Tim Thomerson (Dr. Moriarty), Gwynne Gilford (Anne), Linda Kerridge (Marilyn), Morgan Paull (Gary Bially), Eve Brent Ashe (Aunt Stella). Directed by Vernon Zimmerman. Produced by George G. Braunstein and Ron Hamady. Screenplay by Zimmerman.

It will probably help to be a movie buff if you find yourself watching *Fade to Black*. This is a weird, uneven, generally intriguing thriller about a young man whose fantasy life is totally controlled by images from movies. He works in a Los Angeles film exchange, checking and shipping movie prints, and at night he comes home to his museumlike room in the home of his aunt—a shrill harridan who would feel less secure in her wheelchair if she had ever seen *Kiss of Death*.

The young man is played with a kind of creepy power by Dennis Christopher, in a role completely opposite from his performance as the hero of *Breaking Away*. He is lonely, socially isolated, hostile. He has memorized every movie ever made, although when he bets money on a trivia question, it's one with a ridiculously easy answer: He wants to know Humphrey Bogart's full name in *Casablanca*. Everybody knows that one.

Things start going wrong in the kid's life. His boss gets on his case at work. His aunt is impossible. He makes a date with a young girl (Linda Kerridge) who looks just like Marilyn Monroe, and then he thinks she stood him up. This is too much all at once, and the kid goes berserk.

In a scene we know is inevitable, he mimics Richard Widmark in *Kiss of Death* and pushes his aunt down the stairs. Then he begins masquerading as his other movie heroes—Hopalong Cassidy, James Cagney, the Mummy—and wiping out the rest of his opposition. These scenes are handled by director Vernon Zimmerman with a mixture of reality and stylized fantasy. For example, when Hoppy gets in a shoot-out, the scene is staged and lit like a movie, which heightens the effect. But it's not lit like a Hopalong Cassidy movie; it's lit to backlight and isolate the hero, and that, no doubt, is the kid's own fantasy.

I don't want to give away too many of the movie's surprises, although if you're a movie buff you'll anticipate a lot of them. The climax, though, is a bravura piece of stylistic overkill, with Christopher creeping around of the roof of Hollywood's Chinese Theater, looking like a cross between the Phantom of the Opera and Cary Grant in *To Catch a Thief*.

What's the point of all this? Just pure escapist silliness, I suppose. But I was rather moved by the Christopher character's loneliness in the earlier scenes (later, he's frankly just a caricature manipulated by the plot). I also liked the way that some of the minor roles, including Kerridge's were handled to develop the humanity of the characters rather than just the stereotypes.

The Falcon and the Snowman
★ ★ ★ ★
R, 131 m., 1985

Timothy Hutton (Christopher Boyce), Sean Penn (Daulton Lee), Pat Hingle (Mr. Boyce), Joyce Van Patten (Mrs. Boyce), David Suchet (Alex), Boris Leskin (Mikhail). Directed by John Schlesinger and produced by Gabriel Katska and Schlesinger. Screenplay by Steven Saillian.

A few years ago there were stories in the papers about a couple of California kids who were caught selling government secrets to the Russians. The stories had an air of unreality about them. Here were a couple of middle-class young men from suburban backgrounds, who were prosecuted as spies and traitors and who hardly seemed to have it quite clear in their own minds how they had gotten into the spy business. One of the many strengths of *The Falcon and the Snowman* is that it succeeds, in an admirably matter-of-fact way, in showing us exactly how these two young men got in way over their heads. This is a movie about spies, but it is not a thriller in any routine sense of the word; it's just the meticulously observant record of how naiveté, inexperience, misplaced idealism, and greed led to one of the most peculiar cases of treason in American history.

The movie stars Timothy Hutton as Christopher Boyce, a seminarian who has a crisis of conscience, drops out of school, and ends up working almost by accident for a message-routing center of the CIA. Sean Penn is his best friend, Daulton Lee. Years ago, they were altar boys together, but in recent times their paths have diverged; while Boyce was studying for the priesthood, Lee was setting himself up as a drug dealer. By the time we meet them, Boyce is earnest and clean-cut, just the kind of young man the CIA might be looking for (it doesn't hurt that his father is a former FBI man). And Lee, with a mustache that makes him look like a failed creep, is a jumpy, paranoid drug dealer who is one step ahead of the law.

The whole caper begins so simply. Boyce, reading the messages he is paid to receive and forward, learns that the CIA is engaged in dirty tricks designed to influence elections in Australia. He is deeply offended to learn that his government would be interfering in the affairs of another state, and the more he thinks about it, the more he wants to do something. For example, supply the messages to the Russians. He doesn't want to be a Russian *spy*, you understand, just to bring this injustice to light. Lee has some contacts in Mexico, where he buys drugs. One day, in a deceptively casual conversation by the side of a backyard swimming pool, the two friends decide to go into partnership to sell the information to the Soviet Embassy in Mexico City. Lee takes the documents south and launches them both on an adventure that is a lark at first, and then a challenge, and finally just a very, very bad dream.

These two young men have one basic problem. They are amateurs. The Russians don't necessarily like that any better than the Americans would; indeed, even though the Russians are happy to have the secrets that are for sale, there is a definite sense in some scenes that the key Russian contact agent, played by David Suchet, is almost offended by the sloppy way Penn deals in espionage. The only thing Penn seems really serious about is the money.

The Falcon and the Snowman never steps wrong, but it is best when it deals with the relationship between the two young American spies. The movie was directed by John Schlesinger, an Englishman whose understanding of American characters was most unforgettably demonstrated in *Midnight Cowboy*, and I was reminded of Joe Buck and

Ratso Rizzo from that movie as I watched this one. There is even a quiet, understated quote to link Ratso with the Penn character: a moment in a parking garage when Penn defies a car to pull in front of him, and we're reminded of Ratso crossing a Manhattan street and hurling the line "I'm *walking* here!" at a taxi that dares to cut him off. Instead of relying on traditional methods for creating the suspense in spy movies, this one uses the energy generated between the two very different characters, as the all-American Boyce gradually begins to understand that his partner is out of control. *The Falcon and the Snowman*, like most good movies, is not really about its plot but about its characters. These two young men could just as easily be selling stolen IBM programs to Apple, instead of CIA messages to the Russians; the point is that they begin with one set of motives and then the implacable real world supplies them with another, harder, more unforgiving set of realities.

Just as with *Midnight Cowboy*, it's hard to say who gives the better performance this time: Sean Penn, with his twitching intensity as he angles for respect from the Russians, or Timothy Hutton, the straight man, earnestly telling his girlfriend that she should remember he really loves her—"no matter what you may hear about me in a few days from now."

Falling in Love ★ ★
PG-13, 106 m., 1984

Robert De Niro (Frank Raftis), Meryl Streep (Molly Gilmore), Ann Kaczmarek (Ann Raftis), David Clennon (Brian Gilmore), Harvey Keitel (Ed Lasky). Directed by Ulu Grosbard and produced by Marvin Worth.

This movie is the clearest case I've seen in a long time of the war between movie stars and the scripts they are given. The movie is a love story. The stars are Robert De Niro and Meryl Streep—arguably the two most distinguished American movie actors under fifty. They have a genuine chemistry together on the screen and undeniable charisma. And that's it in this movie, which gives them not one memorable line of dialogue, not one inventive situation, not one moment when we don't groan at the startling array of clichés they have to march through.

Falling in Love is nothing if not upfront about its intentions. It wants to be a 1940s romance, and it makes that bountifully clear by making the first encounter between the characters a Meet Cute. Meet Cutes are what Hollywood calls those clichéd scenes where Rosalind Russell and Cary Grant are both leaving Macy's at the same time; they run into each other, drop their packages, and bump heads as they awkwardly bend over to pick them up. Would you believe that is *exactly* how the Meet Cute works in this movie? De Niro and Streep are at a bookstore, not a department store, but as their packages drop, the movie almost could use a subtitle with the cross-reference to other films.

I'm sure there was some sort of story conference about how it would be fun to reprise a classic Meet Cute. I'm sure they had a lot of story conferences on this movie, giving one another pep talks about how the movie's total lack of substance was really a style decision. But it's just a cop-out. How can you put Streep and De Niro in a movie and not give them characters to play or interesting things to say? It's a waste of resources.

The movie's story involves two people who commute to New York on the same train. After their "Meet Cute," they are attracted to each other by instant chemistry. They meet again. There is a little awkward conversational jostling, and before long they're embarked on a chaste year-long affair in which they have lunch, go to Chinatown, visit tall buildings and trendy art galleries, and find mutual support while Streep's father dies. Art galleries and Chinatown are almost obligatory in movies like this. All true love affairs must begin with a mutual return to the infantile, as the lovestruck new partners buy hot dogs from vendors and watch the ice skating in Rockefeller Center and in other ways symbolically reenact the necessity of reliving their entire lives, from childhood on, in the company of this treasured new person.

Fine. Except that in all romances worthy of the name, there sooner or later comes a meeting of the minds: There are those rushed, excited conversations in which the two lovers realize that they are both brilliant, both insightful, both witty, and both sharing a viewpoint so unique that the rest of the world will never quite understand it. *Falling in Love* has no such passages. The dialogue is unremittingly, perhaps deliberately, banal. The funniest line in the movie ("How much do you weigh?") is inspired by the characters' inability to think of anything to say. We learn nothing of substance about them. They are provided with spouses who are ciphers, with personalities that are shallow and narcissistic, with crises that depend upon a manipulative script.

And as if all of that were not bad enough, the movie also resorts to Idiot Plot techniques to squeeze out an infuriating ending. A final farewell between the lovers is prevented because of faulty communications. A later reunion takes place when there is only one fact that each lover needs to know—that the other is separated or divorced. Incredibly, neither character makes this revelation, because to supply that single essential fact would spoil *Falling in Love*'s manipulative and shameless ending.

Incredibly, there are passages when this movie works. They are entirely due to the chemistry, the genuine human qualities of Streep and De Niro. They carry the plot and the dimwit dialogue because of the goodwill they've built up with us, and because of their own magnetism, their ability to invest worthless dialogue with a certain personal charm. *Falling in Love* will serve as a definitive example of good performances in a bad movie.

Fame ★ ★ ★ ½
R, 133 m., 1980

Eddie Barth (Angelo), Irene Cara (Coco), Lee Curreri (Bruno), Laura Dean (Lisa), Antonia Franceschi (Hilary), Boyd Gaines (Michael), Albert Hague (Shorofsky), Tresa Hughes (Mrs. Finsecker). Directed and produced by David De Silva and Alan Marshall. Screenplay by Christopher Gore.

Mrs. Seward, the draconian rhetoric teacher who drilled literacy into generations of Urbana (Ill.) High School students, used to tell us we were having the best four years of our lives. We groaned. *Fame* is a movie that she might have enjoyed. It's about a dozen or so talented kids who enter New York's High School of the Performing Arts as freshmen and emerge four years later as future Freddie

Prinzes and Benny Goodmans, Leonard Bernsteins and Mrs. Sewards.

Fame is a genuine treasure, moving and entertaining, a movie that understands being a teen-ager as well as *Breaking Away* did, but studies its characters in a completely different milieu. It's the other side of the coin: A big-city, aggressive, cranked-up movie to play against the quieter traditions of *Breaking Away*'s small Indiana college town. *Fame* is all New York City. It's populated by rich kids, ghetto kids, kids with real talent, and kids with mothers who think they have real talent. They all go into the hopper, into a high school of kids who are worked harder because they're "special"— even if they're secretly not so sure they're so special.

The movie has the kind of sensitivity to the real lives of real people that we don't get much in Hollywood productions anymore. Anyone who ever went to high school will recognize some of *Fame*'s characters: the quiet little girl who blossoms, the class genius who locks himself up in the basement with his electronic equipment, the kid who can't read but is a naturally gifted performer, the wiseass, the self-destructive type, the sexpot, the rich kid, and on and on. The cast has been recruited from New York's most talented young performers, some of them almost playing themselves. The teachers are familiar too: self-sacrificing, perfectionist, cranky, love-hate objects.

If the character types seem familiar, the movie's way of telling their stories is not. This isn't a movie that locks its characters into a conventional plot. Instead, it fragments the experiences of four years into dozens of vignettes, loosely organized into sections titled "The Auditions," "Freshman Year," and so on. We get to know the characters and their personalities gradually, as we see them in various situations. The effect is a little like high school itself; you come in as a total stranger and by the time you leave, the school has become your world.

If the kids in *Fame* are like high school kids anywhere, they're also different because they *are* talented, and the movie's at its best when it examines the special pressures on young people who are more talented than they are mature, experienced, or sure of themselves. The ghost that hovers over everyone in this school is a former graduate, Freddie Prinze, who had the talent but never figured out how to handle it.

The movie's director, Alan Parker, seems to have a knack for isolating just those moments in the lives of his characters when growth, challenge, and talent are all on the line at once. Where did he find his insights into talented young people? Probably while he was directing his first film, the wonderful *Bugsy Malone* (1976), which was a gangster musical with an all-kid cast. *Fame* is a perfect title for this movie; it establishes an ironic distance between where these kids are now and where they'd like to be someday, and then there's also the haunting suggestion that some of the ones who find fame will be able to handle it, and some will not.

Fanny and Alexander ★ ★ ★ ★
R, 197 m., 1983

Pernilla Allwin (Fanny Ekdahl), Bertil Guve (Alexander Ekdahl), Jan Malmsjo (Bishop Vergerus), Erland Josephson (Isak Jacobi), Kabi Laretei (Aunt Emma), Gunn Wallgren (Helena Ekdahl), Ewa Froling (Emilie Ekdahl), Gunnar Bjornstrand (Filip Landahl). Directed by Ingmar Bergman and produced by Jorn Donner. Screenplay by Bergman.

There was a time when Ingmar Bergman wanted to make films reflecting the whole of human experience. He asked the big questions about death, sex, and God, and he wasn't afraid of the big, dramatic image, either. Who else (except Woody Allen) has had the temerity to show a man playing chess with Death? Bergman was swinging for the fences in those deliberately big, important films. But he has discovered that a better way to encompass all human experience is to be specific about a small part of it and let the audience draw its own conclusions. In *The Seventh Seal* (1956), he portrayed Death as a symbolic grim reaper. But in *Cries and Whispers* (1973), by showing one particular woman dying painfully while her sisters and her maid stood by helplessly, he said infinitely more about death.

His film *Fanny and Alexander* is one of the most detailed and specific he's ever made, and therefore one of the most universal. It comes directly out of his experiences as a Swede in his mid-sixties who was born into a world of rigid religious belief, grew up in a world of war and turmoil, and is now old enough, wise enough, and resigned enough to develop a sort of philosophical mysticism about life. In its chronology, the film covers only a handful of years. But in its buried implications about life, I believe, it traces the development of Bergman's thought from his school days until the day before yesterday.

Fanny and Alexander is a long film that contains many characters and many events. Very simply: In a Swedish provincial town in the early years of this century, two children are growing up within the bosom of a large, jolly extended family. Their father dies and their mother remarries. Their new stepfather is a stern, authoritarian clergyman who means well but is absolutely incapable of understanding the feelings of others. Escape from his household leads them, by an indirect path, into the life of an old Jewish antique dealer whose life still has room for the mysticism and magic of an earlier time. Not everything is explained by the end of the film, but everything is reconciled.

Bergman has confessed that a great deal of the movie is autobiographical—if not literally, then in terms of its feelings. He had, for example, a father who was a strict clergyman. But it's too easy to assume that the bishop in the movie represents only Bergman's father: Can he not also represent Bergman himself, who is seen within the circle of his collaborators as an authoritarian figure with a tendency to know what is right for everyone else? Bergman has hinted that there's a little of himself, indeed, in *all* the male characters in his movie. Looking for Bergman's autobiography in his characters is one thing. I think we also can see *Fanny and Alexander* as the autobiography of his career. The warm humanism of the early scenes reflects his own beginnings in naturalism. The stern aestheticism of the middle scenes reflects his own middle period, with its obsession with both philosophical and stylistic black-and-white. The last third of the film, like the last third of his career, admits that there are more things in heaven and on Earth than dreamed of in his philosophy.

Fanny and Alexander is a big, exciting, ambitious film—more of a beginning than, as Bergman claims, the summary of his career. If you've followed him on his long trek of discovery, this will feel like a film of resolution. If you're coming fresh to Bergman, it may, paradoxically, seem to burst with the sort of invention we associate with young first-time directors. It's a film for all seasons.

Farewell, My Lovely ★ ★ ★ ★
R, 95 m., 1975

Robert Mitchum (Philip Marlowe), Charlotte Rampling (Velma), John Ireland (Lieutenant Nulty), Sylvia Miles (Mrs. Nulty), Jack O'Halloran (Moose Malloy), Anthony Zerbe (Brunette), Harry Dean Stanton (Billy Rolfe), Walter McGinn (Tommy Ray). Directed by Dick Richards and produced by George Pappas and Jerry Bruckheimer. Screenplay by David Zelag Goodman.

Los Angeles, 1941. A run-down street of seedy shop fronts and blinking neon signs. Music from a lonely horn. The camera pans up to a second-story window of a flophouse. In the window, his hat pushed back, his tie undone, Philip Marlowe lights another cigarette and waits for the cops to arrive. He is ready to tell his story.

These opening shots are so evocative of Raymond Chandler's immortal Marlowe, archetypical private eye, haunting the underbelly of Los Angeles, that if we're Chandler fans we hold our breath. Is the ambience going to be maintained, or will this be another campy ripoff? Half an hour into the movie, we relax. *Farewell, My Lovely* never steps wrong. It is, indeed, the most evocative of all the private detective movies we have had in the last few years. It is not as great as Roman Polanski's *Chinatown*, which was concerned with larger subjects, but in the genre itself there hasn't been anything this good since Hollywood was doing Philip Marlowe the first time around. One reason is that Dick Richards, the director, takes his material and character absolutely seriously. He is not uneasy with it, as Robert Altman was when he had Elliott Gould flirt with seriousness in *The Long Goodbye*. Richards doesn't hedge his bet.

And neither does Robert Mitchum, in what becomes his definitive performance. Mitchum is one of the great screen presences. He was born to play the weary, cynical, doggedly romantic Marlowe. His voice and his face and the way he lights his cigarette are all exactly right, and seem totally effortless. That's his trademark. In a good Mitchum performance, we are never aware he is acting. And it is only when we measure the distances between his characters that we can see what he is doing. Mitchum is at home on the kinds of streets Philip Marlowe worked: streets of one-room furnished flats and pink stucco hotels, out-of-town newsstands and seedy bars, and always the drowsy commonness of the flat lands leading up to the baroque mansions in the hills and canyons.

Farewell, My Lovely, gets all of this just right—Angelo Graham's art direction is a triumph—and then places Mitchum's Marlowe in the center of it and leads him through one of Chandler's tortuous plots. Although everything does finally tie together in this one (as it never did in Chandler's labyrinthine *The Big Sleep*), it doesn't matter that much. What's important is the gallery of characters Marlowe encounters, each grotesque and beautiful in his own way. The most touching is Moose Malloy, played by an ex-prizefighter named Jack O'Halloran. Moose towers over everyone in the film, both in stature and in the immensity of his need. Seven years ago he fell in love with a hooker named Velma and they were going to be married, but something went wrong during a bank job, and Moose took the rap. When he gets out of prison, he hires Marlowe to find his Velma.

Marlowe's quest for Velma, a faded memory from a hopeless love affair, leads him, as we might have known, into a case a lot larger and more important than he could have suspected. There is an odyssey through a lurid whorehouse and a killing in a ghetto bar, and a midnight rendezvous that ends in another death, and always there is Lieutenant Nulty, of the Los Angeles Police Department, trying to figure out why Marlowe winds up attached to so many dead bodies. Richards's approach, with screenplay by David Zelag Goodman, is to start the story at the end with Marlowe trying to explain things to Nulty and then flash back to the beginning and let Marlowe elaborate on the story voice-over. It is a strategy that is often distracting in movies. But not this time, because it bor-

rows from Chandler's own first-person narrative. And it provides great one-liners, as when the elusive Velma (Charlotte Rampling) sizes Marlowe up and down and he says, "She threw me a look I caught in my hip pocket."

Farewell, My Lovely is a great entertainment and a celebration of Robert Mitchum's absolute originality. The day after you view it, you might find yourself quoting lines to friends, which is always the test in these cases, because most of the time private-eye stories have no meaning at all unless it is in the way their heroes behave in the face of the most unsettling revelations about human nature. This time Philip Marlowe behaves very well.

Fast Times at Ridgemont High ★
R, 92 m., 1982

Sean Penn (Jeff Spicoli), Jennifer Jason Leigh (Stacy Hamilton), Judge Reinhold (Brad Hamilton), Robert Romanus (Mike Damone), Brian Backer (Rat Ratner), Phoebe Cates (Linda Barrett). Directed by Amy Heckerling and produced by Art Linson and Irving Azoff. Screenplay by Cameron Crowe.

How could they do this to Jennifer Jason Leigh? How could they put such a fresh and cheerful person into such a scuz-pit of a movie? Don't they know they have a star on their hands? I didn't even know who Leigh was when I walked into *Fast Times at Ridgemont High,* and yet I was completely won over by her. She contained so much life and light that she was a joy to behold. And then she and everybody else in this so-called comedy is invited to plunge into offensive vulgarity. Let me make myself clear. I am not against vulgarity as a subject for a movie comedy. Sometimes I treasure it, when it's used with inspiration, as in *The Producers* or *National Lampoon's Animal House.* But vulgarity is a very tricky thing to handle in a comedy; tone is everything, and the makers of *Fast Times at Ridgemont High* have an absolute gift for taking potentially funny situations and turning them into general embarrassment. They're tone-deaf.

The movie's another one of those adolescent sex romps, such as *Porky's* and *Animal House,* in which part of the humor comes from raunchy situations and dialogue. This movie is *so* raunchy, however, that the audience can't quite believe it. I went to a sneak preview thrown by a rock radio station, and the audience had come for a good time. But during a scene involving some extremely frank talk about certain popular methods of sexual behavior, even the rock fans were grossed out. There's a difference between raunchiness and gynecological detail.

The movie's cast struggles valiantly through all this dreck. Rarely have I seen so many attractive young performers invited to appear in so many unattractive scenes. Leigh, for example, plays a virginal young student at Ridgemont High. She's curious about sex, and so the script immediately turns her into a promiscuous sex machine who will go to bed with anybody. And then her sexual experiences all turn out to have an unnecessary element of realism, so that we have to see her humiliated, disappointed, and embarrassed. Whatever happened to upbeat sex? Whatever happened to love and lust and romance, and scenes where good-looking kids had a little joy and excitement in life, instead of all this grungy downbeat humiliation? Why does someone as pretty as Leigh have to have her nudity exploited in shots where the only point is to show her ill-at-ease?

If this movie had been directed by a man, I'd call it sexist. It was directed by a woman, Amy Heckerling—and it's sexist all the same. It clunks to a halt now and then for some heartfelt, badly handled material about pregnancy and abortion. I suppose that's Heckerling paying dues to some misconception of the women's movement. But for the most part this movie just exploits its performers by trying to walk a tightrope between comedy and sexploitation.

In addition to Leigh's work, however, there are some other good performances. Sean Penn is perfect as the pot-smoking space cadet who has been stoned since the third grade. Phoebe Cates is breathtaking as the more experienced girl who gives Leigh those distasteful lessons in love. Judge Reinhold has fun as a perennial fast-food cook who rebels against the silly uniforms he's supposed to wear. Ray Walston is suitably hateful as the dictatorial history teacher, Mr. Hand. But this movie could have been a *lot* more fun if it hadn't chosen to confuse embarrassment with humor. The unnecessary detail about sexual functions isn't funny, it's distasteful. Leigh looks so young, fresh, cheerful, and innocent that we don't laugh when she gets into unhappy scenes with men—we wince. The whole movie is a failure of taste, tone, and nerve—the waste of a good cast on erratic, offensive material that hasn't been thought through, or maybe even thought about.

The Final Conflict (Omen III) ★ ★
R, 108 m., 1981

Sam Neill (Damien), Rossano Brazzi (De Carlo), Don Gordon (Dean), Lisa Harrow (Kate), Barnaby Holm (Peter), Mason Adams (President). Directed by Graham Baker and produced by Harvey Bernhard and Mace Neufeld. Screenplay by Andrew Birkin.

The first ten minutes of *The Final Conflict* are such a masterful job of storytelling that I dared to hope that the *Omen* trilogy had pulled itself out of the bag. The story is told in images without dialogue. An earth-moving machine in Chicago digs up seven ancient daggers. A workman carries the daggers home and pawns them. An antique dealer buys the daggers from the pawnshop. They go on auction and are eventually carried to an old monastery in Italy, where the abbot solemnly prays before them. These are the daggers, we learn, that are necessary to kill the antichrist.

This is a terrific opening. But, alas, the moment *The Final Conflict* turns to dialogue and a plot, it loses its inspiration. If Armageddon is as boring as this movie, we'll need a program to tell the players. Loyal students of the *Omen* trilogy will know, of course, that this final conflict has been brewing for a long time—ever since 1976, when the original and rather effective *The Omen* was released. In that one, the U.S. ambassador to Great Britain adopted a child who, we learned, was the devil reincarnate. In *Damien: Omen II* (1978), the kid grew up, went to a military school, and set the stage for his eventual confrontation with the forces of good. A subplot was introduced, involving Thorne Industries, a multinational conglomerate with plans to dominate mankind by controlling the Third World's food supply. As *The Final*

Conflict opens, the adopted son (now played by Sam Neill) is in command of Thorne Industries, and is himself named ambassador to Great Britain—as well as chairman of the United Nations Youth Committee.

He does not make a very good youth chairman. Shortly after moving to England he learns that Christ has been reborn, and orders his flunkies at Thorne to kill all the male children born between midnight and 6 A.M. on the suspected day. That includes the son of his most trusted assistant, but so carelessly is this movie assembled that we're never quite sure if the associate (a) knows and believes his boss is the son of Satan, (b) is a diabolical creation himself, or (c) is just on the payroll. *Somebody* on the staff must be in full sympathy with Damien, however, because in the attic of the U.S. Embassy in London's Berkeley Square he has a room devoted to the Black Mass, including a grotesque wooden effigy of the crucifixion. I found myself thinking irreverent thoughts, like, what did they tell the movers as they were carting that crucifix upstairs?

So it goes. In addition to its opening sequence, *The Final Conflict* has one other great scene involving a fox hunt and a plot by the priests of the Italian monastery to lure Damien away from the hunt and kill him. This scene is wonderfully staged and edited. But the movie is otherwise a growing disappointment, as we realize that the apocalyptic confrontation between the forces of good and evil is being reduced to a bunch of guys with Italian accents running around trying to stab Damien in the back.

I would not, of course, dream of revealing this movie's ending. But it's not cheating to say how disappointed I was, as Damien slinks through an abandoned cathedral screaming the equivalent of "Come on out, Nazarene! Come out and fight!" And the last scenes are a disappointing anticlimax that raise once again the ancient question: Why is evil always so much more colorful than good in the movies?

The Final Countdown ★ ★
PG, 92 m., 1980

Kirk Douglas (Captain Yelland), Martin Sheen (Warren Lasky), Katharine Ross (Laurel Scott), James Farentino (Commander Owens), Ron O'Neal (Commander Thurman), Charles Curning (Senator Chapman). Directed by Don Taylor and produced by Peter Vincent Douglas. Screenplay by David Ambrose, Gerry Davis, Thomas Hunter, and Peter Powell.

Logic is a dangerous thing to apply to science fiction. It hardly matters in *The Final Countdown*, in which the aircraft carrier *Nimitz* sails through a whirlpool in time and is thrown back forty years to the day before Pearl Harbor. It's an appealing idea: A nuclear-powered carrier with a full complement of jet warplanes, right off Pearl and knowing the Japanese attack plans. Unfortunately, the movie makes such a mess of it that the biggest element of interest is the aircraft carrier itself. The movie was shot on board, with Navy cooperation, and the operations of the carrier are shown in interesting detail.

Just try to forget the plot. It has the *Nimitz* sailing through clear waters when suddenly a gigantic whirlpool appears in the sky. This is apparently a gateway into the past, although it looks more like a rejected test run for Disney's *Black Hole*. Thrown back to 1940, the ship is in a position to alter the course of history. Will it destroy the Japanese air fleet? *Ha.* We know it can't—because, in the future the *Nimitz* was thrown back from, it didn't, or hadn't. Anyway, just before the zero hour, the *Nimitz* is hurled back into 1980 by another whirlpool. But it leaves two people back there in 1940.

And that sets up this insoluble time-travel paradox: If a guy from 1980 travels forty years back in time, and then lives for another forty years, could he have a meeting with hiFPL is snatched back to 1980, they'd be left flying around the Pacific with no place to land.) The movie dodges all sorts of fundamental questions like that, and it moves so slowly, alas, that we have lots of time to ponder them.

Still, the footage aboard the carrier is good. We get an interesting notion of life on ship, and we see lots of takeoffs and even an emergency landing. This is the kind of movie that some kids would probably enjoy—it's filled with technology, special effects, and action. But it just doesn't make any sense. And it lacks the wit to have fun with its time travel paradoxes, as the wonderful *Time After Time* did. It just plows ahead. Or behind. Or somewhere.

Firefox ★ ★ ★ ½
PG, 136 m., 1982

Clint Eastwood (Mitchell Gant), Freddie Jones (Kenneth Aubrey), David Huffman (Buckholz), Warren Clarke (Pavel Upenskoy), Ronald Lacey (Semelovsky), Kenneth Colley (Colonel Kontarsky), Stefan Schnabel (First Secretary). Directed and produced by Clint Eastwood. Screenplay by Alex Lasker and Wendell Wellman.

Clint Eastwood's *Firefox* is a slick, muscular thriller that combines espionage with science fiction. The movie works like a well-crafted machine, and it's *about* a well-crafted machine. The *Firefox* of the title is a top-secret Russian warplane capable of flying six times the speed of sound while remaining invisible on radar. Eastwood's mission, if he chooses to accept it: Infiltrate the Soviet Union disguised as a Las Vegas drug smuggler, and then steal the Firefox by flying it to the West.

This is one of those basic movie plots that can generate a lot of entertainment if it's handled properly. *Firefox* knows the territory. It complicates things slightly by making Eastwood a Vietnam veteran who is sometimes overcome by the hallucination that he's still in combat. The movie calls it Post-Combat Stress Syndrome. But the CIA man who recruits him explains that the government isn't much worried, because you don't have the syndrome while you're *in* combat, you see, but only afterward. Somebody ought to compile a textbook of psychology as practiced in movies.

Anyway, Eastwood trains for the mission, is disguised with a mustache and horn-rim glasses, and survives some uncomfortable moments at Moscow customs before he makes it into Russia. Then he makes contact with a confederation of spies and double agents who lead him to a Jewish dissident who is such a brilliant scientist that he is still being allowed to work on Firefox. Why does the dissident *want* to work on it? Because he knows how Eastwood could steal the plane. All of these scenes include obligatory shots, which are kind of fun to anticipate, if you're a fan of the Alistair Maclean–James Bond– "Mission: Impossible"–*Guns of Navarone* genre. The one indispensable scene is probably the Introduction of the MacGuffin. A MacGuffin, you will remember, was what Alfred Hitchcock called that element of the plot that everybody thinks is important. In this case, it's the Firefox, a long, sleek, cruel-looking machine that looks like a cross between a guided missle and a DeLorean. Eastwood and the camera circle it lovingly; this is the sexiest shot in a movie without a romantic subplot. The movie's climax involves Eastwood's attempt to fly this plane north to the Arctic Circle, make a refueling rendezvous, and then take it on home. His flight is intercut with comic opera scenes involving members of the Russian high command, who argue and bicker while looming over an illuminated map that casts an eerie underlight on their faces, making them look like ghouls from old E.C. comics.

Does Eastwood make it out in one piece? Does he bring along the plane? I wouldn't dream of giving away the plot. But I will say that the movie's climax is a sensational high-altitude dogfight between two different Firefoxes, and that as Eastwood occupies the Firefox cockpit, surrounded by video screens and computer displays of flight patterns and missile trajectories, it looks as if Dirty Harry has died and gone to Atari heaven. The special effects are really pretty good in this movie. The planes looked surprisingly real to me, and the choreography of the dogfight was not only realistic but understandable. There's one sensational chase sequence that's an homage to *Star Wars*. Remember the *Star Wars* scene where the two ships chased each other between the towering walls of the city in space? Eastwood and his Russian pursuer rocket through a crevice between two ice cliffs, and it looks great even while we're realizing it's logically impossible. I guess that goes for the whole movie.

Firestarter ★ ★
R, 115 m., 1984

David Keith (Andrew McGee), Drew Barrymore (Charlie McGee), Freddie Jones (Dr. Wanless), Martin Sheen (Captain Hollister), George C. Scott (John Rainbird), Art Carney (Irv Manders), Louise Fletcher (Norma Manders). Directed by Mark L. Lester and produced by Frank Capra, Jr. Screenplay by Stanley Mann.

Firestarter contains a little girl who can start fires with her mind; her father, whose own ESP causes him to have brain hemorrhages; an Indian child molester who is a CIA killer; a black scientist; a kindly farmer; a government bureaucrat; and a brilliant scientist whose experiments kill 75 percent of his subjects but leave the others with powers beyond the imagination of mortal man. The most astonishing thing in the movie, however, is how boring it is.

The little girl is played by Drew Barrymore, from *E. T.*, where she was the kid sister. Her father is played by David Keith, who was Richard Gere's buddy in *An Officer and a Gentleman.* The child molester is played by George C. Scott. The farmer is Art Carney. And so on. There isn't a role in this movie not filled by a capable actor. And there's not a character in this movie that is convincing, even for a moment, nor a line in this movie that even experienced performers can make real.

Firestarter was the fifth movie in a year that was based on a best-selling thriller by Stephen King. The others were *Christine, Cujo, The Dead Zone,* and *Children of the Corn.* The best of those—and the one most similar to *Firestarter*—is *The Dead Zone,* which starred Christopher Walken as a man cursed with the ability to foretell the future. The movie approached Walken as an ordinary man burdened with a power that should belong only to God, and allowed us to empathize with his terrible gift. But in *Firestarter,* we don't feel sorry for Barrymore because she's never developed as a believable little girl—just a plot gimmick. She gets mad, her eyes narrow, and things catch on fire. Her father is even less interesting; although he can use ESP to hypnotize people to obey his will, he gets a nosebleed every time he does it, and the way he clasps his hands to his head and strains makes ESP look like physical labor.

Of the other characters, the most totally confused is John Rainbird, the Indian played by Scott. Rainbird shows every sign of being a character who was rewritten so extensively that finally nothing was left except the notes. He's an Indian, I guess, judging by his name and ponytail. He wants the little girl because he dreams of killing her with one karate blow to the nose. He has a couple of gruesomely detailed speeches in which he outlines this ambition, but the movie spares us the sight of Scott carrying out his plan. Thanks for small favors. The film's crucial flaw is the lack of a strong point to the story. A little girl has her dangerous power, some government agents want to examine her, others want to destroy her, and things catch on fire. That's about it.

First Blood ★ ★ ★
R, 94 m., 1982

Sylvester Stallone (Rambo), Richard Crenna (Trautman), Brian Dennehy (Teasle), David Caruso (Mitch). Directed by Ted Kotcheff and produced by Buzz Feitshans. Screenplay by Michael Kozoll, William Sackheim, and Q. Moonblood.

Sylvester Stallone is one of the great physical actors in the movies, with a gift for throwing himself so fearlessly into an action scene that we can't understand why somebody doesn't *really* get hurt. When he explodes near the beginning of *First Blood,* hurling cops aside and breaking out of a jail with his fists and speed, it's such a convincing demonstration of physical strength and agility that we never question the scene's implausibility. In fact, although almost all of *First Blood* is implausible, because it's Stallone on the screen, we'll buy it.

What we can't buy in this movie is the message. It's handled in too heavy-handed a way. Stallone plays a returned Vietnam veteran, a Green Beret skilled in the art of jungle survival and fighting, and after a small-town police force sadistically mishandles him, he declares war on the cops. All of this is set up in scenes of great physical power and strength—and the central sections of the movie, with Stallone and the cops stalking each other through the forests of the Pacific

Northwest, have a lot of authority. But then the movie comes down to a face-off between Stallone and his old Green Beret commander (Richard Crenna), and the screenplay gives Stallone a long, impassioned speech to deliver, a speech in which he cries out against the injustices done to him and against the hippies who demonstrated at the airport when he returned from the war, etc. This is all old, familiar material from a dozen other films—clichés recycled as formula. Bruce Dern did it in *Coming Home* and William Devane in *Rolling Thunder*. Stallone is made to say things that would have much better been implied; Robert De Niro, in *Taxi Driver*, also plays a violent character who was obviously scarred by Vietnam, but the movie wisely never makes him talk about what happened to him. Some things are scarier and more emotionally moving when they're left unsaid.

So the ending doesn't work in *First Blood*. It doesn't necessarily work as action, either. By the end of the film, Stallone has taken on a whole town and has become a one-man army, laying siege to the police station and the hardware store and exploding the pumps at the gas station. This sort of spectacular conclusion has become so commonplace in action movies that I kind of wonder, sometimes, what it would be like to see one end with a whimper rather than a bang.

Until the last twenty or thirty minutes, however, *First Blood* is a very good movie, well-paced, and well-acted not only by Stallone (who invests an unlikely character with great authority) but also by Crenna and Brian Dennehy, as the police chief. The best scenes come as Stallone's on the run in the forest, using a hunting knife with a compass in the handle, and living off the land. At one point he's trapped on a cliffside by a police helicopter, and we really feel for this character who has been hunted down through no real fault of his own. We feel more deeply for him then, in fact, than we do later when he puts his grievances into words. Stallone creates the character and sells the situation with his presence itself. The screenplay should have stopped while it was ahead.

Firstborn ★ ★
PG, 100 m., 1984

Teri Garr (Wendy Livingston), Peter Weller (Sam), Christopher Collet (Jake Livingston), Corey Haim (Brian Livingston). Directed by Michael Apted and produced by Paul Junger Witt and Tony Thomas. Screenplay by Ron Koslow.

Firstborn has such a sudden and unnecessary breakdown that it almost makes you wonder how the movie's ending was decided upon. Was there a final failure of will? The movie creates such an urgent situation, and fills it with such interesting characters, that when everything goes wrong at the end I felt more than disappointed, I felt cheated.

The movie is about a quiet and happy little suburban family that is violated by the appearance of the wrong man at the wrong time. The family consists of a divorced mother (Teri Garr) and her two sons. The man is Garr's new lover, and he arrives almost in response to a crisis in her life—when her ex-husband, a man she still loves, suddenly decides to remarry. On the rebound, she comes home with a young man (Peter Weller) whom she says she loves. Well, maybe she *does* love him. Love is blind. But her sons are not blind—especially not the older teen-ager (Christopher Collet), who spots this guy right away for a phony. Weller announces that he has lots of big plans for his new family. He and Garr are going to open a home security service. Or maybe a restaurant. He has lots of ideas. All he needs is capital.

Meanwhile, he spends all day sitting around the house, watching TV, and raiding the icebox. And when Collet challenges him too closely about his plans, he slaps the kid just a little too hard on the back, and tells him to get off his case. Collet tries to talk to his mom, but she won't listen. She's under this guy's spell, and it gets even worse when he turns out to be a small-time drug dealer and Garr begins to experiment with cocaine.

Up until about this point in the movie, *Firstborn* has been a very accurately observed family drama, one that even bears comparison to *Ordinary People*. The performances are strong, the plot moves with a compelling simplicity, and the dialogue shows a good ear for the way the movie's different kinds of characters might really speak. I was experiencing that special confidence you feel when a movie is making the right choices: This was going to be a good one.

It did not, alas, turn out to be so good. Having raised its issues, having trapped the children in a cruel dilemma (how can they turn in the boyfriend without implicating their mother in a drug case?), having created in a dramatic form the kind of problem that does confront real families, *Firstborn* throws away all its good work on a canned, formula ending.

Would you believe a chase and a fight? Would you believe the little brother coming to the rescue with a baseball bat? Would you believe a three-dimensional, sensitive family drama that tries to resolve itself like a TV action show? The climactic scenes in *Firstborn* are so dismally predictable that I even got a little angry. The movie had been so good that somehow it didn't have the right to evade all the issues it had raised and just turn into a suburban thriller.

What happened? Did somebody think the ending would be commercial? Did they think it would save a problematical movie from becoming too "serious"? Maybe so. But how could mistakes that basic be made by the same people with the taste to make the opening and middle segments of this movie? Love isn't all that's blind.

Fitzcarraldo ★ ★ ★ ★
PG, 157 m., 1982

Klaus Kinski (Fitzcarraldo), Claudia Cardinale (Molly), Jose Lewgoy (Don Aquilino), Miguel Angel Fuentes (Cholo). Directed by Werner Herzog. Screenplay by Herzog.

Werner Herzog's *Fitzcarraldo* is a movie in the great tradition of grandiose cinematic visions. Like Coppola's *Apocalypse Now* or Kubrick's *2001*, it is a quest film in which the hero's quest is scarcely more mad than the filmmaker's. Movies like this exist on a plane apart from ordinary films. There is a sense in which *Fitzcarraldo* is not altogether successful—it is too long, we could say, or too meandering—but it is still a film that I would not have missed for the world. The movie is the story of a dreamer named Brian Sweeney Fitzgerald, whose name has been simplified to "Fitzcarraldo" by the Indians and Spanish who inhabit his godforsaken corner of South America. He loves opera. He spends his days making a little money from an ice factory and his nights dreaming up new schemes. One of them, a plan to build a railroad across the continent, has already failed. Now he is ready with another: He seriously intends to build an opera house in the rain jungle, twelve hundred miles upstream from the civilized coast, and to bring Enrico Caruso there to sing an opera.

If his plan is mad, his method for carrying it out is madness of another dimension. Looking at the map, he becomes obsessed with the fact that a nearby river system offers access to hundreds of thousands of square miles of potential trading customers—if only a modern steamship could be introduced into that system. There is a point, he notices, where the other river is separated only by a thin finger of land from a river that already is navigated by boats. His inspiration: Drag a steamship across land to the other river, float it, set up a thriving trade, and use the profits to build the opera house—and then bring in Caruso! This scheme is so unlikely that perhaps we should not be surprised that Herzog's story is based on the case of a real Irish entrepreneur who tried to do exactly that.

The historical Irishman was at least wise enough to disassemble his boat before carting it across land. In Herzog's movie, however, Fitzcarraldo determines to drag the boat up one hill and down the other side in one piece. He enlists engineers to devise a system of blocks-and-pulleys that will do the trick, and he hires the local Indians to work the levers with their own muscle power. And it is here that we arrive at the thing about *Fitzcarraldo* that transcends all understanding: Werner Herzog determined to literally drag a real steamship up a real hill, using real tackle and hiring the local Indians! To produce the movie, he decided to do personally what even the original Fitzgerald never attempted.

Herzog finally settled on the right actor to play Fitzcarraldo, author of this plan: Klaus Kinski, the shock-haired German who starred in Herzog's *Aguirre, the Wrath of God* and *Nosferatu,* is back again to mastermind the effort. Kinski is perfectly cast. Herzog's original choice for the role was Jason Robards, who is also gifted at conveying a consuming passion, but Kinski, wild-eyed and ferocious, consumes the screen. There are other characters important to the story, especially Claudia Cardinale as the madam who loves Fitzcarraldo and helps finance his attempt, but without Kinski at the core it's doubtful this story would work.

The story of Herzog's own production is itself well-known, and has been told in Les Blank's *Burden of Dreams*, a brilliant documentary about the filming. It's possible that every moment of *Fitzcarraldo* is colored by our knowledge that Herzog was "really" doing the things we see Fitzcarraldo do. (The movie uses no special effects, no models, no opticals, no miniatures.) Perhaps we're even tempted to give the movie extra points because of Herzog's ordeal in the jungle. But *Fitzcarraldo* is not all sweat and madness. It contains great poetic images of the sort Herzog is famous for: An old phonograph playing a Caruso record on the desk of a boat spinning out of control into a rapids; Fitzcarraldo frantically oaring a little rowboat down a jungle river to be in time to hear an opera; and of course the immensely impressive sight of that actual steamship, resting halfway up a hillside.

Fitzcarraldo is not a perfect movie, and it never comes together into a unified statement. It *is* meandering, and it is slow and formless at times. Perhaps the conception was just too large for Herzog to shape. The movie does not approach perfection as *Aguirre* did. But as a document of a quest and a dream, and as the record of man's audacity and foolish, visionary heroism, there has never been another movie like it.

Five Easy Pieces ★ ★ ★ ★
R, 98 m., 1970

Jack Nicholson (Robert Dupea), Karen Black (Rayette), Susan Anspach (Catherine), Billy Green Bush (Elton), Helena Kallianiotes (Hitchhiker), Ralph Waite (Carl Dupea), William Challee (Nicholas Dupea), John Ryan (Spicer). Directed by Bob Rafelson and produced by Richard Wechsler and Rafelson. Screenplay by Adrien Joyce.

The title of *Five Easy Pieces* refers not to the women its hero makes along the road, for there are only three, but to a book of piano exercises he owned as a child. The film, one of the best American films, is about the distance between that boy, practicing to become a concert pianist, and the need he feels twenty years later to disguise himself as an oil field rigger. When we sense the boy, tormented and insecure, trapped inside the adult man, *Five Easy Pieces* becomes a masterpiece of heartbreaking intensity.

At the outset, we meet only the man—played by Jack Nicholson with the same miraculous offhandedness that brought *Easy Rider* to life. He's an irresponsible roustabout, making his way through the oil fields, sleeping with a waitress (Karen Black) whose every daydreaming moment is filled with admiration for Miss Tammy Wynette. The man's name is Robert Eroica Dupea. He was named after Beethoven's Third Symphony and he spends his evenings bowling and his nights wearily agreeing that, yes, his girl sings "Stand By Your Man" just like Tammy.

In these first marvelous scenes, director Bob Rafelson calls our attention to the grimy life textures and the shabby hopes of these decent middle Americans. They live in a landscape of motels, highways, TV dinners, dust, and jealousy, and so do we all, but they seem to have nothing else: Dupea's friends are arrested at the mental and emotional level of about age seventeen; he isn't, but thinks or hopes he is.

Dupea discovers his girl is pregnant (his friend Elton breaks the news out in the field, suggesting maybe it would be good to marry her and settle down). He walks out on her in a rage, has a meaningless little affair with a slut from the bowling alley, and then discovers more or less by accident that his father is dying. His father, we discover, is a musical genius who moved his family to an island and tried to raise them as Socrates might have. Dupea feels himself to be the only failure.

The movie bares its heart in the scenes on the island, where Dupea makes an awkward effort to communicate with his dying father. The island is peopled with eccentrics, mostly Dupea's own family, but including a few strays. Among their number is a beautiful young girl who's come to the island to study piano with Dupea's supercilious brother. Dupea seduces this girl, who apparently suggests the early life he has abandoned. He does it by playing the piano; but when she says she's moved, he says he isn't—that he played better as a child and that the piece was easy anyway.

This is possibly the moment when his nerve fails and he condemns himself, consciously, to a life of self-defined failure. The movie ends, after several more scenes, on a note of ambiguity; he is either freeing himself from the waitress or, on the other hand, he is setting off on a journey even deeper into anonymity. It's impossible to say, and it doesn't matter much. What matters is the character during the time covered by the film: a time when Dupea tentatively reapproaches his past and then rejects it, not out of pride, but out of fear.

The movie is joyously alive to the road life of its hero. We follow him through bars and bowling alleys, motels and mobile homes, and we find him rebelling against lower-middle-class values even as he embraces them. In one magical scene, he leaps from his car in a traffic jam and starts playing the piano on the truck in front of him; the scene sounds forced, described this way, but Rafelson and Nicholson never force anything, and never have to. Robert Eroica Dupea is one of the most unforgettable characters in American movies.

The Flamingo Kid ★ ★ ★ ½
PG-13, 100 m., 1984

Matt Dillon (Jeffrey Willis), Hector Elizondo (Arthur Willis), Molly McCarthy (Ruth Willis), Martha Gehman (Nikki Willis), Richard Crenna (Phil Brody), Jessica Walter (Phyllis Brody), Carole R. Davis (Joyce Brody). Directed by Garry Marshall and produced by Michael Phillips. Screenplay by Neal and Garry Marshall.

"When I was eighteen, my father was ignorant on a great many subjects," Mark Twain once said, "but by the time I was twenty-five, it was amazing the things the old man had learned." Here is a movie that condenses that process into one summer. The summer begins with a kid from a poor Brooklyn neighborhood taking a job as a cabana boy at a posh beach club out on Long Island. That's against the advice of his father, a plumber, who wants his son to get a job where he can learn about hard work. By the middle of the summer, the kid has started to idolize a flashy car dealer who's the champion of the gin rummy tables. By Labor Day, he has found out more about the car dealer than he wanted to know. And he has come to love and understand his father in a new way.

The Flamingo Kid stars Matt Dillon as the teen-ager, Hector Elizondo as his father, and Richard Crenna as the car dealer. There are other characters—in particular, a bikinied goddess who helps sell Matt on life at the beach—but these are the three characters who stand at the heart of the story. Elizondo is a hard-working man who still remembers how to dream, but knows that life has few openings for dreamers. In some of the movie's most poetic passages, he reveals a lifelong obsession with ships, and the ways of harbor pilots. Crenna, on the other hand, is a man who firmly believes "You are what you wear," and values his status as the club's gin rummy champion as if it really meant something.

Dillon is a revelation in this movie. Perhaps because of his name, Matt Dillon has risked being confused with your average teen-age idol, the kind the pimple magazines put on their covers. Yet he has been an extraordinarily sensitive actor ever since his first appearance, in the unsung 1977 movie about alienated teen-agers, *Over the Edge*. In two movies based on novels by S.E. Hinton, *Tex* and *Rumble Fish*, he had the kind of clarity, the uncluttered relationship with the camera, that you see in only a handful of actors: He was a natural. He is here, too. His role in *The Flamingo Kid* could easily have been turned into an anthology of twitches and psychic anguish as he wrestles with the meaning of life. But Dillon has the kind of acting intelligence that allows him to play each scene for no more than that particular scene is really about; he's not trying to summarize the message in every speech. That gives him an ease, an ability to play the teen-age hero as if every day were a whole summer long.

We fall into the rhythm of the beach club. Into the sunny days where all the members have lots of time to know and envy each other, and time is so plentiful that it can take hours for a nasty rumor to sweep through the cabanas. Dillon hurries from one member to another with drinks, towels, club sandwiches, messages. He feels acutely that he does not belong at this level of society—and when Richard Crenna takes notice of him, and even more when Crenna's daughter invites him home for dinner, Dillon feels that he's cutting loose from the boring life back in Brooklyn. But this will be a summer of learning, and by autumn he will have learned how wise and loving his own father is, and how easy it is to be deceived by surfaces. Along the way to that lesson, *The Flamingo Kid* has a lot of fun (I hope I haven't made this social comedy sound dreary), and at the end it has a surprisingly emotional impact.

Flash Gordon ★ ★ ½
PG, 110 m., 1980

Sam J. Jones (Flash Gordon), Melody Anderson (Dale Arden), Topol (Dr. Zarkov), Max von Sydow (Emperor Ming), Ornella Muti (Princess Aura), Timothy Dalton (Prince Barin), Mariangela Melato (Kala). Directed by Mike Hodges and produced by Dino De Laurentiis. Screenplay by Lorenzo Semple, Jr.

Flash Gordon opens with an ominous crisis facing mankind, but Earth scientists are playing it cool: A NASA spokesman denies that there's anything unusual about an unexpected total eclipse of the sun. Unusual? That the moon is out of its orbit? Ha! It takes a mad scientist like Dr. Hans Zarkov to realize that the Earth is under attack, and speed to the rescue in his private space ship—with Flash Gordon and Dale Arden aboard as unwilling passengers. This new Dino De Laurentiis production is true to the tacky pop origins of the Flash Gordon comic strip and the serials starring Buster Crabbe. At a time when *Star Wars* and its spinoffs have inspired special-effects men to bust a gut making their interplanetary adventures look real, *Flash Gordon* is cheerfully willing to look as phony as it is.

You *can* make a city float in the clouds and look marginally realistic (as in *The Empire Strikes Back*), but there's something sort of fun about the *Flash Gordon* city that floats in the clouds and looks like a large miniature

model floating in fake clouds. And as the spaceships lumbered past on the screen, I really wouldn't have minded if they'd left a tube of model airplane glue lying in the lower left-hand corner.

Flash Gordon is played for laughs, and wisely so. It is no more sophisticated than the comic strip it's based on, and that takes the curse off of material that was old before it was born. This is space opera, a genre invented by Edgar Rice Burroughs, Hugo Gernsback and other men of unlimited imagination harnessed to limited skills. It's fun to see it done with energy and love and without the pseudo-meaningful apparatus of the Force and the Trekkie Power.

The plot is simple: The Emperor Ming (Max von Sydow), bored with life in the universe, decides to pick on Earth. After warming up with a few hurricanes and earthquakes, he sends the moon spinning down toward the planet. Meanwhile, Zarkov, Flash (Sam J. Jones, Bo Derek's husband in *10*) and Dale (Melody Anderson) crash-land in Ming's imperial space city. There are intrigues afoot, but meanwhile Dale catches Ming's eye, he determines to marry her, and Flash finds himself fighting for his life with a gladiator.

Mike Hodges, the British director hired by De Laurentiis to orchestrate this comic space opera, is true to the visual tradition of the original serials: Everyone is dressed in capes and ridiculous boots and headdresses, and stands around on the command decks of ornate spaceships. There's an imperial court to applaud and boo at the appropriate times. And there's a cliff-hanging showdown when the Hawk Men, looking amazingly like the winged angels in De Laurentiis's production of *Barbarella* (1968), engage the crew of a space ship in hand-to-hand battle (you know there's something lacking with the Ming technology when the commander of the rocket ship shouts, "Stand by to the repel invaders!"). Is all of this ridiculous? Of course. Is it fun? Yeah, sort of, it is.

A Flash of Green ★ ★ ★
NO MPAA RATING; 121 m., 1985

Ed Harris (Jimmy Wing), Blair Brown (Kat Hubble), Richard Jordan (Elmo Bliss), George Coe (Brian Haas), Joan Goodfellow (Mitchie), Jean De Baer (Jackie Halley). Directed by Victor Nunez and produced by Richard Jordan. Screenplay by Nunez.

A Flash of Green is based on a novel by John D. MacDonald, and like a lot of his stories, it seems to be about the plot but is really about the characters. We start with a story about saving an unspoiled bay from greedy developers, and we end with a story about a man trying to save himself from his own greed. It's a relief, halfway through the movie, to realize it's not going to be about how the good guys win and the bad guys don't turn the grasslands into parking lots. Instead, it's going to be about a complicated relationship involving a newspaper reporter, his conscience, and the woman he loves.

The reporter is played by Ed Harris, who has never been better in a movie. He's not one of those hotshot journalists the movies like to fabricate, but a small-town journeyman who keeps a low profile, gets his job done, and in his own quiet way knows where all the bodies are buried. He gets a tip one day: Grassy Bay, the beautiful nature preserve, is once again being threatened by the schemes of Elmo Bliss (Richard Jordan), the rich and ambitious local developer.

He passes the tip along to Kat Hubble (Blair Brown), the woman who led the last fight to save the bay. He loves Kat Hubble. They've both known that for a long time, but the situation is complicated by Harris's own wife, who has been slowly dying for months, and by the fact that Kat is a recent widow. Harris has another problem. He needs money, and when Elmo Bliss offers to cut him in for a piece of the action, he agrees. Is that a contradiction? *A Flash of Green* is attentive to the compromises of daily life, and it understands how people can be complicated enough to hold two opposed ideas at the same time. Harris knows that what he is doing is wrong, that it is a betrayal of his friends, and yet he does it because it seems necessary.

Most movie newspapermen are portrayed as either heroes or creeps. Either they win the Pulitzer, or they violate somebody's privacy. The Harris character is seen more carefully, as a hard-working small-town guy who has lost a lot of his illusions. The developer, played by Richard Jordan, also is seen as a specific case. He isn't simply a wheeler-dealer, but a man who has more ambition than taste, and who can convince himself that it'll be good for everybody if Grassy Bay is filled in. And the Blair Brown character is complex, too; she understands the sexual attraction that exists between herself and Harris, but she doesn't confuse it with love, because it's not love, it's simply unfinished business.

A Flash of Green was directed by Victor Nunez, who also made *Gal Young Un*. Once again, he would rather explore his characters than send them spinning through some meaningless plot. Nunez lives near the Florida locations of this movie, and he has achieved a real sense of place. We feel the moist heat of the long summer nights, the cynical ways in which everybody knows everybody else's business, the urgency of unfulfilled people who can smell money, and think it means success.

Flashdance ★ ½
R, 96 m., 1983

Jennifer Beals (Alex), Michael Nouri (Nicky), Belinda Bauer (Katie Hurley), Lilia Skala (Hanna Long). Directed by Adrian Lyne and produced by Don Simpson and Jerry Bruckheimer. Screenplay by Tom Hedley and Joe Eszterhas.

I have a friend who has a simple test for a movie: Is this movie as interesting as the same things would be, happening in real life? A lot of movies aren't, and *Flashdance* sure isn't. If this movie had spent just a little more effort getting to know the heroine of its story, and a little less time trying to rip off *Saturday Night Fever*, it might have been a much better film.

My friend's simple test applies to this movie in another way: The movie is *not* as interesting as the real-life story of Jennifer Beals, the young actress who stars in it. Beals launched a career as a model (covers on *Town & Country* and *Vogue*) at the age of 15, after being discovered by Chicago photographer Victor Skrebneski. She enrolled in Yale, took some acting classes in New York, went to an audition, and won this role. The irony is that her story, simply and directly told, might have been a lot more interesting than the story of *Flashdance*, which is so loaded down with artificial screenplay contrivances and flashy production numbers that it's waterlogged. This is one of those movies that goes for a slice of life and ends up with three pies.

Jennifer Beals plays Alex, an eighteen-year-old who is a welder by day, *and* a go-go dancer by night, *and* dreams of being a ballet star, *and* falls in love with the Porsche-driving boss of the construction company. These are a lot of "character details" even if she *didn't* also have a saintly old woman as a mentor, a big slobbering dog as a friend, a bicycle she rides all over Pittsburgh, a loft the size of a sweatshop, a sister who ice skates, a grumpy old pop, *and* the ability to take off her bra without removing her sweatshirt. This poor kid is so busy performing the pieces of business supplied to her by the manic screenwriters that she never gets a chance to develop a character.

Meanwhile, the movie has a disconcerting way of getting sidetracked with big dance scenes. The heroine works in the most improbable working-class bar ever put on film, a joint named Mawby's that has a clientele out of Miller's Beer TV ads, stage lighting reminiscent of Vegas, go-go dancers who change their expensive costumes every night, *and* put on punk rock extravaganzas, *and* never take off all their clothes, *and* never get shouted at by the customers for not doing so.

Flashdance is like a movie that won a free ninety-minute shopping spree in the Hollywood supermarket. The director (Adrian Lyne, of the much better *Foxes*) and his collaborators race crazily down the aisles, grabbing a piece of *Saturday Night Fever*, a slice of *Urban Cowboy*, a quart of *Marty*, and a two-pound box of "Archie Bunker's Place." The result is great sound and flashdance, signifying nothing. But Jennifer Beals shouldn't feel bad. She is a natural talent, she is fresh and engaging here, and only needs to find an agent with a natural talent for turning down scripts.

Fletch ★ ★ ½
PG, 110 m., 1985

Chevy Chase (I.M. Fletcher), Joe Don Baker (Chief Karlin), Dana Wheeler-Nicholson (Gail Stanwyk), Richard Libertini (Walker), Tim Matheson (Alan Stanwyck), M. Emmet Walsh (Dr. Dolan). Directed by Michael Ritchie and produced by Alan Greisman and Peter Douglas. Screenplay by Andrew Bergman.

Why did Chevy Chase want to play I.M. Fletcher, the laconic hero of Gregory McDonald's best sellers? Was it because Chase saw a way to bring Fletch to life? Or was it because Chase thought Fletch was very much like himself? The problem with *Fletch* is that the central performance is an anthology of Chevy Chase mannerisms in search of a character. Other elements in the movie are pretty good: the supporting characters, the ingenious plot, the unexpected locations. But whenever the movie threatens to work, there's Chevy Chase with his monotone, deadpan cynicism, distancing himself from the material.

Fletch is not the first movie that Chase has undercut with his mannerisms, but it is the best one—since *Foul Play*, anyway. His problem as an actor is that he perfected a personal style on "Saturday Night Live" all those many years ago, and has never been able to work outside of it. The basic Chevy Chase personality functions well at the length of a TV sketch, when there's no time to create a new character, but in a movie it grows deadening. *Fletch* is filled with a series of extraordinary situations, and Chase seems to react to all of them with the same wry dubiousness. His character this time is an investigative reporter for a Los Angeles newspaper. Deep into an investigation of drug traffic on the city's beaches, Fletch is approached by a young man (Tim Matheson) with a simple proposition: He wants to be killed. The story is that Matheson is dying of cancer and wants to die violently so his family can qualify for enlarged insurance benefits, but Fletch doesn't buy it. Something's fishy, and Fletch pretends to take the job, while conducting his own investigation.

The case leads him to an extraordinary series of interesting characters; the film's director, Michael Ritchie is good at sketching human originals, and we meet an aging farm couple in Utah, a manic editor, a no-nonsense police chief, a mysterious drug dealer, a slimy doctor, a beautiful wife, and a lot of mean dogs. Every one of the characters is played well, with the little details that Ritchie loves: The scene on a farmhouse porch in Utah is filled with such sly, quiet social satire that it could stand by itself. The movie's physical comedy is good, too. A scene where Fletch breaks into a realtor's office—scaling a fence and outsmarting vicious attack dogs—is constructed so carefully out of comedy and violence that it's a little masterpiece of editing.

The problem is, Chase's performance tends to reduce all the scenes to the same level, at least as far as he's concerned. He projects such an inflexible mask of cool detachment, of ironic running commentary, that we're prevented from identifying with him. If he thinks this is all just a little too silly for words, what are we to think? If we're more involved in the action than he is, does that make us chumps? *Fletch* needed an actor more interested in playing the character than in playing himself.

The Fog ★ ★
R, 91 m., 1980

Adrienne Barbeau (Stevie Wayne), Hal Holbrook (Father Malone), Janet Leigh (Kathy Williams), Jamie Lee Curtis (Elizabeth Solley), John Houseman (Machen), Tommy Atkins (Nick Castle), Nancy Loomis (Sandy Fadel). Directed by John Carpenter and produced by Debra Hill. Screenplay by Carpenter and Hill.

The problem is with the fog. It must have seemed like an inspired idea to make a horror movie in which clouds of fog would be the menace, but the idea just doesn't work out in *The Fog*, John Carpenter's next thriller after *Halloween*. The movie's made with style and energy, but it needs a better villain.

And it also needs a slightly more plausible plot. We don't really care about the logic of the plot in horror movies, of course, but there has to be *some* plausibility, just so we know what the rules are. Carpenter's fog—which contains the ghosts of murdered sailors—is too unpredictable. When it rolls in,

it's likely to kill anyone, no matter whether or not their ancestors were responsible for killing the sailors one hundred years ago.

It's easy to see, though, why this project must have been appealing to Carpenter, a talented young filmmaker who built a cult audience with the low-budget genre films *Dark Star* and *Assault on Precinct 13* before breaking through to enormous ratings with the made-for-TV *Elvis*. Carpenter's *Halloween* was one of the major box office successes of 1979 (*Variety* called it the most profitable independent film ever made) and it demonstrated his favorite approach: He likes films that manipulate audiences, films designed, quite simply, to cause emotions—and his favorite response is shock.

The Fog basically has the same structure as *Halloween*. It gives us a small American town. It introduces a few of its inhabitants, especially isolated women. It establishes a threat. And then the rest of the movie is devoted to scenes in which the threat either does or does not destroy its intended victims.

Very simple. The threat need not even be believable; *Halloween*'s psychotic killer, wrapped in sheets and apparently invulnerable, just kept on coming while a platoon of baby-sitters bit the dust. But *Halloween*'s killer was a person, and had at least a bit of personal background (we saw a traumatic scene from his childhood and heard a psychiatrist describe him as evil incarnate).

The narrative background in *The Fog* is presented stylishly—John Houseman tells a ghost story around a campfire on the beach, little kids listen with their mouths hanging open, we learn that shipwrecked sailors were murdered near this town a century ago, and that they vowed to return one hundred years later. And, of course, tonight's the night.

But when the sailors' ghosts return, wrapped in fog, we can't figure out what their motives are. Do they want to kill the descendants of their murderers? Are they angry at the town itself? Are they indeed *there* in the fog, or are the victims hallucinating?

We wouldn't care about the answers to these questions if *The Fog* were as scary as *Halloween*. But because *The Fog* has a historical plot, because its events are inspired by the past, it should make more sense. A sentient fog may be photogenic (and this is a good-looking movie), but can we identify with it? Is it the kind of villain we love to hate? Not really.

Fool for Love ★ ★ ★
R, 107 m., 1985

Sam Shepard (Eddie), Kim Basinger (May), Harry Dean Stanton (Old Man), Randy Quaid (Martin). Directed by Robert Altman and produced by Menahem Golan and Yoram Globus. Screenplay by Sam Shepard.

At the center of Sam Shepard's *Fool for Love* are two people whose hurts are so deep, whose angers are so real, that they can barely talk about what they really feel. That does not stop them from talking, on and on into the hurtful night, and eventually we can put together their stories, using what they have said, and especially what they have not said.

One of the characters is a blonde slattern named May, whose natural beauty has been rearranged into a parody of the classic movie baby doll—Brigitte Bardot, say. The other character is named Eddie, and he is a cowboy who drives through the empty Texas reaches in the obligatory pickup truck with the obligatory rifle rack behind his head and the obligatory horse trailer behind. One night May is working behind the counter of a restaurant in a crumbling motel, and she sees Eddie's pickup coming down the road. She runs and hides. Standing in the shadows of the rundown motel is an older man (Harry Dean Stanton) who simply waits and watches.

Shepard's method is direct. He allows his characters to talk around what they're really thinking, and occasionally the talk escalates into brief, incisive bursts of action—even violence. Eventually we learn that the older man is the father of both Eddie and May, that they had different mothers, that the old man commuted between two families, and that Eddie and May eventually met under circumstances that were later determined to be incestuous.

These developments would provide the ingredients for a basic story of redneck passion, and there are times when *Fool for Love* wants to strike those very notes. We feel we might be looking at the characters in a story by William Faulkner or Erskine Caldwell,

and the visual compositions look inspired by the lurid covers of 1940s paperback novels. The deliberately trashy surface, however, conceals deeper levels of feeling, and by the end of *Fool for Love* we have witnessed some sort of classic tragedy, set there in the Texas backlands.

Robert Altman's movie version of Shepard's play stars Shepard himself, in a strong performance as Eddie. But he doesn't dominate the story as much as you might think. The central performance in the movie is really Kim Basinger's, as May. Although she has played sexpots before—has indeed specialized in them—nothing prepared me for the dimensions she was able to find in this one. What's astonishing is that *Fool for Love* is essentially a male drama, told from a male point of view, and yet Basinger is able to suggest so much with her performance that she steals the center of the stage right away from the man who wrote the lines and is playing opposite her.

Part of her impact is probably because the director is Altman. Few other major directors are more interested in women, and in his films like *Thieves Like Us, Three Women*, and *Come Back to the 5 & Dime, Jimmy Dean, Jimmy Dean*, he has shown women in settings very similar to this one: unfulfilled women, conscious of the waste of their lives, living in backwaters where their primary pastime is to await the decisions of men.

Altman does a brilliant job of visualizing this particular backwater. From the opening aerial shots of the godforsaken motel, he creates a tangibly real, dusty, forlorn world. Some of his shots are so beautiful it's hard to figure how he obtained them: That ominous dark sky lowering over the motel, for example, looks almost like a painting. Altman is also up to some of the same visual tricks he used in *Jimmy Dean*, including the use of windows and mirrors to give us two planes of action at the same time. And he has a wonderfully subtle way of showing us the Harry Dean Stanton character in both the past and the present.

This is Altman's fourth movie in a row based on a play. It comes after *Jimmy Dean, Streamers*, and the extraordinary *Secret Honor*, about Richard Nixon (he has filmed three other plays for cable television). After a career as one of the most free-swinging of all modern movie directors *(M*A*S*H, McCabe and Mrs. Miller, Nashville)* it is interesting to see him embracing the discipline of a play script. Having made movies that were all over the map, he now inhabits interiors—of rooms, and of people's minds. With *Fool for Love,* he has succeeded on two levels that seem opposed to each other. He has made a melodrama, almost a soap opera, in which the characters achieve a kind of nobility.

Footloose ★ ½
PG, 106 m., 1984

Kevin Bacon (Ren), Lori Singer (Ariel), John Lithgow (Reverend Moore). Directed by Herbert Ross and produced by Lewis J. Rachmil and Craig Zadan. Screenplay by Dean Pitchford.

Footloose is a seriously confused movie that tries to do three things, and does all of them badly. It wants to tell the story of a conflict in a town, it wants to introduce some flashy teen-age characters, and part of the time it wants to be a music video. It's possible that no movie with this many agendas *can* be good; maybe somebody should have decided, early on, exactly what the movie was supposed to be about. The film tells the story of a Chicago kid named Ren (Kevin Bacon), who has a fashionable haircut and likes to dance. He moves with his mother to a small town named Bomont, which is somewhere in the Midwest, although I seriously doubt a town like this exists anywhere outside of standard movie clichés. The old fuddies in Bomont have imposed a total ban on rock 'n' roll and dancing. The ban is led by an uptight preacher named Shaw Moore (John Lithgow), who is still grieving because he lost a child in a car wreck five years ago. To the Reverend Moore, dancing and rock lead to booze and drugs.

Ren falls in love with the preacher's daughter (Lori Singer). He also has the usual standard showdowns with the locals, including the high school bully. Ren decides what this town needs is a dance. His assignment, should he choose to accept it, is to (1) win the approval of the preacher and the town council to allow dancing, (2) beat up the bully,

and (3) star in at least three segments of the movie that can be used as TV music videos. The basic conflict in this movie was not new when the *Beach Party* gang discovered it. Remember Annette and Frankie trying to persuade the old folks to let them hold a dance on the beach? If the movie had only relaxed and allowed itself to admit how silly the situation is, it could have been more fun. Instead, it gets bogged down in the peculiar personality of the preacher, who is played by Lithgow as a man of agonizing complexity.

Footloose makes one huge, inexplicable error with the Lithgow character. It sets him up as an unyielding reactionary, and then lets him change his mind 180 degrees without a word of explanation. In one scene, the preacher's daughter confronts her dad in church and announces she isn't a virgin (the movie never remembers to tell us whether she really is or not). The preacher turns livid, starts to scream, and then is interrupted by news that they're burning books down at the library. In the *very next scene,* the preacher is arguing against the book burners—and before long, without any meaningful transitional scenes, he has caved in to the idea of the dance. It's cheating to set up Lithgow as the enemy and then turn him into a friend without a word of explanation.

I mentioned the flashy teen-age characters. The one who gave me the most trouble was that preacher's daughter. She enjoys suicidal games of chicken, like balancing with her legs on the doors of a speeding car and a speeding truck while a speeding semi bears down on her. This trick is, of course, impossible to do in real life, and so it simultaneously makes her into an idiot and a stuntwoman. As for the music video scenes: On three different occasions, the movie switches gears and goes into prepackaged MTV-type production numbers, with the fancy photography and the flashy quick cuts. These scenes may play well on TV, but they break what little reality the story has, and expose *Footloose* as a collection of unrelated ingredients that someone thought would be exploitable.

For Your Eyes Only ★ ★
PG, 127 m., 1981

Roger Moore (James Bond), Carole Bouquet (Melina), Topol (Columbo), Julian Glover (Kristatos), Cassandra Harris (Lisl), Janet Brown (Prime Minister). Directed by John Glen and produced by Albert R. Broccoli. Screenplay by Richard Malbaum and Michael Wilson.

For Your Eyes Only is a competent James Bond thriller, well-crafted, a respectable product from the 007 production line. But it's no more than that. It doesn't have the special sly humor of the Sean Connery Bonds, of course, but also doesn't have the visual splendor of such Roger Moore Bonds as *The Spy Who Loved Me*, or special effects to equal *Moonraker*. And in this era of jolting, inspired visual effects from George Lucas and Steven Spielberg, it's just not quite in the same league. That will no doubt come as a shock to Producer Albert (Cubby) Broccoli, who has made the James Bond series his life's work.

Broccoli and his late partner, Harry Saltzman, all but invented the genre that Hollywood calls "event films" or "special effects films." The ingredients, which Bond popularized and others imitated, always included supervillains, sensational stunts, sex, absurd plots to destroy or rule the world and, of course, a hero. The 007 epics held the patent on that formula in the late '60s and early '70s, but they are growing dated. *For Your Eyes Only* doesn't have any surprises. We've seen all the big scenes before, and when the villains turn out to be headquartered in an impregnable mountaintop fortress, we yawn. After *Where Eagles Dare* and *The Guns of Navarone* and the hollow Japanese volcano that Bond himself once infiltrated, let's face it: When you've seen one impregnable mountaintop fortress, you've seen 'em all.

The movie opens with James Bond trapped inside a remote-controlled helicopter being guided by a bald sadist in a wheelchair. After Bond triumphs, the incident is never referred to again. *This* movie involves the loss of the secret British code controlling submarine-based missiles. The Russians would like to have it. Bond's mission: Retrieve the control console from a ship sunk in the Aegean. The movie breaks down into a series of set-pieces. Bond and his latest Bondgirl (long-haired, undemonstrative Carole Bouquet) dive in a mini-sub, engage in a complicated chase through the back roads of Greece, crawl through the sunken wreck in wet suits, are nearly drowned and blown up, etc. For variety, Bond and Bouquet are dragged behind a powerboat as shark bait, and then Bond scales the fortress mountain. A fortress guard spots Bond dangling from a rope thousands of feet in the air. What does he do? Does he just cut the rope? No, sir, the guard descends part way to tantalize Bond by letting him drop a little at a time. The rest is predictable.

In a movie of respectable craftsmanship and moderate pleasures, there's one obvious disappointment. The relationship between Roger Moore and Carole Bouquet is never worked out in an interesting way. Since the days when he was played by Sean Connery, agent 007 has always had a dry, quiet, humorous way with women. Roger Moore has risen to the same challenge, notably opposite Barbara Bach in *The Spy Who Loved Me*. But Moore and Bouquet have no real chemistry in *For Your Eyes Only*. There's none of that kidding byplay. It's too routine. The whole movie is too routine.

The Formula ★ ★
R, 117 m., 1980

George C. Scott (Detective), Marlon Brando (Adam Steifel), Marthe Keller (Lisa), John Gielgud (Dr. Esau), G.D. Spradlin (Clements). Directed by John Avildsen and produced and written by Steve Shagan.

One of the ironies of *The Formula* is that if it had only been made from an old Hollywood formula—*any* formula—we might have been able to understand it better. As it stands, it's so thoroughly baffling that we find ourselves asking, not only who-did-it, but what they did, and who they were. The movie is no help. Since *The Formula* is intended as a thriller, its completely muddled plot is a disaster: There can be no joy in unraveling a plot that is a mystery even to itself.

The movie's based on Steve Shagan's best-selling novel, which began with the premise that the Nazis discovered a cheap formula for synthetic fuel thirty-five years ago, and that the giant oil corporations have been suppressing it ever since. In the movie, the oil companies are represented by Marlon Brando, who appears in three fascinating scenes and leaves us wishing for more. The good guys are boiled down in the person of George C. Scott, as a Los Angeles detective who starts out investigating the murder of a friend and stumbles onto a trail that leads him to Europe and possessors of that secret formula.

Of *that* much I'm sure. Various other questions remain unanswered. For example, in Europe Scott takes up with a young lady who seems to be on the same side he's on. She's played by Marthe Keller as the same sort of beautiful international enigma she has played before. But what's she *really* up to? In interviews, Steve Shagan explains that she's from the Palestine Liberation Organization. In the movie, we learn she has guilt feelings because her Nazi father murdered Jews. Then why would she be in the PLO? It hardly matters, since her affiliation, if any, is never made clear in the movie.

There are other puzzles. As Scott tracks down the formula, everyone he talks to is killed almost immediately after he talks to them. Why? Because he's being led on a wild goose chase, and each character is eliminated after serving his function? Because the killers are trying to discourage Scott—and just can't seem to kill him, too? It's a mystery. I must also admit that at the movie's end, I still did not know for sure who was doing the shooting. I assumed it was a conspiracy by Brando's oil company, but I couldn't be sure.

The Formula apparently is a mess because of a post-production fight between Shagan, as writer-producer, and John Avildsen, as director; they exchanged acrimonious letters in the *Los Angeles Times,* and Avildsen failed in an attempt to have his name removed from the picture. They way they tell it, Avildsen wanted the movie to make more sense as a thriller, while Shagan was more concerned with his "message."

Well. One of the problems with his message is that it is not based on fact; it's a fantasy. Even though it may be true that the multinational oil companies try to manipulate the energy market, it is apparently not true that a formula exists that could turn coal into cheap synthetic fuel. Yet the movie's publicity calls the existence of a secret Nazi formula a "proven fact."

I have here an article from the November 1980 issue of *Science* magazine, noting that the "synthesis used by the Germans are more in the nature of textbook processes than Mobil secrets" and that the film, "as history, is bunkum."

If the film cannot be taken seriously as an exposé, and it is hopelessly confused as a thriller, what's left? Two marvelous performances. Scott, as the detective, is a harried, tired, deeply cynical man who fills the crevices of his role with an actor's details that make the cop a human being. Brando, who designed his makeup to resemble Occidental Oil's Armand Hammer, has a great speech at the end of the film and several other classic lines ranging from "You're missing the point—we *are* the Arabs," to the succinct offer "Milk Dud?" What happens during *The Formula* is that we eventually give up trying to make any sense out of the movie and content ourselves with regarding these performances. They are subtle and lovingly crafted, and it is just too bad there's no substance surrounding them.

Fort Apache, The Bronx ★ ★
R, 123 m., 1981

Paul Newman (Murphy), Edward Asner (Connolly), Ken Wahl (Corelli), Danny Aiello (Morgan), Rachel Ticotin (Isabella), Pam Grier (Charlotte), Kathleen Beller (Theresa). Directed by Daniel Petrie and produced by Martin Richards and Tom Fiorello. Screenplay by Heywood Gould.

It's sort of insidious, the way a formula can take over and smother a good idea for a movie. *Fort Apache, The Bronx* apparently began as such an idea. It's said to be based on the experiences of a couple of real cops in the worst area of New York's Bronx. The area looks like a bomb site, with burned-out buildings and people. The filmmakers wanted to go into this area and use a police story as a framework for showing how people live and suffer there, and how public agencies such as the police grow frustrated trying to deal with an impossible situation. That was their intention, anyway. What they came out with is the most complete collection of cop-movie clichés since John Wayne played a Chicago cop in *McQ*.

There were authentic perceptions and ideas available to this film—and you can see them on the screen. You can see them in the look of some of the shots, tracking across the urban wasteland, and in the sound and feel of a scene where a pimp beats and berates one of his girls, and the grim humor of a scene where a thief outruns a cop—who pauses, gasping for breath, and lights a cigarette.

But then there's a story line that keeps getting in the way. There are too many scenes that are necessary to the plot but not to the movie, scenes where the life of the movie stops so story details can be filled in. And we realize that somehow Hollywood hasn't wanted to get *too* close to this material. Instead, it has borrowed a look of grim authenticity and grafted it to assorted cop show situations.

The movie stars Paul Newman. He's good in his role, as a cop named Murphy who simultaneously falls in love with a nurse, witnesses his fellow officers committing a murder, and has a battle of will with his commanding officer. The chief is played by Edward Asner, who is in the movie so briefly that, effective as he is, we have trouble remembering he's a cop. He's still Lou Grant, barking orders in the sqaud room instead of the city room.

The movie has several story threads that lead nowhere. One involves Pam Grier, as a junkie prostitute who wanders the streets in a daze, kills a couple of cops—and then turns out to have been basically a walk-on, and *not* the key to the movie's mysteries. There are also several whole scenes that seem to have been put in without much purpose, including one in which Newman and his partner try to talk a transvestite out of jumping off a building, and another in which Newman delivers a baby. Then there's a big climactic scene, with drug dealers holed up with hostages and the SWAT boys (and Newman, of course) crashing through windows on the ends of ropes.

These scenes all seem to be in the movie because the filmmakers thought they belonged in any self-respecting cop movie. Too bad. The purely human story in this movie would have been much more interest-

ing. It involves Newman's relationship with the Puerto Rican nurse (wonderfully well-played by Rachel Ticotin) and the crisis of conscience he goes through about whether to turn in his fellow officers after he saw them throw a kid off a roof.

Do the filmmakers feel we're not ready for issues like that, served straight? Do we need violence and action to keep our attention? Is our attention span so short that no strand of character development can be followed for long without throwing in some kind of sensational diversion? I hope not. To throw in all the stock characters and shopworn situations from old TV cop shows is an insult to the abilities of the actors and to the real lives this movie pretends to reflect.

48 Hours ★ ★ ★ ½
R, 100 m., 1982

Nick Nolte (Cates), Eddie Murphy (Reggie), James Remar (Ganz), Sonny Landham (Billy Bear), Annette O'Toole (Elaine). Directed by Walter Hill and produced by Lawrence Gordon and Joel Silver. Screenplay by Roger Spottiswoode, Hill, Larry Gross, and Steven E. de Souza.

Sometimes an actor becomes a star in just one scene. Jack Nicholson did it in *Easy Rider*, wearing the football helmet on the back of the motorcycle. It happened to Faye Dunaway when she looked sleepily out of a screen window at Warren Beatty in *Bonnie and Clyde*. And in *48 Hours*, it happens to Eddie Murphy. His unforgettable scene comes about halfway through *48 Hours*. He plays a convict who has done thirty months for theft and will do six more unless he helps out Nick Nolte, a hungover hot dog of a detective who's on the trail of some cop killers. Nolte has sprung Murphy from jail for forty-eight hours, with the promise of freedom if they get the killers. Murphy thinks there's a bartender who may have some information. The thing is, the bar is a redneck country joint, the kind where urban cowboys drink out of longneck bottles and salute the Confederate flag on the wall. Murphy has been jiving Nolte about how he can handle any situation. Nolte gives him a chance. And Murphy, impersonating a police officer, walks into that bar, takes command, totally intimidates everybody, and gets his information. It's a great scene—the mirror image of that scene in *The French Connection* where Gene Hackman, as Popeye Doyle, intimidated the black regulars in a Harlem bar.

Murphy has other good moments in this movie, and so does Nolte, who gives a wonderful performance as a cynical, irresponsible, and immature cop who's always telling lies to his girlfriend and sneaking a jolt of whiskey out of his personal flask. The two men start out suspicious of each other in this movie and work up to a warm dislike. But eventually, grudgingly, a kind of respect starts to grow.

The movie's story is nothing to write home about. It's pretty routine. What makes the movie special is how it's made. Nolte and Murphy are good, and their dialogue is good, too—quirky and funny. Character actor James Remar makes a really slimy killer, genuinely evil. Annette O'Toole gets third billing as Nolte's lover, but it's another one of those thankless women's roles. Not only could O'Toole have phoned it in—she does, spending most of her scenes on the telephone calling Nolte a no-good bum. The direction is by Walter Hill, who has never been any good at scenes involving women and doesn't improve this time. What he is good at is action, male camaraderie and atmosphere. His movies almost always feature at least one beautifully choreographed, unbelievably violent fight scene (remember Charles Bronson's bare-knuckle fight in *Hard Times?*), and the fight scene this time is exhausting.

Where Hill grows in this movie is in his ability to create characters. In a lot of his earlier movies *(The Warriors, The Driver, Long Riders, Southern Comfort)* he preferred men who were symbols, who represented things and so didn't have to be human. In *48 Hours,* Nolte and Murphy are human, vulnerable, and touching. Also mean, violent, and chauvinistic. It's that kind of movie.

Four Friends ★ ★ ★ ★
R, 114 m., 1981

Craig Wasson (Danilo Prozor), Jodi Thelen (Georgia Miles), Jim Metzler (Tom Donaldson), Michael Huddleston (David Levine), Reed Birney (Louie Carnahan), Julie Murray (Adrienne Carnahan), Miklos Simon (Mr. Prozor). Directed by Arthur Penn and produced by Penn and Gene Lasko. Screenplay by Steven Tesich.

Somewhere in the middle of *My Dinner with André,* Andre Gregory wonders aloud if it's not possible that the 1960s were the last decade when we were all truly alive—that since then we've sunk into a bemused state of self-hypnosis, placated by consumer goods and given the illusion of excitement by television. Walking out of *Four Friends,* I had some of the same thoughts. This movie brings the almost unbelievable contradictions of that decade into sharp relief, not as nostalgia or as a re-creation of times past, but as a reliving of all of the agony and freedom of the weirdest ten years any of us is likely to witness.

The movie is told in the form of a loose-knit autobiography, somewhat inspired by the experiences of Steve Tesich, the son of Yugoslavian parents who moved to this country as a boy and lived in the neighborhoods of East Chicago, Indiana, that provide the film's locations. If the film is his emotional autobiography, it is also perhaps the intellectual autobiography of Arthur Penn, the film's director, whose *Bonnie and Clyde* was the best American film of the 1960s and whose *Alice's Restaurant* (1970) was an earlier examination of that wonderful and haunted time.

Their movie tells the stories of four friends. When we meet them, they're entering their senior year of high school. It is 1961. That is so long ago that nobody has yet heard of the Beatles. One of the friends is a young woman (Jodi Thelen), who imagines she is the reincarnation of Isadora Duncan, and who strikes attitudes and poses in an attempt to appear altogether too much of an artistic genius for East Chicago to contain. The other three friends are male classmates. They all love the girl in one way or another, or perhaps it's just that they've never seen anyone like her before. In the ten years to follow, these four people will have lives that were not imaginable in 1961. They will have the opportunity to break out of the sedate conservatism of the Eisenhower era and into the decade of "alternative life-styles."

The movie is ambitious. It wants to take us on a tour of some of the things that happened in the 1960s, and some of the ways four midwestern kids might have responded to them. It also wants to be a meditation on love, and on how love changes during the course of a decade. When Thelen turns up at the bedroom window of her "real" true love (Craig Wasson) early in the movie and cheerfully offers to sleep with him, Wasson refuses, not only because he's a high school kid who's a little afraid of her—but also because he's too much in love with his idea of her to want to make it real. By the time they finally do come back together, years later, they've both been through bad scenes, through madness, drug abuse, and the trauma of the war in Vietnam. They have also grown up, some. The wonder is not that *Four Friends* covers so much ground, but that it makes many of its scenes so memorable that we learn more even about the supporting characters than we expect to.

There are individual scenes in this movie that are just right. One of them involves a crowd of kids walking home in the dusk after school. Another happens between Wasson and Miklos Simon, who plays his gruff, defensive Yugoslavian father, and who finally, painfully, breaks down and smiles after a poker-faced lifetime. A relationship between Wasson and a dying college classmate (Reed Birney) is well drawn, to remind us of undergraduate friendships based on idealism and mutual discovery. And the scene where Wasson and Thelen see each other after many years is handled tenderly and with just the right notes of irony.

Four Friends is a very good movie. Like *Breaking Away*, the story of growing up in Bloomington, Indiana (for which Tesich also wrote the original screenplay), this is a movie that remembers times past with such clarity that there are times it seems to be making it all up. Did we really say those things? Make those assumptions? Live on the edge of what seemed to be a society gone both free and mad at once? Some critics have said the people and events in this movie are not plausible. I don't know if they're denying the movie's truth, or arguing that from a 1980s point of view the '60s were just a bad dream. Or a good one.

The Fox and the Hound ★ ★ ★
G, 83 m., 1981

With the voices of Pearl Bailey (Big Mama), Kurt Russell (Copper), Mickey Rooney (Tod), Sandy Duncan (Vixey), Pat Buttram (Chief), Jack Albertson (Slade). Directed by Art Stevens, Ted Berman, and Richard Rich and produced by Wolfgang Reitherman and Stevens. Screenplay by Larry Clemmons and others.

In all the old familiar ways, *The Fox and the Hound* looks like a traditional production from Walt Disney animators. In has cute little animals and wise old owls. It has a villain in the shape of a mountainous grizzly bear, and comic relief in a long-standing feud between a woodpecker and a caterpillar. And it has songs that contain such uncontroversial wishes as, "If only the world wouldn't get in the way . . . If only the world would let us play." And yet, for all of its familiar qualities, this movie marks something of a departure for the Disney studio, and its movement is in an interesting direction. *The Fox and the Hound* is one of those relatively rare Disney animated features that contains a useful lesson for its younger audiences. It's not just cute animals and frightening adventures and a happy ending; it's also a rather thoughtful meditation on how society determines our behavior.

The movie is a fable about a small puppy named Tod and an orphaned fox named Copper. At the outset we sense something unusual—after the camera traces a gloomy path through the shadows of the forest, a mother fox and her baby come running terrified out of the woods, chased by hunters and hounds. Will the mother and child escape? They almost do. But then the mother hides her baby and sacrifices her life to draw attention away from him. This is the cruel world, without any magical cartoon escapes.

The little fox is taken under the wing, so to speak, by wise old Big Mama Owl, who arranges for the baby to be adopted by a kindly farm woman. It's at this point that the puppy comes into the plot. Puppy and fox become great friends in their childhoods and pledge to be loyal to each other forevermore. But then the quickly growing hound is taken away to be trained as a hunter, and the next time the two friends meet, the hound is savagely trying to chase down the fox. After they are almost killed by the bear, there is a reconciliation of sorts. They realize (and perhaps the kids in the audience will realize, too) how quickly our better impulses can be drowned out by the noise of society. The message is not heavy-handed, nor does it need to be, because the lessons in the movie are so firmly illustrated by the lives of the animals.

Although *The Fox and the Hound* is the first Disney animated feature to have been made mostly by a newer generation of artists at the studio, the film's look still is in the tradition of *The Rescuers* (1977) and other Disney work in the 1970s. That means we don't get the painstaking, frame-by-frame animation of individual leaves and flowers and birds that made *Snow White* magical back when animator man-hours were cheaper. But we do get a lot of life and energy on the screen.

The star of the movie's sound track is Pearl Bailey as Big Mama Owl. She sings three songs, dispenses advice with a free hand, and struts around in the forest as a sort of feathered Ann Landers. The animators have done a wonderful job of giving their cartoon owl some of Pearlie Mae's personality traits, but the two leading characters (with Mickey Rooney as the fox and Kurt Russell as the hound) are more straightforward.

The bottom line, I suppose, is: Will kids like this movie? And the answer is, sure, I think so. It's a fast-moving, colorful story, and as I watched the animated images on the screen, I was suddenly reminded of a curious belief I held when I was a kid. I believed that cartoons looked more real than "live" features, because everything on the screen had sharper edges. I outgrew my notion, but I'm not sure that represents progress.

Foxes ★ ★ ★
R, 106 m., 1980

Jodie Foster (Jeanie), Scott Baio (Brad), Sally Kellerman (Mary), Randy Quaid (Jay), Lois Smith (Mrs. Axman), Adam Faith (Bryan), Cherie Currie (Annie), Marilyn Kagan (Madge), Kandice Stroh (Dierdre). Directed by Adrian Lyne and produced by David Puttnam and Gerald Ayres. Screenplay by Ayres.

God help us if many American teen-agers are like the ones in this movie—but God love *them*, for that matter, for surviving in the teen-age subculture of Los Angeles. *Foxes* is a movie about four teen-age girls who live in the San Fernando Valley, who come from broken or unhappy homes, who are surrounded by a teen-age subculture of sex, dope, booze, and rock and roll . . . and who aren't bad kids, not really.

They run in a pack, sleeping over at each other's homes, going to school together, hanging out together, forming a substitute family because home doesn't provide a traditional one. They form the fierce loyalties that all teen-agers depend upon—loyalties of friendship that run deeper than the instant romances and sudden crushes that are a dime a dozen. They live in a world where sixteen-year-old kids are somehow expected to live in adult society, make decisions about adult vices, and yet not be adult. That's what's scariest about *Foxes:* Our knowledge that alcohol, pot, and pills *are* available to teen-agers unwise enough to go looking for them, and that they can provide emotional overloads far beyond the ability of the kids to cope.

One of the kids in the movie does cope fairly well, though. She's Jeanie, played by Jodie Foster as a sort of teen-age mother hen, a young girl who's got problems of her own but is intelligent, balanced, and enough of a survivor to clearly see the mistakes the others are making. That doesn't mean she rejects her friends. She runs with the pack and she takes her chances, but she's not clearly doomed. And some of the others are.

The movie follows its four foxes through several days and several adventures. It's a loosely structured film, deliberately episodic to suggest the shapeless form of these teen-agers' typical days and nights. Things happen on impulse. Stuff comes up. Kids stay out all night, or run away, or get drunk, or get involved in what's supposed to be a civilized dinner party until it's crashed by a mob of greasers.

The subject of the movie is the way these events are seen so very differently by the kids and their parents. And at the heart of the movie is one particular, wonderful, and complicated parent-child relationship, between Jodie Foster and Sally Kellerman. They only have a few extended scenes together, but the material is written and acted with such sensitivity that we really understand the relationship. And we understand Kellerman, as an attractive woman in her thirties, divorced from a rock promoter, who is trying to raise a sixteen-year-old, attend college, and still have a love life of her own. Kellerman has a line that evokes whole lives, when she talks about "all those desperately lonely, divorced UCLA undergraduates."

The parallels here are obvious. The Kellerman character, we suspect, got swept up in the rock and drug subculture, got married too young, got pregnant immediately, and now, the mother of a sixteen-year-old, is *still* in the process of growing up herself. She doesn't want her kid to go through what she went through. But kids grow up so fast these days that, oddly enough, these two women are almost in the same boat.

Foxes is an ambitious movie, not an exploitation picture. It's a lot more serious, for example, than the hit *Little Darlings*. It contains the sounds and rhythms of real teenage lives; it was written and directed after a lot of research, and is acted by kids who are to one degree or another playing themselves. The movie's a rare attempt to provide a portrait of the way teen-agers really do live today in some suburban cultures.

Frances ★ ★ ★ ½
R, 139 m., 1983

Jessica Lange (Frances Farmer), Sam Shepard (Harry York), Bart Burns (Farmer). Directed by Graeme Clifford and produced by Jonathan Sanger. Screenplay by Eric Bergren, Christopher Devore, and Nicholas Kazan.

Graeme Clifford's *Frances* tells the story of a small-town girl who tasted the glory of Hollywood and the exhilaration of Broadway and then went on to lead a life during which everything went wrong. It is a tragedy without a villain, a sad story with no moral except that there, but for the grace of God, go we. The movie is about Frances Farmer, a beautiful and talented movie star from the 1930s and 1940s who had a streak of independence

and a compulsion toward self-destruction, and who went about as high and about as low as it is possible to go in one lifetime. She came out of Seattle as a high school essay-contest winner and budding intellectual. She was talented and pretty enough to make her way fairly easily into show business, where she immediately gravitated to the left-wing precincts of the Group Theater and such landmark productions as Clifford Odets's *Waiting for Lefty*. She also became a movie star, and there was a time when her star shone so brightly that it seemed it would last forever.

It did not. She was a stubborn, opinionated star who fought with the studio system, defied the bosses, drank too much, took too many pills, and got into too much trouble. Her strong-willed mother stepped in to help her, and that's when Frances's troubles really began. The mother orchestrated a series of hospitalizations in bizarre mental institutions, where Frances Farmer was brutally mistreated and finally, horrifyingly, lobotomized. She ended her days as a vague, pleasant middle-age woman who did a talk show in Indianapolis and finally died of alcoholism.

Jessica Lange plays Frances Farmer in a performance that is so driven, that contains so many different facets of a complex personality, that we feel she has an intuitive understanding of this tragic woman. She is just as good when she portrays Farmer as an uncertain, appealing teen-ager from the Northwest as she is when she plays her much later, snarling at a hairdresser and screaming at her mother. All of those contradictions were inside Farmer, and if she had learned to hide or deal with some of them she might have lived a happier life.

The story of Frances Farmer makes a fascinating movie, if only because it's such a contrast to standard show-business biographies. They usually come in two speeds: rags to riches, or rags to riches to victim. *Frances* never really lays blame for the tragedy of Farmer's life. It presents a number of causes for Farmer's destruction. (A short list might include her combative personality, her shrewish mother, the studio system, betrayal by her lovers, alcoholism, drug abuse, psychiatric malpractice, and the predations of a mad lobotomist.) But the movie never comes right out and says what it believes "caused" Farmer's tragedy. That is good, I think, because no simple explanation will do for Farmer's life. The movie is told from her point of view, and from where she stood, she was surrounded. On one day she had one enemy, and on another day, another enemy. Always, of course, her worst enemy was herself. The movie doesn't let us off the hook by giving us someone to blame. Instead, it insists on being a bleak tragedy, and it argues that sometimes it is quite possible for everything to go wrong. Since most movies are at least optimistic enough to provide a *cause* for human tragedy, this one is sort of daring.

It is also well made by Clifford, whose credits as a film editor include such virtuoso work as *McCabe and Mrs. Miller* and *Don't Look Now.* In his debut as a director Clifford has made a period picture that wears its period so easily that we're not distracted by it, a movie that is bleak without being unwatchable.

There are a few problems with his structure, most of them centering around an incompletely explained friend of Farmer's, played by Sam Shepard as a guy who seems to drift into her life whenever the plot requires him. Kim Stanley plays Farmer's mother on a rather thankless note of shrillness, and the lobotomist in the picture seems to have wandered over from a nearby horror film. (He apparently gave the same impression in real life.) But Lange provides a strong emotional center for the film, and when it is over we're left with the feeling that Farmer never really got a chance to be who she should have been, or to do what she should have done. She had every gift she needed in life except for luck, useful friends, and an instinct for survival. She could have been one of the greatest movie stars of her time. As it is, when I was asked to name a few of Frances Farmer's best films, I had to admit that, offhand, I couldn't think of one.

Fraternity Vacation ★
R, 95 m., 1985

Stephen Geofferys (Wendell Tvedt), Sherre J. Wilson (Ashley Taylor), Cameron Dye (Joe Gillespie), Leigh McCloskey (Chas). Directed by James Frawley and produced by Robert C. Peters. Screenplay by Lindsay Harrison.

No women are hacked to pieces in *Fraternity Vacation*, but they are the victims of violence all the same—the kind of violence that denies them the opportunity to be as interesting, as aggressive, and as free to choose as all the guys in this brain-damaged film. Their basic role here is to be the prizes in a male sexual competition. Since the guys in this movie are shallow, narcissistic, self-obsessed dummies, to be the prize is to lose the game, but in a movie like this, those are the rules.

The film takes place in Palm Springs, during spring break, when a bunch of fraternity boys from Iowa descend on the town. Why Palm Springs and not Fort Lauderdale? Because Palm Springs is closer to Hollywood, and therefore a cheaper place to make a movie, that's why. So the movie glosses over the fact that Palm Springs is the most boring town in America for anyone who does not play golf and/or know Bob Hope or Betty Ford. In the movie, the college students cruise up and down the main drag in their convertibles, checking out the action, and we meet the main players. On one side there are three fraternity brothers—two jocks and a nerd. On the other side, two jocks from a rival fraternity. Everybody is out to get laid, of course, and that leads to the movie's painfully offensive opening sex scene.

You've got to see this episode to believe what pathological attitudes the movie has about women. Let me set the scene. The guys from the rival fraternity—let's call them the bad guys—have brought along a couple of girlfriends, and convince them to stage a practical joke to make the good guys think they're going to get lucky. So the women go up to the good guys' room, make out for a while, completely strip, and then play the "joke" by pretending they have herpes. What a ton of fun. Consider: What's essentially happening, in this jocular, happy-go-lucky scene, is that the girlfriends are asked to behave like hookers, and they agree. You think that's bad? Get this: After that scene, the two women *are never seen again in this movie!* They are simply dropped as characters—and as girlfriends, too, I guess. how would you feel if you were an actress auditioning for a part, and the good news was you were the girlfriend of the star, and the bad news was that after you stripped and made a herpes joke, you disappeared from the movie?

Meanwhile, the arena of sexual competition changes. There's a beautiful, mysterious blonde (Sherre J. Taylor) at poolside, and all the guys lust after her. So, they make a $1,000 bet about who will be the first to get her in the sack. The rest of the movie consists of the idiotic things all five guys do to impress the blonde. At the end of the film, of course, it's not the jocks but the nerd who wins out. Who said this movie doesn't have a conscience?

Don't get me wrong. I have nothing against dumb sex comedies. All I object to is the fact that *Fraternity Vacation* is playing with half a deck—the male half. The men are the characters and the women are the objects. That's probably because the movie was made by men who lacked the imagination to get outside their own fat heads and imagine what it might be like to be a woman—not a woman in real life, mind you, but even a woman in their trashy little movie. Think how much more interesting it could have been if the women, as well as the men, were allowed to lust, to scheme, to make bets, to have competitions, and to do all sorts of fun things, instead of just tanning themselves by the side of the pool. Of course, that would be another movie. Maybe even another universe.

The French Lieutenant's Woman
★ ★ ★ ½
R, 124 m., 1981

Meryl Streep (Sarah and Anna), Jeremy Irons (Charles and Mike), Hilton McRae (Sam), Emily Morgan (Mary), Charlotte Mitchell (Mrs. Tranter), Lynsey Baxter (Ernestina). Directed by Karol Reisz and produced by Leon Clore. Screenplay by Harold Pinter.

Reading the last one hundred pages of John Fowles's *The French Lieutenant's Woman* is like being caught in a fictional labyrinth. We think we know where we stand in the story, and who the characters are and what possibilities are open to them, and then Fowles begins an astonishing series of surprises. He turns his story inside out, suggesting first one ending, then another, always in a way that forces us to rethink everything that has gone before. That complex structure was long thought to make Fowles's novel unfilmable. How could his fictional surprises, depending on the relationship between reader and omniscient narrator, be translated into the more literal nature of film? One of the directors who tried to lick *The French Lieutenant's Woman* was John Frankenheimer, who complained: "There is no way you can film the book. You can tell the same story in a movie, of course, but not in the same way. And how Fowles tells his story is what makes the book so good." That seemed to be the final verdict, until the British playwright Harold Pinter tackled the project.

Pinter's previous screenplays, such as *The Accident* and *The Go-Between*, are known for a mastery of ambiguity, for a willingness to approach the audience on more than one level of reality, and what he and director Karel Reisz have done with their film, *The French Lieutenant's Woman*, is both simple and brilliant. They have frankly discarded the multi-layered fictional devices of John Fowles, and tried to create a new cinematic approach that will achieve the same ambiguity. Fowles made us stand at a distance from his two doomed lovers, Sarah and Charles. He told their story, of a passion that was forbidden by the full weight of Victorian convention, and then he invited us to stand back and view that passion in terms of facts and statistics about . . . well, Victorian passions in general. Pinter and Reisz create a similar distance in their movie by telling us two parallel stories. In one of them, Sarah Woodruff (Meryl Streep) still keeps her forlorn vigil for the French lieutenant who loved and abandoned her, and she still plays her intriguing cat-and-mouse game with the obsessed young man (Jeremy Irons) who must possess her.

In the other story, set in the present, two actors named Anna and Mike are playing Sarah and Charles. And Anna and Mike are also having a forbidden affair, albeit a more conventional one. For the length of the movie's shooting schedule, they are lovers offscreen as well as on. But eventually Mike will return to his family and Anna to her lover.

This is a device that works, I think. Frankenheimer was right in arguing that just *telling* the Victorian love story would leave you with . . . just a Victorian love story. The modern framing story places the Victorian lovers in ironic relief. Everything they say and do has another level of meaning, because we know the "real" relationship between the actors themselves. Reisz opens his film with a shot that boldly states his approach: We see Streep in costume for her role as Sarah, attended by a movie makeup woman. A clapboard marks the scene, and *then* Streep walks into the movie's re-creation of the British coastal village of Lyme Regis.

"It's only a movie," this shot informs us. But, of course, it's *all* only a movie, including the story about the modern actors. And this confusion of fact and fiction interlocks perfectly with the psychological games played in the Victorian story by Sarah Woodruff herself.

The French lieutenant's woman is one of the most intriguing characters in recent fiction. She is not only apparently the victim of Victorian sexism, but also (as Charles discovers) its manipulator and master. She cleverly uses the conventions that would limit her, as a means of obtaining personal freedom and power over men. At least that is one way to look at what she does. Readers of the novel will know there are others.

The French Lieutenant's Woman is a beautiful film to look at, and remarkably well-acted. Streep was showered with praise for her remarkable double performance, and she deserved it. She is offhandedly contemporary one moment, and then gloriously, theatrically Victorian the next. Opposite her, Jeremy Irons is authoritative and convincingly bedeviled as the man who is frustrated by both of Streep's characters. The movie's a challenge to our intelligence, takes delight in playing with our expectations, and has one other considerable achievement as well: It entertains admirers of Fowles's novel, but does not reveal the book's secrets. If you see the movie, the book will still surprise you, and that's as it should be.

Frenzy ★ ★ ★ ★
R, 116 m., 1972

Jon Finch (Richard Blaney), Barry Foster (Rusk), Barbara Leigh-Hunt (Brenda Blaney), Anna Massey (Babs Mulligan), Alec McGowen (Chief Inspector Oxford), Vivien Merchant (Mrs. Oxford). Directed by Alfred Hitchcock. Associate producer William Hill. Screenplay by Anthony Schaffer.

Alfred Hitchcock's *Frenzy* is a return to old forms by the master of suspense, whose newer forms have pleased movie critics but not his public. This is the kind of thriller Hitchcock was making in the 1940s, filled with macabre details, incongruous humor, and the desperation of a man convicted of a crime he didn't commit.

The only 1970s details are the violence and the nudity (both approached with a certain grisly abandon that has us imagining *Psycho* without the shower curtain). It's almost as if Hitchcock, at seventy-three, was consciously attempting to do once again what he did better than anyone else. His films since *Psycho* struck out into unfamiliar territory and even got him involved in the Cold War *(Torn Curtain)* and the fringes of fantasy *(The Birds)*. Here he's back at his old stand.

Frenzy, which allegedly has a loose connection with a real criminal case, involves us in the exploits of a murderer known as The Necktie Killer (Barry Foster). And involvement is the sensation we feel, I think, since we know his identity from the beginning and sometimes cannot help identifying with him. There is a scene, for example, in which he inadvertently gets himself trapped in the back of a potato truck with a sack containing the body of his latest victim. We know he is a slimy bastard, but somehow we're sweating along with him as he crawls through the potatoes trying to regain a bit of incriminating evidence. He is the killer but, as is frequently the case with Hitchcock, another man seems much more guilty. This is Richard Blaney (Jon Finch), an ex-RAF hero who is down on his luck and has just lost his job. Through a series of unhappy coincidences which I'd better not give away, he's caught red-handed with the evidence while the killer walks away.

Hitchcock sets his action in the crowded back alleys of Covent Garden, where fruit and vegetable vendors rub shoulders with prostitutes, third-rate gangsters, bookies, and barmaids. A lot of the action takes place in a pub, and somehow Hitchcock gets more feeling for the location into his films than he usually does. With a lot of Hitchcock, you have the impression every frame has been meticulously prepared. This time, the smell and tide of humanity slops over. (There is even one tide in the movie which does a little slopping over humanity itself—but never mind.)

It's delicious to watch Hitchcock using the camera. Not a shot is wasted, and there is one elaborate sequence in which the killer goes upstairs with his victim. The camera precedes them up the stairs, watches them go in a door, and then backs down the stairs, alone, and across the street to look at the outside of the house. This shot is not for a moment a gimmick; the melancholy of the withdrawing camera movement is one of the most touching effects in the film, despite the fact that no people inhabit it.

There's a lot of humor, too, including two hilarious gourmet meals served to the Chief Inspector (Alec McGowen) by his wife (Vivien Merchant). There is suspense, and local color ("It's been too long since the Christie murders; a good colorful crime spree is good for tourism") and, always, Hitchcock smacking his lips and rubbing his hands and delighting in his naughtiness.

Friday the 13th, Part II ½ ★
R, 87 m., 1981*

Amy Steel (Ginny), John Furey (Paul), Adrienne King (Alice), Kirsten Baker (Terry). Directed and produced by Steve Miner. Screenplay by Ron Kurz.

I saw *Friday the 13th Part II* at the Virginia Theater, a former vaudeville house in my hometown of Champaign-Urbana, Illinois. The late show was half-filled with high school and college students, and as the lights went down I experienced a brief wave of nostalgia. In this very theater, on countless Friday nights, I'd gone with a date to the movies. My nostalgia lasted for the first two minutes of the movie.

The pretitle sequence showed one of the heroines of the original *Friday the 13th*, alone at home. She has nightmares, wakes up, undresses, is stalked by the camera, hears a noise in the kitchen. She tiptoes into the kitchen. Through the open window, a cat springs into the room. The audience screamed loudly and happily: It's fun to be scared. Then an unidentified man sunk an

ice pick into the girl's brain, and, for me, the fun stopped.

The audience, however, carried on. It is a tradition to be loud during these movies, I guess. After a batch of young counselors turns up for training at a summer camp, a girl goes out walking alone at night. Everybody in the audience imitated hoot-owls and hyenas. Another girl went to her room and started to undress. Five guys sitting together started a chant: "We want boobs!"

The plot: In the original movie, a summer camp staff was wiped out by a demented woman whose son had been allowed to drown by incompetent camp counselors. At the end of that film, the mother was decapitated by the young woman who is killed with an ice pick at the beginning of *Part II*. The legend grows that the son, Jason, did *not* really drown, but survived, and lurks in the woods waiting to take his vengeance against the killer of his mother . . . and against camp couselors in general, I guess.

That sets up the film. The counselors are introduced, very briefly, and then some of them go into town for a beer and the rest stay at the camp to make out with each other. A mystery assailant prowls around the main cabin. We see only his shadow and his shoes. One by one, he picks off the kids. He sinks a machete into the brain of a kid in a wheelchair. He surprises a boy and a girl making love, and nails them to a bunk with a spear through both their bodies. When the other kids return to the camp, it's their turn. After almost everyone has been killed in a disgusting and violent way, one girl chews up the assailant with a chain saw, *after* which we discover the mummies in his cabin in the woods, *after* which he jumps through a window at the girl, etc.

This movie is a cross between the Mad Slasher and Dead Teen-ager genres; about two dozen movies a year feature a mad killer going berserk, and they're all about as bad as this one. Some have a little more plot, some have a little less. It doesn't matter.

Sinking into my seat in this movie theater from my childhood, I remembered the movie fantasies when I was a kid. They involved teen-agers who fell in love, made out with each other, customized their cars, listened to rock and roll, and were rebels without causes. Neither the kids in those movies nor the kids watching them would have understood a world view in which the primary function of teen-agers is to be hacked to death.

*This review will suffice for the *Friday the 13th* film of your choice.

The Friends of Eddie Coyle ★ ★ ★ ★
R, 102 m., 1973

Robert Mitchum (Eddie Coyle), Peter Boyle (Dillon), Richard Jordan (Dave Foley), Steven Keats (Jackie), Alex Rocco (Scalise), Joe Santos (Artie Van). Directed by Peter Yates and produced and written by Paul Monash.

Someone remarks of Eddie, about halfway through *The Friends of Eddie Coyle*, that for a two-bit hood, he has fingers in a lot of pies. Too many, as it turns out. Without ever rising to the top, Eddie has been employed in organized crime for most of his life. He's kind of a utility infielder, ready to trade in some hot guns, drive a hijacked truck, or generally make himself useful.

Eddie got the nickname "Fingers" some years ago after a gun deal. The buyers he supplied got caught. Their friends slammed Eddie's fingers in a drawer. He understood. There is a certain code without which it would be simply impossible to go on doing business.

But as the movie opens, Eddie is in trouble, and it looks like he'll have to break the code. He's facing a two-year stretch in New Hampshire, and he wants out of it. He doesn't want to leave his wife and kids and see them go on welfare. He is, at heart, just a small businessman; he deals in crime but is profoundly middle class. He thinks maybe he can make a deal with the state's attorney and have a few good words put in for him up in New Hampshire.

The movie is as simple as that. It's not a high-strung gangster film, it doesn't have a lot of overt excitement in it, and it doesn't go in for much violence. He gives us a man, invites our sympathy for him, and then watches almost sadly as his time runs out. And *The Friends of Eddie Coyle* works so well because Eddie is played by Robert Mitchum, and Mitchum has perhaps never been better.

He has always been one of our best screen actors: sardonic, masculine, quick-witted, but slow to reveal himself. He has never been in an absolutely great film; he doesn't have masterpieces behind him like Brando or Cary Grant. More than half his films have been conventional action melodramas, and it is a rare summer without at least one movie in which Mitchum wears a sombrero and lights bombs with his cigar. But give him a character and the room to develop it, and what he does is wonderful. Eddie Coyle is made for him: a weary middle-aged man, but tough and proud; a man who has been hurt too often in life not to respect pain; a man who will take chances to protect his own territory.

The movie is drawn from a knowledgeable novel by George V. Higgins, himself a state's attorney, and has been directed by one of the masters of this sort of thing, Peter Yates (*Robbery, Bullitt*). Paul Monash's screenplay stays close to the real-life Massachusetts texture of the novel, and the dialogue sounds right. The story isn't developed in the usual movie way, with lots of importance being given to intricacies of plot; instead, Eddie's dilemma occurs to him as it occurs to us, and we watch him struggle with it.

If the movie has a flaw, it's that we don't really care that much about the bank robberies that are counterpointed with Eddie's situation. We're interested in him. We can get the bank robberies in any summer's caper picture. It's strange that a movie's interest should fall off during its action scenes. But this is Eddie Coyle's picture, and Mitchum's.

Fright Night ★ ★ ★
R, 106 m., 1985

Roddy McDowall (Peter Vincent), Chris Sarandon (Jerry, the Vampire), William Ragsdale (Charley), Amanda Bearse (Amy), Stephen Geoffreys (Evil Ed). Directed by Tom Holland and produced by Herb Jaffe. Screenplay by Holland.

The best line in *Fright Night* belongs to Roddy McDowall, who plays a broken-down old hambone actor who used to star in vampire movies. "The kids today," he complains, "don't have the patience for vampires. They want to see some mad slasher running around and chopping off heads." He's right. Vampires, who are doomed to live forever, have outlived their fashion. They've been replaced by guys in ski masks who hack their way through Dead Teen-ager Movies.

Fright Night is an attempt to correct that situation. It stars William Ragsdale as an impressionable teen-ager who becomes convinced that vampires have moved in next door. It doesn't take a detective to figure that out. The vampires almost flaunt their unholy natures, performing weird rites in front of open windows and disposing of the bodies of their victims in plastic garbage bags. They are safe in the knowledge that nobody believes in vampires anymore.

The kid calls the cops. The vampires have a plausible explanation for their activities. The kid claims there has to be a coffin somewhere down in the basement. The cops warn him to stop wasting their time. And then, when the vampires start getting really threatening, the kid has no place to turn—except to old Peter Vincent (McDowall), the former B-movie actor who has just been fired from his TV job as host of the local Creature Features.

McDowall knows all about vampires: How to detect them, how to repel them, how to kill them. He also knows all about being behind on the rent, being evicted, and being out of work. For 500 bucks, he agrees to have a go at the vampires, and that sets up the second half of *Fright Night*.

The first part of the movie is basically funny. The second half unleashes lots of spectacular special effects devised by Richard Edlund, the same man who created the effects for *Ghostbusters*. Since part of the fun with vampire movies is how bad the special effects usually are, Edlund has to walk a narrow line, and he does. He gives us satisfactory scenes of transformations and decompositions, and seems to know his way around vampires, but he doesn't overwhelm the action.

The center of the movie, however, is the Roddy McDowall character, whose name, Peter Vincent, is obviously supposed to remind us of Peter Cushing and Vincent Price. Throw in Christopher Lee, and you'd have a quorum. McDowall's performance is wickedly funny, and he must have enjoyed it, chewing the scenery on his horror movie TV program and then chewing real scenery

down in the vampire's basement. *Fright Night* is not a distinguished movie, but it has a lot of fun being undistinguished.

The Gambler ★ ★ ★ ★
R, 111 m., 1974

James Caan (Axel), Paul Sorvino (Hips), Lauren Hutton (Billie), Morris Carnovsky (A.R. Lowenthal), Jacqueline Brooks (Naomi), Burt Young (Carmine). Directed by Karel Reisz and produced by Irwin Winkler and Robert Chartoff. Screenplay by James Toback.

"Jeez, Axel, I never seen such bad cards," Axel Freed's friend tells him consolingly. They're standing in the kitchen of a New York apartment, and gray dawn is seeping through the smoke. Axel has never seen such bad cards either. His disbelief that anyone could draw so many lousy poker hands in a row has led him finally $44,000 into debt. He doesn't have the money, but it's been a bigtime game, and he has to find it somewhere or be in heavy trouble.

And that's how Karel Reisz's *The Gambler* begins: with a problem. The way Axel solves his problem is only fairly difficult. He borrows the money from his mother, who is a doctor. But then we discover that his problem is greater than his debt, because there is some final compulsion within him that won't let him pay back the money. He needs to lose, to feel risk, to place himself in danger. He needs to gamble away the forty-four grand on even more hopeless bets because in a way it isn't gambling that's his obsession—it's danger itself.

"I play in order to lose," he tells his bookie at one point. "That's what gets my juice going. If I only bet on the games I know, I could at least break even." But he doesn't want that. At one point, he's driven to bet money he doesn't really have on college basketball games picked almost at random out of the sports pages.

And yet Axel Freed is not simply a gambler, but a very complicated man in his mid-thirties who earns his living as a university literature teacher. He teaches Dostoyevsky, William Carlos Williams, Thoreau. But he doesn't seem to teach their works so much as what he finds in them to justify his own obsessions. One of the students in his class has Axel figured out so completely that she always has the right answer, when he asks what Thoreau is saying, or what Dostoyevsky is saying. They're saying, as Axel reads them, to take risks, to put the self on the line.

"Buffalo Bill's defunct," he says, quoting the e e cummings poem, and the death of the nineteenth century age of heroes obsesses him. In that earlier age, he could have tested himself more directly. His grandfather came to America flat broke, fought and killed to establish himself, and still is a man of enormous vitality at the age of eighty. The old man is respectable now (he owns a chain of furniture stores), but the legend of his youth fascinates Axel, who recites it poetically at the eightieth-birthday party.

Axel finds nothing in 1974 to test himself against, however. He has to find his own dangers, to court and seduce them. And the ultimate risk in his life as a gambler is that behind his friendly bookies and betting cronies is the implacable presence of the Mafia, the guys who take his bets like him, but if he doesn't pay, there's nothing they can do. "It's out of my hands," his pal Hips explains. "A bad gambling debt has got to be taken care of." And that adds an additional dimension to *The Gambler*, which begins as a portrait of Axel Freed's personality, develops into the story of his world, and then pays off as a thriller. We become so absolutely contained by Axel's problems and dangers that they seem like our own. There's a scene where he soaks in the bathtub and listens to the last minutes of a basketball game, and another scene where he sits in the stands and watches a basketball game he has tried to fix (while a couple of hit men watch him), and these scenes have a quality of tension almost impossible to sustain.

But Reisz sustains them, and makes them all the more real because he doesn't populate the rest of his movie with stock characters. Axel Freed, as played by James Caan, is himself a totally convincing personality, and original. He doesn't derive from other gambling movies or even from other roles he's played.

And the people around him also are specific, original creations. His mother Naomi (Jacqueline Brooks) is a competent, independent person who gives him the money

because she fears for his life, and yet understands that his problem is deeper than gambling. His grandfather, marvelously played by Morris Carnovsky, is able to imply by his behavior why he fascinates Axel so. The various bookies and collectors he comes across aren't Mafia stereotypes. They enforce more in sorrow than in anger. Only his girlfriend (Lauren Hutton) fails to seem very real. Here's still another demonstration of the inability of contemporary movies to give us three-dimensional women under thirty.

There's a scene in *The Gambler* that has James Caan on screen all by himself for two minutes, locked in a basement room, waiting to meet a Mafia boss who will arguably instruct that his legs be broken. In another movie, the scene could have seemed too long, too eventless.

But Reisz, Caan, and screenwriter James Toback have constructed the character and the movie so convincingly that the scene not only works, but works two ways: first as suspense, and then as character revelation. Because as we look into Axel Freed's caged eyes we see a person who is scared to death and yet stubbornly ready for this moment he has brought down upon himself.

Gandhi ★ ★ ★ ★
PG, 188 m., 1983

Ben Kingsley (Mahatma Gandhi), Candice Bergen (Margaret Bourke-White), Edward Fox (General Dyer), John Gielgud (Lord Irwin), Trevor Howard (Judge Broomfield), John Mills (The Viceroy) Martin Sheen (Walker), Rohini Hattangady (Kasturba Ghandi), Ian Charleson (Charlie Andrews), Athol Fugard (General Smuts). Directed and produced by Richard Attenborough. Screenplay by John Briley.

In the middle of this epic film there is a quiet, small scene that helps explain why *Gandhi* is such a remarkable experience. Mahatma Gandhi, at the height of his power and his fame, stands by the side of a lake with his wife of many years. Together, for the benefit of a visitor from the West, they reenact their marriage vows. They do it with solemnity, quiet warmth, and perhaps just a touch of shyness; they are simultaneously demonstrating an aspect of Indian culture and touching on something very personal to them both. At the end of the ceremony, Gandhi says, "We were thirteen at the time." He shrugs. The marriage had been arranged. Gandhi and his wife had not been in love, had not been old enough for love, and yet love had grown between them. But that is not really the point of the scene. The point, I think, comes in the quiet smile with which Gandhi says the words. At that moment we believe that he is fully and truly human, and at that moment, a turning point in the film, *Gandhi* declares that it is not only a historical record but a breathing, living document.

This is the sort of rare epic film that spans the decades, that uses the proverbial cast of thousands, and yet follows a human thread from beginning to end: *Gandhi* is no more overwhelmed by the scope of its production than was Gandhi overwhelmed by all the glory of the British Empire. The movie earns comparison with two classic works by David Lean, *Lawrence of Arabia* and *Dr. Zhivago*, in its ability to paint a strong human story on a very large canvas.

The movie is a labor of love by Sir Richard Attenborough, who struggled for years to get financing for his huge but "non-commercial" project. Various actors were considered over the years for the all-important title role, but the actor who was finally chosen, Ben Kingsley, makes the role so completely his own that there is a genuine feeling that the spirit of Gandhi is on the screen. Kingsley's performance is powerful without being loud or histrionic; he is almost always quiet, observant, and soft-spoken on the screen, and yet his performance comes across with such might that we realize, afterward, that the sheer moral force of Gandhi must have been behind the words. Apart from all its other qualities, what makes this movie special is that it was obviously made by people who believed in it.

The movie begins in the early years of the century, in South Africa, where Gandhi was born and spent the first decades of his life. He was trained as a lawyer and received his degree, but, degree or not, he was a target of South Africa's system of racial segregation, in which Indians (even though they are Caucasian, and thus should "qualify") are denied full citizenship and manhood.

Gandhi's reaction to the system is, at first, almost naive; an early scene on a train doesn't quite work only because we can't believe the adult Gandhi would still be so ill-informed about the racial code of South Africa. But Gandhi's response sets the tone of the film. He is nonviolent but firm. He is sure where the right lies in every situation, and he will uphold it in total disregard for the possible consequences to himself.

Before long Gandhi is in India, a nation of hundreds of millions, ruled by a relative handful of British. They rule almost by divine right, shouldering the "white man's burden" even though they have not quite been requested to do so by the Indians. Gandhi realizes that Indians have been made into second-class citizens in their own country, and he begins a program of civil disobedience that is at first ignored by the British, then scorned, and finally, reluctantly, dealt with, sometimes by subterfuge, sometimes by brutality. Scenes in this central passage of the movie make it clear that nonviolent protests could contain a great deal of violence. There is a shattering scene in which wave after wave of Gandhi's followers march forward to be beaten to the ground by British clubs. Through it all, Gandhi maintains a certain detachment; he is convinced he is right, convinced that violence is not an answer, convinced that sheer moral example can free his nation—as it did. "You have been guests in our home long enough," he tells the British, "Now we would like for you to leave."

The movie is populated with many familiar faces, surrounding the newcomer Kingsley. Where would the British cinema be without its dependable, sturdy, absolutely authoritative generation of great character actors like Trevor Howard (as a British judge), John Mills (the British viceroy), John Gielgud, and Michael Hordern? There are also such younger actors as Ian Bannen, Edward Fox, Ian Charleson, and, from America, Martin Sheen as a reporter and Candice Bergen as the photographer Margaret Bourke-White.

Gandhi stands at the quiet center. And Ben Kingsley's performance finds the right note and stays with it. There are complexities here; *Gandhi* is not simply a moral story with a happy ending, and the tragedy of the bloodshed between the Hindu and Buddhist populations of liberated India is addressed, as is the partition of India and Pakistan, which we can almost literally feel breaking Gandhi's heart.

I imagine that for many Americans, Mahatma Gandhi remains a dimly understood historical figure. I suspect a lot of us know he was a great Indian leader without quite knowing why and—such is our ignorance of Eastern history and culture—we may not fully realize that his movement did indeed liberate India, in one of the greatest political and economic victories of all time, achieved through nonviolent principles. What is important about this film is not that it serves as a history lesson (although it does) but that, at a time when the threat of nuclear holocaust hangs ominously in the air, it reminds us that we are, after all, human, and thus capable of the most extraordinary and wonderful achievements, simply through the use of our imagination, our will, and our sense of right.

Gates of Heaven ★ ★ ★ ★
NO MPAA RATING, 85 m, 1978 ✓

A documentary produced, directed, and written by Errol Morris.

There are many invitations to laughter during this remarkable documentary, but what *Gates of Heaven* finally made me feel was an aching poignancy about its subjects. They say you can make a great documentary about almost anything, if only you see it well enough and truly, and this film proves it. *Gates of Heaven*, which has no connection with the unfortunate *Heaven's Gate*, is a documentary about pet cemeteries and their owners. It was filmed in Southern California, so of course we immediately anticipate a sardonic look at peculiarities of the Moonbeam State. But then *Gates of Heaven* grows ever so much more complicated and frightening, until at the end it is about such large issues as love, immortality, failure, and the dogged elusiveness of the American Dream.

The film was made by a California filmmaker named Errol Morris, and it has been the subject of notoriety because Werner Herzog, the West German director, promised to eat his shoe if Morris ever finished it. Morris did finish it, and at the film's pre-

miere in Berkeley, Herzog indeed boiled and ate his shoe.

Gates of Heaven is so rich and thought-provoking, it achieves so much while seeming to strain so little, that it stays in your mind for tantalizing days. It opens with a monologue by a kind-looking, somewhat heavyset paraplegic, with a slight lisp that makes him sound like a kid. His name is Floyd McClure. Ever since his pet dog was run over years ago by a Model A Ford, he has dreamed of establishing a pet cemetery. The movie develops and follows his dream, showing the forlorn, bare patch of land where he founded his cemetery at the intersection of two superhighways. Then, with cunning drama, it gradually reveals that the cemetery went bankrupt and the remains of 450 animals had to be dug up. Various people contribute to the story: One of McClure's investors, a partner, two of the women whose pets were buried in his cemetery, and an unforgettable old woman named Florence Rasmussen, who starts on the subject of pets, and switches, with considerable fire, to her no-account son. Then the action shifts north to the Napa Valley, where a go-getter named Cal Harberts has absorbed what remained of McClure's dream (and the 450 dead pets) into his own pet cemetery, the Bubbling Well Pet Memorial Park. It is here that the movie grows heartbreaking, painting a portrait of a life-style that looks chillingly forlorn, and of the people who live it with relentless faith in positive thinking.

Harberts, a patriarch, runs his pet cemetery with two sons, Phil and Dan. Phil, the older one, has returned home after a period spent selling insurance in Salt Lake City. He speaks of having been overworked. Morris lets the camera stay on Phil as he solemnly explains his motivational techniques, and his method of impressing a new client by filling his office with salesmanship trophies. He has read all of Clement Stone's books on "Positive Mental Attitude," and has a framed picture of Stone on his wall. Phil looks neat, presentable, capable. He talks reassuringly of his positive approach to things, "mentally wise." Then we meet the younger brother, Dan, who composes songs and plays them on his guitar. In the late afternoon, when no one is at the pet cemetery, he hooks up his 100-watt speakers and blasts his songs all over the valley. He has a wispy mustache and looks like a hippie. The family hierarchy is clear. Cal, in the words of Phil, is "El Presidento." Then Dan comes next, because he has worked at the cemetery longer. Phil, the golden boy, the positive thinker, is maintaining his P.M.A. in the face of having had to leave an insurance business in Salt Lake City to return home as third in command at a pet cemetery.

The cemetery itself is bleak and barren, its markers informing us, "God is love; dog is god backwards." An American flag flies over the little graves. Floyd McClure tells us at the beginning of the film that pets are put on Earth for two reasons: to love and to be loved. At the end of this mysterious and great movie, we observe the people who guard and maintain their graves, and who themselves seem unloved and very lonely. One of the last images is of old Cal, the patriarch, wheeling past on his forklift, a collie-sized coffin in its grasp.

The Gauntlet ★ ★ ★
R, 111 m., 1977

Clint Eastwood (Ben Shockley), Sondra Locke (Gus Mally), Pat Hingle (Josephson), William Prince (Blakelock), Bill McKinney (Constable), Michael Cavanaugh (Feyderspiel). Directed by Clint Eastwood and produced by Robert Daley. Screenplay by Michael Butler and Dennis Shryack.

The Gauntlet is classic Clint Eastwood: fast, furious, and funny. It tells a cheerfully preposterous story with great energy and a lot of style, and nobody seems more at home in this sort of action movie than Eastwood. He plays a cop again this time, but not a supercop like Dirty Harry Callahan. He's a detective from Phoenix, and no hero: He drives up in front of police headquarters, opens his car door, and a whisky bottle crashes to the street.

Eastwood hasn't compiled the most stellar record in the department, but somehow the police commissioner thinks he's the right man for the next assignment: Fly to Las Vegas, take custody of a hooker there, and bring her back to Phoenix to be a witness in an important court case. It sounds routine to Eastwood, until he flies to Vegas, takes custody, and discovers that the Mafia is quoting sixty-to-one odds against his witness leaving Nevada alive. Maybe, he begins to suspect, this isn't a totally typical witness . . . .

The witness (played by Sondra Locke) isn't a totally typical hooker, either. She's a college graduate, spunky, pleasant. She tells Eastwood he'd be wise to catch the next flight home, because there's a contract out on her. Eastwood's too stubborn. He's taken the assignment and he'll carry it out through hell and high water (which turn out to be just about the only two things he doesn't have to survive on this mission).

The return trip gets off to a slightly shaky start when they survive an auto bomb. Then, after Eastwood commandeers an ambulance, they're involved in a high-speed chase with three gunmen. They take refuge in Locke's house, which is promptly surrounded by dozens of police marksmen, who open fire, achieving overkill so completely that (in one of the movie's many mixtures of humor and violence), the house simply topples over. Still ahead of them are nights in the desert, an encounter with Hell's Angels, a fight on a moving freight train, a chase in which their motorcycle is pursued by a rifle marksman in a helicopter . . . and then the grand finale, in which Eastwood hijacks a passenger bus, armor-plates it, and drives himself and his witness through downtown Phoenix against a hail of machine-gun fire. You see what I mean about the plot's being cheerfully preposterous.

Eastwood directed himself again this time, and he's a good action craftsman (as *The Outlaw Josey Wales* demonstrated). He's also good at developing relationships; despite the movie's barrage of violence, there's a nice pacing as his cop and hooker slog through their ordeals and begin to like and respect one another. As in most Eastwood movies, by the way, the woman's role is a good one: Eastwood has such a macho image that maybe people haven't noticed that his female sidekicks (like Tyne Daly, Dirty Harry's partner in *The Enforcer*) have minds of their own and are never intended to be merely decorative.

The Gauntlet will no doubt be attacked in various quarters because of its violence, but it's a harmless, pop-art type of violence, often with a comic quality. The wall of gunfire during the final bus ride up the steps of the Hall of Justice, for example, is an extravaganza of sound and action during which, incredibly, no one is killed. Eastwood himself fires his pistol only twice: once at a door, and once at a gas tank.

George Stevens: A Filmmaker's Journey ★ ★ ★ ½
PG, 113 m., 1985

A documentary written, produced, and directed by George Stevens, Jr. Edited by Catherine Shields. Music by Carl Davis.

The last shot of *Citizen Kane* showed the dead tycoon's storerooms, vast spaces filled with the jumble of a lifetime. One of the early shots in this documentary about George Stevens has something of the same quality. We see the memorabilia of his long career: cowboy hats, leather-bound scripts, cans of film, albums of photographs, Oscars, diaries, belt buckles—everything with a story, and half the stories already forgotten.

The voice on the sound track is the filmmaker's son, telling us about his famous father. One of the things the father told him, one day when they were driving past the warehouse where all of these memories were stored, was, "That'll all be yours when I'm gone." As he rummaged through the souvenirs of his father's lifetime, he made some extraordinary discoveries: Not only the prints and scripts of such classics as *Giant, A Place in the Sun*, and *Alice Adams*, but also documentary footage of Stevens on the set of his movies, and rare color footage Stevens shot for himself while he was leading a newsreel unit during World War II.

More than most men, Stevens seems to have been concerned to leave behind a record of his career. He began in movies almost at the beginning, as an assistant on the early silent films, and his first work as a director was on the Laurel and Hardy films. We see some of his earliest footage, and then we begin to hear the voices of the people who knew him then, and worked with him: Old directors like Rouben Mamoulian and John Huston, stars like Katharine Hepburn and Warren Beatty, writers like Irwin Shaw. Hepburn gave Stevens his real start, rescuing him from grade B features and second-unit work because she was impressed by his enthusiasm for *Alice Adams*. It became his first prestigious production, but then there was a flood of others: the definitive Astaire-Rogers musical *Swing Time*, the audacious *Gunga Din*, and *Woman of the Year*, and Stevens began to build a reputation as a man who saw his own way through the standard scripts he was handed, freeing his actors so that *Gunga Din*, for example, became a high-spirited comic masterpiece instead of just another swashbuckler.

The film contains a lot of home movies and private documentary footage; Stevens shot the only color footage of the landing at Normandy, and we also see moments of Stevens at work, always quietly professional, thoughtful, not the flamboyant self-promoter so many other directors of his generation became. Stevens, more than anyone else, fashioned the image of James Dean. He directed some of Elizabeth Taylor's most memorable scenes. And he pressed on in the face of daunting odds to direct such movies as *The Greatest Story Ever Told*. Shooting in Utah, he was faced with the first snowstorms in a generation, and when he asked the cast and crew to pitch in and shovel snow, they respected him enough that they did it.

A Filmmaker's Journey is a film biography of a movie director, and it inevitably shares some of the conventions of the genre. We see the clips of great scenes, we hear the memories of old colleagues. Two things distinguish the film: The quiet professionalism with which the materials have been edited together, and the feeling that George Stevens, Jr., really is engaging in a rediscovery of his father through the making of this film. By the end of the film, we are less aware of George Stevens as a filmmaker than as a good and gifted man who happened to use movies as a means of expressing his gifts.

Ghost Story ★ ★ ★
R, 110 m., 1981

Fred Astaire (Ricky Hawthorne), Melvyn Douglas (John Jeffrey), Douglas Fairbanks, Jr. (Edward Wanderly), John Houseman (Sears James), Craig Wasson (Don/David), Alice Krige (Alma/Eva), Patricia Neal (Stella). Directed by John Irvin and produced by Burt Weissbourd. Screenplay by Lawrence D. Cohen.

Ghost stories should always begin as this one does, in shadows so deep that the flickering light of the dying fire barely illuminates the apprehensive faces of the listeners. They should be told in an old man's voice, dry as dust. They should be listened to by other men who are so old and so rich that we can only guess at the horrors they have seen. And, of course, ghost stories should be about things that happened long ago to young, passionate lovers who committed unspeakable crimes and have had to live forever after with the knowledge of them. If at all possible, some of the characters should be living in this life, filled with guilt, while others should be living the half-lives of the Undead, filled with hatred and revenge.

Peter Straub's best-selling novel *Ghost Story* contained all of those elements, and so I plugged away at it for what must have been hundreds of pages before his unspeakable prose finally got to me. At least, he knows how to make a good story, if not how to tell it, and that is one way in which the book and the movie of *Ghost Story* differ. The movie is told with style. It goes without saying that style is the most important single element in every ghost story, since without it even the most ominous events disintegrate into silliness. And *Ghost Story*, perhaps aware that if characters talk too much they disperse the tension, adopts a very economical story-telling approach. Dialogue comes in short, straightforward sentences. Background is provided without being allowed to distract from the main event. The characters are established with quick, subtle strokes. This is a good movie.

The story involves four very old men, who have formed a club to tell each other ghost stories. The casting is crucial here, and the movie's glory is in the performances and presences of Fred Astaire, the late Melvyn Douglas, Douglas Fairbanks, Jr., and John Houseman. What a crowd.

There is also a young protagonist (Craig Wasson), who has a dual role as Fairbanks's twin sons. When one comes to a dreadful end, the other begins to suspect that a mysterious woman may have something to do with it. And indeed she may. I would not dream of even hinting at exactly what connection this young woman (played with creepy charm by Alice Krige) might have with the four old

men, but of course there is a connection. The movie flashes back fifty or sixty years to establish the connection, but its scariest scenes are in the present. They involve a wonderful haunted house, a long-drowned auto, a series of horrendous accidents, a group of ghostly manifestations, and a truly horrible vengeance wreaked upon the living by the not-exactly-dead.

If you like ghost stories, you will appreciate that they cannot be told with all sorts of ridiculous skeletons leaping out of closets, as in Abbott and Costello. They must be told largely in terms of fearful and nostalgic memory, since (by definition) a ghost is a ghost because of something that once happened that shouldn't have happened. *Ghost Story* understands that, and restrains its performers so that the horror of the ghost is hardly more transparent than they are.

Ghostbusters ★ ★ ★ ½
PG, 107 m., 1984

Bill Murray (Venkman), Dan Aykroyd (Stantz), Harold Ramis (Spengler), Sigourney Weaver (Dana), Ernie Hudson (Winston), Rick Moranis (Louis). Directed and produced by Ivan Reitman. Screenplay by Dan Aykroyd and Harold Ramis.

Ghostbusters is a head-on collision between two comic approaches that have rarely worked together very successfully. This time, they do. It's (1) a special effects blockbuster, and (2) a sly dialogue movie, in which everybody talks to each other like smart graduate students who are in on the joke. In the movie's climactic scenes, an apocalyptic psychic mindquake is rocking Manhattan, and the experts talk like Bob and Ray.

This movie is an exception to the general rule that big special effects can wreck a comedy. Special effects require painstaking detail work. Comedy requires spontaneity and improvisation—or at least that's what it should feel like, no matter how much work has gone into it. In movies like Steven Spielberg's *1941*, the awesome scale of the special effects dominated everything else; we couldn't laugh because we were holding our breath. Not this time. *Ghostbusters* has a lot of neat effects, some of them mind-boggling, others just quick little throwaways, as when a transparent green slime monster gobbles up a mouthful of hot dogs. No matter what effects are being used, they're placed at the service of the actors; instead of feeling as if the characters have been carefully posed in front of special effects, we feel they're winging this adventure as they go along.

The movie stars Bill Murray, Dan Aykroyd, and Harold Ramis, three graduates of the Second City/*National Lampoon/* "Saturday Night Live" tradition. They're funny, but they're not afraid to reveal that they're also quick-witted and intelligent; their dialogue puts nice little spins on American clichés, and it uses understatement, irony, in-jokes, vast cynicism, and cheerful goofiness. Rarely has a movie this expensive provided so many quotable lines.

The plot, such as it is, involves an epidemic of psychic nuisance reports in Manhattan. Murray, Ramis, and Aykroyd, defrocked parapsychologists whose university experiments have been exposed as pure boondoggle, create a company named Ghostbusters and offer to speed to the rescue like a supernatural version of the Orkin man. Business is bad until Sigourney Weaver notices that the eggs in her kitchen are frying themselves. Her next-door neighbor, Rick Moranis, notices horrifying monsters in the apartment hallways. They both apparently live in a building that serves as a conduit to the next world. The ghostbusters ride to the rescue, armed with nuclear-powered backpacks. There is a lot of talk about arcane details of psychic lore (most of which the ghostbusters are inventing on the spot), and then an earthshaking showdown between good and evil, during which Manhattan is menaced by a monster that is twenty stories high, and about which I cannot say one more word without spoiling the movie's best visual moment.

Ghostbusters is one of those rare movies where the original, fragile comic vision has survived a multimillion-dollar production. It is not a complete vindication for big-budget comedies, since it's still true, as a general rule, that the more you spend, the fewer laughs you get. But it uses its money wisely, and when that, ahem, monster marches down a Manhattan avenue and climbs the side of a skyscraper . . . we're glad they spent the money for the special effects because it gets one of the biggest laughs in a long time.

Ginger and Fred ★ ★
PG-13, 126 m., 1986 ✔

Giulietta Masina (Amelia), Marcello Mastroianni (Pippo), Franco Fabrizi (TV Host), Frederick Ledebur (Admiral), Augusto Poderosi (Transvestite). Directed by Federico Fellini and produced by Alberto Grimaldi. Screenplay by Fellini, Tonino Guerra, and Tullio Pinelli.

It's been said that any frame of a movie by Federico Fellini is instantly recognizable, that he is one of the few filmmakers with such a distinctive visual universe. That's true, but it is also probably a mixed blessing. *Ginger and Fred*, for example, is so clearly derivative of Fellini's other movies that we keep waiting to find out why he wanted to make it. If he's only going to repeat himself, why bother?

The movie stars two of Fellini's most familiar actors, Marcello Mastroianni and Giulietta Masina (the director's real-life wife), in the story of a couple of has-beens, a dance team who were briefly popular, years ago, and have not seen each other since they broke up. Their names are Amelia and Pippo, but they were known in their old days as "Fred and Ginger," because they hoped, forlornly, to become the Italian equivalents of Astaire and Rogers.

Now they have been brought together for a final reunion, under the sponsorship of an Italian television program. Although the ads for this movie claim that it contains Fellini's view of television, the TV show resembles no other program ever seen before on any station in any country. What it does resemble is a review of the visual extravaganzas from many of Fellini's earlier films. If you recall the ecclesiastical fashion show from *Fellini Roma* or the menageries of bizarre characters from most of his films, you'll recognize them again this time. The TV program is allegedly a nostalgia revue, but the nostalgia is mostly on Fellini's part, as he stages a roll-call from his earlier work.

In the midst of the human menagerie, there is some attempt to tell the story of Ginger and Fred. We learn that their professional partnership broke up over personal problems, that Fred once attempted to commit suicide over Ginger, that the years have left them with at least the shadow of their old grace and shabby magic. They are booked into adjoining rooms in a Rome hotel, and share some sad memories before trying to get their act together and take it on the road for one last time.

The chaos surrounding the television program—both the rehearsals and the broadcast—reminded me a little of 8½, Fellini's masterpiece about a movie project that was careening out of control. What's missing here is any sense that Fellini really understands television; he seems to stage his TV show as a live stage show with cameras, and there are so many interruptions and asides and power blackouts that the actual program, if it were really being broadcast, would last for days. Instead of satirizing television as he sees it, he reinterprets television as a Fellini film—and ends up, ironically, satirizing himself.

There are moments in *Ginger and Fred* that act as poignant reminders of great Fellini films from the past. There are reminders of the circus all through the film, and of course a pseudo circus parade to close it. There are transvestites and ringmasters and eccentrics and grotesques, and we imagine that again this time, Fellini held a casting call for all of the weirdest people in Rome. And there is, of course, that distinctive Fellini sound track, the lush, romantic, wall-to-wall music; Nino Rota has died and so the composer this time is Nicola Piovani, but the sound is the same.

The real problem is with the central characters. Mastroianni's best work for Fellini has been done when he was "really" playing Fellini himself, as in *La Dolce Vita*, 8½, and even the weaker *City of Women*. Here he is playing a clearly fictional character, and we never really get a sense for the person behind this performance. Who is he? What has he been doing for the last thirty years? Curiously, Mastroianni and Fellini never really convinced me that this man named Pippo was really even in show business; he never has the old trouper's spirit, and seems more like a tired businessman, pressed into service for some sort of charity event.

Masina is better. I did believe her as an old song-and-dancer, and I enjoyed the remind-

ers of her sad, faded romanticism; she plays a woman similar to her last Fellini character, all those years ago in *Juliet of the Spirits* (1963), an ordinary, everyday woman a little dazzled by all the razzmatazz around her.

What never happens is a sense of the real relationship between these two characters. They go through the motions, in the midst of the usual Fellini circus. Their climactic scene, their song-and-dance on national television, is sort of sweet, but it's not the kind of payoff the movie needs. Fellini never seems to know where he's going in this movie, and when he gets there, he seems puzzled by his destination.

Gloria ★ ★ ★
PG, 123 m., 1980

Gena Rowlands (Gloria Swenson), John Adames (Phil), Buck Henry (Jack), Julie Carmen (Jeri Dawn). Directed by John Cassavetes and produced by Sam Shaw. Screenplay by Cassavetes.

Well, it's a cute idea for a movie, and maybe that's why they've had this particular idea so often. You start with tough-talking, streetwise gangster types, you hook them up with a little kid, you put them in fear of their lives, and then you milk the situation for poignancy, pathos, excitement, comedy, and anything else that turns up. It's the basic situation of *Little Miss Marker*, the Damon Runyon story that has been filmed three times. And now John Cassavetes tells it again in *Gloria*. The twists this time: The tough-talking gangster type is a woman, and the kid is Puerto Rican. Cassavetes has cast his wife, Gena Rowlands, in the title role, and it's an infectious performance—if infectious is the word to describe a chain-smoking dame who charges around town in her high heels, dragging a kid behind her.

The kid is also well cast. He's a youngster named John Adames who has dark hair and big eyes and a way of delivering his dialogue as if daring you to change one single word. Precisely because the material of this movie is so familiar, almost everything depends on the performances. And that's where Cassavetes saves the material and redeems the corniness of his story. Rowlands propels the action with such appealing nervous energy that we don't have the heart to stop and think how silly everything is.

The movie begins with a two-bit hoodlum (Buck Henry, an inexplicable casting choice) barricaded in an apartment with his Puerto Rican wife (Julie Carmen) and their kids. Men are going to come through the door at any moment with guns blazing. There's a knock on the door. It's Rowlands, as the neighbor, with the somehow inevitable name of Gloria Swenson. She wants to borrow sugar. She winds up with the kid. She doesn't want the kid. She doesn't like kids, she tells Henry: "Especially your kids." But the kid tags along. There's a shoot-out, the kid's family is dead, and things get even more complicated when it turns out that Henry gave his kid a notebook that has information in it the mob will kill to retrieve. That's the premise for the rest of the movie, which is a cat-and-mouse chase through the sleazier districts of New York and New Jersey.

Cassavetes has a nice eye for locale. There's a crummy flophouse where the clerk tells Rowlands, "Just pick a room. They're all open." There's a garishly decorated love nest that Rowlands occasionally occupies with a mobster. There are bus stations, back alleys, dimly lit hallways, and the kinds of bars that open at dawn and do most of their business by 9 A.M. (That provides one of the movie's best scenes. Gloria and the kid argue, Gloria tells the kid to split if that's the way he feels, and then she marches into the bar, orders a beer, lights a cigarette and says to the bartender: "Listen. There are reasons why I can't turn around and look . . . but is there a little kid heading in here?").

Cassavetes remains one of the most consistently interesting Hollywood mavericks. He makes money by acting, and immediately spends it producing his own films. Most of them are passionately indulgent of the actors, who sometimes repay his indulgence with inspired performances. Rowlands won an Oscar nomination for Cassavetes's *A Woman Under the Influence.* His next picture starred Ben Gazzara in *The Murder of a Chinese Bookie* (1978), which has become an unseen, lost film—better, if the truth be known, than *Gloria*, which is fun and engaging but slight. What saves this movie is Cassavetes's reliance on a tried-and-true plot construction. For once, his characters aren't all over the map in nonstop dialogue, as they were in *Husbands*, the talkathon he made in 1970 with Peter Falk, Gazzara, and himself. *Gloria* is tough, sweet, and goofy.

The Go-Between ★ ★ ★½
PG, 116 m., 1971

Julie Christie (Marian), Alan Bates (Ted Burgess), Dominic Guard (Leo, as a Boy), Margaret Leighton (Leo, as a Man), Michael Gough (Mr. Maudsley). Directed by Joseph Losey and produced by John Heyman. Screenplay by Harold Pinter.

There was a time, fairly recent, when the British upper classes thought it was a shade embarrassing to have to work for a living. Boys from middle-class families might attend the same school as upper-class boys, but they were tarnished, somehow, by their parents' direct contact with money. Money was something that needed to pass through a few sets of intervening hands, to let the sweat dry, before it could be spent by the aristocracy.

In a famous essay about English boarding schools, George Orwell delineated this delicate, cruel class distinction. He came from a white-collar family that made less than many blue-collar families, and yet had to present certain "standards" to the world. One of these was the necessity to send its children away to schools which, although they were shabby by Eton standards, were at least private. The children were the ones who suffered directly at the hands of class snobbism, of course, and sometimes their personalities were marked for life.

Joseph Losey's *The Go-Between* is about class distinction and its warping effect upon the life of one small boy. The story is set in the days before World War I, privileged days that seemed to stretch endlessly before the British upper class. The boy, Leo, comes to spend a summer holiday at the home of a rich friend. And he falls in hopeless schoolboy love with the friend's older sister (Julie Christie).

The sister is engaged to marry well, but she is in love with a roughshod tenant farmer (Alan Bates), and she enlists the boy to carry messages back and forth between them. The boy has only a shadowy notion at first about the significance of the messages, but during the summer he is sharply disillusioned about love, fidelity, and his own place in the great scheme of things.

Losey and his screenwriter, Harold Pinter, are terribly observant about small nuances of class. In the family's matriarch (Margaret Leighton) they give us a woman who seems to support the British class system all by herself, simply through her belief in it. They show a father and a fiancé who are aware of the girl's affair with the farmer, but do nothing about it. They are confident she will do the "right thing" in the end, and she does. "Why don't you marry Ted," the boy asks the young woman. "Because I can't," she replies. "Then why are you marrying Trimmington?" "Because I must."

She understands, and she is tough enough to endure. Indeed, at the end of the film she turns up years later as an old lady very much in the image of her mother. The victim is the boy, who is scarred sexually and emotionally by his summer experience. When we see him at the film's end, he is a sort of bloodless eunuch, called in to perform one last errand for the woman.

Losey's production is elegantly costumed and mounted and has the same eye for details of character that distinguished his two previous films with Pinter (*The Servant* and *Accident*). One visual device is distracting, however, he keeps giving us short flash-forwards to the end of the film. On the one hand, this eventually gives the ending away. On the other, it imposes a ponderous significance on the events that go before, diluting their freshness.

If the film had been told in straight chronology followed by an epilogue, it would have been more effective. In fact, the epilogue could have been lost altogether with no trouble; everything that will become of this boy in his adult life is already there, by implication, at the end of his summer holiday.

The Godfather ★ ★ ★ ★
R, 171 m., 1972

Marlon Brando (Don Vito Corleone), Al Pacino (Michael Corleone), James Caan (Sonny Corleone), Robert Duvall (Tom Hagen), Richard Castellano (Clemenza). Directed by Francis Ford Coppola and produced by Albert S. Ruddy. Screenplay by Mario Puzo.

We know from Gay Talese's book *Honor Thy Father* that being a professional mobster isn't all sunshine and roses. More often, it's the boredom of stuffy rooms and a bad diet of carry-out food, punctuated by brief, terrible bursts of violence. This is exactly the feel of *The Godfather*, which brushes aside the flashy glamour of the traditional gangster picture and gives us what's left: fierce tribal loyalties, deadly little neighborhood quarrels in Brooklyn, and a form of vengeance to match every affront.

The remarkable thing about Mario Puzo's novel was the way it seemed to be told from the inside out; he didn't give us a world of international intrigue, but a private club as constricted as the seventh grade. Everybody knew everybody else and had a pretty shrewd hunch what they were up to.

The movie (based on a script labored over for some time by Puzo and then finally given form, I suspect, by director Francis Ford Coppola) gets the same feel. We tend to identify with Don Corleone's family not because we dig gang wars, but because we have been with them from the beginning, watching them wait for battle while sitting at the kitchen table and eating chow mein out of paper cartons.

The Godfather himself is not even the central character in the drama. That position goes to the youngest, brightest son, Michael, who understands the nature of his father's position while revising his old-fashioned ways. The Godfather's role in the family enterprise is described by his name; he stands outside the next generation which will carry on and, hopefully, angle the family into legitimate enterprises.

Those who have read the novel may be surprised to find Michael at the center of the movie, instead of Don Corleone. In fact, this is simply an economical way for Coppola to get at the heart of the Puzo story, which dealt with the transfer of power within the family. Marlon Brando, who plays the Godfather as a shrewd, unbreakable old man, actually has the character lead in the movie; Al Pacino, with a brilliantly developed performance as Michael, is the lead.

But Brando's performance is a skillful throwaway, even though it earned him an Academy Award for best actor. His voice is wheezy and whispery, and his physical movements deliberately lack precision; the effect is of a man so accustomed to power that he no longer needs to remind others. Brando does look the part of old Don Corleone, mostly because of acting and partly because of the makeup, although he seems to have stuffed a little too much cotton into his jowls, making his lower face immobile.

The best of the actors supply one example after another of inspired casting. Although *The Godfather* is a long, minutely detailed movie of some three hours, there naturally isn't time to go into the backgrounds and identities of such characters as Clemenza, the family lieutenant; Jack Woltz, the movie czar; Luca Brasi, the loyal professional killer; McCluskey, the crooked cop, and the rest. Coppola and producer Al Ruddy skirt this problem with understated typecasting. As the Irish cop, for example, they simply slide in Sterling Hayden and let the character go about his business. Richard Castellano is an unshakable Clemenza. John Marley makes a perfectly hateful Hollywood mogul (and, yes, he still wakes up to find he'll have to cancel his day at the races).

The success of *The Godfather* as a novel was largely due to a series of unforgettable scenes. Puzo is a good storyteller, but no great shakes as a writer. The movie gives almost everything in the novel except the gynecological repair job. It doesn't miss a single killing; it opens with the wedding of Don Corleone's daughter (and attendant upstairs activity); and there are the right number of auto bombs, double crosses, and garretings.

Coppola has found a style and a visual look for all this material so *The Godfather* becomes something of a rarity: a really good movie squeezed from a bestseller. The decision to shoot everything in period decor (the middle and late 1940s) was crucial; if they'd tried to save money as they originally planned, by

bringing everything up-to-date, the movie simply wouldn't have worked. But it's uncannily successful as a period piece, filled with sleek, bulging limousines and postwar fedoras. Coppola and his cinematographer, Gordon Willis, also do some interesting things with the color photography. The earlier scenes have a reddish-brown tint, slightly overexposed and feeling like nothing so much as a 1946 newspaper rotogravure supplement.

Although the movie is three hours long, it absorbs us so effectively it never has to hurry. There is something in the measured passage of time as Don Corleone hands over his reins of power that would have made a shorter, faster moving film unseemly. Even at this length, there are characters in relationships you can't quite understand unless you've read the novel. Or perhaps you can, just by the way the characters look at each other.

The Godfather, Part II ★ ★ ★
R, 200 m., 1974

Al Pacino (Michael), Robert Duvall (Tom Hagen), Diane Keaton (Kay), Robert De Niro (Don Vito Corleone), John Cazale (Fredo), Lee Strasberg (Hyman Roth), G. D. Spradlin (Senator Geary). Directed by Francis Ford Coppola and produced by Gray Frederickson and Fred Ross. Screenplay by Coppola and Mario Puzo.

Moving through the deep shadows and heavy glooms of his vast estate, Michael Corleone presides over the destruction of his own spirit in *The Godfather, Part II*. The character we recall from *The Godfather* as the best and brightest of Don Vito's sons, the one who went to college and enlisted in the Marines, grows into a cold and ruthless man, obsessed with power. The film's closing scenes give us first a memory of a long-ago family dinner, and then Michael at mid-life, cruel, closed, and lonely. He's clearly intended as a tragic figure.

The Corleone saga, as painted by Francis Ford Coppola and Mario Puzo in two films totaling nearly seven hours, has been a sort of success story in reverse. In a crazy way, *The Godfather* and its sequel belong in the same category with those other epics of immigrant achievement in America, *The Emigrants* and *The New Land*. The Corleone family worked hard, was ambitious, remembered friends, never forgave disloyalty, and started from humble beginnings to become the most powerful Mafia organization in the country. If it were not that the family business was crime, these films could be an inspiration for us all.

Coppola seems to hold a certain ambivalence toward his material. Don Vito Corleone as portrayed by Marlon Brando in *The Godfather* was a man of honor and dignity, and it was difficult not to sympathize with him, playing with his grandchild in the garden, at peace after a long lifetime of murder, extortion, and the rackets. What exactly were we supposed to think about him? How did Coppola feel toward the Godfather?

The Godfather, Part II moves both forward and backward in time from the events in *The Godfather*, in an attempt to resolve our feelings about the Corleones. In doing so, it provides for itself a structural weakness from which the film never recovers, but it does something even more disappointing: It reveals a certain simplicity in Coppola's notions of motivation and characterization that wasn't there in the elegant masterpiece of his earlier film.

He gives us, first of all, the opening chapters in Don Vito's life. His family is killed by a Mafia don in Sicily, he comes to America at the age of nine, he grows up (to be played by Robert De Niro), and edges into a career of crime, first as a penny-ante crook and then as a neighborhood arranger and power broker: a man, as the movie never tires of reminding us, of respect.

This story, of Don Vito's younger days, occupies perhaps a fourth of the film's 200 minutes. Coppola devotes the rest to Michael Corleone, who has taken over the family's business after his father's death, has pulled out of New York, and consolidated operations in Nevada, and has ambitions to expand in Florida and Cuba. Michael is played, again and brilliantly, by Al Pacino, and among the other familiar faces are Robert Duvall as Tom Hagen, the family's lawyer; Diane Keaton as Michael's increasingly despairing wife Kay; and John Cazale as the weak older brother Fredo.

Coppola handles a lot of this material very well. As in the earlier film, he reveals himself as a master of mood, atmosphere, and

period. And his exposition is inventive and subtle. The film requires the intelligent participation of the viewer; as Michael attempts to discover who betrayed him and attempted his assassination, he tells different stories to different people, keeping his own counsel, and we have to think as he does so we can tell the truth from the lies.

Pacino is very good at suggesting the furies and passions that lie just beneath his character's controlled exterior. He gives us a Michael who took over the family with the intention of making it "legitimate" in five years, but who is drawn more and more deeply into a byzantine web of deceit and betrayal, all papered over with code words like respect, honor, and gratitude. By the film's end he has been abandoned by almost everyone except those who work for him and fear him, and he is a very lonely man.

But what was his sin? It was not, as we might have imagined or hoped, that he presided over a bloody enterprise of murder and destruction. No, Michael's fault seems to be pride. He has lost the common touch, the dignity he should have inherited from his father. And because he has misplaced his humanity he must suffer.

Coppola suggests this by contrast. His scenes about Don Vito's early life could almost be taken as a campaign biography, and in the most unfortunate flashbacks we're given the young Vito intervening on behalf of a poor widow who is being evicted from her apartment. The don seems more like a precinct captain than a gangster, and we're left with the unsettling impression that Coppola thinks things would have turned out all right for Michael if he'd had the old man's touch.

The flashbacks give Coppola the greatest difficulty in maintaining his pace and narrative force. The story of Michael, told chronologically and without the other material, would have had really substantial impact, but Coppola prevents our complete involvement by breaking the tension. The flashbacks to New York in the early 1900s have a different, a nostalgic tone, and the audience has to keep shifting gears. Coppola was reportedly advised by friends to forget the Don Vito material and stick with Michael, and that was good advice.

There's also some evidence in the film that

Coppola never completely mastered the chaotic mass of material in his screenplay. Some scenes seem oddly pointless (why do we get almost no sense of Michael's actual dealings in Cuba, but lots of expensive footage about the night of Castro's takeover?), and others seem not completely explained (I am still not quite sure who really did order that attempted garroting in the Brooklyn saloon).

What we're left with, then, are a lot of good scenes and good performances set in the midst of a mass of undisciplined material and handicapped by plot construction that prevents the story from ever really building.

There is, for example, the brilliant audacity of the first communion party for Michael's son, which Coppola directs as counterpoint to the wedding scene that opened *The Godfather*. There is Lee Strasberg's two-edged performance as Hyman Roth, the boss of the Florida and Cuban operations; Strasberg gives us a soft-spoken, almost kindly old man, and then reveals his steel-hard interior. There is Coppola's use of sudden, brutal bursts of violence to punctuate the film's brooding progress. There is Pacino, suggesting everything, telling nothing.

But Coppola is unable to draw all this together and make it work on the level of simple, absorbing narrative. The stunning text of *The Godfather* is replaced in *Part II* with prologues, epilogues, footnotes, and good intentions.

The Gods Must Be Crazy ★ ★ ★
PG, 109 m., 1984

N!xau (Xi), Marius Weyers (Andrew Steyn), Sandra Prinsloo (Kate Thompson), Louw Verwey (Sam Boga), James Uys (The Reverend). Directed and produced by Jamie Uys. Screenplay by Uys.

Here's a movie that begins with a Coke bottle falling from the heavens, and ends with a Jeep up in a tree. *The Gods Must Be Crazy* is a South African movie that arrived in Europe with little fanfare in 1982, broke box office records in Japan and South America and all over Europe, and even became a cult hit here in North America, where there has not been much of a demand for comedies from South Africa.

The film begins in the Kalahari Desert. A pilot in a private plane throws his empty Coke bottle out of the window. It lands near a Bushman who is on a hunting expedition. He has never seen anything like it before. He takes it back to his tribe, where it is put to dozens of uses: It becomes a musical instrument, a patternmaker, a fire starter, a cooking utensil, and, most of all, an object of bitter controversy. Everybody in the tribe ends up fighting over the bottle, and so the Bushman, played by the Xhosa actor N!xau (the exclamation point represents a click), decides there is only one thing to do: He must return the bottle to the gods. This decision sends him on a long odyssey toward more settled lands on the edges of the desert, where the movie develops into a somewhat more conventional comedy.

We meet some of the new characters: A would-be schoolteacher, a goofy biologist, and an insurgent leader. They are all intent on their own lives and plans, but in one way or another, the Xhosa and his Coke bottle bring them together into unexpected combinations. And the director, Jamie Uys, has the patience to develop some really elaborate sight gags, which require a lot of preparation but pay off with big laughs—particularly the sequence with an indecisive, back-and-forth Jeep.

The star of the movie is N!xau, who is so forthright and cheerful and sensible that his very presence makes some of the gags pay off. In any slapstick comedy, the gags must rest on a solid basis of logic: It's not funny to watch people being ridiculous, but it is funny to watch people doing the next logical thing, and turning out to be ridiculous. N!xau, because he approaches Western society without preconceptions, and bases all of his actions on logical conclusions, brings into relief a lot of the little tics and assumptions of everyday life. I think that reveals the thought that went into this movie: It might be easy to make a farce about screwball happenings in the desert, but it's a lot harder to create a funny interaction between nature and human nature. This movie's a nice little treasure.

Godspell ★ ★ ★ ★
G, 102 m., 1973 ✓

Victor Garber (Jesus), David Haskell (John, Judas), Jerry Sroka (Jerry), Lynne Thigpen (Lynne), Katie Hanley (Katie), Robin Lamont (Robin), Gilmer McCormick (Gilmer), Joanne Jonas (Joanne), Merrell Jackson (Merrell), Jeffrey Mylett (Jeffrey). Directed by David Greene.

The thing about *Godspell* that caught my heart was its simplicity, its refusal to pretend to be anything more than it is. It's not a message for our times, or a movie to cash in on the Jesus movement, or even quite a youth movie. It's a series of stories and songs, like the Bible is, and it's told with the directness that simple stories need: with no tricks, no intellectual gadgets, and a lot of openness.

This was the quality that attracted me to the stage version. I had to be almost dragged to the play, because its subject matter sounded so depressingly contemporary. But after I finally got into the theatre and sat down and let *Godspell* relax me, I found myself simply letting it happen. For a musical based on the Gospel according to St. Matthew, *Godspell* is strangly irreverent, wacky, and endearing.

The stage version has been opened up into a movie by taking the whole of New York as a set. Except for the scenes at the beginning and end—which show the city as a temple of mammon and a rat nest—the movie is populated only by its cast; we don't see anybody else, and the ten kids dance, sing, and act out parables in such unlikely places as the World Trade Center and a tugboat. This is a new use for New York, which looks unusually clean; even its tacky skyscrapers edge toward grandeur when the vast long shots engulf them.

Against this wilderness of steel and concrete, the characters come on like kids at a junior high reunion, clothed in comic book colors and bright tattered rags. Only two have names: Jesus, and a character who plays both John (who ushered Jesus into the Bible) and Judas (who hastened him out). The other eight characters, who seem to represent an on-the-spot gathering of disciples, are just themselves.

What's nice about the casting—which gives us all new faces—is that the characters don't look like professional stage youths. Remember *West Side Story*, where all the allegedly teen-age dancers looked like hardened theatrical professionals in greaser wigs? *Godspell*'s cast is not only young but is allowed to look like a collection of individuals. These could conceivably be real people, and their freshness helps put the material over even when it seems pretty obvious. For some blessed reason the director, David Greene, has resisted any temptation to make the movie visually fancy. With material of this sort, there must have been an impulse to go for TV-commercial trendiness, but Greene's style is unforced, and goes well with the movie's freshness and basic colors.

The movie characters, like the stage characters, are given little watercolor designs on their faces by Jesus. A girl gets a little yellow flower, a boy gets a tiny red star, and so on. It was necessary in the stage version to exaggerate this makeup to make it visible, but the movie underplays it and it was gentle and nice. It occurred to me, about an hour into the film, that maybe young people will pick up on this. Tattoos were big in the 70s—little butterflies and stars—so why not face-paint zigzags and pinwheels and flowers? Anything to brighten up this miserable world: Which is what *Godspell* is saying, anyway.

Godzilla 1985 ★
PG, 91 m., 1985

Raymond Burr (Steve Martin), Keiju Kobayashi (Prime Minister), Ken Tanaka (Reporter), Yasuko Sawaguchi (Naoko). Directed by Kohji Hashimoto and R.J. Kizer and produced by Tomoyuki Tanaka and Anthony Randel. Screenplay by Shuichi Nagahara and Lisa Tomei.

The "Good Bad Movie" is by now an accepted item of cultural history, and we are all familiar with the theory that a movie can be so bad that it's good. Just consider *Infra-Man*. To really qualify as a GBM, however, a movie must *think* that it is good; part of the fun is watching it struggle to be other than it is. The fatal flaw in *Godzilla 1985* is that it is a bad movie with aspirations of being a good bad movie.

My clues in arriving at this conclusion are many. The filmmakers must have known that the original *Godzilla* (1956) had many loyal fans all over the world who treasured the absurd dialogue, the bad lip-synching, the unbelievable special effects, the phony profundity. So they have deliberately gone after the same inept feeling in *Godzilla 1985*. Examples:

Dialogue: It is so consistently bad that the entire screenplay could be submitted as an example. My favorite moment occurs when the hero and heroine are clutching each other on the top floor of a skyscraper being torn apart by Godzilla and the professor leaps into the shot, says, "What has happened here?" and leaps out again without waiting for an answer.

Lip-synching: Especially in the opening shots, there seems to be a subtle effort to exaggerate the bad coordination between what we see and what we hear. All lip-synch is a little off, of course, but this movie seems to be going for condescending laughs from knowledgeable filmgoers.

Special effects: When Godzilla marches on Tokyo, the buildings are the usual fake miniature models, made out of paint and cardboard. The tipoff is when he rips a wall off a high-rise, and nothing falls out. That's because there is nothing inside. Godzilla himself also undergoes bewildering changes in size. At one point, he's small enough to peer into the window of a ship; a little later, he's so tall that he knocks over sixty-story buildings. Curiously, his feet, when seen in close-up mashing cars and things, always seem to be the same size.

Phony profundity: This is Raymond Burr's department, and it is a thankless task. He is in the movie, I suppose, as the only living link with the 1956 classic (apart from Godzilla, of course). His scenes were apparently all shot in a few days. He wears the same wardrobe and the same expression, and steps forward out of the shadows to utter inanities such as, "That will never stop Godzilla," and, "Those weapons of war will only anger Godzilla." At no time is he involved dramatically in the adventure. In a career that has contained many highs and many lows, this is not one of Raymond Burr's finest hours.

Godzilla is said to be popular in Japan because he touches a nerve: He is a monster created by radioactivity, the destructive heritage of World War II. There have been a lot of Godzilla adventures since the original one in 1956 (my favorite is *Godzilla Versus the Smog Monster*), but this is the first one made by Toho, the studio that launched the series.

The message seems to be as bleak as ever: "So long as mankind continues to defy the forces of nature (a narrator intones), we will be visited by catastrophes like hurricanes, tidal waves, and Godzilla." And, for that matter, as long as Toho continues to heed the call of the marketplace, we will be visited by catastrophes like *Godzilla 1985*.

The Goodbye Girl ★ ★ ★
PG, 110 m., 1977

Richard Dreyfuss (Elliott Garfield), Marsha Mason (Paula McFadden), Quinn Cummings (Lucy McFadden), Paul Benedict (Mark), Barbara Rhoades (Donna), Theresa Merritt (Mrs. Crosby). Directed by Herbert Ross and produced by Ray Stark. Screenplay by Neil Simon.

Neil Simon's *The Goodbye Girl* is a funny movie with its heart finally in the right place, but all sorts of unacknowledged complications lurk just beneath its polished surface. The surface is pure Simon, which means that it's a funny-sad-tough-warm story about basically nice people who are given just three snappy one-liners too many to be totally human. But this time Simon has slipped in some subtleties we might miss the first time around.

The story's about three people we can instantly identify with. There's the former actress (Marsha Mason) and her cute ten-year-old daughter (Quinn Cummings), and the would-be actor from Chicago (Richard Dreyfuss). Until the moment before the movie opens, Miss Mason has been living with another actor in an apartment on New York's Upper East Side, where apartments are harder to find than cabs, which are harder to find than plumbers who make house calls on Sunday (which is a Simon kind of progression).

Miss Mason and her daughter come home to find that her roommate, that rat, has jumped the boat. He leaves a note explaining that he's got a great role in the new Bertolucci picture in Europe—and lotsa luck, kid. That's bad enough. Worse is when she finds out that the apartment has been sublet to this actor from Chicago, who's paid three months' rent and, reasonably enough, expects to move in, especially since at the moment he's standing in the rain.

After the two of them shout at each other for a sufficient period of time, she does allow him to move in (he gets the smaller bedroom). And then we know the basic plot structure: Total warfare in the apartment will de-escalate into a guarded truce, followed by alternating forays of warmth and decency, until the kid acts as a catalyst and they fall in love.

Wonderful. Not so wonderful is the way the Marsha Mason character is written and acted. She's hardly ever sympathetic. Sure, she's been burned by a lot of guys—but she's so hard-edged you wonder how she met them in the first place. She sees the situation strictly in economic terms, consistently behaves as a bitch, and gives Dreyfuss no reason for getting to like her.

Dreyfuss, on the other hand, is great. Eccentric, yes, since Simon always gives his characters off-the-wall touches to make them human (he meditates, plays his guitar in the middle of the night, sleeps in the nude, eats health food, etc.). But he's a nice guy. He's trapped in this weird off-off-off-Broadway production of Shakespeare's *Richard III*, and the director is convinced Richard should be played as a gay (the scenes involving the production, performance, and reception of the play are the funniest in a movie since Mel Brooks staged *Springtime for Hitler*). He fears, rightly, that the play could be the end of his New York career, and his fears are played against the unsympathetic Mason character and her basically lovable daughter.

He finally wins the mother through her child ("Listen, I can't stand you, but you got a ten-year-old in there I'm nuts about . . ."). But why does he want to? Simon short-circuits the first scene in which Mason says a decent and warm word by having Dreyfuss fall asleep so he doesn't hear it. He never really provides the dialogue and situations we need to *like* the female character—and so, in a funny way, we *aren't* rooting for them to get together. When they do, though, the movie works best. The first hour is awkward at times and never quite involving, but some of the later scenes, especially a

dinner on a rooftop and the way Dreyfuss receives the disastrous reviews of his play, are really fine. It's strange: We leave the movie having enjoyed its conclusion so much that we almost forgot our earlier reservations. But they were there, and they were real.

The Goonies ★ ★ ★
PG, 114 m., 1985

Sean Astin (Mikey), Josh Brolin (Brand), Jeff Cohen (Chunk), Corey Feldman (Mouth), Kerri Green (Andy), Martha Plimpton (Stef), and Ke Huy Quan (Data). Directed by Richard Donner and produced by Donner and Harvey Bernhard. Executive producer, Steven Spielberg. Screenplay by Chris Columbus.

The Goonies is a smooth mixture of the usual ingredients from Steven Spielberg action movies, made special because of the high-energy performances of the kids who have the adventures. It's a fantastical story of buried pirate treasure, told with a slice-of-life approach that lets these kids use words Bogart didn't know in *Casablanca*. There used to be children's movies and adult movies. Now Spielberg has found an in-between niche, for young teen-agers who have fairly sophisticated tastes in horror. He supervises the formula and oversees the production, assigning the direction to stylish action veterans (this time, it's Richard Donner, of *Superman* and *Ladyhawke*).

Goonies, like *Gremlins*, walks a thin line between the cheerful and the gruesome, and the very scenes the adults might object to are the ones the kids will like the best: Spielberg is congratulating them on their ability to take the heavy-duty stuff. The movie begins with an assortment of engaging boys, including a smart kid, a kid with braces, a fat kid, an older brother, and an Asian kid whose clothing conceals numerous inventions. Along the way they pick up a couple of girls, whose function is to swap spit and get bats in their hair. The kids find an old treasure map and blunder into the hideout of a desperate gang of criminals—two brothers, led by a Ma Barker type. There is a third brother, a Quasimodish freak, who is kept chained down in the cellar, where he watches TV. The tunnels to the treasure begin under the hideout. The kids find the tunnels while fleeing from the bad guys, and then go looking for the treasure with the crooks on their tails. There are lots of special effects and among the set pieces are the same kinds of booby traps that Indiana Jones survived in *Raiders* (falling boulders, sharp spikes), and a toboggan ride on a water chute that will remind you of the runaway train in *The Temple of Doom.*

If the ingredients are familiar from Spielberg's high-powered action movies, the kids are inspired by *E. T.* The single most important line of dialogue in any Spielberg movie is probably the line in *E. T.* when one kid calls another kid "penis-breath." The dialogue hears and acknowledges the precocious way that kids incorporate vulgarity into their conversations, especially with each other; the line in *E. T.* created such a shock of recognition that the laughs swept away any objections.

This time, his kids say "shit" a lot, and it is a measure of Spielberg's insight that the word draws only a PG rating for the movie; Spielberg no doubt argues that most kids talk like that half the time, and he is right. His technique is to take his 13- and 14-year-olds and let them act a little older than their age. It's more refreshing than the old Disney technique, which was to take characters of all ages and have them behave as if they were 12.

Another Spielberg trademark, faithfully achieved by Donner, is a breakneck narrative speed. More things happen in this movie than in six ordinary action films. There's not just a thrill a minute; there's a thrill, a laugh, a shock, and a special effect. The screenplay has all the kids talking all at once, all the time, and there were times, especially in the first reel, when I couldn't understand much of what they were saying. The movie needs to be played loud, and with extra treble.

During *Goonies*, I was often exhilarated by what was happening. Afterwards, I was less enthusiastic. The movie is totally manipulative, which would be okay, except it doesn't have the lift of a film like *E. T.* It has the high energy without the sweetness. It uses what it knows about kids to churn them up, while *E. T.* gave them things to think about, the values to enjoy. *Goonies*, like *Gremlins*, shows that Spielberg and his direc-

tors are absolute masters of how to excite and involve an audience. *E. T.* was more like *Close Encounters;* it didn't simply want us to feel, but also to wonder, and to dream.

Gorky Park ★ ★ ★ ½
R, 128 m., 1983

William Hurt (Arkady Renko), Lee Marvin (Jack Osborne), Joanna Pakula (Irina), Brian Dennehy (Kirwell), Ian Bannen (Iamskoy). Directed by Michael Apted and produced by Gene Kirkwood and Howard W. Koch, Jr. Screenplay by Dennis Potter.

Mystery fans talk about the "police procedural," a crime novel that follows police work, step by meticulous step, from the opening of a case to its eventual resolution. The crimes aren't always solved, but then the solution isn't really the point. Instead, "procedurals" are a way to study human nature under stress, to see how a society works from the inside out and the bottom up. There are procedurals set all over the world, from Ed McBain's 87th Precinct on the East coast to the Martin Beck thrillers in Stockholm, but Martin Cruz Smith's *Gorky Park* was the first good police procedural set in Russia. It used the procedural approach to show us an honest cop under pressure, a system that functioned only through corruption, and a conflict between socialism and Russia's homegrown capitalism.

This is the movie of that book, and it has all of the same strengths. It begins with a shocking murder (three corpses found frozen in the snow with their faces and fingerprints removed). There are no clues. A police inspector named Renko (William Hurt) is assigned to the case, and makes it his personal crusade. He recruits a physical anthropologist to try to re-create the missing faces on the bodies. He prowls the black market, where deals are made in Western currency. He meets a beautiful young woman and a mysterious American businessman. And he learns about the obsessive power of sable fur coats.

The investigation of the crime has a fascination of its own, but what makes *Gorky Park* really interesting is its views of Soviet cops, criminals, bureaucrats, and ordinary citizens. As Renko gets closer and closer to a solution to the case, his investigation leads him to powerful circles in the Soviet Union. And his heart, of course, leads him closer to the girl, who may have all of the necessary information but has been so warped by paranoia that she refuses to betray those she thinks are her friends.

The movie is directed with efficiency by Michael *(Coal Miner's Daughter)* Apted, who knows that pacing is indispensable to a procedural. Too long a pause for anything—romance, detail, speculation, explanation—and the spell is broken. He uses actors who are able to bring fully realized characters to the screen, so we don't have to stand around waiting for introductions. That involves a certain amount of typecasting. Lee Marvin, gravel-voiced, white-haired, expensively dressed, is perfect for the businessman. Joanna Pakula, a young Polish actress in her first Western role, is beautiful, vulnerable, wide-eyed, and fresh—and as an exile stranded in Paris when her Warsaw theater was closed by Poland's martial law, she doesn't have to fake her paranoia about the Soviet state.

William Hurt, as Renko, is probably the key to the picture. He makes this cop into a particular kind of person, cold, at times willfully blinded by duty, sublimating his feelings in his profession, until this case breaks him wide open. By the end of *Gorky Park*, we realize that it's not the solution that matters, but what the case itself forces the people to discover about themselves.

The Great Gatsby ★ ★ ½
PG, 146 m., 1974

Robert Redford (Gatsby), Mia Farrow (Daisy Buchanan), Bruce Dern (Tom Buchanan), Karen Black (Myrtle Wilson), Scott Wilson (George Wilson), Sam Waterston (Nick Carraway), Lois Chiles (Jordan Baker), Howard Da Silva (Meyer Wolfsheim), Robert Blossom (Mr. Gatz), Edward Hermann (Klipspringer). Directed by Jack Clayton and produced by David Merrick. Screenplay by Francis Ford Coppola.

The Great Gatsby is a superficially beautiful hunk of a movie with nothing much in common with the spirit of F. Scott Fitzgerald's novel. I wonder what Fitzgerald, whose prose was so graceful, so elegantly controlled, would have made of it: of the willingness to spend so much time and energy on exterior effect while never penetrating to the souls of the characters. It would take about the same time to read Fitzgerald's novel as to view this movie—and that's what I'd recommend.

The movie is "faithful" to the novel with a vengeance—to what happens in the novel, that is, and not to the feel, mood, and spirit of it. Yet I've never thought the events in *The Great Gatsby* were that important to the novel's success; Fitzgerald, who came out of St. Paul to personify the romance of an age, was writing in a way about himself when he created Gatsby. The mundane Midwestern origins had been replaced by a new persona, by a flash and charisma that sometimes only concealed the despair underneath. For Fitzgerald, there was always something unattainable; and for Gatsby, it was Daisy Buchanan, the lost love of his youth, forever symbolized by that winking green beacon at the end of her dock.

The beacon and the other Fitzgerald symbols are in this movie version, but they communicate about as much as the great stone heads on Easter Island. They're memorials to a novel in which they had meaning. The art director and set decorator seem to have ripped whole pages out of Fitzgerald and gone to work to improve on his descriptions. Daisy and her husband, the ruthless millionaire Tom Buchanan, live almost drowning in whites, yellows, and ennui. Tom's mistress Myrtle and her husband, the shabby filling station owner George, live in a wasteland of ashes in Fitzgerald's novel; in the movie, they seem to have landed on the moon.

All of this unfeeling physical excess might have been overcome by performances. But the director, Jack Clayton, having assembled a promising cast, fails to exploit them very well. When the casting of Robert Redford as Jay Gatsby was announced, I objected because he didn't fit my notion of Gatsby: He was too substantial, too assured, even too handsome. I saw him as Tom Buchanan, and somebody else as Gatsby (Jack Nicholson, maybe, or Bruce Dern—who plays Tom). Having seen the movie, I think maybe I was wrong: Redford could have played Gatsby. I'm not even sure it's his fault he doesn't. The first time Clayton shows us Gatsby, it's a low angle shot of a massive figure seen against the night sky and framed by marble: This isn't the romantic Gatsby on his doomed quest, it's Charles Foster Kane. A scene where Gatsby reaches out as if to snatch the green beacon in his hand is true to the book, but the movie's literal showing of it looks silly.

These hints of things to come lead up to two essential scenes in which Clayton fails to give us a Gatsby we care about. The first is the initial meeting between Gatsby and Nick (Gatsby wants Nick, his neighbor and Daisy's cousin, to invite her to tea so they can meet again). Redford is so inarticulate and formal in this scene with Nick that we laugh; it's the first time we hear him talk, and he's so mannered that the acting upstages the content of the scene. Doesn't that have to be Clayton's fault? We know Redford has range enough to have played the scene in several better ways. And then the actul reunion between Gatsby and Daisy—the moment on which the rest of the movie is going to depend—gives us Gatsby's toothpaste grin and Daisy's stunned reaction and holds both for so long that any tension reduces itself to the ridiculous. It doesn't even feel as if Gatsby's happy to see Daisy—more that he assumes she's overjoyed to see him.

The message of the novel, if I read it correctly, is that Gatsby, despite his dealings with gamblers and bootleggers, is a romantic, naive, and heroic product of the Midwest—and that his idealism is doomed in any confrontation with the reckless wealth of the Buchanans. This doesn't come through in the movie. When Nick, at his last meeting with Gatsby, tells him how much he admires him ("You're worth the whole crowd of them"), we frankly don't know why unless we've read the book. Oh, we're *told*, to be sure: The sound track contains narration by Nick that is based pretty closely on his narration in the novel. But we don't feel. We've been distanced by the movie's overproduction. Even the actors seem somewhat cowed by the occasion; an exception is Bruce Dern, who just goes ahead and gives us a convincing Tom Buchanan. We don't have to be told the ways in which Tom is indifferent to human feeling, because we can sense them. But we can't penetrate the mystery of

Gatsby. Nor, to be honest, can we quite understand what's so special about Daisy Buchanan. Not as she's played by Mia Farrow, all squeaks and narcissism and empty sophistication. In the novel, Gatsby never understands that he is too good for Daisy. In the movie, we never understand why he thought she was good enough for him. And that's what's missing.

That, and one other small item: How could a screenplay that plundered Fitzgerald's novel so literally, that quoted so much of the narration and dialogue, have ended with a rinky-dink version of "Ain't We Got Fun" instead of the most famous last sentence of any novel of the century? Maybe because the movie doesn't ever come close to understanding it: "And so we beat on, boats against the current, borne back ceaselessly into the past."

The Great Muppet Caper ★ ★
G, 95 m., 1981

Charles Grodin (Nicky), Diana Rigg (Lady Holiday). With the Muppets and their performers: Jim Henson, Frank Oz, Dave Goetz, Jerry Holson, and Richard Hunt. Cameo appearances by Robert Morley, Peter Ustinov, and Jack Warden. Directed by Jim Henson and produced by Frank Oz. Screenplay by Tom Patchett, Jay Tarses, Jerry Juhl, and Jack Rose.

The Muppets are a wonderful creation, but they lose their special quality in *The Great Muppet Caper.* They behave like clones of other popular kiddie superstars—like the basic cartoon heroes they once seemed destined to replace. Jim Henson's original inspiration with the Muppets was to invest them with very real human qualities: Miss Piggy's vanity and insecurity, Kermit's insouciant inquisitiveness, Fozzie's fuzzy desire to be loved, and so on. Then he involved them in situations that revolved around their personalities, so that the kids who watched them could perhaps learn something about human nature. A lot of suspense during a Muppet story depended on how a particular Muppet would *feel* about something.

That was the approach of many of the Muppet TV episodes and of the original *Muppet Movie* (1979). This time, though,

Henson and his associates haven't developed a screenplay that pays attention to the Muppet personalities. Instead, they ship them to England and dump them into a basic caper plot, treating them every bit as much like a formula as James Bond. This won't do. We don't care about some dumb diamond the size of a baseball, and as Muppet fans we're probably also indifferent to Henson's ambition to satirize old movie genres.

When he gives us a Busby Berkeley-like water ballet starring Miss Piggy, our reaction is complex. We think (a) that kids in the audience won't know what is being satirized and (b) that Miss Piggy's fantasies have become less fun as they reveal less vulnerability. And as for Miss Piggy herself . . . I really hate to say this, but she's not nearly as appealing in *The Great Muppet Caper* as she's always been before. She is also alarmingly thinner. Are we witnessing the Hollywoodization of Miss Piggy? Is she perhaps beginning to believe her own publicity? She's less vulnerable this time, less touching, with fewer instantly recognizable human frailties.

The movie involves a Muppet expedition to London, a near-affair between Charles Grodin and Miss Piggy, and some missing jewels. It also features some cameo appearances by familiar stars, but Henson seems content that the stars are merely in his movie; he doesn't use them with comic imagination. Example: When the Muppets crash-land in the middle of a British pond, they're greeted by British Airways' TV spokesman Robert Morley. But Morley plays the scene absolutely straight. Here was a great chance to have fun with Morley's TV ads: He could have brusquely informed the Muppets that hotels were $400 a night, there were no theater tickets available, not a single rental car was to be had for miles around, and that, frankly, the British wished their American cousins would stay at home.

The lack of a cutting edge hurts this movie. It's too nice, too routine, too predictable, and too safe.

The Great Santini ★ ★ ★ ★
PG, 118 m., 1980

Robert Duvall (Bull Meechum), Blythe Danner (Lillian Meechum), Michael O'Keefe (Ben Meechum), Lisa Jane Persky (Mary Anne Meechum), Stan Shaw (Toomer Smalls), Theresa Merritt (Arrabelle Smalls). Directed by Lewis John Carlino and produced by Charles A. Pratt. Screenplay by Carlino.

Like almost all of my favorite films, *The Great Santini* is about people more than it's about a story. It's a study of several characters, most unforgettably the Great Santini himself—played by Robert Duvall. Despite his name, he is not a magician or an acrobat but a lieutenant colonel in the Marines with the real name of Bull Meechum. He sees himself as the Great Santini, an ace pilot, great Marine, heroic husband and father and, in general, a sterling man among men. His family is expected to go along with this— and to go along with him, as he's transferred to a duty camp in South Carolina in the early 1960s.

There are five other members of the Meechum family. His wife (Blythe Danner) is a sweet Southern girl who calls her kids "sugar" and understands her maverick husband with a love that is deep but unforgiving. His oldest son (Michael O'Keefe) is just turning eighteen and learning to stand up to a father who issues "direct orders," calls everyone "sports fan," and expects to be called "sir." There are two more daughters and a son, but the movie's main relationship is between the father and the oldest boy.

Santini, you understand, is one hell of a guy. All he understands is competition. He's a royal pain in the ass to his Marine superiors, because he's always pulling damn fool stunts and making a spectacle out of himself. But he's a great pilot and he's said to be a good leader (even though his first briefing session for the men under him in South Carolina leaves them totally bewildered). Santini wants to win at everything, even backyard basketball with his son.

But the son is learning to be his own man. And there's a subplot involving a friendship between O'Keefe and the intense actor Stan Shaw, who plays the son of the family's black maid. Marine kids grow up nowhere and everywhere, we learn, and in South Carolina these two kids go shrimping together, trade lore together, become friends. It's a nice relationship, although a little tangential to the main thrust of the movie.

It's Robert Duvall who really makes the movie live—Duvall and Blythe Danner in a stunning performance that nothing she's done before (in *1776, Hearts of the West,* etc.) prepares us for. Although *The Great Santini* is set about ten years before *Apocalypse Now,* Duvall is playing essentially the same character in both films—we remember his great scene in *Apocalypse,* shouting that napalm smells to him like victory, as he gives his gung-ho speeches in this movie.

Duvall and O'Keefe go hard at each other, in the father-son confrontation, and there's an especially painful scene where the father bounces a basketball off his son's head, egging him on. But this movie is essentially a comedy—a serious, tender one, like *Breaking Away,* which is also about a son getting to know his father.

There are wonderful little moments in the dialogue (as when the Great Santini's daughter wonders aloud if females are allowed full Meechum family status, or are only sort of one-celled Meechums). There are moments straight out of left field, as when Duvall and the family's new maid (the formidable Theresa Merritt) get into an impromptu shoulder-punching contest. There are moments so unpredictable and yet so natural they feel just like the spontaneity of life itself. And the movie's conclusion is the same way: sentimental without being corny, a tearjerker with dignity.

The Great Santini is a movie to seek out and to treasure.

Gregory's Girl ★ ★ ★
PG, 93 m., 1982

Gordon John Sinclair (Gregory), Dee Hepburn (Dorothy), Chic Murray (Headmaster), Jake D'Arcy (Phil), Alex Norton (Alec), John Bott (Alistair). Directed by Bill Forsyth and produced by Clive Parsons and Davina Boling. Screenplay by Forsyth.

There was a little item in the paper not long ago that should have been front page news. It was about a survey reporting that physically handsome men were less successful in business, made less money, married younger, and had less "desirable" spouses than men of average or below-average looks. The sociologists who announced these conclusions speculated that the handsome guys

tended to get sidetracked in high school, spending more time on social life and less time on studies; they tended to depend on their golden boy charm instead of plowing ahead through college; and they tended, because they were more sexually active at younger ages, to marry sooner and therefore to marry women who were looking for marriage rather than careers. On the average, therefore, the weird kid with acne who's president of Chem Club will do better in the long run than the prom king.

Bill Forsyth's *Gregory's Girl* is a charming, innocent, very funny little movie about the weird kid. It is set in Scotland, where the teen-agers are quieter, more civilized and more naive than, let's say, those in *The Class of 1984.* And it is about Gregory (Gordon John Sinclair), a gangling adolescent who has started to shoot up all of a sudden and finds he is hopelessly uncoordinated on the soccer field. Gregory looks sort of like an immensely likable stork. He loses his place on the soccer team to another student who is a good deal faster and more coordinated. The other student happens to be a girl. Her name is Dorothy (Dee Hepburn), and Gregory instantly falls deeply in love with her. Nothing like this has ever hit him before, and romance becomes for him almost a physical illness. Dorothy is sweet to him, but distant, because she not only suspects Gregory's feelings but is way ahead of him in her analysis of the whole situation.

The movie takes place mostly in a pleasant suburb of Glasgow, where the kids hang about and trade endless speculation on the impossibility of being sixteen and happy at the same time. Gregory turns for romantic advice to his younger sister, who is much more interested in ice cream. His sister, in fact, is oblivious to boys, although one pays her an earnest compliment: "She's only ten, but she has the body of a woman of thirteen." Meanwhile, Gregory consoles his best friend, who is fifteen and a half and has never known love.

This movie is a reminder that we tend to forget a lot of things about adolescence. For example: That it is no use telling a teen-ager what his faults are, because he is painfully aware of every possible fault in the minutest detail; that boys are absolutely helpless in the throes of teen-age romance, whereas girls tend to retain at least some perspective; that it is an unwritten law of the universe that no sixteen-year-old ever falls instantly in love with the right person at the right time.

The movie has a lot of gentle, civilized fun with insights like that. And along the way, Gregory the stork is led on a wild goose chase with a swan at the end. The movie contains so much wisdom about being alive and teenaged and vulnerable that maybe it would even be painful for a teen-ager to see it; it's not much help, when you're suffering from those feelings of low self-esteem and an absolutely hopeless crush, to realize that not only are you in pain and suffering an emotional turmoil, but you're not even unique. Maybe only grown-ups should see this movie. You know, people who have gotten over the pains of unrequited love (hollow laugh).

Gremlins ★ ★ ★
PG, 111 m., 1984

Hoyt Axton (Rand Peltzer), Zach Galligan (Billy), Phoebe Cates (Kate), Scott Brady (Sheriff Frank), Polly Holliday (Mrs. Deagle). Directed by Joe Dante and produced by Michael Finnell. Executive producer Steven Spielberg. Screenplay by Chris Columbus.

Gremlins is a confrontation between Norman Rockwell's vision of Christmas and Hollywood's vision of the blood-sucking monkeys of voodoo island. It's fun. On the one hand, you have an idyllic American small town, with Burger Kings and Sears stores clustered merrily around the village square, and on the other hand you have a plague of reprehensible little beasties who behave like a rodent road company of Marlon Brando's motorcycle gang in *The Wild One*.

The whole movie is a sly series of send-ups, inspired by movie scenes so basic they reside permanently in our subconscious. The opening scene, for example, involves a visit to your basic Mysterious Little Shop in Chinatown, where, as we all know, the ordinary rules of the visible universe cease to operate and magic is a reality. Later on, after a kid's father buys him a cute little gremlin in Chinatown, we have a new version of your basic Puppy for Christmas Scene. Then there are such basic movie characters as the

Zany Inventor, the Blustering Sheriff, the Clean-Cut Kid, the Cute Girlfriend, and, of course, the Old Bag.

The first half of the movie is the best. That's when we meet the little gremlins, which are unbearably cute and look like a cross between a Pekingese, Yoda from *Empire*, the Ewoks from *Jedi*, and kittens. They have impossibly big eyes, they're cuddly and friendly, and they would make ideal pets except for the fact that they hate bright lights, should not be allowed to get wet, and must never be fed after midnight. Well, of course, it's *always* after midnight; that's the tip-off that this isn't a retread of *E.T.* but comes from an older tradition, the fairy tale or magic story. And in the second half of the movie, after the gremlins have gotten wet, been fed after midnight, etc., they turn into truly hateful creatures that look like the monster in *Alien*.

The movie exploits every trick in the monster-movie book. We have scenes where monsters pop up in the foreground, and others where they stalk us in the background, and others when they drop into the frame and scare the Shinola out of everybody. And the movie itself turns nasty, especially in a scene involving a monster that gets slammed in a microwave oven, and another one where a wide-eyed teen-age girl (Phoebe Cates) explains why she hates Christmas. Her story is in the great tradition of 1950s sick jokes, and as for the microwave scene, I had a queasy feeling that before long we'd be reading newspaper stories about kids who went home and tried the same thing with the family cat.

Gremlins was hailed as another *E.T.* It's not. It's in a different tradition. At the level of Serious Film Criticism, it's a meditation on the myths in our movies: Christmas, families, monsters, retail stores, movies, boogeymen. At the level of Pop Moviegoing, it's a sophisticated, witty B movie, in which the monsters are devouring not only the defenseless town, but decades of defenseless clichés. But don't go if you still believe in Santa Claus.

The Grey Fox ★ ★ ★ ½
PG, 92 m., 1983

Richard Farnsworth (Bill Miner), Jackie Burroughs (Kate Flynn), Wayne Robson (Shorty), Ken Pogue (Jack Budd). Directed by Phillip Borsos and produced by Peter O'Brian. Screenplay by John Hunter.

Here's a lovely adventure: a movie about a stubborn, indomitable character who robs people because that's what he knows best. A man should work at his craft, shouldn't he? *The Grey Fox* tells the story of Bill Miner, a man who was thrown into prison in the heyday of the Old West, was kept behind bars for thirty-three years, and who finally emerged, confused but interested, into the twentieth century, where the movie begins in 1901. Bill Miner robbed stagecoaches. What's he supposed to do with a train? He's a whiskery old man, stubborn as a mule, and his pride hasn't grown any smaller during those years in jail. He heads for his sister's place to look for work and a roof over his head, but he doesn't get along with his brother-in-law and he also doesn't much like picking oysters for a living. He leaves. He hits the road, drifting aimlessly, a man without a mission—until the night in 1903 when he sees Edwin S. Porter's *The Great Train Robbery*. That famous movie is only eleven minutes long, but long enough to make everything absolutely clear to Miner, who realizes he has a new calling in life, as a train robber.

All of this could, of course, be an innocuous Disney movie, but it's well-written and directed, and what gives it zest and joy is the performance by Richard Farnsworth, who plays Miner. Maybe you'll recognize Farnsworth when you see him on the screen. Maybe not. His life has been one of those careers that makes you realize Hollywood is a company town, where you can make a living for years and never be a star. Farnsworth has been in more than 300 movies. He was a stuntman for thirty years. He's had speaking roles in movies ranging from *The Cowboys* to *Resurrection*. He was even in "Roots" on TV. And yet there is absolutely no mention of his name in Leslie Halliwell's *Filmgoer's Companion*. Farnsworth is one of those unstudied, graceful, absolutely natural actors who has spent a

lifetime behaving exactly as he feels. I think he is incapable of a false or a dishonest moment. He makes Miner so proud, so vulnerable, such a noble rascal, that the whole movie becomes just a little more complex because he's in it.

There's one scene where you can really see Farnsworth's gift for conviction. It's a love scene with a feminist lady photographer named Kate Flynn (Jackie Burroughs), who is touring the West to document its changing times. Bill and Kate are instantly attracted to one another. And their love scene together is a warm, amusing masterpiece of quiet affection. Miner doesn't deny his age; he triumphs with it. He's not handsome but he's damned attractive, and knows it. Kate Flynn can see that this man has six times the worth of an ordinary man, and adores him. The scene is a treasure, even when you don't know whether to laugh or cry.

The director, Phillip Borsos, is able to make this a human story and still keep it exciting as an action picture. And he gives it a certain documentary feel; *The Grey Fox* is apparently based, to some degree, on truth. That doesn't matter half as much as that Farnsworth bases his performance on how he sees the truth of Bill Miner.

Greystoke ★ ★ ★
PG, 129 m., 1984

Christopher Lambert (Tarzan), Ralph Richardson (Earl of Greystoke), Ian Holm (Captain D'Arnot), Andie MacDowell (Jane Porter). Directed by Hugh Hudson and produced by Hudson and Stanley S. Canter. Screenplay by P.H. Vazak and Michael Austin.

One of the most unforgettable mothers in the history of literature is named Kala, and she is an ape. Some people will immediately know that Kala is the great ape who adopted a shipwrecked orphan and raised him as her own, until he became Tarzan, Lord of the Apes. Other people will not know that, and for them, the movie *Greystoke* may be missing a certain resonance. I think it helps, in seeing this movie, to draw on a background of rainy Saturday afternoons when you were ten and had your nose buried in *Tarzan* books.

Greystoke, the Legend of Tarzan, Lord of the

Apes is the most faithful film adaptation of the Tarzan legend ever made. That isn't saying much, because most of the forty or so Tarzan movies were laughable quickies with Tarzan trying not to be upstaged by cute chimps. *Greystoke* takes the legend seriously, and it's worthy of being taken seriously, I think, because the story of Tarzan has become one of the most durable of all the myths of the twentieth century. The obvious challenge for this movie is to convince an audience that it is actually looking at a little human baby being nurtured by wild animals. *Greystoke* passes that test. The movie combines footage of real animals with footage of human actors disguised by the special effects makeup of Rick Baker, and I was hard-pressed to tell the difference. The movie has an extended opening sequence that takes place entirely in the jungle, without spoken dialogue, and that captures the central mystery of the Tarzan legend as well as anything I've ever seen.

Unfortunately, there's one other aspect of Tarzan that *Greystoke* doesn't capture as well. The Tarzan adventures were all inspired by the imagination of a pulp writer named Edgar Rice Burroughs, who was not a stylist or a philosopher but was certainly a great plotter and knew how to entangle Tarzan in cliff-hanging melodrama. *Greystoke* isn't melodrama and doesn't try to be, and I missed that. After the great early jungle scenes, it has the grown-up Tarzan (Christopher Lambert) being discovered by a Belgian explorer (Ian Holm) who returns him to his ancestral Scottish home, Greystoke Manor, where he meets his grandfather (Ralph Richardson) and also a young lady named Jane (Andie MacDowell). The movie has fun showing Tarzan's introduction to civilization; there's a spine-tingling moment when he growls into Jane's ear. The characters also are well-drawn, especially Ralph Richardson's Earl of Greystoke, who childishly slides down a staircase on a silver tray, and who has a touching death scene that was acted not long before Richardson himself died.

But where's the action? Shouldn't there be some sort of pulp subplot about the ant men, or the jewels of Opar, or a wild elephant on a rampage? *Greystoke* is the story of the legend of Tarzan, but it doesn't contain an adventure *involving* Tarzan. Who would have guessed there'd ever be a respectable Tarzan movie?

Hair ★ ★ ★ ★
R, 118 m., 1979

John Savage (Claude), Beverly D'Angelo (Sheila), Dorsey Wright (Hud), Cheryl Barnes (Hud's Fiancee), Treat Williams (Berger), Annie Golden (Jeannie), Don Dacus (Woof). Directed by Milos Forman and produced by Lester Persky and Michael Butler. Screenplay by Michael Weller.

I walked into *Hair* with the gravest doubts that this artifact of 1960s social shock would transfer to our current, sleepier times. In the 1960s we went to angry musicals; now we line up for *La Cage aux Folles*. My doubts disappeared with the surge and bold authority of the first musical statement: *This is the dawning of the Age of Aquarius!*

So maybe it isn't, really, and maybe the sun set on that particular age back around the time they pinched the Watergate burglars. But Milos Forman's *Hair* opens with such confidence and joy, moves so swiftly and sustains itself so well that I wonder why I had any doubts. *Hair* is, amazingly, not a period piece but a freshly conceived and staged memory of the tribulations of the mid-sixties.

It is also a terrific musical. The songs, of course, were good to begin with: The glory of "Hair" and "Let the Sun Shine In" and "Age of Aquarius" and the sly, silly warmth of "Black Boys/White Boys." But to the original music, the film version adds a story that works well with it, airy and open photography, and glorious choreography by Twyla Tharp.

I said I lost my doubts about *Hair* during "Age of Aquarius." To be more precise, they disappeared during Tharp's opening scene in Central Park, when the dancers were joined by the horses of mounted policemen. Anyone who can sit through that opening dance sequence and not be thrilled should give up musicals.

The original play, you may recall, didn't exactly have what you could call much of a plot. The screenplay, by Michael Weller, remedies that, but not too much. Weller provides a framework structured around the experiences of a young Midwestern farmboy (John Savage) who takes the bus to Manhattan to be inducted into the army and makes instant friends with a family of hippies living in Central Park.

Savage is just right as the shy, introspective kid who feels suspicious of the hippies—and, indeed, of any alternative lifestyle. But he knows nobody else in New York, so he hangs around with these kids and suddenly a vision enters his life: a beautiful girl on horseback (Beverly D'Angelo), a debutante passing through Central Park and probably out of his life.

She comes from an incredibly wealthy family, he learns. They have nothing in common. But she's drawn, sort of, to the easy freedom of the hippies. And the leader of the hippies (Treat Williams, of *Jesus Christ Superstar*) leads them all in a high-spirited invasion of the girl's debutante party. It's one of the movie's best scenes, somehow finding a fresh way to handle the old cliché of the uninvited street people at a millionaire's party.

The movie also evokes the stylistic artifacts of the flower power time. The love beads and vests and headbands and fringed jackets and all the other styles that were only yesterday, already look more dated than costumes from the 1940s. And it remembers the conflicts in lifestyles, mostly strikingly in scenes between the young black man (Dorsey Wright) who has joined the hippies, and the mother of his child (Cheryl Barnes), whom he left behind.

The movie's final sequences center on Savage's induction, leading to the hilarious "Black Boys/White Boys" number, an omnisexual showstopper. Twyla Tharp's choreography here is wonderfully happy and grin-inducing, as enlisted men rub legs under the table.

This number, like a lot of the movie, is loosely structured around the political attitudes of the Vietnam era, but the politics isn't heavy-handed. The movie's ideas are handled with grace and style. And it's interesting how it recalls *Hair*'s myths of the 1960s—especially the image of the youth culture as a repository, simultaneously, of ancient American values and the new values aborning in the Age of Aquarius.

That this time and spirit could be evoked

so well and so naturally is a tribute to the director, Forman. His accomplishment is all the more remarkable when you reflect that when *Hair* first occupied a stage, the Russians were in the process of occupying Forman's native Czechoslovakia, and he was in the process of becoming a filmmaker without a country.

He has since, however, shown an uncanny feeling for the textures of American life, in his *Taking Off*, with its runaway children; in his *One Flew Over the Cuckoo's Nest*, and now in *Hair*. Maybe it's just as well that this version had to wait a decade to be filmed so Forman could be hired to do it. He brings life to the musical form in the same way that *West Side Story* did, the last time everyone was saying the movie musical was dead.

Halloween ★ ★ ★ ★
R, 93 m., 1978

With Donald Pleasence, Jamie Lee Curtis, P.J. Soles, and Nancy Loomis. Directed by John Carpenter and produced by Irving Yablans. Screenplay by Carpenter and Debra Hill.

"I enjoy playing the audience like a piano."—Alfred Hitchcock

So does John Carpenter. *Halloween* is an absolutely merciless thriller, a movie so violent and scary that, yes, I *would* compare it to *Psycho*. It's a terrifying and creepy film about what one of the characters calls Evil Personified. Right. And that leads us to the one small piece of plot I'm going to describe. There's this six-year-old kid who commits a murder right at the beginning of the movie, and is sent away, and is described by his psychiatrist as someone he spent eight years trying to help, and then the next seven years trying to keep locked up. But the guy escapes. And he returns on Halloween to the same town and the same street where he committed his first murder. And while the local babysitters telephone their boyfriends and watch *The Thing* on television, he goes back into action.

Period: That's all I'm going to describe, because *Halloween* is a visceral experience—we aren't seeing the movie, we're having it happen to us. It's frightening. Maybe you don't like movies that are *really* scary: Then don't see this one. Seeing it, I was reminded of the favorable review I gave a few years ago to *The Last House on the Left*, another really terrifying thriller. Readers wrote to ask how I could possibly support such a movie. But it wasn't that I was supporting it so much as that I was describing it: You don't want to be scared? Don't see it. Credit must be paid to filmmakers who make the effort to really frighten us, to make a good thriller when quite possibly a bad one might have made as much money. Hitchcock is acknowledged as a master of suspense; it's hypocrisy to disapprove of other directors in the same genre who want to scare us too.

It's easy to create violence on the screen, but it's hard to do it well. Carpenter is uncannily skilled, for example, at the use of foregrounds in his compositions, and everyone who likes thrillers knows that foregrounds are crucial: The camera establishes the situation, and then it pans to one side, and something unexpectedly looms up in the foreground. Usually it's a tree or a door or a bush. Not always. And it's interesting how he paints his victims. They're all ordinary, everyday people—nobody's supposed to be the star and have a big scene and win an Academy Award. The performances are all the more absorbing because of that; the movie's a slice of life that is carefully painted (in drab daylights and impenetrable nighttimes) before its human monster enters the scene.

We see movies for a lot of reasons. Sometimes we want to be amused. Sometimes we want to escape. Sometimes we want to laugh, or cry, or see sunsets. And sometimes we want to be scared. I'd like to be clear about this. If you don't want to have a really terrifying experience, don't see *Halloween*.

Halloween II ★ ★
R, 92 m., 1981

Jamie Lee Curtis (Laurie), Donald Pleasence (Sam Loomis), Charles Cyphers (Leigh Brackett), Dick Warlock (The Shape). Directed by Rich Rosenthal and produced by Debra Hill and John Carpenter. Written by Hill and Carpenter.

It's a little sad to witness a fall from greatness, and that's what we get in *Halloween II*.

John Carpenter's original 1978 *Halloween* was one of the most effective horror films ever made, a scarifying fable of a mad-dog killer's progress through a small Illinois town on Halloween. That movie inspired countless imitations, each one worse than the last, until the sight of a woman's throat being slashed became ten times more common in the movies than the sight of a kiss.

Mad Slasher Movies, they were called, and they became a genre of their own, even inspiring a book of pseudoscholarship, *Splatter Movies*, by John McCarty. His definition of a Splatter Film is concise and disheartening, and bears quoting: "[They] aim not to scare their audiences, necessarily, nor to drive them to the edge of their seats in suspense, but to *mortify* them with scenes of explicit gore. In splatter movies, mutilation is indeed the message—many times the only one."

Halloween II fits this description precisely. It is not a horror film but a geek show. It is technically a sequel, but it doesn't even attempt to do justice to the original. Instead, it tries to outdo all the other violent *Halloween* rip-offs of the last several years. The movie does not have the artistry or the imagination of the original, but it does have new technology: For those like McCarty who keep records of such things, this movie has the first close-up I can remember of a hypodermic needle being inserted into an eyeball. We see that twice. It mortifies the viewer nicely, just as scenes in Splatter Movies are supposed to do. There are a few other moments of passable originality, as when the killer disfigures the face of a beautiful woman by plunging her repeatedly into the scalding water of a whirlpool bath. But for the most part, *Halloween II* is a retread of *Halloween* without that movie's craft, exquisite timing, and thorough understanding of horror.

The movie begins just where the last one left off—with some of the same footage, indeed. The mysterious, invincible killer (who escaped from an institution earlier that Halloween day) has just tried to kill Jamie Lee Curtis. But Donald Pleasence, a psychiatrist who has decided the killer is literally inhuman, fires six bullets at close range. The killer is down, but not out. As the first movie ended, his body had disappeared. As this one opens, he's on the prowl again, still shuffling after screaming women at the same maddening slow pace.

The plot of *Halloween II* absolutely depends, of course, on our old friend the Idiot Plot which requires that everyone in the movie behave at all times like an idiot. That's necessary because if anyone were to use common sense, the problem would be solved and the movie would be over. So Jamie Lee Curtis and other young women consistently run into traps where the killer can corner them. In the first film, Jamie Lee locked herself in an upstairs closet. This time, it's a basement boiler room. The movie's other idiotic masterstroke comes when Curtis and a young kid are hiding in a car parked outside, and the kid slumps forward and honks the horn, revealing his hiding place. Inspired. The killer keeps coming. He's relentless. So is the movie. It uses the standard horror formula: Cause a false alarm, get a laugh, and then spring violence on the audience. You know how it works. The heroine opens a creaking door into a dark room and peers inside. A hand claps her on the shoulder. The audience screams. But whaddya know, it's only the friendly teen-age intern. Laughter. *Then* the killer strikes.

This can get monotonous. But since most of this movie takes place in a hospital, the killer has lots of props to work with. I've already mentioned the whirlpool bath and the needles. Another particularly nasty gimmick is the intravenous tube. The killer uses it to drain the blood from one of his victims. That's gruesome, but give the filmmakers credit. They use that gimmick to deliver the one scene I've been impatiently expecting for years and years in gore films: Finally, one of the characters kills himself by slipping on the wet blood and hitting his head on the floor. Sooner or later, it had to happen.

Halloween III ★ ½
R, 98 m., 1982

Tom Atkins (Dr. Challis), Stacey Nelkin (Ellie Grimbridge), Dan O'Herlihy (Conal Cochran), Ralph Strait (Buddy). Directed by Tommy Lee Wallace and produced by Debra Hill and John Carpenter. Screenplay by Wallace.

There are a lot of problems with *Halloween III*, but the most basic one is that I could never figure out what the villain wanted to accomplish if he got his way. His scheme is easy enough to figure: He wants to sell millions of Halloween masks to the nation's kiddies and then brainwash them to put them on at the same time, whereupon laser beams at the base of the neck will fry the tykes. Meanwhile, he runs a factory that turns out lifelike robots. What's his plan? Kill the kids and replace them with robots? Why?

A half-baked scheme like that feels right at home in *Halloween III*, which is a low-rent thriller from the first frame. This is one of those Identikit movies, assembled out of familiar parts from other, better movies. It begins at the end of *Halloween II*, when the monster was burned up in the hospital parking lot, but it's not still another retread of the invincible monster. In fact, the monster is forgotten, except for a lab technician who spends the whole movie sifting through his ashes. Instead, the plot follows the young daughter (Stacey Nelkin) of one of the victims, who ran a toy shop. She enlists the aid of a local doctor (Tom Atkins), and they retrace her father's steps back to an ominous toy factory run by Dan O'Herlihy. The factory has the whole town bugged and under surveillance, and the factory's guards are androids who crush their victims' heads with their hands.

Like a lot of horror movies in this age of self-conscious filmmaking, *Halloween III* is filled with references to other movies. The friendly motel owner in the company town, for example, is dressed as a dead ringer for Henry Fonda in *On Golden Pond*. The scene where the bugs and snakes crawl out of the crushed skull is a cross-reference, sort of, to *The Thing*—the last movie by John Carpenter, whose original *Halloween* was incomparably better than Parts II and III. But the funniest reference comes when the hero and heroine break into O'Herlihy's factory and are captured. Then the demented toymaker takes them on a tour of his facility, while explaining his diabolical scheme. He's got an obligatory underground mad scientist laboratory, and we know the approach by heart from all the James Bond movies: White-coated technicians scurry around with clipboards, while the boss arranges a demonstration of the weird method of killing that will soon be tried on our heroes. The funny part is that the underground lab is so cheesy. It consists of a few TV monitors on high-tech bookshelves and a papier-mâché mock-up of one of the stones from Stonehenge. (If you can figure out what Stonehenge has to do with this movie, you're smarter than anyone in it.) Next, there are lots of shots of the guy and girl running from O'Herlihy's henchmen. These are all obligatory shots where the man grabs the woman's hand and yanks her along, she of course being too dumb to run from danger on her own.(Cf. "Me-Push-Pull-You," in the Glossary.)

The one saving grace in *Halloween III* is Stacey Nelkin, who plays the heroine. She has one of those rich voices that makes you wish she had more to say and in a better role. But watch her, too, in the reaction shots: When she's not talking, she's listening. She has a kind of rapt, yet humorous, attention that I thought was really fetching. Too bad she plays her last scene without a head.

Hannah and Her Sisters ★ ★ ★ ★
PG-13, 107 m., 1985 ✓

Woody Allen (Mickey), Michael Caine (Elliot), Mia Farrow (Hannah), Carrie Fisher (April), Barbara Hershey (Lee), Lloyd Nolan (Hannah's Father), Maureen O'Sullivan (Hannah's Mother), Daniel Stern (Dusty), Max von Sydow (Frederick), Dianne Wiest (Holly). Directed by Woody Allen and produced by Robert Greenhut. Screenplay by Allen.

Woody Allen's *Hannah and Her Sisters*, the best movie he has ever made, is organized like an episodic novel, with acute self-contained vignettes adding up to the big picture.

Each section begins with a title or quotation on the screen, white against black, making the movie feel like a stately progression through the lives of its characters. Then the structure is exploded, time and again, by the energy and the passion of those characters: an accountant in love with his wife's sister, a TV executive who fears he is going to die, a woman whose cocaine habit has made her life a tightrope of fear, an artist who pretends to be strong but depends pitifully on his girlfriend.

By the end of the movie, the section titles and quotations have made an ironic point: We try to organize our lives according to what we have read and learned and believed in, but our plans are lost in a tumult of emotion.

The movie spans two years in the lives of its large cast of characters—New Yorkers who labor in Manhattan's two sexiest industries, art and money. It begins and ends at family Thanksgiving dinners, with the dinner in the middle of the film acting as a turning point for several lives.

It is hard to say who the most important characters are, but my memory keeps returning to Elliot, the accountant played by Michael Caine, and Lee, the artist's girlfriend, played by Barbara Hershey. Elliot is married to Hannah (Mia Farrow), but has been blind-sided with a sudden passion for Lee. She lives in a loft with the tortured artist Frederick (Max von Sydow), who treats her like his child or his student. He is so isolated from ordinary human contact that she is actually his last remaining link with reality.

Lee and Hannah have a third sister, Holly (Dianne Wiest). They form parts of a whole. Hannah is the competent, nurturing one. Lee is the emotional, sensuous earth mother. Holly is a bundle of tics and insecurities. When they meet for lunch and the camera circles them curiously, we sense that in some ways the movie knows them better than they will ever know themselves. And to talk about the movie that way is to suggest the presence of the most important two characters in the movie, whom I will describe as Woody Allen and Mickey.

Mickey is the character played by Allen; he is a neurotic TV executive who lives in constant fear of death or disease. He was married to Hannah at one time. Even after Hannah's marriage to Elliot, Mickey remains a member of the family, circling its security with a winsome yearning to belong.

The family itself centers on the three women's parents, played by Maureen O'Sullivan and Lloyd Nolan as an aging showbusiness couple who have spent decades in loving warfare over his cheating and her drinking and their mutual career decisions.

If Mickey is the character played by Woody Allen in the movie, Allen also provides another, second character in a more subtle way. The entire movie is told through his eyes and his sensibility; not Mickey's, but Allen's. From his earlier movies, especially *Annie Hall* and *Manhattan*, we have learned to recognize the tone of voice, the style of approach.

Allen approaches his material as a very bright, ironic, fussy, fearful outsider; his constant complaint is that it's all very well for these people to engage in their lives and plans and adulteries because they do not share his problem, which is that he sees through everything, and what he sees on the other side of everything is certain death and disappointment.

Allen's writing and directing style is so strong and assured in this film that the actual filmmaking itself becomes a narrative voice, just as we sense Henry James behind all of his novels, or William Faulkner and Iris Murdoch, behind theirs.

The movie is not a comedy, but it contains big laughs, and it is not a tragedy, although it could be if we thought about it long enough. It suggests that modern big-city lives are so busy, so distracted, so filled with ambition and complication that there isn't time to stop and absorb the meaning of things. Neither tragedy nor comedy can find a place to stand; there are too many other guests at the party.

And yet, on reflection, there is a tragedy buried in *Hannah and Her Sisters*, and that is the fact of Mickey's status as the perennial outsider. The others get on with their lives, but Mickey is stuck with his complaints. Not only is he certain there is no afterlife, he is very afraid that this life might also be a sham. How he ever married Hannah in the first place is a mystery; it must have been an intermediate step on his journey to his true role in life, as the ex-husband and hanger-on.

There is a scene in the movie where Michael Caine confronts Barbara Hershey and tells her that he loves her. She is stunned, does not know what to say, but does not categorically deny that she has feelings for him. After she leaves him, he stands alone on the street, ecstatic, his face glowing, saying "I've got my answer! I've got my answer!"

Underlying all of *Hannah and Her Sisters* is the envy of Mickey (and Woody) that anyone could actually be happy enough and lucky

enough to make such a statement. And yet, by the end of the movie, in his own way, Mickey has his answer, too.

Hardcore ★ ★ ★ ★
R, 106 m., 1979

George C. Scott (Jake VanDorn), Peter Boyle (Andy Mast), Season Hubley (Niki), Dick Sargent (Wes DeJong), Leonard Gaines (Ramada), David Nichols (Kurt), Gary Rand Graham (Tod), Larry Block (Burrows). Directed by Paul Schrader and produced by Buzz Feitshans. Screenplay by Schrader.

Hardcore is said to be the story of a father's search for a daughter who has disappeared into the underworld of pornography and prostitution. That does indeed describe its beginning and ending. But there are moments in between when it becomes something much more interesting: The story of a tentative, trusting human relationship between the father and the young prostitute he enlists in his search.

The man is played by George C. Scott, the girl by Season Hubley. They have moments in the movie when they talk, really talk, about what's important to them—and we're reminded of how much movie dialogue just repeats itself, movie after movie, year after year. There's a scene in *Hardcore* where the man (who is a strict Calvinist) and the prostitute (who began selling herself in her early teens) talk about sex, religion, and morality, and we're almost startled by the belief and simple poetry in their words.

This relationship, between two people with nothing in common, who meet at an intersection in a society where many have nothing in common, is at the heart of the movie, and makes it important. It is preceded and followed by another of those story ideas that Paul Schrader seems to generate so easily. His movies are about people with values, in conflict with society. He wrote *Taxi Driver* and *Rolling Thunder* and wrote and directed *Blue Collar*. All three are about people prepared to defend (with violence, if necessary) their steadfast beliefs.

The Scott character is a fundamentalist from Grand Rapids, Michigan—Schrader's own hometown. The opening scenes establish the family setting, at Christmas, with a fairly thick theological debate going on around the dinner table. (The small boy listening so solemnly, Schrader has said, can be taken for himself.) A few days later, Scott's daughter leaves home for a church rally in California. She never returns. Scott hires a private detective (Peter Boyle) to try to find her, and Boyle does find her—in an 8-millimeter porno movie. Can it be traced? Boyle says not: "Nobody made it. Nobody sold it. Nobody *sees* it. It doesn't exist."

But Scott vows to follow his daughter into the sexual underworld and bring her back. His efforts to trace her, through San Francisco and Los Angeles and San Diego, make *Hardcore* into a sneakily fascinating guided tour through massage parlors, whorehouses, and the world of porno movies. Schrader sometimes seems to be having it both ways, here: Scott is repelled by the sex scenes he explores, but is the movie?

That doesn't matter so much after he meets Niki (Season Hubley), who might know some people who might know where his daughter is. She is in many ways like all the other lost young girls who drift to California and disappear. But she has intelligence and a certain insight into why she does what she does, and so their talks together become occasions for mutual analysis.

She has a deep psychological need for a father figure, a need she thinks Scott can meet. She also has insights into Scott's own character, insights his life hasn't previously made clear to him. There's a scene near the waterfront in San Diego that perfectly illuminates both of their personalities, and we realize how rare it is for the movies to show us people who are speaking in real words about real things.

The movie's ending is a mess, a combination of cheap thrills, a chase, and a shootout, as if Schrader wasn't quite sure how to escape from the depths he found. The film's last ten minutes, in fact, are mostly action, the automatic resolution of the plot; the relationship between Scott and Hubley ends without being resolved, and in bringing his story to a "satisfactory" conclusion, Schrader doesn't speak to the deeper and more human themes he's introduced. Too bad. But *Hardcore*, flawed and uneven, contains moments of pure revelation.

Harlan County, U.S.A. ★ ★ ★ ★
PG, 103 m., 1976

A documentary directed and produced by Barbara Kopple.

One moment among many in *Harlan County, U.S.A.*: The striking miners are holding an all-day rally and picnic. A big tent has been pitched, and it's filled with people—some of them familiar to us by now, others new. There are speeches and songs and union battle cries, and then an old woman takes the microphone. The words she sings are familiar: *They say in Harlan County, there are no neutrals there. You'll either be a union man or a thug for Sheriff Blair.* And then the whole tent-full joins in the chorus: *Which side are you on?*

The woman who is leading the singing wrote the song fifty years ago, during an earlier strike in the county the miners call "Bloody Harlan." And here it is 1973, in a county where the right of workers to organize has presumably long since been won, and the song is not being sung out of nostalgia. It is being sung by striking coal miners in Harlan County, where it still applies.

That's the most uncomfortable lesson we learn in Barbara Kopple's magnificent documentary: That there are still jobs for scabs and strike breakers, that union organizers still get shot at and sometimes get killed, and that in Harlan County, Kentucky, it still matters very much which side you're on. And so a song we know best from old Pete Seeger records suddenly proves itself still frighteningly relevant.

The movie, which won the 1976 Academy Award for best feature-length documentary, was shot over a period of eighteen months in eastern Kentucky, after the miners at the Brookside mine voted to join the United Mine Workers. The Duke Power Company refused to sign the UMW contract, fought the strike, and was fought in turn by the miners and—most particularly—their wives.

Barbara Kopple and her crew stayed in Harlan County during that entire time, living in the miners' homes and recording the day-by-day progress of the strike. It was a tumultuous period, especially since the mine workers' union itself was deep in the midst of the Tony Boyle-Jock Yablonsky affair. But what emerges from the film is not just a document of a strike, but an affecting, unforgettable portrait of a community.

The cameras go down into the mines to show us the work, which is backbreaking, dirty, and brutal. We get to meet many of the miners, and to notice a curious thing about the older ones: They tend to talk little, as if their attentions are turned inward to the source of the determination that takes them back down the mine every day. Their wives, on the other hand, seem born to lead strikes. The film shows them setting up committees, organizing picket lines, facing (and sometimes reciprocating) violence, and becoming eloquent orators.

Ms. Kopple is a feminist, and her work includes *Year of the Women.* In *Harlan County,* though, she doesn't seem to have gone looking for examples of capable, competent, strong women: They were simply inescapable. There are talents, energies, and intelligences revealed in this film that could, if we would tap them, transform legislatures and bring wholesale quantities of common sense to public life. There are tacticians, strategists, and philosophers in *Harlan County, U.S.A.* who make the UMW theoreticians look tame—and the company spokesmen look callow and inane.

The movie is a great American document, but it's also entertaining; Kopple structures her material to provide tension, brief but vivid characterizations, and dramatic confrontations (including one incredibly charged moment when the sheriff attempts to lead a caravan of scabs past the picket line). There are gunshots in the film, and a death, and also many moments of simple warmth and laughter. The many union songs on the sound track provide a historical context, and also help Kopple achieve a fluid editing rhythm. And most of all there are the people in the film, those amazing people, so proud and self-reliant and brave.

Harold and Maude ★ ½
PG, 92 m., 1971

Ruth Gordon (Maude), Bud Cort (Harold), Vivian Pickles (Mrs. Chasen), Cyril Cusack (Glaucus), Charles Tyner (Uncle Victor), Ellen Geer (Sunshine Dare). Directed by Hal Ashby and produced by Colin Higgins and Charles Mulverhill. Screenplay by Higgins.

Death can be as funny as most things in life, I suppose, but not the way Harold and Maude go about it. They meet because they're both funeral freaks, and one day their eyes lock over a grave. They fall into conversation after Maude steals Harold's hearse and offers him a ride. Harold drives a hearse, by the way, because he is fascinated by death, particularly his own. So fascinated that maybe the only reason he doesn't kill himself is that suicide would put an end to his suicide fantasies. You can see that Harold is a young man with a problem.

Now Maude, on the other hand, is seventy-nine years young, and has what is known in the trade as a lust for life. She lives in a railroad car, spends her afternoons uprooting city trees and returning them to the forest, and in general is an all-round booster of the life force. She goes to funerals because there is a time to live and a time to die, and she wants to be on time.

The word has gotten out that *Harold and Maude* is the story of a love affair between these two people. It is not, so necrophiliacs please stay cool. It is about how Harold annoys (yes, annoys would be the word) his mother by staging a staggering variety of suicide attempts. Let's see. There's immolation, hanging, whacking off his arm with a meat cleaver, driving his car over a cliff, drowning, and if I missed one, never mind. But his mother is merely annoyed. She takes a morning dip in the swimming pool, for example, and when she comes upon Harold's body floating face down, she merely swims another lap. Talk about exercise freaks.

Harold's mother figures maybe what Harold needs is a little female companionship. She signs him up with a computer dating service, but the girls are sort of put off when he sets himself afire on their date, and things like that. Maude, on the other hand, doesn't seem to mind. As played by Ruth Gordon, she is the same wise-cracking operator out of the side of the mouth that we met in *Rosemary's Baby.* When a traffic cop stops her for being in possession of a stolen truck, a stolen car, and a stolen shovel, she apologizes and then drives away. When he catches up with her again, she steals his motorcycle. You see what an indomitable sort she is.

Harold is played by Bud Cort, the round-eyed and solemn-mouthed announcer over the PA system in $M*A*S*H$. He is even rounder and more solemn this time, having perfected a funeral droop of the lower lip. It is hard to get very much animation into a character who is obsessed with his own oblivion, but Cort doesn't even try.

And so what we get, finally, is a movie of attitudes. Harold is death, Maude life, and they manage to make the two seem so similar that life's hardly worth the extra bother. The visual style makes everyone look fresh from the Wax Museum, and all the movie lacks is a lot of day-old gardenias and lilies and roses in the lobby, filling the place with a cloying sweet smell. Nothing more to report today. Harold doesn't even make pallbearer.

Harry and Tonto ★ ★ ★ ★
PG, 115 m., 1974

Art Carney (Harry), Ellen Burstyn (Shirley), Chief Dan George (Indian), Geraldine Fitzgerald (Jessie). Directed and produced by Paul Mazursky. Screenplay by Mazursky and Josh Greenfield.

Paul Mazursky's *Harry and Tonto* tells the story of a feisty seventy-two-year-old who is carried forcibly from his New York apartment one step ahead of the wrecker's ball. He was happy with his life in the city (apart from the four muggings so far this year) and content to talk to his old cronies and to his cat, Tonto. But life without a home isn't easy. He goes for a while to live with his son on Long Island, where he's welcomed, sort of, into a household on the edge of insanity. One of his grandsons thinks the other one is crazy. The other won't respond because, you see, he has taken a vow of silence. Harry sizes up the situation, packs Tonto in a carrying case, and hits the road. The road becomes a strange and wonderful place for Harry, mostly because of his own resilient personality. He's played by Art Carney as a man of calm philosophy, gentle humor, and an acceptance of the ways people can be. He is also not a man in a hurry. When he can't carry Tonto onto an airplane, he takes the bus. When the bus can't wait for Tonto to

relieve himself, he buys a used car and picks up hitchhikers.

One of them is a young girl who becomes his friend. She talks of her life, and he talks of his, including his long-ago romance with a member of the Isadora Duncan troupe. The last he'd heard of her, she was living in Peru, Indiana, as the wife of a pharmacist. The girl talks him into stopping in Indiana and looking the old woman up. And he does so, in a scene of rare warmth and tenderness. The woman, Jessie (played by Geraldine Fitzgerald), has a very shaky memory, but she does recall being a dancer, and in the calm of the recreation room at her nursing home, the old couple dances together one last time.

And then Harry's back on the road to Chicago, where he has a daughter who runs a bookstore. He spends a few days with her, walking on the beach and talking things over. His silent grandson has broken his vow and flown to Chicago to try to talk the old man into coming back to New York. But, no, Harry doesn't think he will. ("You're talking now?" he asks his grandson. "Garbo speaks," the kid shrugs.)

He heads vaguely westward. His young hitchhiker has fallen in love with his grandson, and they think they'll aim for a commune in Colorado. Harry gives them a lift because that's more or less where he's going, but he declines, just now, to join the commune. He gives them his car, hitches a ride with a Las Vegas hooker, is (to his vast surprise) seduced by her, has a good time in Vegas, and, alas, is arrested for having a few too many.

This leads to the film's most hilarious scene. Harry is tossed into a cell already occupied by an ancient Indian (Chief Dan George) who has been arrested for practicing medicine without a license. The two old men gravely discuss recent television shows and the problem of bursitis, and the chief cures Harry's aching shoulder in return for an electric blender. Chief Dan George is so solemn, so understated, with Mazursky's dialogue that the result is a great comic scene.

Harry and Tonto drift on West toward the Pacific, and we begin to get the sense that this hasn't been your ordinary road picture, but a sort of farewell voyage by a warm and good old man who is still, at seventy-two, capable of being thankful for the small astonishments offered by life. The achievement is partly Mazursky's, partly Carney's.

Mazursky has established himself as the master of a kind of cinema he calls "serious comedy"—movies that make us laugh and yet have a special attitude toward their material and American society. His earlier films have included *Bob & Carol & Ted & Alice* and the remarkable *Blume in Love.*

Art Carney has, of course, fashioned a distinguished career for himself on the stage after all those years as Norton on "The Honeymooners." Here, he flowers as a movie star. The performance is totally original, all his own, and worthy of the Academy Award it received. It's not easy to make comedies that work as drama, too. But Carney's acting is so perceptive that it helps this material succeed.

Heart Beat ★ ★ ½
R, 109 m., 1980

Nick Nolte (Neal Cassady), Sissy Spacek (Carolyn Cassady), John Heard (Jack Kerouac). Directed by John Byrum and produced by Alen Greisman and Michael Shamberg. Screenplay by Byrum.

Jack Kerouac's novel *On the Road* announced an end to the Eisenhower years and the beginning of the narcissistic, rebellious sixties. It told the story of the first beatniks, those dropouts from the middle class who rode the highways from Maine to Mexico and raised hell, wrote poetry, loved unwisely, drank too well, and did the basic engineering on the life-style that would eventually be run to exhaustion by the hippies. Kerouac's novel starred a heroic proto-beat named Dean Moriarty, based on the legendary underground figure Neal Cassady. In *Heart Beat* we get the story of Neal and Jack and Neal's wife. Sort of.

The movie's based on a memoir written a few years ago by Carolyn Cassady, who was not one of the heroes of *On the Road,* and who, it now appears, had good reason to be less than enchanted with the beatnik lifestyle. The wives of famous men often have unique outlooks on their wonderful opportunities to live so close to greatness; when Bennett Cerf, visiting the James Joyces in Paris, described Joyce as a genius, Mrs. Joyce dryly replied, "That's all very well for *you* to say—*you* don't have to live with the bloody man." Carolyn Cassady's *Heart Beat* comes from the same fervent neighborhood of the soul.

But this movie is another matter altogether. How closely it resembles the facts I cannot say, but it paints a portrait of Jack and Neal as good buddies who drank, sang, hitchhiked, lied, and fought their way around the America of the late 1940s (Kerouac described himself and Cassady as "furtives"), and then both fell in love with Carolyn. She married Neal, who stayed at home, sometimes, between time on the road with Jack and a great deal of additional time spent on applied research into alcoholism. Jack was a drunk, too, and a lot of the movie deals with their attempts to patch things together in the little postwar suburban house in San Francisco where Carolyn tried to maintain a home.

This is not exactly the story we have in memory from the Kerouac legend, and there were long stretches of *Heart Beat* during which I found myself wishing instead for a film version of *On the Road.* That's unfair, I guess—but what is director John Byrum trying to do in *this* movie? I'm not sure. The movie's a triumph of art direction, all right; the locations, clothes, lighting, moods, music, and whole tones of the performances are designed to throw a kind of nostalgic drop cloth over the story, and we're constantly invited to read greater significance into dialogue and gestures because they took place during those now-lost times.

Fine, except that the significance doesn't seem to be there. *Heart Beat* seems to exist almost entirely as a matter of style. The characters are wonderfully well played by Nick Nolte, Sissy Spacek, and John Heard—they have scenes together in which the round-robin of everyday dialogue is almost poetic—but nobody has given their characters anything to do except to be. They exist, we watch them, the decor is inspired, that's it.

The attempts to add other characters from the period are mostly misguided. A character named Ira, inspired by Allen Ginsberg (who forbade use of his name), is so awkwardly drawn he comes off as a fifties' satire of a beatnik poet. Jazz musicians are so artfully "cool" they're paralytic. Jack and Neal move through the worlds of coffee houses and jazz clubs as if they were backdrops, not habitations.

What finally happens is that the whole period—the conformist fifties as well as the rebellious beats—gets frozen into the same flashback. *Everything* becomes part of the film's nostalgic memory. The film seems to treasure the conformity of American mainstream society if only because it provides such an ideal contrast to Neal and Jack. This movie treats its events as so long ago, so finished and done with and bathed in a yellowing afterglow, that we don't sense the very passion and rebelliousness it's supposed to be about. What an irony for the first serious film about the Beats.

Heartbreakers ★ ★ ★ ½
R, 98 m, 1985

Peter Coyote (Arthur Blue), Nick Mancuso (Eli Kahn), Carole Laure (Liliane), Max Gail (King), Carol Wayne (Cathy), James Laurenson (Terry Ray), Jamie Rose (Libby), Kathryn Harrold (Syd). Directed by Bobby Roth and produced by Bob Weis and Roth. Screenplay by Roth.

You can only play the field so long. Then you get stuck in it. You become a person so adept at avoiding commitment that it eventually becomes impossible for you to change your own rules, and so there you are, trapped in your precious freedom. Bobby Roth's *Heartbreakers* is about a group of people like that, a mixed bag of loners that includes a couple of artists, a businessman, a gallery owner, an aerobics instructor, and a model who specializes in telephone sex. During the course of a few weeks, their lives cross in ways that make it particularly hard for each one of them to deny his own unhappiness.

The movie stars Peter Coyote as an angry young artist and Nick Mancuso as his best friend, a businessman who is confused about women and a great many other things. They've been pals for a long time, through good times and bad, but the one thing they've never been able to do is break down and talk about what they're really feeling. During the course of the film, they both fall in love with a beautiful young woman (Carole Laure) who works in an art gallery,

and whose body is available but whose mind always seems to be somewhere else.

These three characters are in a movie populated with a lot of other interesting characters, the sort of mixed bag of people who find themselves thrown together in a big city like Los Angeles. Kathryn Harrold plays Coyote's long-time lover, who finally can't take his irresponsibility any longer and moves in with another artist (Charles King), who is big and powerful but surprisingly gentle—his character is developed against type, in interesting ways. Jamie Rose plays an aerobics instructor who is attracted to Mancuso, but he is attracted to Laure, although not in a way that is likely to get him anywhere.

All of the threads of these lives seem to come together during one long night that Mancuso and Coyote spend with the busty, mid-thirties blonde who models for Coyote's kinky paintings. She is played by Carol Wayne, who had regular walk-ons on the Johnny Carson program until she drowned in Mexico not long after completing her work on this movie. Her performance is so good, so heartbreaking, if you will, that it pulls the whole movie together; her character's willingness to talk about what she really feels places the other characters in strong contrast.

When we first see her, she's an enigma at the edge of the screen—a seemingly dumb blonde who dresses up in leather to model for Coyote's strange, angry paintings. Later, the two men, adrift and unhappy about their respective love lives, end up in her apartment, and what begins as a *ménage à trois* ends up as her own startlingly direct confessional. She makes a frank assessment of her body, her appearance, her prospects. She talks about what she hoped for from life, and what she has received. There is an uncanny feeling that, to some degree, we are listening here to the real Carol Wayne, the real person beneath the image on the Carson show. It is one of the best movie scenes in a long time.

The rest of the movie is also very good, in the way it examines the complex relationships in its Los Angeles world of art, sex, and business, and in the way it shows how arid the Mancuso-Coyote buddy relationship is. The people in this movie might seem glamorous if you glimpsed just a small corner of their lives. But *Heartbreakers* sees them whole, and mercilessly.

Heartland ★ ★ ★ ★
PG, 95 m., 1981

Conchata Ferrell (Elinore Randall), Rip Torn (Clyde Stewart), Barry Primus (Jack), Lilia Skala (Grandma), Megan Folsom (Jerrine). Directed by Richard Pearce and produced by Annick Smith, Michael Hausman, and Beth Ferris. Screenplay by Ferris.

Richard Pearce's *Heartland* is a big, robust, joyous movie about people who make other movie heroes look tentative. It takes place in 1910, out in the unsettled frontier lands of Wyoming, and it's about a determined young widow who packs up her daughter and moves out West to take a job as the housekeeper on a ranch. At first she is completely baffled by the rancher who has hired her ("I can't talk about anything with that man"), but in the end she marries him and digs in to fight an endless battle with the seasons, the land, and the banks.

A movie newcomer named Conchata Ferrell plays the widow, Elinore Randall. She's a big-boned, clear-eyed, wide-hipped woman of about thirty who makes us realize that most of the women in Westerns look as if they're about to collapse under the strain. She is extremely clear about her motivations. She gives a full day's work for a full day's pay, but she is tired of working for others, and would like to own her own land someday. She does not, however, speak endlessly about her beliefs and ambitions, because *Heartland* is a movie of few words. That is partly because of the character of Clyde Stewart (Rip Torn), the rancher she goes to work for. He hardly ever says anything. He is a hard man, a realist who knows that the undisciplined Western land can break his back. But he is not unkind, and in the scene where he finally proposes to marry her, his choice of words contains understated wit that makes us smile.

Everything in this movie affirms life. Perhaps that is why *Heartland* can also be so unblinking in its consideration of death. The American West was not settled by people who spent all their time baking peach cobbler and knitting samplers, and this movie contains several scenes that will shock some audiences because of their forthright realism. We see a pig slaughtered, a calf birthed, cattle skinned, and a half-dead horse left out in the blizzard because there is simply nothing to feed it.

All of *Heartland* is stunningly photographed on and around a Montana ranch. (The movie is based on the real life of a settler named Elinore Randall Stewart.) It contains countless small details of farming life, put in not for "atmosphere" but because they work better than dialogue to flesh out the characters. The desolation of the frontier is suggested in small vignettes, such as one involving a family that could get this far and no farther, and lives huddled inside a small wagon. Among the many scenes that delight us with their freshness is one moment right after the wedding, when Ferrell realizes she got married wearing her apron and work boots, and another when she is about to give birth and her husband rides off into the storm to fetch the midwife from the next farm. We settle back here in anticipation of the obligatory scene in which the midwife arrives and immediately orders everyone to boil hot water, lots of it—but this time we're surprised. The husband returns alone; the midwife was not at her farm. Quiet little developments like that help expose the weight of cliché that holds down most Westerns.

In a movie filled with wonderful things, the very best thing in *Heartland* is Conchata Ferrell's voice. It is strong, confident, clear as a bell, and naturally musical. It is a fine instrument, bringing authenticity to every word it says. It puts this movie to a test, because we could not quite accept that voice saying words that sounded phony and contrived. In *Heartland*, we never have to.

Heat and Dust ★ ★ ★
R, 130 m., 1983

Julie Christie (Anne), Zakir Hussain (Inder Lal), Greta Scacchi (Olivia), Shashi Kapoor (The Nawab). Directed by James Ivory and produced by Ismail Merchant. Screenplay by Ruth Prawer Jhabvala.

Forster suggested in *A Passage to India* that the subcontinent would forever be beyond the understanding of Western minds, and that attempts to impose European ways upon it were bound to be futile and likely to be ridiculous. *Heat and Dust* makes the same argument by telling us two love stories, one set in the 1920s, the other set in the present day.

The heroine of the earlier love story is Olivia Rivers (Greta Scacchi), a free spirit whose independent ways do not fit in with the hidebound values of the British. Her husband demands that she conform, that she stay with the other British wives, share their values and interests, and keep India itself at arm's length. Olivia does not see it that way. She explores on her own. She becomes fascinated by India. Eventually she has an affair with the local Nawab (Shashi Kapoor), who is beguiling, attractive, cheerfully sophisticated, and possibly a murderer. When she becomes pregnant with his child, the whole fabric of British-Indian relationships is torn, because—depending on the point of view—*both* of the lovers have lowered themselves.

The second love story involves Olivia's great-niece, Anne (Julie Christie). Fascinated by hints about the long-ago family scandal, she follows Olivia's footsteps out to India and does her own exploring and has her own affair. There comes a moment in the movie when we realize, with a little shock, what the movie is really about. It's an effective scene; soon after Anne arrives at a decision about her own pregnancy, she visits the isolated cottage where the disgraced Olivia went to spend her confinement.

As Anne dreamily moves among the memories of the past, we realize that India and England, the East and the West, are not quite the issues here: that both women were made social outcasts from both societies in two different periods, simply because of biological facts. East is East and West is West, and never the twain shall meet—except possibly in a shared enthusiasm for sexist double standards.

Heat and Dust contains wonderful sights and sounds and textures. It is seductive, treating both of its love stories with seriousness; these are not romances, but decisions to dissent. It is fully at home in its times and places (the director, James Ivory, and the producer, Ismail Merchant, have spent twenty years making films about the British in India). And when it is over, we're a little surprised to find that it is angry, too.

Angry that women of every class and every system, women British and Indian, women of the 1920s and of the 1980s, are always just not quite the same caste as men.

Heaven Help Us ★ ★ ½
R, 103 m., 1985

Andrew McCarthy (Michael Dunn), Mary Stuart Masterson (Danni), Kevin Dillon (Rooney), Malcolm Danare (Caesar), Donald Sutherland (Brother Thadeus), John Heard (Brother Timothy). Directed by Michael Dinner and produced by Don Wigutow and Mark Carliner. Screenplay by Charles Purpura.

If you remember those little clickers that the nuns used to use, you'll know why I liked the beginning of *Heaven Help Us* so much—and why I had such mixed feelings about the rest of it. The clickers were dime-store crickets that made a nice, loud click, perfect for signaling a First Communion class so all the kids would stand up at the same time, and kneel at the same time, and start filing down the aisle together. In an opening scene of the movie, a kid has his own clicker, and uses it to sabotage the nun's signals, so that the whole class is bobbing like a yo-yo. I thought that was funny, and I thought it set the tone for an affectionate, nostalgic, funny look back at Catholic school education in Brooklyn in the 1960s—sort of a cross between *Do Black Patent Leather Shoes Really Reflect Up?* and *Sister Mary Agnes Explains It All for You.* Unfortunately, what the movie turns into is more like a cross between *Stalag 17* and *Porky's,* as sadistic teachers beat every last glimmer of spirit out of students, and kids establish new indoor records in self-abuse.

Because *Heaven Help Us* does not have the slightest ambition to be a serious movie about Catholic high schools, I can't understand why the classroom scenes are so overplayed. As the sadistic teaching brother (Jay Patterson) slams his students against the blackboard, all we're really watching is a lapse in judgment by the moviemakers. The scenes are so ugly and depressing that they throw the rest of the movie out of balance. And that's too bad, because here and there in this movie are moments of real insight and memory. There's a special charm in the sweet, shy romance between a student (Andrew McCarthy) and the daughter (Mary Stuart Masterson) of the local soda fountain owner. I also liked the character named Caesar (Malcolm Danare), who pretends to be a snotty intellectual, as a defense against the heat he gets because he's smart.

The strange thing about the movie is the way the moments of inspiration raise our hopes, and then disappoint them. Take the scene where the school plays host to the nearby Catholic girls' school at a dance. The boys and girls are lined up on opposite sides of the room, and then an earnest little priest (Wallace Shawn, from *My Dinner with André*) stands up on the stage and delivers a lecture on "The Evils of Lust," gradually warming to his subject. The idea of the scene is funny, and it has a certain amount of underlying truth (I remember a priest once warning my class, "Never touch yourselves, boys"—without telling us where). But Shawn's speech climbs to such a hysterical pitch that it goes over the top, and the humor is lost; it simply becomes weird behavior.

Heaven Help Us has assembled a lot of the right elements for a movie about a Catholic boys' high school—the locations, the actors, and a lot of the right memories. But it has not found its tone. Maybe the filmmakers just never did really decide what they thought about the subject. For their penance, they should see *Rock and Roll High School*.

Heaven's Gate ½ ★
R, 220 m., 1981

Kris Kristofferson (Averill), Christopher Walken (Champion), John Hurt (Irvine), Sam Waterston (Canton), Brad Dourif (Eggleston), Isabelle Huppert (Ella), Joseph Cotten (Reverend Doctor), Jeff Bridges (John), Gordana Rashovich (Widow Kovach). Directed by Michael Cimino and produced by Joann Carelli. Screenplay by Cimino.

We begin with a fundamental question: Why is *Heaven's Gate* so painful and unpleasant to look at? I'm not referring to its content, but to its actual visual texture: This is one of the ugliest films I believe I have ever seen. Its director, Michael Cimino, opens his story at Harvard, continues it in Montana, and closes it aboard a ship. And yet a grim industrial pall hangs low over everything. There are clouds and billows of dirty yellow smoke in every shot that can possibly justify it, and when he runs out of smoke he gives us fog and such incredible amounts of dust that there are whole scenes where we can barely see anything. That's not enough. Cimino also shoots his picture in a maddening soft focus that makes the people and places in this movie sometimes almost impossible to *see*. And then he goes after the colors. There's not a single primary color in this movie, only dingy washed-out sepia tones.

I know, I know: He's trying to demystify the West, and all those other things hotshot directors try to do when they don't really want to make a Western. But this movie is a study in wretched excess. It is so smoky, so dusty, so foggy, so unfocused and so brownish yellow that you want to try Windex on the screen. A director is in deep trouble when we do not even enjoy the primary act of looking at his picture.

But Cimino's in deeper trouble still. *Heaven's Gate* has, of course, become a notorious picture, a boondoggle that cost something like $36 million and was yanked out of its New York opening run after the critics ran gagging from the theater. Its running time, at that point, was more than four hours. Perhaps length was the problem? Cimino went back to the editing room, while a United Artists executive complained that the film had been "destroyed" by an unfairly negative review by *New York Times* critic Vincent Canby. Brother Canby was only doing his job. If the film was formless at four hours, it was insipid at 140 minutes. At either length it is so incompetently photographed and edited that there are times when we are not even sure which character we are looking at. Christopher Walken is in several of the initial Western scenes before he finally gets a closeup and we see who he is. John Hurt wanders through various scenes to no avail. Kris Kristofferson is the star of the movie, and is never allowed to generate enough character for us to miss him, should he disappear.

The opening scenes are set at Harvard (well, they were actually shot in England, but never mind). They show Kristofferson, Hurt, and other idealistic young men graduating in 1870 and setting off to civilize a nation. Kristofferson decides to go West, to help develop the territory. He explains this decision in a narration, and the movie might have benefited if he'd narrated the whole thing, explaining as he went along. Out West, as a lawman, he learns of a plot by the cattlebreeders' association to hire a private army and assassinate 125 newly arrived European immigrants who are, it is claimed, anarchists, killers, and thieves. Most of the movie will be about this plot, Kristofferson's attempts to stop it, Walken's involvement in it, and the involvement of both Kristofferson and Walken in the private life of a young Montana madam (Isabelle Huppert).

In a movie where nothing is handled well, the immigrants are handled very badly. Cimino sees them as a mob. They march onscreen, babble excitedly in foreign tongues, and rush off wildly in all directions. By the movie's end, we can identify only one of them for sure. She is the Widow Kovach, whose husband was shot dead near the beginning of the film. That makes her the emblem of the immigrants' suffering. Every time she steps forward out of the mob, somebody respectfully murmurs "Widow Kovach!" in the subtitles. While the foreigners are hanging onto Widow Kovach's every insight, the cattlemen are holding meetings in private clubs and offering to pay their mercenaries $5 a day plus expenses and $50 for every other foreigner shot or hung. I am sure of those terms because they are repeated endlessly throughout a movie that cares to make almost nothing else clear.

The ridiculous scenes are endless. Samples: Walken, surrounded by gunmen and trapped in a burning cabin, scribbles a farewell note in which he observes that he is trapped in the burning cabin, and then he signs his full name so that there will be no doubt who the note was from. Kristofferson, discovering Huppert being gang-raped by several men, leaps in with six-guns in both hands and shoots all the men, including those aboard Huppert, without injuring her. In a big battle scene, men make armored wagons out of logs and push them forward into the line of fire, even though anyone could ride around behind and shoot them. There is more. There is much more. It all adds up to a great deal less. This movie is $36 million thrown to the winds. It is the most scandalous cinematic waste I have ever seen, and remember, I've seen *Paint Your Wagon*.

The Heavenly Kid ★
PG-13, 92 m., 1985

Lewis Smith (Bobby), Jason Gedrick (Lenny), Jane Kaczmarek (Emily), Richard Mulligan (Rafferty), Mark Metcalf (Joe), Beau Dremann (McIntyre). Directed by Cary Medoway and produced by Mort Engleberg. Screenplay by Medoway and Martin Copeland.

It's not the idea. It's what you do with the idea. Consider these two movie scenarios:

1. A teen-ager from the present makes friends with a mad scientist, who has invented a time-travel machine. The kid is transported back in time to the 1950s, where he meets his own parents when they were teen-agers, and tries to help his dad stop being a wimp. Life in the fifties looks weird to a 1980s teen-ager, but he's able to teach the kids a thing or two—including a hard-driving rock and roll guitar style.

2. A teen-ager from the 1950s dies and goes to Purgatory, where he makes friends with a weird old guy who runs everything. The old guy assigns the kid to a mission in the future. He is to return to Earth in the 1980s, to help a modern teen-age kid stop being a wimp. Life in the eighties looks weird to a 1950s teenager, but he's able to teach the kids a things or two—like how to customize an old Chevy, and wear black leather jackets and act cool.

If you were a motion picture executive, how would you choose between these two outlines? I'd toss a coin. But the first scenario became *Back to the Future*, one of the most successful 1985 releases. And the second one is *The Heavenly Kid*, a comedy of crushing idiocy, papered with clichés from wall to wall.

The movie stars Lewis Smith in the title role, as Bobby Fontana, a James Dean clone who dies in a game of chicken when he fails to get out of his car before it goes over a cliff. He wakes up in Purgatory, which is an endless subway loop with only one stop. It's got a café that claims "we never close." He believes it. An old guy (Richard Mulligan, who was Dudley Moore's boss in *Mickey and Maude*) tells him he has to earn the right to

"Uptown" by doing a good deed on earth. And the assignment is to be a friend to a hopeless wimp named Lenny (Jason Gedrick), who is the victim of all the bullies at school.

The heavenly kid comes down to earth and befriends Lenny by teaching him how to be a circa-1957 hood. He's gotta learn how to smoke, and how to pick up girls, and how to customize a Chevy convertible. Amazingly, Bobby's lessons work, and Lenny starts making progress. It might have been fun to take the other route, and show how obsolete Bobby's 1959 macho strategies seem in these liberated times, but this isn't a movie that wants to risk anything as complicated as irony.

The deadly thing about the movie is its absolute predictability. I like to be surprised in movies. I like it when the filmmakers put an extra spin on things, and show me a development I didn't expect. In *The Heavenly Kid*, we anticipate whole entire passages of dialogue. And the movie's big secret (the true identity of Lenny) will be a secret only for anyone who misses the movie's first two reels (which might not be a bad idea).

Maybe it's unfair to compare this film with *Back to the Future*. But psychologically, it's no wonder *Back to the Future* seems funnier than *The Heavenly Kid*. Average moviegoers are under twenty. What would seem funnier to them? A movie where today's teen-ager finds out how funny his parents were, or a movie where a teen-ager from their parents' generation finds out how funny today's teen-agers are? Case closed.

High Anxiety ★ ★ ½
PG, 92 m., 1978

Mel Brooks (Dr. Thorndyke), Madeline Kahn (Victoria Brisbane), Cloris Leachman (Nurse Diesel), Harvey Korman (Dr. Montague), Ron Carey (Brophy), Howard Morris (Professor Lillolman), Murphy Dunne (Piano Player), Ira Miller (Psychiatrist). Directed and produced by Mel Brooks. Screenplay by Brooks, Ron Clark, Rudy DeLuca, and Barry Levinson.

One of the problems with Mel Brooks's *High Anxiety* is that it picks a tricky target: It's a spoof of the work of Alfred Hitchcock, but Hitchcock's films are often funny themselves. And satire works best when its target is self-important. It's easy for the *National Lampoon* to take on the *Reader's Digest*. But can you imagine a satire *of* the *National Lampoon?*

Almost all of Hitchcock's fifty-three or so films have their great moments of wit. And wit—the ability to share a sense of subtle fun with an audience—is not exactly Mel Brooks's strong point. He takes such key Hitchcock moments as the shower scene from *Psycho*, the climbing scene from *Vertigo*, and the shooting in *North by Northwest* and he clobbers them. It's not satire; it's overkill. Maybe it wasn't such a hot idea for Brooks to spoof Hitchcock in the first place. What he's done, though, is to go ahead and take the Hitchcock material, and almost bury his own comic talent in the attempt to fit things into his satirical formula. The best moments in *High Anxiety* come not when Brooks is being assaulted in the shower with a rolled-up newspaper, but when Brooks leaves Hitchcock altogether and does his own crazy, brilliant stuff.

Take, for example, a moment when dramatic music overwhelms the sound track while Brooks and his chauffeur are driving down a Los Angeles freeway. They look at each other, puzzled, and then we see the Los Angeles Symphony Orchestra performing in a bus in the next lane. Sure, he's pulled the same gag before (Count Basie turning up in the desert in *Blazing Saddles)*, but it still works. Another Brooks specialty that works again this time is the casting of Cloris Leachman in variations of a neo-Nazi sadist. In *Young Frankenstein*, she was Frau Blucher, whose very name made horses whinny with fright. Now she's Nurse Diesel, sinister presence at the Institute for the Very, *Very* Nervous, where Brooks has been hired as the new director. She has a closet full of whips and chains, and walks around as if her nurse's uniform covered a cast-iron corset. It's funny . . . but because it comes from Brooks and Leachman, not because it has much to do with Hitchcock.

Here's an example of why Hitchcock is so spoof-proof. At the end of *High Anxiety*, a victim dangles from the top of a tower for what seems like minutes on end, hanging at times by a single leg. Brooks is having fun with the way Hitchcock plays with his scenes of climactic violence. Fine. But remember

Hitchcock's wonderful 1972 movie *Frenzy?* There's that strangling in it that goes on and on and on, played very straight, until we finally realize that Hitchcock is slyly giving us our money's worth by playing with the scene beyond all the possibilities of realism.

Brooks has made a specialty of movie satires: *Blazing Saddles, Young Frankenstein,* and *Silent Movie.* But they took on well-chosen targets. It's one thing to kid the self-conscious seriousness of a Western or a horror movie. It's another to take on a director of such sophistication that half the audience won't even get the in-jokes the other half is laughing at.

High Road to China ★ ★
PG, 107 m., 1983

Tom Selleck (O'Malley), Bess Armstrong (Eve), Jack Weston (Struts), Wilford Brimley (Bradley Tozer), Robert Morely (Bentik). Directed by Brian G. Hutton and produced by Fred Weintraub. Screenplay by Sandra Weintraub Roland and S. Lee Rogostin.

Word has it that Tom Selleck was Steven Spielberg's first choice for the lead in *Raiders of the Lost Ark,* and that Harrison Ford got the job at the last minute. I wonder if that left Selleck walking around frustrated, still wanting to play someone like Indiana Jones. That would be one explanation for *High Road to China,* an unconvincing, harmless action movie that at its best is a pale echo of *Raiders.* The movie stars Selleck as a freelance pilot who gives flying lessons at a field outside Istanbul. The year is 1920. The movie never pauses to explain how he finds enough customers to support himself by giving lessons in Turkey in 1920. It's too busy introducing Selleck to Bess Armstrong, a plucky American rich kid who has to prove that her daddy is alive or lose an inheritance of millions. Armstrong hires Selleck and his sidekick, Jack Weston, to fly off in the general direction of Tibet, where she thinks her father might be running a border war.

Well, that's the premise. What we get then is a series of more-or-less predictable scenes in which our heroes fly over mountains and deserts, sit by campfires, barely escape from the clutches of hostile Arabs, Turks, Tartars, and Mongolians, and eventually find her father. He's played by the wonderful char-acter actor Wilford Brimley. (He played the federal attorney who came in and settled everybody's hash in the climactic scenes of *Absence of Malice.*) And he's masterminding the defense of a Tibetan hill town against the onslaughts of the barbarians below.

There has to be conflict in a movie like this, and so, of course, there is. Selleck and Armstrong start out hating each other. She gets one of his planes destroyed. Jack Weston has to stay behind. Selleck and Armstrong fly off together, have some close calls, and eventually fall in love. The movie gives them a lot of time to exchange wisecracks, tender and otherwise, and then they get to play one of my all-time favorite obligatory scenes. I call it the We're Alive! Let's Kiss! Scene. You've seen it in a hundred movies. It always starts with the hero and heroine up on their elbows in a shallow ditch. People are shooting at them. A bullet throws up a cloud of dirt, inches from their faces. They tumble down for cover, wind up in each other's arms, and zowie! All those repressed passions explode, and we realize (with well-concealed surprise) that their wisecracks disguised a growing love. Every movie star should play this scene at least once, at the most.

High Road to China is not a terrible movie, but it's a lifeless one. It follows some of the forms of *Raiders of the Lost Ark* without ever finding the comic rhythms. It's directed at a nice, steady pace, but without flair and without the feeling that anything's being risked. And it tells such an absolutely standard story that we never fear for the characters and we hardly ever believe them.

History of the World—Part I ★ ★
R, 90 m., 1981

Mel Brooks (Moses, Comicus, Torquemada, Jacques, Louis XVI), Dom DeLuise (Nero), Madeline Kahn (Empress Nympho), Harvey Korman (Count De Monet), Cloris Leachman (Madame Defarge), Ron Carey (Swiftus), Mary-Margaret Humes (Miriam). Directed and produced by Mel Brooks. Screenplay by Brooks.

Mel Brooks's movie *History of the World—Part I* is a rambling, undisciplined, sometimes embarrassing failure from one of the most gifted comic filmmakers around. What went wrong? Brooks never seems to have a clear idea of the rationale of his movie—so there's no confident narrative impetus to carry it along. His "history" framework doesn't have an approach or point of view; it's basically just a laundry-line for whatever gags he can hang on it.

What *is* this bizarre grab bag? Is it a parody of old Biblical, Roman, and French historical epics? Sometimes. Is it one-shot, comedy revue blackouts? Sometimes. Is it satire aimed at pompous targets? Sometimes. But most of the time it's basically just expensive sets sitting around waiting for Brooks to do something funny in front of them.

Brooks seems to rely on his own spontaneous comic genius in this film, and genius, even when you have it, is not something to be relied upon. He provides isolated moments that are indeed hilarious, moments that find an inspired image and zing us with it (as when a slave boogies through the streets of ancient Rome with a loud transistor radio glued to his ear). But as the movie creeps on, we realize that the inspirations are going to be rare, and that Brooks has not bothered to create a framework for the movie or to people it with characters. It's all just cardboard comic cutouts.

The film has another serious problem: It is in unfunny bad taste. That sounds strange coming from me. I've always enjoyed Brooks's ventures into taboo subject matter, and I still think his "Springtime for Hitler" from *The Producers* and the celebrated campfire scene in *Blazing Saddles* were hilarious. He seemed to be demonstrating that you could get away with almost anything in a movie, if you made it funny enough. (Told that *The Producers* was vulgar, he once responded loftily, "It rises *below* vulgarity.") But this time, the things he's trying to get away with aren't funny. There is, for example, the movie's tiresome series of jokes about urination. There must be comic possibilities in the subject (and he finds one when he shows a Stone Age critic's method of reviewing a cave painting), but there is nothing inherently funny about urination, and Brooks proves it here, again and again.

There also is nothing inherently funny about Jews, Catholics, nuns, blacks, and gays. They can all conceivably provide the makings of comedy, of course, but in *History*

of the World Brooks doesn't have the patience to introduce a character and then create a comic situation *about* him. He introduces the character and expects us to laugh at the character himself. Example. Instead of developing a comic situation around Orthodox Jews, he simply shows us some, complete with beards and hats, their heads stuck through a stockade, and expects us to laugh. But while we might laugh with Brooks at a comic situation, we have no reason to laugh *at* people just because of their appearance or religion.

The same thing goes wrong with Brooks's big production number in this movie, "The Inquisition," featuring a song-and-dance team of medieval monks, and a chorus line of nuns who splash in a pool, Busby Berkeley-style. We're supposed to laugh at the shocking juxtaposition of religious images and Hollywood corn. But Brooks never gives us an additional comic level, one where he's making funny points about the images. When he dresses up like a monk and then dances like Donald O'Connor, that's only funny for a second. If we knew anything about the monk as a comic character, the scene could build. Instead, it just continues.

History of the World—Part I was fairly expensive to produce, but it exists on the level of quick, disposable, television. It thumbs its nose at icons that have lost their taboo value for most of us, and between the occasional good laughs, we're a little embarrassed that the movie is so dumb and predictable. God knows Mel Brooks is straining for yuks up there on the screen, but he's like the life of the party who still has the lampshade on his head when everybody else is ready to go home.

The Hitcher   no stars
R, 98 m., 1985

C. Thomas Howell (Jim Halsey), Rutger Hauer (John Ryder), Jennifer Jason Leigh (Nash). Directed by Robert Holman and produced by Kip Oham. Screenplay by Eric Red.

The Hitcher begins and ends with the same sound, of a match being struck and flaring into flame. At the beginning of the film, the sound is made by the villain, a hitchhiker who is a mass-murderer. At the end of the film, the sound is made by the hero, a young man whose life has been spared so that he can become the special victim of the hitchhiker. The movie seems to be telling us, by the use of the sounds and in several other ways, that the killer and the hero have developed some kind of deep bond through their experiences together. The victim's identification with his torturer is not a new phenomenon. In many of the hostage cases in recent years, some of the captives have adopted the viewpoints of their jailers. What is particularly sick about *The Hitcher* is that the killer is not given a viewpoint, a grudge, or indeed even a motive. He is deliberately presented as a man without a past, without a history, who simply and cruelly hurts and kills people. Although he spares the movie's young hero, he puts him through a terrible ordeal, framing him as a mass murderer and trapping him in a Kafkaesque web of evidence, until even the hero himself despairs of getting anyone to tell his story.

At the end of the movie, there is of course a scene of vengeance, in which the two men meet in final combat. And yet this showdown does not represent a fight between good and evil, because the movie suggests—and one of the characters even says—that there is something weird going on between the two men. The implication is that they have formed some kind of half-acknowledged sadomasochistic relationship. The death of the villain is not the hero's revenge, but the conclusion that the villain has been setting up for himself all along.

This unhealthy bond between the young hero (played by C. Thomas Howell) and the older killer (the cold-eyed Rutger Hauer) is developed in a movie which proves a horrible fate for its only major female character. As Howell flees down desert highways from the violence of Hauer, he is befriended by a young waitress (Jennifer Jason Leigh). She believes that he is innocent, and goes on the run with him. But the movie does not develop into a standard story of teen-agers in love.

The Howell character scarcely seems to notice Leigh as a human being; of course, he has a great deal else on his mind. She wants to sleep with him one night, but the scene is only a set-up for a later scene in which Hauer slips into her bed. And her death—she is tied hand and foot between two giant trucks and pulled in two—is so grotesquely out of proportion with the main business of this movie that it suggests a deep sickness at the screenplay stage.

There are other disgusting moments, as when a police dog feasts on the blood dripping from its master's neck, or when Howell finds a human finger in his french fries. Nothing else quite betrays the cynicism of this movie, however, as the scene in which Jennifer Jason Leigh and Howell are being chased by a helicopter, which is shot down in flames by Hauer. This scene takes on a grisly double meaning when you reflect that Leigh is the daughter of Vic Morrow, the actor who died in a tragic helicopter stunt gone wrong.

The Hitcher grants the Hauer character almost supernatural powers; he always seems to anticipate what Howell will do next. Although that makes the movie impossible to accept on a realistic level, it didn't bother me. I could see that the film was meant as an allegory, not a documentary. But on its own terms, this movie is diseased and corrupt. I would have admired it more if it had found the courage to acknowledge the real relationship it was portraying between Howell and Rutger, but no: It prefers to disguise itself as a violent thriller, and on that level it is reprehensible.

The Home and the World ★ ★ ★
NO MPAA RATING; 130 m., 1986 ✔

Soumitra Chatterjee (Sandip), Victor Banerjee (Nikhil), Swatilekha Chatterjee (Bimala), Gopa Aich (Sister-in-law), Jennifer Kapoor (Miss Gilly). Directed by Satyajit Ray and produced by the National Film Development Corporation of India. Screenplay by Ray.

The very first thing we learn in Satyajit Ray's *The Home and the World* is that Bimala, his heroine, has exchanged the home of her parents for the home of her husband, in the inner apartments of his Bengal palace. She lives in *purdah*, the Hindu custom of cloistering women. Nikhil, the maharaja who is her husband, is the only man she has ever seen. She saw him first on their wedding day. She is content with her life and has no desire to walk down the long corridor, bathed in sunlight falling through stained glass, that leads to the outer apartments and then to the world.

But her husband has other ideas. The year is 1908, and he is a modern Indian who has been educated in England. His wife loves him, but he reasons that her love is meaningless if she cannot compare him with other men. At his wish, she begins to take lessons from an English governess, and after ten years, she takes the momentous walk down that corridor to the outside.

Nikhil wants her to meet his best friend, Sandip, a charismatic nationalist leader who is staying as a guest in the palace. Sandip is leading a boycott against traders who sell imported goods; he is opposed to the British policy of dividing Bengal and setting Hindu against Moslem. He also is something of a fraud who borrows money from Nikhil and soon begins to borrow the affections of his wife.

Bimala is swept away by Sandip. His passion and his politics are a contrast to her quiet, passive husband. His compliments overwhelm her. They do not exactly have an affair, not by Western standards—their first kiss comes after years of mounting romantic tension—but it is clear to everyone, even Nikhil, that the two of them are in love.

Nikhil does nothing. He is an intelligent, reasonable man who sees everything in the light of such quiet reason that action seems almost beyond him. For example, although he is content to have Sandip, the revolutionary, live in his palace, he opposes most of Sandip's policies. He knows that the traders in foreign goods are mostly Moslems, very poor, and that the boycott will only serve to drive a wedge between the two communities. Yet he stands by while Sandip makes speeches and leads parades.

The real story of the movie takes place, meanwhile, within Bimala's heart and mind. Over a period of years, she grows out of the restraints of *purdah*, but her formative years were all spent in seclusion, and only gradually does she find the confidence to act according to her beliefs. She is totally taken in by the charming Sandip. She even takes money from her husband's safe to feed Sandip's taste for first-class travel. And all the time her husband stands by, his detachment becoming one of the fascinations of the movie.

The Home and the World is based on a novel of the same name by the Hindu writer Rabindranath Tagore, a Nobel Prize winner. Satyajit Ray, the greatest Indian director, was a young man when he first wrote a screenplay based on the novel, but it has taken him thirty-five years to film it. It is a contemplative movie—quiet, slow, a series of conversations punctuated by sudden bursts of activity.

The suspense in the movie and the drama all form around the changing character of Bimala, the wife. We see her move from total seclusion to the ability to act recklessly and with courage. The character is played by Swatilekha Chatterjee, a gravely beautiful, full-figured woman, whose eyes are able to suggest great passions inside a cautious exterior.

The radical leader is played by Soumitra Chatterjee, a veteran of Ray's films all the way back to the Apu Trilogy, and the husband is played by Victor Banerjee, who was so different—so excitable and brash—as Dr. Aziz in David Lean's *A Passage to India*. Together, they form a small group of ideas and emotions, growing and shifting, mirroring in their secluded chambers the violent changes in India.

Honkytonk Man ★ ★ ★
PG, 123 m., 1982

Clint Eastwood (Red Stovall), Kyle Eastwood (Whit), John McIntire (Grandpa), Alexa Kenin (Marlene), Verna Bloom (Emmy). Directed and produced by Clint Eastwood.

Clint Eastwood produced and directed *Honkytonk Man*, and stars in it as a Depression-era loser who drifts through the South with his young nephew, aiming eventually to get to Nashville and maybe get on the Grand Ol' Opry. The movie's credits say the screenplay is by Clancy Carlile, based on his own novel, but in speculating on what drew Eastwood to this project, I came across this entry in Ephraim Katz's *Film Encyclopedia:*

"Eastwood, Clint. Actor, director. Born on May 31, 1930, in San Francisco. A child of the Depression, he spent his early boyhood trailing a father who pumped gas along dusty roads all over the West Coast . . ."

The entry goes on to list the usual odd jobs (logger, steel-furnace stoker) that all actors seem to hold down on their way to stardom, but I'd read enough to support my intuition that *Honkytonk Man* means a lot to Eastwood in ways that may not be immediately apparent. This is a sweet, whimsical, low-key movie, a movie that makes you feel good without pressing you too hard. It provides Eastwood with a screen character who is the complete opposite of the patented Eastwood tough guys and provides a role of nearly equal importance for his son, Kyle, as a serious, independent and utterly engaging young nephew named Whit. What happens to them on the road is not quite as important in this movie as what happens between them.

The movie starts with Eastwood drunk behind the wheel of a big 1930s touring car, knocking over the windmill on his latest return to the old homestead. He's sort of a Hank Williams type. His family has seen this act before. They put him to bed and hide the bottle. The next day, with an ominous cough, Eastwood talks about his dream of heading for Nashville and cashing in some old IOUs. He's a singer and a songwriter, luckless but not untalented, and he thinks he could make it onto the Opry. He wants to take the kid along. After some hesitation, the kid's mother (Verna Bloom) agrees, mostly because she hopes her son can ride herd on Eastwood and keep him reasonably sober. She makes her son promise not to drink or fool around with women (thus putting her finger unerringly on one thing he did the night before, and another that he hopes to do as soon as possible). Old grandpa (John McIntire) also decides to go along for the ride; he's got some people in Tennessee he hasn't seen in forty years.

The road part of the picture is picaresque, photographed through a haze of romance and nostalgia, and spiced up with a visit to a gambling house and an encounter with a very individualistic young woman (Alexa Kenin) who also decides to join the traveling party. She has an amazing gift for couching the most ordinary sentiments in romantic prose. The movie's best scenes are the ones Eastwood plays in Nashville, during an audition at the Opry and, later, in a recording studio. He sings his songs with the kind of bone-weariness that doesn't hurt the right kind of country song, and there's a special

moment in the studio when a supporting musician lends a hand. The movie turns out to be about realizing your dreams after all, which is sort of a surprise in a story where even the high points are only bittersweet.

This is a special movie. In making it, Eastwood was obviously moving away from his Dirty Harry image, but that's nothing new; his spectacular success in violent movies tends to distract us from his intriguing and challenging career as the director and star of such offbeat projects as *Bronco Billy* and *Play Misty For Me.* He seems to have a personal stake in this story, and we begin to feel it, too. Sometimes the simplest country songs are just telling the facts.

Howling II ★
R, 91 m., 1986

Sybil Danning (Stirbà), Christopher Lee (Stefan), Annie McEnroe (Jenny), Reb Brown (Ben), Marsha A. Hunt (Mariana), Judd Owen (Vlad). Directed by Philippe Mora and produced by Steven Lane. Screenplay by Robert Sarno and Gary Brandner.

There is a moment in *Howling II* when Sybil Danning and two other werewolves revert to their native state. Fangs grow from their mouths, their nails turn into claws, and they are covered with fur. Then they have a *ménage à trois,* snarling and snapping at each other and raking each other with their claws, in what must be the most unintentionally funny movie scene of the week.

You do not see scenes like this in other movies. You do not see a lot of well-known actresses appearing in them. Let us therefore speak in praise of Sybil Danning. I have interviewed her three times, and have always found her with one of the best senses of humor in Hollywood. She appears in movies like this for the money, of course, but also (I suspect) because she laughs out loud when she reads the scripts.

I'd like to check out Danning's closets at home. If they let her keep the costumes from her movies, I'll bet she has quite a collection. For example, the cloak that Lou Ferrigno made her wear in *Hercules and the Seven Gladiators,* because her muscles were distracting from his. Or the Rambo gear she wears in the intros to her "Adventure Video" series.

From this movie alone, not counting the wolf fur, there's her Flash Gordon outfit, with the low-cut bronze breastplates and the pushup armor. And then there's the slightly more formal leather gear she wears to receive Christopher Lee, who has come to do battle with her. It's only suitable, of course, to dress up for Christopher Lee, who has been in so many vampire and werewolf movies that a Hollywood traffic cop once pulled him over and asked him if he should be driving in the daylight.

In *Howling II*, which is not the worst movie Danning has made (though it is close), she plays Stirba, bisexual queen witch of Transylvania. There have been a lot of versions of Transylvania in the movies, but check this one out: Transylvania consists of a special effects drawing of a castle on a hill, and a single street set showing some painted backdrops, a few doors, and what looks like an ethnic food fair—the Taste of Transylvania.

Into this dread kingdom, on what is described as "The Feast of a New Full Moon," venture the heroes of the movie. There's Christopher Lee as the expert werewolf-killer, and Reb Brown as the brother of a TV anchorwoman who turned into a werewoman during a newscast, grew fur and fangs and attacked a cameraman. This was, of course, a great tragedy for the TV station. It didn't take place during one of the Nielsen ratings sweep periods.

Anyway, once the heroes have arrived in Transylvania, they get involved in the strange rituals of the cult of Stirba. Although the rituals, like the rest of the movie, are impenetrable and amazingly inept (a werewolf movie is not, after all, the hardest thing in the world to make), I have to concede that no one presides over a ritual quite as well as Sybil Danning, especially when she is savagely ripping open the bodice of her dress. She rips the dress so dramatically, in fact, that the shot is repeated twice during the closing credits, providing the movie with its second and third interesting moments.

The Hunger ★ ½
R, 100 m., 1983

Catherine Deneuve (Miriam), David Bowie (John), Susan Sarandon (Sarah), Cliff De Young (Tom). Directed by Tony Scott. Screenplay by Ivan Davis and Michael Thomas.

The Hunger is an agonizingly bad vampire movie, circling around an exquisitely effective sex scene. Sorry, but that's the way it is, and I have to be honest. The seduction scene involves Catherine Deneuve, as an age-old vampire, and Susan Sarandon, as her latest victim. There was a great deal of controversy while the movie was being made (all sorts of rumors about closed sets, etc.), but the scene as it now appears isn't raunchy or *too* explicit—just sort of dreamily erotic. I mention the scene so prominently because it's one of the few scenes that really work in *The Hunger*, a movie that has been so ruthlessly overproduced that it's all flash and style and no story. Well, there's probably a story moping about somewhere within all the set decoration. It seems to involve Deneuve as a vampire of vaguely Egyptian origins, whose latest partner (David Bowie) is giving out on her after three or four centuries.

After an initial orgy of fancy camerawork, the movie settles down into the story of Bowie's final days. He has that chronic vampire disease where you age suddenly. He needs a lot of blood to keep going. He appeals to a medical researcher (Sarandon) for help, but she brushes him off, and by the time she realizes he's serious, he looks like Methuselah. Then Sarandon visits the lavish town house where Deneuve and Bowie live, and that's where a glass of sherry leads to the seduction scene.

I've got to be honest about this scene. Part of its interest lies in the fact that Catherine Deneuve *herself*, and Susan Sarandon *herself*, are acting in the scene. That gives it a level of reality that would be lacking in a porno film, even a much more explicit one. Because we know that famous actresses don't usually agree to appear in scenes such as this, we're aware of the chance they're taking—and the documentary reality of the scene gives it an effectiveness all its own. Deneuve, of course, has made a career out of the contrast between her cool, perfect beauty and the strange, erotic predicaments her characters get involved in. (Remember *Belle de Jour?*) Sarandon's scene by the window in *Atlantic City*, bathing herself with lemons, created great sultriness. But *The Hunger* approaches its big scene on an altogether different level, with understatement, awkward little pauses in conversation, and a canny awareness of our own curiosity about whether Deneuve and Sarandon really will go ahead with this scene, or whether the director will cut away to the usual curtains blowing in the wind.

Well, he doesn't, but it's about the only time in the whole movie there aren't curtains blowing in the wind. This movie has so much would-be elegance and visual class that it never quite happens as a dramatic event. There's so much cross-cutting, so many memories, so many apparent flashbacks, that the real drama is lost—the drama of a living human being seduced into vampirism. In Herzog's *Nosferatu*, we felt some of the blood-scented lure of eternal death-in-life. Here, it's just—how would an ad put it?—Catherine Deneuve for Dracula.

I Never Promised You a Rose Garden
★ ★ ★
R, 90 m., 1977

Kathleen Quinlan (Deborah), Bibi Andersson (Dr. Fried), Ben Piazza (Mr. Blake), Lorraine Gary (Mrs. Blake), Michael McGuire (McPherson), Reni Santoni (Hobbs), Susan Tyrrell (Kitty), Robert Viharo (Anterrabae). Directed by Anthony Page and produced by Terence F. Deane, Daniel H. Blatt, and Michael Hausman. Screenplay by Gavin Lambert and Lewis John Carlino.

I'm becoming suspicious of movies that assure us mental illness can be cured if the victim "wants" to be cured, or assume that mental illness is not illness at all—because in an insane world the only sane people are the crazies. *I Never Promised You a Rose Garden* doesn't altogether avoid the first assumption, but it firmly rejects the second, and it gives us a heroine so convincingly real we finally believe perhaps she *could* cure herself.

The heroine is well known to the millions of readers of Joanne Greenberg's novel, which began as a cult paperback and became a durable bestseller. She is Deborah, sixteen, schizophrenic, child of an affluent home,

but inhabitant of a personal fantasy. After a suicide attempt, she spends three years in a mental institution, coming close to self-destruction more than once, but finally surviving through her own efforts and those of a psychiatrist who really attempts to understand her.

We are given only sketchy information about what drove her to attempt suicide— her parents didn't understand her, she's filled with guilt because she believes she tried to kill a younger sister—but her fantasies are shown in much greater detail. As visualized in the film, they seem to be inspired by the paintings of Frank Frazetta: A race of muscular young people, clothed in furs and feathers, ride giant horses across the desert and want her to join them.

This alternative universe is so much more romantic and seductive than the real world, which for Deborah becomes Ward D of the mental institution. It's a women's ward, filled with the "worst" cases. Some of the patients do indeed seem to be totally within their private hells, but others (like the loud and often cheerful Kitty) have a reservoir of common sense. Deborah is wary, here, and often silent; she's properly afraid of the sinister male attendant Hobbs, but the turning point in her cure comes when she can admit of the other attendant, McPherson: "I like him. He treats me like I'm a real person." That touch of reality from outside is the first crack in the totality of her fantasies.

The psychiatrist is Dr. Fried, played by Bibi Andersson with sympathy and fortitude: She listens, encourages, supports, suggests, doesn't push. And over a period of three years Deborah is finally able to open herself to the world outside her dreams, to send her phantom gods galloping out into the desert without her.

I Never Promised You a Rose Garden has been compared, of course, to *One Flew Over the Cuckoo's Nest*, which first defied a kind of unwritten Hollywood superstition. That superstition was that movies about mental illness wouldn't succeed at the box office, that they were too depressing. *Cuckoo's Nest* wasn't filmed for years because of that taboo, and *Rose Garden* probably couldn't have been made if it hadn't been for *Cuckoo's Nest*'s great success.

One big difference between the two

movies is that R.P. McMurphy, in *Cuckoo*, was, in fact, sane. Deborah is not. *Cuckoo* celebrates McMurphy's cosmic sanity, and so has room for the dimensions of Jack Nicholson's manic performance. *Rose Garden* celebrates, instead, very small victories (and one of its most poignant moments comes when Deborah, burning herself with a cigarette, realizes with triumph that she actually feels pain—that her mind has let the reality in).

This is difficult material to bring to life, but a young actress named Kathleen Quinlan does it with heart and sensitivity. There were opportunities here for climbing the walls and chewing the scenery, I suppose, but her performance always finds the correct and convincing human note.

And it's the skill with which Miss Quinlan (and Bibi Andersson) follow that thread of characterization that makes the movie work. Otherwise, those desert fantasies and all those feathers and fur might have been fatally distracting. But because Deborah seems to regard them with a sober fatalism, we can almost accept them; and because she never expresses any emotions that don't seem to grow right out of the situations she finds herself in, we always accept her.

I Never Sang for My Father ★ ★ ★ ★
PG, 92 m., 1971

Melvyn Douglas (Tom), Gene Hackman (Gene), Dorothy Stickney (Margaret), Estelle Parsons (Alice, The Sister), Elizabeth Hubbard (Peggy). Directed and produced by Gilbert Cates. Screenplay by Robert Anderson.

At the beginning and again at the end of *I Never Sang for My Father*, we see a grainy snapshot of an old man and a middle-aged man, arms thrown about each other's shoulders, peering uncertainly into the camera as if they're not quite sure what drew them out into the sunshine to pose this day. And we hear Gene Hackman's voice: "Death ends a life. But it does not end a relationship." This film takes that simple fact and uses it to make a poignant and ultimately tragic statement about parents and children, life and death, and all the words that go unspoken. The man is played by Melvyn Douglas, and Hackman plays his son, and the film is about

the fierce love they bear for each other, and about their inability to communicate that love, or very much of anything else.

The story takes place at a time when the old man's life is ending, but he won't admit it, and when the younger man's life is about to permit a new beginning. The old man is eighty-one, and a long time ago he was the mayor and the school board president—one of the town's most important citizens. But now he has largely been forgotten, left to live a comfortable life in the rambling old family home. He lives there with his wife and his memories, and a fierce possessiveness for his son.

What he wants from the son is a show of devotion. He doesn't communicate with him; indeed, he spends a lot of time falling asleep in front of the television set. But he wants him there, almost as a hostage, because he has a hunger for affection left over from his own neglected childhood. The son tries to go through the motions. But his own wife died a year ago, and now, at forty-four, he has decided to marry a woman doctor who lives in California. This will mean leaving the hometown, and that would be heresy to his father.

The situation becomes urgent when the old man's wife dies. He seems to accept the death as an inconvenience, transferring his grief to memories of his own mother's death half a century before. But his dependence upon his son becomes almost total. His daughter (Estelle Parsons) comes home for the funeral; in a fit of rage, the old man had banished her for marrying a Jew. Now she explains to Hackman, with an objectivity that sounds cruel but springs from love, that an arrangement is going to have to be made about their father. He can't live in the big house by himself.

The trouble is, his pride makes him refuse to hire the housekeeper he could easily afford. He expects his son to watch over him. And Hackman has not gathered the courage to reveal his marriage plans. He goes to look at a couple of old peoples' homes, but he finds them depressing and he knows his father would never, ever, go to one. So there you have the son's dilemma. The father should not live alone. A nursing home seems impossible. For a moment, the children consider gaining power of attorney and insisting on a housekeeper. But then, in a scene of remarkable emotional impact, the son watches as his father finally breaks down and reveals his grief, and the son invites him to come and live in California. But that, of course, is also unacceptable to the old man, whose pride will not allow him to admit that others could make his decisions, and whose stubbornness makes him insist on having everything his way, no matter what.

These bare bones of plot hardly give any hint of the power of this film. I've suggested something of what it's about, but almost nothing about the way the writing, the direction, and the performances come together to create one of the most unforgettably human films I can remember.

Robert Anderson's screenplay is from his autobiographical play, and it rings with truth. His dialogue is direct and revealing, without the "literary" touches or sophistication that could have sabotaged the characters. Eugene O'Neill was writing a different kind of dialogue for different purposes in *Long Day's Journey into Night*, a somewhat similar work that comes to mind. But for Anderson's story, which depends on everyday realism and would find symbolism dangerous, the unadorned dialogue is essential.

Gilbert Cates's direction also respects the fact that this is a movie about visual style or any other fashionably cinematic self-consciousness. With the exception of an inappropriate song which sneaks onto the sound track near the film's beginning, Cates has directed solely to get those magnificent performances onto the screen as movingly as possible. Much of the film is just between the two of them and the characters seem to work so well because Douglas and Hackman respond to each other in every shot; the effect is not of acting, but as if the story were happening right now while we see it.

The film tells us that death ends a life, but not a relationship. That's true of all close and deep human relationships; when one person dies, the other continues long afterwards to wonder what could have been said between them, but wasn't.

I Never Sang for My Father has the courage to remain open-ended; the father dies, but the problems between father and son remain unresolved. That is really more tragic than the fact of death, because death is natural, but human nature cries out that parents and children should understand each other.

I Spit on Your Grave   no stars
R, 98 m., 1980

With Camille Keaton, Eron Tabor, Richard Pace, and Anthony Nichols. Directed by Meir Zarchi and produced by Joseph Zbeda. Screenplay by Zarchi.

I Spit on Your Grave is a vile bag of garbage that is so sick, reprehensible, and contemptible that I can hardly believe it played in respectable theaters. But it did. Attending it was one of the most depressing experiences of my life.

This is a film without a shred of artistic distinction. It lacks even simple craftsmanship. There was no possible motive for exhibiting it, other than the totally cynical hope that it might make money. And it did make money: When I saw it at 11:20 A.M. on a Monday, the theater contained a larger crowd than usual.

It was not just a large crowd, it was a profoundly disturbing one. I do not often attribute motives to audience members, nor do I try to read their minds, but the people who were sitting around me on that Monday morning made it easy for me to know what they were thinking. They talked out loud. And if they seriously believed the things they were saying, they were vicarious sex criminals.

The story of *I Spit on Your Grave* is told with moronic simplicity. A girl goes for a vacation in the woods. She sunbathes by a river. Two men speed by in a powerboat. They harass her. Later, they tow her boat to a rendezvous with two of their buddies. They strip the girl, beat her, and rape her again. She crawls home. They are already there, beat her some more, and rape her again.

Two weeks later, somewhat recovered, the girl lures one of the men out to her house, pretends to seduce him, and hangs him. She lures out another man and castrates him, leaving him to bleed to death in a bathtub. She kills the third man with an axe and disembowels the fourth with an outboard engine. End of movie.

These horrible events are shown with an absolute minimum of dialogue, which is so poorly recorded that it often cannot be heard. There is no attempt to develop the personalities of the characters—they are, simply, a girl and four men, one of them mentally retarded. The movie is nothing more or less than a series of attacks on the girl and then her attacks on the men, interrupted only by an unbelievably grotesque and inappropriate scene in which she enters a church and asks forgiveness for the murders she plans to commit.

How did the audience react to all of this? Those who were vocal seemed to be eating it up. The middle-aged, white-haired man two seats down from me, for example, talked aloud. After the first rape: "That was a good one!" After the second: "That'll show her!" After the third: "I've seen some good ones, but this is the best." When the tables turned and the woman started her killing spree, a woman in the back row shouted: "Cut him up, sister!" In several scenes, the other three men tried to force the retarded man to attack the girl. This inspired a lot of laughter and encouragement from the audience.

I wanted to turn to the man next to me and tell him his remarks were disgusting, but I did not. To hold his opinions at his age, he must already have suffered a fundamental loss of decent human feelings. I would have liked to talk with the woman in the back row, the one with the feminist solidarity for the movie's heroine. I wanted to ask if she'd been appalled by the movie's hour of rape scenes. As it was, at the film's end I walked out of the theater quickly, feeling unclean, ashamed, and depressed.

This movie is an expression of the most diseased and perverted darker human natures. Because it is made artlessly, it flaunts its motives: There is no reason to see this movie except to be entertained by the sight of sadism and suffering. As a critic, I have never condemned the use of violence in films if I felt the filmmakers had an artistic reason for employing it. *I Spit on Your Grave* does not. It is a geek show. I wonder if its exhibitors saw it before they decided to play it, and if they felt as unclean afterward as I did.

Iceman ★ ★ ★ ★
PG, 99 m., 1984

Timothy Hutton (Dr. Shephard), John Lone (Iceman), Lindsay Crouse (Dr. Diane Brady). Directed by Fred Schepisi and produced by Norman Jewison and Patrick Palmer. Screenplay by John Drimmer and Chip Proser.

Iceman begins in almost exactly the same way as both versions of *The Thing*, with a team of Arctic scientists chopping a frozen mammal out of the ice. But somehow we're more interested in this discovery because the frozen object isn't simply a gimmick at the beginning of a horror picture; it is presented with real curiosity and awe.

What is it? As a helicopter lifts the discovery aloft, we can glimpse its vague, shadowy outline through the block of 40,000-year-old ice. It seems almost to be a man, with its arms outstretched. If we remember Fellini's *La Dolce Vita*, we're reminded of its famous opening scene, as the helicopter flew above Rome with the statue of Christ. In both cases, a contrast is made between the technological gimmicks of man and an age-old mystery. In both cases, also, we're aware that we are in the hands of a master director. *Iceman* is by Fred Schepisi, the Australian who made *The Chant of Jimmy Blacksmith* and Willie Nelson's *Barbarosa*. Both of those movies were about men who lived entirely apart from modern society, according to rules of their own, rules that we eventually realized made perfect sense (to them, at least). Now Schepisi has taken that story idea as far as it will go.

The block of ice is thawed. As each drop of water trickles down a stainless-steel table to the floor, we feel a real excitement. We're about to discover something, just as we were when the apes found the monolith in *2001*. Inside the block of ice is a Neanderthal man, perfectly preserved, frozen in an instant with his hands pushing out and his mouth open in a prehistoric cry of protest. Such a discovery is at least theoretically possible; mastodons have been found in Russia, frozen so quickly in a sudden global catastrophe that the buttercups in their stomachs had still not been digested. Why not a man? Of course, the man's cell tissue would have been destroyed by the freezing process, right? Not according to *Iceman*, which advances an ingenious theory.

The scene in which the Neanderthal is brought back to life is one of those emergency room dramas we're familiar with from the TV medical shows, with medics pounding on the chest and administering electrical shocks. Then the movie leaves the familiar, and begins an intriguing journey into the past of the man. The Neanderthal (his name sounds like "Charlie") is placed in a controlled environment. Two scientists (Timothy Hutton and Lindsay Crouse) establish a relationship with him. Elementary communication is started—although here the movie makes a basic error in showing the scientists teaching Charlie to speak English, when of course they would want to learn his language instead.

The rest of the movie develops a theory about how Charlie was frozen and what he was looking for when that surprising event took place. There is also an argument between two branches of science: Those who are more interested in what they can learn from Charlie's body and those who want to understand his mind. This conflict seems to have been put in to generate suspense (certainly no responsible scientist, presented with a living Neanderthal man, would suggest any experiment that would endanger his life). But never mind; before it turns into conflict between good and evil, *Iceman* departs in an unexpected, mystical direction.

This movie is spellbinding storytelling. It begins with such a simple premise and creates such a genuinely intriguing situation that we're not just entertained, we're drawn into the argument. What we feel about Charlie reflects what we feel about ourselves. And what he knows—that we've forgotten—illuminates the line between man the firebuilder, and man the stargazer. Think how much more interesting *The Thing* would have been if its frozen life form had been investigated rather than destroyed, and you have an idea of *Iceman*'s appeal.

The Idolmaker ★ ★ ★
PG, 117 m., 1980

Ray Sharkey (Vince Vacarri), Tovah Feldshuh (Brenda Roberts), Peter Gallagher (Cesare), Paul Land (Tommy Dee), Joe Pantoliano (Gino Pilate). Directed by Taylor Hackford and produced by Gene Kirkwood and Howard W. Koch, Jr. Screenplay by Edward Di Lorenzo.

At the core of *The Idolmaker*, making it a better film than it might otherwise have been, is the hungry, lonely ego of the movie's hero, Vince Vacarri. He has all the skills necessary to become a rock 'n' roll idol, especially in the late-1950s world of Top Forty payola and prefabricated stars. But he doesn't have the looks. He so desperately wants stardom, though, that he tries to have it vicariously, through the "idols" he painstakingly manufactures. Maybe that makes *The Idolmaker* sound more serious than it is, but it's that core of obsession in the Ray Sharkey performance that takes a movie that might have been routine and makes it interesting. This is not a dazzlingly original idea, but the movie understands its passions well enough to entertain us with them.

The "idolmaker" of the title is based, I understand, on the real-life character of Bob Marcucci (listed as the film's "technical adviser"). He is the Philadelphia Svengali who discovered, coached, and managed Frankie Avalon and Fabian, quarterbacking them to stardom. If this movie can be believed, he was a rock 'n' roll puppetmaster, supplying the lines, the songs, the delivery and—most importantly—the stage mannerisms and "look" of his personalities.

The movie moves the story to Brooklyn, and borrows heavily from the clichés of show-biz rags to riches movies: Not only is it lonely at the top in this movie . . . it's lonely at the bottom, too, for practice. The Sharkey character manufactures his first rock star (Paul Land) out of a little raw talent, an unshaped stage presence, and sheer energy. One of the movie's most engaging scenes shows Land at a high school record hop, doggedly pantomiming his first record while Sharkey, backstage, goes through the same motions.

Land does a good job of playing the movie's first rock singer—a spoiled, egotistical creation renamed "Tommy Dee." We can predict what will happen. He'll be pushed to the top by Sharkey, develop an inflated opinion of himself, and think he did it all alone. That's exactly what happens, but Land moves through these stages with a conviction that makes them seem fairly new, even while we're recognizing them.

Meanwhile, Sharkey has another discovery waiting in the wings. He spots a busboy (Peter Gallagher) in his brother's restaurant. The guy can't keep time, can't sing, and has one enormous hairy eyebrow all the way across his face. No problem: Sharkey pounds rhythm into him, grooms him, renames him Caesare and fast-talks him onto the movie's version of "American Bandstand." It turns out that this kid *does* have a natural rapport with the prepubescent girls in his audiences, and he's on his way.

None of this would work if *The Idolmaker* didn't have convincing actors playing the two rock singers. It does. Land and Gallagher can sing and move well enough to convince us they're plausible teen idols. They can also act well enough to modulate their stage performances—they start out terrible and work their way up to levels that Fabian himself must only have dreamed about. And the movie has fun with its production numbers. The songs are all standard late-fifties rock dreck (but newly composed for the movie), but the stage performances are a little sneaky. They're not as ridiculous as many of the late-fifties adolescent heroes actually were; they seem to owe a lot not only to Elvis (naturally) but also to such performers of a decade later as Mick Jagger.

All of this is not to say that *The Idolmaker* is a masterpiece. But it is a well-crafted movie that works, that entertains, and that pulls us through its pretty standard material with the magnetism of the Ray Sharkey performance. Because we sense his hungers, his isolations, and his compulsive needs, we buy scenes that might otherwise have been unworkable.

The Incredible Shrinking Woman
★ ★ ½
PG, 88 m., 1981

Lily Tomlin (Pat Kramer and Judith Beasley), Charles Grodin (Vance Kramer), Ned Beatty (Dan Beame), Henry Gibson (Dr. Nortz). Directed by Joel Schumacher and produced by Hank Moonjean. Screenplay by Jane Wagner.

This is a terrific movie for kids and teenagers. It's a melancholy fact of the times we live in that any movie of even moderate ambition is supposed to become a blockbuster—and that "family movies," with few exceptions, are inane, innocent, and boring. But *The Incredible Shrinking Woman* is not inane, is sometimes wickedly knowing, and is only periodically boring. It strikes a note of quiet desperation that appeals to the teen-ager in all of us. When Lily Tomlin's character has shrunk to twenty-four inches in height and is desperately screaming for help because she is about to be flushed down the garbage disposal unit— who among us cannot say he has felt exactly the same way?

I suppose that at some basic level *The Incredible Shirnking Woman* is a protest against the lot of the housewife in American society. As Lily Tomlin slaves away in her suburban dream home, her husband (Charles Grodin) gets big raises and promotions for advertising home-care products. And eventually one of those products (was it the dye? detergent? glue?) causes Lily Tomlin to start shrinking. One of the intriguing things about the movie is that the smaller Tomlin gets, the more people treat her like a child. She even winds up living in a doll's house. I would like to argue that this is a dilemma not limited to housewives. A lot of people know this feeling. Kids can identify with the maddening sensation that they are smaller than everyone else in the world and *no one is listening!* Teen-agers have grown accustomed to being stuck down the garbage disposal of life: Nobody wants them around, and most people would probably like to hit a switch and make them disappear.

So there's a certain poignant comedy in *The Incredible Shrinking Woman* that strikes some chords. The movie is also funny in its visual approach, showing us a suburban world in which everything is done in hideously jolly colors and everybody, even the TV anchorman, wears peach blazers. America in this movie looks like a gigantic paint-color chart.

It's too bad, I suppose, that *The Incredible*

Shrinking Woman succeeds on the levels I've mentioned without ever breaking through to become a really inspired comedy. Lily Tomlin is such a funny woman that we expect her to hit home runs in every movie. She doesn't in this one, but she does something almost as hard. She creates a character that is halfway believable, in the midst of chaos. She causes us to feel a certain comic sympathy for her plight. And, for that matter, she inhabits a plight that is interesting. Most "family movies" these days are uninspired, moronic, and directed and acted without any visible style. *The Incredible Shrinking Woman* at least has an intelligence behind it. It is engaging a lot of the time and funny some of the time, especially when a gorilla helps the two-inch-tall Tomlin escape from captivity.

Indiana Jones and the Temple of Doom ★ ★ ★ ★
PG, 118 m., 1984 ✔

Harrison Ford (Indiana Jones), Kate Capshaw (Willie Scott), Ke Huy Quan (Short Round), Amrish Puri (Mola Ram), Philip Stone (Captain Blumburtt), Roshan Seth (Chattar Lal). Directed by Steven Spielberg and produced by George Lucas. Screenplay by Willard Huyck and Gloria Katz.

Steven Spielberg's *Indiana Jones and the Temple of Doom* is one of the greatest Bruised Forearm Movies ever made. You know what a Bruised Forearm Movie is. That's the kind of movie where your date is always grabbing your forearm in a viselike grip, as unbearable excitement unfolds on the screen. After the movie is over, you've had a great time but your arm is black-and-blue for a week. This movie is one of the most relentlessly nonstop action pictures ever made, with a virtuoso series of climactic sequences that must last an hour and never stop for a second. It's a roller coaster ride, a visual extravaganza, a technical triumph, and a whole lot of fun. And it's not simply a retread of *Raiders of the Lost Ark*, the first Indiana Jones movie. It works in a different way, and borrows from different traditions.

Raiders was inspired by Saturday afternoon serials. It was a series of cliffhanging predicaments, strung out along the way as Indiana Jones traveled from San Francisco to Tibet, Egypt, and other romantic locales. It was an exotic road picture. *Indiana Jones* mostly takes place on one location, and belongs more to the great tradition of the Impregnable Fortress Impregnated. You know the kind of fortress I'm talking about. You see them all the time in James Bond pictures. They involve unbelievably bizarre hideaways, usually buried under the earth, beneath the sea, on the moon, or inside a volcano. They are ruled over by megalomaniac zealots who dream of conquest, and they're fueled by slave labor. Our first glimpse of an Impregnable Fortress is always the same: An ominous long shot, with Wagnerian music, as identically uniformed functionaries hurry about their appointed tasks.

The role of the hero in a movie like this is to enter the fortress, steal the prize, and get away in one piece. This task always involves great difficulty, horrendous surprises, unspeakable dangers, and a virtuoso chase sequence. The very last shots at the end of the sequence are obligatory: The fortress must be destroyed. Hopefully, there will be great walls of flame and water, engulfing the bad guys as the heroes race to freedom, inches ahead of certain death.

But enough of intellectual film criticism. Let's get back to Indiana Jones. As *Temple of Doom* opens, Indiana is in a nightclub somewhere in Shanghai. Killers are after him. He escapes in the nick of time, taking along a beautiful nightclub floozy (Kate Capshaw), and accompanied by his trusty young sidekick, Short Round (Ke Huy Quan). Their getaway leads them into a series of adventures: A flight over the Himalayas, a breathtaking escape from a crashing plane, and a meeting with a village leader who begs Indiana to find and return the village's precious magic jewel—a stone which disappeared along with all of the village's children. Indiana is a plucky chap and agrees. Then there's a dinner in the palace of a sinister local lord. The dinner scene, by the way, also is lifted from James Bond, where it's an obligatory part of every adventure: James is always promised a sure death, but treated first to an elegant dinner with his host, who boasts of his power and takes inordinate pride in being a sophisticated host. After Indiana and Willie retire for the night, there's the movie's only slow sequence, in which such matters as love are discussed. (Make some popcorn.) Then the movie's second half opens with a breathtaking series of adventures involving the mines beneath the palace—mines that have been turned into a vision of hell.

The set design, art direction, special effects, and sound effects inside this underground Hades are among the most impressive achievements in the whole history of Raiders and Bond-style thrillers. As dozens of little kids work on chain gangs, the evil maharajah keeps them in slavery by using the sinister powers of the missing jewel and its two mates. Indiana and his friends look on in astonishment, and then Indiana attempts to steal back the jewel. Some of the film's great setpieces now take place: Human victims are lowered into a subterranean volcano in a steel cage, weird rituals are celebrated, and there is a chase scene involving the mine's miniature railway. This chase has to be seen to be believed. Spielberg has obviously studied Buster Keaton's *The General*, that silent classic that solved the obvious logistic problem of a chase on railway tracks (i.e., what to do about the fact that one train seemingly always has to be behind the other one). As Indiana and friends hurtle in the little out-of-control mine car, the pursuers are behind, ahead, above, below, and beside them, and the scene will wring you out and leave you breathless. *Indiana Jones and the Temple of Doom* makes no apologies for being exactly what it is: Exhilarating, manic, wildly imaginative escapism.

No apologies are necessary. This is the most cheerfully exciting, bizarre, goofy, romantic adventure movie since *Raiders*, and it is high praise to say that it's not so much a sequel as an equal. It's quite an experience. You stagger out with a silly grin—and a bruised forearm, of course.

Infra-Man ★ ★ ½
PG, 92 m., 1976

Li Hsiu-hsien, Wang Hsieh, Yuan Man-tzu, Terry Liu, Tsen Shu-yi, Huang Chien-lung, Lu Sheng. Directed by Hua Shan and produced by Rumme Shaw.

Within the first four minutes of *Infra-Man*, (a) a giant flying lizard attacks a school bus, (b) the Earth cracks open, (c) Hong Kong is destroyed by flames, (d) mountains disintegrate to reveal the forms of reptilian monsters with blinking yellow eyes, (e) the Professor announces that a twenty-million-year-old woman is unleashing the hibernating monsters upon civilization, (f) the Science Headquarters is shaken by a second quake, (g) the Mutants awake, and (h) the Professor, obviously shaken, informs a secret meeting of world leaders, "This situation is so bad that it is the worst that ever has been!"

No doubt about it: This is a case for Infra-Man. In his secret laboratory far beneath the Science Headquarters, the Professor explains to a brave volunteer: "We will wire your arms and legs with powerful transistors and death rays. You will be powered by a tiny nuclear reactor. Unfortunately, the operation will be very painful and you may die."

And so we're off and running, in the best movie of its kind since *Invasion of the Bee Girls*. I'm a pushover for monster movies anyway, but *Infra-Man* has it all: Horrendous octopus men, a gigantic beetle man with three eyes who sprays his victims with sticky cocoons, savage robots with coiled spring necks that can extend ten feet, a venomous little critter that looks like a hairy mutant footstool, elaborately staged karate fights, underground throne rooms, damsels in distress, exploding volcanoes, and a whip-cracking villainess named Princess Dragon Mom (Philip Wylie, please note).

The movie's totally, almost joyfully absurd, and a victim of John Carter's Syndrome. You remember J.C.S., based on the logical oversight in Edgar Rice Burrough's books about John Carter of Mars. After whole chapters of galloping across the Martian desert on his Martian steed and fighting off enemies in sword fights, John Carter finally says to hell with it, pulls out a ray gun, and fries everybody.

Same here. Gigantic mutant monsters with built-in death rays attack Infra-Man, who can hurl lightning bolts from the soles of his feet, and what do they do? They have a karate fight. After ten minutes of chopping and socking and doing acrobatic flips, THEN they zap each other.

No matter, *Intra-Man* contains terrific moments. In one cliff-hanging scene, for example, the Professor has Infra-Man wired up on the operating table when Science Headquarters is attacked by gigantic mutant arms. That's right, arms: no body, just arms. The arms squirm all over the headquarters, knocking off the power supply. The Professor shouts into his radio: "You have one minute to restore power before Infra-Man dies!"

His aide struggles toward a red power switch. He is knocked unconscious by an arm. Shot of a stopwatch ticking away the seconds. He regains consciousness, struggles some more. The arm attacks again. With ten seconds to go, soldiers burst into the room with a power saw and cut the arm in half. The switch is thrown and Infra-Man lives.

There are other good things. Lines like, "We are doing this for the children of the world." Or, "The clouds will cut off the sun and deprive Infra-Man of his power source." Or, "Drop the Earthling to her doom—she will melt at 3,000 degrees." The movie even looks good: It's a classy, slick production by the Shaw Brothers, the Hong Kong kung fu kings. When they stop making movies like *Infra-Man*, a little light will go out of the world.

Insignificance ★ ★ ★
R, 110 m., 1985

Theresa Russell (The Actress), Tony Curtis (The Senator), Gary Busey (The Ballplayer), Michael Emil (The Professor), Will Sampson (Elevator Man). Directed by Nicholas Roeg and produced by Jeremy Thomas. Screenplay by Terry Johnson.

The premise is not too unlikely. Imagine that during one hot and steamy night in a New York City hotel room, the lives of these people crossed paths: Marilyn Monroe, Senator Joe McCarthy, Joe DiMaggio, and Albert Einstein. The key linking element is, of course, Monroe, a woman of such undefinable and ethereal appeal that her real life did indeed encompass such husbands as DiMaggio and Arthur Miller, such admirers as Norman Mailer and Laurence Olivier, such friends as Jack Kennedy and Robert Mitchum. Her address book, which disappeared mysteriously after she died, no doubt included names from such unexpected corners of America that DiMaggio, Einstein, and McCarthy would only have been starters.

But imagine, all the same, that long and steamy night and that hotel room, and you have the substance of *Insignificance*, which was first a play on the London stage and is now one of the last sorts of films I would have expected Nicholas Roeg to direct. Roeg is a master of baroque visuals and tangled plot lines. His *Don't Look Now* still has people trying to explain that Venetian dwarf in the red raincoat, and his credits include at least one good film, *Eureka*, that was not quite sure whether it was a dream.

Insignificance is a film in which almost all the audacity is contained by the premise— that these four most famous figures of the 1950s met during one long night. Grant Roeg that much, and he gives us a fairly realistic film of most of the rest of the way. The characters are never actually given their real names in the film, but there seems to be little doubt who they're meant to be, especially when Einstein and Monroe work out the theory of relativity together, using a flashlight, a few simple props, and some almost perfect dialogue.

Monroe is played in the film by Theresa Russell, who is *still* only about twenty-six years old, and who already has appeared in such landmarks as *Straight Time*, *The Last Tycoon*, and *Bad Timing*. She doesn't really look very much like Monroe, but what does it matter? The blonde hair and the red lips are there, and so is the manner, which has been imitated so often, and so badly, that the imitators prove that Monroe was a special case. Russell doesn't imitate. She builds her performance from the ground up, and it works to hold the movie together.

Tony Curtis has a lot of fun as the hard-drinking, paranoic senator. He has turned, in his middle years, into a glorious ham, willing to take the chance of appearing ridiculous in order to reach for the farther edges of a performance. His theories about the Russians in this film are little masterpieces of dialogue. Gary Busey is the ballplayer, stolid and not quite comprehending his famous wife, and Michael Emil is a wonderful Einstein, sweet and childlike, and closest of all of them to Monroe's own personality.

I am not quite sure, however, what the point of the movie is. It's more of an acting and writing tour de force than a statement on sports, politics, sex symbol, or relativity. It begins by imagining its remarkable meetings, and ends by having created them. It's all process, no outcome. I think in this case that's OK.

Interiors ★ ★ ★ ★
PG, 93 m., 1978

Kristin Griffith (Flyn), Marybeth Hurt (Joey), Richard Jordan (Frederick), Diane Keaton (Renata), E.G. Marshall (Arthur), Geraldine Page (Eve), Maureen Stapleton (Pearl), Sam Waterston (Mike). Directed by Woody Allen and produced by Charles H. Joffe. Screenplay by Allen.

Yes, the opening *does* remind us of Bergman: The static shots, held for a moment's contemplation, of the rooms and possessions of a family. But then people enter the rooms, and their lives and voices have a particularly American animation; Woody Allen is right to say that his drama, *Interiors*, belongs more in the tradition of Eugene O'Neill than of Ingmar Bergman. But what's this? Here we have a *Woody Allen* film, and we're talking about O'Neill and Bergman and traditions and influences? Yes, and correctly. Allen, whose comedies have been among the cheerful tonics of recent years, is astonishingly assured in his first drama.

He gives us a time of crisis in a family, and develops it in counterpoint with the countless smaller joys and crises that are a family. He is very spare: Every scene counts, and the dialogue has the precision of a J.D. Salinger short story. There's nothing thrown in for effect unless the effect contributes specifically to the direction of the complete film.

Allen's central character is the family's mother, Eve, played by Geraldine Page as a heartbreaking showdown between total self-confidence in the past and catastrophic breakdown in the present. She is a designer, and her rooms are some, but not all, of the interiors of the title. She aims for a cool perfectionism in her rooms, for grays and greens and pale blues, for a look of irreproachable sterility. Her science and art is to know the correct place for a lamp, within a fraction of an inch.

She is married to a wealthy lawyer (E.G. Marshall). She has three daughters: A poet (Diane Keaton), a movie star (Kristin

Griffith), and a searcher for meaningful occupation (Marybeth Hurt). Keaton lives with an alcoholic would-be novelist (Richard Jordan). Hurt lives with a filmmaker (Sam Waterston). Marshall announces that he wants a trial separation from Page, and later introduces a woman he's met on a cruise and wants to marry (Maureen Stapleton).

There you have them, the eight people of this movie. Allen, who thought nothing in *Annie Hall* of producing Marshall McLuhan from behind a theater lobby display for a comic walk-on, isolates his characters in *Interiors* so thoroughly, we're reminded of O'Neill's family in *Long Day's Journey Into Night*, coming and going in an old house with no access to any world outside.

There are hurts in this family that have been buried for years, and guilts that still hold it together. One daughter finally blurts out an accusation against her mother, who had thought herself so perfect and yet was as capable as anyone of pettiness and cruelty. We get the feeling, indeed, that the family has been together much too long, and that family life is not necessarily a blessing.

If there is a common wish shared by all the characters in the film, it's to live a life of their own. The father, defending to his daughters his decision to marry a woman they call a "vulgarian," argues not unreasonably that he's paid the bills and maintained the household for years—that now, in his early sixties, he's *earned* his right to some years of his own choosing.

The others have earned their rights, too, but each at the expense of the others. That is how each sees it, anyway. The same charge passes again and again around the family circle: That if the others had not been so demanding, or selfish, or jealous, or vindictive, then *this* person would have been set free to realize himself or herself.

Allen treats these themes in scenes that have an elegant economy of expression. The scene around the dinner table, for example, as the father announces his decision to leave, is handled in a way that etches the feelings of every member of the family, in just the right tones of anger, disbelief, or defiance. Scenes involving the daughters and their men suggest in different ways that the problems of this family will not end in this generation.

The funniest and saddest scene begins

with the father's second marriage; Maureen Stapleton is wonderful as the "vulgarian," sweeping in with her red gown and finding Page's rooms "so gray. . . ." The dinner table conversation this time allows Allen to regard the Stapleton character with a mixture of tenderness and satire so delicately balanced, it's virtuoso.

The wonderment is that it's "serious." Yes, it is, but to be serious is not always to be good, and a movie both serious and bad is a great depression for everyone. *Interiors* becomes serious by intently observing complex adults as they fend and cope, blame and justify. Because it illuminates some of the ways we all act, it is serious but not depressing; when it's over, we may even find ourselves quietly cheered that Allen has seen so clearly how things can be.

Into the Night ★
R, 117 m., 1985

Jeff Goldblum (Ed Okin), Michelle Pfeiffer (Diana), Richard Farnsworth (Jack Caper), Irene Papas (Shaheen), Kathryn Harrold (Christie), Paul Mazursky (Bud Herman), Bruce McGill (Brother Elvis), David Bowie (Colin Morris). Directed by John Landis and produced by George Folsey, Jr., and Ron Koslow. Screenplay by Koslow.

Into the Night is a fitfully funny, aimless, unnecessary thriller. That would not necessarily be enough to make it a bad movie; *Beverly Hills Cop* is also fitfully funny, aimless, and unnecessary, but it is also a more successful movie because it has a sense of style and because it has Eddie Murphy at its center. This movie has no center, even though the wonderful actor Jeff Goldblum was available to supply one. I have a theory about that.

The movie was directed by John Landis, who has filled it with countless cameo appearances. Everybody knows that a lot of Hollywood directors have walk-ons in *Into the Night*, but that's just the beginning. Everybody and his cousin dirfts through this movie. And I have a notion that the set began to resemble a party, with a different guest list every day. As Landis played host and tried to make all of his nonactors feel comfortable,

some degree of vital tension was lost. Creating the experience became more important than making the movie. Look at the guest list. Among the directors who appear in the film are David Cronenberg, Colin Higgins, Daniel Petrie, Paul Mazursky, Paul Bartel, Don Siegel, Jim Henson, Amy Heckerling, Roger Vadim, Lawrence Kasdan, Jonathan Demme, Carl Gottleib, and Landis himself. Not sure who all of them are? That's all right; they probably had a great time at the Director's Guild screening. Other bit players in the film include actors Dan Ackroyd, Vera Miles, Clu Gulanger, and Irene Papas, cinematographer Robert Paynter, publicist Saul Kahan, car dealer Cal Worthington, rock star David Bowie, writer Waldo Salt, computer software expert Hadi Sadjadi, body-builder Jake Steinfeld, cartoonist Bruce McGill (who is very good as an Elvis freak), special effects makeup artist Rick Baker, country singer Carl Perkins, assistant director David Sosna, second assistant cameraman Christopher George, sound mixer William B. Kaplan, and makeup man Wes Dawn. And I'll bet I missed a few.

What's the idea here? To make a home movie? If I had been the agent for one of the stars, like Goldblum, Michelle Pfeiffer, Richard Farnsworth, or Kathryn Harrold, I think I would have protested to the front office that Landis was engaging in cinematic autoeroticism and that my clients were getting lost in the middle of the family reunion.

The irony is that *Into the Night* opens so promisingly. Goldblum plays an aerospace engineer who is unhappily married, unhappily employed, depressed, and restless. When he finds out his wife is having an affair, he gets up in the middle of the night and drives his car to the airport—planning to fly off into the night. At this point, wonderful things could have happened. Instead, Michelle Pfeiffer lands on the hood of his car, pursued by four murderous Arabs. Goldblum saves her life and gets caught in an intrigue involving stolen jewels, black-market con games, and an international network of thieves. And the movie gets reduced to a mindless, shapeless mess, with the Arabs chasing him around in a Mercedes, looking like the Four Stooges. There was never a moment when I cared about the plot. And there have been so many chase scenes in the movies that Hollywood should open a franchise: Chase 'n' Shoot, regular or crispy, with or without cheesecake.

Landis is not a bad director. Look at his credits like *Animal House, The Blues Brothers*, and *Trading Places*. Some of the scenes in this movie work, including a funny beachfront episode with Mazursky and Harrold, Farnsworth's touching work as a dying old man and McGill's hilarious supporting role as an angry Elvis imitator. Maybe what the movie needed was more professional discipline and less geniality. As a rule, it's probably better to throw the party after the filming is finished.

Invasion USA ½ ★
R, 108 m., 1985

Chuck Norris (Matt Hunter), Richard Lynch (Rostov), Melissa Prophet (McGuire), Alexander Zale (Nikko). Directed by Joseph Zito and produced by Menahem Golan and Yoram Globus. Screenplay by James Bruner and Chuck Norris.

You'd think maybe Chuck Norris would want to follow up his great action movie *Code of Silence* with another winner, but you'd be wrong. *Invasion U.S.A.* is a brain-damaged, idiotic thriller, not bad enough to be laughable. The movie is a production of the Cannon Group, which sometimes makes good movies and more often makes junk like this. The theory is that a big-name star like Norris will help the movie make money in the Third World. That theory has all but destroyed the box-office credibility of Charles Bronson, and Norris seems to be following in the same footsteps.

In *Code of Silence* he played a well-written character in a well-constructed story, and there were lots of thrilling stunts and good supporting performances. In *Invasion U.S.A.* he hardly even interacts with other people on the screen. He simply steps into the frame when needed and blows somebody away.

The movie is about an invasion of the United States by several boatloads of vicious killers, who come from somewhere (Cuba, maybe?) and leave their amphibious vehicles on the beach. They pile into a caravan of rented trucks and vans and spread out across Florida, using grenades, machine-guns, and bazookas to destroy anything that looks remotely like a wholesome American image. Examples: School buses full of kids; shopping malls; church services; and even suburban families decorating Christmas trees while singing "Hark! The Herald Angels Sing!"

The theory is that their random violence will unleash anarchy upon America, the rule of law will collapse, and government will fall, and then they will take over. Who are they? Their leader, named Rostov, sometimes seems Russian, usually sounds American. His followers are sometimes Oriental, sometimes Latino, usually anonymous.

Chuck Norris works for "the agency," and is brought out of retirement to fight the threat, but as usual he insists on two specific working conditions: He works alone, and he drives his own pickup truck. (In one scene, he drives the truck through the wall of a shopping mall and mows down several terrorists, miraculously not hitting any civilians in the process.) He says as little as possible, and the role has no particular individual characteristics. He's just a mindless violence symbol.

He isn't the only one with no dimensions. The movie's worst, most thankless role goes to Melissa Prophet, who plays a newspaper reporter. She stands around at the scenes of all the many violent crimes in this movie, snapping photographs and being angry. (Like many photographers in the movies, she acts as if photography consists of pointing the camera in the direction of the action and recording the largest possible view.)

This woman is angry at everyone. She spouts off to cops, badmouths security guards, and when Norris saves her life from savage terrorists she brushes his hand off her sleeve and bitterly snarls, "Thanks a lot, cowboy!" Never in the movie does she write or file a story or a photograph, and (this is most amazing) at no point does her presence in the movie make the slightest difference. She never interacts with anybody else for any purpose. She just stands around with her camera, being mad.

Is this a bad movie? Real bad.

Irreconcilable Differences ★ ★ ★ ½
PG, 112 m., 1984

Ryan O'Neal (Albert Brodsky), Shelley Long (Lucy Van Patten Brodsky), Drew Barrymore (Casey Brodsky), Sam Wanamaker (David Kessler), Allen Garfield (Phil Hanner), Hortensia Colorado (Maria Hernandez). Directed by Charles Shyer and produced by Arlene Sellers and Alex Winitsky. Screenplay by Nancy Myers and Shyer.

The opening moments of *Irreconcilable Differences* are not promising. A lawyer is advising his client about divorce—and when we see the client, she turns out to be a little girl. Her plan is to divorce her parents, because they have (she stumbles over the word) ir . . . ir . . . rec . . . concilable differences. Right away, I was bracing myself for one of those smarmy movies about cute kids and mean parents. I could foresee the series this movie would inspire: "Kids' Court," with a different little plaintiff every week. It turns out that I was too cynical. *Irreconcilable Differences* is sometimes cute, and is about mean parents, but it also is one of the funnier and more intelligent movies of 1984, and if viewers can work their way past the ungainly title, they're likely to have a surprisingly good time.

The movie stars Drew Barrymore as the little girl. You may remember her from *E. T.*, when she hid E.T. in the closet with her stuffed animals. She has grown up just a little, but she still has that slight lisp and that air of preternaturally concentrated seriousness: She is the right actress for this role precisely because she approaches it with such grave calm. A kid trying to be funny would be a mistake. Her parents are played by Shelley Long of "Cheers," who is one of my favorite actresses, and Ryan O'Neal, who is not usually one of my favorite actors but is right for this role and good in it. They have a Meet-Cute while he is hitchhiking and she is returning her car to her tall, muscular boyfriend. It's love at first sight, even after Bink, the boyfriend, bursts into their motel room and figures out that his engagement is over.

O'Neal plans to be a great movie director. (His character seems inspired by Peter Bogdanovich, right down to the style of his glasses.) Long starts out to be a helpful wife

and good mother, but then, after O'Neal's career hits the skids, she has great success as a writer. The point is that one parent or the other is always so busy, so successful, so much in demand, that the little girl gets overlooked. The only place she really feels loved and comfortable is when she goes home with the family's Mexican maid. So the kid sues for divorce. She wants to give the maid custody of herself. The parents are shocked. The media have a circus. The plot drifts dangerously toward a series of stagy confrontations, but avoids the obvious: This movie has been written with so much wit and imagination that even obligatory scenes have a certain freshness and style.

It also has a real edge, even a suggestion of bitterness, in its scenes about Hollywood. Although *Irreconcilable Differences* is a movie about family life, it's also a perceptive portrait of success and failure in Hollywood, with a good ear for the way people use the language of Leo Buscaglia to describe the behavior of Machiavelli.

The Drew Barrymore character sees right through all of this. She doesn't care about careers, she wants to be given a happy home and her minimum daily requirement of love, and, in a way, the movie is about how Hollywood (and American success in general) tends to cut adults off from the natural functions of parents. The theory is that kids will wait but a deal won't. Actually, it's just the opposite.

Jagged Edge ★ ★ ★ ½
R, 108 m., 1985

Glenn Close (Teddy Barnes), Jeff Bridges (Jack Forester), Peter Coyote (Thomas Krasny), Robert Loggia (Sam Ransom). Directed by Richard Marquand and produced by Martin Ransohoff. Screenplay by Joe Eszterhas.

Directors like to talk about playing the audience like a piano, about making movies that are efficient machines for assaulting our emotions. *Jagged Edge* is a movie like that, a murder thriller which dangles one clue after another before our eyes, daring us to decide who committed the murder. The machinery in this movie is so efficient that we don't know the answer until the very last shot—

and I'll be getting back to that last shot in a moment.

The film stars Jeff Bridges as a powerful San Francisco publisher whose wife is brutally murdered in their isolated oceanside home. After an investigation reveals that he stood to inherit his wife's entire fortune, he is arrested and charged with the murder. Glenn Close plays his defense attorney. At first, she insists she has retired from courtroom cases, but then Bridges convinces her that he is innocent. And before long, she is also convinced that they are in love.

The Close character stands at the center of the film. Is she defending the man she loves against the unjust charges against him? Or is she defending a cold-blooded killer, who might murder her just as he murdered his wife? There are moments in *Jagged Edge* when each of these possibilities seems convincing, but most of the time we just don't know. There's a lot of evidence on both sides.

Close's courtroom opponent is the assistant D.A. (Peter Coyote). They worked together a few years ago on a case where, she believes, he concealed evidence in order to win a conviction. Is he concealing evidence this time? There comes a time when we think he may be. And by then the film's tension is so tightly wound that we, and Close, don't know what to believe.

Jagged Edge is supremely effective at what it sets out to do—toy with the audience. It's another effective thriller from Richard Marquand, who made *Eye of the Needle*. The performances are good and the plot is watertight, as a whodunit must be. I have only one quarrel with the film, but it's a fairly substantial one. The movie *only* wants to keep us guessing. The characters are developed only in ways intended to string us along. Any behavior is possible if it will further the plot. There's no sense of reality beneath the gleaming surface.

Even that would be all right, if the movie didn't reveal the identity of the real killer in the final shot. Here's my theory: In a movie which exists only to tantalize us with clues and deceptive evidence, we *shouldn't* find out who the killer was—because that should be what we're arguing about as we leave the theater. Once the killer is unmasked, his crime reflects on everything else we know

about his character, and that's more realism than you really need in a well-oiled machine.

NOTE: As this movie went into wide release, a strange thing happened. People started to get confused about the identity of the real killer. Even though there is a close-up of his face, the shot is taken from such an oblique angle that some viewers were confused, and I got letters and phone calls suggesting at least three possible villains. I imagine a VCR freeze-frame will solve the mystery.

Jaws ★ ★ ★ ★
PG, 124 m., 1975

Roy Scheider (Brody), Robert Shaw (Quint), Richard Dreyfuss (Hooper), Lorraine Gary (Ellen Brody), Murray Hamilton (Mayor). Directed by Steven Spielberg and produced by Richard Zanuck and David Brown. Screenplay by Peter Benchley and Carl Gottleib.

Steven Spielberg's *Jaws* is a sensationally effective action picture—a scary thriller that works all the better because it's populated with characters that have been developed into human beings we get to know and care about. It's a film that's as frightening as *The Exorcist*, and yet it's a nicer kind of fright, somehow more fun because we're being scared by an outdoor-adventure saga instead of by a brimstone-and-vomit devil.

The story, as I guess everyone knows by now, involves a series of attacks on swimmers by a great white shark, the response of the threatened resort island to its loss of tourist business, and, finally, the epic attempt by three men to track the shark and kill it. There are no doubt supposed to be all sorts of levels of meanings in such an archetypal story, but Spielberg wisely decides not to underline any of them. This is an action film content to stay entirely within the perimeters of its story, and none of the characters has to wade through speeches expounding on the significance of it all. Spielberg is very good, though, at presenting those characters in a way that makes them individuals. Before the three men get on that leaky old boat and go forth to do battle with what amounts to an elemental natural force, we know them well enough to be genuinely interested in the ways they'll respond. There's Brody (Roy Scheider), the police chief, who came to the island from New York looking, so he thought, for a change from the fears of the city. There's Quint (Robert Shaw), a caricature of the crusty old seafaring salt, who has a very particular personal reason for hating sharks. And there's Hooper (Richard Dreyfuss), the rich kid turned oceanographer, who knows best of all what a shark can do to a man, and yet is willing to get into the water with one.

All three performances are really fine. Scheider is the character most of us identify with. He's actually scared of the water, doesn't like to swim and, when he sees the giant shark swim past the boat for the first time, we believe him when he informs Quint, very sincerely, "We need a bigger boat." Shaw brings a degree of cheerful exaggeration to his role as Quint, stomping around like a cross between Captain Queeg and Captain Hook, and then delivering a compelling five-minute monologue about the time the *Indianapolis* went down and he was one of more than 1,000 men in the water. By the time rescue came, two-thirds of them had been killed by sharks.

Probably the most inspired piece of casting in the movie is the use of Richard Dreyfuss as the oceanographer. He made this film soon after playing the driven, scheming, overwhelmingly ambitious title character in *The Apprenticeship of Duddy Kravitz,* and the nice kid, college-bound, in *American Graffiti.* Here he looks properly young, engaging, and scholarly, and introduces the technical material about sharks in a way that reinforces our elemental fear of them.

Which brings us to the shark itself. Some of the footage in the film is of an actual great white shark. The rest uses a mechanical shark patterned on the real thing. The illusion is complete. We see the shark close up, we look in its relentless eye, and it just plain feels like a shark. *Jaws* is a great adventure movie of the kind we don't get very often any more. It's clean-cut adventure, without the gratuitous violence of so many action pictures. It has the necessary amount of blood and guts to work—but none extra. And it's one hell of a good story, brilliantly told.

The Jazz Singer ★
PG, 115 m., 1980

Neil Diamond (Jess Robin), Laurence Olivier (Cantor Rabinovitch), Lucie Arnaz (Molly Bell), Catlin Adams (Rivka Rabinovitch). Directed by Richard Fleischer and produced by Jerry Leider. Screenplay by Herbert Baker.

The Jazz Singer has so many things wrong with it that a review threatens to become a list. Let me start with the most obvious: This movie is about a man who is at least twenty years too old for such things to be happening to him. *The Jazz Singer* looks ridiculous giving us Neil Diamond going through an adolescent crisis.

The movie is a remake, of course, of Al Jolson's 1927 *The Jazz Singer,* which was the first commercially successful talking picture. The remake has played with time in an interesting way: It sets the story in the present, but it places the characters in some kind of time warp. Their behavior seems decades out of date, and some scenes are totally inexplicable in *any* context. For example: In the film, Diamond plays a young Jewish cantor at his father's synagogue. He is married, and he appears settled down to a lifetime of religion. But he also writes songs for a black group—and when one of the quartet gets sick, Diamond takes his place, appearing in a black nightclub in blackface. Oh yeah? This scene is probably supposed to be homage to Jolson's blackface performance of "Mammy" in the original, but what it does now is get the movie off to an unintentionally hilarious start.

The bulk of the movie concerns Diamond's decision to leave New York, his father, and his wife, and go to Los Angeles, where he hopes to break into the music industry. This whole business of leaving the nest, of breaking the ties with his father, seems so strange in a middle-aged character: Diamond is just too old to play these scenes. But no matter; the movie is ridiculous for lots of other reasons.

When he arrives in L.A., for example, he's instantly "discovered" in a recording studio by Lucie Arnaz, who plays an agent and is filled with energy and spunk—she's the best thing in the movie. She thinks he has promise, so she gets him a job as the opening act for a comic. This gives Diamond a chance to sing, and his onstage appearances, I guess, are supposed to be the big deal in this movie. Because of that, the film sacrifices any attempt to present them realistically: For his West Coast debut as a warm-up for a comic, Diamond is backed up by dozens of onstage musicians, which look like the L.A. Philharmonic and, at union scale, would cost thousands of dollars. Sure.

The plot plods relentlessly onward. Laurence Olivier plays the aging father in the film, in a performance that seems based on that tortured German accent he also used in *The Boys from Brazil, Marathon Man* and *A Little Romance:* Is it too much to hope that Sir Laurence will return to the English language sometime soon? Father and son fight, split, grudgingly meet again, hold a tearful reunion—all in scenes of deadly predictability. One sequence that is not predictable has Neil Diamond abandoning (the now pregnant) Lucie Arnaz in order to hit the highway and become a road-show Kristofferson. This stretch of the film, with Diamond self-consciously lonely and hurting, is supposed to be affecting, but is misfires, it drips with so much narcissism.

But then Diamond's whole presence in this movie is offensively narcissistic. His songs are melodramatic, interchangeable, self-aggrandizing groans and anguished shouts, backed protectively by expensive and cloying instrumentation. His dramatic presence also looks overprotected, as if nobody was willing to risk offending him by asking him to seem involved, caring, and engaged.

Diamond plays the whole movie looking at people's third shirt buttons, as if he can't be bothered to meet their eyes and relate with them. It's strange about the Diamond performance: It's not just that he can't act. It's that he sends out creepy vibes. He seems self-absorbed, closed off, grandiose, out of touch with his immediate surroundings. His fans apparently think Neil Diamond songs celebrate worthy human qualities. I think they describe conditions suitable for treatment.

Jeremiah Johnson ★ ★ ★
PG, 108 m., 1972

Robert Redford (Jeremiah Johnson), Will Geer (Bear Claw), Stefan Gierasch (Del Gue), Allyn Ann McLerie (Crazy Woman), Delle Bolton (Swan), Charles Tyner (Robidoux). Directed by Sydney Pollack and produced by Joe Wizan. Screenplay by John Milius and Edward Anhalt.

If Thoreau had been a violent man, angry and unforgiving, *Jeremiah Johnson* might have been made from one of his books. Like *Walden*, it's the story of a man who goes alone into the wilderness to live by his hands and wits. It is good at showing us this man and the ways by which he survives; but not so good when it ventures into Indian myth and magic, and edges up to vast universal questions.

There's a sense in which movies like this should be rough-hewn and a little inarticulate. When a man makes up his mind to go into the mountains and say to hell with civilization, it's cheating a little to frame him against spectacular landscapes as if he were a particularly heroic tour guide. It may also be cheating to cast Robert Redford in the title role; he projects a kind of intellectual, winsome handsomeness that doesn't really belong in such a simple character.

Still, the movie does approach its subject with a certain dogged honesty; it agrees for the most part to coexist with the rhythms of the wilderness, and not go for big, phony climaxes (it is so studiously low-keyed, indeed, that it seems to end four or five times before it really does). The humor is direct and folksy, as when an old trapper asks Jeremiah if he can skin a grizzly. Jeremiah says he can, and so the trapper lures a grizzly into the cabin with Jeremiah, jumps out the back window and shouts, "Start skinnin'!"

The humor is direct, and so is the violence. Director Sydney Pollack approaches his scenes head-on. He doesn't deal in the choreography of violence, like Peckinpah, or the fetish of violence, like the Kubrick of *A Clockwork Orange*. Instead, his violent scenes are brutally short and forcible. Death occurs suddenly, and is absorbed by the emptiness of the mountain range.

The story follows Jeremiah as he makes a roughly circular journey through high mountain ranges and passes. He nearly starves the first winter, until the old trapper (Will Geer, looking like Father Christmas in his fur parka) has mercy on him. He forms brief friendships and partnerships with some of the other outcasts of the mountains; he has hostile encounters with Crow Indians and friendly ones with Flatheads; and as the result of a misunderstanding he finds himself married to the daughter of a Flathead chief. The marriage sets up the movie's most absorbing sequences. Jeremiah has earlier become a sort of guardian for a young boy, and now the three of them set up housekeeping. Pollack gets a kind of poetic documentary rhythm going as they clear a space, cut some trees, and build a cabin. Their long weeks of work are followed by a clumsy football game in which the three of them, so different from one another, show that they've become a family.

It is after this section of the movie that things begin to go a little wrong. Without telling you everything that happens (because that would remove the necessary shock value), I can say that Jeremiah runs up against a host of impenetrable wilderness mysteries, undying Indian blood feuds and, yes, fate itself. In the end he becomes a mysterious and legendary figure, a man of the mountains, who is too symbolic to suit me.

Still, as the portrait of a man who turns his back on society, *Jeremiah Johnson* is a finely felt and beautiful film. And the scenery is particularly beautiful. I say that with a certain sense of pain; I made a vow never to praise a movie because "the scenery is beautiful." The scenery is beautiful in movies. Liking a movie because of its beautiful scenery is like buying a car because its tires are round. And yet . . . the movie was shot on location in the national forests of Utah, and there are moments in it that make *Doctor Zhivago* look cramped for space.

The Jewel of the Nile ★ ★ ★
PG, 105 m., 1985

Michael Douglas (Jack Colton), Kathleen Turner (Joan Wilder), Danny DeVito (Ralph), Avner Eisenberg (Holy Man), Spiros Focas (Omar). Directed by Lewis Teague and produced by Michael Douglas. Screenplay by Mark Rosenthal and Lawrence Konner.

The Jewel of the Nile is more silliness in the tradition of *Romancing the Stone*, which in its turn was a funny action comedy inspired by the Indiana Jones epics. We walk into the theater expecting absolutely nothing of substance, and that's exactly what we get, served up with high style. The movie reassembles three key cast members—Michael Douglas, Kathleen Turner, and Danny DeVito—and goes on to a fourth inspired casting decision with the addition of Avner Eisenberg as a holy man of gentle goofiness.

Movie industry gossip had it that Kathleen Turner didn't particularly want to make this sequel, and that even Michael Douglas, who produces as well as stars, thought it might be best to quit while he was ahead. But the original contract specified a sequel, and it's to everybody's credit that *The Jewel of the Nile* is an ambitious and elaborate attempt to repeat the success of the first movie; it's not just a ripoff.

Even so, it lacks some of the pleasures of *Romancing*, especially the development of the romance between Douglas and Turner. This time, as the movie opens, they're old friends, unwinding in Cannes and reminiscing about the good times they had in South America. Perhaps sensing that there is nowhere to go with this essentially stable relationship, the movie plunges them almost immediately into Middle East intrigue.

A fabulously wealthy Arab (Spiros Focas) invites Turner to travel with him to his homeland, for reasons as vague as they are fascinating. Douglas temporarily drops out; after a manufactured spat, he decides he'd rather sail his boat through the Mediterranean. Turner is quickly involved in danger as the Arab reveals plans to usurp the role of a legendary holy man, and Douglas becomes an ally of the great spiritual leader, who is known as the Jewel of the Nile. (Danny DeVito is somewhat lost in all of this, and left for long stretches of the film to wander through the desert and suffer meaningless tortures in lieu of a clearly defined role.)

The Jewel of the Nile expends amazing resources on some of its scenes, including a gigantic spiritual meeting in the desert that is staged as a cross between a rock concert and the Nuremberg Rally. What makes the Middle Eastern stuff work, however, is the performance of Eisenberg, who is a true comic discovery. He has some of the same cynical innocence we sensed in the Harold Ramis character in *Ghostbusters:* he's very wise and very innocent. Some of his best moments involve his bewildering cross-cultural dialogue: he speaks in vast metaphysical concepts which are unexpectedly interrupted with 1985 slang and pop sociology.

Meanwhile, Douglas and Turner have fun with two of the broadest roles in recent memory. They fight, they make up, they wisecrack in the face of calamity. And they make an ideally matched comedy team. Just as Woody Allen and Diane Keaton always seem to be on the same wavelength in their comic dialogues, so do Douglas and Turner, in their own way, seem well matched. It seems clear that they like each other and are having fun during the parade of ludicrous situations in the movie, and their chemistry is sometimes more entertaining than the contrivances of the plot.

My favorite moment between them comes as they hang by their hands over a rat-pit, while acid gnaws away at the ropes which suspend them above certain doom. Sure, this scene owes something to *Raiders of the Lost Ark.* But what's new about it this time is the dialogue, the way they break down and confess they love each other and make marriage plans as death inexorably approaches. And then, when DeVito appears and might possibly save them, there is some business with a ladder that is followed by dialogue so perfectly timed that I laughed not so much in amusement as in delight at how well the mechanisms of the scene fell together.

For all of those pleasures, *The Jewel of the Nile* is a slight and lightweight entertainment. How could it be otherwise? And it is not quite the equal of *Romancing the Stone.* That's not a surprise. For what it is, though, it's fun. And for what it's worth, Douglas and Turner could keep on working in this tradition forever, giving us a 1980s version of the Crosby and Hope *Road* pictures. I guess they don't want to, though, and perhaps that's just as well. What I hope is that a casting director sees Avner Eisenberg for what he is, the most intriguing comedy discovery in a long time.

Jo Jo Dancer, Your Life Is Calling
★ ★ ★
R, 97 m., 1986 ✓

Richard Pryor (Jo Jo), Debbie Allen (Michelle), Paula Kelly (Satin Doll), Billy Eckstine (Johnny Barnett), Art Evans (Arturo), J.J. Barry (Sal), Barbara Williams (Dawn), Carmen McRae (Grandmother), Diahnne Abbott (Mother), Scoey Mitchell (Father), E'Lon Cox (Little Jo Jo). Directed and produced by Richard Pryor. Screenplay by Rocco Urbisci, Paul Mooney, and Pryor.

Richard Pryor says that *Jo Jo Dancer, Your Life Is Calling* is not really his autobiography, and I believe him. But the movie is clearly inspired by the journey he has taken since that day in 1980 when he almost killed himself in a drug-related accident. There is pain in this movie, and truth, and also a lot of warmth and nostalgia. There is a certain incompleteness in the ending of the film, however; it seems to close without a third act. But Pryor has said there may be a sequel, and perhaps that's where the rest of the story will be told.

Jo Jo Dancer begins when its hero already is an entertainment superstar. We track him restlessly around his luxurious Hollywood home as he calls a drug dealer and sets up a party, all the time claiming that he's off drugs. He throws bottles and paraphernalia into the fireplace, screams to himself that he's gotta stop, and then decides to do cocaine one last time. The rest of the scene is borrowed from the headlines, as Jo Jo is raced into an emergency room with burns over most of his body.

He faces a turning point. Will he choose to live, or die? Jo Jo's alter ego separates from his body, looks down at the bandages, and says, "Jo Jo, what have you done to us this time?" And then the alter ego embarks on a trip back through Jo Jo's life and the memories that will die if the body dies.

We see little Jo Jo being raised in a small Ohio town, where his grandmother runs a whorehouse, and his mother is one of the girls. We see the affection he receives, but also the conflicting signals about sex, race, and booze. Later, after his mother has married, there is tension at home after Jo Jo announces that he thinks he could become a nightclub comedian. There are painful scenes of his first stumbling attempts to entertain an audience, and then the night when he talks back to a drunk and begins to find his own onstage voice.

This early show business material supplies the most heartfelt material in the film, and some of its best characters, especially a stripper named Satin Doll (Paula Kelly), who befriends Jo Jo and gets him his first job. Backstage, we meet the boozy old emcee (Art Evans), and the veteran trouper (Billy Eckstine). There is a great sequence where Pryor, dressed in drag, pulls out a fake pistol and tries to bluff the club's Mafia owners into paying him his salary.

There's an abrupt transition from these early scenes, which seem bathed in a glow of nostalgia and gratitude, and later scenes in which Jo Jo starts to make it big and is introduced to the Beverly Hills cocaine scene. Along the way, there have been several wives, one too frightened to leave her hometown, one so mercenary she comes along only for the money, one a white girl who likes cocaine too much. None of the relationships seems real, because Jo Jo doesn't seem real himself.

That's a point Pryor makes at the end of the film, in an onstage routine that represents his comeback nightclub act after he recovers from his accident. These passages are a reminder of *Richard Pryor Live on the Sunset Strip* and *Richard Pryor Here and Now*, his two post-cocaine concert films. He talks about always feeling that he didn't belong, always needing the instant confidence that came from booze and drugs, until finally they took away everything they had promised him.

The problem with the final onstage scene is that it's too self-contained. It doesn't take the dramatic chances that the rest of the movie is so willing to risk. It shows Pryor the performer, instead of continuing the story of Jo Jo the character. The structure of the movie leads us to a place where we expect some sort of redemption and re-evaluation from the character, but it's not there and we miss it. Maybe the sequel will show Jo Jo learning to live without drugs.

All the same, Pryor has taken some major risks in this movie. He has played straight and honest with his story, but he also has shown that he has a real gift as a director; the narrative scenes in the movie have a convic-tion and an interest that grow and hold us. This isn't a heartfelt amateur night, but a film by an artist whose art has become his life.

Johnny Dangerously ★ ★
PG-13, 90 m., 1984

Michael Keaton (Johnny), Joe Piscopo (Danny Vermin), Marilu Henner (Lil), Maureen Stapleton (Mom Kelly), Peter Boyle (Jocko), Griffin Dunne (D.A.), Glynnis O'Connor (Sally). Directed by Amy Heckerling and produced by Michael Hertzberg. Screenplay by Norman Steinberg, Bernie Kukoff, Harry Colomby, and Jeff Harris.

The opening scenes of *Johnny Dangerously* are so funny you just don't see how they can keep it up. And you're right: They can't. But they make a real try. The movie wants to do for gangster films what *Airplane!* did for *Airport*, and *Top Secret* did for spy movies. It has its work cut out; this formula consumes comic inspiration at an exhausting rate, and the gangster movie is not exactly an original target for satire. What distinguishes *Johnny Dangerously* from the other attempts in this direction is the caliber of the actors: This is a high-class cast, having fun with the material, and bringing a certain reality to some of the characters almost in spite of themselves.

Michael Keaton, from *Mr. Mom*, plays Johnny as a sweet, sort of gentle gangster who doesn't see any need to stir things up. His archenemy is Danny Vermin, played by Joe Piscopo, and there are a lot of other inter-esting characters around, including Marilu Henner as a sex bomb who spends some of her most intimate moments on top of a piano; Peter Boyle as an eminently reason-able mob patriarch, and Maureen Stapleton as Johnny's long-suffering mom.

The movie begins with the promise that it will grow into a great comedy. There's a title song out of left field, sung by Weird Al Yankovich, and then we see Johnny as a mid-dle-aged pet store owner, stamping prices on his animals using one of those tape labeling machines they use in grocery stores. A kid tries to shoplift, and that inspires Johnny to remember the days when he began his own career in crime. The flashback then develops more or less along standard gangster movie lines, with of course a comic twist on every cliché. It's a little dizzying trying to spot all of the cameo roles as they go by; everybody who wandered onto the 20th Century Fox lot must have been hired to walk through this movie. But what gradually occurs to us is that we aren't laughing as often; the movie keeps trying, but it runs out of steam.

Too bad. And especially too bad for Joe Piscopo, who is such an accomplished mimic that he once literally had me thinking I was watching Jerry Lewis on "Saturday Night Live." Since masters of disguise are a fixture in gangster movies, why didn't they let Piscopo play a most-wanted criminal who was desperately trying to alter his appearance, and kept running up against incompetent gangland plastic surgeons? He plays Danny Vermin well enough, but the role seems rather limiting.

Johnny Got His Gun ★ ★ ★ ★
R, 111 m., 1971

Timothy Bottoms (Joe Bonham), Kathy Fields (Kareen), Jason Robards (Joe's Father), Diane Varsi (Fourth Nurse), Donald Sutherland (Jesus Christ), Eduard Franz (General Tillery). Directed by Dalton Trumbo and produced by Bruce Campbell. Screenplay by Trumbo.

I've never much liked anti-war films. They've never much stopped war, for one thing. For another, they attract hushed and reverential praise which speaks of their universality and the urgency of their messages. Most anti-war films come so burdened with universality and urgency that the ads for them read like calls to sunrise services.

Dalton Trumbo's *Johnny Got His Gun* smelled like that kind of anti-war film. It came out of the Cannes Film Festival with three awards and a slightly pious aroma, as if it had been made for joyless Student Peace Union types of thirty-five years ago. But it isn't like that at all. Trumbo has taken the most difficult sort of material—the story of a soldier who lost his arms, his legs, and most of his face in a World War I shell burst—and handled it, strange to say, in a way that's not so much anti-war as pro-life. Perhaps that's why I admire it. Instead of belaboring ironic points about the "war to end war," Trumbo remains stubbornly on the human level. He

lets his ideology grow out of his characters, instead of imposing it from above. In this sense, his film resembles Joseph Losey's *King and Country* which also turned its back on the war in order to consider one ordinary, unremarkable soldier.

Trumbo's soldier is Joe Bonham (Timothy Bottoms), who comes from an American background that is clearly modeled on Trumbo's own. The boy works in a bakery, supports his mother and sisters after his father's death, is in love with an open-faced and sweet Irish girl, and enlists in the army because "it's the sort of thing a fellow ought to do, when his country is in trouble." Months later, he's sent on a patrol into no-man's land to bury a corpse that was offending a colonel's nose. A shell lands near him, and he wakes up in a hospital.

The army is convinced he has no conscious mind. They decide to keep him alive simply to learn from him. But he can think, and gradually the enormity of his injuries is revealed to him. He is literally the prisoner of his mind, for years, until he finds a way of communicating with a sympathetic nurse (Diane Varsi).

Trumbo uses flashbacks and fantasies to make Joe alive for us, while he exists in a living death. The most charming flashback is the first, when Joe and his girl kiss in her living room and are interrupted by her father. He's an old Wobbly who sends them both into the bedroom, and there is a love scene of such tenderness and beauty that its echoes resound through the entire film. Other scenes develop Joe's relationship with his father (Jason Robards) and with Jesus Christ (Donald Sutherland), whom he consults in fantasies. Christ really doesn't have much to suggest; he has no answers, in Joe's fantasies, because there are no answers.

The movie ends with no political solutions and without, in fact, even a political position. It simply states a case. Here was a patriotic young man who went off and was grievously wounded for no great reason, and whose conscious mind remains a horrible indictment of the system that sent all the young men away to kill each other. The soldier's own answer to his situation seems like the only possible one. He wants them to put him in a sideshow, where, as a freak, he can cause people a moment's thought about war.

If they won't do that, he wants them to kill him. The army won't do either, of course.

The Journey of Natty Gann ★ ★ ★
PG, 101 m., 1985

Meredith Salenger (Natty Gann), John Cusack (Harry Slade), Ray Wise (Natty's Father). Directed by Jeremy Kagan and produced by Mike Lobell. Screenplay by Jeanne Rosenberg.

There is one sense in which I cannot stand any movie involving a child and an animal. I am acutely aware of the possibilities for manipulating the story in order to gain unearned emotional payoffs. There is another sense in which I cannot resist a story about a child and an animal—if it is done intelligently, bravely, and without cheap sentiment.

The Journey of Natty Gann falls into the second category. It begins with potentially lethal ingredients: A young girl is joined by a glorious wolf on a cross-country odyssey in search of her missing father. Along the way, she is befriended by another teen-age drifter, threatened by tough kids and railway cops, and faced with one setback after another. This is the sort of story that used to be routinely trashed by the Walt Disney people, who would turn it into sentimental melodrama. Amazingly, then, *The Journey of Natty Gann* is a Disney production, more evidence of the fresh winds blowing through the studio.

The movie stars Meredith Salenger, a solemn-faced newcomer, as Natty Gann, the young teen-age daughter of a Chicago working-class stiff (Ray Wise). The time is the Depression. Jobs are scarce and dollars are few. When Wise gets a chance at a good-paying lumberman's job in the Northwest, he decides to take it. The bus is pulling out, Natty is nowhere to be found, and he decides to leave her in the care of a boarding-house owner and send for her later.

It appears to Natty that he is never going to send for her, and the reformatory beckons. She hops on a freight train and heads west in a forlorn search for her father, and most of the movie concerns her adventures along the way. Her great moment comes when she is lost and alone in a rainstorm in a forest, and a wolf approaches her and, amazingly, curls up at her side. With the wolf as a companion, she is understandably protected from many of the dangers of the road, and she makes it out West and also makes a friend, Harry (John Cusack), another teen-ager riding the rails.

The film's photography is magnificent, as the girl, the boy, and the wolf make their way through the Rockies and into the Northwest. More to the point is the relationship between Natty and her wolf. The movie was written by Jeanne Rosenberg, co-author of *The Black Stallion*, and again this time there is a real, fundamental feeling for the reality of a relationship between a human and a beast. The wolf looks longingly into the forest, but stays by the girl's side, and there is a thrilling sequence in which both of them jump a freight train—a close call.

This is the kind of movie that younger teen-agers might like a lot, if they have not already been broken down by the corrupt cynicism of so many Hollywood "teen-age" movies. It is about dreams and fears and dangers, love and determination. And it does justice to those qualities.

Julia ★ ★ ½
PG, 118 m., 1977

Jane Fonda (Lillian), Vanessa Redgrave (Julia), Jason Robards (Hammett), Maximilian Schell (Johann), Hal Holbrook (Alan), Rosemary Murphy (Dottie). Directed by Fred Zinnemann and produced by Richard Roth. Screenplay by Alvin Sargent.

Julia is the story of a fascinating woman, told from the point of view of someone who hardly knew her. That is, I realize, an unkind judgment against Lillian Hellman, whose wartime memoirs provide the inspiration for the story. But this movie's problems start with its point of view, and it never quite recovers from them. The film is structured as a tribute to a memory. We hear the voice of Jane Fonda, as Lillian Hellman, telling us about this great friend of her youth, and how Julia (Vanessa Redgrave) grew up to become a brave and doomed woman. All very well, but the film never really establishes a relationship between the two women; instead, it documents an attitude. To Lillian, Julia is a goddess. But what is Lillian to Julia? A courier, in the movie's long central scene:

Lillian is recruited to carry large sums of Julia's money into pre-war Germany, to buy the freedom of several hundred Jews and other prisoners. But even here, in a scene in a Vienna cafe that contains the longest of the movie's rare stretches of dialogue between Julia and Lillian, confidences are not really exchanged. Julia, who seems to be acting as she feels an Eric Ambler heroine should, doesn't reveal herself except in a sort of understated, heroic posture.

It's awkward, the way the movie has to suspend itself between Julia—its ostensible subject—and Lillian Hellman, its real subject. Jane Fonda provides an interesting portrait of the young woman playwright who banged out her frustrations on the typewriter, who chain-smoked, who drank too much (and lived with Dashiell Hammett, who also drank too much) and who eventually became the legend we know today. We like this Lillian so much, indeed, that we wouldn't at all mind a whole movie about her.

But, no, the movie pretends to be about Julia. And so we get romantic flashbacks, and heroic musings on the sound track, and the one story trying to fit into the other and splitting its seams. The movie's central weakness betrays itself when we compare its two relationships. The one between Lillian and "Dash" is basically intended as background and atmosphere, I suppose, but Fonda and Jason Robards, Jr., make it real. They bring dimensions to it: When Hammett finally bestows his blessings on one of Hellman's plays, we believe the moment.

Between Lillian and Julia, though, there are only two notes. One is childhood idolatry, as in the scene, beautiful to watch but impossible to take seriously, in which the two adolescent girls idealize their emotions. The other is adult role-playing, in which Julia strides purposefully through Oxford, and then through Europe, playing the kind of heroic radical Vanessa Redgrave has sometimes fancied herself. Lillian, at her side, can admire and envy. But she cannot connect.

What you really have, buried deep within the memoir, is the unspoken wish that Lillian had known Julia better. But Julia remains an enigma. We see key moments of Lillian's life—we even see her glorying in her first Broadway success—but the movie's

missing comparable information about Julia. She remains a distant symbol, an example of what women can do, an icon.

Many of the reviews of *Julia* went on and on about the relationship it portrays between two women, and have discovered in the movie all sorts of feminist lessons. That's wishful thinking. The only real relationship in the movie is the man-woman one, and, if anything, *Julia* documents how hard it was forty years ago for two women, even emancipated intellectual women, to meet each other on the level.

Perhaps to cover up that weakness, director Fred Zinnemann provides a long, would-be suspenseful, set-piece in the center of the film, following Lillian as she attempts to smuggle the money into Germany. The caper is so awkwardly acted and directed that we sometimes can't even follow it. The timing is off, the significant glances are insignificant, the adventure seems cooked up to fill screen time.

If *Julia* had been about Julia, that would have been an improvement. If it had been about Lillian, that would have been an inspiration. But how did a movie get made that isn't really about either one of them?

Just Between Friends ★ ½
PG-13, 110 m., 1985

Mary Tyler Moore (Holly Davis), Christine Lahti (Sandy Dunlap), Ted Danson (Chip Davis), Sam Waterston (Harry Crandall), Salome Jens (Helga), Read Morgan (Charlie). Directed by Allan Burns and produced by Edward Teets and Burns. Screenplay by Burns.

The story in *Just Between Friends* could have been interesting, if only the movie knew how to tell it. Watching this film is the damnedest experience, because it labors over the smallest points of the most inconsequential scenes, and then hurries past the big emotional climaxes.

The first hour of the movie is the setup, and there are times when we feel we are watching every single waking moment in the lives of the characters. The second hour is the payoff, filled with shocking developments and revelations, and there are moments when we want to ask the projectionist if maybe he has forgotten a reel.

The movie stars Mary Tyler Moore as a housewife who is married to a seismologist (Ted Danson) and spends her days raising their children and her evenings at aerobics class. One day at the gym, she meets a spunky, independent young woman (Christine Lahti), and they feel an instant affection for one another. They go out for coffee, they talk for hours, and Moore invites Lahti over for dinner.

At this point, there is the first of the movie's shocking revelations. Since it was revealed in commercials for the film, I feel no guilt in telling you that Danson and Lahti are lovers, that Moore doesn't know it, and that when Lahti accepts the invitation to dinner, she has no idea this nice woman is married to her lover. (In a case of misidentification not quite worthy of Elizabethan comedy, she doesn't know his nickname is Chip.)

Now let's back up a second, to a particularly irritating little scene that illustrates what's wrong with this movie. Early in the story, an earthquake shakes California, and Lahti, a TV reporter, goes on the air with lover Danson, the earthquake expert. Meanwhile, at home, Mary Tyler Moore's phone rings just as the interview begins, and although her kids keep shouting at her to come and watch Daddy on TV, she can't get rid of the caller for minute after agonizing minute, until the interview is over. Thus, she doesn't realize that Lahti and her husband have already met.

What's irritating is, we never believe Moore would have that much trouble getting rid of her caller. Why couldn't she just shout, "My husband's on TV—hang on a minute!" By dragging the scene out to an awkward and unconvincing length, the movie makes us restless and frustrated. Sure, it's important to show that Moore doesn't see Lahti and her husband together—otherwise, she'd mention it to Lahti, who would realize this was the wife of her lover. But didn't it occur to anybody that one way to do that was to eliminate the silly scene altogether?

By contrast, consider the scene not long after, in which Lahti arrives at dinner, where Moore hopes to fix her up with their bachelor friend (Sam Waterston). What happens at a dinner party for four, at which the wife is the only one who doesn't know about her husband's affair with the guest? You won't find out in this movie, which uses a few awkward sitcom double-takes, and dumps out. The dinner scene was potentially the centerpiece of the movie, but the movie doesn't have the heart or the imagination to really deal with it.

Later in the film, there is another surprise, which I will not reveal, and then another one. The movie attempts to make a heartwarming statement about the love-hate relationship between these two women who love the same man. But there's no time left. The movie took forty-five minutes to show us the first day of this story, but now it lets months slide past without a blink rather than deal with the implications.

By the end of the movie, we don't believe in the emotional honesty of anything that happens, because it all happens on cue. In fact, it happens on musical cue: The movie's sound track has an irritating habit of tipping us off to emotional changes about to take place. (The movie industry calls movie scores like this one "Mickey Mouse music," because, just like in cartoons, the music faithfully mirrors everything on screen.)

There are a few good things in *Just Between Friends*. One shot in particular, of the two women seen through a doorway, sharing a moment of truth, is so effective it makes its surrounding scenes seem unworthy. Another good scene shows Moore confronting Lahti with her knowledge of her husband's affair.

But why is the rest of the movie so ungainly? Why, in showing that Moore and Lahti instantly like each other, does the director show them exchanging so many superfluous glances at an aerobics class that they seem to be picking each other up? Why is Moore's mother (Jane Greer) able to discover a secret in ten seconds when Moore can't figure it out in ten months?

A movie like this needs a bottom line of plausibility and accuracy if it's going to hold our interest. There are so many logical contradictions in the plot, so many loose ends, so many inexplicable decisions, that we give up. These characters have their hearts in the right place, but are they playing with a full deck?

Kagemusha ★ ★ ★ ★
PG, 160 m., 1980

Tatsuya Nakadai (Shingen and Kagemusha), Tsutomu Yamazaki (Nobukado), Kenichi Hagiwara (Katsuyori), Jinpachi Nezu (Bodyguard), Shuji Otaki (Fire General). Directed by Akira Kurosawa and produced by Kurosawa and Tomoyuki Tanaka. Screenplay by Kurosawa and Masato Ide.

Kagemusha, we learn, means "shadow warrior" in Japanese, and Akira Kurosawa's great film tells the story of a man who becomes the double, or shadow, of a great warrior. It also teaches the lesson that shadows or appearances are as important as reality, but that men cannot count on either shadows or reality.

Kagemusha is a samurai drama by the director who most successfully introduced the genre to the West (with such classics as *The Seven Samurai* and *Yojimbo*), and who, at the age of seventy, made an epic that dares to wonder what meaning the samurai code—or any human code—really has in the life of an individual man. His film is basically the story of one such man, a common thief who, because of his astonishing resemblance to the warlord Shingen, is chosen as Shingen's double. When Shingen is mortally wounded in battle, the great Takeda clan secretly replaces him with the double—so their enemies will not learn that Shingen is dead. Thus begins a period of three years during which the kagemusha is treated by everyone, even his son and his mistresses, as if he were the real Shingen. Only his closest advisers know the truth.

But he is not Lord Shingen. And so every scene is undercut with irony. It is important that both friends and enemies believe Shengen is alive; his appearance, or shadow, creates both the respect of his clan and the caution of his enemies. If he is unmasked, he is useless; as Shingen's double, he can send hundreds of men to be killed, and his own guards will willingly sacrifice their lives for him. But as himself, he is worthless, and when he *is* unmasked, he's banished into the wilderness.

What is Kurosawa saying here? I suspect the answer can be found in a contrast between two kinds of scenes. His film contains epic battle scenes of astonishing beauty and scope. And then there are the intimate scenes in the throne room, the bedroom, the castles, and battlefield camps. The great battle scenes glorify the samurai system. Armies of thousands of men throw themselves heedlessly at death, for the sake of pride. But the intimate scenes undermine that glorious tradition; as everyone holds their breath, Shingen's double is tested in meetings with his son, his mistresses, and his horse. They know him best of all. If they are not fooled, all of the panoply and battlefield courage is meaningless, because the Tanaka clan has lost the leader who is their figurehead; the illusion that he exists creates the clan's reality.

Kurosawa made this film after a decade of personal travail. Although he is often considered the greatest living Japanese director, he was unable to find financial backing in Japan when he first tried to make *Kagemusha*. He made a smaller film, *Dodeskaden*, which was not successful. He tried to commit suicide, but failed. He was backed by the Russians and went to Siberia to make the beautiful *Dersu Uzala* (1976), about a man of the wilderness. But *Kagemusha* remained his obsession, and he was finally able to make it only when Hollywood directors Francis Ford Coppola and George Lucas helped him find U.S. financing.

The film he finally made is simple, bold, and colorful on the surface, but very thoughtful. Kurosawa seems to be saying that great human endeavors (in this case, samurai wars) depend entirely on large numbers of men sharing the same fantasies or beliefs. It is entirely unimportant, he seems to be suggesting, whether or not the beliefs are based on reality—all that matters is that men accept them. But when a belief is shattered, the result is confusion, destruction, and death. At the end of *Kagemusha*, for example, the son of the real Lord Shingen orders his troops into a suicidal charge, and their deaths are not only unnecessary but meaningless, because they are not on behalf of the sacred person of the warlord.

There are great images in this film: Of a breathless courier clattering down countless steps, of men passing in front of a blood-red sunset, of a dying horse on a battlefield. But Kurosawa's last image—of the dying kagemusha floating in the sea, swept by tidal currents past the fallen standard of the Takeda clan—summarizes everything: ideas and men are carried along heedlessly by the currents of time, and historical meaning *seems* to emerge when both happen to be swept in the same way at the same time.

The Karate Kid ★ ★ ★ ★
PG, 126 m., 1984

Ralph Macchio (Daniel), Noriyuki "Pat" Morita (Miyagi), Elisabeth Shue (Ali), Martin Kove (Kreese), William Zabka (Johnny). Directed by John G. Avildsen and produced by Jerry Weintraub. Written by Robert Mark Kamen.

I didn't want to see this movie. I took one look at the title and figured it was either (a) a sequel to *Toenails of Vengeance,* or (b) an adventure pitting Ricky Schroeder against the Megaloth Man. I was completely wrong. *The Karate Kid* was one of the nice surprises of 1984—an exciting, sweet-tempered, heartwarming story with one of the most interesting friendships in a long time. The friends come from different worlds. A kid named Daniel (Ralph Macchio) is a New Jersey teen-ager who moves with his mother to Los Angeles. An old guy named Miyagi (Pat Morita) is the Japanese janitor in their apartment building. When Daniel starts to date the former girlfriend of the toughest kid in the senior class, the kid starts pounding on Daniel's head on a regular basis. Daniel tries to fight back, but this is a Southern California kid, and so of course he has a black belt in karate. Enter Mr. Miyagi, who seems to be a harmless old eccentric with a curious hobby: He tries to catch flies with chopsticks. It turns out that Miyagi is a karate master, a student not only of karate fighting but of the total philosophy of the martial arts. He agrees to take Daniel as his student.

And then begins the wonderful center section of *The Karate Kid,* as the old man and the kid from Jersey become friends. Miyagi's system of karate instruction is offbeat, to say the least. He puts Daniel to work shining cars, painting fences, scrubbing the bottoms of pools. Daniel complains that he isn't learning karate, he's acting as free labor. But there is a system to Mr. Miyagi's training.

The Karate Kid was directed by Ralph Avildsen, who made *Rocky.* It ends with the same sort of climactic fight scene; Daniel faces his enemies in a championship karate tournament. But the heart of this movie isn't in the fight sequences, it's in the relationships. And in addition to Daniel's friendship with Miyagi, there's also a sweet romantic liaison with Ali (Elisabeth Shue), who is your standard girl from the right side of town and has the usual snobbish parents.

Macchio is an unusual, interesting choice for Daniel. He's not the basic handsome Hollywood teen-ager but a thin, tall, intense kid with a way of seeming to talk to himself. His delivery always sounds natural, even offhand; he never seems to be reading a line. He's a good, sound, interesting lead, but the movie really belongs to Pat Morita, an actor who has been around a long time (he was Arnold on "Happy Days") without ever having a role anywhere near this good. Morita makes Miyagi into an example of applied serenity. In a couple of scenes where he has to face down a hostile karate coach, Miyagi's words are so carefully chosen they don't give the other guy any excuse to get violent; Miyagi uses the language as carefully as his hands or arms to ward off blows and gain an advantage. It's refreshing to see a completely original character like this old man. *The Karate Kid* is a sleeper with a title that gives you the wrong idea: It's one of 1984's best movies.

Kerouac ★ ★ ½
NO MPAA RATING, 73 m., 1985

Jack Coulter (Kerouac). With appearances by Carolyn Cassady, Lawrence Ferlinghetti, William S. Burroughs, Allen Ginsberg, and Joyce Johnson. Directed and produced by John Antonelli. Screenplay by John Tytell, Antonelli, and Frank Cervarich.

Jack Kerouac announced the Beat Generation with his 1957 novel *On the Road* and, within a few years, the Beats had metamorphized into hippies and yippies and flower children. What started as a popularization of a Bohemian lifestyle eventually grew into the badge of a generation. But Kerouac himself sat out most of the 1960s, disappearing with consistent desperation into alcohol, and by the time the great anti-establishment beatnik died, his mother was running his checkbook.

What John Antonelli's short documentary *Kerouac* demonstrates more than anything else is the way we adapt legends to our needs. At the time of his great success, Kerouac was seen as a wild rebel, an anarchic poet who flouted convention and churned out great passionate novels. Much was made of his writing style; instead of individual sheets of writing paper, Kerouac used endless paper rolls from the wire services, so he'd never have to slow down to change paper. Modern writers, using word processors, are essentially doing the same thing, only faster—but Kerouac's approach inspired Truman Capote's immortal barb, "That's not writing. It's typing." The robust, cheerful energy of Kerouac's early work was much more than typing, however, and at the end of the Eisenhower 1950s the Beats came like a howling gale of fresh air. Everything seemed to fit together, as the 1950s became the 1960s: Kerouac, modern jazz, Lenny Bruce, Allen Ginsberg's *Howl*, Mailer's *Advertisements for Myself*, Ferlinghetti's City Lights books, the New Journalism at *Esquire*, the experimentation with lifestyle that was shocking then and is now considered a sign of mental health. To the degree that one man can be said to have dramatized the period, that man is probably Jack Kerouac.

The problem was, Jack was a drunk. You can see that awkward fact sneaking around the edges of a lot of the things people say about him in this documentary. They talk about his genius, his good looks, his charm . . . and his drinking. For a time he was a regular guest on TV talk shows (the movie opens with a clip from the Steve Allen program), but then he got to be unreliable, and his confidence vanished, and eventually he vanished, too. Lawrence Ferlinghetti apologizes for sounding harsh, and then says he remembers Kerouac as a drunk at a party, clutching a bottle.

Antonelli's film is studiously noncommittal in the face of the testimony by Kerouac's friends. His approach is an interesting one: He shoots on the locations of Kerouac's childhood, young manhood, and Beat adventures, and uses an actor (Jack Coulter) to represent him. Coulter hardly ever speaks. Instead, the sound track combines narration with on-camera interviews and with selections from Kerouac's prose.

Among the friends who remember him are Carolyn Cassady, who was married to Neal Cassady, the model for Dean Moriarty, the hero of *On the Road*. We also hear from Ginsberg, William S. Burroughs and Joyce Johnson, who was one of the girls Jack loved and left. The film plays something like an educational docudrama, but it's an interesting companion to *Heart Beat*, (see p. 245) the 1979 feature based on Kerouac's life and starring John Heard, Nick Nolte, and Sissy Spacek. It has less of the romance, and more of the unhappy reality, of a man who sent his generation on a voyage of self-discovery, and then hid from himself in a bottle.

The Killing Fields ★ ★ ★ ★
R, 139 m., 1984

Sam Waterston (Sydney Schanberg), Dr. Haing S. Ngor (Dith Pran), John Malkovich (Al Rockoff), Craig T. Nelson (Military Attaché), Athol Fugard (Dr. Sundesval). Directed by Roland Joffe and produced by David Puttnam. Screenplay by Bruce Robinson.

There's a strange thing about stories based on what the movies insist on calling "real life." The haphazard chances of life, the unanticipated twists of fate, have a way of getting smoothed down into Hollywood formulas, so that what might once have happened to a real person begins to look more and more like what might once have happened to John Wayne. One of the risks taken by *The Killing Fields* is to cut loose from that tradition, to tell us a story that does not have a traditional Hollywood structure, and to trust that we'll find the characters so interesting that we won't miss the cliché. It is a risk that works, and that helps make this into a really affecting experience.

The "real life" story behind the movie is by now well-known. Sydney Schanberg, a correspondent for the *New York Times*, covered the invasion of Cambodia with the help of Dith Pran, a local journalist and translator. When the country fell to the communist Khmer Rouge, the lives of all foreigners were immediately at risk, and Schanberg got out along with most of his fellow Western correspondents. He offered Pran a chance to leave with him, but Pran elected to stay. And when the Khmer Rouge drew a bamboo curtain around Cambodia, Pran disappeared into a long silence. Back home in New York, Schanberg did what he could to discover information about his friend; for example, he wrote about four hundred letters to organizations like the Red Cross. But it was a futile exercise, and Schanberg had given up his friend for dead, when one day four years later word came that Pran was still alive and had made it across the border to a refugee camp. The two friends were reunited, in one of the rare happy endings that come out of a period of great suffering.

As a human story, this is a compelling one. As a Hollywood story, it obviously will not do because the last half of the movie is essentially Dith Pran's story, told from his point of view. Hollywood convention has it that the American should fight his way back into the occupied country (accompanied by renegade Green Berets and Hell's Angels, and Rambo, if possible), blast his way into a prison camp, and save his buddy. That was the formula for *Uncommon Valor* and *Missing in Action*, two box-office hits, and in *The Deer Hunter* one friend went back to Vietnam to rescue another. Sitting in New York writing letters is not quite heroism on the same scale. And yet, what else could Schanberg do? And, more to the point, what else could Dith Pran do, in the four years of his disappearance, but try to disguise his origins and his education, and pass as an illiterate peasant—one of the countless prisoners of Khmer Rouge work camps? By telling his story, and by respecting it, *The Killing Fields* becomes a film of an altogether higher order than the Hollywood revenge thrillers.

The movie begins in the early days of the journalistic coverage of Cambodia. We meet Schanberg (Sam Waterston) and Pran (played by Dr. Haing S. Ngor, whose own story is an uncanny parallel to his character's), and we sense the strong friendship and loyalty that they share. We also absorb the conditions in the country, where warehouses full of Coca-Cola are blown up by terrorists who know a symbolic target when they see one. Life is a routine of hanging out at cafes and restaurants and official briefings, punctuated by an occasional trip to the front, where the American view of things does not seem to be reflected by the suffering that the correspondents witness.

The whole atmosphere of this period is suggested most successfully by the character of an American photographer, played by John Malkovich as a cross between a dopehead and a hard-bitten newsman. He is not stirred to action very easily, and still less easily stirred to caring, but when an occasion rises (for example, the need to forge a passport for Pran), he reveals the depth of his feeling. As the Khmer Rouge victory becomes inevitable, there are scenes of incredible tension, especially one in which Dith Pran saves the lives of his friends by some desperate fast talking with the cadres of adolescent rebels who would just as soon shoot them. Then there is the confusion of the evacuation of the U.S. Embassy and a last glimpse of Dith Pran before he disappears for four years.

In a more conventional film, he would, of course, have really disappeared, and we would have followed the point of view of the Schanberg character. But this movie takes the chance of switching points of view in midstream, and the last half of the film belongs to Dith Pran, who sees his country turned into an insane parody of a one-party state, ruled by the Khmer Rouge with instant violence and a savage intolerance for any reminders of the French and American presence of the colonial era. Many of the best scenes in the film's second half are essentially played without dialogue, as Pran works in the fields, disguises his origins, and waits for his chance.

The film is a masterful achievement on all the technical levels—it does an especially good job of convincing us with its Asian locations—but the best moments are the human ones, the conversations, the exchanges of trust, the waiting around, the sudden fear, the quick bursts of violence, the desperation. At the center of many of those scenes is Dr. Haing S. Ngor, a non-actor who was recruited for the role from the ranks of Cambodian refugees in California, and who brings to it a simple sincerity that is absolutely convincing. Sam Waterston is effective in the somewhat thankless role of Sydney Schanberg, and among the carefully drawn vignettes are Craig T. Nelson as a military attaché and Athol Fugard as Dr. Sundesval.

The American experience in Southeast Asia has given us a great film epic *(Apocalypse Now)* and a great drama *(The Deer Hunter)*. Here is the story told a little closer to the ground, of people who were not very important and not very powerful, who got caught up in events that were indifferent to them, but never stopped trying to do their best and their most courageous.

King David ★
PG-13, 114 m., 1985

Richard Gere (David), Luigi Montefiori (Goliath), Jenny Lipman (Abigail), Genevieve Allenbury (Ahinoam), David De Keyser (Ahitophel), John Castle (Abner), Denis Quilley (Samuel), Edward Woodward (Saul). Directed by Bruce Beresford and produced by Martin Elfand. Screenplay by Andrew Birkin and James Costigan.

I don't even mind that *King David* loses interest when David stops sinning and flashes forward to the big deathbed scene. I just wish David had been a more interesting sinner. If there's anything more boring than a scandalous movie with a moral at the end, it's the moral without the scandal. Salome isn't Hollywood's favorite biblical character for nothing.

I suspect this may not be the properly devout note on which to launch a review of *King David,* but what other organizing principle will encompass all those beheadings, Bathsheba's wedding night, *and* David versus Goliath? *King David* is a movie without a single new or interesting idea about its characters—a "Classics Illustrated" version of the Old Testament, with its values so confused that it originally was filmed to be released with an R rating and then was trimmed to a PG-13.

There is something inherently hilarious about the thought of all those Paramount executives, trying to decide which cuts to make: Can you really release a Bible movie where kids under seventeen should be accompanied by their parents or adult guardians? As it is, the PG-13 rating probably reflects unease about the scene in which David enters Jerusalem and is so overcome with emotion that he boogies in his loincloth.

The story told in *King David* is 3,000 years old. But the movie's style is only forty years

old. This is yet another movie about biblical times that has absolutely no curiosity about what it was really like to be alive 3,000 years ago; no imagination about how people looked and behaved then; and, probably worst of all, no feeling for the powerful religious feelings they had.

Imagine, if you will, a group of small, obscure tribes in the deserts of the Middle East. Imagine their awe in the face of their God, their passion in defense of their beliefs, their determination to build a law that would tame a society still based on brute strength. There is a wonderful story there, and I have never seen a movie that told it.

Instead, the movie industry has given us an unrelenting series of set-pieces in which everyone marches about in procession, sits on thrones, and speaks in pseudobiblical solemnities, and doesn't seem to have a spark of passion or an ounce of humor in their entire bodies.

As for this particular movie, what can I say? Richard Gere, who is often interesting because of his audacity (see *American Gigolo* and *Breathless*) sleepwalks through the role of King David. When it comes to the dialogue, he shares with every other actor in the movie a fatal flaw: He says every line as if he knew what line came next. The whole movie projects a feeling of foreknowledge, as if everybody already knew the story; there is no sense of surprise or spontaneity, no sense that these characters are actually living their lives as we watch them. That's underlined by the presence of a narrator who helps the movie skip over enormous chunks of time.

I also had some problems with the movie's set design. Much is made, for example, of a large, elaborate model for a temple that David hopes to build to hold the Ark of the Covenant. The model is too large, too well-built; Gere, circling it, defending it, seems to have wandered in from architecture school. He's too much of an aesthete, instead of projecting the savage ambition of a man who wants to put up a building so he can say he did it.

What's strange is that Gere relates in much the same way to his wives in this movie, approaching them as prospective players in a legend instead of as young women he feels strongly about. Discussions with them take on the flavor of a merger between two fast-selling lines of toy myths. In the real world of 3,000 years ago, isn't it likely that marriages were both more passionate and more cruelly arranged than in this movie?

Just once, I'd like to see a Bible movie that has been entirely reimagined, from beginning to end, with new thoughts about the clothes, and buildings, and manners and even the temper of those days. I'd be happy to make suggestions. Here's one to start with: I'll bet almost anything that at least some of the people who lived 3,000 years ago talked real fast, made clever, offhand comments, and did not know that they were supposed to speak in grave, measured, historical pronouncements. I'll bet there must have been someone who said, "David! You've got to be kidding!"

The King of Comedy ★ ★ ★
PG, 101 m., 1983

Robert De Niro (Rupert Pupkin), Jerry Lewis (Jerry Langford), Diahnne Abbott (Rita), Sandra Bernhard (Masha), Ed Herlihy (Himself). Directed by Martin Scorsese. Screenplay by Paul Zimmerman.

Martin Scorsese's *The King of Comedy* is one of the most arid, painful, wounded movies I've ever seen. It's hard to believe Scorsese made it; instead of the big-city life, the violence and sexuality of his movies like *Taxi Driver* and *Mean Streets*, what we have here is an agonizing portrait of lonely, angry people with their emotions all tightly bottled up. This is a movie that seems ready to explode—but somehow it never does. That lack of release seriously disturbed me the first time I saw *The King of Comedy*. I kept straining forward, waiting for the movie to let loose, and it kept frustrating me. Maybe that was the idea. This is a movie about rejection, with a hero who never admits that he has been rejected, and so there is neither comic nor tragic release—just the postponement of pain.

I left that first screening filled with dislike for the movie. Dislike, but not disinterest. Memories of *The King of Comedy* kept gnawing at me, and when people asked me what I thought about it, I said I wasn't sure. Then I saw the movie a second time, and it seemed to work better for me—maybe because I was able to watch without any expectations. I

knew it wasn't an entertainment, I knew it didn't allow itself any emotional payoffs, I knew the ending was cynical and unsatisfactory, and so, with *those* discoveries no longer to be made, I was free to simply watch what was on the screen.

What I saw the second time, better than the first, were the performances by Robert De Niro, Jerry Lewis, Diahnne Abbott, and Sandra Bernhard, who play the movie's most important characters. They must have been difficult performances to deliver, because there's almost no feedback in this movie. The actors can't bounce emotional energy off each other, because nobody *listens* in this film; everybody's just waiting for the other person to stop talking so they can start. And everybody's so emotionally isolated in this movie that they don't even seem able to guess what they're missing.

The movie stars De Niro, as Rupert Pupkin, a nerdish man in his thirties who fantasizes himself as a television star. He practices in his basement, holding condescending conversations with life-size cardboard cutouts of Liza Minnelli and Jerry Lewis. His dream is to get a stand-up comedy slot on the late-night talk show hosted by Lewis (whose name in the movie is Jerry Langford). The movie opens with Rupert's first meeting with Jerry; he barges into Jerry's limousine and is immediately on an obnoxious first-name basis. Jerry vaguely promises to check out Rupert's comedy routine, and the rest of the movie is devoted to Rupert's single-minded pursuit of fame. He arrives at Jerry's office, is politely brushed off, returns, is ejected, arrives at Jerry's country home with a "date" in tow, is ejected again, and finally decides to kidnap Jerry.

This *sounds* like an entertaining story, I suppose, but Scorsese doesn't direct a single scene for a payoff. The whole movie is an exercise in *cinema interruptus;* even a big scene in a bar, where Rupert triumphantly turns on the TV set to reveal himself on television, is deliberately edited to leave out the payoff shots—reaction shots of the amazed clientele. Scorsese doesn't want laughs in this movie, and he also doesn't want release. The whole movie is about the inability of the characters to get any kind of a positive response to their bids for recognition.

The King of Comedy is not, you may

already have guessed, a fun movie. It is also not a bad movie. It is frustrating to watch, unpleasant to remember, and, in its own way, quite effective. It represents an enormous departure for Scorsese, whose movies teemed with life before he filmed this emotional desert, and whose camera used to prowl restlessly before he nailed it down this time. Scorsese and De Niro are the most creative, productive director/actor team in the movies right now, and the fact that they feel the freedom to make such an odd, stimulating, unsatisfying movie is good news, I guess. But *The King of Comedy* is the kind of film that makes you want to go and see a Scorsese movie.

The King of Marvin Gardens ★ ★ ★
R, 104 m., 1972

Jack Nicholson (David Staebler), Bruce Dern (Jason Staebler), Ellen Burstyn (Sally), Julia Anne Robinson (Jessica), Scatman Crothers (Lewis), Charles Levine (Grandfather). Directed and produced by Bob Rafelson. Screenplay by Jacob Brackman.

Bob Rafelson's *The King of Marvin Gardens* is a perversely satisfying movie—it works after going out of its way not to—and a very eccentric one. It backs into its real subject in much the same way that *Five Easy Pieces*, Rafelson's previous film, did. Only after it's over do some of its scenes and moments fall into place; for much of the way we've been disoriented and the story has been suspended somewhere in midair. As someone wrote about a totally dissimilar movie, Paul Morrissey's *Trash*, it's the kind of film you want to walk out of, and then when it's over you want to see it again.

The movie opens and closes with autobiographical monologues being delivered by an all-night talk jockey (Jack Nicholson) into the loneliness of the FM airwaves. He works in a darkened studio, stopping sometimes to search for words, and it's evident that his broadcasts tear something loose from deep inside. It's possible, indeed, that he says more on the radio (or into his tape recorder) in this movie than he ever gets around to saying in the actual situations he finds himself in. He's tentative, unsure, private. His radio fantasies often involve his brother, Jason (Bruce Dern), who lives in Atlantic City,

New Jersey, and does mysterious but glorious things there. After a long silence, Jason himself calls his brother and tells him to hustle down to Atlantic City because there are big deals cooking. They're going to buy an island near Hawaii and develop it into a resort. Sure.

Most of the movie takes place in Atlantic City, where the metaphor of a Monopoly game is employed a little too persistently, I thought. There's the Boardwalk, of course, and Marvin Gardens itself; but there are also Jason's attempts to buy a hotel, and the fact that he's in jail when we first meet him. This stuff is worked in quietly enough by Jacob Brackman's script, however, that it doesn't really distract.

Jason is living with a blonde on the far side of the hill (Ellen Burstyn) and her stepdaughter, a blonde coming up fast on this side (Julia Anne Robinson). A great deal of the movie is about the unacknowledged sexual competition between the two women, but this (like a few other things) becomes important only gradually. Most of the action seems to involve a disagreement between Jason, who turns out to be a minor hood, the mysterious Lewis, who is the black rackets boss and moneyman in town. Jason's deals are based on reckless confidence in Lewis's money, and Lewis isn't going along.

Until the movie's end, when everything falls together with a really stunning force, Rafelson and Brackman seem to be going for a series of set-pieces. There is an unhappy lobster dinner with two Japanese investors reputed to have money; they wear their lobster-proof bibs happily, but don't come through. There's the matter of the older blonde marching into the hotel next door to take a bath ("Hell, you told me you *owned* the damn place," she says, then Jason explains the deal is still at the stage of "negotiations over language.")

And there is a truly fine scene, almost surrealistic, in which the stepmother concedes the sexual sweepstakes to her stepdaughter and throws all of her clothes and makeup apparatus into a bonfire on the beach. Even her false eyelashes. "They're made out of mink hairs, did you know that?" she says. "For twenty years I've been wearing animal hairs on my face."

The movie's performances are as good as

we've come to expect from the somewhat incestuous BBS Productions. Rafelson had directed three movies for the company before this one, and Nicholson had acted in three and directed one (*Drive, He Said*, in which Dern was wonderfully uptight and focused as the basketball coach). These people have worked together often enough that they have a kind of BBS feel for scenes, if you will; Nicholson and Dern work with each other as easily as any two actors. Ellen Burstyn succeeds in a difficult task; she has to make her performance striking enough to justify the movie's ending, but she can't push *too* far or we'll know too much, too soon.

For the rest, all I can say is that *The King of Marvin Gardens* is an original, individual, and often frustrating movie that takes a lot of chances and wins on about sixty percent of them. There are scenes (including a simulated Miss America pageant in a deserted hall and a horseback confrontation between Nicholson and Dern) that are hopelessly affected. There are others, including Dern's blurted-out declaration of his love for his brother, that are deeply affecting.

Kiss of the Spider Woman ★ ★ ★ ½
R, 119 m., 1985

William Hurt (Luis Molina), Raul Julia (Valentin), Sonia Braga (Leni/Marta/Spider Woman), Jose Lewgoy (Warden). Directed by Hector Babenco and produced by David Weidman. Screenplay by Leonard Schrader.

Kiss of the Spider Woman tells one of those rare and entrancing stories where one thing seems to happen while another thing is really happening. There are passages in the movie that seem to be absolutely self-contained, and then a word or gesture will reveal that they have depths we can only guess. By the end of the film, what started out as a contest between two opposite personalities has expanded into a choice between two completely different attitudes toward life. And the choice is not sexual, although for a long time it seems so. It is between freedom and slavery.

The movie opens in a prison cell, somewhere in South America. A man is telling a story. The story is a lurid intrigue that seems pieced together from fragments and memories of countless old *film noir* melodramas—

from those movies of the 1940s where the woman had lips that could kill, and the men were dying to kiss them. Only gradually does the reality of the film reveal itself: We are in a cramped, depressing prison cell, and the storyteller is a prisoner, trying to pass the days by escaping into fantasy.

His name is Luis. He is played by William Hurt as an affected homosexual, a window dresser who has been jailed for sex offenses. His cellmate is Valentin (Raul Julia), a bearded, macho political prisoner who has nothing but contempt for Luis's stories— not to mention his sexuality and his politics. But as Luis calmly explains, unless someone gives him a key to walk out of his prison, he will continue to escape in any way he can.

As he continues to weave his verbal movie plots, the movie uses fantasy scenes to depict them. There is a Nazi crime melodrama, and a thriller about a spider woman, and the woman in both of them is played by the same actress (Sonia Braga). Later in the film, she will also appear as Valentin's lover; reality and fantasy are by then thoroughly mixed.

What *Kiss of the Spider Woman* at first seems to be about is the changing nature of the relationship between two very different men who have been locked together in the same cell. They are opposites in every way. But they share the same experiences, day after day, and that gives them a common bond. Gradually, an affection grows between them, and we assume that the movie will be about the ways in which they learn to accept each other. Only gradually, mysteriously, do we realize that the movie is about a good deal more. Details of the plot are revealed so subtly and so surprisingly that I will say nothing more, except that the film does not lead in the directions we anticipate.

The performances are wonderful. The director, Hector Babenco, is a Brazilian, but he has directed his American stars in English without falling prey to the occasional loss of tone you sometimes hear as foreigners work in unfamiliar languages. William Hurt, who won the Academy Award and best actor award at Cannes for this film, creates a character utterly unlike anyone else he has ever played—a frankly theatrical character, exaggerated and mannered—and yet he never seems to be reaching for effects. Raul Julia, sweaty and physical in the early scenes, gradually reveals a poetry that makes the whole movie work. And Sonia Braga, called upon to satirize bad acting, makes a perfect spider woman.

Every decade seems to be dominated by the cinema of a different country (in addition to Hollywood, of course, a country of its own). In the 1950s it was Italy. In the 1960s, France. In the 1970s, Germany. In the 1980s, Brazil and Australia seem to be the centers of the most exciting work. Babenco's previous credits include the heartbreaking *Pixote* about a child growing up on the streets of San Paolo. *Kiss of the Spider Woman* is another film of insights and surprises.

Klute ★ ★ ★½
R, 114 m., 1971

Jane Fonda (Bree Daniel), Donald Sutherland (John Klute), Charles Cioffl (Frank Ligouri), Dorothy Tristan (Arlyn Page). Directed and produced by Alan J. Pakula. Screenplay by Andy K. and Dave Lewis.

What is it about Jane Fonda that makes her such a fascinating actress to watch? She has a sort of nervous intensity that keeps her so firmly locked into a film character that the character actually seems distracted by things that come up in the movie. You almost have the feeling, a couple of times in *Klute*, that the Fonda character had other plans and was just leaving the room when this (whatever it is) came up.

The movie is about a skilled, intelligent, cynical, and personally troubled New York call girl who does not, for once, have a heart of gold. She never feels anything when she's with a man, she tells her shrink, but she does experience a sense of professional pride when she's able to satisfy a client. And some of her clients have very complicated needs, which challenge the girl's imaginative acting ability. One old garment industry tycoon, for example, has spent all his life making clothes. But he fantasizes an idealistic sort of pre-World War I existence in Europe, in Vienna maybe, and the girl describes it to him in quiet, warm images while she disrobes. He never touches her.

The girl's name is Bree, and the movie should probably be titled *Bree* instead of *Klute*, because the Fonda character is at the center. John Klute (played by Donald Sutherland) is a policeman who has come to New York, free lance, to try to settle a missing persons case. It appears that the missing man may still be alive, and may be the source of obscene letters and telephone calls Bree has been receiving. Bree initially refuses to talk to Klute, but she eventually does confide in him, mostly because she's frightened by midnight prowlers and wants his protection. The film examines their somewhat strange relationship, and at the same time functions on another level as a somewhat awkward thriller.

There are scary shots of the prowler, for example, and shots of hands gripping a mesh fence—shots that are not very satisfactory because the wrong point of view is established. One thing about a thriller is that the threat should always be seen from the point of view of the threatened. We don't like looking over the killer's shoulder at his victim; shots like that interfere with our desire to identify with the victim and be scared in a satisfactory way.

Klute doesn't scare us very satisfactorily, maybe because it's kind of schizo. The director is Alan Pakula, whose concern is all too much with plot, and it gets in the way of the unusual and interesting relationship between Bree and Klute. But how *do* you develop a relationship between a prostitute with hang-ups and a square suburban cop? *Klute* does it by making the cop into a person of restraint and dignity, a man who is genuinely concerned about this girl he's met. His attitude is what makes their love relationship so absorbing. Usually, in the movies, it's just assumed the lovers were drawn toward each other by magnetism or concealed springs or something.

The scenes between Fonda and Sutherland are very good, then, and Bree is further developed in scenes showing her trying to get out of the trade and into something straight. She takes acting lessons, she auditions to model for cosmetics ads. She talks to her shrink (in scenes that sound improvised and exhibit Fonda's undeniable intelligence).

Intelligence. I suppose that's the word. In *Klute* you don't have two attractive acting vacuums reciting speeches at each other. With Fonda and Sutherland, you have actors who understand and sympathize with their characters, and you have a vehicle worthy of that sort of intelligence. So the fact that the thriller stuff doesn't always work isn't so important.

Koyaanisqatsi ★ ★ ★
NO MPAA RATING, 87 m., 1983

Produced and directed by Godfrey Reggio.

ko·yaa·nis·qatsi, n. (Hopi). 1. crazy life. 2. life in turmoil. 3. life disintegrating. 4. life out of balance. 5. a state of life that calls for another way of living.

I give the definition because it is the key to the movie. Without it, you could make a sincere mistake. *Koyaanisqatsi* opens with magnificent images out of nature: great canyons and limitless deserts and a world without man. Through the use of speeded-up images, clouds climb the sides of mountains and speed across the sky, their shadows painting the landscape. Then the movie turns to images of smokestacks, factories, and expressways. There is an assumption on the part of the filmmaker, Godfrey Reggio, that we'll immediately get the message. And the message, I think, is that nature is wonderful, but that American civilization is a rotten despoiler that is creating a "crazy life."

But I am irreverent, and given to my own thoughts during the film. After I have admired its visionary photography (this is a beautiful movie) and fallen under the spell of its music (an original sound track by the distinguished composer Philip Glass), there is still time to think other thoughts, such as:

This film has one idea, a simplistic one. It contrasts the glory of nature with the mess made by man. But man *is* a messy beast, given to leaving reminders of his presence all over the surface of planet Earth. Although a Hopi word is used to evoke unspoiled nature, no Hopis are seen, and the contrast in the movie doesn't seem to be between American Indian society and Los Angeles expressways, but between expressways and a beautiful world *empty* of man. Thanks, but no thanks.

I had another problem. *All* of the images in this movie are beautiful, even the images of man despoiling the environment. The first shots of smokestacks are no doubt supposed to make us recoil in horror, but actu-

ally I thought they looked rather noble. The shots of the expressways are also two-edged. Given the clue in the title, we can consider them as an example of life out of control. *Or*—and here's the catch—we can marvel at the fast-action photography and reflect about all those people moving so quickly to their thousands of individual destinations. What a piece of work is a man! And what expressways he builds!

Koyaanisqatsi, then, is an invitation to knee-jerk environmentalism of the most sentimental kind. It is all images and music. There is no overt message except the obvious one (the Grand Canyon is prettier than Manhattan). It has been hailed as a vast and sorrowful vision, but to what end? If the people in all those cars on all those expressways are indeed living crazy lives, their problem is not the expressway (which is all that makes life in L.A. manageable) but perhaps social facts such as unemployment, crime, racism, drug abuse, and illiteracy—issues so complicated that a return to nature seems like an elitist joke at their expense. Having said that, let me add that *Koyaanisqatsi* is an impressive visual and listening experience, that Reggio and Glass have made wonderful pictures and sounds, and that this film is a curious throwback to the 1960s, when it would have been a short subject to be viewed through a marijuana haze. Far-out.

La Cage aux Folles ★ ★ ★ ★
R, 91 m., 1979

Ugo Tognazzi (Renato), Michel Serrault (Zaza), Michel Galabru (Charrier), Claire Maurier (Simone), Remy Laurent (Laurent), Benny Luke (Jacob). Directed by Edouard Molinaro and produced by Marcello Danon. Screenplay by Francis Veber and Molinaro.

La Cage aux Folles are "birds of a feather," which are precisely and hilariously what do not flock together in this wonderful comedy from France. It's about the gay owner of a scandalous nightclub in St. Tropez, his transvestite lover, and how the owner reacts after his son returns home one day and announces he's going to marry . . . a girl!

But that's not *really* what it's about: This is basically the first sitcom in drag, and the comic turns in the plot are achieved with such clockwork timing that sometimes we're laughing at what's funny and sometimes we're laughing at the movie's sheer comic invention. This is a great time at the movies.

The nightclub owner is played by Ugo Tognazzi, that grizzled Italian veteran of so many macho roles, and he has lived for twenty years with a drag queen (Michel Serrault) who stars in the club. They're like an old married couple, nostalgic and warm one minute, fighting like cats and dogs the next. Tognazzi sired the son all those years ago and has raised him with the help of "Auntie" Serrault and their live-in "maid," a wickedly funny black transvestite who has perhaps the movie's funniest moment.

Tognazzi and Serrault have trouble at first accepting the notion that their treasured young man is going to get married. They have more trouble, however, accepting the notion that the intended bride is the daughter of the Minister of Moral Standards—and that the in-laws are planning to come to dinner.

This dilemma inspires the film's hilarious middle section, in which Tognazzi's garishly bizarre apartment is severely redecorated in crucifixes and antiques, and Serrault is gently asked by the son if he'd mind being gone for the evening: "I told them my father was a Cultural Attaché; what'll they think when they find out he lives with a drag queen?"

Tognazzi, meanwhile, goes to visit the woman who bore his son two decades ago, to ask her to portray the mother for one night. She agrees. Too bad, because in the course of the uproariously funny dinner party, at least two reputed mothers are produced, one of them suspiciously hairy around the chest.

Describing a comedy is always a risky business; the bare plot outline is, of course, no hint as to how funny a film is, and to steal the jokes is a misdemeanor. What I can say, though, is that La Cage aux Folles gets the audience on its side with immediate ease; it never betrays our confidence; it astonishes us with the inspiration and logic it brings to ringing changes on the basic situation.

And it contains several classic sequences. The best is perhaps the one in which Tognazzi coaches Serrault on how to act "macho," an attribute that apparently consists of knowing how to butter your toast with manly firmness. There's also that extended dinner scene that begins with the

Minister of Moral Standards discovering that . . . Greek boys . . . are doing . . . *something* . . . on his soup plate . . . and builds from there.

Lady Sings the Blues ★ ★ ★
R, 144 m., 1972

Diana Ross (Billie Holiday), Billy Dee Williams (Louis McKay), Richard Pryor (Piano Man), James Callahan (Reg Hanley), Paul Hampton (Harry), Virginia Capers (Mama Holiday). Directed by Sidney J. Furie and produced by Berry Gordy. Screenplay by Terence McCloy, Chris Clark, and Suzanne de Passa.

My first reaction when I learned that Diana Ross had been cast to play Billie Holiday was a quick and simple one: I didn't think she could do it. I knew she could sing, although not as well as Billie Holiday and certainly not in the same way, but I couldn't imagine Diana Ross reaching the emotional highs and lows of one of the more extreme public lives of our times. But the movie was financed by Motown, and Diana Ross was Motown's most cherished property, so maybe the casting made some kind of commercial sense. After all, Sal Mineo played Gene Krupa.

All of those thoughts were wiped out of my mind within the first three or four minutes of *Lady Sings the Blues*, and I was left with a feeling of complete confidence in a dramatic performance. This was one of the great performances of 1972.

And there is no building up to it. The opening scene is one of total and unrelieved anguish; Billie Holiday is locked into prison, destitute and nearly friendless, and desperately needing a fix of heroin. The high, lonely shriek which escapes from Ross in this scene is a call from the soul, and we know this isn't any "screen debut" by a Top 40 star; this is acting.

It was probably inevitable that the movie itself would follow the tried-and-true formula of most of the musical biographies of the last twenty years. The genre is well-established, and since most of the musicians they've made movies about have had unhappy privates lives, there's the problem of making downhill look like uphill, at least sometimes. This is usually handled (and it is again this time) by showing the performer hitting bottom, rebounding into the arms of friends, being nursed back to health, and making a spectacular comeback performance at Carnegie Hall, or at least the Palace. The formula is so firmly established that stars even seem to follow it consciously, and we're left with tantalizing possibilities: Did Judy Garland play the Palace for the last time to give the proper form to her biography? You gotta go out in triumph, no matter what happens before.

Lady Sings the Blues has most of the clichés we expect—but do we really mind clichés in a movie like this? I don't think so. There's the childhood poverty, the searching for love, the unhappy early sexual experiences, the first audition, the big break, the years of climbing to the top, the encounter with hard drugs, the fall, the comeback, the loyal lover . . . we know the scenes by heart.

What brings the movie alive is the performance that Diana Ross, and director Sidney J. Furie, bring to the scenes. As a gangly adolescent set out to work as a maid in a whorehouse, Ross somehow manages to look gangly and adolescent. When she is transformed into a great beauty later in the film, it IS a transformation, because she was brave enough, and good enough, to really look awful at first: "You got a long way to go," the madam tells her accurately, "before anybody gonna pay $2 for an hour of your time."

The movie is filled with many of the great Billie Holiday songs, and Ross handles them in an interesting way. She doesn't sing in her own style, and she never tries to imitate Holiday, but she sings somehow in the manner of Holiday. There is an uncanny echo, a suggestion, and yet the style is a tribute to Billie Holiday, not an impersonation. The songs do slow the movie down quite a bit, and it feels long at over two hours, but the Billie Holiday music is really the occasion, so I suppose I shouldn't complain.

Lassiter ★ ★ ★
R, 100 m., 1984

Tom Selleck (Lassiter), Jane Seymour (Sara), Lauren Hutton (Kari), Bob Hoskins (Becker). Directed by Roger Young and produced by Albert S. Ruddy. Screenplay by David Taylor.

Here's a basic rule about thrillers: Style is a lot more important than plot. What happens isn't nearly as important as how it happens and who it happens to—and if you doubt me, think back over to your favorite James Bond movies. *Lassiter* is a good example. Here's a movie with a plot spun out of thin air. That doesn't matter, though, because the movie is acted and directed with such style that we have fun slogging through the silliness. And part of the fun comes from watching Tom Selleck, the hero of "Magnum, P.I.," in a movie that does him justice. He was wasted in *High Road to China*, which looked like a *Raiders of the Lost Ark* rip-off with Selleck plugged into the Harrison Ford role. *Lassiter* is a movie that seems to have been made with Selleck in mind, and he delivers—he's clearly one of the few actors capable of making the leap from TV to the big screen.

The movie stars Selleck as Nick Lassiter, an American thief in London on the eve of World War II. A hardheaded police inspector (Bob Hoskins) gets the goods on him and makes him a flat offer: Either Lassiter breaks into the German Embassy and steals $10 million in jewels, or he goes into the slammer. Lassiter goes for the jewels. That involves seducing the kinky, sadistic German countess (Lauren Hutton) who has the diamonds in her bedroom inside the well-guarded embassy. The movie misses a bet here: It spends a lot of time establishing the Hutton character (who has an unusual taste for blood), and we see her killing one of her bed partners. Yet when Lassiter finally goes to bed with her, the movie cuts to the morning after instead of showing how he survived the night. And there's no big final confrontation with the countess; at a crucial moment, Lassiter knocks her cold, and that's that.

Other characters are handled more carefully. We meet Lassiter's sweet girlfriend (Jane Seymour, looking more than ever like a perfect porcelain portrait); Hoskins, who played the mob boss in *The Long Good Friday*, and assorted creeps. Selleck occupies this world effortlessly. He is a big man, and yet he moves gracefully, wears a tuxedo well, makes charming small talk, doesn't seem to be straining himself during the fight scenes, and, in general, stands at the center of a lot of action as if he belonged there. He would make a good James Bond. *Lassiter* knows that, and knows that style and movement are a lot more important than making sense of everything. I squirm when the action stops in a thriller while the characters explain everything to one another; I think of those speeches as memos from the screenwriter to the director. *Lassiter* stops for nothing.

The Last Detail ★ ★ ★ ★
R, 104 m., 1974

Otis Young (Mulhall), Jack Nicholson (Buddusky), Randy Quaid (Meadows), Carol Kane (Prostitute), Michael Moriarty (Marine O D). Directed by Hal Ashby and produced by Gerald Ayres. Screenplay by Robert Towne.

Meadows is a big hulk of a kid who compulsively shoplifts candy bars and peanut butter sandwiches and eats them for consolation. He has been in the navy only long enough to get busted for stealing a charity box with forty bucks inside, for which he has been sentenced to eight years in the Portsmouth naval brig. Buddusky and Mulhall are the two navy lifers assigned to transport him to Portsmouth, and *The Last Detail* is the story of how they travel there on a series of trains, buses, and drunks. It's a very good movie—and the best thing in it is Jack Nicholson's performance as Buddusky. Nicholson, always one of the most interesting of actors, does in *The Last Detail* what he did in *Easy Rider.* He creates a character so complete and so complex that we stop thinking about the movie and just watch to see what he'll do next.

What he tries to do is show the kid a good time. Now a good time, by Buddusky's standards, is not everybody's idea of a good time. It involves great volumes of time spent drinking great volumes of beer. It involves bitching about the system instead of doing something about it. But it also involves some small measure of human sympathy: Buddusky is personally affronted that the kid is going to be locked up for eight years before his life as a man has even begun.

Mulhall (Otis Young), the other member of this shore patrol, is a serious black man who has spent a lot of years working for his seniority and his retirement rights, and is not going to forfeit everything just by letting one dumb kid escape. But he goes along, within limits, and they take off the kid's handcuffs and try to give him some taste of life. They get him drunk in Washington and take him to a red-light house in New York—and the funny thing is, the kid goes along mostly to please them.

He might be described as a totally unformed youth. He's played superbly by Randy Quaid, who you might remember as the kid with the bottle in his sport coat pocket in *The Last Picture Show*—the grinning kid in the corner who took Cybill Shepherd skinny-dipping in the next county. His character is the only one that changes in the movie. What happens is that he learns in a very tentative way to assert himself—even to value himself, and make a token protest against his fate.

The direction is by Hal Ashby. How good this movie really is can be gauged by comparing it to *Cinderella Liberty,* another navy movie based on a novel by the same author, Darryl Ponicsan. Both movies have similar world views, and the stories in both move somewhat relentlessly toward inevitable conclusions. But *Cinderella Liberty* just can't be believed, and in *The Last Detail,* we always have the sense that these people are plausible individuals: each limited in his own way, but each somehow coping with life. The movie is ultimately pretty sad, but for most of the way it alternates between being poignant and being very funny. Nicholson plays comedy better than most comedians, because with him the humor seems to well up from the real experiences of his character.

The Last Dragon ★ ★ ½
PG-13, 110 m., 1985

Taimak (Leroy), Vanity (Laura), Julius J. Carry III (Sho'Nuff), Chris Murney (Eddie). Directed by Michael Schultz and produced by Rupert Hitzig. Screenplay by Louis Venosta.

The Last Dragon opens with its hero learning from his karate master that he has at last reached the final level of realization; he no longer needs a master, because what remains to be learned can only be found within himself. When he achieves the final level, he will know it because of a glow all over his body. This is not an idle promise; by the end of the film, the hero glows like somebody who has just tapped into the wrong power lines. Setups like that are obligatory in karate movies;

there's an unwritten law that the movie must begin with five minutes of solemn, portentous philosophy before the action can begin. Once past its prologue, however, *The Last Dragon* turns into a funny, high-energy combination of karate, romance, rock music, and sensational special effects. It's so entertaining that I could almost recommend it—if it weren't for an idiotic subplot about a gangster and his girlfriend, a diversion that brings the movie to a dead halt every eight or nine minutes.

The Last Dragon stars two remarkably attractive and likable actors, who have one name apiece. The hero is played by Taimak, a twenty-year-old karate student who has not acted before, but who has a natural screen presence, and the heroine is Vanity, the rock singer discovered by Prince and used as a warm-up act at some of his concerts prior to the *Purple Rain* tour. Of Vanity, let it be said that she has the sort of rapport with the camera that makes us like her instantly; she has a sunny smile, and an inner happiness, and in the middle of this plot about gangsters and night clubs and bloody fights, she floats serenely, a joy to behold. In the same year, Prince introduced two electrifying actresses, Appolonia Kotero from *Purple Rain*, and now Vanity.

There's another engaging actor in the movie, a man named Julius J. Carry III, who describes himself as the Shogun of Harlem, and who presides over a hilarious early scene where he marches into a movie theater full of Bruce Lee fans and threatens to fight everyone in the house. Taimak is in the front row, so loyal to the Bruce Lee mystique that he's eating his popcorn with chopsticks, and after he has a showdown with the Shogun, it becomes inevitable that they will have to endure a fight to the finish. Meanwhile, Vanity is working as a video disc jockey at a private club, and a gangster (Chris Murney) decrees that she should play a video he has produced, starring his girlfriend (Faith Prince, no relation). Vanity refuses, and she is rescued from the gangster's thugs not once but twice by the brave Taimak, who barehandedly demolishes the hitmen.

That sets up the movie's basic situation: Taimak must defeat both the Shogun and the gangster—and fall in love with the girl, of course. There are also some nice scenes involving Taimak's father, who proudly runs New York's best black pizza parlor, and his little brother, who is a lot more street-smart than the otherworldly karate master.

The Last Dragon surrounds this simple plot with a lot of technology. The movie is backed by Berry Gordy's Motown Records, which has supplied it with a digital sound track, and the scenes in the disco make much use of back-projected music videos and scenes from old Bruce Lee movies. This is an expensive, high tech production. But then there's that whole business of the gangsters. They've been borrowed from a hundred other movies, they say things that have been said a hundred other times, and they walk around draining the movie of its vitality. They're tired old clichés getting in the way of the natural energy of Taimak, Vanity, and the Shogun character. Take out the gangsters, pump up the Shogun role, give Taimak and Vanity a little more screen time, and you'd have a great entertainment instead of simply a great near-miss.

Last House on the Left ★ ★ ★ ½
R, 82 m., 1972

David Hess (Krug), Ludy Gratham (Phyllis), Sandra Cassell (Mari), Marc Sheffler (Junior), Jeramie Rain (Sadie), Fred Lincoln (Weasel), Gaylord St. James (Dr. Collingwood), Cynthia Carr (Mrs. Collingwood). Directed by Wes Craven and produced by Sean S. Cunningham. Screenplay by Craven.

Last House on the Left is a tough, bitter little sleeper of a movie that's about four times as good as you'd expect. There is a moment of such sheer and unexpected terror that it beats anything in the heart-in-the-mouth line since Alan Arkin jumped out of the darkness at Audrey Hepburn in *Wait Until Dark*.

I don't want to give the impression, however, that this is simply a good horror movie. It's horrifying, all right, but in ways that have nothing to do with the supernatural. It's the story of two suburban girls who go into the city for a rock concert, are kidnapped by a gang of sadistic escaped convicts and their sluttish girlfriend, and are raped and murdered. Then, in a coincidence even the killers find extreme, the gang ends up spending the night at the home of one of the girls' parents.

The parents accidentally find out the identities of the killers, because of a stolen locket and some blood-stained clothing in their baggage. Enraged, the father takes on the gang single-handedly and murders them. Does any of this sound familiar? Think for a moment. Setting aside the modern details, this is roughly the plot of Ingmar Bergman's *The Virgin Spring*.

The story is also based on a true incident, we're told at the beginning of the movie, but I have my doubts; I think the producers may simply be trying one of those "only the names have been changed" capers. What does come through in *Last House on the Left* is a powerful narrative, told so directly and strongly that the audience (mostly in the mood for just another good old exploitation film) was rocked back on its psychic heels.

Wes Craven's direction never lets us out from under almost unbearable dramatic tension (except in some silly scenes involving a couple of dumb cops, who overact and seriously affect the plot's credibility). The acting is unmannered and . . . natural, I guess. There's no posturing. There's a good ear for dialogue and nuance. And there is evil in this movie. Not bloody escapism, or a thrill a minute, but a fully developed sense of the vicious natures of the killers. There is no glory in this violence. And Craven has written in a young member of the gang (again borrowed on Bergman's story) who sees the horror as fully as the victims do. This movie covers the same philosophical territory as Sam Peckinpah's *Straw Dogs*, and is more hard-nosed about it: Sure, a man's home is his castle, but who wants to be left with nothing but a castle and a lifetime memory of horror?

The Last Metro ★ ★ ★
NO MPAA RATING, 133 m., 1980

Catherine Deneuve (Marion Steiner), Gerard Depardieu (Bernard Granger), Jean Poiret (Jean-Loup), Heinz Bennent (Lucas Steiner), Andrea Ferreol (Arlette), Paulette Dubost (Germaine), Jean-Louis Richard (Daxlat). Directed by Francois Truffaut. Screenplay by Truffaut, Suzanne Schiffman, and Jean-Claude Grumberg.

Francois Truffaut said he wanted to satisfy three old dreams by making *The Last Metro*. He wanted to take the camera backstage in a theater, to evoke the climate of the Nazi occupation of France, and to give Catherine Deneuve the role of a responsible woman. He has achieved the first and last dreams, but he doesn't evoke the occupation well enough to make *The Last Metro* more than a sentimental fantasy.

The film takes place backstage, and below-stage, at a theater in Paris. The theater's director is German Jew (Heinz Bennent) who already has fled from Nazi Germany and now, with the occupation of Paris, goes into permanent hiding in the basement of his theater. Upstairs, his wife (Deneuve) spreads the rumor that he has fled to South America. Then she relays his instructions as the theater attempts to save itself from bankruptcy by presenting a new production.

There are many other characters in the movie, which at times resembles Truffaut's history of a film production in *Day for Night*. Gerard Depardieu plays the leading man for the new production. The supporting cast includes a young woman who will do anything for a job in the theater, an older woman of ambiguous sexuality, an avuncular stage manager, a gay director, and a powerful critic who is such an evil monster that he must surely have been inspired by a close Truffaut friend. Most of the movie's events take place within the walls of the theater; this is a backstage film, not a war film. We see the rehearsals under way, with Bennent downstairs listening through an air duct. There are the romantic intrigues among the cast members. There are occasional walkthroughs by Nazis. There are moments of great danger, somewhat marred by the fact that Truffaut does not resolve them realistically. And there is an unforgivably sentimental ending that ties up everything without solving anything.

The problem, I think, is that Truffaut sees the Nazi presence in Paris simply as a plot device to create tension within his theatrical troupe. It is ever so much more dramatic if the show must go on despite raids, political directives, and an electrical blackout that requires the stagehands to power a generator by bicycle-power. It's all too cute. Nobody seems to *really* understand that there's a war on out there. And yet, within the unfortunate limitations that Truffaut sets for himself, he does deliver an entertaining movie. Catherine Deneuve is as beautiful as ever, and as enigmatic (it is typical of her performance that at the end we have to wait for the screenplay to tell us who she does, or does not, really love). Depardieu is gangly and sincere, a strong presence. Bennent, as the husband downstairs, is wan and courageous in the Paul Henreid role. And the most fascinating character in the cast is of course the villain, Daxlat, the pro-Nazi critic. He at least seems in touch with the true evil that the others, and Truffaut, see as backdrop.

The Last Picture Show ★ ★ ★ ★
R, 114 m., 1971

Timothy Bottoms (Sonny), Jeff Bridges (Duane), Cybill Shepherd (Jacy Farrow), Ben Johnson (Sam the Lion), Cloris Leachman (Ruth Popper), Ellen Burstyn (Lois Farrow), Ellen Brennan (Genevieve), Bill Thurman (Coach Popper). Directed by Peter Bogdanovich and produced by Bert Schneider and Stephen J. Friedman. Screenplay by Larry McMurty and Bogdanovich.

There was something about going to the movies in the 1950s that will never be the same again. It was the decade of the last gasp of the great American movie-going habit, and before my eyes in the middle 1950s the Saturday kiddie matinee died a lingering death at the Princess Theater on Main Street in Urbana. For five or six years of my life (the years between when I was old enough to go alone, and when TV came to town) Saturday afternoon at the Princess was a descent into a dark magical cave that smelled of Jujubes, melted Dreamsicles, and Crisco in the popcorn machine. It was probably on one of those Saturday afternoons that I formed my first critical opinion, deciding vaguely that there was something about John Wayne that set him apart from ordinary cowboys. The Princess was jammed to the walls with kids every Saturday afternoon, as it had been for years, but then TV came to town and within a year the Princess was no longer an institution. It survived into the early 1960s and then closed, to be reborn a few

years later as the Cinema. The metallic taste of that word, cinema, explains what happened when you put it alongside the name "Princess."

Peter Bogdanovich's *The Last Picture Show* uses the closing of another theater on another Main Street as a motif to frame a great many things that happened to America in the early 1950s. The theater is the Royal, and along with the pool hall and the all-night cafe it supplies what little excitement and community survives in a little West Texas crossroads named Anarene.

All three are owned by Sam the Lion, who is just about the only self-sufficient and self-satisfied man in town. The others are infected by a general malaise, and engage in sexual infidelities partly to remind themselves they're alive. There isn't much else to do in Anarene, no dreams worth dreaming, no new faces, not even a football team that can tackle worth a damn. The nourishing myth of the Western (*Wagonmaster* and *Red River* are among the last offerings at the Royal) is being replaced by nervously hilarious TV programs out of the East, and defeated housewives are reassured they're part of the "Strike It Rich" audience with a heart of gold.

Against this background, we meet two high school seniors named Sonny and Duane, who are the co-captains of the shameful football squad. We learn next to nothing about their home lives, but we hardly notice the omission because their real lives are lived in a pickup truck and a used Mercury. That was the way it was in high school in the 1950s, and probably always will be: A car was a mobile refuge from adults, frustration, and boredom. When people in their thirties say today that sexual liberation is pale compared to a little prayerful groping in the front seat, they are onto something.

During the year of the film's action, the two boys more or less survive coming-of-age. They both fall in love with the school's only beauty, a calculating charmer named Jacy who twists every boy in town around her little finger before taking this skill away with her to Dallas. Sonny breaks up with his gum-chewing girlfriend and has an unresolved affair with the coach's wife, and Duane goes off to fight the Korean War. There are two deaths during the film's year, but no babies are born, and Bogdanovich's final pan shot along Main Street curiously seems to turn it from a real location (which it is) into a half-remembered backdrop from an old movie. *The Last Picture Show* is a great deal more complex than it might at first seem, and this shot suggests something of its buried structure. Every detail of clothing, behavior, background music, and decor is exactly right for 1951—but that still doesn't explain the movie's mystery.

Mike Nichols's *Carnal Knowledge* began with 1949, and yet felt modern. Bogdanovich has been infinitely more subtle in giving his film not only the decor of 1951, but the visual style of a movie that might have been shot in 1951. The montage of cutaway shots at the Christmas dance; the use of an insert of Sonny's foot on the accelerator; the lighting and black and white photography of real locations as if they were sets—everything forms a stylistic whole that works. It isn't just a matter of putting in Jo Stafford and Hank Williams.

The Last Picture Show has been described as an evocation of the classic Hollywood narrative film. It is more than that; it is a belated entry in that age—the best film of 1951, you might say. Using period songs and decor to create nostalgia is familiar enough, but to tunnel down to the visual level and get that right, too, and in a way that will affect audiences even if they aren't aware how, is one hell of a directing accomplishment. Movies create our dreams as well as reflect them, and when we lose the movies we lose the dreams. I wonder if Bogdanovich's film doesn't at last explain what it was that Pauline Kael, and a lot of the rest of us, lost at the movies.

The Last Starfighter ★ ★ ½
PG, 100 m., 1984

Lance Guest (Alex Rogan), Dan O'Herlihy (Grig), Catherine Mary Stewart (Maggie), Barbara Bosson (Jane Rogan), Robert Preston (Centauri). Directed by Nick Castle and produced by Gary Adelson and Edward O. Denault. Screenplay by Jonathan Betuel.

The way to get rich, they say is to invent something that's cheap and habit-forming, and get a patent on it. I guess video games would qualify. Kids pump quarters into them by the hour, turning into video junkies as they watch gorillas climbing little electronic ladders. Are the games educational? Sure, if you want to grow up to be a professional video game player.

Those arcade video games had to come from somewhere, and *The Last Starfighter* has an interesting theory to explain why they seemed to pop up all over the world, almost overnight. They came from outer space. Just as I've always suspected. That's right, they were put on Earth by representatives of the Star League, who use them as testing devices. If you break a record on a video game, they come and get you and turn you into an intergalactic fighter pilot. Meanwhile, your place on Earth is taken by a robot.

The Last Starfighter starts in a trailer camp in California. We know it's in California because all the residents are fugitives from mainstream life-styles. A kid (Lance Guest) lives in the camp and sets a record on a Starfighter game, and a Star League recruiter (Robert Preston) whisks him into outer space to join the battle against the evil race of Ko-Dan. At first the kid is a little reluctant. He'd rather stay on Earth and neck with his girlfriend. But he's persuaded that he's all that stands between the Ko-Dan and intergalactic civilization as we know it. So he agrees to become a Starfighter, and is tutored by a wise old lizard-warrior named Grig, who is played by Dan O'Herlihy in makeup inspired by the heartbreak of psoriasis.

The Last Starfighter is not a terrifically original movie. The video game concept seems inspired by Walt Disney's *Tron*, and the battles in space are such close copies of the Star Wars movies that George Lucas might have a lawsuit. For example, when Grig gives the kids lessons in how to fire from the cockpit of his rocket, the cockpit's swivel chair looks directly inspired by the original *Star Wars*. If the movie isn't original in its special effects, it tries to make up for that in the trailer camp scenes. A large gallery of eccentric supporting actors is trotted onscreen, all with a few colorful lines to say, and there's a subplot about the love affair between the kid's girlfriend and the robot who has replaced the kid (every time the girl tries to lick his ear, he gets a short circuit).

This is all pretty lame material. *The Last Starfighter* is a well-made movie. The special effects are competent. The acting is good, and I enjoyed Robert Preston's fast-talking *Music Man* reprise (we've got trouble, right here in the galaxy) and the gentle wit of Dan O'Herlihy's extraterrestrial. But the final spark was missing, the final burst of inspiration that might have pulled all these concepts and inspirations and retreads together into a good movie.

The Late Show ★ ★ ★ ★
PG, 94 m., 1977

Art Carney (Ira Wells), Lily Tomlin (Margo), Bill Macy (Charlie Hatter), Eugene Roche (Ron Birdwell), Joanna Cassidy (Laura Birdwell), John Considine (Lamar), Howard Duff (Harry Regan), Ruth Nelson (Mrs. Schmidt). Directed by Robert Benton and produced by Robert Altman. Screenplay by Benton.

It's hard enough for a movie to sustain one tone, let alone half a dozen, but that's just what Robert Benton's *The Late Show* does. It's the story of a strangely touching relationship between two people. It's a violent crime melodrama. It's a comedy. It's a commentary on the private eye genre, especially its 1940s manifestations. It's a study of the way older people do a balancing act between weariness and experience. It's a celebration of that uncharted continent, Lily Tomlin.

And most of all, it's a movie that dares a lot, pulls off most of it, and entertains us without insulting our intelligence. What's quietly astonishing is that all of it starts with a woman coming to a private eye about a missing cat. The woman is played by Lily Tomlin, who somehow provides scatterbrained eccentricism with a cutting edge. The cat has been missing a couple of days, and she's worried. The private eye is played by Art Carney, who has seen it all twice, when once would have been too much.

He takes the case maybe because he could use the money, maybe because he's intrigued by the client, maybe because he's bored, maybe because he's been taking cases so long it's second nature. He doesn't give a damn about the cat. But then, in a series of plot developments so labyrinthine we should be taking notes, the missing cat leads to a mysterious robbery, a missing stamp collection, a fence with a house full of stolen goods, and a dead body that's in the . . .

But, no, I won't say where the body is, because the way Benton reveals it and then lets Lily Tomlin discover it (when all she was after was a Coke) is one of the movie's many pleasures. A friend of mine objected to the body, and to the movie's violence, as being unnecessary in a comedy. Well, *The Late Show* is a long way from being only a comedy, and the introductory shot of that body redeems any amount of gratuitous movie violence.

It's the case with most good detective fiction that the puzzle seems impossible to solve until the last chapter, when everything is made transparently clear. That's true here, with Art Carney providing a brilliant analysis of the connections and coincidences just when it's most irrelevant. But the plot's incidental to the movie's center, which has to do with Carney and Lily Tomlin.

You see, they're allowed to be people here. They're allowed to play characters who have no particular connection with clichés or stereotypes or characters who were successful in a box office hit last year. Yes, Carney's a private eye, but a particular one: Overweight and wheezing, hard of hearing, given to comments that only obliquely refer to the problem at hand.

And Lily Tomlin . . . well, her character employs a form of reasoning that has nothing to do with logic but a lot to do with the good reasons we have for behaving as we do. An example. Art Carney pretends to be mortally ill (never mind why). He is not (never mind why). His ruse has saved their lives (never mind how). Lily Tomlin is not pleased: She could have had a heart attack! Does he think it's funny, playing with his own friend's *emotions* that way? Doesn't he have any *consideration*?

Benton's screenplay is filled with lines that perfectly define their moments (and belong so securely to the characters that they seem to come from them, as some of them probably did). The way in which Tomlin explains why today is the *pits*, for example. The way Carney wonders if it would kill her, for chrissakes, to wear a dress once in a while.

The way Carney's sometime partner talks to himself before he dies. The way the fence offers a bribe of a stereo set.

The Late Show is one of three movies from the late seventies that had their spiritual origins in the classic private eye films. The other two were Dick Richard's *Farewell, My Lovely* (in which Robert Mitchum demonstrated that he was born to play Philip Marlowe), and Robert Altman's *The Long Goodbye*, (in which Elliott Gould demonstrated that he was not).

Altman produced *The Late Show*, which is probably another way of saying he made it possible to be filmed, and Benton has brilliantly realized it. Maybe these three films about an all but extinct occupation are telling us something: That the more we become plastic and bland, the more we become fascinated by a strata in our cities we'd like to believe still exists, a society of loners and eccentrics, people brave and crazy and doomed, old private eyes and cat lovers. If they're OK, we're OK.

Legend ★ ★
PG, 89 m., 1986 ✔

Tom Cruise (Jack), Mia Sara (Lili), Tim Curry (Darkness), David Bennent (Gump), Alice Playten (Blix), Billy Barty (Screwball). Directed by Ridley Scott and produced by Arnon Milchan. Screenplay by William Hjortsberg.

Recent movies have created sort of a generic fantasy universe, made out of Muppets and swamps, strange beasts and evil tyrants, damsels and heroic lads, ancient prophecies and mythical legends. It's a world that seems inspired by ingredients from *Lord of the Rings*, the *Star Wars* movies, Dungeons and Dragons gamesmanship, tales of King Arthur, and the latest gimmicks from the special effects people. In a movie that works, these ingredients can be exciting and delightful. *Legend* does not work.

The movie is a big-budget British special effects extravaganza by Ridley Scott, the director of *Alien*. It tells of a time that is long, long ago, when unicorns roam the earth, and the powers of light and darkness are at war. An evil prince named Darkness lives in caverns far beneath the earth, scheming to blot the sun out of the lives of all the planet's creatures, and rule the gloom forever.

Earth itself is a sylvan place, filled with flowers and little glades and grassy clearings—but also with dread swamps and mouldy fens. Young lovers can kiss for an afternoon in a bath of sunshine, but fearsome storms come up suddenly, and lash the land with their fury. A race of evil little druids lives in the woods and spreads mischief wherever they venture. Their favorite pastime is frightening the unicorns.

Into this setting come our heroes, Jack and Lili. Jack (Tom Cruise) is a hero whose mission in life is to vanquish Darkness and allow the sun to prevail. Lili (Mia Sara) is the young woman he meets and falls in love with, but who is lured into the underworld and seduced by an exotic priestess into seemingly becoming evil. Will Jack save Lili and defeat Darkness? Or will the movie end unhappily? Can we vote more than once?

Let it be said that *Legend* is an impressive technical achievement. Ridley Scott is a perfectionist who takes infinite pains to make things look right. One problem is, the world of *Legend* is *itself* wrong for this material. To some degree, this is a fairy tale, and it needs a certain lightness of tone, a plucky cheerfulness, to really work. Like so many of the other recent sword and sorcery movies, it is so effective in rendering evil, so good at depicting the dire, bleak fates facing the heroes, that it's too dreary and gloomy for its own good.

Performances tend to get lost in productions like this. I particularly noticed how easily Tom Cruise got buried in the role of Jack. Here is the talented young actor from *Risky Business* where he came across as a genuine individual, and this time he's so overwhelmed by sets and special effects that his character could be played by anybody. Tim Curry, from *Rocky Horror Picture Show*, makes an effective Darkness—I liked his style—but, once again, the makeup people have done such a good job with his blazing eyes and gigantic horns that, in a way, almost any actor could be lurking inside there somewhere (only Curry's sensuous lips give him away).

Despite all its sound and fury, *Legend* is finally just a movie I didn't care very much about. All of the special effects in the world, and all of the makeup, and all of the great Muppet creatures, can't save a movie that has no clear idea of its own mission, and no joy in its own accomplishments.

Let's Spend the Night Together
★ ★ ½
PG, 94 m., 1983

Featuring The Rolling Stones. Directed by Hal Ashby and produced by Ronald L. Schwary.

It all comes down to the difference between a "concert film" and a documentary. *Let's Spend the Night Together* is essentially a concert film—a film recording an "ideal" Rolling Stones concert, put together out of footage shot at several outdoor and indoor Stones concerts. If that's what you want, enjoy this movie. I wanted more. I would have been interested in a film exploring the phenomenon of the Rolling Stones, who bill themselves as the greatest rock 'n' roll band in the world, and are certainly the most durable. I would have liked to know more about the staging of a modern rock concert, which is arguably the most sensually overpowering nonwartime spectacle in human history, and which may have been invented, in form and in its focus on a single charismatic individual, at Hitler's mass rallies. I would have liked to know more about Mick Jagger; how does it feel for an educated, literate, civilized man in his early forties, with a head for figures and a gift for contracts and negotiations, to strut with a codpiece before tens of thousands of screaming, drug-crazed fans?

Let's Spend the Night Together does not answer these questions—nor, to be fair, was it intended to. It is wall-to-wall music. The movie sells well in home video form; it's a cinematic Top Forty with Jagger and the Stones performing many of their best-known hits. But after a certain point it grows monotonous. At the beginning of the film I was caught up in the Stones' waves of sound energy, and fascinated by Jagger's exhilarating, limitless onstage energy. By the end of the film I was simply stunned, and not even "(Can't Get No) Satisfaction" could quite rouse me.

The movie was directed by Hal Ashby, a feature director whose credits include *Shampoo* and *The Last Detail*. It was reportedly photographed with twenty-one cameras, under the direction of cinematographers Caleb Deschanel and Gerald Feil. They've got a lot of good stuff on film, but they haven't broken any new ground. The best rock documentary is still *Woodstock* (1970), and the best concert film is probably Bette Midler's *Divine Madness* (1980). The Stones have been filmed more powerfully before, too, in *Gimme Shelter*, the stunning 1969 documentary of the Stones' Altamont concert, at which a man was killed.

The worst passages in *Let's Spend the Night Together* are the songs in which Ashby and his collaborators try to get seriously symbolic. There is, for example, a montage of images from a suffering world: starving children, a Buddhist monk immolating himself, the skeleton-like bodies of famine victims, decapitated heads of political prisoners, etc. The idea, I guess, is to provide visual counterpoint to the Stones' apocalyptic images. The effect is disgusting; this particular movie has not earned the right to exploit those real images.

The best passages involve Jagger, who is just about the whole show, with the exception of a truncated Keith Richards solo and a strange interlude during which would-be beauty queens invade the stage and dance along to "Honky Tonk Woman." Jagger is, as always, the arrogant hermaphrodite, strutting proudly before his fans and conducting the songs, the band, and the audience with his perfectly timed body movements. There is an exciting moment when he climbs down into the crowd and, carrying a hand-held mike, sings as he is lifted on a surge of security guards from one side of the auditorium to another.

It's fun, but it's about the only time we see the audience in this movie; Ashby apparently made a directorial decision to keep the audience in long-shot, making them into a collective, pulsating mass. But that limits his possibilities for setting up visual rhythms in his editing. In such landmarks rock films as *A Hard Day's Night* (1964) and *Woodstock*, the audience provided not only counterpoint but also emotional feedback. *Let's Spend the Night Together* seems to have been pretty closely calculated as just simply the record of a performance, and if that's what you want, that's what you get.

Lianna ★ ★ ★ ½
R, 110 m., 1983

Linda Griffiths (Lianna), Jane Hallaren (Ruth), Jon DeVries (Dick), Jo Henderson (Sandy), John Sayles (Jerry). Directed by John Sayles. Produced by Jeffrey Nelson and Maggie Renzi. Screenplay by Sayles.

Movies are good at showing us people who make great changes in their lives, but not so good at showing us the consequences of those changes. It's easier to present the sudden dramatic revelation than to follow through into all the messy complications in everyday life. John Sayles's *Lianna*, the story of a woman who discovers in her early thirties that she is a lesbian, follows through. Instead of being the simple, dramatic story of a woman who "comes out," it is the complex, interesting story of what happens then.

The woman is named Lianna (Linda Griffiths). When she was an undergraduate, she fell in love with her teacher—a pattern she is about to repeat. Her husband is a film professor and the father of their two small children. He tends to treat her like one of the children, lecturing to the general audience at the dinner table as if his wife was about as bright as the kids. He is a boor. Lianna, unhappy, tries to change her life. She signs up for a night class in child psychology, and finds herself attracted to the professor, a woman who has a quick sense of humor and really seems to care about her students.

The woman, Ruth (Jane Hallaren), has been a lesbian for years, and is attracted to Lianna. But it is Lianna who makes the first, subtle moves, staying after class for a moment's chat, just as perhaps she did years ago with her husband. The two women become lovers fairly quickly, and although there are love scenes, the movie is not really about that side of their relationship. If *Personal Best* was an exploration of the physical aspects of lesbianism, *Lianna* explores the consequences. They are many. Lianna's husband throws her out and tries to block access to their children. Lianna's oldest friend, Sandy, is suddenly cold and distant. Ruth, a little surprised at the intensity of the affair, confesses that she has a long-standing relationship with another woman in another city. Lianna rents a room off-campus and begins a life-style that is free, yes, but also lonely and filled with guilt.

As *Lianna* looks into the large and small things that have changed in the life of its heroine, we become increasingly aware of the perception of the filmmaker, John Sayles, who wrote, directed, and edited. In this movie and his previous work, *Return of the Secaucus Seven*, he seems in touch with the kinds of changes that some Americans in their thirties are going through; his movies are cinematic versions of Gail Sheehey's *Passages*. He is attentive to what is said, what is worn, what attitudes are taken, what goes unsaid—and he is particularly interested, in both movies, in the ways that a generation raised to "do your own thing" now tries to decide when personal freedom ends and responsibility begins.

It's in that particular area that *Lianna* is a little shaky. It never quite dealt, I thought, with the issue of Lianna's two children. Although Lianna's lover is a child psychologist and Lianna herself seems to be a responsible and loving mother as the film opens, the kids are sort of left hanging. There are a couple of brief scenes with the kids, but no real resolution of the questions that a newly gay mother would have to answer. (Since the husband is presented as such a twerp, this absence of follow through is doubly bothering.) Still, in many other scenes, including two in which Lianna has a subtly class-conscious affair with a woman in the armed services, *Lianna* is an intelligent, perceptive movie. And the performances, especially by Griffiths and Hallaren, are so specific that we're never looking at "lesbians"—only at people.

Little Big Man ★ ★ ★ ★
PG, 157 m., 1971

Dustin Hoffman (Jack Crabb), Faye Dunaway (Mrs. Pendrake), Martin Balsam (Merriweather), Richard Mulligan (General Custer), Chief Dan George (Old Lodge Skins), Jeff Corey (Wild Bill Hickok). Directed by Arthur Penn and produced by Stuart Millar. Screenplay by Calder Willingham.

Arthur Penn's *Little Big Man* is an endlessly entertaining attempt to spin an epic in the form of a yarn. It mostly works. When it doesn't—when there's a failure of tone or an overdrawn caricature—it regroups cheerfully and plunges ahead. We're disposed to go along; all good storytellers tell stretchers once in a while, and circle back to be sure we got the good parts.

It is the very folksiness of Penn's film that makes it, finally, such a perceptive and important statement about Indians, the West, and the American dream. There's no stridency, no preaching, no deep-voiced narrators making sure we got the point of the last massacre. All the events happened long, long ago, and they're related by a 121-year-old man who just wants to pass the story along. The yarn is the most flexible of story forms. Its teller can pause to repeat a point; he can hurry ahead ten years; he can forget an entire epoch in remembering the legend of a single man. He doesn't capture the history of a time, but its flavor. *Little Big Man* gives us the flavor of the Cheyenne nation before white men brought uncivilization to the West. Its hero, played by Dustin Hoffman, is no hero at all but merely a survivor.

Hoffman, or Little Big Man, gets around pretty well. He touches all the bases of the Western myth. He was brought West as a settler, raised as a Cheyenne, tried his hand at gunfighting and medicine shows, scouted for the cavalry, experimented with the hermit life, was married twice, survived Custer's Last Stand, and sat at the foot of an old man named Old Lodge Skins, who instructed him in the Cheyenne view of creation.

Old Lodge Skins played by Chief Dan George with such serenity and conviction that an Academy Award was mentioned, doesn't preach the Cheyenne philosophy. It is part of him. It's all the more a part of him because Penn has allowed the Indians in the film to speak ordinary, idiomatic English. Most movie Indians have had to express themselves with an "um" at the end of every other word: "Swap-um wampum plenty soon," etc. The Indians in *Little Big Man* have dialogue reflecting the idiomatic richness of Indian tongues; when Old Lodge Skins simply refers to Cheyennes as "the

Human Beings," the phrase is literal and meaningful and we don't laugh.

Despite Old Lodge Skins, however, Little Big Man doesn't make it as an Indian, or as a white man, either, or as anything else he tries. He looks, listens, remembers, and survives, which is his function. The protagonists in the film are two ideas of civilization: the Indian's and the white man's. Custer stages his bloody massacres and is massacred in turn, and we know that the Indians will eventually be destroyed as an organic community and shunted off to reservations. But the film's movement is circular, and so is its belief about Indians.

Penn has adopted the yarn form for a reason. All the characters who appear in the early stages of the film come back in the later stages, fulfilled. The preacher's wife returns as a prostitute. The medicine-quack, already lacking an arm, loses a leg (physician, heal thyself). Wild Bill Hickok decays from a has-been to a freak show attraction. Custer fades from glory to madness. Only Old Lodge Skins makes it through to the end not merely intact, but improved.

His survival is reflected in the film's structure. Most films, especially ones with violence, have their climax at the end. Penn puts his near at the center; it is Custer's massacre of an Indian village, and Little Big Man sees his Indian wife killed and his baby's head blown off. Penn can control violence as well as any American director (remember *Bonnie and Clyde* and *The Left Handed Gun*). He does here. The final massacre of Custer and his men is deliberately muted, so it doesn't distract from Old Lodge Skins's "death" scene.

But Custer stays dead, and Old Lodge Skins doesn't quite die ("I was afraid it would turn out this way"). So he leaves the place of death and invites Little Big Man home to have something to eat. Custer's civilization will eventually win, but Old Lodge Skins's will prevail. William Faulkner observed in his Nobel Prize speech that man will probably endure—but will he prevail? It's probably no accident that we don't smile when Old Lodge Skins explains the difference between Custer and the Human Beings.

Little Darlings ★ ★
R, 95 m., 1980

Tatum O'Neal (Ferris), Kristy McNichol (Angel), Armand Assante (Gary), Matt Dillon (Randy), Maggie Blye (Ms. Bright), Krista Errickson (Cinder). Directed by Ronald F. Maxwell and produced by Stephen J. Friedman. Screenplay by Kimi Peck and Dalene Young.

There's one moment in *Little Darlings* that very nearly redeems a lot of the movie's weaknesses. It belongs to the young actress Kristy McNichol. She plays a fifteen-year-old who has just experienced sex for the first time. It was not, of course, quite like she expected it to be. She sits quietly in a corner of a deserted summer cottage, her thoughts a million miles away from her teen-age boyfriend. At last she says, "I feel so lonely."

The feelings implied in that single line of dialogue are completely true to the scene and to the character. She is lonely because she has suddenly and rather unhappily passed on from the ranks of pubescent girls. She is now an individual, possessed of the sometimes uncomfortable freedom to make decisions. Sexual intercourse, she tells the boy, "made me feel like you could see right through me." She slept with him for childish reasons, but now, we feel, she will never approach the decision so casually again.

Because this key scene is played so honestly (and because another key scene involving Tatum O'Neal is also written and acted with sensitivity), *Little Darlings* earns the right to its subject matter—even though some of the scenes unashamedly exploit the subject matter.

The movie is about two fifteen-year-old girls at summer camp, and how they're egged on into a bet about who will be the first to lose her virginity. The movie begins with inexperienced teen-agers who have an uninformed, frivolous attitude toward sex, and it moves rather awkwardly through would-be comic scenes in which O'Neal and McNichol attempt to seduce their target males and win the bet. But the scenes in which they actually confront the realities of sex are handled so thoughtfully and tastefully that they almost seem to belong to another movie.

That's possibly because *Little Darlings*

really wanted to be two movies at once: A fairly serious film about teen-agers and sex, but also a box-office winner like *Animal House* or *Meatballs*. That's why we get awkwardly forced comedy like the food-fight scene. The movie also suffers from uncertain direction. When O'Neal and McNichol first meet on the bus to camp, for example, the way in which they get involved in a fight is very unconvincing. Their whole personal feud, in fact, feels phony, and parts of this movie are so badly handled that we can only marvel that *Little Darlings* somehow does succeed in treating the awesome and scary subject of sexual initiation with some of the dignity it deserves.

The Little Drummer Girl ★ ★
R, 155 m., 1984

Diane Keaton (Charlie), Yorgo Voyagis (Joseph), Klaus Kinski (Kurtz), Sami Frey (Khalil). Directed by George Roy Hill and produced by Robert L. Crawford. Screenplay by Loring Mandel.

The Little Drummer Girl lacks the two essential qualities it needs to work: It's not comprehensible, and it's not involving. They made a real effort to pull of the daunting task of filming John Le Carre's labyrinthine bestseller, but the movie doesn't work. It is so jammed with characters and incidents and mystifications that everything seems to get equal, cursory attention. And not a single one of the characters comes alive. Not Kurtz, the brusque, scarred, touchingly human chief of Israeli intelligence, who was my favorite character in the book. Not Charlie, the American actress who is recruited by the Israelis to play a dangerous double game with a Palestinian terrorist. And certainly not Joseph, the man who is delegated to make Charlie fall in love with him. Those three characters, Kurtz and Charlie especially, are among the most vivid creations in recent fiction. In this movie version they are pale shadows of the people I imagined as I was turning the pages.

At least I have the advantage of having read the novel. If you haven't read the book, I suspect that a lot of *The Little Drummer Girl* will escape you, unless you focus on every piece of information with unwavering attention. The book was long and complicated, weaving a story of intrigue, double-cross, and betrayal. The movie is relatively long, but not long enough to do justice to Le Carre's plot. What's amazing is how many plot details are in the movie. Most of the characters turn up (even such minor walk-ons as Charlie's agent and the fake Red Cross men), and most of the twists and turns of the events are here. But the movie maintains a breathless pace to squeeze everything in; at the end we're stunned with information, but not moved by emotion. There is no time to linger on the emotional significance of the story—and surely what distinguished the Le Carre book was the way it combined a topical thriller with a deeper appreciation of the human issues involved in the Middle East.

Because the screenplay doesn't really provide the characters with time and space to grow and breathe, it may be unfair to criticize the actors: How much can you do with the Cliff's Notes edition of a story? Nevertheless, the movie has crucial failures in the two key roles. Diane Keaton's Charlie is not young enough, passionate enough or, if I may say so, sluttish enough, to recapture the wild, sloppy character in Le Carre's book. And Klaus Kinski's performance as Kurtz seems intended for a standard thriller. There is no sense of the man's past, of his intelligence, of his torn emotions, of the doubts he has about the job that Charlie is being asked to do.

What would have helped? Maybe the director, George Roy Hill, could have pared the story down to one specific element, such as Charlie's recruitment, training, and mission. Maybe we didn't need the scenes involving the capture of the red Mercedes, or the surveillance in the town square, or the stuff about Charlie's theatrical career in London. Even then, we'd be left with performances that did not resonate. It's not that Keaton and Kinski are bad actors, just that they were miscast. Unfortunately, there has hardly been another novel in recent years for which the casting of the movie version was more crucial.

Local Hero ★ ★ ★ ★
PG, 112 m., 1983

Burt Lancaster (Happer), Peter Riegert (Mac), Peter Capaldi (Danny), Fulton McKay (Ben), Denis Lawson (Urquhart). Directed by Bill Forsyth and produced by David Puttnam. Screenplay by Forsyth.

Here is a small film to treasure; a loving, funny, understated portrait of a small Scottish town and its encounter with a giant oil company. The town is tucked away in a sparkling little bay, and is so small that everybody is well aware of everybody else's foibles. The oil company is run by an eccentric billionaire (Burt Lancaster) who would really rather have a comet named after him than own all the oil in the world. And what could have been a standard plot about conglomerates and ecology, etc., turns instead into a wicked study of human nature.

The movie opens in Houston, but quickly moves to the fishing village of Ferness. The oil company assigns an earnest young American (Peter Riegert) and a whimsical Scot (Peter Capaldi) to go to Ferness, and buy it up, lock, stock, and beachline, for a North Sea oil-refining complex. This is a simpler job than it appears, since a lot of the locals are all too willing to soak the oil company for its millions of dollars, sell the beach, and go in search of the bright lights of Edinburgh. But there are complications. One of them is old Ben, the cheerful philosopher who lives in a shack on the beach. It turns out that the beach has been the legal property of Ben's family for four centuries, ever since an ancestor did a favor for the king. And Ben doesn't want to sell: "Who'd look after the beach then? It would go to pieces in a short matter of time."

The local negotiations are handled by the innkeeper, Urquhart (Denis Lawson). He also is the accountant, and sort of the mayor, I guess, and is so much in love with his pretty wife that they're forever dashing upstairs for a quickie. Meanwhile, Riegert and Capaldi fall under the spell of the town, settle into its rhythms, become wrapped up in its intrigues, and, in general, are co-opted by a place whose charms are seductive.

What makes this material really work is the low-key approach of the writer-director, Bill Forsyth, who also made the charming

Gregory's Girl and has the patience to let his characters gradually reveal themselves to the camera. He never hurries, and as a result, *Local Hero* never drags: Nothing is more absorbing than human personalities, developed with love and humor. Some of the payoffs in this film are sly and subtle, and others generate big laughs. Forsyth's big scenes are his little ones, including a heartfelt, whiskey-soaked talk between the American and the innkeeper, and a scene where the visitors walk on the beach and talk about the meaning of life. By the time Burt Lancaster reappears at the end of the film, to personally handle the negotiations with old Ben, *Local Hero* could hardly have anything but a happy ending. But it's a fairly close call.

Lone Wolf McQuade ★ ★ ★ ½
107 m., 1983

Chuck Norris (J.J. McQuade), David Carradine (Rawley), Barbara Carrera (Lola), Robert Beltran (Kayo Ramas), Sharon Farrell (Molly), Leon Isaac Kennedy (Jackson). Directed by Steve Carver.

To really understand *Lone Wolf McQuade*, you have to go back to those original spaghetti Westerns that made Clint Eastwood a star. They weren't great movies, and some critics attacked them for trashing the classic forms of the Western. But they had presence, style, and energy, and at the center of them they had a perfectly realized hero in Clint Eastwood. He was called The Man With No Name. He dealt violence with implacable fury. He stood at the middle of the maelstrom and remained untouched. And, in his own way, he was powerfully charismatic. Eastwood and Sergio Leone, his director, created a new kind of Western, pared down to its bare essentials of men and guns, horses and deserts, sweat and flies, and rotgut.

Now comes Chuck Norris. He's been in a series of karate and kung fu movies that were almost always better than average—but not a lot better than average. (The best of them was *Eye for an Eye*, directed by Steve Carver, who also directed *McQuade*.) The most you could say for a Chuck Norris film was that it did not have downright contempt for its action audiences; it tried to be better than

the interchangeable chop-socky movies from Hong Kong, and Norris made an energetic, likable star. What Norris was really looking for in all those pictures, I guess, was the right character. Like Eastwood's Man With No Name, he needed a personality that would fit, that would contain his kung fu skills and allow him ways of expression not limited to flying fists and deadly elbows. That's what he's found in *Lone Wolf McQuade*.

This is an action movie. It makes no apology for that. But it's high-style action. Norris plays J.J. McQuade, a renegade modern-day Texas Ranger who walks alone, likes to work with machine guns, deals out justice on the spot, and hardly ever says much of anything. The movie surrounds him with a gallery of interesting characters, played by colorful stars: David Carradine is Rawley, the evil local criminal and karate master; Barbara Carrera is lovely, as usual, as Carradine's wife and Norris's mistress; Robert Beltran plays Kaya Ramas, Norris's Mexican-American sidekick; Leon Issac Kennedy is the federal officer; grizzled L.Q. Jones lopes through a few scenes; and Sharon Farrell is counterpoint as Norris's former wife. All of these people are thrown together into a plot that is, of course, essentially meaningless. But the movie respects the plot, and keeps it moving, and a lot of excitement is generated.

Series characters always have one archetypal scene. With Eastwood, it was the time he killed three men with one bullet. Lone Wolf McQuade has a classic. He's shot. They think he's dead. They bury him in his supercharged, customized pickup truck. He comes to. Pours a beer over his head. Floors the accelerator and drives that mother right out of the grave. You get the idea.

The Lonely Guy ★ ½
R, 91 m., 1984

Steve Martin (Larry), Charles Grodin (Warren), Judith Ivey (Iris), Steve Lawrence (Jack), Robyn Douglass (Danielle), Dr. Joyce Brothers (Herself). Directed and produced by Arthur Hiller. Screenplay by Ed Weinberger and Stan Daniels.

I saw *The Lonely Guy* all by myself. It was one of those Saturday afternoons where the snow is coming down gray and mean, and you can't even get a decent recorded message on the answering machines of strangers.

There was a warm glow coming out of the windows of a tanning parlor. At a table in the window of a hot dog joint, three bums were laughing warmly, sharing a joke and a cup of coffee. I stuck my hands down deep into the pockets of my jeans and hunched my shoulders against the cold. I tried to force a smile to my frozen lips: Hey, I was going to the movies!

I walked up to the ticket booth of the Esquire theater and with a flourish presented my Plitt Theaters pass. "What's this?" asked the ticket person. "A pass to the Plitt Theaters," I said. "I don't know," the person said. "I'll have to phone and check it out." I turned my back to the wind until the pass was verified, and then walked into the theater's priceless and irreplaceable Art Deco lobby, which cheered me somewhat.

"It's a shame they're tearing this theatre down," said a young woman to her date, as they swept past me on their way to the street. I ordered a box of popcorn, and went into the theater.

"Good luck," an usher told me. "You're going to need it."

He was right. *The Lonely Guy* is the kind of movie that seems to have been made to play in empty theaters on overcast January afternoons. It stars Steve Martin, an actor who inspires in me the same feelings that fingernails on blackboards inspire in other people. He plays a lonely guy. His girl leaves him, and he keeps losing the phone number of the only girl in New York who will talk to him. This could have been fun, if the movie were only a little more upbeat about his loneliness. But it isn't. *The Lonely Guy* is a dreary slog through morose situations, made all the worse by Martin's deadpan delivery, his slightly off-balance sense of timing, and his ability to make you cringe with his self-debasing smarminess. In a movie crawling with bad scenes, the worst is probably the bedroom scene with Iris (Judith Ivey), the above-mentioned only girl in New York who will talk to him. She has never had an orgasm. He convinces her that she will have an orgasm every time he sneezes. She fakes it by screaming "gesundheit!"

The Lonely Guy is the kind of movie that inspires you to distract yourself by counting the commercial products visible on the screen, and speculating about whether their manufacturers paid fees to have them worked into the movie. I counted two Diet 7-Ups, two Tabs, and Steve Martin.

The Lonely Lady ½★
R, 92 m., 1983

Pia Zadora (Jerilee Randall), Lloyd Bochner (Walter Thornton), Bibi Besch (Veronica Randall), Joseph Cali (Dacosta), Anthony Holland (Guy). Directed by Peter Sasdy and produced by Robert R. Weston. Screenplay by John Kershaw and Shawn Randall.

If *The Lonely Lady* had even a shred of style and humor, it could qualify as the worst movie of 1983. Unfortunately, it's not that good. It's a dog-eat-dog world, and it's not enough to be merely awful. You need something to set yourself apart. Pia Zadora tries, and she has pluck, but she's just not bad enough all by herself. The movie is bad in all the usual ways, and it would be easy enough to simply list them: The overacting, the use of "voice-over" narration to bridge awkward chasms between scenes, the predictable plot. But why don't we take all of those things for granted and move on to the truly unspeakable things in this movie. We could make a list:

1. I suppose it was necessary to have a scene in which the heroine is cruelly treated by men. But (a) couldn't they have thought of something other than rape by a garden hose, and (b) shouldn't such a traumatic event have had some *effect* on the character?

2. After the rape, Pia is seen being comforted in bed by her mother and a doctor. A single thread of stage makeup, representing blood, has trickled out of her mouth and dried. It is left in place for the entire scene, suggesting that at no point did the doctor, her mother, or any other medical personnel or family member care enough to disturb the makeup in order to make the scene realistic by wiping away the blood.

3. Proper nouns are missing from this movie. It seems to exist in a generic alternative universe in which nothing has its own name. The Oscars are known as "these awards" or "the awards." After Pia and her

first lover leave a movie, they have this con-versation: "I liked him better." "I liked her better." No him or her is identified. This is the kind of conversation that results when a screenplay says, *They leave the theater and briefly discuss the movie,* but the screenplay doesn't care what movie they saw.

4. The movie has no time for emotional transitions. When Pia marries the successful Hollywood writer, he is attentive and caring in one scene, and a sadist in the next, simply because the plot requires him to act that way. No motivation. When Pia goes crazy, it's not so much in reaction to what's been happening to her (she survived the garden hose with nary a backward glance) but because the script requires it, so that, later, she can pull herself back together again just as arbitrarily.

5. The movie's whole plot hinges on Pia's ability to rewrite a scene better than her jeal-ous writer-husband. When the star of her husband's movie weeps that she can't play a certain graveyard scene, Pia whips out the portable typewriter and writes brilliant new dialogue for the star. What, you may ask, does Pia write? Here's what: She has the grieving widow kneel by the side of the open grave and cry out (are you ready for this?) "Why? Why!!!"

That's it. That's the brilliant dialogue. And it can be used for more than death scenes, let me tell you. In fact, I left this movie saying to myself, "Why? Why!!!"

The Long Good Friday ★ ★ ★ ★
R, 118 m., 1982

Bob Hoskins (Harold Shand), Helen Mirrin (Victoria), Eddie Constantine (Charlie), Derek Thompson (Jeff), Bryan Marshall (Harris), Paul Freeman (Collin). Directed by John Mackenzie and produced by Barry Hanson. Screenplay by Barrie Keeffe.

Harold is as hard as a rock and he will crush you. He runs the London docks and he wants to put together the biggest real estate deal in Europe. He has Mafia money from America and the tacit cooperation of the London criminal organization. He's short, barrel-chested, with his thinning hair combed forward above a round face and teeth that always seem to be grinding. He cannot believe that in one weekend his whole world can come apart. Harold Shand is a

hood, but he lives in a penthouse, anchors a world-class yacht in the Thames, has the love of an intelligent and tactful mistress and talks obsessively about the ten years of peace he has helped negotiate in the London underground. Then a bomb blows up his Rolls Royce, killing his chauffeur. Another bomb demolishes the lovingly restored land-mark pub he owns. A third bomb is found inside Harold's Mayfair casino, but fails to detonate. Who is after him? Who is his enemy? And why has the enemy chosen this worst of all possible times to come after him—the Easter weekend when an Ameri-can Mafioso is in town to consider investing millions in his real estate project?

The Long Good Friday, which is a master-ful and very tough piece of filmmaking, eventually does answer these questions. But the point of the film isn't to analyze Harold Shand's problems. It's to present a portrait of this man. And I have rarely seen a movie character so completely alive. Shand is an evil, cruel, sadistic man. But he's a mass of contradictions, and there are times when we understand him so completely we almost feel affectionate. He's such a character, such an overcompensating Cockney, sensitive to the slightest affront, able to strike fear in the hearts of killers, but a pushover when his mistress raises her voice to him. Shand is played by a compact, muscular actor named Bob Hoskins, in the most-praised film per-formance of the year from England. Hoskins has the energy and the freshness of a younger Michael Caine, if not the good looks, of course. There are scenes where he hangs his enemies upside down from meat hooks and questions them about the bombings, and other scenes, moments later, where he sol-emnly kids with the neighborhood juvenile delinquents and tries to soft-talk the Ameri-can out of his millions.

He's an operator. He's a con man who has muscled his way to the top by knowing exactly how things work and what buttons to push, and now here he is, impotent before this faceless enemy. *The Long Good Friday* tells his story in a rather indirect way, open-ing with a montage of seemingly unrelated events, held together by a hypnotic music theme. Everything is eventually explained. It's all a big misunderstanding, based on stu-pid decisions taken by Shand's underlings and misinterpreted by the IRA. But although we know the real story, and Harold Shand does, the IRA never does—and the movie's final shots are, quite simply, extraordinary close-ups, held for a long time, of Shand's ratlike face in close-up, as his eyes shift from side to side, and his mouth breaks into a terrified grin, and he realizes how it feels to get a dose of his own medicine. This movie is one amazing piece of work, not only for the Hoskins performance but also for the energy of the filmmaking, the power of the music, and, oddly enough, for the engaging quality of its sometimes very violent sense of humor.

The Long Goodbye ★ ★ ★
R, 112 m., 1973

Elliott Gould (Philip Marlowe), Nina van Pallandt (Eileen Wade), Sterling Hayden (Roger Wade), Mark Rydell (Marty Augustine), Henry Gibson (Dr. Verringer), David Arkin (Harry). Directed by Robert Altman and produced by Elliott Kastner. Screenplay by Leigh Brackett.

Robert Altman's *The Long Goodbye* attempts to do a very interesting thing. It tries to be all genre and no story, and it almost works. It makes no serious effort to reproduce the Raymond Chandler detective novel it's based on; instead, it just takes all the characters out of that novel and lets them stew together in something that feels like a private-eye movie.

The private eye is, I suppose, a fairly obsolete institution in our society. I'm not talking about the divorce case specialists and the missing persons guys; I'm thinking of the Chandler, Dashiell Hammett, Ross Mac-Donald kind of hired eye whose occupation takes him into glamorous danger and who subscribes to a weary private credo. The private eye as a fiction device was essentially a way to open doors; the best novels of Chandler and the others are simply hooks for a cynical morality.

Altman seems to understand this. He knows we don't care any more about the plot than he does; he agrees with Hitchcock that it doesn't even matter what the plot is about (as long as it's something). The important thing is the way the characters spar with each other. But Altman has added a twist: Instead of making his private eye into a cool, compe-

tent professional, he makes him into a 1950s anachronism. Philip Marlowe has been in a lot of movies, but never one in which he was more confused than he is in this one.

The story, or whatever you want to call it, involves a murder, a missing person, and an alcoholic writer with a bewitching blonde wife. There are also some gangsters and a cat. The writer and his wife are played with really fine style by Sterling Hayden and Nina van Pallandt—who not only demonstrates that she can act, but also that a real woman is infinitely more interesting on the screen than some starlet beauty-school graduate who should be leading the pompon team.

The middle of this mess is inhabited by Elliott Gould, as the chain-smoking, mumbling, disorganized Marlowe. It's a good performance, particularly the virtuoso ten-minute stretch at the beginning of the movie when he goes out to buy food for his cat. Gould has enough of the paranoid in his acting style to really put over Altman's revised view of the private eye.

Altman doesn't string his scenes together to tell a taut story, but he directs each scene as if he were. There's an especially memorable scene involving Philip Marlowe and a gangster (played by Mark Rydell, who is usually a director). The gangster smacks his girlfriend with a pop bottle and then snarls at Marlowe: "Now that's someone I *love*. Think what could happen to you." The scene sounds rather grim in print, I know, but in the movie it has a kind of hard-boiled desperation to it. It feels like it belongs in a private eye's life and so does the whole movie—right up to the ending, which is really off the wall.

Looking for Mr. Goodbar ★ ★ ★
R, 136 m., 1977

Diane Keaton (Theresa), Tuesday Weld (Katherine), William Atherton (James), Richard Kiley (Mr. Dunn), Richard Gere (Tony), Alan Feinstein (Martin), Tom Berenger (Gary), Priscilla Pointer (Mrs. Dunn). Directed by Richard Brooks and produced by Freddie Fields. Screenplay by Brooks.

There's one crucial thing that *Looking for Mr. Goodbar* doesn't make clear: Just because you find Mr. Goodbar doesn't necessarily mean you were looking for him. The heroine of Judith Rossner's bestseller *was* looking. Theresa was turned on to a particular flavor of self-destructive sexual experience, one involving possible danger to herself, and she played a role in bringing about her own death.

In Richard Brooks's film version, that masochistic impulse isn't considered as openly. He gives us a Theresa who drinks too much, sleeps around too much, and takes too many drugs—but she seems more of a hedonist than a masochist. She's looking for a combination of good times, good sex, and a father figure, for psychological reasons the movie makes all too abundantly clear. But she isn't looking for danger, mistreatment, or death. Maybe Brooks thought audiences would find Rossner's masochistic heroine too hard to understand. He has rewritten the story, in any event, into a cautionary lesson: Promiscuous young women who frequent pick-up bars and go home with strangers are likely to get into trouble.

Brooks hasn't improved the story by changing its focus, and he's distracted from the heart of the narrative by several unnecessary scenes. Theresa's fantasies, for example, are handled in ways that annoy viewers more than they intrigue them. And her home life—its broadly painted Freudian details right out of soap operas—could have just simply been dropped.

But, all the same, Brooks hasn't directed a bad picture. *Looking for Mr. Goodbar* is very much worth seeing, particularly for the Diane Keaton performance. And it's not fair to praise her while damning Brooks (as so many critics have done). Brooks and Keaton must have worked together to create such a great performance; it's just a shame that it's surrounded by perhaps half an hour of material that only distracts.

The performance creates a character who would have been unthinkable in the movies of thirty years ago: A young woman who spends her days teaching first grade to a classroom of deaf-mutes and her nights making herself available in singles bars. Women weren't allowed to be that complicated in the "women's pictures" that *Mr. Goodbar* has come such a long way from. They were ladies or they were tramps. Now they're allowed to

be both, which has done wonders for the quality of the tramps you meet these days.

Diane Keaton suggests the motivation for her character almost independently from all those heavy-handed scenes in which her father stomps around the living room, and we get flashbacks of her tragic childhood. She suggests that Theresa is driven by a need to communicate on her own terms—and that those terms require her to have an advantage. She's great in a classroom of deaf-mutes, and great, too, with the men she picks up—men who are inarticulate because of insecurity, cultural short-changing, or too much booze. She delights in working people over verbally—in kidding them, mocking them, putting them down, playing games with them. On the physical level, though, she needs constant reassurance.

This Theresa is a different woman from the Judith Rossner character, but she's an interesting one. And Keaton plays her wonderfully, with a light touch you'd think would be impossible with this material. She's always moving. She choreographs every situation, and only eventually do we realize she's dancing out of the way. Her voice is liquid and funny, tossing off asides because they cut more deeply that way. The performance and the character are fully realized, even in this movie that finds room for so many loose ends and dead ends.

Then there's that ending that bothers me. On a New Year's Eve, she makes a fatal decision in choosing the next guy she's going to take home. *We* know she's made the wrong decision because Brooks abandons her point of view to show us a scene in which the guy is established as unbalanced and hostile. But she doesn't know that and gets killed because she doesn't. Her lack of knowledge is exactly the issue here: In the book, Theresa might have picked up the guy *because* she knew he'd be trouble.

What we get (and I quote from someone walking out of the screening ahead of me) is "another one of those movies that are supposed to be all filled with significance because the person gets killed at the end." What we might have gotten is a movie about a character obsessed, and fascinated, by what the end might be. Even a movie about how she got to be that way.

The Lords of Discipline ★ ★
R, 103 m., 1983

David Keith (Will), Robert Prosky (Bear), G.D. Spradlin (General Durrell), Barbara Babcock (Abigail), Michael Biehn (Alexander), Rick Rossovich (Pig), Mark Breland (Pearce). Directed by Frank Roddam and produced by Herb Jaffe and Gabriel Katzka. Screenplay by Thomas Pope and Lloyd Fonvielle.

I knew the military school in *Taps* (1981) was a fiction, but I didn't mind, because it was a fiction that worked to support a group of compelling characters. I also know that the military school in *The Lords of Discipline* is a fiction, and this time I *do* mind, because the whole function of the school here is to provide a framework for a nasty, cruel little thriller.

The movie takes place in the South, in the mid-1960s. A famous private military academy is struggling to haul itself into the twentieth century. A few cadets have been admitted who "don't belong," including a kid too gauche to fit in with the polished cadets, and another kid who is the school's first black. The story is told mostly through the eyes of one cadet who stands up for the underdogs. He's played by David Keith, who was the naval officer's candidate who hanged himself in *An Officer and a Gentleman*.

The school is a little odd. Although it has a magnificent, galleried library (where secret notes are hidden in the pages of Spengler's *The Decline of the West*), it apparently has no classrooms, no academic program, and no faculty members except two: the school's president, a slimy retired general (G.D. Spradlin), and a crusty old colonel named Bear (Robert Prosky), who lights a cigar every time he has anything to say. Keith is elected head of the cadet corps and determines to protect the rights of the misfit and the black. But then he begins to hear about a mysterious organization named "The Ten," a secret society within the school; its origins lost in the mists of time, its duty to "protect" the school's sacred honor against contamination by undesirable elements. Before long, it's Keith against "The Ten."

The Lords of Discipline starts out fairly well, and David Keith and the other actors in the movie are good, convincing performers. So it's only gradually that we realize the movie is essentially a ridiculous revenge melodrama. There's a scene where a cadet plunges to his death from the top of a school building, but that's nothing compared to the really creepy scenes where the black student is cut with a razor blade, attacked in a shower, and finally—in an offensively gratuitous scene—kidnapped, held in an old plantation, and tortured with electrical charges to his genitals. There's a funny thing about the way the movie handles that scene. David Keith tracks down the kidnappers, looks in a window, sees the electrical shock torture, sees the masked members of "The Ten" pour gasoline over the helpless student, sees them set a rag on fire and dangle it over him, watches all that happen, and *then* tries to stop the torture. Why didn't he act sooner? I'm afraid the answer, a sick one, is that the movie was so happy to linger over the scene that it didn't want to interrupt the sadism with a quick rescue. This is not a nice movie.

Lost in America ★ ★ ★ ★
R, 90 m., 1985

Albert Brooks (David Howard), Julie Hagerty (Linda Howard), Garry K. Marshall (Casino Boss), Art Frankel (Job Counselor). Directed by Albert Brooks and produced by Marty Katz. Screenplay by Brooks and Monica Johnson.

Every time I see a Winnebago motor home, I have the same fantasy as the hero of *Lost in America*. In my dream, I quit my job, sell everything I own, buy the Winnebago, and hit the open road. Where do I go? Look for me in the weather reports. I'll be parked by the side of a mountain stream, listening to Mozart on compact discs. All I'll need is a wok and a paperback.

In *Lost in America*, Albert Brooks plays an advertising executive in his thirties who realizes that dream. He leaves his job, talks his wife into quitting hers, and they point their Winnebago down that long, lonesome highway. This is not, however, a remake of *The Long, Long Trailer*. Brooks puts a different spin on things. For example, when movie characters leave their jobs, it's usually because they've been fired, they've decided to take an ethical stand, or the company has gone broke. Only in a movie by Brooks would the hero quit to protest a "lateral transfer" to New York. There's something intrinsically comic about that: He's taking a stand, all right, but it's a narcissistic one. He's quitting because he wants to stay in Los Angeles, he thinks he deserves to be named vice president, and he doesn't like the traffic in New York.

Lost in America is being called a yuppie comedy, but it's really about the much more universal subjects of greed, hedonism, and panic. What makes it so funny is how much we can identify with it. Brooks plays a character who is making a lot of money, but not enough; who lives in a big house, but is outgrowing it; who drives an expensive car, but not a Mercedes-Benz; who is a top executive, but not a vice president. In short, he is a desperate man, trapped by his own expectations.

On the morning of his last day at work, he puts everything on hold while he has a long, luxurious telephone conversation with a Mercedes dealer. Brooks has great telephone scenes in all of his movies, but this one perfectly captures the nuances of consumerism. He asks how much the car will cost—including *everything*. Dealer prep, license, sticker, add-ons, extras, *everything*. The dealer names a price.

"That's *everything?*" Brooks asks.

"Except leather," the dealer says.

"For what I'm paying, I don't get leather?" Brooks asks, aghast.

"You get Mercedes leather."

"*Mercedes* leather? What's that?"

"Thick vinyl."

This is the kind of world Brooks is up against. A few minutes later, he's called into the boss's office and told that he will not get the promotion he thinks he deserves. Instead, he's going to New York to handle the Ford account. Brooks quits, and a few scenes later, he and his wife (Julie Hagerty) are tooling the big Winnebago into Las Vegas. They have enough money, he conservatively estimates, to stay on the road for the rest of their lives. That's before she loses their nest egg at the roulette tables.

Lost in America doesn't tell a story so much as assemble a series of self-contained

comic scenes, and the movie's next scene is probably the best one in the movie. Brooks the adman tries to talk a casino owner (Garry K. Marshall) into giving back the money. It doesn't work, but Brooks keeps pushing, trying to sell the casino on improving its image ("I'm a high-paid advertising consultant. These are professional opinions you're getting.") There are other great scenes, as the desperate couple tries to find work to support themselves: An interview with an unemployment counselor, who listens, baffled, to Brooks explaining why he left a $100,000-a-year job because he couldn't "find himself." And Brooks's wife introducing her new boss, a teen-age boy.

Lost in America has one strange flaw. It doesn't seem to come to a conclusion. It just sort of ends in midstream, as if the final scenes were never shot. I don't know if that's the actual case, but I do wish the movie had been longer and had arrived at some sort of final destination. What we do get, however, is observant and very funny. Brooks is especially good at hearing exactly how people talk, and how that reveals things about themselves. Take that line about "Mercedes leather." A lot of people would be very happy to sit on "Mercedes leather." But not a Mercedes owner, of course. How did Joni Mitchell put it? "Don't it always seem to go, that you don't know what you've got, till it's gone."

Louie Bluie ★ ★ ★ ½
NO MPAA RATING, 75 m., 1985

A documentary featuring Howard Armstrong and Ted Bogan. Directed and produced by Terry Zwigoff.

It was back in 1970 when the Earl called me up and said I should be at his bar on Monday night because he had something special, a band called Martin, Bogan, and the Armstrongs. "Don't ask any questions," he said. "Just be here." I was there, and I returned week after week for more than a year, along with a loyal cult who packed the place.

Martin, Bogan, and one of the Armstrongs were black men in their sixties and seventies (the other Armstrong, a son, played bass). They looked like a blues band, but they didn't play the blues, and in fact it was hard to figure out exactly what they did play. They did all the Mills Brothers standards, such as "Lazy River" and "Paper Doll," and they sang "Lady Be Good" and an unprintable version of "Sweet Georgia Brown." Howard Armstrong stood up and did fiddle solos on songs such as "Turkey in the Straw," and brought the house down.

Sixteen years later, those Monday sessions blur into a smoky series of hot summer nights when the sweet lyrics of Armstrong's fiddle danced above Martin's guitar and Bogan's mandolin, and they took turns on the vocals, including Martin's composition of "The Barnyard Dance" and Armstrong's pseudo-Hawaiian love songs. Toward the end of the evening, Ted Bogan would sing "Summertime" with such unadorned purity that you knew, quite simply, that you would never, ever, hear that great song sung better by anyone, anywhere.

Martin, Bogan, and the Armstrongs stopped playing together in the mid-1970s, and a few years later the Earl of Old Town closed its doors. When I would run into Earl Pionke, I would ask him about them and he would have vague reports that they were in Detroit, or Tennessee. Then word came that Carl Martin, who always scowled the fiercest when he was singing the funniest lyrics, had died.

And that was the situation when I went to the 1985 Telluride Film Festival, up in the San Juan range of the Rockies, and there on Main Street I saw Howard Armstrong with his beret and all that hip jewelry around his neck, checking out the scene and giving free advice to Ted Bogan, who was nodding and not listening, just like he always did when Armstrong talked to him during the sets at the Earl.

The story of how they got to Telluride is an amazing one, and it explains the existence of *Louie Bluie*, an equally amazing music documentary film.

Terry Zwigoff, a music lover who went on to produce and direct *Louie Bluie*, was an avid collector of old jazz and blues recordings. He liked the sound on an old 1930s disc that was by somebody named Louie Bluie who never recorded before or since, and after years of searching he found out that Louie Bluie was Howard Armstrong, and his group, one of the first (and now one of the

last) of the traditional black string bands, was still around.

Zwigoff tracked down Armstrong, who had moved to Detroit, and talked Armstrong and Bogan into appearing in a film, and *Louie Bluie* is that film, filled with music and life and humor, but also with an extraordinary portrait of Howard Armstrong, who is an artist, poet, composer, violin virtuoso, storyteller, and tireless womanizer (according to many of his stories).

The movie is loose and disjointed, and makes little effort to be a documentary about anything. Mostly, it just follows Armstrong around as he plays music with Bogan, visits his Tennessee childhood home, and philosophizes on music, love, and life. The film occasionally turns to the pages of the semipornographic journals Armstrong has kept through the years, filled with lurid cartoons and bawdy poems and his observations of life. Armstrong is a natural artist, and he remembers making his first colors out of dyes wrung out of crepe paper.

There is a lot of music in the movie, including some I could do without. (Armstrong likes his Hawaiian and German songs much better than I do.) There is also an enigma to consider: the relationship of Bogan and Armstrong, who have known each other and played together for almost seventy years, despite the fact that Armstrong is almost always on Bogan's case, and Bogan's eyes always seem to be looking for the nearest exit. *Louie Bluie* peers into the areas where nothing is certain, except that these people live and strive and laugh and make music. It is a wonderful film.

Love Letters ★ ★ ★ ½
R, 98 m., 1984

Jamie Lee Curtis (Anna), James Keach (Oliver), Amy Madigan (Wendy), Matt Clark (Mr. Winter). Directed by Amy Jones and produced by Roger Corman. Screenplay by Jones.

Love Letters teaches this lesson: Passion can exist between two people who know their relationship is wrong, but love cannot exist, because love demands to know that it is right. The movie stars Jamie Lee Curtis, in the best performance she has ever given, as Anna, a bright young woman who has an affair with a married man. She tries to make herself see their relationship as existing above conventional morality, but she can't, not after she sees the man's wife and kids.

The affair begins at a crossroads in her life. She's an announcer for a public radio station in San Francisco, and within a period of a few weeks her mother dies, and she gets a job offer from a larger station. She doesn't take the job, though, because something else happens. She meets a photographer (James Keach), who is a sensitive, intelligent, married man, and feels powerfully drawn to him. And she finds her mother's love letters, which reveal that her mother once had an affair. The old letters are used as a counterpoint to the events in the present. They're read on the sound track in the voice of the man who wrote them—a man we don't meet until the movie is almost over. They are letters about love, separation, loneliness, and loyalty. Anna learns to her astonishment that her mother continued the affair for years and years during her marriage, finally ending it only because she had decided to stay with her husband.

We meet the husband, Anna's father. He is a self-pitying alcoholic who believes he was never good enough for Anna's mother, and who smothers Anna with neurotic demands. What happens then is fascinating, and the movie treats it with great intelligence. Anna is already attracted to the James Keach character. Now, reading the old love letters, she begins to develop a romantic idea about affairs. She hates her father, and so, perhaps, did her mother. Her mother cheated on her father—and so will she, by having an affair with Keach. She will become the same kind of noble, romantic outsider that the author of the love letters must have been.

All of this is handled with as much subtlety as Ingmar Bergman brought to similar situations in *Scenes from a Marriage*. This isn't a soap opera romance; it's an investigation into how we can intellectualize our way into situations where our passions are likely to take over. Anna and the photographer spend happy times together. They are "in love." Anna thinks she only wants an affair, but she grows possessive in spite of herself. And when she spies on Keach's family, she sees that his wife is a good woman and there

is love in their home. Her life refuses to parallel the love letters.

Love Letters was written and directed by Amy Jones, whose previous credit was *The Slumber Party Massacre*. This is perhaps another case of a young filmmaker beginning with exploitation movies and finally getting the chance to do ambitious work. What she accomplishes here is wonderful. She creates a story of passion that is as absorbing as a thriller. She makes a movie of ideas that never, ever, seems to be just a message picture. And she gives Jamie Lee Curtis the best dramatic role of her career; this role, side-by-side with Curtis's inspired comic acting in *Trading Places*, shows her with a range we couldn't have guessed from all her horror pictures. *Love Letters* is one of those treasures that slips through once in a while: A movie that's as smart as we are, that never goes for cheap shots, that's about passion but never blinded by it.

Love Story ★ ★ ★ ★
PG, 100 m., 1970

Ali MacGraw (Jenny Cavilleri), Ryan O'Neal (Oliver Barrett IV), Ray Milland (Oliver Barrett III), John Marley (Phil Cavilleri). Directed by Arthur Hiller and produced by Howard G. Minsky. Screenplay by Erich Segal.

I read *Love Story* one morning in about fourteen minutes flat, out of simple curiosity. I wanted to discover why five and a half million people had actually bought it. I wasn't successful. I was so put off by Erich Segal's writing style, in fact, that I hardly wanted to see the movie at all. Segal's prose style is so revoltingly coy—sort of a cross between a parody of Hemingway and the instructions on a soup can—that his story is fatally infected.

The fact is, however, that the film of *Love Story* is infinitely better than the book. I think it has something to do with the quiet taste of Arthur Hiller, its director, who has put in all the things that Segal thought he was being clever to leave out. Things like color, character, personality, detail, and background. The interesting thing is that Hiller has saved the movie without substantially changing anything in the book. Both the screenplay and the novel were written at the same time, I understand, and if you've read the book, you've essentially read the screenplay. Nothing much is changed except the last meeting between Oliver and his father; Hiller felt the movie should end with the boy alone, and he was right. Otherwise, he's used Segal's situations and dialogue throughout. But the Segal characters, on paper, were so devoid of any personality that they might actually have been transparent. Ali MacGraw and Ryan O'Neal, who play the lovers on film, bring them to life in a way the novel didn't even attempt. They do it simply by being there, and having personalities.

The story by now is so well-known that there's no point in summarizing it for you. I would like to consider, however, the implications of *Love Story* as a three-, four- or five-handkerchief movie, a movie that wants viewers to cry at the end. Is this an unworthy purpose? Does the movie become unworthy, as *Newsweek* thought it did, simply because it has been mechanically contrived to tell us a beautiful, tragic tale? I don't think so. There's nothing contemptible about being moved to joy by a musical, to terror by a thriller, to excitement by a Western. Why shouldn't we get a little misty during a story about young lovers separated by death?

Hiller earns our emotional response because of the way he's directed the movie. The Segal book was so patently contrived to force those tears, and moved toward that object with such humorless determination, that it must have actually disgusted a lot of readers. The movie is mostly about life, however, and not death. And because Hiller makes the lovers into individuals, of course we're moved by the film's conclusion. Why not?

Love Streams ★ ★ ★ ★
PG-13, 141 m., 1984

Gena Rowlands (Sarah Lawson), John Cassavetes (Robert Harmon), Diahnne Abbott (Susan), Seymour Cassel (Jack Lawson), Margaret Abbott (Margarita). Directed by John Cassavetes and produced by Menachem Golan and Yoram Globus. Screenplay by Ted Allan and Cassavetes.

John Cassavetes's *Love Streams* is the kind of movie where a woman brings home two horses, a goat, a duck, some chickens, a dog,

and a parrot, and you don't have the feeling that the screenplay is going for cheap laughs. In fact, there's a tightening in your throat as you realize how desperate an act you're witnessing, and how unhappy a person is getting out of the taxi with all those animals. The menagerie scene occurs rather late in the film, after we've already locked into Cassavetes's method. This is a movie about mad people, and they are going to be acting in crazy ways, but the movie isn't going to let us off the hook by making them funny or picaresque or even symbolic (as in *King of Hearts*). They are, quite simply, desperate.

The brother, Robert (played by Cassavetes), is a writer who lives up in the Hollywood Hills in one of those houses that looks like *Architectural Digest* Visits a Motel. He writes trashy novels about bad women. A parade of hookers marches through his life; he gathers them by the taxi load, almost as a hobby, and dismisses them with lots of meaningless words about how he loves them, and how they're sweethearts and babies and dolls. The circular drive in front of his house is constantly filled with the cars of the lonely and the desperate. He is an alcoholic who stays up for two or three days at a stretch, as if terrified of missing one single unhappy moment. The sister, Sarah (Gena Rowlands), is as possessive as her brother is evasive. She is in the process of a messy divorce from her husband (Seymour Gassel), and her daughter is in flight from her. Rowlands thinks that maybe she can buy love: First she buys the animals, later she talks about buying her brother a baby, because that's what he "needs."

At least Cassavetes and Rowlands can communicate. They share perfect trust, although it is the trust of two people in the same trap. There are other characters in the movie that Cassavetes talks at and around, but not with. They include a bemused young singer (Diahnne Abbott) who goes out with Cassavetes but looks at him as if he were capable of imploding, and a former wife (Michele Conway) who turns up one day on the doorstep with a small boy and tells him: "This is your son." The way Cassavetes handles this news is typical of the movie. The woman wonders if maybe he could baby sit for a weekend. He says he will. He brings the kid into the house, scares him away, chases him halfway down Laurel Canyon, brings him back, pours him a beer, has a heart-to-heart about "Women, Life and Marriage," and then asks the kid if he'd like to go to Vegas. Cut to Vegas. Cassavetes dumps the kid in a hotel room and goes out partying all night. He is incapable of any appropriate response to a situation requiring him to care about another human being. He fills his life with noise, hookers, emergencies, and booze to drown out the insistent whisper of duty.

The movie is exasperating, because we never know where we stand or what will happen next. I think that's one of its strengths: There's an exhilaration in this roller coaster ride through scenes that come out of nowhere. This is not a docudrama or a little psychological playlet with a lesson to be learned. It is a raw, spontaneous life, and when we laugh (as in the scene where Cassavetes summons a doctor to the side of the unconscious Rowlands), we wince.

Viewers raised on trained and tame movies may be uncomfortable in the world of Cassavetes; his films are built around lots of talk and the waving of arms and the invoking of the gods. Cassavetes has been making these passionate personal movies for twenty-five years, ever since his *Shadows* helped create American underground movies. His titles include *Minnie and Moskowitz* (in which Rowlands and Cassel got married), *Faces, A Woman Under the Influence, The Killing of a Chinese Bookie, Gloria, Opening Night,* and *Husbands.* Sometimes (as in *Husbands*) the wild truth-telling approach evaporates into a lot of empty talk and play-acting. In *Love Streams,* it works.

Lovesick ★ ★ ★
PG, 94 m., 1983

Dudley Moore (Saul Benjamin), Elizabeth McGovern (Chloe Allen), Alec Guinness (Sigmund Freud), Wallace Shawn (Otto Jaffe), Ron Silver (Ted Caruso), Larry Rivers (Jac Applezweig), John Huston (Dr. Geller). Directed by Marshall Brickman and produced by Charles Okun. Screenplay by Brickman.

The notion of a psychiatrist falling in love with his patient is not exactly new, but there are whole moments at a time when it *seems* new in *Lovesick,* a comedy where the psychiatrist is played by Dudley Moore and his

patient is Elizabeth McGovern. They should not fall in love. It is against all the rules. It is also in violation of all the ethics of Moore's profession. But what is he to do when she turns those wide, grave eyes upon him and asks for his help? Moore actually hears about McGovern before he meets her. He gets a visit from a colleague (Wallace Shawn, who had dinner with André). Shawn needs help. He's head over heels with the woman and can't stop himself. Moore disapproves, until Shawn leaves and he himself meets McGovern. Then he is instantly smitten.

The scene in which he is smitten illustrates some of the best and worst qualities of this movie. Dudley Moore is very good at what directors call "reaction shots"—shots where we watch an actor watching someone else. In *Lovesick,* Moore's reactions as he gazes upon McGovern are comic and helpless. Her close-ups are fun, too. We find ourselves in sympathy with them. But the development of the scene is interrupted by an annoying device used throughout the film by Marshall Brickman, the director. He stops everything for a fantasy sequence in which Moore imagines that he goes around his desk and kisses McGovern, and that she responds, and that Sigmund Freud magically appears to chastise him.

Brickman, who has written for Woody Allen, may be developing a device here that was first used in *Annie Hall.* (Remember the scene where Marshall McLuhan appeared in a theater lobby and answered a man's question?) Here, though, it doesn't work. Freud (played by Alec Guinness) appears several times during the movie, and although the gimmick no doubt seemed like a clever way to illustrate the subconscious, it brings everything grinding to a dead standstill.

It's not fatal, though, to a movie with a lot of other nice things in it. I really enjoyed the rapport between Moore and McGovern—she so limpid in her unstudied sexuality; he so dreadfully serious about the burden of his love—as if the fact that he loves her is a cross he must bear. The movie is populated with a lot of interesting supporting performances, too. In fact, you can tell it's a New York film, and you can almost guess that it comes from someone in the Woody Allen orbit because of the fun it has with celebrity cameos; the actors, professional and not, who appear in this film include not only Shawn but Alan King, artist Larry Rivers, director Gene Saks, playwright Renee Taylor, director John Huston, and several actual New York shrinks.

Lovesick isn't a great comedy but it's not a bad one. And it's a reminder that Dudley Moore is a gifted and very likable comic actor. I suppose that like all great comedians, he has urges to play serious roles, but after the dreadful *Six Weeks* (in which his principal mistake was to appear), here he is in the lovesick territory of *10* and *Arthur.* It's where he belongs.

Lucas ★ ★ ★ ★
PG-13, 99 m., 1985

Corey Haim (Lucas), Kerri Green (Maggie), Charlie Sheen (Cappie), Courtney Thorne-Smith (Alise), Guy Bond (Coach). Directed by David Seltzer and produced by Lawrence Gordon and David Nicksay. Screenplay by Seltzer.

The first loves of early adolescence are so powerful because they are not based on romance, but on ideals. When they are thirteen and fourteen, boys and girls do not fall in love with one another because of all the usual reasons that are celebrated in love songs; they fall in love because the other person is perfect. Not smart or popular or good-looking, but *perfect,* the embodiment of all good.

The very name of the loved one becomes a holy name, as you can see in *Lucas,* when the hero says, "Maggie. Is that short for Margaret?" And then hugs himself to find that it is, because he suddenly realizes that Margaret is the most wonderful name in all the world.

Everybody grows up, and sooner or later love becomes an experience that has limits and reasons. *Lucas* is a movie that takes place before that happens. It is about a very smart kid who looks a little too short and a little too young to be in high school, and when you tell him that, he nods and solemnly explains that he is "accelerated."

One summer day, while riding his bike through the leafy green of a suburb north of Chicago, he sees a red-haired girl practicing her tennis swing. He stops to speak to her, and before long they are fast friends who sit cross-legged in the grass, knees touching knees, and talk about things that begin with capital letters, like Life and Society and Art.

Lucas loves Maggie, but she is just a little older and more mature than he, and has her eye on a member of the football team. Lucas believes, of course, that the whole value system of football and cheerleaders and pep rallies is corrupt. Maggie says she agrees. But how can she argue when the football hero notices her, breaks up with his girlfriend, and asks her if he can have a kiss?

To describe this situation is to make *Lucas* sound like just one more film about teen-age romance. But it would be tragic if this film got lost in the shuffle of "teen-age movies." This is a movie that is as pure and true to the adolescent experience as Truffaut's *The 400 Blows.* It is true because it assumes all of its characters are intelligent, and do not want to hurt one another, and will refuse to go along with the stupid, painful conformity of high school.

The film centers around the character of Lucas, a skinny kid with glasses and a shock of unruly hair and a gift for trying to talk himself into situations where he doesn't belong. Lucas is played by Corey Haim, who was Sally Field's son in *Murphy's Romance,* and he does not give one of those cute little boy performances that get on your nerves. He creates one of the most three-dimensional, complicated, interesting characters of any age in any recent movie, and if he can continue to act this well he will never become a half-forgotten child star but will continue to grow into an important actor. He is that good.

But the film's other two major actors are just as effective. Kerri Green, who was in *The Goonies,* is so subtle and sensitive as Maggie that you realize she isn't just acting, she understands this character in her heart. As the football hero, Charlie Sheen in some ways has the most difficult role, because we're primed to see him in terms of clichés— the jock who comes along and wins the heart of the girl. Sheen doesn't play the character even remotely that way. It is a surprise to find that he loves Lucas, that he protects him from the goons at school, that although he has won Maggie away from Lucas, he cares very deeply about sparing the kid's feelings.

The last third of the movie revolves

around a football game. So many films have ended with the "big match" or the "big game," that my heart started to sink when I saw the game being set up. Surely *Lucas* wasn't going to throw away all its great dialogue and inspired acting on another formula ending? Amazingly, the movie negotiates the football game without falling into predictability. Lucas finds himself in uniform and on the field under the most extraordinary circumstances, but they are plausible circumstances, and what happens then can hardly be predicted.

There are half a dozen scenes in the movie so well-done that they could make little short films of their own. They include: The time Lucas and Maggie listen to classical music and discuss her name; the scene between Maggie and the football hero in the high school's laundry room; the scene in which Lucas is humiliated at a school assembly, and turns the situation to his advantage; the way in which he takes the news that he will not be going to the dance with Maggie; and the very last scene in the whole movie, which is one of those moments of perfect vindication that makes you want to cry.

Lucas was written and directed by David Seltzer, who has obviously put his heart into the film. He has also used an enormous amount of sensibility. In a world where Hollywood has cheapened the teen-age years into predictable vulgarity, he has remembered how urgent, how innocent, and how idealistic those years can be. He has put values into this movie. It is about teen-agers who are learning how to be good to each other, to care, and not simply to be filled with egotism, lust, and selfishness—which is all most Hollywood movies think teen-agers can experience. *Lucas* is one of the year's best films.

Lust in the Dust ★ ★
R, 90 m., 1985

Tab Hunter (Abel), Divine (Rosie), Lainie Kazan (Marguerite), Geoffrey Lewis (Hard Case), Cesar Romero (Father Garcia), Gina Gallego (Ninfa). Directed by Paul Bartel and produced by Allan Glaser and Tab Hunter. Screenplay by Philip John Taylor.

Lust in the Dust would have worked better with Divine in the Tab Hunter role. Divine was born to play Tab Hunter, a claim Hunter himself has not been able to make for several years. And Divine wouldn't have made the mistake Hunter makes, of playing his Western gunslinger as a Clint Eastwood type. Divine would have chewed the scenery before shooting at it, and *Lust in the Dust* might have been funny all the way through, instead of just for the first twenty minutes.

The movie is a comedy Western, deliberately camp, starring Tab Hunter as a silent cowboy with no name, Divine as a hapless wanderer in the desert who wants to be a saloon singer, and Lainie Kazan as the owner of the only saloon in the miserable little town of Chili Verde. Divine is, of course, the well-known transvestite who has starred in lots of John Waters's movies (including *Polyester*, where the audience was issued Scratch 'n' Sniff cards). Divine usually goes for hysterical overacting, but this time she plays a timid, wistful soul, and it doesn't work as well. We need her slinging people out the saloon doors.

The movie is apparently intended as a satire on several different classic Westerns, including *Duel in the Sun*, but a funny thing happens at about the halfway point: It settles down and starts to get involved in its story. And since we don't care about the story, that's a mistake. The movie should have continued to go for the one-liners. As it is, we get this impenetrable story about a missing treasure map, and when they find the map, believe me, it's not a pretty sight.

Good things in the movie include a rousing, high-spirited performance by Kazan, who has abandoned forever her former images and has developed into an effective comedy performer; a TV producer should take a look at this movie and develop a sitcom around her (but not a comedy Western, please!). Hunter underplays until he is almost not present in some of the scenes, Divine is misused. Cesar Romero is a distraction as the local priest, and a young saloon waitress (Gina Gallego) has what used to be called the Lainie Kazan role.

The movie was directed by Paul Bartel, whose previous credit is *Eating Raoul*. Like most of the people associated with the movie, including Tab Hunter (who shares the producer's credit), he seems convinced that simply combining Divine, Kazan, and

Hunter in the same room would create a fissionable comic mass. Before he shut the door, he should have also thrown in a screenplay.

M*A*S*H ★ ★ ★ ★
R, 116 m., 1970

Donald Sutherland (Hawkeye), Elliott Gould (Trapper John), Tom Skerritt (Duke), Sally Kellerman (Hot Lips Hoolihan), Robert Duvall (Major Burns), Jo Ann Pflug (Lieutenant Dish), Rene Auberjonois (Dago Red). Directed by Robert Altman and produced by Ingo Preminger. Screenplay by Ring Lardner, Jr.

One of the reasons M*A*S*H is so funny is that it's so desperate. It is set in a surgical hospital just behind the front lines in Korea, and it is drenched in blood. The surgeons work rapidly and with a gory detachment, sawing off legs and tying up arteries, and making their work possible by pretending they don't care. And when they are at last out of the operating tent, they devote their lives to remaining sane. The way they do that, in M*A*S*H, is to be almost metaphysically cruel. There is something about war that inspires practical jokes and the heroes (Donald Sutherland, Elliott Gould, and cronies) are inspired and utterly heartless. They sneak a microphone under the bed of Major "Hot Lips" Hoolihan, and broadcast her lovemaking to the entire camp. They drug a general and photograph him in a brothel.

We laugh, not because M*A*S*H is Sgt. Bilko for adults, but because it is so true to the unadmitted sadist in all of us. There is perhaps nothing so exquisite as achieving (as the country song has it) sweet mental revenge against someone we hate with particular dedication. And it is the flat-out, poker-faced hatred in M*A*S*H that makes it work. Most comedies want us to laugh at things that aren't really funny; in this one we laugh precisely because they're not funny. We laugh, that we may not cry.

But none of this philosophy comes close to the insane logic of M*A*S*H, which is achieved through a peculiar marriage of cinematography, acting, directing, and writing. The movie depends upon timing and tone to be funny. I had an opportunity to read the original script, and I found it uninteresting.

It would have been a failure, if it had been directed like most comedies; but Ring Lardner, Jr., wrote it, I suspect, for exactly the approach Robert Altman used in his direction, and so the angle of a glance or the timing of a pause is funnier than any number of conventional gag lines. This is true, for example, in the football game between the surgeons and the general's team. The movie assumes, first of all, that we are intimate with the rules of football. We are. The game then becomes doubly funny, not just because the M*A*S*H boys have recruited a former pro as a ringer for their side, but because their victory depends upon legal cheating (how about a center-eligible play?). The audience's laughter is triumphant, because our guys have outsmarted the other guys. Another movie might have gone for purely physical humor in the scene (big guy walks over little guy, etc.) and blown it.

The performances have a lot to do with the movie's success. Elliott Gould and Donald Sutherland are two genuinely funny actors; they don't have to make themselves ridiculous to get a laugh. They're funny because their humor comes so directly from their personalities. They underplay everything (and Sutherland and Gould trying to downstage each other could eventually lead to complete paralysis).

Strangely enough, they're convincing as surgeons. During operations, covered with blood and gore, they mutter their way through running commentaries that sound totally professional. Sawing and hacking away at a parade of bodies, they should be driving us away, but they don't. We can take the unusually high gore-level in M*A*S*H because it is originally part of the movie's logic. If the surgeons didn't have to face the daily list of maimed and mutilated bodies, none of the rest of their lives would make any sense. When they are matter-of-factly cruel to "Hot Lips" Hoolihan, we cannot quite separate that from the matter-of-fact way they've got to put wounded bodies back together again. "Hot Lips," who is all Army professionalism and objectivity, is less human because the suffering doesn't reach her.

I think perhaps that's what the movie is about. Gould and Sutherland and the members of their merry band of pranksters are offended because the Army regulars don't feel deeply enough. "Hot Lips" is concerned with protocol, but not with war. And so the surgeons, dancing on the brink of crack-ups, dedicate themselves to making her *feel* something. Her façade offends them; no one could be unaffected by the work of this hospital, but she is. And so if they can crack her defenses and reduce her to their own level of dedicated cynicism, the number of suffering human beings in the camp will go up by one. And even if they fail, they can have a hell of a lot of fun trying. Also, of course, it's a distraction.

Mad Max Beyond Thunderdome
★ ★ ★ ★
R, 115 m., 1985

Mel Gibson (Mad Max), Tina Turner (Aunty Entity), Frank Thring (Collector), Angelo Rossitto (Master), Paul Larsson (Blaster), Angry Anderson (Ironbar). Directed and produced by George Miller. Co-directed by George Ogilvie. Screenplay by Miller and Terry Hayes.

It's not supposed to happen this way. Sequels are not supposed to be better than the movies that inspired them. The third movie in a series isn't supposed to create a world more complex, more visionary, and more entertaining than the first two. Sequels are supposed to be creative voids. But now here is *Mad Max Beyond Thunderdome*, not only the best of the three Mad Max movies, but one of the best films of 1985.

From its opening shot of a bizarre vehicle being pulled by camels through the desert, *Mad Max Three* places us more firmly within its apocalyptic postnuclear world than ever before. We are some years in the future; how many, it is hard to say, but so few years that the frames and sheet metal of 1985 automobiles are still being salvaged for makeshift new vehicles of bizarre design. And yet enough years that a new society is taking shape. The bombs have fallen, the world's petroleum supplies have been destroyed, and in the deserts of Australia, mankind has found a new set of rules and started on a new game.

The driver of the camels is Mad Max (Mel Gibson), former cop, now sort of a free-lance nomad. After his vehicle is stolen and he is

left in the desert to die, he makes his way somehow to Bartertown, a quasi-Casablanca hammered together out of spare parts. Bartertown is where you go to buy, trade, or sell anything—or anybody. It is supervised by a Sydney Greenstreet-style fat man named the Collector (Frank Thring), and ruled by an imperious queen named Aunty Entity (Tina Turner).

And it is powered by an energy source that is, in its own way, a compelling argument against nuclear war: In chambers beneath Bartertown, countless pigs live and eat and defecate, and from their waste products, Turner's soldiers generate methane gas. This leads to some of the movie's most memorable moments, as Mad Max and others wade knee-deep in piggy-do.

Tina Turner herself lives far above the masses, in a birds'-nest throne room perched high overhead. And as Mad Max first visits Turner's sky palace, I began to realize how completely the director, George Miller, had imagined this future world. It has the crowding and the variety of a movie crossroads, but it also has a riot of hairstyles and costume design, as if these desperate creatures could pause from the daily struggle for survival only long enough to invent new punk fashions. After the clothes, the hair, the crowding, the incessant activity, the spendthrift way in which Miller fills his screen with throwaway details, Bartertown becomes much more than a movie set—it's an astounding address of the imagination, a place as real as Bogart's Casablanca or Orson Welles's Xanadu or the Vienna of *The Third Man*. That was even before the movie introduced me to Thunderdome, the arena for Bartertown's hand-to-hand battles to the death.

Thunderdome is the first really original movie idea about how to stage a fight since we got the first karate movies. The "dome" is a giant upside-down framework bowl. The spectators scurry up the sides of the bowl, and look down on the fighters. But the combatants are not limited to fighting on the floor of the arena. They are placed on harnesses with long elastic straps, so that they can leap from top to bottom and from side to side with great lethal bounds. Thunderdome is to fighting as three-dimensional chess is to a flat board. And the weapons available to the fighters are hung from the inside of the dome: Cleavers, broadaxes, sledge-hammers, the inevitable chainsaw.

It is into Thunderdome that Mad Max goes for his showdown with Aunty Entity's greatest warrior, and George Miller's most original creation, a character named Master-Blaster, who is actually two people. Blaster is a giant hulk of a man in an iron mask. Master is a dwarf who rides him like a chariot, standing in an iron harness above his shoulders. The fight between Mad Max and Master-Blaster is one of the great creative action scenes in the movies.

There is a lot more in *Mad Max Beyond Thunderdome*. The descent into the pig world, for example, and the visit to a sort of postwar hippie commune, and of course the inevitable final chase scene, involving car, train, truck, cycle, and incredible stunts. This is a movie that strains at the leash of the possible, a movie of great visionary wonders.

Making Love ★ ★
R, 111 m., 1982

Michael Ontkean (Zack), Kate Jackson (Claire), Harry Hamlin (Bart), Wendy Hiller (Winnie). Directed by Arthur Hiller and produced by Allen Adler and Daniel Melnick. Screenplay by Barry Sandler.

Arthur Hiller's *Making Love* tells the story of a couple that has been married for eight years—happily married, according to the evidence—when the husband has an affair with another man, discovers that he is gay, and decides to leave his wife. *Making Love* is limited primarily to the characters' sexual identities. There would be no movie if the husband were not homosexual; this film has nothing else to be about. Its characters, as written, aren't open to the surprises of real life, because the movie is single-mindedly about the specific nature of their sexual dilemma.

Since we already know the secrets when we start watching *Making Love* (the ads summarized the plot), we feel locked in; there's nothing to do but wait while the movie marches through its lockstep development. The stages are predictable: (a) introduction of the ideal marriage; (b) the husband's secret homosexual desires; (c) the other man; (d) passion and deception; (e) the revelation scene; (f) unhappiness and acceptance; followed by (g) a brave new tomorrow.

Every scene and almost every line seems to be programmed to make an obvious point. This movie has some of the worst dialogue one can imagine:

She: "What about passion?"
He: "What about support?"
She: "What about betrayal?"

The movie stars Kate Jackson as the wife, Michael Ontkean as her husband, and Harry Hamlin as the homosexual writer Ontkean falls in love with. Jackson's a TV executive, Ontkean's a young doctor, and their marriage (pre-Hamlin) exists in one of those Hollywood wonderlands in which young couples figure they can meet the mortgage payments if they start brown-bagging their lunch. No attempt is made to present the marriage in messy human terms; it has to be boringly happy so that Jackson can be amazed when her husband walks out.

And walk out Ontkean does, after some preliminary false starts. He visits a couple of gay bars populated exclusively by extras who look as if they should be posing for an *Ah! Men!* catalog. He drives down an alley lined with shoulder-to-shoulder hustlers. Then Hamlin comes into his office for a physical exam (the most cursory and incompetent such exam, incidentally, ever presented in a movie). Ontkean is attracted, asks him out to dinner, and the rest is predictable, right down to the obligatory scene in which Jackson tears her husband's clothes out of the closet and throws them on the floor.

Making Love is essentially a TV docudrama, in which the subject is announced loud and clear at the outset and there are no surprises. People have described the movie to me in one sentence as "Kate Jackson finds out her husband is a homosexual," and they haven't left out much.

The Man Who Loved Women ★ ★
R, 118 m., 1983

Burt Reynolds (David), Julie Andrews (Marianna), Kim Basinger (Louise), Marilu Henner (Agnes). Directed by Blake Edwards and produced by Edwards and Tony Adams. Screenplay by Edwards, Milton Wexler, and Geoffrey Edwards.

Here is a sad movie with a funny movie inside trying to get out. The sad movie tells the story of a man who is utterly obsessed with women. He thinks he loves them, but he's not a lover, he's a collector. He goes to see an analyst, but that doesn't help because he falls in love with her. Beautiful women make him restless. He letches and dreams, pursues and fantasizes, until finally his obsession kills him. Because his funeral opens the movie, I have not given away very much. This movie is not only sad, it's also insincere and dishonest.

The funny movie inside is another matter. It's about how Burt Reynolds goes to Texas and is seduced by a sex-mad temptress whose husband is a jealous oil millionaire. She likes risk. Her encounters with Reynolds take place during cocktail parties, horse races, and on the highway. Because she is truly a sensuous woman (especially as played, with great wit, by Kim Basinger), these encounters take on a kind of surrealism. And Basinger drapes her body on Reynolds with a bold sort of leaning maneuver that would create obsession in a man of stone.

The Texas movie is funny. It reminds us of some of the best farcical work by Blake Edwards, the director, whose movies include 10 and Victor/Victoria. Unfortunately, the Texas sequence lasts only thirty minutes or so, and the rest of the movie is an uncomfortable mixture of psycho-babble, fake sincerity, and scenes we are supposed to take seriously even though they contain obviously impossible elements. Reynolds plays a man who, we are told, loves women too much. At his funeral, they turn out by the dozens. But nowhere in the movie do we really see him *loving* a woman. He courts them. He is nice to them. He kids with them. He goes to bed with them. He tries to be protective toward a young hooker. But he's not a lover, he's a perfect host.

This is a portrait of a lonely man. The problem with a man who loves *all* women is that he can never love *a* woman. There is always another one demanding his attention and requiring his care. When the analyst (played by Julie Andrews) makes her smarmy little speech about how he *really* and *truly* loved all of those women, each in her own way, she speaks like no woman I know.

If she truly loved Reynolds and felt he truly loved her, and if she had half the brains you need to get out of Analysis 101, she would have (a) been a little hurt, (b) a little jealous, and (c) deeply suspicious of the health of his motives.

This movie is a remake, by the way, of a little-seen 1977 Francois Truffaut film. In the Truffaut, the man was seen as something of a victim, suffering from an incurable obsession that was almost a disease. The tip-off to the phoniness of the Reynolds version is that the movie seems to be recommending the disease.

The Man Who Would Be King
★ ★ ★ ★
PG, 129 m., 1975

Sean Connery (Daniel Dravot), Michael Caine (Peachy Carnahan), Christopher Plummer (Kipling), Saeed Jaffrey (Billy Fish), Shakira Caine (Roxanne). Directed by John Huston and produced by John Foreman. Screenplay by Huston and Gladys Hill.

John Huston's *The Man Who Would Be King* is swashbuckling adventure, pure and simple, from the hand of a master. It's unabashed and thrilling and fun. The movie invites comparison with the great action films like *Gunga Din* and *Mutiny on the Bounty,* and with Huston's own classic *Treasure of the Sierra Madre:* We get strong characterizations, we get excitement, we even get to laugh every once in a while.

The action epics of the last twenty years seem to have lost their sense of humor; it's as if once the budget goes over five million dollars, directors think they have to be deadly serious. *Lawrence of Arabia* was a great movie, but introspective and solemn, and efforts such as *Dr. Zhivago* and *War and Peace* never dared to smile. Huston's movie isn't like that. It reflects his personality and his own best films; it's open, sweeping, and lusty—and we walk out feeling exhilarated.

Huston waited a long time to make this film, and its history is a Hollywood legend. He originally cast Bogart and Gable, but then Bogart died. In the early 1960s, he planned to make it with Gable and Michael Caine—but then Gable died, and the project was shelved until 1975. Maybe it's just as well. We need movies like this more now than we did years ago, when Hollywood wasn't shy about straightforward action films. And Huston's eventual casting of Michael Caine and Sean Connery is exactly right.

They work together so well, they interact so easily and with such camaraderie, that watching them is a pleasure. They never allow themselves to be used merely as larger-than-life heroes, photographed against vast landscapes. Kipling's story, and Huston's interpretation of it, requires a lot more than that; it requires acting of a subtle and difficult sort, even if the sheer energy of the movie makes it look easy.

The two of them play former British soldiers who vow to march off into Afghanistan or somewhere and find a kingdom not yet touched by civilization. With their guns and training, they think they'll be able to take over pretty easily, manipulate the local high priests, and set themselves up as rulers. They tell their plan to an obscure colonial editor named Kipling (played very nicely by Christopher Plummer) and then they set off into the mountains. After the obligatory close calls, including an avalanche that somehow saves their lives, they find their lost land and it's just as they expected it would be.

The natives aren't too excited by their new rulers at first, but a lucky Masonic key chain saves the day—never mind how—and Connery finds himself worshiped as a deity. He even gets to like it, and condescends to Caine, who remains a Cockney and unimpressed. The movie proceeds with impossible coincidences, untold riches, romances and betrayals, and heroic last words and—best of all—some genuinely witty scenes between Connery and Caine, and when it's over we haven't learned a single thing worth knowing and there's not even a moral, to speak of, but we've had fun. It's great that someone still has the gift of making movies like this; even Huston, after thirty years, must have wondered whether he still knew how.

The Man With Two Brains ★ ★
R, 91 m., 1983

Steve Martin (Dr. Hfuhruhurr), Kathleen Turner (Dolores), David Warner (Dr. Necessiter), Paul Benedits (Butler). Directed by Carl Reiner and produced by David V. Picker and William E. McEuen. Written by Reiner, Steve Martin, and George Gipe.

Steve Martin and Carl Reiner continue their tour of ancient movie genres with *The Man With Two Brains*, which does for Mad Scientist movies what *Dead Men Don't Wear Plaid* did for private eye pictures, which is to say, not very much. Some of the gags depend on a familiarity with classics like *Donovan's Brain, Bride of Frankenstein*—and even, in this case, Mel Brooks's *Young Frankenstein*. Other gags depend on Steve Martin's comic personality, as a guy whose elevator doesn't go all the way to the top floor. I've never found Steve Martin irresistibly funny. There's something stolid about his approach to humor, something deliberately half-paced and mannered that seems designed to be subtly irritating. I guess it's a tribute to *The Man With Two Brains* that I found myself laughing a fair amount of the time, despite my feelings about Martin. This is not a great comedy but it has scenes that don't know that.

Martin plays a brain surgeon named Dr. Michael Hfuhruhurr. The moment I heard the name I knew we were in trouble, and, sure enough, the movie never tires of making jokes based on his funny name. Since the First Law of Comedy should be *No funny names are funny unless they are used by W.C. Fields or Groucho Marx*, the name jokes are an exercise in futility. Hfuhruhurr has perfected something called the cranial screw-top method of brain surgery, and uses it to save the life of a beautiful young woman (Kathleen Turner) whom he's hit with his Mercedes. The woman, alas, turns out to be a gold digger. She seduces the gardener but refuses to have sex with Hfuhruhurr, who in his frustration falls in love with the brain of another young woman—a brain that has been pickled in a jar in the Vienna laboratory of the eccentric Dr. Necessiter (David Warner).

And so on. The movie uses the basic approach established by Brooks in *Young Frankenstein:* sight gags, cross-references, scatalogical puns, broad plotting, running gags, and so on. It filters its material through Martin's peculiar style, which is, I think, not light-footed enough. Martin is the kind of comedian who chews every line, lingering even on the throwaways.

Turner, seen in *Body Heat*, has a nice teasing quality as the hot-and-cold sexpot. David Warner (remember him from *Morgan* all those years ago?) makes a suitably cadaverous mad scientist. But the cast somehow seems underpopulated, and the characters are underdeveloped. That's one of the weaknesses of genre satires: The filmmakers depend on our knowledge of past characters as a substitute for creating new ones. And since comedy grows out of inappropriate behavior, and our notions of inappropriate behavior depend on what we know about people, the jokes all boil down to the fact that the characters in old Mad Scientist movies wouldn't behave like the characters in this one. So what?

Manhattan ★ ★ ★ ½
R, 96 m., 1979

Woody Allen (Isaac Davis), Diane Keaton (Mary Wilke), Michael Murphy (Yale), Mariel Hemingway (Tracy), Meryl Streep (Jill), Anne Byrne (Emily), Karen Ludwig (Connie), Michael O'Donoghue (Dennis). Directed by Woody Allen and produced by Charles H. Joffe. Screenplay by Allen and Marshall Brickman.

The overture is filled with brash confidence: Gershwin's "Rhapsody in Blue," played over powerful black-and-white visions of Manhattan and its skyline, and the mighty bridges leaping out to it from the provinces. The voice is filled with uncertainty and hesitation: "Chapter One. . . ."

The voice is Woody Allen's, of course, and we find ourselves laughing—actually laughing *already*—on the words "Chapter One," because the Allen character is so firmly established in our imaginations that we supply the rest of the joke ourselves. "Chapter One," yes, but Woody's the definitive vulnerable artist with giant dreams, and so of course he begins with confidence but will be mired in self-doubt long, long before Chapter Two.

A great deal of the success of Allen's *Manhattan* depends on how well he has established that Woody persona. Because we believe we know him (or the character he plays), we supply additional dimensions to the situations on the screen. A movie that might seem sketchily fleshed-out in other hands becomes a great deal more resonant in Allen's: This is a variation on a familiar theme.

And the Gershwin is a masterstroke. Woody Allen populates his film with people who are at odds with their own visions of themselves. They've been so sold, indeed, on the necessity of seeming true and grave and ethical that even their affairs, their deceptions, have to be discussed in terms of "values" and "meanings"—the dialogue in this film was learned in psychoanalysis. Their rationalizations double back upon themselves, and then, clear as a bell on the sound track, there are the Gershwin songs. "S'Wonderful" and "Embraceable You" and "Sweet and Low Down" and "I've Got a Crush on You" . . . written as if love were *simple*, for chrissakes, and you actually could "fall" in love when we all know it's more a matter of pulling yourself up, hand over hand, out of a pit of snapping emotions. In Allen's earlier films, middle-class society was usually the contrast to the Woody character's hang-ups and fantasies. This time, brilliantly, he sets his entire story in a "real" world—and uses the music as the counterpoint. No wonder it's deliberately loud and dominating; Gershwin is the second most important person in this film.

Allen's humor has always been based on the contrast between his character ("Woody," spectacled, anemic, a slob, incredibly bright and verbal, tortured by self-doubt) and his goals (writing a great novel, being like Bogart, winning the love of beautiful women). The fact that he thinks he can achieve his dreams (or that he *pretends* he thinks he can) makes him lovable. It is amazing, for example, how many women believe they are unique because they find Woody sexy.

What Allen does in *Manhattan* is to treat both the Woody character and the goals with more realism, and to deal with them in an urban social setting we can recognize. He was already doing this in *Annie Hall*, the comedy the critics said was "really" serious—as if comedy were not already serious enough. His earlier movies were made from farce, slapstick, stand-up verbal wit, satire, and the appeal of the Woody character. *Annie Hall* and *Manhattan* are made from his observations about the way we talk and behave, and the fearsome distances between what we say and what we mean, and how we behave and how we mean to behave.

The story follows several characters through several affairs. Woody himslf is twice-divorced as the movie opens—most recently from a lesbian who is writing a book that will tell all about their marriage. He is having an affair with a seventeen-year-old girl (Mariel Hemingway). His best friend, Yale (Michael Murphy), is married and is having an affair with a girl he met at a party (Diane Keaton). But Murphy has doubts about the relationship, and so subtly tries to shift Keaton to Allen, who in the meantime thinks he wants to ditch the seventeen-year-old. Inevitably, Woody and Keaton begin to fall in love, and their courtship is photographed against magnificent Manhattan backdrops. And once this is all set up, of course, it goes topsy-turvy.

The relationships aren't really the point of the movie: It's more about what people say during relationships—or, to put it more bluntly, it's about how people lie by technically telling the truth. *Manhattan* is one of the few movies that could survive a sound track of its dialogue; a lot of it, by Allen and Marshall Brickman, has the kind of convoluted intellectual cynicism of the early Nichols and May (and a lot of the rest of it consists of great one-liners).

Manhattan has been almost routinely praised by the New York critics as "better than *Annie Hall.*" I don't think so. I think it goes wrong in the very things the New York critics like the most—when, in the last forty-five minutes or so, Allen does a subtle turn on his material and gets serious about it. I'm most disturbed by the final scene between Woody and Mariel Hemingway. It's not really thought out; Allen hasn't found the line between the irony the scene needs and the sentiment he wants his character to feel. The later scenes involving the Michael Murphy character are also not as good as the early ones; the character is not seen correctly for humor, but hasn't been developed completely enough to bear the burden of confession.

And yet this is a very good movie. Woody Allen is . . . Woody, sublimely. Diane Kea-

ton gives us a fresh and nicely edged New York intellectual. And Mariel Hemingway deserves some kind of special award for what's in some ways the most difficult role in the film. It wouldn't do, you see, for the love scenes between Woody and Mariel to feel awkward or to hint at cradle-snatching or an unhealthy interest on Woody's part in innocent young girls. But they don't feel that way: Hemingway's character has a certain grave intelligence, a quietly fierce pride, that, strangely enough, suggest that even at seventeen she's one Woody should be thinking of during Gershwin's "Someone to Watch Over Me."

Note: The video version of Manhattan *was released with black bands at the top and bottom to preserve the wide-screen composition of the film. This unusual decision reflects Allen's perfectionism—and provides an eye-opening demonstration of how much is lost when other wide-screen formats are squeezed into the video frame.*

The Manhattan Project ★ ★ ★ ★
PG-13, 118 m., 1986 ✔

John Lithgow (John Mathewson), Christopher Collet (Paul Stephens), Cynthia Nixon (Jenny Anderman), Jill Eikenberry (Elizabeth Stephens). Directed by Marshall Brickman and produced by Brickman and Jennifer Ogden. Screenplay by Brickman and Thomas Baum.

The kid is really smart, but like a lot of smart kids he has learned to hide it, to lay back and observe and keep his thoughts to himself. When the new scientist arrives in town and starts to date the kid's mother, and then tries to make pals by taking the kid on a tour of the research lab where he works, the kid keeps his eyes open and his mouth shut. But he knows the lab is devoted to nuclear weapons research, and he's kind of insulted that the scientist would try to deceive him.

That's the setup for *The Manhattan Project*, a clever, funny, and very skillful thriller about how the kid builds his own atomic bomb. This is not, however, another one of those teen-age movies about bright kids and science projects. There have been some good movies in that genre—I liked *WarGames* and *Real Genius*—but this isn't really a teen-age movie at all, it's a thriller. And it's one of those thrillers that stays as close as possible to the everyday lives of convincing people, so that the movie's frightening aspects are convincing.

The kid is played by Christopher Collet. He is very, very smart. We know that not just because we are told so, but because the movie has lots of subtle, sometimes funny little ways of demonstrating it—as when the kid solves a puzzle in three seconds flat, just as we were trying to understand it.

The kid lives with his mother (Jill Eikenberry) in an upstate New York college town. John Lithgow plays the scientist who moves into the town and starts to date Eikenberry and makes friends with the kid. The movie is very sophisticated about the relationship between Collet and Lithgow. This isn't a case of the two men competing for the affections of the mother; indeed, there are times when these two bright, lonely males seem to have more in common with each other.

In particular, the Lithgow character isn't allowed to fall into clichés. He isn't a mad scientist, and he isn't a heartless intellectual: He's just a smart man trying to do his job well and still have some measure of simple human pleasure.

After Collet is given his tour of the "research center," he tells his girlfriend (Cynthia Nixon) that he's a little insulted that they thought they could fool him. He knows a bomb factory when he sees one. And so, to prove various things to various people, the kid figures out a way to sneak into the plant, steal some plutonium, and build his own nuclear bomb. He wants to enter it in a New York City science fair.

I love it when movies get very detailed about clever schemes for outsmarting people. *The Manhattan Project* invites us to figure out things along with Collet, as he uses his girlfriend as a decoy and outsmarts the security guards at the plant. Inside, he has it all figured out: how to baffle the automatic alarms, how to anticipate what the guards are going to do, how to get in and out without being detected.

The long closing sequence is probably too predictable, as Lithgow and the federal authorities try to convince the kid to take his bomb out of the science fair and allow them to disarm it before he vaporizes the city.

Even here, the movie doesn't depend on ordinary thriller strategies; a lot depends not only on the relationship between the kid and the scientist, but on how they think alike and share some of the same goals.

The Manhattan Project was co-written and directed by Marshall Brickman, the sometime Woody Allen collaborator (*Annie Hall, Manhattan*) whose own films include *Lovesick* and *Simon*. This movie announces his arrival into the first ranks of skilled American directors. It's a *tour de force*, the way he combines everyday personality conflicts with a funny, oddball style of seeing things, and wraps up the whole package into a tense and effective thriller. It's not often that one movie contains so many different kinds of pleasures.

Marie ★ ★ ★
PG-13, 113 m., 1985

Sissy Spacek (Marie Ragghianti), Jeff Daniels (Eddie Sisk), Keith Szarabajka (Kevin McCormack), Morgan Freeman (Charles Traughber), Fred Thompson (Himself), Lisa Banes (Toni Greer). Directed by Roger Donaldson and produced by Frank Capra, Jr. Screenplay by John Griley.

The true story of Marie Ragghianti is one of those lives they ought to make a movie about, and this time they did. Marie was a young Tennessee woman who broke out of a marriage with a wife-beater and somehow managed to put herself through school while raising her kids, including a chronically ill little boy. Then she got involved on the edges of the state political world, caught the eye of an assistant to the governor, was given a state job, and worked her way up to head of the state parole board.

If the story ended there, however, it probably wouldn't have made a movie. What makes Marie's story extraordinary is that she discovered corruption in the parole system, and she blew the whistle on the grafters. As a result of her testimony, a Tennessee governor and other officials were sentenced to the very prisons they sought to control. And Marie emerged as a heroine, although not without some dicey moments when it looked as if the governor's powerful cronies would be able to paint her as a heavy drinker who fudged on her expense accounts.

Marie's story falls within a fairly new tradition of American movies, of the humble young woman with pluck who struggles against the system and takes a stand for what she believes in. The stars of the genre are Sally Field *(Norma Rae, Places in the Heart,)* Jessica Lange *(Country)*, and, of course, Sissy Spacek, who can add *Marie* to a list that includes *Coal Miner's Daughter, Raggedy Man, Missing,* and *The River.*

Marie Ragghianti is the sort of character we are not surprised to find Spacek playing, and indeed there are few surprises in the movie once we understand the direction the story is taking. But Spacek is such a good actress, so well grounded in the particular traits of her characters, that it doesn't matter if she has played this sort of role before, because she does it so well this time.

She is helped, too, by the direction of Roger Donaldson, the New Zealander whose little-seen *Smash Palace* is one of the best movies ever made about the tensions surrounding an unhappy marriage, and the pressures it puts on children. Some of the same situations happen in the course of this story.

What happens to Marie is that she breaks out of one marriage to find herself in another situation where a man wants to call all the shots. The second man is Eddie Sisk, the governor's special assistant, whose job is to casually arrange special understandings and favors without involving the governor directly. Sisk is the man who gets Marie her job, and he is eventually the one who threatens to take it away. Sisk is played by Jeff Daniels, who was Debra Winger's husband in *Terms of Endearment,* and again this time he projects an uncanny combination of smooth charm and concealed deceptiveness.

The story is told as a counterpoint between Marie's political adventures and her problems in raising her family. I, for one, could have done with less about the sick little boy, who was never quite right after he swallowed a pistachio shell as an infant. I have no doubt that Marie did struggle heroically with her family, but the movie's medical emergencies and races to the hospital belong in a different sort of movie. Here, they make us wonder what *All the President's Men* would have been like if Woodward and Bernstein had spent half their time at bedside.

That problem aside, *Marie* is an absorbing movie about a brave woman. My only complaint is that it's too predictable. There's never really any doubt in our minds that Marie will do the right thing. Perhaps some sort of suggestion of earlier weakness would have helped; if we could see Marie overcoming a tendency to cave in and compromise, then there would be more suspense. As it is, *Marie* does a good job of telling a straightforward and somewhat inevitable story.

Mask ★ ★ ★ ½
PG-13, 120 m., 1985

Cher (Rusty Dennis), Eric Stoltz (Rocky Dennis), Sam Elliott (Gar), Estelle Getty (Evelyn), Richard Dysart (Abe), Laura Dern (Diana). Directed by Peter Bogdanovich and produced by Martin Starger. Screenplay by Anna Hamilton Phelan.

When we see him for the first time, it's a glimpse through his bedroom window, half-reflected in a mirror. A second later, we see him more clearly, this teen-age boy with the strange face. We are shocked for a second, until he starts to talk, and then, without effort, we accept him as a normal kid who has had an abnormal thing happen to him. The name of his disease is craniodiaphyseal dyaplasia, and it causes calcium deposits on his skull that force his face out of shape. "What's the matter?" he likes to ask. "You never seen anyone from the planet Vulcan before?"

The kid's name is Rocky Dennis, and his mother is named Rusty. She is not your normal mom, either. She rides with a motorcycle gang, abuses drugs, shacks up with gang members, and has no visible means of employment. But within about ten minutes, we know that she is the ideal mom for Rocky. That's in the scene where the school principal suggests that Rocky would be better off in a "special" school, and she tells the principal he is a jerk, her son is a good student with good grades, and here is the name of her lawyer.

Movies don't often grab us as quickly as *Mask* does. The story of Rocky and Rusty is absorbing from the very first, maybe because the movie doesn't waste a lot of time wringing its hands over Rocky's fate. *Mask* lands on its feet, running. The director,

Peter Bogdanovich, moves directly to the center of Rocky's life—his mother, his baseball cards, his cocky bravado, his growing awareness of girls. Bogdanovich handles *Mask* a lot differently than a made-for-TV movie would have, with TV's disease-of-the-week approach. This isn't the story of a disease, but the story of some people. And the most extraordinary person in the movie, surprisingly, is not Rocky, but his mother. Rusty Dennis is played by Cher as a complicated, angry, high-energy woman with a great capacity to love her son and encourage him to live as fully as he can. Rocky is a great kid, but because he succeeds so well at being a teen-ager, he is not a special case like, say, the Elephant Man. He is a kid with a handicap. It is a tribute to Eric Stoltz, who plays the role beneath the completely convincing makeup of Michael Westmore, that we accept him on his own terms.

Cher, on the other hand, makes Rusty Dennis into one of the most interesting movie characters in a long time. She is up front about her life-style, and when her son protests about her drinking and drugging, she tells him to butt out of her business. She rides with the motorcycle gang, but is growing unhappy with her promiscuity, and is relieved when the guy she really loves (Sam Elliott) comes back from a trip and moves in. She is also finally able to clean up her act, and stop drinking and using, after Rocky asks her to; she loves him that much.

Mask is based on a true story, and that doesn't come as a surprise: Hollywood wouldn't have the nerve to make a fictional tearjerker like this. The emotional peak of the movie comes during a summer that Rocky spends as an assistant at a camp for the blind. He falls in love with a blind teen-ager (Laura Dern), who feels his face and says he looks all right to her, and they have some of that special time together that only teen-agers can have: time when love doesn't mean sex so much as it means perfect agreement on the really important issues, like Truth and Beauty. Then the girl's parents come to pick her up, and their reaction to Rocky comes as a shock to us, a reminder of how completely we had accepted him.

Mask is a wonderful movie, a story of high spirits and hope and courage. It has some songs in it, by Bob Seger, and there was a lot of publicity about the fact that Peter Bogdanovich would rather the songs were by Bruce Springsteen. Let me put it this way: This is a movie that doesn't depend on its sound track. It works because of the people it's about, not because of the music they listen to.

Maxie ½ ★
PG, 98 m., 1985

Glenn Close (Jan/Maxie), Mandy Patinkin (Nick), Ruth Gordon (Mrs. Lavin), Bernard Hughes (Bishop Campbell), Valerie Curtin (Miss Sheffer), Googy Gress (Father Jerome). Directed by Paul Aaron and produced by Carter De Haven. Screenplay by Patricia Resnick.

Jan is an absolutely normal San Francisco woman. She lives in a big landmark Victorian house, she's married to a librarian, and she works as the secretary to the local Catholic bishop. (So far, all that's wrong with this picture is the landmark Victorian house, which Jan and her husband, Nick, could not afford unless he owned the library and she were the bishop.) One day they are stripping wallpaper from the walls and they discover a message that was left more than sixty years ago by Maxie, a flapper who once lived in the house. We know the message is from Maxie because Ruth Gordon, the next-door neighbor, drops in and tells them Maxie once had a bit role in a silent film and then died tragically at a young age.

Jan and Nick do what any normal couple would do. They rent a videocassette of the old silent film. And apparently their act of seeing Maxie's old performance, in Maxie's old house, causes the psychic energies to flow in such a way that Maxie appears and possesses Jan's body. Jan begins to talk in Maxie's penetrating nasal screech and she starts using a lot of 1920s slang, but she still looks exactly like Glenn Close, who plays both Jan and Maxie.

Nick (played by Mandy Patinkin) does not at first figure out what is happening. This leads to some embarrassment, as when Maxie suddenly occupies Jan's body during an office party and throws her drink down the dress of Nick's boss (Valerie Curtin, as a sex-mad harridan).

There are other horrible moments, as

when Jan becomes Maxie at bedtime, and when Maxie forces Jan to audition for a TV commercial. Maxie can be shocking, but she is not anywhere near as shocking as the utter, complete lack of wit and intelligence in this movie, which goes its entire length without producing one single clever twist on its boring premise.

As a service to the screenwriter and director, I herewith supply some ideas they might have used: (1) Jan becoming Maxie *during* sex, to Nick's consternation; (2) The bishop turning out to be Maxie's old beau, before he went into the seminary; (3) Maxie in a San Francisco leather bar; (4) Nick preferring Maxie to boring old Jan; (5) Nick being possessed by Maxie's old boyfriend, who goes after her, only to find the boring Yuppie, Jan, in his arms; (6) Maxie enlisting her friends from the Other Side to possess everyone else at the office party, so that W.C. Fields is talking with Calvin Coolidge, etc.

I offer these possibilities only to illuminate the fact that *Maxie* does as little with its original inspiration as is humanly possible. This is the sort of movie where, if Maxie had any brains, she'd appear in Jan's body, take one look at the script, and decide she was better off dead.

McCabe and Mrs. Miller ★ ★ ★ ★
R, 120 m., 1971

Warren Beatty (McCabe), Julie Christie (Mrs. Miller), Rene Auberjonois (Shehan), Hugh Millais (Butler), Michael Murphy (Sears), William Devane (Lawyer). Directed by Robert Altman and produced by David Foster and Mitchell Brower. Screenplay by Altman and Brian McKay.

McCabe rides into the town of Presbyterian Church under a lowering sky, dismounts, takes off his buffalo-hide coat, puts on his bowler hat, and mumbles something under his breath that we can't quite make out, but the tone of voice is clear enough. This time, he's not going to let the bastards grind him down. He steps off through the mud puddles to the only local saloon, throws a cloth on the table, and takes out a pack of cards, to start again. His plan is to build a whorehouse with a bathhouse out in back, and get rich. By the end of the movie, he will have been offered $6,250 for his holdings, and he will be sitting

thoughtfully in a snowbank, dead, as if thinking it all over.

And yet Robert Altman's *McCabe and Mrs. Miller* doesn't depend on that final death for its meaning. It doesn't kill a character just to get a trendy existential feel about the meaninglessness of it all. No, McCabe doesn't find it meaningless at all, and once Mrs. Miller explains the mistake he made in his reasoning, he rides all the way into the next town to try to sell his holdings for half what he was asking, because he'd rather not die.

Death is very final in this Western, because the movie is about life. Most Westerns are about killing and getting killed, which means they're not about life and death at all. We spend a time in the life of a small frontier town, which grows up before our eyes out of raw, unpainted lumber and tubercular canvas tents. We get to know the town pretty well, because Altman has a gift for making movies that seem to eavesdrop on activity that would have been taking place anyway.

That was what happened in $M*A*S*H$, where a lot of time didn't have to be wasted in introducing the characters and explaining the relationships between them, because the characters already knew who they were and how they felt about each other. In a lot of movies, an actor appears on the screen and has no identity at all until somebody calls him "Smith" or "Slim," and then he's Smith or Slim. In *McCabe and Mrs. Miller,* Altman uses a tactfully unobtrusive camera, a distinctive conversational style of dialogue, and the fluid movements of his actors to give us people who are characters from the moment we see them; we have the sense that when they leave camera range they're still thinking, humming, scratching, chewing, and nodding to each other in the street.

McCabe and Mrs. Miller are an organic part of this community. We are aware, of course, that they're played by Warren Beatty and Julie Christie, but rarely have stars been used so completely for their talents rather than their fame. We don't ever think much about McCabe being Warren Beatty, and Mrs. Miller being Julie Christie; they're there along with everybody else in town, and the movie just happens to be about their lives.

Because the movie is about a period in the lives of several people (and not about a series of events that occur to one-dimensional characters), McCabe and Mrs. Miller change during the course of the story. Mrs. Miller is a tough Cockney madam who convinces McCabe that he needs a competent manager for his whorehouse: How would *he* ever know enough about managing women? He agrees, and she lives up to her promise, and they're well on their way to making enough money for her to get out of this dump of a mining town and back to San Francisco, where, she believes, a woman of her caliber belongs.

All of this happens in an indoor sort of a way, and by that I don't mean that the movie looks like it was shot on a sound stage. The outdoors is always there, and people are always coming in out of it and shaking the rain from their hats, and we see the trees whipping in the wind through the windows. But it's a wet autumn and then a cold winter, so people naturally congregate in saloons and grocery stores and whorehouses, and the climate forces a sense of community. Then the enforcers come to town: The suave, Scottish-accented Butler, who kills people who won't sell out to the Company, and his two sidekicks. One of them is slack-jawed and mean, and the other is a nervous blond kid with the bare makings of a mustache. On the suspension bridge that gets you across the river to the general store, he kills another kid — a rawboned, easygoing country kid with a friendly smile—and it is one of the most affecting and powerful deaths there ever has been in a Western.

The final hunt for McCabe takes place in almost deserted streets, because the church is burning down and everybody is out at the edge of town trying to save it. The church burns during a ghostly, heavy daylight snowstorm: fire and ice. And McCabe almost gets away. Mrs. Miller, who allowed him into her bed but always, except once, demanded five dollars for the privilege, caught on long before he did that the Company would rather kill him than go up $2,000. She is down at the foot of town, in Chinatown, lost in an opium dream while the snow drifts against his body. *McCabe and Mrs. Miller* is like no other Western ever made.

Mean Streets ★ ★ ★ ★
R, 110 m., 1974

Robert De Niro (Johnny Boy), Harvey Keitel (Charlie). Directed by Martin Scorsese and produced by Jonathan T. Taplin. Screenplay by Scorsese and Mardik Martin.

Martin Scorsese's *Mean Streets* isn't so much a gangster movie as a perceptive, sympathetic, finally tragic story about how it is to grow up in a gangster environment. Its characters (like Scorsese himself) have grown up in New York's Little Italy, and they understand everything about that small slice of human society except how to survive in it. The two most important characters, Charlie and Johnny Boy, move through the Mafia environment almost because it's expected of them. Charlie is a Catholic with pathological guilt complexes, but because the mob is the family business, he never quite forces himself to make the connection between right and wrong and what he does. Not that he's very good at being a Mafioso: He's twenty-seven, but he still lives at home; he's a collector for his uncle's protection racket, but the collections don't bring in much. If he has any luck at all, he will be able to take over a bankrupt restaurant.

He is, at least fitfully, a realist. Johnny Boy, on the other hand, is a violent, uncontrolled product of romanticized notions of criminal street life. Little Italy is all around him, and yet he seems to have formed his style and borrowed half his vocabulary from the movies. He contains great and ugly passions, and can find no way to release them except in sudden violent bursts. Charlie is in love with Johnny Boy's sister, and he also feels a dogged sense of responsibility for Johnny Boy: He goes up on a roof one night when Johnny is shooting out streetlights and talks him down. At least Johnny releases his angers in overt ways. Charlie suppresses everything, and sometimes in desperation passes his hand through a flame and wonders about the fires of hell. He takes his Catholicism literally.

Scorsese places these characters in a perfectly realized world of boredom and small joys, sudden assaults, the possibility of death, and the certainty of mediocrity. He shot on location in Little Italy, where he was born and where he seems to know every nuance of architecture and personality, and his story isn't built like a conventional drama: It emerges from the daily lives of the characters. They hang out. They go to the movies. They eat, they drink, they get in sudden fights that end as quickly as a summer storm. Scorsese photographs them with fiercely driven visual style. We never have the sense of a scene being set up and then played out; his characters hurry to their dooms while the camera tries to keep pace. There's an improvisational feel even in scenes that we know, because of their structure, couldn't have been improvised.

Scorsese got the same feel in his first feature, *Who's That Knocking at My Door?* (1967). *Mean Streets* is a sequel, and Scorsese gives us the same leading actor (Harvey Keitel) to assure the continuity. In the earlier film, he was still on the edge of life, of sex, of violence. Now he has been plunged in, and he isn't equal to the experience. He's not tough enough to be a Mafia collector (and not strong enough to resist). Johnny Boy is played by Robert De Niro and it's a marvelous performance, filled with urgency and restless desperation.

The movie's scenes of violence are especially effective because of the way Scorsese stages them. We don't get spectacular effects and skillfully choreographed struggles. Instead, there's something realistically clumsy about the fights in this movie. A scene in a pool hall, in particular, is just right in the way it shows its characters fighting and yet mindful of their suits (possibly the only suits they have). The whole movie feels like life in New York; there are scenes in a sleazy nightclub, on fire escapes, and in bars, and they all feel as if Scorsese has been there.

Melvin and Howard ★ ★ ★ ½
R, 95 m., 1980

Paul Le Mat (Melvin Dummar), Jason Robards (Howard Hughes), Mary Steenburgen (Lynda Dummar), Pamela Reed (Bonnie Dummar), Michael J. Pollard (Little Red), Charles Napier (Man with Envelope), Robert Ridgely (TV Host), Melvin Dummar (Depot Counterman). Directed by Jonathan Demme and produced by Art Linson and Don Phillips. Screenplay by Bo Goldman.

Melvin Dummar is the man who claimed he gave a lift to a doddering old hitchhiker, loaned him a quarter, and was left $156 million in the hitchhiker's will. If he was telling the truth, the hitchhiker was Howard Hughes. But Jonathan Demme's wonderful comedy *Melvin and Howard* doesn't depend on whether the so-called Mormon Will was really written by Hughes. That hardly matters. This is the story of a life lived at the other end of the financial ladder from Hughes. It sees Dummar as the kind of American hero who is celebrated for being so extraordinarily ordinary.

For what, after all, constitutes heroism? And why shouldn't Dummar be considered a hero? We learn from this movie that he ventured single-handedly into the jungle of American consumerism, and lived. We see his major battles. Here's a guy who was married three times (twice to the same woman, the second time with the "Hawaiian War Chant" playing in an all-night Vegas chapel). He had three cars and a boat repossessed, he went from being Milkman of the Month to hauling his first wife off a go-go stage, he loved his children, did not drink or smoke, and stood at the brink of losing his gas station franchise on the very day when a tall, blond stranger dropped what looked a lot like Hughes's last will and testament into his life.

The genius of *Melvin and Howard* is that it is about Melvin, not Howard. The film begins and ends with scenes involving the Hughes character, who is played by Jason Robards as a desert rat with fading memories of happiness. Dummar stops in the desert to answer a call of nature, finds Hughes lying in the sagebrush, gives him a ride in his pickup truck, and gets him to sing. For reasons of his own, Hughes sings "Bye, Bye Blackbird": *Got no one to love and understand me . . . oh, what hard-luck stories they all hand me.*

Robards is a chillingly effective Hughes. But this movie belongs to Paul Le Mat, as Dummar. Le Mat played the round-faced hot-rodder in *American Graffiti*, and Dummar is the kind of guy that character might have grown up to be. He is pleasant, genial, simple of speech, crafty of mind, always looking for an angle. He angles for Milkman of the Month, he plots to get his wife on a TV game show, he writes songs like "Santa's Souped-Up Sleigh," he plays the slots at Vegas and goes through his life asking only for a few small scores.

When he gets a big score—named the beneficiary of a $156 million will that seems to have been signed by Hughes—he hardly knows what to do. Long-lost relatives and new-found friends turn up by the dozens, and press conferences are held in front of his gas station. There is a court trial, but the movie never really addresses itself to the details of the Hughes will court case. It goes instead for the drama and for the effect on Dummar and his family.

This is a slice of American life. It shows the flip side of Gary Gilmore's Utah. It is a world of mobile homes, Pop Tarts, dust, kids, and dreams of glory. It's pretty clear how this movie got made. The producers started with the notion that the story of the mysterious Hughes will might make a good courtroom thriller. Well, maybe it would have. But my hunch is that when they met Dummar, they had the good sense to realize that they could get a better—and certainly a funnier—story out of what happened to him between the day he met Hughes and the day the will was discovered. Dummar is the kind of guy who thinks they oughta make a movie out of his life. This time, he was right.

Mephisto ★ ★ ★ ★
NO MPAA RATING, 135 m., 1981

Klaus Maria Brandauer (Henrik Hofgon), Krystyna Janda (Barbara Bruckner), Ildiko Bansagi (Nicolette Von Hiebuhr), Karin Boyd (Juliette Martens). Directed and produced by Istvan Szabo. Screenplay by Szabo and Peter Dobel.

There are times in *Mephisto* when the hero tries to explain himself by saying that he's only an actor, and he has that almost right. *All* he is, is an actor. It's not his fault that the Nazis have come to power, and that as a German speaking actor he must choose between becoming a Nazi and being exiled into a foreign land without jobs for German actors. As long as he is acting, as long as he is not called upon to risk his real feelings, this man can act his way into the hearts of women,

audiences, and the Nazi power structure. This is the story of a man who plays his life wearing masks, fearing that if the last mask is removed, he will have no face.

The actor is played by Klaus Maria Brandauer in one of the greatest movie performances I've ever seen. The character, Henrik, is not sympathetic, and yet we identify with him because he shares so many of our own weaknesses and fears. Henrik is not a very good actor or a very good human being, but he is good enough to get by in ordinary times. As the movie opens, he's a socialist, interested in all the most progressive new causes, and is even the proud lover of a black woman. By the end of the film, he has learned that his liberalism was a taste, not a conviction, and that he will do anything, flatter anybody, make any compromise, just to hear applause, even though he knows the applause comes from fools.

Mephisto does an uncanny job of creating its period, of showing us Hamburg and Berlin from the 1920s to the 1940s. And I've never seen a movie that does a better job of showing the seductive Nazi practice of providing party members with theatrical costumes, titles, and pageantry. In this movie, not being a Nazi is like being at a black tie ball in a brown corduroy suit. Hofgon, the actor, is drawn to this world like a magnet. From his ambitious beginnings in the provincial German theater, he works his way up into more important roles and laterally into more important society. All of his progress is based on lies. He marries a woman he does not love, because her father can do him some good. When the rise of the Nazis destroys his father-in-law's power, he leaves his wife. He continues all this time to maintain his affair with his black mistress. He has a modest, but undeniable, talent as an actor, but prostitutes it by playing his favorite role, Mephistopheles in *Faust*, not as he could but as he calculates he should.

The obvious parallel here is between the hero of this film and the figure of tragedy who sold his soul to the devil. But *Mephisto* doesn't depend upon easy parallels to make its point. This is a human story, and as the actor in this movie makes his way to the top of the Nazi propaganda structure and the bottom of his own soul, the movie is both merciless and understanding. This is a weak and shameful man, the film seems to say, but then it cautions us against throwing the first stone.

Mephisto is not a German but a Hungarian movie, directed by the talented Istvan Szabo, who has led his country's cinema from relative obscurity to its present position as one of the best and most innovative film industries in Europe. Szabo, in his way, has made a companion film to Fassbinder's *The Marriage of Maria Braun*. The Szabo film shows a man compromising his way to the top by lying to himself and everybody else, and throwing aside all moral standards. It ends as World War II is under way. The Fassbinder film begins after the destruction of the war, showing a woman clawing her way out of the rubble and repeating the same process of compromise, lies, and unquestioning materialism.

Both the man in the Szabo film and the woman in the Fassbinder film maintain one love affair all through everything, using their love (he for a black woman, she for a convict) as a sort of token contempt for a society whose corrupt values they otherwise completely accept. The fact that they *can* still love, of course, makes it impossible for them to quite deceive themselves. That is the price they pay for their deals with the devil.

Merry Christmas, Mr. Lawrence
★ ★ ½
R, 122 m., 1983

David Bowie (Celliers) Tom Conti (Colonel Lawrence), Ryuichi Sakamoto (Captain Yonoi), Takeshi (Sergeant Hara), Jack Thompson (Hicksley-Ellis). Directed by Nagisa Oshima and produced by Jeremy Thomas. Screenplay by Oshima and Paul Mayersberg.

Here's a movie that is even stranger than it was intended to be. *Merry Christmas, Mr. Lawrence* is about a clash between two cultures (British and Japanese) and two styles of military service (patriotic and pragmatic). That would be enough for any movie, and there are scenes when it *is* enough, and the movie works pretty well. But then the movie makes another contrast that doesn't work so well, a contrast between basic views of theatrical acting styles. British tradition suggests that, everything else being equal,

actors should behave as if they were real people in a real situation. The Japanese tend toward a more overwrought acting style, made of screams and grimaces, histrionics and dramatizations. Each tradition works well enough in a movie where it is the only tradition. But in a movie where British and Japanese are on the screen at the same time and are apparently sharing the same reality, the results look odd, and eventually undermine the film. We wonder, in some small irreverent corner of our minds, whether the soft-spoken British *notice* that the Japanese rant and rave over everything, including the weather, and whether the Japanese, in turn, find the British catatonic.

The movie is by Nagisa Oshima, the best-known of the younger Japanese directors, whose notorious *In the Realm of the Senses* (1976) began with a love affair between a businessman and a geisha and ended in a bloodbath of castration and suicide. He is clearly fascinated by relationships between authorities and victims, and that's the subject here. The time is 1942, in a Japanese prison camp on Java, and the story concentrates on two pairs of officers. The British are Celliers (David Bowie), very upper crust, duty-bound, guilt-ridden, and Lawrence (Tom Conti), sensitive, bilingual, trying to translate not only the words but the values of the two races. The Japanese are Yonoi (Ryuichi Sakamoto) of the warrior class, filled with pride and glory, and Hara (Takeshi), a sort of Japanese Falstaff with a streak of sadism. How these two pairs get along together will determine the fate of the British (which is complicated by their nominal leader, a blustering bully played by Jack Thompson).

The movie develops the situation in a series of scenes that owe something to *Bridge Over the River Kwai*. Rules are made, forgotten, broken, then strictly enforced. Enemies admit at weak moments that we are all human beings, after all. But then there's a breach of protocol and a crackdown from the top. The most rigid officers on each side (Celliers and Yonoi) have a sort of admiration for each other, which turns into a contest of wills. This is interesting material, especially since Oshima plunges a little more deeply into the psychology of his characters than your average prisoner-of-war movie is likely to. There are hints of a homosexual attraction between Celliers and Yonoi, eventually leading to one of the movie's most awkward moments—a parting in which the British soldier actually seems to be saying that both sides were right in the war and both sides were wrong.

It's awkward, not because of the subject matter, because of the contrasting acting styles. Here are two men trying to communicate in a touchy area and they behave as if they're from different planets. The overstatement in the Japanese acting ruins the scene. It's strange: Japanese acting styles never bother me in all-Japanese movies (especially not when they're modulated, as in the contemporary films of Kurosawa). It's only when you have actors who are clearly on different wavelengths that the Japanese histrionics become distracting. What this movie needed was a diplomatic acting coach.

Metropolis ★ ★ ★ ★
NO MPAA RATING, 120 m., 1926,
1984 (Sound version)

Alfred Abel (Leader), Gustav Frohlich (His Son), Brigitte Helm (Maria), Rudolf Klein-Rogge (Rotwang), Heinrich George (Foreman). Directed by Fritz Lang. Screenplay by Lang and Thea Von Harbou. New sound track by Giorgio Moroder.

Fritz Lang's 1926 film *Metropolis* is one of the great achievements in the silent era, a work so audacious in its vision and so angry in its message that it is, if anything, more powerful today than when it was made. But it is rarely seen today; even in the era of insatiable home TV watching, silent films are condemned to the hinterlands of film societies and classrooms.

That is a great loss. Lang's movie is one of the great overwrought fantasies of German Expressionism, a story of a monstrous twenty-first-century city in which the workers labor like robots in their subterranean factories, while the privileged classes dance the night away, far above. The plot is broad melodrama: The son of the ruler of Metropolis visits the underground city and falls in love with a revolutionary named Maria, who makes impassioned speeches against the tyrants above. But the ruler orders a mad scientist to provide his new robot with Maria's face, creating a false Maria who will mislead the workers. Some of the individual scenes are amazing in their visual power, especially our first sight of the workers marching to their jobs, and a bizarre Art Deco factory wall where the humans are treated as parts of the machines. The movie was widely influential: The scene where the robot is turned into the false Maria was the inspiration for all the 1930s transformations of Frankenstein's monsters. Yet the original *Metropolis* is hardly known to today's filmgoers.

But now Giorgio Moroder, the composer of "Flashdance—What a Feeling" and the sound tracks for such movies as *Cat People*, has resurrected *Metropolis*, discovered or reconstructed some of its missing scenes, added some color tinting, and released it with a sound track of 1984 pop music. When this version of the movie was premiered at the 1984 Cannes Film Festival, it was sold primarily for its possibilities as a midnight cult film. In some sort of weird cultural inversion, Pat Benatar and Adam Ant would be used to sell Fritz Lang.

After you've seen the film with its new sound track, however, the notion seems almost sane. Silent films have always been accompanied by some sort of musical accompaniment—everything from orchestras to solo pianos. And in recent years such silent classes as *Napoleon* and *Peter Pan* have been resurrected with new scores. This is even the second time around for *Metropolis*, which was given a track of electronic music by the BBC in the 1970s. Moroder, however, has gone all the way and tarted up *Metropolis* with the same kinds of songs you'd expect to hear on MTV—he treats *Metropolis* like a music video. The film is too strong and original to be reduced to a formula, however; it absorbs the sound track, instead of being dominated by it, and the result is a film that works and a sound track that is an addition.

Some purists will not approve of Moroder's choice in music. Kevin Thomas of the *Los Angeles Times* was especially offended by the use of songs with words ("which sound especially silly because they're so painfully redundant"), but the words didn't bother me because, frankly, I didn't find myself listening to them. They are part of the background, and Fritz Lang's great film, so lovingly reconstructed, is the magnificent foreground.

Micki & Maude ★ ★ ★ ★
PG-13, 115 m., 1984

Dudley Moore (Rob Salinger), Amy Irving (Maude Salinger), Ann Reinking (Micki Salinger), Richard Mulligan (Leo Brody), Lu Leonard (Nurse Verbeck). Directed by Blake Edwards and produced by Tony Adams. Screenplay by Jonathan Reynolds.

The key to the whole thing is Dudley Moore's absolutely and unquestioned sincerity. He loves both women. He would do anything to avoid hurting either woman. He wants to do the right thing but, more than that, he wants to do the kind thing. And that is how he ends up in a maternity ward with two wives who are both presenting him with baby children. If it were not for those good qualities in Moore's character, qualities this movie goes to great lengths to establish, *Micki & Maude* would run the risk of turning into tasteless and even cruel slapstick. After all, these are serious matters we're talking about. But the triumph of the movie is that it identifies so closely with Moore's desperation and his essentially sincere motivation that we understand the lengths to which he is driven. That makes the movie's inevitable climax even funnier.

As the movie opens, Moore is happily married to an assistant district attorney (Ann Reinking) who has no desire to have children. Children are, however, the only thing in life that Moore himself desires; apart from that one void, his life is full and happy. He works as a reporter for one of those TV magazine shows where weird people talk earnestly about their constitutional rights to be weird: For example, nudists defend their right to bear arms. Then he meets a special person, a cello player (Amy Irving) who has stepped in at the last moment to play a big concert. She thinks he has beautiful eyes, he smiles, it's love, and within a few weeks Moore and Irving are talking about how they'd like to have kids. Then Irving gets pregnant. Moore decides to do the only right thing, and divorce the wife he loves to marry the pregnant girlfriend that he also loves. But then his wife announces that she's preg-

nant, and Moore turns, in this crisis of conscience, to his best friend, a TV producer wonderfully played by Richard Mulligan. There is obviously only one thing he can do: become a bigamist.

Micki & Maude was directed by Blake Edwards, who also directed Moore in *10*, and who knows how to build a slapstick climax by one subtle development after another. There is, for example, the fact that Irving's father happens to be a professional wrestler, with a lot of friends who are even taller and meaner than he is. There is the problem that Moore's original in-laws happen past the church where he is having his second wedding. Edwards has a way of applying absolute logic to insane situations, so we learn, for example, that after Moore tells one wife he works days and the other one he works nights, his schedule works out in such a way that he begins to get too much sleep.

Dudley Moore is developing into one of the great movie comedians of his generation. *Micki & Maude* goes on the list with *10* and *Arthur* as screwball classics. Moore has another side as an actor, a sweeter, more serious side, that shows up in good movies like *Romantic Comedy* and bad ones like *Six Weeks*, but it's when he's in a screwball comedy, doing his specialty of absolutely sincere desperation, that he reaches genius. For example: The last twenty minutes of *Micki & Maude*, as the two pregnant women move inexorably forward on their collision course, represents a kind of filmmaking that is as hard to do as anything you'll ever see on a screen. The timing has to be flawless. So does the logic: One loose end, and the inevitability of a slapstick situation is undermined. Edwards and Moore are working at the top of their forms here, and the result is a pure, classic slapstick that makes *Micki & Maude* a real treasure.

A Midsummer Night's Sex Comedy ★ ★
PG, 88 m., 1982

Woody Allen (Andrew), Mia Farrow (Ariel), Jose Ferrer (Leopold), Julie Hagerty (Dulcy), Tony Roberts (Maxwell), Mary Steenburgen (Adrian). Directed by Woody Allen and produced by Robert Greenhut. Screenplay by Allen.

The further north you go in summer, the longer the twilight lingers, until night is but a finger drawn between the dusk and the dawn. Such nights in northern climes are times of revelry, when lads and maids frolic in the underbrush to the pipes of Pan. Woody Allen's *A Midsummer Night's Sex Comedy* sneaks up rather suspiciously on this tradition; his men and women are rationalists, belong to such professions as finance, medicine, and psychiatry, and are nonchalant in the face of such modern inventions as flying bicycles. And yet here they all are, out in the country for the weekend. They gather at a little cottage somewhere in upstate New York, arriving by carriage or primitive auto, and in no time at all they are deeply unhappy about each other's sex lives. The host and hostess are Woody Allen and Mary Steenburgen. He is a stockbroker and she is his shy and sweet wife. The guests include Jose Ferrer, as an egotistical scientist, Mia Farrow, as his fiancée, Tony Roberts as a doctor, and Julie Hagerty as his abundantly sexed nurse.

During the course of their long weekend, many themes emerge, but the most common one is the enigma of male jealousy. Look at these three men, each one paired with the wonderful woman of his dreams. Allen, a part-time crackpot inventor, has a wife who loyally supports his experiments. Ferrer, an aging genius with a monstrous ego, has a beautiful young woman to hang on his arm. Roberts, an insatiable satyr, has a nubile nurse panting with desire. Are all three men happy and satiated? Not a chance. It is the most inevitable thing in the world that each man should be consumed with lust for one or more of the other women. It is not enough to have a bird in the hand; one must also have another bird in the bush. Or, as David Merrick once observed, "It is not enough for me to succeed. My enemies must fail."

From this simple and intriguing little situation, Woody Allen spins a rondelet of sexual intrigue and frustration. The basic developments: Allen pines away with the thought that he could once have made love to Farrow, but declined the chance. Ferrer conspires to meet Hagerty in the woods. Roberts attempts to seduce Farrow. And, through it all, Steenburgen steadfastly hopes for the best from everybody. To pass the time in between assignations and intrigues, the couples picnic, go for walks in the woods and express curiosity in Allen's latest inventions, which, in addition to the flying bicycle, include a metal sphere that can provide a magic lantern show that remembers the past and foresees the future.

This all sounds very charming and whimsical, and it is—almost paralyzingly so. *A Midsummer Night's Sex Comedy* is so low-key, so sweet and offhand and slight, there are times when it hardly even seems happy to be a movie. I am not quite sure what Allen had in mind when he conceived this material, but in addition to the echoes of Shakespeare and of Bergman's *Smiles of a Summer Night*, there are suggestions of John Cheever's Wapshots, Doctorow's *Ragtime* and Jean Renoir films in which nice people do nice things to little avail. This is not a "Woody Allen film," then. It is not a brash comedy, it does not really contain the Woody Allen persona, and I guess Woody wanted it that way; he says he wants to try new things instead of giving people the same old stuff all the time. It is our misfortune that he arrived at that decision just after making *Annie Hall* and *Manhattan*, two wonderful films that brought his same old stuff to an exciting new plateau.

Now, with *Stardust Memories* and this film, he seems rudderless. I don't object to *A Midsummer Night's Sex Comedy* on grounds that it's different from his earlier films, but on the more fundamental ground that it's adrift. There doesn't seem to be a driving idea behind it, a confident tone to give us the sure notion that Allen knows what he wants to do here. It's a tip-off that the story is lacking in both sex and comedy. If the film seems at a loss to know where to turn next, the ending is particularly unsatisfactory. It involves a moment of fantasy or spirituality in which one of the movie's most rational characters dies and turns into a spirit of light, and bobs away on the twilight breeze. I don't object to the development itself, but to the way Allen handles it, so briefly and incompletely that it ends the film with what can only be described as a whimsical anticlimax.

There are nice small moments here and reflective, quiet performances, and a few laughs and smiles. But when we see Woody pedaling furiously to spin the helicopter blades of his flying bicycle, we're reminded of what we're missing. Woody doesn't have to be funny in every shot and he doesn't have to become another Mel Brooks, but he should allow himself to be funny when he feels like it, without apology, instead of receding into cuteness. I had the feeling during the film that Woody Allen was soft-pedaling his talent, was sitting on his comic gift, was trying to be somebody that he is not—and that, even if he were, would not be half as wonderful a piece of work as the real Woody Allen.

Mishima ★ ★ ★ ★
R, 121 m., 1985

Ken Ogato (Yukio Mishima), Mashayuki Shionoya (Morita), Hiroshi Mikami (First Cadet), Naoko Otani (Mother). Directed by Paul Schrader and produced by Mata Yamamoto and Tom Luddy. Screenplay by Paul and Leonard Schrader.

The Japanese author Yukio Mishima seems to have thought of his life as a work of art, and more than anyone since Hemingway he got other people to think of it that way, too. He was a brilliant self-promoter who not only wrote important novels and plays, but also cultivated the press, posed for beefcake photographs, and founded his own private army. He was an advocate of a return to medieval Japanese values, considered himself a samurai, and died on schedule and according to his own plan: After occupying an Army garrison with some of his soldiers, he disemboweled himself while being beheaded by a follower.

Mishima's life obviously supplies the materials for a sensationalistic film. Paul Schrader has not made one. Instead, his *Mishima* takes this most flamboyant of writers and translates his life into a carefully structured examination of three different Mishimas: Public, private, and literary.

The film begins with the public Mishima, a literary superstar who begins the last day of his life by ritualistically donning the uniform of his private army. From time to time during the film, we return to moments from that final day, as Mishima is jammed somewhat inelegantly into a tiny car and driven by his followers to an appointment with a Japanese

general. The film ends with Mishima holding the general hostage, and winning the right to address the troops of the garrison (who must have been just as astonished as if Norman Mailer turned up at West Point). Although the film ends with Mishima's ritual suicide, it is not shown in the graphic detail that's popular in recent films; Schrader wisely realizes that too much blood would destroy the mood of his film and distract attention from the idea behind Mishima's death.

Mishima's last day is counterpointed with black-and-white sequences showing his childhood and adolescence, and with gloriously stylized color dramatizations of scenes from his novels, *Temple of the Golden Pavilion*, *Kyoko's House*, and *Runaway Horses*. The scenes from the novels were visualized by designer Eiko Ishioka, who seems to have been inspired by fantasy scenes from early Technicolor musicals. They don't summarize Mishima's novels so much as give us an idea about them; as we see the ritualistic aspects of his fantasies, we are seeing Japan through his eyes, as he wished it to be.

The black-and-white biographical sequences show a little boy growing up into a complicated man. Young Yukio, raised by his mother and his grandmother, was a lonely outcast with a painful stammer, and we can see in the insecurities of his youth impulses that led him to build his muscles, to leap for literary glory, and to wrap himself in the samurai ethic.

Mishima is a rather glorious project, in these days of pragmatic commercialism and rank cynicism in the movie industry. Although a sensationalized version of his life might have had potential at the box office (and although Schrader, author of *Taxi Driver*, director of *American Gigolo*, would have been quite capable of directing it), this is a much more ambitious and intellectual film.

It challenges us to think about Mishima, instead of simply observing the strange channels of his life. What did he prove, on the day when his life ended according to plan? That he was willing to pay the ultimate price to transform his life into an artistic statement—and also, perhaps, that some of his genius was madness. Was it worth it? Who can say who is not Mishima?

Missing ★ ★ ★
R, 122 m., 1982

Jack Lemmon (Ed Horman), Sissy Spacek (Beth Horman), Melanie Mayron (Terry Simon), John Shea (Charles Horman), Charles Cioffi (Capt. Tower), David Clennon (Consul Putnam). Directed by Constantin Costa-Gavras and produced by Edward and Mildred Lewis. Screenplay by Costa-Gavras and Donald Stewart.

Much has already been written about the bravery of *Missing*, which dares, we are told, to make a specific attack on American policies in Chile during and after the Allende regime. I wish the movie had been even braver—brave enough to risk a clear, unequivocal, uncompromised statement of its beliefs, instead of losing itself in a cluttered mishmash of stylistic excesses. This movie might have *really* been powerful, if it could have gotten out of its own way.

The story involves the disappearance in the early 1970s of a young American journalist in a country (not named) that is obviously intended to be Chile. The young man and his wife (played by John Shea and Sissy Spacek) have gone down there to live, write, and absorb the local color. But then a civil war breaks out, martial law is declared, troops roam the streets, and one day soldiers come and take the young man away. The movie is the record of the frustrating attempts by Spacek and her father-in-law (Jack Lemmon) to discover what happened to the missing man. It suggests that the young American might have been on some sort of informal hit list of left-wing foreign journalists, that he was taken away and killed, and that (this is the controversial part) American embassy officials knew about his fate and may even have been involved in approving his death.

If that was indeed the case, then it is a cause for great anger and dismay. And the best scenes in *Missing*—the ones that make this movie worth seeing despite its shortcomings—are the ones in which Spacek and Lemmon hack their way through a bureaucratic jungle in an attempt to get someone to make a simple statement of fact. Those scenes are masterful. The U.S. embassy officials are painted as dishonest weasels, shuffling papers, promising immediate action, and lying through their teeth. Lemmon and Spacek are about as good an example of Ordinary Americans as you can find in a movie, and their flat voices and stubborn determination and even their initial dislike for one another all ring exactly true. If *Missing* had started with the disappearance of the young man, and had followed Spacek and Lemmon in a straightforward narrative as they searched for him, this movie might have generated overwhelming tension and anger. But the movie never develops the power it should have had, because the director, Constantin Costa-Gavras, either lacked confidence in the strength of his story, or had too much confidence in his own stylistic virtuosity. He has achieved the unhappy feat of upstaging his own movie, losing it in a thicket of visual and editing stunts.

Let's begin with the most annoying example of his meddling. *Missing* contains scenes that take place before the young man disappears. We see his domestic happiness with his wife and friends, we see him reading from *The Little Prince* and making plans for the future. The fact that this material is in the movie suggests, at least, that the story is being told by an omniscient author, one who can also tell us, if he wishes to, what happened to the victim. But he does not. Costa-Gavras shows us all sorts of ominous warnings of approaching trouble (including a lot of loose talk by American military men who are not supposed to be in the country, but are, and all but claim credit for a coup). He shows us a tragic aftermath of martial law, guns in the streets, vigilante justice, and the chilling sight of row after row of dead young men, summarily executed by the new junta. But he does not show us what happened to make the film's hero disappear. Or, rather, he shows us several versions—visual fantasies in which the young husband is arrested at home by a lot of soldiers, or a few, and is taken away in this way or that. These versions are pegged to the unreliable eyewitness accounts of the people who live across the street. They dramatize an uncertain human fate in a time of upheaval, but they also distract fatally from the flow of the film.

By the time *Missing* begins its crucial last half-hour, a strange thing has happened. We care about this dead American, and his wife and father, almost *despite* the movie. The performances of Spacek and Lemmon carry us along through the movie's undisciplined stylistic displays. But at the end of the film, there isn't the instant discharge of anger we felt at the end of Costa-Gavras's great Z (1968), because the narrative juggernaut of that film has been traded in for what is basically just a fancy meditation on the nature of reality. Something happened to the missing young man (his story is based on real events). Somebody was guilty, and somebody was lying, and he was indeed killed. But *Missing* loses its way on the road to those conclusions, and at the end Lemmon and Spacek seem almost to mourn alone, while the crew is busy looking for its next shot.

Mommie Dearest ★
PG, 129 m., 1981

Faye Dunaway (Joan Crawford), Diana Scarwid (Christina, adult), Steve Forrest (Greg Savitt), Howard Da Silva (L.B. Mayer), Mara Hobel (Christina, child), Autanya Alda (Carol Ann). Directed by Frank Perry and produced by Frank Yablans. Screenplay by Yablans, Perry, Tracy Hotchner, and Robert Getchell.

I can't imagine who would want to subject themselves to this movie. *Mommie Dearest* is a painful experience that drones on endlessly, as Joan Crawford's relationship with her daughter, Christina, disintegrates from cruelty through jealousy into pathos. It is unremittingly depressing, not to any purpose of drama or entertainment, but just to depress. It left me feeling creepy. The movie was inspired, of course, by a best-selling memoir in which adopted daughter Christina Crawford portrayed her moviestar mother as a grasping, sadistic, alcoholic wretch whose own insecurities and monstrous ego made life miserable for everyone around her. I have no idea if the book's portrait is an accurate one, but the movie is faithful to it in one key sense: It made life miserable for me.

Mommie Dearest repeats the same basic dramatic situation again and again. Baby Christina tries to do the right thing, tries to be a good girl, tries to please Mommie, but Mommie is a manic-depressive who alternates between brief triumphs and long savage tirades, infecting her daughter with resentment and guilt. In scene after scene, we are invited to watch as Joan Crawford screams at Christina, chops her hair with scissors, beats her with a wire coat hanger and, on an especially bad day, tackles her across an end table, hurls her to the carpet, bangs her head against the floor, and tries to choke her to death. Who wants to watch this?

This material is presented essentially as sensationalism. The movie makes no attempt to draw psychological insights from the life of its Joan Crawford—not even through the shorthand Freudianism much beloved by Hollywood. Mommie is a monster, that's all, and there's some mention of her unhappy childhood. Christina is a brave, smiling, pretty, long-suffering dope who might inspire more sympathy if she were not directed (in both her childhood and adult versions) to be distant and veiled.

The movie doesn't even make narrative sense. Success follows crisis without any pattern. At one moment, Joan is in triumph after winning the Oscar for *Mildred Pierce*. In the very next scene she goes so berserk we want to scrape her off the screen with a spatula. The scenes don't build, they just happen. Another example: After an especially ugly fight, Joan sends Christina to a convent school. There's a scene where the mother superior welcomes her and promises to reform her. One scene later, Christina checks out of the school, and the nun wishes her godspeed. No mention of what happened in the school, how it affected Christina, or whether the nun changed her opinion of the girl.

The movie also offers few insights into Crawford's relationships with others. There's a loyal housekeeper, but never a scene where Crawford speaks personally with her. There is a lover and a third husband, both enigmas. Crawford's acting career is treated mostly in ellipses. The sets look absolutely great, Faye Dunaway's impersonation of Crawford is stunningly suggestive and convincing, and little Mara Hobel, as Baby Christina, handles several difficult moments very well. But to what end? *Mommie Dearest* is a movie that knows exactly how it wants to look, but has no idea what it wants to make us feel.

The Money Pit ★
PG-13, 90 m., 1986 ✔

Tom Hanks (Walter Fielding), Shelley Long (Anna Crowley), Alexander Godunov (Max Beissart), Maureen Stapleton (Estelle), Joe Mantegna (Art Shirk), Philip Bosco (Curly Shirk), Josh Mostell (Schnittman), Yakov Smirnoff (Shatov). Directed by Richard Benjamin and produced by Frank Marshall, Kathleen Kennedy, and Art Levinson. Screenplay by David Giler.

In a movie called *Big Deal on Madonna Street*, a gang of crooks was trying to break through a wall into a bank building. They rigged up a system that was going to penetrate the wall, and braced it against another wall, and of course it was the other wall that collapsed. Their surprise when that happened was one of the biggest laughs in the movie.

However, if the entire movie had consisted of the same gag, repeated over and over again, with the gadget breaking through the wrong wall a dozen times, I think the original laughter would have eventually collapsed into quiet desperation. That is what happens with *The Money Pit*, a movie that contains one funny scene, and more than an hour of running time to kill.

The movie stars Tom Hanks and Shelley Long as a couple who need to find a house in a hurry. They've been living in the Manhattan apartment of her former husband (Alexander Godunov, as a symphony conductor), but now he throws them out and they take the only place they can find—a country estate at a suspiciously low price. Sure, it needs a little work. All older houses need a little work. But Hanks begins to suspect something is seriously wrong when he slams the front door, and it falls off its hinges.

Ha, ha. In the course of this movie, we will also see a staircase collapse, a bathtub fall through the floor, and several walls reduced to piles of rubble. That's before the craftsmen arrive to repair the building. They have a standard answer to how long everything will take: "Two weeks," they say, snickering up their sleeves. They demand cash advances and then drive off in their Cadillacs and Porsches, maybe never to be seen again.

If the movie had made the carpenters, plumbers, and electricians into interesting characters, it might have been able to save itself. But one contractor (Joe Mantegna) is onscreen so little he seems like an afterthought, and the other one (Philip Bosco) is never developed into much more than a genial presence.

Instead, we get one monotonous sight gag after another. The most irritating is the one where Hanks falls through the floor and is pinned, halfway down, by a rug. He can't move. All he can do is scream for help, but when Long finally arrives at the house, he screams all the wrong things, until we aren't laughing, we're groaning. Didn't it occur to anybody that the smarter the characters were, the funnier their troubles would be? Make them into idiots, and who cares if their house falls down?

There is just the beginning of a comic idea with the Godunov character. He exhibits a certain wry charm, as a conceited conductor who thinks himself to be altogether the most brilliant person in the world. His scenes with Shelley Long are among the movie's few pleasant interludes, if only because he's so cheerful about his absolute cynicism.

But the house is a disaster in more ways than one. Sure, it's a triumph of art direction. The Hollywood artisans who designed it deserve some sort of medal, for the neat stunts they think up and the great tricks they're able to pull. There is even one sustained Rube Goldberg-type gag that is really funny, as an incredible chain of events unfolds with meticulous precision. But one gag does not a comedy make, and if they'd spent the time on the characters that they spent on building the house, they might have really had something here.

Monsignor ★
R, 122 m., 1982

Christopher Reeve (Flaherty), Genevieve Bujold (Clara), Fernando Rey (Santoni). Directed by Frank Perry and produced by Frank Yablans. Screenplay by Abraham Polonsky and Wendell Mayes.

Monsignor is the most cynical movie ever made about organized religion. I include in that statement the anticlerical broadsides by Luis Bunuel, who attacked Catholicism with shocking imagery and gleefully flaunted his atheism but at least took the Roman Catholic

Church seriously enough to treat it as a worthy adversary. *Monsignor* uses the Vatican only for a storyline—and doesn't even get a good one.

The movie takes place during World War II, when the Italian-dominated Vatican establishment, racked by in-fighting, imports a young Irish-Catholic priest (Christopher Reeve) from America. He's said to be a good accountant. He sure is. Under the sponsorship of the Vatican Secretary of State (Fernando Rey), he concocts a plan to finance the bankrupt Vatican by selling fifty thousand cartons of American cigarettes a week to the Mafia-controlled black market. This is obviously a bright young man, destined to rise in the church hierarchy. Unfortunately, despite his promising start in illegal profiteering, he turns out to have a character defect: He lusts after a young nun (Genevieve Bujold), and they have an affair.

There follows a confusing flash-forward to a point some years in the future, after Reeve has allowed $400 million of the church's money to be lost in reckless stock market speculation. *This* time, has he gone too far? Not really. At the movie's end, he's exchanging confidences with his old sponsor, who has just been elected pope. As you may already have gathered, the Catholics in this movie do everything but pray. The church is seen as a venal, corrupt, dishonest institution—I think. (The strange thing is that Reeve maintains such a veneer of saintliness through the movie that at times we really believe his sophistry as he's defending his black market sales.) I do not object to the filmmaker's desire to make a film of overwhelming cynicism about the Vatican power structure. I simply object to the film they have made.

It appears to have no purpose. It doesn't condemn dishonesty, yet neither does it applaud unscrupulous schemery. It doesn't bemoan low human weaknesses, nor does it contain heroes. In the case of the affair between the priest and the nun, it doesn't even take a stand! The flash-forward avoids the necessity of even *finishing* that aspect of the story. There are a few good things in *Monsignor*. The movie is populated with good performances in the character roles, especially by Fernando Rey (who once

played one of Bunuel's anticlerical clerics), by Robert Prosky (he's an American cardinal here, and was superb as the mob fixer in *Thief*) and by Leonardo Cimino as a pope who looks uncannily like E.T. and looks forward to his own death with a grim humor. These performances, alas, do not occur in an engaging screenplay; the most cynical thing in this cynical movie is that it doesn't even bother to put its nihilistic characters in a comprehensible story.

Monty Python's Meaning of Life
★ ★ ½
R, 103 m., 1983

Written and starring: Graham Chapman, John Cleese, Terry Gilliam, Eric Idle, Terry Jones, and Michael Palin. Directed by Terry Jones and produced by John Goldstone.

Halfway through *Monty Python's Meaning of Life*, the thought struck me that One-Upmanship was a British discovery. You remember, of course, the book and movie *(School for Scoundrels)* inspired by Stephen Potter's theory of One-Upmanship, in which the goal of the practitioner was to One-Up his daily associates and, if possible, the world. A modern example:

Victim: I've just been reading Gabriel Garcia Marquez's *Chronicle of a Death Foretold* in *Vanity Fair* magazine.

One-Upman: Really? I'm afraid I missed it.

Victim: But Garcia Marquez is brilliant.

One-Upman: No doubt, dear fellow, but my subscription ran out in 1939.

I use this illustration as an approach to *Monty Python's Meaning of Life*, which is a movie that seems consumed with a desire to push us too far. This movie is so far beyond good taste, and so cheerfully beyond, that we almost feel we're being One-Upped if we allow ourselves to be offended. Take, for example, the scene featuring projectile vomiting. We don't get just a little vomit in the scene, as we saw in *The Exorcist*. No sir, we get gallons of vomit, streams of it, all a vile yellow color, sprayed all over everybody and everything in a formal dining room. The first reaction of the non-Upman is *"Yech!"* But I think the Python gang is working at another level. And, given the weakness of movie critics for discussing what "level" a movie "works" on, I find myself almost compelled to ask myself, "At what 'level' *does* the projectile vomiting 'work'?" And I think the Python One-Up reply would be, dear fellow, that it rises above vulgarity and stakes out territory in the surrealistic. Anyone who takes the vomiting literally has missed the joke; the scene isn't about vomiting, but about the lengths to which Python will go for a laugh.

There are other scenes in equally poor taste in this movie, which has a little something to offend everybody. And I mean *really* offend them: This isn't a Mel Brooks movie, with friendly little ethnic in-jokes. It's a barbed, uncompromising attack on generally observed community standards. Does the attack work? Only occasionally. The opening sequence of the film is one of its best, showing the overworked old clerks in an insurance company staging a mutiny. After they've gained control of their shabby old stone building, the movie does a brilliant turn into surrealism, the building becomes a ship, and the clerks weigh anchor and set sail against the fleets of modern high-rises, firing their filing cabinets like cannons. It's a wonderful sequence.

I also liked a scene set on a military parade ground, and a joke involving a tankful of fish, and a cheerfully unfair rugby match between two teams, one made up of twelve small schoolboys, the other with eighteen schoolmasters, all huge. Balanced against these bright moments is the goriest scene in Python history, showing a liver being removed from a transplant "volunteer" by brute force. There are also a lot of religious jokes, some straightforward sexism, and the above-mentioned vomiting sequence.

By admitting to being offended by some of the stuff in this movie, I've been One-Upped. By liking the funny stuff, I've been One-Upped again. ("But you liked the jokes that were in good taste? Jolly good!") But I'm a good loser, and I don't mind being One-Upped. In fact, let's say this is a tennis match, and the Pythons are the winners. Here, I'll hold down the net while they jump over to shake hands with me. Whoops!

Moonlighting ★ ★ ★ ★
PG, 97 m., 1982

Jeremy Irons (Nowak), Eugene Lipinski (Banaszak), Jiri Stanislav (Wolski), Eugeniusz Haczkiewicz (Kudaj). Directed by Jerzy Skolimowski and produced by Mark Shivas and Skolimowski. Screenplay by Skolimowski.

Moonlighting is a wickedly pointed movie that takes a simple little story, tells it with humor and truth, and turns it into a knife in the side of the Polish government. In its own way, this response to the crushing of Solidarity is as powerful as Andrezej Wajda's *Man of Iron*. It also is more fun. The movie takes place in London, during the weeks just before and after the banning of the Solidarity movement in Poland. It begins, actually, in Warsaw, with a mystifying scene in which a group of plotters are scheming to smuggle some hardware past British customs. They're plotters, all right; their plot is to move into a small house in London and remodel it, knocking out walls, painting ceilings, making it into a showplace for the Polish government official who has purchased it. The official's plan is simplicity itself: By bringing Polish workers to London on tourist visas, he can get the remodeling done for a fraction of what British workman would cost him. At the same time, the workers can earn good wages that they can take back to Poland and buy bicycles with. The only thing nobody counts on is the upheaval after Solidarity is crushed and travel to and from Poland is strictly regulated.

Jeremy Irons, of *The French Lieutenant's Woman*, plays the lead in the film. He's the only Polish workman who can speak English. Acting as foreman, he guides his team of men through the pitfalls of London and safely into the house they're going to remodel. He advises them to keep a low profile, while he ventures out to buy the groceries and (not incidentally) to read the newspapers. When he finds out about the crisis in Poland, he keeps it a secret from his comrades. The daily life of the renovation project falls into a pattern, which the film's director, Jerzy Skolimowski, intercuts with the adventures of his hero. Jeremy Irons begins to steal things: newspapers, bicycles, frozen turkeys. He concocts an elaborate scheme to defraud the local supermarket, and some of the movie's best scenes involve the subtle timing of his shoplifting scam, which involves the misrepresentation of cash-register receipts. He needs to steal food because he's running out of money, and he knows his group can't easily go home again. There's also a quietly hilarious, and slightly sad, episode involving a salesgirl in a blue jeans store. Irons, pretending to be more naive than he is, tries to pick the girl up. She's having none of it.

Moonlighting invites all kinds of interpretations. You can take this simple story and set it against the events of the last two years, and see it as a kind of parable. Your interpretation is as good as mine. Is the house itself Poland, and the workmen Solidarity—rebuilding it from within, before an authoritarian outside force intervenes? Or is this movie about the heresy of substituting Western values (and jeans and turkeys) for a home-grown orientation? Or is it about the manipulation of the working classes by the intelligentsia? Or is it simply a frontal attack on the Communist Party bosses who live high off the hog while the workers are supposed to follow the rules?

Like all good parables, *Moonlighting* contains not one but many possibilities. What needs to be insisted upon, however, is how much *fun* this movie is. Skolimowski, a Pole who has lived and worked in England for several years, began writing this film on the day that Solidarity was crushed, and he filmed it, on a small budget and with a small crew, in less than two months: He had it ready for the 1982 Cannes Film Festival where it was a major success. It's successful, I think, because it tells an interesting narrative in a straightforward way. Skolimowski is a natural storyteller. You can interpret and discuss *Moonlighting* all night. During the movie, you'll be more interested in whether Irons gets away with that frozen turkey.

Moscow on the Hudson ★ ★ ★ ★
R, 115 m., 1984

Robin Williams (Vladimir Ivanoff), Maria Conchita Alonso (Lucia Lombardo), Cleavant Derricks (Witherspoon), Alejandro Rey (Orlando Ramirez). Directed and produced by Paul Mazursky. Screenplay by Mazursky and Leon Capetanos.

Mike Royko likes to make fun of foreign-born taxi drivers. He uses a lot of phonetic spellings to show how funny dey speeka da Engleesh. Maybe he's missing out on some good conversations. Have you ever *talked* to a taxi driver from Iran or Pakistan or Africa? I have, and usually I hear a fascinating story about a man who has fled from poverty or persecution, who in some cases has left behind a thriving business, and who is starting out all over again in this country. I also usually get the name of a good restaurant.

I thought of some of those experiences while I was watching Paul Mazursky's *Moscow on the Hudson*, a wonderful movie about a man who defects to the United States. His name is Vladimir Ivanoff, he plays the saxophone in a Russian circus, and when the circus visits New York, he falls in love with the United States and defects by turning himself in to a security guard at Bloomingdale's. The Russian is played by Robin Williams, who disappears so completely into his quirky, lovable, complicated character that he's quite plausible as a Russian. The movie opens with his life in Moscow, a city of overcrowded apartments, bureaucratic red tape, long lines for consumer goods, secret pleasures like jazz records, and shortages so acute that toilet paper has turned into a currency of its own. The early scenes are eerily convincing, partly because Williams plays them in Russian. This isn't one of those movies where everybody somehow speaks English. The turning point of the movie occurs in Bloomingdale's, as so many turning points do, and Ivanoff makes two friends right there on the spot: Witherspoon, the black security guard (Cleavant Derricks) and Lucia, the Italian salesclerk (Maria Conchita Alonso).

They're a tip-off to an interesting casting decision by Mazursky, who populates his movie almost entirely with ethnic and racial minorities. In addition to the black and the Italian, there's a Korean taxi driver, a Cuban lawyer, a Chinese anchorwoman, all of them reminders that all of us, except for American Indians, came from somewhere else. Ivanoff moves in with the security guard's family, which greatly resembles the one he left behind in Moscow, right down to the pious grandfather. He gets a job selling hot dogs from a pushcart, he works his way up to driving a limousine, and he falls in love with the salesclerk from Italy. That doesn't go so well. She dreams of marrying a "real American," and Ivanoff, even after he trims his beard, will not quite do.

Moscow on the Hudson is the kind of movie that Paul Mazursky does especially well. It's a comedy that finds most of its laughs in the close observations of human behavior, and that finds its story in a contemporary subject Mazursky has some thoughts about. In that, it's like his earlier films *An Unmarried Woman* (women's liberation), *Harry and Tonto* (growing old), *Blume in Love* (marriage in the age of doing your own thing), and *Bob & Carol and Ted & Alice* (encounter groups). It is also a rarity, a patriotic film that has a liberal, rather than a conservative, heart. It made me feel good to be an American, and good that Vladimir Ivanoff was going to be one, too.

Motel Hell ★ ★ ★
R, 106 m., 1980

Rory Calhoun (Farmer Vincent), Paul Linke (Bruce Smith), Nancy Parsons (Ida Smith), Nina Axelrod (Terry), Wolfman Jack (Reverend Billy), Elaine Joyce (Edith Olson). Directed by Kevin Connor and produced by Steven-Charles Jaffe and Robert Jaffe. Screenplay by Jaffe and Jaffe.

Motel Hell satirizes a whole sub-basement genre of American movies that a lot of lucky people may never even have seen. I call them Sleazoid Movies; films that deliberately test our sensibilities, and our stomachs, by the subhuman and nauseating behavior of the characters on the screen. The genre includes *The Texas Chainsaw Massacre, The Hills Have Eyes, The Honeymoon Killers, Night of the Living Dead,* and *Last House on the Left.*

These films are not to be confused with those of a neighboring genre, the Women in Danger films, which spew hatred of women. Sleazoid movies seem to exist on the edge of self-parody, and their ambition is to be to the cinema what the geek show is to the circus. They're not antiwoman, they're antitaste, and their characters sink into moronic, bestial savagery. They touch on the ultimate horror of people degraded into subhuman, animalistic behavior. Some of these films, I should add, are not without merit—although this isn't the place to launch into a defense of them.

What *Motel Hell* brings to this genre is the refreshing sound of laughter. This movie *is* disgusting, of course; it's impossible to satirize this material, I imagine, without presenting the subject matter you're satirizing. But *Motel Hell* is not nearly as gruesome as the films it satirizes, and it finds the right stylistic note for its central characters, who are simple, cheerful, smiling, earnest, and resourceful cannibals.

Motel Hell (the second "e" on the neon sign has gone out) is a ramshackle place that seems to be located in the same redneck backwoods where Russ Meyer's characters all live. It is operated by friendly Farmer Vincent (Rory Calhoun) and his sister (Nancy Parsons). The district is patrolled, none too adroitly, by a relative (Paul Linke), who is the sheriff, but sees nothing wrong with burying the victims of a motorcycle crash without benefit of investigation or autopsy.

That's just as well, because Farmer Vincent's specialty is burying people. He just doesn't wait until they're dead. He waylays unsuspecting travelers, knocks them unconscious, buries them up to their necks in his secret garden, fattens them up with cattle feed, and then slaughters them, smokes them in his smokehouse, and sells them as sausage at his roadside stand. His cheerful motto: "It takes all kinds of critters . . . to make Farmer Vincent's fritters."

All right now, of *course* this is disgusting. But hold on just a dagbone minute, as Farmer Vincent might say. It isn't simply the subject matter of Sleazoid Movies that makes them reprehensible, it's their low opinion of human nature, their acquiesence in the proposition that the world is essentially an evil place. *Motel Hell,* with Rory Calhoun looking like a Norman Rockwell model in his bib overalls, pushes this material so far in such unlikely directions that, incredibly, it works as satire. A lot of horror movies used to work that way. We went to be scared, sure, but we also went to laugh, enjoying the delicious self-indulgence with which Vincent Price or Christopher Lee hammed it up. But horror movies stopped being funny. And now they're mostly just depressing, disgusting exercises in depravity.

Motel Hell is a welcome change-of-pace; it's to *Chainsaw Massacre* as *Airplane!* is to *Airport*. It has some great moments, including a duel fought with chainsaws, a hero swinging to the rescue on a meathook, and Farmer Vincent's dying confession of the shameful secret that he concealed for years. These moments illuminate the movie's basic and not very profound insight, which is that most of the sleazoids would be a lot more fun if they didn't take themselves with such gruesome solemnity.

Mother's Day   no stars
R, 98 m., 1980

With Nancy Hendrickson, Deborah Luce, Tiana Pierce, Holden McQuire, Billy Ray McQuade, and Rose Ross.

Mother's Day is a reprehensible specimen of the geek film, so-called because such films are about the activities of that subcategory of humans formerly found in the carnival sideshows, biting the heads off chickens. Like the geeks of old, a film such as this will stoop to anything in its attempt to disgust its audiences. And the audiences for geek films are not easily disgusted. After the first five minutes of *Mother's Day*—after the shot of blood spurting from the severed neck of the movie's first victim—I was ready to walk out. But no, that would have been too easy. I determined to stick this one out.

The plot: A demented old woman lives in a shack in the woods with her two cretinous sons. Their entertainment is to capture unwary campers and torture, rape, and kill them for the delight of their mother. In between, they behave like pigs. A typical dinner scene involves one of the sons shooting a can of pressurized cheese whip down his throat.

Near the beginning of the film (but after the first beheading), three young women, former college classmates, go camping in the woods. They are imprisoned inside their sleeping bags and dragged back to the shack, where they are assaulted, raped, cut up, beaten, and forced to watch unspeakable acts. The mother cackles with glee. The actresses scream relentlessly.

Later in the film, after one of the girls is dead, the two survivors come back for revenge. (This sort of "eye for an eye" conclusion is apparently a ghastly attempt at fairness on the part of the geeks who make these movies.) The girls get their revenge. In one sequence, one of the sons is stabbed with a hatchet. His brother has a can of Drano poured down his throat, and is hit over the head with a television set. Viewers can look in through the TV screen as the victim is electrocuted. The question of why anybody of any age would possibly want to see this film remains without an answer.

Mr. Mom ★ ★
PG, 92 m., 1983

Michael Keaton (Jack), Teri Garr (Caroline), Frederick Koehler (Alex), Taliesin Jaffe (Kenny), Martin Mull (Ron). Directed by Stan Dragoti and produced by Lynn Loring and Lauren Shuler. Screenplay by John Hughes.

People have been living through the basic idea of *Mr. Mom* for years. It's too bad this movie doesn't feel more like their lives and less like the pilot for a TV sitcom. The movie's about a well-paid Ford executive who gets laid off and can't find work. Then his wife finds a job at an advertising agency, and her years of experience in "the front lines of consumerism" make her a big hit with the clients. Meanwhile, her husband stays home to keep house and raise the children. There are so many genuine comedy ideas (and not a few provocative ones) rising out of this situation that it's hard to see how the filmmakers could go wrong. But go wrong they do, with gimmicky sight gags and awkward fantasy sequences, stock characters, and unbelievable situations. What a lost opportunity.

That's especially true because the cast is so promising. Michael Keaton, a kinetic young actor who gives the uncanny impression of being able to think faster than he can talk, plays the husband. Teri Garr, Dustin Hoffman's other girlfriend in *Tootsie*, is the wife. And Martin Mull is the snaky president of the advertising agency, with plans for promoting Garr into his own life. Now if they'd taken these characters and their situation and followed through on the implications, on a believable level, they might have come up with a true human comedy. Instead, everything is pushed too far, situations are overwritten and overdirected, and the movie is desperate enough to throw in vacuum cleaners with minds of their own, seductive next-door neighbors, and a team of local repairmen who show up on cue and seem straight out of TV commercials.

God knows there's enough in ordinary housework to make a comedy out of, especially if the hotshot husband is trying to learn how to run the house. Do we really need the scene in which he cheerfully puts four cups of detergent into the washer? Enough real things can go wrong around the house without the movie needing a monosyllabic female TV repairman and an exterminator who's afraid of bugs.

Meanwhile, at the ad agency, Teri Garr also is having her problems with a script that strives for the predictable. She's brought into a conference on a tuna account. The agency's failed campaign presentations line the walls. She shoots them down and comes up with a bright idea: Offer a big discount for the duration of the recession. Brilliant, eh? Except, wait a minute, the other campaigns on the bulletin board don't even look like professional presentations; they look like scrawls out of *Mad* magazine. And her bright idea is obviously only in the movie because if she *has* a bright idea, you see, she'll get the job and attract the boss. No attempt is made to be perceptive or original about the idea of a housewife returning to the job wars as an ad executive.

Mr. Mom gives itself away with its title, I think. The title was so obviously a Concept, a brief encapsulation of what the movie would be "about," that all the script needed to deliver was manufactured, artificial situations inspired, not by the experiences of joblessness or role-reversal, but by memories of old TV shows. They had a great idea here. It's too bad they didn't follow it through on a human level, instead of making it feel made-up and artificial and twice-removed from the everyday experience it pretends to be about.

The Muppet Movie ★ ★ ★ ½
G, 94 m., 1979

Jim Henson (Kermit, Rowlf, Dr. Teeth, and Waldorf), Frank Oz (Miss Piggy, Fozzie Bear, Animal, and Sam), Jerry Nelson (Floyd Pepper, Crazy Harry, Robin the Frog, and Lew Zealand), Richard Hunt (Scooter, Statler, Janice, Sweetums, and Beaker), Dave Goelz (The Great Gonza, Zoot, and Dr. Bunsen Honeydew). Directed by James Frawley and produced by Jim Henson. Screenplay by Jerry Juhl and Jack Burns.

Jolson sang, Barrymore spoke, Garbo laughed, and now Kermit the Frog rides a bicycle. *The Muppet Movie* not only stars the Muppets but, for the first time, shows us their feet. And if you can figure out how they were able to show Kermit pedaling across the screen, then you are less a romantic than I am: I prefer to believe he did it himself.

He's pedaling on his way to Hollywood, and *The Muppet Movie* itself is one of those origin stories so beloved by comic books. We've learned how Spiderman came into his extraordinary powers, and now here are the earliest days of the Muppets.

Kermit, we learn, was born in a swamp. Well, maybe we coulda guessed it. And he was born with an ability somewhat unusual to frogs: a talent for playing the guitar. We encounter him sitting on a log and singing one of the movie's several Paul Williams songs, and for just a second we wonder where Jim Henson is. That's because Kermit is quite clearly surrounded by water, and we can't for the life of us figure out where they hid the Muppeteer.

It turns out Henson was sitting in a watertight compartment and communicating with the rest of the crew via walkie-talkie, and that Kermit's hands on the banjo were animated by remote control, and that all sorts of technology went into making the Muppets move, but after that first second we quit wondering: This is magic, after all, so who *wants* to know where Henson is?

Dom DeLuise, on the other hand, wants to know where Kermit is. DeLuise comes rowing through the swamp in a rowboat and hears Kermit's song and reveals himself to be a big Hollywood agent with a copy of *Variety* in his boat. And, wouldn't you know, *Variety* has an ad for singing frogs in it. So of course

Kermit leaves his swamp behind and commences a cross-country odyssey to Hollywood to make his audition.

He makes his trip mostly in a late-1940s Studebaker, one of those models that looked like it was going in both directions simultaneously, and the trip would have been a happy one except for one thing: Kermit is pursued by an evil fast-food magnate (Charles Durning) who wants him to sign on as the trademark of a chain of French-fried frogs' legs restaurants. It is one of the movie's more poignant ironies that no sooner does Kermit obtain legs than humans find an unsavory use for them.

Durning and DeLuise are two of the several humans in the film. The format makes absolutely no distinction between the Muppets and other forms of life, so we meet such humans as Mel Brooks, Bob Hope, Carol Kane, Steve Martin, Richard Pryor, Telly Savalas, Orson Welles, and, in their last film appearance before their deaths, Edgar Bergen and Charlie McCarthy.

We also meet, of course, Miss Piggy, who falls instantly and incurably in love with Kermit. And we get to know all the Muppets better than we could on their television show. They turn out, somehow, to have many of the same emotions and motivations that we do. They are vain and hopeful, selfish and generous, complicated and true. They mirror ourselves, except that they're a little nicer.

The Muppets Take Manhattan ★ ★ ★
G, 94 m., 1984

With guest stars Dabney Coleman, Joan Rivers, Liza Minelli, and John Landis. Directed by Frank Oz and produced by David Lazer. Written by Oz and Jim Henson.

Dear Kermit,

I hope you will take this in the right spirit. I know you've been tortured for some years now by an identity crisis, ever since you were discovered sitting on that log down in the swamp, strumming on your ukulele. Stardom happened almost overnight, and here you are in your third starring vehicle, *The Muppets Take Manhattan.* Yet you still don't know who you really are.

You are obviously not a frog. You have none of the attributes of a frog, except for your appearance and your name. In your first film, *The Muppet Movie,* you were sort of a greenish overgrown pop singer, an amphibian Frankie Avalon. In your second movie, *The Great Muppet Caper,* you were cast adrift in a plot that really belonged to the human guest stars. You basically had a supporting role, making the humans look good. Only in *The Muppets Take Manhattan,* your third film, do you really seem to come into your own. You take charge. You are the central figure in the plot, you do not allow yourself to get shouldered aside by Miss Piggy, and you seem thoroughly at home with the requirements of genre, stereotype, and cliché. In the 1940s, you would have been under contract to MGM.

The plot of your movie has been seen before. I doubt if that will come as news to you. *The Muppets Take Manhattan* is yet another retread of the reliable old formula in which somebody says "Hey, gang! Our senior class musical show is so good, I'll bet we could be stars on Broadway!" The fact that this plot is not original does not deter you, Kermit, nor should it. It's still a good plot.

I liked the scenes in which you persevered. I liked the way you went to New York and challenged the stubborn agents like Dabney Coleman, and upstaged Liza Minnelli in Sardi's. I especially liked the scenes where you supported yourself by waiting tables in a greasy spoon cafe with rats in the kitchen and a Greek owner who specialized in philosophical statements that didn't make any sense. I even liked Miss Piggy's scenes, especially her childhood memories. I gasped at the wedding scene, in which you finally married her. I refrained from speculating about your wedding night—and speculation is all your G-rated movie left me with.

In short, I liked just about everything about your movie. But what I liked best was your discovery of self. Kermit, you are no longer a frog with an identity crisis. You've found the right persona, old boy, and it will see you through a dozen more movies. It was clear to me from the moment you took your curtain call and basked in the spotlight. Kermit, this may come as a shock, but you're Mickey Rooney in a frog suit. Think about it. You're short. You're cute. You never say die. You keep smilin'. You have a philosophy for everything. You appear only in wholesome, G-rated movies. And sex bombs like Liza Minnelli only kiss you on the cheek.

One word of advice. Dump Miss Piggy. Stage a talent search for a Liza Minnelli Muppet. Mickey Rooney made a lot of movies with Liza's mother before you were hatched, Kermit, and now it's your turn. Move fast, kid, before you croak.

Murder on the Orient Express ★ ★ ★
PG, 128 m., 1974

Albert Finney (Hercule Poirot), Lauren Bacall (Mrs. Hubbard), Martin Balsam (Blanchi), Ingrid Bergman (Greta Ohlsson), Jacqueline Bisset (Countess Andrenyi), Jean-Pierre Cassel (Pierre Paul Michel), Sean Connery (Colonel Arbuthnot), John Gielgud (Beddoes), Wendy Hiller (Princess Dragomiroff), Anthony Perkins (Hector McQueen), Vanessa Redgrave (Mary Debenham), Richard Widmark (Ratchett), Rachel Roberts (Hildegarde Schmitt), Michael York (Count Andrenyi). Directed by Sidney Lumet and produced by John Brabourne and Richard Goodwin. Screenplay by Paul Deim.

There is a cry of alarm, some muffled French, a coming and a going in the corridor. Hercule Poirot, adjusting the devices that keep his hair slicked down and his mustache curled up, pauses for a moment in his train compartment. He lifts an eyebrow. He looks out into the hallway. He shrugs. The next morning, it's revealed that Ratchett, the hateful American millionaire, has been stabbed to death in his sleep. This is quite obviously a case for Poirot, the most famous detective in the world, and, over breakfast, he agrees to accept it. The list of suspects is long, but limited: It includes everybody on board the crack Orient Express, en route from Istanbul to Calais, and currently brought to a standstill by an avalanche of snow that has fallen across the track. Poirot arranges to begin a series of interviews and plunges himself (and the rest of us) into a net of intrigue so deep, so deceptive, and so labyrinthine that only Agatha Christie would have woven it. *Murder on the Orient Express* is a splendidly entertaining movie of the sort that isn't made any more: It's a classical whodunit, with all the clues planted and all of them visible, and it's peopled with a large and expensive collection of stars. Albert Finney, who plays Poirot, is the most impressive, largely because we can never for a moment be sure that he *is* Finney. His hair is slicked down to a patent-leather shine, his eyes have somehow become beady and suspicious, his French mustache is constantly quivering with alarm (real and pretended), and he scurries up and down the train like a paranoid crab. The performance is brilliant, and it's high comedy.

So is the movie, although it's careful never to make its essentially comic intentions get in the way of Miss Christie's well-oiled mystery. This isn't a "thriller," because we're not thrilled, or scared—only amused. The murder itself has a certain antiseptic, ritualistic quality, and the investigation is an exercise in sophisticated cross-examination and sputters of indignation. What I liked best about this movie is its style, both the deliberately old-fashioned visual strategies used by director Sidney Lumet, and the cheerful overacting of the dozen or more suspects.

They form a suitably bizarre menagerie and at first glance have nothing in common with one another. Bear with me please, and I'll work my way through the all-stars: Lauren Bacall is a particularly obnoxious American, Ingrid Bergman is an African missionary, Michael York and Jacqueline Bisset are Hungarian royalty, Jean-Pierre Cassel is the conductor, Sean Connery is an English officer returning from India, Vanessa Redgrave is his constant companion, John Gielgud is a veddy, veddy proper manservant to millionaire Richard Widmark, Wendy Hiller is an aloof Russian aristocrat, Anthony Perkins is Widmark's secretary, Rachel Roberts is a neo-Nazi ladies' maid, Martin Balsam is a director of the railroad line, and there are, believe it or not, others also under suspicion.

There are obviously big technical problems here: More than a dozen characters have to be introduced and kept alive, a very complicated plot has to be unraveled, and everything must take place within the claustrophobic confines of the railway car. Lumet overcomes his difficulties in great style, and we're never for a moment confused (except when we're supposed to be, which is most of the time).

There is hardly anything more I can tell you, or even hint, about the plot, except that nothing is as it seems (and you knew that already about a movie based on an Agatha Christie book). The movie provides a good time, high style, a loving salute to an earlier period of filmmaking, and an unexpected bonus: It ends with a very long scene in which Poirot asks everyone to be silent, please, while he explains his various theories of the case. He does so in great detail, and it's fun of a rather malicious sort watching a dozen high-priced stars keep their mouths shut and just listen while Finney masterfully dominates the scene.

Murphy's Romance ★ ★ ★
PG-13, 107 m., 1985

Sally Field (Emma Moriarty), James Garner (Murphy Jones), Brian Kerwin (Bobby Jack), Corey Haim (Jake), Dennis Burkley (Freeman Coverly), Georgann Johnson (Margaret). Directed by Martin Ritt and produced by Laura Ziskin. Screenplay by Harriet Frank, Jr., and Irving Ravetch.

From the moment Sally Field pilots her battered old pickup into town and parks her kid out at the farm and walks into James Garner's drugstore and they lay eyes on each other for the first time, it's pretty clear that they are going to have to fall in love with each other and get married. All you have to do is look at them to see that.

Murphy's Romance takes almost two hours to arrive at the conclusion that takes us two minutes, but that doesn't mean this is a predictable movie. The whole point of this movie is how it looks at those characters, and listens to them, and allows them to live in a specific time and place. If they knew what we know, it would spoil all the fun, as they flirt and pout and spar and circle each other, and survive the sudden and unexpected appearance of Sally Field's no-good ex-husband.

His name is Bobby Jack, and Field describes him in a sentence: "How come you were never as good on your feet as you were between the sheets?" He's an immature, sweet-talking con man without a responsible bone in his body. He turns up one day, and moves in, and Field lets him stay because it means a lot to their son, Jake.

At first it appears that Bobby Jack's arrival is going to cause problems for the budding relationship between Emma and Murphy (Field and Garner). But Emma keeps on inviting Murphy to stay to dinner, and Murphy reads the situation correctly: Emma may be stuck with Bobby Jack, but she is stuck on Murphy.

Murphy is quite a guy. He figures he has a lot of knowledge about human nature, and he's not shy about sharing it. He doesn't take himself too seriously, but he likes to pretend that he does. He speaks thoughtfully, moves deliberately, and lets you know what a character he is by parking his mint-condition 1928 Studebaker out in front of his drugstore. Garner plays this character in more or less his usual acting style, but he has been given such quietly offbeat dialogue by the screenwriters, Harriet Frank, Jr., and Irving Ravetch, that he comes across as a true original.

Sally Field is also not particularly original in her approach to the character Emma, who is a close relative of other Field heroines: plucky, quietly sensible in the face of calamity. Originality is not called for in this performance, anyway; it would have been a mistake to turn Emma into a colorful character, instead of letting her proceed at her own speed. In the movie's key series of scenes—where Bobby Jack makes his move and Emma sneezes at him and then a surprise visitor turns up from Tulsa—the movie is saved from melodrama only by Field's matter-of-fact ability to take things as they come.

Then comes the ending, which is one of the most carefully and lovingly written passages in any recent movie. Much depends on exactly what Emma and Murphy say to each other, and how they say it, and what they don't say. The movie gets it all right.

Murphy's Romance was directed by Martin Ritt, who also directed Field's Oscar-winning performance in *Norma Rae* (and worked with her again in the less-than-successful *Back Roads*). Ritt specializes in movies about the rural South and Southwest (his credits also include *Sounder, Hud,* and *Conrack*), and one of the strengths of *Murphy's Romance* is the freedom he feels to simply pause, occasionally, and soak in the local color. Two examples: Listen carefully to the man who calls the bingo numbers, and the old man Murphy gives a lift to one day. They have particular voices and deliberate word choices, and they seem completely authentic. So, to a surprising degree, does the whole movie.

The Music Lovers ★ ★
R, 122 m., 1971

Richard Chamberlain (Tchaikovsky), Glenda Jackson (Nina Milukova), Max Adrian (Nicholas Rubenstein), Christopher Gable (Count Chiluvsky), Isabella Teleznska (Madame Von Meck). Directed and produced by Ken Russell. Screenplay by Melvyn Bragg.

Ken Russell's *The Music Lovers* is an involved and garish private fantasy which Russell, alas, presents to us as the life of Tchaikovsky. Poor Tchaikovsky. I know it is against the rules to complain that this or that detail may not be precisely accurate, or that Tchaikovsky may not have been dealt with in the fairest possible manner. I know, because I get letters from graduate students, that I must resolutely examine the film itself—or the "film itself" as they put it—and put aside considerations from real life. What difference does it matter whether Tchaikovsky actually existed as Russell portrays him—as long as Russell has made a good film?

Well, I suppose there's something to be said for that point of view, had Russell made a good film and not said it was about Tchaikovsky. But *The Music Lovers* is libelous not only to the composer but to his music. I am no composer, Lord knows, but I have a notion that even the greatest of composers must have spent most of their time hard at work composing. I doubt whether their great works came to them, full-blown, in moments of sexual, religious, political, or sporting ecstasy. I doubt whether any great work in any field of art "comes" to anybody. Great novels are not produced by automatic writing, so why should great symphonies be?

Russell apparently thinks they are. And so although his film is more visually daring and more sexually explicit than other biographies of composers, it rests on the same fallacious assumption: That a sunset, or a woman (or a man, in Tchaikovsky's case), or

a famous naval victory, or something could inspire the composer to sit down and dash off a few inspired moments.

Lest you accuse me of exaggerating, let me just mention that Tchaikovsky's mental image, when the cannons roar in the "1812 Overture," is supposed to be a friend's head being blown off. Better we should have a movie in which Russell's image, during the same passage, is of his own head being blown off. We would save the head for last, of course, in order to deal with lesser extremities of the minor works.

The Music Lovers is totally irresponsible, then, as a film about, or inspired by, or parallel to, or bearing a vague resemblance to, Tchaikovsky, his life and times. It is not, however, a complete failure. Ken Russell is a most deviously baroque director, sucking us down with him into his ornate fantasies of decadent interior decoration, until every fringe on every curtain has a fringe of its own, and the characters have fringes, too, and the characters elbow their way through a grotesque jungle of candlesticks, potted plant stands, incense sticks, old champagne bottles, and gilt edges, and it is almost certain that something is happening in the movie. But what?

My Beautiful Laundrette ★ ★ ★
R, 93 m., 1986 ✓

Daniel Day Lewis (Johnny), Saeed Jaffrey (Nasser), Roshan Seth (Papa), Gordon Warnecke (Omar), Shirley Ann Field (Rachel), Rita Wolf (Tania). Directed by Stephen Frears and produced by Sarah Radclyffe and Tim Bevan. Screenplay by Hanif Kureishi.

When people told me they'd seen *My Beautiful Laundrette* and it was a good movie, I had a tendency to believe them, for who would dare to make a bad movie with such an uncommercial title? The launderette in question is a storefront operation in one of the seedier areas of London, and it is losing money when a rich Pakistani decides to entrust its management to his nephew. But this is not the saga of a launderette. It is the story of two kinds of outsiders in modern London.

The film opens with some uneventful days in the life of its hero, Omar, who is a young man in need of a job. His father is an alcoholic journalist, once important and successful, now never far from the gin bottle. His uncle Nasser is one of the more successful members of the Pakistani community in London, a businessman who owns a chain of parking garages and storefront retail shops. He enjoys success in British terms: He has a big house in the country, an expensive car, and a British mistress.

Because a man cannot stand by and see a member of his family fail for lack of opportunity, he gives Omar a job in a parking garage, and later turns the launderette over to him. He also suggests that Omar should get married, perhaps even to his own daughter.

There is some doubt, however, about whether Omar will ever get married. Earlier in the film, we have witnessed a strange scene. Omar and friends have been stopped by a gang of punk neofascist Paki bashers, when Omar walks up fearlessly to their leader, Johnny, and greet him with affection. We discover that the two young men had been lovers, and before long Johnny abandons his gang to join with Omar in the operation of the launderette.

My Beautiful Laundrette refuses to commit its plot to any particular agenda, and I found that interesting. It's not about whether Johnny and Omar will remain lovers, and it's not about whether the launderette will be a success, and it's not about the drunken father or even about Nasser's daughter, who is so bored and desperate that during a cocktail party she goes outside and bares her breasts to Omar through the French doors: Anything to get away from the small talk.

The movie is not concerned with plot, but with giving us a feeling for the society its characters inhabit. Modern Britain is a study in contrasts, between rich and poor, between upper and lower classes, between native British and the various immigrant groups—some of which, like the Pakistanis, have started to prosper. To this mixture, the movie adds the conflict between straight and gay.

Their relationship encompasses some subtleties which the movie handles with great delicacy. Although Omar is a member of a non-white immigrant group and Johnny is Anglo-Saxon, the realities of their lives are

that Omar will probably turn out to be more successful and prosperous than Johnny. He has the advantage of his uncle's capital, his family connections, and his own gift at business. Johnny is a true outsider with small prospects of success.

There is another outsider in the movie who shares his dilemma. She is Rachel, Nasser's British mistress. Nasser remains married to his Pakistani wife, and although the two women are more or less known to one another, he keeps them in separate compartments of his life. There is a moment, though, during the opening ceremonies at the launderette, when the two women are accidentally in the same room at the same time, and it results in an extraordinary speech by Rachel, who with pride and dignity defends her position as Nasser's mistress by describing herself as a woman who has never had a break in life, who has always had to ask for what she wanted, and who deserves some small measure of happiness, just like everybody else.

A movie like this lives or dies with its performances, and the actors in *My Beautiful Laundrette* are a fascinating group of unknowns, with one exception—Shirley Anne Field, who plays Rachel, and who may be familiar from *Saturday Night and Sunday Morning* and other British films.

The character of Johnny may cause you to blink, if you've seen the wonderful *A Room with a View;* he is played by Daniel Day Lewis, the same actor who in that film plays the heroine's affected fiancé Cecil. Seeing these two performances side by side is an affirmation of the miracle of acting: That one man could play these two opposites is astonishing.

Omar is played by Gordon Warnecke, an actor unknown to me, as a bright but passive youth who hasn't yet figured out the strategy by which he will approach the world. He is a blank slate, pleasant, agreeable, not readily showing the sorrows and angers that we figure ought to be inside there somewhere. The most expansive character in the movie is Nasser (Saeed Jaffrey), an engaging hedonist who doesn't see why everyone shouldn't enjoy life with the cynical good cheer he possesses.

The viewer is likely to go through a curious process while watching this film. At first there is unfamiliarity: Who are these people, and where do they come from, and what sort of society do they occupy in England? We get oriented fairly quickly, and understand the values that are at work. Then we begin to wonder what the movie is about. It is with some relief that we realize it isn't "about" anything; it's simply some weeks spent with some characters in a way that tells us more about some aspects of modern Britain than we've seen before.

I mentioned *A Room with a View* because of the link with Daniel Day Lewis. There is another link between the two films. They are both about the possibility of opening up views—of being able to see through a window out of your own life and into other possibilities. Both films argue that you have a choice. You can accept your class, social position, race, sexuality, or prejudices as absolutes, and live entirely inside them. Or you can look out the window, or maybe even walk out the door.

My Bodyguard ★ ★ ★ ½
PG, 97 m., 1980

Chris Makepeace (Clifford), Adam Baldwin (Linderman), Matt Dillon (Moody), Ruth Gordon (Gramma), Martin Mull (Mr. Peache), John Houseman (Dobbs), Paul Quandt (Carson), Craig Richard Nelson (Griffith). Directed by Tony Bill and produced by Don Devlin. Screenplay by Alan Ormsby.

There is a terrifying moment in adolescence when suddenly some of the kids are twice as big as the rest of the kids. It is terrifying for everybody: For the kids who are suddenly tall and gangling, and for the kids who are still small and are getting beat up all the time. *My Bodyguard* places that moment in a Chicago high school and gives us a kid who tries to think his way out of it.

The kid's name is Clifford. He has everything going against him. He's smart, he's new in the school, he's slightly built. As he's played by Chris Makepeace, he is also one of the most engaging teen-age characters I've seen in the movies in a long time. Too many movie teen-agers have been sex-crazed (*Little Darlings*), animalistic food-fighters (*Meat Balls*), or hopelessly romanticized (*The Blue Lagoon*). Clifford is basically just your normal, average kid.

He has just moved to Chicago with his family. His father (Martin Mull) is the new resident manager of the Ambassador East Hotel. His grandmother (Ruth Gordon) hangs out in the lobby and picks up old men in the bar. Life is great, backstage at a hotel (he gets his meals in the kitchen or sometimes in the Pump Room). But it's not so great at school. The movie sends Clifford to Lake View High School, where he's immediately shaken down for his lunch money.

The extortionist (Matt Dillon) is the kind of kid we all remember from high school. He's handsome in an oily way, he's going through a severe case of adolescent sadism, he's basically a coward. His threat is that unless Clifford pays protection money, he'll sic the dreaded Linderman on him.

Linderman (Adam Baldwin) is a school legend, a big, hulking kid who allegedly killed his brother, raped a teacher, hit a cop, you name it. The movie's inspiration is to have Clifford *think* his way out of his dilemma—neutralizing Linderman by hiring him as a bodyguard. This is genius, and there's a wonderful scene where Clifford springs Linderman on the rest of the kids.

Then the movie takes an interesting turn. Clifford and Linderman become friends, and we learn some of the unhappy facts of Linderman's life. It turns out Linderman isn't the Incredible Hulk after all—he's just another kid going through growing pains and some personal tragedy. This whole middle stretch is the best part of the movie, developing a friendship in a perceptive and gentle way that's almost shocking in comparison with the idiotic, violent teen-agers so many movies have given us.

The ending is predictable (it's a showdown between Linderman and another tough kid). And there are some distractions along the way from Clifford's family. Martin Mull makes an interesting hotel manager, whimsical and charming. But the movie gets off track when it follows Ruth Gordon through some of her adventures, including a romantic collision with a hotel executive played by John Houseman. These scenes just don't seem part of the same movie: The hotel stuff is sitcom, while the stuff in the high school is fresh and inventive.

That seems to apply to the performances, too. One of the strengths of *My Bodyguard* is in the casting of the younger performers—Chris Makepeace, Adam Baldwin, Matt Dillon. They look right for their parts, but, more to the point, they *feel* right. Dillon exudes creepiness, Makepeace is plausible while thinking on his feet, Linderman is convincingly vulnerable and confused, and there's another kid, the solemn-faced, wide-eyed Paul Quandt, who steals a couple of scenes with his absolute certainty that the worst is yet to come.

My Bodyguard is a small treasure, a movie about believable characters in an unusual situation. It doesn't pretend to be absolutely realistic, and the dynamics of its big city high school are simplified for the purposes of the story. But this movie is fun to watch because it touches memories that are shared by most of us, and because its young characters are recognizable individuals, and not simplified cartoon figures like so many movie teen-agers.

My Brilliant Career ★ ★ ★ ½
NO MPAA RATING, 101 m., 1980

Judy Davis (Sybylia Melvyn), Sam Neill (Harry Beecham), Wendy Hughes (Aunt Helen), Robert Grubb (Frank Hawden), Max Cullen (Mr. McSwat), Pat Kennedy (Aunt Gussie). Directed by Gillian Armstrong and produced by Margaret Fink. Screenplay by Eleanor Witcombe.

What magic is it that sometimes allows young girls in backward districts to guess that they need not play along with the general ideas about a "woman's role"? I ask because three of my favorite writers—and now a fourth—discovered, more or less by themselves, that the possibilities in their lives were unlimited.

Two of the writers are famous: Willa Cather, who wrote of independent young women in Nebraska and points west, and Doris Lessing, whose *Children of Violence* series chronicles the liberation of a young woman from Rhodesia. The other two writers are not so well known, but the parallels in their lives are so astonishing that I'd like to sketch them, briefly, before moving on to an extraordinary film, *My Brilliant Career.* Their names are Olive Schreiner and Miles Franklin. They both led isolated childhoods in the nineteenth century, in the backwaters

of the British Empire. And they both wrote novels about those lives at a very early age.

Olive Schreiner was raised on a farm in the Orange Free State, in South Africa. She learned Afrikaans along with English, read the Bible daily, and in her mid-teens wrote a classic novel, *The Story of an African Farm*. It was about the awakening of the spirit of a teen-age girl (herself, obviously) who did not see why her life had to be so limited just because she was a woman. Schreiner's later life was spent in intellectual and feminist circles in London (and for a time she filled the challenging position of being Havelock Ellis's mistress).

The other writer is someone I've just learned about recently: Miles Franklin, born in 1879 in rural Australia and raised on an isolated country station in the outback. At the age of sixteen she wrote a novel about her experiences, *My Brilliant Career.* It was published six years later in Edinburgh. Like Schreiner, Franklin became a feminist, traveled abroad in her twenties (and came to Chicago, where she and Alice Henry organized the Women's Trade Union League).

The Story of an African Farm is an established literary classic. *My Brilliant Career,* on the other hand, was relatively forgotten until a group of Australian women filmmakers made it into this remarkable film. It tells the story of a restless, high-spirited young woman whose temperament just isn't suited to the leftover Victorian standards of Australian country districts in the 1890s.

Franklin's novel is successful as a movie primarily because of a brilliant casting discovery. Judy Davis, who plays the film's heroine, is so fresh, unique, irreverent, and winning that she makes this material live. She's a young actress from Perth, a sometime pop and jazz singer, who was reportedly the second choice for the film's lead; if that's so, it was a completely fortunate second choice.

My Brilliant Career could have been just another feminist film. The director, Gillian Armstrong, could have gone to great lengths to explain the thinking and motivations of her character—and bored us in the meantime. But she doesn't. Instead, she makes her points through Judy Davis's presence and personality.

This isn't a movie that ends with any final answers or conclusions. Instead, it's about a young woman in a painful and continuing process of indecision. She's not considered by her family to be an ideal young woman at all—she's too independent, untamed, unreconciled to a woman's role. She doesn't automatically swoon at the attentions of every young man in the district. She's red-haired, freckled, feisty.

These qualities do appeal, however, to one young neighboring man, a farmer who's of two minds about her: He finds her independence appealing, and yet he tends to share the prevailing view about proper behavior for women. Can he overcome his narrow view and accept her? He does propose marriage. Can she overcome her headstrong independence and accept him? That's the film's key question, and *My Brilliant Career* is wise in never quite answering it.

The film is beautiful to look at. It was filmed on location in the outback, in warm natural colors, and the costumes and settings meticulously establish the period. But Judy Davis's performance establishes it even more, because she creates a complicated character so naturally that we feel the conflicts instead of having to understand them intellectually. This is the best kind of movie of ideas, in which the movie supplies the people and emotions and *we* come up with the conclusions.

My Dinner with André ★ ★ ★ ★
NO MPAA RATING, 110 m., 1981

Wallace Shawn (Wally), André Gregory (André), Jean Lenauer (Waiter), Roy Butler (Bartender). Directed by Louis Malle and produced by George W. George and Beverly Karp. Screenplay by Shawn and Gregory.

The idea is astonishing in its audacity: a film of two friends talking, just simply talking—but with passion, wit, scandal, whimsy, vision, hope, and despair—for 110 minutes. It sounds at first like one of those underground films of the 1960s, in which great length and minimal content somehow interacted in the dope-addled brains of the audience to provide the impression of deep if somehow elusive profundity. *My Dinner with André* is not like that. It doesn't use all of those words as a stunt. They are alive on the screen, breathing, pulsing, reminding us of endless, impassioned conversations we've had with those few friends worth talking with for hours and hours. Underneath all the other fascinating things in this film beats the tide of friendship, of two people with a genuine interest in one another.

The two people are André Gregory and Wallace Shawn. Those are their real names, and also their names in the movie. I suppose they are playing themselves. As the film opens, Shawn travels across New York City to meet Gregory for dinner, and his thoughts provide us with background: His friend Gregory is a New York theater director, well-known into the 1970s, who dropped out for five years and traveled around the world. Now Gregory has returned, with wondrous tales of strange experiences. Shawn has spent the same years in New York, finding uncertain success as an author and playwright. They sit down for dinner in an elegant restaurant. We do not see the other customers. The bartender is a wraith in the background, the waiter is the sort of presence they were waiting for in *Waiting for Godot*. The friends order dinner, and then, as it is served and they eat and drink, they talk.

What conversation! André Gregory does most of the talking, and he is a spellbinding conversationalist, able to weave mental images not only out of his experiences, but also out of his ideas. He explains that he had become dissatisfied with life, restless, filled with anomie and discontent. He accepted an invitation to join an experimental theater group in Poland. It was *very* experimental, tending toward rituals in the woods under the full moon.

From Poland, he traveled around the world, meeting a series of people who were seriously and creatively exploring the ways in which they could experience the material world. They (and Gregory) literally believed in mind over matter, and as Gregory describes a monk who was able to stand his entire body weight on his fingertips, we visualize that man and in some strange way (so hypnotic is the tale) we share the experience.

One of the gifts of *My Dinner with André* is that we share so many of the experiences. Although most of the movie literally consists of two men talking, here's a strange thing: *We* do not spend the movie just passively listening to them talk. At first, director Louis Malle's sedate series of images (close-ups, two-shots, reacton shots) calls attention to itself, but as Gregory continues to talk, the very simplicity of the visual style renders it invisible. And like the listeners at the feet of a master storyteller, we find ourselves visualizing what Gregory describes, until this film is as filled with visual images as a radio play—*more* filled, perhaps, than a conventional feature film.

What Gregory and Shawn talk about is, quite simply, many of the things on our minds these days. We've passed through Tom Wolfe's Me Decade and find ourselves in a decade during which there will apparently be less for everybody. The two friends talk about inner journeys—not in the mystical, vague terms of magazines you don't want to be seen reading on the bus, but in terms of trying to live better lives, of learning to listen to what others are really saying, of breaking the shackles of conventional ideas about our bodies and allowing them to more fully sense the outer world.

The movie is not ponderous, annoyingly profound, or abstract. It is about living, and Gregory seems to have lived fully in his five years of dropping out. Shawn is the character who seems more like us. He listens, he nods eagerly, he is willing to learn, but— something holds him back. Pragmatic questions keep asking themselves. He can't buy Gregory's vision, not all the way. He'd like to, but this is a real world we have to live in, after all, and if we all danced with the druids in the forests of Poland, what would happen to the market for fortune cookies?

The film's end is beautiful and inexplicably moving. Shawn returns home by taxi through the midnight streets of New York. Having spent hours with Gregory on a wild conversational flight, he is now reminded of scenes from his childhood. In *that* store, his father bought him shoes. In that one, he bought ice cream with a girl friend. The utter simplicity of his memories acts to dramatize the fragility and great preciousness of life. He has learned his friend's lesson.

My Favorite Year ★ ★ ★ ½
PG, 92 m., 1982

Peter O'Toole (Alan Swann), Mark Linn-Baker (Benjy Stone), Jessica Harper (K.C. Downing), Joseph Bologna (King Kaiser), Lainie Kazan (Belle Corroca), Lou Jacobi (Uncle Morty). Directed by Richard Benjamin and produced by Michael Gruskoff. Screenplay by Norman Steinberg and Dennis Palumbo.

"Live? I can't go on *live!!* I'm a movie star—not an actor!"

Alan Swann is imploring them: Say it isn't so! He's an alcoholic British matinee idol, veteran of countless swashbuckling epics in which he faced fleets of pirates and waves of savage barbarians. Now he is being asked to accept the worst challenge of all: to appear on live television.

My Favorite Year is the story of an era when most television was live, and the great television stars were inventing the medium out of their own imaginations every Saturday night. The year is 1950. The program is "King Kaiser's Comedy Hour," obviously inspired by the old Sid Caesar and Imogene Coca programs. The British star, Alan Swann, is played by Peter O'Toole, but he could be Errol Flynn or John Barrymore or even O'Toole himself. The movie is told from the point of view of a young production assistant named Benjy (Mark Linn-Baker). His job is to shadow the great Alan Swann, get him everything he wants except booze, keep him out of trouble, and deliver him intact to the studio in time for the broadcast. Along the way, Benjy adds a priority of his own, his continuing courtship of his would-be girlfriend, K.C. (Jessica Harper).

Through Benjy's eyes, we see Swann as the great man he was, as the pathetic drunk he is, and as the hero he could become—if he survives the live telecast. We also gain some understanding of King Kaiser (Joseph Bologna), who is a big, beefy, not-too-bright guy who has an absolutely accurate understanding of his own comic talent. Translated, that means he knows what will work. What will get a laugh. He has no taste, of course; when he offends a girl, he sends her steaks instead of flowers, and he sends a business associate a gift of tires. But he's a physical comedian with a gift for pumping the laughter out of this frail new medium, and he's backed up by a whole crew of talented writers.

Swann, meanwhile, is backed up only by memories of his greatness and fears of performing in front of a live audience. But as O'Toole plays this character, he becomes one of the great comic inventions of recent movies. Swann is a drunk, but he has an uncanny ability to pass from coma through courtliness to heroics without ever quite seeming to gain consciousness. A character like Swann could probably only be played by someone who is both a great actor and a great ham, and O'Toole is both.

My Favorite Year is not a perfect movie. I could have done without the entire romantic subplot between Benjy and K.C. But I liked the movie's ability to move from one unexpected comic situation to another. That produces one of the best scenes, when Benjy takes Swann home to Brooklyn to meet his mother and weird Uncle Morty (Lainie Kazan and Lou Jacobi in hilarious performances). There is, to be sure, a force running through the movie's disorganization, and that force is O'Toole's charisma. He is so completely charming, so doomed, so funny, and so pathetically invincible as Swann that this movie succeeds despite its occasional unnecessary scenes.

Nashville ★ ★ ★ ★
R, 159 m., 1975

Henry Gibson (Haven Hamilton), Ronee Blakely (Barbara Jean), Timothy Brown (Tommy Brown), Gwen Welles (Sueleen Gay), Michael Murphy (John Triplette), Shelley Duvall (L.A. Joan), Lily Tomlin (Linnea Reese), Ned Beatty (Delbert Reese), Scott Glenn (Pfc. Glenn Kelly), Keith Carradine (Tom Frank), Geraldine Chaplin (Opal), Karen Black (Connie White), Barbara Harris (Albuquerque). Directed and produced by Robert Altman. Screenplay by Joan Tewkesbury.

Robert Altman's *Nashville*, which was the best American movie since *Bonnie and Clyde*, creates in the relationships of nearly two dozen characters a microcosm of who we were and what we were up to in the 1970s. It's a film about the losers and the winners, the drifters and the stars in Nashville, and

the most complete expression yet of not only the genius but also the humanity of Altman, who sees people with his camera in such a way as to enlarge our own experience. Sure, it's only a movie. But after I saw it I felt more alive, I felt I understood more about people, I felt somehow wiser. It's that good a movie.

The movie doesn't have a star. It does not, indeed, even have a lead role. Instead, Altman creates a world, a community in which some people know each other and others don't, in which people are likely to meet before they understand the ways in which their lives are related. And he does it all so easily, or seems to, that watching *Nashville* is as easy as breathing and as hard to stop. Altman is the best natural filmmaker since Fellini.

One of the funny things about *Nashville* is that most of the characters never have entrances. They're just sort of there. At times, we're watching an important character and don't even know, yet, why he's important, but Altman's storytelling is so clear in his own mind, his mastery of this complex wealth of material is so complete, that we're never for a moment confused or even curious. We feel secure in his hands, and apart from anything else, *Nashville* is a vurtuoso display of narrative mastery.

It concerns several days and nights in the lives of a very mixed bag of Nashville locals and visitors, all of whom, like the city itself, are obsessed with country music. Tennessee is in the midst of a presidential primary, and all over Nashville, there are the posters and sound trucks of a quasipopulist candidate, Hal Philip Walker, who seems like a cross between George Wallace and George McGovern. We never meet Walker, but we meet both his local organizer and a John Lindsay-type PR man. They're trying to round up country-western talent for a big benefit, and their efforts provide a thread around which some of the story is loosely wound.

But there are many stories here, and in the way he sees their connections, Altman makes a subtle but shrewd comment about the ways in which we are all stuck in this thing together. There are the veteran country stars like Haven Hamilton (Henry Gibson), who wears gaudy white costumes, is self-conscious about his short stature, is painfully earnest about recording a painfully banal Bicentennial song, and who, down deep, is basically just a good old boy. There is the reigning queen of country music, Barbara Jean (Ronee Blakely), who returns in triumph to Nashville after treatment at a burn center in Atlanta for unspecified injuries incurred from a fire baton (she's met at the airport by a phalanx of girls from TIT—the Tennessee Institute of Twirling—only to collapse again). There is the corrupted, decadent rock star, played by Keith Carradine, who is so ruthless in his sexual aggression, so evil in his need to hurt women, that he telephones one woman while another is still just leaving his bed, in order to wound both of them.

But these characters are just examples of the people we meet in *Nashville*, not the leads. Everyone is more or less equal in this film, because Altman sees them all with a judicious and ultimately sympathetic eye. The film is filled with perfectly observed little moments: The starstruck young soldier keeping a silent vigil by the bedside of Barbara Jean; the campaign manager doing a double-take when he discovers he's just shaken the hand of Elliott Gould ("a fairly well-known actor," Haven Hamilton explains, "and he used to be married to Barbra Streisand"); the awestruck BBC reporter describing America in breathless, hilarious hyperbole; the way a middle-aged mother of two deaf children (Lily Tomlin) shyly waits for an assignation with a rock singer; the birdbrained cheerfulness with which a young groupie (Shelley Duvall) comes to town to visit her dying aunt and never does see her, being distracted by every male over the age of sixteen that she mets.

The film circles around three motifs without, thankfully, ever feeling it has to make a definitive statement about any of them. Since they're all still very open subjects, that's just as well. What Altman does is suggest the ways in which we deal with them—really, in unrehearsed everyday life, not thematically, as in the movies. The motifs are success, women, and politics.

Success: It can be studied most fruitfully in the carefully observed pecking order of the country-and-western performers. There are ones at the top, so successful they can afford to be generous, expansive, well-liked.

There are the younger ones in the middle, jockeying for position. There are what can only be described as the professional musicians at the bottom, playing thanklessly but well in the bars and clubs where the stars come to unwind after the show. And at the very bottom, there are those who aspire to be musicians but have no talent at all, like a waitress (Gwen Welles) who comes to sing at a smoker, is forced to strip, and, in one of the film's moments of heartbreaking truthfulness, disdainfully flings at the roomful of men the sweat socks she had stuffed into her brassiere.

Women: God, but Altman cares for them while seeing their predicament so clearly. The women in *Nashville* inhabit a world largely unaffected by the feminist revolution, as most women do. They are prized for their talent, for their beauty, for their services in bed, but not once in this movie for themselves. And yet Altman suggests their complexities in ways that movies rarely have done before. The Lily Tomlin character, in particular, forces us to consider her real human needs and impulses as she goes to meet the worthless rock singer (and we remember a luminous scene during which she and her deaf son discussed his swimming class). Part of the movie's method is to establish characters in one context and then place them in another, so that we can see how personality—indeed, basic identity itself—is constant but must sometimes be concealed for the sake of survival or even simple happiness.

Politics: I won't be giving very much away by revealing that there is an attempted assassination in *Nashville*. The assassin, a loner who takes a room in a boarding house, is clearly telegraphed by Altman. It's not Altman's style to surprise us with plot. He'd rather surprise us by revelations of character. At this late date after November 22, 1963, and all the other days of infamy, I wouldn't have thought it possible that a film could have anything new or very interesting to say on assassination, but *Nashville* does, and the film's closing minutes, with Barbara Harris finding herself, to her astonishment, on stage and singing, "It Don't Worry Me," are unforgettable and heartbreaking. *Nashville*, which seems so unstructured as it begins, reveals itself in this final sequence to have had a deep and very profound structure—but one of emotions, not ideas.

This is a film about America. It deals with our myths, our hungers, our ambitions, and our sense of self. It knows how we talk and how we behave, and it doesn't flatter us but it does love us.

National Lampoon's Animal House
★ ★ ★ ★
R, 109 m., 1978

John Belushi (Bluto), Tim Matheson (Otter), John Vernon (Dean Wormer), Verna Bloom (Mrs. Wormer), Thomas Hulce (Pinto), Cesare Danova (Mayor), Donald Sutherland (Jennings), Mary Louise Weller (Mandy), Stephen Furst (Flounder), Mark Metcalf (Neidermeier). Directed by John Landis and produced by Marry Simmons and Ivan Reitman. Screenplay by Harold Ramis, Douglas Kenney, and Chris Miller.

"What we need right now," Otter tells his fraternity brothers, "is a stupid, futile gesture on someone's part." And no fraternity on campus—on any campus—is better qualified to provide such a gesture than the Deltas. They have the title role in *National Lampoon's Animal House*, which remembers all the way back to 1962, when college was simpler, beer was cheaper, and girls were harder to seduce.

The movie is vulgar, raunchy, ribald, and occasionally scatological. It is also the funniest comedy since Mel Brooks made *The Producers. Animal House* is funny for some of the same reasons the *National Lampoon* is funny (and Second City and Saturday Night Live are funny): Because it finds some kind of precarious balance between insanity and accuracy, between cheerfully wretched excess and an ability to reproduce the most revealing nuances of human behavior.

In one sense there has never been a campus like this movie's Faber University, which was apparently founded by the lead pencil tycoon and has as its motto "Knowledge is Good." In another sense, Faber University is a microcosm of . . . I was going to say *our society*, but why get serious? Let someone else discuss the symbolism of Bluto's ability to crush a beer can against his forehead.

Bluto is, of course, the most animalistic of the Deltas. He's played by John Belushi, and

the performance is all the more remarkable because Bluto has hardly any dialogue. He isn't a talker, he's an event. His best scenes are played in silence (as when he lasciviously scales a ladder to peek at a sorority pillow fight).

Bluto and his brothers are engaged in a holding action against civilization. They are in favor of beer, women, song, motorcycles, *Playboy* centerfolds, and making rude noises. They are opposed to studying, serious thought, the Dean, the regulations governing fraternities, and, most especially, the disgusting behavior of the Omegas—a house so respectable it has even given an ROTC commander to the world.

The movie was written by *National Lampoon* contributors (including Harold Ramis, who was in Second City at the same time Belushi was), and was directed by John Landis. It's like an end run around Hollywood's traditional notions of comedy. It's anarchic, messy, and filled with energy. It assaults us. Part of the movie's impact comes from its sheer level of manic energy: When beer kegs and Hell's Angels come bursting through the windows of the Delta House, the anarchy is infectious. But the movie's better made (and better acted) than we might at first realize. It takes skill to create this sort of comic pitch, and the movie's filled with characters that are sketched a little more absorbingly than they had to be, and acted with perception.

For example: Tim Matheson, as Otter, the ladies' man, achieves a kind of grace in his obsession. John Vernon, as the Dean of Students, has a blue-eyed, rulebook hatefulness that's inspired. Verna Bloom, as his dipsomaniacal wife, has just the right balance of cynicism and desperation. Donald Sutherland, a paranoic early sixties pothead, nods solemnly at sophomoric truisms and admits he's as bored by Milton as everyone else. And stalking through everything is Bluto, almost a natural force: He lusts, he thirsts, he consumes cafeterias full of food, and he pours an entire fifth of Jack Daniels into his mouth, belches, and observes, "Thanks. I needed that."

He has, as I suggested, little dialogue. But it is telling. When the Delta House is kicked off campus and the Deltas are thrown out of school, he makes, in a moment of silence, a philosophical observation: "Seven years down the drain." What the situation requires, of course, is a stupid, futile gesture on someone's part.

The Natural ★ ★
PG, 134 m., 1984

Robert Redford (Roy Hobbs), Robert Duvall (Max Mercy), Glenn Close (Iris Gaines), Kim Basinger (Memo Paris), Wilford Brimley (Pop Fisher), Barbara Hershey (Harriet Bird), Robert Prosky (The Judge), Richard Farnsworth (Red Blow). Directed by Barry Levinson and produced by Mark Johnson. Screenplay by Roger Towne and Phil Dusenberry.

Why didn't they make a baseball picture? Why did *The Natural* have to be turned into idolatry on behalf of Robert Redford? Why did a perfectly good story, filled with interesting people, have to be made into one man's ascension to the godlike, especially when no effort is made to give that ascension meaning? And were the most important people in the god-man's life kept mostly off-screen so they wouldn't upstage him?

Let's begin at the end of *The Natural*. Redford plays Roy Hobbs, a middle-aged ballplayer making his comeback. It's the last out of the last inning of the crucial play-off game, and everything depends on him. He's been in a slump. Can his childhood sweetheart, Iris Gaines (Glenn Close), snap him out of it? She sends him a note revealing that her child is his son. The fact that he has not already figured this out is incredible. But he is inspired by the revelation. He steps to the plate. He has been having some trouble with his stomach. Some trouble, all right. A stain of blood spreads on his baseball shirt. It's a pretty badly bleeding stomach when it bleeds right through the skin. Roy swats a homer that hits the lights, and they all explode into fireworks, showering fiery stars upon him as he makes the rounds. In the epilogue, Roy plays catch with Iris and their son—a son who has not been allowed a single onscreen word—and a woman whose role has been to sit in the stands, wreathed in ethereal light, and inspire him.

Come on, give us a break. The last shot is cheap and phony. Either he hits the homer and then dies, or his bleeding was just a false alarm. If the bleeding was a false alarm, then everything else in the movie was false, too. But I guess that doesn't matter, because *The Natural* gives every sign of a story that's been seriously meddled with. Redford has been placed so firmly in the foreground that the prime consideration is to show him in a noble light. The people in his life—baseball players, mistresses, gamblers, crooks, sportswriters—seem grateful to share the frame with him. In case we miss the point, Redford is consistently backlit to turn his golden hair into a saintly halo.

The Natural could have been a decent movie. One reason that it is not: Of all its characters, the only one we don't want to know more about is Roy Hobbs. I'd love to get to know Pop Fisher (Wilford Brimley), the cynical, old team manager. Robert Duvall, as the evil sportswriter, Max Mercy, has had his part cut so badly that we only know he's evil because he practically tells us. Richard Farnsworth, as a kindly coach, has a smile that's more genuine than anything else in the movie. But you have to look quick. And what's with Glenn Close? She's the childhood sweetheart who doesn't hear from Roy after an accident changes the course of his life. Then she turns up years later, and when she stands up in the bleachers she is surrounded by blinding light: "Our Lady of Extra Innings." In the few moments she's allowed alone with Roy, she strikes us as complicated, tender, and forgiving. But even the crucial fact of her life—that she has borne this man's son—is used as a plot gimmick. If *The Natural* were about human beings and not a demigod, Glenn Close and Robert Redford would have spoken together, in the same room, using real words, about their child. Not in this movie.

As for the baseball, the movie isn't even subtle. When a team is losing, it makes Little League errors. When it's winning, the hits are so accurate they even smash the bad guy's windows. There's not a second of real baseball strategy in the whole film. The message is: Baseball is purely and simply a matter of divine intervention. At about the 130-minute mark, I got the idea that God's only begotten son was playing right field for the New York team.

Neighbors ★ ★ ★
R, 90 m., 1981

John Belushi (Earl Keese), Kathryn Walker (Enid Keese), Cathy Moriarty (Ramona), Dan Aykroyd (Vic). Directed by John G. Avildsen and produced by Richard D. Zanuck and David Brown. Screenplay by Larry Gelbart.

If there's one quality that middle-class Americans have in common, it's a tendency to be rigidly polite in the face of absolutely unacceptable behavior. Confronted with obnoxious rudeness, we freeze up, we get a nervous little smile, we allow our eyes to focus on the middle distance, and we cannot believe this is happening to us. It's part of our desire to avoid a scene. We'd rather choke to death in a restaurant than break a plate to attract attention. *Neighbors* is about one such man, Earl Keese (John Belushi). He is a pleasant, low-key dumpling of a fellow. He lives an uneventful life with an uneventful wife (Kathryn Walker). Then the neighbors move in, and there goes the neighborhood. They are everything we dread in neighbors. They are loud. They are blatant freeloaders. The man (Dan Aykroyd) is gung-ho macho. The woman (Cathy Moriarty, from *Raging Bull*) is oversexed and underloved. They park some kind of customized truck on their front lawn. They invite themselves to dinner.

There are compensations. For example, the woman seems to be a nymphomaniac. That would be more of a compensation for Earl if he were not terrified of aggressive woman. Earl has not the slightest notion of how to deal with these next-door maniacs, and his wife's no help: She puts on her best smile and tries to handle the situation as if everyone were playing by Emily Post's rules. The story of the Keeses and their weird neighbors was first told in Thomas Berger's novel. It was obviously a launching pad for a movie, but what sort of movie? The relationships among these neighbors depend almost entirely on the chemistry of casting: For example, obnoxious Richard Benjamin could have moved in next to meek Donald Sutherland. In *Neighbors*, however, we get Belushi and Aykroyd. I think it was brilliant casting, especially since they divided the roles somewhat against our expectations. Belushi, the most animalistic animal in *Animal House*, plays the mild-mannered Keese. And Aykroyd, who often plays straight-arrows, makes the new neighbor into a loud neo-fascist with a back slap that can kill.

The movie slides easily from its opening slices of life into a surburban nightmare. We know things are strange right at the start, when Aykroyd extorts money from Belushi to get a carry-out Italian dinner, and then secretly cooks the spaghetti right in his own kitchen. Belushi sneaks out into the night to spy on Aykroyd and catches him faking it with Ragu, but is too intimidated to say anything. The whole movie goes like that, with Belushi so intimidated that he hardly protests even when he finds himself sinking into quicksand.

Meanwhile, the women are making their own strange arrangements, especially after the Keese's college-age daughter (Lauren-Marie Taylor) comes home from school and begins attracting Moriarty's attention. The movie operates as a satire of social expectations, using polite clichés as counterpoint to deadly insults (all delivered in pleasant conversational tones).

The first hour of *Neighbors* is probably more fun than the second, if only because the plot developments come as a series of surprises. After a while, the bizarre logic of the movie becomes more predictable. But *Neighbors* is a truly interesting comedy, an offbeat experiment in hallucinatory black humor. It grows on you.

Network ★ ★ ★ ★
R, 121 m, 1976

Faye Dunaway (Diana Christenson), William Holden (Alex Schumacher), Peter Finch (Howard Beale), Robert Duvall (Frank Hackett), Wesley Addy (Nelson Chaney), Ned Beatty (Arthur Jensen). Directed by Sidney Lumet and produced by Howard Gottfried. Screenplay by Paddy Chayefsky.

There's a moment near the beginning of *Network* that has us thinking this will be the definitive indictment of national television we've been promised. A veteran anchorman has been fired because he's over the hill and drinking too much and, even worse, because his ratings have gone down. He announces his firing on his program, observes that broadcasting has been his whole life, and adds that he plans to kill himself on the air in two weeks. We cut to the control room, where the directors and technicians are obsessed with getting into the network feed on time. There are commercials that have to be fit in, the anchorman has to finish at the right moment, the buttons have to be pushed, and the station break has to be timed correctly. Everything goes fine. "Uh," says somebody, "did you hear what Howard just said?" Apparently nobody else had.

They were all consumed with form, with being sure the commercials were played in the right order and that the sesgment was the correct length. What was happening—that a man has lost his career and was losing his mind—passed right by. It wasn't their job to listen to Howard, just as it wasn't his job to run the control board. And what *Network* seems to be telling us is that television itself is like that: An economic process in the blind pursuit of ratings and technical precision, in which excellence is as accidental as banality.

If the whole movie had stayed with this theme, we might have had a very bitter little classic here. As it is, we have a supremely well-acted, intelligent film that tries for too much, that attacks not only television but also most of the other ills of the 1970s. We are asked to laugh at, be moved by, or get angry about such a long list of subjects: Sexism and ageism and revolutionary ripoffs and upper-middle-class anomie and capitalist exploitation and Neilsen ratings and psychics and that perennial standby, the failure to communicate. Paddy Chayefsky's script isn't a bad one, but he finally loses control of it. There's just too much he wanted to say. By the movie's end, the anchorman is obviously totally insane and is being exploited by blindly ambitious programmers on the one hand and corrupt businessmen on the other, and the scale of evil is so vast we've lost track of the human values.

And yet, still, what a rich and interesting movie this is. Lumet's direction is so taut, that maybe we don't realize that it leaves some unfinished business. It attempts to deal with a brief, cheerless love affair between Holden and Dunaway, but doesn't really allow us to understand it. It attempts to suggest that multinational corporations are the only true contemporary government, but

does so in a scene that slips too broadly into satire, so that we're not sure Chayefsky means it. It deals with Holden's relationship with his wife of twenty-five years, but inconclusively.

But then there are scenes in the movie that are absolutely chilling. We watch Peter Finch cracking up on the air, and we remind ourselves that *this* isn't satire, it was a style as long ago as Jack Paar. We can believe that audiences would tune in to a news program that's half happy talk and half freak show, because audiences *are* tuning in to programs like that. We can believe in the movie's "Ecumenical Liberation Army" because nothing along those lines will amaze us after Patty Hearst. And we can believe that the Faye Dunaway character could be totally cut off from her emotional and sexual roots, could be fanatically obsessed with her job, because jobs as competitive as hers almost require that. Twenty-five years ago, this movie would have seemed like a fantasy; now it's barely ahead of the facts.

So the movie's flawed. So it leaves us with loose ends and questions. That finally doesn't bother me, because what it does accomplish is done so well, is seen so sharply, is presented so unforgivingly, that *Network* will outlive a lot of tidier movies. And it won several Academy Awards, including those for Peter Finch, awarded posthumously as best actor; Chayevsky for his screenplay; Beatrice Straight, as best supporting actress; and Faye Dunaway, as best actress. Watch her closely as they're deciding what will finally have to be done about their controversial anchorman. The scene would be hard to believe—if she weren't in it.

Never Say Never Again ★ ★ ★ ½
PG, 137 m., 1983

Sean Connery (James Bond), Klaus Maria Brandauer (Largo), Max von Sydow (Blofeld), Barbara Carrera (Fatima Blush), Kim Basinger (Domino), Bernie Casey (Felix Leiter). Directed by Irwin Kershner and produced by Jack Schwartzman. Screenplay by Lorenzo Semple, Jr.

Ah, yes, James, it is good to have you back again. It is good to see the way you smile from under lowered eyebrows, and the way you bark commands in a sudden emergency, and it is good to see the way you look at women. Other secret agents may undress women with their eyes. You are more gallant. You undress them, and then thoughtfully dress them again. You are a rogue with the instincts of a gentleman.

It has been several years since Sean Connery hung it up as James Bond, several years since *Diamonds Are Forever,* and Connery's announcement that he would "never again" play special agent 007. What complex instincts caused him to have one more fling at the role, I cannot guess. Perhaps it was one morning in front of the mirror, as he pulled in his gut and reflected that he was in pretty damn fine shape for a man over fifty. And then, with a bow in the direction of his friend Roger Moore, who has made his own niche as a different kind of Bond, Sean Connery went back on assignment again.

The movie is called *Never Say Never Again.* The title has nothing to do with the movie—except why Connery made it—but never mind, nothing in this movie has much to do with anything else. It's another one of those Bond plots in which the basic ingredients are thrown together more or less in fancy. We begin with a threat (SPECTRE has stolen two nuclear missiles and is holding the world at ransom). We continue with Bond, his newest gadgets, his mission briefing. We meet the beautiful women who will figure in the plot (Barbara Carrera as terrorist Fatima Blush; Kim Basinger as the innocent mistress of the evil Largo). We meet the villains (Max van Sydow as Blofeld; Klaus Maria Brandauer as Largo). We visit exotic locations, we survive near-misses, and Bond spars with the evil woman and redeems the good one. All basic.

What makes *Never Say Never Again* more fun than most of the Bonds is more complex than that. For one thing, there's more of a human element in the movie, and it comes from Klaus Maria Brandauer, as Largo. Brandauer is a wonderful actor, and he chooses not to play the villian as a cliché. Instead, he brings a certain poignancy and charm to Largo, and since Connery always has been a particularly human James Bond, the emotional stakes are more convincing this time.

Sean Connery says he'll never make another James Bond movie, and maybe I believe him. But the fact that he made this one, so many years later, is one of those small show-business miracles. There was never a Beatles reunion. Bob Dylan and Joan Baez don't appear on the same stage anymore. But here, by God, is Sean Connery as Sir James Bond. Good work, 007.

The Neverending Story ★ ★ ★
PG, 94 m., 1984

Barret Oliver (Bastian), Noah Hathaway (Atreyu), Tami Stronach (Empress), Moses Gunn (Cairon). Directed by Wolfgang Petersen and produced by Bernd Eichinger and Dieter Geissler. Screenplay by Petersen and Weigel.

How's this for a threat? The kingdom of Fantasia is about to be wiped out, and the enemy isn't an evil wizard or a thermonuclear device, it's Nothingness. That's right, an inexorable wave of Nothingness is sweeping over the kingdom, destroying everything in its path. Were children's movies this nihilistic in the old days?

The only thing standing between Fantasia and Nothingness is the faith of a small boy named Bastian (Barret Oliver). He discovers the kingdom in a magical bookstore, and as he begins to read the adventure between the covers, it becomes so real that the people in the story know about Bastian. How could that be? Well, that's the very first question Bastian asks. This is a modern kid with quite a healthy amount of skepticism, but what can he do when he turns the page and the Child Empress (Tami Stronach) is begging him to give her a name so that Fantasia can be saved?

The idea of the story within a story is one of the nice touches in *The Neverending Story.* Another one is the idea of a child's faith being able to change the course of fate. Maybe not since the kids in the audience were asked to save Tinker Bell in *Peter Pan* has the outcome of a story been left so clearly up to a child's willingness to believe. There is a lot we have to believe in *The Neverending Story,* and that's the other great strength of this movie. It contains some of the more inventive special effects work of a time when battles in outer space, etc., have grown routine. Look for example, at *The Last Starfighter,* where the special effects are competent but never original—all the visual concepts are ripped off from *Star Wars*—and then look at this movie, where an entirely new world has been created.

The world of Fantasia contains creatures inspired by Alice in Wonderland (a little man atop a racing snail), the Muppets (a cute dragon-dog that can fly), and probably B.C. (a giant made of stone, who snacks on quartz and rumbles around on his granite tricycle). Many of the special effects involve sophisticated use of Muppet-like creatures (there are scenes that reminded me of *The Dark Crystal*). They are, in a way, more convincing than animation, because they exist in three dimensions and have the same depth as their human co-stars. And that illusion, in turn, helps reinforce the more conventional effects like animation, back projection, and so on. The world of this movie looks like a very particular place, and the art direction involved a lot of imagination. The movie's director, Wolfgang Petersen, is accustomed to creating worlds in small places; his last film, *Das Boot (The Boat)*, took place almost entirely within a submarine.

Within the world of Fantasia, a young hero (Noah Hathaway) is assigned to complete a hazardous quest, sneak past the dreaded portals of some stone amazons, and reach the Ivory Tower, where he will receive further instructions from the empress. In most movies, this quest would be told in a straightforward way, without the surrounding story about the other little boy who is reading the book. But *The Neverending Story* is *about* the unfolding of a story, and so the framing device of the kid hidden in his school attic, breathlessly turning the pages, is interesting. It lets kids know that the story isn't just somehow happening, that storytelling is a neverending act of the imagination.

New York, New York ★ ★ ★
PG, 163 m., 1977

Liza Minnelli (Francine Evans), Robert De Niro (Jimmy Doyle), Lionel Stander (Tony Harwell), Barry Primus (Paul Wilson), Mary Kay Place (Berenice), Georgie Auld (Frankie Harte). Directed by Martin Scorsese and produced by Irwin Winkler and Robert Chartoff. Screenplay by Earl MacRauch and Mardik Martin.

Martin Scorsese's *New York, New York* never pulls itself together into a coherent whole, but if we forgive the movie its confusions we're left with a good time. In other words: Abandon your expectations of an orderly plot, and you'll end up humming the title song. The movie's a vast, rambling, nostalgic expedition back into the big band era, and a celebration of the considerable talents of Liza Minnelli and Robert De Niro.

She plays a sweet kid with a big voice who starts as a band vocalist and ends up as a movie star. He plays an immature, aggressive, very talented saxophone player whose social life centers around the saloon fights. A generation before Punk Rock, here's Punk Swing. They get married for reasons the movie never makes quite clear (oh, they're in love, all right, but he's so weird it's a miracle she'll have him). And then their marriage starts to disintegrate for reasons well hallowed in show biz biographies: Her success, his insecurity, his drinking, their child.

De Niro comes on as certifiably loony from the start, and some of the movie's best scenes are counterpoint between his clowning and her rather touching acceptance of it. Maybe because he's really shy underneath, he likes to overact in social situations. He's egotistical, self-centered, inconsiderate, and all sorts of other things she should leave him because of, and there are times when the Minnelli character is so heroically patient that it's gotta be love. The movie doesn't really explore the nuances of their personalities, though; the characters are seen mostly by their surfaces, and they inhabit a cheerfully phony Hollywood back-lot New York. Scorsese, who knows how to shoot New York in California so it looks real (see *Mean Streets*), is going for a frankly movie feel with his sets and decors, and especially with his colors, which tend toward lurid rotogravure.

The look is right for the movie's musical scenes, and there are a lot of them: We start with a loving re-creation of V-J Day, with Tommy Dorsey's orchestra playing all the obligatory standards and De Niro trying with desperate zeal to pick up Minnelli. And then maybe half of the movie from then on will be music, mostly very good music (the movie's new songs deserve comparison with the old standards), and wonderfully performed. That Liza Minnelli has not been making an annual musical for the last decade is our loss; she's hauntingly good and so much more, well, human than Barbra Streisand.

It's a good thing the movie inhabits a familiar genre, though, because the fact that we've seen dozens of other musical biographies helps us fill in the gaps in this one. And there are a lot of them; the movie originally came in at something like four hours, and the cuts necessary to get it down to a more commercial length are responsible for a lot of confusion. The confusions, as I've suggested, can be forgiven because the movie has so many good things in it. And in the video version, to make amends, they've put back two musical numbers that weren't seen in the theater. But the ending is still puzzling. We've seen De Niro, totally unable to deal with the fact that he's become a father, tearfully (and amusingly) end their marriage right there in the maternity ward. Six years pass, there are Liza's great final production numbers, and then they have a backstage reunion after her night of triumph. Great, we're thinking, we've been here before, we relish the obligatory romantic reunion scene in the dressing room. But, no, he leaves. Then he calls her from a pay phone: He can't stand the people she's with, but would she like to sneak out, meet by the stage door, eat some Chinese food, and talk about themselves? Sure, she would. He waits outside the door. She approaches it from inside, pauses, sees no one there, and goes back to her dressing room. End of movie (with a nicely evocative night street scene). But did she change her mind and *decide* not to go out and meet him, or did she expect him to be waiting *inside* the door—and assume the cocky S.O.B. had stood her up again? This particular confusion is hard to forgive.

So the movie's flawed. It's not Scorsese's best work, or De Niro's (there are scenes in which his personality quirks and bizarre behavior make him seem uncannily like his Travis Bickle in Scorsese's *Taxi Driver*). Liza Minnelli's musical numbers are wondrous, as I've said, but the movie doesn't provide her with a character as fully understood as *Cabaret* did. So I guess we go to *New York, New York* to enjoy the good parts, and spend

just a moment regretting the absence of a whole.

Nine ½ Weeks ★ ★ ★ ½
R, 113 m., 1985

Kim Basinger (Elizabeth), Mickey Rourke (John). Directed by Adrian Lyne and produced by Anthony Rufus Isaacs and Zalman King. Screenplay by Patricia Knop, King, and Sarah Kernochan.

Nine ½ Weeks arrived in a shroud of mystery and scandal, already notorious as the most explicitly sexual big-budget movie since *Last Tango in Paris*. I went expecting erotic brinksmanship (how far *will* its famous stars go in the name of their art?) and came away surprised by how thoughtful the movie is, how clearly it sees exactly what really happens between its characters.

That's not to say the movie isn't sexy. I suppose a project of this sort depends crucially on the chemistry between its actors, and Kim Basinger and Mickey Rourke develop an erotic tension in this movie that is convincing, complicated, and sensual.

In the film, they play strangers who meet one day in a Chinese grocery store in Manhattan—Elizabeth, the smart, pretty assistant in a Soho art gallery, and John, the smiling, enigmatic commodities broker. Their first meeting is crucial to the entire film, and it is a quiet masterpiece of implication. She waits by a counter. Senses someone is standing behind her. Turns, and meets his eyes. He smiles. She turns away. Is obviously surprised by how much power was in their exchange of glances. She hesitates, turns back, meets his eyes again, almost boldly, and then turns away again. And a few minutes later looks at him very curiously as he walks away along the street.

They meet again, of course, and that is the beginning of their relationship, as chronicled first in a best-selling novel and now in this movie by Adrian Lyne, the director of *Flashdance*. It is clear from the start that they aren't going to follow an orthodox pattern of courtship and romance. He offers her, quite boldly, an experimental erotic relationship. The first time he touches her seriously, it is to tie a blindfold around her eyes. They advance into arenas of lovemaking often described in the letters column in *Penthouse* magazine, and Elizabeth, for the most part, is prepared to let John call all the shots. He wants to be in control, and as she surrenders to him, she abandons herself into dreamy erotic absentmindedness.

John is nothing if not inventive. In one scene, he blindfolds her and feeds her all kinds of strange foods, sweet and sour, different textures, each one a surprise to her lips, and it's astonishing the way the movie makes this visual scene so tactile. John calls her at unexpected times, orders her to unorthodox rendezvous, and as she follows his instructions they both seem to retreat more deeply into their obsession.

The movie contrasts their private life with the everyday world of her work: With the small talk and gossip of the art gallery, with a visit she pays to an old artist who lives like a hermit in the woods, with the intrigue as her ex-husband dates another woman in the gallery. This everyday material is an interesting strategy: It makes it clear that the private life of Elizabeth and John is a conscious game they're playing outside of the real world, and not just a fantasy in a movie where reality has been placed on hold.

Eventually, it is Elizabeth's hold on the real world that redeems the movie—makes it more than just a soft-core escapade—and sets up the thoughtful and surprising conclusion. So long as it is understood that she and John are engaged in a form of a game, and are conspiring in a sort of master-slave relationship for their mutual entertainment, Elizabeth has no serious objections. But as some of John's games grow more challenging to her own self-respect, she rebels. Does he want to engage her mind and body in an erotic sport, or does he really want to edge her closer to self-debasement? There are two times that Elizabeth draws the line, and a third time when she chooses her own independence and self-respect over what begins to look like his sickness.

That's what makes the movie fascinating: Not that it shows these two people entering a bizarre sexual relationship, but because it shows the woman deciding for herself what she will, and will not, agree to. At the end of Nine ½ Weeks, there is an argument, not for sexual liberation, but for sexual responsibility.

I have a few problems with certain scenes in the film. There is a moment when John and Elizabeth run through the midnight streets of a dangerous area of Manhattan, chased by hostile people, and finally take refuge in a passageway where they make love in the rain. The scene owes more to improbable gymnastic events than to the actual capabilities of the human body.

There is another scene in which John and Elizabeth go into a harness shop, and John selects and purchases a whip, while the shop employees do double-takes and Elizabeth stands wide-eyed, while he whooshes it through the air. There is no subsequent scene in which the whip is used. I do not argue that there should be; I only argue that in a movie like this, to buy a whip and not use it is like Camille coughing in the first reel and not dying in the last.

Any story like Nine ½ Weeks risks becoming very ridiculous. The actors are taking a chance in appearing in it. Plots like this make audiences nervous, and if the movie doesn't walk a fine line between the plausible and the bizarre, it will only find the absurd. A lot of the success of Nine ½ Weeks is because Rourke and Basinger made the characters and their relationship convincing.

Rourke's strategy is to never tell us too much. He cloaks himself in mystery, partly for her fascination, partly because his whole approach depends on his remaining a stranger. Basinger's strategy is equally effective, and more complicated. Physically, she looks sensuous and luscious; if you saw her in Fool for Love, you won't be surprised by the force of her appearance here. But if she'd just presented herself as the delectable object of all of these experiments, this would have been a modeling job, not an acting job.

In the early scenes, while she's at work in the gallery, she does a wonderful job of seeming distracted by this new relationship; her eyes cloud over and her attention strays. But one of the fascinations of the movie is the way her personality gradually emerges and finds strength, so that the ending of the film belongs completely to her.

The Hitcher, is also about a sadomasochistic relationship between a stronger personality and a weaker one. Because it lacks the honesty to declare what it is really about, and because it romanticizes the cruel acts of its characters, it left me feeling only disgust and disquiet. *Nine ½ Weeks* is not only a better film, but a more humanistic one, in which it is argued that sexual experimentation is one thing, but the real human personality is something else, something incomparably deeper and more valuable—and more erotic.

1984 ★ ★ ★ ½
R, 117 m., 1984

John Hurt (Winston Smith), Richard Burton (O'Brien), Suzanna Hamilton (Julia), Cyril Cusack (Charrington), Gregor Fisher (Parsons). Directed by Michael Radford and produced by Simon Perry. Screenplay by Radford.

George Orwell made no secret of the fact that his novel *1984* was not really about the future but about the very time he wrote it in, the bleak years after World War II when England shivered in poverty and hunger. In a novel where passion is depicted as a crime, the greatest passion is expressed, not for sex, but for contraband strawberry jam, coffee, and chocolate. What Orwell feared, when he wrote his novel in 1948, was that Hitlerism, Stalinism, centralism, and conformity would catch hold and turn the world into a totalitarian prison camp. It is hard, looking around the globe, to say that he was altogether wrong.

Michael Radford's brilliant film of Orwell's vision does a good job of finding that line between the "future" world of 1984 and the grim postwar world in which Orwell wrote. The movie's 1984 is like a year arrived at through a time warp, an alternative reality that looks constructed out of old radio tubes and smashed office furniture. There is not a single prop in this movie that you couldn't buy in a junkyard, and yet the visual result is uncanny: Orwell's hero, Winston Smith, lives in a world of grim and crushing inhumanity, of bombed factories, bug-infested bedrooms, and citizens desperate for the most simple pleasures.

The film opens with Smith rewriting history: His task is to change obsolete government documents so that they reflect current reality. He methodically scratches out old headlines, obliterates the photographs of newly made "unpersons," and attends mass rallies at which the worship of Big Brother

alternates with numbing reports of the endless world war that is still going on somewhere, involving somebody. Into Smith's world comes a girl, Julia, who slips him a note of stunning force. The note says, "I love you." Smith and Julia become revolutionaries by making love, walking in the countryside, and eating strawberry jam. Then Smith is summoned to the office of O'Brien, a high official of the "inner party," who seems to be a revolutionary too, and gives him the banned writings of an enemy of the state.

This story is, of course, well known. *1984* must be one of the most widely read novels of our time. What is remarkable about the movie is how completely it satisfied my feelings about the book; the movie looks, feels, and almost tastes and smells like Orwell's bleak and angry vision. John Hurt, with his scrawny body and lined and weary face, makes the perfect Winston Smith; and Richard Burton, looking so old and weary in this film that it is little wonder he died soon after finishing it, is the immensely cynical O'Brien, who feels close to people only while he is torturing them. Suzanna Hamilton is Julia, a fierce little war orphan whose rebellion is basically inspired by her hungers.

Radford's style in the movie is an interesting experiment. Like Chaplin in *Modern Times*, he uses passages of dialogue that are not meant to be understood—nonsense words and phrases, garbled as they are transmitted over Big Brother's primitive TV, and yet listened to no more or less urgently than the messages that say something. The 1954 film version of Orwell's novel turned it into a cautionary, simplistic science fiction tale. This version penetrates much more deeply into the novel's heart of darkness.

Nine to Five ★ ★ ★
PG, 111 m., 1980

Jane Fonda (Judy Bernly), Lily Tomlin (Violet Newstead), Dolly Parton (Doralee Rhodes), Dabney Coleman (Franklin Hart, Jr.), Sterling Hayden (Tinsworthy), Elizabeth Wilson (Roz). Directed by Colin Higgins and produced by Bruce Gilbert. Screenplay by Higgins and Patricia Resnick.

Nine to Five is a good-hearted, simple-minded comedy that will win a place in film history, I suspect, primarily because it contains the movie debut of Dolly Parton. She is a natural-born movie star, a performer who holds our attention so easily that it's hard to believe it's her first film. The movie has some funny moments, and then it has some major ingredients that don't work, including some of its fantasy sequences. But then it also has Dolly Parton. And she contains so much energy, so much life and unstudied natural exuberance that watching her do anything in this movie is a pleasure. Because there have been so many Dolly Parton jokes (and doubtless will be so many more), I had better say that I'm not referring to her sex appeal or chest measurements. Indeed, she hardly seems to exist as a sexual being in the movie. She exists on another plane, as Monroe did: She is a center of life on the screen.

But excuse me for a moment while I regain my composure. *Nine to Five* itself is pleasant entertainment, and I liked it, despite its uneven qualities and a plot that's almost too preposterous for the material. The movie exists in the tradition of 1940s screwball comedies. It's about improbable events happening to people who are comic caricatures of their types, and, like those Forties movies, it also has a dash of social commentary. The message has to do with women's liberation and, specifically, with the role of women in large corporate offices. Jane Fonda, Lily Tomlin, and Dolly Parton all work in the same office. Tomlin is the efficient office manager. Fonda is the newcomer, trying out her first job after a divorce. Parton is the boss's secretary, and everybody in the office thinks she's having an affair with the boss. So the other women won't speak to her.

The villain is the boss himself. Played by Dabney Coleman, he's a self-righteous prig with a great and sincere lust for Dolly Parton. She's having none of it. After the movie introduces a few social issues (day care, staggered work hours, equal pay, merit promotion), the movie develops into a bizarre plot to kidnap Coleman in an attempt to win equal rights. He winds up swinging from the ceiling of his bedroom, attached by wires to a garage-door opener. Serves him right, the M.C.P. This whole kidnapping sequence move so far toward unrestrained farce that it damages the movie's marginally plausible opening scenes. But perhaps we don't really care. We learn right away that this is deliberately a lightweight film, despite its superstructure of social significance. And, making the necessary concessions, we simply enjoy it.

What I enjoyed most, as you have already guessed, was Dolly Parton. Is she an actress? Yes, definitely, I'd say, although I am not at all sure how wide a range of roles she might be able to play. She's perfect for this one—which was, of course, custom-made for her. But watch her in the scenes where she's not speaking, where the action is elsewhere. She's always in character, always reacting, always generating so much energy we expect her to fly apart. There's a scene on a hospital bench, for example, where Tomlin is convinced she's poisoned the boss, and Fonda is consoling her. Watch Dolly. She's bouncing in and out, irrepressibly. What is involved here is probably something other than "acting." It has to do with what Bernard Shaw called the "life force," that dynamo of energy that some people seem to possess so bountifully. Dolly Parton simply seems to be having a great time, ready to sweep everyone else up in her enthusiasm, her concern, her energy. It's some show.

Nomads ★ ½
R, 103m., 1985

Pierce Brosnan (Pommier), Lesley-Anne Down (Flax), Anna-Maria Montecelli (Niki), Adam Ant (Number One), Hector Mercado (Ponytail), Josie Cotton (Silver Ring), Mary Woronov (Dirty Blonde). Directed by John McTiernan and produced by George Pappas and Cassian Elwes. Screenplay by McTiernan.

I would like to describe the plot of *Nomads*, but my space is limited. Maybe I can give it a try. A French anthropologist (Pierce Brosnan) moves to Los Angeles with his wife. Their new home is immediately made the target of a roaming band of fierce street people who dress in leather and chains and paint slogans on garage walls. The anthropologist discovers that these people are not your average big-city vandals, but an urban version of the Innuat. And, about halfway through the movie, we learn what the Innuat are. According to old Eskimo legends, they are nomadic spirits who wander the earth in human form, spreading evil.

That is not the complicated part of the plot. The hard part is what we have to slog through before we find out about Innuats. The movie starts with Lesley-Anne Down as an emergency room doctor. A deranged patient (Brosnan) is brought in, and handcuffed to the bed. Everybody thinks he's on a bad drug trip, but no, it's simpler than that; he has gone stark raving mad. He keeps screaming the same phrase in French: "N'y sont pas, sont des Innuat." This translates as: "They are not there; they are Innuat." But nobody can figure that out, because they don't know "Innuat" is an Eskimo word, you see, and they simply think his French is bad.

That reminds me of a classic story from the Cannes Film Festival a few years back, when Rex Reed got an engraved invitation in French. The only word he could read was "Eskimo." He had heard that there was a great new Eskimo film in the festival, however, and so at midnight he went bravely out into the rainy night and got a cab and went to the address on the invitation, only to discover that he was a guest at the opening of an Eskimo Pie ice cream store.

Now you may argue, not unreasonably, that my story has little to do with Nomads. True. But it has at least as much to do with Nomads as the ancient Eskimo myth of the Innuat. Nomads is a very confused movie, especially after the berserk Brosnan leaps out of his manacles and bites Lesley-Anne Down on the neck, transferring all of his memories into her head, so that she goes crazy and relives all of Brosnan's traumatic experiences with the Innuat.

This grows very confusing for Brosnan's wife (Anna-Maria Montecelli), who does not understand why Down is telling her things only Brosnan would know. It is also very confusing for the audience, because the movie keeps switching signals on us. Sometimes we see Down and then we get a point-of-view shot that is supposed to be inside her head but looking out through Brosnan's eyes. Sometimes we see Brosnan from the outside. Sometimes that means we are looking at the

real Brosnan, and sometimes it doesn't. We'd really be confused, if we gave a damn.

But we don't. The movie tells one of those stories where the characters have only themselves to blame, for going out into dark nights and looking for trouble with the Innuat and not getting on the next plane back to France. Everybody in this movie gets what's coming to them, except for Lesley-Anne Down, and even she should have been smart enough not to shine her flashlight in the eyes of a man who was foaming at the mouth.

Nomads does, however, have one great shot. An Innuat on a motorcycle is chasing the two women down a lonely interstate highway. Suddenly, the Innuat turns back, and the camera pans slowly to reveal a highway sign: The California State Line. Apparently Nevada is not loony enough for the Innuat. And so the lonely Innuat wheels his motorcycle around, and drives slowly back to Los Angeles, where, in keeping with the ancient Eskimo legend, his spirit will haunt the backlots of Hollywood, waiting for another movie that wouldn't be quite bad enough without him.

Norma Rae ★ ★ ★
PG, 114 m., 1979

Sally Field (Norma Rae), Ron Liebman (Reuben), Beau Bridges (Sonny), Pat Hingle (Father), Barbara Baxley (Mother), Gail Strickland (Bonnie). Directed by Martin Ritt and produced by Tamara Asseyev and Alex Rose. Screenplay by Irving Ravetch and Harriet Frank, Jr.

We're sometimes unfair to our movie actresses, and Sally Field's extraordinary performance in Norma Rae helps dramatize it. Most new actresses come up through television and its lame-brained sexist stereotyping. And most of the female TV stars have their moment of glory and then become unfairly categorized in our memories. Be honest: Didn't we think of Sally Field as the Flying Nun before this Oscar-winning performance?

For any actress, an opportunity to star on TV has to be great. But the opportunity to escape TV and appear in a challenging movie has to be a godsend. Jill Clayburgh got her chance with An Unmarried Woman. Here it's

Sally Field's turn. And as the plain-spoken, spunky Southern textile worker in Martin Ritt's *Norma Rae,* she quite simply surpassed our expectations.

The performance is at the heart of the movie, because this isn't a film about labor unions or mill working conditions; it's about a woman of thirty-one learning to grow into her own potential.

She has a couple of kids—one out of wedlock, the other orphaned by a brawling father—and a few boyfriends here and there, and she's never taken much time to think about the value of her life. Like everyone in the town, she works in the textile mill, which has no union, pays minimum wages, has few benefits, and does little or nothing about brown lung disease.

Then a union organizer (Ron Liebman) from New York turns up in town. He finds precious little support, and almost none from Norma Rae; she's too absorbed in a whirlwind courtship and marriage with a local good ol' boy (Beau Bridges) who promises to bring his check home on Fridays and not chase around. She marries him, mostly out of affection and convenience.

But then the organizer begins to make a little sense to her. She grows less blind to the conditions at the mill. She gets angry when her father drops dead on an assembly line. She goes to a couple of meetings at which Liebman harangues his handful of recruits. She becomes a recruit herself, a volunteer organizer, and eventually it's taking up all of her time.

Her new husband complains—but both she and the movie tend to ignore him. The marriage, indeed, seems almost peripheral to the movie's central story, which is about the way she slowly opens her eyes to herself and her world. Liebman puts it simply: "You're too smart to do what you're doing to yourself."

She eventually agrees. And we're sort of set up for a situation where Norma Rae and the organizer fall in love with each other. But they don't; the movie is steadfast in its determination to show Norma Rae growing because of her own thought and will—not under the influence of yet another sexual liaison.

That's what makes the movie so special. It has all sorts of plot problems (especially involving the marriage), and there are scenes that don't quite fit together, and moments that don't sound right. But the character of Norma Rae is so deeply seen and realized, and played by Sally Field with such conviction, that we accept her in spite of our doubts about other things. In the tenth year of her acting career, Sally Field has made a remarkable debut.

North Dallas Forty ★ ★ ★ ½
R, 117 m., 1979

Nick Nolte (Phil Elliott), Mac Davis (Maxwell), Charles Durning (Coach Johnson), Dayle Haddon (Charlotte), Bo Svenson (Jo Bob), Steve Forrest (Conrad Hunter), G.D. Spradlin (B.A.), John Matuszak (O.W. Shaddock). Directed by Ted Kotcheff and produced by Frank Yablans. Screenplay by Yablans, Kotcheff, and Peter Gent.

North Dallas Forty is about pro football the way *Network* was about television. It's about the ways large and competitive institutions grind up people and spit them out. The guy who gets spit out in this movie is Phil Elliott, whose coach tells him he has the best hands in football, but a "bad attitude." Elliott is played by Nick Nolte in a muscular and compelling performance: After this movie, people began to take Nolte seriously.

The movie is not really a sports film. It doesn't share the patented formula of the routine sports movie, in which everything depends on the bravura final match, or game, or race. The film does lead up to an important game, yes—North Dallas plays Chicago for a divisional championship—but by then we're so involved in the human drama that we almost don't care who wins.

The drama revolves around the Nolte character and his best friend, a quarterback played by Mac Davis. They play football very hard and very well. Off the field, they regard the business of football with a profound cynicism, and they assault themselves with boozing, drugs, all-night partying, and bleak thoughts about what they will do when the day comes when they finally cannot play any longer.

Characters in the movie talk, at times, about words like "play" and "game." Is professional football a game? Not according to John Matuszak, in real life an Oakland

Raider, who in one of the movie's most electrifying scenes has a shouting match with a coach in the locker room. At *some* point, he screams, football for the players must be more than a business—must be a cause, a spirit. In the fourth quarter, when you're cold and hurt and exhausted, the game plan means nothing, but your desire means everything.

The North Dallas management doesn't quite see it that way. The owners and coaches are detached, scientific, quite prepared to see a player shoot up pain-killers and run the risk of permanently crippling himself. Nolte himself is prepared to do that. But the management doesn't like him. He's a wiseass. He has the wrong attitude. He's childish. Their ideal football player would be someone like the fearsome Jo Bob Priddy (Bo Svenson), who is not in fact as good a player as Nolte, but has a magnificently simpleminded "correct" attitude.

The pressures put Nolte in a vise: He loves playing, he cannot envision himself not playing, he even understands the management attitude if only they knew it. But age and wear and cynicism are closing in, and he finds himself, half astonished, in love with a woman. She represents a kind of settling down that football has given him license to avoid, and the movie uses the relationship as a counterpoint to a week of training and a climactic game.

The football scenes are brutally real; the locker room scenes are totally authentic. There are obscenities and violence and pain, and a clear view of how the "adults"—the coaches—manipulate their strong, fearsome, and intimidated employees. "*We're* not the team," Nolte shouts at the owner. "*You're* the team. We're only the equipment—like the jockstraps and the helmets."

The movie is funny at times, especially during the lecture meetings where the players, openly contemptuous, listen to such dim inspirational insights as that, if God had really meant all men to be equal, he wouldn't have called us the human "race." God, for example, clearly meant for North Dallas to be more equal than Chicago.

Those kinds of details, and the scenes of the players' agents and the parties and the practice sessions, have a convincing documentary feel. Holding it all together, making

it work, forcing us to get involved, is the Nolte character. It's a tribute to this movie that we would probably care as much about Nolte if he were *not* a football player. What he's facing is common in so many parts of American society; in so many of the things we do and the jobs we have, at some ultimate level we are just simply part of somebody else's business.

Nosferatu ★ ★ ★ ★
R, 63 m., 1979

Klaus Kinski (Count Dracula), Isabelle Adjani (Lucy Harker), Bruno Ganz (Jonathan Harker). Directed, produced, and written by Werner Herzog.

Set aside for the moment the details of the Dracula story. They've lost their meaning. They've been run through a thousand vampire movies too many. It's as easy these days to play Dracula as Santa Claus. The suit comes with the job. The kids sit on your knee and you ask them what they want and this year they want blood.

Consider instead Count Dracula. He bears a terrible cross but he lives in a wonderful sphere. He comes backed by music of the masters and dresses in red and black, the colors De Sade found finally the most restful. Dracula's shame as he exchanges intimacies and elegant courtesies with you is that tonight or sometime soon he will need to drink your blood. What an embarrassing thing to know about someone else.

Werner Herzog's *Nosferatu* concerns itself with such knowledge. *Nosferatu*. A word for *the vampire*. English permits "vampire movies"—but a "nosferatu movie?" Say "vampire" and your lips must grin. The other word looks like sucking lemons. Perfect. There is nothing pleasant about Herzog's vampire, and this isn't a movie for Creature Feature fans. There are movies for people who like to yuk it up and make barfing sounds, God love 'em, while Christopher Lee lets the blood dribble down his chin, but they're not the audience for *Nosferatu*. This movie isn't even scary. It's so slow it's meditative at times, but it is the most evocative series of images centered around the idea of the vampire that I have ever seen—since F. W. Murnau's *Nosferatu*, which was made in 1922.

That is why we're wise to forget the details of the basic Dracula story. *Nosferatu* doesn't pay them heed. It is about the mood and *style* of vampirism, about the terrible seductive pity of it all. There is a beautiful passage early in the film showing the hero, Jonathan Harker, traveling from his home village to the castle of Dracula. The count has summoned him because he is considering the purchase of another home. Harker makes the journey by horse path. He enters into a high mountain pass filled with tenuous cloud layers that drift by a little too fast, as if God were sucking in his breath. The music is *not* your standard creepy Loony Tunes, but a fierce melody of exhilaration and dread. Deeper and deeper rides Harker into the cold gray flint of the peaks. Some will say this passage goes on too long and that nothing happens during it. I wish the whole movie were this empty.

Before long, we are regarding the count himself. He is played totally without ego by Klaus Kinski. The *count* has a monstrous ego, of course—it is Kinski who has none. There is never a moment when we sense this actor enjoying what a fine juicy cornpone role he has, with fangs and long sharp fingernails and a cape to swirl. No, Kinski has grown far too old inside to play Dracula like that: He makes his body and gaunt skull transparent, so the role can flicker through.

Sit through *Nosferatu* twice, or three times. Cleanse yourself of the expectation that things will happen. Get with the flow. This movie works like an LP record: You can't love the music until you've heard the words so often they're sounds. It's in German with English subtitles. It would be just fine with no subtitles, dubbed into an unknown tongue. The need to know what Dracula is saying at any given moment is a bourgeois affectation. Dracula is *always* saying, "I am speaking with you now as a meaningless courtesy in preface to the unspeakable event that we both know is going to take place between us sooner rather than later."

Off Beat ★ ★ ★ ½
PG, 93 m., 1986

Judge Reinhold (Joe Gower), Meg Tilly (Rachel Wareham), Cleavant Derricks (Abe Washington), Joe Mantegna (Pete Peterson), Jacques D'Amboise (August), Amy Wright (Mary Ellen), John Turturro (Pepper), Harvey Keitel (Bank Robber), Julie Bovasso (Mrs. Wareham). Directed by Michel Dinner and produced by Joe Roth and Harry Ufland. Screenplay by Mark Medoff.

It's been a long time since I've found the characters in a comedy as sympathetic as they are in *Off Beat*. So many recent American comedies seem to hate their heroes, to want to make fun of them, but here is a movie about sweet, likable people who get into a funny situation and watch it grow funnier the more they try to escape from it. *Off Beat* is a movie with a sharp edge and more than a little hostility, but the overall feeling is sort of warm and romantic.

It's about this librarian named Joe (Judge Reinhold) who is going nowhere with his life. He puts on his roller skates and rolls back and forth in the stacks of the New York Public Library, feeding a conveyor belt with books for people he never sees. His promotion is blocked by the hateful Mr. Pepper (John Turturro), who is a Pee Wee Herman clone; his girlfriend has just left him, and he spends his evenings drowning his sorrows, drinking with his best friend, a black cop named Washington (Cleavant Derricks).

One day he screws up one of Washington's undercover assignments, and so he owes him one. And here is what Washington wants him to do: Having been assigned to audition for the dance line in a police department charity show, he wants Joe to go to the audition for him. Joe protests, but it's no use, and that's how he gets into the peculiar position of impersonating a police officer *and* a dancer, both at once.

The audition is not a happy event. Most of the cops are angry about having to be there. Joe figures he can flunk the audition, and that'll be that, but then his eyes meet the eyes of a high-spirited woman cop (Meg Tilly), and he decides to stick around. *Off Beat* will be the story of their love affair, cross-cut with such other matters as a bank robbery, backstage intrigue at the library, the hostility of the other cops, and the problems Joe walks into by wearing a police uniform around the streets of New York.

The movie has a more ingenious plot than is usually the case in modern comedies; it's not just a straight line from beginning to end, but a series of little character studies and quiet dialogue passages and small insights into human nature. Holding the elements together is the strong chemistry between Judge Reinhold (who was Eddie Murphy's partner in *Beverly Hills Cop*) and Meg Tilly (who won an Academy Award nomination for *Agnes of God*, but is ten or twenty times more interesting in this film). What's nice is that they approach each other out of vulnerability. There isn't that feeling you sometimes get with the big stars, that *of course* people are going to be attracted to them. They both seem a little flattered to be so much in love. It creates a good feeling.

But the movie isn't all sweetness. It contains one of the single most explosive and surprising comic moments of any movie in a long time, when a hostile cop delivers a brutal insult to Meg Tilly, and she responds appropriately. More than that I won't say, but the moment gets a laugh that grows out of shock, surprise, and the perfect timing of what happens.

Off Beat is filled with good character actors, bringing more dimensions to their characters than the roles might otherwise permit. Among them are Harvey Keitel as a bank robber, Julie Bovasso as Tilly's mother, and Joe Mantegna as a cop who hates ballet instructors.

At the center of everything, Reinhold and Tilly make a wonderful romantic couple. There is a real magic about the scene where they have a quiet dinner and then begin to dance. Reinhold became a star of sorts in *Beverly Hills Cop*, just by having a good role in a hit movie, but this time he carries the show, and gives promise of being around for a long time, probably in more of these Everyman roles that Jack Lemmon plays so well. Meg Tilly has been in wildly uneven movies over the years (and I was not one of the admirers of *Agnes of God*, her most prestigious film to date). This time, allowed to play a fairly tough and complicated character, she suddenly blossoms. She's never been more appealing.

Off Beat probably sounds contrived. The plot is filled with predictable devices and contrived meetings and wild coincidences, and elements that seem borrowed from other films. What's surprising is how original it all

seems, maybe because the director, Michael Dinner, seems to really care for his characters.

An Officer and a Gentleman
★ ★ ★ ★
R, 126 m., 1982

Richard Gere (Zack Mayo), Debra Winger (Paula Pokrifki), Lou Gossett, Jr. (Sergeant Foley), David Keith (Sid Worley), Robert Loggia (Byron Mayo), Lisa Blount (Lynette), Lisa Eilbacher (Casey Seeger). Directed by Taylor Hackford and produced by Martin Elfand. Screenplay by Douglas Day Stewart.

An Officer and a Gentleman is the best movie about love that I've seen in a long time. Maybe that's because it's not about "love" as a Hollywood concept, but about love as growth, as learning to accept other people for who and what they are. There's romance in this movie, all right, and some unusually erotic sex, but what makes the film so special is that the sex and everything else is presented within the context of its characters finding out who they are, what they stand for—and what they will *not* stand for.

The movie takes place in and around a Naval Aviation Officer Candidate School in Washington state. Every thirteen weeks, a new group of young men and women come here to see if they can survive a grueling session of physical and academic training. If they pass, they graduate to flight school. About half fail. Across Puget Sound, the local young women hope for a chance to meet an eligible future officer. They dream of becoming officers' wives, and in some of their families, we learn, this dream has persisted for two generations.

After the first month of training, there is a Regimental Ball. The women turn out with hope in their hearts and are sized up by the candidates. A man and a woman (Richard Gere and Debra Winger) pair off. We know more about them than they know about one another. He is a loner and a loser, whose mother died when he was young and whose father is a drunk. She is the daughter of an officer candidate who loved and left her mother twenty years before. They dance, they talk, they begin to date, they fall in love. She would like to marry him, but she refuses to do what the other local girls are willing to do—get pregnant or fake pregnancy to trap a future officer. For his part, the man is afraid of commitment, afraid of love, incapable of admitting that he cares for someone. All he wants is a nice, simple affair, and a clean break at the end of OCS.

This love story is told in counterpoint with others. There's the parallel affair between another candidate and another local girl. She *is* willing to trap her man. His problem is, he really loves her. He's under the thumb of his family, but he's willing to do the right thing, if she'll give him the chance.

All of the off-base romances are backdrops for the main event, which is the training program. The candidates are under the supervision of a tough drill sergeant (Lou Gossett, Jr.) who has seen them come and seen them go and is absolutely uncompromising in his standards. There's a love-hate relationship between the sergeant and his trainees, especially the rebellious, resentful Gere. And Gossett does such a fine job of fine-tuning the line between his professional standards and his personal emotions that the performance deserves its Academy Award.

The movie's method is essentially to follow its characters through the thirteen weeks, watching them as they change and grow. That does wonders for the love stories, because by the end of the film we know these people well enough to care about their decisions and to have an opinion about what they should do. In the case of Gere and Winger, the romance is absolutely absorbing because it's so true to life, right down to the pride that causes these two to pretend they don't care for each other as much as they really do. When it looks as if Gere is going to throw it all away—is going to turn his back on a good woman who loves him, just because he's too insecure to deal with her love—the movie isn't just playing with emotions, it's being very perceptive about human behavior.

But maybe I'm being too analytical about why *An Officer and a Gentleman* is so good. This is a wonderful movie precisely because it's so willing to deal with matters of the heart. Love stories are among the rarest of movies these days (and when we finally get one, it's likely to involve an extra-terrestrial). Maybe they're rare because writers and filmmakers no longer believe they understand what goes on between modern men and women. *An Officer and a Gentleman* takes chances, takes the time to know and develop its characters, and by the time this movie's wonderful last scene comes along, we know exactly what's happening, and why, and it makes us very happy.

Oh, God! ★ ★ ★ ½
PG, 104 m., 1977

George Burns (God), John Denver (Jerry Landers), Teri Garr (Bonnie Landers), Donald Pleasence (Dr. Harmon), Ralph Bellamy (Sam Raven), William Daniels (George Summers), Paul Sorvino (Reverend Williams), Dinah Shore (Dinah). Directed by Carl Reiner and produced by Jerry Weintraub. Screenplay by Larry Gelbart.

Carl Reiner's *Oh, God!* is a treasure of a movie: A sly, civilized, quietly funny speculation on what might happen if God endeavored to present himself in the flesh yet once again to forgetful Man. He comes back this time looking and talking a great deal like George Burns, an improvement on his earlier cinematic incarnations. And as his contact on Earth, he selects a common man — John Denver, to the manner born.

Part of the movie's charm is in the way it surprises us by treating its subject matter with affection and respect. I went expecting blasphemous jokes and cheap shots at religion, since serious subjects so rarely make it into comedies these days except as targets. But no: *Oh, God!* is lighthearted, satirical, and humorous and (that rarest of qualities) in good taste.

It also makes you feel good, in the way some of the Frank Capra comedies did. The John Denver character becomes a contemporary version of Mr. Smith, John Doe, Mr. Deeds, and those other Capra heroes who prevailed because they were decent, honest, and true. Once Denver gets over his initial astonishment at being selected as God's spokesman, he makes a good job of it, justifying God's faith in the common man, which He, after all, put into production.

God is careful, throughout the movie, to make his reasoning clear. Why did he pick Denver? "You're like the lady who's the millionth person across the bridge and gets to meet the governor. You're better than some people, and worse than others, but you came

across the bridge at the right time." The
message God wants to remind His creatures
of is a simple one: That things *can* turn out
all right, although they will not necessarily
or automatically do so. That we have everything here on Earth that we need to bring a
happy ending to our story. And that we
should try being a little nicer to one another.

Carl Reiner's credits as a director include
the immortal *Where's Poppa?* (1970), a masterpiece of comic bad taste. So there was reason to anticipate a showdown again this time
between the sacred and the profane. As an
idea, indeed, *Oh, God!* must have seemed
almost impossibly supplied with ways to go
wrong. But it doesn't. Reiner is superb at
establishing the right tone for this very difficult material, and the casting of George
Burns as God is an inspiration.

"I took this form," God explains,
"because if I showed myself to you as I am,
you wouldn't be able to comprehend me."
He chose his form well. God, as Burns,
recalls some of his miracles (the 1969 Mets),
some of his mistakes (tobacco, giraffes, and
avocados—"I made the seeds too big"), and
some common misconceptions about Himself ("To tell you the truth, I spent the first
five days thinking and created everything on
the sixth"). And he has such quiet authority,
such wonderfully understated humor, such
presence. John Denver, too, is well-cast: Sincere, believable, with that face so open and
goofy. They work with Reiner, and with
Larry Gelbart's screenplay, to create a movie
that takes a really risky comic gamble, and
wins.

Oh, God! Book II ★ ★
PG, 94 m., 1980

George Burns (God), Louanne (Tracy),
Suzanne Pleshette (Paula), David Birney
(Don), John Louie (Shingo), Anthony
Holland (Dr. Newell). Directed and produced
by Gilbert Cates. Screenplay by John
Greenfield, Hal Goldman, Fred S. Fox,
Seaman Jacobs, and Melissa Miller.

Oh, God! Book II qualifies as a sequel only
because of its title and the irreplaceable presence of George Burns in the title role. Otherwise, it seems to have lost faith in the film it's
based on. It begins with the same great idea
for a movie (what would happen if God per-

sonally came down to earth and got involved
in the affairs of men?), but it winds up as a
third-rate situation comedy, using its subject
as a gimmick.

Neither of the *Oh, God!* movies is, of
course, seriously religious; they create God
as a sort of ancient Will Rogers on a Christmas card by Norman Rockwell, and then
give him lots of cute lines and paradoxical
comic insights. But the original film—with
God appearing to a supermarket manager
played by John Denver—did at least follow
through on its basic premise. What if God
really did turn up in the checkout line? How
do you behave when God blows the whistle
and challenges you to test his rules?

Oh, God! Book II doesn't seem willing to
devote a whole movie to the same subject; it
uses God as basically just a *deus ex machina*.
He is, of course, enormously appealing, and
George Burns is rich and understated in the
role. But after he appears to a little girl
named Tracy (played by a very little actress
named Louanne), the movie uses him as a
springboard for scenes involving the little
girl, her parents, her school, her psychiatrist—everything except what we'd really
enjoy—more scenes with God.

Tracy's basic problem, it appears, is that
she can see God and talk with him, but
nobody else can. Her parents and teachers
think she's talking to herself. God asks her to
organize an advertising campaign to pro-
mote his image on earth, and she comes up
with a slogan ("Think God") which her little
playmates plaster on every open space in
town. But, meanwhile, a psychiatrist
(Anthony Holland) determines that Tracy's
got serious problems.

There are other sitcom-style distractions.
Tracy's parents (Suzanne Pleshette and
David Birney) are divorced. Tracy doesn't
like her daddy's new girlfriend. The principal at school is a meanie. And so on. The
movie's screenplay was written by no less
than five collaborators, but they were so
bankrupt of ideas that some scenes have a
quiet desperation to them. For example:
There's an awkward TV newscast staged in
the movie, with Hugh Downs as the avuncular anchorman and none other than Dr.
Joyce Brothers giving her opinion that little
Tracy may, indeed, have seen God. It would
be sad enough if the movie were using

Downs and Brothers for laughs—but, God help us, they're brought in as authority figures.

There is, however, one additional small treasure in this movie, a supporting performance by Mari Gorman, who steals every scene she's in, playing Tracy's grade school teacher, Miss Hudson. She has a weird kind of off-balance walk and out-of-time speaking style that's infectious and funny. It's amazing that a movie so devoid of comic imagination would allow itself to play around with such an offbeat supporting performance. If Gorman had played, say, Tracy's mother—and if the rest of the movie had been equally willing to take chances with its approach—*Book II* could have been worth seeing.

Oh, God! You Devil ★ ★ ★ ½
PG, 96 m., 1984

George Burns (God and Harry), Ted Wass (Bobby Shelton), Roxanne Hart (Wendy), Ron Silver (Gary). Directed by Paul Bogart and produced by Robert M. Sherman. Screenplay by Andrew Bergman.

The *God* pictures are ideal for sequels; after all, the leading character has no beginning and no end. But sequels have a way of ripping off profitable ideas without anything new to say. They grow so dreary and pale that we forget why we liked the original picture in the first place. That's why *Oh, God! You Devil* is such a delight. Here is George Burns's third God movie, and not only does it have as much humor, warmth, and good cheer as the first—it actually has a better story. The story involves a young man who was placed under God's protection when he was a little baby; he had a fever, and his father's prayers were answered. The kid has grown up into an unsuccessful musician, and one day while he's performing at some dumb wedding reception, he meets an unusual guest, one Harry O. Tophet, who is, of course, the devil. Harry makes the kid an offer he should, but does not, refuse, and before long the kid is the top rock superstar in the world.

Of course, there's a catch. He has to assume the identity of another musician—an existing superstar whose deal with the devil has just run out. And worst of all, he has to remember his previous life, including the wife he loved and the child they were expecting. This whole balancing act between success and loss is unexpectedly touching, and gives the movie a genuine human heart.

Meanwhile, the devil basks in his acquisition, and then God gets into the act when the rock star prays to be released from his deal with the devil.

It's here that we get what we've been waiting for all through the picture, the scenes where God and the devil, both played by George Burns, appear on the same screen. Dual appearances through trick photography are, of course, an old Hollywood standby, but what's fun here is the way Burns plays scenes with himself: This casting was made in heaven.

Oh, God! You Devil has two different kinds of successful elements. The Burns stuff is all superb, especially when the devil reflects whimsically about the evils he's unleashed upon the earth. But the other story—the story starring Ted Wass as the condemned rock star—has an authenticity of its own. Like Warren Beatty's *Heaven Can Wait*, it starts with a fantastical idea and then develops it along plausible human lines. For the first time in the God pictures, we care so much about the human characters that it really does make a difference what God does; it's not just a celestial vaudeville act.

On Golden Pond ★ ★ ★ ★
PG, 109 m., 1981

Katharine Hepburn (Ethel Thayer), Henry Fonda (Norman Thayer, Jr.), Jane Fonda (Chelsea), Doug McKeon (Billy Ray), Dabney Coleman (Bill Ray). Directed by Mark Rydell and produced by Bruce Gilbert. Screenplay by Ernest Thompson.

Simple affection is so rare in the movies. Shyness and resentment are also seldom seen. Love is much talked-about, but how often do we really believe that the characters are in love and not simply in a pleasant state of lust and like? Fragile emotions are hard to portray in a movie, and the movies that reach for them are more daring, really, than movies that bludgeon us with things like anger and revenge, which are easy to portray.

On Golden Pond is a treasure for many reasons, but the best one, I think, is that I could believe it. I could believe in its major characters and their relationships, and in the things they felt for one another, and there were moments when the movie was witness to human growth and change. I left the theater feeling good and warm, and with a certain resolve to try to mend my own relationships and learn to start listening better. All of those achievements are small miracles for any movie, but especially for this one, which began as a formula stage play and still contains situations and characters that are constructed completely out of cardboard.

The story of *On Golden Pond* begins with the arrival of an old, long-married couple (Henry Fonda and Katharine Hepburn) at the lakeside cottage where they have summered for many years. They know each other very well. Hepburn, of course, knows Fonda better than he knows her—or himself, for that matter. Fonda is a crotchety, grouchy old professor whose facade conceals a great deal of shyness, we suspect. Hepburn knows that. Before long, three more people turn up at the pond: Their daughter (Jane Fonda), her fiancé (Dabney Coleman), and his son (Doug McKeon).

That's the first act. In the second act, the conflicts are established. Jane Fonda feels that her father has never really given her her due—he wanted a son, or perhaps he never really understood how to be a father, anyway. Jane tells her parents that she's spending a month in Europe with Coleman, and, ah, would it be all right if they left the kid at the lake? Hepburn talks the old man into it. In the central passages of the movie, the old man and the kid grudgingly move toward some kind of communication and trust. There is a crisis involving a boating accident, and a resolution that brings everybody a lot closer to the realization that life is a precious and fragile thing. Through learning to relate to the young boy, old Fonda learns, belatedly, how to also trust his own daughter and communicate with her: The kid provides Henry with practice at how to be a father. There is eventually the sort of happy ending that some people cry through.

Viewed simply as a stage plot, *On Golden Pond* is so predictable we can almost hear the gears squeaking. Forty-five minutes into the movie, almost everyone in the audience can probably predict more or less what is going to happen to the characters, emotionally.

And yet *On Golden Pond* transcends its predictability and the transparent role of the young boy, and becomes a film with passages of greatness.

This is because of the acting, first of all, but also because Ernest Thompson, who wrote such a formula play, has furnished it with several wonderful scenes. A conversation between old Henry Fonda and young Coleman is an early indication that this is going to be an unusual movie: A man who is forty-five asks a man who is eighty for permission to sleep in the same room with the man's daughter, and after the old man takes the question as an excuse for some cruel putdowns, the conversation takes an altogether unexpected twist into words of simple truth. That is a good scene. So are some of the conversations between Hepburn and Fonda. And so are some remarkable scenes involving the boating accident, in which there is no doubt that Hepburn, at her age, is doing some of her own stunts. It's at moments like this that stardom, acting ability, character, situation—and what the audience already knows about the actors—all come together into an irreplaceable combination.

As everybody knows, this is the first film in which Hepburn and the two Fondas have acted in any combination with one another. Some reviews actually seem to dismiss the casting as a stunt. I believe it adds immeasurably to the film's effect. If Hepburn and Henry Fonda are legends, seen in the twilight of their lives, and if we've heard that Jane and Henry have had some of the same problems offscreen that they have in this story—does that make the movie simple gossip? No, not if the movie deals honestly with the problems, as this one does. As people, they have apparently learned something about loving and caring that, as actors, they are able to communicate, even through the medium of this imperfect script. Watching the movie, I felt I was witnessing something rare and valuable.

On the Edge ★ ★ ★ ½
PG-13, 112 m., 1986 ✓

Bruce Dern (Wes Holman), John Marley (Elmo Glidden), Bill Bailey (Flash), Jim Haynie (Owen Riley). Directed by Rob Nilsson and produced by Jeffrey Hayes and Nilsson. Screenplay by Nilsson.

There is some mention that Wes Holman has been coaching for the last twenty years, but more likely he has been brooding. He is a thin, wiry man with a bushy beard and burning eyes. When we see him for the first time, he is watching some runners race up the side of a mountain. Just by the way he looks at the mountain, we can tell how important it is to him. Of course, the dramatic music doesn't hurt.

As Wes Holman was turning to walk back down the road, I was settling down into my seat, convinced that I was doomed to witness yet another formula sports picture. The film would follow Holman's masochistic training regime, and then the climax would be his amazing comeback and victory. It would all be very predictable, I thought, but I was wrong. On the Edge may have a familiar formula, but it is an angry, original, unpredictable movie. And it's not about winning. It's about the reasons that athletes carry in their hearts after all strength and reason have fled.

The movie stars Bruce Dern, in one of his best performances, as Holman, a great runner who was banned from amateur athletics twenty years ago after he attempted to expose clandestine payoffs to athletes. He was no more dishonest than anyone else, but he rocked the boat, insisting that amateurism in athletics was the way the rich kept the poor from competing.

Now the runner has come back to prove something. He wants to run the Cielo-Sea Race, the second oldest in America, a grueling race over the mountains from Mill Valley to the Pacific. It's a point-to-point race, which means the runner can follow any path he chooses, as long as he passes a few checkpoints. Holman, running in the older-than-forty age group, figures he can win the race, especially if he can persuade his old coach to help him.

The coach is played magnificently by the late John Marley, in his last role. He is one of the two great old men in the movie. The other, playing Holman's father, is the West Coast radical union organizer Bill Bailey, in his first dramatic role. The age shift in this movie is interesting; instead of a kid with a father figure, Holman is a bitter, grown man who wants to prove something once again to the men who were so important to him years ago.

The middle portions of the movie alternate between the training sequences and episodes from Holman's private life. He moves into makeshift quarters on an old dredging boat. He visits his father's junkyard and sits down to eat with a table full of old leftists. He spends time in the bar where his old coach hangs out. The movie creates a real sense of place: These aren't Hollywood locations but rooms where human voices sound at home.

The race is as exciting as it should be. But the ending is something else again. Never mind who wins. At the end, it's not winning that counts. It's making a statement about sports, about why hundreds of people train for a year so that one of them can win and the rest can lose. The last few minutes of On the Edge are surprisingly moving, as the film makes its point with great dramatic images.

On the Edge was directed by Rob Nilsson, whose earlier credits include Northern Lights, the independent film about the farmer-labor movement in Minnesota. Here he combines his politics with adequate financing and creates a powerful movie. What's best about it is that the sports don't overwhelm everything else. Winning is not the only thing for Wes Holman and his friends. Or, to be more precise, placing first is not the same as winning.

On the Road Again ★ ★ ★
PG, 119 m., 1980

Willie Nelson (Buck), Dyan Cannon (Viv), Amy Irving (Lily), Slim Pickens (Garland), Joey Floyd (Jamie), Mickey Rooney, Jr. (Cotton). Directed by Jerry Schatzberg and produced by Sydney Pollack and Gene Taft. Screenplay by Carol Sobieski, William D. Wittliff, and John Binder.

The plot of Willie Nelson's Honeysuckle Rose* is just a slight touch familiar, maybe because it's straight out of your basic country and western song. To wit: The hero, a veteran country singer still poised at the brink of stardom after twenty-five years on the road, won't listen to his wife's pleas that he leave the road and settle down with her and their son. Meanwhile, the band's guitarist, who is also the singer's best friend, retires. A replacement is needed, and the singer hires the best friend's daughter.

She is a shapely young lady who has had a crush on the singer since she was knee-high to a grasshopper. Once they go out on the road again, the singer and the best friend's daughter start sleeping with one another. This situation causes anguish for the singer, the daughter, the best friend, the wife, the son, and the band. But after going down to Mexico to slug back some tequila and think it over, the singer returns to his wife and the best friend's daughter wisely observes: "Anything that hurts this many people can't be right."

This story is totally predictable from the opening scenes of *Honeysuckle Rose*, which is a disappointment; the movie is sly and entertaining, but it could have been better. Still, it has its charms, and one is certainly the presence of Willie Nelson himself, making his starring debut at the age of forty-seven and not looking a day over sixty. He's grizzled, grinning, sweet-voiced and pleasant, and a very engaging actor. (He gave promise of that with a single one-liner in his screen debut in *Electric Horseman*, expressing his poignant desire for the kind of girl who could suck the chrome off a trailer hitch.)

The movie also surrounds Nelson with an interesting cast: Dyan Cannon is wonderful as Willie's long-suffering wife, a sexy fortyish earth-woman with streaked hair and a wardrobe from L.L. Bean. She survives the test of her big scene, an archetypical C&W confrontation in which she charges onstage to denounce her husband and his new girlfriend.

Amy Irving is not quite so well-cast as the girlfriend; she has too many scenes in which she gazes adoringly at Willie—who, on the other hand, hardly ever gazes adoringly at her. Slim Pickens, who should be registered as a national historical place, is great as the best friend. And there is a hilarious bit part, a fatuous country singer, played by Mickey Rooney, Jr.

Mercifully, the movie doesn't drag out its tale of heartbreak into a C&W soap opera. Instead, director Jerry Schatzberg *(Scarecrow)* uses an easy-going documentary style to show us life on the band bus, at a family reunion, and backstage at big concerts. All of these scenes are filled to overflowing with colors; this is one of the cheeriest, brightest looking movies I've ever seen, starting with Willie's own amazing costumes and including the spectrum at the concerts, reunions, picnics, etc. Half the movie seems to be shot during parties, and although we enjoy the texture and detail we sometimes wonder why so little seems to be happening.

The movie remains resolutely at the level of superficial cliché, resisting any temptation to make a serious statement about the character's hard-drinking, self-destructive life-style; this isn't a movie like *Payday*, in which Rip Torn re-created the last days of the dying Hank Williams. *Honeysuckle Rose* has the kind of problems that can be resolved with an onstage reconciliation in the last scene: Willie and Dyan singing a duet together and everybody knowing things will turn out all right.

If there's an edge of disappointment coming out of the movie, maybe it's inspired by that simplicity of approach to complicated problems. Willie Nelson has lived a long time, experienced a lot, and suffered a certain amount on his way to his current success, and my hunch is that he knows a lot more about his character's problems in this movie than he lets on. Maybe the idea was to film the legend and save the man for later.

*Retitled *On the Road Again* for TV and cassette.

Once Upon a Time in America
★ — short version
★ ★ ★ ★ — original version
R, 137 m., 227 m., 1984

Robert De Niro (Noodles), James Woods (Max), Elizabeth McGovern (Deborah), Treat Williams (Jimmy), Tuesday Weld (Carol), Burt Young (Joe). Directed by Sergio Leone and produced by Arnon Milchan. Screenplay by L. Benvenuti, P. De Bernardo, E. Medioli, F. Arcalli, F. Ferrini, Leone, and S. Kaminski.

This was a murdered movie, now brought back to life on cassette. Sergio Leone's *Once*

Upon a Time in America, which in its intended 227-minute version is an epic poem of violence and greed, was chopped by ninety minutes for U.S. theatrical release into an incomprehensible mess without texture, timing, mood, or sense. The rest of the world saw the original film, which I saw at the Cannes Film Festival. In America, a tragic decision was made. When the full-length version (now available in cassette form) played at the 1984 Cannes Film Festival, I wrote:

"Is the film too long? Yes and no. Yes, in the sense that it takes real concentration to understand Leone's story construction, in which everything may or may not be an opium dream, a nightmare, a memory, or a flashback, and that we have to keep track of characters and relationships over fifty years. No, in the sense that the movie is compulsively and continuously watchable and that the audience did not stir or grow restless as the epic unfolded."

The movie tells the story of five decades in the lives of four gangsters from New York City—childhood friends who are merciless criminals almost from the first, but who have a special bond of loyalty to each other. When one of them breaks that bond, or thinks he does, he is haunted by guilt until late in his life, when he discovers that he was not the betrayer but the betrayed. Leone's original version tells this story in a complex series of flashbacks, memories, and dreams. The film opens with two scenes of terrifying violence, moves to an opium den where the Robert De Niro character is seeking to escape the consequences of his action, and then establishes its tone with a scene of great power: A ceaselessly ringing telephone, ringing forever in the conscience of a man who called the cops and betrayed his friends. The film moves back and forth in a tapestry of episodes, which all fit together into an emotional whole. There are times when we don't understand exactly what is happening, but never a time when we don't feel confidence in the film's narrative.

That version was not seen in American theaters, although it is now available on cassette. Instead, the whole structure of flashbacks was junked. The telephone rings once. The poetic transitions are gone. The movie has been wrenched into apparent chronolog-

ical order, scenes have been thrown out by the handful, relationships are now inexplicable, and the audience is likely to spend much of its time in complete bewilderment. It is a great irony that this botched editing job was intended to "clarify" the film.

Here are some of the specific problems with the shortened version. A speakeasy scene comes before a newspaper headline announces that Prohibition has been ratified. Prohibition is then repealed, on what feels like the next day but must be six years later. Two gangsters talk about robbing a bank in front of a woman who has never been seen before in the film; they've removed the scene explaining who she is. A labor leader turns up, unexplained, and involves the gangsters in an inexplicable situation. He later sells out, but to whom? Men come to kill De Niro's girlfriend, a character we've hardly met, and we don't know if they come from the mob or the police. And here's a real howler: At the end of the shortened version, De Niro leaves a room he has never seen before by walking through a secret panel in the wall. How did he know it was there? In the long version, he was told it was there. In the short version, his startling exit shows simple contempt for the audience.

Many of the film's most beautiful shots are missing from the short version, among them a bravura moment when a flash-forward is signaled by the unexpected appearance of a Frisbee, and another where the past becomes the present as the Beatles' "Yesterday" sneaks into the sound track. Relationships are truncated, scenes are squeezed of life, and I defy anyone to understand the plot of the short version. The original *Once Upon a Time in America* gets a four-star rating. The shorter version is a travesty.

One Flew Over the Cuckoo's Nest
★ ★ ★
R, 129 m., 1975

Jack Nicholson (R.P. McMurphy), Louise Fletcher (Nurse Ratched), Will Sampson (The Chief), William Redfield (Harding), Brad Dourif (Billy), Sydney Lassick (Cheswick), Scatman Crothers (Turkle), Dean R. Brooks (Dr. Spivey), Danny DeVito (Martini). Directed by Milos Forman and produced by Saul Zaentz and Michael Douglas.

Screenplay by Lawrence Hauben and Bo Goldman.

Milos Forman's *One Flew Over the Cuckoo's Nest* is a film so good in so many of its parts that there's a temptation to forgive it when it goes wrong. But it does go wrong, insisting on making larger points than its story really should carry, so that at the end, the human qualities of the characters get lost in the significance of it all. And yet there are those moments of brilliance. If Forman was preaching a parable, the audience seemed in total agreement with it, and I found that a little depressing: It's a lot easier to make noble points about fighting the establishment, about refusing to surrender yourself to the system, than it is to closely observe the ways real people behave when they're placed in an environment like a mental institution.

That sort of observation, when it's allowed to happen, is what's best about *One Flew Over the Cuckoo's Nest*. We meet a classic outsider—R.P. McMurphy, a quintessentially sane convict sent to the institution as a punishment for troublemaking—whose charisma and gall allow him to break through to a group of patients who've mostly fallen into a drugged lethargy. Their passive existence is reinforced by the unsmiling, domineering Nurse Ratched, who lines them up for compulsory tranquilizers and then leads them through group therapy in a stupor.

McMurphy has no insights into the nature of mental illness, which is his blessing. He's an extroverted, life-loving force of nature who sees his fellow patients as teammates, and defines the game as the systematic defiance of Nurse Ratched and the system she personifies. In many of the best scenes in the film, this defiance takes the shape of spontaneous and even innocent little rebellions: During exercise period, the patients mill around aimlessly on a basketball court until McMurphy hilariously tries to get a game going.

He also makes bets and outrageous dares, and does some rudimentary political organizing. He needs the votes of ten patients, out of a possible eighteen, to get the ward schedule changed so they can all watch the World Series—and his victory is in overcoming the indifference the others feel not only toward the Series but toward existence itself.

McMurphy is the life force, the will to prevail, set down in the midst of a community of the defeated. And he's personified and made totally credible by Jack Nicholson, in another of the remarkable performances that have made him the most interesting actor to emerge in the last two decades. Nicholson, manically trying to teach basketball to an Indian (Will Sampson) who hasn't even spoken in twelve years, sometimes succeeds in translating the meaning of the movie and Ken Kesey's novel into a series of direct, physical demonstrations.

That's when the movie works, and what it's best at. If Forman had stayed at that level—introducing his characters and making them real, and then seeing how they changed as they bounced off one another—*One Flew Over the Cuckoo's Nest* might have been a great film. It's a good one as it is, but we can see the machinery working. Take, for example, the all-night orgy that finally hands McMurphy over to his doom. He's smuggled booze and broads into the ward, and everyone gets drunk, and then the hapless Billy (Brad Dourif) is cheerfully bundled into a bedroom with a willing girl. Billy stutters so badly he can hardly talk, but he's engaging and intelligent, and we suspect his problems are not incurable. The next morning, as Nurse Ratched surveys the damage, Billy at first defies her (speaking without a stutter, which is too obvious) and then caves in when she threatens to tell his mother what he's done. Nurse Ratched and Billy's mother are old friends, you see (again, too obvious, pinning the rap on Freud and Mom). Billy commits suicide, and we're invited to stand around his pitiful corpse and see the injustice of it all—when all we've really seen is the plot forcing an implausible development out of unwilling subject matter.

Another scene that just doesn't work, because it's too heavily burdened with its purpose, occurs when McMurphy escapes, commandeers a school bus, and takes all the inmates of the ward on a fishing trip in a stolen boat. The scene causes an almost embarrassing break in the movie—it's Forman's first serious misstep—because it's an idealized fantasy in the midst of realism. By now, we've met the characters, we know them in the context of hospital politics, and when they're set down on the boat deck, they just don't belong there. The ward is the arena in which they'll win or lose, and it's not playing fair—to them, as characters—to give them a fishing trip.

Even as I'm making these observations, though, I can't get out of my mind the tumultuous response that *Cuckoo's Nest* received from its original audiences. Even the most obvious, necessary and sobering scenes—as when McMurphy tries to strangle Nurse Ratched to death—were received, not seriously, but with sophomoric cheers and applause. Maybe that's the way to get the most out of the movie—see it as a simple-minded antiestablishment parable—but I hope not. I think there are long stretches of a very good film to be found in the midst of Forman's ultimate failure, and I hope they don't get drowned in the applause for the bad stuff that plays to the galleries.

One from the Heart ★ ★
PG, 98 m., 1982

Frederic Forrest (Hank), Teri Garr (Frannie), Raul Julia (Ray), Nastassja Kinski (Leila), Lainie Kazan (Maggie), Harry Dean Stanton (Moe). Directed by Francis Ford Coppola and produced by Bernard Gersten.

Arriving after two years of sound and fury, after all the news items on the financial pages and alarms and excursions in the movie trade press, Francis Ford Coppola's *One from the Heart* is an interesting production but not a good movie. From Coppola, the brilliant orchestrator of *Apocalypse Now* and the God-father films, it is a major disappointment. This must be the first movie in history to arrive with more publicity about its production techniques than about its stars. Everybody knows that Coppola used experimental video equipment to view and edit his movie, sealing himself into a trailer jammed with electronic gear so that he could see on TV what the camera operator was seeing through the lens. Of course the film itself was photographed on the same old celluloid that the movies have been using forever; Coppola used TV primarily as a device to speed up the process of viewing each shot and trying out various editing combinations. (Or, as an industry wisecrack had it, "He took an $8 million project and used the latest

advances in video to bring it in for $23 million.")

If *One from the Heart* is the sort of film this process inspires, then Coppola should abandon it. But of course the process is neutral; films live or die according to an inner rhythm of their own. The most dismal thing about *One from the Heart* is that it lacks those rhythms. It is a ballet of graceful and complex camera movements occupying magnificent sets, and somehow the characters get lost in the process. There was never a moment in this film when I cared about what was happening to the people in it, and only one moment (a cameo by Allen Goorwitz as an irate restaurant owner) when I felt that an actor's spontaneity was able to sneak past Coppola's smothering style and into the audience.

The storyteller of *The Godfather* has become a technician here. There are chilling parallels between Coppola's obsessive control of this film and the character of Harry Caulfield, the wiretapper in Coppola's *The Conversation* (1973), who cared only about technical results and refused to let himself think about human consequences. Movies are a lot of different things, but most of the best ones are about people and for people, and *One from the Heart* pays little heed to the complexities of the human heart. Indeed, it seems almost on guard against the actors who occupy its carefully architectured scenes. They are hardly ever allowed to dominate. They are figures in a larger pattern, one that diminishes them, that sees them as part of the furniture. They aren't given many close-ups; they're often bathed in garish red glows or sickly blues and greens; they're placed in front of distractingly flamboyant sets or lost in badly choreographed crowds, and sometimes they're cut off in the middle of an emotion or a piece of business because the relentlessly programmed camera has business elsewhere.

I've neglected, in fact, to name the actors, or describe the characters they play. That's not so much of an oversight in a review of a film like this. The two main characters (Teri Garr and Frederic Forrest) inhabit a Las Vegas of disappointment, ennui, and glittering lights. For a brief time, they break out of their humdrum lives and meet new lovers (Raul Julia and Nastassja Kinski) who tease them with dreams and fantasies. The underlying story notion, I suppose, is that ordinary little people have a great night on the town, but the night and the town in Coppola's production so overwhelm them that they remain ordinary little people throughout.

There are small pleasures in this movie. One is Harry Dean Stanton's walk-through as the seedy owner of a junkyard, although Coppola resists showing us Stanton's most effective tool, his expressive eyes. Kinski, as a circus tightrope walker, has a beauty much more mature than in *Tess* and a wonderful moment when she explains "to make a circus girl disappear, all you have to do is blink your eyes." Garr is winsome, but her role makes her thanklessly passive, and Forrest (the Oscar nominee from *The Rose*) is almost transparent here, he's given such a nebbish to play.

One Magic Christmas ★ ★
G, 89 m., 1985

Mary Steenburgen (Ginnie), Gary Basaraba (Jack), Harry Dean Stanton (Gideon the Angel), Arthur Hill (Caleb), Elizabeth Harnois (Abbie), Robbie Magwood (Cal). Directed by Philip Borsos and produced by Peter O'Brien and Fred Roos. Screenplay by Thomas Meehan.

This is very unfortunate. What we have here is a movie with an intelligent screenplay, wonderful performances, and skillful direction, but it is a tactical miscalculation from beginning to end. The name of the movie is *One Magic Christmas*, it comes from the folks at Walt Disney, and although it eventually arrives at a sort of happy ending, first it spends ninety minutes telling a sad, sad story. Since the movie was presumably made for family audiences, why did it have to be about all of the most tragic things that can happen to a family?

Let me make a depressing list of what happens (and if you plan to see the movie, maybe you'd better read no further—unless you are trying to decide whether kids will like it).

The movie is about the Grainger family, Mom and Dad and two kids, who live in a nice house on a nice street in a nice city. Then Dad loses his job. Since they live in a company house, they have to be out by January 1.

That means Christmas season is spent packing and planning to move. Just to make sure we don't miss the point, a Scrooge from the company comes around to show the house to the next people who will be moving in.

Well, at least the Graingers have a little money in the bank. Mr. Grainger (Gary Basaraba) goes to the bank to take out $200 for Christmas presents. But then we meet a desperate man (Wayne Robson) who is also out of work and broke, and who tells his little son to wait for him at the bus station. The man sticks up the bank and shoots Mr. Grainger dead. Then he steals Mr. Grainger's car for the getaway. The Grainger kids, Abbie and Cal, are in the back seat, so they are kidnapped. There is more bad news. The car plunges through a bridge railing, and the kids are drowned. (Meanwhile, the bad man's little boy is presumably still waiting at the bus station—a loose end the movie leaves hanging.)

This is a pretty desperate story for a Christmas movie to be telling. But, to be sure, there is another level to the story. The Graingers' neighborhood is being watched over by the Archangel Gideon (Harry Dean Stanton), who is sad because Mrs. Grainger (the wonderful Mary Steenburgen) does not share the spirit of Christmas. Her lack of faith is sort of what's caused all the family's problems, I guess. And at the end of the movie, after the kids have been resurrected through one of the angel's miracles, Abbie gets to go to the North Pole and meet Santa Claus in person, after which her dad is brought back to life, too.

A lot of love and effort obviously went into this movie. The direction is by Philip Borsos, who made the memorable *Grey Fox*. His images develop a real bittersweet resonance. Steenburgen finds just the right notes as the mom who doesn't believe in Christmas. She isn't mean, just cynical and tired. Arthur Hill is fine as a kindly old great-granddad, and Gary Basaraba has a nice winsome quality as he talks about wanting to open a bicycle repair shop. I am not sure exactly what I think about Harry Dean Stanton's archangel. He is sad-faced and tender, all right, but he looks just like the kind of a guy that our parents told us never to talk to.

Anyway, all of these people work hard and carefully, and produce an intelligent and sensitive movie. For adults and older family members, it will probably work pretty well. But a Disney movie named *One Magic Christmas* will attract little kids, and I don't think too many sugarplums are going to be dancing in their dreams after this one.

$1,000,000 Duck ★
G, 92 m., 1971

Dean Jones (Albert Dooley), Sandy Duncan (Katie Dooley), Tony Roberts (Fred), Lee Montgomery (Jimmy). Directed by Vince McEveety and produced by Bill Anderson. Screenplay by Roswell Rogers.

Walt Disney's *$1,000,000 Duck* is one of the most profoundly stupid movies I've ever seen. It is a movie about a duck that gets an overdose of radiation and starts laying golden eggs. It is also about the people who won the duck, and about how greed and avarice appear in their lives, and about the lesson in love and understanding that the father gets when his son runs away with the duck and becomes trapped on a ladder between the ledges of two tall buildings, and about how the father gets a fair trial from the American judiciary system.

The people in this movie inhabit a universe of clean little 1940s bungalows with rose trellises, and there's a mean neighbor next door and some teen-agers down the street who are always souping up their hot rod. This universe looks vaguely familiar, and you wonder where you've seen it before. It certainly doesn't exist in the current American space-time continuum, but maybe . . . And then you recognize the universe. The reason you had trouble before was that you'd never seen the *whole* universe before, but only its laundry room. This is the universe of those sweet, simple folks who live in TV soap ads. They mean well, poor souls, and they dress neatly and keep a cheery smile, but they must have been shortchanged in the smarts department because all they care about in this life is how white their whites get. At night they have surrealistic dreams in which their towels come out whiter and whiter and whiter until the whole laundry room is filled with dazzling metaphysical sunlight, and (at last!) their towels are clean and their sins forgiven.

The woman in the family in the movie has apparently survived nine years of marriage since she has an eight-year-old son, but her survival must have been a matter of blind luck. She makes applesauce with garlic in it because she doesn't know any better, and she takes a golden egg down to the bank when her checking account gets overdrawn. Being married to such a mentality would be wearing to her husband, you imagine; he is a young scientist engaged in teaching rabbits and ducks to walk down the ramp and through the maze and push the right button and be rewarded with rabbit food or duck food.

There was a Stan Freberg record once about a rat who was put through this ordeal. Over drawbridges. Up ramps. Through doors, past dead ends. Across the moat. Up the ladder. And finally, finally . . . when the exhausted rodent reached his objective and punched the right button, do you know what came out of the little door for him to eat? One single chlorophyl gum ball.

The Onion Field ★ ★ ★ ★
R, 126 m., 1979

John Savage (Karl Hettinger), James Woods (Greg Powell), Franklyn Seales (Jimmy Smith), Ted Danson (Ian Campbell), Ronny Cox (Pierce Brooks), David Huffman (Phil Halpin), Christopher Lloyd (Jailhouse Lawyer), Diane Hull (Helen Hettinger), Priscilla Pointer (Chrissie Campbell). Directed by Harold Becker and produced by Walter Coblenz. Screenplay by Joseph Wambaugh.

Since *The Onion Field* will inevitably inspire comparisons with *In Cold Blood*, we might as well begin with a basic one: Both the book and the film of *In Cold Blood* restructured the order of real events in order to use the actual murders as a climax. The storytellers were having it both ways, by conveying dismay at the killings while at the same time using them for essentially fictional shock value.

The Onion Field does not do that. It is also based on real events—the 1963 kidnappings of Los Angeles police officers Karl Hettinger and Ian Campbell, and the eventual cold-blooded murder of Campbell. But Joseph Wambaugh, who wrote the book and personally controlled the film production, didn't reorder the facts to give us a dramatic burst of gunfire at the end. Instead, he places the deadly event of the murder in an onion field at about where it should occur, midway between the criminal preparations that led up to it and the longest single criminal court case in California history, which lasted more than seven years.

For Wambaugh (himself a former policeman), the trial, too, was a crime—and the fact of Campbell's murder had to be considered in the context of the legal travesties that followed it. That attention to the larger context of the kidnap-killing is one thing that makes The Onion Field so much more than another cop drama. This movie is about people, about how they behave and why, and about how small accidents and miscalculations can place people in situations they never dreamed of. Life is a very fragile thing; The Onion Field knows that in its bones.

The film moves betwen two basic, completely dissimilar, sets of characters: the two police officers, and the two third-rate hoods who would eventually be convicted of the crime. The cops aren't seen in quite the same sharp focus as the criminals—perhaps because, until the night of the onion field, little they had done in their lives had prepared them for what would follow.

Campbell (Ted Danson), the one who is killed, is seen almost as a memory: a tall, good-looking, black-haired Scottish-American with an obsession for bagpipes. Hettinger (John Savage from The Deer Hunter) is seen at the beginning as a cheerful, open-faced young man who will only later, after the onion field, develop very deep hurts and complications.

The hoods are seen more clearly. There's Greg Powell (James Woods), a street-wise smartass with a quick line of talk and an ability to paint situations so other people see them his way. And then there's Jimmy Smith (Franklyn Seales), a disturbed, insecure young black who is a perfect recruit for Powell. They make a suitable team. Powell creates criminal scenarios out of his fantasies; Smith finds them real enough to follow; and in some convoluted way Powell then follows Smith into them.

The Onion Field makes these two characters startlingly convincing: It paints their manners, their speech, their environment,

their indecisions in such a way that we can almost understand them as they blunder stupidly into their crimes.

It never quite captures the personality of Campbell, the man who will be killed, but in the aftermath of the killing it begins to develop disturbing insights into Hettinger, the survivor. In a dozen subtle ways he becomes an outcast in the department (he senses, perhaps correctly, that the other cops wonder how he could allow his partner to be killed). Eventually, punishing himself, seeking guilt, he becomes a shoplifter, and is caught and fired from the force. Savage's handling of a scene of near-suicide, late in the film, is so frightening we can hardly stand to watch it.

Those events take place as The Onion Field explores the bureaucratic nightmare of the criminal courts system. The case dragged on and on and on—Hettinger was called upon to testify in more than six different trials—and plea bargaining, delays, and continuances, and legal loopholes made the case into an impossible (and almost insoluble) tangle.

So there is a lot of ground for The Onion Field to cover. It covers it remarkably well, working both as a narrative and as Wambaugh's cry of protest against the complicated and maddening workings of the courts. The movie is actually a vindication for Wambaugh: He was so displeased with the Hollywood and TV treatments of his novels (especially The Choirboys) that he said he would never let this factual story be made into a movie unless he controlled the production.

He did, and he has made it into a strong and honorable film. His instinct in going with Harold Becker, a commercial director with little previous feature experience, was obviously a good one; the movie's craftsmanship is unobtrusive but fine. And the performances (especially James Woods's as Greg Powell) bring the characters into heartbreaking reality. This is a movie that, once seen, cannot be set aside.

Only When I Laugh ★
R, 120 m., 1981

Marsha Mason (Georgia), Kristy McNichol (Polly), James Coco (Jimmy), Joan Hackett (Toby), David Dukes (David). Directed by Glenn Jordan and produced by Roger M. Rothstein and Neil Simon. Screenplay by Simon.

Neil Simon's *Only When I Laugh* is basically a movie about a woman who is recovering from alcoholism, although the film also provides us with a lonely homosexual, a disturbed teen-ager, a fortyish woman losing her husband, and a *Looking for Mr. Goodbar* scene in which protagonist Marsha Mason is assaulted and raped. It comes billed as one of Neil Simon's "serious" films. That means that it is about serious subjects. It does not mean Simon examines them seriously. The film should have contained half so many problems if he hoped to provide us with insights into them. But Simon uses misfortunes as a way of creating characters. If he can create an "alcoholic," then he doesn't have to create a three-dimensional person for his film. He can just fill out the person's life with predictable crises from the disease. The same with the film's homosexual, who can complain of loneliness, rejection, feelings of inadequacy—can do everything, indeed, except be gay onscreen.

There are times, as a result, when *Only When I Laugh* seems like a series of characters reporting to headquarters. Many of the big moments take place offscreen, and then the movie stars turn up onscreen to tell us about them. Maybe that is not so bad. In the scenes where Simon does try to grapple with his film's issues, he exhibits little understanding. Take, for example, the business of his central character's alcoholism. The movie's heroine, played by Simon's wife, Marsha Mason, is an actress who is just being released from a rehabilitation program when the movie opens. The doctor congratulates her on her wonderful progress. Then she hits the streets, where her entire program for maintaining sobriety seems to consist of (a) keeping up a brave front, (b) looking noble, (c) wallowing in self-pity with the encouragement of her neurotic friends, (d) quickly walking past bars, and

(e) gulping a drink the moment things start to go wrong.

No wonder she gets drunk again. That's predictable, but couldn't Simon have spared us a lapse scene reminiscent of *The Fatal Glass of Beer?* At one point, a glass of wine looms so menacingly on a piano top in the foreground that we think this is a Hitchcock film and that the booze must be poisoned. (In other shots in the same scene, the continuity is so sloppy that the glass disappears from the piano, but never mind.) Simon and Mason must not drink, know little about drinking, and less about how to stop drinking. If Simon had cared enough to look into the subject, he might, given his undeniable comic gifts, have been inspired to write some really good stuff about the joys and pitfalls of sobriety. (Can you imagine a Neil Simon version of an AA meeting?)

But Simon's not that interested in any of the problems he hauls onscreen in *Only When I Laugh.* He'll settle for maudlin mother-daughter confrontations, cozy, clichéd scenes of "understanding" between Mason and her gay friend (James Coco), and histrionics from another friend (Joan Hackett) who comes undone upon turning forty. The only genuine moments amid the phony landscapes of this film come from Kristy McNichol, who turns in a wonderful performance as Mason's daughter. McNichol carries conviction. She suggests the real passions and hurts that her character must feel. The other people in the movie seem to be drawn from superficial medical-advice columns, advice for the lovelorn, and the character insights of popular songs. Anyone consulting this movie for insights into alcoholism would be better off asking a bartender.

Ordinary People ★ ★ ★ ★
R, 125 m., 1980

Donald Sutherland (Calvin), Mary Tyler Moore (Beth), Judd Hirsch (Berger), Timothy Hutton (Conrad), M. Emmet Walsh (Swim Coach), Elizabeth McGovern (Jeannine), Dinah Manoff (Karen). Directed by Robert Redford and produced by Ronald L. Schwary. Screenplay by Alvin Sargent.

Families can go along for years without ever facing the underlying problems in their relationships. But sometimes a tragedy can bring everything out in the open, all of a sudden and painfully, just when everyone's most vulnerable. Robert Redford's *Ordinary People* begins at a time like that for a family that loses its older son in a boating accident. That leaves three still living at home in a perfectly manicured suburban existence, and the movie is about how they finally have to deal with the ways they really feel about one another.

There's the surviving son, who always lived in his big brother's shadow, who tried to commit suicide after the accident, who has now just returned from a psychiatric hospital. There's the father, a successful Chicago attorney who has always taken the love of his family for granted. There's the wife, an expensively maintained, perfectly groomed, cheerful homemaker whom "everyone loves." The movie begins just as all of this is falling apart.

The movie's central problems circle almost fearfully around the complexities of love. The parents and their remaining child all "love" one another, of course. But the father's love for the son is sincere yet also inarticulate, almost shy. The son's love for his mother is blocked by his belief that she doesn't really love him—she only loved the dead brother. And the love between the two parents is one of those permanent facts that both take for granted and neither has ever really tested.

Ordinary People begins with this three-way emotional standoff and develops it through the autumn and winter of one year. And what I admire most about the film is that it really *does* develop its characters and the changes they go through. So many family dramas begin with a "problem" and then examine its social implications in that frustrating semifactual, docudrama format that's big on TV. *Ordinary People* isn't a docudrama; it's the story of these people and their situation, and it shows them doing what's most difficult to show in fiction—it shows them changing, learning, and growing.

At the center of the change is the surviving son, Conrad, played by a wonderfully natural young actor named Timothy Hutton. He is absolutely tortured as the film begins; his life is ruled by fear, low self-esteem, and the

correct perception that he is not loved by his mother. He starts going to a psychiatrist (Judd Hirsch) after school. Things are hard for this kid. He blames himself for his brother's death. He's a semi-outcast at school because of his suicide attempt and hospitalization. He does have a few friends—a girl he met at the hospital, and another girl who stands behind him at choir practice and who would, in a normal year, naturally become his girlfriend. But there's so much turmoil at home.

The turmoil centers around the mother (Mary Tyler Moore, inspired casting for this particular role, in which the character masks her inner sterility behind a facade of cheerful suburban perfection). She does a wonderful job of running her house, which looks like it's out of the pages of *Better Homes and Gardens*. She's active in community affairs, she's an organizer, she's an ideal wife and mother—except that at some fundamental level she's selfish, she can't really give of herself, and she *has*, in fact, always loved the dead older son more. The father (Donald Sutherland) is one of those men who wants to do and feel the right things, in his own awkward way. The change he goes through during the movie is one of the saddest ones: Realizing his wife cannot truly care for others, he questions his own love for her for the first time in their marriage.

The sessions of psychiatric therapy are supposed to contain the moments of the film's most visible insights, I suppose. But even more effective, for me, were the scenes involving the kid and his two teen-age girlfriends. The girl from the hospital (Dinah Manoff) is cheerful, bright, but somehow running from something. The girl from choir practice (Elizabeth McGovern) is straightforward, sympathetic, able to be honest. In trying to figure them out, Conrad gets help in figuring himself out.

Director Redford places all these events in a suburban world that is seen with an understated matter-of-factness. There are no cheap shots against suburban life-styles or affluence or mannerisms: The problems of the people in this movie aren't caused by their milieu, but grow out of themselves. And, like it or not, the participants have to deal with them. That's what sets the film apart from the sophisticated suburban soap opera it could easily have become. Each character in this movie is given the dramatic opportunity to look inside himself, to question his *own* motives as well as the motives of others, and to try to improve his own ways of dealing with a troubled situation. Two of the characters do learn how to adjust; the third doesn't. It's not often we get characters who face those kinds of challenges on the screen, nor directors who seek them out. *Ordinary People* is an intelligent, perceptive, and deeply moving film.

Out of Africa ★ ★ ★ ★
PG, 153 m., 1985

Meryl Streep (Karen), Robert Redford (Denys), Klaus-Maria Brandauer (Bror), Michael Kitchen (Berkeley), Malick Bowens (Farah), Joseph Thiaka (Kamante), Stephen Kinyanjui (Kinyanjui), Michael Gough (Delamere), Suzanna Hamilton (Felicity). Directed and produced by Sydney Pollack. Screenplay by Kurt Luedtke.

Earlier, there was a moment when a lioness seemed about to attack, but did not. The baroness had been riding her horse on the veld, had dismounted, had lost her rifle when the horse bolted. Now the lioness seemed about to charge, when behind her a calm voice advised the baroness not to move one inch. "She'll go away," the voice said, and indeed the lioness did skulk away after satisfying its curiosity.

That scene sets up the central moment in Sydney Pollack's *Out of Africa*, which comes somewhat later in the film. The baroness is on safari with the man who owned the cool voice, a big-game hunter named Denys. They happen upon a pride of lions. Once again, the man assumes charge. He will protect them. But then a lion unexpectedly charges from another direction, and it is up to the baroness to fell it, with one shot that must not miss, and does not. After the man and woman are safe, the man sees that the woman has bitten her lip in anxiety. He reaches out and touches the blood. Then they hold each other tightly.

If you can sense the passion in that scene, then you may share my enjoyment of *Out of Africa*, which is one of the great recent epic romances. The baroness is played by Meryl Streep. The hunter is Robert Redford.

These are high-voltage stars, and when their chemistry is wrong for romances (as Streep's was for *Falling in Love*, and Redford's for *The Natural*), it is very wrong. This time, it is right.

The movie is based on the life and writings of Baroness Karen Blixen, a Danish woman who, despairing that she would be single forever, married her lover's brother, moved to Kenya in East Africa, ran a coffee plantation on the slopes of Kilimanjaro, and later, when the plantation was bankrupt and the dream was finished, wrote books about her experiences under the name Isak Dinesen.

Her books are glories—especially *Out of Africa* and *Seven Gothic Tales*—but they are not the entire inspiration for this movie. What we have here is an old-fashioned, intelligent, thoughtful love story, told with enough care and attention that we really get involved in the passions between the characters.

In addition to the people Streep and Redford play, there is a third major character, Bror, the man she marries, played by Klaus Maria Brandauer. He is a smiling, smooth-faced, enigmatic man, who likes her well enough, after his fashion, but never seems quite equal to her spirit. After he gives her syphilis and she returns to Denmark for treatment, she is just barely able to tolerate his behavior—after all, he did not ask to marry her—until a New Year's Eve when he flaunts his infidelity, and she asks him to move out.

He turns up once more, asking for money, after Redford has moved his things into the baroness's farmhouse. The two men have a classic exchange. Brandauer: "You should have asked permission." Redford: "I did. She said yes."

The movie takes place during that strange blip in history when the countries of East Africa—Kenya, Uganda, the Rhodesias—were attracting waves of European settlers discontented with life at home in the years around World War I. The best land available to them was in the so-called white highlands of Kenya, so high up the air was cooler and there were fewer insects, and some luck could be had with cattle and certain crops.

The settlers who lived there soon settled into a hard-drinking, high-living regime that has been documented in many books and novels; they were sort of "Dallas" crossed with *Mandingo*. The movie steers relatively clear of the social life, except for a scene where Streep is snubbed at the local club, a few other scenes in town, and an extraordinary moment when she goes down on her knees before the British governor to plead for land for the Africans who live on her bankrupt farm.

Before that moment, she has not seemed particularly interested in Africans, except for an old overseer who becomes a close friend (and this is not true to the spirit of her book, where Africans are of great importance to her). Instead, she is much more involved in the waves of passion that sweep over the veld, as Redford passes through her life like a comet on a trajectory of its own.

He wants to move "his things" in, but does not want to move himself in. He wants commitment, but personal freedom. His ambiguity toward her is something like his ambiguity toward the land, which he penetrates with truck and airplane, leading tours while all the time bemoaning the loss of the virgin veld. Because *Out of Africa* is intelligently written, directed, and acted, however, we do not see his behavior as simply willful and spoiled, but as part of the contradictions he needs to stay an individual in a land where white society is strictly regimented.

The Baroness Blixen needs no such shields; she embodies sufficient contradictions on her own. In a land where whites are foreigners, she is a foreign white. She writes and thinks instead of gossiping and drinking. She runs her own farm. She scorns local gossip. In this hunter, she finds a spirit equal to her own, which is eventually the undoing of their relationship.

Out of Africa is a great movie to look at, breathtakingly filmed on location. It is a movie with the courage to be about complex, sweeping emotions, and to use the star power of its actors without apology. Sydney Pollack has worked with Redford before—notably in another big-sky epic, *Jeremiah Johnson*. He understands the special, somewhat fragile mystique of his star, who has a tendency to seem overprotective of his own image. In the wrong hands, Redford can look narcissistic. This time, he seems to have much to be narcissistic about.

Out of the Blue ★ ★ ★ ½
R, 94 m., 1982

Linda Manz (CeBe), Dennis Hopper (Don), Sharon Farrell (Kathy), Raymond Burr (Dr. Brean), Don Gordon (Charlie). Directed by Dennis Hopper and produced by Gary Jules Jouvenat. Screenplay by Leonard Yakir and Brenda Nielson.

Out of the Blue is one of the unsung treasures of independent films, a showcase for the maverick talents of two movie rebels: veteran actor Dennis Hopper, of *Easy Rider* and *Rebel Without a Cause*, and young, tough-talking Linda Manz, whose debut in *Days of Heaven* was so heartbreaking. Made in 1982, it never got a chance in commercial theaters. The movie is Hopper's comeback as a director. After the enormous international success of *Easy Rider* (1969) and the resounding thud of his next directorial effort, *Last Movie* (1971), he didn't direct again until this movie (he acted, in such films as *The American Friend* and *Apocalypse Now*). Originally hired just to act in *Out of the Blue*, he took over two weeks into production, rewrote the screenplay, found new locations and made this movie into a bitter, unforgettable poem about alienation.

Hopper is one of the movie's stars, playing an alcoholic truck driver whose semi-rig crashes into a school bus, kills children, and sends him to jail for six years. Manz plays his daughter, a leather-jacketed, punk teen-ager who combs her hair with shoe polish and does Elvis imitations. Her mother is played by Sharon Farrell as a small-town waitress who tries a reconciliation with Hopper when he gets out of prison but is undercut by her drug addiction. Manz is the centerpiece of the film. As she demonstrated in the magnificent pastoral romance *Days of Heaven*, she has a presence all her own. She's tough and hard-edged and yet vulnerable, and in this movie we can sometimes see the scared little kid beneath the punk bravado. She lives in a world of fantasy. All but barricaded into her room, surrounded by posters of Elvis and other teen heroes, she practices her guitar (she isn't very good) and dresses up in her dad's leather jacket. He's a hero to her. She doesn't buy the story that he was responsible for the deaths of those kids. And when he finally gets out of prison, she has a father at last—but only for a few days.

Hopper's touch as a director is especially strong in a pathetic scene of reunion, including the family's day at the overcast, gloomy beach, and a "party" that turns into a violent brawl dominated by the Hopper character's drunken friend (Don Gordon). The movie escalates so relentlessly toward its violent, nihilistic conclusion that when it comes, we believe it. This is a very good movie that simply got overlooked. When it premiered at the 1980 Cannes Film Festival, it caused a considerable sensation, and Manz was mentioned as a front-runner for the best actress award. But back in North America, the film's Canadian backers had difficulties in making a distribution deal, and the film slipped through the cracks.

The Outlaw Josey Wales ★ ★ ★
PG, 135 m., 1976

Clint Eastwood (Josey), Chief Dan George (The Old Indian), Sondra Locke (The Girl), John Vernon (Fletcher). Directed by Clint Eastwood and produced by Robert Daley. Screenplay by Phil Kaufman.

Clint Eastwood's *The Outlaw Josey Wales* is a strange and daring Western that brings together two of the genre's usually incompatible story lines. On the one hand, it's about a loner, a man of action and few words, who turns his back on civilization and lights out for the Indian nations. On the other hand, it's about a group of people heading West who meet along the trail and cast their destinies together. What happens next is supposed to be against the rules in Westerns, as if *Jeremiah Johnson* were crossed with *Stagecoach:* Eastwood, the loner, becomes the group's leader and father figure.

We meet his character, Josey Wales, just after the Civil War. He's an unreconstructed Southerner, bitter about the atrocities he's witnessed, refusing to surrender. When Northern troops cold-bloodedly murder some of his comrades, he mows down the Yankees with a Gatling gun and becomes a fugitive. So far, we're on familiar ground; Eastwood plays essentially the same character he's been developing since the *Dollar*

Westerns. He says little, keeps his face in the shadows, has an almost godlike personal invulnerability, and lives by a code we have to intuit because he'd die rather than explain it aloud.

But then this character begins to come across other drifters and refugees in the unsettled postwar West. The first is an old Indian, played by Chief Dan George with such wonderfully understated wit that there should have been an Oscar nomination around somewhere. "I myself never surrendered," he explains to Josey Wales. "But they got my horse, and *it* surrendered." George achieves the same magical effect here that he did in *Harry and Tonto*, trading Mixmasters for Indian medicine in a jail cell: He's funny and dignified at once. He joins up with the outlaw Eastwood, and their relationship is a reminder of all those great second bananas from the Westerns of the 1940s—the grizzled old characters played by Gabby Hayes and Smiley Burnette. But Chief Dan George brings an aura to his role that audiences seem to respond to viscerally. He has his problems (he's humiliated, as an Indian, that he's grown so old he can no longer sneak up behind people), but he has a humanity that's just there, glowing. He's as open with his personality as Josey Wales is closed; it's a nice match.

Various, and inexhaustible, bounty hunters are constantly on the outlaw's trail, despite the Eastwood ability (in this movie as before) to wipe out six, eight, ten bad guys before they can get off a shot. Eastwood keeps moving West, picking up along the way a young Indian girl and then the survivors of a Kansas family nearly wiped out on their quest for El Dorado. The relationships in the group are easily established or implied. There's not a lot of talking, but everybody understands each other.

Eastwood is such a taciturn and action-oriented performer that it's easy to overlook the fact that he directs many of his movies—and many of the best, most intelligent ones. Here, with the moody, gloomily beautiful, photography of Bruce Surtees, he creates a magnificent Western feeling.

Pale Rider ★ ★ ★
R, 113 m., 1985

Clint Eastwood (Preacher), Michael Moriarty (Hull Barret), Carrie Snodgress (Sarah Wheeler), Christopher Penn (Josh LaHood), Richard Dysart (Coy LaHood), Sydney Penny (Megan Wheeler), Richard Kiel (Club), Doug McGrath (Spider). Directed and produced by Clint Eastwood. Screenplay by Michael Butler and Dennis Shryack.

Clint Eastwood has become an actor whose moods and silences are so well-known that the slightest suggestion will do to convey an emotion. No actor is more aware of his own instrument, and Eastwood demonstrates that in *Pale Rider*, a film he dominates so completely that only later do we realize how little we really saw of him.

Instead of filling each scene with his own image and dialogue, Eastwood uses sleight of hand: We are shown his eyes, or a corner of his mouth, or his face in a shadow, or his figure with strong light behind it. He has few words. The other characters in the movie project their emotions upon him. He may indeed be the Pale Rider suggested in the title, whose name was death, but he may also be an avenging spirit, come back from the grave to confront the man who murdered him. One of the subtlest things in the movie is the way it plays with the possibility that Eastwood's character may be a ghost, or at least something other than an ordinary mortal.

Other things in the movie are not so subtle. In its broad outlines, *Pale Rider* is a traditional Western, with a story that has been told, in one form or another, a thousand times before. In a small California mining town, some independent miners have staked a claim to a promising lode. The town is ruled by a cabal of evil men, revolving around the local banker and the marshal, who is his hired gun. The banker would like to buy out the little miners, but, lacking that, he will use force to drive them off their land and claim it for his company.

Into this hotbed rides the lone figure of Eastwood, wearing a clerical collar and preferring to be called "Preacher." There are people here he seems to know from before. The marshal, for example, seems to be trying to remember where he has previously

encountered this man. Eastwood moves in with the small miners, and becomes close with one group: a miner (Michael Moriarty) who lives with a woman (Carrie Snodgress) and her daughter (Sydney Penny). He urges the miners to take a stand and defend their land, and agrees to help them. That sets the stage for a series of violent confrontations.

As the film's director, Eastwood has done some interesting things with his vision of the West. Instead of making the miners' shacks into early American antique exhibits, he shows them as small and sparse. The sources of light are almost all from the outside. Interiors are dark and gloomy, and the sun is blinding in its intensity. The Eastwood character himself is almost always backlit, so we have to strain to see him, and this strategy makes him more mysterious and fascinating than any dialogue could have.

There are some moments when the movie's myth-making becomes self-conscious. In one scene, for example, the marshal's gunmen enter a restaurant and empty their guns into the chair where Eastwood had been sitting moments before. He is no longer there; can't they see that? In the final shoot-out, the Preacher has a magical ability to dematerialize, confounding the bad guys, and one shot (of a hand with a gun emerging from a water trough) should have been eliminated—it spoils the logic of the scene. But *Pale Rider* is, overall, a considerable achievement, a classic Western of style and excitement. Many of the greatest Westerns grew out of a director's profound understanding of the screen presence of his actors; consider, for example, John Ford's films with John Wayne and Henry Fonda. In *Pale Rider*, Clint Eastwood is the director, and having directed himself in nine previous films, he understands so well how he works on the screen that the movie has a resonance that probably was not even there in the screenplay.

The Paper Chase ★ ★ ★ ★
PG, 111 m., 1973

Timothy Bottoms (Hart), Lindsay Wagner (Susan), John Houseman (Kingsfield), Graham Beckel (Ford), Edward Herrmann (Anderson), Bob Lydiard (O'Connor). Directed by James Bridges and produced by

Robert C. Thompson and Rodrick Paul.
Screenplay by Bridges.

The Paper Chase is about an aggressive, very bright, terribly engaging first-year student at Harvard Law School. The movie respects its hero, respects the school, and most of all respects the venerable Professor Kingsfield, tyrant of contract law.

Kingsfield is really the movie's central character, even though John Houseman gets supporting billing for the role. Everything centers around his absolute dictatorship in the classroom and his icy reserve at all other times. He's the kind of teacher who inspires total dread in his students, and at the same time a measure of hero worship; he doesn't just know contract law, he wrote the book.

Into his classroom every autumn come several dozen would-be Harvard law graduates, who fall into the categories we all remember from school: (a) the drones, who get everything right but will go forth to lead lives of impeccable mediocrity; (b) the truly intelligent, who will pass or fail entirely on the basis of whether they're able to put up with the crap; (c) those with photographic memories, who can remember everything but connect nothing; (d) the students whose dogged earnestness will somehow pull them through; and (e) the doomed.

One of each of these types is in the study group of Hart, the movie's hero, and the one who is truly intelligent. He's a graduate of the University of Minnesota and somewhat out of place among the Ivy League types, but he does well in class because he really cares about the law. He also cares about Kingsfield, to the degree that he breaks into the library archives to examine the master's very own undergraduate notes.

Hart is played by Timothy Bottoms, the star of *The Last Picture Show*. Bottoms is an awfully good actor, and so natural and unaffected that he shows up the mannerisms of actors like Dustin Hoffman or Jon Voight. Bottoms never seems to try; he's just there, complete and convincing. He falls in love, fatefully, with Susan (Lindsay Wagner), who turns out to be, even more fatefully, Kingsfield's daughter. Their relationship is a little hard to follow in the film; we aren't sure why she treats him the way she does—after all, she loves the guy—and the movie jerks abruptly in bringing them back together after a split-up.

But that isn't fatal because the fundamental relationship in the movie is between Hart and Kingsfield. The crusty old professor obviously appreciates the intelligence and independence of his prize student, but he hardly ever lets his affection show; there's a great scene in the classroom where he calls Hart forward, offers him a dime, and says: "Call your mother and tell her you will never be a lawyer." Houseman is able to project subtleties of character even while appearing stiff and unrelenting; it's a performance of Academy Award quality, and resulted in an Oscar for Best Supporting Actor.

Lindsay Wagner, as the daughter, is also a surprise; she made her movie debut in the unfortunate *Two People*, which had Peter Fonda as a conscience-stricken Army deserter. She wasn't able to make much of an impression in that one, but *The Paper Chase* establishes her as an actress with class and the saving grace of humor.

What's best about the movie is that it considers interesting adults—young and old—in an intelligent manner. After it's over we almost feel relief; there are so many movies about clods reacting moronically to romantic and/or violent situations. But we hardly ever get movies about people who seem engaging enough to spend half an hour talking with (what would you say to Charles Bronson?). Here's one that works.

Paris, Texas ★ ★ ★ ★
R, 145 m., 1984

Harry Dean Stanton (Travis), Nastassja Kinski (Jane), Hunter Carson (Their Son), Dean Stockwell (Walt), Aurore Clement (Anne), Bernhard Wicki (Dr. Ulmer). Directed by Wim Wenders and produced by Don Guest. Screenplay by Sam Shepard.

A man walks alone in the desert. He has no memory, no past, no future. He finds an isolated settlement where the doctor, another exile, a German, makes some calls. Eventually the man's brother comes to take him back home again. Before we think about this as the beginning of a story, let's think about it very specifically as the first twenty minutes of a movie. When I was watching *Paris, Texas* for the first time, my immediate reaction to the film's opening scenes was one of intrigue: I had no good guesses about where this movie was headed, and that, in itself, was exciting, because in this most pragmatic of times, even the best movies seem to be intended as predictable consumer products. If you see a lot of movies, you can sit there watching the screen and guessing what will happen next, and be right most of the time. That's not the case with *Paris, Texas*. This is a defiantly individual film, about loss and loneliness and eccentricity. We haven't met the characters before in a dozen other films. To some people, that can be disconcerting; I've actually read reviews of *Paris, Texas* complaining because the man in the desert is German, and that another character is French. Is it written that the people in movies have to be Middle Americans, like refugees from a sitcom?

The characters in this movie come out of the imagination of Sam Shepard, the playwright of rage and alienation, and Wim Wenders, a West German director who often makes "road movies," in which lost men look for answers in the vastness of great American cities. The lost man is played this time by Harry Dean Stanton, the most forlorn and angry of all great American character actors. We never do find out what personal cataclysm led to his walk in the desert, but as his memory begins to return, we learn how much he has lost. He was married, once, and had a little boy. The boy has been raised in the last several years by Stanton's brother (Dean Stockwell) and sister-in-law (Aurore Clement). Stanton's young wife (Nastassja Kinski) seems to have disappeared entirely in the years of his exile. The little boy is played by Hunter Carson, in one of the least affected, most convincing juvenile performances in a long time. He is more or less a typical American kid, despite the strange adults in his life. He meets Stanton and accepts him as a second father, but of course he thinks of Stockwell and Clement as his family. Stanton has a mad dream of finding his wife and putting the pieces of his past back together again. He goes looking, and finds Kinski behind the one-way mirror of one of those sad sex emporiums where men pay to talk to women on the telephone. *Paris, Texas* is more concerned with exploring emotions than with telling a story.

This isn't a movie about missing persons, but about missing feelings. The images in the film show people framed by the vast, impersonal forms of modern architecture; the cities seem as empty as the desert did in the opening sequence. And yet this film is not the standard attack on American alienation. It seems fascinated by America, by our music, by the size of our cities, and a land so big that a man like the Stanton character might easily get misplaced. Stanton's name in the movie is Travis, and that reminds us not only of Travis McGee, the private eye who specialized in helping lost souls, but also of lots of American Westerns in which things were simpler, and you knew who your enemy was. It is a name out of American pop culture, and the movie is a reminder that all three of the great German New Wave directors—Herzog, Fassbinder, and Wenders—have been fascinated by American rock music, American fashions, American mythology.

This is Wenders's fourth film shot at least partly in America (the others were *Alice in the Cities*, *The American Friend*, and *Hammett*). It also bears traces of *Kings of the Road*, his German road movie in which two men meet by chance and travel for a time together, united by their mutual inability to love and understand women. But it is better than those movies—it's his best work so far—because it links the unforgettable images to a spare, perfectly heard American idiom. The Sam Shepard dialogue has a way of allowing characters to tell us almost nothing about themselves, except for their most banal beliefs and their deepest fears.

Paris, Texas is a movie with the kind of passion and willingness to experiment that was more common fifteen years ago than it is now. It has more links with films like *Five Easy Pieces* and *Easy Rider* and *Midnight Cowboy*, than with the slick arcade games that are the box office winners of the 1980s. It is true, deep, and brilliant.

A Passage to India ★ ★ ★ ★
PG, 160 m., 1984

Judy Davis (Adela Quested), Victor Banerjee (Dr. Aziz), Peggy Ashcroft (Mrs. Moore), Alec Guinness (Godbole) James Fox (Fielding), Nigel Havers (Ronny Heaslop).

Directed by David Lean and produced by John Brabourne and Richard Goodwin. Screenplay by Lean.

"Only connect!"—E.M. Forster

That is the advice he gives us in *Howard's End*, and then, in *A Passage to India*, he creates a world in which there are no connections, where Indians and Englishmen speak the same language but do not understand each other, where it doesn't matter what you say in the famous Marabar Caves, since all that comes back is a hollow, mocking, echo. Forster's novel is one of the literary landmarks of this century, and now David Lean has made it into one of the greatest screen adaptations I have ever seen.

Great novels do not usually translate well to the screen. They are too filled with ambiguities, and movies have a way of making all their images seem like literal fact. *A Passage to India* is especially tricky, because the central event in the novel is something that happens offstage, or never happens at all—take your choice. On a hot, muggy day, the eager Dr. Aziz leads an expedition to the Marabar Caves. One by one, members of the party drop out, until finally only Miss Quested, from England, is left. And so the Indian man and the British woman climb the last path alone, at a time when England's rule of India was based on an ingrained, semiofficial racism, and some British, at least, nodded approvingly at Kipling's "East is East, and West is West, and never the twain shall meet."

In Forster's novel, it is never clear exactly what it was that happened to Miss Quested after she wandered alone into one of the caves. David Lean's film leaves that question equally open. But because he is dealing with a visual medium, he cannot make it a mystery where Dr. Aziz is at the time; if you are offstage in a novel, you can be anywhere, but if you are offstage in a movie, you are definitely not where the camera is looking. So in the film version we know, or think we know, that Dr. Aziz is innocent of the charges later brought against him—of the attempted rape of Miss Quested.

The charges and the trial fill the second half of Lean's *A Passage to India*. Lean brings us to that point by a series of perfectly modulated, quietly tension-filled scenes in which Miss Quested (Judy Davis) and the kindly Mrs. Moore (Peggy Ashcroft) sail to India, where Miss Quested is engaged to marry the priggish local British magistrate in a provincial backwater. Both women want to see the "real India"—a wish that is either completely lacking among the locals, or is manfully repressed. Mrs. Moore goes walking by a temple pool by moonlight, and meets the earnest young Dr. Aziz, who is captivated by her gentle kindness. Miss Quested wanders by accident into the ruins of another temple, populated by sensuous and erotic statuary, tumbled together, overgrown by vegetation.

Miss Quested's temple visit is not in Forster, but has been added by Lean (who wrote his own screenplay). It accomplishes just what it needed, suggesting that in Miss Quested the forces of sensuality and repression run a great deal more deeply than her sexually constipated fiancé is ever likely to suspect. Meanwhile, we meet some of the other local characters, including Dr. Godbole (Alec Guinness), who meets every crisis with perfect equanimity, and who believes that what will be, will be. This philosophy sounds like recycled fortune cookies but turns out, in the end, to have been the simple truth. We also meet Fielding (James Fox), one of those tall, lonely middle-aged Englishmen who hang about the edges of stories set in the Empire, waiting until their destiny commands them to take a firm stand.

Lean places these characters in one of the most beautiful canvases he has ever drawn (and this is the man who directed *Dr. Zhivago* and *Lawrence of Arabia*). He doesn't see the India travel posters and lurid postcards, but the India of a Victorian watercolorist like Edward Lear, who placed enigmatic little human figures here and there in spectacular landscapes that never seemed to be quite finished. Lean makes India look like an amazing, beautiful place that an Englishman can never quite put his finger on—which is, of course, the lesson Miss Quested learns in the caves.

David Lean is a meticulous craftsman, famous for going to any lengths to make every shot look just the way he thinks it should. His actors here are encouraged to give sound, thoughtful, unflashy performances (Guinness strains at the bit), and his screenplay is a model of clarity: By the end of this movie we know these people so well, and understand them so thoroughly, that only the most reckless among us would want to go back and have a closer look at those caves.

Patton ★ ★ ★ ★
PG, 171 m., 1970

George C. Scott (Patton), Karl Malden (Bradley), Stephen Young (Captain Hansen), Michael Strong (General Carver), Karl Michel Vogler (Rommel), Michael Bates (Montgomery). Directed by Franklin J. Schaffner and produced by Frank McCarthy. Screenplay by Francis Ford Coppola.

We have all of these things buried inside of us, waiting for a movie like *Patton* to release them. The reflex patriotism of World War II is still there, we discover, Vietnam has soured us on war, but not on that war. There is a small corner of our being that will always be thrilled by Patton's dash across Europe after the Germans, and we are still a little bit in admiration of heroes on his arrogant scale. And that is why, make no mistake, *Patton* is not an antiwar film. If I read one, I read half a dozen tortuous liberal rationalizations for this movie, written by people who liked it but felt guilty afterward. *Patton* is really against war, they said; by taking us almost inside the soul of the most fanatically military of all America's generals, *Patton* was supposed to fill us with distaste for militarism. It does not, of course. But neither is it a very hawklike movie. It is such an extraordinarily intelligent film, so sure of its purpose, that it makes war its medium but not its subject. It is not about war but about Patton at war, and it is one of the best screen biographies ever made.

Patton once said something to the effect that war was the supreme human activity because it forced men to operate at the ultimate limit of their abilities. This is not a very good justification for war, but it is a supreme test for men, and the action in *Patton* all takes place at the delicate balance point where the war meets the man. That was a basically brilliant idea in Francis Ford Coppola's original screenplay, but what makes it work so well in *Patton* is the performance of George C. Scott. He is absorbed into the role, and com-mands it. He is such a good actor that the movie doesn't have to explain a lot of things; we feel we know Patton and so we're sure of our footing. That's good, because it frees director Franklin J. Schaffner from a lot of cluttering props and plot lines. *Patton* is almost three hours long but it is a surprisingly uncomplicated movie, telling its story with clean, simple scenes and shots. Schaffner is at home here; one of the best things about his *Planet of the Apes* was the simplicity of style he found for it. If *Planet* had gotten complicated, we would have laughed at it.

The simplicity of *Patton* does not lead to any loss of subtlety; just the reverse. Because we are freed from those semiobligatory junk scenes that clutter up most war movies (the wife at home, the "human interest" drained from ethnic character actors, the battle scenes that are allowed to run too long because they cost so much) we can concentrate on the man, and we can even begin to believe we understand a warrior like this one. Because it's no good being hypocritical, I guess. Generals should be generals, and not lovable quasi-political figures like Ike or MacArthur. Patton's life was war (and how sad that really was) but he was honest enough to admit it, and the movie takes its stand on that point. And so although we deplore war we find ourselves respecting the movie; *Patton* is written and directed with integrity.

Beyond that, it's an awfully good movie, and one of its best features is the way it gets its laughs. There aren't any cheap laughs in *Patton*, but there are a lot of earned ones, all serving to flesh in our idea of this brilliant, obsessed man. And a lot of the humor is simply there, embodied in the Scott performance. It turns out *Patton* is exactly the war movie we didn't realize how much we wanted to see.

Pennies from Heaven ★ ★
R, 107 m., 1981

Steve Martin (Arthur), Bernadette Peters (Eileen), Christopher Walken (Tom), Jessica Harper (Joan), Vernel Barneris (Accordion Man). Directed by Herbert Ross and produced by Nora Kay and Ross. Screenplay by Dennis Potter.

Pennies from Heaven is dazzling and disappointing in equal measure. It's a musical with an idea, and ideas usually have been deadly to the musical, that most gloriously heedless of movie genres. The idea this time is that there was a great contrast between the grim reality of the Depression era, and the mindless song-and-dance of the era's favorite escapist entertainment, the musical. Well, so there was, and *viva la difference*.

Pennies from Heaven illustrates its insight by setting up a brutal constrast between its dramatic scenes and its musical numbers. The story in this film is relentlessly downbeat, cruel, and occasionally twisted: A miserable marriage leads to a cheerless love affair, both based on the sexual humiliation of women. Then, just as we are primed to hurl ourselves out of the window, the characters undergo a transmogrification into inhabitants of an upbeat 1930s musical. The voices of Bing Crosby, Connie Boswell, Fred Astaire, and other Depression recording artists issue from their mouths, and they dance their way through the most dazzling production numbers since Busby Berkeley.

The movie keeps cutting back and forth between its mean-spirited narrative and the empty-headed perfection of its musical numbers until we're as dispirited as the characters. We get it: Nothing is real except pain, and anyone who dares to sing "Let's Face the Music and Dance" is sooner or later going to have to face the music. It is the structure of *Pennies from Heaven* that works most fatally against the film. A few key scenes contrasting grim reality and movie escapism would have made the point, but two hours of contrast simply destroy our ability to get into the movie and enjoy it. The movie constantly shatters its own reality—which is, admittedly, a daring thing for a $25 million musical to do, but in this case is not a very good idea.

Original ads placed the emphasis on the movie's musical numbers and its stars, especially sheet music salesman Steve Martin and his schoolteacher mistress, Bernadette Peters (there was less emphasis on Jessica Harper, who plays Martin's desperately hapless wife). Hollywood is always pragmatic in these matters: If the filmmakers haven't made the film the studio had in mind, the studio simply advertises the film they wish had been made. That led to some thoroughly puzzled audiences, as Martin fans lined up for a wild and crazy musical and discovered they were in a musical that wanted to subvert musicals. Some of the scenes in *Pennies from Heaven* are very hard to take, especially one in which Harper pathetically tries to cater to Martin's favorite fetish, which is lipstick on the nipples; this is the most embarrassing and gratuitously cruel scene I've seen in a long time.

On the other hand, *Pennies* also contains musical scenes that are wonderfully entertaining, even if the movie has a way of ending them with emotional crash landings. The choreography has been referred to as a Busby Berkeley parody, but it's not parody, it's homage, and never have I seen such well-drilled troupes of chorus girls, song-and-dance men, and even well-scrubbed little toddlers lined up at dozens of baby grand pianos.

The production values in this movie are superb, and it's great to look at, not only during the musical interludes but even in the dramatic moments. Many of the compositions are borrowed from famous paintings or photographs of the time.

The problem is, *Pennies from Heaven* is all flash and style and no heart. That's the problem with the Steve Martin performance, too: He provides a technically excellent performance that does not seem to be inhabited by a person. Bernadette Peters has a winning way with the schoolteacher, all curls and sweetness and shattered hopes, but the emotional reality of the other characters is consistently undermined by the movie's lame-brained determination to interrupt each happy moment with a grim one, and vice versa, until we're emotionally shellshocked. Just imagine if the creativity, energy, work, talent, and money that went into *Pennies from Heaven* had been devoted instead to a cheerful film on the same topic. Boy, would we need it now.

Perfect ★ ½
R, 120 m., 1985

John Travolta (Adam), Jamie Lee Curtis (Jessie), Jann Wenner (Mark Roth), Anne De Salvo (Frankie), Marilu Henner (Sally), Laraine Newman (Linda), Matthew Reed (Roger), Kenneth Welsh (McKenzie).

Produced and directed by James Bridges.
Screenplay by Aaron Latham and Bridges.

They say you never enjoy a movie about a
subject you know something about. You
keep spotting the flaws instead of enjoying
the story. Maybe that's my problem with
Perfect, a movie that is about journalism and
health clubs. I know something about journalism and nothing about health clubs, and I
hated the movie's journalism scenes, but I
thought Jamie Lee Curtis was really hot as
the aerobics instructor.

The movie stars John Travolta as a *Rolling
Stone* reporter who goes to Los Angeles to
research an article about health clubs as the
singles bars of the 1980s. At the same time,
he's doing an exclusive interview with a
white-collar criminal who bears a strong
resemblance to John DeLorean. In L.A., at
a health club called the Sports Connection,
he meets Jamie Lee Curtis, falls in love with
her, and tries to interview her. But she's been
burned before by investigative reporters,
and she won't talk to him. Their courtship
turns into a protracted agony for them, and
for the viewer. They like each other. They
have a lot in common. They go out on a date,
Travolta produces the tape recorder. She gets
mad at him and goes home. They make up.
They kiss. His tape recorder is on. She
throws him out of her car. They start talking
again. And so on, endlessly as Travolta plays
the first reporter in history who would rather
boogie with his Sony than with Jamie Lee
Curtis.

The Travolta character is inspired by
Aaron Latham, a *Rolling Stone* reporter who
wrote the "Urban Cowboy" article for *Rolling Stone,* and recycled it into the Travolta
movie of the same name. The director of
both films is James Bridges. The reason the
Latham-Travolta-Bridges combination
doesn't work this time is that the material
hasn't been transformed into fiction. With
Urban Cowboy, the filmmakers used
Latham's articles to make a movie about an
urban cowboy. With *Perfect*, we get a movie
about the writing of the articles. If they'd
gone one step further, eliminated the scenes
about the journalism, and made the movie
about the Jamie Lee Curtis character, the
formula might have worked again.

Instead, the movie scurries distractingly

from one subplot to another. There are
three: (1) the Travolta-Curtis relationship,
with a backdrop of health clubs; (2) the
McKenzie case, about a businessman busted
for drug sales; and (3) the *Rolling Stone*
scenes, with the magazine's publisher, Jann
Wenner, playing himself. The stuff about the
businessman feels shoehorned into an overcrowded plot, and could have been eliminated. The *Rolling Stone* material is
distracting because the Wenner character
behaves in such a shockingly unethical manner that if he weren't in the movie, he'd be
suing it. (At one point, he orders Travolta's
article to be totally rewritten and sensationalized, without the knowledge or con-
sent of the author.)

The movie's strategic mistake is to be
about journalism instead of about health
clubs. Its most interesting scenes involve
people from the Sports Connection (or the
"Sports Erection," as Travolta nicknames
it). We meet a busty brunette (Marilu Henner) who's the star of the club's social whirl;
an insecure young woman (Laraine Newman) who believes that aerobics and plastic
surgery could someday make her "perfect";
and an assortment of other body worshipers
who are most comfortable in front of mirrors. Curtis is a queen in this world; as the
club's most popular aerobics instructor, she
has a circle of groupies and commands a bigger salary.

When the movie deals with the little universe inside the health club, it's fascinating—especially when Jamie Lee is onscreen,
because of her electrifying performance.
Travolta can also be electrifying, but his performance is so laid-back it doesn't much
matter; he seems to be doing a Carl Bern-
stein/Dustin Hoffman number. Cub reporters are warned not to make themselves the
stars of their stories. *Perfect* needed the same
advice.

Performance ★ ★ ½
R, 105 m., 1970

James Fox (Charles), Mick Jagger (Turner),
Anita Pallenberg (Pherber), Michele Breton
(Lucy), Ann Sidney (Dana), John Bindon
(Moody). Directed by Donald Cammell and
Nicolas Roeg. Screenplay by Cammell.

Performance is a bizarre, disconnected

attempt to link the inhabitants of two kinds of London underworlds: pop stars and gangsters. It isn't altogether successful, largely because it tries too hard and doesn't pace itself to let its effects sink in. But it does have a kind of frantic energy, and it introduced Mick Jagger in a role that reinforced his stage image without copying it. The movie is really about images anyway. On its most fundamental plot level, it's about a gangster (James Fox) who is trying to disguise himself so that he can slip out of England on a forged passport. He meets the Jagger character by accident when he takes a basement room in a boarding house.

Jagger is introduced as a top star of two or three years ago who has "retired" and hidden away to work on his memoirs or something. Mostly he seems to have submerged himself in a hedonistic existence with two girls, a variety of drugs, and a cloying assortment of Eastern artifacts. Almost every shot in his apartment is aimed past candles, incense, wall hangings, tapestries, and all that, and half the time we're even getting the Turkish rug reflected in the mirror.

This is not exactly the environment your everyday white-collar gangster feels at home in, but Fox plays a strange character who never feels at home anywhere. His workaday style is to beat and threaten potential "protection" customers. But despite his enthusiasm, he isn't really accepted even by the boss (every gangster has a boss) and his associates. So Jagger's little corner of London seems much like any other to him, affording a hideout until he can get the passport and fly to New York. Alas, Jagger doesn't see it that way, and over the course of a day or two, the gangster is sucked down into a psychedelic whirlpool with Jagger and the two girls. One of them feeds him a hallucinogenic mushroom, after which the other dresses him in the unisex clothes they all wear, and then we get a lot of obligatory psychedelic photography showing the poor guy losing his identity, or his values, or in any event his inclination to escape.

The movie is so nervously edited that it doesn't stay around to develop the effects it introduces. That was a tendency with many semi-experimental British films of the early seventies; they were so concerned with reminding us they're movies that they don't do the work movies should. The first half of the movie is especially distracting. But after the gangster and the pop star meet, the editing and the story settle into a kind of consistency.

The surprise of the movie, and the reason to see it, is Mick Jagger's performance. It isn't simply good; it's a comment on his life and style. The ads emphasized his unisex appearance, and the role does so even more. When he slicks back his hair during a psychedelic fantasy, and seems to adopt the gangster's lifestyle, we're looking at acting insights of a very complex psychological order. Other than that, the movie is neither very good nor very bad. Interesting.

Personal Best ★ ★ ★ ★
R, 124 m., 1982

Mariel Hemingway (Chris Cahill), Patrice Donnelly (Tory Skinner), Scott Glenn (Coach), Kenny Moore (Denny Stites). Directed and produced by Robert Towne. Screenplay by Towne.

Robert Towne's *Personal Best* tells the story of two women who are competitors for pentathlete berths on the 1980 U.S. Olympics team—the team that did not go to Moscow. The women are attracted to one another almost at first sight, and what begins as a tentative exploration develops into a love relationship. Then the romance gets mixed up with the ferocity of top-level sports competition.

What distinguishes *Personal Best* is that it creates *specific* characters—flesh-and-blood people with interesting personalities, people I cared about. *Personal Best* also seems knowledgeable about its two subjects, which are the weather of these women's hearts, and the world of Olympic sports competition.

It is a movie containing the spontaneity of life. It's about living, breathing, changeable people and because their relationships seems to be so deeply felt, so important to them, we're fascinated by what may happen next. The movie stars Mariel Hemingway and Patrice Donnelly as the two women track stars, Scott Glenn as their coach, and Kenny Moore as the Olympic swimmer who falls in love with Hemingway late in the film. These four people are so right for the roles it's almost scary; it makes us sense the difference between performances that are technically excellent and other performances, like these, that may sometimes be technically rough but always find the correct emotional note.

Mariel Hemingway plays a young, naive natural athlete. We sense that she always has been under the coaching thumb of her father, a perfectionist, and that her physical excellence has been won at the cost of emotional maturity. She knows everything about working out, and next to nothing about her heart, her sexuality, her own identity. She loses an important race at a preliminary meet, is sharply handled by the father, gets sick to her stomach, is obviously emotionally distraught.

Patrice Donnelly, as a more experienced athlete, tries to comfort the younger girl. In a dormitory room that night, they talk. Donnelly shares whatever wisdom she has about training and running and winning. They smoke a joint. They kid around. They arm wrestle. At this point, watching the film, I had an interesting experience. I did not already know that the characters in the film were homosexual, but I found myself thinking that the scene was so erotically charged that, "if Hollywood could be honest," it would develop into a love scene. Just then, it did! "This is scary," Donnelly says, and then she kisses Hemingway, who returns the kiss.

Personal Best is not simply about their romance, however, It is about any relationship in which the trust necessary for love is made to compete with the total egotism necessary for championship sports. *Can* two people love each other, and at the same time compete for the same berth on an Olympic team? Scott Glenn, the coach, doesn't think so. He accepts the fact of his two stars' homosexuality, but what bothers him is a suspicion that Donnelly may be using emotional blackmail to undercut Hemingway's performance.

This is a very physical movie, one of the healthiest and sweatiest celebrations of physical exertion I can remember. There is a lot of nudity in the film—not only erotic nudity, although there is some of that, but also locker room and steam room nudity, and messing around nudity that has an unashamed, kidding freshness to it. One scene that shocks some viewers occurs between Mariel Hemingway and Kenny Moore, when he gets up to go to the bathroom and she decides to follow along; the scene is typical of the kind of unforced, natural spontaneity in the whole film. The characters in *Personal Best* seem to be free to have real feelings. It is filled with the uncertainties, risks, cares, and rewards of real life, and it considers its characters' hearts and minds, and sees their sexuality as an expression of their true feelings for each other.

Phar Lap ★ ★ ★
PG, 107 m., 1985

Tom Burlinson (Tommy Woodcock), Ron Liebman (Dave Davis), Martin Vaughan (Harry Telford), Judy Morris (Bea Davis), James Steele (Jim Pike), Celia de Burgh (Vi Telford), Georgia Carr (Emma). Directed by Simon Wincer and produced by John Sexton. Screenplay by David Williamson.

For ordinary people, *Phar Lap* sounds less like a racehorse than like a great little Thai restaurant. That's probably why this intelligent, exciting movie sat on the shelf for two years. It has a title that makes your eyes go out of focus.

Phar Lap tells the story of a horse that ran too fast for its own good, and died in 1932 under circumstances that are still controversial in the world of racing. Bought cheap in New Zealand as a colt by a trainer who thought the horse had good bloodlines, Phar Lap lost his first four races and then began to win. Urged on by a stable boy who loved him, the horse came to dominate Australian racing so completely that the gamblers grew restless: How could you make money on a race that wasn't really a contest?

The horse was raced carrying more and more weight, but continued to win, and on one unlucky weekend bankrupted half the bookies in Sydney. It became clear that Phar Lap was simply too good to continue racing in Australia, and the racing establishment complained about his "freakish" speed. His owner decided to bring the horse to the Northern Hemisphere for the richest race in the world, in Agua Caliente, Mexico. And then the threats began from the American underworld: A horse that was "too good" would not make for good horse races.

The movie tells this story while avoiding the usual clichés that encumber all racing pictures (the film, for example, does *not* end with a big race). It also avoids some of the human clichés that seem to surround all movie horses. Phar Lap's first trainer, for example, is a man who has the foresight and faith to stick with the horse, but is nevertheless such a mean taskmaster that the horse will not win for him. The stable boy (Tom Burlinson), who *can* communicate with the horse, does so not simply with heart, but also with a good deal of calculation. And the horse's owner (Ron Leibman) pulls off the neat trick of throwing one race and still remaining sort of a semihero.

Phar Lap is unique among racehorse movies because it gives real attention to the lore and knowledge of trainers. The horse is seen not as some sort of heroic, lovable demigod, but as a gifted animal whose speed creates all sorts of tactical problems. The movie is about a lot more than whether Phar Lap will win the big race, and the movie's human stories deal directly with the horse; even the trainer's romance is seen, not as a distraction from the story, but as part of it.

Phar Lap is the most expensive movie ever made in Australia, where the horse's name is still remembered and where the movie cleaned up at the box office. If it had been given a different title, the movie might have had a chance here; it's part of the recent tradition of quality films from Australia, beautifully photographed, well acted, not insulting to our intelligence. But who ever heard of going to see a movie named *Phar Lap?*

Picnic at Hanging Rock ★ ★ ★ ½
PG, 110 m., 1980

Rachel Roberts (Miss Appleyard), Dominic Guard (Fitzhubert), Helen Morse (Dianne), Jacki Weaver (Minnie). Directed by Peter Weir and produced by James and Hal McElroy. Screenplay by Cliff Green.

Peter Weir's *Picnic at Hanging Rock* has something of the same sense of mystery and buried terror as Antonioni's *L'Aventura*— another film about a sudden and disquieting disappearance. But it's more lush and seductive than Antonioni's spare black-and-white images: Weir films an Australian landscape that could be prehistoric, that suggests that men have not come this way before . . . and that, quite possibly, they should not have come this time.

"This time" is 1900, when much of Australia remained unseen by European eyes, but when a staid and proper version of European culture had been established at such places as Appleyard College, presented here as a boarding school for proper young ladies. As is almost always the case in movies about proper boarding schools, an undercurrent of repressed sexuality runs through Appleyard, and especially through the person of its headmistress (Rachel Roberts).

We get a preliminary sense of that in the film's opening scenes, which show several of the young ladies preparing to spend the day picnicking at nearby Hanging Rock, a geological outcropping from time immemorial. And then there is the picnic itself, with the girls in their bonnets and parasols and immaculate white dresses, dappled in sunlight.

The film moves here at a deliberately lazy pace. The sun beats down, insects drone— and four of the young ladies, having climbed halfway up into the rock passages, are overcome by torpor. When they awake, three of them climb farther on, never to be seen again. The fourth, badly frightened, returns to the main group. A search is set into motion, and the local constable questions witnesses who saw the young girls later on in the day, but the mystery of their disappearance remains unsolved.

It's that very inconclusiveness, linked with later scenes in which the cruel nature of the headmistress is developed, that make *Picnic at Hanging Rock* so haunting. What's going on here, we ask, knowing there is no possible answer and half-pleased by the enigma. The film opens itself to our interpretations: Is the disappearance a punishment, real or imagined, for the girls' stirring sexuality? Is it a rebuke from the ancient landscape against the brash inroads of civilization? Or is it, as it was in the famous

Antonioni film, a statement of nihilism: These people have disappeared, so might we, it all matters nothing, life goes on meaninglessly. *Picnic at Hanging Rock* of course subscribes to none of those readings or to any reading. I've heard its ending described as inconclusive (it is) and frustrating (ditto). But *why not?* Do we want a rational explanation? Arrest and trial for vagabond kidnappers? An autopsy revealing broken necks? Poisonous snakes named as the culprits? If this film *had* a rational and tidy conclusion, it would be a good deal less interesting. But as a tantalizing puzzle, a tease, a suggestion of forbidden answer just out of earshot, it works hypnotically and very nicely indeed.

Places in the Heart ★ ★ ★
PG, 110 m., 1984

Sally Field (Edna Spaulding), John Malkovich (Mr. Will), Danny Glover (Mose), Lindsay Crouse (Margaret Lomax), Ed Harris (Wayne Lomax), Amy Madigan (Viola Kelsey). Directed by Robert Benton and produced by Arlene Donovan. Screenplay by Benton.

The places referred to in the title of Robert Benton's movie are, he has said, places that he holds sacred in his own heart: The small town in Texas where he grew up, various friends and relatives he remembers from those days, the little boy that he once was, and the things that happened or almost happened. His memories provide the material for a wonderful movie, and he has made it, but unfortunately he hasn't stopped at that. He has gone on to include too much. He tells a central story of great power, and then keeps leaving it to catch us up with minor characters we never care about.

The main story stars Sally Field as a sheriff's widow who learns from the banker that times are hard and she should sell her farm and maybe board her kids with somebody else. She refuses. She will keep the farm and keep the kids, thank you, although she's not sure just how that will work. Then a black hobo comes knocking at the back door, asking for food, and he sort of insists that he is just the man to plant her acreage in cotton and farm it. He knows all there is to know about cotton. Since Field has no choice, she takes the man at his word, and he plants the

cotton. Meanwhile, the banker, trying to solve a family problem and maybe help her at the same time, brings around a blind relative named Mr. Will, who will be a paying boarder. The three adults and the two kids form a little family that pulls together to make that farm work—and that is the central story of *Places in the Heart*.

Unfortunately, there are other stories. We meet Field's sister (Lindsay Crouse), and her brother-in-law (Ed Harris), and the local woman (Amy Madigan) he's having an affair with. Their stories function as counterpoint to the drama on the farm, but who cares? We learn just enough about the other characters to suspect that there might be a movie in their stories—but not this one, please, when their adulteries and betrayals have nothing to do with the main story.

Places in the Heart is the kind of movie where people tend to dismiss the parts they don't like. I've seen some reviews where the story of Field and the farm is the only part of the movie the critics refer to, as if Crouse, Harris, and Madigan had slipped their minds. That's wishful thinking. The subplot is there, and it's an unnecessary distraction, and it robs the movie of a lot of the sheer narrative power it would have had otherwise. It also robs us of a chance to learn more about the relationships among Field, the black farmer (Danny Glover), and the blind boarder (John Malkovich). What a group of unforgettable characters! What do they talk about in their evenings at home? Do they ever get into politics or philosophy? This is Texas in the Depression: How do they think the neighbors like the idea of a black man helping a white woman farm her land? The movie spends so much time watching the hanky-panky at the dances in town that when the Ku Klux Klan suddenly turns up in the movie, it's like it dropped out of a tree.

The movie's last scene has caused a lot of comment. It is a dreamy, idealistic fantasy in which all the characters in the film—friends and enemies, wives and mistresses, living and dead, black and white—take communion together at a church service. This is a scene of great vision and power, but it's too strong for the movie it concludes. *Places in the Heart* can't support such an ending, because it hasn't led up to it with a narrative that was straight and well-aimed as an arrow. The story was on the farm and not in the town, and although the last scene tries to draw them together, you can't summarize things that have nothing in common.

Play It Again, Sam ★ ★ ★
PG, 85 m., 1972

Woody Allen (Allan), Diane Keaton (Linda), Tony Roberts (Dick), Jerry Lacy (Bogart), Susan Anspach (Nancy), Jennifer Salt (Sharon), Joy Bang (Julie), Viva (Jennifer). Directed by Herbert Ross and produced by Arthur P. Jacobs. Screenplay by Woody Allen.

Allan lives in an apartment furnished with movie trivia. He sleeps beneath a poster for *Across the Pacific*, shaves with *Casablanca* reflected in the mirror, and fries his eggs across from *The Big Sleep*. There is not a place in the apartment from which the names Mary Astor and Sydney Greenstreet cannot be read. He is a Humphrey Bogart fan. He is more than that. He is a Humphrey Bogart pupil.

Allan's wife moved out some weeks ago and is suing for divorce, so now there are only the two people living in the apartment: Allan and Bogie. Whenever Allan reaches a crisis in his life, Bogie appears. His snapbrim is pulled down low over his eyes, and the collar is turned up on his trench coat, and there is a gat in his pocket and a Chesterfield in his mug.

"Tell her your life has changed since you met her," Bogie advises. Allan turns toward the lovely brunette sitting next to him on the sofa. He turns back to Bogie. "She won't fall for that!" Allan says. "Oh no?" says Bogie. "Try it and see."

This is pretty high-class advice, but Allan is a mess around girls. He's your average, ordinary movie freak, perfectly at home in the dark cave of a revival theater, watching the airport scene from *Casablanca*. But get him away from the movies and he gets . . . nervous. His friends try to take him to the beach. "I hate the beach! I hate the sun!" he cries. "I'm pale and I'm redheaded! I don't tan—I stroke!"

You can see that he has problems, even with Bogie on his side. His friends, Linda and Dick, try to fix him up with girls, but he

splashes himself with too much Canoe and then destroys his furniture during a seizure of nonchalance. After a while it begins to occur to him that he's in love with Linda, and she likes him, and Dick is always on the phone making real estate deals.

All of this is slightly less mad than your usual Woody Allen comedy, maybe because *Play It Again, Sam* is based on Woody's Broadway play, and with a play it's a little hard to work in material like a Howard Cosell play-by-play of an assassination in South America. Still, as comedies go, this is a very funny one. Woody Allen is one of those rare comedians who understands that humor can be based on pathos as well as sadism. While the high-pressure comics overwhelm us with aggressive humor, Woody is off in the bathroom somewhere being attacked by a hairdryer.

The notion of using a Bogart character is surprisingly successful. The Bogie imitation by Jerry Lacy is good, if not great, and the movie begins and ends with variations on that great *Casablanca* ending. That, and the movie's rather conventional Broadway plot structure, give it more coherence than the previous Woody Allen films, *Take the Money and Run* and *Bananas*. Maybe the movie has too much coherence, and the plot is too predictable; that's a weakness of films based on well-made Broadway plays. Still, that's hardly a serious complaint about something as funny as *Play It Again, Sam*.

Play Misty for Me ★ ★ ★ ★
R, 102 m., 1971

Clint Eastwood (Disc Jockey), Jessica Walter (Strange Woman), Donna Mills (Girlfriend), Don Siegel (Bartender). Directed by Clint Eastwood and produced by Robert Daley. Screenplay by Jo Heims and Dean Reisner.

The girl calls up every night at about the same time and asks the disc jockey to play "Misty" for her. Some nights he does. He's the all-night man on a small station in Carmel who plays records, reads poems, and hopes to make it someday in the big city. After work (and before work, for that matter) he drinks free at bars around town, places he sometimes mentions on the air. He had a steady girl for a while, but he's been free-lancing recently, and one night he picks up a girl in a bar. Or maybe she picks him up. She's the girl who likes "Misty." She is also mad. She insinuates herself into his life with a passionate jealousy, and we gradually come to understand that she is capable of violence. At the same time, the disc jockey's old love turns up in town, and he wants nothing more than to allow himself, finally, to quit playing the field and marry her. But the new girl doesn't see it that way. And she has this thing for knives.

Play Misty for Me is not the artistic equal of *Psycho*, but in the business of collecting an audience into the palm of its hand and then squeezing hard, it is supreme. It doesn't depend on a lot of surprises to maintain the suspense. There ARE some surprises, sure, but mostly the film's terror comes from the fact that the strange woman is capable of anything.

The movie was Clint Eastwood's debut as a director, and it was a good beginning. He must have learned a lot during seventeen years of working for other directors. In particular, he must have learned a lot from Don Siegel, who directed his previous four movies and has a bit part (the bartender) in this one. There is no wasted energy in *Play Misty for Me*. Everything contributes to the accumulation of terror, until even the ordinary, daytime scenes seem to have unspeakable things lurking beneath them.

In this connection, Eastwood succeeds in filming the first Semi-Obligatory Lyrical Interlude that works. The Semi-OLI, you'll recall, is the scene where the boy and girl walk in the meadow and there's a hit song on the sound track. In Eastwood's movie, he walks in the meadow with the girl, but the scene has been prepared so carefully that the meadow looks ominous. The grass looks muddy, the shadows are deep, the sky is gray, and there is a chill in the air. The whole visual style of the movie is strangely threatening.

The movie revolves around the character of the girl, who is played with an unnerving effectiveness by Jessica Walter. She is something like flypaper; the more you struggle against her personality, the more tightly you're held. Clint Eastwood, in directing himself, shows that he understands his unique movie personality. He is strong but somehow passive, he possesses strength but

keeps it coiled inside. And so the movie, by refusing to release any emotion at all until the very end, absolutely wrings us dry. There is no purpose to a suspense thriller, I suppose, except to involve us, scare us, to give us moments of vicarious terror. *Play Misty for Me* does that with an almost cruel efficiency.

Plenty ★ ★ ★ ½
R, 119 m., 1985

Meryl Streep (Susan), Charles Dance (Raymond), Tracey Ullman (Alice), John Gielgud (Darwin), Sting (Mick), Ian McKellen (Sir Andrew), Sam Neill (Lazar). Directed by Fred Schepisi and produced by Edward R. Pressman and Joseph Papp. Screenplay by David Hare.

At the end of World War II, a young woman stands on a hilltop in France and, as the sun bathes her in golden light, she says, "There will be days and days and days like this." That image provides the last shot in *Plenty*, which is the story of how very wrong she was.

The woman is Susan Traherne, a young English fighter in the French Resistance. She is not very seasoned and perhaps not very good at her job, but she stays alive behind enemy lines and she has a brief, poignant love affair with one of the men who parachuted down out of the night sky to fight the Germans.

The movie opens with her days in France. It follows her through the next fifteen or twenty years, and ends with that painful flashback to a day when she thought the future had nothing but good things for her. But nothing else in her life is ever as important, as ennobling or as much fun as the war. She is, perhaps, a little mad. She confesses at one point that she has a problem: "Sometimes I like to lose control."

The movie stars Meryl Streep as Susan and it is a performance of great subtlety; it is hard to play an unbalanced, neurotic, self-destructive woman, and do it with such gentleness and charm. Susan is often very pleasant to be around for the other characters in *Plenty*, and when she is letting herself lose control, she doesn't do it in the style of those patented movie mad scenes in which eyes roll and teeth are bared. She does it with an almost winsome urgency.

When she returns to England after the war, Susan makes friends almost at once. One of them is Alice (Tracey Ullman), a round-faced, grinning imp who seems born to the role of best pal. Another is Raymond (Charles Dance), a foreign service officer who is at first fascinated by her free, Bohemian lifestyle, and then marries her and becomes her lifelong enabler, putting up a wall of patience and almost saintly tolerance around her outbursts.

It is hard to say exactly what it is that troubles Susan. At first, David Hare's screenplay leads us to her own interpretation: That after the glory and excitement of the war, after the heroism and romance, it is impossible for her to return to civilian life and suffer the boring conversations of polite society. Later, we begin to realize there is something a little willful, a little cruel, in the way she embarrasses her husband on important occasions, always seeking to say the wrong thing at the wrong time. Finally, we tend to agree with him when he explodes that she is cruel and brutish, and ungrateful to those who have put up with her.

But then there is an epilogue—a strange, furtive meeting with the boy, the parachutist, she made love with twenty years earlier. It is bathed in the cold, greenish-gray light of the saddest part of an autumn afternoon, and there is such desperation in the way they both realize that nothing will ever, ever touch them again the way the war did.

Plenty is finally not a statement about war, or foreign service, or the British middle class, but simply the story of this flawed woman who once lived intensely, and now feels that she is hardly living at all.

The performances in the movie supply one brilliant solo after another; most of the big moments come as characters dominate the scenes they are in. Streep creates a whole character around a woman who could have simply been a catalog of symptoms. Charles Dance has a thankless role, I suppose, as her long-suffering husband, but manages to suggest that he is decent as well as duped. Sting plays a nondescript young man who unsuccessfully attempts to father her child. John Gielgud has three brief scenes and steals them all.

The movie is written, acted, and directed (by Fred Schepisi) as a surface of literacy and brittle wit, beneath which lives the realization that life can sometimes be pointless and empty and sad—and that there can be days and days and days like that.

Police Academy   no stars
R, 97 m., 1984

Steve Guttenberg (Carey Mahoney), Kim Cattrall (Karen Thompson), G.W. Bailey (Lieutenant Harris), Bubba Smith (Moses Hightower), Georgina Spelvin (Hooker). Directed by Hugh Wilson and produced by Paul Maslansky. Screenplay by Neal Israel, Pat Proft, and Wilson.

Once upon a time there was a movie named *Airplane!* which had a clever notion: Wouldn't it be fun to satirize all of those *Airport* movies by combining their clichés into one gloriously confused mess, typecasting the movie with walking stereotypes, and going for every corny gag in the book? They were right. It was a great idea, and it made a very funny movie. It also inspired a dreary series of clones and rip-offs, including *Young Doctors in Love* and *Jekyll and Hyde—Together Again*. Now comes without any doubt the absolute pits of this genre, the least funny movie that could possibly have been inspired by *Airplane!* or any other movie.

It's really something. It's so bad, maybe you should pool your money and draw straws and send one of the guys off to rent it so that in the future, whenever you think you're sitting through a bad comedy, he could shake his head, and chuckle tolerantly, and explain that you don't know what bad is. This is the kind of movie where they'll bring a couple of characters onscreen and begin to set up a joke, and then, just when you realize you can predict exactly what's going to happen . . . not only doesn't it happen, but nothing happens—they just cut to some different characters! If there's anything worse than a punch line that doesn't work, it's a movie that doesn't even bother to put the punch lines in.

Among the many questions raised by *Police Academy*, the easiest is: What genre does this movie think it's satirizing? Are there any other movies about police academies? That hardly matters, since the academy in this movie resembles no police academy known to modern man, and seems, indeed, to be modeled after a cross between basic training and prep school. All of the trainee cops live on campus together, in big dorms. The head of the academy is sort of like the headmaster. The campus is green and leafy and peaceful and altogether unlike, I suspect, the training experience undergone by any real police officers.

In a movie this bad, one plot element is really idiotic. It involves the casting of Bubba Smith as a giant black recruit who only has to look at a guy, and his knees start to tremble. This is funny? Don't they know that in comedy, you need a twist—like, why not make Bubba Smith a pathological coward who's afraid of everybody? Now right there is one good idea more than you can find in this entire movie.

Poltergeist ★ ★ ★
PG, 114 m., 1982

Craig T. Nelson (Steve), Jobeth Williams (Diane), Beatrice Straight (Dr. Lesh), Dominique Dunne (Dana), Oliver Robins (Robbie), Heather O'Rourke (Carol Anne). Directed by Tobe Hooper and produced by Steven Spielberg and Frank Marshall. Screenply by Spielberg, Michael Grais, and Mark Victor.

Special effects in the movies have grown so skilled, sensational, and scary that they sometimes upstage the human actors. And they often cost a lot more. In *Poltergeist*, for example, the cast is made up of relatively unknown performers, but that's all right because the real stars are producer Steven Spielberg *(Raiders of the Lost Ark)*, director Tobe Hooper *(The Texas Chainsaw Massacre)*, and their reputations for special effects and realistic violence. Their names on this horror film suggest that its technology will be impeccable. And they don't disappoint us. This is the movie *The Amityville Horror* dreamed of being. It begins with the same ingredients (a happy American family, living in a big, comfortable house). It provides similar warnings of doom (household objects move by themselves, the weather seems different around the house than anywhere else). And it ends with a similar apocalypse (spirits take total possession of the house, and terrorize the family). Even some

of the special effects are quite similar, as when greasy goo begins to ooze around the edges of a doorjamb.

But *Poltergeist* is an effective thriller, not so much because of the special effects, as because Hooper and Spielberg have tried to see the movie's strange events through the eyes of the family members, instead of just standing back and letting the special effects overwhelm the cast along with the audience. The movie takes place in Spielberg's favorite terrain, the American suburb (also the locale of parts of *Close Encounters, Jaws,* and *E. T.*). The haunted house doesn't have seven gables, but it does have a two-car garage. It is occupied by a fairly normal family (two parents, three kids) and the movie begins on a somewhat hopeful note with the playing of "The Star Spangled Banner" as a TV station signs off.

The opening visuals, however, are somewhat ominous. They're an extreme close-up of a TV screen, filled with the usual patriotic images (Iwo Jima, the Lincoln Memorial). Why so close? We're almost being invited to look between the dots on the screen and see something else. And indeed, the family's youngest daughter, an open-faced, long-haired, innocent little cherub, begins to talk to the screen. She's in touch with the "TV people." Before long she disappears from this plane of existence and goes to live with the TV people, wherever they are. Weird events begin to happen in the house. An old tree behaves ominously. The swimming pool seems to have a mind of its own. And the villains are the same people who were the bad guys in Spielberg's *Jaws*—the real estate developers. This time, instead of encouraging people to go back into the water, they're building a subdivision on top of an old graveyard.

This is all ridiculous, but Hooper and Spielberg hold our interest by observing the everyday rituals of this family so closely that, since the family seems real, the weird events take on a certain credibility by association. That's during the first hour of the movie. Then all hell breaks loose, and the movie begins to operate on the same plane as *Alien* or *Altered States*, as a shocking special effects sound-and-light show. A closet seems to exist in another dimension. The swimming pool is filled with grasping, despairing forms of the undead. The search for the missing little girl involves a professional psionics expert, and a lady dwarf who specializes in "cleaning" haunted homes. Nobody ever does decide whether a poltergeist really is involved in the events in the house, or who the poltergeist may be, but if that doesn't prevent them from naming the movie *Poltergeist* I guess it shouldn't keep us from enjoying it.

The Pope of Greenwich Village

★ ★ ★

R, 122 m., 1984

Eric Roberts (Paulie), Mickey Rourke (Charlie), Daryl Hannah (Diane), Geraldine Page (Mrs. Ritter), Kenneth McMillan (Barney), Tony Musante (Pete), Burt Young (Bedbug Eddie). Directed by Stuart Rosenberg and produced by Gene Kirkwood. Screenplay by Vincent Patrick.

Everybody is very ethnic in *The Pope of Greenwich Village*. They all wave their hands a lot, and hang out on street corners, and have uncles in the Mafia. They have such bonds of blood brotherhood, a cousin to them is closer than your mother is to you. And they've always got some kind of con game going on the side. Take Paulie, for example. He knows this racehorse that's selling for $15,000, only the joke is, this is a champion horse because it was sired with sperm stolen directly from the winner of the Belmont. Paulie explains about the horse while he has his mouth full of a hero sandwich that's a yard long. His cousin, Charlie, tells him he's crazy. That is a compliment in this family.

Paulie and Charlie have just been fired from their jobs at a restaurant for stealing from the management. Charlie is hard up. He can no longer support his girlfriend, a long-limbed, blonde aerobics instructor who seems attracted to his exotic ethnic charm. Paulie has the answer to their problems. He will buy the future champion racehorse with money from a juice loan and then pay off the loan by cracking a safe he has heard about. There is only one problem with this plan. The safe belongs to the Mafia godfather of Greenwich Village, and if he finds out who did it, not even Paulie's uncle in the Mafia can save them. Meanwhile, Charlie's

girlfriend is pregnant, Paulie's car has been towed, a cop has killed himself falling down an elevator shaft, and on the sound track Frank Sinatra is singing "Summer Wind."

The Pope of Greenwich Village bills itself as a drama and is structured like a crime thriller, but I categorize it as basically a Behavior Movie. The real subject of the movie is the behavior of the characters, and the story is essentially an excuse for showboat performances. This movie is an actor's dream, and the actors involved are Eric Roberts, fresh from his triumph in *STAR 80*, as Paulie; Mickey Rourke, the hero of *Diner*, as Charlie; Daryl Hannah, right after her hit in *Splash*, as the aerobics instructor; and the usual supporting types like Tony Musante as the uncle, Burt Young—stuffing his face with pasta—as the godfather, and Geraldine Page as the tough-talking mother of the dead cop. Also, Kenneth McMillan has a well-acted key role as an old safecracker who gets caught in the middle of the whole deal.

There are times when *The Pope of Greenwich Village* seems to aspire to some great meaning, some insight into crime like *The Godfather* had. But the tip-off is the last shot, where the boys have a happy-go-lucky walk down the street and into a freeze-frame, while Sinatra is trotted out for his third encore. This movie is not really about anything except behavior, and the only human drama in it is the story of the safecracker and his family. That doesn't mean it's not worth seeing. The behavior is well-observed, although Eric Roberts has a tendency to go over the top in his mannered performance, and the last two scenes are highly unlikely. It's worth seeing for the acting, and it's got some good laughs in it, and New York is colorfully observed, but don't tell me this movie is about human nature, because it's not; it's about acting.

Popeye ★ ★ ★ ½

PG, 114 m., 1980

Robin Williams (Popeye), Shelly Duvall (Olive Oyl), Ray Walston (Poopdeck Pappy), Paul Dooley (Wimpy), Paul L. Smith (Bluto), Richard Libertini (Geezil). Directed by Robert Altman and produced by Robert Evans. Screenplay by Jules Feiffer.

One of Robert Altman's trademarks is the way he creates whole new worlds in his movies—worlds where we somehow don't believe that life ends at the edge of the screen, worlds in which the main characters are surrounded by other people plunging ahead at the business of living. That gift for populating new places is one of the richest treasures in *Popeye*, Altman's musical comedy. He takes one of the most artificial and limiting of art forms—the comic strip—and raises it to the level of high comedy and high spirits.

And yet *Popeye* nevertheless remains true to its origin on the comic page, and in those classic cartoons by Max Fleischer. A review of this film almost has to start with the work of Wolf Kroeger, the production designer, who created an astonishingly detailed and rich set on the movie's Malta locations. Most of the action takes place in a ramshackle fishing hamlet—"Sweethaven"—where the streets run at crazy angles up the hillsides, and the rooming houses and saloons lean together dangerously.

Sweethaven has been populated by actors who look, or are made to look, so much like their funny-page originals that it's hardly even jarring that they're *not* cartoons. Audiences immediately notice the immense forearms on Robin Williams, who plays Popeye; they're big, brawny, and completely convincing. But so is Williams's perpetual squint and his lopsided smile. Shelly Duvall, the star of so many other Altman films, is perfect here as Olive Oyl, the role she was born to play. She brings to Olive a certain . . . dignity, you might say. She's not lightly scorned, and although she may tear apart a room in an unsuccessful attempt to open the curtains, she is fearless in the face of her terrifying fiancé, Bluto. The list continues: Paul Smith (the torturer in *Midnight Express*) looks ferociously Bluto-like, and Paul Dooley (the father in *Breaking Away*) is a perfect Wimpy, forever curiously sniffing a hamburger with a connoisseur's fanatic passion. Even the little baby, Swee' Pea, played by Altman's grandson, Wesley Ivan Hurt, looks like typecasting.

But it's not enough that the characters and the locations look their parts. Altman has breathed life into this material, and he hasn't done it by pretending it's camp, either. He organizes a screenful of activity, so carefully choreographed that it's a delight, for example to watch the moves as the guests in Olive's rooming house make stabs at the plates of food on the table.

There are several set pieces. One involves Popeye's arrival at Sweethaven, another a stop on his lonely quest for his long-lost father. Another is the big wedding day for Bluto and Olive Oyl, with Olive among the missing and Bluto's temper growing until steam jets from his ears. There is the excursion to the amusement pier, and the melee at the dinner table, and the revelation of the true identity of a mysterious admiral, and the kidnapping of Swee' Pea, and then the kidnapping of Olive Oyl and her subsequent wrestling match with a savage octopus.

The movie's songs, by Harry Nilssen, fit into all of this quite effortlessly. Instead of having everything come to a halt for the musical set pieces, Altman stitches them into the fabric. Robin Williams sings Popeye's anthem, "I Yam What I Yam" with a growling old sea dog's stubborness. Bluto's "I'm Mean" has an undeniable conviction, and so does Olive Oyl's song to Bluto, "He's Large." Shelly Duvall's performance as Olive Oyl also benefits from the amazingly ungainly walking style she brings to the movie.

Popeye, then, is lots of fun. It suggests that it *is* possible to take the broad strokes of a comic strip and turn them into sophisticated entertainment. What's needed is the right attitude toward the material. If Altman and his people had been the slightest bit condescending toward Popeye, the movie might have crash-landed. But it's clear that this movie has an affection for Popeye, and so much regard for the sailor man that it even bothers to reveal the real truth about his opinion of spinach.

Porky's ★ ½
R, 94 m., 1982

Dan Monahan (Pee Wee), Mark Herrier (Billy), Wyatt Knight (Tommy), Roger Wilson (Mickey), Kim Cattrall (Honeywell), Alex Karras (Sheriff), Susan Clark (Cherry Forever), Nancy Parsons (Ms. Balbricker). Directed by Bob Clark and produced by Don Carmody and Clark.

Porky's is another raunchy teen-age sex-and-food-fight movies. The whole genre seems fixated on the late 1950s and early 1960s, when the filmmakers, no doubt, were teen-agers. Do today's teenagers really identify with jokes about locker rooms, Trojans, boobs, jockstraps, killer-dyke gym coaches, and barfing? Well, yes, probably they do. Teen-agers seem to occupy a time warp of eternally unchanging preoccupations. Hollywood originally entered that world with a certain innocence in the late 1950s with Pat Boone and beach part movies. That innocence is now long, long ago. Since *American Graffiti, National Lampoon's Animal House*, and *Meatballs*, the A.C.N.E.S. movie has turned cynical. You remember what A.C.N.E.S. stands for. It's an acronym for any movie about the dreaded Adolescent Character's Neurotic Eroticism Syndrome.

In *Porky's*, the male characters are neurotic about the usual three subjects: the size, experience, and health of their reproductive organs. The female characters, on the other hand, are seen almost entirely as an undiscovered species from a lost continent. They're whispered about, speculated about, spied upon, victimized, and, in general, feared. And it's not only Ms. Balbricker, the juggernaut gym coach, who's a heavy. All of the women in this movie are weird. One howls like a dog during sexual intercourse. Others lure unsuspecting horny teen-age boys into rooms with trapdoors, and dump them into alligator-infested waters.

In fact, the strangest thing about *Porky's* is how much it hates women. The only close friendships in the movie are between men. The movie even takes certain scenes that are usually clichés for female characters and assigns them to men. For example, you can hardly make a movie like this without a scene in which someone's caught nude in public. Remember Hot Lips in *M*A*S*H?* In *Porky's*, it's a kid named Pee Wee. He's caught with his pants down, chased into the woods, picked up by the cops, and deposited at the local drive-in hamburger stand, where he poses like September Morn.

Since the movie doesn't like women, its sex scenes all create fear and hostility, which prevents them from being funny (sex scenes *about* fear and hostility, on the other hand, can be very funny). Even in an easy scene

like the one where the guys spy on the girls in the locker room, the director, Bob Clark, blows it. Peeping-tom scenes can be very funny (remember John Belushi on the ladder in *Animal House?*). Here, it's just smarmy. There's one other problem. None of the male actors in this movie look, sound, or act like teen-agers. They all look like overgrown preppies at their fraternity pledge class's fifth reunion. Jokes based on embarrassment never work unless we can identify with the embarrassed character. Here, the actors all seem to be just acting.

I see that I have neglected to summarize the plot of *Porky's*. And I don't think I will. I don't feel like writing one more sentence (which is, to be sure, all it would take).

The Postman Always Rings Twice
★ ★ ½
R, 122 m., 1981

Jack Nicholson (Frank Chambers), Jessica Lange (Cora Papadakis), John Colicos (Nick Papadakis), Michael Lerner (Katz), John P. Ryan (Kennedy), Anjelica Huston (Madge). Directed by Bob Rafelson and produced by Charles Mulvehill and Rafelson. Screenplay by David Mamet.

The Postman Always Rings Twice is an absolutely superb mounting of a hollow and disappointing production. It shows a technical mastery of filmmaking, and we are dazzled by the performances, the atmosphere, the mood of mounting violence. But by the second hour of the film we've lost our bearings: What is this movie *saying* about its characters? What does it feel and believe about them? Why was it necessary to tell their stories? The movie is based on a hardboiled, classic novel by James M. Cain, which has already inspired three previous films, including the famous 1946 John Garfield version. It isn't difficult to guess why the director, Bob Rafelson, wanted to make it again. On the basis of his key scenes, he was attracted by the physical violence in the story and he felt that in 1981 he could deal more frankly with Cain's sexual savagery.

He was right. His film contains passages of unusual physical power, including one in which Jack Nicholson and Jessica Lange make love (if that is the word) on a kitchen table. Nicholson plays a Depression-era drifter in the film, a cheap thief, and a con man. Lange is the bored and sensuous cook in a short-order joint run by her much older Greek husband, John Colicos. Passion flares between Nicholson and Lange almost the moment they first see one another, and their lovemaking is quick, brutal, uncontrolled, and animalistic.

Eventually, they kill Colicos—although not without the greatest difficulties. This is one of those films where blood, violence, and sheer weight of human bodies are made into Hitchcockian embarrassments. And then the two lovers are put on trial, are freed through a cynical arrangement between opposing insurance companies, and then arrive at an ironic fate. Along the way, there is a brief and totally inexplicable appearance by a woman lion tamer (Anjelica Huston), who seems to be visiting from another movie.

The movie is a triumph of atmosphere. Every last weathered Coke sign, every old auto and old overcoat and old cliché have been put in with loving care. And the performances have been cranked up to levels of trembling intensity. Jessica Lange, first seen in *King Kong*, this time submits to the embrace of a wanton monster. Jack Nicholson has never been seedier, shiftier, more driven. John Colicos, as the simple, alcoholic, ambitious Greek-American, provides a wonderfully textured performance. And yet, there is no feeling of tragedy in Colicos's death. No feeling of greatness in the romantic compulsion of Lange and Nicholson. No way to tell what the movie believes about their acquittal and eventual fate. A movie such as *Bonnie and Clyde* comes to mind. It also dealt with passion, crime, and money, but so clearly that at the end of the film we felt we knew the dying characters.

We never know the people in *The Postman Always Rings Twice*. They are kept rigidly imprisoned within a tradition of absolute naturalism: They exist, they eat, they sleep, they act. That would be acceptable if the filmmakers could stand outside their characters and have feelings about them. But I never believed that was the case. Rafelson and his collaborators have gone to infinite pains, successfully, to create a film that is wonderfully achieved on the level of produc-

tion. But they have not filled it with the purposes of its characters.

Power ★ ★ ½
R, 111 m., 1985

Richard Gere (Pete St. John), Julie Christie (Ellen Freeman), Gene Hackman (Wilfred Buckley), Kate Capshaw (Sydney Betterman), Denzel Washington (Arnold Billings), E.G. Marshall (Sam Hastings). Directed by Sidney Lumet and produced by Renee Schisgal and Mark Tarlov. Screenplay by David Himmelstein.

When Sidney Lumet released *Network* back in 1976, I saw it at a screening with a lot of television news people, who walked out of the movie shaking their heads in wonderment and admitting that Lumet had, by and large, gotten it right. After all the Hollywood flights of fancy about TV news, here was a movie with some real insights.

Now Lumet has made a movie named *Power* about the world of professional political campaign organizers, and he seems to have gotten this one right, too. The movie exudes a sense of authenticity, of a subject researched well. The major difference, however, between *Network* and *Power* is that *Network* had a plot and *Power* does not.

The movie stars Richard Gere as Pete St. John, campaign strategist and hired gun. During the course of the movie, he will mastermind campaigns in New Mexico, Washington, and Ohio—where his man is a cynical stooge for the big oil companies. We will see him filming TV commercials, and coaching his clients about the way to behave during press conferences, and fighting the opposition's dirty tricks with some of his own.

We will also look into his private life, into his relationship with his sexy, accommodating assistant (Kate Capshaw) and his weary, philosophical former wife (Julie Christie). And we will see him survive a moment of truth with the aging, alcoholic strategist (Gene Hackman) who gave him his start in the business.

Because these relationships are so well-written and acted, and because *Power* seems based on a wealth of research about the world of campaign professionals, the movie builds up considerable momentum during its first hour. There's a sense of excitement, of identification with this man who is being driven by his own energy, ambition, and cynicism. The opening titles show Gere compulsively beating out a rhythm with drumsticks, and his whole life has the same staccato urgency.

During the second half of the movie, however, a growing disappointment sets in. *Power* is too episodic. It doesn't really declare itself to be about any particular story, any single clear-cut issue. The mechanics of plot can sometimes be overdone, but here I found myself missing those basic mechanics: I learned about these people and their world, but I didn't know what I wanted to have happen at the movie's end. Should Gere lose because of his cynicism? Win because of his skill?

There does come a moment of truth, as Gere loses all faith in his corrupt candidate and bursts into the room where Hackman is coaching the opposition—a hapless, idealistic college professor with no chance of success. Gere implores the man to forget all strategy and simply tell the truth, and there are echoes here of the famous moment in *Network* when the anchorman asks his viewers to shout out that they're mad as hell, and they aren't going to take it anymore.

Unfortunately, the very idealism of the scene in *Power* is undermined by the movie's cool professionalism: We think we've learned enough about the campaign business to know that Gere's strategy won't work.

There were a lot of things I liked about this movie. One of them was the quiet, affectionate scene between Christie and Gere, when they were at last able to talk openly, even fondly, of the reasons they broke up their marriage. Another one was an angry meeting between Gere and Hackman. And there were some fascinating passages in which Gere took a hopelessly inept candidate and re-edited his TV spots to make him look somewhat less inept.

But the movie itself seems to sense that it's going nowhere. The climax is a pointless, frustrating montage of images. It's a good montage, but it belongs somewhere in the middle of the movie; it states the problem, but not the solution or even the lack of a solution. The movie seems to be asking us to

skake our heads in disillusionment, but I was more puzzled than disillusioned.

Lumet is known for his work with actors, and for his sure touch when he casts a movie. Reflect on how wise his choices were when he put Peter Finch and William Holden in *Network*, and Al Pacino in *Dog Day Afternoon*. In *Power*, the obvious question is, how well does Richard Gere play a political professional? Gere is a good actor—he has demonstrated that time and again—but there is something about his smoothness, his good looks, his occasional narcissism, that alerts audiences to look for chinks in his performances.

I would have preferred an older, grittier, wearier character in the Pete St. John role—maybe Hackman. But I found myself accepting Gere in this unlikely role, and I reflected that he, like Nick Nolte, will only get better in the movies as he gets older and as some of the youthful glamour fades.

As for the movie, it's smart, it's knowledgeable, sometimes it's funny, occasionally it is very touching, and I learned something from it. That is almost enough, I suppose; it's more than most movies provide. But at the end of the film, I found myself asking what it had really been about. As that infuriating montage played on the screen, I was still waiting for the ending, for the winners and the losers. Isn't that, finally, what political campaigns are all about?

Pretty Baby ★ ★ ★
R, 109 m., 1978

Brooke Shields (Violet), Keith Carradine (Bellocq), Susan Sarandon (Hattie), Frances Faye (Nell), Antonio Fargas (Professor), Matthew Anton (Red Top), Diana Scarwid (Frieda). Directed and produced by Louis Malle. Screenplay by Polly Platt.

Louis Malle's *Pretty Baby* was a pleasant surprise: After all the controversy and scandal surrounding its production, it turned out to be a good-hearted, good-looking, quietly elegiac movie. That was a coup for Malle, who sometimes seemed to dare himself to find acceptable ways of filming unacceptable subjects.

His subject this time is a twelve-year-old girl who is raised in the New Orleans brothel where her mother works. She plays in the garden, she rides a pony, she likes ragtime music, and one day she's auctioned off to the man who will deflower her. This is, of course, tragically perverted, but *Pretty Baby* itself is not a perverted film: It looks soberly, and with a good deal of compassion, at its period of history and the people who occupied it.

The pretty baby of the title is named Violet, and is played by Brooke Shields, as an extraordinarily beautiful child. Before anyone had seen *Pretty Baby,* Malle was being accused of exploiting that fact. But he's thoughtful and almost cautious in his approach: Given the film's subject matter and its obligatory sex scenes, Malle shows taste and restraint. And Shields really creates a character here; her subtlety and depth are astonishing.

Malle places her in an extraordinarily well-realized world, the Storyville section of New Orleans, circa 1917. The movie pays infinite attention to detail, and looks and feels accurate: We get to know the brothel so well, with its curving staircases and baroque furnishings, we almost feel we live there too. And we get to know the people, too, especially the strange and cynical brothel-keeper Madame Nell (Frances Faye), who observes at one point in her gravelly voice: "I am old. And I know one thing: Life is very long." An almost opaque line, but she invests it with infinite weariness.

She also keeps a well-run establishment, populated by hookers like Violet's mother Hattie (Susan Sarandon), who dreams of escaping from the life and eventually succeeds: She marries a prosperous businessman from St. Louis, and moves north. She wants to take her daughter with her, but Violet won't go: For her, this house *is* a home. Violet has in the meantime gained a protector and confidant: Bellocq (Keith Carradine), the silent, eccentric photographer. He seems at first to feel no passion at all, as he takes his infinite pains to arrange the lights and shadows in which he poses the prostitutes. There is, we feel, the possibility that he's asexual. But he does have a special feeling for Violet. And on the night she is auctioned off, there are two long, anguished close-ups: Of Bellocq, and of the house's black piano player (Antonio Fargas). Both of them clearly feel the auction is an outrage.

Neither one speaks out. They are both creatures of Storyville, and know how things are done.

After Hattie goes north, Violet stays in the house for a time, and then goes to live with Bellocq. Their relationship is, of course, a strange one, made more complicated by the fact that this experienced twelve-year-old prostitute is still just a little girl. One of the film's most heartbreaking scenes has Violet sitting under a tree, playing with her doll. She is pretending that the doll is herself and that she is her mother. There's such a curious mixture of resentment and envy in her game that we cringe.

Pretty Baby has been attacked in some quarters as child porn. It's not. It's an evocation of a time and a place and a sad chapter of Americana. The ragtime music and the blues that fill its sound track take on a deeper meaning, in the context of the story, and we are reminded that the artists who sang "Do You Know What It Means to Miss New Orleans?" knew very well, and perhaps for that reason missed it less than their listeners.

Pretty in Pink ★ ★ ★
PG-13, 96 m., 1985

Molly Ringwald (Andie Walsh), Harry Dean Stanton (Jack Walsh), Jon Cryer (Duckie Dale), Andrew McCarthy (Blane McDonoug), Annie Potts (Iona), James Spader (Steff McKee). Directed by Howard Deutch and produced by Lauren Shuler. Screenplay by John Hughes.

Although *Pretty in Pink* contains several scenes that are a great deal more dramatic, my favorite moments were the quietest ones, in which nothing was being said because a boy was trying to get up the courage to ask a girl out on a date, and she knew it, and he knew it, and still nothing was happening.

To be able to listen to such a silence is to understand the central dilemma of adolescence, which is that one's dreams are so much larger than one's confidence. *Pretty in Pink* is a movie that pays attention to such things. And although it is not a great movie, it contains some moments when the audience is likely to think, yes, being sixteen was exactly like that.

The movie stars Molly Ringwald as Andie Walsh, a poor girl from the wrong side of the tracks. Her mother bailed out of her life some years earlier, and she lives with her unemployed father (Harry Dean Stanton), whose first words after she wakes him one morning are, "Where am I?" Andie works in a record store in a downtown mall and wears fashions that seem thrown together by a collision between a Goodwill store and a 1950s revival.

Andie attends a high school where most of the kids are wealthy snobs, and she has a crush on a rich kid named Blane (Andrew McCarthy). Her best friends are Duckie (Jon Cryer), who is a case study of the kind of teenage boy who thinks he can clown his way into a girl's heart, and Iona (Annie Potts), a thirtyish sprite who affects one radical hairstyle after another.

The movie's plot is old, old, old. It's about how the rich boy and the poor girl love each other, but the rich kid's friends are snobs, and the poor girl doesn't want anyone to know what a shabby home she lives in, and about how they do find true love after all. Since the basic truths in the movie apply to all teen-agers, rich and poor, I wish the filmmakers had found a new plot to go along with them. Perhaps they could have made the lovers come from different ethnic groups, which wouldn't have been all that original, either, but at least would have avoided one more recycling of ancient Horatio Alger stories.

There is one other major problem with the movie, and that involves the character of Steff McKee (James Spader), the effete, chain-smoking rich snot who is Blane's best friend. He has been turned down several times by Andie and now pretends to be appalled that Blane would want to go out with such a "mutant." His snobbery almost shipwrecks the romance. Steff does have one great line of dialogue: "Money really means nothing to me. Do you think I'd treat my parents' house this way if it did?" But, as played by Spader, he looks much too old to be a teen-ager, and his scenes play uneasily for that reason. He seems more like a sinister twenty-five-year-old still lurking in the high school corridors, the Ghost of Proms Past.

Those objections noted, *Pretty in Pink* is a heartwarming and mostly truthful movie, with some nice touches of humor. The movie was written by John Hughes, who repeats the basic situation of his *Sixteen Candles*, which also starred Molly Ringwald as a girl who had a crush on a senior boy, and whose best friend was the class geek. But Ringwald grows with every movie into an actress who can project poignancy and vulnerability without seeming corny or coy, and her scenes here with Cryer and Potts have one moment of small truth after another.

The nicest surprise in the movie is the character created by Potts. The first time we see her, she's dressed in leather and chains, but the next time, she wears one of those beehive hairdos from the early 1960s. She is constantly experimenting with her "look," and when she finally settles on conservative good taste, the choice seems like her most radical so far.

Pretty in Pink is evidence, I suppose, that there must be a reason why certain old stories never seem to die. We know all the clichés, we can predict half of the developments. But at the end, when this boy and this girl, who are so obviously intended for one another, finally get together, there is great satisfaction. There also is the sense that Molly Ringwald just might have that subtle magic that will allow her, like young Elizabeth Taylor, to grow into an actress who will keep on breaking and mending boys' hearts for a long time.

Prince of the City ★ ★ ★ ★
R, 167 m., 1981

Treat Williams (Daniel Ciello), Jerry Orbach (Gus Levy), Richard Foronjy (Joe Marinaro), Don Billett (Bill Mayo), Jenny Marino (Dom Bando), Bob Balaban (Sentimassino), Lindsay Crouse (Carla Ciello). Directed by Sidney Lumet and produced by Burtt Harris. Screenplay by Jay Presson Allen and Lumet.

He will not rat on his partners. This is his bottom line. He will talk to investigators about all the other guys he knows things about. He will talk about how narcotics cops get involved in the narcotics traffic, how they buy information with drugs, how they string out addicts and use them as informers, how they keep some of the money and some of the drugs after big busts. He will tell what he knows about how the other cops do these things. But he will not talk about his partners in his own unit. This is his code, and, of course, he is going to have to break it.

That is the central situation of Sidney Lumet's *Prince of the City.* While you are watching it, it's a movie about cops, drugs, and New York City, in that order. After the film starts to turn itself over in your mind, it becomes a much deeper piece, a film about how difficult it is to go straight in a crooked world without hurting people you love.

Drugs are a rotten business. They corrupt everyone they come into contact with, because they set up needs so urgent that all other considerations are forgotten. For addicts, the need is for the drug itself. For others, the needs are more complex. The members of the special police drug unit in *Prince of the City,* for example, take on an envied departmental status because of their assignment. They have no hours, no beats, no uniforms. They are elite free-lancers, modern knights riding out into the drug underworld and establishing their own rules. They do not look at it this way, but their status depends on drugs. If there were no drugs and no addicts, there would be no narcs, no princes of the city. Of course, their jobs are also cold, dirty, lonely, dangerous, thankless, and never finished. That is the other side of the deal, and that helps explain why they will sometimes keep the money they confiscate in a drug bust. It's as if they're levying their own fines. It also explains why they sometimes supply informers with drugs: They know better than anyone how horrible the addict's life can be. "A junkie can break your heart," the hero of this movie says at one point, and by the movie's end we understand what he means.

The film is based on a book by Robert Daley about Bob Leuci, a New York cop who cooperated with a 1971 investigation of police corruption. In the movie, Leuci is called Ciello, and he is played by Treat Williams in a demanding and grueling performance. Williams is almost always onscreen, and almost always in situations of extreme stress, fatigue, and emotional turmoil. We see him coming apart before our eyes. He falls to pieces not simply because of his job, or because of his decision to testify, but because he is in an inexorable trap and he *will* sooner or later have to hurt his partners.

This is a movie that literally hinges on the issue of perjury. And Sidney Lumet and his co-writer, Jay Presson Allen, have a great deal of respect for the legal questions involved. There is a sustained scene in this movie that is one of the most spellbinding I can imagine, and it consists entirely of government lawyers debating whether a given situation justifies a charge of perjury. Rarely are ethical issues discussed in such detail in a movie, and hardly ever so effectively.

Prince of the City is a very good movie and, like some of its characters, it wants to break your heart. Maybe it will. It is about the ways in which a corrupt modern city makes it almost impossible for a man to be true to the law, his ideals, and his friends, all at the same time. The movie has no answers. Only horrible alternatives.

Private Benjamin ★ ★ ★
R, 110 m., 1980

Goldie Hawn (Judy Benjamin), Eileen Brennan (Captain Lewis), Armand Assante (Henri Tremont), Robert Webber (Colonel Thornbush), Sam Wanamaker (Teddy Benjamin), Barbara Barrie (Harriet Benjamin), Harry Dean Stanton (Sergeant Ballard), Albert Brooks (Yale Goodman). Directed by Howard Zieff and written and produced by Nancy Meyers, Charles Shyer, and Harvey Miller.

Howard Zieff's *Private Benjamin* is an appealing, infectious comedy starring Goldie Hawn as Judy Benjamin, a Jewish-American princess, breathless with joy on the day of her second marriage. She has a real catch: He's named Yale, he's a professional man, he wants his study done in mushroom colors. Alas, he dies in the throes of passion on his wedding night (something his grieving mother discovers when Judy solemnly repeats his last words). And Judy goes into mourning.

What's she to do? She calls in to an all-night talk show and is promised a solution by another caller. The next day, we meet the guy with the answer. Played by Harry Dean Stanton, that wonderful character actor who could be Robert Mitchum's sneaky cousin, the guy turns out to be an Army recruiter. And he solemnly paints a picture of Army life that has Judy signing up. Her subsequent shocks of discovery provide the great laughs of the movie's best scenes. She solemnly explains to a captain (Eileen Brennan) that she *did* sign up with the Army, yes, but with another Army. Where, she asks, are the private condo living quarters the recruiter promised her? And surely the Army could have afforded some draperies? In no time at all, she's cleaning the latrines with her electric toothbrush.

This is an inspired idea for a movie comedy, and Goldie Hawn has a lot of fun with it. She finds just the right note for her performance, poised halfway between the avaricious and the slack-jawed, the calculating and the innocent. She makes some kind of impression on everyone she runs up against (or into), especially Robert Webber as the square-jawed Colonel Thornbush, commander of the Army's elite paratroop unit, the Thornbushers.

It's at about this point that the movie seems to lose its unique comic direction and turn into a more or less predictable combination of service comedy and romantic farce. After Judy's parents try to rescue her from the Army, she suddenly decides to stay and stick it out. She turns into a passable soldier. She almost inadvertently captures the entire Red team and makes them Blue prisoners of war during war games. And she is invited to join the Thornbushers by Colonel Thornbush himself (who turns out to have an alternative in mind if Judy doesn't want to jump at 13,000 feet).

Along the way, she meets a sexy and eligible French bachelor who's a gynecologist. After she blackmails Thornbush into sending her to Allied Army headquarters in Paris, she falls in love with the Frenchman (Armand Assante), and gets involved in Gallic romantic intrigues. It turns out that her would-be third husband is more interested in Sunday morning soccer games and cute little downstairs maids than in the kind of marriage Judy Benjamin was brought up to desire.

This stuff is occasionally funny, but it's kind of predictable. It turns *Private Benjamin* into areas that are too familiar: We've all seen the comic situations that grow out of the courtship with the Frenchman, and we'd really rather have seen more stuff of Private Benjamin in the Army. The movie would have been better off sticking with Goldie

Hawn as a female Beetle Bailey and forgetting about the changes that allow her to find self-respect, deal with the Frenchman, etc. Still, *Private Benjamin* is refreshing and fun. Goldie Hawn, who is a true comic actress, makes an original, appealing character out of Judy Benjamin, and so the movie feels alive—not just an exercise in gags and situations.

Prizzi's Honor ★ ★ ★ ★
R, 129 m., 1985

Jack Nicholson (Charley Partanna), Kathleen Turner (Irene Walker), Anjelica Huston (Maerose), Robert Loggia (Eduardo Prizzi), John Randolph (Pop Partanna), William Hickey (Don Carrado Prizzi), Lee Richardson (Dominic). Directed by John Huston and produced by John Foreman. Screenplay by Richard Condon and Janet Roach.

John Huston's *Prizzi's Honor* marches like weird and gloomy clockwork to its relentless conclusion, and half of the time, we're laughing. This is the most bizarre comedy in many a month; a movie so dark, so cynical, and so funny that perhaps only Jack Nicholson and Kathleen Turner could have kept straight faces during the love scenes. They do. They play two professional Mafia killers who meet, fall in love, marry, and find out that the mob may not be big enough for both of them.

Nicholson plays Charley Partanna, a soldier in the proud Prizzi family, rulers of the East Coast, enforcers of criminal order. The godfather of the Prizzis, Don Corrado, is a mean little old man who looks like he has been freeze-dried by the lifelong ordeal of draining every ounce of humanity out of his wizened body. To Don Corrado (William Hickey), nothing is more important than the Prizzis' honor—not even another Prizzi. Charley Partanna is the Don's grandson. He has been raised in this ethic, and accepts it. He kills without remorse. He follows orders. Only occasionally does he disobey the family's instructions, as when he broke his engagement with Maerose Prizzi (Anjelica Huston), his cousin. She then brought disgrace upon herself and, as the movie opens, is in the fourth year of self-imposed exile. But she is a Prizzi, and does not forget, or forgive.

The movie opens like *The Godfather*, at a wedding. Charley's eyes roam around the church. In the choir loft, he sees a beautiful blonde (Kathleen Turner). She looks like an angel. At the reception, he dances with her once, and then she disappears. Later that day, there is a mob killing. Determined to find out the name of the blonde angel, Charley discovers even more—that she was the California hitman, brought in to do the job. He turns to Maerose for advice. She counsels him to go ahead: After all, it's good to have interests in common with your wife.

Charley flies to the coast, setting up a running gag as they establish a transcontinental commute. There is instant, electrifying chemistry between the two of them, and the odd thing is, it seems halfway plausible. They're opposites, but they attract. Nicholson plays his hood as a tough Brooklynite; he uses a stiff upper lip, like Bogart, and sounds simple and implacable. Turner, who is flowering as a wonderful comic actress, plays her Mafia killer like a bright, cheery hostess. She could be selling cosmetics.

What happens between them is best not explained here, since the unfolding of the plot is one of the movie's delights. The story is by Richard Condon, a novelist who delights in devious plot construction, and here he takes two absolutes—romantic love and the Prizzis' honor—and arranges a collision between them. Because all of the motivations are so direct and logical, the movie is able to make the most shocking decisions seem inevitable.

John Huston directed this film right after *Under the Volcano*, and what other director could have put those two back-to-back? It is one of his very best films, perhaps because he made it with friends; Condon is an old pal from Ireland, Anjelica Huston is, of course, his daughter, and Nicholson has long been Anjelica's lover. Together they have taken a strange plot, peopled it with carefully overwrought characters, and made *Prizzi's Honor* into a treasure.

Protocol ★ ★ ½
PG, 96 m., 1984

Goldie Hawn (Sunny), Chris Sarandon (Michael), Richard Romanus (Emir), André Gregory (Nawaf), Gail Strickland (Mrs. St. John), Cliff De Young (Hilley). Directed by Herbert Ross and produced by Anthea Sylbert. Screenplay by Buck Henry.

The first hour of *Protocol* is so much fun, and the Goldie Hawn character is such an engaging original, that at first I couldn't believe they were going to throw away all that work by going for a standard Hollywood ending. But they did. You know a movie's in trouble when they stop dealing with the characters and start throwing things at the screen.

Maybe it's just that they started with such a good premise, such a good first and second act, that they never got around to ending the movie. *Protocol* begins with Goldie as a cocktail waitress who dresses like a big bird every night to entertain the regulars in a sleazy nightclub. She's broke and without prospects. But then one night she pushes to the front of a crowd, and when a guy pulls out a gun, she wrestles him to the ground and saves the life of the leader of an obscure Arab oil sheikdom. She is, in the process, wounded in the nether regions, and when she becomes a national heroine and the star of TV interview shows, the Arab leader falls in love with her and the White House decides to hire her as a protocol officer and more or less give her to the sheik.

The setup for the film has a lot of charm, with Goldie as a goofy heroine who rooms with a couple of gay men and asks them thoughtfully, "Do you think I might be one of those people who is referred to as cute, but none too heavy in the brains department?" Her first televised press conference after the foiled assassination is probably the movie's high point; she answers each question with such refreshing directness that she becomes an overnight star. It's right after the press conference that the movie reaches its turning point: Should it continue to develop this story along the lines of more or less realistic comedy, or should it go for the bizarre and the slapstick? It makes the second choice. We meet the sheik (Richard Romanus) and his chief aide (André Gregory), and the usual clichés about Arabs start to fly thick and fast. Goldie soon finds herself in the Middle East as a prospective harem wife. Some of this stuff is funny, but the movie really falls apart when it moves back to Washington and Goldie invites the Arabs to a party in her old nightclub.

One of the things Hollywood has trouble learning is that wild party scenes are almost never funny (*Bachelor Party* was an exception). *Protocol*'s party scene fills the screen with the standard clichés: The Arabs, visiting Japanese businessmen, Hell's Angels, shocked diplomats, S&M couples, waitresses dressed like giraffes, and so on. It's not funny, it's desperate. We look at a lot of people going nuts and breaking glasses over each other's heads, and it's like the movie is pleading artistic bankruptcy.

There's more: A Capra-style ending, with Goldie making a patriotic, tear-jerking speech before a congressional hearing and then running for public office. None of this has much to do with the genuine comic premises that were set up at the beginning. Why couldn't they have followed Hawn's character into the labyrinth of real diplomatic protocol, and created original characters instead of off-the-shelf stereotypes? Why do so many Hollywood movies these days feel they have to go berserk in the last half hour, instead of putting in the groundwork to create a situation we care about and a conclusion that makes a difference? The character that Goldie Hawn creates in this movie is so refreshing and so interesting that they should have gone ahead and made the extra effort and written an intelligent screenplay about her.

Psycho II ★ ★ ½
R, 113 m., 1983

Anthony Perkins (Norman Bates), Vera Miles (Lila), Meg Tilly (Mary), Robert Loggia (Dr. Raymond), Dennis Franz (Toomey), Hugh Gillan (Sheriff Hunt). Directed by Richard Franklin and produced by Hilton A. Green. Screenplay by Tom Holland.

The first thing is to put Alfred Hitchcock's original 1960 *Psycho* right out of your mind. There will never be another movie like it, and no sequel could possibly capture its unique charms. If you've seen *Psycho* a dozen times and can recite the shots in the shower scene by heart, *Psycho II* is just not going to do it for you. But if you can accept this 1983 movie on its own terms, as a fresh start, and put your memories of Hitchcock on hold, then *Psycho II* begins to work. It's too heavy on plot and too willing to cheat

about its plot to be really successful, but it does have its moments, and it's better than your average, run-of-the-mill slasher movie.

Norman Bates, having been judged not guilty by reason of insanity back in 1960, has responded well to psychiatric treatment. He is released. Because of a "state budget cutback," however, there will be no halfway house to ease his transition back into society's mainstream, and no social worker to drop in from time to time. Instead, Norman's all on his own—and he moves back into that Gothic house of horrors up on the hill above the Bates Motel. The movie's homecoming scenes strike a nerve. After all, that *is* the Bates Motel, and few images of Sir Alfred's long career have remained more indelibly etched in the memories of moviegoers. Perkins plays Bates about the same as the last time we saw him, with perhaps a few additional twitches. But he's a more sympathetic character this time, more mellow, more subdued. He still is, of course, as nutty as a fruitcake. He gets a job washing dishes at the local diner, and he makes friends with a waitress named Mary (Meg Tilly), who agrees to move into the Bates home and become his roommate. And then, in Norman's words, it starts again. His "mother," long dead (as we have every reason to recall), begins telephoning him. There are some unexplained murders. The plot thickens, but I'll end my description right here, to preserve the movie's many, many, many, secrets.

Is *Psycho II* worth seeing? It is a craftsmanlike piece of filmmaking with a suitably flaky performance by Perkins, but it isn't really a sequel to *Psycho*. It continues the story, but not the spell. And it never really establishes the other characters very well. Meg Tilly, as Norman's friend, is too laid-back and dreamy to hold her own against Norman Bates *and* a fresh slasher mystery. Vera Miles, as a woman with a fierce hatred of Norman, never quite crosses the line from indignation to insanity. In a movie full of half-sketched characters and half-explained developments, Norman Bates is just too mesmerizing to fit in very easily. But then I should have guessed the sequel wouldn't make it—right from the pretitle sequence, in which Hitchcock's original shower scene is shown, but is allowed to end before the shot of the blood going down the drain! Is nothing sacred?

Psycho III ★ ★ ★
R, 93 m., 1986 ✔

Anthony Perkins (Norman Bates), Diana Scarwid (Maureen), Jeff Fahey (Duane), Roberta Maxwell (Tracy), Hugh Gillin (Sheriff Hunt), Lee Garlington (Myrna). Directed by Anthony Perkins and produced by Hilton A. Green. Screenplay by Charles Edward Pogue.

How well we remember Norman Bates. Tens of thousands of movie characters have come and gone since 1960, when he made his first appearance in *Psycho*, and yet he still remains so vivid in the memory, such a sharp image among all the others that have gone out of focus.

Most movies are disposable. *Psycho* supplied us with the furnishings for nightmares. "Dear Mr. Hitchcock," a mother wrote the master, "after seeing your movie my daughter is afraid to take a shower. What should I do?" Send her to the dry cleaners, Hitch advised her.

In *Psycho III*, there is one startling shot that completely understands Norman Bates. Up in the old gothic horror house on the hill, he has found a note from his mother, asking him to meet her in Cabin Number Twelve. We know that although his mother may have frequent conversations with him, she is in no condition to write him a note. Norman knows that, too. He stuffed her himself. As he walks down the steps and along the front of the Bates Motel toward his rendezvous, the camera tracks along with him, one unbroken shot, and his face is a twitching mask of fear.

The face belongs to Anthony Perkins, who is better than any other actor at reflecting the demons within. Although his facial expressions in the shot are not subtle, he isn't overacting; he projects such turmoil that we almost sympathize with him. And that is the real secret of Norman Bates, and one of the reasons that *Psycho III* works as a movie: Norman is not a mad-dog killer, a wholesale slasher like the amoral villains of the Dead Teen-ager Movies. He is at war with himself. He is divided. He, Norman Bates, wants to do the right thing, to be pleasant and quiet and pass without notice. But also inside of him is the voice of his mother, fiercely urging him to kill.

At the beginning of *Psycho III*, only a short time has passed since the end of *Psycho II*. In a nearby convent, a young novice (Diana Scarwid) blames herself when an older nun falls to her death. She runs out into the night, gets a ride with a sinister motorist (Jeff Fahey), and ends up at the Bates Motel. Fahey arrives there, too, and is hired as a night clerk. Other people also turn up: an investigative reporter who wants to do a story on Norman; a local woman who gets drunk and is picked up by Fahey; and finally a crowd of rowdies back for their high school reunion.

By the end of the movie, many of these people will be dead—and because this is a tragedy, not a horror story, some of the dead ones won't deserve it, and others will survive unfairly.

The movie was directed by Perkins, in his filmmaking debut. I was surprised by what a good job he does. Any movie named *Psycho III* is going to be compared to the Hitchcock original, but Perkins isn't an imitator. He has his own agenda. He has lived with Norman Bates all these years, and he has some ideas about him, and although the movie doesn't apologize for Norman, it does pity him. For the first time, I was able to see that the true horror in the *Psycho* movies isn't what Norman does—but the fact that he is compelled to do it.

There are a couple of scenes that remind us directly of Hitchcock, especially the scene where the local sheriff dips into the ice chest on a hot day, and doesn't notice that some of the cubes he's popping into his mouth have blood on them. Perkins permits himself a certain amount of that macabre humor, as when he talks about his hobby ("stuffing things") and when he analyzes his own case for the benefit of the visiting journalist. But the movie also pays its dues as a thriller, and there is one shocking scene that is as arbitrary, unexpected, tragic, and unfair as the shower scene in *Psycho*. Only one, but then one of those scenes is enough for any movie.

Pumping Iron II: The Women
★ ★ ★ ½
NO MPAA RATING, 130 m., 1985 ✔

Featuring Lori Bowen, Carla Dunlap, Bev Francis, and Rachel McLish. Directed and produced by George Butler and written by Charles Gaines.

The music is *Also Sprach Zarathustra*, the theme of *2001: A Space Odyssey*. From a concealed staircase at the back of the stage, an awesome human figure emerges. The backlighting makes it hard to discern: Is this Arnold Schwarzenegger? Sylvester Stallone? Not even close. This is Bev Francis, an Australian-born power-lifter who is the most muscular woman in the world.

The idea of women with big muscles is still a little strange. Spending some time with the stars of *Pumping Iron II: The Women* at the 1985 Cannes Film Festival, I was struck by the reactions they inspired from people on the street, who stopped, turned, and stared at these women with broad shoulders and huge biceps. Until the last few years, crowds at Cannes have traditionally been drawn by women with exaggerated feminine physiologies; now here were women from the covers of muscle magazines, and the French, usually so blasé, simply did not know how to react.

At first sight, there is something disturbing about a woman with massive muscles. She is not merely androgynous, a combination of the sexes like an Audrey Hepburn or a Mick Jagger, but more like a man with a woman's face. We are so trained to equate muscles with men, softness and slight build with women, that it seems nature has made a mistake. The impulse is to reject musclewomen as freaks, and that is probably going to be the first reaction of viewers to *Pumping Iron II*, a companion to the original *Pumping Iron*, which made Schwarzenegger a star. The intriguing thing about the movie is how it alters our original reactions, involving us in the sport of women's body-building, using the clichés of all sports to make us fans of this one, until by the end of the movie we're watching the 1983 International Women's Body-Building Competition with a connoisseur's eye. If we don't know how we feel about women with muscles, neither do the

judges; the entry of Bev Francis into the competition inspires a philosophical debate about the definition of "femininity."

Because Francis is by far more muscular than any other woman in the competition—including former champions Rachel McLish and Carla Dunlap—she should be the obvious favorite, but some of the judges say she doesn't look like a woman. Should she? Is this a body-building competition, or a beauty pageant? McLish, with her Farrah Fawcett hairstyle and rhinestone bra, has an obvious cheesecake appeal. Dunlap, Lori Bowen, and others in the finals are good-looking women. Francis looks like she belongs on the wrestling team. Her entry forces the judges—a hopelessly inept group—to define their terms. Meanwhile, we go backstage. George Butler, who has directed both *Pumping Iron* films, makes no pretense that his films are *cinéma vérité*. The documentary is scripted, in the sense that scenes are set up to dramatize Butler's points—even though the subjects and their dialogue are "real." We see Francis training in Australia, Dunlap talking with her mother, Bowen confessing that she idolizes Rachel McLish, and McLish tying body-building into born-again Christianity.

There are the obligatory gymnasium scenes, as the women work out, and the movie makes no secret of the narcissism implied by the sport. The real competition is with the mirror. The stage competition, at Caesar's Palace in Las Vegas, is more of a performance. The women line up, pair off for comparisons, are judged singly and in groups, displaying their basic muscle groups. The contest is so frankly obsessed with the details of these physical bodies that it seems like a particularly honest Miss America competition: They all know what they're onstage for, and there are no essays to write or songs to sing.

If anything sets the muscle-women apart from the Miss Americas, however, it's their intelligence. Miss Americas almost always share a stunning gift for the banal, for rehearsed clichés from civics class. The body-builders are, without exception, after all, articulate about what they are doing, and why. It has taken them, after all, a great deal more effort over a much longer time to get to *their* championship competition, and they have had to spend much of that time defending the very idea of their sport.

They are also, I thought, more articulate than most other athletes of either sex. Most competitive sports come already packaged with a complete set of rationales and clichés; nobody asks a football player to defend *the idea* of football. Nobody asks Chris Evert if she thinks playing tennis means she doesn't really want to be a woman. Body-building is a sport that seems to be about defining muscles, but *Pumping Iron II* shows that it is at least as much about defining attitudes and definitions of sexuality. You walk into this movie expecting to see a lot of sweat, and you walk out with more to think about than you bargained for.

Purple Hearts ½ ★
R, 115 m., 1984

Ken Wahl (Don Jardian), Cheryl Ladd (Deborah Solomon), Stephen Lee (Wizard), Drew Snyder (Colonel Larrimore), David Harris (Haynes). Directed and produced by Sidney J. Furie. Screenplay by Furie and Rick Natkin.

Remember those movie ads that used to show two lovers in the foreground, and a whole war in the background? You know, where the whole world was a stage, and millions of people were fighting and dying so that these two goofballs could swap spit? I thought they'd stopped making movies like that, but nope: *Purple Hearts* dedicates itself to all the Purple Heart winners of Vietnam, and then turns that war into a lonely hearts club for a couple of lovesick medics.

The characters:

Dr. Don Jardian (Ken Wahl), Navy battlefield surgeon, attached to the Marines. A gruff cynic until he looks up during a tricky operation and sees, above her surgical mask, the eyes of . . .

Deborah Solomon (Cheryl Ladd), Navy nurse, who has already lost a husband in this war, and is not willing to risk her heart one more time on a man who could be killed, breaking it again.

Jardian is in the front lines, up to his elbows in blood, performing major surgery on an assembly line. Then one critically wounded soldier comes in, and Jardian's superior predicts the soldier will die. Jardian

doesn't think so—not if the kid can get the latest treatment at a good hospital. So he commandeers a plane, escorts the wounded soldier to a hospital in Da Nang, and meets Nurse Solomon. The soldier dies. *C'est la guerre.* The doctor and nurse fall in love. He makes a proposition. She rejects it. Disconsolate, he flies back into danger—or, as John Wayne once put it, he steers into harm's way. Later, they meet again and this time they make love. In the morning, though, she announces that they cannot have an affair because she doesn't want to "commit" herself and have another broken heart, etc. She explains that they can always treasure the memory of last night. Thanks a lot, Nurse Solomon.

Jardian volunteers for heavy-duty frontline combat assignments. There is then a great deal of rugged battle footage, in which inflamed waves of Viet Cong charge American machine gun positions. The combat looks about as authentic as in John Wayne's *The Green Berets* (which ended, you will recall, with the Duke standing on the beach, silhouetted against a sun that had to be setting in the East). Anyway, Jardian is shot down behind enemy lines and has to trek back 150 miles through the jungle with a wounded comrade on his back. Meanwhile, Nurse Solomon hears he's dead. Also meanwhile, something happens so that when Jardian returns to base, *he* thinks *she's* dead. Not since *Romeo and Juliet* has the old They-Both-Think-the-Other-One-is-Dead ploy been milked so shamelessly.

This isn't war, this is bad plotting. And this isn't romance, it's soap opera. The last half-hour of the movie is an exercise in complete frustration for the audience: We cut back and forth between the doctor and the nurse in such a way that we know everything about both of them, and they know nothing about each other. It's the kind of movie where you want to shout advice at the screen. What's disappointing is that *Purple Hearts* comes from director Sidney J. Furie, who also made *The Boys in Company C*, a Vietnam film I admired very much. It was lean and angry and filled with a bitter humor. *Purple Hearts* is just romantic goo and impossible coincidence. The boys in Company C would have thrown beer bottles at the screen.

The Purple Rose of Cairo ★ ★ ★ ★
PG, 87 m., 1985

Mia Farrow (Cecilia), Jeff Daniels (Tom Baxter/Gil Shepherd), Danny Aiello (Monk), Van Johnson (Larry), Alexander H. Cohen (Raoul Hirsh). Directed by Woody Allen and produced by Robert Greenhut. Screenplay by Allen.

About twenty minutes into Woody Allen's *The Purple Rose of Cairo*, an extraordinary event takes place. A young woman has been going to see the same movie over and over again, because of her infatuation with the movie's hero. From his vantage point up on the screen, the hero notices her out in the audience. He strikes up a conversation, she smiles and shyly responds, and he abruptly steps off the screen and into her life. No explanation is offered for this miraculous event, but then perhaps none is needed: Don't we spend our lives waiting for the same thing to happen to us in the movies?

Life, of course, is never as simple and dreamy as the movies, and so the hero's bold act has alarming consequences. The movie's other characters are still stranded up there on the screen, feeling angry and left out. The Hollywood studio is aghast that its characters would suddenly develop minds of their own. The actor who *played* the hero is particularly upset, because now there are two of him walking around, one wearing a pith helmet. Things are simple only in the lives of the hero and the woman, who convince themselves that they *can* simply walk off into the sunset, and get away with this thing.

The Purple Rose of Cairo is audacious and witty and has a lot of good laughs in it, but the best thing about the movie is the way Woody Allen uses it to toy with the very essence of reality and fantasy. The movie is so cheerful and open that it took me a day or two, after I'd seen it, to realize how deeply Allen has reached this time. If it is true, and I think it is, that most of the time we go to the movies in order to experience brief lives that are not our own, then Allen is demonstrating what a tricky self-deception we practice. Those movie lives consist of *only* what is on the screen, and if we start thinking that real life can be the same way, we are in for a cruel awakening.

The woman in the movie is played by Mia Farrow as a sweet, rather baffled small-town waitress whose big, shiftless lug of a husband bats her around. She is a good candidate for the magic of the movies. Up on the screen, sophisticated people have cocktails and plan trips down the Nile and are recognized by the doormen in nightclubs. The hero in the movie is played by Jeff Daniels (who was Debra Winger's husband in *Terms of Endearment*). He is a genial, open-faced smoothie with all the right moves, but he has a problem: He *only* knows what his character knows in the movie, and his experience is literally limited to what happens to his character in the plot. This can cause problems. He's great at talking sweetly to a woman, and holding hands, and kissing—but just when the crucial moment arrives, the movie fades out, and therefore, alas, so does he.

Many of Allen's best moments come from exploring the paradox that the movie character knows nothing of real life. For example, he can drive a car, because he drives one in the movie, but he can't start a car, because he doesn't turn on the ignition in the movie. Mia Farrow thinks maybe they can work this out. They can learn from each other. He can learn real life, and she can learn the romance of the movies. The problem is, both of them are now living in real life, where studio moguls and angry actors and snoopy reporters are making their life miserable.

Allen's buried subject in *The Purple Rose of Cairo* is, I think, related to the subjects of his less successful movies, *Stardust Memories* (1980) and *Zelig* (1983). He is interested in the conflicts involving who you want to be, and who other people want you to be. *Stardust* was about a celebrity whose fame prevented people from relating to anything but his image. *Zelig*, the other side of the coin, was about a man whose anonymity was so profound that he could gain an identity only by absorbing one from the people around him. In *Purple Rose*, the movie hero has the first problem, and the woman in the audience has the second, and when they get together, they still don't make one whole person, just two sad halves.

Purple Rose is delightful from beginning to end, not only because of the clarity and charm with which Daniels and Farrow explore the problems of their characters, but also because the movie is so intelligent. It's not brainy or intellectual—no one in the whole movie speaks with more complexity than your average 1930s movie hero—but the movie is filled with wit and invention, and Allen trusts us to find the ironies, relish the contradictions, and figure things out for ourselves. While we do that, he makes us laugh and he makes us think, and when you get right down to it, forget about the fantasies; those are two of the most exciting things that could happen to anybody in a movie. The more you think about *The Purple Rose of Cairo*, and about the movies, and about why you go to the movies, the deeper the damned thing gets.

Q ★ ★ ½
R, 92 m., 1982

Michael Moriarty (Quinn), Candy Clark (Girlfriend), David Carradine (Detective), Richard Roundtree (Detective), Ed Kovens (Crook). Directed by Larry Cohen and produced by Samuel Z. Arkoff. Screenplay by Cohen.

A few days after *Q* was screened at the Cannes Film Festival (under its original title, *The Winged Serpent*), the following conversation took place between Samuel Z. Arkoff, the film's producer, and Rex Reed, the critic:

> *Reed:* Sam! I just saw *The Winged Serpent!* What a surprise! All that dreck—and right in the middle of it, a great Method performance by Michael Moriarty!
> *Arkoff:* The dreck was my idea.

I believe him. Arkoff has been producing films for thirty years now, and even if he *was* honored with a retrospective at the Museum of Modern Art, his heart still lies with shots of a giant flying lizard attacking a woman in a bikini on top of a Manhattan skyscraper. He's just that kinda guy. There are, in fact, several shots in *Q* that owe their ancestry to Sam Arkoff. I am aware, of course, that Larry Cohen gets credit for having written and directed this movie, but where would Cohen or any other director be without the rich heritage of a quarter-century of American-International Pictures made by Sam Arkoff? Here are examples of the shots I have in mind:

- The camera looks straight down at terrified citizens fleeing from a menace. They run crazily across the street. Some run away from the camera, some toward it, so that you can't tell for sure where the menace is, and the shot can be intercut with shots of a menace approaching from any direction.
- The hero empties his machine gun into the giant serpent and turns away from a window to issue orders: "Everybody hold your positions!" Just then the serpent reappears behind him.
- There are False Serpent Alarms in which people get hit from behind by toy birds, chairs, and their boyfriends.
- David Carradine says, "He doesn't die easy."

You get the idea. *Q* is another silly monster movie. But think how long it's *been* since we had another silly monster movie. There was a time during the golden age of Sam Arkoff's career when there were lots of monster movies. Remember, for example, *Attack of the Crab Monsters*, *The Viking Women and the Sea Serpent*, *Creature from the Haunted Sea*, and *Wasp Woman*. But in the last few years Creature Features have been replaced by Dead Teen-ager Movies, and instead of awful special effects of a monster going berserk, we get worse shots of a homicidal maniac going berserk.

Q returns to the basic formula, in which a prehistoric creature terrorizes the city. In this case, the creature is a Quetzalcoatl, a mythical Aztec monster with wings *and* four claws. It apparently has been brought back into existence in connection with some shady human sacrifices at the Museum of National History (although this particular subplot is very muddled). It lives in a nest at the top of the Chrysler Building, lays eggs, and terrorizes helpless New Yorkers, who are not sure if this is a real monster or another crazy circulation stunt by Rupert Murdoch.

Rex Reed was right, though, about the Method performance by Michael Moriarty. In the middle of this exploitation movie, there's Moriarty, rolling his eyes, improvising dialogue, and acting creepy. He's fun to watch, especially in the scene where he names his terms for leading the cops to the lizard. The cast also includes David Carradine, Richard Roundtree, and Candy Clark, good actors all, but you have to be *awfully* good not to be upstaged by the death throes of a dying Quetzalcoatl.

Still to be answered: How did *one* Quetzalcoatl get pregnant?

Quest for Fire ★ ★ ★ ½
R, 100 m., 1982

Everett McGill (Noah), Ron Perlman (Amoukar), Nameer El-Kadi (Gaw), Rae Dawn Chong (Ika). Directed by Jean-Jacques Annaud and produced by John Kemeny and Denis Heroux. Screenplay by Gerard Brach.

There are basically two ways to regard *Quest for Fire*. The movie is either (a) the moving story of how scattered tribes of very early men developed some of the traits that made them human, or (b) a laughable caveman picture in which a lot of lantern-jawed actors jump around in animal skins, snarling and swinging clubs at one another. During the movie's opening scenes, I found myself seeing it in the second way, as a borderline comedy. But then these characters and their quest began to grow on me, and by the time the movie was over I cared very much about how their lives would turn out.

Other viewers report some of the same confusion. The movie has been compared with such varied works of art as *2001: A Space Odyssey* and *Alley Oop*. The question, I suppose, is whether you can make your own leap of imagination into the world of the movie—whether you're willing to identify with these beetle-browed ancestors who made more important discoveries, in their way, than all of the Nobel laureates put together. I found I *was* willing, and I was a little surprised at how much affection the movie generated.

Quest for Fire was shot on rugged locations in Canada and Scotland and takes place at the dawn of man. It introduces us to a tribe of primitive men who guard their most precious possession, which is fire. They know how to tend it and how to use it, but not how to make it. And after a jealous tribe of less-advanced creatures attacks them and destroys their fire, three men set out on an odyssey to seek another tribe that possesses fire and to steal it from them. Along the way, there are terrifying adventures. A saber-toothed tiger chases the men up into a tree

and keeps them there for days. On another occasion, the heroes are trapped between an unfriendly tribe of apes and a herd of mastodons. In each situation, the men realize that simply running away won't work; they can't run fast or far enough. And so they slowly and painfully figure out a solution to their dilemma. Climbing the tree, for example, is rather obvious, but their solution to the mastodon problem is a brave inspiration.

Eventually the men discover another tribe, a more advanced tribe that lives in primitive huts and knows how to make fire and has even developed arts (they decorate themselves with mud, and their clay pots have drawings of animals scratched on them). The leader of the wanderers lusts after one of the women of the new tribe, and after a strange initiation ceremony he has sex with her. Soon he will make one of his greatest discoveries: The difference between lust and love and how it leads to the difference between isolation—and loneliness.

Quest for Fire compresses prehistory quite radically, of course. It's a little much to expect that one man in one span of a few weeks could make the scientific, emotional, and tactical discoveries that take place in the movie. Our progress as a race must have been slower than that (although Loren Eiseley writes in his books of the amazing explosion of the size of the human brain in just a handful of generations). *Quest for Fire* isn't science, though, it's an imaginary re-creation of our past, and it uses history for inspiration, not as a data source. The only two technical advisers listed in the credits are, appropriately, a novelist and a scientific popularizer: Anthony Burgess created the special primitive languages in the film, and Desmond Morris choreographed the body language and gestures.

I suggested earlier that there's probably a temptation to laugh during *Quest for Fire*, especially during such touchy scenes as the one in which early woman teaches early man that it *wasn't* as good for her as it was for him. I smiled during those scenes. But, thinking over my response, I realize that I wasn't smiling at the movie, but at the behavior of the characters. Man is a comic beast. For all of our dignity, we are very simple in many of our wants and desires, and as we crawled out of the primeval sludge and started our long trek toward civilization, there must have been many more moments of comedy than of nobility.

Quest for Fire cheerfully acknowledges that, and indeed some of its best scenes involve man's discovery of laughter. When one of the primitive tribesmen is hit on the head by a small falling stone, the woman from the other tribe laughs and laughs. Our heroes are puzzled: They haven't heard such a noise before. But it strikes some sort of deep chord, I guess, because later, one of the tribesmen deliberately drops a small stone on his friend's head, and then everybody laughs: The three men together with the woman who taught them laughter. That's human. The guy who got hit on the head is, of course, a little slow to join in the laughter, but finally he goes along with the joke. That's civilization.

Quicksilver ★ ★
PG, 106 m., 1985

Kevin Bacon (Jack Casey), Jami Gertz (Terri), Paul Rodriguez (Hector), Rudy Ramos (Gypsy), Andrew Smith (Gabe Kaplan), Gerald S. O'Laughlin (Mr. Casey), Larry Fishburne (Voodoo). Directed by Tom Donnelly and produced by Michael Rachmil and Daniel Melnick. Screenplay by Donnelly.

Quicksilver is a collision between realism and gloss, between a story that demands to be told at street-level, and a style that looks inspired by music videos. The movie has moments when it comes to life, when it threatens to tell a story about interesting people, and then it wanders off into inane scenes designed only to sell records. Isn't it time for the movies to stop being an advertising medium for the music industry?

The story is *Trading Places* told backwards. A rich young commodities broker named Jack Casey (Kevin Bacon) loses his entire fortune on a bad day on the trading floor. Instead of starting over, he decides to drop out, and after weeks of wandering the streets he gets a job with a bicycle messenger service. It suits him fine. He likes the freedom of riding the streets, of choosing his own routes, of not wearing a suit and tie, of moving freely through the city as a free-lance observer. And he likes some of the people he

meets at the messenger service, especially Terri (Jami Gertz), a spunky brunette.

But life on the streets is not without its down side. The messengers are sometimes used as a low-rent, low-risk delivery service for drug dealers, and a slimeboat named Voodoo (Larry Fishburne) starts using Terri to run his drugs. To her, a job's a job, but Bacon starts feeling protective toward her, and knows how much of a danger Voodoo really is.

Meanwhile, there's a subplot. A fellow messenger named Hector (Paul Rodriguez) dreams of putting together enough money to retire his bicycle and buy his own hot-dog cart. Bacon decides to try a comeback in the markets, using Hector's money to run up enough of a profit to buy the cart. This is, of course, another thinly disguised example of the CLIDVIC Syndrome (the Climb from Despair to Victory), which has been cloned into countless new movies from the *Rocky* formula. But the movie isn't content with one standard ending; it has two. After the climax on the trading floor, there's another one, a chase scene.

There once was a time when movies introduced us to characters and then solved their problems in human terms. Now it's all technology. Here's a guy who drops out of high finance and becomes a bicycle messenger, and what's the solution to his problem? Why, he has to win a deadly chase to the death with a drug dealer, naturally. After he survives the chase, the movie ends, having provided us with something that felt like an ending but wasn't one.

In between, *Quicksilver* misses other chances to connect. For example, the most touching moment in the whole movie comes early, when Bacon confesses to his father that he's lost not only all of his own money, but also his parents' nest egg. His father acts tough and brave, and urges him to go back in the ring and keep fighting. But then Bacon leaves home and returns unexpectedly to find his father sitting at the dining room table, his face in his hands, weeping in despair. This is such a compelling scene that it's frustrating when the movie never follows up on it; the parents disappear for a long stretch, and then are handled with a line of dialogue ("I'm giving this money to my father").

I guess there wasn't time for another visit to the family home, what with all the MTV scenes of messengers doing wheelies to rock music (one of the songs is actually subtitled "Dueling Bikes"). Based on the evidence on the screen, my guess is that *Quicksilver* started out as a complex screenplay about complicated people—and that the only way it could be sold was to tart it up with lots of high-tech style. The story is so interesting, and Bacon and the other actors are so capable, that if this movie had been two hours out of their lives, I would have found it compelling. What we get, though, is thirty-five minutes of their lives and a lot of recycled visual clichés.

Racing with the Moon ★ ★ ★ ½
PG, 108 m., 1984

Sean Penn (Hopper), Elizabeth McGovern (Caddie), Nicholas Cage (Nicky), Suzanne Adkinson (Sally), Julie Phillips (Alice). Directed by Richard Benjamin and produced by Alain Bernheim and John Kohn. Screenplay by Steven Kloves.

I'd like to start with a hypothetical question: How long has it been since you went to a movie that ended with the words "I love you"? For me, it had been a very long time, and one of the simpler pleasures of *Racing with the Moon* was to observe the movie marching inevitably toward those three words. A deeper pleasure was that the movie arrived there with grace and charm.

The story takes place in California in 1943, with the United States at war and teen-agers volunteering for the service. We meet a couple of high school kids, Hopper and Nicky, who are pinspotters down at the bowling alley and otherwise spend their time cutting classes, shooting pool, hitching rides on trains, and talking about the meaning of life. We are reminded of Tom and Huck. One night Hopper goes to the movies. His eyes meet the girl who is selling him his ticket, and he is thunderstruck by her. Her name is Caddie. Nicky already has a girlfriend, a plump little blonde named Sally. Hopper starts a campaign to win Caddie's heart, by slipping her flowers anonymously and tracking her down in the high school library. It

appears that Caddie is a rich kid who lives in the house on the hill. But she likes Hopper anyway, and he likes her, and *Racing with the Moon* turns into a love story.

So far, what we have here is a movie that could go in several different directions. It could be sappy, it could be great, it could be dripping with so much nostalgia that it would feel like a memory even while we were watching it. *Racing with the Moon* doesn't fall into the *Summer of '42* nostalgia trap, but tries to be honest with its romantic characters. The performers are probably the reason that approach works so well. The three leading actors are Sean Penn and Elizabeth McGovern, as the young lovers, and Nicholas Cage, as Penn's friend. It's a pleasure to watch them work.

Penn, in particular, shows a whole side we didn't see in movies like *Bad Boys* or, needless to say, *Fast Times at Ridgemont High*. He's somehow better-looking than before, and more relaxed and confident. He doesn't come across with a lot of distracting self-importance. He plays the kind of kid who uses a rough exterior—smoking and shooting pool—as a kind of cover-up for the intelligence and sensitivity underneath, and one of the movie's best quiet moments comes when he reveals how well he can play the piano. McGovern, who had such a sweet face and such a wicked charm as the mistress in *Ragtime*, seems younger here. She has a secret she keeps from Penn, but only because she loves him. The way she plays against him is fun to watch: She's not a flirt and she's not coy, but instead she's open with this kid and has fun teasing him; there's a scene where she sets him up for a date with her girlfriend, and it's written and choreographed so carefully that it takes you back to any soda fountain you may ever have inhabited. Cage is good, too, reckless and self-destructive and dreamy, and by the end of the movie we really have a feeling for their complex relationships with each other.

Racing with the Moon is a movie like *Valley Girl* or *Baby, It's You*, a movie that is interested in teen-agers and willing to listen to how they talk and to observe, with great tenderness, the fragility and importance of their first big loves. It's easy to end a movie with "I love you," but it's hard to get there honestly.

Raggedy Man ★ ★ ★ ½
PG, 94 m., 1981

Sissy Spacek (Nita), Eric Roberts (Teddy), Sam Shepard (Bailey), R.G. Armstrong (Rigby). Directed by Jack Fisk and produced by Burt Weissbourd and William D. Wittliff. Screenplay by Wittliff.

Raggedy Man remembers the small-town years of World War II so exactly that, although not yet born when the war broke out, I found myself remembering things I didn't even know I knew. Things like the way kids zoomed around dusty backyards, making their arms into airplane wings and imitating the noises of dive bombers. Like the Andrews Sisters singing "Rum and Coca-Cola" on the radio. Like the absolutely correct detail of a plaster-of-paris plaque on the wall, with a child's hand print immortalized on it. Remember?

Sissy Spacek stars as the sole switchboard operator of a small-town telephone company somewhere in the wilds of Texas. She lives in a small white frame house with a slamming screen door, and tries to raise her two sons, who are almost too small to support such grown-up names as Henry and Harry. The question of her husband is a mystery. Spacek hates her job, but she can't leave it: Mr. Rigby, the president of the telephone company, barks that this is wartime and her job is "frozen." Right, and she's frozen in it, until one day a young sailor (Eric Roberts) comes looking for a pay phone so he can call home. He's got a few days' leave, and has hitchhiked for hundreds of miles on the hopes of seeing his fiancée. The phone call reveals that she has taken up with a new beau. Roberts is crestfallen. Spacek kindly offers him some coffee. More or less, a little at a time, they fall in love.

These surface events of small-town life are wonderfully observed in *Raggedy Man*, which never pushes the romance between Spacek and Roberts too far: They remain decent, sensitive, courteous people, a little shy in the presence of large emotions. The town gossips about the woman taking up with the sailor, but people will gossip. (Nobody knows that better than the telephone operator!) Unfortunately, *Raggedy Man* has a whole additional level of plotting that is not nearly as rewarding as the events

I've already described. There is, for example, the mystery of the "raggedy man" himself, a strange, scarecrow character who hangs about in the background of several scenes and has a disconcerting way of disappearing just when you want to get a closer look at him. There's also the matter of the town louts, who inhabit the beer hall and lust after the slim, young telephone operator.

These two plot strands lead up to a climactic ending that, quite frankly, I thought was unnecessary. Without giving away several secrets that the movie itself takes very seriously, I can say that *Raggedy Man* would have pleased me more if it had completely avoided its violent conclusion—and if the raggedy man himself had been left totally out of the story, the movie, and especially the symbolism.

Such regrets still leave my affection for this movie pretty much untouched. The Sissy Spacek performance is a small jewel: She has the words, the movements, the very tilt of her face, down just right. There's a scene where she puts music on the radio and dances with a broom, and another scene where she has a serious talk with her two little boys, and they're nearly perfect scenes. So is another one, where Roberts takes the two boys to a carnival. Roberts himself is a revelation: He is often overwrought in his acting; here, playing more quietly, he expresses great reserve of tenderness and strength, and is very effective.

Raggedy Man was Sissy Spacek's first movie after she won the Academy Award for *Coal Miner's Daughter*, and the first movie directed by her husband, Jack Fisk. (She met him when he was the art director for her first starring movie, *Badlands*, back in 1973.) The movie was made with a lot of love and startlingly fresh memories of the early 1940s, and reminds us once again that Spacek is a treasure.

Raging Bull ★ ★ ★ ★
R, 119 m., 1980

Robert De Niro (Jake La Motta), Cathy Moriarty (Vickie La Motta), Joe Pesci (Joey), Frank Vincent (Salvy), Nicholas Colasanto (Tommy Como), Theresa Saldana (Lenore), Frank Adonis (Patsy), Mario Gallo (Mario). Directed by Martin Scorsese and produced

by Irwin Winkler and Robert Chartoff.
Screenplay by Paul Schrader and Mardik
Martin.

Martin Scorsese's *Raging Bull* is a movie
about brute force, anger, and grief. It is also,
like several of Scorsese's other movies, about
a man's inability to understand a woman
except in terms of the only two roles he
knows how to assign her: virgin or whore.
There is no room inside the mind of the
prizefighter in this movie for the notion that
a woman might be a friend, a lover, or a partner. She is only, to begin with, an inaccessible sexual fantasy. And then, after he has
essed her, she becomes tarnished by sex.
Insecure in his own manhood, the man
becomes obsessed by jealousy—and releases
his jealousy in violence.

It is a vicious circle. Freud called it the
"madonna-whore complex." Groucho Marx
put it somewhat differently: "I wouldn't
belong to any club that would have me as a
member." It amounts to a man having such
low self-esteem that he (a) cannot respect a
woman who would sleep with him, and (b) is
convinced that, given the choice, she would
rather be sleeping with someone else. I'm
making a point of the way *Raging Bull*
equates sexuality and violence because one of
the criticisms of this movie is that we never
really get to know the central character. I
don't agree with that. I think Scorsese and
Robert De Niro do a fearless job of showing
us the precise feelings of their central character, the former boxing champion Jake
La Motta.

It is true that the character never tells us
what he's feeling, that he is not introspective,
that his dialogue is mostly limited to
expressions of desire, fear, hatred, and jealousy. But these very limitations—these stone
walls separating the character from the
world of ordinary feelings—tell us all we
need to know, especially when they're
reflected back at him by the other people in
his life. Especially his brother and his wife,
Vickie.

Raging Bull is based, we are told, on the
life of La Motta, who came out of the slums
of the Bronx to become middleweight champion in the 1940s, who made and squandered
millions of dollars, who became a pathetic
stand-up comedian, and finally spent time in

a prison for corrupting the morals of an
underage girl. Is this the real La Motta? We
cannot know for sure, though La Motta was
closely involved with the production. What's
perhaps more to the point is that Scorsese
and his principal collaborators, actor Robert
De Niro and screenwriter Paul Schrader,
were attracted to this material. All three
seem fascinated by the lives of tortured, violent, guilt-ridden characters; their previous
three-way collaboration was the movie *Taxi
Driver*.

Scorsese's very first film, *Who's That
Knocking at My Door* (1967), starred Harvey
Keitel as a kid from Little Italy who fell in
love with a girl but could not handle the facts
of her previous sexual experience. In its
sequel, *Mean Streets* (1972), the same hang-
up was explored, as it was in *Taxi Driver*,
where the De Niro character's madonna-
whore complex tortured him in sick relationships with an inaccessible, icy blonde,
and with a young prostitute. Now the filmmakers have returned to the same ground, in
a film deliberately intended to strip away
everything but the raw surges of guilt, jealousy, and rage coursing through La Motta's
extremely limited imagination.

Raging Bull remains close to its three basic
elements: a man, a woman, and prizefighting. La Motta is portrayed as a punk kid,
stubborn, strong, and narrow. He gets
involved in boxing, and he is good at it. He
gets married, but his wife seems almost an
afterthought. Then one day he sees a girl at a
municipal swimming pool and is transfixed
by her. The girl is named Vickie, and she is
played by Cathy Moriarty as an intriguing
mixture of unstudied teen-ager, self-reliant
survivor, and somewhat calculated slut.

La Motta wins and marries her. Then he
becomes consumed by the conviction she is
cheating on him. Scorsese finds a way to
visually suggest his jealousy: From
La Motta's point of view, Vickie sometimes
floats in slow motion toward another man.
The technique fixes the moment in our
minds; we share La Motta's exaggeration of
an innocent event. And we share, too, the
La Motta character's limited and tragic
hang-ups. This man we see is not, I think,
supposed to be any more subtle than he
seems. He does not have additional
"qualities" to share with us. He is an engine

driven by his own rage. The equation between his prizefighting and his sexuality is inescapable, and we see the trap he's in: La Motta is the victim of base needs and instincts that, in his case, are not accompanied by the insights and maturity necessary for him to cope with them. The raging bull. The poor sap.

Ragtime ★ ★ ★ ½
PG, 156 m., 1981

Howard E. Rollins, Jr. (Coalhouse Walker), James Cagney (Rhinelander Waldo), Brad Dourif (Younger Brother), Mary Steenburgen (Mother), James Olson (Father), Elizabeth McGovern (Evelyn Nesbit), Kenneth McMillan (Willie Conklin), Pat O'Brien (Delmas), Mandy Patinkin (Tateh), Moses Gunn (Booker T. Washington). Directed by Milos Forman and produced by Dino De Laurentiis. Screenplay by Michael Weller.

Milos Forman apparently made a basic decision very early in his production of E.L. Doctorow's best-selling novel, *Ragtime*. He decided to set aside the book's kaleidoscopic jumble of people, places, and things, and concentrate on just one of the several narrative threads. Instead of telling dozens of stories, his film is mostly concerned with the story of Coalhouse Walker, Jr., a black piano player who insists that justice be done after he is insulted by some yahoo volunteer firemen.

Doctorow's novel was an inspired juggling act involving both actual and fictional characters, who sometimes met in imaginary scenes of good wit and imagery. The Coalhouse story was more or less equal with several others. A film faithful to the book would have had people walking in and out of each other's lives in an astonishing series of coincidences. That might have been a good film, too. It might have looked a little like Robert Altman's *Nashville* or *Buffalo Bill*, and indeed Altman was the first filmmaker signed to direct *Ragtime*. But we will never see what Altman might have done, and Forman decided to do something different. He traces the ways in which Coalhouse Walker enters and affects the lives of an upstate New York family in the first decade of the century. The family lives in White Plains, N.Y., in a vast and airy old frame manor, and it consists of Father, Mother, and Younger Brother, with walk-ons by a grandfather and a young son.

For Younger Brother, the sirens of the big city call, in the form of an infatuation with the chorus girl Evelyn Nesbit (Elizabeth McGovern). That's before the saga of Coalhouse Walker alters his life. Coalhouse (in a superb performance by Howard E. Rollins, Jr.) meets the family by accident, or maybe by fate. A young black woman gives birth to Coalhouse's son, and then the family takes in both the woman and her son, hiring her as their maid. Coalhouse comes calling. He wants to marry the mother of his child. He has earned enough money. Everything's all set for the ceremony, when an event takes place that changes everything. The local volunteer firemen, enraged that a black man would own his own Model T, block the car's way in front of their station. They pile horse manure on the front seat. And Coalhouse, quite simply, cannot rest until he sees his car restored to him in its original condition.

The story develops quickly into a confrontation. Coalhouse barricades himself into New York's J. Pierpont Morgan Library, and issues a set of demands. The library is surrounded by police and guardsmen, led by Police Commissioner Rhinelander Waldo (the great James Cagney, out of retirement). Father (James Olson) gets drawn into negotiations, and Younger Brother (Brad Dourif) is actually one of Coalhouse's lieutenants, in blackface disguise. Meanwhile, Mother is running off with a bearded immigrant who started out making cutout silhouettes on the streets and is now one of the first film directors.

The story of *Ragtime*, then, is essentially the story of Coalhouse Walker, Jr. Forman, a Czechoslovakian with an usually keen eye for American society—his credits include *One Flew Over the Cuckoo's Nest* and *Hair!*—has made a film about black pride and rage and . . . not *only* white racism, which we sort of expect, but also white liberalism.

The great achievement of *Ragtime* is in its performances, especially Rollins and the changes he goes through in this story, from youthful romantic love to an impassioned cry "Lord, why did you fill me with such rage?" Olson, quiet and self-effacing, is subtly powerful as Father. Mary Steenburgen is clear-voiced, primly ethical Mother who springs a big surprise on everyone. Pat O'Brien has two great scenes as a corrupt, world-weary lawyer. Kenneth McMillan blusters and threatens as the racist fire chief. And when Cagney tells him "people tell me . . . you're slime," there is the resonance of movie legend in his voice.

Ragtime is a loving, beautifully mounted, graceful film that creates its characters with great clarity. We understand where everyone stands, and most of the time we even know why. Forman surrounds them with some of the other characters from the Doctorow novel (including Harry Houdini, Teddy Roosevelt, and Norman Mailer as the architect Sanford White), but in the film they're just atmosphere—window dressing. Forman's decision to stick with the story of Coalhouse is vindicated, because he tells it so well.

Raiders of the Lost Ark ★ ★ ★ ★
PG, 115 m., 1981

Harrison Ford (Indy), Ronald Lacey (Teht), John Rhys-Davies (Sallah), Karen Allen (Marion), Wolf Kahler (Dietrich). Directed by Steven Spielberg and produced by Frank Marshall. Executive producers, George Lucas and Howard Kazanjian. Screenplay by Lucas and Phillip Kaufman.

Raiders of the Lost Ark is an out-of-body experience, a movie of glorious imagination and breakneck speed that grabs you in the first shot, hurtles you through a series of incredible adventures, and deposits you back in reality two hours later—breathless, dizzy, wrung-out, and with a silly grin on your face. This movie celebrates the stories we spent our adolescence searching for in the pulp adventure magazines, in the novels of Edgar Rice Burroughs, in comics—even in the movies. There used to be a magazine named *Thrilling Wonder Stories*, and every shot in *Raiders of the Lost Ark* looks like one of its covers. It's the kind of movie where the hero gets out of bed wondering what daring exploits and astonishing, cliff-hanging, death-defying threats he will have to survive in the next ten seconds.

It's actually more than a movie; it's a catalog of adventure. For locations, it ticks off the jungles of South America, the hin-

terlands of Tibet, the deserts of Egypt, a hidden submarine base, an isolated island, a forgotten tomb—no, make that *two* forgotten tombs—and an American anthropology classroom. For villains, it has sadistic Nazis, slimy gravediggers, drunken Sherpas, and scheming Frenchmen. For threats, it climaxes with the wrath of God, and leads up to that spectacular development by easy stages, with tarantulas, runaway boulders, hidden spears, falling rock slabs, burning airplanes, runaway trucks, sealed tombs, and snakes. Lots of snakes. For modes of conveyance, it looks like one of those old world's fair panoramas of transportation: It has horse carts, biplanes, motorcycles, submarines, ships, horse, trains, and trucks. No bicycles.

For heroes, it has Indiana Jones (Harrison Ford) and his former and future girlfriend, Marion (Karen Allen). She's the kind of girl . . . well, to make a long story short, when they first met ten years ago, Indiana deflowered her, and that made her so mad at men that she moved to the mountains of Tibet, opened a bar, and started nightly drinking contests with the Sherpas. She'll never forgive him, almost.

The time is 1936. Indy is an American anthropologist who learns that the Nazis think they've discovered the long-lost resting place of the Ark of the Covenant, the golden casket used by the ancient Hebrews to hold the Ten Commandments. Indy's mission: Beat the Nazis to the prize. He flies to Tibet, collects Marion and a priceless medallion that holds the secret of the Ark's location, and then tries to outsmart the Nazis. What is a little amazing about *Raiders of the Lost Ark* is that this plot somehow holds together and makes some sense, even though it functions primarily as a framework for the most incredible series of action and stunt set-pieces I've ever seen in a movie. Indiana and Marion spend the entire film hanging by their fingernails—literally, at one point, over a pit of poisonous snakes.

They survive a series of gruesome and dreadful traps, pitfalls, double-crosses, ambushes, and fates worse than death (of which this movie suggests several). And Indiana engages in the best chase scene I've seen in a film. (I include, in second place, the chase from *The French Connection*, with *Bullitt* in third.) The chase involves a truck, three jeeps, a horse, a motorcycle, and an awesomely difficult stunt in which a character is required to make a 360-degree turn of the speeding truck. All of these spectacles are achieved with flawless movie technology brought to a combination of stunts, special visual effects, and sheer sweat. The makers of this film have covered similar ground before, if perhaps never so fluently; George Lucas, the executive producer, gave birth to the *Star Wars* movies, and Steven Spielberg, the director, made *Jaws* and *Close Encounters*. The rest of the all-star crew's work includes photography by veteran British cinematographer Douglas Slocombe, appropriately stirring and haunting music by *Star Wars* composer John Williams, sets by *Star Wars* production designer Norman Reynolds and art director Les Dilley, and countless wonderments by Richard Edlund, who supervised the visual effects.

Two things, however, make *Raiders of the Lost Ark* more than just a technological triumph: its sense of humor and the droll style of its characters. This is often a funny movie, but it doesn't get many of its laughs with dialogue and only a few with obvious gags (although the biggest laugh comes from the oldest and most obvious gag, involving a swordsman and a marksman). We find ourselves laughing in surprise, in relief, in incredulity at the movie's ability to pile one incident upon another in an inexhaustible series of inventions. And the personalities of the central characters are enormously winning. Harrison Ford, as Indy Jones, does not do a reprise of his *Star Wars* work. Instead he creates a taciturn, understated, stubborn character who might be the Humphrey Bogart of *Treasure of the Sierra Madre* with his tongue in his cheek. He survives fires, crushings, shootings, burnings. He really hates snakes. Karen Allen plays the female lead with a resilient toughness that develops its own charm. She can handle herself in any situation. She *really* hates snakes.

Raiders of the Lost Ark is a swashbuckling adventure epic in the tradition of *Star Wars*, *Superman*, the James Bond pictures, and all the other multimillion-dollar special effects extravaganzas. It wants only to entertain. It succeeds. Watch it with someone you know fairly well. There will be times during the film when it will be necessary to grab somebody.

Rambo: First Blood Part II ★ ★ ★
R, 90 m., 1985

Sylvester Stallone (Rambo), Richard Crenna (Trautman), Charles Napier (Murdock), Steven Berkoff (Podovsky). Directed by George P. Cosmatos and produced by Buzz Feitshans. Screenplay by Stallone and James Cameron.

Rambo, subtitled *First Blood Part II* and continuing the adventures of Sylvester Stallone's one-man army, is two movies in one. First there's a hard-boiled, high-energy, violent action picture, which will probably find a large and enthusiastic audience. Lurking beneath the action is a political statement accusing the U.S. government of such base political motives that I was, quite simply, astonished. *Rambo* is not left wing or right wing, but belongs to the paranoid wing of American politics, in which villains left and right crawl under the covers together and conspire to annihilate John Rambo.

If you saw the original *First Blood*, which was a big hit, you remember Rambo. He is a returned Vietnam hero, a superbly trained fighting machine who is considered by his superior officers to be the finest soldier they have ever seen. But Rambo becomes unhinged by civilian life, and by the insults which he believes society is heaping on men like himself, who risked their lives to fight the war. So Rambo reverts to his military training and turns into a one-man army dedicated to destroying the establishment that does not honor him.

At the end of *First Blood*, Rambo was captured after blowing up half a town and wiping out countless civilian and military authorities. If anyone had been keeping count, he would have qualified as the nation's most prolific mass killer. In the opening scenes of *Rambo*, he is breaking rocks on a chain gang when his old superior officer (Richard Crenna) arrives with a mission: Rambo is needed to parachute into Southeast Asia and scout out a suspected POW compound holding missing Americans. Any questions, Rambo? "Only one," he tells Crenna. "This time, do we get to win?"

His question places *Rambo* squarely within the revisionist genre of Vietnam movies, in which the war is refought with a happy ending. *Uncommon Valor*, the two *Missing in Action* movies, and this film are all about missions to free American MIAs and kill countless Asian soldiers. The basic assumption is that we lost the war because "the politicians" prevented men like Rambo from doing what they were trained to do. And indeed, again this time he has his hands tied: he's only supposed to take pictures, not engage in violence. Needless to say, if they only want pictures, they've picked the wrong mass murderer for the job.

Rambo's mission is outlined by a suspicious American intelligence officer (the square-jawed, rugged Charles Napier, a favorite of Russ Meyer *and* Jonathan Demme). Only after Rambo parachutes into the night does it become clear that Napier doesn't really want the mission to succeed. In logic so impenetrable that I would love to have somebody run it past me again, the movie argues that it would be politically embarrassing for American MIAs to be found at this late date, and that therefore it would be best if Rambo's mission fails. If he *does* come back with photos, they'll be suppressed. In that case, I was wondering, why sponsor the mission in the first place—and especially with a loose cannon like Rambo? No matter; the movie turns into an efficient action picture, with Rambo wiping out legions of North Vietnamese and Russians with a variety of weapons, including explosive-tipped arrows. Back at headquarters, Napier does all he can to sabotage the mission, but it becomes clear that Rambo could have won the Vietnam war by himself, had he been unleashed, and everything leads to a big climax, a helicopter dogfight. The strange thing about *Rambo* is that it works despite its politics. Its conspiracy theory is so angry and so unlikely that we tend to ignore it, sit back, and enjoy the action.

Ran ★ ★ ★ ★
R, 160 m., 1985 ✔

Tatsuya Nakadai (Lord Hidetora), Akira Terao (Taro, Eldest Son), Jinpachi Nezu (Jiro, Second Son), Daisuke Ryn (Sahuro, Youngest Son), Mjeko Harada (Lady Kaede, Taro's Wife), Yoshiko Miyazaki (Lady Sue, Jiro's Wife), Masayuki Yui (Tango, Hidetora's Servant), Peter (Kyoami, The Fool). Directed by Akira Kurosawa and produced by Serge Silberman and Masato Hara. Screenplay by Hideo Oquino, Masato Ide, and Kurosawa.

One of the early reviews of Akira Kurosawa's *Ran* said that he could not possibly have directed it at an earlier age. My first impression was to question that act of critical omnipotence. Who is to say Kurosawa couldn't have made this film at fifty or sixty, instead of at seventy-five, as he has? But then I thought longer about *Ran*, which is based on Shakespeare's *King Lear* and on a similar medieval samurai legend. And I thought about Laurence Olivier's Lear and about the *Lear* I recently saw starring Douglas Campbell and I realized that age is probably a prerequisite to fully understanding this character. Dustin Hoffman might be able to play Willy Loman by aging himself with makeup, but he will have to wait another twenty years to play Lear.

The character contains great paradoxes, but they are not the paradoxes of youth; they spring from long habit. Lear has the arrogance of great power, long held. He has wide knowledge of the world. Yet he is curiously innocent when it comes to his own children; he thinks they can do no wrong, can be trusted to carry out his plans. At the end, when his dreams have been broken, the character has the touching quality of a childlike innocence that can see breath on lips that are forever sealed, and can dream of an existence beyond the cruelties of man. Playing Lear is not a technical exercise. I wonder if a man can do it who has not had great disappointments and long dark nights of the soul.

Kurosawa has lived through those bad times. Here is one of the greatest directors of all time, out of fashion in his own country, suffering from depression, nearly blind. He prepared this film for ten years, drawing hundreds of sketches showing every shot, hardly expecting that the money would ever be found to allow him to make the film. But a deal was finally put together by Serge Silberman, the old French producer who backed the later films of Luis Bunuel (who could also have given us a distinctive Lear). Silberman risked his own money; this is the most expensive Japanese film ever made, and, yes, perhaps Kurosawa could not have made it until he was seventy-five.

The story is familiar. An old lord decides to retire from daily control of his kingdom, yet still keep all the trappings of his power. He will divide his kingdom in three parts among his children. In *Ran*, they are sons, not daughters. First, he requires a ritual statement of love. The youngest son cannot abide the hypocrisy, and stays silent. And so on.

The Japanese legend which Kurosawa draws from contains a famous illustration in which the old lord takes three arrows and demonstrates that when they are bundled, they cannot be broken, but taken one at a time, they are weak. He wishes his sons to remain allies, so they will be strong, but of course they begin to fight, and civil war breaks out as the old lord begins his forlorn journey from one castle to another, gradually being stripped of his soldiers, his pride, his sanity.

Nobody can film an epic battle scene like Kurosawa. He has already abundantly demonstrated that in *The Seven Samurai*, in *Yojimbo*, in *Kagemusha*. In *Ran*, the great bloody battles are counterpointed with scenes of a chamber quality, as deep hatreds and lusts are seen to grow behind the castle's walls.

King Lear is a play that centers obsessively around words expressing negatives. "Nothing? Nothing will come of nothing!" "Never, never, never." "No, no, no, no, no." They express in deep anguish the king's realization that what has been taken apart will never be put together again, that his beloved child is dead and will breathe no more, that his pride and folly have put an end to his happiness. Kurosawa's film expresses that despair perhaps more deeply than a Western film might; the samurai costumes, the makeup inspired by Noh drama, give the story a freshness that removes it from all our earlier associations.

Ran is a great, glorious achievement. Kurosawa must often have associated himself with the old lord as he tried to put this film together, but in the end he has triumphed, and the image I have of him, at seventy-five, is of three arrows bundled together.

The Razor's Edge ★ ★ ½
PG-13, 130 m., 1984

Bill Murray (Larry Darrell), Theresa Russell (Sophie), Catherine Hicks (Isabel), Denholm Elliott (Elliot Templeton), James Keach (Gray Maturin), Brian Doyle-Murray (Piedmont). Directed by John Byrum and written by Byrum and Bill Murray. Produced by Robert P. Marcucci and Harry Benn.

Here is the story of a man who can never quite get back to a suburban frame of mind after he's seen World War I. The man is born into a world of lawn parties, polo ponies, and rich relatives who wave benignly from the shade of a cocktail shaker. He volunteers to be an ambulance driver in the war, sees death and despair, and comes back home to tell his fiancée that they'd better postpone the wedding: He wants to live in Paris for a while and find himself.

The Razor's Edge then tells a standard story of self-discovery in which the young man drops out, becomes a bohemian in the Paris of the 1920s, works as a coal miner, and takes a passage to India to discover the meaning of life. He actually gets all the way to a mountaintop, signs on with a monastery, and spends some time as a contemplative monk, before discovering within himself only a desire to return to Paris. His fiancée comes to Paris. He courts her, but is not ready to marry her. Another American woman, a wild young thing whose husband and child have been killed in a motor crash, joins them in Paris and is quickly swept into a world of drunkenness and drugs. The young man discovers that he loves this woman and tries to save her, but by the end of the film, having stared death in the face in the war and regarded infinity from a mountaintop, he realizes that nothing really makes any difference.

In other words, this is your standard 1960s hippie drama, moved back in time and adapted from the great novel by Somerset Maugham. If the movie really had a sense of its time (if it seemed to know that it took place in an era when the characters were much more unusual than they would be today), the hero's odyssey would mean more. But the flaw in this movie is that the hero is too passive, too contained, too rich in self-irony, to really sweep us along in his quest.

And that, I'm afraid, is the fault of Bill Murray, who plays the hero as if fate is a comedian and he is the straight man. Murray, who is usually such a superb actor, has taken the wrong path in this performance, giving us moments when everybody in the film and in the audience is moved, except Murray. There are times when he seems downright obstinate in his performance, giving us a ramrod posture, a poker face, and eyes that will not let us inside. Perhaps, in his desire to make a break with the comic roles we know him for, he was overreacting. That makes even more curious the moments in the film when he allows himself to be funny: The comic side of his character doesn't seem to be coming out of anything.

The movie has other flaws. It is more interested in showing him going to India than in really dealing with what he might have discovered there. It is fascinated by the character of the dissipated young woman (a wonderful performance by Theresa Russell), but never lets us really see the ex-fiancée (Catherine Hicks) as anything more than a predestined ex-fiancée. A rich uncle (Denholm Elliott) who lives in Paris is seen just enough to become intriguing, but not enough to be understood: Why did *he* become an expatriate?

The Razor's Edge is far from being a bad movie. Some of the scenes are very good, especially the uncle's deathbed farewell and Murray's first attempts to sober up Russell. But at the end I didn't feel engaged. I didn't feel that the hero's attention had been quite focused during his quest for the meaning of life. He didn't seem to be a searcher, but more of a bystander, shoulders thrown back, deadpan expression in place, waiting to see if life could make him care.

Re-Animator ★ ★ ★
NO MPAA RATING, 95 m., 1985

Jeffrey Combs (Herbert West), Bruce Abbott (Dan Cain), Barbara Crampton (Megan Halsey), David Gale (Dr. Carl Hill), Robert Sampson (Dean Halsey), Gerry Glack (Mace), Carolyn Purdy-Gordon (Dr. Harrod). Directed by Stuart Gordon and produced by Brian Yuzna. Screenplay by Dennis Paoli, William J. Morris, and Gordon.

One of the most boring experiences on Earth

is a trash movie without the courage of its lack of convictions. If it only wants to be cynical, it becomes lifeless in every moment—a bad dream on the screen. One of the pleasures of the movies, however, is to find a movie that chooses a disreputable genre and then tries with all its might to transcend the genre, to go over the top into some kind of artistic vision, however weird.

Stuart Gordon's *Re-Animator* is a pleasure like that, a frankly gory horror movie that finds a rhythm and a style that make it work in a cockeyed, offbeat sort of way. It's charged up by the tension between the director's desire to make a good movie and his realization that few movies about mad scientists and dead body parts are ever likely to be very good. The temptation is to take a camp approach to the material, to mock it, as Paul Morrissey did in *Andy Warhol's Frankenstein*. Gordon resists that temptation, and creates a livid, bloody, deadpan exercise in the theater of the undead.

Seeing this movie at the Cannes Film Festival, I walked in with no particular expectations, except that I hoped *Re-Animator* would be better than the festival's run-of-the-mill exploitation films. I walked out somewhat surprised and reinvigorated (if not re-animated) by a movie that had the audience emitting taxi whistles and wild goat cries. In its own way, on its own terms, in its corrupt genre, this movie worked as well as any other movie in the festival.

I was reminded of Pauline Kael's sane observation: "The movies are so rarely great art, that if we can't appreciate great trash, there is little reason for us to go."

The movie's story involves . . . but why bother? In the ads, the hero was described as having a good head on his shoulders, and another one in the laboratory dish in front of him. That more or less captures the essence of *Re-Animator*. Driven by an insane desire to vindicate himself by creating living beings out of dead body parts, a scientist uses his intelligence to burrow more and more deeply into sheer madness.

Gordon's direction, and particularly his use of special effects, will come as no surprise to anyone who saw his famous *Warp* trilogy onstage. He borrows from the traditions of comic-book art and B-grade thrillers, using his special effects not as set pieces for us to study, but as dazzling throwaways as the action hurtles ahead. By the end of the film, we are keenly aware that nothing of consequence has happened, but so what? We have been assaulted by a lurid imagination, amazed by unspeakable sights, blind-sided by the movie's curiously dry sense of humor. I guess that's our money's worth.

Real Genius ★ ★ ★ ½
PG-13, 105 m., 1985

Val Kilmer (Chris Knight), William Atherton (Professor Hathaway), Gabe Jarret (Mitch), Michelle Meyrink (Jordan Cochran), Jonathan Gries (Laslo [recluse]), Robert Prescott (Kent Torokvei), Severn Darden (Dr. Meredith). Directed by Martha Coolidge and produced by Brian Grazer. Screenplay by Neal Israel, Pat Profit, and Peter Torokvei.

It is probably not true that all American college students have been lobotomized and pumped full of sex hormones, although most movies treat them that way. Some students are more like the ones we meet in *Real Genius.* They are smart but socially uncertain and relativity is easier for them to understand than what to say on a first date. This is the first movie in a long time that's set on a college campus where the students are supposed to be intelligent. The campus is apparently Cal Tech, and the students are the next generation of great physicists, the kind who will write papers proving that everything we know is wrong.

The movie involves the saga of Mitch (Gabe Jarret), a brilliant high school student whose Science Fair project has revised the theory of laser beam technology. He is personally recruited by Prof. Hathaway (William Atherton), a famous physics professor who wants the kid to work in his personal laboratory. Once on campus, the kid meets the legendary Chris Knight (Val Kilmer), who was the most brilliant freshman in history, and who is now a junior whose mind is beginning to be cluttered by mischief. The two students room together—and there seems to be a third person in the room, a strange, wraith-like bearded figure who disappears into the clothes closet, and doesn't seem to be there when the door is flung open.

The professor is running a scam. He has a Defense Department contract for a sophisticated laser device so accurate that it could incinerate a single man on earth from a base in orbit. The professor is using his students as slave labor to do most of the work on the project while ripping off the government grant to build himself a new house. The students, meanwhile, have no idea they're working on a weapons system, and are more interested in using laser beams to lead everyone to a "Tanning Invitational" they've set up by turning a lecture hall into a swimming pool.

Real Genius allows every one of its characters the freedom to be complicated and quirky and individual. That's especially true of Jordan (Michelle Meyrink), a hyperactive woman student who talks all the time and never sleeps and knits things without even thinking about it, and follows Mitch into the john because she's so busy explaining something that she doesn't even notice what he's doing. I could recognize students like this from my own undergraduate days. One of the most familiar types on campus (and one of the rarest in the movies) is the self-styled eccentric, who develops a complex of weird personality traits as a way of clearing space and defining himself.

Real Genius was directed by Martha Coolidge, who made *Valley Girl,* one of the best and most perceptive recent teen-age movies. What I like best about her is that she gives her characters the freedom to be themselves. They don't have to be John Belushi clones, or fraternity jocks, or dumb coeds. They can flourish in all of their infinite variety, as young people with a world of possibilities and a lot of strange, beautiful notions. *Real Genius* contains many pleasures, but one of the best is its conviction that the American campus contains life as we know it.

Red Sonja ★ ½
PG-13, 91 m., 1985

Arnold Schwarzenegger (Kalidor), Brigitte Nielsen (Red Sonja), Sandahl Bergman (Queen Gedren), Paul Smith (Falkon), Ernie Reyes, Jr. (Tarn). Directed by Richard Fleischer and produced by Christian Ferry. Screenplay by Clive Exton and George MacDonald Fraser.

If I were writing a screenplay like this, I would be laughing out loud:

Red Sonja's house is in flames. Murderers have killed her family, defiled her, and set her lands on fire. She lies unconscious on the ground. A wavy white mist in vaguely human form appears in the trees, and says, "Sonja! You are suffering!"

At this point (which is about sixty seconds into *Red Sonja*), all that could save the movie would be for Sonja to look up and say, "Only when I laugh." But Sonja, alas, lacks such wit, and so she sets off to avenge her dead sister, her pillaged lands, and her lost honor. There is a hard road ahead of her.

First, she must learn the ways of the sword from the Grandmaster, a character who looks like a cross between Fu Manchu and Clara Peller (the "Where's the beef?" lady). He tells her, "To be a great swordsman . . . you need a great sword." She nods intently, and selects one from the stock he has on hand. Then she rides out of the amphitheater by passing beneath a statue of the Buddha, who was squatting in such a familiar position that I instinctively knew why he looked so contented.

Along the way, Red Sonja meets Kalidor, a muscular swordsman with a great sword. They encounter a little emperor and his valet, who does not carry a great sword but does have several small knives. They enter the temple of Queen Gedren, who has stolen a glowing emerald talisman that (so it is spoken) will destroy the world in thirteen days, by flood and earthquake. Sonja has met Gedren before. As the voice of the wraithlike white mist reminded her: "Queen Gedren desired you. But she filled you with repugnance. So you struck out at her, scarring her face."

There are many battles with the great swords. There are also bottomless pits, exploding mountains, falling trap doors, savage warriors, and, of course, floods and earthquakes. But what could be more earth-shaking than the love story?

Kalidor loves Red Sonja. He wants to kiss her. She rebuffs his advance, and says, "I have vowed to love no man who cannot defeat me in battle." This is a tough one for Kalidor. He knits his brow and puzzles it out. "But . . . if I defeat you," he says, "then you will be dead . . . and then how will I love

you?" His logic is irrefutable, but they fight anyway.

Red Sonja is one of the ranking goofy movies of our time. The ads feature Arnold Schwarzenegger, but the real star of the movie is Brigitte Nielsen, a tall Danish model who looks just great. The exact time frame of the story is a little hard to figure out, but using the evidence on the screen, I have been able to narrow it down to the epoch between the rise of Buddhism and the year brass brassieres went out of style.

Reds ★ ★ ★ ½
PG, 200 m., 1981

Warren Beatty (John Reed), Diane Keaton (Louise Bryant), Edward Herrmann (Max Eastman), Jerzy Kosinski (Zinoviev), Jack Nicholson (Eugene O'Neill), Maureen Stapleton (Emma Goldman), Paul Sorvino (Louis Fraina), Gene Hackman (Pete Van Wherry). Directed and produced by Warren Beatty. Screenplay by Beatty and Trevor Griffiths.

The original John Reed was a dashing young man from Portland who knew a good story when he found one, and, when he found himself in the midst of the Bolshevik revolution, wrote a book called *Ten Days That Shook the World* and made himself a famous journalist. He never quite got it right again after that. He became embroiled in the American left-wing politics of the 1920s, participated in fights between factions of the Socialist Party and the new American Communist Party, and finally returned to Moscow on a series of noble fool's errands that led up, one way or another, to his death from tuberculosis and kidney failure in a Russian hospital. He is the only American buried within the Kremlin walls.

That is Reed's story in a nutshell. But if you look a little more deeply you find a man who was more than a political creature. He was also a man who wanted to be where the action was, a radical young intellectual who was in the middle of everything in the years after World War I, when Greenwich Village was in a creative ferment and American society seemed, for a brief moment, to be overturning itself. It is that personal, human John Reed that Warren Beatty's *Reds* takes as its subject, although there is a lot, and maybe too much, of the political John Reed as well. The movie never succeeds in convincing us that the feuds between the American socialist parties were much more than personality conflicts and ego-bruisings, so audiences can hardly be expected to care which faction is "the" American party of the left.

What audiences can, and possibly will, care about, however, is a traditional Hollywood romantic epic, a love story written on the canvas of history, as they used to say in the ads. And *Reds* provides that with glorious romanticism, surprising intelligence, and a consistent wit. It is the thinking man's *Dr. Zhivago*, told from the other side, of course. The love story stars Warren Beatty and Diane Keaton, who might seem just a tad unlikely as casting choices, but who are immediately engaging and then grow into solid, plausible people on the screen. Keaton is a particular surprise. I had somehow gotten into the habit of expecting her to be a touchy New Yorker, sweet, scared, and intellectual. Here, as a Portland dentist's wife who runs away with John Reed and eventually follows him halfway around the world, through blizzards and prisons and across icy steppes, she is just what she needs to be: plucky, healthy, exasperated, loyal, and funny.

Beatty, as John Reed, is also surprising. I expected him to play Reed as a serious, noble, heroic man for all seasons, and so he does, sometimes. But there is in Warren Beatty's screen persona a persistent irony, a way of kidding his own seriousness, that takes the edge off a potentially pretentious character and makes him into one of God's fools. Beatty plays Reed but does not beatify him: He permits the silliness and boyishness to coexist with the self-conscious historical mission.

The action in the movie takes Reed to Russia and back again to Portland, and off again with Louise Bryant (Keaton), and then there is a lengthy pause in Greenwich Village and time enough for Louise to have a sad little love affair with the morosely alcoholic playwright Eugene O'Neill (Jack Nicholson). Then there are other missions to Moscow, and heated political debates in New York basements, and at one point I'm afraid I entirely lost track of exactly why Reed was running behind a horsecart in the middle of some forgotten battle in an obscure backwater of the Russian empire. The fact is, Reed's motivation from moment to moment is not the point of the picture. The point is that a revolution is happening, human societies are being swept aside, a new class is in control—or so it seems—and for an insatiably curious young man, that is exhilirating, and it is enough.

The heart of the film is in the relationship between Reed and Bryant. There is an interesting attempt to consider her problems as well as his. She leaves Portland because she is sick unto death of small talk. She wants to get involved in politics, in art, in what's happening: She is so inexorably drawn to Greenwich Village that if Reed had not taken her there, she might have gone on her own. If she was a radical in Portland, however, she is an Oregonian in the Village, and she cannot compete conversationally with such experienced fast-talkers as the anarchist Emma Goldman (Maureen Stapleton). In fact, no one seems to listen to her or pay much heed, except for sad Eugene O'Neill, who is brave enough to love her but not smart enough to keep it to himself. The ways in which she edges toward O'Neill, and then loyally returns to Reed, create an emotional density around her character that makes it really *mean* something when she and Reed embrace at last in a wonderful tear-jerking scene in the Russian train station.

The whole movie finally comes down to the fact that the characters matter to us. Beatty may be fascinated by the ins and outs of American left-wing politics sixty years ago, but he is not so idealistic as to believe an American mass audience can be inspired to care as deeply. So he gives us people. And they are seen here with such warmth and affection that we sense new dimensions not only in Beatty and Keaton, but especially in Nicholson. In *Reds*, understating his desire, apologizing for his passion, hanging around Louise, handing her a poem, throwing her out of his life, he is quieter but much more passionate than in the overwrought *The Postman Always Rings Twice*.

As as for Beatty, *Reds* is his bravura turn. He got the idea, nurtured it for a decade, found the financing, wrote most of the script, produced, and directed and starred and still found enough artistic detachment to make his Reed into a flawed, fascinating enigma instead of a boring archetypal hero. I liked this movie. I felt a real fondness for it. It was quite a subject to spring on the capitalist Hollywood movie system, and maybe only Beatty could have raised $35 million to make a movie about a man who hated millionaires. I noticed, here at the end of the credits, a wonderful line that reads: *Copyright © MCMLXXXI Barclays Mercantile Industrial Finance Limited.* John Reed would have loved that.

Repo Man ★ ★ ★
R, 92 m., 1984

Harry Dean Stanton (Bud), Emilio Estevez (Otto), Tracey Walter (Miller), Olivia Barash (Leila). Directed by Alex Cox and produced by Jonathan Wacks and Peter McCarthy. Screenplay by Cox.

Repo Man is one of those movies that slips through the cracks and gives us all a little weirdo fun. It is the first movie I know about that combines (1) punk teen-agers, (2) automobile repossessors, and (3) aliens from outer space. This is the kind of movie that baffles Hollywood, because it isn't made from any known formula and doesn't follow the rules. The movie begins with a mad scientist careening down a New Mexico road in his Chevy Malibu. He is stopped by a cop, who finds some really strange things happening in the car's trunk. Then the action moves to Los Angeles, where a punk kid (Emilio Estevez) is passing the time by going to dances and banging his head against other kids' heads, to demonstrate his affection.

The kid runs into a guy named Bud (Harry Dean Stanton), who is an auto repossessor. Bud tricks the kid into driving a repo car for him, and before long the kid is a full-time auto repossessor, learning the ropes. The ropes are pretty tough. Repo men, we learn, live their lives on the edge, operating under extreme tension that is caused partly by their working conditions and partly because as Stanton explains, "I've never known a repo man who didn't use a lot of speed." Harry Dean Stanton is one of the treasures of American movies. He has appeared in a lot of films without becoming a big star, but he has that total cynicism that

brings jobs like repo into focus. In the movie, he and Estevez make a nice team; the beaten veteran and the cocky kid, and they cruise the streets looking for cars.

Meanwhile (and here I will be careful to respect some surprises in the story), the government is looking for that Chevy Malibu, because it is connected to the possibility that alien beings have visited the Earth. The feds put out a $10,000 reward for the car, which makes it the jackpot every repo man in L.A. is looking for. Hot on the trail of the car, Stanton and Estevez get into a duel with the famed Rodriguez brothers, known as the bandits of repo. All of this works very nicely, but what's best about *Repo Man* is its sly sense of humor. There are a lot of running gags in the movie, and the best of them involves generic food labels, of all things. (There is a moment involving some food in a refrigerator that gave me one of the biggest laughs I'd had at the movies in a long time.) The movie also has a special way of looking at Los Angeles, seeing it through Harry Dean Stanton's eyes as a wasteland of human ambitions where a few bucks can be made by the quick, the bitter, and the sly.

I saw *Repo Man* near the end of a busy stretch on the movie beat: Three days during which I saw more relentlessly bad movies than during any comparable period in memory. Most of those bad movies were so cynically constructed out of formula ideas and "commercial" ingredients that watching them was an ordeal. *Repo Man* comes out of left field, has no big stars, didn't cost much, takes chances, dares to be unconventional, is funny, and works. There is a lesson here.

Return of the Jedi ★ ★ ★ ★
PG, 133 m., 1983

Mark Hamill (Luke Skywalker), Harrison Ford (Han Solo), Carrie Fisher (Princess Leia), Billy Dee Williams (Lando Calrissian), Anthony Daniels (C-3PO), David Prowse (Darth Vader), James Earl Jones (Vader's Voice), Alec Guinness (Obi-Wan Kenobi). Directed by Richard Marquand and produced by Howard Kazanjian. Screenplay by Lawrence Kasdan and George Lucas.

Here is just one small moment in *Return of the Jedi*, a moment you could miss if you looked away from the screen, but a moment that helps explain the special magic of the Star Wars movies. Luke Skywalker is engaged in a ferocious battle in the dungeons beneath the throne room of the loathsome Jabba the Hutt. His adversary is a slimy, gruesome, reptilian monster made of warts and teeth. Things are looking bad when suddenly the monster is crushed beneath a falling door. And then (here is the small moment) there's a shot of the monster's keeper, a muscle-bound jailer, who rushes forward in tears. He is brokenhearted at the destruction of his pet. Everybody loves somebody.

It is that extra level of detail that makes the Star Wars pictures much more than just space operas. Other movies might approach the special effects. Other action pictures might approximate the sense of swashbuckling adventure. But in *Return of the Jedi*, as in *Star Wars* and *The Empire Strikes Back*, there's such a wonderful density to the canvas. Things are happening all over. They're pouring forth from imaginations so fertile that, yes, we do halfway believe in this crazy Galactic Empire long ago and far, far away.

Return of the Jedi is both a familiar movie and a new one. It concludes the stories of the major human characters in the saga, particularly Skywalker, Han Solo, Princess Leia, and Darth Vader. It revisits other characters who seem either more or less than human, including Ben (Obi-Wan Kenobi), Yoda, Chewbacca, and the beloved robots C-3PO and R2-D2. If George Lucas persists in his plan to make nine Star Wars movies, this will nevertheless be the last we'll see of Luke, Han, and Leia, although the robots will be present in all the films.

The story in the Star Wars movies is, however, only part of the film—and a less crucial element as time goes by. What *Jedi* is really giving us is a picaresque journey through imagination, and an introduction to forms of life less mundane than our own. In *Jedi*, we encounter several unforgettable characters, including the evil Jabba the Hutt, who is a cross between a toad and the Cheshire cat; the lovable, cuddly Ewoks, the furry inhabitants of the "forest moon of Endor"; a fearsome desert monster made of sand and teeth, and hateful little ratlike creatures that scurry about the corners of the frame. And there is an admiral for the Alliance who looks like

the missing link between Tyrannosaurus Rex and Charles de Gaulle.

One thing the Star Wars movies never do is waste a lot of time on introductions. Unlike a lot of special effects and monster movies, where new creatures are introduced with laborious setups, *Jedi* immediately plunges its alien beasts into the thick of the action. Maybe that's why the film has such a sense of visual richness. Jabba's throne room, for example, is populated with several weird creatures, some of them only half-glimpsed in the corner of the frame. The camera in *Jedi* slides casually past forms of life that would provide the centerpiece for lesser movies.

The movie also has, of course, more of the amazing battles in outer space—the intergalactic video games that have been a trademark since *Star Wars*. And *Jedi* finds an interesting variation on that chase sequence in *Star Wars* where the space cruisers hurtled through the narrow canyons on the surface of the Death Star. This time, there's a breakneck chase through a forest, aboard airborne motorcycles. After several of the bad guys have run into trees and gotten creamed, you pause to ask yourself why they couldn't have simply flown *above* the treetops . . . but never mind, it wouldn't have been as much fun that way.

And *Return of the Jedi* is fun, magnificent fun. The movie is a complete entertainment, a feast for the eyes and a delight for the fancy. It's a little amazing how Lucas and his associates keep topping themselves. From the point of view of simple moviemaking logistics, there is an awesome amount of work on the screen in *Jedi* (twice as many visual effects as *Star Wars* in the space battles, Lucas claims). The fact that the makers of *Jedi* are able to emerge intact from their task, having created a very special work of the imagination, is the sort of miracle that perhaps Obi-Wan would know something about.

Return of the Living Dead ★ ★ ★
R, 90 m., 1985

Clu Gulager (Burt), James Karen (Frank), Don Calfa (Ernie), Thom Mathews (Freddy), Beverly Randolph (Tina), Miguel A. Nunez (Spider). Directed by Dan O'Bannon and produced by Tom Fox and Graham Henderson. Screenplay by O'Bannon.

Not many movies have the nerve to name their sources right there in the dialogue, so you can make your own comparisons. *Return of the Living Dead* makes no secret of its inspiration. The movie opens with a teenager going to work in one of those supply houses that ship cadavers and skeletons to scientists, and in no time at all the man who runs the company is leaning over the desk and asking if the kid has ever seen *Night of the Living Dead*. Because it wasn't just a movie, see? It was the truth. But the government tried to cover it up, and he can prove it, because they bottled up those zombies in airtight canisters—*and they're down in the basement right now.*

This is probably as elegant a way as any to rip off *Night of the Living Dead*—admitting your sources and going on from there. *Return of the Living Dead* is not a sequel to George Romero's first two Living Dead movies, and in fact there is some sort of irony in the fact that it opened at the same time as *Day of the Dead*, which was a Romero sequel, but not a very satisfactory one. *Return* is the directorial debut of Dan O'Bannon, a sometime collaborator with John Carpenter, and the co-author of the screenplay for *Alien*. It is not a great creative breakthrough, but it is a satisfactory ghoul movie, moving with precision from the funny opening scenes through the obligatory middle passages of pseudo-science, and on to the barf-bag climax.

The ghouls in all of these movies perform more or less the same function. They shuffle inexorably toward the camera, drawn by their insatiable appetite for human flesh. The tasks of the living characters in the movie are threefold: (1) to attempt to destroy or control the monsters; (2) to flee the monsters in panic; and (3) to become the monsters.

O'Bannon's *Return* handles the third requirement in a scene that has a certain charm. The teen-ager and the cadaver wholesaler have been overrun by ghouls. The virus, or whatever it is, has infected their whole laboratory, and the two humans come down with what seems to be a cold. Then the muscular pains get intense, and they start shivering. Their friends call the paramedics. An on-the-spot physical exam turns up some alarming symptoms. Both men have no pulse, and their body temperatures are the same as room temperature. The muscle pains? Rigor mortis. In other words, they are dead. They take this information pretty hard.

Meanwhile, *Return* supplies the usual grisly special effects. The lab stock includes "split dogs," sort of cross-sections of dead dogs that have been preserved as lab specimens. The Living Dead disease strikes them, and they begin to crawl about. Nothing will stop them—not even skewering. Indeed, the severed limbs of the ghouls have a life of their own. And, inexorably, the ghouls take over.

What's the bottom line on a movie like this? If you are below a certain age, I suppose it's scary, and the R rating is richly deserved. To hardened veterans of ghoul movies, however, a sort of connoisseurship develops. *Return* is a movie with some nice, droll opening scenes and the obligatory horrible climax. It doesn't make the mistake of *Day of the Dead*—talking too much. It's kind of a sensation-machine, made out of the usual ingredients, and the real question is whether it's done with style. It is.

Return of the Secaucus Seven ★ ★ ★
NO MPAA RATING, 110 m., 1981

Mark Arnott (Jeff), Gordon Clapp (Chip), Maggie Cousineau-Arndt (Frances), Adam Le Fevre (J.T.), Bruce MacDonald (Mike), Jean Passanante (Irene), John Sayles (Howie), Maggie Renzi (Katie). Directed and written by John Sayles. Produced by William Aydelott and Jeffrey Nelson.

A friend asked me what *Return of the Secaucus Seven* was about. "It's the story of your life," I said.

"*My* life?"

Well, and my life, too. Everybody's life who was younger once and demonstrated against one thing or another, and is older now and stumped for the moment by the curiosity that the most outspoken advocate of change in our society is Ronald Reagan. The movie tells the story of a group of friends who set out during the late 1960s to join the March on the Pentagon, and were arrested in Secaucus, New Jersey, on charges they still do not fully understand. So they didn't make it to the Pentagon, where their brain power might have made the difference in Abbie Hoffman's plan to levitate that building.

Those were strange times. Even Norman Mailer, in his *Armies of the Night,* reported that when the Yippies started to chant and meditate and try to levitate the Pentagon, he looked to see if it had started to rise: An unlikely event, of course, but one that a reporter would always kick himself for if he had missed it. Years have passed since those days. The original members of the Secaucus Seven have grown older now, can taste their thirtieth birthdays, and as the movie opens have gathered for a weekend reunion in the country. The film tells the story of their weekend, as they take their measure and remember the 1960s.

The Sixties. A director once told me that he had been interviewed by a group of college editors, one of whom asked him, "Was drug usage really prevalent back in the 1960s?" He didn't know whether to laugh or cry. The Secaucus Seven has the same choice. They are never again going to be as young as they were, but they still remember their days of activism so sharply that they refuse to cut loose from them. These days, people still go through their thirtieth birthday crisis, all right, but they seem to hold it on their fortieth birthday.

The Secaucus Seven has grown slightly, with the addition of spouses, lovers, and even children. They gather to play basketball, sing songs, get drunk, fight, break up, and sleep together—or apart. In mood, the film resembles Alain Tanner's wonderful *Jonah Who Will Be 25 in the Year 2000.* Some of the Seven have become fairly successful: There are a congressional aide and a medical student. There is also a kid who is still trying to make it as a folk singer, an occupation that no longer pays very well even if he had the talent, which he does not. And another who has chosen to stay in the old hometown and pump gas.

John Sayles, who wrote and directed the movie, made it as a labor of love (and financed it by writing the screenplays for *Piranha* and *Alligator,* so he may still not quite have evened the scales). He alternates among the various couples and groupings

and intrigues, and at first the movie is frankly confusing. We can't keep everybody straight, and there's too much explanation of who they all are and what they've all done. Before long, though, we have everyone sorted out. We know the relationships. And we grow quietly grateful that Sayles has chosen not to pack his weekend reunion with a series of dramatic confrontations and crises. There are no overdoses, suicides, or murders. Only the adjustments such a weekend would be expected to bring, and the inevitable bitterness when one couple has broken up, and the old and new lovers have to confront one another.

This is not a perfect film. Odds and ends stick out, and some scenes have a certain gracelessness. But it is an absorbing film that contains shrewd observations about human nature, and more than its share of humor. We leave with mixed feelings: We feel like we've attended that reunion, and at the same time we're relieved that we did not. It is easier to be young if your friends don't age on you.

Return to Oz ★ ★
PG, 110 m., 1985

Fairuza Balk (Dorothy), Nicol Williamson (Worley/King), Jean Marsh (Nurse Wilson/Mombi), Piper Laurie (Aunt Em), Matt Clark (Uncle Henry). Directed by Walter Murch and produced by Paul Maslansky. Screenplay by Murch and Gill Dennis.

Somewhere between the sweetness of *The Wizard of Oz* and the astonishing special effects of *Return to Oz,* something got lost. I think it was innocence. Maybe it was the ability to dream like a child. Here is an expensive, ambitious movie that wants to continue the story of Dorothy's adventures in Oz. It throws great resources and remarkable craftsmanship into the task. And it has no idea what made *The Wizard of Oz* such a special movie.

The original *Wizard* was good not only because of the performances, the music, and the land of Oz, but also because it contained reassuring news for children: Even the most dreaded wizards might turn out to be just as timid and frightened as anyone else. This new film, *Return to Oz,* has a more ominous message: It's a cruel world, in which dreadful forces run loose, and little girls are right to be timid and frightened. The first *Wizard* was deliciously scary. *Return* is just plain scary.

In the opening scenes, Dorothy has returned from Oz to Kansas, but still remembers her adventures and misses her friends. Aunt Em is concerned that the child is ruining her health with daydreams. So she bundles Dorothy into a wagon and takes her miles away to a clinic run by a sinister doctor and a forbidding nurse. Aunt Em leaves Dorothy *alone* there, and says she'll be back the next day. Dorothy is shown to a stark, forbidding room. She hears ominous noises, echoing down the long, dark corridors. Then they come for her, strap her to a cot, wheel her into the operating room, and prepare to give her electroshock therapy.

Is this bad enough? It gets worse. An enormous storm comes up, lightning and thunder split the skies, there is a terrible flood, and Dorothy is swept away. When she regains consciousness, she's in Oz—but not the Oz we remember, of yellow brick roads and Munchkins and fairy-tale architecture. This looks like a post-nuclear Oz. The road has been ripped up. The landscape is a barren desert. Instead of Munchkins, there are Wheelies, which are dreadful creatures with wheels for their hands and feet. (They look like the latest ride at a leather theme park.)

Worst of all, the very stones can talk. Rock walls open up dreadful faces and rumble threats at Dorothy. The wall-creatures are led by the Nome King, a fearsome face of infinite expressions, who roars and threatens and brings rocks hailing down all over Oz. As we watch the Nome King, something bothers us, and I think it's this: In the original *Wizard*, the dreaded ruler was invisible and turned out to be a phony. The Nome King is real—in Oz, anyway.

Dorothy finds some friends in Oz, but they are pale imitations of the Scarecrow, the Tin Man, and the Cowardly Lion. She meets a stick man with a pumpkin head; a stuffed moose that can fly, and a walking copper teapot that looks ripped off from *Star Wars*. They aren't much help, perhaps because they are seen as gimmicks rather than as distinct personalities.

Return to Oz is a considerable technical achievement. The Nome King and the Talking Rocks are the work of Will Vinton,

whose "Claymation" process (stop-action photography of modeling clay) won an Oscar a few years ago. The other special effects are equally impressive. Fairuza Balk, who plays Dorothy, is not another Judy Garland—but who could be? She's a spunky little girl who does her best. But the story of *Return to Oz* is so mean-spirited and dreary that it overwhelms everything else. The original movie took Dorothy and the audience a long way from Kansas. This movie is a long way from Oz.

Rhinestone ★
PG, 111 m., 1984

Sylvester Stallone (Martinelli), Dolly Parton (Jake Ferris), Richard Farnsworth (Noah Ferris), Ron Liebman (Freddie). Directed by Bob Clark and produced by Howard Smith and Marvin Worth. Screenplay by Phil Alden Robinson and Sylvester Stallone.

Rhinestone takes two of the most interesting actors in the movies and puts them into a movie they're expected to carry with sheer charm. There are times when they almost pull it off. Sure, Dolly Parton has wonderful energy and a great voice, and sure, Sylvester Stallone has a gift for ham-bone physical comedy. But this movie is so thin they both seem curiously absent. The screenplay allegedly is based on the song "Rhinestone Cowboy," but that will come as a surprise to the ghost of George Bernard Shaw, who first wrote this story as *Pygmalion*, and to Lerner and Loewe, who turned it into *My Fair Lady.* This time Dolly Parton has the Henry Higgins role. She bets a New York nightclub owner that she can take any guy off the streets and turn him into a country singer in two weeks. Along comes Stallone, driving his Yellow Cab as if he were auditioning for *Cannonball Run.* Dolly talks him into the experiment and takes him down home to Tennessee, where her daddy (Richard Farnsworth) is a country musician.

The center part of the film—the country "training" sessions—could have been fun if they'd been written with a satiric edge. Unfortunately, they seem to have been written with a blunt instrument. Dolly explains that the way to "walk country" is to pretend you have jock itch. Stallone needs to have this concept explained to him. Meanwhile, of course, they fall in love, and have a sex scene so tame that Miss Piggy goes further with Kermit. There is a dumb subplot involving Dolly's old boyfriend, and a couple of idiotic fight scenes, and then of course the big lame-brained showdown in the New York country music club. What we become agonizingly aware of, after a while, is how little Dolly Parton is singing. She has a great voice, filled with character and with little quirks and riffs and inflections that find their way around the words, but in *Rhinestone* we get shortchanged. And Stallone's overacting as her would-be partner is embarrassing.

One final fashion note. Dolly Parton is, of course, justly famous for her figure. It is presented in this movie with as much rigidity as the exhibit of presidential wives' inaugural gowns in the Smithsonian. The fabrics and colors change, but the basic design configuration remains identical in one dress after another, until her bosom takes on a sort of objective unreality, like Mr. Spock's ears.

Rich and Famous ★ ★ ½
R, 117 m., 1981

Jacqueline Bisset (Liz Hamilton), Candice Bergen (Merry Noel Black), David Selby (Doug Black), Hart Bochner (Chris Adams), Steven Hill (Jules Levi). Directed by George Cukor and produced by William Allyn. Screenplay by Gerald Ayres.

The lesson of *Rich and Famous* is that, although a woman cannot be too thin or too rich, she *can* be too famous. The movie stars Jacqueline Bisset and Candice Bergen as college classmates who become writers (Bisset, a serious intellectual writer and Bergen, an author of trashy bestsellers) and who maintain their friendship over the years. What threatens them most is fame, because fame seems to make the men in their lives a little goofy, and goofy men are their downfall. This film is a real curiosity. It's a good-bad movie, like *The Other Side of Midnight* or *The Greek Tycoon*. It contains scenes that make you want to squirm because of their awkwardness and awfulness, and yet you don't want to look away and you're not bored. The movie has the courage to go to extremes, and some of those extremes may not be art but are certainly unforgettable.

Take, for example, Candice Bergen's performance as Merry Noel Black. She's one of those tawny, plump Southern belles with a Betty Crocker hairstyle and a dirty mind. She marries well and lives on the beach and dashes off a scandalous book about her neighbors in the Malibu colony. It becomes a bestseller, and we are tantalized by hints that Bergen's character is "really" Jacqueline Susann or Judith Krantz. It doesn't matter. Bergen's performance is in the inimitable style of the late Ms. Susann, who once leaned across a luncheon table, took my hand, and informed me seriously: "You know, Roger, I've never met a dog I didn't like." Bergen plays the role broadly and with vulgar abandon, sometimes to great comic effect (although you know that with a name like "Merry Noel," she's going to have some real depressions around Christmas). Her performance is in counterpoint with the character played by Jacqueline Bisset. Bisset's character at times seems inspired by Mary McCarthy or Susan Sontag (and at other times, particularly when she is making love to strange men in airplane restrooms, seems inspired by Emmanuelle).

While Bergen grinds out the potboilers, Bisset writes one great book, and then seizes up with a severe case of writer's block. She can't write that second book, but she preaches to Bergen about honesty. Bergen somewhere dredges up the resources to write her own honest book—even, amazingly, a good book—and it's nominated for a national award. With perfect soap opera inevitability, Bisset is on the jury to award the prize. That leads into the second half of the movie, an extended sojourn in New York and thereabouts, where books are upstaged by Bisset's compulsion for strange sex. She rejects a seduction attempt from a young *Rolling Stone* reporter, but later that same day makes love with an even younger man who's a gigolo. The eroticism in that scene is particularly effective, and somewhat surprising, considering that the director is the eighty-two-year-old George Cukor. But later, when Bisset, to her amazement, falls in love with the *Rolling Stone* reporter, we're confused, because in a major casting blunder, the reporter and the gigolo look so much alike that we can't tell them apart.

No matter. The movie forges ahead

through tempestuous fights and tearful reconciliations, while Bergen's alcoholic ex-husband makes a pass at Bisset, and Bergen tries to bribe all of New York to win the book prize. I was not (and am not) sure what this movie was trying to tell me about the two characters—perhaps that if you stay in touch with someone for twenty years, you can be absolutely sure that at the end of that time you still will be in touch.

Insights into human nature don't seem to be the point of the movie, anyway. It's a slick, trashy, entertaining melodrama, with too many dumb scenes to qualify as successful. A film critic for one of the national newsweeklies said, in reviewing this film, that he has a friend who has a rule: He only attends movies that are in color and are about rich people. I deplore the attitude behind that statement, but in a crazy way, I absolutely understand it.

Richard Pryor Here and Now
★ ★ ★ ★
R, 94 m., 1983

A documentary written and directed by Richard Pryor and produced by Bob Parkinson and Andy Friendly.

Is there anyone else in America who could have pulled off this film? *Richard Pryor Here and Now* is a documentary of one man talking. Pryor walks onto the stage of the Saenger Theater in New Orleans, establishes an immediate rapport with the audience, and away he goes. At the end of the movie we have been wrung out with laughter—and with a few other things, too, because Pryor is more than a comedian in this film: He's a social commentator and a man talking honestly about himself.

This is Pryor's third concert film. The first one, *Richard Pryor Live in Concert*, was made before he set himself on fire while free-basing cocaine. The second, *Richard Pryor Live on the Sunset Strip* (1982), recorded his first filmed concert after the accident, and included his description of Jim Brown's attempts to talk him out of drug use, and Pryor's own now-famous dialogue with cocaine. In *Here and Now*, filmed in August 1983 with Brown as executive producer, Pryor firmly says he hasn't used drugs or alcohol for seven months. The arithmetic

would seem to suggest that he hadn't stopped using everything when he made the second film, or that he had a relapse after his initial hospitalization. I mention that only because the Richard Pryor we see on screen in *Here and Now* has obviously found some kind of peace with himself that was lacking in the *Sunset Strip* film.

He can smile more easily. He doesn't have to reach for effects. He handles audience interruptions with grace and cool. He is the master of his instrument. And he takes bigger chances. Some of his material covers familiar ground—sex, booze, race, marriages. But all along he's showing his gift for populating the stage with a lot of different characters. He goes in and out of accents, body language, and characters, giving us confused drunks, defensive husbands, shrill wives, uptight WASPs, impenetrable Africans ("Everybody speaks English," one tells him in Zimbabwe, "but what language do you speak at *home?*"). And then at the end of his act, he goes into an extended characterization of a street black shooting heroin. In this character are humor and pain, self-deception and touching honesty, and the end of the sketch comes closer to tragedy than it does to comedy.

Pryor is a spokesman for our dreams and fears, the things we find funny and the things we're frightened of. He has assumed a role that has previously been filled by such comedians as Will Rogers, Lenny Bruce, Mort Sahl, and Woody Allen—all men who, as Rogers put it, talked about what they'd just seen in the papers. Pryor works off issues and subjects that are absolutely current, and he addresses them with a humor that is aimed so well, we duck. His story could have gone either way. He could have been killed in that wasteful accident. But he was not, and now, given a second chance, he is paying his dues.

Richard Pryor Live on the Sunset Strip
★ ★ ★ ★
R, 82 m., 1982

Directed by Joe Layton and produced by Richard Pryor.

At the beginning of this film, Richard Pryor is clearly nervous. He is back on a stage for the first time since he set himself on fire.

That means he is working with the stand-up comedian's greatest handicap, the audience's awareness of his vulnerability. Whatever else they do, comics must project utter confidence in their material, and when Pryor had his accident, he also had his whole hip image blown out from under him. So it's a shaky start. He begins by almost defiantly using the word "fuck" as an incantation, employing it not so much for shock value (does it still have any?) as for punctuation. His timing is a little off. He is not, at first, the supremely confident, cocky Richard Pryor of his earlier films. But as he gets rolling, as he populates the stage with a whole series of characters, we watch the emergence of a Richard Pryor who is older, wiser, and funnier than before. And the last fifty or sixty minutes of this film are extraordinary.

Richard Pryor Live on the Sunset Strip was filmed at the Hollywood Palladium, down at the unfashionable east end of that legendary street of rock clubs, restaurants, hookers and heroes, hot-pillow motels, and some of the most expensive real estate in the world. The movie opens with a montage of the strip's neon signs (including the Chateau Marmont, where John Belushi died). Then it cuts inside to the Palladium auditorium, and Pryor walks onstage and lays claim to being the most talented one-man stage show in existence right now.

His gift is to be funny and painfully self-analytical at the same time. Like Bill Cosby, he gets a lot of his material out of memories of growing up black in America. But he sees deeper than Cosby, and his vignettes capture small truths and build them into an attitude. In the brilliant middle sections of this film, he uses just his own voice and body to create little one-act plays, such as the one where he recalls working in a Mafia-owned nightclub in Ohio. In that one, his Italian-American-gangster accent is perfectly heard; in another skit, about the animals in Africa, he turns into a gifted physical comedian, getting laughs out of his impressions of the movements of gazelles, water buffaloes, and lions—and ending with a hilarious observation of the body language of two whites passing each other on the street in black Africa. The whole middle passage of the film is that good. The last twenty minutes is one of the most remarkable marriages of comedy and truth I have ever seen. He talks with great honesty about his drug addiction, his accident, and how his life has changed since he stopped using drugs. He confesses that in the three weeks before his accident, he holed up alone in his room with his cocaine pipe, which talked to him in reassuring, seductive tones uncannily like Richard Nixon's. Then a friend, the actor Jim Brown, came to see him, and asked him flat-out, "Whatcha gonna do?" There was nothing he wanted to do but hide in drugs. What he finally did was set himself on fire.

I saw the film the same day that actor Shay Duffin opened his one-man evening with Brendan Behan at the Apollo Theater Center in Chicago. The papers that day carried the news that Belushi had overdosed. Behan, of course, killed himself with alcohol. Some day, inevitably, an actor will give us an evening with John Belushi. The dramatic structure is all there, for the Behans and Belushis: The genius, the laughter, and the doomed drive to self-destruction. Watching *Richard Pryor Live on the Sunset Strip*, a breathtaking performance by a man who came within a hair of killing himself with drugs, was like a gift, as if Pryor had come back from the dead to perform in his own one-man memory of himself. It is good we still have him. He is better than ever.

The Right Stuff ★ ★ ★ ★
PG, 193 m., 1983

Sam Shepard (Chuck Yeager), Ed Harris (John Glenn), Fred Ward (Gus Grissom), Dennis Quaid (Gordon Cooper), Scott Glenn (Alan Shepard), Barbara Hershey (Glennis Yeager), Mary Jo Deschanel (Annie Glenn), Pamela Reed (Trudy Cooper). Directed by Philip Kaufman and produced by Irwin Winkler and Robert Chartoff. Screenplay by Kaufman.

At the beginning of *The Right Stuff,* a cowboy reins in his horse and regards a strange sight in the middle of the desert: the X-1 rocket plane, built to break the sound barrier. At the end of the film, the seven Mercury astronauts are cheered in the Houston Astrodome at a Texas barbecue thrown by Lyndon B. Johnson. The contrast between those two images contains the message of *The Right Stuff,* I think, and the message is that Americans still have the right stuff, but we've changed our idea of what it is.

The original American heroes were loners. The cowboy is the perfect example. He was silhouetted against the horizon and he rode into town by himself and if he had a sidekick, the sidekick's job was to admire him. The new American heroes are team players. No wonder Westerns aren't made much anymore; cowboys don't play on teams. The cowboy at the beginning of *The Right Stuff* is Chuck Yeager, the legendary lone-wolf test pilot who survived the horrifying death rate among early test pilots (more than sixty were killed in a single month) and did fly the X-1 faster than the speed of sound. The movie begins with that victory, and then moves on another ten years to the day when the Russians sent up Sputnik, and the Eisenhower administration hustled to get back into the space race.

The astronauts who eventually rode the first Mercury capsules into space may not have been that much different from Chuck Yeager. As they're portrayed in the movie, anyway, Gus Grissom, Scott Carpenter, and Gordon Cooper seem to have some of the same stuff as Yeager. But the astronauts were more than pilots; they were a public-relations image, and the movie shows sincere, smooth-talking John Glenn becoming their unofficial spokesman. The X-1 flew in secrecy, but the Mercury flights were telecast, and we were entering a whole new era, the selling of space. There was a lot going on, and there's a lot going on in the movie, too. *The Right Stuff* is an adventure film, a special effects film, a social commentary, and a satire. That the writer-director, Philip Kaufman, is able to get so much into a little more than three hours is impressive. That he also has organized this material into one of the best recent American movies is astonishing. *The Right Stuff* gives itself the freedom to move around in moods and styles, from a broadly based lampoon of government functionaries to Yeager's spare, taciturn manner and Glenn's wonderment at the sights outside his capsule window.

The Right Stuff has been a landmark movie in a lot of careers. It announces Kaufman's arrival in the ranks of major directors. It contains uniformly interesting performances by a whole list of unknown or little-known actors, including Ed Harris (Glenn), Scott Glenn (Alan Shepard), Fred Ward (Grissom), and Dennis Quaid (Cooper). It confirms the strong and sometimes almost mystical screen presence of playwright Sam Shepard, who played Yeager. And it joins a short list of recent American movies that might be called experimental epics: movies that have an ambitious reach through time and subject matter, that spend freely for locations or special effects, but that consider each scene as intently as an art film. *The Right Stuff* goes on that list with *The Godfather, Nashville, Apocalypse Now*, and maybe *Patton* and *Close Encounters*. It's a great film.

Risky Business ★ ★ ★ ★
R, 96 m., 1983

Tom Cruise (Joel), Rebecca De Mornay (Lana), Curtis Armstrong (Miles), Bronson Pinchot (Barry), Joe Pantoliano (Guido). Directed by Paul Brickman and produced by Joe Avnet and Steve Tisch. Screenplay by Brickman.

Risky Business is a movie about male adolescent guilt. In other words, it's a comedy. It's funny because it deals with subjects that are so touchy, so fraught with emotional pain, that unless we laugh there's hardly any way we can deal with them—especially if we are now, or ever were, a teen-age boy. The teenager in the movie is named Joel. His family lives in a suburb on Chicago's North Shore. It's the sort of family that has three cars: the family station wagon, Mom's car, and Dad's Porsche. As the movie opens, Mom and Dad are going off on vacation to a sun-drenched consumer paradise and their only son, Joel, is being left alone at home. It's a busy time in Joel's life. He's got college board exams, an interview with a Princeton admissions officer, and finals at high school.

It gets to be an even busier time after his parents leave. Joel gets involved in an ascending pyramid of trouble. He calls a number in one of those sex-contact magazines and meets a young hooker who moves into the house. He runs afoul of the girl's pimp. His mother's expensive Steuben egg is stolen. His dad's Porsche ends up in Lake Michigan. The family home turns into a brothel. He blows two finals. And so on.

This description may make *Risky Business* sound like a predictable sitcom. It is not. It is one of the smartest, funniest, most perceptive satires in a long time. It not only invites comparison with *The Graduate*, it earns it. Here is a great comedy about teen-age sex.

The very best thing about the movie is its dialogue. Paul Brickman, who wrote and directed, has an ear so good that he knows what to leave out. This is one of those movies where a few words or a single line says everything that needs to be said, implies everything that needs to be implied, *and* gets a laugh. When the hooker tells the kid, "Oh, Joel, go to school. Learn something," the precise inflection of those words defines their relationship for the next three scenes.

The next best thing about the movie is the casting. Rebecca De Mornay somehow manages to take that thankless role, the hooker with a heart of gold, and turn it into a very specific character. She isn't all good and she isn't all clichés: she's a very complicated young woman with quirks and insecurities and a wayward ability to love. I became quietly astounded when I realized that this movie was going to create an original, *interesting* relationship involving a teen-ager and a hooker. The teen-age kid, in what will be called the Dustin Hoffman role, is played by Tom Cruise, who also knows how to imply a whole world by what he won't say, can't feel, and doesn't understand.

This is a movie of new faces and inspired insights and genuine laughs. It's hard to make a good movie and harder to make a good comedy and almost impossible to make a satire of such popular but mysterious obsessions as guilt, greed, lust, and secrecy. This movie knows what goes on behind the closed bathroom doors of the American dream.

The River ★ ★
PG-13, 122 m., 1985

Mel Gibson (Tom Garvey), Sissy Spacek (Mae Garvey), Scott Glenn (Joe Wade), Shane Bailey (Lewis Garvey), Becky Jo Lynch (Beth Garvey), Don Hood (Senator Neiswinder). Directed by Mark Rydell and produced by Edward Lewis and Robert Cortes. Screenplay by Robert Dillon and Julian Barry.

The River has some basic problems anyway, but it might have seemed like a much fresher film if it had not been the third of Hollywood's "save the farm" movies released between September 1984 and January 1985. Like *Places in the Heart* and *Country*, it tells the story of brave, stubborn farmers who are determined not to lose their family land to the bankers. The farmers in this film have their own unique challenge—the farm is next to a river that tends to overflow—but *The River* also has a lot in common with the earlier films, including two crucial scenes that are astonishingly similar to ones in *Country*. It is some kind of cosmic bad joke on the makers of *The River*, who worked hard and earnestly on what is essentially a good film, that it came third in the parade.

The movie contains a heartfelt performance by Sissy Spacek as the Tennessee farm wife; an adequate performance by Mel Gibson as her husband; and a scene-stealing performance by Scott Glenn as the local financier who wants to buy up all the land in the valley, dam the river, and generate some jobs with cheap hydroelectric power. (The crucial flaw in the movie's plot is that Glenn's ideas, which are supposed to make him the bad guy, sound like simple common sense.) As the movie opens, Gibson is fighting the river and almost is trapped and drowned beneath a bulldozer. We remember the opening scene in *Country*, where the son of the family is almost suffocated in an overturned load of grain, and *The River* suffers in comparison: A secondary character might be killed in an opening scene, but hardly the male lead.

Then life settles down on the farm, and we get to know the Spacek and Gibson characters and their small children. These scenes of simple domestic life are good ones; a kitchen love scene between Gibson and Spacek is warm, true, and electrifying. But then the farm gets caught in a credit crunch, and Gibson goes off to work as a scab at a struck steel mill in Birmingham, Alabama. It's here that we begin to notice a fairly heavy touch in the screenplay. After a frightened deer wanders into the mill, the strike-breakers take pity on the animal, surround it, and lead it to safety.

A memorable image, which is ruined because in the very next scene, the striking workers do exactly the same favor for the scabs.

Meanwhile, back on the farm, an auction is broken up by the chants of fellow farmers, expressing solidarity: "No sale! No sale!" This scene is just like the one in *Country.* Feeling a certain amount of *déjà vu*, we listen to Scott Glenn's reasons that Gibson and Spacek should sell their farm: "Sooner or later, you'll have to. The river will flood again, or there'll be a drought, or a surplus."

I don't think the movie wants us to believe him, but he has logic on his side. You know a movie's got problems when you find yourself wishing the heroes would agree with the villain.

Of the three "save the farm" movies, which one wins the sweepstakes? My vote goes to *Country,* which is the most concerned with actual farm problems, with the credit crunch brought on by low-priced farm loans in the 1970s and falling market prices in the 1980s—and which contains the best performance, Jessica Lange's. *Places in the Heart* is more of a human fable, more concerned with its characters than with actual farm problems, but it placed second. *The River* feels too contrived in comparison with the genuine emotion of *Places* and the authentic politics of *Country.*

The Road Warrior ★ ★ ★ ½
R, 97 m., 1982

Mel Gibson (Max), Bruce Spence (Gyro Captain), Vernon Wells (Wez), Emil Minty (Feral Kid), Virginia Hey (Warrior Woman). Directed by George Miller and produced by Byron Kennedy. Screenplay by Terry Hayes, Miller, and Brian Hannant.

The Road Warrior is a film of pure action, of kinetic energy organized around the barest possible bones of a plot. It has a vision of a violent future world, but it doesn't develop that vision with characters and dialogue. It would rather plunge headlong into one of the most relentlessly aggressive movies ever made. I walked out of *The Road Warrior* a little dizzy and with my ears still ringing from the roar of the sound track; I can't say I "enjoyed" the film, but I'll hardly forget it. The movie takes place at a point in the future when civilization has collapsed, anarchy and violence reign in the world, and roaming bands of marauders kill each other for the few remaining stores of gasoline. The vehicles of these future warriors are leftovers from the world we live in now. There are motorcycles and semi-trailer trucks and oil tankers that are familiar from the highways of 1982, but there are also bizarre customized racing cars, of which the most fearsome has two steel posts on its front to which enemies can be strapped (if the car crashes, the enemies are the first to die).

The road warriors of the title take their costumes and codes of conduct from a rummage sale of legends, myths, and genres: They look and act like Hell's Angels, samurai warriors, kamikaze pilots, street-gang members, cowboys, cops, and race drivers. They speak hardly at all; the movie's hero, Max, has perhaps two hundred words. Max is played by Mel Gibson, an Australian actor who starred in *Gallipoli.* Before that, he made *Mad Max* for the makers of *The Road Warrior,* and that film was a low-budget forerunner to this extravaganza of action and violence. Max's role in *The Road Warrior* is to behave something like a heroic cowboy might have in a classic Western. He happens upon a small band of people who are trying to protect their supplies of gasoline from the attacks of warriors who have them surrounded. Max volunteers to drive a tanker full of gasoline through the surrounding warriors and take it a few hundred miles to the coast, where they all hope to find safety. After this premise is established with a great deal of symbolism, ritual, and violence (and so few words that sometimes we have to guess what's happening), the movie arrives at its true guts. The set piece in *The Road Warrior* is an unbelievably well-sustained chase sequence that lasts for the last third of the film, as Max and his semi-trailer run a gauntlet of everything the savages can throw at them.

The director of *The Road Warrior,* George Miller, compares this chase sequence to Buster Keaton's *The General,* and I can see what he means. Although *The General* is comedic, it's also very exciting, as Keaton, playing the engineer of a speeding locomotive, runs an endless series of variations on the basic possibilities of two trains and several sets of railroad tracks. In *The Road Warrior*, there is basically a truck and a road. The pursuers and defenders have various kinds of cars and trucks to chase or defend the main truck, and the whole chase proceeds at breakneck speed as quasi-gladiators leap through the air from one racing truck to another, more often than not being crushed beneath the wheels. The special effects and stunts in this movie are spectacular; *The Road Warrior* goes on a short list with *Bullitt*, *The French Connection*, and the truck chase in *Raiders of the Lost Ark* as among the great chase films of modern years.

What is the point of the movie? Everyone is free to interpret the action, I suppose, but I prefer to avoid thinking about the implications of gasoline shortages and the collapse of Western civilization, and to experience the movie instead as pure sensation. The filmmakers have imagined a fictional world. It operates according to its special rules and values, and we experience it. The experience is frightening, sometimes disgusting, and (if the truth be told) exhilarating. This is very skillful filmmaking, and *The Road Warrior* is a movie like no other.

Rocky ★ ★ ★ ★
PG, 119 m., 1976

Sylvester Stallone (Rocky), Talia Shire (Adrian), Burt Young (Paulie), Carl Weathers (Apollo Creed), Burgess Meredith (Mickey), Frank Stallone (Timekeeper). Directed by John Avildsen and produced by Robert Chartoff and Irwin Winkler. Screenplay by Sylvester Stallone.

She sits, tearful and crumpled, in a corner of her little bedroom. Her brother has torn apart the living room with a baseball bat. Rocky, the guy she has fallen in love with, comes into the room.

"Do you want a roommate?" she asks shyly, almost whispering.

"Absolutely," says Rocky.

Which is exactly what he should say, and how he should say it, and why *Rocky* is such an immensely involving movie. Its story, about a punk club fighter from the back streets of Philly who gets a crack at the world championship, has been told a hundred times before. A description of it would sound like a cliché from beginning to end.

But *Rocky* isn't about a story, it's about a hero. And it's inhabited with supreme confidence by a star.

His name is Sylvester Stallone, and, yes, in 1976 he did remind me of the young Marlon Brando. How many actors have come and gone and been forgotten who were supposed to be the "new Brando," while Brando endured? And yet in *Rocky* he provides shivers of recognition reaching back to *A Streetcar Named Desire*. He's tough, he's tender, he talks in a growl, and hides behind cruelty and is a champion at heart. "I coulda been a contender," Brando says in *On the Waterfront*. This movie takes up from there.

It inhabits a curiously deserted Philadelphia: There aren't any cars parked on the slum street where Rocky lives or the slightest sign that anyone else lives there. His world is a small one. By day, he works as an enforcer for a small-time juice man, offering to break a man's thumbs over a matter of $70 ("I'll bandage it!" cries the guy. "It'll *look* broke"). In his spare time, he works out at Mickey's gym. He coulda been good, but he smokes and drinks beer and screws around. And yet there's a secret life behind his facade. He is awkwardly in love with a painfully shy girl (Talia Shire) who works in the corner pet shop. He has a couple of turtles at home, named Cuff and Link, and a goldfish named Moby Dick. After he wins forty bucks one night for taking a terrible battering in the ring, he comes home and tells the turtles: "If you guys could sing and dance, I wouldn't have to go through this crap." When the girl asks him why he boxes, he explains: "Because I can't sing and dance."

The movie ventures into fantasy when the world heavyweight champion (Carl Weathers, as a character with a certain similarity to Muhammad Ali) decides to schedule a New Year's Eve bout with a total unknown—to prove that America is still a land of opportunity. Rocky gets picked because of his nickname, the Italian Stallion; the champ likes the racial contrast. And even *here* the movie looks like a genre fight picture from the 1940s, right down to the plucky little gymnasium manager (Burgess Meredith) who puts Rocky through training, and right down to the lonely morning ritual of rising at four, drinking six raw eggs, and going out to do roadwork. What makes the movie extraordinary is that it doesn't try to surprise us with an original plot, with twists and complications; it wants to involve us on an elemental, a sometimes savage, level. It's about heroism and realizing your potential, about taking your best shot and sticking by your girl. It sounds not only clichéd but corny—and yet it's not, not a bit, because it really does work on those levels. It involves us emotionally, it makes us commit ourselves: We find, maybe to our surprise after remaining detached during so many movies, that this time we *care*.

The credit for that has to be passed around. A lot of it goes to Stallone when he wrote this story and then peddled it around Hollywood for years before he could sell it. He must have known it would work because he could see himself in the role, could imagine the conviction he's bringing to it, and I can't think of another actor who could quite have pulled off this performance. There's that exhilarating moment when Stallone, in training, runs up the steps of Philadelphia's art museum, leaps into the air, shakes his fist at the city, and you know he's sending a message to the whole movie industry.

The director is John Avildsen, who made *Joe* and then another movie about a loser who tried to find the resources to start again, *Save the Tiger*. Avildsen correctly isolates Rocky in his urban environment, because this movie shouldn't have a documentary feel, with people hanging out of every window: It's a legend, it's about little people, but it's bigger than life, and you have to set them apart visually so you can isolate them morally.

And then there's Talia Shire, as the girl (she was the hapless sister of the Corleone boys in *The Godfather*). When she hesitates before kissing Rocky for the first time, it's a moment so poignant it's like no other. And Burt Young as her brother—defeated and resentful, loyal and bitter, caring about people enough to hurt them just to draw attention to his grief. There's all that, and then there's the fight that ends the film. By now, everyone knows who wins, but the scenes before the fight set us up for it so completely, so emotionally, that when it's over we've had it. We're drained.

Rocky II ★ ★ ★
PG, 119 m., 1979

Sylvester Stallone (Rocky Balboa), Talia Shire (Adrian), Burt Young (Paulie), Carl Weathers (Apollo Creed), Burgess Meredith (Mickey), Tony Burton (Apollo's Trainer). Directed by Sylvester Stallone and produced by Irwin Winkler and Robert Chartoff. Screenplay by Stallone.

Rocky II isn't the movie the first *Rocky* was—what could equal that original burst of vitality?—but it's a well-crafted sequel with a lot of the same appeal, and with a climactic fight scene that's sensationally effective. 1979 was a year of sequels and prequels and remakes, and, as they go, this is one of the best.

That's because it's legitimately a sequel: It continues the story and further develops the characters, instead of just ripping off a successful formula. At the end of *Rocky* we wanted to know what came next, and now we do. That's a lot different from something like *Beyond the Poseidon Adventure*, which essentially just repeats the original movie.

Rocky II begins exactly where the first movie ended, with Rocky Balboa's once-in-a-million shot at the heavyweight title. Sylvester Stallone, who directed this time as well as writing and starring, is wise to quote from that fight footage. It's a reminder of the extraordinary impact of *Rocky*, which took a tired old Hollywood genre and brilliantly rediscovered its strength.

Stallone then gives us a scene that speaks directly to our memories of the first movie. After their mutual battering, both Rocky and heavyweight champ Apollo Creed are hospitalized. And in the middle of the night Rocky opens Apollo's door and says, "Apollo? You awake?" Yeah. "Can I ask you somethin'?" Yeah. "Did you give me your best shot?" Yeah, I did. "Thank you."

Rocky's life changes dramatically, of course, after his moral victory in the fight. He's badgered by agents who want him to endorse products and do TV commercials (and he does at least one, holding a club and wearing a leopard skin and standing in a cage to endorse a men's after-shave). One of the first things he does, of course, is to marry his girl friend Adrian (Talia Shire). They buy a car and a house. And Rocky looks around for a job.

His problem is that he can't fight again. Doctor's orders: He suffered damage to his eyes, and another fight could lead to blindness. But Rocky Balboa can't really *do* anything but fight. After a couple of menial jobs, he goes back to the gym run by his trainer, Mickey (played by Burgess Meredith in a jolly, scenery-chewing performance). These scenes—interlaced with Adrian's pregnancy and the birth of their son, Rocky, Jr. (with an astonishing head of hair)—head up to a sustained stretch of soap opera. Adrian goes into a coma. Rocky goes into a depression. Apollo Creed, driven by the need to clear his reputation, taunts Rocky for another fight in newspaper ads.

This is all pretty obvious stuff, and if it were handled with less care we might be tempted to laugh at the clichés. But Stallone as a writer has a way of getting away with things. He tells stories that are simple, basic, and human; he doesn't apologize for them, and he plays them with a conviction that makes them work.

He is also interesting as a director. The first *Rocky* was directed by John Avildsen, who placed it in a Philadelphia landscape deliberately kept barren of people who didn't figure in the story. The streets were empty, and the result was curiously effective: The characters gained a mythic stature because they were kept in relief and not marched through crowds of extras.

Stallone uses that same approach in *Rocky II*. But he also introduces an element of highly personal humor that first surfaced in *Paradise Alley* (1978), which he also wrote and directed. He likes characters who are offbeat and cheerfully grotesque. He likes scenes that are allowed to drift from realism into comic exaggeration. He likes to view life at an angle.

Paradise Alley gave us three heroic, crazy, goofy brothers, and scenes like the one in which the organ grinder's monkey is kept captive in the bathroom. *Rocky II* has fun with the wedding scene, with the absurd TV commercials, and especially with the night of the big fight. Instead of going for conventional devices to build the tension, Stallone cuts between drama and comedy, between the mounting excitement inside the fight arena and Rocky's leisurely progress through the city. Apollo Creed is sweating it out in his dressing room, but Rocky Balboa's stopping off at a parish hall for a quick blessing from the priest.

Then comes the fight scene. I wouldn't dream, of course, of telling you who wins. But the scene itself is terrific action footage, and Stallone's occasional use of slow motion seems to work here; in *Paradise Alley*'s closing fight, it was distracting and excessive. *Rocky II* tells the story crisply and with style, and keeps us hooked even during the soap opera stuff.

But almost any sequel to an enormous hit movie has this problem: We are already familiar with the qualities that made the original extraordinary. *Rocky* introduced us to this strange, eccentric, funny-talking, big lug from Philly who had turtles named Cuff and Link and a dog named Butkus, and was in love with the shy girl who worked at the pet store. It showed us Rocky's one-time shot at the big time. It established a fictional world that was fresh.

Rocky II can't do those things. It doesn't have the advantage of novelty. If you liked *Rocky*, you'll certainly want to see *Rocky II*. But the impact just can't be quite the same. Maybe that's why it's so good to have the fight scene at the end: It has such sheer animal intensity that it's got us cheering, just like the first time around.

Romancing the Stone ★ ★ ★
PG, 106 m., 1984

Michael Douglas (Jack Colton), Kathleen Turner (Joan Wilder), Danny DeVito (Thug), Alfonso Arau (Juan), Manuel Ojeda (Zolo). Directed by Robert Zemeckis and produced by Michael Douglas. Screenplay by Diane Thomas.

It may have an awkward title, but *Romancing the Stone* is a silly, high-spirited chase picture that takes us, as they say, from the canyons of Manhattan to the steaming jungles of South America. The movie's about a New York woman who writes romantic thrillers in which the hungry lips of lovers devour each other as the sun sinks over the dead bodies of their enemies. Then she gets involved in a real-life thriller, which is filled with cliffhanging predicaments just like the ones she writes about. The writer, played by Kathleen Turner, uses her novels as a form of escape. Throbbing loins may melt together on her pages, but not in her life. Then she gets a desperate message from her sister in South America: Unless she flies to Cartagena with a treasure map showing the location of a priceless green jewel, her sister will be killed.

What follows is an adventure that will remind a lot of people of *Raiders of the Lost Ark*, but it will be a pleasant memory. After all the *Raiders* rip-offs, it's fun to find an adventure film that deserves the comparison, that has the same spirit and sense of humor. Turner lands in Colombia, and almost instantly becomes part of the plans of a whole lineup of desperadoes. There are the local police, the local thugs, the local mountain bandits, and the local hero, a guy named Jack Colton, who is played by Michael Douglas.

Movies like this work best if they have original inspirations about the ways in which the heroes can die. I rather liked the pit full of snarling alligators, for example. They also work well if the villains are colorful, desperate, and easy to tell apart. They are. Danny DeVito, from TV's "Taxi," plays a Peter Lorre type, complete with a white tropical suit and a hat that keeps getting trampled in the mud. He's a gangster from up north, determined to follow Turner to the jewel. There's also a suave local paramilitary hero named Zolo (Manuel Ojeda), who wears a French Foreign Legion cap and lusts after not only Turner's treasure map but all of her other treasures. And Alfonso Arau plays a rural bandito who turns out to have memorized all of Turner's thrillers.

Movies like this have a tendency to turn into a long series of scenes where the man grabs the woman by the hand and leads her away from danger at a desperate run. I always hate scenes like that. Why can't the woman run by herself? Don't they both have a better chance if the guy doesn't have to always be dragging her? What we're really seeing is leftover sexism from the days when women were portrayed as hapless victims. *Romancing the Stone* doesn't have too many scenes like that. It begins by being entirely about the woman, and although Douglas takes charge after they meet, that's basically

because he knows the local territory. Their relationship is on an equal footing, and so is their love affair. We get the feeling they really care about each other, and so the romance isn't just a distraction from the action.

A Room with a View ★ ★ ★ ★
PG-13, 110 m., 1985 ✔

Maggie Smith (Charlotte Bartlett), Helena Bonham-Carter (Lucy Honeychurch), Denholm Elliott (Mr. Emerson), Julian Sands (George Emerson), Daniel Day Lewis (Cecil Vyse), Simon Callow (Reverend Beebe), Judi Dench (Miss Lavish), Rosemary Leach (Mrs. Honeychurch). Directed by James Ivory and produced by Ismail Merchant. Screenplay by Ruth Prawer Jhabvala.

My favorite character in *A Room with a View* is George Emerson, the earnest, passionate young man whose heart beats fiercely with love for Lucy Honeychurch. She is a most respectable young woman from a good family, who has been taken to Italy on the grand tour, with a lady companion, Miss Bartlett. Lucy meets George and his father in their *pensione*. A few days later, while standing in the middle of a waving field of grass, the sun bathing the landscape in a yellow joy, she is kissed by George Emerson, most unexpectedly. He does not ask her permission. He does not begin with small talk. He takes her and kisses her, and for him, something "great and important" has happened between them.

Lucy Honeychurch is not so sure. She catches her breath, and Miss Bartlett appears on top of a hill and summons her back to tea, and a few months later, in England, Lucy announces her engagement to Cecil Vyse, who is a prig. Cecil is the sort of man who would never play tennis, who wears a *pince-nez*, who oils his hair, and who thinks that girls are nice because they like to listen to him read aloud. Cecil does not have many clues as to what else girls might be nice for.

Meanwhile, George Emerson and his father—who is an idealist, a dreamer, and a follower of Thoreau—take a cottage in the neighborhood. And one day George kisses Lucy again. He then delivers himself of an astonishing speech, in which he explains that love exists between them. (Not love but

Love—you can hear the capital letter in his voice.) Lucy must not marry Cecil, he explains, for Cecil does not understand women and will never understand Lucy, and wants her only for an ornament. George, on the other hand, wants her as his partner in the great adventure of life.

George does not have many big scenes, other than those two. The rest of the time, he keeps a low profile and says little. But his function is clear: He is the source of passion in a society that is otherwise tightly bound up in convention, timidity, and dryness. He is the man to break the chains, to say what he thinks, to free Lucy's spirit. And that he does, with great energy and efficiency. George is my favorite character because he is such a strange bird, so intense, so filled with conviction, so convinced of Lucy's worth.

A Room with a View is the story of George and Lucy, but it is also an attack on the British class system. In the opening scenes of the movie, Lucy and Miss Bartlett have been given a room in the Italian *pensione* that does not have a view. Dear old Mr. Emerson insists that the women take his rooms, which have a view. By the end of the film, George will have offered Lucy a view out of the room of her own life. She has been living a suffocating, proper existence—and he will open the window for her. That's what's exhilarating about the film, that it is not only about perplexing and eccentric characters, it's about how they can change their lives.

The movie has been adapted from the E.M. Forster novel by three filmmakers who have specialized recently in film adaptations of literary works: Director James Ivory, producer Ismail Merchant, and screenwriter Ruth Prawer Jhabvala. Their other recent credits include *The Bostonians, The Europeans,* and *Heat and Dust.* This is the best film they have ever made.

It is an intellectual film, but intellectual about emotions: it encourages us to think about how we feel, instead of simply acting on our feelings. It shows us a young woman, Lucy Honeychurch, who is about to marry the wrong man—not because of her passion, but because of her lack of thought. Only think about your passion, the movie argues, and you will throw over Cecil and marry George. Usually thought and passion are

opposed in the movies; this time it's entertaining to find them on the same side.

The story moves at a deliberate pace, with occasionally dramatic interruptions for great passion. The dialogue is stately and abstract, except when all of a sudden it turns direct and honest. The performances are perfectly balanced between the heart and the mind. At the center of everything stands Lucy, who is played by Helena Bonham-Carter, that darkbrowed, stubborn little girl from *Lady Jane.* Maggie Smith is wonderfully dotty as her companion. Denholm Elliott, the most dependable of all British character actors, steals scene after scene as George's freethinking father ("Leave me my portrait of Thoreau," he insists, as they are moving from their cottage). Julian Sands is the intense young George and Daniel Day Lewis creates a foppish masterpiece in his performance as Cecil; give him a monocle and a butterfly, and he could be on the cover of the *New Yorker.*

A Room with a View enjoys its storytelling so much that I enjoyed the very process of it; the story moved slowly, it seemed, for the same reason you try to make ice cream last—because it's so good.

The Rose ★ ★ ★
R, 134 m., 1979

Bette Midler (Rose), Alan Bates (Rudge), Frederic Forrest (Dyer), Harry Dean Stanton (Billy Ray), Barry Primus (Dennis), David Keith (Mal). Directed by Mark Rydell and produced by Martin Worth and Aaron Russo. Screenplay by Bill Kerby and Bo Goldman.

If *The Rose* accomplished nothing else, it would deserve praise for frustrating our national desire to turn the deaths of celebrities into entertainment events. It has gotten to the point in recent years where a popular singer can hardly hope to make it without being dead, and the hot thing for Hollywood lawyers is to put together a portfolio of superstar estates.

The Elvis Industry, balanced precariously between idolatry and necrophilia, is particularly depressing, but count our dead heroes: Jim Croce, Jimi Hendrix, Jim Morrison, Buddy Holly, Otis Redding, Janis Joplin . . . and there was that stir several years ago when yearning Beatles fans tried to bury Paul McCartney the better to praise him.

The girl rock-and-roll singer portrayed by Bette Midler in *The Rose* is officially not Janis Joplin, of course; Midler and director Mark Rydell say they drew from lots of sources, and the movie shows that they did. But the popular conception is that Bette's playing Janis, and audiences are going to *The Rose* to get the lowdown on she and Bobby McGee. The reaction after the movie is over is fascinating: It's a downer, some people complain. Too depressing. You see how fickle we are with our fads. We want movies celebrating the early deaths of our heroes—but they shouldn't be too glum. It's on record that Joplin went to her doom speeded by drugs and Southern Comfort, but maybe what the fans want now is a remake of *Heaven Can Wait*, with Warren Beatty greeting her in heaven.

The Rose is not that movie, and fans hoping to chuckle along at good ol' Rose as she self-destructs will be disappointed. This movie about the pressures of rock stardom and its road tours is told from the inside in two ways: Midler and the filmmakers know what it's like because they've been there, and the movie also concentrates on staying mostly inside the Rose character's head.

Rose, in the movie, is a junkie, a drunk, dependent on uppers, downers, and levelers (she is also, I should probably add, capable of having a good time, able to belt out some terrific performances, and not totally wasted until the end). The movie suggests some of the reasons for her shotgun addictions, but most people use drugs and booze, of course, not because of the personality and behavioral "reasons" so beloved by the social help experts but—quite simply—because they got addicted, and now can't stop. Telling someone he can beat a habit once he understands "why" he's using something is as cruel as telling a man with a broken leg that he can walk if he understands his bone structure.

The Rose seems to understand this. It is intelligent on the subject of addictions, and its insights are reflected in an interesting stylistic strategy. People on booze or certain drugs develop a tunnel vision in dealing with their environment: They focus on what's important to them at a given moment, and screen out the distractions.

The Rose handles its locations and supporting characters in that way, from Rose's point of view, so that cast members swim in and out of focus and we're seduced into Rose's state of mind. That makes the movie's gradual descent from good times into disquiet, pity, doom, and silence an especially effective one.

But some people say they don't like it, it's depressing. One is tempted to wonder what they expected (how do you base a comedy on Janis Joplin?), but maybe it's not their fault. We've been so brainwashed by the Elvis Industry and its lesser clones that we expect dead stars to come in a nice-smelling package. Used to be fans just identified with their heroes. Now they want the final word.

Runaway Train ★ ★ ★ ★
R, 111 m., 1985

Jon Voight (Manny), Eric Roberts (Buck), Rebecca De Mornay (Sara), Kyle T. Heffner (Frank Barstow), John P. Ryan (Ranken), Kenneth McMillan (Eddie). Directed by Andrei Konchalovsky and produced by Menahem Golan and Yoram Globus. Screenplay by Djordje Milicevic, Paul Zindel, and Edward Bunker.

The great adventure movies have all been stories of character, not just tales of action. One of the great losses in the movies of recent years has been that sense of real character: One-dimensional people insert themselves into chases and explosions, and the mindless spectacle on the screen is supposed to replace the presence of plausible human beings.

Runaway Train is a reminder that the great adventures are great because they happen to people we care about. That was true of *The African Queen*, and of *Stagecoach*, and of *The Seven Samurai*, three movies that would otherwise seem to have little in common. And it is also true of this tale of two desperate convicts on board a train that is hurtling through the snows of Alaska.

The movie stars Jon Voight and Eric Roberts, who were both nominated for Oscars. They are two actors with dramatically different styles. Voight is always internalized and moody; Roberts has a collection of verbal and physical tics that are usually irritating, and are sometimes meant to be.

Here they are both correctly cast, as two convicts in a maximum-security prison in Alaska, who escape through a drain tunnel and then blunder onto the train that takes them on their hellbound mission.

Voight plays Manny, a convict who is so distrusted by the warden that his cell doors have been welded shut for three years. "He's not a human being—he's an animal," the warden says, and this is not just stock dialogue, but the thesis on which the whole movie will rest. Roberts is Buck, a trusty who works for the prison laundry. The warden is Barstow (Kyle T. Heffner), and he has a personal grudge against Manny. In fact, he releases him from solitary in the wicked hope that Manny will try to escape—he's done it before—and that will give Barstow license to kill him.

The opening passages are intense, but somewhat routine; they're out of the basic kit of prison movie clichés. Then the two convicts escape, and stumble by luck into one of the back cabs of a train that consists of four locomotives linked together. The train starts, the engineer suddenly collapses with a heart attack, and the movie's epic journey has begun.

Runaway Train is based on an original screenplay by the Japanese master Akira Kurosawa, whose best movies use the actors as a means of studying character. After some rewriting, *Runaway Train* was directed by Andrei Konchalovsky, the emigré Russian who figures so memorably (under a pseudonym) as Shirley MacLaine's lover in her bestseller *Dancing in the Light*. He has given the story the kind of wildness and passion it requires; this isn't a high-tech Hollywood adventure movie, but a raw saga that works close to the floor.

Once the train has started to move, the movie follows three threads. One involves the three people on the train (the two men discover after a while that a woman crew member, played by Rebecca De Mornay, is also on board, and also powerless to stop the engines). The second thread involves the railway dispatchers, who quarrel over a computer system that may possibly have the ability to clear the tracks ahead of the runaway. The third involves the ferocious determination of Barstow, the warden, to track the train by helicopter, and kill the men inside.

Those elements might be enough to make *Runaway Train* a superior action movie. What makes it more than that is the dynamic inside the cab of the train. Voight is seen as a man who is intelligent enough to realize how desperate the situation is—because he has been caught not just in a physical trap, but also in a psychological one. In an impassioned speech that may be the best single scene he has ever played, he tries to explain to Roberts how limited their choices are in life. He uses a story of a man with a broom to create a parable about the impossibility of living as a free man.

The Roberts character does not quite understand the story. He is a wild man of limited intelligence, and prison life has made him dangerous—he acts without regard for the consequences. When these two men are joined by a woman, it is not just a plot gimmick; her role as an outsider gives them an audience and a mirror.

The action sequences in the movie are stunning. Frequently, in recent movies, I've seen truly spectacular stunts and not been much excited, because I knew they were stunts. All I could appreciate was their smoothness of execution. In *Runaway Train*, as the characters try to climb along the sides of the ice-covered locomotive, as the train crashes through barriers and other trains, as men dangle from helicopters and try to kill the convicts, there is such a raw, uncluttered desperation in the feats that they put slick Hollywood stunts to shame.

The ending of the movie is astonishing in its emotional impact. I will not describe it. All I will say is that Konchalovsky has found the perfect visual image to express the ideas in his film. Instead of a speech, we get a picture, and the picture says everything that needs to be said. Afterwards, just as the screen goes dark, there are a couple of lines from Shakespeare that may resonate more deeply the more you think about the Voight character. This was one of the year's best.

Ruthless People ★ ★ ★ ½
R, 93 m., 1986 ✔

Danny DeVito (Sam Stone), Bette Midler (Barbara Stone), Judge Reinhold (Ken Kessler), Helen Slater (Sandy Kessler), Anita Morris (Carol). Directed by Jim Abrahams,

David Zucker, and Jerry Zucker and produced by Michael Peyser. Screenplay by Dale Launer.

It is hard to play a lovable villain, and Danny DeVito does it so easily. His eyes narrow, his voice deepens, and he speaks with great earnestness and sincerity about his selfish schemes and vile designs. *Ruthless People* opens as DeVito is having lunch with his mistress, and we can see that this is a man filled with passion. In this case, the passion is hatred for his wife and for all that she stands for, and for all that her rich father stands for, and even for all that her poodle stands for.

DeVito is the mainspring of *Ruthless People,* the engine of murderous intensity right at the center. His passion is so palpable that it adds weight to all the other performances in the movie. If we can believe he really wants to kill his wife, then we can believe he would not pay the ransom if she were kidnapped, which is the movie's comic premise.

It is, indeed, a pleasure to watch his face as he receives the first call from the kidnappers and they threaten to kill his wife if he doesn't follow every single one of their instructions to the letter. As he agrees to their stipulations, one after another, a wondrous calm spreads over his face, and the scene builds to a perfect climax.

The wife is played by Bette Midler, who makes her first entrance kicking and screaming inside a burlap bag. She has been kidnapped by Judge Reinhold and Helen Slater, who want to get even with DeVito, a clothing manufacturer who has ripped off their designs. It's a juicy role for Midler, a first cousin to the airhead housewife she played in *Down and Out in Beverly Hills,* and she milks it for all it's worth, turning into an exercise freak while being held captive in a basement.

The movie doesn't depend on just the one inspiration—the husband who doesn't want to ransom his wife. It has lots of other ideas and characters that fit together like a clockwork mechanism. We have the mistress (Anita Morris) and her boyfriend (Bill Pullman), who is not playing with a full deck. And then there are the police chief (William G. Schilling), who backs himself into an embarrassing situation, and a mad slasher (J.E. Freeman), who picks the wrong victim when he comes after Midler.

The movie is slapstick with a deft character touch here and there. It's hard to keep all the characters and plot lines alive at once, but *Ruthless People* does it, and at the end I felt grateful for its goofiness.

The discovery in the movie is DeVito. After seeing him on television's "Taxi" and here and there in character roles, I began to notice how good he was in *Romancing the Stone.* Then came his great performance in *Wise Guys,* opposite Joe Piscopo, and now this second virtuoso performance in a row.

He is, of course, very short, but there's a funny thing about his stature: It seems to be a fact of his body, not his mind or personality. In close-ups and whenever he speaks, he has so much force that he can easily command his scenes. He never seems to be compensating; he seems to be holding back. Like British actor Bob Hoskins, who is also shorter than most of the people in most of his scenes, he has a way of making the taller people around him seem unsure of what to do with their legs.

DeVito is a great joy to watch in this movie, as the turns of the plot catch him in one dilemma and then another. First he wants the kidnappers to kill his wife. Then, when he is charged with faking her kidnapping, he wants to ransom her. All along, there's a running gag as he negotiates the ransom price, and Midler has a great moment when she learns that her husband is trying to buy her back—at a discount. *Ruthless People* is made out of good performances, a script of diabolical ingenuity, and a whole lot of silliness.

St. Elmo's Fire ★ ½
R, 110 m., 1985

Emilio Estevez (Kirbo), Rob Lowe (Billy), Andrew McCarthy (Kevin), Demi Moore (Jules), Judd Nelson (Alex), Ally Sheedy (Leslie), Mare Winningham (Wendy), Martin Balsam (Mr. Beamish). Directed by Joel Schumacher and produced by Lauren Schuler. Screenplay by Schumacher and Carl Kurlander.

St. Elmo's Fire tells the story of a crowd of twits in their early twenties who consider each other friends, which is questionable, and unique, which is amazing. Filled with their own self-importance, they march through the bars and bedrooms of Georgetown, auditioning for a series that could be called "Grandchildren of Dynasty." The movie has lots of those scenes in which characters discuss the Meaning of Life, which would be OK, except the screenplay has no ideas on the subject.

The film stars some of the best and brightest actors of the new generation, in a movie they will be advised to drop from their resumes. Here is the roll call of the cast, all members of what Hollywood calls the "Brat Pack": Rob Lowe, Ally Sheedy, Emilio Estevez, Demi Moore, Judd Nelson, Mare Winningham, Andrew McCarthy.

Three of these actors (Estevez, Nelson, Sheedy) were together in *The Breakfast Club*, which was about high school students. They said in interviews at the time that they were looking forward to playing their "own age" in this film, which is about a group of friends one year out of college. But the characters in *St. Elmo's Fire* are not as mature and interesting as the teen-agers in *The Breakfast Club*.

As the movie opens, the friends are raising hell in a bar. Then we get to meet them. There's the coke-head (Moore) who's sleeping with the bank president; the waiter (Estevez) who is obsessed with a slightly older woman; the social worker who is still a virgin (Winningham); the drunk (Lowe); the stud (Nelson); the good girl (Sheedy); and the guy (McCarthy) who loves his best friend's girl. They're all on the first rungs of the ladder to success, as congressional aides, law clerks, etc. But their real lives are lived at night, when they party, carouse, weep, double-cross, lie, cheat, and talk about love. (The movie's theory of love, incidentally, is that love sucks—this is the least convincing movie about romance I've ever seen.)

None of the actors is untalented, but most of them are in the wrong movie. Most grievously misused is Estevez, whose character moons after a pretty intern, and follows her to ski resorts and fancy parties, where he stands around like a wet puppy. His character seems to exist on a different level of reality than the others in this movie.

The most convincing character is probably the coke-head, played by Demi Moore.

As she grows more dependent on the drug, she goes deeper into debt, sleeps with her boss to raise money, is fired, and finally ends up shivering on the floor of her apartment, which is empty because the finance company has just hauled away the furniture. If the movie had wanted to make a statement about drugs, here was its chance, but all the movie really wants to do is provide us with a series of sensational soap-opera predicaments.

St. Elmo's Fire really made me angry, and what made me angriest was the smarmy air of self-congratulation it's cloaked in. The director and co-writer, Joel Schumacher, obviously thinks he's making some kind of statement about the generation in its early twenties, but all he's really saying is that he cannot imagine these people as three-dimensional human beings, and so has to fall back on melodrama, clichés, and such a cynical view of love between the sexes that it hardly seems worth the effort.

Note: For a good movie on the same subject, also starring Lowe and Moore, see About Last Night. . . .

Salvador ★ ★ ★
R, 125 m., 1986 ✔

James Woods (Richard Boyle), James Belushi (Dr. Rock), Michael Murphy (Ambassador Kelly), John Savage (John Cassady), Elepedia Carrillo (Maria), Tony Plana (Major Max), Colby Chester (Jack Morgan), Cynthia Gibb (Cathy Moore). Directed by Oliver Stone and produced by Gerald Green and Stone. Screenplay by Stone and Richard Boyle.

Given the headlines, you might perhaps think *Salvador* was a controversial movie about America's role in Central America, but actually it's a throwback to a different kind of picture, to the Hunter Thompson story *Where the Buffalo Roam*, where hard-living journalists hit the road in a showdown between a scoop and an overdose. The movie has an undercurrent of seriousness, and it is not happy about the chaos which we are helping to subsidize, but basically it's a character study—a portrait of a couple of burnt-out free-lancers trying to keep their heads above the water.

The movie stars James Woods, that master

of nervous paranoia, as a foreign correspondent who has hit bottom. He's drinking, drugging, unemployed, living off past glories. When all hell breaks loose in Central America, he figures it's a good story, since he still has some contacts down there. So he enlists his best friend, a spaced-out disc jockey (James Belushi), and they load up with beer and drive their jalopy down through Mexico to where the action is.

The heart of the movie is in their relationship, and I kept being reminded of another Hunter Thompson saga, his book *Fear and Loathing in Las Vegas*, where the journalist and his lawyer drove their car through the desert, where drug-induced dragons seemed to swoop at them out of the sky. *Salvador* is a movie about real events as seen through the eyes of characters who have set themselves adrift from reality. That's what makes it so interesting.

Once they're at their destination, Woods and Belushi start looking up Woods's old contacts, who include a neofascist general, several bartenders, and an old girlfriend. Woods makes a stab at being a correspondent—he's always on long distance to New York, trying to get credentials from a reputable news-gathering agency—while Belushi settles into the local routine of bars and loose women.

A plot of sorts emerges, along with the usual characters we expect in a story like this—the American generals and embassy spokesmen and CIA types. Woods and Belushi hurry off recklessly in all directions, keep finding themselves surrounded by the wrong people, and escape with their lives only because Woods is such a con artist.

And he is. This is the sort of role James Woods was born to play, with his glibness, his wary eyes, and the endless cigarettes. There is an utter cynicism just beneath the surface of his character, the cynicism of a journalist who has traveled so far, seen so much, and used so many chemicals that every story is just a new version of how everybody gets screwed. That's why there is a special interest in the love affair in this movie, between Woods and Elepedia Carrillo, as the local woman Maria, the woman he truly loves but who lives by a code of Catholicism and respectability—a code that seems constantly in danger of being overwhelmed by events.

The central scene in the movie is possibly the one where Woods goes to confession. He has decided to marry the woman, in order to get her out of the country before all hell breaks loose. She insists on a church wedding. And so we get an extraordinary closeup of Woods's face as he talks with the priest, and tries to make some sort of a bargain between Catholic requirements and his own total ignorance of conventional morality.

Meanwhile, we meet some of the other people on the scene, including John Savage, as a great war photographer, and Michael Murphy, as the American ambassador, a tortured liberal who speaks of peace and freedom while the CIA goes about its usual business right under his nose. The subplot involving the Savage character is not very successful. I can see what they're doing, trying to set him up as a dedicated photojournalist who will risk his life for a great picture, but when he finally does come to his personal turning point, it's for a photo even the audience knows isn't great: A shot of an airplane swooping out of the sky. Without context, it could be any airplane, flying out of any sky.

Salvador is long and disjointed, and tries to tell too many stories for its length. A scene where Woods debates policy with the American officials sounds tacked-on, as if the director and co-writer, Oliver Stone, was afraid of not making his point. But the heart of the movie is fascinating. And the heart consists of Woods and Belushi, two losers set adrift in a world they never made, trying to play games by everybody else's rules.

Santa Claus: The Movie ★ ★ ½
PG, 112 m., 1985 ✓

Dudley Moore (Patch), John Lithgow (B.Z.), David Huddleston (Claus), Burgess Meredith (Ancient Elf), Judy Cornwell (Anya), Jeffrey Kramer (Towzer). Directed by Jeannot Szwarc and produced by Ilya Salkind and Pierre Spengler. Screenplay by David Newman.

It seems strange at first that the producers of the Superman movies would move on to an epic about Santa Claus. But in a way it makes sense. Both Superman and Santa are legendary superheroes, able to cure our pains through magical intervention. Both of them can fly through the air. Both have large supporting casts: Superman has Lois Lane, Jimmy Olsen, and Perry White, and Santa has Mrs. Claus, the elves, and, of course, Dasher and Donner and Blitzen.

Ilya Salkind, the co-producer of the Superman movies, has extended the similarities by making *Santa Claus: The Movie* roughly similar in shape and form to a Superman epic. The key element in the lives of superheroes is their origin (somehow, they are rarely simply born to humble folk). Superman came from Krypton, and Claus, we learn, was a kindly middle-aged man who was loved by everybody in the neighborhood because he went out in blizzards with a sleigh full of toys.

Near the beginning of the movie, Claus ventures out into one blizzard too many, and freezes. But then he is spirited mysteriously to the North Pole, where he learns that he will get a new name—Santa Claus—and new duties, as the superpower of Christmas Eve.

The movie does an interesting job of visualizing Santa's workshop, and introducing the residents there. The elves seem to have a sort of craft guild. Burgess Meredith, wearing a white beard several yards long, plays the Ancient Elf, who briefs Claus on his duties. Dudley Moore is Patch, the chief elf, who is not as efficient as he should be. There are long rows of new toys, all made in a sturdy, old-fashioned way out of wood and nails. There's not a piece of plastic or polyurethane in sight.

Alas, Patch gets ideas for speeding up production and, before long, the wheels are falling off children's wagons all over the world. Patch leaves the North Pole in disgrace, and soon meets a crooked toy manufacturer (John Lithgow), who makes dangerous toys. For me, the high point of the movie was a Senate hearing where a shocked Senate aide emptied out the stuffings of one of Lithgow's toy animals. What had he stuffed it with? Why, nails and rusty razor blades and shards of glass, of course!

Lithgow is supposed to be in the great tradition of superhero villains, like Gene Hackman's Lex Luthor in *Superman*, or all of the bizarre enemies Batman had to face. Lithgow gives a nice hateful performance, but the villain is not drawn big enough, and he doesn't have enough to do. Indeed, the central weakness of *Santa Claus: The Movie* is its lack of real conflict. The movie needs a super-Scrooge and all it gets is the kind of bad guy Ralph Nader might have invented. The biggest crisis in the movie is when a couple of reindeer come down with runny noses.

The good thing about the movie is the special effects. The Salkinds and their associates have by now figured out exactly how to make it look like somebody is flying, and when Santa's sleigh makes a run past the Brooklyn Bridge, it's a pretty sight. Little kids will like it, and, indeed, little kids will probably like most of the movie. The weakness is that larger kids and parents, deputized to watch it with the little ones, are likely to find a lot of it a little thin.

Saturday Night Fever ★ ★ ★ ½
R, 118 m., 1977

John Travolta (Tony Manero), Karen Gorney (Stephanie), Barry Miller (Bobby C), Joseph Cali (Joey), Paul Paps (Double J), Donna Pescow (Annette). Directed by John Badham and produced by Robert Stigwood. Screenplay by Norman Wexler.

Each night I ask the stars up above:
Why must I be a teen-ager in love?
                    —Dion and the Belmonts

Saturday Night Fever is an especially hard-edged case and a very good movie. It's about a bunch of Brooklyn kids who aren't exactly delinquents but are fearsomely tough and cynical and raise a lot of hell on Saturday nights. They live for Saturday night, in fact: They hang their gold chains around their necks and put on the new shirts they bought with their Friday paychecks, and they head for a place called Disco 2001, and they take pills and drink and, as Leo Sayer put it, dance the night away. Occasionally they go out to the parking lot for a session in the back seat with a girl.

John Travolta is the center of the crowd: He's Tony Manero, the best dancer, the best looker, the guy with the most confidence. His life is just as screwed up as everyone else's, but they don't know that, and they tell him: "You know somethin', Tony? You always seem to be in control."

He is not. He works all week at a paint and hardware store and comes home to a family that worships his older brother, who is a priest. The family's sketched briefly right at the beginning in a dinner scene which, like the whole movie, is able to walk the tightrope between what's funny and what's pathetic.

We meet Tony's friends and the girls that hang around them, and we are reminded that feminism has not yet conquered Brooklyn. Some of the girls, especially a spunky little number named Annette (Donna Pescow), worship Tony. He dances with Annette because she's a good dancer, but he tries to keep her at arm's length otherwise. He's caught in a sexist vise: Because he likes her, he doesn't want to sleep with her, because then how could he respect her? The female world is divided, he explains, between nice girls and tramps. She accepts his reasoning and makes her choice.

The Brooklyn we see in *Saturday Night Fever* reminds us a lot of New York's Little Italy as Martin Scorsese saw it in *Who's That Knocking at My Door?* and *Mean Streets.* The characters are similar: They have few aims or ambitions and little hope of breaking out to the larger world of success—a world symbolized for them by Manhattan, and the Brooklyn Bridge reaching out powerfully toward it. But *Saturday Night Fever* isn't as serious as the Scorsese films. It does, after all, have almost wall-to-wall music in it (mostly by the Bee Gees, but including even "Disco Duck"). And there are the funny scenes (like the one where Travolta shouts at his father: "You hit my hair!") to balance the tragic and self-destructive ones.

There's also a hint of *Rocky,* whose poster Travolta's character has on his bedroom wall. Travolta meets a Brooklyn girl (Karen Gorney) who's made it in Manhattan, sort of, as a secretary. She comes back to Brooklyn to dance, and they team up to enter a $500 disco contest. They win it, too, but not before winning has become meaningless to Travolta. Their relationship is interesting because Travolta sees Miss Gorney not so much as a girl (although he thinks she's beautiful) but as an example of how *he* might escape Brooklyn.

The movie's musical and dancing sequences are dazzling. Travolta and Miss Gorney are great together, and Travolta does one solo (in an unbroken shot) that the audiences cheered for. The movie was directed by John Badham (*The Bingo Long Traveling All-Stars*), and his camera occupies the dance floor so well that we really do understand the lure of the disco world, for all of the emptiness and cruelty the characters find there.

Say Amen, Somebody ★ ★ ★ ★
G, 100 m., 1983

Featuring Willie May Ford Smith, Thomas A. Dorsey, Sallie Martin, the Barrett Sisters, Edward and Edgar O'Neal, and Zella Jackson Price. Directed by George Nierenberg and produced by George and Karen Nierenberg.

Say Amen, Somebody is one of the most joyful movies I've ever seen. It is also one of the best musicals and one of the most interesting documentaries. And it's a terrific good time. The movie is about gospel music, and it's filled with gospel music. It's sung by some of the pioneers of modern gospel, who are now in their seventies and eighties, and it's sung by some of the rising younger stars, and it's sung by choirs of kids. It's sung in churches and around the dining room table; with orchestras and a capella; by an old man named Thomas A. Dorsey in front of thousands of people, and by Dorsey standing all by himself in his own backyard. The music in *Say Amen, Somebody* is as exciting and uplifting as any music I've ever heard on film.

The people in this movie are something, too. The filmmaker, a young New Yorker named George T. Nierenberg, starts by introducing us to two pioneers of modern gospel: Mother Willie May Ford Smith, who is seventy-nine, and Professor Dorsey, who is eighty-three. She was one of the first gospel soloists; he is known as the Father of Gospel Music. The film opens at tributes to the two of them—Mother Smith in a St. Louis church, Dorsey at a Houston convention—and then Nierenberg cuts back and forth between their memories, their families, their music, and the music sung in tribute to them by younger performers.

That keeps the movie from seeming too much like the wrong kind of documentary— the kind that feels like an educational film and is filled with boring lists of dates and places. *Say Amen, Somebody* never stops moving, and even the dates and places are open to controversy (there's a hilarious sequence in which Dorsey and Mother Smith disagree very pointedly over exactly which of them convened the first gospel convention).

What's amazing in all of the musical sequences is the quality of the sound. A lot of documentaries use "available sound," picked up by microphones more appropriate for the television news. This movie's concerts are miked by up to eight microphones, and the Dolby system is used to produce full stereo sound that really rocks. Run it through your stereo speakers, and play it loud.

Willie May Ford Smith comes across in this movie as an extraordinary woman, spiritual, filled with love and power. Dorsey and his longtime business manager, Sallie Martin, come across at first as a little crusty, but then there's a remarkable scene where they sing along, softly, with one of Dorsey's old records. By the end of the film, when the ailing Dorsey insists on walking under his own steam to the front of the gospel convention in Houston, and leading the delegates in a hymn, we have come to see his strength and humanity. Just in case Smith and Dorsey seem too noble, the film uses a lot of mighty soul music as a counterpoint, particularly in the scenes shot during a tribute to Mother Smith at a St. Louis Baptist church. We see Delois Barrett Campbell and the Barrett Sisters, a Chicago-based trio who have enormous musical energy; the O'Neal Twins, Edward and Edgar, whose "Jesus Dropped the Charges" is a show-stopper; Zella Jackson Price, a younger singer who turns to Mother Smith for advice; the Interfaith Choir, and lots of other singers.

Say Amen, Somebody is the kind of movie that isn't made very often, because it takes an unusual combination of skills. The filmmaker has to be able to identify and find his subjects, win their confidence, follow them around, and then also find the technical skill to really capture what makes them special. Nierenberg's achievement here is a masterpiece of research, diligence, and direction. But his work would be meaningless if the movie didn't convey the spirit of the people in it, and *Say Amen, Somebody* does that with great and mighty joy. This is a great experience.

Scarface ★ ★ ★ ★
R, 170 m., 1983

Al Pacino (Tony Montana), Steven Bauer (Manny Ray), Michelle Pfeiffer (Elvira), Mary Elizabeth Mastrantonio (Gina), Robert Loggia (Frank Lopez). Directed by Brian De Palma and produced by Martin Bregman. Screenplay by Oliver Stone.

The interesting thing is the way Tony Montana stays in the memory, taking on the dimensions of a real, tortured person. Most thrillers use interchangeable characters, and most gangster movies are more interested in action than personality, but *Scarface* is one of those special movies, like *The Godfather*, that is willing to take a flawed, evil man and allow him to be human. Maybe it's no coincidence that Montana is played by Al Pacino, the same actor who played Michael Corleone. Montana is a punk from Cuba. The opening scene of the movie informs us that when Cuban refugees were allowed to come to America in 1981, Fidel Castro had his own little private revenge and cleaned out his prison cells, sending us criminals along with his weary and huddled masses. We see Montana trying to bluff his way through an interrogation by U.S. federal agents, and that's basically what he'll do for the whole movie: bluff. He has no real character and no real courage, although for a short time cocaine gives him the illusion of both.

Scarface takes its title from the 1932 Howard Hawks movie, which was inspired by the career of Al Capone. That Hawks film was the most violent gangster film of its time, and this 1983 film by Brian De Palma also has been surrounded by a controversy over its violence, but in both movies the violence grows out of the lives of the characters; it isn't used for thrills but for a sort of harrowing lesson about self-destruction. Both movies are about the rise and fall of a gangster, and they both make much of the hero's neurotic obsession with his sister, but the 1983 *Scarface* isn't a remake, and it owes more to *The Godfather* than to Hawks.

That's because it sees its criminal so clearly as a person with a popular product to sell, working in a society that wants to buy. In the old days it was booze. For the Corleones, it was gambling and prostitution. Now it's cocaine. The message for the dealer remains the same: Only a fool gets hooked on his own goods. For Tony Montana, the choices seem simple at first. He can work hard, be honest, and make a humble wage as a dishwasher. Or he can work for organized crime, make himself more vicious than his competitors and get the big cars, the beautiful women, and the boot-licking attention from nightclub doormen. He doesn't wash many dishes.

As Montana works his way into the south Florida illegal drug trade, the movie observes him with almost anthropological detachment. This isn't one of those movies where the characters all come with labels attached ("boss," "lieutenant," "hit man") and behave exactly as we expect them to. De Palma and his writer, Oliver Stone, have created a gallery of specific individuals and one of the fascinations of the movie is that we aren't watching crime-movie clichés, we're watching people who are criminals.

Al Pacino does not make Montana into a sympathetic character, but he does make him into somebody we can identify with, in a horrified way, if only because of his perfectly understandable motivations. Wouldn't we all like to be rich and powerful, have desirable sex partners, live in a mansion, be catered to by faithful servants—and hardly have to work? Well, yeah, now that you mention it. Dealing drugs offers the possibility of such a life-style, but it also involves selling your soul. Montana gets it all and he loses it all. That's predictable. What is original about this movie is the attention it gives to how little Montana enjoys it while he has it. Two scenes are truly pathetic; in one of them, he sits in a nightclub with his blonde mistress and his faithful sidekick, and he's so wiped out on cocaine that the only emotions he can really feel are impatience and boredom. In the other one, trying for a desperate transfusion of energy, he plunges his face into a pile of cocaine and inhales as if he were a drowning man.

Scarface understands this criminal personality, with its links between laziness and ruthlessness, grandiosity and low self-esteem, pipe dreams and a chronic inability

to be happy. It's also an exciting crime picture, in the tradition of the 1932 movie. And, like the Godfather movies, it's a gallery of wonderful supporting performances: Steven Bauer as a sidekick, Michelle Pfeiffer as a woman whose need for drugs leads her from one wrong lover to another, Robert Loggia as a mob boss who isn't quite vicious enough, and Mary Elizabeth Mastrantonio, as Pacino's kid sister who wants the right to self-destruct in the manner of her own choosing. These are the people Tony Montana deserves in his life, and *Scarface* is a wonderful portrait of a real louse.

Scenes from a Marriage ★ ★ ★ ★
PG, 168 m., 1974

Liv Ullmann (Marianne), Erland Josephson (Johan), Bibi Andersson (Katarina), Jan Malmslo (Peter). Directed and written by Ingmar Bergman.

They have reached a truce which they call happiness. When we first meet them, they're being interviewed for some sort of newspaper article, and they agree that after ten years of marriage, they're a truly happy couple. The husband, Johan, is most sure: He is successful in his work, in love with his wife, the father of two daughters, liked by his friends, considered on all sides to be a decent chap. His wife, Marianne, listens more tentatively. When it is her turn, she says she is happy, too, although in her work she would like to move in the direction of—but then she's interrupted for a photograph. We are never quite sure what she might have said, had she been allowed to speak as long as her husband. And, truth to tell, he doesn't seem to care much himself. Although theirs is, of course, a perfect marriage.

And so begins one of the truest, most luminous love stories ever made, Ingmar Bergman's *Scenes from a Marriage*. The marriage of Johan and Marianne will disintegrate soon after the film begins, but their love will not. They will fight and curse each other, and it will be a wicked divorce, but in some fundamental way they have touched, really touched, and the memory of that touching will be something to hold to all of their days.

Bergman has been working for years with the theme of communication between two people. At one time, he referred to it as "the agony of the couple." And who can forget the terrible recriminations and psychic bloodshed of the couples in *Winter Light* or *The Passion of Anna?* And here he seems finally to have resolved his crisis.

The years that preceded the making of this film saw a remarkable conciliation going on within the work of this great artist. In *Cries and Whispers*, he was at last able to face the fact of death in a world where God seemed silent. And now, in this almost heartbreaking masterpiece, he has dealt with his fear that all men are, indeed, islands. The film (168 minutes, skillfully and without distraction edited down from six, fifty-minute Swedish television programs) took him four months to make, he has said, but a lifetime to experience.

His married couple are Swedish upper-middle-class. He is a professor, she is a lawyer specializing in family problems (for which, read divorce). They have two daughters, who remain offscreen. They are intelligent, independent. She truly believes their marriage is a happy one (although she doesn't much enjoy sex). One evening, he comes to their summer cottage and confesses that he has gone and fallen in love with someone else. There is nothing to be done about it. He must leave her.

The way in which his wife reacts to this information displays the almost infinite range of Liv Ullmann, who is a beautiful soul and a gifted performer. Her husband (Erland Josephson) has left her literally without an alternative ("You have shut me out. How can I help us?") and still she loves him. She fears that he will bring unhappiness upon himself.

But he does leave, and the film's form is a sometimes harsh, sometimes gentle, ultimately romantic (in an adult and realistic way) view of the stages of this relationship. At first, their sexual attraction for each other remains, even though they bitterly resent each other because of mutual hurts and recriminations. The frustrations they feel about themselves are taken out on each other. At one point, he beats her and weeps for himself, and we've never seen such despair on the screen. But the passage of time dulls the immediate hurt and the feeling of betrayal. And at last, they are able to meet as fond friends and even to make love, as if visiting an old home they'd once been cozy in.

They drift apart, they marry other people (who also remain offscreen), they meet from time to time.

Ten years after the film has opened, they find themselves in Stockholm while both their spouses are out of the country, and, as a nostalgic lark, decide to spend a weekend in their old summer cottage. But it's haunted with memories, and they go to a cottage nearby.

In the last section of the film (subtitled "In the Middle of the Night in a Dark House"), Marianne awakens screaming with a nightmare, and Johan holds her.

And this is twenty years after they were married, and ten years after they were divorced, and they are in middle age now but in the night still fond and frightened lovers holding on for reassurance.

And that is what Bergman has been able to accept, the source of his reconciliation: Beyond love, beyond marriage, beyond the selfishness that destroys love, beyond the centrifugal force that sends egos whirling away from each other and prevents enduring relationships—beyond all these things, there still remains what we know of each other, that we care about each other, that in twenty years these people have touched and known so deeply that they still remember, and still need.

Marianne and Johan are only married for the first part of this film, but the rest of it is also scenes from their marriage.

Secret Honor ★ ★ ★ ★
NO MPAA RATING, 90 m., 1984

Philip Baker Hall (Nixon). Directed and produced by Robert Altman. Screenplay by Donald Freed and Arnold M. Stone.

The most tantalizing images in Woodward and Bernstein's *The Final Days* were those stories of a drunken Richard M. Nixon, falling to his knees in the White House, embarrassing Henry Kissinger with a display of self-pity and pathos. Was the book accurate? Even Kissinger said he had no idea who the authors' sources were (heh, heh). But as Watergate fades into history, and as revisionist historians begin to suggest that Nixon might after all have been a great president—apart from the scandals, of course—our curiosity remains. What were the real secrets of this most complex president? Robert Altman's *Secret Honor,* which is one of the most scathing, lacerating and brilliant movies of 1984, attempts to answer our questions. The film is a work of fiction. An actor is employed to impersonate Nixon. But all of the names and many of the facts are real, and the film gives us the uncanny sensation that we are watching a man in the act of exposing his soul.

The action takes place in Nixon's private office, at some point after his resignation. The shelves are lined with books, and with a four-screen video monitor for the security system. The desk top is weighted down with brass and gold. From the walls, portraits peer down. Eisenhower, Lincoln, Washington, Woodrow Wilson, Kissinger. Nixon begins by fiddling with his tape recorder; there is a little joke in the fact that he doesn't know quite how to run it. Then he begins to talk. He talks for ninety minutes. That bare description may make *Secret Honor* sound like *My Dinner with André,* but rarely have I seen ninety more compelling minutes on the screen. Nixon is portrayed by Philip Baker Hall, an actor previously unknown to me, with such savage intensity, such passion, such venom, such scandal, that we cannot turn away. Hall looks a little like the real Nixon; he could be a cousin, and he sounds a little like him. That's close enough. This is not an impersonation, it's a performance.

What Nixon the character has to say may or may not be true. He makes shocking revelations. Watergate was staged to draw attention away from more serious, even treasonous, activities. Kissinger was on the payroll of the Shah of Iran, and supplied the Shah with young boys during his visits to New York. Marilyn Monroe was indeed murdered by the CIA, and so on. These speculations are interwoven with stories we recognize as part of the official Nixon biography: the letter to his mother, signed "Your faithful dog, Richard"; the feeling about his family and his humble beginnings; his hatred for the Eastern Establishment, which he feels has scorned him.

Truth and fiction mix together into a tapestry of life. We get the sensation of a man pouring out all of his secrets after a lifetime of repression. His sentences rush out, disorganized, disconnected, under tremendous pressure, interrupted by four-letter words that serve almost as punctuation. After a while the specific details don't matter so much; what we are hearing is a scream of a brilliant, gifted man who is tortured by the notion that fate might have made him a loser.

A strange thing happened to me as I watched this film. I knew it was fiction. I didn't approach it in the spirit of learning the "truth about Nixon." But as a movie, it created a deeper truth, an artistic truth, and after *Secret Honor* was over, you know what? I had a deeper sympathy for Richard Nixon than I have ever had before.

Shaft ★ ★ ½
R, 98 m., 1971

Richard Roundtree (Shaft), Moses Gunn (Boss), Gwenn Mitchell (Ellie), Christopher St. John (Militant). Directed by Gordon Parks and produced by Joel Freeman. Screenplay by Ernest Tidyman and John D.F. Black.

Gordon Parks's *Shaft* gave us the first really convincing black private eye. Movies about private detectives have always been among my favorites—they seem to be better than most other formula movies—and John Shaft, as played by Richard Roundtree, belongs in the honorable tradition of Philip Marlowe, Sam Spade, Lew Archer, and company. He belongs because, like them, he keeps no regular company. Private eyes (in the movies, anyway) are loners in a way that defines the word. They live in dingy walk-up offices, sipping bourbon from the office bottles and waiting for the phone to ring.

These may all be clichés, but, hell, a private-eye movie without clichés wouldn't be worth the price of admission. We don't go to Westerns to see cowboys riding ostriches. The strength of Parks's movie is his willingness to let his hero fully inhabit the private-eye genre, with all of its obligatory violence, blood, obscenity, and plot gimmicks. The weakness of *Shaft,* I suspect, is that Parks is not very eager to inhabit that world along with his hero.

Gordon Parks was the first black director to make a major studio film, and his *The Learning Tree* (1969) was a deeply felt, lyrically beautiful film that was, maybe, just too simple and honest to be commercial. It didn't find a large audience, and I suspect that Parks turned next to *Shaft* for commercial survival.

The nice thing about *Shaft* is that it savors the private-eye genre, and takes special delight in wringing new twists out of the traditional relationship between the private eye and the boys down at homicide. The story covers some of the same ground as *Cotton Comes to Harlem*, but in a different way. Shaft is brought in by a Harlem rackets boss (Moses Gunn) whose traditional slice of power is being threatened by the Mafia. They don't want a partnership anymore, so they kidnap the boss's daughter. Shaft's job is to get her back.

His adventures along the way include a thoroughly unpleasant encounter with a white pick-up, who is insulted because all black exploitation movies have to insult at least one white pick-up (and why not? Fair is fair). The climax involves a complicated plan with Shaft and his allies swinging from ropes and using firehoses to accomplish with five people in five minutes what could have been done with one, in one. Parks isn't especially good at action direction, but the heart of a private-eye movie is in the mood scenes, anyway, and he supplies a scene in a bar and another one with the Harlem rackets boss that are very nice.

Sharky's Machine ★ ★ ★
R, 119 m., 1981

Burt Reynolds (Sharky), Rachel Ward (Dominoe), Vittorio Gassman (Victor), Brian Keith (Papa), Charles Durning (Frisco). Directed by Burt Reynolds and produced by Hank Moonjean. Screenplay by Gerald Di Pago.

Sharky's Machine contains all of the ingredients of a tough, violent, cynical big-city cop movie, but what makes it intriguing is the way the Burt Reynolds character plays against those conventions. His name is Sharky. As the movie opens, he's an undercover narcotics cop. He blows a big case and is demoted to the vice squad—which is a bawdy, brawling, vocal gang of misfits who act like a cross between "Hill Street Blues" and a Joseph Wambaugh nightmare.

Sharky is not happy in vice. He is, in fact, not happy anywhere, not until a young woman named Dominoe enters his life. She is a hooker. She also seems to be involved with some snaky big-money characters, and so Sharky places her under twenty-four hour surveillance. That involves moving several cops, telescopes, cameras, and bugging devices into the high-rise opposite her apartment. The cops set up housekeeping and settle down for a long wait. And it's here that the movie begins to really involve us. Reynolds, as Sharky, falls in love with the woman. It is a voyeuristic love, involving spying and eavesdropping, and Sharky is not a voyeur—so it is particularly painful for him to witness the woman's sexual involvement with others.

The central scenes of the movie, involving the call girl's private life and the probing eyes of Sharky, could easily have become tawdry—could have disintegrated into a peep show. That doesn't happen, partly because Reynolds (who also directed the film) doesn't provide cheap displays of flesh, but also because the call girl is played by British actress Rachel Ward, who brings poignancy and restraint to the role. She plays a hooker who's not a tramp. She has a husky voice and an astonishing body, but there's an innocence in her manner. Later, we discover that she has been in virtual bondage to her pimp since she was an infant. She knows no other life. This is a setup of sorts, a device in the plot to allow the female lead to be both prostitute and victim, but it clarifies the relationship between Reynolds and Ward. And when they fall in love, as they inevitably do, it provides some leftover innocence to be celebrated.

Reynolds surrounds this central relationship with a lot of cops, known as Sharky's Machine. They are played by actors who have played a lot of other cops in a lot of other movies—Brian Keith, Charles Durning—and by Bernie Casey, who is playing his first cop but does it with special grace. There's a long scene in the film, reportedly improvised, in which Casey tells Reynolds what it felt like, the first time he was shot. We are reminded that cops in the movies hardly ever talk about being shot.

Sharky's Machine has a lot of plot, most of it inspired by the original novel by William Diehl. Maybe it has too much plot for a movie that Reynolds has referred to as *Dirty Harry Goes to Atlanta*. But this is an ambitious film; it's as if something inside Reynolds was chafing at the insipid roles he was playing in one car-chase movie after another. He doesn't walk through this movie, and he doesn't allow himself the cozy little touches that break the mood while they're letting the audience know how much fun Burt is having.

The result of his ambition and restraint is a movie much more interesting than most cop thrillers. *Sharky's Machine* does have a lot of action, including an extended, exhausting, brutal shoot-out at the end. But it also has the special qualities of the relationship between Reynolds and Ward (more fully developed than the camaraderie between Reynolds and Catherine Deneuve, as another hooker in another thriller, *Hustle*, in 1974). As a director, Reynolds allows himself a few excesses (one howler is the dramatic cut from a sex scene to the phallic glory of the Peachtree Plaza Hotel). But he's put a lot of his ambition in this movie, and it reminds us that there is a fine actor within the star of *Cannonball Run*.

Sheena, Queen of the Jungle ★
PG, 117 m., 1984

Tanya Roberts (Sheena), Ted Wass (Vic Casey), Donovan Scott (Fletcher), Elizabeth of Toro (Shaman), Trevor Thomas (Prince Otwani). Directed by John Guillermin and produced by Paul Aratow. Screenplay by David Newman and Lorenzo Semple, Jr.

How can this be? I casually reached over to the old reference shelf, to find some old references to *Sheena, Queen of the Jungle*, the jungle heroine who inflamed the pubescent fantasies of lads in the early 1950s. And not only wasn't there an entry in Halliwell's *Filmgoer's Companion*, but neither the *Oxford Companion of Film* nor *The Film Encyclopedia* had ever heard of Sheena. Could this be because Sheena spent most of her time on television, where she was once played by the one, the only, Irish McCallum? I dunno, but I think they're missing a bet in Oxford if they don't have a Sheena festival right away.

I mention my old memories because the movie *Sheena* seems likely to provide me with few new memories. The movie stars Tanya Roberts as the legendary blonde jungle girl. After Sheena's parents are killed in a cave-in, she is adopted by the beautiful Shaman (played by the fashion model Elizabeth of Toro, who undoubtedly taught Sheena all about makeup, explaining Sheena's plucked eyebrows and purple eye shadow, there in the midst of the trees). Shaman's tribe considers Sheena a god, and she learns to talk to the animals, ride a zebra bareback, and fashion crude jungle bikinis out of only those simple materials one finds in a boutique. Then an American TV crew comes to the jungle to film an interview with an African prince, who is also a place kicker for a U.S. pro football team. The prince is behind a plot to assassinate his brother, the king, and the TV crew stumbles into the story and over Sheena, who the prince's jealous girlfriend has vowed to kill.

Are you following all this? Anyway, Sheena and the anchorman (Ted Wass) disappear into the jungle, where the clichés of male superiority *instantly* take hold. Get this. The clod of an anchorman, faced with a woman who can tame zebras and talk to the elephants, tells this magnificent wild creature that, and I quote, what he'd like to do is take her to Wall Street and show her the World Trade Center while they both eat peanuts.

Anyway, *Sheena* contains all too little of Sheena at some times, and all too much at others. Let me explain. The whole dumb plot about the palace coup, the evil prince, etc., is given a lot of screen time, even though it is awesomely uninteresting. Sheena, who might have been presented as sort of a female Greystoke, a real jungle creature, meanwhile takes nude baths in waterfalls and learns that American men do rude things like pressing their lips against hers. The nudity in the movie is extensive enough to raise eyebrows over its PG rating.

Is there anything good about *Sheena*? Yeah, the animals are fun to watch, especially the lions. But Tanya Roberts is about as convincing, swinging from those vines, as Carol Burnett would have been. And come to think of it, Sheena, Queen of the Jungle, is the kind of character that, in our time, perhaps only Carol Burnett could play.

Shoah ★ ★ ★ ★
NO MPAA RATING; 563 m. on five cassettes, 1986

A documentary directed and produced by Claude Lanzmann.

For more than nine hours I sat and watched a film named *Shoah*, and when it was over, I sat for a while longer and simply stared into space, trying to understand my emotions. I had seen a memory of the most debased chapter in human history. But I had also seen a film that affirmed life so passionately that I did not know where to turn with my confused feelings. There is no proper response to this film. It is an enormous fact, a 563-minute howl of pain and anger in the face of genocide. It is one of the noblest films ever made.

The film's title is a Hebrew word for chaos or annihilation—for the Holocaust. The film is a documentary, but it does not contain images from the 1940s. There are no old newsreel shots, no interviews with the survivors of the death camps, no coverage of the war crimes trials. All of the movie was photographed in the last five or six years by a man named Claude Lanzmann, who went looking for eyewitnesses to Hitler's "Final Solution." He is surprisingly successful in finding people who were there, who saw and heard what went on. Some of them, a tiny handful, are Jewish survivors of the camps. The rest are mostly old people, German and Polish, some who worked in the camps, others who were in a position to observe what happened.

They talk and talk. *Shoah* is a torrent of words, and yet the overwhelming impression, when it is over, is one of silence. Lanzmann intercuts two kinds of images. He shows the faces of his witnesses. And then he uses quiet pastoral scenes of the places where the deaths took place. Steam engines move massively through the Polish countryside, down the same tracks where trains took countless Jews, gypsies, Poles, homosexuals, and other so-called undesirables to their deaths. Cameras pan silently across pastures, while we learn that underneath the tranquility are mass graves. Sometimes the image is of a group of people, gathered in a doorway, or in front of a church, or in a restaurant kitchen.

Lanzmann is a patient interrogator. We see him in the corners of some of his shots, a tall, lanky man, informally dressed, chain-smoking. He wants to know the details. He doesn't ask large, profound questions about the meaning of the extermination of millions of people. He asks little questions. In one of the most chilling sequences in the film, he talks to Abraham Bomba, today a barber in Tel Aviv. Bomba was one of the Jewish barbers ordered to cut off the hair of Jewish women before they were killed in Treblinka. His assignment suggests the shattering question: How can a woman's hair be worth more than her life? But Lanzmann does not ask overwhelming and unanswerable questions like this. These are the sorts of questions he asks:

You cut with what? With scissors?
There were no mirrors?
You said there were about sixteen barbers? You cut the hair of how many women in one batch?

The barber tries to answer. As he talks, he has a customer in his chair, and he snips at the customer's hair almost obsessively, making tiny movements with his scissors, as if trying to use the haircut as a way to avoid the questions. Their conversation finally arrives at this exchange, after he says he cannot talk any more:

A. I can't. It's too horrible. Please.
Q. *We have to do it. You know it.*
A. I won't be able to do it.
Q. *You have to do it. I know it's very hard. I know and I apologize.*
A. Don't make me go on, please.
Q. *Please. We must go on.*

Lanzmann is cruel, but he is correct. He must go on. It is necessary to make this record before all of those who were witnesses to the Holocaust have died.

His methods in obtaining the interviews were sometimes underhanded. He uses a concealed television camera to record the faces of some of the old Nazi officials whom he interviews, and we look over the shoulders of the TV technicians in a van parked outside the buildings where they live. We see the old men nonchalantly pulling down charts from the wall to explain the layout of a death camp, and we hear their voices, and at one point when a Nazi asks for reassurance that the conversation is private, Lanzmann provides it. He will go to any length to obtain this testimony.

He does not, however, make any attempt to arrange his material into a chronology, an objective, factual record of how the "Final Solution" began, continued, and was finally terminated by the end of the war. He uses a more poetic, mosaic approach, moving according to rhythms only he understands among the only three kinds of faces we see in this film: survivors, murderers, and bystanders. As their testimony is intercut with the scenes of train tracks, steam engines, abandoned buildings, and empty fields, we are left with enough time to think our own thoughts, to meditate, to wonder.

This is a long movie but not a slow one, and in its words it creates something of the same phenomenon I experienced while watching *My Dinner with André*. The words themselves create images in the imagination, as they might in a radio play. Consider the images summoned by these words, spoken by Filip Muller, a Czech Jew assigned to work at the doors of the gas chambers, a man who survived five waves of liquidations at Auschwitz:

A. You see, once the gas was poured in, it worked like this: It rose from the ground upwards. And in the terrible struggle that followed—because it was a struggle—the lights were switched off in the gas chambers. It was dark, no one could see, so the strongest people tried to climb higher. Because they probably realized that the higher they got, the more air there was. They could breathe better. That caused the struggle. Secondly, most people tried to push their way to the door. It was psychological; they knew where the door was; maybe they could force their way out. It was instinctive, a death struggle. Which is why children and weaker people and the aged always wound up at the bottom. The strongest were on top. Because in the death struggle, a father didn't realize his son lay beneath him.

Q. *And when the doors were opened?*

A. They fell out. People fell out like blocks of stone, like rocks falling out of a truck.

The images evoked by his words are inutterably painful. What is remarkable, on reflection, is that Muller is describing a struggle that neither he nor anyone else now alive ever saw. I realized, at the end of his words, that a fundamental change had taken place in the way I personally visualized the gas chambers. Always before, in reading about them or hearing about them, my point of view was outside, looking in. Muller put me inside.

That is what this whole movie does, and it is probably the most important thing it does. It changes our point of view about the Holocaust. After nine hours of *Shoah*, the Holocaust is no longer a subject, a chapter of history, a phenomenon. It is an environment. It is around us. Ordinary people speak in ordinary voices of days that had become ordinary to them. A railroad engineer who drove the trains to Treblinka is asked if he could hear the screams of the people in the cars behind his locomotive:

A. Obviously, since the locomotive was next to the cars. They screamed, asked for water. The screams from the cars closest to the locomotives could be heard very well.

Q. *Can one get used to that?*

A. No, it was extremely distressing. He knew the people behind him were human, like him. The Germans gave him and the other workers vodka to drink. Without drinking, they couldn't have done it.

Some of the strangest passages in the film are the interviews with the officials who were running the camps and making the "Final Solution" work smoothly and efficiently. None of them, at least by their testimony, seem to have witnessed the whole picture. They only participated in a small part of it, doing their little jobs in their little corners. If they are to be believed, they didn't personally kill anybody, they just did small portions of larger tasks, and somehow all of the tasks, when added up and completed, resulted in people dying. Here is the man who scheduled the trains that took the Jews to die:

Q. *You never saw a train?*

A. No, never. We had so much work, I never left my desk. We worked day and night.

And here is a man who lived 150 feet from a church where Jews were rounded up, held, and then marched into gas vans for the trip to the crematoriums:

Q. *Did you see the gas vans?*

A. No—yes, from the outside. They shuttled back and forth. I never looked inside; I didn't see Jews.

What is so important about *Shoah* is that the voices are heard of people who did see, who did understand, who did comprehend, who were there, who know that the Holocaust happened, who tell us with their voices and with their eyes that genocide occurred in our time, in our civilization.

There is a tendency while watching *Shoah* to try to put a distance between yourself and the events on the screen. These things happened, after all, forty or forty-five years ago. Most of those now alive have been born since the events happened. Then, while I was watching the film, came a chilling moment. A name flashed on the screen in the subtitles, the name of one of the commandants at Treblinka death camp. At first I thought the name was "Ebert"—my name. Then I realized it was "Eberl." I felt a moment of relief, and then a moment of intense introspection as I realized that it made no difference what the subtitle said. The message of this film (if we believe in the brotherhood of man) is that these crimes were committed by people like us, against people like us.

But there is an even deeper message as well, and it is contained in the testimony of Filip Muller, the Jew who stood at the door of a crematorium and watched as the victims walked in to die. One day some of the victims, Czech Jews, began to sing. They sang two songs: "The Hatikvah," and the Czech national anthem. They affirmed that they were Jews and that they were Czechs. They denied Hitler, who would have them be one but not the other. Muller speaks:

That was happening to my countrymen, and I realized that my life had become meaningless. (His eyes fill with tears.) Why go on living? For what? So I went into the gas chamber with them, resolved to die. With them. Suddenly, some who recognized me came up to me. . . . A small group of women approached. They looked at me and said, right there in the gas chamber . . .

Q. *You were inside the gas chamber?*

A. Yes. One of them said: "So you want to die. But that's senseless. Your death won't give us back our lives. That's no way. You must get out of here alive, you must bear witness to our suffering and to the injustice done to us."

And that is the final message of this extraordinary film. It is not a documentary,

not journalism, not propaganda, not political. It is an act of witness. In it, Claude Lanzmann celebrates the priceless gift that sets man apart from animals and makes us human, and gives us hope: the ability for one generation to tell the next what it has learned.

Shoot the Moon ★ ★ ★ ½
R, 124 m., 1982

Albert Finney (George Dunlap), Diane Keaton (Faith Dunlap), Karen Allen (Sandy), Peter Weller (Frank), Dana Hill (Sherry). Directed by Alan Parker and produced by Alan Marshall. Screenplay by Bo Goldman.

Alan Parker's *Shoot the Moon* is a film that sometimes keeps its painful secrets even from itself. It opens with a shot of a man in agony. In another room, his wife, surrounded by four noisy daughters, dresses for a dinner that evening at which the man will be honored. The man has to pull himself together. His voice is choking with tears, he telephones the woman he loves and tells her how hard it will be to get through the evening without her. Then he puts on his rumpled tuxedo and marches out to do battle. As we watch this scene, we assume that the movie will answer several of the questions it raises, such as: What went wrong in the marriage? Why is the man in such agony? What is the nature of his love for the other woman? One of the surprises in *Shoot the Moon* is that none of these questions is ever quite answered, and we are asked to fill in the gaps ourselves.

That is not necessarily a flaw in the film. *Shoot the Moon* is not the historical record of this marriage, but the emotional history. It starts with what should be a happy marriage. A writer of books (Albert Finney) lives with his beautiful, funky wife (Diane Keaton) and their four rambunctious daughters in a converted farmhouse somewhere in Marin County, California. Their house is one of those warm battle zones filled with books, miscellaneous furniture, and the paraphernalia for vast projects half-completed. We learn that the marriage has gone disastrously wrong. That the man is determined to stalk out and be with his new woman. That the wife, after a period of anger and mourning, is prepared to react to this decision by almost deliberately having an affair with the loutish but well-meaning young man who comes to build a tennis court. That the husband and wife still harbor fugitive feelings of love and passion for another.

We never really learn how the marriage went wrong. There is the usual talk about how one partner was not given the room to grow, or the other did not have enough "space"—concepts that love would render meaningless, but that divorce makes into savagely defended positions. We also learn just a tantalizing little about the two new lovers. Albert Finney's new woman (Karen Allen) is so cynical about their relationship in one scene that we wonder if their affair will soon end (we never learn). Diane Keaton's new man (Peter Weller) is so emotionally stiff, so closed-off, that we don't know for a long time whether Keaton really likes him, or simply desires him sexually and wants to use him to spite her husband.

Does it matter that the movie doesn't want to provide insights in these areas? I think it does. When Ingmar Bergman covered similar grounds in his *Scenes from a Marriage*, he provided us with enough concrete information about the issues in the marriage that it was possible for us to discuss the relationship afterward, taking sides, seeing both points of view. After *Shoot the Moon*, we don't discuss the relationship, we discuss our questions about it. And yet this is sometimes an extraordinary movie. Despite its flaws, despite its gaps, despite two key scenes that are dreadfully wrong, *Shoot the Moon* contains a raw emotional power of the sort we rarely see in domestic dramas.

The film's basic conflict is within Albert Finney's mind. He can no longer stay with his wife, he must leave and be with the other woman, and yet he still wants to own the family and possessions he has left behind. He doesn't want his ex-wife dating other men. He wants to observe the birthday of an eldest daughter (Dana Hill) who hates him and resents his behavior. He remodeled the house with his own hands, and cannot bear to see another man working on it. In one scene of heartbreaking power, he breaks into his own house and finds himself beating his daughter because he loves her so much and she will not love him.

In scenes like that (and in the quiet scenes

where Hill asks, "Why did Daddy leave us?" and Keaton answers, "I don't think he left you; I think he left me"), *Shoot the Moon* is a great film. In scenes like the one where they fight in a restaurant, or argue in court, it ranges from the miscalculated to the disastrous. *Shoot the Moon* is a rare, good film, and yet, afterward, most of my thoughts were about how it might have been better. It is frustrating to feel that the filmmakers knew their characters intimately, but chose to reveal them only in part.

Shooting Party ★ ★ ★
NO MPAA RATING; 97 m., 1985

James Mason (Sir Randolph Nettleby), Edward Fox (Lord Gilbert Hartlip), Dorothy Tutin (Lady Nettleby), Cheryl Campbell (Lady Hartlip), John Gielgud (Cornelius Cardew), Gordon Jackson (Tom Harker), Rupert Frazer (Lionel Stephens), Joris Stuyck (Count Tibor). Directed by Alan Bridges and produced by Geoffrey Reeve. Screenplay by Julian Bond.

The Shooting Party begins, with suitable irony, in the days just before World War I, when the British upper class was able to look out over a world that seemed secure, prosperous, and unchanging. A group of guests arrives at a country home for a weekend of shooting, and by the end of the weekend a tragedy has occurred, and even the narrator can see the storms of Europe gathering on the horizon. There are many similarities here to Jean Renoir's great film *The Rules of the Game*, which showed the French social order breaking up on the eve of World War II, but *The Shooting Party* is smaller, quieter, and gloomier.

The central characters in the movie are two quite different specimens of the aristocracy: Sir Randolph Nettleby, played by James Mason in his last performance, and Lord Hartlip, played by Edward Fox, that tall, diffident British actor who can effortlessly project understated courage, and this time is equally successful at creating understated priggery and evil conceit. Sir Randolph rules with an easy, almost weary charm over his far-flung establishment, which includes not only the usual relatives, guests, and house servants, but also the residents of the rural district, including Tom

Harker (Gordon Jackson), a game-poacher who is nevertheless well-known and liked by everyone. Indeed, when an extra hand is needed to work as a loader and guide, Harker is hired to come along on the shooting party—assisting his betters to do legally in the morning what he himself does illegally at night. The movie develops quietly. There are vignettes of life in the great country house: a masquerade party, the backstairs games of the children, a small boy's love for his pet duck, the sly intrigues and flirtations, the sometimes bitter private conversations between husbands and wives. Sir Randolph lives in this world by habit and custom, as he has for many years, and James Mason brings to the role an air of contented civility. At one point, he is writing in his journal when a grandchild interrupts him. He explains: "It is always good to spend part of each day writing down your thoughts. That way you will not have to bother others with them."

The dialogue in the film is frequently at that level of very quiet, ironic economy. Meanwhile, we grow more familiar with the tensions underlying the shooting party, and particularly a rivalry that grows up between Fox and Lionel Stephens (Rupert Frazer), who boasts that he has shot more birds than Fox, and who also perhaps has started to impress Fox's wife. One morning in the fields, the undeclared contest grows so intense that Fox fires off a final shot after the order has been given to cease firing—and he hits Jackson, the game-poacher, in the face.

All of the film's themes come together in the final scenes, as Mason attempts to comfort Jackson, and as Fox stiffly promises "to make it right—financially, that is." When Mason turns to Fox and says, very quietly, "You were not shooting like a gentleman," there is more violence on the screen than at any time during the shooting.

This is the sort of small, intelligent, and civilized film that we have to find in Europe, because American actors of the same caliber would not want to appear in small roles with so many of their equals. The movie is a reminder that American films are usually about one or two stars and a handful of well-known character actors, while Europeans are still capable of pitching in together for an ensemble piece. There is nothing new in the message of this film, but a great deal of artistry in its telling.

The Shootist ★ ★ ★ ½
PG, 100 m., 1976

John Wayne (The Shootist), Lauren Bacall (The Widow), James Stewart (The Doctor), Ron Howard (The Son), Harry Morgan (The Sheriff), John Carradine (The Undertaker), Hugh O'Brien (The Gambler), Richard Boone (The Gunman). Directed by Don Siegel and produced by M.J. Frankovich and William Seif. Screenplay by Miles Hood.

The old man was around for a long time. When he played the fresh-faced Ringo Kid in *Stagecoach*, back in 1939, he was already thirty-two years old. And I didn't believe it either until I'd counted the credits twice—but *Stagecoach* was his sixtieth film. John Wayne grew, role by role, into the most mythic presence in American movies. Some of the roles were pretty bad ones, but maybe at the time we didn't know that. Maybe at the time we were ten or twelve years old, and it was a Saturday afternoon, and what we registered was that Wayne was up there on the screen, squinting into the sun, making decisions, ready for action. For my generation, while presidents came and went, John Wayne merely grew a little more thoughtful.

He rides onscreen in *The Shootist* afraid that he is dying. Not afraid he'll be killed, but afraid he's dying, which is the last thing we anticipated a John Wayne character would do of his own accord. It is 1901: He has outlived his century. A sawbones in the next state has given him the bad news and now he wants to hear it from the lips of Doc Hostetler, who nursed him back to health after a violent afternoon twenty years ago. And so he rides, the Shootist, into a Carson City to which the Old West has become an embarrassment. The streets are still wide enough to turn a mule train in, but now an abashed little horse trolley runs down the middle of them, and electricity's going to put the horse out of business next year. The pain is way down deep in his back, and he rides on a red velvet cushion he stole out of a whorehouse. It doesn't do a damn bit of good. Hostetler hems and haws and comes out with it: cancer. Two months to live, six weeks, maybe less. In the meantime he can do what he wants. After a while he won't feel like doing much.

In his time, the Shootist shot a lot of men dead. Out at the livery stable, burnt into the leather of his saddle, they find his name: J.B. Books. His arrival in Carson City immediately becomes news. Hostetler steers him over to a boarding house run by the Widow Rogers, who shows him a two dollar room. It'll do fine. Books settles down to die. But all these gunfighters had the same problem: People weren't content to let them die in bed, because they made too good a trophy.

So there is a tricky dilemma: To die with some measure of dignity, and to avoid being shot in the meantime. As the film opens, Books has eight days. You will be surprised with what gentleness and humanity he lives them, before the inevitable gunfire at the end. And unless you have already discovered that John Wayne is an actor as well as a movie star, you will be surprised by the dimensions he provides for J.B. Books.

The movie isn't a bit sentimental. Everybody in town wants the bastard dead, except for the Widow Rogers and her son, Gillom. Even Doc Hostetler, who knows what people can go through toward the end of these illnesses, stops Books at the door and advises him point-blank not to wait around and see how things will eventually feel. The Sheriff is almost cheerful at the prospect of Books's approaching end. The Undertaker offers a free funeral, free tombstone, free casket, free flowers, even two mourners thrown in at no extra charge. "You son of a bitch," Books says, "you aim to do to me what they did with John Wesley Hardin. Lay me out and parade every damn fool in the state past me at a dollar a head, half price for children, and then stuff me in a gunny sack and shovel me under." He is correct.

Still, eight days are enough to establish the beginnings of human contact. The Widow Rogers is appalled at first to have a killer as her paying guest, but an affection and respect grows up between them. Her kid, Gillom, contracts a case of hero worship even while trying to swindle the Shootist out of his horse. And Wayne, as Books, occupies the substantial center of the film. He vows to read a newspaper through from front to back before he dies. He sends his Sunday-go-to-meeting clothes out to the cleaners. And he

challenges three old Carson City enemies to meet him in the saloon at eleven o'clock Monday morning.

It's here that the movie doesn't quite work. We hardly know the three enemies. We don't know why they'd oblige the Shootist's wish to die in a gunfight. We understand his reasoning, but not theirs. And the movie's final scene, in which Gillom Rogers symbolically steps into the Shootist's boots, is just a little too neat to be real. Westerns probably have to end along these lines with confrontations and gunfire and heroism, but *The Shootist* will be remembered for the quieter scenes that came before.

The cast is excellent because it understands the material, and sympathizes with it: James Stewart, as the doctor, and Lauren Bacall, as the widow, play scenes with Wayne that absolutely make us forget we're watching a movie. Gaunt old John Carradine has been an undertaker all his life; finally they cast him as one. Don Siegel's direction reveals a sensitivity we didn't suspect after films like *Dirty Harry*. And observe the way John Wayne says "Good day, Mrs. Rogers" to Lauren Bacall for the last time.

Silent Movie ★ ★ ★ ★
PG, 88 m., 1976

Mel Brooks (Mel Funn), Marty Feldman (Marty Eggs), Dom DeLuise (Dom Bell), Bernadette Peters (Vilma Kaplan), Sid Caesar (Studio Chief), Harold Gould (Engulf), Ron Carey (Devour), Henny Youngman (Fly-in-Soup Man). Directed by Mel Brooks and produced by Michael Hertzorg. Screenplay by Brooks, Ron Clark, Rudy DeLuca, and Barry Levinson.

There's a moment very early in *Silent Movie* (before the opening credits, in fact) when Mel Brooks, Marty Feldman, and Dom DeLuise are tooling through Los Angeles in a tiny sports car. They pass a pregnant lady at a bus stop. "That's a very pregnant lady!" Brooks says (on a title card, of course, since this is a silent movie). "Let's give her a lift!" The lady gets into the back of the car, which tilts back onto its rear wheels. Mel drives off with the front wheels in the air.

This is far from being the funniest scene in a very funny movie, but it helps to illustrate my point, which is that Mel Brooks will do anything for a laugh. Anything. He has no shame. He's an anarchist; his movies inhabit a universe in which everything is possible and the outrageous is probable, and *Silent Movie*, where Brooks has taken a considerably stylistic risk and pulled it off triumphantly, made me laugh a lot. On the Brooks-Laff-O-Meter, I laughed more than in *Young Frankenstein* and about as much as in *Blazing Saddles*, although not, I confess, as much as in *The Producers*.

Silent Movie is not only funny, it's fun. It's clear at almost every moment that the filmmakers had a ball making it. It's set in contemporary Hollywood, where Big Pictures Studio ("If it's a big picture, we've made it") teeters on the edge of bankruptcy and a takeover from the giant Engulf and Devour conglomerate. Enter Mel Funn (Brooks), a once-talented director whose career was cut short by drunkenness, who vows to save the studio by convincing Hollywood's biggest stars to make a silent movie. This is a situation that gives rise to a lot of inside jokes (I wonder whether executives at Gulf and Western, which took over Paramount, will notice any parallels), but the thing about Brooks's inside jokes is that their outsides are funny, too.

The intrepid gang of Mel, Dom, and Marty set out to woo the superstars, materializing in the shower of one (who counts his hands, puzzled, and finds he has eight) and plucking another out of a nightclub audience. (There are several "actual" stars in the movie, but it would be spoiling the fun to name them.) Everything's done amid an encyclopedia of sight gags, old and new, borrowed and with a fly in their soup. There are gags that don't work and stretches of up to a minute, I suppose, when we don't laugh—but even then we're smiling because of Brooks's manic desire to entertain. There's a story about the days, years ago, when Brooks was a writer for Sid Caesar and Caesar would march into the writers' office, pick up their desks, brandish them and shout *"funnier!"* I think the lesson rubbed off.

In a movie filled with great scenes, these moments are classics: The battle with the Coke machine. The behavior with the horse on the merry-go-round. The nightclub scene. The dramatic reaction of Engulf and Devour's board of directors to the photo of sexpot Vilma Kaplan. The fly in the soup. The Pong game in the intensive-care unit. The . . . but space is limited: Perhaps I should mention, though, that the movie isn't really silent. It's filled with wall-to-wall music, sound effects, explosions, whistles, and crashes and, yes, one word.

Silent Running ★ ★ ★ ★
G, 90 m., 1972

Bruce Dern (Lowell), Cliff Potts (Wolf), Ron Rivkin (Barker), Jesse Vint (Keenan), Mark Persons, Steven Brown, Cheryl Sparks, Larry Wisenhunt (Drones). Directed by Douglas Trumbull and produced by Michael Gruskoff. Screenplay by Deric Washburn, Mike Cimino, and Steve Bochco.

In the not very distant future, man has at last finished with Earth. The mountains are leveled and the valleys filled in, and there are no growing plants left to mess things up. Everything is nice and sterile, and man's global housekeeping has achieved total defoliation. Out around the rings of Saturn, a few lonely spaceships keep their vigil. They're interplanetary greenhouses, pointed always toward the sun. Inside their acres and acres of forests, protected by geodesic domes that gather the sunlight, the surviving plants and small animals of Earth grow. There are squirrels and rabbits and moonlit nights when the wind does actually seem to breathe in the trees: a ghostly reminder of the dead forests of Earth.

The keeper of one of these greenhouses, Freeman Lowell, loves the plants and animals with a not terribly acute intelligence. *Silent Running* is his story. In an earlier day, he might have been a forest ranger and happily spent the winter all alone in a tower, spotting forest fires. Now he is millions of miles from Earth, but his thoughts are filled with weedings and prunings, fertilizer and the artificial rainfall.

One day the word comes from Earth: Destroy the greenhouses and return. Lowell cannot bring himself to do this, and so he destroys his fellow crew members instead. Then he hijacks his spaceship and directs it out into the deep galactic night. All of this is told with simplicity and a quiet ecological concern, and it makes *Silent Running* a movie out of the ordinary—especially if you like science fiction.

The director is Douglas Trumbull, a Canadian who designed many of the special effects for Stanley Kubrick's *2001*. Trumbull also did the computers and the underground laboratory for *The Andromeda Strain*, and is one of the best science fiction special effects men. *Silent Running*, which has deep space effects every bit the equal of those in *2001*, also introduces him as an intelligent, if not sensational, director.

The weight of the movie falls on the shoulders of Bruce Dern, who plays the only man in sight during most of the picture. His only companions are Huey, Louie, and Dewey, who are small and uncannily human robots who help with the gardening. They're OK with a trowel but no good at playing poker, as their human boss discovers during a period of boredom.

Dern is a very good, subtle actor, who was about the best thing in Jack Nicholson's directing debut, *Drive, He Said*. Dern played a basketball coach as a man obsessed with the notion of winning—and the deep-space ecologist this time is a quieter variation on the theme.

Silent Running isn't, in the last analysis, a very profound movie, nor does it try to be. (If it had, it could have been a pretentious disaster.) It is about a basically uncomplicated man faced with an awesome, but uncomplicated, situation. Given a choice between the lives of his companions and the lives of Earth's last surviving firs and pines, oaks and elms, and creepers and cantaloupes, he decides for the growing things. After all, there are plenty of men. His problem is that, after a while, he begins to miss them.

Silkwood ★ ★ ★ ★
R, 128 m., 1983

Meryl Streep (Karen Silkwood), Kurt Russell (Drew Stephens), Cher (Dolly Pelliker), Craig T. Nelson (Winston). Directed by Mike Nichols and produced by Nichols and Michael Hausman. Screenplay by Nora Ephron and Alice Arlen.

When the Karen Silkwood story was first being talked about as a movie project, I pictured it as an angry political exposé, maybe *The China Syndrome, Part 2*. There'd be the noble, young nuclear worker, the evil conglomerate, and, looming overhead, the death's-head of a mushroom cloud. That could have been a good movie, but predictable. Mike Nichols's *Silkwood* is not predictable. That's because he's not telling the story of a conspiracy, he's telling the story of a human life. There are villains in his story, but none with motives we can't understand. After Karen is dead and the movie is over, we realize this is a lot more movie than perhaps we were expecting.

Silkwood is the story of some American workers. They happen to work in a Kerr-McGee nuclear plant in Oklahoma, making plutonium fuel rods for nuclear reactors. But they could just as easily be working in a Southern textile mill (there are echoes of *Norma Rae*), or on an assembly line, or for a metropolitan public school district. The movie isn't about plutonium, it's about the American working class. Its villains aren't monsters; they're organization men, labor union hotshots, and people afraid of losing their jobs. As the movie opens, Karen Silkwood fits naturally into this world, and the movie is the story of how she begins to stand out, how she becomes an individual, thinks for herself, and is punished for her freedom. Silkwood is played by Meryl Streep, in another of her great performances, and there's a tiny detail in the first moments of the movie that reveals how completely Streep has thought through the role. Silkwood walks into the factory, punches her time card, automatically looks at her own wristwatch, and then shakes her wrist: It's a self-winding watch, I guess. That little shake of the wrist is an actor's choice. There are a lot of them in this movie, all almost as invisible as the first one; little by little, Streep and her coactors build characters so convincing that we become witnesses instead of merely viewers.

The nuclear plant in the film is behind on an important contract. People are working overtime and corners are being cut. A series of small incidents convinces Karen Silkwood that the compromises are dangerous, that the health of the workers is being needlessly risked, and that the company is turning its back on the falsification of safety and workmanship tests. She approaches the union.

The union sees some publicity in her complaints. She gets a free trip to Washington—her first airplane ride. She meets with some union officials who are much more concerned with publicity than with working conditions, and she has a little affair with one of them. She's no angel. At home in Oklahoma, domestic life resembles a revolving door, with her boyfriend (Kurt Russell) packing up and leaving, and her friend (Cher), a lesbian, inviting a beautician to move in. It's a little amazing that established movie stars like Streep, Russell, and Cher could disappear so completely into the everyday lives of these characters.

The real Karen Silkwood died in a mysterious automobile accident. She was on her way to deliver some documents to a *New York Times* reporter when her car left the road. Was the accident caused in some way? Was she murdered? The movie doesn't say. Nor does it point suspicion only toward the company. At the end there were a lot of people mad at Karen Silkwood. *Silkwood* is the story of an ordinary woman, hard-working and passionate, funny and screwed-up, who made those people mad simply because she told the truth as she saw it and did what she thought was right.

Silverado ★ ★ ★ ½
PG-13, 132 m., 1985

Kevin Kline (Paden), Scott Glenn (Emmett), Kevin Costner (Jake), Danny Glover (Mal), Linda Hunt (Stella), Jeff Goldblum (Slick), Brian Dennehy (Sheriff Cobb), Rosanna Arquette (Hannah), John Cleese (Sheriff Langston). Directed and produced by Lawrence Kasdan. Screenplay by Lawrence Kasdan and Mark Kasdan.

Walking home after the second Western was over at the Princess Theater, we'd play the roles we had seen on the screen. We were seven or eight years old at the time, but we didn't have the slightest difficulty in identifying with the cowboys in the movies. All of their motives were transparently clear to us—except, possibly, why anyone would want to kiss a girl when he could be practicing his lasso tricks instead.

The Westerns I remember from those days have been filtered through a golden haze of time, but the one thing I am sure I remember correctly is that they were fun. They were high-spirited, joyous, anarchic movies in which overgrown adolescents jumped on their horses and whooped and waved their hats in the air, and rode as fast as the wind to the next town and to the next adventure.

Silverado is a Western like that. I mean the comparison to be praise. This movie is more sophisticated and complicated than the Westerns of my childhood, and it is certainly better looking and better acted. But it has the same spirit; it awards itself the carefree freedom of the Western myth itself—the myth of a nation "endlessly realizing Westward," as Robert Frost had it, with limitless miles of prairie and desert and mountain, interrupted only occasionally enough for a dozen men to shoot at each other without all of them necessarily getting hit.

Silverado is the work of Lawrence Kasdan, the man who wrote *Raiders of the Lost Ark*, and it has some of the same reckless brilliance about it. It's the story of four cowboys who join up together, ride into town, refuse to knuckle under to the corrupt sheriff, and end up fighting for justice. This is a story, you will agree, that has been told before. What distinguishes Kasdan's telling of it is the style and energy he brings to the project.

The cowboys include a sweet-faced young man who hopes to make his fortune (Kevin Kline), his goofy brother (Kevin Costner), a black man who vows to avenge his father's murder (Danny Glover), and a taciturn loner (Scott Glenn) who gets restless when he's not a long way from civilization. They meet along the way, after Glenn saves Kline from death in the desert, and together they help Costner escape from jail. Joining up with Glover, they ride on into the next town, Silverado, which is dominated by a slick sheriff (Brian Dennehy) and a gambling saloon run by a formidably competent little woman named Stella (Linda Hunt, in a scene-stealing performance).

I will not tell you too much of what happens next, but then perhaps I do not need to. If you are familiar with the Western, you will be familiar with this one. What may seem a little strange is that, if there is any nostalgia connected to this film, it will be found in our hearts and not in the characters on the screen. Too many Westerns in the last fifteen years have been elegies to a dead past, played out by actors remembering the cowboy roles of their youth (remember, if you can, the last Westerns of Robert Mitchum, William Holden, Randolph Scott, John Wayne, Joel McCrea, Kirk Douglas). *Silverado* contains a group of talented young actors (Scott Glenn, the oldest, is in his forties), and this is not their last Western but, in many cases, their first. The movie is set at the time when the West was still being opened up, when there was still opportunity there, and when the bad guys were still so unsophisticated they could fall for a dumb trick like getting trapped in a box canyon.

What does it prove, this movie about a bunch of cowboys held together by honor, this movie about bartender philosophers, evil sheriffs, and young pioneer women with lines like "My beauty will pass someday, but the land will only grow more beautiful." What does it prove? That the Western myth is most at home in a setting of innocence, that *Silverado* understands that, and that somewhere in our hearts there may still be memories of little boys and girls who chose up sides for who got to be the good guys on the long walk home.

Sixteen Candles ★ ★ ★
PG, 93 m., 1984

Molly Ringwald (Samantha Baker), Anthony Michael Hall (The Geek), Michael Schoeffling (Jake Ryan), Gedde Watanabe (Long Duk Dong), Paul Dooley (Jim Baker). Directed by John Hughes and produced by Hilton A. Green. Screenplay by Hughes.

Sixteen Candles is a sweet and funny movie about two of the worst things that can happen to a girl on her sixteenth birthday: (1) Her grandparents shrieking "Look! She's finally got her boobies!" and (2) her entire family completely and totally forgetting that it's even her birthday. The day goes downhill from there, because of (3) her sister's wedding to a stupid lunkhead, (4) her crush on the best-looking guy in the senior class, and (5) the long, involved story about how a freshman boy named the Geek managed to get possession of a pair of her panties and sell looks at them for a dollar each to all the guys in the locker room.

If *Sixteen Candles* begins to sound a little

like an adolescent raunch movie, maybe it's because I haven't suggested the style in which it's acted and directed. This is a fresh and cheerful movie with a goofy sense of humor and a good ear for how teen-agers talk. It doesn't hate its characters or condescend to them, the way a lot of teen-age movies do; instead, it goes for human comedy and finds it in the everyday lives of the kids in its story.

The movie stars Molly Ringwald as Samantha, a bright-eyed brunette who pulls off the difficult trick of playing a character who takes everything too seriously—without ever taking herself too seriously. The movie's told mostly from her point of view, and it's like *Valley Girl*—it's about young kids who think a lot about sex, but who are shy and inexperienced and unsure and touchingly committed to concepts like True Love. She has a crush on a senior boy named Jake (Michael Schoeffling), who looks like Matt Dillon, of course, and doesn't even know she's alive. Meanwhile, the Geek (Anthony Michael Hall) is in love with her. Also, there are complications involving Jake's stuck-up girlfriend, Samantha's impossible grandparents, various older and younger brothers and sisters, and a foreign exchange student named Long Duk Dong, who apparently has come to this country to major in partying.

Sixteen Candles contains most of the scenes that are obligatory in teen-age movies: The dance, the makeout session, the party that turns into a free-for-all. But writer and director John Hughes doesn't treat them as subjects for exploitation; he *listens* to these kids. For example, on the night of the dance, Samamtha ends up in the shop room with the Geek. They're sitting in the front seat of an old car. The Geek acts as if he's sex-mad. Samantha tells him to get lost. Then, in a real departure for this kind of movie, they really start to talk, and it turns out they're both lonely, insecure, and in need of a good friend.

There are a lot of effective performances in this movie, including Paul Dooley as Samantha's harried father, Blanche Baker as the zonked-out older sister, Hall as the Geek, and Gedde Watanabe as the exchange student (he elevates his role from a potentially offensive stereotype to high comedy). Ringwald provides a perfect center for the story, and her reaction in the first scene with her grandmother is just about worth the price of admission.

Sleeper ★ ★ ★ ½
PG, 88 m., 1973

Woody Allen (Miles Monroe), Diane Keaton (Luna), John Beck (Erno), Marya Small (Dr. Nero). Directed by Woody Allen and produced by Jack Grossberg. Screenplay by Allen and Marshall Brickman.

So how would you feel if your name was Miles Monroe and you ran the Happy Carrot Health Food Store in Greenwich Village and you went into St. Vincent's Hospital for a minor operation one morning and woke up 200 years in the future? And America had become a police state? And the underground wanted to use you because you were the only person alive without an identification number?

What Woody Allen does is scream bloody murder and claim to be a coward: "I'm even beaten up by Quakers." But life becomes a grim struggle, etc., and Woody finds himself at battle with the thought police.

If the plot sounds slightly insane, recollect that one Allen movie began with Howard Cosell doing a play-by-play of an assassination, and another had Woody slapping Listerine under his arms and squirting Right Guard into his mouth before a big date.

Sleeper established Woody Allen as the best comic director and actor in America, a distinction that would mean more if there were more comedies being made. Without making a count, I'd guess that a dozen action movies get made for every comedy, which says more about our taste than our comedians. Mel Brooks only seems to get geared up every three years or so, but Allen is prolific as well as funny.

He gives us moments in Sleeper that are as good as anything since the silent films of Buster Keaton. There is, for example, a scene where a futuristic instant pudding erupts from a mixing bowl and threatens to fill the kitchen; Woody beats it down with a broom. The scene is part of a long sequence in which he has to pretend to be a robot house servant; he lurches about and buzzes and finally tears up the robot assembly line (in a scene like something from Modern Times). Protesting all the way, Allen eventually penetrates into the inner circles of the underground and the government, and discovers the terrible truth about the nation's dictator, known as The Leader.

Nine months earlier, The Leader's home had burned down leaving nothing of The Leader but his nose. Through great medical innovation, the nose has been kept alive ever since, and the plan is to use genetic engineering to grow, or clone, The Leader's body back onto the nose. Inevitably, Allen is mistaken as the chief surgeon.

Whether the movie's Leader bears any relationship to the nation's current chief executive is a secret that only Woody Allen knows; he does not, however, go to many pains to keep it.

There's also a funny satirical scene in which Allen, as a genuine relic of 1973, is asked to identify such artifacts as General de Gaulle, a Playboy centerfold, and a Howard Cosell broadcast ("When people committed great crimes, they were forced to watch that.")

Sleeper is the closest Allen has come to classic slapstick-and-chase comedy, and he's good at it. His earlier films depended more on plot (except for Everything You Always Wanted to Know about Sex).

And sometimes he had a tendency to get a little sentimental as in Take the Money and Run, which opened with a hilarious documentary style biography of its hero, but then got bogged down in a love story that Allen apparently took seriously. (There was even a slow-motion Semi-Obligatory Lyrical Interlude in which Allen and his girl ran through the park and he didn't even seize the opportunity to satirize a Salem commercial.)

This time, though, he moves at breakneck speed and will risk anything, especially the plot, for a gag. Things move so fast we don't even get around to wondering how, in the middle of the movie, Allen got into the Miss America contest . . . and won.

Sleuth ★ ★ ★ ★
PG, 138 m., 1972

Laurence Olivier (Andrew Wyke), Michael Caine (Milo Tindle), Alec Cawthorne (Inspector Doppler), Eve Channing (Marguerite), John Matthews (Sergeant Talvant), Teddy Martin (Constable Higgs). Directed by Joseph L. Mankiewicz and produced by Morton Gottleib. Screenplay by Anthony Shaffer.

We come upon Andrew Wyke, the mystery writer, in an appropriate setting. He's in the middle of his vast garden, which is filled with shrubbery planted to form a maze. There is no way into, or out of, the maze—unless you know the secret. The better we come to know Andrew Wyke, the more this seems like the kind of garden he would have.

Wyke is a game-player. His enormous Tudor country manor is filled with games, robots, performing dolls, dart boards, and chess tables. He also plays games with people. One day poor Milo Tindle comes for a meeting with him. Milo is everything Wyke detests: only half-British, with the wrong accent, and "brand-new country gentleman clothes."

But Milo and Andrew's wife have fallen in love, and they plan to marry. So Andrew has a little scheme he wants to float. He is willing—indeed, happy—to give up his wife, but only if he can be sure she'll stay gone. He wants to be sure Milo can support her, and he suggests that Milo steal the Wyke family jewels and pawn them in Amsterdam. Then Milo will have a small fortune, and Andrew can collect the insurance.

Up to this point, everything in Sleuth seems so matter-of-fact that there's no hint how complicated things will get later on. But they do get complicated, and deadly, and reality begins to seem like a terribly fragile commodity. Andrew and Milo play games of such labyrinthine ferociousness that they eventually seem to forget all about Andrew's wife (and his mistress) and to be totally absorbed with stalking each other in a macabre game of cat and mouse.

Sleuth, a totally engrossing entertainment, is funny and scary by turns, and always superbly theatrical. It's the kind of mystery we keep saying they don't make anymore, but sometimes they do, and the British seem to write them better than anyone. The movie is based on the long-running play by Anthony Shaffer, who also wrote Alfred Hitchcock's Frenzy. Both films have in common a nice flair for dialogue and a delicate counterpoint between the ironic and the gruesome.

What really makes the movie come alive—what makes it work better than the play, really—are the lead performances by Sir Laurence Olivier, Michael Caine, and Alec Cawthorne. Olivier plays the wealthy mystery writer Andrew Wyke as a true-blue British eccentric: His head, like his house, is cluttered with ornate artifacts largely without function. The hero of his detective stories, the wonderfully named St. John Lord Merridewe, is equally dotty. Olivier is clearly having fun in the role, and he throws in all kinds of accents, asides, and nutty pieces of business. Michael Caine, who might seem an unlikely candidate to play Milo Tindle, turns out to be a very good one. He manages somehow to seem smaller and less assured than Olivier (even while he towers over Sir Laurence). And he is strangely touching as he dresses up in an absurd clown's costume to steal the jewels. Inspector Doppler, the kindly old investigator who suspects that Andrew has murdered Milo, is played by Alec Cawthorne, a veteran stage actor making his movie debut.

It's difficult to say more about Sleuth without giving away its plot—which in this case would be a capital offense. Let me just mention that the play makes a remarkably easy transition to the screen because of director Joseph L. Mankiewicz's willingness to respect its timing and dialogue, instead of trying to jazz it up cinematically. And, despite the fact that most of the movie takes place indoors, we never get the sense of visual limitations because Ken Adams's set designs give us such an incredible multitude of things to look at (and through) in the mansion.

Small Change ★ ★ ★ ★
PG, 104 m., 1976

Geory Desmouceaux (Patrick), Philippe Goldman (Julien), Christine Pelle (Madame), Jean-François Stevenin and Chantal Mercier (The Teachers). Directed by François

Truffaut. Screenplay by Truffaut and
Suzanne Schiffman.

There's a moment in François Truffaut's
Small Change that remembers childhood so
well we don't know whether to laugh or cry.
It takes place in a classroom a few minutes
before the bell at the end of the school day.
The class cutup is called on. He doesn't have
the answer (he never does), but as he stands
up his eyes stray to a large clock outside the
window. The hand stands at twenty-eight
minutes past the hour. Click: twenty-nine
minutes. He stalls, he grins, the teacher
repeats the question. Click: thirty past, and
the class bell rings. The kid breaks out in a
triumphant grin as he joins the stampede
from the room.

This moment, like so many in Truffaut's
magical film, has to be seen to be appreci-
ated. He re-creates childhood, and yet he
sees it objectively, too: He remembers not
only the funny moments but the painful
ones. The agony of a first crush. The ordeal
of being the only kid in class so poor he has to
wear the same sweater every day. The painful
earnestness that goes into the recitation of a
dirty joke that neither the teller nor the listeners quite understand.

Truffaut has been over some of this ground
before. His first feature, *The 400 Blows*, told
the painful story of a Paris adolescent caught
between his warring parents and his own
better nature. In *Small Change* he returns to
similar material in a sunnier mood. He tells
the stories of several kids in a French provincial town, and of their parents and teachers.
His method is episodic; only gradually do we
begin to recognize faces, to pick the central
characters out from the rest. He correctly
remembers that childhood itself is episodic:
Each day seems separate from any other,
each new experience is sharply etched, and
important discoveries and revelations
become great events surrounded by a void.
It's the accumulation of all those separate
moments that create, at last, a person.

"Children exist in a state of grace," he has
a character say at one point. "They pass
untouched through dangers that would
destroy an adult." There are several such
hazards in *Small Change*. The most
audacious—Truffaut at his best—involves a
two-year-old child, a kitten, and an open

window on the tenth floor. Truffaut milks
this situation almost shamelessly before
finally giving us the happiest of denoue-
ments. And he exhibits at the same time his
mastery of film; the scene is timed and
played to exist exactly at the border between
comedy and tragedy, and from one moment
to the next we don't know how we should
feel. He's got the audience in his hand.

That's true, too, in a scene involving a little girl who has been made to stay at home as
a punishment. She takes her father's battery-
powered megaphone and announces indignantly to the neighbors around the courtyard
that she is hungry, that her parents have gone
out to a restaurant without her, and that she
has been abandoned. The neighbors lower
her food in a basket: Chicken and fruit but
not, after all, a bottle of red wine one of the
neighborhood kids wanted to put in.

In the midst of these comic episodes, a
more serious story is developed. It's about
the kid who lives in a shack outside of town.
He's abused by his parents, he lives by his
wits, he steals to eat. His mistreatment is
finally found out by his teachers, and leads to
a concluding speech by one of them that's
probably unnecessary but expresses Truffaut's thinking all the same: "If kids had the
vote," the teacher declares, "the world
would be a better and safer place."

Smash Palace ★ ★ ★ ★
R, 100 m., 1982

Bruno Lawrence (Al Shaw), Anna Jemison
(Jacqui Shaw), Greer Robson (Georgie
Shaw), Keith Aberdeen (Ray Foley), Des
Kelly (Tiny). Directed and produced by Roger
Donaldson. Screenplay by Donaldson, Peter
Hansard, and Bruno Lawrence.

Step by step, this powerful movie takes a
man from perfect happiness into a personal
hell. By the end of the film, the man is
behaving irrationally, but here's the frightening thing: Because we've followed him every
step of the way, we have to admit he's behaving as we ourselves might, in the same circumstances. The man in *Smash Palace* is Al
Shaw, a Grand Prix driver who leaves the racing circuit to take over his father's auto
garage in New Zealand. Played by Bruno
Lawrence, Al is a straight-talking, direct
man who enjoys working with his hands and

takes a vast delight in the affections of his wife and the love of his small daughter. It's a long way from the Grand Prix to repairing transmissions, but he's happy with his work and content to raise a family in peace and quiet. His wife (Anna Jemison) is not so content. She wanted him to leave the racing circuit before he was killed, but now, in the quiet backwaters of New Zealand, she is going quietly stir-crazy. She begins an affair with a local cop (Keith Aberdeen) and finally tells her husband she's leaving him. She's moving into town.

Her decision starts him on a series of wrong moves that may seem logical, one by one, but which eventually add up in the minds of others to a simple conclusion: He has lost his reason. He is jealous—of course. He holds a great fury against his wife and the cop. But, much more important, he misses his daughter. He wants custody. But because he acts in ways that are violent and frightening to his wife (and because her lover is on the police force, which must respond to the domestic emergencies he creates), he works himself into a Catch-22: The more he does to take back his daughter, the closer he is to losing her. Finally, he kidnaps her. He takes her out into the woods where they live together for a time in isolation and happiness. It's an idyll that can't last. But *Smash Palace* doesn't lead up to the inevitable violent conclusion we might expect. All along the way, this film prefers the unexpected turns of actual human behavior to the predictable plot developments we might have expected, and, at the end, there's another turn, a fascinating one.

Smash Palace is one of 1982's best films, an examination of much the same ground as *Shoot the Moon,* but a better film, because it has the patience to explore the ways in which people can become consumed by anger (*Shoot the Moon* contented itself with the outward symptoms). One of the reasons the movie works so well is the performances, which are all the stronger because they come from actors we have not seen before. Bruno Lawrence, bald-headed, wiry, tough, and surprisingly tender, is just right as the man who loses his family. Anna Jemison has a difficult assignment as his wife: We're on his side, and yet we see the logic of her moves. Keith Aberdeen is properly tentative as the

other man; he feels love and lust, and yet is not unaware of the unhappiness he is causing. And there's a guy named Des Kelly who plays Tiny, an employee at the Smash Palace who looks on, and sees all, and wishes he knew what to do.

The movie was directed by a young filmmaker named Roger Donaldson, who, in a sense, *is* the New Zealand film industry. He has produced six features for New Zealand television, and his first feature film, *Sleeping Dogs,* starred Warren Oates in a horrifying and plausible fantasy about the American occupation of New Zealand. Now comes this film, so emotionally wise and observant that we learn from it why people sometimes make the front pages with guns in their hands and try to explain that it's all because of love. Love, yes, but also the terrible frustration of trying to control events, to make people do what you want them to do, what you "know" would make them happy—no matter what they think. The hero of *Smash Palace* does not act wisely, but if we are honest, it's hard to see where we might have acted differently.

Smooth Talk ★ ★ ★ ½
R, 92 m., 1986

Laura Dern (Connie), Treat Williams (Arnold Friend), Mary Kay Place (Katherine), Elizabeth Berridge (June), Levon Helm (Harry), Sarah Inglis (Jill). Directed by Joyce Chopra and produced by Martin Rosen. Music by James Taylor. Screenplay by Tom Cole.

There is a certain kind of teen-ager who always seems to be waiting for something. Others live in the moment, but these waiting ones seem to be the victims of time. It stretches before them in long, empty hours. You can look at them and almost literally see the need in their eyes. It is a need to be someone else, somewhere else.

Connie, the heroine in *Smooth Talk,* is a girl like that. She is about fifteen years old, tall, blonde, unformed. At least that is the vision of her we receive the first time we see her. Then there is a transformation scene. She leaves her house, dressed like a teen-ager on the way to a ballgame, and meets her friends at the mall. They go into the ladies' room and apply makeup and mascara and stuff their jackets into their bags, and when they emerge they look like the runners-up in the Madonna lookalike contest. Sexy beyond their own knowledge, they parade through the mall, attracting attention they do not know how to handle. There is a risky, reckless bounce in their step; they are still waiting, but now they seem to know what they are waiting for.

Appearances deceive. Emotionally, Connie is younger than she looks. At home, she suffers because her mother clearly prefers her older sister. She suffers, too, from the well-meaning idiocy of her father, who talks in vague terms of "finally having a home of our own," as if this were Connie's goal, too, and she would always be fifteen and always coming home to it. She looks at her father as if he were speaking a foreign language. He looks at her as if he were seeing someone else. Connie is played by Laura Dern, an actress who seems perfectly suited to this role; she is a chameleon who looks twelve in one shot, eighteen in the next, and is able to suggest the depth of her unhappiness by the way she tries to seem cheerful.

The first hour of *Smooth Talk* is deceptive. Nothing much seems to happen. Connie and her friends hang out. Connie fights with her parents. Connie waits through the long, endless afternoons of summer. This is the set-up for the second half of the movie, which is an astonishing denouement.

Because *Smooth Talk* depends so completely on surprise, it is hard to know how to write about it. Many will be shocked by the movie's ending, and would want to be warned. Others will see it as a modern morality tale, a Grimm story for the late twentieth century, a time when evil seems more banal and seductive than it should. I will walk lightly around the ending without revealing it.

Smooth Talk is based on a short story by Joyce Carol Oates, who so often finds the materials of classic tragedy in the lives of everyday people. Although the movie is shocking, it is not sensational in the way it might have been—if it had been handled as a horror story, say, instead of as a morality play. Oates's story, adapted by Tom Cole and directed by Joyce Chopra, is about a young girl who is surrounded by sexuality, who is curious about it, who flirts dangerously in the wrong places, and who not only learns her lesson, but grows up, all at once, into a different person than she was.

What happens is that a boy (Treat Williams) sees her at the drive-in. He says his name is Arnold Friend, and that he wants to be *her* friend. Everything about this guy is all wrong. He is nowhere near being as young as he says. There is a bad look in his eye. He pals around with another guy, who doesn't say anything, and doesn't need to, because one look at him and you realize he is missing important parts.

Connie walks around in her shorts and halter top, and Arnold Friend watches her. He makes a pass at her, and she puts him off with the kind of cute flirtation that would work with another kid, but Arnold just looks at her—looks through her—and a chill wind seems to blow. One Sunday when Connie is left at home alone and the family is all hours away, Arnold Friend comes to visit. He does not physically rape her. What he does is much worse than that. He talks to her in a way that forever brings an end to her innocence.

Smooth Talk is not a "teen-age movie." It is not, despite its plot, a horror film. It is a study in deviant psychology, and in the power that one person can have over another, especially if they push in the direction where the other person is already headed. The movie is almost uncanny in its self-assurance, in the way it knows that the first hour, where "nothing" happens, is necessary if the pay-off is to be tragic, instead of merely sensational. The movie is also uncanny in what it does with its last three shots. I watched them, and could not believe so much could be implied so simply. Leave the movie before it's over, and you miss almost everything, because what Connie does at the very end of the film is necessary. It makes *Smooth Talk* the story of the process of life, instead of just a sad episode.

A Soldier's Story ★ ★ ½
PG, 99 m., 1984

Howard E. Rollins, Jr. (Captain Davenport), Adolph Caesar (Sergeant Waters), Art Evans (Private Wilkie), David Alan Grier (Corporal Cobb), David Harris (Private Smalls), Denzel Washington (Private Peterson), Patti LaBelle (Big Mary). Directed by Norman Jewison and produced by Jewison, Ronald L. Schwary, and Patrick Palmer. Screenplay by Charles Fuller.

A Soldier's Story is one of those movies that's about less than you might think. It begins with the murder of a black sergeant, who is shot near an Army base in Louisiana in 1944. Suspicion immediately points to the local whites, who are not too happy about all these blacks stationed in their branch of the deep South. An Army lawyer, a captain, is sent from Washington to handle the investigation, and he turns out to be black, too—the first black officer anyone in the movie has ever seen. As he conducts his investigation, we get to meet some of the important characters on the base, from black privates to the white officers who brag about their experiences at "commanding Negroes." Each time the captain conducts an interview, we get a flashback to another version of the events leading up to the murder. And eventually, we find out who committed the crime.

As a storytelling device, this mechanism is excruciating. The problem is in the time structure. If an investigation begins at the present moment and proceeds, suspense can build. But if the truth is going to emerge from a series of flashbacks, then obviously the movie knows who did it, and is withholding the information from us, using it as a hook to get us to sit through all of its other points. *A Soldier's Story* is not really a murder mystery, then. What is it? I guess it's supposed to be a docudrama. A great deal of the plot revolves around the character of the dead man, Sergeant Waters (Adolph Caesar), who is a scrappy little veteran of World War I, and believes that blacks should always behave so as to favorably impress whites and reflect credit upon their race. He is filled with self-hate, and takes it out on the black men under him who are not acting the way he thinks they should.

This fact is gradually revealed in a series of interviews conducted by the lawyer, Captain Davenport, who is played by Howard E. Rollins, Jr. And what a disappointing performance it is, coming from the same actor who won an Academy Award nomination for *Ragtime*. He invests his character with little humanity; he tries to seem dispassionate, curbed, correct, just a little more noble than

anyone else in the picture. The result is such a laid-back performance that the lawyer seems less interested in solving the case than in keeping his cool (the murdered Sergeant Waters would have been proud of him).

The movie ends with a handshake between Davenport and one of the white officers who has made life hard for him. This is a more ironic ending than was perhaps intended, because *A Soldier's Story* was directed by Norman Jewison, the director who ended *In the Heat of the Night* with Sidney Poitier and Rod Steiger shaking hands. The ending worked in 1967, but in 1984 I think we expect a little more. Did this movie have to be so lockstep, so trapped by its mechanical plot, so limited by a murder mystery? What the movie has to say is so pale and limited that, ironically, the most interesting character in the movie is the victim—that black racist sergeant. At least he has fire and life and, misguided as he is, at least he's vital.

Sometimes a Great Notion ★ ★ ★
PG, 114 m., 1971

Paul Newman (Hank), Henry Fonda (Henry), Michael Sarrazin (Dan), Lee Remick (Henry's Wife). Directed by Paul Newman and produced by John Foreman. Screenplay by John Gay.

Paul Newman's *Sometimes a Great Notion* tells sort of an old-fashioned story about prideful clans carving empires out of the wilderness. The characters seem a little familiar, too. Take the three most important. Henry Fonda is the proud old patriarch, Paul Newman is the son who stays at home but makes up his own mind, and Michael Sarrazin is the kid brother who comes back to the land with all sorts of half-baked notions and scores to settle. So far, the relationships remind us of *Hud*.

But then Newman starts tunneling under the material, coming up with all sorts of things we didn't quite expect, and along the way he proves himself (as he did with *Rachel, Rachel*) as a director of sympathy and a sort of lyrical restraint. He rarely pushes scenes to their obvious conclusions, he avoids melodrama, and by the end of *Sometimes a Great Notion*, we somehow come to know the Stamper family better than we expected to.

The story takes place during a timber strike in the Northwest. The local merchants (especially the neurotic fellow who runs the movie theater and the dry cleaners) are going broke because money has dried up. The striking timber workers idly hang around the union office. But the Stamper family continues to work in defiance of the strike, and despite the fact that Fonda has broken half the bones on his left side in an accident.

Sarrazin, Newman's half-brother by Fonda's second wife, comes home to help—and also to mope, to get over a bummer of a year, and to suggest to Newman's wife (Lee Remick) that maybe she should clear out from the obsessed Stamper clan. There are a lot of things left fairly unclear, though; I'm not quite sure what was on Remick's mind during most of the movie. The character is left wavering, and we don't fully understand her relationship to her husband. Newman shortchanges what you might call the indoor scenes in order to give us the lumber business.

The best scene in the film takes place during a day of work. The Stamper men seem terribly small as they bring enormous trees crashing to the ground, wrap chains around them, and load them on trucks with big, musclebound machines. The direction of this scene is superb; the reality and the danger of the huge logs are caught in a way that defines the men and their job better than any dialogue could.

Another scene that reveals Newman's insight as a director takes place at a lumbermen's picnic. Some of the strikers invite some of the Stampers to a game of touch football. The game develops into a brawl, of course, but in an interesting way; instead of going for a hard-action approach to the scene, Newman shoots it in a sort of twilight, bittersweet style. All through the film, he avoids making the strikers into heavies and their hatred for the Stampers seem melodramatic. Instead, they're clumsy, resentful enemies, and when they try to sabotage a Stamper lumber raft, they only wind up drifting out to sea—and having to be rescued by the Stampers.

The movie doesn't seem very sure of what it thinks about the Fonda character's fierce and stubborn pride. The character himself believes all that matters is getting up for another day, and working, and eating, and sleeeping, and getting on with life. Another character, a brother-in-law, has been "saved" at the local fundamentalist church and has a sort of sweet simplicity that seems out of place—until the scene where he dies. He dies in a way that is truly filled with grace and humor, and the scene is one of the several things in *Sometimes a Great Notion* that make it worth seeing, even if its overall design is murky.

Somewhere in Time ★ ★
PG, 103 m., 1980

Christopher Reeve (Richard Collier), Jane Seymour (Elise McKenna), Christopher Plummer (W.F. Robinson), Teresa Wright (Laura Roberts), Bill Erwin (Arthur), Bo Clausen (Man in Elevator). Directed by Jeannot Szwarc and produced by Stephen Deutsch. Screenplay by Richard Matheson.

Somewhere in Time wants us to share its sweeping romantic idealism, about a love so great that it spanned the decades and violated the sanctity of time itself. But we keep getting distracted by nagging doubts, like, isn't it a little futile to travel sixty-eight years backward into time for a one-night stand? The movie surrounds its love story with such boring mumbo jumbo about time travel that we finally just don't care.

It didn't have to be that way. The underrated and neglected movie *Time After Time*, which had H.G. Wells and Jack the Ripper traveling forward into modern San Francisco, contained a love story that had a lot of sly fun with the notion of relationships between people of different eras. *Somewhere in Time* has a lot of qualities, but slyness and fun are not two of them. This movie drips with solemnity. It enshrines its lovers in such excessive romantic nobility that Rachmaninoff's "Rhapsody" plays almost every time they're on the screen. This is the kind of romance so sacred, so serious, so awesome, that you have to lower your voice in the presence of it. Romances like that are boring, even to the monstrous egos usually involved in them.

But back to the movie. *Somewhere in Time* stars Christopher Reeve as a playwright who visits the Grand Hotel on Mackinac Island and sees a photograph there of an actress who appeared at the hotel in 1912. He is smitten; no, he is obsessed. He researches the career of the actress, falls in love with her, learns from a pseudoscientific psychology professor that time travel is possible, and hypnotizes himself to travel back to 1912. The movie never makes it clear whether the playwright actually does travel through time, or only hypnotizes himself into thinking he does. It doesn't matter. Once he's back in 1912, or thinks he is, he meets the young actress, who is played by the preternaturally beautiful Jane Seymour. "Is it . . . *you?*" she breathes. It is! It is! A little of this goes a long way, even with Rachmaninoff. Especially with Rachmaninoff.

There is, of course, a villain. He is the young actress's manager, played by Christopher Plummer. He has guided her career since she was sixteen, and now resents the intrusion of this stranger who has come from nowhere, is dressed oddly, and threatens to steal his protégée. There are some intrigues, as the three of them steal about the rooms and grounds of the magnificent Grand Hotel. But there are never any scenes that really deal with the romance between Reeve and Seymour—and, incredibly, the movie avoids the opportunity to exploit in their relationship the fact that Reeve is from the future. All of the delightful revelations and paradoxes that could have resulted from Reeve revealing that fact are simply ignored.

This was Reeve's first movie since *Superman*, and he is not particularly convincing in it. He seems a little stolid, a little ungainly; he's so desperately earnest in his love for this actress that he always seems to be squinting a little. The whole movie is so solemn, so worshipful toward its theme, that it's finally just silly.

Songwriter ★ ★ ★ ½
R, 94 m., 1985

Willie Nelson (Doc Jenkins), Kris Kristofferson (Blackie Buck), Melinda Dillon (Honey Carder), Rip Torn (Dino McLeish), Lesley Ann Warren (Gilda), Richard Sarafian (Rocky Rodeo). Directed by Alan Rudolph and produced by Sydney Pollack. Screenplay by Matthew Leonetti.

Songwriter is one of those movies that grows on you. It doesn't have a big point to prove, and it isn't all locked into the requirements of its plot. It's about spending some time with some country musicians who are not much crazier than most country musicians, and are probably nicer than some. It also has a lot of good music.

The movie stars Willie Nelson as a country songwriter named Doc Jenkins, who has a real bad head for business. One day he gets fast-talked into selling control of his company to a slick operator named Rocky Rodeo (Richard Sarafian). Homeless and betrayed, he turns for support to his best friend, a country music star named Blackie (Kris Kristofferson). Blackie, meanwhile, is being promoted by a sleazy manager named Dino (Rip Torn), who has somewhere found a neurotic young singer named Gilda (Lesley Ann Warren). In an early scene that lets us know this movie is not going to be routine, Blackie tries to foist Gilda off on an audience that has paid to see Blackie, and when the audience rebels, Blackie grabs the mike and starts advising them to commit anatomical impossibilities upon themselves.

During the course of some days and nights on the road and back home in Austin, Doc comes up with a clever scheme. Instead of writing any more songs for the despised Dino, he'll write his songs under a pseudonym, and give them to Gilda to record. Blackie will include Gilda on his next tour, and Dino will get screwed. This seems like a good idea to everybody, especially Gilda, who has a tricky drinking problem and thinks she might be falling in love with Doc.

The movie unwinds casually, introducing us to the other people in the lives of these characters. The most important is Doc's former wife (Melinda Dillon), and the best scene in the movie is where Doc visits her and the kids, and is shy and sweet and tremendously moving. Another good scene is one where Gilda invites Doc into her bed, and he tries to be gentle and tactful in explaining that he doesn't think that's a good idea. Willie Nelson is the key to both of those scenes, and it's interesting how subtle his acting is. Unlike a lot of concert stars whose moves tend to be too large for the intimacy of a movie, Nelson is a gifted, understated actor. Watch the expression on his face as he turns down Gilda; not many actors can say as much with their eyes.

Songwriter was directed by Alan Rudolph, who also made *Choose Me*. Rudolph's teacher was Robert Altman, and, like Altman, he specializes in offbeat rhythms of a group of characters in an unpredictable situation. We never have a clear idea of where *Songwriter* is headed; is it about Doc's love for his first wife, or Gilda's self-destruction, or Rocky Rodeo's con games? It's good that we don't know, because then we don't know what to expect next, and the movie can surprise us.

Both Rudolph and Altman also specialize in unlikely combinations of actors; Kris Kristofferson and Nelson don't, at first, seem to belong in the same movie with Warren, Torn, and Dillon, but watch them work together. One of Torn's great unsung roles was in *Payday*, the movie based on the last days of Hank Williams, Sr. This time, he's like the same character a little further down the road, a little more spaced out. Kristofferson is basically the straight man, the hero's best friend. Nelson sings less and acts more than we expected. And Lesley Ann Warren's performance is endlessly inventive: She takes the fairly standard character of a kooky would-be singer, and makes her into a touching, unforgettable creation.

Sophie's Choice ★ ★ ★ ★
R, 157 m., 1982

Meryl Streep (Sophie), Kevin Kline (Nathan), Peter MacNicol (Stingo), Greta Turken (Leslie Lapidus), Gunther Maria Halmer (Rudolf Hoess). Directed by Alan J. Pakula and produced by Pakula and Keith Barish. Screenplay by Pakula.

Sometimes when you've read the novel, it gets in the way of the images on the screen. You keep remembering how you imagined things. That didn't happen with me during *Sophie's Choice*, because the movie is so perfectly cast and well-imagined that it just takes over and happens to you. It's quite an experience.

The movie stars Meryl Streep as Sophie, a Polish-Catholic woman, who was caught by the Nazis with a contraband ham, was sentenced to a concentration camp, lost her two children there, and then was somehow spared to immigrate to Brooklyn, U.S.A., and to the arms of an eccentric charmer named Nathan. Sophie and Nathan move into an old boardinghouse, and the rooms just below them are taken by Stingo, a jug-eared kid from the South who wants to be a great novelist. As the two lovers play out their doomed, romantic destiny, Stingo falls in love with several things: with his image of himself as a writer, with his idealized vision of Sophie and Nathan's romance, and, inevitably, with Sophie herself.

The movie, like the book, is told with two ñarrators. One is Stingo, who remembers these people from that summer in Brooklyn, and who also remembers himself at that much earlier age. The other narrator, contained within Stingo's story, is Sophie herself, who remembers what happened to her during World War II, and shares her memories with Stingo in a long confessional. Both the book and the movie have long central flashbacks, and neither the book nor the movie is damaged by those diversions, because Sophie's story is so indispensable to Stingo's own growth, from an adolescent dreamer to an artist who can begin to understand human suffering. The book and movie have something else in common. Despite the fact that Sophie's story, her choices, and her fate are all sad, sad stories, there is a lot of exuberance and joy in the telling of them. *Sophie's Choice* begins as a young Southerner's odyssey to the unimaginable North—to that strange land celebrated by his hero, Thomas Wolfe, who took the all-night train to New York with its riches, its women, and its romance. Stingo is absolutely entranced by this plump blonde Polish woman who moves so winningly into his life, and by her intense, brilliant, mad lover.

We almost don't notice, at first, as Stingo's odyssey into adulthood is replaced, in the film, by Sophie's journey back into the painful memories of her past. The movie becomes an act of discovery, as the naive young American, his mind filled with notions of love, death, and honor, becomes the friend of a woman who has seen so much hate, death, and dishonor that the only way she can continue is by blotting out the past, and drinking and loving her way into temporary oblivion. It's basically a three-character movie, and the casting, as I suggested, is just right. Meryl Streep is a wonder as Sophie. She does not quite look or sound or feel like the Meryl Streep we have seen before in *The Deer Hunter* or *Manhattan* or *The French Lieutenant's Woman*. There is something juicier about her this time; she is merrier and sexier, more playful and cheerful in the scenes before she begins to tell Stingo the truth about her past. Streep plays the Brooklyn scenes with an enchanting Polish-American accent (she has the first accent I've ever wanted to hug), and she plays the flashbacks in subtitled German and Polish. There is hardly an emotion that Streep doesn't touch in this movie, and yet we're never aware of her straining. This is one of the most astonishing and yet one of the most unaffected and natural performances I can imagine.

Kevin Kline plays Nathan, the crazy romantic who convinces everyone he's on the brink of finding the cure for polio and who wavers uncertainly between anger and manic exhilaration. Peter MacNicol is Stingo, the kid who is left at the end to tell the story. Kline, MacNicol, and Streep make such good friends in this movie—despite all the suffering they go through—that we really do believe the kid when he refuses to act on an unhappy revelation, insisting, "These are my *friends*. I love them!"

Sophie's Choice is a fine, absorbing, wonderfully acted, heartbreaking movie. It is about three people who are faced with a series of choices, some frivolous, some tragic. As they flounder in the bewilderment of being human in an age of madness, they become our friends, and we love them.

Sounder ★ ★ ★ ★
G, 105 m., 1972

Cicely Tyson (Rebecca Morgan), Paul Winfield (Nathan Lee Morgan), Kevin Hooks (David Lee Morgan), Carmen Mathews (Mrs. Boatwright), Taj Mahal (Ike), James Best (Sheriff Young), Janet MacLachlan (Camille, the Teacher), Sylvia (Kuumba), Williams (Harriet). Directed by Martin Ritt and produced by Robert B. Radnitz. Screenplay by John Alonzo.

Sounder is a story simply told and universally moving. It is one of the most compassionate and truthful of movies, and there's not a level where it doesn't succeed completely. It's one of those rare films that can communicate fully to a child of nine or ten, and yet contains depths and subtleties to engross any adult. The story is so simple because it involves, not so much what people do, but how they change and grow. Not a lot happens on the action level, but there's tremendous psychological movement in *Sounder*, and hardly ever do movies create characters who are so full and real, and relationships that are so loving.

The movie is set in rural Louisiana in about 1933, and involves a black sharecropper family. The boy, David Lee, is twelve or thirteen years old, just the right age to delight in the night-time raccoon hunts he goes on with his father and their hound, Sounder. The hunts are not recreation but necessity. There is no food and no money, and at last, the father steals a ham in desperation. He's sentenced to a year at hard labor, and it's up to the mother and the children (two of them too small to be much help) to get the crop in. They do. "We'll do it, because we have to do it," the mother says.

The boy sets out to find the labor camp where his father is being held. He never does, but he comes across a black school where the teacher talks to him of some of the accomplishments of blacks in America. He decides that he would like to attend her school; by special dispensation, he had been attending a segregated school near his home as sort of a back-row, second-class student.

He returns home, the father returns home, and there is a heartbreaking moment when, for the boy, no school in the world could take him away from this family that loves him. He runs away, filled with angry tears, but his father comes after him and talks to him simply and bluntly: "You lose some of the time what you go after, but you lose all of the time what you don't go after."

The father has a totally realistic understanding of the trap that Southern society set for black sharecroppers, and he is determined to see his son break out of that trap, or else. The scene between the father (Paul Winfield) and the son (Kevin Hooks) is one of the greatest celebrations of the bond between parents and children that I have ever seen in a movie. But it is only one of the scenes like that in *Sounder*.

The mother is played by Cicely Tyson, and it is a wonder to see the subtleties in her performance. We have seen her with her family, and we know her strength and intelligence. Then we see her dealing with the white power structure, and her behavior toward it is in a style born of cynicism and necessity. She will say what they want to hear in order to get what she wants to get.

The story is about love, loss, anger, and hope. That's all, and it's enough; not many movies deal with even one of those subjects with any honesty or power. Hope is probably the emotion evoked most by *Sounder*—the hope of the parents that the school will free their bright and capable son from the dead end of sharecropping; the hope of the teacher, who is representative of the Southern growth of black pride and black studies; and, of course, the boy's hope.

The movie was attacked in a few quarters because of this orientation. It is merely "liberal," some of its critics say. It isn't realistic, it's deceiving. I don't think so. I think it has to be taken as a story about one black family and its struggle. It is, I suppose, a "liberal" film, and that has come to be a bad word in these times when liberalism is supposed to stand for compromise—for good intentions but no action. This movie stands for a lot more than that, and we live in such illiberal times that *Sounder* comes as a reminder of former dreams. It's not surprising that the boy in the movie reminded Mrs. Coretta Scott King of her husband.

This is a film for the family to see. That doesn't mean it's a children's film. The producer, Robert B. Radnitz, has specialized in authentic and serious family films (*A Dog of Flanders, The Other Side of the Mountain*). The director, Martin Ritt, is one of the best American filmmakers (his credits include *Hud, The Molly Maguires,* and *The Great White Hope*), and he has made *Sounder* as a serious and ambitious undertaking. There is no condescension in it, no simplification. The relationship between the man and wife is so completely realized on a mature level that it comes as a shock; we'd forgotten that authentic grown-ups can be portrayed in films. We'd thought, for a moment, that to be a movie adult you had to drive a fast car, be surrounded by sexy dames, and pack an arsenal. *Sounder* proves it isn't so.

Southern Comfort ★ ★ ★
R, 106 m., 1981

Keith Carradine (Spencer), Powers Boothe (Hardin), Fred Ward (Reece), Franklyn Seales (Simms), T.K. Carter (Cribbs), Lewis Smith (Stuckey). Directed by Walter Hill and produced by David Filer. Screenplay by Michael Kane, Hill, and Giler.

Southern Comfort is a well-made film, but it suffers from a certain predictability. I suspect the predictability is part of the movie's point. The film is set in the Cajun country of Louisiana, in 1973, and it follows the fortunes of a National Guard unit that gets lost in the bayous and stumbles into a metaphor for America's involvement in Vietnam.

The movie's approach is direct, and its symbolism is all right there on the surface. From the moment we discover that the guardsmen are firing blanks in their rifles, we somehow know that the movie's going to be about their impotence in a land where they do not belong. And as the weekend soldiers are relentlessly hunted down and massacred by the local Cajuns (who are intimately familiar with the bayou), we think of the uselessness of American technology against the Viet Cong.

The guardsmen are clearly strangers in a strange land, and they make fatal blunders right at the outset. They cut the nets of a Cajun fisherman, they "borrow" three Cajun boats, and they mock the Cajuns by firing blank machine-gun rounds at them. The Cajuns are not amused. By the film's end, guardsmen will have been shot dead, impaled, hung, drowned in quicksand, and attacked by savage dogs. And all the time they try to protect themselves with a parody of military discipline, while they splash in circles and rescue helicopters roar uselessly overhead. All this action is shown with great effect in *Southern Comfort*. The movie portrays the bayous as a world of dangerous beauty. Greens and yellows and browns shimmer in the sunlight, and rare birds call to one another, and the Cajuns slip noiselessly behind trees while the guardsmen wander about making fools and targets of themselves. *Southern Comfort* is a film of drum-tight professionalism.

It is also, unfortunately, so committed to its allegorical vision that it never really comes alive as a story about people. That is the major weakness of its director, the talented young Walter Hill, whose credits include *The Warriors, The Driver,* and *The Long Riders.* He knows how to make a movie look great, and how to fill it with energy and style. But I suspect he is uncertain about the human dimensions of his characters. And to cover that up, he makes them into larger-than-life stick figures, into symbolic units who stand for everything except themselves. That tendency was carried to its extreme in *The Driver,* a thriller in which the characters were given titles (the Driver, the Girl) rather than names. It was also Hill's approach in *The Warriors,* which translated New York gang warfare into the terms of Greek myth. His approach bothered me so much in *The Warriors* that I overlooked, I now believe, some of the real qualities of that film. It bothers me again in *Southern Comfort.*

Who *are* these men? Of the Cajuns we learn nothing: They are invisible assassins. Of the guardsmen, however, we learn little more. One is swollen with authority. One intends to look out for himself. One is weak, one is strong, and only the man played by Keith Carradine seems somewhat balanced and sane. Once we get the psychological labels straight, there are no further surprises. And once we understand the structure of the movie (guardsmen slog through bayous, get picked off one by one), the only remaining question is whether any of them will finally survive.

That's the weakness of the storytelling. The strength of the movie is in its look, in its superb use of its locations, and in Hill's mastery of action sequences that could have been repetitive. The action is also good: The actors are given little scope to play with in their characters, but they do succeed in creating plausible weekend soldiers. "We are the Guard!" they chant, and we believe them. And there is one moment of inspired irony, when they are lost, cold, wet, hungry, and in mortal fear of their lives, and one guy asks, "Why don't we call in the National Guard?"

Splash ★ ½
PG, 111 m., 1984

Tom Hanks (Allen), Daryl Hannah (Madison), Eugene Levy (Walter), John Candy (Freddie). Directed by Ron Howard and produced by Brian Grazer. Screenplay by Lowell Ganz, Babaloo Mandel, and Bruce Jay Friedman.

There is a funny movie lurking at the edges of *Splash,* and sometimes it even sneaks on screen and makes us smile. It's too bad the relentlessly conventional minds that made this movie couldn't have made the leap from sitcom to comedy. They must have thought they had such a great idea (Manhattan bachelor falls in love with mermaid) that they couldn't fail. But great ideas are a dime a dozen. *Splash* tells the story of a young man who is twice saved from drowning by a beautiful young mermaid. She falls in love with him and follows him to Manhattan, where he is a fruit and vegetable wholesaler. He falls in love with her. She can, it appears, metamorphose at will, turning her tail into legs. There are a lot of jokes about her total ignorance about all the ways of civilization. She walks naked onto Ellis Island, for example, and eats lobsters—shell and all.

All right. Now that's the situation. But the situation isn't going to be enough. We need some characters here. The mermaid is just fine. As played by the lovely Daryl Hannah, she is young and healthy and touchingly naive. But what about the guy who falls in love with her? It's here that the movie makes its catastrophic casting mistake. You see, they figured they have a comedy as long as the girl has a tail, and a romance whenever she has legs. So they gave her a romantic leading man when they should have given her a lonely guy who could swim. The leading man is Tom Hanks. He is conventionally handsome and passably appealing, and he would do in a secondary role. He'd be great, for example, as the straight-arrow brother. Instead, they make him the mermaid's lover, and they cast John Candy as the brother.

You remember Candy from SCTV. He is the large, shambling, Charles Laughton-type who has such a natural chrisma that he's funny just standing there. They should have made Candy the lover, and Hanks the brother. Then we'd be on the side of this big lunk who suddenly has a mermaid drop into his life and has to explain her to his creepy, swinging-singles brother. Plus, there's the sweet touch that this transcendently sexy mermaid has fallen for the tubby loser with the heart of lust, and not for his slick brother. See what I mean? Instead, they go the other way. John Candy is not used much in the movie, Tom Hanks comes across as a standard young male lead, and they have to concoct a meaningless and boring subplot in order to make the movie long enough. Don't they know in Hollywood that once all the geniuses think they've finished with the screenplay, you just gotta rotate everything 180 degrees and you got a movie?

Spring Break ★
R, 101 m., 1983

David Knell (Nelson), Perry Lang (Adam), Paul Land (Stu), Steve Bassett (O.T.), Corinne Alphen (Joan). Directed and produced by Sean S. Cunningham. Screenplay by David Smilow.

Styles in exploitation films have a way of changing overnight. Just when I thought I couldn't take one single more Dead Teenager Movie—one more of those hundreds of movies in which screaming teen-agers were chased by maniacs and carved up with hatchets—they stopped making them. That's the good news. The bad news is, Dead Teenager Movies have been replaced by Horny Teen-ager Movies.

The first one was *Porky's*. It went through the roof. Then we got *The Last American Virgin*, *Private Lessons*, *Going All the Way*, and *My Tutor* (which was sort of fun). Here's *Spring Break*, a sex-and-sand epic about the annual mating rituals in Fort Lauderdale. The obvious inspiration for *Spring Break* is all the Beach Party movies from the late 1950s and early 1960s. Here's the most obvious connection between *Spring Break* and the Beach Party flicks: They all have absolutely unnecessary subplots involving idiotic politicians who act like complete nerds and become apoplectic at the thought of kids having any fun. In the late 1950s, that sort of plot was standard. This is the 1980s, and it's absurd. The story this time involves a cloddish senatorial candidate (Donald Symington) who becomes enraged when his son sneaks off to join the gang at Fort Lauderdale. He assigns a bunch of hired goons to patrol the beach and bring back his son.

There's another thing seriously wrong with *Spring Break*. It doesn't know that girls are people, too. It's only about horny teenage boys. Four of them—two studs, two timid kids—become roommates in a motel and go out looking for where the girls are. All four have names, identities, characteristics, etc. The whole movie involves their adventures, their quests for girls, their exploits, their big wins in the belly-flopping contest, etc. The women in their lives are interchangeable, and, as nearly as I can recall, *not one woman in this movie was called by name!*

That's too bad, especially since *Spring Break* costars a young woman named Corinne Alphen, who was *Penthouse's* 1982 Pet of the Year. Sad to say, most of the Pets and Playmates who win movie roles turn out to be sort of self-conscious and untalented as actresses. Not Corinne Alphen. She has a dazzling smile, a great personality, and a relaxed naturalness on the screen that makes the Horny Teen-ager Boys seem all the more gauche.

A funny little movie *might* have been made about her adventures in Fort Lauderdale, "where the boys are." She would have had the personality to carry it. Instead, the lock-step mentalities who made this movie tell their story entirely from a boring male point of view, supply us with male wimps and studs who are equally uninteresting, and view women only as wet T-shirt finalists. What a letdown for horny movie critics.

The Spy Who Loved Me ★ ★ ★ ½
PG, 125 m., 1977

Roger Moore (James Bond), Barbara Bach (Anya Amasova), Curt Jurgens (Stromberg), Richard Kiel (Jaws), Caroline Munro (Naomi), Bernard Lee (M), Desmond Llewelyn (Q), Lois Maxwell (Miss Moneypenny). Directed by Lewis Gilbert and produced by Albert R. Broccoli. Screenplay by Christopher Wood and Richard Maibaum.

The best of the James Bond adventures have always depended on cheerfully silly violence, and *The Spy Who Loved Me* is one of the best. It's heartening to see there's life in the old series yet. The first 007 caper was released twenty-four years ago, and here's Bond back once again with his beautiful girls, his lethal gadgets, and that tuxedo that never seems to wear out no matter how many mountains he climbs or deserts he treks in it.

There have been a lot of obituaries for the 1960s recently, but, no, Virginia, the sixties will never die, not so long as there is another twenty million dollars somewhere in the world to film another James Bond thriller. Bond lives in that yesterday we can vaguely remember: in a world of conspicuous consumption, fast cars, unliberated women, bizarre weapons, man-eating creatures of land, air, and sea, archvillains with German accents, and a British Empire upon which the sun has not yet set, although it's getting rather dusky out. The Bond universe is an anachronism, but one we've grown fond of, and *The Spy Who Loved Me* celebrates it with abundant energy. There was a time there, during some of the middle Bonds, when the series seemed to be losing its nerve, to be apologizing for its excesses. But not this time: *The Spy Who Loved Me* is gloriously ridiculous from beginning to end, and that's as it should be.

The stories in a lot of the Bond movies bear only the most tenuous relationship to the original fantasies of Ian Fleming, and that's especially true here. The plot involves a villain named Stromberg, who has a plan to capture nuclear submarines and use them to start World War III, after which he will rule the Earth from his undersea headquarters. British Agent 007 (Roger Moore) is assigned to trace the missing British sub, and Soviet Agent XXX (Barbara Bach) is after the Russian sub.

The chase leads to all sorts of places: Cairo, the pyramids, the desert, Sardinia. And it features the best would-be Bond-killer since the immortal Odd Job in *Goldfinger*; Stromberg's hired assassin, named Jaws (Richard Kiel) stands seven-feet-two inches tall, has hands about the size of the Sears catalog, and sharp steel teeth that can chomp through wood and steel, attacking sharks and foreign agents.

It's in the showdowns with Jaws that the movie has a lot of its fun. Jaws can tear apart vans, kill a shark one-on-one, hurl Bond through the air with ease, but he keeps get-ting almost killed—and one of the movie's standing jokes is his incredible power of survival. Agents 007 and XXX, meanwhile, make their way through incredible difficulties to the one obligatory scene in every Bond movie—the scene involving a gigantic indoor set where the destruction of the world is being plotted and enemy troops dressed in matching jumpsuits scurry about on catwalks high up under the ceiling.

The movie is jammed with special effects. It contains, in fact, almost as many spectacular stunts and effects as *Star Wars*, although their terrestrial locale may make them seem more routine. There's a car that turns into a submarine, and a tanker that turns into a sub-snatcher, and all sorts of guided missiles and instruments of oceanic warfare and spectacular explosions, and of course the underwater headquarters of the evil Stromberg, with its hungry sharks lurking at the bottom of the elevator shaft. *The Spy Who Loved Me* is in the tradition of the best Bonds: thrilling, sexy, ridiculous, gimmicky, violent, and, what all the Bonds are supposed to be, preposterous escapist fun.

STAR 80 ★ ★ ★ ★
R, 102 m., 1983

Mariel Hemingway (Dorothy Stratten), Eric Roberts (Paul Snider), Cliff Robertson (Hugh Hefner), Carroll Baker (Dorothy's Mother), Roger Rees (Aram Nicholas). Directed by Bob Fosse and produced by Wolfgang Glattes and Kenneth Utt. Screenplay by Fosse.

Bob Fosse dresses all in black and makes films about the demonic undercurrents in our lives. Look at his credits: *Cabaret, Lenny, All That Jazz*, and now *STAR 80*. Although his Broadway musicals have been upbeat entertainment, he seems to see the movie camera as a device for peering into our shames and secrets. *STAR 80* is his most despairing film. After the Nazi decadence of *Cabaret*, after the drug abuse and self-destruction in *Lenny*, and the death-obsessed hero of *All That Jazz*, here is a movie that begins with violent death and burrows deeper. There were times when I could hardly keep my eyes on the screen, and a moment near the end when I seriously asked myself if I wanted to continue watching.

And yet I think this is an important movie. Devastating, violent, hopeless, and important, because it holds a mirror up to a part of the world we live in, and helps us see it more clearly. In particular, it examines the connection between fame and obscurity, between those who have a moment of praise and notoriety, and those who see themselves as condemned to stand always at the edge of the spotlight. Like Martin Scorsese's *Taxi Driver*, it is a movie about being an outsider and about going crazy with the pain of rejection.

The movie tells the story of two young people from Vancouver. One of them was Dorothy Stratten, a shy, pretty blonde who thought her hands and feet were too big, who couldn't understand why anyone would value her, and who was close enough to some sort of idealized North American fantasy that she became the 1979 Playmate of the Year. The other was Paul Snider, a Vancouver small-timer who worked as a salesman, con man, and part-time pimp. When Paul saw Dorothy behind the counter of a hamburger stand, he knew she was his ticket to the big time. Dorothy resisted his compliments at first, but he was so relentless in his adoration that she surrendered to his fantasies. Paul masterminded Dorothy's rise. He arranged the photo session that attracted the eye of *Playboy*'s talent scouts. He bought her dresses and flowers. He pushed her into the limelight and then edged into it next to her. But then she went to Los Angeles and found the real stardust, the flattery of the Playboy Mansion, the attentions of young men whose sports cars were bought with their own money, while Paul's was bought with hers.

Paul had a vanity license plate made: STAR 80. But Dorothy had moved out of his world, had been given a taste of a larger world that, frankly, Paul didn't have the class to appreciate. She fell in love with a movie director. She went out of town on location. She and Paul drifted apart, and he went mad with jealousy and resentment. On August 14, 1980, Dorothy went back to the shabby little North Hollywood bungalow they had rented together, and Paul murdered her.

STAR 80 begins with the murder. Everything else is in flashback, and, therefore, the film has no really happy scenes. Dorothy's triumphs are all stained with our knowledge of what will happen. Every time she smiles, it's poignant. We know Paul will go berserk and kill her, and so we can see from the beginning that he's unbalanced. Fosse knows his material is relentlessly depressing, and so he doesn't try for moments of relief. Although we enter the world of *Playboy* and see Dorothy partying in the mansion and posing in nude modeling sessions, although the whole movie is concerned with aspects of sex, there is never an erotic moment. Fosse keeps his distance, regarding Dorothy more as a case study than as a fantasy. That makes Mariel Hemingway's performance as Dorothy all the more powerful. She has been remade into the sleek, glossy Playmate image, but she still has the adolescent directness and naiveté that she used so well in *Manhattan* and *Personal Best*. She's a big kid. Her eyes open wide when she gets to Los Angeles, and she's impressed by the attention she's receiving. The character she plays is simple, uncomplicated, shallow, and so trusting that she never does realize how dangerous Paul is.

The other performances in the movie are equally strong. Eric Roberts as Paul even succeeds in persuading us to accept him as a suffering human being rather than as a hateful killer. Like Robert De Niro as Travis Bickle in *Taxi Driver*, he fills his role with so much reality that we feel horror, but not blame. Carroll Baker, as Dorothy's mother, is heartbreakingly incapable of connecting in any meaningful way with her daughter.

What is the point of *STAR 80?* I'm not sure, just as I wasn't sure of the points of *In Cold Blood* or *Lacombe, Lucien* or "The Executioner's Song." There is no redemption in the movie, no catharsis. It unblinkingly looks at the short life of a simple, pretty girl, and the tortured man who made her into something he couldn't have, and then killed her for it. The movie seems to be saying: These things happen. After it was over, I felt bad for Dorothy Stratten. In fact, for everybody.

A Star Is Born ★ ★ ★ ★
PG, 175 m., 1954 (1983)

Judy Garland, James Mason, Jack Carson, Tommy Noonan, Charles Bickford. Directed by George Cukor.

A Star Is Born hasn't merely been restored. It has been rediscovered. George Cukor's 1954 movie, which starred James Mason and Judy Garland in the story of Hollywood lives destroyed by alcoholism, always has been considered one of the great tear-jerking Hollywood melodramas, populated with bravura performances. But has it ever been praised for its purely cinematic qualities? I don't think so, and yet it showed Cukor's mastery not only of the big effects, but also of subtle lighting and exquisite compositions. It's an irony, but if Warner Brothers hadn't chopped twenty-seven minutes out of the movie in 1954 and tried to throw them away, the whole movie never would have been rereleased in its current form. It is very good to have the missing footage back, of course, but it's even better to have the whole movie back again, a landmark of Hollywood melodrama.

Although this version is exactly as long as Cukor's final cut in 1954, it doesn't have quite all the footage. Two major production numbers and a charming little scene in a drive-in restaurant were rediscovered by film historian Ron Haver (after months of detective work). Haver also found the movie's complete stereo soundtrack, but about seven minutes of the visual footage seem to be gone forever—and so this restoration uses an effective montage of music, dialogue, and production stills to bridge the gaps. Seeing this version of the movie makes it clear what major surgery was performed by Warner Brothers. The studio chopped out an entire Judy Garland musical number, "Here's What I'm Here For," filled with fire and energy. That's wonderful to have back again, but the other major restored sequence is almost indispensable to the film.

It's a scene from fairly early in the film. The alcoholic movie star (Mason) has convinced the young band vocalist (Garland) to risk everything and try for a movie career. With his support, she's on the brink of stardom. She's recording a song with a studio orchestra, and afterward she rests on a stair-

case with Mason. He proposes marriage. She says he drinks too much. He promises to reform. Neither one realizes that their whole conversation is being recorded by an eavesdropping overhead mike. Then, as a joke by the director, the proposal is played back for all the musicians to hear—and Garland accepts. By taking out that proposal scene, Warner Brothers had a movie that skipped unconvincingly from Garland's movie debut to her elopement with Mason. The earlier missing footage—the scenes represented by the still photos—also represented important bridging material, covering an uncertain period during which Garland thinks Mason has forgotten about her. Without those scenes, the movie skips directly from Garland's early hopes to her first day at the studio, with no period of uncertainty.

The missing scenes are good to have back again. But the movie's central scenes are even better to see again. There is an absolutely brilliantly lit and directed scene in a darkened nightclub, with Garland singing while the camera prowls silently among the musicians' instruments; it's one of the best examples of composition I've ever seen. And near the end of the movie, there's Garland's big, bravura scene, in which she interrupts a big production number for a heart-rending dressing-room conversation with her studio chief (Charles Bickford). And then, of course, there is Mason's sad, lonely walk into the sea, and the movie's unforgettable closing line: "Good evening, everyone. This is Mrs. Norman Maine."

A Star Is Born is one of the rare films that successfully integrate music with drama; it's not exactly a musical, but it has more music than most musicals. It's also not exactly a serious drama—it's too broad and predictable for that—but it's the sort of exaggerated, wide-gauge melodrama that Rainer Werner Fassbinder would experiment with twenty years later; a movie in which larger-than-life characters are used to help us see the melodramatic clichés that we do, indeed, sometimes pattern our own lives after.

I was lucky enough to visit George Cukor at his Hollywood home in December of 1981. He said he had never seen the butchered version of *A Star Is Born* and never would. "If they wanted it shorter," he said, "I could have sweated out twenty-five minutes here and there, and nobody would have missed them. Instead, they took an ax to the movie." George Cukor died on the evening before he was to see a rough version of this restored print. That is sad, but then Cukor, of course, knew what his original movie looked like. Now the rest of us can know, too.

Star Trek: The Motion Picture ★ ★ ★
G, 132 m., 1979

William Shatner (Kirk), Leonard Nimoy (Spock), DeForest Kelley ("Bones" McCoy), James Doohan (Scotty), George Takei (Sulu), Walter Koenig (Chekov). Directed by Robert Wise and produced by Gene Roddenberry. Screenplay by Harold Livingston.

Two things occurred to me as I watched *Star Trek:*
• The producers have succeeded at great expense in creating a toy for the eyes. This movie is fun to watch.
• Epic science fiction stories, with their cosmic themes and fast truths about the nature of mankind, somehow work best when the actors are unknown to us. The presence of the *Star Trek* characters and actors—who have become so familiar to us on television—tends in a strange way to undermine this movie. The audience walks in with a possessive, even patronizing attitude toward Kirk and Spock and Bones, and that interferes with the creation of the "sense of wonder" that science fiction is all about.

Let's begin with the toy for the eyes. The *Star Trek* movie is fairly predictable in its plot. We more or less expected that two of the frequent ingredients in the television episodes would be here, and they are: a confrontation between Starship Enterprise and some sort of alien entity, and a conclusion in which basic human values are affirmed in a hostile universe. In *Star Trek: The Motion Picture,* the alien entity is an unimaginably vast alien spaceship from somewhere out at the edge of the galaxy. The movie opens as it's discovered racing directly toward Earth, and it seems to be hostile. Where has it come from, and what does it want?

The Starship Enterprise, elaborately rebuilt, is assigned to go out to intercept it, with Admiral Kirk, of course, in charge.

And scenes dealing with the Enterprise and the other ship will make up most of the movie—if the special effects aren't good, the movie's not going to work. But they are good, as, indeed, they should be: The first special effects team on this movie was fired, and the film's release was delayed a year while these new effects were devised and photographed. (The effects get better, by the way, as the movie progresses. The alien ship looks great but the spaceports and futuristic cities near the film's beginning loom fairly phony.)

The Enterprise, perhaps deliberately, looks a lot like other spaceships we've seen in *2001, Silent Running, Star Wars,* and *Alien.* Kubrick's space odyssey set a visual style for the genre that still seems to be serviceable. But the look of the other spaceship in *Star Trek* is more awesome and original. It seems to reach indefinitely in all directions, the Enterprise is a mere speck inside of it, and the contents of the alien vessel include images of the stars and planets it has passed en route, as well as enormous rooms or spaces that seem to be states of a computer-mind. This is terrific stuff.

But now we get to the human level (or the half-human level, in the case of Mr. Spock). The characters in this movie are part of our cultural folklore; the *Star Trek* television episodes have been rerun time and time again. Trekkies may be unhappy with me for saying this, but there are ways in which our familiarity with the series works against the effectiveness of this movie. On the one hand we have incomprehensible alien forces and a plot that reaches out to the edge of the galaxy. On the other hand, confronting these vast forces, we have television pop heroes. It's great to enjoy the in-jokes involving the relationships of the Enterprise crew members and it's great that Trekkies can pick up references meant for them, but the extreme familiarity of the Star Trek characters somehow tends to break the illusion in the big scenes involving the alien ship.

Such reservations aside, *Star Trek: The Motion Picture* is probably about as good as we could have expected. It lacks the dazzling brilliance and originality of *2001* (which was an extraordinary one-of-a-kind film). But on its own terms it's a very well-made piece of work, with an interesting premise. The alien spaceship turns out to come from a mechanical or computer civilization, one produced by artificial intelligence and yet poignantly "human" in the sense that it has come all this way to seek out the secrets of its own origins, as we might.

There is, I suspect, a sense in which you can be too sophisticated for your own good when you see a movie like this. Some of the early reviews seemed pretty blasé, as if the critics didn't allow themselves to relish the film before racing out to pigeonhole it. My inclination, as I slid down in my seat and the stereo sound surrounded me, was to relax and let the movie give me a good time. I did and it did.

Star Trek II: The Wrath of Khan
★ ★ ★
PG, 113 m., 1982

William Shatner (Kirk), Leonard Nimoy (Spock), Ricardo Montalban (Khan), DeForest Kelley ("Bones" McCoy), Kirstie Alley (Lieutenant Saavik). Directed by Nicholas Meyer and produced by Robert Sallin. Screenplay by Jack B. Sowards.

The peculiar thing about Spock is that, being Vulcan and therefore possessing no human emotions, he consistently, if dispassionately, behaves as if he possessed very heroic human emotions indeed. He makes a choice in *Star Trek II* that would be made only by a hero, a fool, or a Vulcan. And when he makes his decision, the movie rises to one of its best scenes, because the *Star Trek* stories have always been best when they centered around their characters. Although I liked the special effects in the first movie, they were probably not the point; fans of the TV series wanted to see their favorite characters again, and *Trek II* understood that desire and acted on it.

Time has passed since the last episode. Kirk has retired to an administrative post. Spock is commanding the *Enterprise*, with a lot of new faces in the crew. The ship is conducting tests of the Genesis device, a new invention which, if I understand it correctly, is capable of seeding a barren planet with luxuriant life. (Genesis is actually considered to be a weapon, but the logic escaped

me.) Scouting for barren planets, *Enterprise* discovers one that seems to be dead, but its instruments pick up a small speck of life. Crew members investigate, and find the planet inhabited by an outlaw named Khan, who was exiled there years ago by Kirk, and has brooded of vengeance ever since.

Khan is played as a cauldron of resentment by Ricardo Montalban, and his performance is so strong that he helps illustrate a general principle involving not only *Star Trek* but *Star Wars* and all the epic serials, especially the James Bond movies: Each film is only as good as its villain. Since the heroes and the gimmicks tend to repeat from film to film, only a great villain can transform a good try into a triumph. In a curious way, Khan captures our sympathy, even though he is an evil man who introduces loathesome creatures into the ear canals of two *Enterprise* crew members. Montalban doesn't overact. He plays the character as a man of deeply wounded pride, whose bond of hatred with Admiral Kirk is stronger even than his traditional villain's desire to rule the universe.

There is a battle in outer space in this movie, a particularly inept one that owes more to "Captain Video" than to state-of-the-art special effects. I always love it when they give us spaceships capable of leaping across the universe, and then arm them with weapons so puny that a direct hit merely blows up a few control boards and knocks people off their feet. Somehow, though, I don't much care if the battles aren't that amazing, because the story doesn't depend on them. It's about a sacrifice made by Spock, and it draws on the sentiment and audience identification developed over the years by the TV series.

Perhaps because of that bond, and the sense that an episode may be over but the *Enterprise* will carry on, the movie doesn't feel that it needs an ending in a conventional sense. The film closes with the usual *Star Trek* end narration, all about the ship's mission and its quest, and we are obviously being set up for a sequel. You could almost argue that the last few minutes of *Trek II* are a trailer for *Trek III*, but, no, that wouldn't be in the spirit of the *Enterprise*, would it?

Star Trek III: The Search for Spock
★ ★ ★
PG, 105 m., 1984

William Shatner (Kirk), DeForest Kelley ("Bones" McCoy), James Doohan (Scotty), Walter Koenig (Chekov), George Takei (Sulu), Nichell Nichols (Uhura), Mark Lenard (Sarek), Leonard Nimoy (Spock). Directed by Leonard Nimoy and produced by Harve Bennett. Screenplay by Bennett.

Read no further if you don't want to know whether Mr. Spock is alive at the end of *Star Trek III: The Search for Spock*. But, if you, like me, somehow had the notion that there was a 100 percent chance that they would find Spock (if only so he would be available for *Star Trek IV*), then you will be relieved to learn that his rediscovery and rebirth pay due homage to the complexities of the Vulcan civilization. By the end of this movie, all Mr. Spock has to do is raise one of those famous eyebrows, and the audience cheers.

This is a good but not great *Star Trek* movie, a sort of compromise between the first two. The first film was a *Star Wars* road company that depended on special effects. The second movie, the best one so far, remembered what made the *Star Trek* TV series so special: not its special effects, not its space opera gimmicks, but its use of science fiction as a platform for programs about human nature and the limitations of intelligence. *Star Trek III* looks for a balance between the first two movies. It has some of the philosophizing and some of the space opera, and there is an extended special effects scene on the exploding planet Genesis that's the latest word in fistfights on the crumbling edges of fiery volcanoes.

There is also a great-looking enemy spaceship that resembles a predatory bird in flight (although why ships in the vacuum of space require wings is still, of course, a question *Star Trek* prefers not to answer).* The ship is commanded by the fairly slow-witted Klingon warrior Kruge (played by Christopher Lloyd of "Taxi"), who falls for a neat little double cross that is audacious in its simplicity. The movie's plot involves a loyal attempt by the Enterprise crew to return to the planet Genesis in an attempt to reunite Spock's body and spirit. The alien spaceship is in the same sector, attempting to steal the secret of Genesis, a weapon from the last movie that begins by bringing life to dead planets and goes on from there. The showdown between the Klingons and the Enterprise crew resembles, at times, one of those Westerns where first Bart had the draw on Hoppy and then Hoppy had the draw on Bart, but the struggle to the death between Kirk and Kruge takes place against such a great apocalyptic background that we forgive all.

The best thing the *Star Trek* movies have going for them is our familiarity with the TV series. That makes for a sort of storytelling shorthand. At no point during this film, for example, is it ever explained that Vulcans are creatures of logic, not emotion—although we have to know that in order to understand most of the ending. It's not necessary. These characters are under our skins. They resonate, and a thin role in a given story is reinforced by stronger roles in a dozen others. That's sort of reassuring, as (a fanfare, please) the adventure continues.

*Leonard Nimoy sent me a helpful explanation: "The Klingon Bird of Prey has wings for the same reason that our own space shuttle does. It can land in an earth-like atmosphere."

Star Wars ★ ★ ★ ★
PG, 121 m., 1977

Mark Hamill (Luke Skywalker), Carrie Fisher (Princess Leia), Harrison Ford (Han Solo), Alec Guinness (Obi-Wan Kenobi), David Prowse (Darth Vader), James Earl Jones (Vader's Voice), Kenny Baker (R2D2), Anthony Daniels (C3PO). Directed by George Lucas and produced by Gary Kurtz. Screenplay by Lucas.

Every once in a while I have what I think of as an out-of-the-body experience at a movie. When the ESP people use a phrase like that, they're referring to the sensation of the mind actually leaving the body and spiriting itself off to China or Peoria or a galaxy far, far away. When I use the phrase, I simply mean that my imagination has forgotten it is actually present in a movie theater and thinks it's up there on the screen. In a curious sense, the events in the movie seem real, and I seem to be a part of them.

Star Wars works like that. My list of other

out-of-the-body films is a short and odd one, ranging from the artistry of *Bonnie and Clyde* or *Cries and Whispers* to the slick commercialism of *Jaws* and the brutal strength of *Taxi Driver.* On whatever level (sometimes I'm not at all sure) they engage me so immediately and powerfully that I lose my detachment, my analytical reserve. The movie's *happening,* and it's happening to me.

What makes the *Star Wars* experience unique, though, is that it happens on such an innocent and often funny level. It's usually violence that draws me so deeply into a movie—violence ranging from the psychological torment of a Bergman character to the mindless crunch of a shark's jaws. Maybe movies that scare us find the most direct route to our imaginations. But there's hardly any violence at all in *Star Wars* (and even then it's presented as essentially bloodless swashbuckling). Instead, there's entertainment so direct and simple that all of the complications of the modern movie seem to vaporize.

Star Wars is a fairy tale, a fantasy, a legend, finding its roots in some of our most popular fictions. The golden robot, lion-faced space pilot, and insecure little computer on wheels must have been suggested by the Tin Man, the Cowardly Lion, and the Scarecrow in *The Wizard of Oz.* The journey from one end of the galaxy to another is out of countless thousands of space operas. The hardware is from *Flash Gordon* out of *2001,* the chivalry is from *Robin Hood,* the heroes are from Westerns and the villains are a cross between Nazis and sorcerers. *Star Wars* taps the pulp fantasies buried in our memories, and because it's done so brilliantly, it reactivates old thrills, fears, and exhilarations we thought we'd abandoned when we read our last copy of *Amazing Stories.*

The movie works so well for several reasons, and they don't all have to do with the spectacular special effects. The effects *are* good, yes, but great effects have been used in such movies as *Silent Running* and *Logan's Run* without setting all-time box-office records. No, I think the key to *Star Wars* is more basic than that.

The movie relies on the strength of pure narrative, in the most basic storytelling form known to man, the Journey. All of the best tales we remember from our childhoods had

to do with heroes setting out to travel down roads filled with danger, and hoping to find treasure or heroism at the journey's end. In *Star Wars,* George Lucas takes this simple and powerful framework into outer space, and that is an inspired thing to do, because we no longer have maps on Earth that warn, "Here there be dragons." We can't fall off the edge of the map, as Columbus could, and we can't hope to find new continents of prehistoric monsters or lost tribes ruled by immortal goddesses. Not on Earth, anyway, but anything is possible in space, and Lucas goes right ahead and shows us very nearly everything. We get involved quickly, because the characters in *Star Wars* are so strongly and simply drawn and have so many small foibles and large, futile hopes for us to identify with. And then Lucas does an interesting thing. As he sends his heroes off to cross the universe and do battle with the Forces of Darth Vader, the evil Empire, and the awesome Death Star, he gives us lots of special effects, yes—ships passing into hyperspace, alien planets, an infinity of stars—but we also get a wealth of strange living creatures, and Lucas correctly guesses that they'll be more interesting for us than all the intergalactic hardware.

The most fascinating single scene, for me, was the one set in the bizarre saloon on the planet Alderaan. As that incredible collection of extraterrestrial alcoholics and bug-eyed martini drinkers lined up at the bar, and as Lucas so slyly let them exhibit characteristics that were universally human, I found myself feeling a combination of admiration and delight. *Star Wars* had placed me in the presence of really magical movie invention: Here, all mixed together, were whimsy and fantasy, simple wonderment and quietly sophisticated story-telling.

When Stanley Kubrick was making *2001* twenty years ago, he threw everything he had into the special effects depicting outer space, but he finally decided not to show any aliens at all—because they were impossible to visualize, he thought. But they weren't at all, as *Star Wars* demonstrates, and the movie's delight in the possibilities of alien life forms is at least as much fun as its conflicts between the space cruisers of the Empire and the Rebels.

And perhaps that helps to explain the

movie's one weakness, which is that the final assault on the Death Star is allowed to go on too long. Maybe, having invested so much money and sweat in his special effects, Lucas couldn't bear to see them trimmed. But the magic of *Star Wars* is only dramatized by the special effects; the movie's heart is in its endearingly human (and non-human) people.

Stardust Memories ★ ★
PG, 89 m., 1980

Woody Allen (Sandy), Charlotte Rampling (Dori), Jessica Harper (Violinist), Marie-Christine Barrault (Frenchwoman). Directed by Woody Allen and produced by Robert Greenhut. Screenplay by Allen.

Woody Allen's *Stardust Memories* is a deliberate homage to *8½*, the 1963 film in which Federico Fellini chronicled several days in the life of a filmmaker who had no idea where to turn next. The major difference between the two films is that Fellini's movie was *about* a director bankrupt of new ideas, while Allen's is a movie *by* a director with no new ideas. I know that sounds harsh, especially when applied to one of the few American directors who can be counted on for freshness and intelligence, but *Stardust Memories* is an incomplete, unsatisfying film.

The movie begins by acknowledging its sources of visual inspiration. We see a claustrophobic Allen trapped in a railroad car (that's from the opening of *8½*, with Marcello Mastroianni trapped in an auto), and the harsh black and white lighting and the ticking of a clock on the soundtrack give us a cross-reference to the nightmare that opens Ingmar Bergman's *Wild Strawberries*. Are these the exact scenes Allen had in mind? Probably, but no matter; he clearly intends *Stardust Memories* to be his *8½*, and it develops as a portrait of the artist's complaints.

Most of the action of the film centers around two subjects. The first is a weekend film seminar (obviously patterned after Judith Crist's weekends at Tarrytown, N.Y.), to which the Allen character has been invited. The second subject is a very familiar one, Allen's stormy relationships with women. The subjects blend into the basic complaint of the Woody Allen persona we have to come to know and love, and can be summarized briefly: If I'm so famous and brilliant and everybody loves me, then why doesn't anybody *in particular* love me?

At the film seminar, the Allen character is constantly besieged by groupies. They come in all styles: pathetic young girls who want to sleep with him, fans who want his autograph, weekend culture vultures, and people who spend all their time at one event promoting the next one they're attending. Allen makes his point early, by shooting these unfortunate creatures in close-up with a wide-angle lens that makes them all look like Martians with big noses. They add up to a nightmare, a non-stop invasion of privacy, a shrill chorus of people whose praise for the artist is really a call for attention.

Fine, except what *else* does Allen have to say about them? Nothing. In the Fellini film, the director-hero was surrounded by sycophants, business associates, would-be collaborators, wives, mistresses, old friends, all of whom made calls on his humanity. In the Allen picture, there's no depth, no personal context: They're only making calls on his time. What's more, the Fellini character was at least trying to create something, to harass his badgered brain into some feeble act of thought. But the Allen character expresses only impotence, despair, uncertainty, discouragement. All through the film, Allen keeps talking about diseases, catastrophes, bad luck that befalls even the most successful. Yes, but that's what artists are for: to hurl their imagination, joy, and conviction into the silent maw. Sorry if I got a little carried away. *Stardust Memories* inspires that kind of frustration, though, because it's the first Woody Allen film in which impotence has become the situation rather than the problem. This is a movie about a guy who has given up. His relationships with women illustrate that; after the marvelous and complex women in *Annie Hall* and *Manhattan*, in *Stardust Memories* we get a series of enigmas and we never really feel that Allen is connecting with them. These women don't represent failed relationships, they represent walk-throughs.

Woody Allen has always loved jazz and the great mainstream American popular music. There's a lot of it in *Stardust Memories*, but it doesn't amplify or illustrate the scene this time—it steals them. There's a scene where Allen remembers a wonderful spring morning spent with a former love (Charlotte Rampling), and how he looked up in his apartment to see her there, and for a moment felt that life was perfect. As Allen shows that moment, Louis Armstrong sings "Stardust" on the soundtrack, and something happens that should not be allowed to happen. We find our attention almost entirely on Armstrong's wonderfully loose jazz phrasing.

Stardust Memories is a disappointment. It needs some larger idea, some sort of organizing force, to pull together all these scenes of bitching and moaning, and make them lead somewhere.

Starman ★ ★ ★
PG, 112 m., 1984

Jeff Bridges (Starman), Karen Allen (Jenny Hayden), Charles Martin Smith (Mark Shermin), Richard Jaeckel (George Fox). Directed by John Carpenter and produced by Larry J. Franco. Screenplay by Bruce A. Evans and Raynold Gideon.

Starman begins by reminding us of Voyager, that little spacecraft that is even now speeding beyond the solar system. Remember Carl Sagan on the "Tonight" show, explaining to Johnny about all the messages that were on board, in case someday an alien race found this postcard from Earth? Voyager carried greetings in all of the tongues of man, and there is something inevitable about the scene, early in *Starman*, when we get an extraterrestrial visitor who has studied them carefully, and is able to say "hello" a hundred different ways.

The starman of the title is a ball of glowing light. He, or it, has traveled to Earth in response to the invitation from Voyager, but of course the Air Force treats the spacecraft as a possible invader and shoots missiles at it. Knocked off course, the starman lands in rural Wisconsin, where it becomes the identical clone of a dead house painter. The painter's widow (Karen Allen) is stunned when she sees this creature from beyond the grave. It is even more difficult when she realizes this is not her husband, but something infinitely different that just happens to look exactly like her husband. The visitor is very

smart, but has a lot to learn, and at first it controls its human host body with a lot of awkward lurching. Meanwhile, government officials led by Richard Jaeckel are seeking the extraterrestrial for "security" reasons, and scientist Charles Martin Smith hopes to get there first and record the historic moment of man's first meeting from a race from another world.

All of this seems like a setup for a science-fiction movie, but what's interesting is the way the director, John Carpenter, makes a U-turn and treats *Starman* as a road movie. The visitor (played by Jeff Bridges) forces Allen to start driving in the direction of the Great Meteor Crater, where he has a rendezvous with his ride home. And as the two characters spend time together as refugees from the search parties, they begin to communicate, and the woman's initial hostility turns into respect and finally into love. This is a wonderfully sweet process, especially as Allen and Bridges go about it. *Starman* contains the potential to be a very silly movie, but the two actors have so much sympathy for their characters that the movie, advertised as space fiction, turns into one of 1984's more touching love stories. Meanwhile, Carpenter provides many of the standard scenes from earlier road movies, including a stop in a roadside diner where the alien's uncertain behavior draws attention. And there's an interlude in Vegas where the extraterrestrial tries to outsmart the slots.

The most interesting thing about *Starman* is probably Bridges's approach to playing a creature from another world. The character grows gradually more human as the film moves along, but he is never completely without glitches: His head movements are birdlike, his step is a little uncertain, he speaks as if there were just a millisecond's delay between brain and tongue. Actors sometimes try to change their appearance; Bridges does something trickier, and tries to convince us that Jeff Bridges is not inhabited by himself. I think he succeeds, and that *Starman* makes Voyager seem like a good investment.

Stay Hungry ★ ★ ★
R, 102 m., 1976

Jeff Bridges (Craig Blake), Sally Field (Mary Tate), Arnold Schwarzenegger (Joe Santo), R.G. Armstrong (Thor Erickson), Robert Englund (Franklin), Helena Kallianiotes (Anita), Roger E. Mosley (Newton), Woodrow Parfrey (Uncle Albert), Scatman Crothers (William). Directed by Bob Rafelson and produced by Harold Schneider and Rafelson. Screenplay by Charles Gaines and Rafelson.

Bob Rafelson's *Stay Hungry* is ungainly and confused at times—it stretches its seams a little too much—but it's a breath of fresh air—a quirky, funny, oddball movie about the most unlikely characters ever to be trapped in the same plot. Jeff Bridges plays the lead, an Alabama blueblood of uncounted generations of aristocracy. He's involved in a real estate deal that involves convincing a gymnasium owner to sell his property so a high-rise can go up. Bridges visits the gym, becomes fascinated by the earnest body-builders and fierce female karate instructors and sort of forgets to do anything about the deal. And one of the body-builders (the former Mr. Universe, Arnold Schwarzenegger, who likes to work out in a rubber Batman suit) introduces him to a sweet young thing he can't help falling in love with.

The girl is played by Sally Field, and she's a simple country type who doesn't exactly fit in with Bridges's genteel cousins; she attends a family party dressed in something that looks mail-ordered from Frederick's of Hollywood. Bridges begins to get letters from his Uncle Albert, who points out that this new found interest in muscle-building and girls without any breeding is going to qualify him as the family's first black sheep since the cousin who moved to Puerto Rico and opened a goat farm. Meanwhile, the would-be real estate investors turn out to be mob types with a penchant for sending guys around to wreck the air conditioning.

The movie doesn't concern itself very much with plot; like Rafelson's *Five Easy Pieces* and the underrated *King of Marvin Gardens*, it introduces us to sharply defined, rather odd characters and then lets them mix it up. The movie is episodic, and some of the episodes are brilliant. Among the best is a

scene in which the aged family retainer (Scatman Crothers) announces his resignation and his intention of taking a suit of armor with him, another in which several dozen body-builders race through the startled streets of Birmingham, a harrowing fight scene in a gym in which people throw weights at each other, and a tables-turned situation in which a hooker is forcibly given a massage.

Schwarzenegger, in his first dramatic role, turns in an interesting performance as Bridges's new found buddy. He works out incessantly, speaks in an Austrian accent, and then turns out to be the lead fiddler in a bluegrass band (people in Rafelson movies are always revealing unsuspected musical abilities).

One of the best things about *Stay Hungry* is that we have almost no idea where it's going; it's as free-form as *Nashville* and Rafelson is cheerfully willing to pause here and there for set-pieces like the woman's karate class and the eventual Mr. Universe competition (in which the muscled competitors, back-lit, rise slowly onto a revolving stage in a moment reminiscent of the sunrise in *2001*). When the movie's over, we're still not sure why it was made (maybe it's a subtle comment on Southern class structure—very subtle), but we've had fun and so, it appears, has Rafelson.

Staying Alive ★
PG, 96 m., 1983

John Travolta (Tony Manero), Cynthia Rhodes (Jackie), Finola Hughes (Laura), Julie Bovasso (Mother). Directed by Sylvester Stallone and produced by Robert Stigwood. Screenplay by Stallone and Norman Wexler.

Staying Alive is a big disappointment. This sequel to the gutsy, electric *Saturday Night Fever* is a slick, cinematic jukebox, a series of self-contained song-and-dance sequences that could be cut apart and played forever on MTV. Like *Flashdance*, it isn't really a movie at all, but an endless series of musical interludes between dramatic scenes that aren't there. It's not even as good as *Flashdance*, but it may appeal to the same audience; it's a Walkman for the eyes.

The movie has an extremely simple plot.

Extremely. Six years have passed since Tony Manero (John Travolta) gazed longingly at the lights of Manhattan at the end of *Saturday Night Fever*. Now he lives in a fleabag Manhattan hotel, works as a waiter and a dance instructor, and dates a young dancer (Cynthia Rhodes) with the patience of a saint. He's still a woman-chaser. But he meets a long-haired British dancer (Finola Hughes) who's his match. She's a queen bitch who takes him to bed and jilts him. Meanwhile, he gets a job as a dancer in her new show and when her lead dancer falters, Tony gets the job. Does this all sound familiar?

The movie was co-authored and directed by Sylvester Stallone, and is the first bad movie he's made. He remembers all the moves from his Rocky plots, but he leaves out the heart—and, even worse, he leaves out the characters. Everybody in *Staying Alive* is Identikit. The characters are clichés, their lives clichés, and God knows their dialogue is clichés. The big musical climaxes are interrupted only long enough for people to shout prepackaged emotional countercharges at each other. There is little attempt to approximate human speech. Like the Rocky movies, *Staying Alive* ends with a big, visually explosive climax. It is so ludicrous it has to be seen to be believed. It's opening night on Broadway. Tony Manero not only dances like a hero, he survives a production number of fire, ice, smoke, flashing lights, and laser beams, throws in an improvised solo—and ends triumphantly by holding Finola Hughes above his head with one arm, like a quarry he has tracked and killed. The musical he is allegedly starring in is something called *Satan's Alley*, but it's so laughably gauche it should have been called *Springtime for Tony*. Stallone makes little effort to convince us we're watching a real stage presentation; there are camera effects the audience could never see, montages that create impossible physical moves, and—most inexplicably of all—a vocal track, even though nobody on stage is singing. It's a mess. Travolta's big dance number looks like a high-tech TV auto commercial that got sick to its stomach.

What I really missed in *Staying Alive* was the sense of reality in *Saturday Night Fever*—the sense that Tony came from someplace and was somebody particular. There's no old neighborhood, no vulgar showdowns with his family (he *apologizes* to his mother for his "attitude"!), and no Brooklyn eccentricity. Tony's world has been cloned into a backstage musical. And not a good one.

Still, the movie has one great moment. A victorious Tony says "I want to strut!" and struts across Times Square while the Bee Gees sing "Stayin' Alive." That could have been the first shot of a great movie. It's the last shot of this one.

Stephen King's Silver Bullet ★ ★ ★
R, 95 m., 1985

Gary Busey (Uncle Red), Everett McGill (Reverend Lowe), Corey Haim (Marty Coslaw), Megan Follows (Jane Coslaw), Terry O'Quinn (Sheriff), James Gammon (Arnie Westrum). Directed by Daniel Attias and produced by Martha Schumacher. Screenplay by Stephen King.

Stephen King's Silver Bullet is either the worst movie ever made from a Stephen King story, or the funniest. It is either simply bad, or it is an inspired parody of his whole formula, in which quiet American towns are invaded by unspeakable horrors.

It's a close call, but I think the movie is intentionally funny. And because I laughed longer and louder during this film than during any other comedy I'd seen since *Broadway Danny Rose*, I am going way out on a shaky limb and actually giving the movie a three-star rating, which means I even think you might enjoy it, too.

The movie takes place in 1976, in one of King's patented little American towns. A narrator talks about how quiet and sleepy things used to be—and then, after a few shots of Main Street, we see what really goes on. The town's social life centers around the bar, where mean drunks sit around looking hostile. A decapitated body is found down by the tracks. We meet a local family (named the "Coslaws"—a nice touch, especially if the Potato Salads live next door). One of the kids in the family is in a motorized wheelchair. His uncle is an alcoholic. Worst of all, when the full moon shines, a werewolf breaks into people's homes and rips them to shreds.

Who is the werewolf? I was able to guess

almost the moment he walks onscreen. See how you do. As the werewolf continues his raids, the story centers around the typical family, and especially around the crippled kid, little Marty, whose legs are paralyzed but who is able to use his arms to climb trees and sneak out of the house at night. Marty therefore doesn't need a motorized wheelchair, but the movie goes for some sick jokes as the kid pulls into a gas station to fill his tank.

And then Uncle Red (Gary Busey) gives the kid a great present. A customized, souped-up, hot rod wheelchair named the Silver Bullet (it kills werewolves—get it?). The kid takes off at sixty miles per hour, doing wheelies down the highway, and eventually the movie treats us to the extraordinary sight of the local clergyman in his car, trying to run down the kid in the hot rod wheelchair. This is not an image the movies have previously offered us.

There are all sorts of sly satiric touches in the film. For example, the narrator turns out to be little Marty's sister, Jane Coslaw (Megan Follows). Her voice on the sound track sounds mature and middle aged, and yet, hold on, this movie takes place in 1976, when she's about nine, so she can't be more than eighteen.

The town's local characters are broadly drawn—real broadly. When they form a vigilante posse and go out looking for the werewolf, one guy is scared, and his wife, so help me, says, "Are you going to make lemonade in your pants?" Later, three vigilantes wander into a clearing where the fog is waist-high, and the werewolf strikes from under the fog, dragging them down one at a time.

I know that a case can be made for how bad Silver Bullet is. I agree. It's bad. But it's not routinely bad. It is bad in its own awesomely tasteless and bubble-brained way—so bad, I think every laugh was put in lovingly, by hand. Most horror movies are exercises in unrelieved vulgarity, occasionally interrupted by perfunctory murders. This movie, to borrow an immortal comment by Mel Brooks, "rises below vulgarity." If you are sick up to here of horror movies in general and Stephen King in particular, this is the movie for you. If you have impeccable taste and high artistic standards, why have you read this far in the first place?

Stevie ★ ★ ★
NO MPAA RATING, 102 m., 1981

Glenda Jackson (Stevie Smith), Mona Washbourne (Her Aunt), Alec McCowen (Freddie), Trevor Howard (The Man). Directed and produced by Robert Enders. Screenplay by Hugh Whitemore.

Stevie Smith came across a newspaper clipping one day that told of a man who drowned within a few hundred yards off the shore. The people on the beach saw him waving, and they waved back. The truth, as Stevie expressed it in a famous poem, was the man's problem was just like her own:

I was much too far out all my life
And not waving, but drowning.

In those lines, Stevie Smith made an image of her own life, and it is an image that Glenda Jackson's film *Stevie* expresses with clarity, wit, and love.

Stevie Smith was a British poet of considerable reputation, who died in 1971 at the age of sixty-nine. She spent almost all of her life living in a small home in the London suburb of Palmers Green, where she moved as a child. She worked every day in an office in the city, until her growing reputation as a poet allowed her to take an early retirement. She lived with an old maid aunt, and eventually she became an old maid herself. We watch this process as it is punctuated by a marriage proposal, by a visit to Buckingham Palace for tea with the queen, by a half-hearted suicide attempt. Every night, there was definitely a glass or two or more of sherry, or sometimes gin.

To the world, she must have appeared to be an exemplary example of a talented English eccentric. Her poems were irreverent, sharply satirical, and laconic. She was capable of writing one day:

The Englishwoman is so refined
She has no bosom and no behind.

And on another day, writing about death:

I have a friend
At the end
of the world.
His name is a breath
Of fresh air.

She was not waving, but drowning. The film *Stevie* captures this laconic despair, but it also does a great deal more. It gives us a very particular portrait of a woman's life. The movie is based on a play by Hugh Whitemore, and it contains one of Glenda Jackson's greatest performances. She knows this character well. She played Stevie on the London stage and on a BBC radio production before making this film. She does what great actors can do: She takes a character who might seem uninteresting, and makes us care deeply about the uneventful days of her life.

Although *Stevie* is totally dominated by Jackson's performance, it is not a one-character film by any means. The veteran British actress Mona Washbourne provides a magnificent performance as Stevie's maiden aunt, who is a little dotty and a little giggly and very loving, who likes her glass of sherry and wears flowered print dresses that Stevie says look like a seed catalog illustration titled "They All Came Up." Alec McCowen plays Freddie, the not-so-young man who comes calling, and whose proposal Stevie rejects. And the wonderful Trevor Howard has an ambiguous part as "the man." On one level, "the man" is just someone she met at a literary party and conned into giving her rides to poetry readings. At another level, especially when he is seen by himself, telling us about Stevie and reading some of her lines, he is the understanding, forgiving father figure Stevie never had.

Movies like *Stevie* run the risk of looking like photographs of stage plays, but *Stevie* somehow never feels that way. Even though it uses the artifices of the stage (including remarks addressed by Glenda Jackson directly to the audience), and even though a lot of its dialogue is poetry, *Stevie* always feels as if it occupies this woman's life. She is the poet, we are her confidantes, and it is a privilege to get to know her. I have perhaps given the impression that *Stevie* is grim and depressing. It is not at all. It is very sad at times, of course, but there are other times of good humor and barbed wit, when she's not drowning, but waving.

Stir Crazy ★ ★
R, 111 m., 1980

Gene Wilder (Skip Donahue), Richard Pryor (Harry Monroe), Georg Stanford Brown (Rory), Jobeth Williams (Meredith). Directed by Sidney Poitier and produced by Hannah Weinstein. Screenplay by Bruce Jay Friedman.

Stir Crazy seems to change its mind, halfway through, about the kind of movie it wants to be. It starts strong: It's a comedy that teams up Gene Wilder and Richard Pryor. It gives them crazy things to do, like working as performing chickens, but it also gives them interesting characters. Wilder is a playwright, Pryor is an actor, they're both out of work, and they decide to head West and seek their fortunes.

So far, great—right up to the case of mistaken identities that lands them in court. Their courtroom scene is one of the movie's high points. Their lawyer has persuaded them to plead guilty in hope of a light sentence, but they're given 125 years apiece. Wilder begins a monosyllabic scream: "Wa! Wa! Wa!" Pryor tries to explain that everything was Wilder's idea. The movie has started well and at this point it looks like it could develop into a terrific comedy.

But it doesn't. Instead, once Wilder and Pryor are thrown into prison, it seems to lose its way. There are still some funny scenes to come, especially those involving a gigantic murderer named Grossburger (who is played by Erland Van Lidth de Jeude, the motorcycle gang leader in *The Wanderers*). But, inexplicably, the movie gets bogged down in developing its own plot. That is not always the best thing for a comedy to do, because if we're not laughing it hardly matters what happens to the plot.

But to the plot: The warden of the prison has a long-standing rivalry with another warden, and they bet on the outcome of rodeos held between the inmates at their prisons. After Wilder amazingly turns out to be a "natural cowboy" who can ride any bronco, Wilder and Pryor get involved in a scheme to escape during the prison rodeo. This is a deadly mistake for the movie. We get a long, boring rodeo sequence, intercut with the repetitive process of escape. The escape route involves slipping under a loose board and climbing under the grandstand, and sneaking out of a ventilation panel and into a peanut vendor's wagon, and on and on, and about four different characters travel this route when one would have been plenty.

So that's what's wrong with the construction of this movie. The employment of Wilder and Pryor falls in another category. The movie was directed by Sidney Poitier (this is his fifth directorial job), and either Poitier or the producers made a tactical error in making Wilder the more aggressive character and Pryor the laid-back one. This is casting against type, all right: Wilder is brilliant at being meek and laid-back, and Pryor is a genius when he's allowed to be hyper. But it just doesn't feel right when Wilder goes for the high notes and Pryor hangs back.

And that's a shame, because good comedies are hard to make and this one shows a lot of promise. What went wrong? Maybe everybody got too absorbed in the details of the rodeo and the escape plan? It's possible. But long, complicated courses of action do not necessarily suit themselves to comedy, and when the characters get absorbed in them they're not free to react in comic ways.

Stop Making Sense ★ ★ ★ ½
NO MPAA RATING, 88 m., 1984

With the Talking Heads: David Byrne, Chris Frantz, Jerry Harrison, and Tina Weymouth. Guest musicians: Edna Holt, Lynn Mabry, Steve Scales, Alex Weir, and Bernie Worrell. Directed by Jonathan Demme and produced by Gary Goetzman.

The overwelming impression throughout *Stop Making Sense* is of enormous energy, of life being lived at a joyous high. And it's not the frenetic, jangled-nerves energy of a rock band that's wired; it's the high spirits and good health we associate with artists like Bruce Springsteen. There are a lot of reasons to see concert films, but the only ones that usually get mentioned are the music and the cinematography. This time the actual physical impact of the film is just as exhilarating: Watching the Talking Heads in concert is a little like rock 'n' roll crossed with "Jane Fonda's Workout." The movie was shot during two live performances of the Talking Heads, a New York rock band that centers on the remarkable talent of its lead singer, David Byrne. Like David Bowie, his stage presence shows the influence of mime, and some of his best effects in *Stop Making Sense* are achieved with outsize costumes and

hand-held lights that create shadow plays on the screen behind him.

Given all the showmanship that will develop later during the film, the opening sequences are a low-key, almost anticoncert throwaway. Byrne walks on a bare stage with a ghetto-blaster in his hand, puts it down on the stage, turns it on and sings along with "Psycho Killer." Eventually he is joined onstage by Tina Weymouth on bass. Then stagehands wander out from the wings and being to assemble a platform for drummer Chris Frantz. Gear is moved into place. Electical cables are attached. The backup singers, Edna Holt and Lynn Mabry, appear. And the concert inexorably picks up tempo.

The music of the Talking Heads draws from many sources, in addition to traditional rock 'n' roll. You can hear the echoes, in Byrne's voice, of one of his heroes, country singer Hank Williams. In the music itself, there are elements of reggae and of gospel, especially in the driving repetitions of single phrases that end some of the songs. What is particularly delightful is that the Talking Heads *are* musical: For people who have passed over that invisible divide into the age group when rock sounds like noise, the Heads will sound like music.

The film is good to look at. The director is Jonathan Demme *(Melvin and Howard)*, making his first concert film, and essentially using the visuals of the Talking Heads rather than creating his own. Instead of the standard phony cutaways to the audience (phony because, nine times out of ten, the audience members are not actually reacting to the moment in the music that we're hearing), Demme keeps his cameras trained on the stage. And when Byrne and company use the stage-level lights to create a shadow play behind them, the result is surprisingly more effective than you might imagine: It's a live show with elements of *Metropolis*.

But the film's peak moments come through Byrne's simple physical presence. He jogs in place with his sidemen; he runs around the stage; he seems so happy to be alive and making music. Like Springsteen and Prince, he serves as a reminder of how sour and weary and strung-out many rock bands have become. Starting with Mick Jagger, rock concerts have become, for the performers, as much sporting events as musical and theatrical performances. *Stop Making Sense* understands that with great exuberance.

Straight Time ★ ★ ★ ½
R, 114 m., 1978

Dustin Hoffman (Max Dembo), Theresa Russell (Jenny Mercer), Harry Dean Stanton (Jerry Schue), Gary Busey (Willy Darin), M. Emmet Walsh (Earl Frank), Sandy Baron (Manny). Directed by Ulu Grosbard and produced by Stanley Beck and Tim Zinnemann. Screenplay by Alvin Sargent, Edward Bunker, and Jeffrey Boam.

Straight Time is a great sleeper, a film good enough that we wonder why we didn't hear more about it. So does Dustin Hoffman, who sued Warner Brothers for what he considered the mishandling of the picture. He may have had a point; his performance here as Max Dembo, ex-con turned thief, is one of his very best.

Max gets out of prison determined to go straight. It's not easy. Under the conditions of his parole, for example, he can't take a job that involves the handling of money. But a girl in an employment office does find him a job, at a can company. And when he asks her out to dinner, she accepts. He also finds a room he can afford to rent, and so he's doing fairly well. He's on the road to personal rehabilitation, as his parole officer might put it. The parole officer (M. Emmet Walsh) is not, however, very good at the rehabilitation game. He's mean-spirited, suspicious and sadistic, all behind a large, cynical smile. He busts Max on suspicion of drug use, causing him to lose his job—and that's enough for Max, who returns to the trade he knows best, theft.

Straight Time is based on a novel by an ex-con, and it feels authentic. What especially absorbs us is the way the movie projects the feeling of being a thief—the compulsion, the addiction, the rush of adrenaline, the fear. It's also good at explaining why this guy would be attractive to a girl, and especially the girl at the employment office.

She's played by Theresa Russell, who does a good job of projecting her feelings. She doesn't talk a lot, but she listens well, and she's drawn to the mysteries in Max's character. He wants to keep her out of his jobs but not out of his life, and she is eventually willing to settle for his terms.

Max pulls several jobs. He sticks up a grocery, for example, and then a pawnshop, where he gets the shotgun that will be useful in his stick-ups of a bank and a jewelry store. He enlists old buddies as his accomplices, and Harry Dean Stanton is especially good as an ex-con who almost succeeds in going straight. Stanton's got it all together: A house, a swimming pool, hamburgers grilled on the patio . . . but he can't resist the urgency of Max Dembo's sales pitch.

The robberies themselves have the same sense of manic desperation we felt in *Dog Day Afternoon*. And they have something else, as well: They project the feeling that Max Dembo, without admitting it even to himself, *wants* to get caught again. He lingers. He dawdles. His partner is calling out the number of seconds that have elapsed, as part of their plan to get out before the cops arrive. But Max Dembo isn't listening. Maybe that's part of the emotional payoff he needs, stretching a job to its last second, walking out the back door as the cops come in the front, taunting society while at the same time almost begging for punishment.

Hoffman's performance reminds me of his Ratso Rizzo in *Midnight Cowboy*, especially in his ways of telling the world to go to hell. Ratso was far gone on his own personal death trip, of course, and Max Dembo has whole moments when he rathers enjoys life. But they're similar in their moves, their choices. They belong outside society because it doesn't dare have places for them. Maybe *that's* what turns the girl on; maybe she has a sheltering instinct.

Straight Time exists so close to the drabness and desperation of its story that it might turn some people off. Hoffman must have known that; this is such a personal project that after he bought the original novel he planned to direct it himself before deciding, instead, on the Broadway and sometime movie director Ulu Grosbard. But Hoffman and Grosbard don't change details just to make their movie more palatable. Instead, they stick with Max Dembo, figuring him out, following his impulses, until those oddly disturbing final photographs—his mug shots—with the eyes suggesting that somehow this particular human being was *always* doomed.

Stranger than Paradise ★ ★ ★ ★
R, 90 m., 1984

John Lurie (Willie), Eszter Balint (Eva), Richard Edson (Eddie), Cecillia Stark (Aunt Lottie), Danny Rosen (Billy), Rammellzee (Man with Money), Tom Decillo (Airline Agent). Directed by Jim Jarmusch and produced by Sara Driver. Screenplay by Jarmusch.

Stranger than Paradise is filmed in a series of uninterrupted shots; the picture fades in, we watch the scene, and when the scene is over, there's a fade to black. Then comes the next fade-in. This is not a gimmick, but a visual equivalent of the film's deadpan characters, who take a lot to get excited.

The movie's hero is Willie (John Lurie), who arrived on these shores from Hungary about ten years ago, and has spent the intervening decade perfecting his New York accent and trying to make nothing out of himself. He lives in an apartment where the linoleum is the highlight. On a good day, he'll sleep late, hang out, play a little poker. His cousin Eva arrives from Budapest. This is the last thing he needs, a 16-year-old girl who needs a place to stay. She hates him, too. But she has to kill some time before she goes to Cleveland to live with her aunt Lottie. She has good taste in American music, but not according to him. Willie's friend, Eddie, comes over occasionally and eyeballs Eva. Nothing much happens. She leaves for Cleveland.

The screen is filled with large letters: ONE YEAR LATER. This in itself is funny, that we'd get such a momentous time cue in a movie where who even knows what day it is. Eddie and Willie get in some trouble over a poker game and Eddie suddenly remembers Willie's cousin in Cleveland. They go to see her. It is cold in Cleveland. Eva has bought the American Dream and is working in a fast-food outlet. They all go to look at the lake, which is frozen. Aunt Lottie turns out to make Clara Peller look like Dame Peggy Ashcroft. The guys say to hell with it and head for Florida. Then they come back and get Eva and take her along with them. They

have a postcard that makes Florida look like paradise, but they wind up living at one of those hotels where the permanent guests live in the woodwork. Everything goes sour. Eva wants to go back to Hungary. The guys lose all their money at the dog races. Creeps start hanging around. It will take a miracle to give this movie an upbeat ending. There is a miracle.

Stranger than Paradise is a treasure from one end to the other. I saw it for the first time at the 1984 Cannes Film Festival, where it was having its first public showing. Half the people in the theater probably didn't speak English, but that didn't stop them from giving the movie a standing ovation, and it eventually won the Camera d'Or prize for the best first film. It is like no other film you've seen, and yet you feel right at home in it. It seems to be going nowhere, and knows every step it wants to make. It is a constant, almost kaleidoscopic experience of discovery, and we try to figure out what the film is up to and it just keeps moving steadfastly ahead, fade in, fade out, fade in, fade out, making a mountain out of a molehill.

Streamers ★ ★ ★ ★
R, 118 m., 1984

Matthew Modine (Billy), Michael Wright (Carlyle), Mitchell Lichtenstein (Richie), David Alan Grier (Roger), Guy Boyd (Rooney), George Dzundza (Cokes). Directed by Robert Altman and produced by Altman and Nick H. Mileti. Screenplay by David Rabe.

Robert Altman's *Streamers* is one of the most intense and intimate dramas I've ever seen on film. It's based on the play by David Rabe, about young soldiers waiting around a barracks for their orders to go to Vietnam. Most directors, faced with a play that takes place on one set, find ways to "open it up" and add new locations. Altman has moved in the opposite direction, taking advantage of the one-room set to tighten the play until it squeezes like a vise. Watching this film is such a demanding experience that both times I've seen it, it has been too much for some viewers, and they've left. Those who stay, who survive the difficult passages of violence, will find at the end of the film a conclusion that is so poetic and moving it succeeds in placing the tragedy in perspective.

It is the era of Vietnam. In a barracks somewhere, three young men wait for their orders. They are Billy, who is white and middle-class; Roger, who is black and middle-class; and Richie, a dreamy young man who likes to tease the others with hints that he is a homosexual. The only other occupants of the barracks are two drunken master sergeants, Rooney and Cokes, who are best friends and who are stumbling through idiotic revelry in an attempt to drown the realization that Cokes has leukemia. Into this little world comes Carlyle, an angry young black man who is gay, and whose conversations with Richie will lead the others into anger and denial before the situation finally explodes.

There are some surprises, but the developments in *Streamers* flow so naturally out of the material that its surprises should be left intact. A lot can be said, however, about the acting, Altman's direction, and Rabe's writing. I didn't see this play on stage and don't know how it worked there, but Altman is so completely the visual master of this material that we're drawn into that barracks room and into its rhythms of boredom, drunkenness, and passion.

The actors are all unknown to me, except for George Dzundza, who plays Cokes. They are all so natural that the dialogue has an eerie double quality: We know it's written dialogue because it has a poetry and a drama unlikely in life, but Rabe's ear is so accurate it sounds real, and the performers make it so convincing there's never a false note. The two key performances are by Mitchell Lichtenstein, as Richie, and Michael Wright, as Carlyle. Richie is indeed homosexual, as we realize long before his barracks mates are willing to acknowledge it. He likes to tease the others with insinuations that they may be gay, too. Billy boasts that he is straight, but he protests too much. Roger tries to be a peacekeeper. Then Carlyle wanders in from another unit. He is drunk and angry, collapses, sleeps it off, blearily looks around, figures out Richie, and tries to make a connection.

But there is a lot more going on here than sexual competition. *Streamers* uses both sex and race as foreground subjects while the movie's real subject, war, hovers in the background and in several extraordinary monologues—one about snakes, one about a battle, and one about the realities of parachuting. As the veteran master sergeants make their drunken way through the movie, they drop these hard realities into the lives of the unseasoned kids. And when anger turns to violence and a tragedy occurs, it is up to one of the fat old guys (Dzundza) to deliver a monologue that is one of the most revealing, intimate, honest, and moving speeches I've ever heard.

Streets of Fire ★ ★ ★
PG, 93 m., 1984

Michael Pare (Tom Cody), Diane Lane (Ellen Aim), Amy Madigan (McCoy), Rich Moranis (Billy Fish), William Dafoe (Raven), Deborah Van Valkenburgh (Reva). Directed by Walter Hill and produced by Lawrence Gordon and Joel Silver. Written by Hill and Larry Gross.

Walter Hill's *Streets of Fire* begins by telling us it's a "rock 'n' roll fable . . . from another time, another place." The movie is right on the rock 'n' roll, but the alternative time and place are mysteriously convincing—especially if, like me, you believe the most beautiful postwar American cars were Studebakers. In this world, Studebakers made it. All the cops in this movie drive circa 1950 Studebakers, and all the people in the movie live in the shadow of oppressive elevated tracks, in a shabby, nighttime city inhabited mostly by cops, street gangs, rock fans, and soda jerks.

The movie begins with the kidnapping of a rock singer (Diane Lane), who is muscled off the stage by some Hell's Angels types. But first we get one of the few original approaches to rock concert photography: Full-stage photography of the singers is combined with black foreground silhouettes of the audience, waving their hands and clapping. The effect is a little like a Roger Brown painting, and it works: This looks like it's going to be a new approach to the basic street and rock images. Unfortunately, the movie doesn't live up to its opening. It turns into your basic fable about warring street gangs, with a superman (Michael Pare) and his tough female accomplice (Amy Madigan) breaking into the headquarters of the rival gang and bringing Diane Lane back alive. This ground has been covered before, most obviously in Hill's *The Warriors*, a controversial 1978 thriller that was credited with inspiring more fights in its audience than on the screen.

Hill likes characters who are broadly symbolic. He occasionally gives us people who are individuals (as in his most successful film, *48 Hours*, with Eddie Murphy and Nick Nolte). But mostly he likes characters who stand tall and represent good or evil and settle the matters of the universe with unlimited violence. That's what we get this time. What we also get is some interesting atmosphere, which owes a lot to the art direction and the background musical score by Ry Cooder. Hill came to Chicago to shoot some of his blasted landscapes of barren warehouses under ominous L tracks, and matched them with back-lot sets at Universal that suggest a city where gentrification never caught on. The cops are corrupt in this fictional city, the gangs rule the streets, and there are districts where you've got to be armed.

Side-by-side with this paramilitary society is a world of art nouveau theater marquees, corny soda fountains, and the rock singer's manager (Rick Moranis), who wears checked sport coats and bow ties and looks like the creep of the class of '57. The language is strange, too: It's tough, but not with 1984 toughness. It sounds like the way really mean guys would have talked in the late 1950s, only with a few words different—as if this world evolved a slightly different language. The performances fit this world nicely. The most engaging character is Amy Madigan's McCoy, an Army veteran who smokes cigars, blast bikers to smithereens, and tells Pare he ain't her type. Pare is your basic taciturn, implacable Hill hero, and Diane Lane has so much of the right energy in the opening concert scene that we wonder why there wasn't a lot more rock 'n' roll in the movie. Also more Studebakers, please.

Streetwise ★ ★ ★ ★
R, 92 m., 1985

Directed by Martin Bell and produced by Cheryl McCall. Reported by Mary Ellen Mark.

The mother is being frank about her daughter. She says she knows the girl is working as a prostitute, but she figures "it's just a phase she's going through." Her daughter is about fifteen years old. That is not the most harrowing moment in *Streetwise*, a heartbreaking documentary about the street children of Seattle. There are worse moments, for example the one where a street kid tries to talk to her mother about the fact that her stepfather "was fooling around . . . doing perverted things with me" when she was a baby. "Yes," says the mother philosophically, "but now he's stopped."

The subject of runaway, abducted, and abandoned children has received a lot of attention in the news, but never anything remotely like *Streetwise*, which enters into the lives of these under-age survivors as they fight for life and love on the streets of Seattle. The movie was inspired by a *Life* magazine article on a group of the kids, who, at an age when other kids are in school, are learning to be hookers, thieves, con men, pushers, and junkies. Now comes this movie, which contains extraordinary everyday footage, which the filmmakers obtained by spending months hanging out with the kids, until they gained their trust and their cameras became accepted.

The street kids lead horrifying lives, but sometimes there are moments of acceptance and happiness. They cling to each other. They relate uneasily with a social worker who seems philosophically resigned to the facts of street life. They try to dodge the cops. They live in an abandoned hotel, get money by begging and prostitution, eat by raiding the dumpsters behind restaurants. They even have a system for marking garbage so they don't eat food that's too old.

What is amazing is that some of these kids are still in touch with their parents. One girl shrugs that her mother is off to the woods for a weekend: "I've always known she don't love me or shit. So OK." She hugs herself. Another girl tries to talk to her mother, who says, "Be quiet. I'm drinking." A kid named DeWayne goes to visit his father in prison and gets a long lecture about smoking, drinking, and taking drugs, and a pie-in-the-sky speech about how they're going to open a thrift shop when the old man gets out of prison. The next time we see

DeWayne, it is at his funeral; he hanged himself in a jail cell.

You walk out of *Streetwise* realizing that these aren't bad kids. They are resourceful, tough, and true to their own standards. They break the law, but then how many legal ways are there for fourteen-year-olds to support themselves? They talk about their parents in a matter-of-fact way that, we suspect, covers up great wounds, as when one girl says she's never met her natural father— "unless maybe I dated him once."

Streetwise is surprising for the frankness of the material it contains. How did the filmmakers get these people to say these things, to allow the cameras into their lives? We see moments of intimacy, of violence, of pain. The answer, I suspect, is that a lot of these kids were so starving for attention and affection that by offering both, the filmmakers were able to get whatever they wanted. Some of the scenes are possibly staged, in the sense that the characters are aware they are in a movie, but none of the scenes are false or contrived. These are children living rough in an American city, and you would blame their parents if you didn't see that the parents are just as alienated and hopeless, and that before long these kids will be damaged parents, too.

Stripes ★ ★ ★ ½
R, 105 m., 1981

Bill Murray (John), Harold Ramis (Russell), Warren Oates (Sergeant Hulka), P.J. Soles (Stella), Sean Young (Louise), John Candy (Ox). Directed by Ivan Reitman and produced by Reitman and Dan Goldberg. Screenplay by Goldberg, Len Blum, and Harold Ramis.

Stripes is an anarchic slob movie, a celebration of all that is irreverent, reckless, foolhardy, undisciplined, and occasionally scatalogical. It's a lot of fun. It comes from some of the same people involved in *National Lampoon's Animal House*, and could have been titled *National Lampoon's Animal Army* with little loss of accuracy. As a comedy about a couple of misfits who find themselves in the U.S. Army's basic training program, it obviously resembles Goldie Hawn's *Private Benjamin*. But it doesn't duplicate that wonderful movie; they could play on the same double feature. *Stripes* has the added

advantage of being a whole movie about the Army, rather than half a movie (*Private Benjamin* got sidetracked with Hawn's love affair).

The movie is not only a triumph for its stars (Bill Murray and Harold Ramis) and its director (Ivan Reitman), but a sort of vindication. To explain: Reitman directed, and Murray starred in, the enormously successful *Meatballs*, which was an entertaining enough comedy but awfully ragged. No wonder. It was shot on a shoestring with Canadian tax shelter money. What Murray and Reitman prove this time is that, given a decent budget, they can do superior work— certainly superior to *Meatballs*, for starters. For Harold Ramis, who plays Murray's grave-eyed, flat-voiced, terminally detached partner in *Stripes*, this is a chance, at last, to come out from behind the camera. Ramis and Murray are both former Second City actors, but in Hollywood, Ramis has been typecast as a writer (*Animal House, Meatballs, Caddyshack*), maybe because he sometimes looks too goofy for Hollywood's unimaginative tastes.

In *Stripes*, Murray and Ramis make a wonderful team. Their big strength is restraint. Given the tendency of movies like this to degenerate into undisciplined slapstick, they wisely choose to play their characters as understated, laid-back anarchists. Murray enlists in the Army in a what-the-hell mood after his girlfriend throws him out, and Ramis enlists because one stupid gesture deserves another. They're older than the usual Army recruit, less easily impressed with gung-ho propaganda, and quietly amazed at their drill instructor, Sergeant Hulka, who is played by Warren Oates with tough-as-nails insanity.

The movie has especially good writing in several scenes. My favorite comes near the beginning, during a session when recruits in the new platoon get to know one another. One obviously psycho draftee, who looks like Robert De Niro, quietly announces that if his fellow soldiers touch him, touch his stuff, or interfere in any way with his person or his privacy, he will quite simply be forced to kill them. Sergeant Hulka replies: "Lighten up!"

The movie's plot follows basic training, more or less, during its first hour. Then a romance enters. Murray and Ramis meet a couple of cute young military policewomen (P.J. Soles and Sean Young), and they happily violate every rule in the book. One funny scene: Murray and Soles sneak into the kitchen of the base commander's house and do unprecedented things with kitchen utensils.

It's an unwritten law of these movies that the last half hour has to involve some kind of spectacular development. In *Animal House,* it was the homecoming parade. In *Stripes,* the climax involves the Army's latest secret weapon, which is a computerized, armored, nuclear weapons carrier disguised as a recreational vehicle. Murray's platoon is assigned to go to Europe and test it. Murray, Ramis, and their girls decide to test it during a weekend holiday swing through the Alps. After they inadvertently cross the Iron Curtain, all hell breaks loose.

Stripes is a complete success on its intended level—it's great, irreverent entertainment—but it was successful, too, as a breakthrough for Ramis, Reitman, and Murray, on their way to *Ghostbusters.* Comedy is one of the hardest film genres to work in. Nobody knows all its secrets, not even Woody Allen and Mel Brooks. Here's a comedy from people who know some of the secrets most of the time.

Stripper ★ ★ ★
R, 90 m., 1986

Janette Boyd (Herself), Sara Costa (Herself), Kimberly Holcomb (Danyel), Loree Menton (Mouse), Lisa Suarez (Gio), Ellen Claire McSweeney (Shakto Om), Jamal Rofeh (Club Owner). Directed by Jerome Gary and produced by Gary, Geoff Bartz, and Melvyn J. Estrin.

Why do strippers take off their clothes? Because they are paid to take them off, I imagine, and also perhaps because exhibitionism satisfies some psychological hunger inside of them. The point of a striptease is very basic: the extraordinary fact that a woman walks into a roomful of strangers and undresses. This ritual is eternal. And although there is a lot of talk about the "art" of striptease, no stripper in history, however artistic, has succeeded by starting nude and dressing herself.

Stripper, which pretends to be a documentary about striptease artists, satisfies all the traditional requirements. During the course of the film, several attractive women take off their clothes. The movie claims to be about an international striptease competition being held in Las Vegas. But the contest is being held for only one reason—to provide a framework for this film—and there are many scenes where there doesn't even seem to be an audience.

The movie was directed by Jerome Gary, who also made *Pumping Iron,* and by now his formula is pretty well polished. He "casts" his documentaries by finding likely candidates (he was the first director to make Arnold Schwarzenegger and Lou Ferrigno into stars). Then he sets up some sort of confrontation, such as the strip contest in this film, as a framework for his story. To be sure, the women in this film are real strippers, and that is why the film succeeds in spite of itself. We may not care about the striptease competition and we may not even believe in it, but still the movie has a certain fascination.

A movie camera is an extraordinary device. Point it at something, and it will record what it sees. In the case of *Stripper,* it sees Janette Boyd, a plucky woman in her thirties, who has been a Vegas dancer for years. She saved her money, made wise investments, planned the future for herself and her young daughter, and then was betrayed by a man who took all of her money and ran. We see Kimberly Holcomb, a young woman who soberly discusses her attraction to sadomasochism, and then plans a stage act in which she will use fake blood. We even see her in a supply shop, looking for the right shade of blood.

We learn that most of the good strip clubs in North America are in Canada and that they're booked out of Vancouver. In the movie's most interesting passage, we see a couple of young strippers setting out from Vancouver in a convertible, heading for the vast Northwest. And we see the simple, almost humble bar where they take off their clothes for a week while providing the regulars with what they're starving for.

To our surprise, we find that the regulars—lonely working men—are starving, not for sex, but for conversation, and for the sweetness and the cheerfulness that these young women bring into their lives. We get the impression that if anyone in the bar tried to lay a hand on the girls, the others would throw him out.

I would have preferred an entire film made in the same vein, following the strippers from club to club, finding the parallels between their lives and the lives of the early vaudevillians. Instead, the movie uses all of these scenes as setups, to establish the competitors who will be entering the contest in Vegas.

There are even a few villains, such as Jamal Rofeh, owner of the Body Shop in Los Angeles, who doesn't want to give one of his strippers time off so she can enter the contest. As he tells the girl she can't go, something gnaws at us, and we realize that the scene is obviously staged. (What strip club manager would invite cameras into his office and then forget they were there?)

The contest itself is sort of pathetic. There is some interest in the stagecraft, especially after Boyd hires a metalworker to build a scaffold for her act, in which she impersonates a woman from space. And there is some drama in Holcomb's stage blood. But the judges are never clearly identified, the audience is usually invisible, and the alleged public-address announcer keeps saying phony lines over the loud speaker. (At one point, he announces to everyone, "This is the day before the big event," something the movie audience needs to know but which the actual audience would hardly need to be told.)

The problem with *Stripper* is that stripping is not a competitive sport, but an intensely private one, and there can be no standards by which a stripper can be judged—at least no standards except the private ones that few judges would wish to discuss. The film's framework is phony. But some of the women in this film are manifestly real—complicated and interesting—and they make the movie worth seeing.

The Stuff ★ ½
R, 93 m., 1985

Michael Moriarty (David), Andrea Marcovicci (Nicole), Garrett Morris (Chocolate Chip Charlie), Paul Sorvino (Colonel Spears), Scott Bloom (Jason), Danny Aiello (Vickers).

Directed by Larry Cohen and produced by Paul Kurta. Screenplay by Cohen.

The Stuff is a wildly ambitious movie that fails because it forgets to attend to its bottom line. Before you can make a clever, funny, satirical horror film, first you have to make a horror film. The groundwork in *The Stuff* is so unconvincing that it sabotages all of the good things in the film, including a deadpan performance by Michael Moriarty.

The movie's premise: Some kind of gooey white stuff comes bubbling out of the ground near a petroleum refinery in Alaska. A workman sticks a little of it into his mouth, and, hey, the stuff tastes good. Before long it's in pink and purple containers on the shelves of every grocery store in the country. Seems like people can't get enough of it. They eat it morning, noon, and night. It takes over their whole diet. It's just too damn *good*.

Larry Cohen, the writer and director of *The Stuff*, takes this premise as a springboard for satirical shots at TV commercials, marketing, industrial espionage, and nutrition. One of the many messages in the movie seems to be: Since we don't care about food additives that will kill us eventually, why should we care about a food that doesn't prolong the misery? (Without revealing too much about *The Stuff*, I can say it does for this movie what pods did for *Invasion of the Body Snatchers*.)

Since his first film, *It's Alive* (1976), Cohen has specialized in quasi-realistic horror films. In other words, the basic premise is off the wall, but it's surrounded by three-dimensional characters in plausible situations. That was the case with *Q* (1983), his film about the prehistoric lizard that nested on top of the Chrysler Building, and it's the case this time. Moriarty, a good New York actor, is the star of both films, and in *The Stuff* he plays a low-key good ol' boy named Mo ("My friends call me Mo, because no matter how much I get, I always want mo'"). He's hired by a food company that wants to discover the Stuff's secret, and eventually he stumbles across a whole sci-fi scenario in which people are being converted into Stuffies.

As a basic plot, this never quite works. The Stuff isn't represented in a dramatic way (it looks like the Redi-Whip That Ate the World), and there are distracting glitches like the scene where the kid is trapped inside the tank truck, and we see The Stuff coming after him even though there's no plausible light source. The movie falls completely apart at the end, when Paul Sorvino shows up as a right-wing nut with a private army; he seems left over from a "Saturday Night Live" sketch about the John Birch Society.

The Stuff has moments when it comes alive because of the ingenuity of the actors and Cohen's willingness to have fun with his material. But the story doesn't work and *The Stuff* isn't as interesting as, say, flying lizards; what we have here are a lot of nice touches in search of a movie.

The Stunt Man ★ ★
R, 129 m., 1980

Peter O'Toole (Eli Cross), Steve Railsback (Cameron), Barbara Hershey (Nina Franklin), Allen Goorwitz (Sam), Alex Rocco (Jake), Sharon Farrell (Denise), Adam Roarke (Bailey), Philip Bruns (Ace). Directed and produced by Richard Rush. Screenplay by Lawrence B. Marcus and Rush.

Richard Rush's *The Stunt Man* is like one of those sets of Chinese boxes, each one with another box inside, growing smaller and smaller until finally there is nothing left at all. I don't mean that as a criticism; the film is intended to be seen in that way, as a cinematic puzzle in which there are no answers and the only question is that old standby—what is reality? The movie takes place on the set of a movie, a World War I flying daredevils-type picture of the sort that hasn't been made since *The Blue Max*. Peter O'Toole plays the director of the film-within-the-film, supplying a heavily mannered performance that somehow succeeds in winning us over with its very unlikeliness. He's so very arch and fey that we realize no one like this could really exist—except, possibly, in real life.

This movie set is a chamber of horrors that already has claimed one victim, a stunt man drowned when his car crashed off a bridge. Was his death an accident? Or is O'Toole a maniac who arranged it? Who knows? The movie deliberately teases us with the pos-

sibilities. And then the hero (Steve Railsback) stumbles into the picture and, before long, onto the picture. Railsback is wanted by the cops. He has to hide out. O'Toole discovers his secret and offers him a job, replacing the missing stunt man. Railsback has little choice but to accept, and before long, blackmailed by O'Toole, he's doing the most difficult stunts himself. The only problem is that some of the stunts seem a little too real. Railsback begins to suspect that O'Toole really wants to kill him, either in the service of cinematic art or for some sadistic private purpose. And that is essentially the situation the film repeats, over and over, scene after scene, all the way to the end.

That's what bothered me. I caught on right away (it didn't take much deep thought) that the method of the movie was to deceive and mislead me. Because the ability to do that is completely within the director's ability—because I can know only what he chooses to tell me—I found the movie's approach more frustrating than challenging. *The Stunt Man* is like magic tricks done by a magician in a movie: It doesn't matter how well they're done, or even if they're really done, because cinematic special effects make it all trickery, anyway.

There's a great deal in the film that I admire: that weird O'Toole performance, Railsback's pluckiness not only as a character but also as an actor put through incredible trials, and the movie's stunts themselves. But there were times when I felt cheated. Some of the stunts are staged so that they're not only deceiving to Railsback, as intended, but plainly impossible. And I never understood why O'Toole is lifted in a director's crane even when he wasn't working—and why his offscreen activities were lit like a movie.

The stunts were also sneaky. At one moment in particular, Railsback's on a tower that's blown up in flames. We think there's no way he could have escaped alive—and the movie merely cuts to another shot of him, without explaining his escape. A film that depends on deceiving us has got to play by its own rules. If we are going to be deceived in general, fine, but then we can't be cheated on particulars.

Sudden Impact ★ ★ ★
R, 117 m., 1983

Clint Eastwood (Harry Callahan), Sondra Locke (Jennifer Spencer), Pat Hingle (Chief Jannings), Bradford Dillman (Captain Briggs). Directed and produced by Clint Eastwood. Screenplay by Joseph C. Stinson.

Most of what you hear about pop art and pop culture is pure hype. But there comes a moment about halfway through *Sudden Impact*, a Dirty Harry movie, when you realize that Harry has achieved some kind of legitimate pop status, as the purest distillation in the movies of the spirit of vengeance. To all those cowboy movies we saw in our youth, all those TV westerns and cop dramas and war movies, Dirty Harry has brought a great simplification: A big man, a big gun, a bad guy, and instant justice.

We learned early to cheer when John Wayne shot the bad guys. We cheered when the cavalry turned up, or the Yanks, or the SWAT team. What Eastwood's Dirty Harry movies do is very simple. They reduce the screen time between those cheers to the absolute minimum. *Sudden Impact* is a Dirty Harry movie with only the good parts left in. All the slow stuff, such as character, motivation, atmosphere, and plot, has been pared to exactly the minimum necessary to hold together the violence. This movie has been edited with the economy of a thirty-second commercial. As a result, it's a great audience picture. It's not plausible, it doesn't make much sense, it has a cardboard villain and, for that matter, a hero who exists more as a set of functions (grin, fight, chase, kill) than as a human being. But none of those are valid objections. *Sudden Impact* is more like a music video; it consists only of setups and payoffs, its big scenes are self-contained, it's filled with kinetic energy, and it has a short attention span. That last is very important, because if anyone were really keeping track of what Callahan does in this movie, Harry would be removed from the streets after his third or fourth killing. Dirty Harry movies are like Roadrunner cartoons; the moment a body is dead, it is forgotten, and nobody stands around to dispose of the corpses.

The movie's basically a revenge tragedy. A young woman (Sondra Locke) and her sister are sexually attacked at a carnival by a group of quasi-human bullies. The sister goes nuts, and Locke vows vengeance. One by one, she tracks down the rapists, and murders them by shooting them in the genitals and forehead. Dirty Harry gets assigned to the case, and the rest is a series of violent confrontations. Occasionally there's comic relief, in the form of Harry's meetings with his superiors, and his grim-jawed putdowns of anyone who crosses his path. ("Suck fish heads," he helpfully advises one man.)

If the movie has a weakness, it's the plot. Because I'm not sure the plot is relevant to the success of the film, I'm not sure that's a weakness. The whole business of Locke's revenge is so mechanically established and carried out that it's automatic, and because she has a "good" motive for her murders, she doesn't make an interesting villain. If Eastwood could create a villain as single-minded, violent, economically chiseled, and unremittingly efficient as Dirty Harry Callahan, then we'd be onto something.

Summer of '42 ★ ★ ½
R, 103 m., 1971

Jennifer O'Neill (Dorothy), Gary Grimes (Larmie), Jerry Houser (Oscy), Oliver Conant (Benjie). Directed by Robert Mulligan and produced by Richard A. Roth. Screenplay by Herman Raucher.

Word comes to the woman that her husband has been killed in action, and almost wordlessly she takes the adolescent boy to her bed that very same night. The next day she is gone, leaving behind a note in which she gently declines to comment on the meaning of their experience—suggesting that perhaps, with time, it will take on an appropriate meaning of its own for the boy.

The problem is that it doesn't. Robert Mulligan's *Summer of '42* is constructed to suggest that during that summer an event happened after which the boy was never the same. But we have to be content with an adult narrator who tells us this about himself; we never do learn how the boy, as a boy, put it together for himself. The fault may lie in the movie's obsession with nostalgia. The movie isn't set up to tell a story about a boy who was young in the summer of 1942; it insists on presenting itself, instead, as an adult memory of that long-ago summer. We don't learn very much about the boy because the movie's adult point of view refuses to come to terms with him. Nostalgia is used as a distancing device—to keep us safely insulated from the boy's immediate grief, love, and passion. *Summer of '42* seems to be suggesting, between its frames, that since all these things happened long ago and far away, in a world of meat rationing and old Unguentine ads and black Hudsons with running boards and theories about the care and use of rubbers, that the boy's experience is somehow less intensely human.

The movie fairly drips with what's supposed to pass for taste and restraint; the love scene itself, for example, is filmed in a stubbornly minor key (as if, here again, Mulligan was trying to turn ice into slush, or an immediately felt human experience into a sort of vague and gentle memory). But in the scenes that produce the most laughs—the hero's embarrassment in the drugstore, or his friend's sexual initiation on the beach, or their double date at the movies—*Summer of '42* isn't restrained at all.

That drugstore scene, for example. Second City has had at least two versions of the sketch where an adolescent tries to whisper his order for Trojans to a loud, unsympathetic druggist. This will do as comedy revue material; but *Summer of '42* handles the material on exactly the same level, breaking step with the movie's cadence to get some easy laughs. Same with the double-date scene, which is crude in comparison with Frank Perry's similar scene in *Last Summer.*

What we're left with are some beautifully produced and photographed notes toward a movie. Mulligan has succeeded in convincing us that his movie remembers and understands the wartime summer of 1942. He is very good, too, at trying to convince us that adolescence was somehow more innocent then. But anyone who has ever been an adolescent—and every adult has—will remember that it is hardly ever easy-going, in 1942 or any other year, and that although it may seem innocent when we remember it nostalgically, at the time it felt like an agonizingly prolonged fall from grace.

Sunday Bloody Sunday ★ ★ ★ ★
R, 110 m., 1971

Glenda Jackson (Alex Greville), Peter Finch (Dr. Daniel Hirsh), Murray Head (Bob Elkin), Peggy Ashcroft (Mrs. Greville), Tony Britton (Businessman), Maureice Denham (Mr. Greville). Directed by John Schlesinger and produced by Joseph Janni. Screenplay by Penelope Gilliatt.

The official East Coast line on John Schlesinger's *Sunday Bloody Sunday* was that it is civilized. That judgment was enlisted to carry the critical defense of the movie; and, indeed, how can the decent critic be against a civilized movie about civilized people? My notion, all the same, is that *Sunday Bloody Sunday* is about people who suffer from psychic amputation, not civility, and that this film is not an affirmation but a tragedy.

The story involves three people in a rather novel love triangle: A London doctor in his forties, a divorced woman in her thirties, and the young man they are both in love with. The doctor and the woman know about each other (the young man makes no attempt to keep secrets) but don't seem particularly concerned; they have both made an accommodation in order to have some love instead of none at all.

The screenplay by Penelope Gilliatt takes us through eight or nine days in their lives, while the young man prepares to leave for New York. Both of his lovers will miss him—and he will miss *them*, after his fashion—but he has decided to go, and between them, they don't have enough pull on him to make him want to stay. So the two love affairs approach their ends, while the lovers go about a melancholy daily existence in London.

Both the doctor and the woman are involved in helping people, he by a kind and intelligent approach to his patients, she through working in an employment agency. The boy, on the other hand, seems exclusively preoccupied with the commercial prospects in America for his sculpture (he does things with glass tubes, liquids, and electricity). He isn't concerned with whether his stuff is any good, but whether it will sell to Americans. He doesn't seem to feel very deeply about anything, in fact. He is kind enough and open enough, but there is no dimension to him, as there is to his lovers.

It is with the two older characters that we get to the core of the movie. In a world where everyone loses eventually, they are still survivors. They survive by accommodating themselves to life as it must be lived. The doctor, for example, is not at all personally disturbed by his homosexuality, and yet he doesn't reveal it to his close-knit Jewish family; maintaining relations-as-usual with them is another way for him to survive. The woman tells us late in the film, "Some people believe something is better than nothing, but I'm beginning to believe that nothing can be better than something." Well, maybe so, but we get to know her well enough to suspect that she will settle for something, not nothing, again the next time.

The glory of *Sunday Bloody Sunday* is supposed to be the intelligent, sophisticated—civilized!—way in which these two people gracefully accept the loss of a love they had shared. Well, they *are* graceful as hell about it, and there is a positive glut of being philosophical about the inevitable. But that didn't make me feel better for them, or about them, the way it was supposed to; I felt pity for them. I insist that they would *not* have been so bloody civilized if either one had felt really deeply about the boy. The fact that they were willing to share him is perhaps a clue: They shared him not because they were willing to settle for half, but because they were afraid to try for all. The three-sided arrangement was, in part, a guarantee that no one would get in so deep that being "civilized" wouldn't be protection enough against hurt.

The acting is flawless. The late Peter Finch is the doctor, Glenda Jackson the woman, and Murray Head the young man. They are good to begin with and then just right for Gilliatt's screenplay and Schlesinger's direction. They are set down in a very real and sad London (seen mostly in cold twilights), and surrounded by supporting actors who resonate in a way that fills in all the dimensions of the characters. I think *Sunday Bloody Sunday* is a masterpiece, but I don't think it's about what everybody else seems to think it's about. This is not a movie about the loss of love, but about its absence.

Supergirl ★ ★
PG, 105 m., 1984

Helen Slater (Supergirl), Faye Dunaway (Selena), Peter O'Toole (Zaltar), Mia Farrow (Alura), Brenda Vaccaro (Bianca), Peter Cook (Nigel), Simon Ward (Zor-El). Directed by Jeannot Szwarc and produced by Timothy Burrill. Screenplay by David Odell.

The best way to approach *Supergirl* is through a statement by Clint Eastwood, who once observed that his spaghetti Westerns worked only because he played them completely seriously. In the famous scene where he shoots three guys with one bullet, if the faintest wisp of a smile had creased his lips, the whole power of the scene would have been destroyed. Only by playing it straight did he make the scene work—and it worked, incidentally, as comedy.

Supergirl doesn't know that. When it goes for campy laughs, it falls flat on its face. That also was a tendency the three Superman movies had to fight. The first two Supermans were the best, because they took the essentially silly legend of Superman and played it quasi-seriously. With the second sequel, the stories got goofier, with Richard Pryor going for slapstick. But remember the opening moments of *Superman*, with Marlon Brando as Jor-El, lending an expensive but authentic solemnity to the film? And then the clean-cut Midwestern images of Superman's childhood, with Glenn Ford no less, as his father? By playing the story straight and simple, and allowing the laughs to flow naturally out of the material (as when Clark Kent did a double-take at one of those new-style phone booths), the movie became a popular triumph.

If *Supergirl* had only taken the same approach, it might have been a pretty good movie. But it trivializes itself with an almost suicidal glee. That's a shame, because there's a place, I think, for a female superhero, and Helen Slater, who plays Supergirl, has the kind of freshness, good health, high spirits, and pluck that would be just right for the character. As it is, Slater is the best thing in the film. She shares with Christopher Reeve the ability to wear a funny costume and not look ridiculous. We look at her and we see Supergirl. We look around her and we see the results of a gag-writer's convention.

The movie begins with the usual legend-building. We learn that after the planet Krypton was destroyed, little Superman was not the only survivor. While his rocket sped him toward Earth, another fragment of Krypton was hurtled into inner space, where Zaltar (Peter O'Toole), one of the survivors, created a utopian society. One day, alas, while Supergirl was out playing, she toyed with one of the new world's energy sources, and was transported to Earth, along with the source itself. That creates a giant struggle for possession of the source, which could give its owner the usual dividend, control of the Earth. And it's about here that the movie starts to break down, with the introduction of Faye Dunaway as a mysterious fortune-teller, and the even less-fortunate introduction of Brenda Vaccaro as her sidekick. The relationship between the two women reminds me of *Mommie Dearest* in search of daughters.

The appearance of *Supergirl*, so soon after *Superman III*, is an indication that the producers of the Superman movies have forgotten, if they ever consciously knew it, the real secret of the movies. We do not go to Superman and Supergirl movies to laugh condescendingly at the characters (which is what the writers, directors, and even some of the actors have started to do). We go to recapture some of the lost innocence of the whole notion of superheroes. The gift of Christopher Reeve, in his best scenes and when the filmmakers allow it, is to play Superman without laughing, to take him seriously so that we can have some innocent escapist fun. Helen Slater has the same gift, but is given even less chance to exercise it in *Supergirl*, and the result is an unhappy, unfunny, unexciting movie. Why even go to the trouble of making a movie that feels like it's laughing at itself?

Superman ★ ★ ★ ★
PG, 144 m., 1978

Christopher Reeve (Superman/Clark Kent), Marlon Brando (Jor-El), Gene Hackman (Lex Luthor), Margot Kidder (Lois Lane), Ned Beatty (Otis), Jackie Cooper (Perry White), Glenn Ford (Jonathan Kent), Trevor Howard (First Elder), Valerie Perrine (Miss Teschmacher). Directed by Richard Donner and produced by Pierre Spengler. Screenplay by Mario Puzo, David and Leslie Newman, and Robert Benton.

Superman is a pure delight, a wondrous combination of all the old-fashioned things we never really get tired of: adventure and romance, heroes and villains, earthshaking special effects, and—you know what else? Wit. That surprised me more than anything: That this big budget epic, which was half a decade making its way to the screen, would turn out to have an intelligent sense of humor about itself.

The wit, to be sure, is a little slow in revealing itself. The film's opening scenes combine great intergalactic special effects with ponderous acting and dialogue—most of it from Marlon Brando, who, as Superman's father, sends the kid to Earth in a spaceship that barely survives the destruction of the planet Krypton. Brando was allegedly paid $3 million for his role, or, judging by his dialogue, $500,000 a cliché. After Superbaby survives his space flight and lands in a Midwestern wheat field, however, the movie gets down to earth, too. And it has the surprising ability to have *fun* with its special effects. That's surprising because special effects on this vast scale (falling airliners, derailing passenger trains, subterranean dungeons, cracks in the earth, volcanic eruptions, dams bursting) are so expensive and difficult that it takes a special kind of courage to kid them a little—instead of regarding them with awe, as in the witless *Earthquake*.

The audience finds itself pleasantly surprised, and taken a little off guard; the movie's tremendously exciting in a comic book sort of way (kids will go ape for it), but at the same time it has a sly sophistication, a kidding insight into the material, that makes it, amazingly, a refreshingly offbeat comedy.

Most of the humor centers, of course, around one of the central icons of American popular culture, Superman (who, and I quote from our common memory of hundreds of comic books and radio and TV shows, in his dual identity as Clark Kent is a mild-mannered reporter for the *Daily Planet*). The producers held a worldwide talent search for an actor to play Superman, and although "talent searches" are usually

100 percent horsefeathers, this time, for once, they actually found the right guy.

He is Christopher Reeve. He *looks* like the Superman in the comic books (a fate I would not wish on anybody), but he's also an engaging actor, open and funny in his big love scene with Lois Lane, and then correctly awesome in his showdown with the arch-villain Lex Luthor. Reeve sells the role; wrong casting here would have sunk everything.

And there would have been a lot to sink. *Superman* may have been expensive, all right, but the money's there on the screen. The screenplay was obviously written without the slightest concern for how much it might cost. After Clark Kent goes to work for the *Daily Planet* (and we meet old favorites Perry White, Lois Lane, and Jimmy Olsen), there's a nonstop series of disasters just for openers: Poor Lois finds herself dangling from one seatbelt after her helicopter crashes high atop the Daily Planet Building; Air Force One is struck by lightning and loses an engine; a thief climbs up a building using suction cups, and so on. Superman resolves his emergencies with, well, tact and good manners. He's modest about his abilities. Snaps a salute to the president. Says he's for "truth, justice, and the American Way." And, of course, falls in love with Lois Lane.

She's played by Margot Kidder, and their relationship is subtly, funnily wicked. She lives in a typical girl reporter's apartment (you know, a penthouse high atop a Metropolis skyscraper), and Superman zooms down to offer an exclusive interview and a free flight over Metropolis. Supposing *you're* a girl reporter, and Superman turns up. What would you ask him? So does she.

Meanwhile, the evil Lex Luthor (Gene Hackman) is planning an apocalyptic scheme to destroy the entire West Coast, plus Hackensack, New Jersey. He knows Superman's weak point: the deadly substance Kryptonite. He also knows that Superman cannot see through lead (Lois Lane, alas, forgets). Luthor lives in a subterranean pad that's a comic inspiration: A half-flooded, subterranean train station. Superman drills through the earth for a visit.

But enough of the plot. The movie works so well because of its wit and its special effects. A word more about each. The movie begins with the tremendous advantage that almost everyone in the audience knows the Superman saga from youth. There aren't a lot of explanations needed; that's brilliantly demonstrated in the first scene where Superman tries to change in a phone booth. Christopher Reeve can be allowed to smile, to permit himself a double entendre, to kid himself.

And then the special effects. They're as good in their way as any you've seen, and they come thick and fast. When the screenplay calls for Luthor to create an earthquake and for Superman to try to stop it, the movie doesn't give us a falling bridge or two, it gives us the San Andreas Fault cracking open. No half measures for Superman. The movie is, in fact, a triumph of imagination over both the difficulties of technology and the inhibitions of money. *Superman* wasn't easy to bring to the screen, but the film-makers kept at it until they had it right.

Superman II ★ ★ ★ ★
PG, 127 m., 1981

Christopher Reeve (Superman/Clark Kent), Gene Hackman (Lex Luthor), Ned Beatty (Otis), Margot Kidder (Lois Lane), Jackie Cooper (Perry White), Sarah Douglas (Ursa), Jack O'Halloran (Non), Valerie Perrine (Eve). Directed by Richard Lester and produced by Alexander and Ilya Salkind and Pierre Spengler. Screenplay by Mario Puzo, David Newman, and Leslie Newman.

I thought the original *Superman* was terrific entertainment—and so I was a little startled to discover that I liked *Superman II* even more. Perhaps the secret of the sequel is that it has more faith in Superman. Before the original *Superman* was released in 1978, the producers knew he could carry a speeding locomotive, all right—but could he carry a movie? They weren't sure, and since they were investing millions of dollars in the project, they didn't want to rest a whole movie on the broad shoulders of their unknown star, Christopher Reeve. So they began *Superman* ponderously, on the planet Krypton, with the presence of Marlon Brando as a sort of totem to convince audiences that this movie was big league. They told us of Superman's origins with a solemnity more befitting a god. They were very serious and very symbolic, and it wasn't until Superman came to Earth that the movie really caught fire. *Then*, half an hour or more into its length, it started giving us what we came for: Superman flying around with his red cape, saving mankind.

Superman II begins in midstream, and never looks back (aside from a brief recap of the first movie). In many ways, it's a repeat of the last ninety minutes of the first film. It has the same key characters, including arch-villain Lex Luthor. It continues the love story of Lois Lane and Superman, not to mention the strange relationship of Lois and Clark Kent. It features the return of three villains from Krypton, who when last seen were trapped in a one-dimensional plane of light and cast adrift in space. And it continues those remarkable special effects.

From his earliest days in a comic book, Superman always has been an urban hero. He lived in a universe that was defined by screaming banner headlines and vast symbolic acts, and *Superman II* catches that flavor perfectly with its use of famous landmarks like the Eiffel Tower, the Empire State Building, Niagara Falls, and the Coca-Cola sign in Times Square. He was a pop hero in a pop world, and like Mickey Mouse and the original Coke trademark, he became an instantly recognizable trademark.

That's why the special effects in both *Superman* movies are so crucial. It is a great deal simpler to show a rocket ship against the backdrop of outer space than to show Kryptonian villains hurling a city bus through the air in midtown Manhattan. But the feeling of actuality makes Superman's exploits more fun. It brings the fantastic into our everyday lives; it delights in showing us the reaction of the man on the street to Superman's latest stunt. In the movie, as in the comic book, ordinary citizens seems to spend their days glued to the sidewalk, gazing skyward, and shouting things like "Superman is dead!" or "Superman has saved the world!"

In *Superman II* he saves large portions of the world, all right, but what he preserves most of all is the element of humanity within him. The Superman movies made a basic decision to give Superman and his alter ego, Clark Kent, more human feelings than the character originally possessed. So *Superman*

II has a lot of fun developing his odd dual relationship with Lois Lane. At long, long last, Lois and Superman make love in this movie (after champagne, but discreetly off-screen in Superman's ice palace). But Lois and Clark Kent also spend the night together in highly compromised circumstances, in a Niagara Falls honeymoon haven. And the movie has fun with another one of those ultimate tests that Lois was always throwing at Clark to make him admit he was really Superman. Lois bets her life on it this time, hurling herself into the rapids below Niagara Falls. Either Clark can turn into Superman and save her—or she'll drown. And what then? All I can say is, Clark does *not* turn into Superman.

This scene has a lot of humor in it, and the whole film has more smiles and laughs than the first one. Maybe that's because of a change in directors. Richard Donner, who made the first *Superman* film and did a brilliant job of establishing a basic look for the series, was followed this time by Richard Lester *(A Hard Day's Night, The Three Musketeers)*, and this is some of Lester's best work. He permits satire to make its way into the film more easily. He has a lot of fun with Gene Hackman, as the still-scheming, thin-skinned, egomaniacal Lex Luthor. And he draws out Christopher Reeve, whose performance in the title role is sly, knowing, and yet still appropriately square. This movie's most intriguing insight is that Superman's disguise as Clark Kent isn't a matter of looks as much as of mental attitude: Clark is disguised not by his glasses but by his ordinariness. Beneath his meek exterior, of course, is concealed a superhero. And, the movie subtly hints, isn't that the case with us all?

Superman III ★ ★ ½
PG, 125 m., 1983

Christopher Reeve (Superman/Clark Kent), Richard Pryor (Gus Gorman), Annette O'Toole (Lana Lang), Robert Vaughn (Ross Webster). Directed by Richard Lester and produced by Alexander Salkind. Screenplay by David and Leslie Newman.

Superman III is the kind of movie I feared the original *Superman* would be. It's a cinematic comic book, shallow, silly, filled with stunts and action, without much human interest. What's amazing is that the first two Superman movies avoided that description, creating a fantasy with a certain charm. They could have been manipulative special effects movies, but they were a great deal more. With this third one, maybe they've finally run out of inspiration.

The big news about *Superman III* is, of course, the presence of Richard Pryor in the cast. But Pryor isn't used very well here. He never really emerges as a person we care about. His character and the whole movie seem assembled out of prefabricated pieces. The first two films were too, in a way, but real care was taken with the dialogue, and we could occasionally halfway believe that real people had gotten themselves into this world of fantasy. Not this time. *Superman III* drops most of the threads of the first two movies—including Lois Lane's increasingly complex love affair with Clark Kent and Superman—and goes for the action. There's no real sense of what Superman, or Clark, ever really feels. The running gag about the hero's double identity isn't really exploited this time. The sheer amazingness of Superman isn't explored; the movie and the people in it take this incredible creature for granted. After the bird and the plane, it's "Superman" when it should be SUPERMAN!

The plot involves the usual scheme to control the Earth. The villain this time is Robert Vaughn, as a mad billionaire who wants to use satellites to control the Earth's crops and become even richer. He directs his satellites and weapons systems by computer, and that's how he hooks up with Pryor, as a brilliant, but befuddled, computer programmer. Superman, meanwhile, has a couple of things on his mind. After Lois Lane leaves to go on vacation at the beginning of the movie (in a particularly awkward scene), Clark goes home to his Smallville High School reunion, and has a love affair with Lana Lang (Annette O'Toole). It's sweet, but it's not half as interesting as the Ice Castle footage with Lois Lane in *Superman II*. Then Superman gets zapped with some ersatz Kryptonite and turns into a meanie, which is good for some laughs (as a practical joke, he straightens the Leaning Tower of Pisa).

All of this is sort of fun, and the special effects are sometimes very good, but there's no real sense of wonder in this film—no moments like the scene in *Superman* where California threatened to fall into the sea and Superman turned back time to save humanity. After that, who cares about Robert Vaughn's satellites? Or Richard Pryor's dilemma? Pryor can be a wicked, anarchic comic actor, and that presence would have been welcome here. Instead, like the rest of *Superman III*, he's kind of innocuous.

The Sure Thing ★ ★ ★ ½
PG-13, 94 m., 1985

John Cusack (Walter Gibson), Daphne Zuniga (Alison Bradbury), Anthony Edwards (Lance), Boyd Gaines (Jason), Tim Robbins (Gary Cooper), Lisa Jane Persky (Mary Ann Webster), Vivica Lindfors (Professor), Nicolette Sheridan (Sure Thing). Directed by Rob Reiner and produced by Roger Birnbaum. Screenplay by Steven Bloom and Jonathan Roberts.

The love story is one of Hollywood's missing genres. The movie industry seems better at teen-age movies like *Porky's*, with its sleazy shower scenes, than with screenplays that involve any sort of thought about the love lives of its characters. That's why *The Sure Thing* is a small miracle. Although the hero of this movie is promised by his buddy that he'll be fixed up with a "guaranteed sure thing," the film is not about the sure thing but about how this kid falls genuinely and touchingly into love.

The movie's love story begins in an Eastern college classroom. Walter Gibson (John Cusack) walks into his English class and falls immediately into love with Alison Bradbury (Daphne Zuniga), who is smart and good-looking and not one of your brainless movie broads. He asks her out, but succeeds, of course, in acting like a total nerd, and she invites him to get out of her life. End of act one. In act two, Walter plans to spend his Christmas vacation in Los Angeles, where his buddy says the Sure Thing is eagerly awaiting his arrival. Alison also plans to go to L.A., to visit her fiancé, who is studying to be a boring middle-class vegetable. They both sign up for rides, and, of course, they both wind up in the back seat of the same car. At first they don't talk. They they start to fight. Then they are ditched at the side of the road and have to hitchhike to L.A. together.

I know this is an obvious movie ploy. I know, in fact, that what will happen next is completely predictable: They'll fight, they'll share experiences, they'll suffer together, and eventually they'll fall in love. I know all of these things, and yet I don't care. I don't care because love is always a cliché anyway, and the only thing that makes it endlessly fascinating is that the players are always changing. These two particular characters, Walter and Alison, played by these two gifted young actors, Cusack and Zuniga, make *The Sure Thing* into a special love story.

One of the unique things about the movie is that the characters show a normal shyness about sex. Most movie teen-agers seem to be valedictorians from the Masters & Johnson Institute. They're born knowing more about sex than Rhett Butler would have been able to teach Scarlett O'Hara. They are also, of course, not shy, not insecure, not modest, and occasionally not human. Walter and Alison are closer to real teen-agers, with real doubts and hesitations and uncertainties. The other surprising thing about the film is that it successfully avoids an obligatory sex scene with the Sure Thing (Nicollette Sheridan, in a thankless role). This film is so revolutionary, it believes sex should be accompanied by respect and love! By the end of the movie, when Walter and Alison finally do kiss, it means something. It means more, in fact, than any movie kiss in a long time, because it takes place between two people we've gotten to know and who have gotten to know each other.

The Survivors ★ ½
R, 102 m., 1983

Walter Matthau (Sonny Paluso), Robin Williams (Donald Quinelle), Jerry Reed (Jack Locke), James Wainwright (Wes Huntley). Directed by Michael Ritchie and produced by William Sackheim. Screenplay by Michael Leeson.

Survivalists are very cautious people who have secret hideaways somewhere in the woods, which they've stocked with food, weapons, ammunition, and survival gear. In case of a nuclear attack, they alert each other by CB radio and light out for the trees. *The*

Survivors, which attempts to have fun with their prudence, is an aimless, self-indulgent, confusing comedy that never comes to grips with its material. And it allows Robin Williams to run wild, destroying any marginal credibility the story might have had.

It's a mess. One of the reasons it's a mess is that it doesn't know whether to be a human comedy or a slapstick, satirical comedy. The first approach would have involved creating plausible characters and plugging them into a comic situation. The second approach allows anything to be funny in any way possible. *The Survivors* goes for both approaches simultaneously, which is confusing. For example, after a slapstick opening in which Williams is fired by a trained parrot, there's a scene of social satire set in an unemployment office. Even within scenes, the styles of the actors suggest they think they're in different movies. Walter Matthau manfully acts as if he's in a plausible movie, while Williams mugs, improvises, and randomly alters his accent. See the problem? If it's a "real" world, then Matthau should observe that Williams isn't playing with a full deck. If it's an anarchic satire, then the joke's on Matthau, who does not seem to realize it.

The story involves two newly unemployed men. Williams has been fired by the parrot and Matthau's gas station has been blown up. After they get discouraged by the lines at the unemployment office, they happen to go to the same diner, which is stuck up by a fierce criminal (Jerry Reed). They snatch off his ski mask and see him, and so Reed believes he has to kill these two witnesses. What happens next is very long and involved. Williams signs up for a wilderness survival training course. He hopes to become tough enough to protect himself. Reed and Matthau both find themselves at the same isolated survivalist area. The head survivalist is a reactionary paramilitary nut who believes American society is doomed to collapse. And so on.

This material is the stuff of promising satire, but the movie's director, Michael Ritchie, goes nowhere with it. His parts don't seem to fit together. One moment we'll be getting a heartfelt talk, and the next moment there's a wilderness shoot-out straight out of *The Road Runner*. The story gets so confused that the movie can't even account for why its characters happen to be in the same place at the same time; in desperation, it gives us a scene where Williams actually calls Reed and tells him where he can be found. Uh-huh.

The Survivors wouldn't be such a disappointment if it didn't employ such talented people, and if it weren't directed by Michael Ritchie, whose gift for satirizing American institutions has given us good movies like *Smile*, *The Bad News Bears*, *The Candidate*, and *Semi-Tough*. This time he seems so fast off the starting line he left his screenplay behind.

Swamp Thing ★ ★ ★
R, 102 m., 1982

Louis Jourdan (Arcane), Adrienne Barbeau (Alice), Ray Wise (Dr. Holland), Dick Durock (Swamp Thing), David Hess (Ferret), Nicholas Worth (Brung). Directed by Wes Craven and produced by Benjamin Melniker and Michael Uslan. Screenplay by Craven.

Swamp Thing had already won my heart *before* its moment of greatness, but when that moment came, I knew I'd discovered another one of those movies that fall somewhere between buried treasures and guilty pleasures. The moment comes after Dr. Alec Holland, brilliant scientist, is attacked by thugs, is splashed with his own secret formula, catches on fire, leaps into the swamp, and turns into Swamp Thing when the formula interacts with his body and the vegetation in the swamp. Crawling back onto dry land, Swamp Thing is not recognized by his former girlfriend, the beautiful Alice Cable (Adrienne Barbeau). But after the thugs fill him with machine gun bullets and hack off his left arm, Alice asks, "Does it hurt?" and Swamp Thing replies, "Only when I laugh."

That was the movie's moment of greatness. There are others that come close, as when Swamp Thing, dripping with moss and looking like a bug-eyed spinach soufflé, says "There is great beauty in the swamp . . . if you know where to look." And when the evil villain (Louis Jourdan) drinks the secret formula and confidently waits for it to transform him into a powerful genius, he discovers that the formula doesn't so much *change* you, as develop what is already latent

within you. Therefore, once a horse's ass, *always* a horse's ass.

This is one of those movies like *Infra-Man* or *Invasion of the Bee Girls:* an off-the-wall, eccentric, peculiar movie fueled by the demented obsessions of its makers. *Swamp Thing* first saw the light of day, so to speak, as a hero in a celebrated series of DC Comics. The movie version was written and directed by Wes Craven, who made *Last House on the Left,* a movie I persist in admiring even in the face of universal repugnance. Craven also made *The Hills Have Eyes,* which even I found decadent, and the made-for-NBC movie *Stranger in Our House,* with Linda Blair. This time, with *Swamp Thing,* he betrays a certain gentleness and poetry along with the gore; in fact, this movie is a lot less violent than many others in the same genre. Craven's inspiration seems to come from James Whale's classic *Bride of Frankenstein* (1935), and he pays tribute in scenes where his swamp monster sniffs a flower, admires a young girl's beauty from afar, and looks sadly at a photograph in a locket. *Swamp Thing* doesn't stop there; it also contains an exact visual quote from Russ Meyer's *Lorna,* and a scene in which the jailer in a dungeon cheerfully quotes the title of a Werner Herzog film: "It's every man for himself, and God against all!"

Will you like this film? Yes, probably, if you like monster and horror movies. The movie occupies familiar ground, but it has a freshness and winsome humor to fit it, and Craven moves confidently through the three related genres he's stealing from (monster movies, mad scientist movies and transformation movies—in which people turn into strange beings). There's beauty in this movie, if you know where to look for it.

Swann in Love ★ ★ ★
R, 110 m., 1984

Jeremy Irons (Charles Swann), Ornella Muti (Odette de Crecy), Alain Delon (Baron de Charlus), Fanny Ardant (Duchesse de Guermantes), Marie-Christine Barrault (Madame Verdurin). Directed by Volker Schlondorff and produced by Nicole Stephane. Written by Peter Brook, Jean-Claude Carriere, and Marie-Helene Estienne.

All of the reviews I've read of Volker Schlondorff's *Swann in Love* treat it like a classroom assignment. The movie is described as a version of one of the stories that make up *Remembrance of Things Past*, the epic novel by Marcel Proust, and then the exercise becomes almost academic: "Compare and contrast Proust and Schlondorff, with particular attention to the difference between fiction and the film." Imagine instead, that this is not a film based on a novel, but a new film from an original screenplay. It will immediately seem more lively and accessible. Because not one person in a hundred who sees the film will have read Proust, this is a sensible approach; it does away with the nagging feeling that one should really curl up with those twelve volumes before going to the theater.

Schlondorff's *Swann in Love*—as opposed to Proust's—is the story of a pale young man who goes one day to visit a prostitute, and is actually indifferent to her until she stands him up. Then he becomes obsessed. She is not the right woman for him, but her very wrongness becomes fascinating. Because she is vulgar, because she lies, because she toys with his affection, and most particularly because she lets him smell the orchid in her bodice, she becomes the most important person in the world to him, and he throws his life and reputation at her feet. Proper society, of course, disapproves of his affair—and talks of nothing else. In the elegant salons where ladies and gentlemen gather, Swann is not welcome if he brings along his Odette, but because he cannot be happy without her, this is no punishment. In the most humiliating scenes in the movie, he abjectly follows her through the night, knocks on a door he hopes is hers, and stands in her boudoir while she nonchalantly disrobes and dresses for an appointment with another man.

Casting is everything in a film like this. Jeremy Irons is perfect as Charles Swann, pale, deep-eyed, feverish with passion. This was his third movie (after *The French Lieutenant's Woman* and *Betrayal*) in which love seemed necessary to his nature. We can believe his passion. As Odette, Schlondorff has cast Ornella Muti, who has a sort of languorous bemusement that is maddening: We wonder if she is even capable of understanding that the man before her is mad with love and desire, and then we realize, of course,

that her very *inability* to care is what creates her fatal attraction. *Swann in Love* is a stylish, period love story, surrounding its central characters with still other pathetic seekers of perfection (Alain Delon is wonderful as a gloomy homosexual who pursues an idealized form of misery). Yet at the film's end, we've probably learned nothing except that lovers were as silly in 1875 as they are now. Sillier, perhaps; they had more time.

Sweet Dreams ★ ★
PG-13, 111 m., 1985

Jessica Lange (Patsy Cline), Ed Harris (Charlie Dick), Ann Wedgeworth (Hilda). Directed by Karel Reisz and produced by Bernard Schwartz. Screenplay by Robert Getchell.

Before there was Loretta Lynn, there was Patsy Cline. One of the legends of country music is the story of how they met and overcame their professional rivalries and became friends, after Cline was able to remember her own shaky beginnings in show business and recognize in Lynn the kind of frightened, ambitious country kid that she herself had been. That story was told in *Coal Miner's Daughter* (1980), with Sissy Spacek winning an Oscar as a gangly, shy Loretta Lynn. Now it is told again in *Sweet Dreams*, with Jessica Lange as a stubborn, uncertain Patsy Cline.

Both movies are, of course, about much more than the ways in which Lynn and Cline crossed paths. They are life stories, and it is unfortunately true that some lives make better stories than others. Both films were produced by Bernard Schwartz, and it is no wonder he started with Loretta Lynn, the scrawny redhead from Butcher's Hollow, instead of with Patsy Cline, whose life was drab but unsensational until she fell into a strange fascination for a husband who loved her, beat her, and drank too much. Patsy Cline was a wonderful singer, but her life was a bad country song even before it ended in a plane crash.

Sweet Dreams begins with more energy than it is able to sustain. We see Lange, as Patsy, getting jobs singing country songs like a good little girl, her eyes half-closed as if she's trying to remember the lyrics. We meet Ed Harris, as Charlie Dick, a hard-drinking printer who hears her sing and falls in love with her and sweeps her off her feet with his self-confidence and cocky smile. The epiphany in this movie comes early, as they dance together in the empty parking lot of a roadhouse, underneath a neon rainbow.

Charlie turns out to be an engaging, likable guy who never quite gets his footing in the job market. He drinks too much, gets Cline pregnant, allows her to put her career on hold to become an Army wife. He doesn't mind being supported by her, but he doesn't much like the fact that she gets fame and attention in the process. Cline, meanwhile, begins to grow. Her clothes change first, then her hair, and then the way she thinks about herself, until finally she outgrows Charlie. She taunts him, and he hits her, and then the first of a series of tragedies strikes her. Before long she is dead and the movie is over. There isn't the sense of a well-shaped structure in this movie; there's no clear idea of what the filmmakers thought about Patsy Cline, or what thoughts her life is supposed to inspire.

The performances are good, of course; Harris and Lange in the same movie cannot be uninteresting, although often we have the feeling they brought more to the set every morning than the screenplay did. It is probably inevitable that Lange's performance will be compared with Spacek's. They have a curious sort of synchronicity; in 1984 they both made movies about American farms, and now they have both made movies about country singers who were friends. Lange made the better farm movie. Spacek wins the second round. This sort of comparison is silly, of course, but wasn't it also silly to even make *Sweet Dreams*?

Note: Spacek, who began her career as a singer, sang her own vocals in Coal Miner's Daughter. *Lange, who doesn't claim to be a singer, lip-synchs to Cline's records. At least it's a reminder of what a wonderful voice Patsy Cline had.*

Sweet Liberty ★ ★ ½
PG, 107 m., 1986 ✓

Alan Alda (Michael Burgess), Michael Caine (Elliott James), Michelle Pfeiffer (Faith Healy), Bob Hoskins (Stanley Gould), Lise Hilboldt (Gretchen Carlsen), Lillian Gish (Cecelia Burgess), Saul Rubinek (Bo Hodges). Directed by Alan Alda and produced by Martin Bregman. Screenplay by Alda.

Sweet Liberty tells the story of a Hollywood movie company that arrives in a small Southeastern college town to shoot a film about the Revolutionary War. It also tells three or four other stories, and that is the problem: The movie wants to juggle a lot of characters all at once, but it keeps dropping the most interesting ones.

The movie stars Alan Alda as the local history professor who sold his book to the movies. He didn't exactly expect them to turn it into a scholarly documentary, but he is shocked to see it rewritten into a seamy tale of lust, betrayal, intrigue, and violence. He makes a liaison with the screenwriter (Bob Hoskins), who tutors him in cynicism, and together they try to change some of the worst parts.

Meanwhile, the small town itself is turning into a seamy hotbed of lust, betrayal, and intrigue. Alda has been dating another faculty member (Lise Hilboldt), but then he falls instantly in love with the movie's sexy leading lady (Michelle Pfeiffer). That's sort of all right, because Hilboldt has a fling with the leading man (Michael Caine). And there are subplots involving the director, the local extras, and even Alda's ancient mother (portrayed by the legendary Lillian Gish, who, old as the character is, still plays below her age).

These are a lot of story strands to keep straight, and *Sweet Liberty* doesn't always succeed. I was left with the impression there was more material than the time to deal with it, and I especially wanted to see more of that excellent comic actor, Michael Caine. His character, a shameless philanderer with a streak of poetry in his soul, is so promising that it's a shame he's on screen so infrequently.

Alda wrote and directed the movie, as well as starred in it, and he has some nice touches. I liked the scene in which Caine covered up the unexpected arrival of his wife by taking everybody on a rollercoaster ride. And I liked the next scene, too, where they walk drunkenly through the town late at night, talking about those great romantic truths which always seem so elusive in the morning.

Alda's best-written character in the movie is probably Faith Healy, the sexy actress played by Michelle Pfeiffer—and her performance uses some wonderfully subtle touches, as she moves back and forth between her historical character and her distinctly more cynical modern one. It's here that the movie comes closest to its theme, which is (I think) the ways that adults can deceive themselves even while thinking they are perfectly aware of all their motives.

The Lillian Gish character is a distraction. Her obsession with an old boyfriend is intriguing enough, however, that maybe this particular story should have been lifted completely out of *Sweet Liberty* and made into a movie of its own. There's a great scene where Alda and Hilboldt go to visit the old boyfriend, whose wife complains that the old lady has made their life miserable. It's such a strong scene that, paradoxically, it doesn't belong in this movie; its tone is wrong for the other stuff.

Sweet Liberty will probably play better on TV and video than it did at the theatre, where its episodic structure will be more at home, and it won't be so obvious how all of the little set-pieces don't hang together. Like most movies about movies, it is not very realistic. It's unlikely a big-budget historical movie would use such shabby painted backdrops, and completely impossible for the climactic scene (a sabotaged battle) to unfold the way it does. Few movies have had the patience to show moviemaking the way it really is (Truffaut's *Day for Night* came fairly close), but there are times here when the onscreen director (Saul Rubinek) doesn't even seem convinced of his own authenticity.

Swing Shift ★ ★ ★
PG, 100 m., 1984

Goldie Hawn (Kay Walsh), Kurt Russell (Lucky Lockhart), Christine Lahti (Hazel Zanussi), Fred Ward (Biscuits), Ed Harris (Jack Walsh), Charles Napier (Moon). Directed by Jonathan Demme and produced by Jerry Bick. Screenplay by Rob Morton.

Girl gets husband, girl loses husband, girl gets job. That's basically what happens in *Swing Shift*, a sentimental memory of World War II, when men went to war and their wives and sweethearts manned the production lines. This is a slice-of-life movie, the kind that director Jonathan (*Melvin and Howard*) Demme is good at. It's so nostalgic that even the anger at the end—when the war ends and the women lose their jobs—seems bittersweet.

The movie stars Goldie Hawn as Kay Walsh, a sweet, cheerful, uncomplicated young woman who lives with her husband in a bungalow on a little Los Angeles courtyard. The husband is played by Ed Harris (John Glenn in *The Right Stuff*), and he's an earnest, affectionate stereotype who doesn't want his "honey" working while he's serving in the Navy. But the aircraft factories of Southern California need workers, so she goes to work. Besides, she's lonely.

Her husband is off to sea, and the safety-control inspector is an *awfully* nice guy named Lucky (Kurt Russell). For six months, he asks Kay out for a date. She finally accepts. And then, like so many wartime spouses, she has a lot of explaining to do when her sailor returns.

What's unexpected about *Swing Shift*, and what keeps it from being predictable and makes it special, is that the relationship between Kay and Lucky isn't really at the heart of the movie. That position is reserved for the friendship between Kay and Hazel Zanussi (Christine Lahti), a leggy brunette who lives off the same courtyard and is having her own unhappy affair with a nightclub owner (Fred Ward). There's a real sense of palship and camaraderie in their friendship. The movie's last shot isn't the usual freeze-frame of the boy and the girl, but of Kay and Hazel, hugging each other because everything—even Hazel's one-night stand with Lucky—has been forgiven.

Swing Shift isn't heavily plotted. There's no melodramatic crisis. The movie covers more than four years, and is more interested in giving us a memory of how it felt on the home front than in creating some kind of false drama. Even the scene where Kay's husband finds out about Lucky is handled with such restrained emotion that it's obvious the filmmakers didn't intend this as a movie about passion. Instead, it's about women in a man's world. Kay and Hazel are riveters on a bomber assembly line. They are hazed by the plant's macho veterans, led by Charles Napier. They also learn to support themselves, to think for themselves, and to see themselves differently. There's no suspense and no big emotional payoff, but the movie is always absorbing. The best performance is Lahti as Hazel—tough, vulnerable, cynical, a real pal. This may be the first buddy movie about women.

Sylvester ★ ★ ★
PG, 103 m., 1985

Richard Farnsworth (Foster), Melissa Gilbert (Charlie), Michael Schoeffling (Matt). Directed by Tim Hunter and produced by Martin Jurow. Written by Carol Sobieski.

Hollywood has never exactly had a shortage of movies about teen-age girls and brave horses, and I was not exactly looking forward to *Sylvester*, which stars Melissa Gilbert as a teen-age girl with a horse so brave that its full name is Sylvester Stallone. I was dreading one of those movies where the horse is almost human, and after the girl starts to cry, the horse nudges her and tries to cheer her up. Maybe that's why *Sylvester* came as such a genuine surprise: There is a good movie here, obscured by a tired old formula. Gilbert plays a tough, determined teen-ager who is raising her two younger brothers herself—and trying to keep them out of the hands of court-appointed guardians. Her ambition in life is to train horses, and she starts with Sylvester, an unsophisticated Western bucking horse who does not look like the sort of animal you'd expect to see in the Olympic steeplechase trials.

The complications in the plot are set up right away: The intervention by the court officials, the challenge of training the horse, and the problem of what to do about Gilbert's old boyfriend (Michael Schoeffling), especially since they still love each other. Gilbert turns to a father figure, a grizzled, drunken old cowboy (Richard Farnsworth), who knows all about horses, all about human nature, and even a little bit about teen-age girls. She wants him to provide a home for herself and her brothers, and supervise Sylvester's training sessions. Farnsworth protests: He's already paid his dues as a father and nursemaid. But Gilbert prevails, and the scenes between the two are

charged with the kinds of tension and affection that make even routine situations seem real.

Sylvester contains, of course, the usual number of obligatory scenes. We know we'll see the horse being trained. We know we'll see Gilbert almost breaking her neck. We know we'll see Farnsworth looking at his watch and allowing as how maybe that damned horse *does* have a chance. And we also rather suspect that the horse doesn't get all the way to Kentucky only to lose. The movie doesn't disappoint us at those obligatory moments, but it has a lot of surprises, as well. One of them is the low-key but mature way it treats the romance between Gilbert and Schoeffling. They have a quiet little PG-rated love scene together that is tactful, honest, and, in its own way, rather bold.

Gilbert is best known for her work on TV's "The Little House on the Prairie." This is her first movie. She has real presence, and a much more interesting and resilient acting style than you might expect from someone raised on a network assembly line. *Sylvester* itself probably started out as little more than a classy steeplechase version of *Rocky*, but Gilbert, Farnsworth, and a good script turn it into something surprisingly better.

Taps ★ ★ ★
PG, 126 m., 1981

George C. Scott (General Bache), Timothy Hutton (Brian Moreland), Ronny Cox (Colonel Kerby), Sean Penn (Alex), Tom Cruise (David). Directed by Harold Becker and produced by Stanley R. Jaffe and Howard B. Jaffe. Screenplay by Darryl Ponicsan and Robert Mark Kamen.

Taps is a meditation on two subjects for which some adolescents have a great capacity: idealism and authoritarianism. It takes place in a realistic setting (it was shot on location at Valley Forge Military Academy), but it is not intended as a realistic film. There are all sorts of clues, including the pointed absence of all but one of the academy's adult faculty members, to indicate that *Taps*, like the emotionally similar *Lord of the Flies*, is using its realistic texture as a setting for a fantasy about human nature.

The film begins with an emotionally stirring commencement exercise at Bunker Hill

Military Academy (as the school is called in the film). Sousa marches fill the air, the cadets march around the parade ground looking gloriously proud of themselves, and the reviewing stand is dominated by the legendary old General Harlan Bache, the academy's commander. Bache is played by George C. Scott, and it is probably no accident that his performance in this movie echoes his title role in *Patton* (1970): He is an iron-willed and yet incurably romantic professional soldier.

We soon meet the leading upperclassman, Brian Moreland (Timothy Hutton). He has been selected to lead the cadet corps next year. In one of the most important evenings of his life, he is granted the great privilege of having dinner with old General Bache and sipping some of the old man's brandy. Soon after, however, this whole network of discipline, glory, and tradition is destroyed when it's revealed that the school's pigheaded trustees intend to sell the school and its land to some condominium developers (it is almost worth the price of admission to hear Scott pronouce "condominiums"). Bache is removed from the scene, in a dramatic development I will not reveal. And then Moreland, the cadet commander, takes inventory of the school's supplies of weapons and decides to lead the student body in making a stand for it. They'll take over the school in a military occupation, bar the gates, mount machine guns, and guard posts, and issue a set of demands designed to save the school.

The central passages of *Taps* are devoted to this scheme. The students barricade themselves in the school grounds, the police and National Guard surround the school, and a standoff develops. Meanwhile, within the student body, tensions develop between those kids who are unstable and a little too violent, and those who would secretly rather be on the outside looking in. Hutton, as Moreland, does a lot of learning and soul-searching as he tries to hold his mad scheme together.

There are obviously various problems of plot (such as: Where are the other faculty members? Why are the outside authorities both so stupid and so uncompromising? Why would the trustees have no appreciation of the school's tradition? Why would the grade-school-age cadets be issued live

ammunition?, etc.). These questions do not really matter. *Taps* is basically a character study, a portrait of the personalities engaged in the showdown. And, like *Lord of the Flies*, it observes that adolescent males can easily translate the idealistic lessons they have been taught into a rationale for acting in ways that are rigid, dogmatic, and self-justifying.

Taps works as an uncommonly engrossing story, primarily because the performances are so well done. All of the cadet roles are well-acted, not only by seasoned actors like Hutton (who won an Academy Award for *Ordinary People*) but even by the very young kids who struggle with guns and realities much too large for them. By the film's end, we share their love for their school, we despair at the situation they have gotten themselves into, and we are emotionally involved in the outcome. After the film, there are some ideas to think about, involving the implications when might and right are on the same side—and when they are not.

Tarzan, the Ape Man ★ ★ ½
R, 112 m., 1981

Bo Derek (Jane), Richard Harris (Parker), John Phillip Law (Holt), Miles O'Keefe (Tarzan), Akushula Seleyah (Africa), Steven Strong (Ivory King). Directed and photographed by John Derek and produced by Bo Derek. Screenplay by Tom Rowe and Gary Goddard.

Tarzan, the Ape Man is *The Blue Lagoon* with elephants. Of course it's completely ridiculous, but at the same time it has a certain disarming charm. Sure, it's easy to groan at the secondhand "plot." It's easy to laugh at the clichés and mourn the demotion of Tarzan, who started out in the movies as king of the jungle and now gets fourth billing behind a schoolgirl, an anthropologist, and a wimp. And yet when Tarzan beats his chest and screams and swings to the rescue on a vine, there is something primal happening on the screen. And when Jane and three loyal chimpanzees tenderly bathe the body of the unconscious ape-man, we're getting very close to the reasons why we watch movies, and why there will always be a few movies to reawaken the child within us.

This Bo Derek version of the "Tarzan" legend is allegedly a remake of the MGM version of 1932, starring Johnnie Weiss-muller and Maureen O'Sullivan. Not in that version or in any of the others, however, did Hollywood honestly address the central mystery of the Tarzan story, which is—what, exactly, *was* the intimate relationship between Tarzan and Jane? Were they lovers? Friends? Neighbors? Business partners? They presumably made love in order to pro-duce Boy, but the reproduction took place far, far offscreen. I always thought there was something just a little peculiar about the behavior of Weissmuller, Lex Barker, Gor-don Scott, and other movie Tarzans. There they were, all alone in the jungle with the beautiful Jane, and what did they do? Swing around on vines and talk to the animals. If I'd wanted *Dr. Doolittle*, I would have seen *Dr. Doolittle*.

This 1981 version is nothing if not willing to satisfy our curiosity about sex life in the rain forest. Bo Derek (who stars and pro-duced) and her husband John (who directed and photographed) are frankly interested only in the relationship between Tarzan and Jane. The whole movie is a setup for several steamy scenes of confrontation between the savage, muscular jungle man and the petite young girl with eyes as wide as her shoul-ders. When Tarzan and Jane first meet, the movie all but abandons its plot in favor of foreplay. This is not a movie to waste time on ivory-smuggling, Nazis, cities of gold, ant-men, slave girls, lost safaris, or any of the countless other plot devices Edgar Rice Bur-roughs used as substitutes for interpersonal relationships. It gets right down to business.

The movie opens with a vow by Bo Derek's scientist father (Richard Harris) to lead an expedition to plunder the jungle of its secrets. His real mission: To capture the leg-endary ape-man Tarzan and bring him back to his club—stuffed and mounted, if possi-ble. Harris takes Bo along on his expedition, which also includes John Phillip Law in the role of the wimp assistant. Law has hardly anything to say, and is always the guy who's looking the other way when Tarzan kidnaps Jane. After a series of routine shots of the jungle march, Tarzan *does* meet Jane and finds himself powerfully attracted to her. Harris is of course insane with jealousy: "Do you know what he *really* wants?" he asks Jane. She hopes so.

Tarzan kidnaps Jane, and then the movie boringly intercuts the jealous father search-ing for the curious girl. Harris's role in this movie is as hapless as Jason Robards's role in *The Lone Ranger.* Nobody cares about him, his dialogue is overwrought and underwrit-ten, and every time Tarzan and Jane are poised to jump into the bullrushes, the movie cuts back to Harris, slogging through the jungle and cursing the ape-man.

The story line was ridiculous to begin with, but it goes berserk by the time of the movie's incomprehensible climax in a village of mud worshippers. They capture Derek, smear her with paint, and prepare her for some sort of unspeakable sacrifice before Tarzan gallops to the rescue with a herd of elephants. Those friendly elephants are, of course, part of the Tarzan legend. Tarzan speaks Elephant, and there's always that great moment when he needs help, and the elephants hear his screams and perk up their ears. I've always thought it would be dan-gerous to ask Tarzan for help unless you really wanted it. Say you had a small prob-lem like a missing gourd or a stolen spear, and Tarzan arrived at your village with a herd of elephants to fix things. You'd get your gourd back, maybe, but you'd be cleaning up for weeks.

But never mind. This movie's scenes between Bo Derek, as Jane, and Miles O'Keefe, as a Tarzan who never speaks a word, show them as complete sexual inno-cents, fascinated by the wonderment of each other's bodies. Jane's expression as she looks at the unconscious Tarzan is entrancing. Her unabashed curiosity about him is sexier than any number of steamy sex scenes would have been. Although some of Bo Derek's nude scenes have reportedly been cut from the movie at the insistence of the spoilsport Edgar Rice Burroughs estate, the remaining nude footage is remarkably free of purience. The Tarzan-Jane scenes strike a blow for noble savages, for innocent lust, for animal magnetism, and, indeed, for soft-core porn, which is ever so much sexier than the hard-core variety. If you do not agree with me, you will probably think Bo's banana scene is ridiculous. I prefer to think it was inevitable.

Taxi Driver ★ ★ ★ ★
R, 112 m., 1976

Robert De Niro (Travis Bickle), Jodie Foster (Iris), Albert Brooks (Tom), Harvey Keitel (Sport), Leonard Harris (Palantine), Peter Boyle (Wizard), Cybill Shepherd (Betsy). Directed by Martin Scorsese and produced by Michael Phillips and Julia Phillips. Screenplay by Paul Schrader.

Taxi Driver shouldn't be taken as a New York film; it's not about a city but about the weathers of a man's soul, and out of all New York he selects just those elements that feed and reinforce his obsessions. The man is Travis Bickle, ex-Marine, veteran of Vietnam, composer of dutiful anniversary notes to his parents, taxi driver, killer. The movie rarely strays very far from the personal, highly subjective way in which he sees the city and lets it wound him.

It's a place, first of all, populated with women he cannot have: Unobtainable blonde women who might find him attractive for a moment, who might join him for a cup of coffee, but who eventually will have to shake their heads and sigh, "Oh, Travis!" because they find him . . . well, he's going crazy, but the word they use is "strange." And then, even more cruelly, the city seems filled with men who *can* have these women—men ranging from cloddish political hacks to street-corner pimps who, nevertheless, have in common the mysterious ability to approach a woman without getting everything wrong.

Travis could in theory look for fares anywhere in the city, but he's constantly drawn back to 42nd Street, to Times Square and the whores, street freaks, and porno houses. It's here that an ugly kind of sex comes closest to the surface—the sex of buying, selling, and using people. Travis isn't into that, he hates it, but Times Square feeds his anger. His sexual frustration is channeled into a hatred for the creeps he obsessively observes. He tries to break the cycle—or maybe he just sets himself up to fail again. He sees a beautiful blonde working in the storefront office of a presidential candidate. She goes out with him a couple of times, but the second time he takes her to a hard-core film and she walks out in disgust and won't have any more to do with him. All the same, he calls her for another date, and it's here that we get close to the heart of the movie. The director, Martin Scorsese, gives us a shot of Travis on a pay telephone—and then, as the girl is turning him down, the camera slowly dollies to the right and looks down a long, empty hallway. Pauline Kael's review called this shot—which calls attention to itself—a lapse during which Scorsese was maybe borrowing from Antonioni. Scorsese calls this shot the most important one in the film.

Why? Because, he says, it's as if we can't bear to watch Travis feel the pain of being rejected. This is interesting, because later, when Travis goes on a killing rampage, the camera goes so far as to adopt slow motion so we can see the horror in greater detail. That Scorsese finds the rejection more painful than the murders is fascinating, because it helps to explain Travis Bickle, and perhaps it goes some way toward explaining one kind of urban violence. Travis has been shut out so systematically, so often, from a piece of the action that eventually he has to hit back somehow.

Taxi Driver is a brilliant nightmare and like all nightmares it doesn't tell us half of what we want to know. We're not told where Travis comes from, what his specific problems are, whether his ugly scar came from Vietnam—because this isn't a case study, but a portrait of some days in his life. There's a moment at a political rally when Travis, in dark glasses, smiles in a strange way that reminds us of those photos of Bremer just before he shot Wallace. The moment tells us nothing, and everything: We don't know the specifics of Travis's complaint, but in a chilling way we know what we need to know of him. The film's a masterpiece of suggestive characterization; Scorsese's style selects details that evoke emotions, and that's the effect he wants. The performances are odd and compelling: He goes for moments from his actors, rather than slowly developed characters. It's as if the required emotions were written in the margins of their scripts: Give me anger—fear—dread. Robert De Niro, as Travis Bickle, is as good as Brando at suggesting emotions even while veiling them from us (and in many of his close-ups, Scorsese uses almost subliminal slow motion to draw out the revelations). Cybill Shepherd, as the blonde goddess, is correctly cast, for once, as a glacier slowly receding toward humanity. And there's Jodie Foster, chillingly cast as a twelve-year-old prostitute whom Travis wants to "save." Harvey Keitel, a veteran of all of Scorsese's films (he was the violent maniac in *Alice Doesn't Live Here Anymore)* is the pimp who controls her, and he's got the right kind of toughness that's all bluff.

These people are seen almost in flashes, as if darkness threatens to close over them altogether. *Taxi Driver* is a hell, from the opening shot of a cab emerging from stygian clouds of steam to the climactic killing scene in which the camera finally looks straight down. Scorsese wanted to look away from Travis's rejection; we almost want to look away from his life. But he's there, all right, and he's suffering.

Tell Them Willie Boy Is Here ★ ★ ★ ½
PG, 96 m., 1970

Robert Redford (Cooper), Katharine Ross (Lola), Robert Blake (Willie Boy), Susan Clark (Liz). Directed by Abraham Polonsky and produced by Philip A. Waxman. Screenplay by Polonsky.

Abraham Polonsky's *Tell Them Willie Boy Is Here* is a simple, direct, almost stark retelling of an event that took place in 1909. It's about Willie Boy, a Paiute Indian whose personal fight for freedom was elevated by the press into an Indian uprising against President William Howard Taft. It is also about white racism and Indian pride, and it is no ordinary Western. It marked the resumption of the directorial career of Polonsky, interrupted twenty years earlier by the House Committee on Un-American Activities during the Hollywood witchhunt. Before he was blacklisted in 1950, Polonsky had written Robert Rossen's *Body and Soul* and directed John Garfield in the classic *Force of Evil.*

Polonsky, who also wrote *Willie Boy,* is at pains to tell his story without gimmicks. It's about how Willie Boy (Robert Blake) comes back to the reservation to marry the girl he loves, Lola (Katharine Ross). But her father forbids them to see each other. In a confrontation, Willie Boy kills the father in self-defense and then goes on the run with Lola. The Indians accept the event as "marriage by capture," forced upon Willie Boy because, as he tells Lola, "I've asked for you

the white man's way, and I'm through asking." But Lola, it turns out, was a favorite of the reservation superintendent (Susan Clark), a proper Bostonian who wanted her to be a teacher. At the superintendent's insistence, the sheriff (Robert Redford) gets up a posse and goes after the couple.

Almost all the movie is concerned with the chase, which takes place at a time when President Taft is visiting the area. The president's visit has drawn dozens of newspaper reporters to town, and they sensationalize Willie Boy's case. When Willie Boy accidentally kills one of the members of the posse, an instant "uprising" is born in the papers. Redford wants to forget the whole thing: "It's Indian business, and besides, this posse couldn't catch a dog in the street." But the publicity forces him to keep after Willie Boy, until a final personal confrontation.

Redford gets top billing, and is very good as the sheriff. He has a natural feel for acting in movies; he makes small gestures do the work of large ones, and he can convey a lot of meaning without spelling it out in dialogue. But the film's real star is Robert Blake, who played one of the killers in *In Cold Blood.* Blake is all gristle and nerve and pride, and gained his greatest fame as TV's Barretta.

The movie is paced more slowly than we'd expect for a Western, but then it's not really a Western at all, but a study of personality. There aren't a lot of action scenes and shootouts; this is essentially an essay on the stereotypes by which white men have attempted to justify their theft of the Indian lands and independence. *Tell Them Willie Boy Is Here* works powerfully on that level, and it is impossible to see it without thinking that the same sort of exploitation still goes on today.

10 ★ ★ ★ ★
R, 123 m., 1979

Dudley Moore (George), Julie Andrews (Sam), Bo Derek (Jenny), Robert Webber (Hugh), Dee Wallace (Mary Lewis), Sam Jones (David), Brian Dennehy (Bartender). Directed by Blake Edwards and produced by Edwards and Tony Adams. Screenplay by Edwards.

Blake Edwards's *10* is perhaps the first comedy about terminal yearning. Like all great comedies, it deals with emotions very close to our hearts: In this case, the unutterable poignance of a man's desire for a woman he cannot have. The woman, of course, must be unbelievably desirable (and the hero of *10*, on a scale of 1 to 10, gives this particular woman an 11). It helps, too, if the man is short, forty-two years old, and filled with inchoate longings.

You remember inchoate longings. They used to stalk the pages of novels by Thomas Wolfe, back in the years before the Me Generation and the cult of instant gratification. There used to be a time, incredibly, when you couldn't have something *just because you wanted it*—*10* remembers that time. Its hero, Dudley Moore, begins *10* as a man who seems to have more or less what any man could desire. He is a successful composer. His girl friend is Julie Andrews. He has a great house up in the hills, he drives a Rolls-Royce, he has cable TV with remote tuning.

But then one day, driving his Rolls down Santa Monica Boulevard, he is visited by a vision. She is a preternaturally beautiful young woman in the next car. She turns to regard him, and he is instantly, helplessly, in love. She turns away. She must be about her business. She is dressed in a bridal gown and is on her way to the church to be married.

He follows her. He is stung by a bee in the church. He has six cavities painfully filled by her father, who is a dentist. Groggy from pain pills and brandy, he finds himself aboard an airplane flying to Mexico—where, amazingly, he winds up at the same resort as his ideal woman (and, of course, her husband—one of the vacuous beach-boy types with a smile fit for a Jockey T-shirts model).

Blake Edwards's screenplay now plunges into some slightly more serious waters, where we will not follow. What we're struck with, in *10*, is the uncanny way its humor gets laughs by touching on emotions and yearnings that are very real for us. We identify with the characters in this movie: Their predicaments are funny, yes—but then ours would be, too, if they weren't our own.

The central treasure in the film is the performance by Dudley Moore. There must have been times when Moore wondered if he'd *ever* get the girl. In *10*, he does. He also brings his character such life and dimension that *10* is a lot more than a comedy: It's a study in the follies of human nature.

The girl (the one who scores 11) is played by Bo Derek. She is so desirable, such a pure and cheerful embodiment of carnal perfection, that we're in there with Dudley Moore every step of the way, even when he's slogging it out to Ravel's interminable "Bolero." Julie Andrews has a small but delightful role as the sensible mistress, and the movie also has warm performances by Robert Webber, as Moore's vulnerable gay friend, and by Brian Dennehy, as a particularly understanding bartender in Mexico.

10 is not only one of the best films Blake Edwards has ever made, but was something of a turning point in his career: The previous decade he had alternated between successful Pink Panther movies and non-Panther flops like *The Tamarind Seed*, *The Wild Rovers*, and *The Carey Treatment*. Did he have another good straight movie in him? Yes, as a matter of fact, he did.

Tender Mercies ★ ★ ★
PG, 93 m., 1983

Robert Duvall (Mac Sledge), Tess Harper (Rosa Lee), Betty Buckley (Dixie), Wilford Brimley (Harry), Ellen Barkin (Sue Anne), Allan Hubbard (Sonny). Directed by Bruce Beresford and produced by Philip S. Hobel. Screenplay by Horton Foote.

Tender Mercies visits some fairly familiar movie territory, and achieves some quietly touching effects. The movie's about the rhythms of a small Texas town, and about the struggle of a has-been country singer to regain his self-respect. It might remind you of parts of *The Last Picture Show* and *Honkytonk Man*, with a little bit of *Payday* thrown in (that was the movie starring Rip Torn, based on the last days of the dying Hank Williams, Sr.). This time, the broken-down country singer is named Mac Sledge. He's at the end of his personal road. He was once a big star and a hero to young musicians around the Southwest, but as his final act opens he's sitting in a fleabag motel outside a small Texas town, drinking himself to death, and fighting for the bottle with another guy he hardly even knows.

When he wakes up on the floor the next morning, the other guy is gone and Sledge is hung over, broke, and without prospects. He throws himself on the mercy of the young widow who runs the motel: He'll work for his room and board. She agrees to that, and throws in $2 an hour, but says he can't drink while he's at the motel. He agrees, and that is the day his life turns around and he begins the rebuilding process.

Tender Mercies tells the story of the relationship between the singer and the young widow in a quiet, subtle way; this isn't one of those movies that spells everything out. The key to the movie's tone is in the performance by Robert Duvall as Sledge. Duvall plays him as a bone-weary, seedy, essentially very simple man who needs some values to hold onto. The widow can provide those, and can also provide the stability of a home and family (she has a young son, whose father was killed in Vietnam). What the Duvall character wants to do, essentially, is keep a low profile, work hard, not drink, and forget about the glories of country singing. It's hard for him to remain invisible, though, after the local paper prints a story and the members of a local band start dropping around for advice. There are more complications: Sledge's ex-wife is still touring as a country singer, and would like to turn his eighteen-year-old daughter against him.

What's interesting about *Tender Mercies* is the way it refuses to approach this material as soap opera *or* as drama. The movie's told more like one of those quiet, sly *New Yorker* stories where the big emotional moments sneak up on you, and the effects are achieved indirectly. Sometimes this movie smiles (as in a scene of a double baptism). Sometimes it simply sits there and talks straight (as in a touching speech by Sledge on the meaning of life). Sometimes its low budget allows the seams to show (as in the unconvincing concert scene involving Sledge's wife). But mostly it just lets these stories happen, lets them get to know these people, and see them dealing with life. Some of them get better, and some of them get worse. It's like a country song.

Terms of Endearment ★ ★ ★ ★
PG, 129 m., 1983

Debra Winger (Emma Horton), Shirley MacLaine (Aurora Greenway), Jack Nicholson (Breedlove), Jeff Daniels (Flap Horton), Danny DeVito (Vernon), John Lithgow (Sam Burns). Directed, produced, and written by James L. Brooks.

When families get together to remember their times together, the conversation has a way of moving easily from the tragedies to the funny things. You'll mention someone who has passed away, and there'll be a moment of silence, and then somebody will grin and be reminded of some goofy story. Life always has an unhappy ending, but you can have a lot of fun along the way, and everything doesn't have to be dripping in deep significance.

The most remarkable achievement of *Terms of Endearment*, which is filled with great achievements, is its ability to find the balance between the funny and the sad, between moments of deep truth and other moments of high ridiculousness. A lesser movie would have had trouble moving between the extremes that are visited by this film, but because *Terms of Endearment* understands its characters and loves them, we never have a moment's doubt: What happens next is supposed to happen, because life's like that. *Terms of Endearment* feels as much like life as any movie I can think of. At the same time, it's a triumph of show business, with its high comic style, its flair for bittersweet melodrama, and its star turns for the actors. Maybe the best thing about this movie is the way it combines those two different kinds of filmmaking. This is a movie with bold emotional scenes and big laughs, and at the same time it's so firmly in control of its tone that we believe we are seeing real people.

The movie's about two remarkable women, and their relationships with each other and with the men in their lives. The mother is played by Shirley MacLaine. She's a widow who lives in Houston and hasn't dated a man since her husband died. Maybe she's redirected her sexual desires into the backyard, where her garden has grown so large and elaborate that she either will have to find a man pretty quickly or move to a house with a bigger yard. Her daughter, played by Debra Winger, is one of those people who seems to have been blessed with a sense of life and joy. She marries a guy named Flap who teaches English in a series of Midwestern colleges; she rears three kids and puts up with Flap, who has an eye for coeds.

Back in Houston, her mother finally goes out on a date with the swinging bachelor (Jack Nicholson) who has lived next door for years. He's a hard-drinking, girl-chasing former astronaut with a grin that hints of unspeakable lusts. MacLaine, a lady who surrounds herself with frills and flowers, is appalled by this animalistic man and then touched by him.

There are a couple of other bittersweet relationships in the film. Both mother and daughter have timid, mild-mannered male admirers: MacLaine is followed everywhere by Vernon (Danny DeVito), who asks only to be allowed to gaze upon her, and Winger has a tender, little affair with a banker.

The years pass. Children grow up into adolescence, Flap gets a job as head of the department in Nebraska, the astronaut turns out to have genuine human possibilities of becoming quasi-civilized, and mother and daughter grow into a warmer and deeper relationship. All of this is told in a series of perfectly written, acted, and directed scenes that flow as effortlessly as a perfect day, and then something happens that is totally unexpected, and changes everything. I don't want to suggest what happens. It flows so naturally that it should be allowed to take place.

This is a wonderful film. There isn't a thing that I would change, and I was exhilarated by the freedom it gives itself to move from the high comedy of Nicholson's best moments to the acting of Debra Winger in the closing scenes. She outdoes herself. It's a great performance. And yet it's not a "performance." There are scenes that have such a casual gaiety that acting seems to have nothing to do with it. She doesn't reach for effects, and neither does the film, because it's all right there.

Tess ★ ★ ★ ★
PG, 180 m., 1980

Nastassja Kinski (Tess), Peter Firth (Angel Clare), Leigh Lawson (Alec d'Urberville), Rosemary Martin (Mrs. Durbeyfield), Sylvia Coleridge (Mrs. d'Urberville), John Collin (John Durbeyfield), Tony Church (Parson), Brigid Erin Bates (Girl in Meadow). Directed by Roman Polanski and produced by Claude Berri. Screenplay by Gerard Brach, Polanski, and John Brownjohn.

Roman Polanski's *Tess* is a love song with a tragic ending—the best kind of love song of all, just so long as it's not about ourselves. He tells the story of a beautiful young girl, innocent but not without intelligence, and the way she is gradually destroyed by the exercise of the male ego. The story is all the more touching because it is not an unrelenting descent into gloom, as it might have been in other hands, but a life lived in occasional sight of love and happiness. Tess is forever just on the brink of getting the peace she deserves.

The movie is based on a novel by Thomas Hardy, but Polanski never permits his film to become a Classics Illustrated; this isn't a devout rendering of a literary masterpiece, but a film that lives and breathes and has a quick sympathy for its heroine. Nastassja Kinski is just right for the title role. She has the youth, the freshness, and the naiveté of a Tess, and none of the practiced mannerisms of an actress engaged to "interpret" the role. That's good because Tess is a character who should stick out like a sore thumb in many scenes, and Kinski's occasional shy awkwardness is just right for the story of a girl who attempts to move up in social class on sheer bravado.

The story involves a young girl who will be the victim, the prey, and sometimes the lover of many men, without ever quite understanding what it is that those men want of her. The first man in her life is her father, a drunken farmer named John Durbeyfield, who discovers from the local parson that he is related to the noble local family of d'Urbervilles. The farmer and his wife immediately send their beautiful daughter, Tess, off to confront the d'Urbervilles and perhaps win a position in their household.

Tess is almost immediately seduced by a rakish cousin. She becomes pregnant, and her child dies soon after it is born. She never tells the cousin. But later, after she falls in love with the son of a local minister and marries him, she confesses her past. This is too much for her new husband to bear; he "married down" because he was attracted to Tess's humble origins. But he is not prepared to accept the reality of her past. He leaves on a bizarre mission to South America. Tess, meanwhile, descends to rough manual labor for a few pennies an hour. She is eventually reunited with her cousin (who is not a complete bastard, and complains that he should have been informed of her pregnancy). She becomes his lover. Then the wayward husband returns, and the physical and psychic contest for Tess ends in tragedy.

As a plot, these events would be right at home in any soap opera. But what happens in Polanski's *Tess* is less important than how Tess feels about it, how we feel about it, and how successfully Polanski is able to locate those events in a specific place and time. His movie is set in England, but was actually photographed in France. It is a beautifully visualized period piece that surrounds Tess with the attitudes of her time—attitudes that explain how restricted her behavior must be, and how society views her genuine human emotions as inappropriate. This is a wonderful film; the kind of exploration of doomed young sexuality that, like *Elvira Madigan*, makes us agree that the lovers should never grow old.

Testament ★ ★ ★ ★
PG, 90 m., 1983

Jane Alexander (Carol Wetherly), William Devane (Tom Wetherly), Ross Harris (Brad), Roxana Zal (Mary Liz), Lukas Haas (Scottie), Philip Anglim (Hollis), Leon Ames (Henry Abhart), Rebecca De Mornay (Mother with Baby). Directed by Lynne Littman and produced by Jonathan Bernstein and Littman. Screenplay by John Sacret Young.

Testament may be the first movie in a long time that will make you cry. It made me cry. And seeing it again for a second time, knowing everything that would happen, anticipating each scene before it came, I was affected just as deeply. But the second time I was able to see more clearly that the movie is more than just a devastating experience, that it has a message with a certain hope.

The film is about a suburban American family, and what happens to that family after a nuclear war. It is not a science fiction movie, and it doesn't have any special effects, and there are no big scenes of buildings blowing over or people disintegrating.

We never see a mushroom cloud. We never even know who started the war. Instead, *Testament* is a tragedy about manners: It asks how we might act toward one another, how our values might stand up in the face of an overwhelming catastrophe.

The movie begins with one of those typical families right out of TV commercials. The father (William Devane) is a physical-fitness nut. The mother (Jane Alexander) is loving, funny, and a little harried. The kids include a daughter who practices the piano, a son who races his dad up hills on their ten-speed bikes, and a little boy who guards the "treasure" in the bottom drawer of his chest. The movie follows these people long enough for us to know them, to appreciate their personalities, their good and weak points, and then one sunny afternoon the war starts.

Most of the film is about what happens then. Anarchy does not break out. There is some looting, but it is limited. For the most part, the people in the small northern California town stick together and try to do the best that they can. There are meetings in the church. There are public-health measures. A beloved community leader (Leon Ames, of TV's "Life with Father" many years ago) is a ham-radio operator, and makes contact with a few other places. A decision is made to go ahead with the grade-school play. Life goes on . . . but death invades it, as radiation poisoning begins to take a toll, first on the babies, then on the children, until finally the cemetery is filled and the bodies have to be burned on a pyre.

The movie finds dozens of small details to suggest existence after the bomb. All the kids, for example, take the batteries out of their toys and computer games, and turn them in for emergency use. Gasoline is rationed, and then runs out. The survivors have no garbage collection, no electricity, and, worst of all, no word from elsewhere. The sky gradually grows darker, suggesting realistically that a nuclear war would finally kill us all by raising great clouds of dust that would choke the Earth's vegetation.

In the midst of this devastation, Jane Alexander, as the mother, tries to preserve love and decency. She stands by her children, watches as they grow in response to the challenges, cherishes them as she sees all her dreams for them disappear. It is a great performance, the heart of the film. In fact, Alexander's performance makes the film possible to watch without unbearable heartbreak, because she is brave and decent in the face of horror. And the last scene, in which she expresses such small optimism as is still possible, is one of the most powerful movie scenes I've ever seen.

Tex ★ ★ ★ ★
PG, 103 m., 1982

Matt Dillon (Tex), Jim Metzler (Mason), Meg Tilly (Jamie), Bill McKinney (Pop), Frances Lee McCain (Mrs. Johnson), Ben Johnson (Cole Collins). Directed by Tim Hunter and produced by Ron Miller. Screenplay by Charlie Haas and Hunter.

There is a shock of recognition almost from the beginning of *Tex*, because we're listening to the sound of American voices in an authentically American world, the world of teen-age boys trying to figure things out and make the right decisions. The voices sound right but may be a little unfamiliar, because adolescents on television are often made to talk in pseudo-hip sitcom nonspeak. Here in *Tex* are the clear voices of two young men who are worthy of attention. Their names are Tex and Mason. They're brothers, one about eighteen, the other fourteen and a half. They live by themselves in a rundown house on some land outside a rural suburb of Tulsa. Their father is a rodeo cowboy who hardly ever stops in at home and forgets to send money for weeks at a time. These two kids are raising themselves and doing a pretty good job of it.

The movie tells the story of a couple of weeks in their lives. These are the kinds of weeks when things can go either well or badly—and if they go badly, we sense, Tex could get his whole life off to the wrong start. The brothers are broke. Mason sells their horses to raise money to buy food and get the gas turned back on. That makes Tex angry and sad; he's a kid looking for trouble.

We meet the other people in their world. There's the rich family down the road, dominated by a stern father who makes his teen-agers toe a strict line. His kids are just as unpredictable as anyone else's, but he doesn't believe that. He believes their two undisciplined friends, Tex and Mason, are leading them into trouble and practically dragging them to late-night beer parties. There's another complication. His daughter and Tex are beginning to fall in love.

There's another friend, a local kid who got a girl pregnant, married her, and moved to Tulsa to start a family. He's dealing drugs. Mason knows this intuitively and surely, and knows the kid is heading for trouble. Tex knows it, too, but there comes a time in this story when Tex just doesn't give a damn, and when the drug dealer happens to be there, Tex accepts a ride into Tulsa with him. Tex doesn't do drugs himself, but he gets into a very scary situation with another dealer, and there's a harrowing scene in which Tex wavers just at the brink of getting into serious trouble.

There is more to this movie's story, but the important thing about it isn't what happens, but how it happens. The movie is so accurately acted, especially by Jim Metzler as Mason and Matt Dillon as Tex, that we care more about the characters than about the plot. We can see them learning and growing, and when they have a heart-to-heart talk about "going all the way," we hear authentic teen-agers speaking, not kids who seem to have been raised at Beverly Hills cocktail parties.

Tex is based on a famous novel by S.E. Hinton, who has had two of her other novels filmed by Francis Ford Coppola. She knows a great deal about adolescents, and her work is unaffected by sentimentality and easy romance. It's authentic. But the backgrounds of the two filmmakers are also interesting. Tim Hunter and Charles Haas bought the book and wrote the screenplay, and Hunter directed. Their previous collaboration was a little movie named *Over the Edge*, about teen-agers who feel cornered and persecuted by the rigid middle-class rules of a cardboard Denver suburb. That movie, a small masterpiece containing Matt Dillon's first movie appearance, never got a fair chance in theaters. Now here are Hunter and Haas again, still remembering what it's like to be young, still getting the dialogue and the attitudes, the hang-ups and the dreams, exactly right.

The Texas Chain Saw Massacre ★ ★
R, 87 m., 1974

Paul A. Partain (Frankle), Marilyn Burns (Debbie), Teri McMinn (Other Girl). Directed and produced by Tobe Hooper. Screenplay by Kim Henkel and Hooper.

Now here's a grisly little item. *The Texas Chain Saw Massacre* is as violent and gruesome and blood-soaked as the title promises—a real Grand Guignol of a movie. It's also without any apparent purpose, unless the creation of disgust and fright is a purpose. And yet in its own way, the movie is some kind of weird, off-the-wall achievement. I can't imagine why anyone would want to make a movie like this, and yet it's well-made, well-acted, and all too effective.

The movie's based on factual material, according to the narration that opens it. For all I know, that's true, although I can't recall having heard of these particular crimes, and the distributor provides no documentation. Not that it matters. A true crime movie like Richard Brooks's *In Cold Blood*, which studies the personalities and compulsions of two killers, dealt directly with documented material and was all the more effective for that. But *The Texas Chain Saw Massacre* could have been made up from whole cloth without any apparent difference. No motivation, no background, no speculation on causes is evident anywhere in the film. It's simply an exercise in terror.

It takes place in an isolated area of Texas, which five young people (one of them in a wheelchair) are driving through in their camper van. They pick up a weirdo hitchhiker who carries his charms and magic potions around his neck and who giggles insanely while he cuts himself on the hand and then slices at the paraplegic. They get rid of him, so they think.

But then they take a side trip to a haunted-looking old house, which some of them had been raised in. The two girls laugh as they clamber through the litter on the floor, but one of the guys notices some strange totems and charms which should give him warning. They don't. He and his girlfriend set off for the old swimming hole, find it dried up, and then see a farmhouse nearby. The guy goes to ask about borrowing some gasoline and disappears inside.

His girl gets tired of waiting for him, knocks on the door, and disappears inside, too. A lot of people are going to be disappearing into this house, and its insides are a masterpiece of set decoration and the creation of mood. We see the innocent victims being clubbed on the hand, hung from meat hooks, and gone after with the chain saw.

We see rooms full of strange altars made from human bones, and rooms filled with chicken feathers and charms and weird relics. And gradually we realize that the house is inhabited by a demented family of retarded murderers and grave robbers. When they get fresh victims, they carve them up with great delight. What they do with the bodies is a little obscure, but, uh, they run a barbecue stand down by the road.

One way or another, all the kids get killed by the maniac waving the chain saw—except one girl, who undergoes a night of panic and torture, who escapes not once but twice, who leaps through no fewer than two windows, and who screams endlessly. All of this material, as you can imagine, is scary and unpalatable. But the movie is good technically and with its special effects, and we have to give it grudging admiration on that level, despite all the waving of the chain saw.

There is, for example, an effective montage of quick cuts of the last girl's screaming face and popping eyeballs. There are bizarrely effective performances by the demented family (one of them, of course, turns out to be the hitchhiker, and Grandfather looks like Dustin Hoffman in *Little Big Man*). What we're left with, though, is an effective production in the service of an unnecessary movie.

Horror and exploitation films almost always turn a profit if they're brought in at the right price. So they provide a good starting place for ambitious would-be filmmakers who can't get more conventional projects off the ground. *The Texas Chain Saw Massacre* belongs in a select company (with *Night of the Living Dead* and *Last House on the Left*) of films that are really a lot better than the genre requires. Not, however, that you'd necessarily enjoy seeing it.

That Was Then . . . This Is Now ★ ★
R, 102 m., 1985

Emilio Estevez (Mark Jennings), Craig Sheffer (Bryon Douglas), Barbara Babcock (Mrs. Douglas), Frank Carlson (M & M), Morgan Freeman (Charlie), Kim Delaney (Cathy), Jill Schoelen (Angela). Directed by Christopher Cain and produced by Gary R. Lindberg and John M. Ondov. Screenplay by Emilio Estevez.

Here is a story that starts out to make a point about a troubled teen-ager, and ends up only making some observations. Maybe that's enough, but *That Was Then . . . This Is Now* ends in such a minor key that it seems almost unfinished. Is there a lesson for the movie's anti-hero to learn, or is he doomed to keep repeating the same destructive patterns until he kills himself?

The film tells the story of a young orphan (Emilio Estevez) who has lived for nine years in the home of his best friend (Craig Sheffer) and his mother. They've been inseparable, but now, as the movie opens, they seem to be growing apart. The Estevez character walks around filled with low-grade anger, which expresses itself as restless troublemaking. Eventually he gets involved in dealing some drugs.

We meet the world these kids live in. Sheffer's mother (Barbara Babcock) plays her first scene from a hospital bed, and we fear the worst: This looks like another case of Ali MacGraw's Disease. But then she comes home, and turns into the most cheerful, patient, understanding parent in recent movie history. The two boys lead independent lives, hanging out at a local pool hall where the tough, cynical owner (Morgan Freeman) can sometimes be counted on to loan them his car.

There are romances. Sheffer has been going with the hard-bitten Jill Schoelen, but then he falls for a sweet, more innocent type (Kim Delaney). Her kid brother is a bright malcontent named M & M, and when he starts hanging around with the older boys there is trouble. Estevez eventually supplies M & M with an unnamed drug which causes him to freak out and disappear. Meanwhile, there's trouble on other fronts. There are gang rumbles in parking lots, and a fight that ends in the death of the pool hall owner. And

it's clear that Estevez is behaving in a steadily more antisocial manner.

This story was originally told in a novel by S.E. Hinton, the woman who has become a poet of teen-age alienation (her other filmed novels include *Tex*, *The Outsiders*, and *Rumble Fish*). She specializes in a sort of dreamy realism, in which kids get involved in hard situations but yet somehow maintain their freedom to learn and grow. That doesn't seem to happen this time. The Estevez character seems flawed at the start, and he gets worse, and he ends up in a lot of trouble. The movie's ending could be summarized as sort of a downbeat sigh.

I wanted more. I thought the movie was very good at conveying the day-to-day existence of its characters. They were interesting, and complicated, and I hadn't seen them in a hundred other movies. I didn't exactly expect an upbeat ending from them, a happy conclusion with an uplifting speech at the end. But the movie set me up for some kind of redemption, and it didn't deliver. The message, I guess, is, that was then, this is now, and then was better. When you're a teen-ager, now should be better. If it isn't, there ought to be a pretty good reason why.

That's Dancing! ★ ★ ★
PG, 105 m., 1985

With hosts Mikhail Baryshnikov, Ray Bolger, Sammy Davis, Jr., Gene Kelly, and Liza Minnelli. Directed by Jack Haley, Jr., and produced by David Niven, Jr., and Haley. Screenplay by Haley.

There is a sense in which it is impossible to dislike *That's Dancing!* and another sense in which movies like this—made by splicing together all the "good parts" —are irritating and sort of unfair to the original films. Given the choice of seeing *Singin' in the Rain* again or spending the same amount of time looking at scenes from *Singin'* and maybe sixty other films, I'd rather see the real movie all the way through. But *That's Dancing!* is not setting an either-or test for us; what it basically wants to do is entertain us with a lot of good dance scenes from a lot of good, and bad, movies, and that is such a harmless ambition that I guess we can accept it.

The movie has been put together by Jack Haley, Jr., and David Niven, Jr., and it recycles Haley's formula in *That's Entertainment!* (1973), the original slice-and-dice anthology from Hollywood's golden ages. There also has been a *That's Entertainment II* (or "too," I seem to recall), and the law of diminishing returns is beginning to apply. Sooner or later, we'll get *That's All, Folks!* In the first movie, for example, we got Gene Kelly's immortal title dance number from *Singin' in the Rain;* in the second movie, we got Donald O'Conner's equally immortal "Make 'em Laugh" sequence; and that leaves Kelly and O'Conner's only somewhat immortal "Moses Supposes" number for this film. Pretty soon we're going to be getting *That's What's Left of Entertainment!*

That's Dancing! shares with the earlier movies an irritating compulsion to masquerade as a documentary, which it isn't. The tone is set by Kelly's opening generalizations about the universality of dance, etc., while we see *National Geographic* outtakes of dancing around the world: tribes in Africa, hula skirts in Hawaii, polkas, geisha girls and so on. Kelly is later spelled by such other dance analysts as Liza Minnelli, Ray Bolger, Mikhail Baryshnikov, and Sammy Davis, Jr., all of whom can dance with a great deal more ease than they can recite pseudoprofundities.

There is, however, a lot of good dancing in this movie, including rare silent footage of Isadora Duncan. We see Busby Berkeley's meticulously choreographed dance geometries, the infinite style of Fred Astaire, the brassy joy of Ginger Rogers, the pizazz of Cyd Charisse and Eleanor Powell, a charming duet between Bill "Bojangles" Robinson and Shirley Temple, and a dazzling display by the Nicholas Brothers, who were the inspiration for the dance team played by the Hines brothers in *Cotton Club*. The movie is up-to-date, with John Travolta from *Saturday Night Fever* and footage from breakdance movies, *Flashdance*, and Michael Jackson's *Thriller*. But perhaps its most pleasing single moment is a little soft-shoe by Jimmy Cagney, who was perhaps not the technical equal of Astaire, but was certainly on the same sublime plane when it came to communicating sheer joy.

One of the insights offered in the narration of *That's Dancing!* is that Astaire was responsible for the theory that you should see the entire body of the dancer in most of the shots in a dance scene, and that the scene should be shown in unbroken shots, as much as possible, to preserve the continuity of the dancer's relationship with space and time. That's the kind of seemingly obvious statement that contains a lot of half-baked conclusions. True, you have to see the dancer's whole body to appreciate what he's doing (look at the disastrous choreography in Travolta's *Stayin' Alive*, which inspired Ginger Rogers to call it a dance film—"from the waist up"). But you also need the cutaways to show the faces of the dancers, and the chemistry between them, as when Astaire and Rogers have their enchanted dancing lesson in *Swing Time*. True, shooting the whole thing in one unbroken take preserves the integrity of the visual record—but what about the sensational dance sequences in *Flashdance* that were achieved by literally cutting between different dancers, all doing their own specialty? All that really matters is the end result.

What conclusions can be drawn from the movie's survey of sixty years of dancing on screen? I can think of one, sort of obvious and sort of depressing: Style has gone out of style. New dancers in recent dance movies are in superb physical shape and do amazing things on the screen, but they do not have the magical personal style of an Astaire or a Kelly. They're technicians. And there's another thing: They don't really dance together. A lot of them are soloists, or two soloists sharing the same floor. When Astaire and Rogers danced together, they danced *together.* And that is maybe what dancing is finally all about.

That's Entertainment! ★ ★ ★ ★
G, 132 m., 1974

Selected scenes from MGM musicals between 1929 and 1958, introduced by Frank Sinatra, Fred Astaire, Gene Kelly, Mickey Rooney, Liza Minnelli, Elizabeth Taylor, James Stewart, Donald O'Connor, and others. Written, produced, and directed by Jack Haley, Jr.

It used to be said that the trickiest thing about a musical was to figure out a way for the characters to break gracefully into song. Maybe that was all wrong. Maybe the hardest thing was for them to stop, once the singing had started. That's my notion after seeing *That's Entertainment!*, a magical tour through the greatest musicals produced by the king of Hollywood studios, Metro-Goldwyn-Mayer.

This isn't just a compilation film, with lots of highlights strung together. Those kinds of movies quickly repeat themselves. *That's Entertainment!* is more of a documentary and a eulogy. A documentary of a time that began in 1929 and seemed to end only yesterday, and a eulogy for an art form that will never be again.

Hollywood will continue to make musicals, of course (although, curiously enough, the form never has been very popular overseas). But there will never be musicals like this again, because there won't be the budgets, there won't be the sense of joyous abandon, there won't be so many stars in the same place all at once and—most of all—there won't be the notion that a musical has to be "important."

The various segments of the film are introduced and narrated by MGM stars of the past (Fred Astaire, Gene Kelly), superstars like Frank Sinatra and Elizabeth Taylor, offspring like Liza Minnelli, and even a ringer like Bing Crosby (he was a Paramount star, but never mind). They seem to share a real feeling of nostalgia for MGM, which, in its heyday, was not only a studio, but also a benevolent and protective organization ruled by the paternal Louis B. Mayer. Liza Minnelli sounds at times as if she's narrating a visit to her mother's old high school. The movie avoids the trap of being too worshipful in the face of all this greatness. It's not afraid to kid; we see Clark Gable looking ill at ease as he pretends to enjoy singing and dancing, and we see a hilarious montage of Judy Garland and Mickey Rooney ringing endless changes to the theme, "I know—we'll fix up the old barn and put on a show!"

And then there are the glorious, unforgettable moments from the great musicals. My favorite musical has always been *Singin' in the Rain*, the 1952 comedy about Hollywood's traumatic switch to talkies. *That's Entertainment!* opens with a montage of musicals (neatly surveying three decades of film progress), and later returns to the two most unforgettable numbers in the film:

Gene Kelly sloshing through puddles while singing the title song, and Donald O'Connor in his amazing "Make 'em Laugh," in which he leaps up walls, takes pratfalls, and dives through a set.

There are other great moments: The closing ballet from *An American in Paris*; Nelson Eddy and Jeanette MacDonald being hilariously serious in *Rose Marie*; Astaire and Ginger Rogers, so light-footed they seem to float; Gene Kelly's incredible acrobatics as he does his own stunts, swinging from rooftop to rooftop; William Warfield singing "Old Man River" in *Showboat*; Judy Garland singing "You Made Me Love You" to a montage of stills of Clark Gable; Garland, again, with "Get Happy" (and a vignette of little Liza's first movie appearance, aged about three); the acrobatic woodchopper's scene from *Seven Brides for Seven Brothers*, and even Esther Williams rising from the deep.

The movie's fun from beginning to end. It's not camp, and it's not nostalgia: It's a celebration of a time and place in American movie history when everything came together to make a new art form.

They Shoot Horses, Don't They?
★ ★ ★ ★
PG, 123 m., 1970

Jane Fonda (Gloria), Michael Sarrazin (Robert), Susannah York (Alice), Gig Young (Rocky), Red Buttons (Sailor), Bonnie Bedelia (Ruby), Severn Darden (Cecil). Directed by Sydney Pollack and produced by Irwin Winkler and Robert Chartoff. Screenplay by James Poe and Robert E. Thompson.

Erase the forced smiles from the desperate faces, and what the dance marathons of the 1930s came down to was fairly simple. A roomful of human beings went around and around within four walls for weeks at a time without sleep, populating a circus for others who paid to see them. At the end, those who didn't collapse or drop dead won cash prizes that were good money during the Depression. And the Depression, in an oblique sort of way, was the reason for it all. The marathons offered money to the winners and distraction to everyone else. To be sure, some of the marathons got pretty grim. Contestants tried to dance their way through illnesses and pregnancies, through lice and hallucinations, and the sight of them doing it was part of the show. Beyond the hit tunes and the crepe paper and the free pig as a door prize, there was an elementary sadism in the appeal of the marathons.

Among American spectator sports, they rank with stock car racing. There was always that delicious possibility, you see, that somebody would die. Or freak out. Or stand helplessly while his partner collapsed and he lost the investment of thousands of hours of his life.

They Shoot Horses, Don't They? is a masterful re-creation of the marathon era for audiences that are mostly unfamiliar with it. In addition to everything else it does, *Horses* holds our attention because it tells us something we didn't know about human nature and American society. It tells us a lot more than that, of course, but because it works on this fundamental level as well it is one of the best American movies of the 1970s. It is so good as a movie, indeed, that it doesn't have to bother with explaining the things in my first two paragraphs; they are all there (and that's where I found them), but they are completely incorporated into the structure of the film.

Director Sydney Pollack has built a ballroom and filled it with characters. They come from nowhere, really; Michael Sarrazin is photographed as if he has walked into the ballroom directly from the sea. The characters seem to have no histories, no alternate lives; they exist only within the walls of the ballroom and during the ticking of the official clock. Pollack has simplified the universe. He has got everything in life boiled down to this silly contest; and what he tells us has more to do with lives than contests.

Sarrazin meets Jane Fonda, and they became partners almost absentmindedly; he wasn't even planning on entering a marathon. There are other contestants, particularly Red Buttons and Bonnie Bedelia in splendid supporting performances, and they are whipped around the floor by the false enthusiasm of Gig Young, the master of ceremonies. "Yowzza! Yowzza!" he chants, and all the while he regards the contestants with the peculiarly disinterested curiosity of an exhausted god.

There are not a lot of laughs in *Horses*, because Pollack has directed from the point of view of the contestants. They are bitter beyond any hope of release. The movie's delicately timed pacing and Pollack's visual style work almost stealthily to involve us; we begin to feel the physical weariness and spiritual desperation of the characters.

The movie begins on a note of alienation and spirals down from there. *Horses* provides us no cheap release at the end; and the ending, precisely because it is so obvious, is all the more effective. We knew it was coming. Even the title gave it away. And when it comes, it is effective not because it is a surprise but because it is inevitable. As inevitable as death.

The performances are perfectly matched to Pollack's grim vision. Jane Fonda is hard, unbreakable, filled with hate and fear. Sarrazin can do nothing, really, but stand there and pity her; no one, not even during the Depression, should have to feel so without hope. Red Buttons, as the sailor who's a veteran of other marathons and cheerfully teaches everybody the ropes, reminds us that the great character actor from *Sayonara* still exists, and that comedians are somehow the best in certain tragic roles.

And that's what the movie comes down to, maybe. The characters are comedians trapped in tragic roles. They signed up for the three square meals a day and the crack at the $1,500 prize, and they can stop (after all) whenever they want to. But somehow they can't stop, and as the hundreds and thousands of hours of weariness and futility begin to accumulate, the great dance marathon begins to look more and more like life.

Thief ★ ★ ★ ½
R, 126 m., 1981

James Caan (Frank), Tuesday Weld (Jessie), Willie Nelson (Okla), James Belushi (Barry), Robert Prosky (Leo), Tom Signorelli (Attaglia), John Santucci (Urizzi), Tom Erhart (Judge). Directed by Michael Mann and produced by Jerry Bruckheimer and Ronnie Caan. Screenplay by Mann.

Michael Mann's *Thief* is a film of style, substance, and violently felt emotion, all wrapped up in one of the most intelligent thrillers I've seen. It's one of those films where you feel the authority right away: This movie knows its characters, knows its story, and knows exactly how it wants to tell us about them. At a time when thrillers have been devalued by the routine repetition of the same dumb chases, sex scenes, and gunfights, *Thief* is completely out of the ordinary.

The movie stars James Caan as a man who says he was "raised by the state" and spent eleven years in prison. As the movie opens, he's been free four years, and lives in Chicago. He is a highly skilled professional thief—a trade he learned behind bars from Okla (Willie Nelson), a master thief. The film's opening sequence establishes Caan's expertise as he cracks a safe with a portable drill. Caan sees himself as a completely independent loner. But we see him differently, as a lonely, unloved kid who is hiding out inside an adult body. He's a loner who desperately needs to belong to somebody. He trusts his partner (James Belushi), but that's not enough. He decides, on an almost abstract intellectual level, to fall in love with a cashier (Tuesday Weld), and in one of the movie's best scenes he tells this woman, who is essentially a stranger, all about his life in prison and his plans for the future. She takes his hand and accepts him.

But there is another person who comes into his life: Leo, the master criminal, the fence who sets up heists and hires people to pull them. Leo, in a wonderfully complex performance by the sad-faced Robert Prosky, knows how to enlist Caan: "Let me be your father," he says. "I'll take care of everything." He does. He even supplies Caan and Weld with an illegally obtained baby boy when they're turned down at the adoption agency. But once the thief goes with Leo, his life gets complicated. The cops seem to be on his case. His phone is bugged. Everybody knows his business. The movie leads up to one final caper, a $4 million diamond heist in Los Angeles, and then it ends in a series of double crosses and a rain of violence.

This movie works so well for several reasons. One is that *Thief* is able to convince us that it knows its subject, knows about the methods and criminal personalities of its characters. Another is that it's well cast: Every important performance in this movie

successfully creates a plausible person, instead of the stock-company supporting characters we might have expected. And the film moves at a taut pace, creating tension and anxiety through very effective photography and a wound-up, pulsing score by Tangerine Dream.

If *Thief* has a weak point, it is probably in the handling of the Willie Nelson character. Nelson is set up well: He became Caan's father-figure in prison, Caan loves him more than anybody, and when he goes to visit him in prison they have a conversation that is subtly written to lead by an indirect route to Nelson's understated revelation that he is dying and does not want to die behind bars. This scene is so strong that it sets us up for big things: We expect Willie to get out, get involved in the plot, and be instrumental in the climax. That doesn't happen. There is a very nice courtroom scene, during which you'll have to pay close attention to catch on to the subverbal and illegal conversation conducted between the judge and the lawyer. But then the Nelson character quickly disappears from the movie, and we're surprised and a little disappointed. Willie has played the character so well that we wanted more. But, then, I suppose it is a good thing when a movie creates characters we feel that strongly about, and *Thief* is populated with them. It's a thriller with plausible people in it. How rare.

Thieves Like Us ★ ★ ★ ½
R, 123 m., 1974

Keith Carradine (Bowie), Shelley Duvall (Keechie), John Schuck (Chicamaw), Bert Remsen (T-Dub), Louise Fletcher (Mattie), Ann Latham (Luie). Directed by Robert Altman and produced by Jerry Bick. Screenplay by Calder Willingham, Joan Tewksbury, and Altman.

Like so much of his work, Robert Altman's *Thieves Like Us* has to be approached with a certain amount of imagination. Some movies are content to offer us escapist experiences and hope we'll be satisfied. But you can't sink back and simply absorb an Altman film; he's as concerned with style as subject, and his preoccupation isn't with story or character, but with how he's showing us his tale. That's the case with *Thieves Like Us,* which no doubt has all sorts of weaknesses in character and plot, but which manages a visual strategy so perfectly controlled that we get an uncanny feel for this time and this place. The movie is about a gang of fairly dumb bank robbers, and about how the youngest of them falls in love with a girl, and about how they stick up some banks and listen to the radio and drink Coke and eventually get shot at.

The outline suggests *Bonnie and Clyde*, but *Thieves Like Us* resembles it only in the most general terms of period and setting. The characters are totally different; Bonnie and Clyde were anti-heroes, but this gang of Altman's has no heroism at all. Just a kind of plodding simplicity, punctuated by some of them with violence, and by the boy with a kind of wondering love. They play out their sad little destinies against two backdrops: One is the pastoral feeling of the Southern countryside, and the other is an exactly observed series of interior scenes that recapture just what it was like to drowse through a slow, hot summer Sunday afternoon, with the radio in the background and the kids playing at pretending to do Daddy's job. If Daddy is a bank robber, so what?

The radio is constantly on in the background of *Thieves Like Us*, but it's not used as a source of music as it was in *American Graffiti* or *Mean Streets*. The old shows we hear are not supposed to be heard by Altman's characters; they're like theme music, to be repeated in the film when the same situations occur. "Gangbusters" plays when they rob a bank, for example, even though the bank would have been closed before "Gangbusters" came on. That's OK, because the radio isn't supposed to be realistic; it's Altman's wry, elegiac comment on the distance between radio fantasy and this dusty, slow-witted reality.

At the heart of the movie is a lovely relationship between the young couple, played by Keith Carradine and Shelley Duvall. They've both been in Altman movies before (just about everybody in view here is in his stock company), and it's easy to see why he likes them so. They don't look like movie stars. They share a kind of rangy grace, an ability to project shyness and uncertainty. There's a scene in bed that captures this; it's a two-shot with Keith in the foreground and

Shelley, on her back, eyes to the ceiling, slowly exhaling little plumes of smoke. Nothing is said. The radio plays. Somehow we know just how this quiet, warm moment feels.

The movie's fault is that Altman, having found the perfect means for realizing his story visually, did not spend enough thought, perhaps, on the story itself. *Thieves Like Us* is not another *Bonnie and Clyde*, and yet it does end in a similar way, with a shootout. And by this time, we've seen too many movies that have borrowed that structure; that have counted on the bloody conclusion to lend significance to what went before. In *Thieves Like Us*, there just wasn't that much significance, and I don't think there's meant to be. These are small people in a weary time, robbing banks because that's their occupation, getting shot because that's the law's occupation.

Altman's comment on the people and time is carried out through the way he observes them; if you try to understand his intention by analyzing the story, you won't get far. Audiences have always been so plot-oriented that it's possible they'll just go ahead and think this is a bad movie, without pausing to reflect on its scene after scene of poignant observation. Altman may not tell a story better than any one, but he sees one with great clarity and tenderness.

The Thing ★ ★ ½
R, 108 m., 1982

Kurt Russell (MacReady), Wilford Brimley (Blair), T.K. Carter (Nauls), David Clennon (Palmer), Keith David (Childs), Richard Dysart (Dr. Copper). Directed by John Carpenter and produced by David Foster and Lawrence Turman. Screenplay by Bill Lancaster.

A spaceship crash-lands on Earth countless years ago and is buried under Antarctic ice. It has a creature on board. Modern scientists dig up the creature, thaw it out, and discover too late that it still lives—and has the power to imitate all life-forms. Its desire to live and expand is insatiable. It begins to assume the identities of the scientists at an isolated Antarctic research station. The crucial question becomes: Who is real, and who is the Thing? The original story was called *Who Goes*

There? It was written by John W. Campbell, Jr., in the late 1930s, and it provided such a strong and scary story that it inspired at least four movie versions before this one: The original *The Thing* in 1952, *Invasion of the Body Snatchers* in 1956 and 1978, *Alien* in 1979, and now John Carpenter's 1982 remake, again called *The Thing.*

I mention the previous incarnations of *The Thing* not to demonstrate my mastery of *The Filmgoer's Companion,* but to suggest the many possible approaches to this material. The two 1950s versions, especially *Body Snatchers,* were seen at the time as fables based on McCarthyism; communists, like victims of the Thing, looked, sounded, and acted like your best friend, but they were infected with a deadly secret. *Alien,* set on a spaceship but using the same premise, paid less attention to the "Who Goes There?" idea and more to the special effects: Remember that wicked little creature that tore its way out of the astronaut's stomach? Now comes this elaborate version by John Carpenter, a master of suspense *(Halloween).* His *Thing* depends on its special effects, which are among the most elaborate, nauseating, and horrifying sights yet achieved by Hollywood's new generation of visual magicians. There are times when we seem to be sticking our heads right down into the bloody, stinking maw of the unknown, as the Thing transforms itself into creatures with the body parts of dogs, men, lobsters, and spiders, all wrapped up in gooey intestines.

The Thing is a great barf-bag movie, all right, but is it any good? I found it disappointing, for two reasons: the superficial characterizations and the implausible behavior of the scientists on that icy outpost. Characters have never been Carpenter's strong point; he says he likes his movies to create emotions in his audiences, and I guess he'd rather see us jump six inches than get involved in the personalities of his characters. This time, though, despite some roughed-out typecasting and a few reliable stereotypes (the drunk, the psycho, the hero), he has populated his ice station with people whose primary purpose in life is to get jumped on from behind. The few scenes that develop characterizations are overwhelmed by the scenes in which the men are just setups for an attack by the Thing.

That leads us to the second problem, plausibility. We know that the Thing likes to wait until a character is alone, and then pounce, digest, and imitate him—by the time you see Doc again, is he still Doc, or is he the Thing? Well, the obvious defense against this problem is a watertight buddy system, but, time and time again, Carpenter allows his characters to wander off alone and come back with silly grins on their faces, until we've lost count of who may have been infected, and who hasn't. That takes the fun away.

The Thing is basically, then, just a geek show, a grossout movie in which teenagers can dare one another to watch the screen. There's nothing wrong with that; I like being scared and I *was* scared by many scenes in *The Thing.* But it seems clear that Carpenter made his choice early on to concentrate on the special effects and the technology and to allow the story and people to become secondary. Because this material has been done before, and better, especially in the original *The Thing* and in *Alien,* there's no need to see this version unless you are interested in what the Thing might look like while starting from anonymous greasy organs extruding giant crab legs and transmuting itself into a dog. Amazingly, I'll bet that thousands, if not millions, of moviegoers *are* interested in seeing just that.

This Is Elvis ★ ★ ★ ½
PG, 88 m., 1981

Voices: Elvis (Ral Donner), Joe Esposito (Joe Esposito), Linda Thompson (Linda Thompson), Priscilla Presley (Lisha Sweetnam). Directed, produced, and written by Malcolm Leo and Andrew Solt. Featuring documentary footage of Elvis Presley.

This Is Elvis is the extraordinary record of a man who simultaneously became a great star and was destroyed by alcohol and drug addiction. What is most striking about its documentary footage is that we can almost always see both things happening at once. There is hardly a time when Elvis doesn't appear to be under the influence of mind-altering chemicals, and never a time, not even when he is only weeks from death, when he doesn't possess his special charisma. The movie's lesson is brutal, sad, and inescapable: Elvis Presley was a man who gave joy to a great many people but felt very little of his own, because he became addicted and stayed addicted until the day it killed him.

This movie does not, however, intend to be a documentary about Presley's drug usage. It just turns out that way, because Presley's life turned out that way. The film is a re-creation of his life and image, and uses documentary footage from a wide variety of sources, including Presley's own professionally made home movies. Not all the footage is even really of Presley. Some early childhood scenes are fiction, with a young actor playing Elvis. They don't work, but they're soon over. A few other scenes are also faked, including one shot following Presley into his home on the night he died, and another showing him rushing to his mother's sickbed (the double is an Elvis imitator named Johnny Harra). But the faked footage adds up to only about 10 percent of the movie, and is helpful in maintaining continuity.

The rest of the film's footage is extraordinary, and about half of it has never been seen anywhere. This film isn't just a compilation of old Elvis documentaries. The filmmakers got permission from Presley's manager, Colonel Tom Parker, to use Presley's own private film archives and to shoot inside Graceland, his mansion. They include footage that was not even suspected to exist, including scenes from a birthday party Elvis had in Germany when he was still in the Army (we see a very young Priscilla at the party), scenes of Elvis's parents moving into Graceland, scenes with Elvis clowning around with buddies, and shots taken inside his limousine very near the end, when he was drunk and drugged and obviously very ill. There are also sequences during which we frankly wonder if he will be able to make it onto the stage.

The documentary also includes some of Presley's key television appearances, including his first guest appearances on the old "Dorsey Brothers Bandstand" and the "Ed Sullivan Show" (with Ed assuring America that Elvis was "a real decent, fine boy . . . Elvis, you're thoroughly all right"). There is newsreel footage of Elvis getting out of the Army (and, significantly, observing "it was so cold some nights we had to take bennies to stay awake"). There is an old kinescope,

long thought to be lost, of a TV special hosted by Frank Sinatra to welcome Elvis back to civilian life (and in his duet with Sinatra, Presley is confused and apparently under the influence of tranquilizers).

The young Elvis in this movie is an entertainer of incredible energy and charisma. The charisma stays, but somewhere along the way we notice a change in his behavior, a draining away of cheerfulness, a dreadful secret scourge. And in the film's final scenes, Presley is shockingly ill: He's bloated, his skin is splotchy, he's shaking and dripping with sweat, and, in one very painful sequence shot during a concert, he cannot remember the words to his songs. But he pushes through anyway, and his final renditions of "My Way" and "Are You Lonesome Tonight?" are beautiful and absolutely heartbreaking. He may have lost his mind, but he never lost his voice or his heart.

Elvis Presley should, of course, still be alive. The film interviews his former bodyguards about his drinking and drug usage, and they argue convincingly that they could not stop him from doing what he was determined to do. But an addict, of course, has only two choices, no matter how he might deceive himself that he has many. He can either continue to use, or he can ask for help.

The irony in Presley's case is that his own doctor was apparently the source of most of his drugs. Could Elvis have stopped? Sure. Would he have been alive today? Probably. But he was never able to admit his addiction and find the will to seek help. And he was surrounded by foot-kissers and yes-men. This movie shows the disintegration and death of a talented man who backed himself into a corner. He did it his way.

This Is Spinal Tap ★ ★ ★ ★
R, 87 m., 1984

Rob Reiner (Marty DiBergi), Michael McKean (David St. Huggins), Christopher Guest (Nigel Tufnel), Harry Shearer (Derek Smalls). Directed by Rob Reiner and produced by Karen Murphy. Screenplay by Christopher Guest, Michael McKean, Harry Shearer, and Reiner.

The children born at Woodstock are preparing for the junior prom, and rock 'n' roll is still here to stay. Rock musicians never die, they just fade away, and *This Is Spinal Tap* is a movie about a British rock group that is rocketing to the bottom of the charts.

The movie looks like a documentary filmed during the death throes of a British rock band named Spinal Tap. It is, in fact, a satire. The rock group does not really exist, but the best thing about this film is that it could. The music, the staging, the special effects, the backstage feuding, and the pseudo-profound philosophizing are right out of a hundred other rock groups and a dozen other documentaries about rock.

The group is in the middle of an American tour. The tour is not going well. Spinal Tap was once able to fill giant arenas, but its audiences have grown smaller and smaller, and concert dates are evaporating as the bad news gets around. No wonder. Spinal Tap is a bad rock 'n' roll band. It is derivative, obvious, phony, and pretentious, and it surrounds itself with whatever images seem commercial at the moment (a giant death's-head on stage, for one). The movie is absolutely inspired in the subtle way it establishes Spinal Tap's badness. The satire has a deft, wicked touch. Spinal Tap is not that much worse than, not that much different from, some successful rock bands. A few breaks here or there, a successful album, and they could be back in business. (Proof of that: A sound track album, "Smell the Glove," is getting lots of air play with cuts like "Sex Farm".)

The documentary is narrated by its director, Marty DiBergi, played by Rob Reiner, the director of the real movie. He explains that he was first attracted to the band by its unusual loudness. He follows them on tour, asking profound questions that inspire deep, meaningless answers, and his cameras watch as the group comes unglued. One of the band members brings in a girlfriend from England. She feuds with the group's manager. Bookings are canceled. The record company doesn't like the cover for the group's new album. One disastrous booking takes Spinal Tap to a dance in a hangar on a military base. The movie is brilliant at telling its story through things that happen in the background and at the edges of the picture: By the end of the film, we know as much about the personalities and conflicts of the band members as if the movie had been straight-forward narrative.

There are a lot of great visual jokes, which I don't want to spoil—especially the climax of the band's Stonehenge production number, or another number that involves them being reborn from womblike stage props. There also are moments of inspired satire aimed at previous styles in rock films, as when we get glimpses of Spinal Tap in its earlier incarnations (the band started as sort of a folk group, plunged into the flower-people generation, and was a little late getting into heavy metal, satanism, and punk).

This Is Spinal Tap assumes that audiences will get most of the jokes. I think that's right. "Entertainment Tonight" and music TV and Barbara Walters specials have made show-business trade talk into national gossip, and one of the greatest pleasures of the movie is that it doesn't explain everything. It simply, slyly, destroys one level of rock pomposity after another.

3 Women ★ ★ ★ ★
PG, 125 m., 1977

Sissy Spacek (Pinky), Shelley Duvall (Millie), Janice Rule (Willie), Robert Fortier (Edgar), Ruth Nelson (Mrs. Rose), John Cromwell (Mr. Rose), Craig Richard Nelson (Dr. Maas), Maysie Hoy (Doris). Directed, produced, and written by Robert Altman.

Robert Altman's *3 Women* is, on the one hand, a straightforward portrait of life in a godforsaken California desert community, and, on the other, a mysterious exploration of human personalities. Its specifics are so real you can almost touch them, and its conclusion so surreal we can supply our own.

The community exists somewhere in Southern California, that uncharted continent of discontent and restlessness. Some of its people have put themselves down in a place that contains, so far as we can see, a spa where old people take an arthritis cure, a Western-style bar with a shooting range out back, and a singles residential motel with a swimming pool that has the most unsettling murals on its bottom.

Into this outpost one day comes Pinky (Sissy Spacek), a child-woman so naive, so open, so willing to have enthusiasm, that in another century she might have been a saint, a strange one. She takes a job at the spa and is instructed in her duties by Millie (Shelley Duvall), who is fascinated by the incorrect belief that the men in town are hot for her. Millie recruits Pinky as a roommate in the motel.

This whole stretch of the film—the first hour—is a funny, satirical, and sometimes sad study of the community and its people, who have almost all failed at something else, somewhere else. The dominant male is Edgar (Robert Fortier), a onetime stuntman, now a boozer with a beer bottle permanently in his hand. He's married to Willie (Janice Rule), who never speaks, and is pregnant, and is painting the murals. It's all terrifically new to Pinky: Drinking a beer (which she does as if just discovering the principle of a glass), or moving into Millie's apartment (which she solemnly declares to be the most beautiful place she's ever seen).

Then the film arrives at its center point, one of masked sexual horror. Millie comes home with Edgar and throws Pinky out of their bedroom, and Pinky tries to commit suicide by jumping into the pool. She survives, but as she recovers the film moves from realism to a strange, haunted psychological landscape in which, somehow, Pinky and Millie exchange personalities. *3 Women* isn't Altman out of Freud via *Psychology Today*, and so the movie mercifully doesn't attempt to explain what's happened in logical terms (*any* explanation would be disappointing, I think, compared to the continuing mystery). Somehow we *feel* what's happened, though, even if we can't explain it in so many words.

The movie's been compared to Bergman's *Persona*, another film in which women seem to share personalities, and maybe *Persona*, also so mysterious when we first see it, helps point the way. But I believe Altman has provided his own signposts, in two important scenes, one at the beginning, one at the end, that mirror one another. Millie, teaching Pinky how to exercise the old folks' legs in the hot baths, places Pinky's feet on her stomach and moves them back and forth, just as Pinky sees the apparition of two twins on the other side of the pool.

Later, when the older woman, Willie, is in labor, Millie places her legs in the same way and moves them in the same way, trying to assist the delivery. But the baby is stillborn, and so are the male-female connections in this small society. And so the women symbolically give birth to each other, around and around in a circle, just as (Altman himself suggests) the end of the picture could be seen as the moment just before its beginning.

The movie's story came to Altman during a dream, he's said, and he provides it with a dreamlike tone. The plot connections, which sometimes make little literal sense, do seem to connect emotionally, viscerally, as all things do in dreams. To act in a story like this must be a great deal more difficult than performing straightforward narrative, but Spacek and Duvall go through their changes so well that it's eerie, and unforgettable. So is the film.

THX 1138 ★ ★ ★
PG, 88 m., 1971

Robert Duvall (THX 1138), Donald Pleasence (SEN 5241), Don Pedro Colley (SRT), Maggie McOmie (LUH 3417). Directed by George Lucas and produced by Lawrence Sturhahn. Screenplay by Lucas and Walter Murch.

The brave new world of the American Zoetrope studio began in the late 1960s in San Francisco. Francis Ford Coppola, a young director of promise, persuaded Warner Bros. to help finance and distribute a group of features by the bright new filmmakers he'd gathered around him. Coppola had just finished a successful mainstream production for Warners', *Finian's Rainbow,* and his proposal sounded good in that era of youth films, bike films, trip films, and other high hopes.

The youth film and the others turned out to be lost causes, however, and as the American film industry moved back to traditional narrative pictures, not many of the proposed American Zoetrope films were made, and even fewer ever opened. Warner Bros., having decided to drop the San Francisco experiment, didn't back the surviving features very enthusiastically. The greatest casualty was George Lucas's *THX 1138,* a science fiction parable set in the twenty-fifth century and displaying remarkable visual mastery.

The movie's strength is not in its story but in its unsettling and weirdly effective visual and sound style. The story is standard sci-fi stuff: Five centuries in the future, mankind inhabits vast underground cities which are programmed by computers and policed by robots. The citizens are force-fed drugs to inhibit their passions, but THX 1138 (Robert Duvall) and his mate LUH 3417 (Maggie McOmie) cut down on their drug rations and discover that they have sexual appetites. Worse still, they are in love.

What follows is a battle against the centralized computer system, a few episodes of outsmarting the dumb robot policemen, and a chase scene. None of this is very original, and the whole business of Love versus State is out of Orwell and countless lesser writers. But Lucas doesn't seem to have been very concerned with his plot, anyway. His film was inspired by a student film he did at UCLA, which won the National Student Film Festival in 1968. The student work was sort of a dry run for this one, exploring ways of creating inexpensive but totally convincing special effects for a futuristic society. The experiment was a success; the subterranean laboratories, apartments, and corridors in *THX 1138* have a blinding, white porcelain sameness, and the characters seem to inhabit the future's most spectacular and sanitary bathroom fixtures.

The sound effects add to the illusion of a distant and different society. The dialogue seems half-heard, half-forgotten; people talk in a bemused way, as if the drugs had made them indifferent. Their words are suspended in a muted, echoing atmosphere in which only the computer-programmed recorded announcements seem confident. And the featureless whiteness of this universe stretches away into infinity (especially in the effective scene involving a prison with no walls—how can you escape from a prison that is simply an empty void?). *THX 1138* suffers somewhat from its simple story line, but as a work of visual imagination it's special, and as haunting as parts of *2001, Silent Running,* and *The Andromeda Strain.*

Ticket to Heaven ★ ★ ★ ½
R, 107 m., 1981

Nick Mancuso (David), Saul Rubinek (Larry), Meg Foster (Ingrid), Kim Cattrall (Ruthie), R.H. Thomson (Linc Strunk), Jennifer Dale (Lisa). Directed by Ralph L. Thomas and produced by Vivienne Lebosh.

Ticket to Heaven is about a young man who enters the all-encompassing world of a religious cult. What makes the movie absolutely spellbinding is that it shows us not only how he is recruited into the group, but how *anyone* could be indoctrinated into one of the many cults in America today. This is a movie that has done its research, and it is made with such artistry that we share the experience of the young man.

His name is David. He is played by Nick Mancuso, a powerful young actor, as an independent type who flies from Toronto to San Francisco to discover what has happened to a friend who joined up with the cult. He is welcomed to their communal residence, joins in a meal and some singing, and is asked if he'd like to spend the weekend at a retreat on the group's farm. He would. By the end of the weekend, he is a cult member. Can it happen that fast? I've read stories claiming that some cults need only seventy-two hours to convert almost anyone to their way. The best and the brightest make the best recruits, they say. The movie shows the three techniques used to indoctrinate new members: (1) low-calorie, low-protein diets; (2) sleep deprivation; (3) "love-bombing," which involves constant positive reinforcement, the chanting of slogans and great care *never* to allow the recruit to be alone for a moment.

Although *Ticket to Heaven* does not mention any existing cult by name, it is based on a series of newspaper articles about a former Moonie. The techniques in the film could, I suppose, be used by anybody. What makes the film so interesting is that it's not just a docudrama, not just a sensationalist exposé, but a fully realized drama that involves us on the human level as well as with its documentary material. There are scenes that are absolutely harrowing: an overhead shot of David trying to take a walk by himself and being "joined" by jolly friends; a scene where he guiltily bolts down a forbidden hamburger;

a scene where another cult member whispers one sentence that sounds to us, as much as to David, like shocking heresy. By that point in the film, we actually understand why David has become so zombie-like and unquestioning. We have shared his experience.

The final scenes in the film involve a deprogramming attempt. They are not as absorbing as what went before, if only because they involve an effort of the intellect, instead of an assault on the very personality itself. I've seen *Ticket to Heaven* three times, and at first I thought the film's ending was "weaker" than the rest. Now I wonder. What cults offer is freedom from the personality. They remove from your shoulders the burden of being you. That is a very seductive offer: why else do people also seek freedom from self through drugs, alcohol, and even jogging? As David is seduced into the cult's womb, we also submit vicariously to the experience. We understand its appeal. At the end, as David's reason is appealed to, as his intellect is reawakened, as he is asked to once again take up the burden of being himself, he resists—and maybe we do, too.

Tightrope ★ ★ ★ ½
R, 114 m., 1984

Clint Eastwood (Wes Block), Genevieve Bujold (Beryl Thibodeaux), Dan Hedaya (Detective Molinari), Alison Eastwood (Amanda Block), Jennifer Beck (Penny Block). Directed by Richard Tuggle and produced by Clint Eastwood and Fritz Manes. Screenplay by Tuggle.

Most modern police thrillers are simple-minded manipulations of chases, violence, pop psychology, and characters painted in broad stereotypes. *Tightrope* contains all four of those ingredients, to be sure, but it also contains so much more that it's a throwback to the great cop movies of the 1940s—when the hero wrestled with his conscience as much as with the killer.

The movie stars Clint Eastwood as a New Orleans homicide detective who is as different as possible from Dirty Harry Callahan. The guy's name is Wes Block. His wife has recently left him, and he lives at home with his two young daughters and several dogs. He is a good but flawed cop, with a peculiar hang-up: He likes to make love to women

while they are handcuffed. The movie suggests this is because he feels deeply threatened by women (a good guess, I'd say). Detective Block is well-known to most of the kinkier prostitutes in the French Quarter, but his superiors don't know that when they assign him to a big case: A mad slasher, apparently an ex-cop, is killing hookers in the Quarter. Block's problem is that he cannot easily enter this world as a policeman after having entered it often as a client. His other problem is that when he walks into that world, all of his old urges return.

The police work in *Tightrope* is more or less standard: The interviews of suspects, the paperwork, the scenes where his superiors chew him out for not making more progress on the case. What makes *Tightrope* better than just another police movie are the scenes between Eastwood and the women he encounters. Some of them are hookers. Some are victims. One of them, played by Genevieve Bujold, is a feminist who teaches women's self-defense classes. Block has always been attracted to flashy, gaudy women, like the Quarter's more bizarre prostitutes. We do not know why his wife left him, and we are given no notions of what she was like, but right away we figure that Bujold isn't his type. She's in her mid-thirties, uses no makeup, wears sweat shirts a lot, and isn't easily impressed by cops. But somehow a friendship does begin. And it becomes the counterpoint for the cop's investigation, as he goes deeper into the messy underworld of the crimes—and as more of the evidence seems to suggest that he should be one of the suspects. It's interesting that the movie gives Eastwood two challenges: To solve the murders, and to find a way out of his own hang-ups and back into an emotional state where he can trust a strong woman.

Tightrope may appeal to the Dirty Harry fans, with its sex and violence. But it's a lot more ambitious than the Harry movies, and the relationship between Eastwood and Bujold is more interesting than most recent male-female relationships in the movies, for three reasons: (1) There is something at risk in it, on both sides; (2) it's a learning process, in which Eastwood is the one who must change; (3) it pays off dramatically at the end, when their developing relationship fits into the climax of the investigation. Think how unusual it is for a major male star to appear in a commercial cop picture in which the plot hinges on his ability to accept and respect a woman. Apart from the other good things in *Tightrope*, I admire it for taking chances; Clint Eastwood can get rich making Dirty Harry movies, but he continues to change and experiment, and that makes him the most interesting of the box office megastars.

Time Bandits ★ ★ ★
PG, 98 m., 1981

Craig Warnock (Kevin), John Cleese (Robin Hood), Sean Connery (Agamemnon), Shelley Duvall (Pansy), Ian Holm (Napoleon), Ralph Richardson (Supreme Being). The Dwarfs: David Rappaport (Randall), Kenny Baker (Fidget), Jack Purvis (Wally), Mike Edmonds (Og), Malcolm Dixon (Strutter), Tiny Ross (Vermin). Directed and produced by Terry Gilliam. Screenplay by Michael Palin and Gilliam.

First reactions while viewing *Time Bandits:* It's amazingly well-produced. The historic locations are jammed with character and detail. This is the only live-action movie I've seen that literally looks like pages out of *Heavy Metal* magazine, with kings and swordsmen and wide-eyed little boys and fearsome beasts. *But* the movie's repetitive, monotonous in the midst of all this activity. Basically, it's just a kid and six dwarfs racing breathlessly through one set-piece after another, shouting at one another. I walked out of the screening in an unsettled state of mind. When the lights go up, I'm usually fairly certain whether or not I've seen a good movie. But my reaction to *Time Bandits* was ambiguous. I had great admiration for what was physically placed on the screen; this movie is worth seeing just to *watch*. But I was disappointed by the breathless way the dramatic scenes were handled and by a breakneck pace that undermined the most important element of comedy, which is timing.

Time Bandits is the expensive fantasy by Terry Gilliam, one of the resident geniuses of Monty Python's Flying Circus. It is *not* a Monty Python film. It begins with a little boy who goes up to bed one night and is astonished, as we all would be, when a horseman gallops through his bedroom wall and he is in the middle of a pitched battle. Before long, the little kid has joined up with a band of six intrepid dwarfs, and they've embarked on an odyssey through history. The dwarfs, it appears, have gained possession of a map that gives the location of several holes in time—holes they can pop through in order to drop in on the adventures of Robin Hood, Napoleon, and King Agamemnon, and to sail on the *Titanic's* maiden voyage.

As a plot gimmick, this sets up *Time Bandits* for a series of comic set-pieces as in Mel Brooks's *History of the World—Part I*. But *Time Bandits* isn't revue-style comedy. It's more of a whimsical, fantastic excursion through all those times and places, and all of its events are seen through the wondering eyes of a child. That's where the superb art direction comes in—inspired work by production designer Milly Burns and costume designer Jim Acheson. I've rarely, if ever, seen a live-action movie that looks more like an artist's conception. And yet, admiring all of these good things (and I might also mention several of the performances), I nevertheless left the screening with muted enthusiasm. The movie was somehow all on the same breathless, nonstop emotional level, like an overlong Keystone Kops chase. It didn't pause to savor its delights, except right near the end, when Sir Ralph Richardson lingered lovingly over a walk-on as the Supreme Being. I had to sort things out. And I was helped enormously in that process by the review of *Time Bandits* by Stanley Kauffmann in *The New Republic*. He describes the film, unblinkingly, as a "children's movie." Of course.

There have been so many elaborate big-budget fantasies in recent years, from *Raiders* to *Superman* to *Clash of the Titans*, that we've come to assume that elaborate costume fantasies are aimed at the average eighteen-year-old filmgoer who is trying to recapture his adolescence. These movies have a level of (limited) sophistication and wickedness that is missing in *Time Bandits*. But perhaps *Time Bandits* does work best as just simply a movie for kids. I ran it through my mind that way, wondering how a kid would respond to the costumes, the panoply, the explosions, the horses and heroic figures and, of course, the breathless, nonstop pacing. And I decided that a kid would like it just fine. I'm not sure that's what Gilliam had in mind, but it allows me to recommend the movie—with reservations, but also with admiration.

The Times of Harvey Milk ★ ★ ★ ½
NO MPAA RATING, 87 m., 1985

A documentary by Robert Epstein and Richard Schmiechen, narrated by Harvey Fierstein.

Harvey Milk must have been a great guy. You get the sense watching this documentary about his brief public career that he could appreciate the absurdities of life and enjoy a good laugh at his own expense. He was also serious enough and angry enough about the political issues in his life that he eventually ran for the San Francisco Board of Supervisors and became California's first openly homosexual public official. That victory may have cost him his life.

The Times of Harvey Milk describes the lives and deaths of Milk and Mayor George Moscone, who both were shot dead in 1978 by Dan White, one of Milk's fellow supervisors. It also describes the political and social climate in San Francisco, which during the 1960s and 1970s began to attract growing numbers of gays because of its traditionally permissive attitude. Milk was one of those gays, and in old photographs we see him in his long-haired beatnik and hippie days before he eventually shaved off the beard and opened a camera store in the Castro District. It was from the Castro that Milk ran for office and was defeated three times before finally winning in the same election that placed the first Chinese-American, the first black woman, and the first avowed feminist on the board. Milk was a master at self-promotion, and the movie includes vintage TV news footage showing him campaigning on such issues as "doggy-do," and stepping, with perfect timing, into a strategically placed pile of same at the climax of the interview.

There is a lot of footage of Milk, Moscone, and White (who disapproved of homosexuals but was naive enough to once suggest that the issue be settled by a softball game between his ward and Milk's ward). It is intercut with later interviews with many of Milk's friends, including a veteran leftist who admits that he was prejudiced against gays for a long time, until he met Milk and began to understand the political issues involved. There is a Chinese-American who parallels his own radicalization with Milk's. And there is immensely moving, emotional footage of the two demonstrations inspired by the deaths of Milk and Moscone: a silent, candlelight parade of forty-five-thousand people on the night of their deaths, and an angry night of rioting when White got what was perceived as a lenient sentence.

"If Dan White had only killed George Moscone, he would have gone up for life," one person says in the film. "But he killed a gay, and so they let him off easy." This is not necessarily the case, and the weakest element in *The Times of Harvey Milk* is its willingness to let Milk's friends second-guess the jury, and impugn the jurors' motives.

Many people who observed White's trial believe that White got a light sentence, not because of antigay sentiment, but because of incompetent prosecution. Some of the jurors were presumably available to the filmmakers, and the decision not to let them speak for themselves—to depend instead on the interpretation of Milk's friends and associates—is a serious bias. That objection aside, this is an enormously absorbing film, for the light it sheds on a decade in the life of a great American city and on the lives of Milk and Moscone, who made it a better, and certainly a more interesting, place to live.

The Tin Drum ★ ★
R, 141 m., 1980

David Bennett (Oskar), Mario Adorf (Alfred), Angela Winkler (Agnes), Daniel Olbrychski (Bronski), Katherina Tahlback (Maria), Charles Aznavour (Markus). Directed by Volker Schlondorff and produced by Frank Seitz and Anatole Dauman. Screenplay by Jean-Claude Carriere, Schlondorff, Franz Seitz, and Gunter Grass.

Allegories have trouble standing for something else if they are too convincing as themselves. That is the difficulty with *The Tim Drum*, which is either (a) an allegory about one person's protest against the inhumanity of the world, or (b) the story of an obnoxious little boy. The movie invites us to see the world through the eyes of little Oskar, who on his third birthday refuses to do any more growing up because the world is such a cruel place. My problem is that I kept seeing Oskar not as a symbol of courage but as an unsavory brat; the film's foreground obscured its larger meaning.

So what does that make me? An anti-intellectual philistine? I hope not. But if it does, that's better than caving in to the tumult of praise for *The Tin Drum*, which has shared the Grand Prix at Cannes (with *Apocalypse Now*) and won the Academy Award as best foreign film, and is hailed on all fronts for its brave stand against war and nationalism and in favor of the innocence of childhood. Actually, I don't think little Oskar is at all innocent in this film; a malevolence seems to burn from his eyes, and he's compromised in his rejection of the world's evil by his own behavior as the most spiteful, egocentric, cold, and calculating character in the film (all right: except for Adolf Hitler).

The film has been adapted by the West German filmmaker Volker Schlondorff from the 1959 novel by Gunter Grass, who helped with the screenplay. It chronicles the career of little Oskar, who narrates his own life story starting with his mother's conception in a potato patch. Oskar is born into a world divided; in the years after World War I, both Germans and Poles live in the state of Danzig, where they get along about as well as Catholics and Protestants in Belfast.

Oskar has fathers of both nationalities (for reasons too complicated to explain here), and he is not amused by the nationalistic chauvinism he sees around him. So, on his third birthday, he reaches a conscious decision to stop growing. He provides a plausible explanation for his decision by falling down the basement stairs. And for the rest of the movie he remains arrested in growth: a solemn-faced, beady-eyed little tyke who never goes anywhere without a tin drum which he beats on incessantly. For his other trick, he can scream so loudly that he shatters glass. There is a scene in which Oskar's drum so confuses a Nazi marching band that it switches from a Nazi hymn to "The Blue Danube." The crashing obviousness of this scene aside, I must confess that the symbolism of the drum failed to involve me.

And here we are at the central problem of the movie: Should I decide to take the drum as, say, a child's toy protest against the marching cadences of the German armies? Or should I allow myself to be annoyed by the child's obnoxious habit of banging on it whenever something's not to his liking? Even if I buy the wretched drum as a Moral Symbol, I'm still stuck with the kid as a pious little bastard.

But what about the other people in the movie? Oskar is right at the middle of the tug-of-war over Danzig and, by implication, over Europe. People are choosing up sides between the Poles and the Nazis. Meanwhile, all around him, adult duplicity is a way of life. Oskar's mother, for example, sneaks away on Thursday afternoons for an illicit sexual interlude. Oskar interrupts her dalliance with a scream that supplies work for half the glassmakers in Danzig. Does this make him a socialist or an Oedipus?

Soon after, he finds himself on the road with a troupe of performing midgets. He shatters glasses on cue, marches around in uniform, and listens as the troupe's leader explains that little people have to stay in the spotlight or big people will run the show. This idea is the last one Oskar needs to have implanted in his mind.

The movie juxtaposes Oskar's one-man protest with the horror of World War II. But I am not sure what the juxtaposition means. Did I miss everything? I've taken the story on a literal level, but I don't think that means I misread the film *as it stands*.

If we come in armed with the Grass novel and a sheaf of reviews, it's maybe just possible to discipline ourselves to read *The Tin Drum* as a solemn allegorical statement. But if we take the chance of just watching what's on the screen, Schlondorff never makes the connection. We're stuck with this cretinous little kid, just when Europe has enough trouble of its own.

To Be or Not To Be ★ ★ ★
R, 108 m., 1983

Mel Brooks (Bronski), Anne Bancroft (Anna Bronski), Tim Matheson (Lieutenant Sobinski), Charles Durning (Colonel Erhardt), Jose Ferrer (Professor Siletski). Directed by

Alan Johnson and produced by Mel Brooks. Screenplay by Thomas Meehan and Ronny Graham.

It's an old gag, the one about the actor who is always interrupted in the middle of Hamlet's soliloquy by a guy in the third row who has to go to the john and loudly excuses himself all the way to the end of the row. But I can't think of a better Hamlet for this particular gag than Mel Brooks. "That is the QUESTION!" he bellows, as the guy screws up his timing, his delivery, his concentration. And the punch line is that the guy is actually going backstage to have a quick assignation with the actor's wife.

Mel Brooks loves show business and has worked it into a lot of his movies, most unforgettably in *The Producers*. He also loves musicals and has worked musical numbers into the most unlikely moments in his movies. (Remember Frankenstein's monster doing the soft-shoe?) In *To Be or Not To Be*, Brooks combines a backstage musical with a wartime romance and comes up with an eclectic comedy that races off into several directions, sometimes successfully.

The movie costars Brooks and his wife, Anne Bancroft, working together for the first time on screen as Frederick and (Anna) Bronski, the impresarios of a brave little theatrical troupe in Warsaw on the brink of war. (Anna) Bronski, whose name is in parentheses because her husband has such a big ego, is a femme fatale with an eye for the handsome young servicemen that worship her nightly in the theater. Bronski is an all-over-the-map guy who does Hamlet's soliloquy and stars in a revue called *Naughty Nazis* in the same night and on the same stage. Then the Nazis march into Poland. What can a humble troupe of actors do to stop them? "Nothing!" Bronski declares—but then the troupe gets involved in an elaborate masquerade, pretending to be real Nazis in order to throw Hitler's men off-course and prevent the success of the German plans.

When *To Be or Not To Be* was originally made, by Ernst Lubitsch in 1942, the Nazis *were* in Poland, which gave a certain poignancy to every funny line. Lubitsch's stars were Jack Benny and Carole Lombard, both specialists in underplaying. Brooks and

Bancroft go in the opposite direction, cheerfully allowing farce, slapstick, pratfalls, and puns into the story, until the whole movie seems strung together like one of the revues in Bronski's theater.

The supporting players, given license to overact, have fun. Charles Durning plays a rigid but peculiarly confused Nazi colonel, and Tim Matheson is the young aviator who excuses himself loudly and sneaks backstage to meet Bancroft. The veteran actor Jose Ferrer plays Professor Siletski, a two-faced collaborator.

It will probably always be impossible for Brooks to remain entirely within the dramatic logic of any story, and here he gives himself a lot of freedom with lines like "Sondheim! Send in the clowns!" But *To Be or Not To Be* works as well as a story as any Brooks film since *Young Frankenstein*, and darned if there isn't a little sentiment involved as the impresario and his wife, after years of marriage, surprise each other by actually falling in love.

To Live and Die in L.A. ★ ★ ★ ★
R, 110 m., 1985

William L. Petersen (Richard Chance), Willem Dafoe (Eric Masters), John Pankow (John Vukovich), Debra Feuer (Bianca Torres), John Turturro (Carl Cody), Darlanne Fluegel (Ruth Lanier), Dean Stockwell (Bob Stockwell), Robert Downey (Thomas Bateman). Directed by William Friedkin and produced by Irving H. Levin. Screenplay by Gerald Petievich and Friedkin.

In the hierarchy of great movie chase sequences, the recent landmarks include the chases under the Brooklyn elevated tracks in *The French Connection*, down the hills of San Francisco in *Bullitt*, and through the Paris Metro in *Diva*. Those chases were not only thrilling in their own right, but they reflected the essence of the cities where they took place. Now comes William Friedkin, director of *The French Connection*, with a movie that contains a second chase that belongs on that short list. The movie is set in Los Angeles, and so of course the chase centers around the freeway system.

To Live and Die in L.A. is a law enforcement movie, sort of. It's about Secret Service agents who are on the trail of a counterfeiter who has eluded the law for years, and who flaunts his success. At one point, when undercover agents are negotiating a deal with the counterfeiter in his expensive health club, he boasts, "I've been coming to this gym three times a week for five years. I'm an easy guy to find. People know they can trust me."

Meanwhile, he's asking for a down payment on a sale of bogus bills, and the down payment is larger than the Secret Service can authorize. So, Richard Chance (William L. Peterson), the hot-dog special agent who's the hero of the movie, sets up a dangerous plan to steal the advance money from another crook, and uses it to buy the bogus paper and bust the counterfeiter.

Neat. The whole plot is neat, revolving around a few central emotions—friendship, loyalty, arrogance, anger. By the time the great chase sequence arrives, it isn't just a novelty, tacked onto a movie where it doesn't fit. It's part of the plot. The Secret Service agents bungle *their* crime, the cops come in pursuit, and the chase unfolds in a long, dazzling ballet of timing, speed, and imagination.

The great chases are rarely just chases. They involve some kind of additional element—an unexpected vehicle, an unusual challenge, a strange setting. The car-train chase in *The French Connection* was a masterstroke. In *Diva*, the courier rode his motor scooter into one subway station and out another, bouncing up and down the stairs. Or think of John Ford's sustained stagecoach chase in *Stagecoach*, or the way Buster Keaton orchestrated *The General* so that trains chased each other through a railway system.

The masterstroke in *To Live and Die in L.A.* is that the chase isn't just on a freeway. It goes *the wrong way* down the freeway. I don't know how Friedkin choreographed this scene and I don't want to know. It probably took a lot of money and a lot of drivers. All I know is that there are high-angle shots during the chase during which you can look a long way ahead and see hundreds of cars across four lanes, all heading for the escape car which is aimed at them, full-speed. It is an amazing sequence.

The rest of the movie is also first-rate. The direction is the key. Friedkin has made some

good movies (*The French Connection, The Exorcist, Sorcerer*) and some bad ones (*Cruising, Deal of the Century*). This is his comeback, showing the depth and skill of the early pictures. The central performance is by William L. Petersen, a Chicago stage actor who comes across as tough, wiry, and smart. He has some of the qualities of a Steve McQueen, with more complexity. Another strong performance in the movie is by Willem Dafoe, as the counterfeiter, cool and professional as he discusses the realities of his business.

I like movies which teach me about something, movies which have researched their subject and contain a lot of information, casually contained in between the big dramatic scenes. *To Live and Die in L.A.* seems to know a lot about counterfeiting, and also about the interior policies of the Secret Service. The film isn't just about cops and robbers, but about two systems of doing business, and how one of the systems finds a way to change itself in order to defeat the other. That's interesting. So is the chase.

Tommy ★ ★ ★
PG, 108 m., 1975

Ann-Margret (Nora Walker), Oliver Reed (Frank Hobbs), Roger Daltrey (Tommy), Elton John (Pinball Wizard), Eric Clapton (Preacher), Keith Moon (Uncle Ernie), Jack Nicholson (Specialist), Tina Turner (Acid Queen). The Who: Pete Townshend, John Entwhistle, Daltrey, and Moon. Directed by Ken Russell and produced by Robert Stigwood and Russell. Screenplay by Russell.

Ken Russell's *Tommy* is a case of glorious overkill—a big, brassy, vulgar overproduction that works because it never stops for a breath or a second thought. It's got confidence. It's a blast of wall-to-wall music for almost two hours, and its quietest moment is a Moog-synthesized belch from Oliver Reed that sounds like the Carlsbad Caverns throwing up. There's not the slightest hint of moderation or restraint in the movie, and there shouldn't be. This is Ken Russell giving a Bronx cheer to the most pretentious of the late 1960s rock operas, turning it into a clothesline on which he strings a series of bizarre, manic production numbers. Sit down in front, slide back in your seat, and let it assault you.

The movie's purpose and achievement would be hard to figure out on the basis of what its makers say about it. Pete Townshend, who wrote the original album for the Who, says *Tommy* is an attack on the hypocrisy of organized religion. Ken Russell, who's made a specialty of films about musicians (Tchaikovsky, Mahler, and Liszt), says *Tommy* is the greatest work of art the twentieth century has produced. He was almost certainly misquoted. What he meant to say was that it was a heaven-sent opportunity for him to exercise his gift for going too far, for creating three-ring cinematic circuses with kinky sideshows.

The message of *Tommy*, if any, is contained mostly in the last thirty minutes (of which we could have done without about fifteen). By then the hero (who started out in life as a blind deaf-mute) has become the pinball superstar of all time, even though he can't see the machine. Stardom brings him a fortune, he becomes the leader of a quasireligious cult, regains his senses, and gets his own Tommy T-shirt. But then things get out of hand. Tommy is on the level, but the people around him begin to commercialize on his fame in order to peddle T-shirts, record albums, and other artifacts. Tommy's enraged fans turn on him and what they perceive as his hypocrisy. How the makers of the film feel about this commercialization can be gauged by the prominence with which the end titles inform us that the sound track album is available on Polydor Records. To make money on a rock opera attacking those who would make money on a rock opera: that was the brave moral stand taken by *Tommy*.

But none of this matters, because Russell correctly doesn't give a damn about the material he started with, greatest art work of the century or not, and he just goes ahead and gives us one glorious excess after another. He is aided by his performers, especially Ann-Margret, who is simply great as Tommy's mother. She has one number that begins in an all-white bedroom with her sexy red dress slit up the side to about the collarbone, and ends with her slithering through several hundred pounds of baked beans. It's that kind of movie.

Tommy's odyssey through life is punctuated by encounters with all sorts of weird folks, of whom the most seductive is Tina Turner as the Acid Queen. The scene begins with Tina as the hooker upstairs from the strip parlor operated by Tommy's wicked stepfather, and ends with a psychedelic stainless steel mummy with acid in its veins. This scene is the occasion for Tommy's first smile, as well it might be.

Then there's the great pinball tournament, which is the movie's best single scene: a pulsating, orgiastic turn-on edited with the precision of a machine gun burst. Elton John, wearing skyscraper shoes, is the defending pinball champion. Tommy is the challenger. Russell cuts between the crowds, the arena, and a dizzying series of close-ups of the games (at times, we almost seem to be inside the pinball machines), and the effect is exhilarating and exhausting.

Tootsie ★ ★ ★ ★
PG, 116 m., 1982

Dustin Hoffman (Michael), Jessica Lange (Julie), Charles Durning (Les Nichols), Teri Garr (Sandy), Bill Murray (Roommate), Dabney Coleman (Ron), Doris Belack (Rita), Sydney Pollack (Agent). Directed by Sydney Pollack and produced by Dick Richards. Screenplay by Larry Gelbart.

One of the most endearing things about *Tootsie*, a movie in which Dustin Hoffman plays a middle-aged actress, is that the actress is able to carry most of her own scenes as herself—even if she weren't being played by Hoffman. *Tootsie* works as a story, not as a gimmick. It also works as a lot of other things. *Tootsie* is the kind of Movie with a capital M that they used to make in the 1940s, when they weren't afraid to mix up absurdity with seriousness, social comment with farce, and a little heartfelt tenderness right in there with the laughs. This movie gets you coming and going.

Hoffman stars as Michael Dorsey, a character maybe not unlike Hoffman himself in his younger days. Michael is a New York actor: bright, aggressive, talented—and unemployable. "You mean *nobody in New York* wants to hire me?" he asks his agent, incredulously. "I'd go farther than that, Michael," his agent says. "Nobody in Hollywood wants to hire you, either." Michael has a bad reputation for taking stands, throwing tantrums, and interpreting roles differently than the director. How to get work? He goes with a friend (Teri Garr) to an audition for a soap opera. The character is a middle-age woman hospital administrator. When his friend doesn't get the job, Michael goes home, thinks, decides to dare, and dresses himself as a woman. And, improvising brilliantly, he gets the role.

That leads to *Tootsie's* central question: Can a fortyish New York actor find health, happiness, and romance as a fortyish New York actress? Dustin Hoffman is actually fairly plausible as "Dorothy," the actress. If his voice isn't quite right, a Southern accent allows it to squeak by. The wig and the glasses are a little too much, true, but in an uncanny way the woman played by Hoffman looks like certain actual women who look like drag queens. Dorothy might have trouble passing in Evanston, but in Manhattan, nobody gives her a second look.

Tootsie might have been content to limit itself to the complications of New York life in drag; it could have been *Victor/Victoria Visits Elaine's*. But the movie's a little more ambitious than that. Michael Dorsey finds to his interest and amusement that Dorothy begins to take on a life of her own. She's a liberated eccentric, a woman who seems sort of odd and funny at first, but grows on you and wins your admiration by standing up for what's right. One of the things that bothers Dorothy is the way the soap opera's chauvinist director (Dabney Coleman) mistreats and insults the attractive young actress (Jessica Lange) who plays Julie, a nurse on the show. Dorothy and Julie become friends and finally close confidantes. Dorothy's problem, however, is that the man inside her is gradually growing uncontrollably in love with Julie. There are other complications. Julie's father (Charles Durning), a gruff, friendly, no-nonsense sort, lonely but sweet, falls in love with Dorothy. Michael hardly knows how to deal with all of this, and his roommate (Bill Murray) isn't much help. Surveying Dorothy in one of her new outfits, he observes dryly, "Don't play hard to get."

Tootsie has a lot of fun with its plot complications; we get almost every possible variation on the theme of mistaken sexual identities. The movie also manages to make some lighthearted but well-aimed observations about sexism. It *also* pokes satirical fun at soap operas, New York show business agents, and the Manhattan social pecking-order. *And* it turns out to be a touching love story, after all—so touching that you may be surprised how moved you are at the conclusion of this comedy.

Top Gun ★ ★ ½
PG, 109 m., 1986 ⮑

Tom Cruise (Maverick), Kelly McGillis (Charlie), Val Kilmer (Iceman), Tom Skerritt (Viper), Anthony Edwards (Goose). Directed by Tony Scott and produced by Don Simpson and Jerry Bruckheimer. Screenplay by Jim Cash and Jack Epps, Jr.

In the opening moments of *Top Gun*, an ace Navy pilot flies upside down about eighteen inches above a Russian-built MiG and snaps a Polaroid picture of the enemy pilot. Then he flips him the finger and peels off.

It's a hog-dog stunt, but it makes the pilot (Tom Cruise) famous within the small circle of Navy personnel who are cleared to receive information about close encounters with enemy aircraft. And the pilot, whose code name is Maverick, is selected for the Navy's elite flying school, which is dedicated to the dying art of aerial dogfights. The best graduate from each class at the school is known as "Top Gun."

And there, I think, you have the basic materials of this movie, except, of course, for three more obligatory ingredients in all movies about brave young pilots: (1) the girl, (2) the mystery of the heroic father, and (3) the rivalry with another pilot. It turns out that Maverick's dad was a brilliant Navy jet pilot during the Vietnam era, until he and his plane disappeared in unexplained circumstances. And it also turns out that one of the instructors at the flying school is a pretty young blonde (Kelly McGillis) who wants to know a lot more about how Maverick snapped that other pilot's picture.

Top Gun settles fairly quickly into alternating ground and air scenes, and the simplest way to sum it up is to declare the air scenes brilliant and the earthbound scenes grimly predictable. This movie comes in two parts: It knows exactly what to do with special effects, but doesn't have a clue as to how two people in love might act and talk and think.

Aerial scenes always present a special challenge in a movie. There's the danger that the audience will become spatially disoriented. We're used to seeing things within a frame that respects left and right, up and down, but the fighter pilot lives in a world of 360-degree turns. The remarkable achievement in *Top Gun* is that it presents seven or eight aerial encounters that are so well choreographed that we can actually follow them most of the time, and the movie gives us a good secondhand sense of what it might be like to be in a dogfight.

The movie's first and last sequences involve encounters with enemy planes. Although the planes are MiGs, the movie provides no nationalities for their pilots. We're told the battles take place over the Indian Ocean, and that's it. All of the sequences in between take place at Top Gun school, where Maverick quickly gets locked into a personal duel with another brilliant pilot, Iceman (Val Kilmer). In one sequence after another, the sound track trembles as the sleek planes pursue each other through the clouds, and, yeah, it's exciting. But the love story between Cruise and McGillis is a washout.

It's pale and unconvincing compared with the chemistry between Cruise and Rebecca De Mornay in *Risky Business*, and between McGillis and Harrison Ford in *Witness*—not to mention between Richard Gere and Debra Winger in *An Officer and a Gentleman*, which obviously inspired *Top Gun*. Cruise and McGillis spend a lot of time squinting uneasily at each other and exchanging words as if they were weapons, and when they finally get physical, they look like the stars of one of those sexy perfume ads. There's no flesh and blood here, which is remarkable, given the almost palpable physical presence McGillis had in *Witness*.

In its other ground scenes, the movie seems content to recycle clichés and conventions out of countless other war movies. Wouldn't you know, for example, that Maverick's commanding officer is the only man who knows what happened to the kid's father in Vietnam? And are we surprised when Maverick's best friend dies in his arms? Is there any suspense as Maverick

undergoes his obligatory crisis of conscience, wondering whether he can ever fly again?

Movies like *Top Gun* are hard to review because the good parts are so good and the bad parts are so relentless. The dogfights are absolutely the best since Clint Eastwood's electrifying aerial scenes in *Firefox*. But look out for the scenes where the people talk to one another.

Top Secret! ★ ★ ★ ½
R, 90 m., 1984

Val Kilmer (Nick Rivers), Lucy Gutteridge (Hillary), Omar Sharif (Cedric), Peter Cushing (Bookseller). Directed by Jim Abrahams, David Zucker, and Jerry Zucker and produced by Jon Davison and Hunt Lowry. Written by Abrahams, Zucker and Zucker, with Martyn Burke.

I have a friend who claims he only laughed real loud on five occasions during *Top Secret!* I laughed that much in the first ten minutes. It all depends on your sense of humor. My friend claims that I have a cornpone sense of humor, because of my origins deep in central Illinois. I admit that is true. As a Gemini, however, I contain multitudes, and I also have a highly sophisticated, sharply intellectual sense of humor. Get me in the right mood, and I can laugh all over the map. That's why I liked *Top Secret!* This movie will cheerfully go for a laugh wherever one is even remotely likely to be found. It has political jokes and boob jokes, dog poop jokes, and ballet jokes. It makes fun of two completely different Hollywood genres: the spy movie and the Elvis Presley musical. It contains a political refugee who fled America by balloon during the Carter administration, a member of the French underground named Escargot, and Omar Sharif inside a compacted automobile.

To describe the plot would be an exercise in futility. This movie has no plot. It does not need a plot. One does not attend movies like *Top Secret!* in order to follow the story line. I think you can figure that out right away, in the opening sequence, which is devoted to the sport of "skeet surfin'" and has beach boys on surfboards firing at clay targets. Instead of a plot, it has a funny young actor named Val Kilmer as the hero, a 1950s-style

American rock 'n' roller who is sent on a concert tour behind the Iron Curtain, and manages to reduce East Germany to a shambles while never missing a word of "Tutti Frutti" (he never even stumbles during *a-wop-bop-a-doo bop, a bop-bam-boom*).

The movie is physical humor, sight gags, puns, double meanings, satire, weird choreography, scatological outrages, and inanity. One particular sequence, however, is such an original example of specifically cinematic humor that I'd like to discuss it at length. (Do not read further if you don't like to understand jokes before laughing at them.) The sequence involves a visit by the hero to a Swedish bookshop. Never mind why he goes there. The scene depends for its inspiration on this observation: People who run tape recorders backward often say that English, played backward, sounds like Swedish (especially, of course, to people who do not speak Swedish). What *Top Secret!* does is to film an entire scene and play it backward, so that the dialogue sounds Swedish, and then translate it into English subtitles. This is funny enough at the beginning, but it becomes inspired at the end, when the scene finally gives itself away.

There are other wonderful moments. The dance sequence in the East Berlin nightclub develops into something Groucho Marx would have been proud of. The malt shop musical number demolishes a whole tradition of Elvis Presley numbers. And how the ballerina makes her exit in *Swan Lake* will, I feel confident, be discussed for years wherever codpieces are sold.

Topaz ★ ★ ★ ½
PG, 124 m., 1970

Frederick Stafford (Andre Deverauz), Dany Robin (Nicole, His Wife), John Vernon (Rico Parra), Karin Dor (Juanita), Michel Piccoli (Jacques Granville), Philippe Noiret (Henri Jarre), John Forsythe (Nordstrom). Directed by Alfred Hitchcock. Screenplay by Samuel Taylor.

In some ways *Topaz* is a perfectly typical Alfred Hitchcock movie, but in other ways it's something new and rather unexpected from the master. The Hitchcock style is still there, all right: The action in incongruous places, the montages showing cause and effect, the sinister qualities of everyday objects, the tightly programmed editing style. That's all there and, even if you don't notice it, it works the old Hitchcock tricks on you and you're scared when he wants you to be. But what's new in *Topaz* is Hitchcock's choice of a field of action. He goes much wider this time, using three groups of protagonists instead of one or two central characters, and his subject is nothing less than the spy systems of the Cold War.

Hitchcock claimed, and he was probably telling the truth, that he really didn't care what his movies were about. He approached them scientifically, manipulating his actors to produce the desired effects in the audience. He liked to get suspense when he wanted it; he liked to play an audience like a piano. In most of his movies, then, he ignored the "real" world and made no attempt to show things as they might really happen. He shut everybody into a Hitchcock universe and tried to trap you in it, too.

So his basic theme was usually the same: An innocent man, wrongly accused, is placed in a position where he must clear himself before he is overtaken by either the bad guys or the law. This theme is terribly useful for getting viewers involved and perhaps (psychology aside) that's why Hitchcock likes it. But in *Topaz*, he made one of his occasional excursions into other areas, and this time he went farther afield than he ever did in *Foreign Correspondent* or *The 39 Steps* or *The Birds*.

Properly speaking, *Topaz* doesn't have a hero, although it has two or three characters who function that way occasionally. It doesn't have a hero because it doesn't have a moral point of view; Hitchcock deals with an American-French-Cuban spy network at the time of the Cuban missile crisis, and yet his focus is so firmly on the spies as professionals that we hardly get the feeling we should be for the French or against the Cubans. The plot is complex, with a lot of characters left over from the mediocre Leon Uris novel. The action moves from Washington to New York to Havana to Paris as two spy networks conspire to get information on the missile crisis to either Washington or Moscow. The movie begins with a good chase scene in Denmark, where a high-ranking Russian has defected. It's not a *Bullitt*-type chase with lots of speed and fast cutting, but one of those Hitchcock chases where everyone's forced to walk slowly and act naturally and smile a lot, nervously. The Americans finally get the Russian back to Washington where he reveals information about the Cuban missiles and also about a security leak in Paris.

Hitchcock does a good job of re-creating that far-off time, 1963. There is a fascinating sequence in Harlem where the Cuban UN delegation (remember?) had taken over the Theresa Hotel. The idea is to get some papers to photograph them. Hitchcock uses a remarkable actor, Roscoe Lee Brown, as a black journalist who saunters in and breezes out again with the secrets. Brown's scenes are the most delightful in the movie; for the most part, Hitchcock allowed his actors to remain so wooden they all look alike.

There is then some hanky-panky in Cuba, including the most protracted tearful-death scene in years (the beautiful Karin Dor done in by blue-eyed, sinister John Vernon). And then the action switches to Paris for the complicated conclusion. The interesting thing about that conclusion, by the way, is that Hitchcock goes out on a downbeat. There's no climax, no chase; just the sordid working-out of a messy game of spying. It's a nice, quiet ending, very much in keeping with the film, and *Topaz* is good Hitchcock. When you see it, wait for that scene where Michel Piccoli urges Philippe Noiret to hurry up and drink his cognac, and you tell me if you believe Piccoli expects a visitor.

Trading Places ★ ★ ★ ½
R, 106 m., 1983

Dan Aykroyd (Louis Winthorpe III), Eddie Murphy (Billy Ray Valentine), Ralph Bellamy (Randolph Duke), Don Ameche (Mortimer Duke), Denholm Elliott (Coleman), Jamie Lee Curtis (Ophelia), Jim Belushi (King Kong). Directed by John Landis and produced by Aaron Russo. Screenplay by Timothy Harris and Herschel Weingrod.

Trading Places resembles *Tootsie* and, for that matter, some of the classic Frank Capra and Preston Sturges comedies: It wants to be funny, but it also wants to tell us something about human nature and there are whole stretches when we forget it's a comedy and get involved in the story. And it's a great idea

for a story: A white preppy snot and a black street hustler trade places, and learn new skills they never dreamed existed.

This isn't exactly a new idea for a story (Mark Twain's *The Prince and the Pauper* comes to mind). But like a lot of stories, it depends less on plot than on character, and the characters in *Trading Places* are wonderful comic inventions. Eddie Murphy plays Billy Ray Valentine, the con man who makes his first appearance as a blind, legless veteran. Dan Aykroyd is Louis Winthorpe III, the stuck-up commodities broker. And, in a masterstroke of casting, those aging veterans Ralph Bellamy and Don Ameche are cast as the Duke brothers, incalculably rich men who compete by making little wagers involving human lives.

One day a particularly tempting wager occurs to them. Aykroyd has had Murphy arrested for stealing his briefcase. It's an unfair charge and Murphy is innocent, but Murphy is black and had the misfortune to bump into Aykroyd in front of a snobby club. To Mortimer Duke (Ameche), a believer that enviroment counts for more than heredity, this is a golden opportunity to test his theory. He bets his brother that if Aykroyd and Murphy were to change places, the black street kid would soon be just as good at calling the shots in the commodity markets as the white Ivy Leaguer ever was. Because the Dukes are rich, they can make almost anything happen. They strip Aykroyd of everything—his job, his home, his butler, his fiancée, his limousine, his self-respect. They give Murphy what they've taken from Aykroyd. And the rest of the movie follows the fortunes of the two changelings as they painfully adjust to their new lives, and get involved in a commodities scam the Duke brothers are trying to pull off.

This is good comedy. It's especially good because it doesn't stop with sitcom manipulations of its idea, and it doesn't go only for the obvious points about racial prejudice in America. Instead, it develops the quirks and peculiarities of its characters, so that they're funny because of who they are. This takes a whole additional level of writing on top of the plot-manipulation we usually get in popular comedies, and it takes good direction, too.

But what's most visible in the movie is the

engaging acting. Murphy and Aykroyd are perfect foils for each other in *Trading Places*, because they're both capable of being so specifically eccentric that we're never just looking at a "black" and a "white" (that would make the comedy unworkable). They both play characters with a lot of native intelligence to go along with their prejudices, peculiarities, and personal styles. It's fun to watch them thinking. The supporting cast has also been given detailed attention, instead of being assigned to stand around as stereotypes. Jamie Lee Curtis plays a hooker with a heart of gold and a lot of T-bills; Ameche and Bellamy have a lot of fun with the Duke brothers; and Denholm Elliott successfully plays butler to both Aykroyd and Murphy, which is a stretch. The movie's invention extends all the way to the climactic scenes, which involve, not the usual manic chase, but a commodities scam, a New Year's Eve party on a train, and a gay gorilla.

Tribute ★ ★ ★
PG, 123 m., 1981

Jack Lemmon (Scottie Templeton), Robby Benson (Jud Templeton), Lee Remick (Maggie Stratton), Colleen Dewhurst (Gladys Petrelli), John Marley (Lou Daniels), Kim Cattrall (Sally Haines). Directed by Bob Clark and produced by Joel B. Michaels and Garth H. Drabinski. Screenplay by Bernard Slade.

I am aware that *Tribute* hauls out some of the oldest Broadway clichés in the book, that it shamelessly exploits its melodramatic elements, and that it is not a movie so much as a filmed stage play. And yet if I were to review it just on those grounds, I would be less than honest. In the abstract, *Tribute* may not be a very good film at all. But in its particulars, and in the way they affected me, it is a touching experience.

It's supposed to be cheating to make an admission like that. I myself believe that it is a film's form, more than its message, that makes it great. And yet *Tribute* is not a visually distinguished film. It has been directed, by Bob Clark, as a straightforward job of work. There are long sequences that are obviously just filmed scenes from Bernard Slade's original stage play. Yet the characters transcend these limitations and become people that we care about.

The film is mostly Jack Lemmon's, and he deserved his seventh Academy Award nomination for his performance as Scottie Templeton, the movie's hero. We all know somebody like Scottie—if we are not, God forbid, a little like Scottie ourselves. He's a wisecracking, popular guy with hundreds of deeply intimate passing acquaintances. He also has a few friends. One of them is his business partner (John Marley) and another is his ex-wife (Lee Remick). They love him and stand by him, but he can't allow himself to reveal how much that means to him. He is also hurt by his relationship with his son (Robby Benson), who has the usual collection of post-adolescent grudges against his father. All of these relationships suddenly become much more important when Scottie discovers he is dying. The movie begins at about that point in Scottie's life, and examines how the fact of approaching death changes all of Scottie's ways of dealing with the living.

His son comes home to visit for a few weeks. His wife returns to New York for a college reunion and stays to become involved in the crisis. The friend, Marley, acts as counsel and adjudicator. Other characters pass through, including a young woman (Kim Cattrall) who Scottie thinks would be ideal for his son (after all, she'd previously been ideal for Scottie himself). Veteran playgoers can already predict the obligatory scenes growing out of this situation. Scottie will be brave at first, then angry, then depressed, then willing to reach out to his son, and finally reconciled to his fate. Scottie's friends will rally around. His son will learn to love the old man. Everybody will become more human and sensitive, and the possibility of death will provide an occasion for a celebration of life. Et cetera.

What's amazing is that when these predictable situations appear, the movie makes them work. A great deal of the credit for that belongs to Lemmon and Benson. They are both actors with a familiar schtick by now: Benson trembling with emotions, Lemmon fast-talking his way into sincerity. In *Tribute*, though, the movie's characters are so close to the basic strengths of Lemmon and Benson that everything seems to work.

Take Lemmon, for example. Another actor, playing Scottie Templeton, might simply seem to be saying funny lines, alternating with bittersweet insights. Lemmon makes us believe that they're not lines; they're the way this guy talks. The big emotional changes take place underneath the surface wisecracks, making them all the more poignant. Robby Benson sometimes comes across as too vulnerable, almost affected in his sensitivity. Here, he's good, too: Examine the early scene where his father asks what the hell's going on, and Benson begins, "Let me try to explain about that . . ." with touching formality.

Maybe your reaction to *Tribute* will depend on your state of mind. I know people who say they "saw through it," dismissing it as merely a well-made play. I know others, myself included, who were really touched by it. Perhaps the film works better because it's *willing* to be a bittersweet soap opera. Life itself, after all, is rarely a great directorial achievement, but almost always seems to work on the melodramatic level.

The Trip to Bountiful ★ ★ ★ ½
PG, 106 m., 1985 ✔

Geraldine Page (Mrs. Watts), John Heard (Ludie Watts), Carlin Glynn (Jessie Mae), Richard Bradford (Sheriff), Rebecca De Mornay (Thelma). Directed by Peter Masterson and produced by Sterling Van Wagenen and Horton Foote. Screenplay by Foote.

The thing that saves this movie from sentimentality is that the heroine is a little ornery. She's not just a sweet and gentle little old lady. She's a big old lady, with a streak of stubbornness. And just because she's right doesn't mean she's always all that nice. When *The Trip to Bountiful* tells us that she wants to leave her miserable life in the city and pay one last visit to her childhood country home, somehow we know that the movie won't be over when she hears the birds singing in the trees.

The movie stars the redoubtable Geraldine Page in her Academy Award-winning role as Mrs. Watts, a country woman who has come to live in a cramped city apartment with her son and daughter-in-law. The apartment isn't big enough for two women. They're always on each other's nerves.

The wife, Jessie Mae (Carlin Glynn),

doesn't like Mrs. Watts singing her hymns around the house. Mrs. Watts's strategy is more subtle: She tries to appear long-suffering, a martyr, and she is much given to throwing herself on the couch and pulling a comforter over her head to muffle her sobs.

Both of these women have a pretty good case against each other, but it's Mrs. Watts we sympathize with. She hates life in the city, she knows it's choking her to death, and she wants to pay one final visit to Bountiful, the little town where she was born. So she goes to the train station, but the milk train doesn't stop in Bountiful anymore. So she goes to the bus station and buys a ticket to the nearest large town. This is in Texas in 1947. Because her son and daughter-in-law have gone to the train station to head her off (she's tried to escape before), she makes her getaway.

The whole middle section of the movie is the best, as she meets another traveler on the bus, a young woman named Thelma (Rebecca De Mornay). They sit next to each other during the long, drowsy trip, and they exchange memories and confidences. Thelma is, in a way, only an excuse to give Mrs. Watts someone to talk to, so that we can eavesdrop. Yet De Mornay makes the character so interesting, so young and open-faced, that the relationship between these two women becomes the heart of the movie. Even the ending itself doesn't quite live up to it.

The Trip to Bountiful has a quiet, understated feel for the small towns of its time. The little rural bus station, with its clerk drowsing under a lonely lamp bulb, looks just right, and so do the midnight streets outside. And when the sheriff arrives, alerted to look for a runaway old lady, it's perfect the way he and the ticket agent size up the situation and let Mrs. Watts have her last look at her childhood home.

Then her family arrives: her son Ludie (John Heard) and his wife Jessie Mae. Ludie really has his work cut out with these two women. Both of them live at a time when many women lived their lives through their men, and there is not enough room inside Ludie's simple, desperate soul for both of these women. Yet there is a moment of poetry as she sits on the porch of the old farmhouse and talks about how she almost expected to see her own parents come walking through the door, just as if all those years had never passed, just as if her own lifetime was a dream, and she was still a young girl again.

The Trip to Bountiful was written by Horton Foote, who based it on his own stage play. This is Foote's second recent slice of life from Texas: *Tender Mercies*, the wonderful movie starring Robert Duvall as an alcoholic country singer, was also written by him. You can see that *Bountiful* was based on a play—it falls fairly obviously into three acts—but the rhythms and dialogue come out of unstudied real life. And Geraldine Page inhabits the central role with authority and vinegar. The movie surprises us: It's not really about conflict between the generations, but about the impossibility of really understanding that you are even a member of an older generation, that decades have gone by.

Geraldine Page, who somehow always manages to have a hint of girlishness in her performances, who always seems to be up to something roguish and not ever quite ready to cave in to age, finds just the right notes in the final scenes to tell her son something he might never be able to understand: Someday he will be old, too, and he won't be able to believe it either.

Tron ★ ★ ★ ★
PG, 96 m., 1982

Jeff Bridges (Flynn/Clu), Bruce Boxleitner (Alan/Tron), David Warner (Dillinger/Sark), Cindy Morgan (Lora/Yori), Barnard Hughes (Gibbs/Dumont), Dan Shor (Ram). Directed by Steven Lisberger and produced by Donald Kushner. Screenplay by Lisberger.

The interior of a computer is a fine and private place, but none, I fear, do there embrace, except in *Tron*, a dazzling movie from Walt Disney in which computers have been used to make themselves romantic and glamorous. Here's a technological sound-and-light show that is sensational and brainy, stylish and fun.

The movie addresses itself without apology to the computer generation, embracing the imagery of those arcade video games that parents fear are rotting the minds of their children. If you've never played Pac-Man or Space Invaders or the Tron game itself, you probably are not quite ready to see this movie, which begins with an evil bureaucrat stealing computer programs to make himself look good, and then enters the very mind of a computer itself to engage the villain, the hero, and several highly programmable bystanders in a war of the wills that is governed by the rules of both video games and computer programs.

The villain is a man named Dillinger (David Warner). The hero is a bright kid named Flynn (Jeff Bridges) who created the original programs for five great new video games, including the wonderfully named "Space Paranoia." Dillinger stole Flynn's plans and covered his tracks in the computer. Flynn believes that if he can track down the original program, he can prove Dillinger is a thief. To prevent that, Dillinger uses the very latest computer technology to break Flynn down into a matrix of logical points and insert him *into* the computer, and at that point *Tron* leaves any narrative or visual universe we have ever seen before in a movie and charts its own rather wonderful path.

In an age of amazing special effects, *Tron* is a state-of-the-art movie. It generates not just one imaginary computer universe, but a multitude of them. Using computers as their tools, the Disney filmmakers literally have been able to imagine any fictional landscape, and then have it, through an animated computer program. And they integrate their human actors and the wholly imaginary worlds of Tron so cleverly that I never, ever, got the sensation that I was watching some actor standing in front of, or in the middle of, special effects. The characters *inhabit* this world. And what a world it is! Video gamesmen race each other at blinding speed, hurtling up and down computer grids while the movie shakes with the overkill of Dolby stereo (justified, for once). The characters sneak around the computer's logic guardian terminals, clamber up the sides of memory displays, talk their way past the guardians of forbidden programs, hitch a ride on a power beam, and succeed in entering the mind of the very Master Control Program itself, disabling it with an electronic Frisbee. This is all a whole lot of fun. *Tron* has been conceived and written with a knowledge of computers that it mercifully assumes the audience shares. That doesn't mean we *do* share it, but that we're bright enough to pick it up, and don't have to sit through long, boring explanations of it.

There is one additional observation I have to make about *Tron*, and I don't really want it to sound like a criticism: This is an almost wholly technological movie. Although it's populated by actors who are engaging (Bridges, Cindy Morgan) or sinister (Warner), it is not really a movie about human nature. Like *Star Wars* or *The Empire Strikes Back*, but much more so, this movie is a machine to dazzle and delight us. It is not a human-interest adventure in any generally accepted way. That's all right, of course. It's brilliant at what it does, and in a technical way maybe it's breaking ground for a generation of movies in which computer-generated universes will be the background for mind-generated stories about emotion-generated personalities. All things are possible.

Trouble in Mind ★ ★ ★ ★
R, 111 m., 1985

Kris Kristofferson (Hawk), Keith Carradine (Coop), Lori Singer (Georgia), Genevieve Bujold (Wanda), Joe Morton (Solo), Divine (Hilly Blue), George Kirby (Detective). Directed by Alan Rudolph and produced by Carolyn Pfeiffer and David Blocker. Screenplay by Rudolph.

Here is a movie that takes place within our memories of the movies. The characters and the mysteries and especially the doomed romances are all generated by old films, by remembered worlds of lurid neon signs and deserted areas down by the docks, of sad cafes where losers linger over a cup of coffee, and lonely rooms where the lightbulb is a man's only friend. This is a world for which the saxophone was invented, a world in which the American Motors Javelin was a popular car.

The movie begins with a man being released from prison, of course, and he is dressed in black and has a beard and wears a hat, of course, and is named Hawk, of course, and the first place he goes when he arrives in town is Wanda's Cafe, where Wanda keeps a few rooms upstairs for her old lovers to mend their broken dreams.

The cafe is on a worn-out old brick street down at the wrong end of Rain City. It's the kind of place that doesn't need to advertise, because its customers are drawn there by their fates. One day a young couple turn up in a broken-down camper. The kid is named Coop, and he knows he always gets into trouble when he comes to the city, but he needs to make some money to support his little family. His girlfriend is named Georgia, and she looks way young to have a baby, but there it is, bawling in her arms. She's a blonde with a look in her eyes that makes the Hawk's heart soar.

Coop falls into partnership with the wrong man, a black man named Solo who sits in a back booth at Wanda's Cafe and recites poems about anger and hopelessness. Before long, Coop and Solo are involved in a life of crime, and Hawk is telling Georgia she's living with a loser.

Wanda stands behind the counter and watches all this happen with eyes that have seen a thousand plans go wrong. She hires Georgia as a waitress. That turns Hawk into a regular customer. Wanda knows Hawk is in love with Georgia, because Wanda and Hawk used to be in love with each other, and once you learn to hear that note in a man's voice, you hear it even when he's not singing to you.

Coop and Solo are trying to sell some hot wristwatches. Hilly Blue doesn't like that. Hilly is the boss of the local rackets, and lives in a house that is furnished like the Museum of Modern Art. The best way to describe Hilly Blue is to say that if Sydney Greenstreet could have reproduced by parthenogenesis after radioactive damage to his chromosomes, Hilly would have been the issue.

Trouble in Mind is not a comedy, but it knows that it is funny. It is not a fantasy, and yet strange troops patrol the streets of Rain City, and as many people speak Korean as English. It does not take place in the 1940s, but its characters dress and talk and live as if it did. Could this movie have been made if there had never been any movies starring Richard Widmark, Jack Palance, or Robert Mitchum? Yes, but it wouldn't have had any style.

To really get inside the spirit of *Trouble in Mind*, it would probably help to see *Choose Me* first. Both films are the work of Alan Rudolph, who is creating a visual world as distinctive as Fellini's and as cheerful as

Edward Hopper's. He does an interesting thing. He combines his stylistic excesses with a lot of emotional sincerity, so that we believe these characters are really serious about their hopes, and dreams, even if they do seem to inhabit a world of imagination. Look at it this way. In Woody Allen's *The Purple Rose of Cairo*, a character stepped out of a movie and off the screen and into the life of a woman in the audience. If that had happened in *Trouble in Mind*, the woman would have asked the character why he even bothered.

Sometimes the names of movie actors evoke so many associations that further description is not necessary. Let's see. Hawk is played by Kris Kristofferson. Coop is Keith Carradine. Wanda is Genevieve Bujold. Hilly Blue is the transvestite Divine, but he is not in drag this time, allegedly. Mix them together, light them with neon reds and greens, and add a blonde child-woman (Lori Singer) and a black gangster (Joe Morton) whose shades are his warmest feature, and perhaps you can begin to understand why they call it Rain City.

True Confessions ★ ★ ★
R, 110 m., 1981

Robert De Niro (Des Spellacy), Robert Duvall (Tom Spellacy), Charles Durning (Jack Amsterdam), Ed Flanders (Dan T. Campion), Burgess Meredith (Seamus Fargo). Directed by Ulu Grosbard and produced by Irwin Winkler and Robert Chartoff. Screenplay by John Gregory Dunne and Joan Didion.

True Confessions contains scenes that are just about as good as scenes can be. Then why does the movie leave us disoriented and disappointed, and why does the ending fail dismally? Perhaps because the attentions of the filmmakers were concentrated so fiercely on individual moments that nobody ever stood back to ask what the story was about. It's frustrating to sit through a movie filled with clues and leads and motivations, only to discover at the end that the filmmakers can't be bothered with finishing the story.

The film is about two brothers, one a priest, the other a cop. In a nice insight in casting, Robert De Niro plays the priest and Robert Duvall plays the cop; offhand, we'd expect it to be the other way around, but

Duvall is just right, seedy and wall-faced, as the cop, and after a scene or two we begin to accept De Niro as a priest (although he seems too young for a monsignor).

The brothers live in Los Angeles in 1948. It is a Los Angeles more or less familiar from dozens of other movies, especially *Chinatown* and the Robert Mitchum *Farewell, My Lovely*—a small town, really, where the grafters and the power brokers know each other (and in some cases are each other). The movie's plot is complicated on the surface but simple underneath. It centers around a creep named Amsterdam (Charles Durning), a construction tycoon who got his start as a pimp. Both brothers have had dealings with the man. When Duvall was a vice cop, he helped handle the protection for Amsterdam's whorehouses. Now De Niro, the cardinal's right-hand man, oversees the building projects of the Los Angeles archdiocese. And Amsterdam gets most of the contracts for new schools and hospitals, even though his operation is tainted with scandal.

It's tainted with more than that after the dead body of a young woman is found in a field, cut in two. Duvall's investigation leads to a madam who once took a rap for him, long ago, and to a sleazy L.A. porno filmmaker. Eventually, certain clues point all the way back to Amsterdam. Try to follow this closely: Amsterdam met the girl through a business associate, who met her as a hitchhiker. When he first gave her a lift in his car, De Niro was another passenger. The movie makes a great deal of the fact that the monsignor once shared a car with the "virgin tramp," as the newspapers label the victim. But so what? One of the maddening things about *True Confessions* is that it's shot through with such paranoia that innocent coincidences take on the same weight as evil conspiracies.

The movie's emotional center is in the cop character. He's painted as a man who's not above taking a bribe. But at the same time he has a moral code that's stiffer than his brother's. (The monsignor, for example, isn't above rigging a church raffle so that a city councilman's daughter will win the new car.) What begins to eat away at Duvall is that this Amsterdam, honored as the Catholic Layman of the Year, is a grafter and former pimp. Did he also murder the girl? Duvall frankly doesn't care: The guy is such slime he should be arrested for the crime just on general principles.

True Confessions spends a lot of effort in laying the groundwork for its complex plot, but then it refuses to ever settle things. Instead, there are inane prologues and epilogues showing the two brothers years later, their hair gray, as they sigh philosophically over impending death and shake their heads at the irony and tragedy of it all—whatever it all was.

Since this isn't a thriller, we are invited, I guess, to take it as a cynical meditation on the corruptibility of man. Joan Didion and John Gregory Dunne, who based the screenplay on his novel, see the social institutions in their story as just hiding places for hypocrites and weary, defeated men. But they never follow through on their insights. The movie has, for example, a major subplot involving an old priest (Burgess Meredith) who is being put out to pasture. The priest is evidently a symbol of something, especially since the young De Niro gets the dirty job of firing him. But the movie never comes to terms with this story; it just leaves it sitting there.

At the end of *True Confessions*, we're just sitting there, too. We have been introduced to clearly drawn and well-acted characters, we've entered a period in time that is carefully reconstructed, we've seen moments between men and women that are wonderfully well-observed. But we haven't seen a film that cares to be about anything in particular, to state its case or draw its lines, or be much more than a skilled exercise in style.

Turk 182! ★
PG-13 97 m., 1985

Timothy Hutton (Jimmy Lynch), Robert Urich (Terry Lynch), Kim Cattrall (Danny Boudreau), Robert Culp (Mayor Tyler), Darren McGavin (Detective Kowalski), Peter Boyle (Detective Ryan). Directed by Bob Clark and produced by Ted Field and Rene Dupont. Screenplay by James Gregory Kinston, Denis Hamill, and John Hamill.

Turk 182! tells the story of an angry young man who plays humiliating practical jokes on the mayor of the world's dumbest city—which, for the purposes of this movie, is New York. The city is dumb because not a single one of its citizens can figure out who the mysterious man signing himself *Turk 182!* really is. No, not even the character whose nickname is Turk and whose fire deparment badge is number 182. The inspiration for *Turk 182*'s exploits possibly comes from the Fox, the anti-pollution activist whose exploits were recorded in the early 1970s by Mike Royko. Like the Fox, the Turk is morally indignant, and embarrasses public officials by staging harmless but dramatic stunts. Unlike the Fox, the Turk is trapped in a screenplay that takes this idea and turns it into an insult to the intelligence of the audience.

The movie stars Timothy Hutton in the title role. He is a talented young actor, and you can see that for yourself by watching *The Falcon and the Snowman*. In *Turk 182!* Hutton plays the kid brother of a New York fireman (Robert Urich), who is injured while rescuing a baby girl from a fire. Because Urich was off-duty at the time, he was in violation of department policy and is refused city health benefits. Hutton thinks that stinks. So do I. So would the mayor of New York. That's why the movie rings false from the very first; no mayor of New York would commit political hari-kari by attacking a heroic fireman at a press conference. But this one does. And so Hutton goes underground, displaying the words "Turk 182!" on subway trains, public monuments, and even the Queensboro Bridge. Every time the mayor makes a public appearance, the Turk is there—despite the best efforts of detectives Darren McGavin and Peter Boyle to stop him.

For a change of pace, the movie also throws in scenes involving the brother, who tries to kill himself and spends much of the movie in an unintentionally hilarious head-to-toe cast. And there are lots of authentic, macho New York saloon scenes, in which everybody stands around doing the Miller Time commercials as amateur hour. If the movie wants to reek of New York authenticity, why don't any of its characters have any street-smarts? Example: Although the Queensboro Bridge is placed under police surveillance, Turk 182 not only manages to sabotage a giant electric sign, but also to grease the girders of the bridge so the cops can't climb up and stop him. How much grease would that take? How many people? How much time? In this movie, you don't ask.

The sad thing about *Turk 182!* is that the whole project sounds like a High Concept movie, in which the *idea* of the Turk was allowed to substitute for a story about him. Sure, it would be neat to see a movie about a guy like this. But not this movie.

The Turning Point ★ ★ ★ ½
PG, 119 m., 1977

Anne Bancroft (Emma), Shirley MacLaine (Deedee), Mikhail Baryshnikov (Yuri), Leslie Browne (Emilia), Tom Skerritt (Wayne), Martha Scott (Adelaide). Directed by Herbert Ross and produced by Ross and Arthur Laurents. Screenplay by Laurents.

Perfect movies are very rare, and very easy to write about. Imperfect movies are harder to write about, and the hardest reviews of all are of movies like *The Turning Point* that are touched with greatness and yet keep losing their way. The good things in it are *so* good that you cherish them, and there's the temptation to forgive the lapses.

So let's start with the good. The movie's the story of an old friendship between a great ballerina (Anne Bancroft) and a ballerina (Shirley MacLaine) who might have been great but will never really know for sure. Twenty years have passed since they were both young dancers, and now Miss Bancroft performs in Miss MacLaine's hometown and their friendship reasserts itself. Miss Mac-Laine's daughter is a promising young ballerina—she already has professional experience—and Miss Bancroft arranges for her to join her company.

As Miss MacLaine accompanies her daughter to New York, three themes assert themselves: Miss MacLaine's jealousy, smoldering for twenty years; Miss Bancroft's fear of approaching age and yet her desire to see the young girl succeed; the self-doubt both women have about the choices they made of careers or marriage. These are adult themes, and *The Turning Point* handles them thoughtfully.

It also gives us a love story or two. Miss MacLaine's daughter falls in love with the ballet company's superstar (Mikhail

Baryshnikov, typecast). And during the long summer of the movie's action, Miss Mac-Laine has to deal not only with her own feelings but with her daughter's. We're dealing here with soap opera stuff, but never in a soap opera way. *The Turning Point* confronts its big emotional moments directly and simply, and maybe that's why they affect us so much.

The straightforward dramatic sections of the movie, then, are very well written and acted; Miss Bancroft and Miss MacLaine are particularly good, and then there are sensitive supporting performances by Tom Skerritt, as Miss MacLaine's husband, and by Leslie Browne, the talented young dancer who plays their daughter. When people say they loved *The Turning Point*, they're probably thinking about moments like the one when Miss Bancroft pushes the reluctant and sick young girl back onto the stage, or when the two older women go aside at a party and finally say all the things they've bottled up, or when Miss MacLaine is so touchingly mystified by how she should react to the news of her daughter's first affair.

Those moments are good enough to make the movie. And, of course, there's also a lot of dancing in the film; Baryshnikov is a wonder, and the film's director, Herbert Ross, is a choreographer who knows how to see dance through his camera. But it's during the ballet sequences that the film breaks down, because Ross can photograph the dances so much better than he can work them into his film.

This has been a juicy, realistic, achingly human movie for most of its length, dealing with age and jealousy, love and the cruel demands of great art. So we feel real disappointment when Ross breaks the mood and the flow. He does that most unforgivingly in a sequence where Miss Browne has a triumph onstage, and Ross cuts away to close-ups of Miss MacLaine and Miss Bancroft watching her—while prophetic dialogue from earlier in the film is repeated in flashback on the sound track. Unforgivable. And the movie's climactic dance scenes—the evening at ballet, punctuated by the hoary old gimmick of a hand turning the pages of a program —are fun for ballet fans, yes, but they land with a thud in the middle of the movie's emotional drama.

To sort out my feelings: *The Turning Point*'s story is handled with real care and touches us. The movie's dance sequences are vurtuoso in themselves. But the pieces don't match, and Ross doesn't help by encumbering the dance material with ungainly story devices from the 1930s. You watch this film about a woman wondering if she could have been a great dancer, and you find yourself wondering if it could have been a great film.

Turtle Diary ★ ★ ★ ½
PG-13, 97 m., 1985

Ben Kingsley (William Snow), Glenda Jackson (Neaera Duncan), Michael Gambon (George Fairbairn), Eleanor Bron (Miss Neap), Harriet Walter (Harriet). Directed by John Irvin and produced by Peter Snell. Screenplay by Harold Pinter.

I saw this scene once in the London Zoo. It happened in the gloom of an insect house. Two men stood stooped over, side by side, their hands clasped behind their backs, peering through a glass into the chamber where a rare spider lived. Their faces were bathed in the low red light coming from the enclosure.

As they watched the spider, I watched them, until at last the spider did whatever it was they had been waiting for it to do. Then they stood up, looked briefly at each other, exchanged a matter-of-fact nod, and went their separate ways. London has always seemed to me to be a city of hobbyists and fanatics, experts in obscure specialities. But this moment stands out in particular, as a spider and two voyeurs shared one of the spider's most intimate moments.

Turtle Diary, the quiet, sly, and immensely amusing film from a screenplay by Harold Pinter, begins with two more such devotees. They are obsessed by giant sea turtles. They peek through the glass as the turtles lazily wheel around and around their cramped space in a tank at the London Zoo. They meet again, by chance, in a bookshop way over on the other side of the city, where the man (Ben Kingsley) is a clerk, and the woman (Glenda Jackson) has come to buy a book on turtles. They gradually become aware that they are seeing each other frequently at the turtle house, and then they discover that each has approached the turtles' keeper with the same question: What would it take to steal those giant turtles and set them free in the sea?

Turtle Diary is about a scheme by Kingsley, Jackson, and the zoo curator to do just that. But it is about a great many other things, as well. It is about the strange boarding house where Kingsley lives in company with a jolly landlady, a moody spinster, and a Turk who never cleans up the kitchen after himself. It is about the flat where Jackson lives, alone with her pet water beetle and about the man across the landing who knows a great deal about snails. And it is about the young woman who works with Kingsley in the bookshop, and lusts after him.

In a movie filled with wonderful, small sequences, I think my favorite begins when Kingsley suddenly turns to the young woman and says, out of the clear sky, "That's a pretty dress." In the next scene they are in a pub, in the next scene a restaurant. And if you want to observe the mastery of screen acting, watch the way Kingsley keeps a poker face while discussing his sex life with the woman, and then watch the way he allows himself to smile.

Ben Kingsley's smile, so warm and mysterious, is the sun that shines all through *Turtle Diary*. This is not a predictable movie, and it does not have a predictable structure (it does not even begin to end with the climax of the turtle caper). It is about peculiar people who somewhere find the impulses to do things that make them very happy.

If this movie had been made in America, I fear, it would have turned into a burlesque, with highway cops chasing turtles down the Santa Monica Freeway. *Turtle Diary* could only have been written, directed, and acted in the country where I saw those two strangers wait with such infinite patience for the spider to do its thing.

28 Up ★ ★ ★ ★
NO MPAA RATING, 136 m., 1985 ✓

Featuring Tony Walker, Bruce Balden, Suzanne Dewey, Nicholas Hitchon, Peter Davies, Paul Kligerman, John Brisby, Andrew Brackfield, Charles Furneaux, Neil Hughes, Jackie Bassett, Lynn Johnson, Susan

Sullivan, and Simon Basterfield. Directed by Michael Apted and produced by Margaret Bottomley and Apted.

The child is father of the man.
—William Wordsworth

Somewhere at home are photographs taken when I was a child. A solemn, round-faced little boy gazes out at the camera, and as I look at him I know in my mind that he is me and I am him, but the idea has no reality. I cannot understand the connection, and as I think more deeply about the mystery of the passage of time, I feel a sense of awe.

Watching Michael Apted's documentary *28 Up*, I had that feeling again and again, the awe that time does pass, and that the same individual does pass through it, grows from a child to an adult, becoming someone new over the passage of years, but still containing some of the same atoms and molecules and fears and gifts that were stored in the child.

This film began twenty-eight years ago as a documentary for British television. The assignment for Michael Apted was to interview several seven-year-olds from different British social classes, races, backgrounds, and parts of the country, simply talking with them about what they found important or interesting about their lives. Seven years later, when the subjects were fourteen, Apted tracked them down and interviewed them again. He repeated the process when they were twenty-one, and again when they were twenty-eight, and this film moves back and forth within that material, looking at the same people when they were children, teenagers, young adults and now warily approaching their thirties.

We have always known that the motion picture is a time machine. John Wayne is dead, but the angle of his smile and the squint in his eye will be as familiar to our children as it is to us. Orson Welles is dead, but a hundred years from now the moment will still live when the cat rubs against his shoe in *The Third Man*, and then the light from the window catches his sardonic grin. What is remarkable about *28 Up* is not, however, that the same individuals have been captured at four different moments in their lives. We quickly grow accustomed to that. What is awesome is that we can see so clearly how the seven-year-old became the adoles-

cent, how the teen-ager became the young man or woman, how the adult still contains the seeds of the child.

One sequence follows the lives of three upper-class boys who come from the right families and go to all the right schools. One of the boys is a snot, right from the beginning, and by the time he is twenty-one he is a bit of a reactionary prig. We are not surprised when he declines to be interviewed at twenty-eight; we could see it coming. We are curious, though, about whether he will check back in at thirty-five, perhaps having outlived some of his self-importance.

Another little boy is a winsome loner at seven. At fourteen, he is a dreamy idealist, at twenty-one he is defiant but discontented, and at twenty-eight—in the most unforgettable passage in the film—he is an outcast, a drifter who moves around Great Britain from place to place, sometimes living in a shabby house trailer, still a little puzzled by how he seems to have missed the boat, to never have connected with his society.

There is another little boy who dreams of growing up to be a jockey, and who is a stable boy at fourteen, and does get to be a jockey, briefly, and now drives a cab and finds in his job some of the same personal independence and freedom of movement that he once thought jockeys had. There is a determined young Cockney who is found, years later, happily married and living in Australia and doing well in the building trades. There is a young woman who at twenty-one was clearly an emotional mess, a vague, defiant, bitter, and unhappy person. At twenty-eight, married and with a family, she is a happy and self-assured young woman; the transformation is almost unbelievable.

As the film follows its subjects through the first halves of their lives, our thoughts are divided. We are fascinated by the personal progressions we see on the screen. We are distracted by wonderment about the mystery of the human personality. If we can see so clearly how these children become these adults—was it just as obvious in our own cases? Do we, even now, contain within us our own personal destinies for the next seven years? Is change possible? Is the scenario already written?

I was intending to write that certain groups would be particularly interested in this movie. Teachers, for example, would hardly be able to see *28 Up* without looking at their students in a different, more curious light. Poets and playwrights would learn from this film. So would psychiatrists. But then I realized that *28 Up* is not a film by or for experts. It is superb journalism, showing us these people passing through stages of their lives in such a way that we are challenged to look at our own lives. It is as thought-provoking as any documentary I've ever seen.

I look forward to the next edition of this film, when its subjects are thirty-five. I have hope for some, fear for others. It is almost scary to realize this film has given me a fair chance of predicting what lies ahead for these strangers. I almost understand the motives of those who chose to drop out of the experiment.

Twice in a Lifetime ★ ★ ★ ½
R, 117 m., 1985

Gene Hackman (Harry), Ann-Margaret (Audrey), Ellen Burstyn (Kate), Amy Madigan (Sonny), Ally Sheedy (Helen), Stephen Lang (Keith), Darrell Larson (Jerry), Brian Dennehy (Nick). Directed and produced by Bud Yorkin. Screenplay by Colin Welland.

Everyday American life is so rare in the movies these days that some of the pleasures of *Twice in a Lifetime* are very simple ones, like seeing a family around a dinner table, or watching a kid sister prepare for her wedding day. The rhythms of life and the normal patterns of speech seemed almost unfamiliar, after all the high-tech thrillers and teen-age idiot films I've seen. This film was so sensible, perceptive, and grown-up that I almost looked for the subtitles.

The film stars Gene Hackman as a working man whose marriage is happy in all the official ways, and dead in the personal ways. His wife (Ellen Burstyn) has centered her life entirely around her home and her family to such an extent that on Hackman's birthday she doesn't even want to go out with him. She tells him to go down to the corner tavern and enjoy himself. And she means it. There is a lot missing in this marriage.

At the saloon, Hackman meets the new barmaid (Ann-Margaret) and begins a wary process of falling in love with her. He even-

tually decides to leave his wife and move in with this woman, and this decision causes upheaval throughout his family. His wife is devastated. But the angriest family member is his oldest daughter (Amy Madigan), who bitterly resents the way he's dumping them—especially when her kid sister (Ally Sheedy) is about to get married.

Twice in a Lifetime stacks its cards very carefully. One of the strengths of the movie is that it allows us to see so many points of view. Hackman has not simply dumped his wife for a sex bomb: the Ann-Margaret character has been around the block a few times and operates from a center of quiet realism. It is possibly true that the life and growth has gone out of his marriage. Perhaps he deserves another chance—although the movie is too hasty to assume that his wife does, too, if only she knew it.

The most complicated and interesting character in the movie is Amy Madigan's angry daughter. She's mad about more than the broken marriage. Her husband is out of work, and in her late twenties she feels somewhat trapped by her marriage and children. A lot of her hopes have gone into her kid sister. She wants her to go to college and make a future for herself, but Ally Sheedy is rushing into her own early marriage, blinded by young love.

Madigan acts as the contact point between the various parts of the story: loving her sister, exasperated by her, standing by her mom, resentfully excluding her father. It's quite an assignment, and as she tries to balance all those demands we see one of the most complex movie characters in a long time (have you noticed how many recent movies assign their characters one mood and think that's enough?).

The Gene Hackman and Ann-Margaret characters are complex, too. They are attracted not by lust but by the promise of a new life. They both feel that when they get up in the morning there's nothing to look forward to all day. This movie knows one of the differences between young love and middle-aged love: Kids often are motivated by romance, but people in their forties and fifties sometimes are inspired by the most romantic notion of all—idealism, and the notion that they have found a mate for their minds.

The least-defined character in *Twice in a Lifetime* is the wife, played by Burstyn. Her husband has made his decision and left her to make hers. At first she is simply lost. Eventually she starts picking up the pieces, and she gets a job in the local beauty parlor. She even gets a new hairdo (in one of the movie's most durable clichés). By the end of the film she has started to realize that she, too, was trapped by the marriage. But there is the slightest feeling that her realization owes more to the convenience of the screenplay than to her own growth.

The movie does not have a conventional happy ending. Life will go on, and people will strive, and new routines will replace old ones. The movie has no villains and few heroes. But it has given us several remarkable scenes, especially two confrontations between Madigan and Hackman, one in a bar, the other at a wedding rehearsal, in which the movie shows how much children expect from their parents, and how little the parents often have to give. Growing up is learning that parents are fallible. The people who find that hardest to learn are parents.

Twilight Zone—the Movie

Prologue and Segment 1. Written and directed by John Landis. Starring Dan Aykroyd, Albert Brooks, Vic Morrow, and Doug McGrath. ★ ★
Segment 2. Directed by Steven Spielberg. Written by George Johnson. Starring Scatman Crothers. ★ ½
Segment 3. Directed by Joe Dante. Written by Richard Matheson. Starring Kathleen Quinlan, Jeremy Light, and Kevin McCarthy. ★ ★ ★ ½
Segment 4. Directed by George Miller. Written by Richard Marheson. Starring John Lithgow and Abbe Lane. ★ ★ ★ ½
PG, 101 m., 1983

Produced by Steven Spielberg and inspired by the television series created by Rod Serling.

Every year at Oscar time, somebody comes up with the bright idea of making the Academy Awards into a fair fight. Instead of making the voters choose among five widely different performances, they say, they ought to have five actors playing the same scene. That way you'd really be able to see who was best. It's an impractical idea, but *Twilight Zone—the Movie* does almost the same thing. It takes four stories that are typical of the basic approach of the great "Twilight Zone" TV series, and has four different directors try their hand at recapturing Rod Serling's "wondrous land whose boundaries are that of imagination." And the surprising thing is, the two superstar directors are thoroughly routed by two less-known directors whose previous credits have been horror and action pictures.

The superstars are John *(Blues Brothers)* Landis and Steven *(E. T.)* Spielberg. The relative newcomers are Joe Dante, whose *The Howling* was not my favorite werewolf movie, and George Miller, whose *The Road Warrior* is some kind of a manic classic. Spielberg, who produced the whole project, perhaps sensed that he and Landis had the weakest results, since he assembled the stories in an ascending order of excitement. *Twilight Zone* starts slow, almost grinds to a halt, and then has a fast comeback.

Landis directed the first episode, which stars Vic Morrow in the story of a bigot who is transported back in time to Nazi Germany and Vietnam and forced to swallow his own racist medicine. This segment is predictable, once we know the premise, and Landis does nothing to surprise us. Because we know that Morrow was killed in a helicopter accident during the filming of the segment, an additional pall hangs over the whole story.

Spielberg's segment is next. It stars Scatman Crothers as a mysterious old man who turns up at an old folks' home one day and literally gives the residents what they think they want; to be young again. The easily anticipated lesson is that one lifetime is enough. Spielberg's visual style in this segment is so convoluted and shadowy that the action is hard to follow; the master of clearcut, sharp-edged visuals is trying something that doesn't work.

But then comes Joe Dante's weird, offbeat segment about a traveler (Kathleen Quinlan) who strays off the beaten path and accepts an offer of hospitality from a fresh-faced young kid who looks healthy and harmless. Once Quinlan is inside the roadside farmhouse where the kid lives, however, she's in another dimension—a bizarre world telepathically projected by the boy's imagination. The kid loves video games and TV cartoons, and he's trapped a whole group of adults in his private fantasies. The art direction in this segment is especially good at giving the house interior a wonderland quality.

George Miller's fourth segment stars John Lithgow in a remake of a famous "Twilight Zone" TV story in which a nervous air traveler sees (or imagines that he sees) a little green man hacking away at the engine of his airplane. But there *couldn't* be a little green man out there—could there? The beauty of *Twilight Zone—the Movie* is the same as the secret of the TV series: It takes ordinary people in ordinary situations and then zaps them with "next stop—the Twilight Zone!"

Two English Girls ★ ★ ★ ★
R, 108 m., 1972

Jean-Pierre Leaud (Claude), Kika Markham (Anne Brown), Stacey Tendeter (Muriel Brown), Sylvia Marriott (Mrs. Brown), Marie Mansart (Madame Roc), Phillipe Leotard (Diurka), Mark Peterson (Mr. Flint), Irene Tunc (Ruta). Directed by François Truffaut and produced by Claude Miler. Screenplay by Truffaut and Jean Gruault.

It's wonderful how offhand François Truffaut's best films fall. There doesn't seem to be any great effort being made; he doesn't push for his effects, but lets them flower naturally from the simplicities of his stories. His film, *Two English Girls,* is very much like that. Because he doesn't strain for an emotional tone, he can cover a larger range than the one-note movies. Here he is discrete, even while filming the most explicit scenes he's ever done; he handles sadness gently; he is charming and funny even while he tells us a story that is finally tragic.

The story is from the second novel by Henri-Pierre Roche, who began writing at the age of seventy-four and whose first novel, *Jules and Jim,* provided the inspiration for nearly everyone's favorite Truffaut film. The two novels (and the two films) are variations on the same theme: What a terrible complex emotional experience it is to have to share love.

We would say that both stories involve romantic triangles, but Roche seems to see them more simply (and poignantly) as the shared dilemmas of people caught helplessly in their situations. Nobody sets out deliberately to involve himself in a triangular relationship—not when the love involved is real. It hurts too much.

Truffaut introduces us to Claude, a young French art critic, and then introduces him to Anne Brown, an English girl visiting in Paris. They form a friendship, and the girl invites him to come and visit her mother and sister in Wales. During the visit, he falls in love (or thinks he does) with the sister, Muriel. They want to marry, but they both have poor health, and it is decided to put off the marriage for a year. Claude returns to Paris, where Anne follows after a while, and then they fall into a sexual relationship that passes for a time as love. The virgin Muriel, meanwhile, remains passionately in love with Claude and nearly has an emotional breakdown when she learns that he no longer plans to marry her.

The story, as it unfolds, is involved but never untrue. Love itself is an elusive prize that passes among them; it is their doom that whenever two of them are together, it is the third who possesses love. The film relates love and loss so closely that we almost forgive Claude for his infidelities and stubbornness. Perversely, he wants to be apart from Muriel (and later Anne) so that he can desire her all the more.

If *Two English Girls* resembles *Jules and Jim* in theme, it has an unmistakable stylistic relationship to Truffaut's little-seen masterpiece of 1970, *The Wild Child.* Both films used diaries, journals, and a spoken narration in order to separate us from the immediate experience of the stories. Truffaut wants us to feel that we're being told a fable, a sad winter's tale, that is all the more touching because these events happened long ago and love is trapped irretrievably in the past.

His visual strategy for creating this feeling is another favorite device from *The Wild Child:* the iris shot. (Put simply, this is the use of a slowly contracting circle to bring a shot to an end, instead of a fade or a cut). The iris isolates one element in the picture, somehow making it feel alone and vulnerable—and past. The film is photographed in a low-keyed color, and the sound recording is also a little muted; this isn't a film for emotional highs, we sense, because it's far and away too late for these lost love opportunities to be regained.

The one scene that violates this tone is as necessary as it is effective; when Muriel finally makes love with Claude we feel the terrible force of her passion, pent up for so many years, and then the camera pans to the blood-stained sheet and goes out of focus. Put in so many words, this probably sounds crude and obvious; in fact, this is almost the only red in the film, and is Truffaut's perfect visual metaphor for the fact that these three people have created a lot of their own unhappiness by avoiding or deflecting the consequences of their emotional feelings.

Jules and Jim was a young man's film (Truffaut was twenty-eight when he made it). *Two English Girls* is the film of a man some ten or twelve years down the road; it is still playful and winsome, but it realizes more fully the consequences of an opportunity lost. The final scene shows Claude, fifteen years later, wandering in the garden where he used to walk with Anne and Muriel. There are English children playing there, and he thinks to ask one of them, "Are you Muriel Brown's daughter?" But he doesn't, because . . . well, because.

2010 ★ ★ ★
PG, 157 m., 1984

Roy Scheider (Heywood Floyd), John Lithgow (Curnow), Helen Mirren (Kirbuk), Bob Balaban (Chandra), Keir Dullea (Bowman), Douglas Rain (HAL 9000). Directed and produced by Peter Hyams. Screenplay by Hyams.

All those years ago, when *2001: A Space Odyssey* was first released, I began my review with a few lines from a poem by e.e. cummings:

*I'd rather learn from one bird how to sing
than teach ten thousand stars how not to
dance.*

That was my response to the people who said they couldn't understand *2001*, that it made no sense and that it was one long exercise in self-indulgence by Stanley Kubrick, who had sent a man to the stars, only to abandon him inside some sort of extraterrestrial hotel room. I felt that the poetry of *2001* was precisely in its mystery, and that to explain everything was to ruin everything— like the little boy who cut open his drum to see what made it bang.

2001 came out in the late 1960s, that legendary time when yuppies were still hippies,

and they went to see the movie a dozen times and slipped up to the front of the theater and lay flat on their backs on the floor, so that the sound-and-light trip in the second half of the movie could wash over them and they could stagger to the exits and whisper "far out" to one another in quiet ecstasy. Now comes *2010*, a continuation of the Kubrick film, directed by Peter Hyams, whose background is in more pragmatic projects such as *Outland*, the Sean Connery space station thriller. The screenplay is by Arthur C. Clarke (who, truth to tell, I always have suspected was a little bewildered by what Kubrick did to his original ideas). *2010* is very much a 1980s movie. It doesn't match the poetry and the mystery of the original film, but it does continue the story, and it offers sound, pragmatic explanations for many of the strange and visionary things in *2001* that had us arguing endlessly through the nights of 1968.

This is, in short, a movie that tries to teach 10,000 stars how not to dance. There were times when I almost wanted to cover my ears. Did I really want to know (a) why HAL 9000 disobeyed Dave's orders? or (b) the real reason for the Discovery's original mission? or (c) what the monoliths were trying to tell us? Not exactly. And yet we live in a most practical time, and they say every decade gets the movies it deserves. What we get in *2010* is not an artistic triumph, but it is a triumph of hardware, of special effects, of slick, exciting filmmaking. This is a movie that owes more to George Lucas than to Stanley Kubrick, more to *Star Wars* than to *Also Sprach Zarathustra*. It has an ending that is infuriating, not only in its simplicity, but in its inadequacy to fulfill the sense of anticipation, the sense of wonder we felt at the end of *2001*.

And yet the truth must be told: This is a good movie. Once we've drawn our lines, once we've made it absolutely clear that *2001* continues to stand absolutely alone as one of the greatest movies ever made, once we have freed *2010* of the comparisons with Kubrick's masterpiece, what we are left with is a good-looking, sharp-edged, entertaining, exciting space opera—a superior film of the *Star Trek* genre.

Because *2010* depends so much upon its story, it would be unfair to describe more than the essentials: A joint Soviet-American expedition sets out for the moons of Jupiter to investigate the fate of the Discovery, its crew, and its on-board computer HAL 9000. There is tension on board between the American leader (Roy Scheider) and the Soviet captain (Helen Mirren), and it's made worse because back on Earth, the superpowers are on the brink of nuclear war over Central America. If Kubrick sometimes seemed to be making a bloodless movie with faceless characters, Hyams pays a great deal of attention to story and personality. But only one of the best moments in his movie grows out of character (the touching scene where a Soviet and an American hold onto each other for dear life during a terrifying crisis). The other great moments are special effects achievements: a space walk threatened by vertigo, the awesome presence of Jupiter, and a spectacular flight through the planet's upper atmosphere.

It is possible that *no* conclusion to *2010* could be altogether satisfying, especially to anyone who still remembers the puzzling, awesome simplicity of the Star Child turning to regard us at the end of *2001*. This sequel has its work cut out for it. And the screenplay compounds the difficulty by repeatedly informing us that "something wonderful" is about to happen. After we've been told several times about that wonderful prospect, we're ready for something *really* wonderful, and we don't get it. We get a disappointly mundane conclusion worthy of a 1950s sci-fi movie, not a sequel to *2001*. I, for one, was disappointed that the monoliths would deign to communicate with men at all—let alone that they would use English, or send their messages via a video screen, like the latest generation of cable news.

So. You have to make some distinctions in your mind. In one category, *2001: A Space Odyssey* remains inviolate, one of the handful of true film masterpieces. In a more temporal sphere, *2010* qualifies as superior entertainment, a movie more at home with technique than poetry, with character than with mystery, a movie that explains too much and leaves too little to our sense of wonderment, but a good movie all the same. If I nevertheless sound less than ecstatic, maybe it's because the grave eyes of the *2001* Star Child still haunt me, with their promise that perhaps someday man would learn to teach 10,000 stars how to sing.

Uforia ★ ★ ★ ★
PG, 100 m., 1985

Cindy Williams (Arlene), Harry Dean Stanton (Brother Bud), Fred Ward (Sheldon), Alan Beckwith (Brother Roy), Beverly Hope Atkinson (Naomi), Harry Carey, Jr. (George Martin), Diane Diefendorf (Delores), Robert Gray (Emile). Directed by John Binder and produced by Gordon Wolf. Screenplay by Binder.

I've always wanted to know one of those women you read about in the *National Enquirer*, those intense Midwestern housewives who are sucked up into flying saucers and flown to Mars, where they have their measurements taken, and are told they will be contacted again real soon. It's not that I want to hear about the trip to Mars. I'd just enjoy having her around the house, all filled with a sense of mystery and purpose.

Uforia is a great and goofy comedy about a woman just like that. Her name is Arlene, and she works as a supermarket checker in a backwater town in the Southwest. She reads all the UFO publications and believes every word, and knows in her heart that They are coming. But the movie is not really about whether They come or not. It's about how waiting for Them can give you something wonderful to think about, to pass the time of those dreary, dusty days.

The movie has two other characters who get involved in Arlene's dream. One of them is named Sheldon, and he is the kind of good ol' boy who drives through the desert in a big ol' convertible, with the car on cruise control and his feet propped up on the dashboard and a can of beer in his hand.

The other one is named Brother Bud, a phony faith-healer who conducts revival services in a tent outside of town. When Sheldon sees Arlene at the supermarket, he falls in love, and before long he has settled down, sort of, in her mobile home. Sheldon and Brother Bud are brothers, and Sheldon hires on with Bud to portray a guy whose sick leg gets healed every night. Meanwhile, Arlene's faith grows that the UFO will arrive at any moment.

This is one of those movies where you walk in not expecting much, and then something great happens, and you laugh, and you start paying more attention, and then you realize that a lot of great things are happening, that this is one of those rare movies that really has it. *Uforia* is not just another witless Hollywood laugh machine, but a movie with intelligence and a sly, sardonic style of humor. You don't have to shut down half of your brain in order to endure it.

The casting is just perfect. Cindy Williams is the cornerstone, as Arlene, a woman whose hopes and dreams are too big for the small corner of the Earth she has been given to occupy. She doesn't know what to do when she meets Sheldon (played by Fred Ward, from *Remo Williams* and *The Right Stuff*). She likes this guy and she hasn't had a man in a long time. But, then again, she always gets her heart "broke" when she falls for a guy, and so she prays for guidance and starts on the tequila.

Ward gives a wicked performance as the good ol' boy Sheldon. He's Smokey and the Bandit with brains. He has a couple of double takes in this movie that are worth the price of a ticket. And he's not a male chauvinist pig, although everything in his background probably points him in that direction. He doesn't see Arlene as a conquest, but as just the lady he's been looking for. He gets a little tired of the flying saucer stuff, however.

Harry Dean Stanton plays Brother Bud. This is exactly the kind of role Stanton has been complaining that he's tired of: the weary, alcoholic con man with the jolly cynicism. Yet they keep casting him in these roles, and in *Uforia* you can see why: Nobody does a better job. He has an assistant in the movie, a junior evangelist named Brother Roy (Alan Beckwith), whose face shines with conviction and who is always bathed in wonderment and glory. The quiet, offhand way Stanton deals with him is one of the movie's many treasures.

Uforia didn't have a lot of money and a big ad campaign behind it. It doesn't have big stars, unless you are the kind of movie lover for whom the names Cindy Williams, Harry Dean Stanton, and Fred Ward guarantee a movie will at least be interesting.

Like *Repo Man* and *Turtle Diary* and *Hannah and Her Sisters*, it is willing to go for originality in a world that prizes the entertainment assembly line. I was hugging myself during this movie, because it had so many moments that were just right.

Under Fire ★ ★ ★ ½
R, 128 m., 1983

Nick Nolte (Russell Price), Gene Hackman (Alex Grazier), Joanne Cassidy (Claire), Ed Harris (Oates). Directed by Roger Spottiswoode and produced by Jonathan Taplin. Screenplay by Ron Shelton and Clayton Frohman.

This is the kind of movie that almost always feels phony, but *Under Fire* feels real. It's about American journalists covering guerrilla warfare in Central America, and so right away we expect to see Hollywood stars transplanted to the phony jungles of one of those movie nations with madeup names. Instead, we see Hollywood stars who create characters so convincing we forget they're stars. And the movie names names: It's set in Nicaragua, in 1979, during the fall of the Somoza regime, period.

We meet three journalists who are there to get the story. This is not the first small war they've covered, and indeed we've already seen them packing up and leaving Africa. Now they've got a new story. Nick Nolte is Price, a photographer. Gene Hackman is Grazier, a TV reporter who dreams of becoming an anchorman. Joanna Cassidy is a radio reporter. During the course of the story, Cassidy will fall out of love with Hackman and into love with Nolte. These things happen under deadline pressure. Hackman cares, but not enough to affect his friendship with both of them.

The story is simply told, since *Under Fire* depends more upon moments and atmosphere than on a manufactured plot. During a lull in the action, Hackman heads back for New York and Nolte determines to get an interview with the elusive leader of the guerrillas. He doesn't get an interview, but he begins to develop a sympathy for the rebel cause. He commits the journalistic sin of taking sides, and it leads him, eventually, to a much greater sin: faking a photograph to help the guerrilla forces. That is, of course, wrong. But *Under Fire* shows us a war in which morality is hard to define and harder to practice. One of the key supporting characters in the movie is a mysterious American named Oates (played by Ed Harris). Is he CIA? Apparently. He's always in the thick of the dirty work, however, and if his conscience doesn't bother him, Nolte excuses himself for not taking an ethical stand. There are, in fact, a lot of ethical stands not taken in this movie. It could almost have been written by Graham Greene; it exists in that half-world between exhaustion and exhilaration, between love and cynicism, between covering the war and getting yourself killed. This is tricky ground, and the wrong performances could have made it ridiculous (cf. Richard Gere's sleek sexual athlete in *Beyond the Limit*). The actors in *Under Fire* never step wrong.

Nolte is great to watch as the seedy photographer with the beer gut. Hackman never really convinced me that he could be an anchorman, but he did a better thing. He convinced me that he thought he could be one. Joanna Cassidy takes a role that could have been dismissed as "the girl" and fills it out as a fascinating, textured adult. *Under Fire* surrounds these performances with a vivid sense of place and becomes, somewhat surprisingly, a serious and moving film.

Under the Volcano ★ ★ ★ ★
R, 109 m., 1984

Albert Finney (Geoffrey Firmin), Jacqueline Bisset (Yvonne Firmin), Anthony Andrews (Hugh Firmin), Ignacio Lopez Tarso (Dr. Vigil), Kathy Jurado (Senora Gregoria). Directed by John Huston and produced by Michael Fitzgerald. Screenplay by Guy Gallo.

The consul drinks. He has been drinking for so many years that he has arrived at that peculiar stage in alcoholism where he no longer drinks to get high or to get drunk. He drinks simply to hold himself together and continue to function. He has a muddled theory that he can even "drink himself sober," by which he means that he can sometimes find a lucid window through the fog of his life. *Under the Volcano* is the story of the last day in his drinking.

He lives in Cuernavaca, Mexico, in the years just before World War II. He is not really the British consul anymore: he was only a vice consul, anyway, and now that has been stripped from him, and he simply drinks. He has a few friends and a few acquaintances, and his long days are spent in a drunk's neverending occupation, monitoring his own condition. On this morning, for example, he had a bit too much and passed out in the road. One of those things. Earlier, or later, sometime in there, he had stumbled into a church and prayed for the return of his wife, who had left him. Now he sits on his veranda talking with his half-brother. He turns his head. His wife is standing in the doorway. He turns back. It cannot be her. He looks again. She is still there. Turns away. It cannot be. Looks again. A hallucination. But it persists, and eventually he is forced to admit that his wife has indeed returned, in answer to his prayers.

He drinks. He passes out. He wakes. The three of them set off on a bus journey. A peasant is found dead on a roadside. Later, in a bar, there is an unpleasantness with a whore. Still later, the day ends in a ditch. The consul's day is seen largely through his point of view, and the remarkable thing about *Under the Volcano* is that it doesn't resort to any of the usual tricks that movies use when they portray drunks. There are no trick shots to show hallucinations. No spinning cameras. No games with focus. Instead, the drunkenness in this film is supplied by the remarkably controlled performance of Albert Finney as the consul. He gives the best drunk performance I've ever seen in a film. He doesn't overact, or go for pathos, or pretend to be a character. His focus is on communication. He wants, he desperately desires, to penetrate the alcoholic fog and speak clearly from his heart to those around him. His words come out with a peculiar intensity of focus, as if every one had to be pulled out of the small hidden core of sobriety deep inside his confusion.

The movie is based on the great novel by Malcolm Lowry, who used this day in the life of a drunk as a clothesline on which to hang several themes, including the political disintegration of Mexico in the face of the rising tide of Nazism. John Huston, the surefooted old veteran who directed the film, wisely leaves out the symbols and implications and subtexts and just gives us the man. Lowry's novel was really about alcoholism, anyway; the other materials were not so much subjects as they were attempts by the hero to focus on something between his ears.

The movie belongs to Finney, but mention must be made of Jacqueline Bisset as his wife and Anthony Andrews as his half-brother.

Their treatment of the consul is interesting. They understand him well. They love him (and, we gather, each other). They realize nothing can be done for him. Why do they stay with him? For love, maybe, or loyalty, but also perhaps because they respect the great effort he makes to continue to function, to "carry on," in the face of his disabling illness. Huston, I think, is interested in the same aspect of the story, that within every drunk is a man with self-respect trying to get free.

An Unmarried Woman ★ ★ ★ ★
R, 124 m., 1978

Jill Clayburgh (Erica), Alan Bates (Saul), Michael Murphy (Martin), Lisa Lucas (Patti), Cliff Gorman (Charlie), Pat Quinn (Sue), Kelly Bishop (Elaine), Linda Miller (Jeannette), Andrew Duncan (Bob), Penelope Russianoff (Tanya). Directed by Paul Mazursky and produced by Mazursky and Tony Ray. Screenplay by Mazursky.

It is, Erica thinks, a happy marriage, although perhaps she doesn't think about it much. It's *there*. Her husband is a stockbroker, she works in an art gallery, their daughter is in a private high school, they live in a high-rise and jog along the East River. In the morning there is "Swan Lake" on the FM radio, and the last sight at night is of the closing stock prices on the TV screen. Had she bargained for more?

One day, though, swiftly and cruelly, it all comes to an end: Her husband breaks down in phony tears on the street and confesses he's in love with another woman. A younger woman. And so her happy marriage is over. At home, consumed by anger, grief, and uncertainty, she studies her face in the mirror. It is a good face in its middle thirties, and right now it looks plain scared.

So end the first, crucial passages of Paul Mazursky's *An Unmarried Woman*. They are crucial because we have to understand how *completely* Erica was a married woman if we're to join her on the journey back to being single again. It's a journey that Mazursky makes into one of the funniest, truest, sometimes most heartbreaking movies I've ever seen. And so much of what's best is because of Jill Clayburgh, whose performance is, quite simply, luminous.

We know that almost from the beginning. There's a moment of silence in the morning, right after Erica's husband and daughter have left the house. "Swan Lake" is playing. She's still in bed. She's just made love. She speaks from her imagination: "The ballet world was thrilled last night. . . ." And then she slips out of bed and dances around the living room in her T-shirt and panties, because she's so happy, so alive . . . and at that moment the movie's got us. We're in this thing with Erica to the end.

The going is sometimes pretty rough, especially when she's trying to make sense out of things after her husband (Michael Murphy) leaves her. She gets a lot of support and encouragement from her three best girl friends, and some of the movie's very best scenes take place when they meet for long lunches with lots of white wine, or lie around on long Sunday mornings paging through the *Times* and idly wondering why *their* lives don't seem to contain the style of a Bette Davis or a Katharine Hepburn. And then there are the scenes when she talks things over with her daughter (Lisa Lucas), who's one of those bright, precocious teen-agers who uses understatement and cynicism to conceal how easily she can still be hurt.

After Erica gets over the period where she drinks too much and cries too much and screams at her daughter when she doesn't mean to, she goes to a woman psychiatrist, who explains that men are the problem, yes, but they are not quite yet the enemy. And so Erica, who hasn't slept with any man but her husband for seventeen years, finds herself having lunch in Chinese restaurants with boors who shout orders at waiters and try to kiss her in the back seat of a cab. There's also the self-styled stud (Cliff Gorman) who's been hanging around the art gallery, and she finally does go up to his place—warily, gingerly, but she has to find a way sometime of beginning her life again.

And then one day a British artist is hanging a show at the gallery, and he asks her if she doesn't think one side of the painting is a little low, and she says she thinks the *whole* painting is too low, and he doesn't even seem to have noticed her as he says, "Let's discuss it over lunch." They fall in love. Oh, yes, gloriously, in that kind of love that involves not only great sex but walking down empty streets at dawn, and talking about each other's childhood. The painter is played by Alan Bates, who is cast, well and true, as a man who is perfectly right for her and perfectly wrong for her, both at the same time. *An Unmarried Woman* plays true with all three of its major movements: The marriage, the being single, the falling in love. Mazursky's films have considered the grave and funny business of sex before (most memorably in *Bob & Carol & Ted & Alice* and *Blume in Love*). But he's never before been this successful at really dealing with the complexities and following them through. I wouldn't want to tell you too much about the movie's conclusion, but believe this much: It's honest and it's *right*, because Mazursky and Jill Clayburgh care too much about Erica to dismiss her with a conventional happy ending.

Clayburgh takes chances in this movie. She's out on an emotional limb. She's letting us see and experience things that many actresses simply couldn't reveal. Mazursky takes chances, too. He wants *An Unmarried Woman* to be true, for starters: We have to believe at every moment that life itself is being considered here. But the movie has to be funny, too. He won't settle for less than the truth *and* the humor, and the wonder of *An Unmarried Woman* is that he gets it. I've been reviewing movies for a long time now without ever feeling the need to use dumb lines like "You'll laugh—you'll cry." But I did cry, and I did laugh.

Until September ½★
R, 95 m., 1984

Karen Allen (Mo), Thierry Lhermitte (Xavier). Directed by Richard Marquand. Produced by Michael Gruskoff. Screenplay by Janice L. Graham.

I knew we were in trouble when Karen Allen told Thierry Lhermitte he had the most beautiful eyes she'd ever seen. His eyes looked more to me like the kind of eyes where, when you turned up looking like that, the nuns sent you to see the school nurse. But then perhaps I am being unfair. Perhaps I do not like Thierry Lhermitte. Perhaps I think he is the biggest drip I've seen in a love story in years. He is the kind of romantic leading man who has the audience wondering when the *real* leading man is

going to turn up and wipe this guy out of the picture. But *Until September* denies us that relief. This is a dumb, pointless, boring romance from beginning to end. Some measure of its desperation comes during the French toast scene, where the two lovers discuss the proper way to hold a fork. This is a scene that cries out for a Groucho Marx to pop up at the first mention of a fork, and cackle, "Your place or mine?"

A word about the plot. Karen Allen plays an American tour guide who misses her group's flight to Warsaw. That means she is stuck in Paris for three weeks. She goes to stay in a friend's apartment. Another apartment on the same landing is occupied by Lhermitte, who is an international banker. That means he makes phone calls about "the half-billion line of credit," and then takes the rest of the day off to debate about French toast. A movie like this depends entirely on chemistry, and unfortunately, there's never a moment when I could believe that Allen and Lhermitte were really attracted to each other. They discuss nothing of substance. They share no real confidences. The Allen character occasionally makes a show of being a liberated woman, and yet Lhermitte's big scenes are when he plays the worldly tutor for the wide-eyed female, explaining why different wines come in different kinds of bottles.

There is another fundamental problem with the film: Lhermitte is married and has kids. He believes in "honesty," by which he means he tells Allen about his wife but doesn't tell his wife about Allen because it would hurt her. Mistresses are hurt-proof, apparently. The movie is so manipulative that at the end, after the obligatory running-into-each-other's-arms-at-the-airport scene, we are supposed to be happy that this man has abandoned his family to be with a woman he has nothing of interest to discuss with. Meanwhile, do we see the glories of Paris, at least? Not really. The movie doesn't even manage to make the city into an interesting character. And a visit to the country—a weekend on the Riviera—is so strangely constructed that we have the impression all sorts of things happened in the screenplay that were cut from the film.

Because there are so few adult love stories made, it's a shame that *Until September* didn't try harder and have more intelli gence. It feels like a movie that was conceived right from the beginning as a compilation of clichés. Love itself, of course, often is made up of clichés, but if the chemistry is right, they don't feel like clichés.

Up the Creek ★ ★ ★
R, 95 m., 1984

Tim Matheson (Bob McGraw), Jennifer Runyon (Heather Merriweather), Stephen Furst (Gonzer), Dan Monahan (Max), Sandy Helberg (Irwin), John Hillerman (Dean Burch). Directed by Robert Butler and produced by Michael L. Meltzer. Screenplay by Jim Kouf.

Up the Creek is in the great tradition of the Undergraduate Slob Movie, a genre that was created by *Animal House*, perfected by Bill Murray, and defiled by the 1984 *Where the Boys Are*. We know where we stand right in the first few minutes, when a fat kid throws his sandwich out the car window, it hits a motorcyclist in the face, and the motorcyclist hurtles over a cliff. This is not what you call subtle, but Undergraduate Slob Movies do not quibble.

The movie is about an intercollegiate white-water raft race. The defending champions are from a hard-ass military academy. The favorites are from the Ivy League. Our team is from Lepetoname University, described by its dean as the worst university in the world. (In French, by the way, le petoname is the kind of guy who was sitting around the campfire in *Blazing Saddles*.) This university has never won anything. Its students have transferred to it from dozens of other universities—each. The dean makes them a deal. If they win the race, he will give them the diplomas of their choice.

The Lepetoname team is made up of an all-star Undergraduate Slob Movie cast: Tim Matheson and Stephen Furst are from *Animal House*, Dan Monahan is from *Porky's*, and Sandy Helberg was in *History of the World—Part One*, which was a Historical Slob Movie. They pile into a car and head for the race, accompanied by Chuck the Wonder Dog, a dog who is so instrumental to the success of this movie that I will even give you its real name, which is Jake.

One of the joys of this kind of movie comes during the scenes where we meet the competitors. The guys from the military school are led by an uptight, future general. The guys from the Ivy League are all blond, rich, good-looking, and unscrupulous: They plan to use bombs, torpedoes, and even radio-controlled model airplanes to shoot their enemies out of the water. There is, of course, a big beer blast before the race gets underway. The party scene has been an obligatory element of Undergraduate Slob Movies ever since the toga party in *Animal House*. But there are good parties and bad ones. In *Where the Boys Are*, the party is a shapeless confusion. In *Up the Creek*, it's a funny, sustained sequence that establishes all the important characters and sets up the tension.

There's one other scene in the movie that has to be singled out. That's when one of the Lepetoname team members is kidnapped, and Chuck the Wonder Dog uses charades to explain where he is. That's a great scene—and so, by the way, are the scenes of the actual race itself, where some skillful and difficult photography makes the river and its rapids seem convincingly dangerous. *Up the Creek* belongs to an honorable movie tradition, the slapstick comedy. It is superficial, obvious, vulgar, idiotic, goofy, sexy, and predictable. Those are all, by the way, positive qualities—at least, in an Undergraduate Slob Movie.

Used Cars ★ ★
R, 113 m., 1980

Kurt Russell (Rudy Russo), Jack Warden (The Fuchs Brothers), Gerrit Graham (Jeff), Frank McRae (Jim), Deborah Harmon (Barbara Fuchs). Directed by Robert Zemekis and produced by Bob Gale. Screenplay by Zemekis and Gale.

I wonder where the idea got started that it's intrinsically funny to see cars crashing into each other. It's not. It is also not *more* funny when there are dozens or hundreds of cars; the delicate timing you need for comedy is lost when a scene becomes a logistical demonstration. When it comes to cars in movies, more is less—a lesson *Used Cars* does not demonstrate.

When the movie isn't manipulating cars, it does have its good moments. It involves an ancient family feud between two brothers who own competing used car lots across the street from each other. The brothers, both played by Jack Warden, have been treated differently by fate: One is rich and successful; the other is on his last legs, like the cars on his lot. Warden does a good enough job in the dual role, but I always wonder why dual roles seem like a good idea in the first place. If you want two brothers, why not cast two brothers, and accentuate their differences? Why cast one actor and settle for one tour de force instead of two undistracting performances?

Anyway, the movie's plot thickens when it appears that the rich brother will run the poor brother out of business. The plot, in fact, does more than thicken; it congeals. There are so many different characters and story lines in the movie that it's hard to keep everything straight, and harder still to care.

The great comedies almost always have very simple story structures, upon which complex gags can be elaborated. Remember, for example, Buster Keaton's *The General*, in which magnificent complexities were developed out of a story that essentially amounted to Keaton driving a locomotive from point A to point B and back again. *Used Cars* makes the fatal error of achieving the reverse effect: Simple gags are generated out of bafflingly complex situations.

Meanwhile, back at the used car lot . . . Kurt Russell plays a used car salesman who hopes to save the failing business in order to raise money for his political campaign. Gerrit Graham has some funny moments as a superstitious, sex-mad salesman. Deborah Harmon is the long-lost daughter of the less successful brother; her surprise reappearance gives him an heir just when he needs one the most.

Used Cars was written, directed, and produced by the team of Bob Zemekis and Bob Gale, two young filmmakers who seem to be higher on kinetic energy than on structure and comedic instinct. Their first collaboration, which I really enjoyed, was *I Wanna Hold Your Hand*, a fantasy about the Beatles' first concert in New York. Their next collaboration was the screenplay for Steven Spielberg's unsuccessful *1941*. Next came *Used Cars*. The second and third projects, in particular, are filled with too many ideas, relationships and situations—with plot overkill. And they seem to share the notion that if

something is big enough and expensive enough, it will also be funny enough.

Valley Girl ★ ★ ★
R, 95 m., 1983

Nicholas Cage (Randy), Deborah Foreman (Julie), Elizabeth Dailey (Loryn), Michael Bowen (Tommy), Colleen Camp (Mom), Frederic Forrest (Dad). Directed by Martha Coolidge and produced by Wayne Crawford and Andrew Lane. Screenplay by Crawford and Lane.

Disgruntled and weary after slogging through Sex-Mad Teen-ager Movies, I came upon *Valley Girl* with low expectations. What can you expect from a genre inspired by *Porky's?* But this movie is a little treasure, a funny, sexy, appealing story of a Valley Girl's heartbreaking decision: Should she stick with her boring jock boyfriend, or take a chance on a punk from Hollywood? Having seen many Sex-Mad Teen-ager Movies in which a typical slice of teen-ager life consisted of seducing your teacher, being seduced by your best friend's mom, or driving off to Tijuana in search of hookers, I found *Valley Girl* to be surprisingly convincing in its portrait of kids in love. These *are* kids. They're uncertain about sex, their hearts send out confusing signals, and they're slaves to peer pressure.

The movie stars Deborah Foreman as Julie, a bright, cute high school girl who is in the process of breaking up with her blond jock boyfriend (Michael Gowen). He's gorgeous to look at, but he's boring and conceited and he does the one thing that drives all teen-age girls mad: He sits down next to them in a burger joint and casually helps himself to their lunch. One night at a party, Julie meets Randy (Nicholas Cage). He's a lanky, kind of goofy-looking kid with an appealing, crooked smile. He's also a punk from across the hills in Hollywood. Julie likes him. He makes her laugh. He's tender. It's awesome. She falls in love. And then her friends start working her over with all sorts of dire predictions, such as that she'll be "totally dropped" if she goes out with this grotty punk. Caving in to peer pressure, Julie agrees to go to the prom with the jock. And then there's the big climax where the punk gets his girl.

One of the nicest things about this movie

is that it allows its kids to be intelligent, thoughtful, and self-analytical. Another thing is that it allows the *parents* to be modern parents. Have you ever stopped to think how *dated* all the parents in teen-ager movies are? They seem to have been caught in a time warp with Dagwood and Blondie. In *Valley Girl*, the parents (Frederic Forrest and Colleen Camp) are former hippies from the Woodstock generation, now running a health food restaurant and a little puzzled by their daughter's preppy friends. It's a perfect touch.

And here's one more nice thing about *Valley Girl*. Maybe because it was directed by a woman, Martha Coolidge, this is one of the rare teen-ager movies that doesn't try to get laughs by insulting and embarrassing teen-age girls. Everybody's in the same boat in this movie—boys and girls—and they're all trying to do the right thing and still have a good time. It may be the last thing you'd expect from a movie named *Valley Girl*, but the kids in this movie are human.

The Verdict ★ ★ ★ ★
R, 122 m., 1982

Paul Newman (Frank Galvin), Charlotte Rampling (Laura Fischer), Jack Warden (Mickey Morrissey), James Mason (Ed Concannon), Milo O'Shea (Judge Hoyle), Edward Binns (Bishop Brophy), Julie Bovasso (Maureen Rooney), Lindsay Crouse (Kaitlin Costello). Directed by Sidney Lumet and produced by Richard Zanuck and David Brown. Screenplay by David Mamet.

There is a moment in *The Verdict* when Paul Newman walks into a room and shuts the door and trembles with anxiety and with the inner scream that people should *get off his back*. No one who has ever been seriously hung over or needed a drink will fail to recognize the moment. It is the key to his character in *The Verdict*, a movie about a drinking alcoholic who tries to pull himself together for one last step at salvaging his self-esteem.

Newman plays Frank Galvin, a Boston lawyer who has had his problems over the years—a lost job, a messy divorce, a disbarment hearing, all of them traceable in one way or another to his alcoholism. He has a "drinking problem," as an attorney for the archdiocese delicately phrases it. That

means that he makes an occasional guest appearance at his office and spends the rest of his day playing pinball and drinking beer, and his evening drinking Irish whiskey and looking to see if there isn't at least one last lonely woman in the world who will buy his version of himself in preference to the facts. Galvin's pal, a lawyer named Mickey Morrissey (Jack Warden) has drummed up a little work for him: An open-and-shut malpractice suit against a Catholic hospital in Boston where a young woman was carelessly turned into a vegetable because of a medical oversight. The deal is pretty simple. Galvin can expect to settle out-of-court and pocket a third of the settlement—enough to drink on for what little future he is likely to enjoy.

But Galvin makes the mistake of going to see the young victim in a hospital, where she is alive but in a coma. And something snaps inside of him. He determines to try this case, by God, and to prove that the doctors who took her mind away from her were guilty of incompetence and dishonesty. In Galvin's mind, bringing this case to court is one and the same thing with regaining his self-respect—with emerging from his own alcoholic coma. Galvin's redemption takes place within the framework of a courtroom thriller. The screenplay by David Mamet is a wonder of good dialogue, strongly seen characters, and a structure that pays off in the big courtroom scene—as the genre requires. As a courtroom drama, *The Verdict* is superior work. But the director and the star of this film, Sidney Lumet and Paul Newman, seem to be going for something more; *The Verdict* is more a character study than a thriller, and the buried suspense in this movie is more about Galvin's own life than about his latest case.

Frank Galvin provides Newman with the occasion for one of his great performances. This is the first movie in which Newman has looked a little old, a little tired. There are moments when his face sags and his eyes seem terribly weary, and we can look ahead clearly to the old men he will be playing in ten years' time. Newman always has been an interesting actor, but sometimes his resiliency, his youthful vitality, have obscured his performances; he has a tendency to always look great, and that is not always what the role calls for. This time, he gives us old, bone-tired, hung over, trembling (and heroic) Frank Galvin, and we buy it lock, stock, and shot glass.

The movie is populated with finely tuned supporting performances (many of them by British or Irish actors, playing Bostonians not at all badly). Jack Warden is the old law partner; Charlotte Rampling is the woman, also an alcoholic, with whom Galvin unwisely falls in love; James Mason is the ace lawyer for the archdiocese; Milo O'Shea is the politically connected judge; Wesley Addy provides just the right presence as one of the accused doctors. The performances, the dialogue, and the plot all work together like a rare machine.

But it's that Newman performance that stays in the mind. Some reviewers have found *The Verdict* a little slow-moving, maybe because it doesn't always hum along on the thriller level. But if you bring empathy to the movie, if you allow yourself to think about what Frank Galvin is going through, there's not a moment of this movie that's not absorbing. *The Verdict* has a lot of truth in it, right down to a great final scene in which Newman, still drinking, finds that if you wash it down with booze, victory tastes just like defeat.

Victor/Victoria ★ ★ ★
R, 133 m., 1982

Julie Andrews (Victor/Victoria), James Garner (King), Robert Preston (Toddy), Lesley Ann Warren (Norma), Alex Karras (Squash), John Rhys-Davis (Cassell). Directed by Blake Edwards and produced by Edwards and Tony Adams.

I've always felt this way about female impersonators: They may not be as pretty as women, or sing as well, or wear a dress as well, but you've got to hand it to them; they sure look great and sing pretty—for men. There are no doubt, of course, female impersonators who practice their art so skillfully that they cannot be told apart from real women—but that, of course, misses the point. A drag queen should be maybe 90 percent convincing as a woman, tops, so you can applaud while still knowing it's an act.

Insights like these are crucial to Blake Edwards's *Victor/Victoria*, in which Julie Andrews plays a woman playing a man playing a woman. It's a complicated challenge. If she just comes out as Julie Andrews, then of course she looks just like a woman, because she is one. So when she comes onstage as "Victoria," said to be "Victor" but really (we know) actually Victoria, she has to be an ever-so-slightly imperfect woman, to sell the premise that she's a man. Whether she succeeds is the source of a lot of comedy in this movie, which is a lighthearted meditation on how ridiculous we can sometimes become when we take sex too seriously.

The movie is made in the spirit of classic movie sex farces, and is in fact based on one (a 1933 German film named *Viktor und Viktoria*, which I haven't seen). Its more recent inspiration is probably *La Cage Aux Folles*, an enormous success that gave Hollywood courage to try this offbeat material. In the movie, Andrews is a starving singer, out of work, down to her last franc, when she meets a charming old fraud named Toddy, who is gay, and who is played by Robert Preston in the spirit of Ethel Mertz on "I Love Lucy." Preston is kind, friendly, plucky, and comes up with the most outrageous schemes to solve problems that wouldn't be half so complicated if he weren't on the case. In this case, he has a brainstorm: Since there's no market for girl singers, but a constant demand for female impersonators, why shouldn't Andrews assume a false identity and pretend to be a drag queen? "But they'll *know* I'm not a man!" she wails. "Of course!" Preston says triumphantly.

The plot thickens when James Garner, as a Chicago nightclub operator, wanders into Victor/Victoria's nightclub act and falls in love with him/her. Garner refuses to believe that lovely creature is a man. He's right, but if Andrews admits it, she's out of work. Meanwhile, Garner's blonde girlfriend (Lesley Ann Warren) is consumed by jealousy, and intrigue grows between Preston and Alex Karras, who plays Garner's bodyguard. Edwards develops this situation as farce, with lots of gags depending on split-second timing and characters being in the wrong hotel rooms at the right time. He also throws in several nightclub brawls, which aren't very funny, but which don't much matter. What makes the material work is not only the fact that it is funny (which it is), but that it's about likable people.

The three most difficult roles belong to Preston, Garner, and Karras, who must walk a tightrope of uncertain sexual identity without even appearing to condescend to their material. They never do. Because they all seem to be people first and genders second, they see the humor in their bewildering situation as quickly as anyone, and their cheerful ability to rise to a series of implausible occasions makes *Victor/Victoria* not only a funny movie, but, unexpectedly, a warm and friendly one.

Videodrome ★ ½
R, 87 m., 1983

James Woods (Max Renn), Sonja Smith (Bianca O'Blivion), Deborah Harry (Nicki Brand), Peter Dvorsky (Harlan), Jack Creley (Brian O'Blivion). Directed by David Cronenberg and produced by Claude Heroux. Screenplay by Cronenberg.

The colors in *Videodrome* are mostly shades of dried blood. The characters are bitter and hateful, the images are nauseating, and the ending is bleak enough that when the screen fades to black it's a relief. This is the kind of movie that makes you want to see a different movie. Yet the film has its interesting qualities. If the director, David Cronenberg, had been prepared to allow just a little humanity and humor into what is basically a good idea for a screenplay, *Videodrome* might have worked. But it's relentlessly grim. The movie stars James Woods as a fly-by-night cable TV operator who starts fooling around with a saucer antenna and picks up a cable show that isn't listed in any of the guides. It's pretty rough stuff: Women being tortured and killed. Where does it come from? He tracks it down to Pittsburgh. Meanwhile, some of the scenarios from the weird cable network start getting instant replays in his own bedroom. His girlfriend, Deborah Harry (formerly of the rock group Blondie), makes kinky suggestions and eventually burns herself with a cigarette, in a scene I could easily have lived without.

Woods is a video freak. Come to think of it, he's almost always a freak of one sort or another in the movies; he gets the roles that are too weird for Bruce Dern, and he usually does a great job with them (I especially liked his work as the psychopathic cop-killer in

The Onion Field). This time, he's one of those video junkies who talks like the letters column of *BYTE* magazine. He becomes fascinated by the Pittsburgh operation and eventually goes there, tracking down a strange skid-row establishment named the Cathode Ray Mission, where bums get a TV set instead of a soup line. What's going on here? What's the master plan of the mysterious Brian O'Blivion, who runs the mission and the underground cable show? (And why, while we're at it, don't directors ever learn that few things make a character less interesting than a funny name?) Without giving away too many of O'Blivion's secrets, I can say that his sexy daughter (Sonja Smith) is the true force behind the Videodrome conspiracy.

I suppose there's a serious subtext lurking in *Videodrome*. The movie symbolizes television as a consuming, engulfing, devouring monster—most memorably in scenes where Woods's TV set turns into a sort of living, pulsing version of Deborah Harry. Television has been seen as a sinister force before, but never this sinister. As I was watching this parade of horrors, I began to wonder why Cronenberg is so unremittingly negative in his filmmaking. His movies are soaked with gloom and defeatism, with ugly images and worthless characters. It's a world view, I guess, but even the most pessimistic director in the history of movies, Luis Bunuel, sometimes found a way to express his bitterness as a joke. *Videodrome*, whatever its qualities, has got to be one of the least entertaining movies ever made.

Violets Are Blue ★ ★ ★
PG-13, 88 m., 1986 ✔

Sissy Spacek (Gussie Sawyer), Kevin Kline (Henry Squires), Bonnie Bedelia (Ruth Squires), Jim Standiford (Addy Squires), John Kellogg (Ralph Sawyer), Augusta Dabney (Ethel Sawyer). Directed by Jack Fisk and produced by Mary Kay Powell. Screenplay by Naomi Foner.

Violets Are Blue is sort of a high school reunion for the heart, a movie about one of those moments that everybody has, where you meet the person you loved when you were seventeen, and now you are thirty-three, and a lot of your life's history has been written. And yet, as your eyes meet, your last kiss is as clear as yesterday.

The movie opens around a campfire on an island off the Maryland coast. Sitting on a blanket are two teen-agers—Gussie and Henry, high school sweethearts, facing the future with doubt in their eyes. Henry (Kevin Kline) is going off to college. Gussie (Sissy Spacek) wants to be an airline flight attendant. They love each other, and say all the correct words about how they will keep in touch and meet again and that this parting of the ways is only temporary. Then they go off to whatever life holds in store for them.

Henry's father dies, and he takes over the family business—the little local newspaper in the Maryland coastal resort where he lives. He gets married and has a son. Gussie gets her wings, starts taking photos for the airline's in-flight magazine, and eventually becomes a world-famous photographer. Then one summer, fifteen years later, she comes home for a vacation.

It is inevitable that they will meet again. In fact, their eyes meet across a long distance during a local boat race. Gussie goes down to the newspaper office to see Henry again, and there is an immediate tension in the air between them, a realization that in one way or another they are going to have to deal with some unfinished business.

Henry invites Gussie over to his house for dinner. Henry's wife Ruth (Bonnie Bedelia) does her best to keep the atmosphere light, and their son Addy (Jim Standiford) asks lots of questions about Gussie's work. But the atmosphere grows more and more awkward, until it becomes clear that Gussie will have to leave early—that she and Henry have an agenda that does not include his family.

This is a difficult scene that is handled with quiet confidence by the director, Jack Fisk; contrast it with the badly handled similar scene in *Just Between Friends*, where everything leads up to the embarrassing dinner table confrontation, and then the movie chickens out and never shows us what happens.

Violets Are Blue establishes its events within a vivid sense of time and place. We get a real feel for the close-knit seaside community, where Gussie's father (John Kellogg) operates the bumper cars and lives in a frame house just down the street. Everybody knows everybody else's business in this little town, and her father tells Gussie one day, with gruffness and love, that she has no business fooling around with a married man. But Gussie can't help herself. She made a choice—career instead of family—but now she has seen the man who could have been her husband, seen the boy who could have been her son—and she wants it both ways.

Although the characters of Gussie and Henry are played with great subtlety and warmth by Spacek and Kline, the best scenes in the movie belong to two of the supporting actors, Bonnie Bedelia as Ruth, Henry's wife, and Kellogg as Gussie's father. They stand up for what they believe in. They refuse to cave in to easy notions of romance or love or inevitability. Bedelia stands in her kitchen one day and clearly, unforgivingly lays out for her husband what his choices are, and it's perhaps the key scene in the whole movie.

What's interesting about *Violets Are Blue* is that it's not necessarily the movie we expect it to be, and Spacek doesn't necessarily play the role we expect from her. It's a movie about adults making some hard choices, facing some inflexible realities in their lives, and when it's over we realize it caused us to think about a couple of things: Not only the road not chosen, which is what we begin by thinking about, but also the road that we have chosen, and our responsibilities to it.

Vision Quest ★ ★ ★ ½
R, 108 m., 1985

Matthew Modine (Louden Swain), Linda Fiorentino (Carla), Michael Schoeffling (Kuch), Ronny Cox (Louden's Dad), Harold Sylvester (Tanneran), Charles Hallahan (Coach), R.H. Thomson (Kevin), J.C. Quinn (Elmo), Frank Jasper (Shute). Directed by Harold Becker and produced by Jon Peters and Peter Guber. Screenplay by Darryl Poniscan.

We think we know the story pretty well already: Young wrestler has two dreams: (a) to win the state championship, and (b) to win the love of a girl. The defending state champion is a man-mountain who carries telephone poles to the top of stadiums. The girl is an independent drifter who is twenty years old and doesn't take the hero seriously. By the end of the movie, the only suspense is whether it will end with a victory in bed or in the ring. Although *Vision Quest* sticks pretty close to that outline, it is nevertheless a movie with some nice surprises, mostly because it takes the time to create some interesting characters. The movie's hero, Louden Swain, is probably the closest thing to a standard movie character, but Matthew Modine plays him with such an ingratiating freshness that he makes the character quirky and interesting, almost in spite of the script.

The other people in the movie are all real originals. They include Louden's father (Ronny Cox), who has lost the family farm and his wife, but still retains the respect of his son; Louden's best pal (Michael Schoeffling), who bills himself as a "half-Indian spiritual adviser"; a black history teacher (Harold Sylvester) who cares about Louden and listens to him; an alcoholic short-order cook (J.C. Quinn) who works in the kitchen of the hotel where Louden's a bellboy, and a wrestling coach (Charles Hallahan) who has mixed feelings about Louden's drive to get down to the 168-pound class so he can wrestle the toughest wrestler in the state. All of those characters are written, directed, and acted just a little differently than we might expect; they have small roles, but they don't think small thoughts.

And then there is the movie's most original creation, the twenty-year-old drifter, Carla (Linda Fiorentino). Without having met the actress, it's impossible for me to speculate on how much of Carla is original work and how much is Fiorentino's personality. What comes across, though, is a woman who is enigmatic without being egotistical, detached without being cold, self-reliant without being suspicious. She has a way of talking—kind of deliberately objective—that makes you listen to everything she says.

All of these people live in Spokane, which looks sort of wet and dark in many scenes, and feels like a place that prizes individuality. Instead of silhouetting the Modine character against the city and a lot of humble supporting roles, and turning him into a Rocky of wrestlers, the movie takes time to place the character in the city and in the lives of the other people. We begin to value his relationships, and it really means something when the short-order cook puts on a clean shirt and goes to the big wrestling meet.

The movie's plot doesn't really equal its characters. After the Rocky movies and *Breaking Away* and *The Karate Kid* and a dozen other movies with essentially the same last scene, it's hard to care about the outcome of the big fight, or race, or match, because, let's face it, we know the hero's going to win. Just once, why couldn't they give us characters as interesting as the ones in *Vision Quest*, in a movie where they'd be set free from the same tired old plot and allowed to live?

Walkabout ★ ★ ★
PG, 95 m., 1971

Jenny Agutter (The Girl), Lucien John (Brother), David Gumpilil (Aborigine), John Mellon (Father). Directed by Nicholas Roeg and produced by Si Litvinoff. Screenplay by Edward Bond.

It is possible to consider *Walkabout* entirely as the story it seems to be: The story of a fourteen-year-old girl and her little brother, who are abandoned in the Australian outback and then saved through the natural skills of a young aborigine boy. It is simpler and easier to consider it on that level, too, because *Walkabout* is a superb work of storytelling and its material is effortlessly fascinating. There's also a tendency (unfortunate, probably) to read *Walkabout* as a catchall of symbols and metaphors, in which the Noble Savage and his natural life are tested and found superior to civilization and cities. The movie does, indeed, make this comparison several times. Hundreds of miles from help, the girl turns on her portable radio to hear a philosopher observe: "It is now possible to state that 'that is' is." Well, this isn't exactly helpful, and so we laugh. And more adolescent viewers may have to stifle a sigh and a tear when the girl is seen, at the movie's end, married to a cloddish office clerk and nostalgically remembering her idyllic days in the desert.

The contrast between civilization and man's more natural states is well-drawn in the movie, and will interest serious-minded younger people (just as, at the level of pure story, *Walkabout* will probably fascinate kids). But I don't think it's fruitful to draw all the parallels and then piously conclude that we would all be better off far from the city, sipping water from the ground, and spearing kangaroos for lunch. That sort of comparison doesn't really get you anywhere and leaves you with a movie that doesn't tell you more than you already knew. I think there's more than that to *Walkabout*. And I'm going to have a hard time expressing that additional dimension for you, because it doesn't quite exist in the universe of words. Even in these days of film experiments, most movies have their centers in the worlds of plots and characters. But *Walkabout* . . .

Well, to begin with, the film was directed and photographed by Nicholas Roeg, the cinematographer of *Petulia* and many other British films. Roeg's first stab at direction was as co-director of *Performance*. This was his first work as an individual. I persisted in seeing *Performance* on the level of its perfectly silly plot, and on that level it was a wretched movie indeed. People told me I should forget the plot and simply enjoy the movie itself, but I have a built-in resistance to that notion, usually. Perhaps I should have listened. Because Roeg's *Walkabout* is a very rare example of that kind of movie, in which the "civilized" characters and the aborigine exist in a wilderness that isn't really a wilderness but more of an indefinite place for the story to be told. Roeg's desert in *Walkabout* is like Beckett's stage for *Waiting for Godot*. That is, it's nowhere in particular, and everywhere.

Roeg's photography reinforces this notion. He is careful to keep us at a distance from the physical sufferings of his characters. To be sure, they have blisters and parched lips, but he pulls up well short of the usual clichés of suffering in the desert. And his cinematography (and John Barry's otherworldly music) make the desert seem a mystical place, a place for visions. So that the whole film becomes mystical, a dream, and the suicides which frame it set the boundaries of reality. Within them, what happens between the boy and the girl, and the boy and the little brother, is not merely "communication" or "survival" or "cooperation," but the same kind of life-enhancement that you imagine people feel when they go into the woods and eat berries and bring the full focus of their intelligence

to bear on the problem of co-existing with nature.

WarGames ★ ★ ★ ★
PG, 110 m., 1983

Matthew Broderick (David), Dabney Coleman (McKittrick), John Wood (Falken), Ally Sheedy (Jennifer), Barry Corbin (General Beringer). Directed by John Badham and produced by Harold Schneider. Screenplay by Lawrence Lasker and Walter F. Parkes.

Sooner or later, a self-satisfied, sublimely confident computer is going to blow us all off the face of the planet. That is the message of *WarGames*, a scary and intelligent thriller that is one of the best films of 1983. The movie stars Matthew Broderick as a bright high school senior who spends a lot of time locked in his bedroom with his home computer. He speaks computerese well enough to dial by telephone into the computer at his school and change grades. But he's ready for bigger game. He reads about a toy company that's introducing a new computer game. He programs his computer for a random search of telephone numbers in the company's area code, looking for a number that answers with a computer tone. Eventually, he connects with a computer. Unfortunately, the computer he connects with does not belong to a toy company. It belongs to the Defense Department, and its mission is to coordinate early warning systems and nuclear deterrents in the case of World War III. The kid challenges the computer to play a game called "Global Thermonuclear Warfare," and it cheerfully agrees.

As a premise for a thriller, this is a masterstroke. The movie, however, could easily go wrong by bogging us down in impenetrable computerese, or by ignoring the technical details altogether and giving us a *Fail Safe* retread. *WarGames* makes neither mistake. It convinces us that it knows computers, and it makes its knowledge into an amazingly entertaining thriller. (Note: I do not claim the movie is *accurate* about computers—only convincing.) I've described only the opening gambits of the plot, and I will reveal no more. It's too much fun watching the story unwind. Another one of the pleasures of the movie is the way it takes cardboard characters and fleshes them out. Two in particular:

the civilian chief of the U.S. computer operation, played by Dabney Coleman as a man who has his own little weakness for simple logic, and the Air Force general in charge of the war room, played by Barry Corbin as a military man who argues that men, not computers, should make the final nuclear decisions.

WarGames was directed by John Badham, best known for *Saturday Night Fever* and *Blue Thunder,* a thriller that I found considerably less convincing on the technical level. There's not a scene here where Badham doesn't seem to know what he's doing, weaving a complex web of computerese, personalities, and puzzles; the movie absorbs us on emotional and intellectual levels at the same time. And the ending, a moment of blinding and yet utterly elementary insight, is wonderful.

The Weavers: Wasn't That a Time!
★ ★ ★ ★
PG, 78 m., 1982

Featuring Lee Hays, Ronnie Gilbert, Fred Hellerman, and Pete Seeger. Directed by Jim Brown and produced by Brown, George Stoney, and Harold Leventhal.

Here is one of the most joyous musical documentaries in a long time, a celebration of the music and the singers that made up the Weavers. There are, I suppose, a lot of people who don't know who the Weavers were, but for a time in the fifties they were the top pop quartet in America, and for twenty years their recordings were a key influence on modern American folk music.

The owners of old Weavers record albums treasure them. I have four or five, and when things get depressing and the sky turns overcast and grim, I like to play one of them. There's just something magical about the joy with which the Weavers sing "Goodnight, Irene" or "Kisses Sweeter than Wine" or "The Sloop John B." or "This Land is Your Land."

The Weavers reached their popular peak in the fifties, with a string of Top Ten hits, which also included "On Top of Old Smokey," "Tzena, Tzena," and "If I Had a Hammer" (which was written by the Weavers, and not, as many people believe, by Bob Dylan). The height of their popularity unfortunately coincided with the height of McCarthyism, and the Weavers, all of them longtime left-wing activists, were blacklisted. They couldn't get jobs on television or in nightclubs, and their records were banned.

For several years in the late fifties, the group existed primarily on records. And the artists went their separate ways: Ronnie Gilbert into theater, Fred Hellerman into San Franciso-area media projects, Pete Seeger into a successful solo concert career, and Lee Hays into semi-retirement on his New England farm.

There were many calls for a Weavers reunion (in some circles, an event more fervently desired than the Beatles reunion). And in May of 1980, Lee Hays himself convened such a reunion, inviting the other Weavers and their families and friends to a picnic on his farm. As they sat around and sang and played, the idea of a public reunion began to take shape, and on November 28 and 29 of 1980, they held one last historic concert at Carnegie Hall.

The Weavers: Wasn't That a Time! is not simply a concert film, however, but a documentary about the Weavers. The director, Jim Brown, was a neighbor of Hays, and grew to admire the old man who kept on singing after his legs were amputated for diabetes and his heart needed a pacemaker.

Brown's film begins with the picnic at Hays's farm, flashes back to newsreel and archive footage of the Weavers in their prime, and then concludes with the concert in Carnegie Hall. It is impossible not to feel a lump in your throat as the Weavers gather once again on stage, and it's hard not to tap your feet when they start to sing.

Seeing this film is a wonderful experience. I'd recommend it wholeheartedly to those who don't know about the Weavers. I imagine that Weavers fans won't need any encouragement.

A Wedding ★ ★ ★ ½
PG, 125 m., 1978

Desi Arnaz, Jr. (Dino Corelli), Carol Burnett (Tulip Brenner), Geraldine Chaplin (Rita Billingsley), Howard Duff (Dr. Meecham), Mia Farrow (Buffy Brenner), Vittorio Gassman (Luigi Corelli), Lillian Gish (Nettie

Sloan), Lauren Hutton (Photographer), Viveca Lindfors (Ingrid Hellstrom), Pat McCormick (MacKenzie Goddard), Dina Merrill (Antoinette Goddard), Nina Van Pallandt (Regina Corelli). Directed and produced by Robert Altman. Screenplay by John Considine, Patricia Resnick, Allan Nicholls, and Altman.

The two families in Robert Altman's *A Wedding* live right there in the closets with their skeletons. They present a cheerful facade to the outer world, of old Lake Forest money on the one hand and new Southern money on the other. But just beneath the surface there are jealousies and greeds and hates, and the random dirty tricks of fate.

Altman plunges gleefully into this wealth of material; there are forty-eight characters in his movie, give or take a few, and by the film's end we know them all. We may not know them *well*—at weddings there are always unidentified cousins over in the corner—but we can place them, and chart the lines of power and passion that run among them. And some of them are drawn as well as Altman has drawn anyone.

That's because *A Wedding* is a lot deeper and more ambitious than we might at first expect. It begins in comedy, it moves into realms of social observation, it descends into personal revelations that are sometimes tragic, sometimes comic . . . and then it ends in a way that turns everything back upon itself. The more you think about what Altman's done, the more impressive his accomplishment becomes.

A Wedding aims to upset our expectations. It takes our society's most fertile source of cliches and stereotypes—a society wedding—and then chisels away at it with maniacal and sometimes savage satire. Nobody gets away: not the bride and groom, so seemingly "ideal;" not the loving parents on either side; not the relatives, with their little dramas that are no doubt played out on every family occasion, and not even the staff of wedding coordinators, chefs, photographers, musicians, and other accomplices.

Altman begins in solemnity and ceremony, with the high Episcopalian wedding. Desi Arnaz, Jr., and Amy Stryker, as the wedding couple, are all but lost in the chaos: The bishop fumbles his lines, a camera crew maneuvers awkwardly behind the palms and, meanwhile, back at the mansion, the groom's grandmother (Lillian Gish) drops dead of anticipated mortification.

Her death is concealed when the wedding party returns to the mansion: Concealed from the family and from the single guest who turns up for the magnificently catered affair. Altman introduces us almost effortlessly to the house jammed with people; his compositions allow characters to be established in the backgrounds while the plot is being pushed ahead in the foreground, so it's as if we're wandering around the house like everyone else.

There are any number of subplots. The parents of the groom are Nina Van Pallandt, whose drug habit is ministered to by the family doctor, and Vittorio Gassman, an Italian who seems to have sinister associations in his past. The bride's parents are Carol Burnett, all sweetness and convention until—gasp!—she's wooed by one of the guests, and Paul Dooley, vulgar, hard-drinking, with a tad too much affection for his youngest daughter (Mia Farrow).

Farrow, it develops, is pregnant—by her sister's new husband, perhaps, or (it develops) by any other member of his class at military school. Other characters reveal themselves as drunks, unreconstructed Communists, secret weepers, fountains of jealousy, reservoirs of lust, or advocates of diverse sexual proclivities.

This is the sort of material that easily lends itself to farce, and, when it does, Altman cheerfully follows. But he leads in other directions, as well. He moves so slyly from one note to another that when Pat McCormick attempts a clumsy seduction of Carol Burnett, we're moved simultaneously by comedy and pathos. And there are scenes of extraordinary emotional complexity, as when a singalong is organized in the basement dining room, or when Nina Van Pallandt tearfully and defiantly reviews the terms under which she's lived her marriage.

Like Altman's other movies with lots of characters (*M*A*S*H, McCabe and Mrs. Miller,* the incomparable *Nashville*), *A Wedding* doesn't fit easily into established feature film categories. For some viewers, it won't satisfy; it doesn't set up situations and then resolve them in standard ways. It's got all the disorganization and contradictions of life—and then Altman almost mystically gives everything a deeper meaning by the catastrophic surprise he springs on us near the end.

A Week's Vacation ★ ★ ★ ½
NO MPAA RATING, 102 m., 1980

Nathalie Baye (Laurence Cuers), Gerard Lanvin (Pierre). Directed by Bertrand Tavernier. Screenplay by Tavernier, Colo Tavernier, and Marie-Francoise Hans.

It's nothing special, just an overcast day in Lyons when everybody's going to work just as usual. A car pulls out of the stream of traffic, and a young woman gets out. Her name is Laurence, she is a schoolteacher, and this day she does not feel like teaching school. It is more than that: She cannot. There is no particular crisis. A great tragedy has not descended on her life. In fact, things are going fairly well. She is thirty-one years old, she lives with her boyfriend, she has been teaching at the same school for ten years. It is simply that large and inarticulate emotions are welling up inside her, and she is desperately unhappy. She goes to see her doctor, and he prescribes a week's vacation.

A Week's Vacation is as simple, and as complicated, as that. It was directed by Bertrand Tavernier, the gifted French filmmaker who has made his hometown of Lyons the locale for some of his best work, including The Clockmaker (1974). That movie was based on a novel by Georges Simenon, and A Week's Vacation could well have been; it has the same matter-of-fact fascination with the great depths and unexpected secrets in the lives of people who outwardly seem ordinary. A Week's Vacation follows the schoolteacher, played by Nathalie Baye, as she spends her week of freedom wandering without a plan through her city, her past, and her sexuality. She meets a friendly café owner and talks to him. She goes out to the country to visit her father, who is so old he has surely discovered the answer to the puzzle of life, but it has made him speechless. Returning to the city, she has an embarrassing encounter. The café owner, mistaking her friendliness for sexual interest, tries to kiss her. She was not thinking along those lines. As they both try to free

themselves from the awkward situation, as he damns himself for being such a fool, there comes a turning point in her week's vacation: It seems to me that this foolish encounter, this mundane sexual pass based on mistaken assumptions, is the catalyst she needs to get back into life again.

What is best about Tavernier is his feeling for the ordinary currents of everyday life. He creates such empathy between his audiences and his characters that when they fall into a reverie, we have no difficulty imagining their thoughts. In A Week's Vacation, he has taken the occasional feeling we all have that we just can't go on any longer, not because of sadness or illness or tragedy, but simply because we have forgotten why we set out in the first place on this journey of life. And he has shown us the answer. The key is in that funny, embarrassing, fumbling little attempt at a kiss: We keep on plugging away because we never know when someone might decide to kiss us, and, better still, because it's so interesting to see how we'll react.

Weird Science ★ ★ ★ ½
PG-13, 94 m., 1985

Anthony Michael Hall (Gary), Kelly LeBrock (Lisa), Ilan Mitchell-Smith (Wyatt), Bill Paxton (Chet), Suzanne Snyder (Deb), Judie Aronson (Hilly). Directed by John Hughes and produced by Joel Silver. Screenplay by Hughes.

Weird Science combines two great traditions in popular entertainment: Inflamed male teen-age fantasies and Frankenstein's monster. Then it crosses them with a new myth, of the teen-age computer geniuses who lock themselves in their bedrooms, hunch over their computer keyboards, and write programs that can change the universe.

In the movie's opening scenes, a couple of bright kids write a program with their specifications for a perfect woman. They feed in centerfolds and magazine covers, measurements and parameters. Then, for additional brain power, they tap into a giant government computer. And at exactly that instant, lightning strikes (just as it did in The Bride of Frankenstein), and out of the mix of bytes and kilowatts steps . . . a perfect woman.

She is played by Kelly LeBrock in the movie, and she has full, sensuous lips, and a throaty English accent, and a lot of style. She is a little more than the kids had bargained on. For one thing, she isn't an idealized Playmate, all staples and no brains, but an intelligent, sensitive woman who sees right through these teen-age boys and tries to do them some good.

That's why *Weird Science* is funnier, and a little deeper, than the predictable story it might have been. The movie is the third success in a row for John Hughes, a director who specializes in films about how teenagers really talk and think. His two earlier films were *Sixteen Candles* and *The Breakfast Club*, and they both featured a young actor named Anthony Michael Hall, who is the costar of *Weird Science*.

Hall was the geek in *Sixteen Candles* and the intellectual in *Breakfast Club*, and I like John Hughes's definition of a geek: "A geek is a guy who has everything going for him, but he's just too young. By contrast, a nerd will be a nerd all of his life." Hall talks fast, with a sprung rhythm that lets you feel you can hear him thinking. He has the ordinary lusts of a teen-age boy, but once he invents this perfect woman, he is quick to catch on to the advantages: For example, your status in high school is sure to change dramatically if a gorgeous model thinks you're the max.

Hughes's earlier teen-age films depended mostly on character and dialogue (which was fine). This one has a lot of special effects, including some reverse photography that plays tricks with time. But the center of the film is the simple, almost elementary insight that fantasies can be hazardous: You've got to be careful what you ask for, because you might get it. Kelly LeBrock is wonderful as the fantasy woman, because she plays the character, not for sex, but for warmth and an almost motherly affection for these two kids. "All you have to do is command me," she says at one point. "You created me. You are my master." It could be soft porn, but the way she says it, her voice has a wink.

Wetherby ★ ★ ★ ★
R, 97 m., 1985 ✓

Vanessa Redgrave (Jean Travers), Ian Holm (Stanley Pilborough), Judi Dench (Marcia Pilborough), Marjorie Yates (Verity Braithwaite), Tim McInnerny (John Morgan), Suzanna Hamilton (Karen Creasy), Joely Richardson (Young Jean). Directed by David Hare and produced by Simon Relph. Screenplay by Hare.

A man kills himself among strangers. They never knew who he was, and they do not know why he chose to die. A man dying among strangers is like a tree falling unobserved in the forest. Death, especially suicide, requires resonance from those who knew the living person before it can be assigned its proper meaning. That is why *Wetherby* is such a haunting film, because it dares to suggest that the death of the stranger is important to everyone it touches—because it forces them to decide how alive they really are.

The movie begins with a woman who is living a sort of dead life. Her name is Jean Travers (played by Vanessa Redgrave); she was once in love with a young man who went off to fight the war and was killed. He was not killed gloriously, but stupidly, while getting involved in someone else's drunken quarrel, but he was dead all the same. As the movie opens, Jean has been teaching school in the small town of Wetherby, where her life is on hold. She doesn't walk around in a state of depression, she does have friends, she is a good teacher, but she is not engaged in life because she put all of her passion into the boy who died so many years ago.

One night she throws a small dinner party. Everyone drinks wine and sits around late, talking. One of the men at the table, John Morgan, sits mute all evening and finally makes a short speech about pain and love and honesty that sounds as if every word were written with his own bitter tears. The next day, John Morgan comes back to Jean's house, sits down for a cup of tea, and kills himself. A funny thing comes out in the investigation: John Morgan was not known to any of the people at the dinner party. Apparently he invited himself.

The film moves from this beginning into an examination of the people who were touched by the death. In addition to Jean, there are the Pilboroughs (Ian Holm and Judi Dench), the local constable (Tom Wilkinson), and a young woman (Suzanna Hamilton) who knew the dead man. Some small suspense develops for a while when it appears that Jean spent some time upstairs with John Morgan during the evening of her party—but that, and many other things, seem to be dead ends.

The movie flashes back into events in Jean's youth, and she is played as a young girl by Joely Richardson, Redgrave's daughter. There is an innocence and tenderness in those early scenes, as young Jean and her boyfriend kiss and neck and make promises, and as Jean gradually realizes that she is looking forward to marriage but he is much more excited by the prospect of putting on a uniform and going overseas. He goes overseas, and in some ways this movie is about the fact that Jean has become a middle-aged woman still waiting for him to come back.

Wetherby was written and directed by David Hare, who also wrote the film *Plenty.* Both films are about women who were never able to fully live their lives after what happened to them during the War. I admire both films, but I found *Wetherby* more moving, because the heroine of *Plenty* was essentially a disturbed woman using her war memories as a crutch, and Jean Travers is a whole and healthy woman who only needs to give herself the permission to live. I left the movie thinking that was the lesson she learned from John Morgan. Hoping so, anyway.

Where the Boys Are ½ ★
R, 93 m., 1984

Lisa Hartman (Jennie), Russell Todd (Scott), Lorna Luft (Carole), Wendy Schaal (Sandra), Howard McGillin (Chip) Lynn-Holly Johnson (Laurie). Directed by Hy Averback and produced by Allan Carr. Screenplay by Jeff Burkhart, Stu Krieger, and Carr.

Close your eyes and you can hear her even now. It's 1960 and you're parked in the Steak n' Shake in your red and white Chevy convertible and on the radio, Connie Francis is singing "Where the Boys Are." It's a love song to a time and a place. And as you tip the curb girl a dime, you close your eyes, and dream about pointing that Chevy right down Route 45 to Fort Lauderdale.

There is a certain innocence in that vision. A certain wistful optimism that maybe in Fort Lauderdale, or somewhere, somehow, sometime, you'll meet that special girl who will look into your eyes and whisper "I know" when you say you love her. It's a kind of innocent, romantic vision that has nothing to do with the 1984 movie also named *Where the Boys Are*, which is an exercise in exhausted cynicism. This movie has nothing to do with the song and the 1960 movie whose name it appropriates. It isn't a sequel and isn't a remake and isn't, in fact, much of anything. The press release contains this priceless line: "Allan Carr is producing *'Where the Boys Are'* from a screenplay based on an original story idea by himself, Jeff Burkhart, and Stu Krieger." What could the original story idea have been? "Hey, Jeff and Stu, let's write a new movie called 'Where the Boys Are'!" Don't laugh. People have made millions in Hollywood with even less-inspired story ideas. Also with even more-inspired ideas, of course, like this one I've just had: Hey, Allan, Jeff, and Stu—let's not rip-off that old title!

The movie stars a cast of aging would-be college kids who do, indeed, head south for Fort Lauderdale for the annual college week in the sun. But their sexual appetites are considerably more decadent than those of the 1960 cast. Before this movie is over, we will witness:

• Four college girls practicing foreplay with an inflatable male doll, which explodes during an experiment in nipple-biting.

• A girl who dreams of making it with a Conan-type body builder, only to find, when she arrives at Conan's apartment, that he is a male prostitute. What does she do then? Walk out in horror and disgust? No, she orders him to disrobe and then tells him he doesn't measure up.

There's also an idiotic subplot out of left field, about a wimpy concert pianist and his domineering mother, and how the whole gang crashes a lawn party at his mother's waterfront mansion. And the usual "Hot Bod" contests and drunken orgies, all written, acted, and directed at such a plodding pace that Valium seems to be the week's drug of choice.

Where the Buffalo Roam ★ ★
R, 98 m., 1980

Peter Boyle (Lazlo), Bill Murray (Hunter S. Thompson), Bruno Kirby (Marty Lewis), Rene Auberjonois (Harris of the Post), R.G.

Armstrong (Judge Simpson), Danny Goldman (Porter). Directed and produced by Art Linson. Screenplay by John Kaye.

Dr. Hunter S. Thompson is the high priest of Gonzo journalism, a reporting style in which the reporter throws himself wildly into the event he is reporting, so that in a way he becomes the event. Karl Lazlo (not his real name) was a Mexican-American attorney Thompson met in the late 1960s and immortalized in *Fear and Loathing in Las Vegas*, a book in which, "speaking as your attorney," Lazlo regularly advised his client to ingest large quantities of booze, drugs, and pills. The purpose: to ward off paranoia and insanity as the two engaged on a drunken odyssey through the craziness of the Vegas Strip.

The Vegas book was followed by *Fear and Loathing on the Campaign Trail*, in which Thompson terrorized the 1972 presidential campaign as a correspondent for *Rolling Stone*. His mere presence was enough to cause terror in the hearts of advance men. The last appearance—or rather disappearance—of Lazlo in Thompson's writing is in "The Banshee Screams for Buffalo Meat," a 1976 *Rolling Stone* article in which the doctor speculates that his attorney has disappeared for good and been murdered.

Where the Buffalo Roam is a comedy inspired by the relationship between Thompson (Bill Murray) and Lazlo (Peter Boyle). The credits say it's "based on the twisted legend of Dr. Hunter S. Thompson." The doctor has become an American folk legend not only through his increasingly infrequent and incoherent *Rolling Stone* articles, but also through his frequent walk-ons (as Duke) in the comic strip Doonesbury. We know his uniform: eyeshade, cigarette holder, garish Hawaiian shirt, Bermuda shorts, bottle of Wild Turkey or similar beverage.

In Doonesbury, the character fights crisis with paranoia. In real life, Thompson has proven no more immune to the effects of alcohol and drug addiction than anybody else, and lives in isolation in his cabin in Woody Creek, Colorado, where he has written almost nothing worth reading since his original brilliant books. He seems to be spending these latter days of his fame having almost as much fun as Brendan Behan did.

But *Where the Buffalo Roam* is a celebration of the self-created public legend of Hunter Thompson, with no insights or hints into the dark night of his soul. That's a legitimate approach, and there are times during the movie when it works: There are really funny moments here, as when we learn that Thompson's dog has been trained to go berserk at the mention of the name Nixon, or when Thompson covers the Super Bowl by staging a football game in his hotel suite, or when he pulls a gun on a telephone, or turns a hospital room into an orgy, or attempts to impersonate a correspondent from the *Washington Post*. An amazing number of these scenes are inspired by real life—although it was Senator George McGovern, not Richard Nixon, who found himself being interviewed by Thompson while standing at a urinal.

We laugh at a lot of these moments; this is the kind of bad movie that's almost worth seeing. But there are large things wrong with *Where the Buffalo Roam*. One of them is its depiction of the relationship between Thompson and Lazlo. That's what the movie is supposed to be about, and yet we never discover why these two characters like one another. What *is* their relationship, aside from the coincidence that they happen to get stoned or drunk together under bizarre circumstances? Are they even really friends? Because the movie's central relationship just isn't there, the events don't matter so much: We get bizarre episodes but no insights.

The other problem is that the Dr. Thompson character never seems to really feel the effects of the chemicals he hurls so recklessly at his system. Murray plays Thompson well, but in a mostly one-level performance: He walks through the most insane situations with a quizzical monotone, a gift for understatement, a drug-induced trance. Any real person drinking and drugging like Thompson would have an occasional high, and a more than occasional disastrous low. Here he has neither.

And so the movie fails to deal convincingly with either Thompson's addictions or with his friendship with Lazlo. It becomes just a series of set-pieces, oft-told tales about the wild and crazy things he's done while he was zonked. We wish him well, but we end up wondering, a little cynically, if Thompson has had as much fun destroying himself as we've had watching him.

Where the Green Ants Dream ★ ★ ★
NO MPAA RATING, 100 m., 1985 ✔

Bruce Spence (Geologist), Wandjuk Marika (Tribal Elder), Roy Marika (Dayipu), Ray Barrett (Cole, Foreman), Norman Kaye (Mining, Vice President), Colleen Clifford (Widow). Directed by Werner Herzog and produced by Lucki Stipetic. Screenplay by Herzog.

Werner Herzog believes in the voodoo of locations, in the possibility that if he shoots a movie in the right place and at the right time, the reality of the location itself will seep into the film and make it more real. He has filmed on the slopes of active volcanoes and a thousand miles up the Amazon, and in his new movie, *Where the Green Ants Dream,* he goes to a godforsaken, heat-baked stretch of Australian Outback. This is grim territory, but it is sacred land to the Aborigines, who believe that this is the place where the green ants go to dream, and that if their dreams are disturbed, unspeakable calamities will rain down on future generations. The Aborigines' belief is not shared by a giant mining company, which wants to tear open the soil and search for uranium.

As the movie opens, the company is in the process of setting off explosions, so geologists can listen to the echoes and choose likely mining sites. The Aborigines sit passively in the way of the explosions, refusing to move, insisting that the ants must not be awakened. We meet the characters on both sides: the tall, gangly mining engineer, the implacable tribal leaders, the supercilious president of the mining company, and the assorted eccentrics who have washed up on this desert shore.

Herzog has said that he thinks in images, not ideas, and that if he can find the correct pictures for a film, he's not concerned about its message. In *Where the Green Ants Dream,* his images include an old woman sitting patiently in the Outback, an opened can of dog food on the ground in front of her, waiting for a pet dog that has been lost in a mine shaft. Then we see a group of Aborigines sit-ting in the aisle of a supermarket, on the exact spot where the last tree in the district once stood; it was the tree under which the men of the tribe once stood to "dream" their children before conceiving them. We also see an extraordinary landscape, almost lunar in its barren loneliness.

We do not see any ants, but then perhaps that is part of Herzog's plan. One of the strangest things about this film (strange if you are not familiar with Herzog, who is the strangest of all living directors) is that noth-ing in this movie is based on anthropological fact. The beliefs, customs, and behavior of the Aborigines, for example, are not inspired by research into their actual lives—but are a fiction, made up by Herzog for his screen-play. The confrontation between the mining company and the Aborigines is likewise not based on yesterday's headlines, but is sym-bolic, representing for Herzog similar "real" stories, but in a more dramatic form. Even the details about the life cycles of the ants are made up; Herzog has no idea if there are really ants in the Outback.

But there is a reality, nevertheless, in this odd film, and it comes out of the two con-flicting sets of beliefs. The Aborigines sit and wait, inspired by deep currents of faith and tradition, and the engineers are always in motion, convinced that success lies in industry and activity. The conflict is every-where in the world today, and Herzog didn't need to make it up, only to find the pictures for it.

White Nights ★ ★
PG-13, 135 m., 1985

Mikhail Baryshnikov (Nikolai), Gregory Hines (Raymond), Jerzy Skolimowski (Colonel Chaiko), Helen Mirren (Galina Ivanova), Geraldine Page (Anne Wyatt), Isabella Rossellini (Darya). Directed by Taylor Hackford and produced by Hackford and William S. Gilmore. Screenplay by James Goldman and Eric Hughes.

White Nights tells such a tortuous story there's only one way to account for it: This screenplay was dreamed up to accommodate two dancers with little else in common. If the movie had allowed them to truly communi-cate about (and through) their dancing, that might have been enough. But *White Nights* has been made in a cynical world where it is actually believed that a dance movie will interest more people if it is also a thriller: a *pas de deux* between the CIA and the KGB, if you will.

The movie tells the story of a Soviet ballet dancer who has defected to America and an American tap dancer who has defected to the Soviet Union. The Russian is on a flight to Japan when the jet is forced to crash-land in Siberia, and so he is once again in the hands of the society he has rejected. The Soviets do not imprison him, however; they hope to score a propaganda victory by re-program-ming him to accept his Russian homeland once again. And one of the ways they hope to do this is to send him to live with the Ameri-can dancer and his Russian-born wife.

The Soviet dancer is played by Mikhail Baryshnikov, once of the Kirov, and the American is played by Gregory Hines, recently of *The Cotton Club*. It is tempting to wonder what sort of a movie might have resulted if they had just been allowed to dance for two hours, but that, I suppose, is too much to hope for. They do find time for several remarkable dance sequences in *White Nights*, and those are the major reasons to see the movie. (The minor reasons include the luminous presence of Isabella Rossellini as Hines's wife, and the superior special effects of the airplane crash scene.)

Baryshnikov opens the movie dancing opposite Florence Faure in Roland Petit's ballet *The Young Man and Death*. It is an extraordinary performance, filled with ath-letic grace, as in one dazzling moment when he climbs onto a chair back, rides it to the floor and continues effortlessly. Hines has a no-less-amazing sequence in which he uses words and dance to explain to Baryshnikov why he chose to leave the United States and settle in the Soviet Union. The moments when the two dancers are together on the screen are the moments when the movie is alive.

All around them, alas, is a drippy thriller plot, made out of recycled political intrigue. Jerzy Skolimowski, the Polish director of *Moonlighting*, plays a Soviet intelligence offi-cial who masterminds the would-be rehabilitation of Baryshnikov. As he attempts to spy and eavesdrop on the danc-ers' activities, the movie takes on a kind of grim monotony that's the opposite of the energy in the dances.

Incredibly, in a film filled with so much grace, the story finally comes down to an awkward action scene in which Baryshnikov, Hines, and Rossellini try to slide down a rope to freedom. As nearly as I could figure out, two of them subsequently re-enter the very building they have just escaped from. Simultaneously, there is an unbelievable tac-tic in which the Soviet eavesdroppers are fooled by a tape recording. Give us a break.

There are two romantic relationships in the movie, which hardly has time for them. Hines and Rossellini are shown in an uneasy alliance: They know they love each other, but they have never reconciled the way they feel about their different societies. Helen Mirren turns up as Baryshnikov's former lover, a dance partner he left behind without a word when he had the opportunity to defect. Now she is a powerful figure in the Soviet dance bureaucracy, the head of the Kirov, and he has a chance to rehabilitate his reputation by staging a comeback on her stage. As if the movie were not already clut-tered, Geraldine Page has the thankless role of Baryshnikov's American agent, forever hectoring the officials at the U.S. Embassy.

White Nights is made by people who seem much more comfortable with dance than with the requirements of the Hollywood thriller. It comes to life in the dance sequences, and then drifts away again. Watching it, I was reminded of nothing so much as those old Ed Sullivan TV shows in which culture was sugar-coated. Watch this ballet dancer, Sullivan would promise us, and Sophie Tucker will be out in a minute.

Wildcats ★ ½
R, 107 m., 1985

Goldie Hawn (Molly), Swoosie Kurtz (Verna), Robin Lively (Alice), Brandy Gold (Marian), James Keach (Frank), Jan Hooks (Stephanie), Bruce McGill (Darwell), Nipsy Russell (Edwards), Tab Thacker (Finch), Scott Eng (Lineman). Directed by Michael Ritchie and produced by Anthea Sylbert. Screenplay by Ezra Sacks.

Wildcats is allegedly about Goldie Hawn's attempts to find success as the coach of a boys' high school football team. But most of the big scenes and almost all of the dialogue in the movie are assigned to her grown-up friends, and the team gets lost in the shuffle—it's the gimmick, not the subject of this movie. With the exception of a Refrigerator clone (Tab Thacker) who plays the tallest and fattest member of her team, Goldie's players are sort of a faceless mass that mills around on cue.

The movie was directed by Michael Ritchie, the same man who made *The Bad News Bears* ten years ago. That was a movie where we really cared about the members of the team—a movie that was about a coach and a team. *Wildcats* is about how spunky Goldie Hawn is, and how cute it's supposed to be that this little woman can make all those great big football players do what she says.

See what happened here? The filmmakers, the producers, and Hawn herself bought the premise instead of looking for the plot. The problem with the movie is that they started with a character description instead of with a story. The fact that Goldie plays a boys' football coach is not in itself interesting. Her relationship with the team would have been interesting, if they'd developed one.

But, no, they thought they had everything they needed. They thought they could clone *Rocky* one more time. At the end of *Wildcats*, whaddaya know, Goldie's team beats its cross-town rivals. I've seen that ending before. I saw the winning football game at the end of *The Best of Times*, and the winning hockey match at the end of *Youngblood*, and God knows how many winning bicycle races and wrestling matches—not to mention *Rocky IV*, of course. The formula is becoming an insidious force in the movie industry; it convinces producers that they have a plot when in fact all they have is a boring structure to trap their characters.

I mentioned that the movie doesn't make much of an effort to make the football players into individuals. Instead, it gives us an astonishingly uninteresting subplot, in which Goldie Hawn's ex-husband (James Keach) threatens to win custody of his daughters because of Goldie's alleged misconduct. (Her players drink beer in her house and make out with their girlfriends, etc., which would be ludicrous except that

the players are mostly black, and the movie supples a wholly unnecessary streak of implied racism in the Keach character.)

Wildcats is clearly an attempt by Hawn to repeat a formula that was wonderfully successful in *Private Benjamin:* Wide-eyed Goldie copes with the real world. It was less successful in *Protocol*, and now it's worn out altogether.

Willard ★ ★
PG, 95 m., 1971

Bruce Davison (Willard Stiles), Elsa Lanchester (Mrs. Stiles), Ernest Borgnine (Martin), Sondra Locke (Gin). Directed by Daniel Mann and produced by Mort Briskin. Screenplay by Gilbert A. Ralston.

Willard is about rats, and about a young man who likes rats and has a mysterious ability to communicate with rats. I hate rats. I also hate spiders. I hate spiders even more than rats, although rats are more dangerous, because of my anthropomorphic bias. But more of that later.

Willard, as I discovered, isn't actually about rats at all. It is a typical Horatio Alger story ("Jed the Poorhouse Boy," if I recollect correctly, or maybe "Do and Dare, or A Brave Boy's Fight for Fortune"), with rats playing more prominent supporting roles than they customarily did in Horatio Alger (where they were limited to run-ons).

The story concerns the plight of plucky young Willard, whose father was cheated out of the family business by the evil Mr. Martin. Willard had counted on inheriting the family concern, but now finds himself a lowly stockboy, the butt of Mr. Martin's cruel jests. Willard and his mother inhabit the old family home, where his mother is bedridden with a disease brought on by the family reversals, and as he struggles to keep a roof over his dear old mother's head, the heartless Mr. Martin weaves an evil scheme to foreclose on the mortgage, tear down the old homestead, and make a killing in real estate. Bad luck on this scale inevitably makes Willard broody, so imagine his delight when he discovers that he can communicate with rats. He discovers, but we don't. I guess you just tickle them and feed them Dog Chow and they like you.

Anyway, Willard has revenge on the evil

Mr. Martin by training a bunch of rats to disrupt a garden party on the occasion of Mr. Martin's wedding anniversary. These days, when there are so few banker's daughters in runaway carriages, direct action seems to be the best policy. Willard's rats bust up the party, and Willard makes special friends of two rats who get upstairs privileges and don't have to stay in the basement. Meanwhile, his mother dies, although not of being eaten alive by rats. I wonder if they missed a bet there.

Willard's rats reproduce and train themselves at such a furious rate that Willard eventually has more rats than he exactly needs, and he gets a little uneasy about the size of his army. One is reminded of Gandhi seeing his troops march past, and running to get at the head of them because he was, after all, their leader. The rats eventually get their opportunity to dine on Mr. Martin (exhibiting the curious ability of being able to fly through the air—almost as if they were being tossed onscreen by a prop man). And then . . .

But I should leave the ending to your imagination. I want to consider, instead, the sociological and psychological implications of Willard. What is it in this film that touches some deep-buried nerve in the public psyche? Why does wholesome family entertainment fade away, while rats make millions? I've thought long and deeply on this subject, believe me, and I've reached a conclusion at last. People have waited a long time to see Ernest Borgnine eaten alive by rats, and now that they have their chance they aren't going to blow it.

Willie and Phil ★ ★ ★
R, 116 m., 1980

Michael Ontkean (Willie), Margot Kidder (Jeannette), Ray Sharkey (Phil), Jan Miner (Mrs. Kaufman), Tom Brennan (Mr. Kaufman), Julie Bovasso (Mrs. D'Amico), Louis Guss (Mr. D'Amico), Kathleen Maguire (Mrs. Sutherland). Directed and written by Paul Mazursky and produced by Mazursky and Tony Ray.

Willie and Phil meet after a screening of Truffaut's *Jules and Jim*, which is a movie about two good friends and how they both fall in love with the same woman, who

becomes the third good friend. Shortly after they see the movie, in Greenwich Village in 1970, Willie and Phil meet Jeannette, and then the three of them spend the 1970s working out their own version of a triangle.

If Paul Mazursky's *Willie and Phil* is supposed to be a psychologically plausible telling of this story, then it doesn't work. The movie gives away its own game right at the beginning, with the reference to *Jules and Jim*. These aren't real people in this movie; they're characters. They don't inhabit life, they inhabit Mazursky's screenplay—which takes them on a guided tour of the cults, fads, human potential movements, and alternative life-styles of the decade during which zucchini replaced Faulkner as the most popular subject on campus.

But I don't think *Willie and Phil* was intended to work on a realistic level, or that we're intended to believe that Willie, Phil, and Jeannette are making free choices throughout the movie. In a subtle, understated sort of way, Mazursky is giving us a movie that hovers between a satirical revue and a series of life-style vignettes. The characters in his movie are almost exhausted by the end of the decade (weren't we all?). Not only have they experimented with various combinations of commitments to one another, but they've also tried out most of the popular 1970s belief systems.

Willie (Michael Ontkean) is a high school teacher as the movie opens, but he wants to be more, to feel deeply, to think on more exalted levels, and his journey through the decade takes him into radicalism, back to the earth, and all the way to India for lessons in meditation. Phil (Ray Sharkey) says he wants love and security, but he holds himself at arm's length from Jeannette and other possible sources of love. Unable to communicate, he channels all of his energy into making it in the communications industries. Jeannette (Margot Kidder) . . . well, what does she want? To love, to be loved, to be possessed, to be free, to commit, but not to be trapped, to . . . have kids? A career? Willie? Phil?

I think Mazursky's suggesting something interesting about the 1970s. It was a decade without a consuming passion, without an overall subject or tone. Every decade from the 1920s to the 1960s had an overriding theme, at least in our collective national imagination, but in the 1970s we went on lifestyle shopping trips, searching for an impossible combination of life choices that would be morally good, politically correct, personally entertaining, and outperform the market—all at once.

And what were we left with in the 1980s? Confusion, vague apprehension, lack of faith in belief systems, EPA mileage estimates, megavitamins as the last blameless conspicuous consumption, and, echoing somewhere in the back of our minds, Peggy Lee singing "Is That All There Is?" How'd we get stuck? Why'd we wind up with a sense of impending doom when we tried every possible superficial substitute for profound change? Mazursky finds this note and strikes it in *Willie and Phil*, and that's what's best about his movie.

But like the decade itself, *Willie and Phil* is not completely substantial or satisfying. What redeems it, curiously, are the scenes involving Willie's Jewish parents, Phil's Italian parents, and Jeannette's Southern mother. Their scenes are reactions to what's happening to their kids in the 1970s, and they work like field trips from other decades. The parents observe, try to understand, are baffled, react with resentment, anger, love, confusion. I loved it when the Italian mother, trying to figure out how Jeannette was going to sleep with her boyfriend in the house of her ex-husband while the ex-husband bunked downstairs and the parents took the guest room, got up, said it was all just too complicated for her, and left for the airport. That's sort of the motif for this movie.

Willie Wonka and the Chocolate Factory ★ ★ ★ ★
G, 98 m., 1971

Gene Wilder (Willie Wonka), Jack Albertson (Grandpa Joe), Peter Ostrum (Charlie), Michael Bollner (Augustus Gloop), Aubrey Wood (Mr. Bill), Gunter Meissner (Mr. Slugwork). Directed by Mel Stuart and produced by Stan Margulies and David L. Wolper. Screenplay by Roald Dahl.

Kids are not stupid. They are among the sharpest, cleverest, most eagle-eyed creatures on God's Earth, and very little escapes their notice. You may not have observed that your neighbor is still using his snow tires in mid-July, but every four-year-old on the block has, and kids pay the same attention to detail when they go to the movies. They don't miss a thing, and they have an instinctive contempt for shoddy and shabby work. I make this observation because nine out of ten children's movies are stupid, witless, and display contempt for their audiences, and that's why kids hate them. Is that all parents want from kids' movies? That they not have anything bad in them? Shouldn't they have something good in them—some life, imagination, fantasy, inventiveness, something to tickle the imagination? If a movie isn't going to do your kids any good, why let them watch it? Just to kill a Saturday afternoon? That shows a subtle kind of contempt for a child's mind, I think.

All of this is preface to a simple statement: *Willie Wonka and the Chocolate Factory* is probably the best film of its sort since *The Wizard of Oz*. It is everything that family movies usually claim to be, but aren't: Delightful, funny, scary, exciting, and, most of all, a genuine work of imagination. *Willie Wonka* is such a surely and wonderfully spun fantasy that it works on all kinds of minds, and it is fascinating because, like all classic fantasy, it is fascinated with itself.

It's based on the well-known Roald Dahl children's book, and it was financed by the Quaker Oats Company as an experiment in providing high-quality family entertainment. It succeeds. It doesn't cut corners and go for cheap shortcuts like Disney. It provides a first-rate cast (Gene Wilder as the compulsively distrustful chocolate manufacturer, Jack Albertson as the game old grandfather), a first-rate production, and—I keep coming back to this—genuine imagination.

The story, like all good fantasies, is about a picaresque journey. Willie Wonka is the world's greatest chocolate manufacturer, and he distributes five golden passes good for a trip through his factory and a lifetime supply of chocolate. Each pass goes to a kid, who may bring an adult along, and our hero Charlie (a poor but honest newsboy who supports four grandparents and his mother) wins the last one.

The other four kids are hateful in one way or another, and come to dreadful ends. One falls into the chocolate lake and is whisked into the bowels of the factory. He shouldn't have been a pig. Another is vain enough to try Wonka's new teleportation invention, and winds up six inches tall—but the taffy-pulling machine will soon have him back to size, right? If these fates seem a little gruesome to you, reflect that all great children's tales are a little gruesome, from the Brothers Grimm to Alice to Snow White, and certainly not excluding Mother Goose. Kids are not sugar and spice, not very often, and they appreciate the poetic justice when a bad kid gets what's coming to him.

Winter of Our Dreams ★ ★ ★
R, 89 m., 1983

Judy Davis (Lou), Bryan Brown (Rob), Cathy Downes (Gretel), Baz Luhrmann (Pete). Directed by John Duigan and produced by Richard Mason. Screenplay by Duigan.

Rob runs a bookstore and lives in one of those houses where the bedrooms hang under the eaves; one false move and you dash your brains out onto the living room floor below. Lou is a prostitute who lives on the streets. They both once had a friend named Lisa, back in the late 1960s when they were all part of the Australian protest movement. Now Lisa has been murdered, and Lou, searching for a meaning in her life or death, runs into Rob again. She thinks he's a trick. He thinks she's an interesting, complicated person who deserves his attention. I think she's closer to the mark.

This is the setup for *Winter of Our Dreams,* an Australian film starring two popular Australian new wave actors, Judy Davis (of *My Brilliant Career*) and Bryan Brown (of *Breaker Morant* and TV's "A Town Like Alice"). Davis brought a kind of wiry, feisty intelligence to *My Brilliant Career,* playing an Australian farm woman who rather felt she would do things her own way. She's wonderful this time, in a completely different role as an insecure, distrustful, skinny street waif. It's Brown who is the trouble. Maybe it's the performance, maybe it's the character, or maybe it's Brown, but I've rarely seen a more closed-off person on the screen. When the story calls for him to reach out to Davis, we feel he's holding his nose. Sometimes there are movies where the leading actors cannot stand one another (Ken Wahl said he was only able to kiss Bette Midler in *Jinxed!* by thinking of his dog), and maybe Brown just couldn't express the feelings that were in the script. But I was never really convinced that he cared for Davis.

That's less of a handicap later in the movie, however, when the Brown character is *required* to draw back from any involvement with this pathetic street kid. The relationships in *Winter of Our Dreams* are very tangled—maybe too tangled. Brown's character has been married for six years to Gretel (Kathy Downes), a handsome, smart woman who has a lover. They have an open marriage, and there's no objection when Brown brings Davis home for the night. Davis, taking this all in, can't understand it. Trying to learn how to feel again, she can't understand why anyone would deliberately trivialize his feelings. The key passages in the film involve Brown's discovery that Davis is a heroin junkie, and then her tortured period of drug withdrawal. They are both pretending to care for one another, and after Davis gets straight maybe Brown will become her lover, while his wife disappears into the woodwork. That is not, however, even remotely in the cards, and there's a painful scene during a party at Brown's house, where Davis realizes that Brown is *very* married, open marriage or not.

There seem to be two movements in *Winter of Our Dreams.* One is Davis's movement away from the cynicism and despair of prostitution, and back toward an ability to care for another person. The other is Brown's initial concern for this girl, and then his retreat back into his shell. Davis performs her movement magnificently. Brown didn't win my sympathy for a moment. What just barely saves this film is the fact that we're not *supposed* to like the Brown character. As for Davis, she's a wonder.

Wise Guys ★ ★ ★ ½
R, 92 m., 1986 ✓

Danny DeVito (Harry Valentini), Joe Piscopo (Moe Dickstein), Harvey Keitel (Bobby DiLea), Ray Sharkey (Marco), Dan Hedaya (Tony Castelo), Captain Lou Albano (Fixer), Julie Bovasso (Lil Dickstein), Patti LuPone (Wanda Valentini). Directed by Brian

DePalma and produced by Aaron Russo.
Screenplay by George Gallo.

Wise Guys tells the story of Harry and Moe,
two low-level hoodlums who become the toys
of the Mafia gods. They're just ordinary
guys, working stiffs who live next door to
each other in houses tucked under a New
Jersey expressway. They dream of the day
when they'll be assigned to really important
jobs, like shaking down widows. But when
the godfather holds his morning staff meetings in the back booth of his favorite restaurant, these guys get humiliated: Their job is
to pick up the boss's laundry.

The two friends are played by Joe Piscopo,
as Moe Dickstein, and Danny DeVito, as
Harry Valentini. They move with easy familiarity through the world of the mob; sometimes the little guys get the best view. They
all know so much, in fact, that when they
screw up, when they do something that is
very, very bad, they don't even have to be
told they're dead. It goes without saying.

Here's what they do. They go to the track
with Fixer, the mob's chief enforcer (played
by Captain Lou Albano, the gigantic professional wrestler). Their assignment is to place
a bet for Tony, the boss (Dan Hedaya).
DeVito gets to thinking, which is always
dangerous. The boss has been betting on the
wrong horses for weeks. They could be
heroes by placing the money on the nose of
the horse that DeVito knows will win. Better
still, they could get rich by betting on the
winning horse and then letting Fixer and the
boss believe the money was lost.

This is a great plan, except unfortunately,
this is the one day that the boss's horse comes
in first, and so DeVito and Piscopo have lost
the boss hundreds of thousands of dollars.
This is bad. It is so bad that DeVito is
plunged into a lobster tank at the restaurant,
and Piscopo is suspended over a pit full of
attack dogs. Then the boss thinks up their
real punishment: He will secretly assign each
one of them to kill the other one. It's here
that the movie really gets rolling. The two
wise guys hit the road, looking for safety,
looking for a mob elder statesman who can
bargain for their safety. And we begin to realize that the movie is filled with an inexhaustible supply of great character actors, that we

are going to meet a lot of people in this story,
and they are all going to be memorable.

In New Jersey, there was Hedaya as the
boss, clean-shaven and slick, and Albano as
Fixer, in one of the year's great supporting
roles. Then, in Atlantic City, we meet the
casino manager Bobby DiLea, played by the
great Harvey Keitel. He doesn't want anyone to get killed in his casino, and once
Harry and Moe check into the penthouse
suite (using Fixer's stolen credit card), he
knows he is going to have to be very lucky to
keep that from happening. Very lucky, or
very weird.

Wise Guys is an abundant movie, filled
with ideas and gags and great characters. It
never runs dry. It never has the desperation
of so many gangster comedies, which seem
to be marching over the same tired ground.
This movie was made with joy, and you can
feel it in the sense of all the actors working at
the top of their form.

The movie was directed by Brian
DePalma, who specializes in movies about
crime and whose credits include *Scarface*,
Body Double, and *Dressed to Kill*. I admired
all those movies—indeed, I think DePalma
is one of the best stylists at work right now—
but I wouldn't have suspected that he had
this comedy in him. His early credits include
such problematic comedies as *Hi, Mom!*
(which was one of Robert De Niro's first
movie jobs), but here's this polished, confident comedy that never seems to step wrong.

A lot of the credit goes to Piscopo and
DeVito, who develop an instant, easy camaraderie. I really did feel that they care for
each other. I liked the way DeVito waved his
arms and demanded attention, and the way
Piscopo played his slightly slower, sweeter,
dumber pal. DeVito has been good in other
recent movies (such as *Romancing the Stone*),
but this is the first time he's been at the top of
the cast, and really free to show his stuff. He
is inspired: This could be a new beginning
for his career. Piscopo, from "Saturday
Night Live," has worked less in the movies,
and has always seemed in search of a character. Here he finds one.

And then there's that gallery of supporting
performances. Albano is so fearsome as
Fixer that I found myself laughing at a time I
don't think was supposed to be funny:
There's a reference to "Mrs. Fixer." Keitel is

suave and sinister as the casino boss, always staying within character, playing it straight, not going for laughs, and so getting more of them.

Laughter doesn't come out of formula, or stupidity, or the manipulation of things that worked before in other films. It comes out of characters and performances, out of people who have some measure of reality, and whose dilemmas we can share. *Wise Guys* is broad and farcical, but there's not a moment when Moe and Harry stop being lovable, and even sort of believable.

Without a Trace ★ ★ ★ ½
PG, 119 m., 1983

Kate Nelligan (Susan Selky), Judd Hirsch (Menetti), David Dukes (Graham Selky), Stockard Channing (Jocelyn). Directed and produced by Stanley Jaffe. Screenplay by Beth Gutcheon.

"A woman's bravery and a police detective's relentless search for her missing son provide the elements of suspenseful human drama in *Without a Trace.*"

—Press release

They have it exactly wrong. The press release describes what might have happened to this story if it had been turned into one of those TV docudramas where every emotion is predictably computed. What makes *Without a Trace* interesting is that it's *not* predictable, because it goes with the ebbs and flows of imperfect human beings. It's not about a woman's bravery but about her intelligence and vulnerability. It's not about a detective's relentless search, but about routine police work, made up of realism and hunches.

Without a Trace opens with a sequence that is very painful, since we know from the movie's title what's about to happen. A young mother (Kate Nelligan), who lives alone with her first-grader, gets him up, gets him his breakfast, scolds him for feeding his breakfast to the dog, tells him he's a good boy, and sends him off to school. He's almost
alk alone to school,
d there's a crossing
to school herself.
r at Columbia Uni-
and waits for her

child. He's late. She makes a call. He never arrived at the school. She calls the police and a search begins at once, but her son has apparently disappeared into thin air. There are door-to-door canvasses, helicopter searches, anonymous phone calls, predictions by psychics, and a neighborhood campaign to put "missing" posters in store windows. But there is no little boy.

One of the unexpected things about *Without a Trace* is that it's not really about the police search for the child. Instead, it's about what happens to people when tragedy turns into open-ended frustration. The mother waits and waits. The detective in charge of the case (Judd Hirsch) follows up leads and does all the things a competent cop is supposed to do. The city lends its resources and pays for an expensive investigation. But everything leads to nothing.

The central passages of the film are the best, as Nelligan plays an intelligent, civilized woman fighting to keep control. She feels rage, yes, but she is a rational person and she tries to behave reasonably. Underneath, she is deeply grieving. It takes her best friend (Stockard Channing) to suggest, after several months, that perhaps it is time to give up and admit that the little boy must be dead. It's time to let go of the past and rebuild her own life. Nelligan rejects that reasoning. And the movie remains neutral. What *is* the right answer: Should she accept what looks like the inevitable, or should she continue to hope? Nelligan's performance grows immensely subtle at this point. We can almost read her mind, and what we are reading is a battle between instinct and intelligence, between common sense and a mother's love.

Then a "suspect" is arrested—a gay sadomasochist. The circumstantial evidence against him is overwhelming. But Nelligan refuses to be bullied into agreement by a police department eager to close its books on the case. She becomes convinced that the man is innocent. And *Without a Trace*, which could so easily have been just another police drama, grows into a thought-provoking movie about how we behave, and why. It asks hard questions. It also has its moments of joy, but it earns every one of them.

Witness ★ ★ ★ ★
R, 120 m., 1985

Harrison Ford (John Book), Kelly McGillis (Rachel), Josef Sommer (Schaeffer), Lukas Haas (Samuel), Alexander Godunov (Daniel Hochleitner). Directed by Peter Weir and produced by Edward S. Feldman. Screenplay by Earl Wallace.

Witness comes billed as a thriller, but it's so much more than a thriller that I wish they hadn't even used the word "murder" in the ads. This is, first of all, an electrifying and poignant love story. Then it is a movie about the choices we make in life and the choices that other people make for us. Only then is it a thriller—one that Alfred Hitchcock would have been proud to make.

The movie's first act sets up the plot, leaving it a lot of time to deal with the characters and learn about them. The film begins on an Amish settlement in Pennsylvania, where for two hundred years a self-sufficient religious community has proudly held onto the ways of their ancestors. The Amish are deeply suspicious of outsiders and stubbornly dedicated to their rural life-style, with its horses and carriages, its communal barn-raisings, its gas lanterns instead of electricity, hooks instead of buttons.

An Amish man dies. His widow and young son leave on a train journey. In the train station in Philadelphia, the little boy witnesses a murder. Harrison Ford plays the tough big-city detective who gets assigned to the case. He stages lineups, hoping the kid can spot the murderer. He shows the kid mug shots. Then it turns out that the police department itself is implicated in the killing. Ford is nearly murdered in an ambush. His life, and the lives of the widow and her son, are in immediate danger. He manages to drive them all back to the Amish lands of Pennsylvania before collapsing from loss of blood.

And it's at this point, really, that the movie begins. Up until the return to Pennsylvania, *Witness* has been a slick, superior thriller. Now it turns into an intelligent and perceptive love story. It's not one of those romances where the man and woman fall into each other's arms because their hormones are programmed that way. It's about two independent, complicated people who begin to love each other because they have shared danger, they work well together, they respect each other—*and* because their physical attraction for each other is so strong it almost becomes another character in the movie.

Witness was directed by Peter Weir, the gifted Australian director of *The Year of Living Dangerously*. He has a strong and sure feeling for places, for the land, for the way that people build their self-regard by the way they do their work.

In the whole middle section of this movie, he shows the man from the city and the simple Amish woman within the context of the Amish community. It is masterful filmmaking. The thriller elements alone would command our attention. The love story by itself would be exciting. The ways of life in the Amish community are so well-observed that they have a documentary feel. But all three elements work together so well that something organic is happening here; we're *inside* this story.

Harrison Ford has never given a better performance in a movie. Kelly McGillis, the young actress who plays the Amish widow, has a kind of luminous simplicity about her; it is refreshing and even subtly erotic to see a woman who doesn't subscribe to all the standard man-woman programmed responses of modern society.

The love that begins to grow between them is not made out of clichés; the cultural gulf that separates them is at least as important to both of them as the feelings they have. When they finally kiss, it is a glorious, sensuous moment, because this kiss is a sharing of trust and passion, not just another plug-in element from your standard kit of movie images.

We have been getting so many pallid, bloodless little movies—mostly recycled teen-age exploitation films made by ambitious young stylists without a thought in their heads—that *Witness* is like a fresh new day. It is a movie about adults, whose lives have dignity and whose choices matter to them. And it is also one hell of a thriller.

A Woman Under the Influence

★ ★ ★ ★

R, 155 m., 1975

Peter Falk (Nick Longhetti), Gena Rowlands (Mabel Longhetti), Katherine Cassavetes (Mama Longhetti), Lady Rowlands (Martha Mortensen), Fred Draper (George Mortensen). Directed by John Cassavetes and produced by Sam Shaw. Screenplay by Cassavetes.

John Cassavetes's *A Woman Under the Influence* gives us a woman whose influences only gradually reveal themselves. And as they do, they give us insight not only into one specific, brilliantly created, woman, but into some of the problems of surviving in a society where very few people are free to be themselves. The woman is Mabel Longhetti, wife and mother and (in some very small, shy, and faraway corner) herself. Her husband, Nick, is the head of a construction gang and a gregarious type with an expansive nature; he's likely to bring his whole crew home at 7 A.M. for a spaghetti dinner.

Mabel isn't gregarious, but she tries. She tries too hard, and that's her problem. She desperately wants to please her husband, and when they're alone, she does. They get along, and they do love one another. But when people are around, she gets a little wacky. The mannerisms, the strange personal little ways she has of expressing herself, get out of scale. She's not sure how to act, because she's not sure who she is. "I'll be whatever you want me to be," she tells Nick, and he tells her to be herself. But who is that?

The film takes place before and after six months she spends in a mental institution. Her husband has her committed, reluctantly, after she begins to crack up. There have been some indications that she's in trouble. She behaves strangely when some neighbor children are brought over to stay for a while with her own, and the neighbor is afraid to leave his kids because of the way she's acting. But what, exactly, is "strange"? Well she's insecure, hyper, manic. She laughs too much and pushes too hard. She's not good with other people around. So her husband does what he thinks he has to do and commits her. But what about him? What kind of a guy is he? It's here that *A Woman*

Under the Influence gets to be complicated, involved, and fascinating—a revelation. Because if Mabel is disturbed, then so is he. He's as crazy as she is, maybe more so. But because he's a man and has channels for his craziness, he stays at home and she gets sent away.

Their ways with kids, for example, are revealing. She feels insecure around them. She's not confident enough to be a mother, and almost wants to be another kid. But the father, when he takes over the responsibility of raising them, yanks them out of school in the middle of the day and drags them, bewildered, to the seashore for the most depressing, compulsory day at the beach we can imagine. And then on the way home, he lets them share a six-pack with him. If Mabel wants to be one of the kids, Nick wants them to be three of the boys.

I don't suppose (although I'm not sure) that real families like this exist, and I don't think Cassavetes wants us to take the film as a literal record. The characters are larger than life (although not less convincing because of that), and their loves and rages, their fights and moments of tenderness, exist at exhausting levels of emotion.

Nick, as played by Peter Falk, shouts and storms and is always on. Mabel (Gena Rowlands, who won an Oscar nomination), seems so touchingly vulnerable to every kind of influence around her that we don't want to tap her, because she might fall apart. Because their personalities are so open, so visible, we see what might be hidden in a quieter, tidier film: that Nick no less than Mabel is trapped in a society where people are assigned roles, duties, and even personalities that have little to do with what they really think and who they really are. This is where Cassavetes is strongest as a writer and filmmaker: at creating specific characters and then sticking with them through long, painful, uncompromising scenes until we know them well enough to read them, to predict what they'll do next, and even to begin to understand why.

Mabel and Nick and their relatives and friends are fully realized, convincing, fictional creations, even though Cassavetes does sometimes deliberately push them into extreme situations. There's a scene, for example, where Nick goes almost berserk in throwing a party for Mabel, who's due home from the institution, then tells all the non-family guests to leave immediately and then berates the family, and Mabel, and himself, in a painful confrontation around the dining room table. The scene's just too extreme to take literally. But as psychodrama, or whatever you want to call it, it abandons any niceties or evasions and deals directly with what the characters are really thinking.

There's also the scenes of great quiet comedy, as when one of Nick's co-workers somehow dumps his entire plate of spaghetti into his lap and the others battle between decorous table manners and their desire to laugh. There's Gena Rowlands's incredible command of her physical acting resources to communicate what Mable feels at times when she's too unsure or intimidated to say. There's Falk, in a performance totally unlike his Columbo, creating this character who's so tender, so much in love, and so screwed up. I have a friend who said, after seeing *A Woman Under the Influence*, that she was so affected, she didn't know whether to cry or throw up. Well, sometimes that's the choice life presents you with—along with the laughs.

Woodstock ★ ★ ★ ★
R, 180 m., 1970

Featuring Richie Havens, Joan Baez, Joe Cocker, Santana, The Who, Sha-Na-Na, Ten Years After, John Sebastian, Crosby, Stills & Nash, Country Joe and The Fish, Arlo Guthrie, Sly and the Family Stone, and Jimi Hendrix. Directed by Michael Wadleigh and produced by Bob Maurice.

Defense Attorney: "Where do you live?"
Abbie Hoffman: "I live in Woodstock nation."
Defense Attorney: "Will you tell the court and the jury where it is?"
Abbie Hoffman: "Yes, it is a nation of alienated young people. We carry it around with us as a state of mind, in the same way the Sioux Indians carry the Sioux nation with them. . . ."

Michael Wadleigh's *Woodstock* is an archaeological study of that nation, which existed for three days in 1969. Because of this movie, the Woodstock state of mind now has its own history, folklore, myth. In terms of

evoking the style and feel of a mass historical event, *Woodstock* may be the best documentary ever made in America. But don't see it for that reason; see it because it is so good to see.

It has a lot of music in it, photographed in an incredible intimacy with the performers, but it's not by any means only a rock-music movie. It's a documentary about the highs and lows of a society that formed itself briefly at Woodstock before moving on. It covers that civilization completely, showing how the musicians sang to it and the Hog Farm fed it and the Port-O-San man provided it with toilet facilities.

And it shows how 400,000 young people formed the third largest city in New York State, and ran it for a weekend with no violence, in a spirit of informal cooperation. The spirit survived even though Woodstock was declared a "disaster area," and a thunderstorm soaked everyone to the skin, and the food ran out. The remarkable thing about Wadleigh's film is that it succeeds so completely in making us feel how it must have been to be there. It does that to the limits that a movie can.

Woodstock does what all good documentaries do. It is a bringer of news. It reports, it shows, it records, and it interprets. It gives us maybe sixty percent music and forty percent on the people who were there, and that is a good ratio, I think. The music is very much part of the event, especially since Wadleigh and his editors have allowed each performer's set to grow and build and double back on itself without interference. That is what rock music in concert is all about, as I understand it. Rock on records is another matter, usually, but in the free form of a concert like Woodstock, the whole point is that the performers and their audience are into a back-and-forth thing from which a totally new performance can emerge.

We get that feeling from Jimi Hendrix when he improvises a guitar arrangement of "The Star Spangled Banner," rockets bursting in air and all. We get it from Country Joe, poker-faced, leading the crowd through the anti-Vietnam "I Feel Like I'm Fixin' to Die Rag." We get it in the raunchy 1950s vulgarity of Sha-Na-Na doing a tightly choreographed version of "At the Hop." And we get it so strongly that some kind of strange sensation inhabits our spine, when Joe Cocker and everybody else in the whole Woodstock nation sings "With a Little Help from My Friends."

This sort of participation can happen at a live concert, and often enough it does. But it is hard to get on film, harder than it looks. It is captured in *Woodstock*, maybe because Wadleigh's crew understood the music better and had the resources to shoot 120 miles of film with sixteen cameras. This gave them miles and hours of film to throw away, but it also gave them a choice when they got into the editing room. They weren't stuck with one camera pointed at one performer; they could cut to reaction shots, to multiple images, to simultaneous close-ups when two members of a band did a mutual improvisation.

And of course they always had the option of remaining simple, even shy, when the material called for it. One of the most moving moments of the film, for me, is Joan Baez singing the old Wobbly song "Joe Hill," and then rapping about her husband David, and then putting down the guitar and singing "Swing Low, Sweet Chariot," with that voice which is surely the purest and sweetest of our generation. Wadleigh and company had the integrity to let her just sing it. No tricks. No fancy camera angles. Just Joan Baez all alone on a pitch-black screen.

But then when the occasion warrants it, they let everything hang out. When Santana gets to their intricate rhythm thing, Wadleigh goes to a triple-screen and frames the drummer with two bongo players. All in synchronized sound (which is not anywhere near as easy as it sounds under outdoor concert conditions). And the editing rhythm follows the tense, driving Santana lead. The thing about this movie, somehow, is that the people who made it were right there, right on top of what the performers were doing.

Watch, for example, the way Richie Havens is handled. He is supposed to be more or less a folk singer—a powerful one, but still within the realm of folk and not rock. So you would think maybe he's seem slightly less there than the hard-rock people? Not at all, because Wadleigh's crew went after the power in Havens's performance, and when they got it they stuck so close to it visually that in his second song, "Freedom,"

we get moved by folk in the way we ordinarily expect to be moved by rock.

We see Havens backstage, tired, even a little down. Then he starts singing, and we don't see his face again, but his thumb on the guitar strings, punishing them. And then (in an unbroken shot) down to his foot in a sandal, pounding with the beat, and then the fingers, and then the foot, and only then the face, and now this is a totally transformed Richie Havens, and we are so close to him, we see he doesn't have any upper teeth. Not that it matters; but we don't usually get that close to anybody in a movie.

Moving along with the music, paralleling it sometimes on a split screen, are the more traditionally documentary aspects of *Woodstock*. There are the townspeople, split between those who are mean and ordinary and closed off, and those like the man who says, "Kids are hungry, you gotta feed 'em. Right?" And the farmer who made his land available. And kids skinny-dipping, and turning on, and eating and sleeping.

Wadleigh never forces this material. His movie is curiously objective, in fact. Not neutral; he's clearly with the kids. But objective; showing what's there without getting himself in the way, so that the experience comes through directly.

With all that film to choose from in the editing room, he was able to give us dozens of tiny unrehearsed moments that sum up the Woodstock feeling. The skinny-dipping, for example, is free and unself-conscious, and we can see that. But how good it is to see that kid sitting on a stump in the water and turning to the camera and saying, "Man, a year ago I never would have believed this was the way to swim. But, man, this *is* the way to swim."

What you're left with finally, though, are the people. I almost said the "kids," but that wouldn't include the friendly chief of police, or the farmer, or Hugh Romney from the Hog Farm ("Folks, we're planning breakfast in bed for 400,000 people"), or the Port-O-San man, or the townspeople who took carloads of food to the park.

Wadleigh and his team have recorded all the levels. The children. The dogs (who were allowed to run loose in this nation). The freaks and the straights. The people of religion (Swami Gi and three nuns giving the peace sing). The cops (eating Popsicles). The Army (dropping blankets, food, and flowers from helicopters). *Woodstock* is a beautiful, complete, moving, ultimately great film, and now that many years have come to pass and the Woodstock generation is attacked for being just as uptight as all the rest of the generations, it's good to have this movie around to show that, just for a weekend anyway, that wasn't altogether the case.

The World According to Garp ★ ★ ★
R, 126 m., 1982

Robin Williams (Garp), Mary Beth Hurt (Helen Holm), Glenn Close (Jenny Fields), John Lithgow (Roberta), Hume Cronyn (Mr. Fields), Jessica Tandy (Mrs. Fields), Swoozie Kurtz (Hooker), Amanda Plummer (Ellen James). Directed by George Roy Hill and produced by Hill and Robert L. Crawford. Screenplay by Steve Tesich.

John Irving's best-selling novel, *The World According to Garp*, was cruel, annoying, and smug. I kept wanting to give it to my cats. But it was wonderfully well-written and was probably intended to inspire some of those negative reactions in the reader. The movie version of *Garp*, however, left me entertained but unmoved, and perhaps the movie's basic failing is that it did not inspire me to walk out on it. Something has to be wrong with a film that can take material as intractable as *Garp* and make it palatable.

Like a lot of movie versions of novels, the film of *Garp* has not reinterpreted the material in its own terms. Indeed, it doesn't interpret it at all. It simply reproduces many of the characters and events in the novel, as if the point in bringing *Garp* to the screen was to provide a visual aid for the novel's readers. With the book we at least know how we feel during the saga of Garp's unlikely life; the movie lives entirely within its moments, keeping us entirely inside a series of self-contained scenes.

The story of Garp is by now part of best-selling folklore. We know that Garp's mother was an eccentric nurse, a cross between a saint and a nuisance, and that Garp was fathered in a military hospital atop the unconscious body of a brain-damaged tech-

nical sergeant. That's how much use Garp's mother, Jenny Fields, had for men. The movie, like the book, follows Garp from this anticlimactic beginning through a lifetime during which he is constantly overshadowed by his mother, surrounded by other strange women and women-surrogates, and asks for himself, his wife and children only uneventful peace and a small measure of happiness.

A great deal happens, however, to disturb the peace and prevent the happiness. Garp is accident-prone, and sadness and disaster surround him. Assassinations, bizarre airplane crashes, and auto mishaps are part of his daily routine. His universe seems to have been wound backward.

The movie's method in regarding the nihilism of his life is a simple one. It alternates two kinds of scenes: those in which very strange people do very strange things while pretending to be sane, and those in which all of the dreams of those people, and Garp, are shattered in instants of violence and tragedy.

What are we to think of these people and the events in their lives? The novel *The World According to Garp* was (I *think*) a tragicomic counterpoint between the collapse of middle-class family values and the rise of random violence in our society. A protest against that violence provides the most memorable image in the book, the creation of the Ellen James Society, a group of women who cut out their tongues in protest against what happened to Ellen James, who had her tongue cut out by a man. The bizarre behavior of the people in the novel, particularly Garp's mother and the members of the Ellen Jamesians, is a cross between activism and insanity, and there is the clear suggestion that without such behavior to hold them together, all of these people would be unable to cope at all and would sign themselves into the nearest institution. As a vision of modern American life, *Garp* is bleak, but it has something to say.

The movie, however, seems to believe that the book's characters and events are somehow real, or, to put it another way, that the *point* of the book is to describe these colorful characters and their unlikely behavior, just as Melville described the cannibals in *Typee*. Although Robin Williams plays Garp as a relatively plausible, sometimes ordinary person, the movie never seems bothered by the jarring contrast between his cheerful pluckiness and the anarchy around him.

That created the following dilemma for me. While I watched *Garp,* I enjoyed it. I thought the acting was unconventional and absorbing (especially by Williams, by Glenn Close as his mother, and by John Lithgow as a transsexual). I thought the visualization of the events, by director George Roy Hill, was fresh and consistently interesting. But when the movie was over, my immediate response was not at all what it should have been. All I could find to ask myself was: What the hell was *that* all about?

Xanadu ★ ★
PG, 93 m., 1980

Olivia Newton-John (Kira), Gene Kelly (Danny McGuire), Michael Beck (Sonny Malone). Directed by Robert Greenwald and produced by Lawrence Gordon. Screenplay by Richard Christian Danus and Marc Reid Rubel.

Xanadu is a mushy and limp musical fantasy, so insubstantial it evaporates before our eyes. It's one of those rare movies in which every scene seems to be the final scene; it's all ends and no beginnings, right up to its actual end, which is a cheat. There are, however, a few—a very few—reasons to see *Xanadu,* which I list herewith: (1) Olivia Newton-John is a great-looking woman, brimming with high spirits, (2) Gene Kelly has a few good moments, (3) the sound track includes "Magic," and (4) it's not as bad as *Can't Stop the Music.*

It is pretty bad, though. And yet it begins with an inspiration that I found appealing. It gives us a young man (Michael Beck) who falls in love with the dazzling fantasy figure (Newton-John) who keeps popping up in his life. Beck works as a commercial artist, designing record album covers, and when he tries to include Olivia in one of his paintings he gets into trouble at work.

That's okay, because he's met this nice older guy (Gene Kelly) who's very rich and wants to open a nightclub like the one he had back in New York in the 1940s. Kelly used to be a sideman in the Glenn Miller Orchestra, and in a quietly charming fantasy scene, he sings a duet with his old flame, the girl singer

in the old Miller band—who, lo and behold, is Olivia Newton-John.

That means both men are in love with the same dream girl, who, we discover, is not of this earth. They team up to convert a rundown old wrestling amphitheater into Xanadu, a nightclub that will combine the music of the 1940s and 1980s. And that is the whole weight of the movie's ideas, except for a scene where Michael Beck visits Olivia in heaven, which looks like a computer-generated disco light show.

Musicals have been made with thinner plot lines than this one, but rarely with less style. The movie is muddy, it's underlit, characters are constantly disappearing into shadows, there's no zest to the movie's look. Even worse, I'm afraid, is the choreography by Kenny Ortega and Jerry Trent, especially as it's viewed by Victor Kemper's camera. The dance numbers in this movie do not seem to have been conceived for film.

For example: When Beck and Kelly visit the empty amphitheater, Kelly envisions a forties band in one corner and an eighties rock group in another. The movie gives us one of each: Andrews Sisters clones in close harmony, and the Electric Light Orchestra in full explosion. Then the two bandstands are moved together so that they blend and everyone is on one bandstand, singing one song. It's a great idea, but the way this movie handles it, it's an incomprehensible traffic jam with dozens of superfluous performers milling about.

The Ortega-Trent choreography of some of the other numbers is just as bad. They keep giving us five lines of dancers and then shooting at eye level, so that instead of seeing patterns we see confusing cattle calls. The dancers in the background muddy the movements of the foreground. It's a free-for-all.

The movie approaches desperation at times in its attempt to be all things to all audiences. Not only do we get the 1940s swing era, but a contemporary sequence starts with disco, goes to hard rock, provides an especially ludicrous country and western sequence, and moves on into prefabricated New Wave. There are times when *Xanadu* doesn't even feel like a movie fantasy, but like a shopping list of marketable pop images. Samuel Taylor Coleridge dreamed the poem Xanadu but woke up before it was over, a possibility overlooked by the makers of this film.

The Year of Living Dangerously
★ ★ ★ ★
PG, 114 m., 1983

Mel Gibson (Guy Hamilton), Linda Hunt (Billy Kwan), Sigourney Weaver (Jill Bryant), Michael Murphy (Pete Curtis), Noel Ferrier (Wally O'Sullivan), Bill Kerr (Colonel Henderson). Directed by Peter Weir and produced by Jim McElroy. Screenplay by David Williamson, Weir, and C.J. Koch.

The Year of Living Dangerously achieves one of the best re-creations of an exotic locale I've ever seen in a movie. It takes us to Indonesia in the middle 1960s, a time when the Sukarno regime was shaky and the war in Vietnam was just heating up. It moves us into the life of a foreign correspondent, a radio reporter from Australia who has just arrived in Jakarta, and who thrives in an atmosphere heady with danger. How is this atmosphere created by Peter Weir, the director? He plunges into it headfirst. He doesn't pause for travelogue shots. He thrusts us immediately into the middle of the action—into a community of expatriates, journalists, and embassy people who hang out in the same bars, restaurants, and clubs, and speculate hungrily on the possibility that Sukarno might be deposed. That would be a really big story, a corrective for their vague feelings of being stuck in a backwater.

Guy Hamilton, the journalist (Mel Gibson), is a lanky, Kennedyesque, chain-smoking young man who has a fix on excitement. He doesn't know the ropes in Indonesia, but he learns them quickly enough, from a dwarfish character named Billy Kwan. Billy is half-Oriental and half-European, and knows everybody and can tell you where all the bodies are buried. He has a warm smile and a way of encouraging you to do your best, and if you sometimes suspect he has unorthodox political connections—well, he hasn't crossed you yet. In all the diplomatic receptions he's a familiar sight in his gaudy tropical shirts. *The Year of Living Dangerously* follows Guy and Billy as they become friends, and something more than friends; they begin to share a common humanity and respect. Billy gets Guy a good interview with

the local Communist Party chief. He even introduces Guy to Jill Bryant (Sigourney Weaver), a British attaché with two weeks left on her tour. As the revolution creeps closer, as the stories get bigger, Guy and Jill become lovers and Billy, who once proposed to Jill, begins to feel pushed aside.

This sounds, no doubt, like a foreign correspondent plot from the 1940s. It is not. *The Year of Living Dangerously* is a wonderfully complex film about personalities more than events, and we really share the feeling of living in that place, at that time. It does for Indonesia what Bogdanovich's *Saint Jack* did for Singapore. The direction is masterful; Weir (whose credits include *Picnic at Hanging Rock*) is as good with quiet little scenes (like Billy's visit to a dying child) as big, violent ones (like a thrilling attempt by Guy and Billy to film a riot).

The performances of the movie are a good fit with Weir's direction, and his casting of the Billy Kwan character is a key to how the film works. Billy, so small and mercurial, likable and complicated and exotic, makes Indonesia seem more foreign and intriguing than any number of standard travelogue shots possibly could. That means that when the travelogue shots *do* come (and they do, breathtakingly, when Gibson makes a trip into the countryside), they're not just scenery; they do their work for the film because Weir has so convincingly placed us in Indonesia. Billy Kwan is played, astonishingly, by a woman—Linda Hunt, a New York stage actress who enters the role so fully that it never occurs to us that she is not a man. This is what great acting is, a magical transformation of one person into another. Mel Gibson (of *The Road Warrior*) is just right as a basically conventional guy with an obsessive streak of risk-taking. Sigourney Weaver has a less interesting role but is always an interesting actress. This is a wonderfully absorbing film.

The Year of the Quiet Sun ★ ★ ★ ★
PG, 106 m., 1986 ✓

Scott Wilson (Norman), Maja Komorowska (Emilia), Hanna Skarzanka (Mother), Ewa Dalkowska (Stella). Directed and written by Krzysztof Zanussi.

Imagine a landscape which seems to contain

no joy. A soldier has been assigned here, far from his home. He is an uncomplicated man, not young anymore, who has never really felt that he belonged to anyone. Also living here is a single woman, not young, who tends to her dying mother in the home they have scraped together out of the rubble. It is shortly after the end of World War II.

The woman speaks Polish. She lives in an area of Europe that is perhaps Poland, perhaps Germany, depending on how the politicians are drawing their lines on the map. There was a time when she and her mother lived comfortably and were respectable, and now there is the terrible shame of having to wear torn clothes and live in a few rooms of a house that is falling to pieces. After the long years of war, there is no lightness in her life, no joy except for one thing: Sometimes she finds a little time to paint.

The soldier sees her painting. He is touched by her determination to find some small beauty in this landscape. They communicate awkwardly, because neither speaks the other's language. They talk with their eyes. The soldier has little to do—there are times when he seems half-forgotten in this backwater—and he begins to court the woman. With his GI's pay and privileges, he is rich by the local standards, and he is able to help her. Soon he asks the woman to marry him.

There is a problem. The woman will not leave her mother. She cannot leave her here to fend for herself in brutal poverty. The mother sees this, but also sees that, for her daughter, this man represents a chance for escape and happiness. So the mother tries to make the escape possible. But there is the suggestion that escape from this life will never be possible, that the war went on too long, and the suffering was too great, and the reality of present poverty is too crushing, for the woman to summon the imagination to see how it could be different.

The Year of the Quiet Sun is by Krzysztof Zanussi, the Polish director who is arguably the best filmmaker in Europe right now. It stars one of his favorite actresses, Maja Komorowska, as the younger woman, and the American actor Scott Wilson (still best known for *In Cold Blood*) as the lonely GI. This is a small, quiet film of enormous power. It is not generated by any genre, by any plot that we can anticipate; it is the particular story of the people in this time and place. It doesn't even make a statement, really; given the fact of the war and its aftermath, Zanussi has no suggestions to make, and simply wants to tell the story of these people whose human needs persist despite everything.

I have no insights into the personal lives of Komorowska or Wilson, but I imagine they must have some source from which to draw the sadness that they project in this film. There are scenes that entirely depend on their ability to find the strength to smile, to hope for a moment that their lives can be better, and the way they do that is enormously convincing.

Although a movie like this doesn't usually find a large audience, it represents what I find most valuable about filmmaking, the ability to record the emotions during precise moments in the lives of other people. It's not the story that matters here, and it's not even all that important whether the man and woman do marry, and he takes her back to his farm in the Midwest. What's important is that they succeed, across the barriers of language and culture, in insisting on their right to be happy together no matter what.

Yentl ★ ★ ★ ½
PG, 134 m., 1983

Yentl (Barbra Streisand), Mandy Patinkin (Avigdor), Amy Irving (Hadass), Nehemiah Persoff (Papa). Directed and produced by Barbra Streisand. Screenplay by Jack Rosenthal and Streisand.

To give you a notion of the special magic of *Yentl*, I'd like to start with the following complicated situation:

Yentl, a young Jewish girl, wants to be a scholar. But girls are not permitted to study books. So she disguises herself as a boy, and is accepted by a community of scholars. She falls in love with one of them. He thinks she is a boy. He is in love with a local girl. The girl's father will not let him marry her. So he convinces Yentl to marry his girlfriend, so that at least he can visit the two people he cares for most deeply. (The girlfriend, remember this, thinks Yentl is a boy.) Yentl and the girl are wed. At first Yentl manages to disguise her true sex. But eventually she realizes that she must reveal the truth. That is the central situation in *Yentl*. And when the critical moment came when Yentl had to decide what to do, I was quietly astonished to realize that I did not have the slightest idea how this situation was going to turn out, and that I really cared about it.

I was astonished because, quite frankly, I expected *Yentl* to be some kind of schmaltzy formula romance in which Yentl's "secret identity" was sort of a running gag. You know, like one of those plot points they use for Broadway musicals where the audience is really there to hear the songs and see the costumes. But *Yentl* takes its masquerade seriously, it treats its romances with the respect due to genuine emotion, and its performances are so good that, yes, I really did care.

Yentl is Barbra Streisand's dream movie. She had been trying to make it for ten years, ever since she bought the rights to the Isaac Bashevis Singer story it's based on. Hollywood told her she was crazy. Hollywood was right—on the irrefutable logical ground that a woman in her forties can hardly be expected to be convincing as a seventeen-year-old boy. Streisand persisted. She worked on this movie four years, as producer, director, cowriter, and star. And she has pulled it off with great style and heart. She doesn't really look like a seventeen-year-old boy in this movie, that's true. We have to sort of suspend our disbelief a little. But she *does* look seventeen, and that's without a lot of trick lighting and funny filters on the lens, too. And she sings like an angel.

Yentl is a movie with a great middle. The beginning is too heavy-handed in establishing the customs against women scholars (an itinerant book salesman actually shouts, "Serious books for men . . . picture books for women"). And the ending, with Yentl sailing off for America, seemed like a cheat; I missed the final scene between Yentl and her "bride." But the middle 100 minutes of the movie are charming and moving and surprisingly interesting. A lot of the charm comes from the cheerful high energy of the actors, not only Streisand (who gives her best performance) but also Mandy Patinkin, as her long-suffering roommate, and Amy Irving, as the girl Patinkin loves and Streisand marries.

There are, obviously, a lot of tricky scenes involving this triangle, but the movie handles them all with taste, tact, and humor. It's pretty obvious what strategy Streisand and her collaborators used in approaching the scenes where Yentl pretends to be a boy. They began by asking what the scene would mean if she *were* a male, and then they simply played it that way, allowing the ironic emotional commentaries to make themselves.

There was speculation from Hollywood that *Yentl* would be "too Jewish" for middle-American audiences. I don't think so. Like all great fables, it grows out of a particular time and place, but it takes its strength from universal sorts of feelings. At one time or another, almost everyone has wanted to do something and been told they couldn't, and almost everyone has loved the wrong person for the right reason. That's the emotional ground that *Yentl* covers, and it always has its heart in the right place.

Young Doctors in Love ★ ★
R, 96 m., 1982

Michael McKean (Dr. August), Sean Young (Dr. Brody), Harry Dean Stanton (Dr. Ludwig), Patrick MacNee (Dr. Jacobs), Hector Elizondo (Angelo), Dabney Coleman (Dr. Prang). Directed by Garry Marshall and produced by Jerry Bruckheimer. Screenplay by Michael Elias and Rich Eustis.

The basic joke in *Young Doctors in Love* was anticipated five years ago, in Mel Brooks's *Silent Movie*. Remember the scene where Brooks and his cohorts stand by Sid Caesar's bedside, watching his heartbeat reflected on a television monitor, when suddenly the heart beep turns into a Pong game? That combination of gallows humor and contemporary cross-references is repeated again and again in *Young Doctors in Love*, and it's finally not very funny. Yet the movie sounds like a good idea. Maybe it was a good idea, lost in the execution. *Young Doctors in Love* has as its modest ambition to be to "General Hospital" what *Airplane!* was to the *Airport* movies and ABC's "Police Squad" was to TV cop shows. Maybe there are two problems here: (1) It is rather hard to outflank "General Hospital," a parody of itself, and (2) If you do, you wind up skirting the edges of very unpleasant comic material about blood and death. Hospitals are just not very funny.

The movie takes place in a loony Los Angeles city hospital, where we meet all the standard types: the monomaniac surgeon, the befuddled chief of staff, and sex-and-dope crazed interns and nurses, and the ambitious young medical students in their first year of residence. There also are several long-running gags, the unfunniest being about a hit man who is turned into the hapless victim of accidents and near-fatal emergency treatments. The movie looks at times like a real-life version of one of those drawings by *Mad* magazine's Jack Davis, in which lunatics chase each other in circles.

Are there funny moments in the middle of the chaos? Yes, there are. There is, in fact, one wonderfully funny moment, starring that superb character actor Harry Dean Stanton, he of the long face, the quivering eyelids, and the perpetual hangover. He attempts to explain the secretion of bodily fluids to the amazed young medical students, and by the time he is finished with his amazing catalog, there is not an orifice left untapped.

That's a great scene, and Dabney Coleman has some nice moments as the egotistical surgeon, obviously modeled on the sorts of Texas super doctors who do most of their operations on the cover of *Life* magazine. Coleman reminds us again here of his versatility; his roles also have included the boss in *9 to 5* and Jane Fonda's fiancé in *On Golden Pond*. But for the rest, *Young Doctors in Love* is not very funny and not very inventive. God knows it tries. Like *Airplane!*, it spends its energy trying to wedge laughs into every crevice of the plot. There are some nice moments, especially a gag about *E.T.* But most of the time I wasn't laughing, and toward the end I wasn't even smiling. When a comedy goes wrong, it goes very wrong. *Young Doctors in Love* goes very wrong.

Young Frankenstein ★ ★ ★ ★
PG, 108 m., 1974

Gene Wilder (Dr. Frankenstein), Peter Boyle (His Monster), Madeline Kahn (Elizabeth), Cloris Leachman (Frau Blucher), Gene Hackman (Blind Man). Directed by Mel Brooks and produced by Michael Gruskoff. Screenplay by Gene Wilder and Brooks.

The moment, when it comes, has the inevitability of comic genius. Young Victor Frankenstein, grandson of the count who started it all, returns by rail to his ancestral home. As the train pulls into the station, he spots a kid on the platform, lowers the window, and asks: "Pardon me, boy; is this the Transylvania station?" It is, and director Mel Brooks is home with *Young Frankenstein*, his most disciplined and visually inventive film (it also happens to be very funny). Victor is a professor in a New York medical school, trying to live down the family name and giving hilarious demonstrations of the difference between voluntary and involuntary reflexes. He stabs himself in the process, dismisses the class, and is visited by an ancient family retainer with his grandfather's will.

Frankenstein quickly returns to Transylvania and the old ancestral castle, where he is awaited by the faithful houseboy Igor, the voluptuous lab assistant Elizabeth, and the mysterious housekeeper Frau Blucher, whose very name causes horses to rear in fright. The young man had always rejected his grandfather's medical experiments as impossible, but he changes his mind after he discovers a book entitled *How I Did It* by Victor Frankenstein. Now all that's involved is a little grave-robbing and a trip to the handy local Brain Depository, and the Frankenstein family is back in business.

In his two best comedies, before this, *The Producers* and *Blazing Saddles*, Brooks revealed a rare comic anarchy. His movies weren't just funny, they were aggressive and subversive, making us laugh even when we really should have been offended. (Explaining this process, Brooks once loftily declared, "My movies rise below vulgarity.") *Young Frankenstein* is as funny as we expect a Mel Brooks comedy to be, but it's more than that: It shows artistic growth and a more sure-handed control of the material by a director who once seemed willing to do literally anything for a laugh. It's more confident and less breathless.

That's partly because the very genre he's satirizing gives him a strong narrative he can play against. Brooks's targets are James Whale's *Frankenstein* (1931) and *Bride of Frankenstein* (1935), the first the most influential and the second probably the best of the 1930s Hollywood horror movies. Brooks uses carefully controlled black-and-white photography that catches the feel of the earlier films. He uses old-fashioned visual devices and obvious special effects (the train ride is a study in manufactured studio scenes). He adjusts the music to the right degree of squeakiness. And he even rented the original *Frankenstein* laboratory, with its zaps of electricity, high-voltage special effects, and elevator platform to intercept lightning bolts.

So the movie is a send-up of a style and not just of the material (as Paul Morrissey's dreadful *Andy Warhol's Frankenstein*). It looks right, which makes it funnier. And then, paradoxically, it works on a couple of levels: first as comedy, and then as a weirdly touching story in its own right. A lot of the credit for that goes to the performances of Gene Wilder, as young Frankenstein, and Peter Boyle as the monster. They act broadly when it's required, but they also contribute tremendous subtlety and control. Boyle somehow manages to be hilarious and pathetic at the same time.

There are set-pieces in the movie that deserve comparison with the most famous scenes in *The Producers*. Demonstrating that he has civilized his monster, for example, Frankenstein and the creature do a soft-shoe number in black tie and tails. Wandering in the woods, the monster comes across a poor, blind monk (Gene Hackman, very good) who offers hospitality and winds up scalding, burning, and frightening the poor creature half to death.

There are also the obligatory town meetings, lynch mobs, police investigations, laboratory experiments, love scenes, and a cheerfully ribald preoccupation with a key area of the monster's stitched-together anatomy. From its opening title (which manages to satirize *Frankenstein* and *Citizen Kane* at the same time) to its closing, uh, refrain, *Young Frankenstein* is not only a Mel Brooks movie but also a loving commentary on our love-hate affairs with monsters. This time, the monster even gets to have a little love-hate affair of his own.

Young Sherlock Holmes ★ ★ ★
PG-13, 109 m., 1985

Nicholas Rowe (Holmes), Alan Cox (Watson), Sophie Ward (Elizabeth), Anthony Higgins (Rathe), Susan Fleetwood (Mrs. Dribb), Freddie Jones (Cragwitch), Nigel Stock (Waxflatter). Directed by Barry Levinson and produced by Mark Johnson. Executive producer, Steven Spielberg. Screenplay by Chris Columbus.

It really does make sense, once you've overcome the novelty of the idea, that Sherlock Holmes and John H. Watson originally met while at school. Their friendship is the sort of immature bond that can best be forged between adolescents, based on Watson's hero worship and Holmes's need for an admiring audience. There has always been something of the eternal teen-ager about Holmes and Watson, especially in their love of gadgets and mysteries and technical intricacies, and their complete bafflement when faced with such complex subjects as human nature, for example, or women.

Young Sherlock Holmes suggests that Holmes and Watson met in their middle teens, at an English public school, and that Holmes solved his first case at about the same time. This theory involves a rewriting of their historic first meeting, but the movie suggests that it set a pattern for many more meetings to come: Watson blunders into the orbit of the supercilious Holmes, who casually inspects him and uses a few elementary clues to tell him everything about himself.

The school they attend is one of those havens of eccentricity that have been celebrated in English fiction since time immemorial. It is run by Rathe (Anthony Higgins), a bright young man, but it is also inhabited by old professor Waxflatter (Nigel Stock), a retired don who hopes to invent the first airplane, and who regularly launches unsuccessful flights from the tops of the school buildings.

Holmes and Watson look, as schoolboys, like younger versions of the men they would someday become. Holmes (Nicholas Rowe) is tall, slender, and taciturn, and Watson (Alan Cox) is short and round and nearsighted. Watson is in every sense the new boy, always available to run an errand for the adored Holmes, to provide a cheering section, and to chronicle the great man's adventures.

The plot of *Young Sherlock Holmes* seems constructed out of odds and ends of several stories by Arthur Conan Doyle. For unknown reasons, several men with no apparent connection to one another die under mysterious circumstances. To Watson's amazement, Holmes finds the missing connection, determines that they have died while hallucinating, identifies the hallucinatory drug and its means of attack, and arrives at a likely suspect.

If these story elements seem typical of Conan Doyle, there is also a lot in this movie that can be traced directly to the work of Steven Spielberg, the executive producer. The teen-age heroes, for example, are not only inspired by Holmes and Watson, but are cousins of the young characters in *The Goonies*. The fascination with lighter-than-air flight leads to a closing scene that reminded me of *E. T.* And the villain's secret temple, with its ritual of human sacrifice, was not unlike scenes in both Indiana Jones movies.

It also doesn't take a Sherlock Holmes to identify the one element of *Young Sherlock Holmes* that definitely doesn't fit; that's the character of Elizabeth, a fetching young girl played by Sophie Ward. She is the granddaughter of the mad inventor, and also lives at the school, and we are asked to believe that young Holmes has had a schoolboy crush on her. I personally do not believe that Sherlock Holmes, the great investigator, ever even began to penetrate the mystery of women, but the movie just barely gets away with the character of Elizabeth by having Holmes swear there will never be another woman for him, for the rest of his life.

The elaborate special effects also seem a little out of place in a Sherlock Holmes movie, although I'm willing to forgive them because they were fun. The traditional world of Holmes (in the movies, anyway) has been limited to fogbound streets, speeding carriages, smoky sitting rooms, and the homes and laboratories of suspects. In this film, we get a series of hallucinations that are represented by fancy special effects, and then there's the pseudo-Egyptian temple of doom at the end.

The effects were supplied by Industrial Light & Magic, the George Lucas brain trust, and the best one is a computer-animated stained-glass window that fights a duel with Holmes. I liked the effect, but I would have liked it more if, at the end of the movie, Holmes had drawn Watson aside, and, using a few elementary observations on the apparent movement of the stained glass, had deduced the eventual invention of computers.

Youngblood ★ ★
PG-13, 110 m., 1985

Rob Lowe (Dean Youngblood), Cynthia Gibb (Jessie Chadwick), Patrick Swayze (Derek Sutton), Ed Lauter (Murray Chadwick), Eric Nesterenko (Blane Youngblood), George Finn (Racki). Directed by Peter Markle and produced by Peter Bart and Patrick Wells. Screenplay by Markle.

Youngblood is not a bad movie, and indeed has moments of real conviction. But it is doomed by its plot, which is yet another example of what I like to call the Climb from Despair to Victory (CLIDVIC, rhymes with Kid Pic).

By now, we know the formula by heart: The hero tries to win, but is soundly defeated by the evil superman on the other side. He goes into exile, trains until he drops, gets advice from a wise old father figure, and then, in the last scene, makes his big comeback and publicly humiliates the enemy. And gets the girl, of course.

This is the plot of the *Rocky* movies and also countless teen-age wrestling, bicycle-racing, and karate movies. *Youngblood* takes it north of the border into the world of small-time Canadian professional hockey. At first, it's interesting just to look at the locations—the seedy ice rinks and shabby rooming houses. But eventually the dead weight of the CLIDVIC formula begins to weigh heavily on our minds, and we realize we are sentenced to yet another slog through the same old plot.

Youngblood stars Rob Lowe in the title role. He's a farm kid who dreams of playing professional hockey. His dad (played by the hockey great Eric Nesterenko) discourages him, but his brother offers to do his chores on the farm, and so Youngblood tries out for a minor league Canadian team.

The best scenes in *Youngblood* are these early ones, as the hero meets the hard-as-nails coach (Ed Lauter) and gets his first look at the evil, sadistic Racki (George Finn), a bearded ice demon who delights in playing dirty and trying to kill his opponents. Even here, the movie has serious lapses in tone.

There's an unnecessary scene where Youngblood is seduced by his hot-blooded landlady, and another one where he's trapped in a public corridor of the stadium wearing nothing but his jockstrap. These scenes are so obviously set up as cheap shots that they undermine the integrity of the scenes that are intended seriously.

By the middle of the film, we are deep into the CLIDVIC formula. Racki has almost killed one of Youngblood's teammates. Youngblood returns to the farm, where his father (working in the great tradition of Burgess Meredith in the *Rocky* movies and Pat Morita in *The Karate Kid*) puts him into training and teaches him age-old wisdom. Then, of course, it's time for Big Game, in which the kid will make his comeback and the evil Racki will eat ice.

Lowe apparently worked hard to prepare for *Youngblood*. He does a lot of his own skating, for which I give him credit. But I think the actors have been let down by the screenplay, which has them doing all the work. If Rob Lowe had to learn to play hockey, was it too much to ask Peter Markle, the writer-director, to write an original screenplay instead of the umpteenth ripoff of CLIDVIC?

Zabriskie Point ★ ★
R, 111 m., 1970

Mark Frechette (Mark), Daria Halprin (Daria), Paul Fix (Café Owner), Rod Taylor (Lee Allen). Directed by Michelangelo Antonioni and produced by Carlo Ponti. Screenplay by Fred Gardner, Sam Shepard, Tonino Guerra, Clare Peplo, and Antonioni.

One of the most unpleasant conventions of movie shorthand is that when adults are happy they act like children. The hero and heroine fall in love, and lickety-split the camera goes all mushy and they race through the park, fly kites, feed the swans in the cemetery, and (most important of all) giggle as the mustard drips out of their hot dogs. I've yet to see one of these sequences that didn't end with the lovers buying hot dogs from that bushy-haired Italian vendor whose specialty is peddling drippy hot dogs to lovers. Turns out the guy's name is Antonioni, and watch it, you're getting that stuff all over your Berkeley sweatshirt.

Michelangelo Antonioni is a fitfully brilliant director whose best, and basic, insight is that the fashionable cultivation of boredom can break down our ability to feel and love. In the 1950s, it seemed to him, people became so shy of spontaneity that they lost the knack. His characters were so alienated and spiritually exhausted they could hardly even get through breakfast together.

We loved it. *Eclipse* (1962) had us leaving the theater feeling deliciously betrayed and alone. *Blow Up* (1967) was even better. It was set in swinging London and left us feeling betrayed, alone, and with-it. In between, Antonioni gave us *The Red Desert* (1964), possibly the most passive and empty serious movie of the decade. That was Antonioni's thing, anyway, and he knew where he was going with it. But something (the enthusiasm young people had for *Blow Up* maybe) caused him to fall victim to that plague of personal directors, involvement. He had been getting his material out of his own instincts, but now he decided to do a "committed" movie about American society and the radical movement.

I suspect the project itself was exactly counter to his talents. He is not remotely an activist in his personal style, and I have a notion he recoils from people who raise their voices in public disagreement. But he decided to make *Zabriskie Point* anyway and cast his lot with the militants, who cast it right back at him. This is such a silly and stupid movie, all burdened down with ideological luggage it clearly doesn't understand, that our immediate reaction is pity. His earlier films have made us think of Antonioni as vulnerable; he shouldn't have exposed himself like this.

The director who made Monica Vitti seem so incredibly alone is incapable, in *Zabriskie Point*, of making his young characters seem even slightly together. Their voices are empty; they have no resonance as human beings. They don't play to each other, but to vague narcissistic conceptions of themselves. They wouldn't even meet were it not for a preposterous Hollywood coincidence. After the hero rejects radical rhetoric (just like that), he decides to try direct personal action and there's a clumsy sequence during which he maybe kills a policeman (the murder in this one is as iffy as the one in *Blow Up*). Then the hero steals an airplane, flies into the desert, sees the girl's 1952 Buick, buzzes it a couple of times, lands, and they go into the desert and make love. They make love, in fact, at Zabriskie Point, which is the lowest point in the United States. That is just as symbolic as Mount Whitney, which is the highest, but colder.

The love scenes are obnoxiously true to all the corrupt love scenes Antonioni copies them from. There is no feeling of liberation, or delight, or anything else other than a long, ridiculous time when lots of people roll around in the sand. Then, let's see, the hero paints the airplane in psychedelic colors, flies it back to Los Angeles, and is killed by cops. Period. The movie is not this uncomplicated, but it is certainly this simple. Antonioni attempts to flesh it out with thousands of yards of outdoor billboards, which are supposed to show America being corrupted by advertising and capitalism, I guess.

The fact is, Antonioni has no feeling for young people. In his European films, he allowed his characters to behave mostly as adults. But in *Zabriskie Point* we get kids who fall in love and act like kids (running up and down sand dunes, etc.) and the sight is even more depressing than adults doing it. He has tried to make a serious movie and hasn't even achieved a beach-party level of insight.

Zelig ★ ★ ★
PG, 79 m., 1983

Woody Allen (Leonard Zelig), Mia Farrow (Dr. Fletcher). Interviews: Susan Sontag, Irving Howe, Saul Bellow, Bricktop, Bruno Bettelheim, Professor John Morton Blum. Directed by Woody Allen. Produced by Robert Greenhut. Screenplay by Allen.

Woody Allen's *Zelig* represents an intriguing idea for a movie, and it has been made with great ingenuity and technical brilliance. That's almost enough. In fact, if *Zelig* were only about an hour long, it would be enough, but the unwritten code of feature films requires that it be longer, and finally there is just so much Zelig that we say enough, already.

The movie is a fake documentary, a film that claims to tell the story of Leonard Zelig, a once-famous American who suffered from a most curious disease: He was a human chameleon. He was so eager to please, so loath to give offense, so willing to blend right in, that perhaps some change took place at a cellular level, and Zelig began to take on the social, intellectual, and even physical characteristics of people that he spent time with. Put him with a psychiatrist, and he began to discuss complexes. Put him next to a Chinese man, and he began to look Oriental. This ability to fit right in propelled Zelig, we are told, to the heights of fame in the earlier decades of this century. He hobnobbed with presidents, was honored by ticker-tape parades, and his case was debated by learned societies. *Zelig* at first seems to be simply the documentary record of Zelig's case, but then another level begins to sneak in.

We are introduced (always through the documentary means of newsreel film, still photos, old radio broadcasts, and narration) to one Dr. Eudora Fletcher, who is a psychiatrist. She takes Zelig as a patient, and eventually they fall in love (we can see it happening, by implication, in documentary footage that apparently concerns other matters). The best thing about *Zelig*, apart from its technical accomplishment, is the way Woody Allen develops the human story of his hero; we get a portrait of a life and a poignant dilemma, peeking out from behind the documentary façade. The technical approach of *Zelig* has been experimented with before, most memorably in the fictional *March of Time* newsreel that introduced *Citizen Kane*. In that movie, we saw Charles Foster Kane apparently standing on balconies with Hitler and talking with Mussolini. In *Zelig*, the actors (Woody Allen, Mia Farrow, and dozens more) are so successfully integrated into old footage that we give up trying to tell the real from the fictional.

Zelig is a technical success, and it is also a success as a statement: Allen has a lot to say here about the nature of celebrity, science, and the American melting pot. He has also made an essay about film itself; the way that *Zelig*'s documentary material goes at right angles to its human story makes us think about the line between documentary and poetic "truth."

But the problem is, all of those achievements are easily accomplished at less length than the movie takes. The basic visual approach is clear from the first frames, and although it continues to impress us, it ceases after a while to amaze us. The emerging of Zelig's personality is intriguing, but the documentary framework allows it to emerge only so far, and no farther. We're left wanting more of Zelig and less of the movie's method; the movie is a technical masterpiece, but in artistic and comic terms, only pretty good.

Zorro, the Gay Blade ★ ★
PG, 96 m., 1981

George Hamilton (Don Diego/Bunny), Lauren Hutton (Charlotte), Brenda Vaccaro (Florinda), Ron Liebman (Esteban), Donovan Scott (Paco), James Booth (Velasquez). Directed by Peter Medak and produced by George Hamilton and E.O. Erickson. Screenplay by Hal Dresner.

It is hard to reconstruct these fragments from the memories of childhood but as nearly as I can remember, the Zorro craze came after the Davy Crockett craze and before Elvis. Kids made Z-marks everywhere—on walls, fences, blackboards, and with ballpoints on the shirts of the kids sitting in front of them—and my personal notion is that Datsun sells half of their Z-cars to guys harboring sublimated Zorro fantasies.

Here's the curious thing. I remember a lot about Zorro. I even remember that he was once played by Clayton Moore, who got to keep wearing his Lone Ranger mask. But I cannot remember if the Zorro movies were ever supposed to be funny. I assume that the Zorros played by Douglas Fairbanks, Tyrone Power, and John Carroll were more or less serious, within the broad outlines of the adventure genre. But what about all the Zorro movies and TV shows that Guy Williams made for Disney? Were we laughing at him, or with him?

I ask because I am just as confused after seeing *Zorro, the Gay Blade*, which stars George Hamilton in a dual role as Don Diego Vega and his twin brother, Bunny. (The brother was originally a Vega, too, but after enlisting in the British Navy he changed his name to Bunny Wigglesworth.) This movie is, of course, intended as a comedy, and it has some funny moments. But it's just not successful, and I think the reason is that Hamilton never for a second plays Zorro as if he were really playing Zorro. We could laugh at the previous movie Zorros because they were so serious about their ridiculous codes and vows and pledges of loyalty and chivalric passions. They were funny as long as they played it straight. But when a movie sets out a create a funny Zorro, that's bringing coals to Newcastle. By playing every scene for laughs, Hamilton has nothing to play against.

Zorro, the Gay Blade was no doubt inspired by the enormous success of Hamilton's spoof of a durable Hollywood character, when he played Dracula in *Love at First Bite* (1979). Hamilton demonstrated in that movie, and demonstrates again in this one, that he is a gifted comic actor. He can have fun with his improbably handsome appearance, he can poke fun at his character's vanity, and he can look convincing enough as Zorro (or Dracula) to remind us of the quintessential Hollywood leading men whose footsteps he is stalking.

But . . . should Zorro be funny because of his puffed-up self-importance, or because his role in life is inescapably ridiculous any way you look at it? Should he be funny because of what he is (my theory), or what he does (this movie's theory)? A funnier comedy might have been made out of a more genuinely satirical examination of the Zorro character. Instead, this one provides Zorro with a gay brother who's a screamingly limp-wristed stereotype, and then goes for jokes that are disappointingly predictable. It also gives him a leading lady (Lauren Hutton) who has all she can do to play her role at all, much less play it satirically. And it never provides a comprehensive story to hold the jokes together. Too bad. I think I remember now: We laughed more at the old Zorros, because they didn't know they were funny.

Afterword

Judging the Classics

Are these the sixteen greatest films of all time, or do 122 of the world's film critics only think they are?

1. *Citizen Kane* (Orson Welles, U.S.)
2. *The Rules of the Game* (Jean Renoir, France)
3. (tie) *The Seven Samurai* (Akira Kurosawa, Japan)
   Singin' in the Rain (Stanley Donen and Gene Kelly, U.S.)
5. *8½* (Federico Fellini, Italy)
6. *Battleship Potemkin* (Sergei Eisenstein, USSR)
7. (tie) *L'Avventura* (Michelangelo Antonioni, Italy)
   The Magnificent Ambersons (Orson Welles, U.S.)
9. (tie) *Vertigo* (Alfred Hitchcock, U.S.)
   The General (Buster Keaton, U.S.)
   The Searchers (John Ford, U.S.)
12. (tie) *2001: A Space Odyssey* (Stanley Kubrick, Great Britain)
   Andrei Roublev (Andrei Tarkovsky, USSR)
14. (tie) *Greed* (Erich von Stroheim, U.S.)
   Jules and Jim (Francois Truffaut, France)
   The Third Man (Carol Reed, Great Britain)

Those sixteen films were the 1982 winners of the fourth International Critics' Poll, conducted every ten years by *Sight & Sound*, the authoritative film quarterly published by the British Film Institute. The magazine's instructions to critics voting from all over the world were simple: "Personal choices of the films which have seemed most significant or relevant to you, which you have enjoyed or admired most. Ten titles only, please, in alphabetical order or in order of preference, of films made anywhere, at any time."

The *Sight & Sound* poll is to movies what the wire service polls are to college sports and the Dow Jones average is to the stock market. It represents an imperfect, subjective, unscientific, and highly influential sampling of the critical stock of the great films and filmmakers of the world. And when the 1982 results were announced, they created shock waves, at least in that little corner of the world where such things matter.

The big news in the 1982 poll was the surprising critical devaluation of the work of Ingmar Bergman, the great Swedish filmmaker whose name seems almost synonymous with cinematic art. In the 1972 poll, Bergman and Orson Welles were the only directors to place two films on the list.[1] This year, Welles's *Citizen Kane* and *Magnificent Ambersons* remain, but Bergman is missing; his *Persona* (tied for fifth in 1972) and *Wild Strawberries* (tied for tenth) dropped off the list altogether, and his more recent contenders, especially *Cries and Whispers* and *Autumn Sonata*, failed to place.

Maybe that was just a statistical aberration? Perhaps Bergman's support was so widely distributed among his more than forty films that no single Bergman movie had the votes to make the list? Not so. In a separate compilation, *Sight & Sound* totaled all of the times any film by a director was voted for. In 1972, Bergman placed a strong third on that list; his thirty-seven votes were close behind Welles's forty-six and Jean Renoir's forty-one. By 1982, Bergman's total vote didn't even qualify him for the top ten![2]

Why did Bergman drop so suddenly from the pantheon? My guess is that the jury changed. In 1972, a majority of the voters would still have belonged to what science-fiction fans call the "sercon" party; they would have been serious, constructive critics looking for meaning, significance, and Art. By 1982, the film generation of the 1960s would have joined in the balloting, probably with a preference for "movies" over "cinema." Perhaps Bergman seemed too heavily laden with symbolism and angst for them, and they wanted to make room for a Western or a musical. Bergman is gone, but not forgotten; look for him on the 1992 list.

Other conclusions from the 1982 balloting:

—Orson Welles continues to stand astride the world of film as an undisputed colossus—at least, as far as the film critics are concerned. Despite the fact that his most important work was done more than forty years ago (*Kane* and *Ambersons* are his first two films), he has strengthened his position since 1972; both times, Welles and *Kane* placed ahead of Renoir and *Rules*, but in 1982, it was a landslide.

Citizen Kane is, of course, widely described as the greatest film ever made— so frequently, and by so many different people, that it has moved into the same quasi-official stratosphere as *King Lear* or Beethoven's Fifth Symphony. What is remarkable is that in 1952, when *Sight & Sound* first conducted its poll, *Citizen Kane* didn't even make the list![3] In 1952, *Citizen Kane* was a masterpiece much talked about but rarely seen, after its original 1941 release was botched. (Because the Hollywood establishment feared to offend publishing

---

[1]The top ten, 1972: *Citizen Kane, Rules of the Game, Battleship Potemkin, 8½, L'Avventura* tied with Dreyer's *The Passion of Joan of Arc, The General* tied with *The Magnificent Ambersons, Ugetsu Monogatari* tied with *Wild Strawberries*.

[2]Voting by directors, 1982: Orson Welles, 71; Jean Renoir, 51; Charles Chaplin, 37; John Ford, 34; Luis Bunuel and Akira Kurosawa, both 33; Federico Fellini and Alfred Hitchcock, both 32; Jean-Luc Godard and Buster Keaton, both 30.

[3]The top four films in 1952, according to both the magazine poll and a vote of filmmakers at the Brussels World Fair, were De Sica's *Bicycle Thief,* Chaplin's *City Lights* and *Gold Rush,* and Eisenstein's *Battleship Potemkin*.

tycoon William Randolph Hearst, whose life inspired Kane's, the major theater chains wouldn't touch the film, and it got scattered release; not until 1957, when a new print was widely distributed, did the film win really wide audiences.)

Why is the film so widely admired? "Citizen Kane is perhaps the one American talking picture that seems as fresh now as the day it opened. It may even seem fresher," Pauline Kael wrote in the opening words of her landmark *The Citizen Kane Book*. If you do not believe her, see it for yourself. The film is endlessly inventive as it circles closer and closer to the mystery of a man's life, a mystery that seems to be summed up by his dying word, "Rosebud."[4] One reason the film always seems fresh is that we never know what's coming next; the film has such an unpredictable structure, leaping about in Kane's life and from flashback to flashback, that it is all but impossible to remember what will follow. I have seen *Citizen Kane* at least thirty times, and yet when I walk in on the middle of a screening, or start my tape at random, I am unable to remember for sure what will come next.

—*The Seven Samurai* and *Singin' in the Rain*, were not even also-rans in 1972; this time, they tied for third. *Seven Samurai*, a saga about medieval warlords that introduced Toshiro Mifune to world movie audiences and inspired the Hollywood remake *The Magnificent Seven*, became the only film on the list from Japan, one of the great centers of cinema; last time, Japan was represented by Mizoguchi's *Ugetsu Monogatari*, the story of a poor man's infatuation with a dreamlike geisha. *Singin' in the Rain* is routinely called the best of the Hollywood musicals, and its high place is a tribute to the whole genre.

—Two veteran Hollywood filmmakers who died in the decade between the polls made it into the top ten. Alfred Hitchcock's *Vertigo* and John Ford's *The Searchers*, were runners-up in 1972, possibly because both directors had been so prolific and made so many great films that no single title could gather a following. By 1982, the consensus was in.

Many movie buffs would name *Rear Window*, *Psycho*, or *Notorious* as Hitchcock's best picture, but *Vertigo*, starring James Stewart and Kim Novak in the story of a man obsessed with a woman he thinks is dead, has been named by Hitchcock's biographers as perhaps his most personal work. Because the copyrights to *Vertigo* and four other Hitchcock titles (*Rope*, *The Man Who Knew Too Much*, *Rear Window*, and *The Trouble with Harry*) were owned by Hitchcock's estate, they had not been publicly screened for years when the 1982 poll was held. In 1984, however, they were bought from the estate by Universal, and are all now available in video.

The Searchers is not everybody's favorite film by the man who once said "My name is Ford. I make Westerns." Some viewers would name *Stagecoach*, *My Darling Clementine*, or *Three Godfathers*. Many critics have questions about the

---

[4]But who heard him say "rosebud"? Although Kane's butler claims late in the film that he heard it, the death chamber seems empty except for the lonely tycoon. A nurse enters after he drops the paperweight.

plot of *The Searchers*, which has John Wayne so appalled when his niece is kidnapped by Indians that he spends five years in the wilderness on a relentless, obsessive search for her. They see the film as a racist portrait of Indians and a male chauvinist story, in which the real importance of the girl (played by Natalie Wood) is as a pawn for the men in the film. Still, *The Searchers* has inspired the stories of many other films, notably Martin Scorsese's *Taxi Driver* and Paul Schrader's *Hardcore*.

—The battle of the two greatest silent clowns continues in the 1982 results. Buster Keaton's *The General*, an amazingly ambitious epic in which he played the engineer of a lengendary Civil War train, slipped from eighth to ninth. Chaplin failed to place any titles on the list, but in the closely bunched vote by directors, he placed somewhat higher than Keaton—third, with thirty-seven votes, to ninth, with thirty. Perhaps the totals reflect the consensus that *The General* is Keaton's greatest film, and an inability to choose among such Chaplin masterpieces as *The Gold Rush*, *City Lights*, and *Modern Times*. Since most silent films are out of copyright, they can be purchased fairly cheaply in video, often under $20.

Is the *Sight & Sound* poll all that important? It's like the football coaches' poll: Everybody cares when it comes out, nobody can remember it by next year. The real importance is that if you set out to see every film on it, you will see sixteen great films, and each one will suggest avenues for further investigation, a few of which I cheerfully outline below, only occasionally venturing from the sublime to the ridiculous:

AFTER SEEING	THEN VIEW	BECAUSE
Citizen Kane	*Providence*	Similar opening shots, narrative ideas
Rules of the Game	*The Grand Illusion*	After and before
The Seven Samurai	*The Magnificent Seven*	The remake
Singin' in the Rain	*An American in Paris*	Gene Kelly
8½	*Day for Night*	Lives of a director
Battleship Potemkin	*Das Boot*	Under pressure
L'Avventura	*Blow Up*	Missing persons
The Magnificent Ambersons	*Breaking Away*	Family life in Indiana
Vertigo	*Body Double*	De Palma's homage
The General	*Modern Times*	Man over machines
The Searchers	*Taxi Driver*	Same underlying story
2001	*My Dinner with André*	"If we could really understand the cigar store next door—wouldn't that be as amazing as climbing Everest?"
Andrei Roublev	*The Seventh Seal*	Medieval legends
Greed	*Sunset Boulevard*	von Stroheim

| *Jules and Jim* | *Two English Girls* | Same author, same director, two approaches |
| *The Third Man* | *Night and the City* | Postwar locations, similar feel |

I'm not sure this chart has the slightest significance, but drawing it up was amusing, and it duplicated one of the pleasures that the VCR has brought into my life—the random walk through movie history, with one film leading to another, one vision suggesting another. It is probably true that some of the films on the list are not available in most video stores; this might be the occasion for a call to Home Film Festival (1-800-258-3456), which rents hard-to-find classics by mail. Or it might be an occasion for a random walk in another direction altogether. Have fun.

My Ten Great Films, and Why

What are my own nominations for the ten best films of all time? Making such a list is, of course, a form of gamesmanship, and the list is sure to change from day to day. On the day in 1982 when I drew up my list for *Sight & Sound,* these were the titles I decided upon, listed alphabetically:

Aguirre, the Wrath of God. Werner Herzog believes we are starving for images in these modern times, and that without them, we will die. His *Aguirre,* one of the great, mad, passionate, foolhardy masterpieces—as reckless and as brilliant as *Greed* or *Apocalypse Now*—stars Klaus Kinski in the story of a member of Pizarro's expedition to find the lost El Dorado. After the main body turns back, Aguirre presses on with a small band of followers, all of them weighted down by the armor which is suicidal in the rain forest. Among the film's great images, are the first, of a string of desperate men winding their way down an unimaginably long mountain path, and one of the last, of Aguirre on a raft overrun by chattering monkeys. Herzog believes in the voodoo of locations, and shot this film deep in the Amazon jungle. There is a legend that Kinski threatened to walk off the film, and Herzog held a gun to him and said he would shoot him if he left. It is probably only an apocraphal story, but neither Herzog nor Kinski denies it.

Bonnie and Clyde. Arthur Penn's film still seems to have the same freshness, after eighteen years, that Kael talks about with *Kane.* It works as comedy, as tragedy, as entertainment, as a meditation on the place of guns and violence in American society. And it was perfectly cast; Warren Beatty and Faye Dunaway have become icons as Clyde and Bonnie, but remember, too, Michael J. Pollard as C.W. Moss, Gene Hackman as Buck Barrow (his first major role), Estelle Parsons as Buck's wife Blanche, Gene Wilder as the hapless undertaker taken along for the ride, and Dub Taylor as C.W.'s greedy father. Scene after scene plays with perfect, almost dreamlike, emotional control: Clyde and the tenant farmer shooting out windows, the cloud passing in front of the sun and shadowing Bonnie and Clyde in the wheat field, Bonnie's farewell to her mother, C.W. parking the getaway car, Blanche screaming and running across the lawn with a spatula in her hand, Buck's dying delirium, and of course the final scene, which has been copied in so many other movies it has become a cliché, except here, where it retains all of its power.

Casablanca. I saw it again recently, at the University of Colorado, where I go every year to take a week and study a film shot-by-shot with a stop-action film analyzer. I was struck once again by what a perfect love story there is here, requiring the lovers to be true to their ideas of each other by choosing a greater good than love. The supporting characters (Claude Rains, Sidney Greenstreet, Peter Lorre, and, always, Dooley Wilson) transform what was, after all, only a set on the back lot at the Burbank Studios and turn it into a teeming, conspiring, colorful Casablanca.

The key to the movie's drama is Bogart's gradual transition, from a man who "sticks his neck out for no one" to a man who embraces once again the ideals of his youth. In remembering *Casablanca,* we think of it as a love story between Bogart and Bergman. (The pale Paul Henreid, as the freedom fighter Victor Laslo, is permitted a chaste peck on Bergman's cheek, and scarcely has the presence in the film to qualify as the third point of a love triangle.) But see the film again and you may be surprised at how bitter Bogart is when he sees Bergman again. His cruelty to her in the late-night drunk scene in Rick's Place is painful—because we see how much it hurts both of them. Only gradually does Bogart come around to the right feelings, and the right decisions. *Casablanca* is not the story of lost love, but of rediscovered idealism.

Citizen Kane. Of course. But for the little touches as well as for the big ones. For Kane's shadow-play with his hands the first time he meets Susan Alexander. For Kane applauding alone, defiantly, maniacally, after Susan's opera debut. For the remarkable visual illusion in Thatcher's office, when Kane, brought in to sign away his empire, is first seen in the foreground in front of what look like normal windows—and then, as Kane walks into the background of the shot, they are revealed as giant cathedral-scale windows, and Kane is diminished into a miniature. And for Mr. Bernstein's sad and wonderful line, "One day, back in 1896, I was crossing over to Jersey on a ferry, and as we pulled out, there was another ferry pulling in, and on it there was a girl waiting to get off. A white dress she had on. She was carrying a white parasol. I only saw her for one second. She didn't see me at all, but I'll bet a month hasn't gone by since, that I haven't thought of that girl." The power of that line is such that, in the years since I first heard it, I'll bet a month hasn't gone by that I haven't thought of it.

La Dolce Vita. Federico Fellini's 1959 film is a page-marker in my own life. It tells the story of a gossip columnist named Marcello, who roams the night world of Rome's Via Veneto, pursuing dreams of fame and sex and money, promising himself and his friend Steiner that someday he will write a great novel. Marcello seems almost afraid to stop moving, for fear that the silence of the emptiness of his life will overwhelm him. Fellini's great images come in profusion: The bearded dancer in the nightclub, lit from beneath as if from hell; the bas reliefs on the walls of the villa, each ancient Roman face the exact duplicate of a guest at the party; the Christ statue carried by helicopter over

Rome; the cat and the fountain at dawn; the children running here and there in the rain, taunting the sick and dying with their sudden sightings of the Virgin Mary. Marcello is thirty in the film. When I first saw it, I was twenty, and it represented a great and wonderful world I wanted to enter. When I was thirty and saw it again, it represented the trap I was in. I saw it again at forty, and saw it as what I had survived and perhaps even learned from. This is, I believe, Fellini's best film, too often overlooked on the short lists of unquestionably great films.

Notorious. This is my favorite Hitchcock film, and the best love story he ever told. In some ways, its triangle resembles *Casablanca*'s; Cary Grant, like Humphrey Bogart, loves Ingrid Bergman but is cruel to her because he feels she has been unfaithful to him—and all the time Bergman has chosen the greater good. Although Claude Rains, the other man who loves Bergman, plays a Nazi in this film, he is in many ways more sympathetic than the cool Paul Henreid in *Casablanca*. He does, after all, really love her—and he will be denied her love, along with so many other things in his life, because of his monstrous mother and his fatal politics. The film is filled with great shots: The introduction of Cary Grant, seen from behind but nevertheless the focus of attention; an overview of an entrance hall, with the camera moving in one unbroken take to a close-up of a key in a hand; the inexorable procession down the stairs and past the Nazis waiting at the bottom. (For fun, and to reveal one of Hitchcock's secrets, watch for the one scene where Cary Grant completely ascends the staircase in Rains's home, and count the number of steps he takes. Then, in the scene where Grant, Bergman, Rains, and Madame Constantine descend the stairs, count how many steps they descend. Hitchcock prolongs the suspense by editing to add extra steps.)

Persona. Ingmar Bergman's 1967 film has been described as almost impossible to understand, but perhaps it can be approached, instead, as a very simple story. An actress, horrified by the suffering in the world, simply stops speaking one day. She is sent by her therapist to spend some time in the country with a nurse. During their months together, a strange personalities transference takes place, until the impressionable young nurse forgets exactly who she is—and then remembers again, when the spell is broken. The film itself "breaks" in the middle, as if the pain from the shard of glass has broken the power of fiction to contain it. The scene of the merging faces is famous (Liv Ullmann and Bibi Andersson told me they had no idea Bergman was going to do it), but even more mysterious is the dream sequence in which both women seem to share the actress's husband. The long monologue about the encounter with the boys on the beach has a strange after-effect; although it is only described, never seen, we visualize it so strongly that, months later, we may swear it was in the film.

Taxi Driver. I think Martin Scorsese's work is the best American film made since I've been reviewing movies, and Robert De Niro's performance as Travis

Bickle, the lonely, violent taxi driver, has entered into folklore ("You talking to *me*?"). The film is visually fascinating, especially the repeated motif of over-head shots (a hack license, junk food, guns on a bed, push-ups, the final killing scene) that Scorsese says has a sacramental significance for him. American his-tory has been rewritten by the loners like Travis who have come out of the woodwork: Oswald, Ruby, Ray, Sirhan, and, a colossal irony, John Hinckley, who shot at President Reagan because of his obsession with Jodie Foster in this film. Some said the film inspired his actions. I would say it predicted them, because the real-life Hinckley bore such an unsettlingly similarity to Bickle. If any film can explain to us how and why our society has created creatures like Travis Bickle, and can help us to enter their savagely narrow, driven visions, *Taxi Driver* can; it is a film to place beside the novel *Crime and Punishment* for its knowledge of a deviant personality.

The Third Man. I would have thought this was a great film anyway, but seeing it for the first time in a little cinema on the Left Bank, on a rainy Paris day, on my first trip to Europe, made it, on that day, a perfect film, and ever since it has occupied a special place in my memory. Once again, a story of doomed love; Joseph Cotten, as Holly Martin, the author of trash Westerns, journeys to postwar Vienna to find his best friend, Orson Welles as Harry Lime ("lie-me"). He discovers that Lime is dead, but meets his girl (Alida Valli), and falls in love with her, and finds that she still loves Lime—no matter that his black market penicillin killed innocent children. It's as if Bergman stayed with Rains in *Notorious,* or moved in with Greenstreet in *Casablanca.* Carol Reed's images are remarkable: The balloon man's shadow on the wall, Orson Welles's first entrance (which is the greatest entrance in the history of the movies), Welles approaching almost sideways across the amusement park, the chase in the sewers, and, of course, the great final shot and the perfect emotional para-bola described as Cotten throws away his cigarette. The line about the cuckoo clocks is justly famous; I also like "Is that what you say when someone dies? How inconvenient?"

2001. One of the greatest stores of powerful, mysterious images in all of film history. What the film means, what it says, no longer matters to me so much (although like all critics I have a detailed explanation, if you have an evening to spare sometime). What is important here is the sense of wonder. The bone transforms itself into a spaceship, the Strauss waltzes are incongruously appro-priate for the sexually charged moment when the ship penetrates the space sta-tion, and the appearances of the monolith are so disturbing that you realize the utter strangeness of man's right angles and straight lines amid the careless jum-ble of nature.

Eliot said he would show us fear in a handful of dust, and Stanley Kubrick shows us infinity in a bedroom, a glass of red wine, and a few green peas. The ending sequence of his film is so great because it does not dare to imagine what other intelligences would look or think like; he shows us a man placed by them, whatever they are, in a room of man's own tradition—and that is so much more frightening than any fantastical alternative. The sequel, *2010*, is a superior space action picture, and I praised it for that. But in explaining the mysteries of *2001*, it diminishes them. e e cummings, who said he'd rather learn from one bird how to sing than teach ten thousand stars how not to dance, wrote in those words the definitive review of both pictures.

In fact, he wrote in those words the definitive review of a lot of pictures.

The Basic Video Library

If I were choosing a basic library of movies on videocassette I would begin with *Citizen Kane*, the most inexhaustible film yet made in America, and go on from there. And that is exactly what I've done here, starting with a dozen categories of film and limiting myself to three choices in each category.

This is not a list of the greatest films of all time (for that list, which contains a few of the same titles, see page 615). It is weighted toward American films, because most subtitled films are still so dauntingly hard to read on the small screen. And it is weighted, also, toward more recent films, since those are the easiest to find in video stores.

The question I've asked myself in selecting every one of my ideal titles is, does the film really stand up to repeated viewing? Is it still fresh and alive the ninth time around? Here are some films that passed those tests:

1. Family and children's films

The Wizard of Oz remains agelessly wonderful. Some sort of magical enchantment must have fallen over MGM when they produced this film, which is made up of so many parts that are all exactly right. If small children could only begin their film experiences with this film, instead of first having their imaginations deadened by countless hours of low-grade Saturday morning animated TV violence, that would be a nice little gift for their spirits. Next on my list would be *E. T.*, which will eventually be released on video, and which is probably the most completely satisfying fantasy since *The Wizard of Oz*. Every family movie library needs at least one film about horses, either *National Velvet* or *The Black Stallion*. And an animated feature. Probably *Pinocchio*.

2. Comedy

Saving Chaplin and Keaton for the silent category, I'd lead this section of the shelf with the single funniest move I've seen since I've been a film critic. That would be Mel Brooks's *The Producers*, with its sublimely demented relationship between Zero Mostel as a crooked Broadway producer who fleeces little old ladies, and Gene Wilder as a timid accountant who is taught that if you've got it, flaunt it. Next, something by the Marx Brothers, probably *Room Service* or *A Night at the Opera*. And then one of those omnibus tapes of W.C. Fields's short subjects, or maybe Fields in *The Bank Dick*. And then Robert Altman's *M*A*S*H*, the funniest movie released since *The Producers*, even though it is much more than "just" a comedy.

3. Crime or film noir

My favorite here is *The Third Man*, which views its bleak vision of human nature through the eyes of a man who stubbornly remains a romantic until his dream is finally crushed in the last, unforgettable, shot. Orson Welles has the most unforgettable entrance in movie history, and one of the best lines of dialogue—the one about the cuckoo clocks. Next in this category, Hitchcock's *Notorious*, for the exquisitely painful way in which the romance between Cary Grant and Ingrid Bergman is played against Grant's low opinion of Bergman, Claude Rains's doomed love for her, and Bergman's own despair. The third film would be the greatest of all crime epics, Francis Coppola's *The Godfather*, with its dark passions and operatic sense of fate. For a modern tribute to the classic noir film, *Farewell, My Lovely* or *Trouble in Mind*.

4. Documentaries

Here I am passing over an obvious choice, the noble nine-hour French film *Shoah*, because its running time makes it so prohibitively expensive that the best bet is obviously to tape it off the air from PBS. Instead, I'd select three personal favorites: Michael Wadleigh's *Woodstock*, which can now be seen, fifteen years later, to capture the unique time of the late 1960s as no other film has; Errol Morris's *Gates of Heaven*, a very odd, challenging, eccentric movie about some people involved in the success and failure of two pet cemeteries; and George Nirenberg's *Say Amen, Somebody*, a documentary about the pioneers of black gospel music that is so joyous that it's just about impossible not to feel better after you've seen it.

5. Drama

Martin Scorsese's *Taxi Driver* is the best American film made since I've been a movie critic. Robert De Niro's title performance stands as one of the most agonizingly painful examinations of character ever put on screen; his Travis Bickle is a composite of all the twisted, unhappy assassins who have stepped out of the shadows since Lee Harvey Oswald so cruelly changed our history in Dallas in 1963. Next on my list, Francis Coppola's *Apocalypse Now*, which created its picture of the war in Vietnam out of contrasting images: gunboats pulling water-skiers, Playboy bunnies fired on by enemy rockets, helicoptors attacking to the music of Wagner. My third drama would be Arthur Penn's *Bonnie and Clyde*, starring Warren Beatty and Faye Dunaway in a perfectly realized story of how two fairly incompetent bank robbers were able to inflame the fancies of the media, until their fame led to their deaths.

6. Foreign films

Here we are at sea when we enter the average video store. Many dealers carry few foreign films, and they present an unhappy choice between subtitles we can't read, and dubbing we can't bear to listen to. We need titles at least as big, for example, as the typefaces used to identify news anchors. In the meantime, my choices would be films that are great to look at even if you can't read the titles. For example, something by Fellini, probably *La Dolce Vita* or *Amarcord*. Something by Kurosawa, whose great *Ikiru* contains too many subtitles, but whose *Seven Samurai* does not. And perhaps one of Bergman's most visual films, such as *The Seventh Seal*.

7. Musicals
Singin' in the Rain, of course. Everybody's favorite musical, and no wonder, since it contains so much happiness and such great music within a plot about the birth of the talkies. Then I'd choose one of the great Astaire-Rogers collaborations, probably *Top Hat* or *Swing Time*. And then the Beatles in *A Hard Day's Night*.

8. Romance
Romance, for me, means not merely a love story, but a love story told against the backdrop of exciting events, in the midst of which, as Bogie once said, "the problems of a couple of little people like you and me don't amount to a hill of beans." Ah, but they do, and precisely because love affirms itself in the face of history, those movies are all the more romantic. So, *Casablanca* first on the list, because of its perfect marriage of time and place and character and that song that Dooley Wilson doesn't think he quite remembers. And then Bogart again, this time with Hepburn in *The African Queen*, one of the greatest of all romantic adventures. And also on the list, *Gone With The Wind*, about which I suspect no explanation is necessary.

9. Social issues
This category may seem unexpected, but the movies have been an effective tool for political content ever since the first blockbuster, *Birth of a Nation*. *The Grapes of Wrath* might be an obvious choice, and so would movies like *Gandhi* or *Z*. But I've chosen three titles you might not immediately think about: Gregory Nava and Anna Thomas's *El Norte*, about the long trek of a Guatemalan brother and sister up through Mexico to the promised land of Los Angeles; Robert Altman's *Nashville*, which was released in the bicentennial year of 1976 and painted a huge canvas of beliefs and behaviors that were in the air at that time; and Lynne Lipton's heartbreaking *Testament*, starring Jane Alexander as a California suburban mother struggling to hold her family together in the aftermath of nuclear war.

10. Special effects
This category could just as well be labeled "science fiction." It reflects the explosion in elaborate, spellbinding visual effects that was set in motion by Stanley Kubrick's *2001* and has continued most notably in the works of Steven

Spielberg and George Lucas. That just about tips my hand; my selections would be *2001: A Space Odyssey, Raiders of the Lost Ark,* and your choice of the *Star Wars* movies. The problem here, of course, is that the limitations of the television screen are especially frustrating when you're dealing with the vast visions contained in these movies. The electronics companies keep promising high-quality giant-screen TV. These movies need it.

11. Silent films

One of the best things about silent films, from the collector's point of view, is that they're often out of copyright, and therefore cheap to purchase. The bad news is that literally anyone can start selling inferior copies of the silent classics, and so it's best to spend a little more for a cassette with a respectable pedigree. My choices here would be a Buster Keaton (*The General,* with its endlessly inventive locomotive chase), a Charlie Chaplin (your choice; mine would be *Modern Times*), a D.W. Griffith (*Birth of a Nation* for its technical excellence but not for its reactionary social vision), and Eisenstein's *Battleship Potemkin,* widely considered the greatest of all silent dramas.

12. Westerns

Here is a category where everyone has strong personal favorites, and so I feel safe in passing over such obvious choices as *Stagecoach* and *High Noon* to list my own favorites: John Ford's *The Searchers,* with John Wayne in an obsessive search for a niece kidnapped by Indians; Ford's *My Darling Clementine,* for its rich retelling of the Wyatt Earp legend and for Henry Fonda's classic haircut scene; and Sam Peckinpah's *The Wild Bunch,* which mourned the passing of cowboys and gunfighters and, in retrospect, seems to have marked the end of the Western as a major genre.

And then, of course, to end where we began, Orson Welles's *Citizen Kane.* One of the mysteries of this film is in its seemingly mercurial story structure. The film's intricate structure of flashbacks and memories makes its examination of a man's life seem new every time I see it.

Every great film, for that matter, should seem new every time you see it. I think most of the films on my list will pass that test.

Thirteen for Halloween

Here are thirteen movies you might want to rent for Halloween.

The main requirement for a Halloween movie is that it scares us. But fright is an emotion that can be so easily evoked in the movies that most of the time it's not even worthy of the name. In making up this list of thirteen recommended Halloween movies, then, I decided simple fright wasn't enough.

Most of these movies are scary, but they are more than that: They are amazing. They take us beyond the plane of natural events and into a world of conjecture and surprise, imagination and dread—a world where everything we believe is open to question. Along with the scary films, I've also included a few spoofs and comedies, which are sometimes a little scary, too.

All of these films are available for rental on videocassette.

1. *Altered States* (R)

Here is one of the weirdest movies ever made, a pyrotechnic excursion back to the dawn of time and the birth of life, told as a scientific thriller, crossed with a love story, and with a farce thrown in. The movie stars William Hurt, an actor who likes to take chances and has never taken bigger ones than in *Altered States*, where at one point he turns into an ape and is chased by the campus security guards. It costars Blair Brown, a wife so devoted that she wades knee-high into a pool of glowing protoplasm and tries to drag her husband out alive—even after he's filed for divorce.

Altered States was directed by Ken Russell, whose movies often are exercises in bizarre excess, but who outdoes himself this time. His starting point is the research by Dr. John Lilly, the scientist who isolates his subjects in total immersion tanks—absolutely lightproof boxes filled with room-temperature salt water—so that they float in the darkness and lose all track of space and time. In the movie, Hurt combines the immersion tank with the sacred mushrooms of an Indian tribe and embarks on a voyage into the heart of the universe.

2. *Blood Simple* (R)

This movie begins with a murder, and plays with that murder as a dog might worry a bone. By the end of the film, the first death has generated several others, but that's nothing compared to what's being experienced by the characters who are left alive. The movie keys off of some of our basic nightmares: (1) We keep washing our hands, but there's still blood on them; (2) we know we committed a murder, but we can't remember why; (3) we fear we've overlooked a tiny detail that will condemn us.

Blood Simple begins with a scummy bar owner paying a sleazy private eye to murder his wife. This murder, if it had been carried out on schedule, would have been a relatively straightforward crime. But the private eye figures out a way to make more money on the deal (and more than this I cannot tell, because so much of *Blood Simple* depends on the surprises in the plot).

The movie's high point is an exercise in the virtuosity of suspense. The filmmakers, Ethan and Joel Coen, begin with an empty room. They isolate some of the characters there, they put a killer outside and then they develop this situation until an incredible moment when one of the bad guys reaches around the corner of a windowsill and one of the most intensely painful passages in movie history begins.

3. *The Bride of Frankenstein* (PG)

This is one of the most imitated classics in the whole history of supernatural films. Watch it as a triple feature with Mel Brooks's *Young Frankenstein* and Wes Craven's *Swamp Thing*, and you'll see different versions of many of the same scenes.

The Bride of Frankenstein is the best of all the Frankenstein movies because the director, James Whale, correctly saw that the character who suffers the most in the movie is the monster himself. What harm does he do, compared with the pain he experiences? And did he ask to be born into this world, anyway? The poignance of the quiet little scene with the child is a counterpoint to all the images we've ever had about Frankenstein's dread creation.

The key scene is the moment when the scientist elevates the body of the bride (Elsa Lancaster) up on a platform to the sky and the lightning courses through her veins. This scene has been copied countless times, but it still retains its elemental force in *Bride*, because the sound, the look of the laboratory, the intensity of the experiment and the ethereal quality of the resurrected woman all come together in a way that is eerily convincing.

4. *Cat People* (R)

This story has its origins in the dim mists of prehistory, when leopards ruled the Earth. The first few human beings were terrified of their feline masters and made an accommodation with them, sacrificing their women to the leopards. But the leopards did not eat the sacrifices, they mated with them—and the result was a race of cat people, who look like ordinary humans except for a certain feline look in the eye, a spring in the step, and a disconcerting tendency to turn into black leopards during sexual intercourse.

As Paul Schrader's movie opens, only two cat people are left alive, a brother and a sister (Nastassja Kinski and Malcolm McDowell). Kinski lives in New Orleans, where she engages the obsessive attention of a zookeeper (John Heard), who thinks he recognizes in her the same thing that fascinates him about the big cats in their cages. Kinski faces a difficult choice: She loves the zookeeper, but, for her, to love someone is to kill them. Then there also is the strange relationship she has with her brother. Kinski is something in this movie. Faced with countless opportunities to overact, she simply relaxes and plays a leopard.

Cat People cuts back and forth between the seamy reality of modern New Orleans and the wind-swept red deserts of prehistory, when leopards ruled their domain. It does what many good horror films do (including *The Exorcist* and *The Dead Zone*): It combines everyday realism in the little things with giant visionary dreads in the big things. To the degree that the details are realistic, the big picture is simply that much more frightening.

5. *Dawn of the Dead*   (R)

The best of George Romero's Ghoul Trilogy, this movie lacks the raw force of his original *Night of the Living Dead*, but makes up for it with its mocking vision of American suburbia. The story begins some weeks after the first film, which, you will recall, dealt with a plague that sent dead bodies lurching and moaning through the night, their flesh hanging in shreds as they desperately sought living victims to devour.

In *Dawn of the Dead*, a patrol party finds a group of the ghouls in a suburban shopping center, where they provide a grim contrast to the display of middle-class prosperity. Stumbling and snuffling, they try to make their way up the down escalator, while Muzak plays in the background, and the automated mall hums with its air conditioning and fluorescent lighting.

6. *The Dead Zone*   (R)

This is the best movie ever made from a Stephen King story—and, for some reason, one of the most obscure. Even a movie like *Cujo* made more money than this sensitive, complex supernatural thriller, which contains a Christopher Walken performance that deserves comparison with his work in *The Deer Hunter.*

Walken plays a man who is leading a fairly ordinary life until he is injured in an accident and goes into a coma for five years. When he emerges, his girlfriend (Brooke Adams) has married someone else, his friends have made new friends, his life is a series of loose ends. And there is something else. He has the psychic gift of precognition. He knows what will happen to people, and in a world like ours this can be a horrible gift.

The key to the movie's success is in the way it creates believable characters. It would simply be a gimmick movie if I didn't believe in this man and his dilemma. But I did, and so I found myself genuinely moved by his sense of loss, isolation, and sorrow.

7. *The Exorcist*   (R)

William Friedkin's 1974 thriller remains one of the standards by which three-dimensional horror movies are measured. That's because the movie is so firmly rooted in its sense of time and place that it even makes its sense of evil more real. Satan and his emissaries become a palpable threat in this film because they enter lives that are otherwise so relatively normal.

When people remember *The Exorcist,* they remember the moments when the movie freaked out: the rotating head, the ugly words emerging from the little girl, the green vomit. These special effects take less screen time than we imagine, however, and much of the movie is taken up with the speculations of ordinary people who are faced with the possibility that the next world does exist, and that it is a place with devils as well as angels. In inspiring its audiences to think personally about spiritual subjects, the movie probably was as effective as more respectable films like Bergman's *The Seventh Seal.* This is not only one of the scariest and most explicit films on this list, but also one of the most intelligent.

8. *Gremlins* (PG)

It's almost as if *Gremlins* divides in the middle. The first half is an anthology of warm, reassuring clichés: small towns, Christmas, pets for the kids, and that inevitable little shop on a side street in Chinatown where magic is a reality. It's in such a shop that the first gremlin is purchased—a small, cute, furry, and harmless little animal. But then we learn the three laws for the care of gremlins. Never let them get wet, never expose them to daylight, and never feed them after midnight.

Well, of course in one sense it's *always* after midnight, and before long the cute fur-balls have turned into the nastiest little beasts since that thing in *Alien* with all the teeth. And then the movie turns mean, too, with such notorious scenes as the gremlin in the microwave oven. This movie is like a practical joke on Norman Rockwell. It's also a satire on all the B movies about small towns invaded by strange creatures. And it's a lot of fun, especially during Phoebe Cates's infamous monologue about Santa Claus.

9. *Halloween* (R)

John Carpenter's 1978 film is, quite simply, one of the scariest movies ever made. Although it has been ripped off countless times in the last eight years (most obviously by its own inferior sequels), *Halloween* remains a landmark. Its most lasting legacy probably is its central character, the unstoppable psychotic killer who terrorizes a small town and who just keeps on coming, no matter what the terrified locals throw at him. (Jason, the creature in the hockey mask in the unspeakably bad *Friday the 13th* films, is a direct steal.)

The movie stars Jamie Lee Curtis, whose good performance is one reason the film is so effective. She plays a baby-sitter in a small Illinois town, a young woman who only gradually realizes that the tricks are for real this Halloween. As her friends are murdered, one after another, she struggles to keep her presence of mind, and the movie comes down to a contest between the killer's murderous hatred and her own cool intelligence.

Carpenter's direction is a major element in the suspense. *Halloween* depends, of course, on the basic visual strategy in which we can see behind the heroine, so we know more about her danger than she does. But it also uses a lot of other effective compositions, including a truly unsettling use of light and shadow in a scene where Curtis hides from the monster in a closet, and his shadow obscures the light coming in through the slats in the door.

10. *Nosferatu* (R)
There are two movies named *Nosferatu*, but the one I think you'll be able to find in your local video store is the modern, 1978 version by Werner Herzog. It stars Klaus Kinski as one of the most tortured vampires in movie history, and Bruno Ganz as the man who goes looking for him. What he finds is a man who really does seem to suffer from some strange disease of vampirism. Unlike most movie vampires, who usually seem to be having a fairly good time in between their opening screams and the final stake through their heart, Kinski seems weighted down by the heavy burden of immortality.

The original *Nosferatu* was made by Germany's F.W. Murnau in the 1920s, and unmistakably influenced the entire vampire genre, deciding how we think of vampires to this day. Herzog, another German, wanted to make a modern retelling of the original film, and one of the interesting things about this Kinski version is that it was literally shot in some of the same locations as the original. It is deep and brooding and obsessed—not lightweight vampire entertainment—but it is never uninteresting to look at.

11. *Poltergeist* (PG)
This is the movie *The Amityville Horror* dreamed of being. It begins in the same way, with an ordinary family living in an ordinary home, and it proceeds in the same way as horrible supernatural events begin to make their lives unbearable. The special effects in both movies look equally gimmicky (especially when the mother in *Poltergeist* grimly marches into the fourth dimension to rescue her child).

But *Poltergeist* has a certain insane conviction to go along with its stunts, and there are times when its world is very convincing, as when the swimming pool develops a mind of its own. The movie never does decide if a poltergeist really was responsible for the happenings inside the house, but by the time the movie's over, we're so stunned by the pyrotechnics that we hardly care. If it wasn't a poltergeist, it must have been something even worse.

12. *Swamp Thing* (R)
This is one of those movies that falls somewhere between a guilty pleasure and a holiday from sanity. It's the story of a scientist who is working on a secret formula, is attacked by thugs, is splashed with his formula, catches fire, jumps into the swamp, and turns into Swamp Thing when the formula interacts with the water to cover him in a green, slimy mat of vegetation. This is only the start of his troubles. After he is machine-gunned and his left arm is hacked off, he meets his former girlfriend, who does not recognize him. But when she asks if it hurts, he replies, "Only when I laugh."

The character of *Swamp Thing* itself is recycled out of old comic books, but the movie seems more influenced by *Bride of Frankenstein*, especially in a scene where Swamp Thing reveals that he has emotions. He sniffs a flower, he looks sadly at a photograph in a locket, he admires a young girl from afar but knows he cannot go closer without frightening her. This movie is a curious mixture of satire, comedy, exploitation, and genuine pathos.

13. *Young Frankenstein*   (PG)
Here is another film influenced by *The Bride of Frankenstein*. And not simply influenced, but sometimes directly recycled. When you watch the two films together, you get the weirdest feeling that you're recognizing something similar, and you're right. When Mel Brooks was preparing his film, he wanted to have a mad scientist's laboratory complete with all the inexplicable electrical equipment in the earlier film. And, to his amazement, he found that the original equipment was still in storage, in the garage of the man who designed it. So, the labs in both movies are built out of the same props.

The movie itself is one of the funniest comedies of modern times, with Gene Wilder's manic performance as Frankenstein's nephew, and Peter Boyle's oddly touching work as the monster. This movie and *The Producers* are Mel Brooks's best films, and in both films he not only made a comedy but also told a story that had a momentum of its own. My favorite moment is probably the scene involving the revolving bookcase, where Wilder gets stuck and gives *very careful* instructions.

Glossary of Movie Terms

The basic movie reference books are filled with definitions of terms like *close-up* and *auteur theory.* Nobody needs to know those words. What you need is the *Movie Home Companion* Glossary of Terms for the Cinema of the 1980s. What follows is an attempt to compile such a list—a practical, everyday guide to enhance your moviegoing pleasure and help you categorize what you find on the screen.

A.C.N.E. Acronym for Adolescent Character's Neurotic Envy Syndrome, which usually afflicts shrill teen-age blondes in movies about how the good girl wins the hero away from the syndrome sufferer. See *Secret Admirer.*

Ali MacGraw's Disease. Movie illness in which only symptom is that the sufferer grows more beautiful as death approaches.

Ark Movie. Dependable genre in which a mixed bag of characters are trapped on a colorful mode of transportation. Examples: *Airport* (airplane), *The Poseidon Adventure* (ocean liner), *Marooned* (space satellite), *The Cassandra Crossing* (train), *The Hindenberg* (dirigible), *The Taking of Pelham One Two Three* (subway train), and of course the best of them all, *Stagecoach.*

Beginning, The. Word used in the titles of sequels to movies in which everyone was killed at the end of the original movie, making an ordinary sequel impossible. Explains to knowledgeable filmgoers that the movie will concern, for example, what happened in the Amityville house *before* the Lutzes moved in. See also: *The First Chapter, The Early Days,* etc.

Balloon Rule. No good movie has ever contained a hot-air balloon.

Box Rule. Useful rule-of-thumb about movie advertisements which have a row of little boxes across the bottom, each one showing the face of a different international star and the name of a character (i.e., "Curt Jurgens as the Commandant"). The rule states: Automatically avoid such films. Example: *The Cassandra Crossing, Force 10 from Navarone,* most films made from Agatha Christie novels.

Brotman's Law. "If nothing has happened by the end of the first reel, nothing is going to happen." (Named for Chicago movie exhibitor Oscar Brotman.)

Crash Scene. Alternative to dialogue; substitute for Burt Reynolds's continuing growth as an actor.

Chop-Socky Movie. Any film involving a karate fight and including the dialogue, "Ha! Ha! Now you die!"

CLIDVIC (Climb from Despair to Victory). Formula for *Rocky* and all the *Rocky* rip-offs. Breaks plot into three parts: (1) Defeat and despair;

(2) Rigorous training, usually to would-be MTV videos; (3) Victory, preferably ending in freeze-frame of triumphant hero.

Dead Teen-ager Movie. Generic term for any movie primarily concerned with killing teen-agers, without regard for logic, plot, performance, humor, etc. Often imitated, never worse than in the *Friday the 13th* sequels.

Docudrama. TV term for extended-length program which stars a disease or social problem and co-stars performers willing to give interviews on how they experienced personal growth through their dramatic contact with same.

Fallacy of the Predictable Tree: The logical error committed every time the good guy is able to predict *exactly* what the bad guy is going to do. For example, in *First Blood*, law enforcement officials are searching the woods for John Rambo. One pauses under a tree. Rambo drops on him. Question: Out of all the trees in the forest, how did Rambo know the guy would pause under that very one?

First Law of Funny Names. No names are funny unless used by W.C. Fields or Groucho Marx. Funny names, in general, are a sign of desperation at the screenplay level. See "Dr. Hfuhruhurr" in *The Man With Two Brains*.

"Food Fight!" Dialogue which replaced "Westward ho!" as American movies ended the long frontier trek and began to look inward for sources of inspiration.

"Fruit Cart!" An expletive used by knowledgeable film buffs during any chase scene involving a foreign or ethnic locale, reflecting their certainty that a fruit cart will be overturned during the chase, and an angry peddler will run into the middle of the street to shake his fist at the departing Porsche.

"Hay Wagon!" Rural version of "Fruit cart!" (q.v.). At the beginning of chase scenes through colorful ethnic locales, knowledgeable film buffs anticipate the inevitable scene in which the speeding sports car will get stuck on a narrow country lane behind a wagon overloaded with hay.

Hollywood Car. Looks like a normal automobile, but backfires after being purchased from used car lot by movie heroine who is starting out again in life and is on her own this time.

Horny Teen-ager Movie. Any film primarily concerned with teen-age sexual hungers, usually male. Replaced, to a degree, by Dead Teen-ager Movies (q.v.), but always popular with middle-aged movie executives, who like to explain to their seventeen-year-old starlets why the logic of the dramatic situation and the teachings of Strasberg and Stanislavsky require them to remove their brassieres.

Idiot Plot. Any plot containing problems which would be solved instantly if all of the characters were not idiots. Originally defined by Damon Knight.

Impregnable Fortress Impregnated. Indispensable scene in all James Bond movies and many other action pictures, especially war films. The IFI sequence begins early in the picture, with long shots of a faraway fortress and Wagnerian music on the sound track. Eventually the hero gains entry to the fortress, which is inevitably manned by technological clones in designer uniforms. Sequence ends with destruction of fortress, as clones futilely attempt to save their marvelous machines. See *The Guns of Navarone*, etc.

Intelligence. In most movies, "all that separates us from the apes." In *Sheena, Queen of the Jungle*, what we have in common with them.

Kookalouris. Name for a large sheet of cardboard or plywood with holes in it, which is moved back and forth in front of a light to illuminate a character's face with moving light patterns. Popular in the 1930s; back in style again with the movies of Steven Spielberg, who uses a kookalouris with underlighting to show faces that seem to be illuminated by reflections from pots of gold, buckets of diamonds, pools of fire, pirate maps, and radioactive kidneys.

Mad Slasher Movies. Movies starring a mad-dog killer who runs amok, slashing all of the other characters. The killer is frequently masked (as in *Halloween* and *Friday the 13th*), not because a serious actor would be ashamed to be seen in the role, but because then no actor at all is required; the only skills necessary are the ability to wear a mask and wield a machete. For additional reading, see *Splatter Movies*, by John ("multilation is the message") McCarty.

Make My Day. First line of movie dialogue quoted at a presidential press conference since Jimmy Carter said, "I'll never lie to you."

Me-Push-Pull-You. Literal translation of the body language in many Hollywood action pictures, in which, as the hero and heroine flee from danger, the man takes the woman's hand and pulls her along meekly behind him. This convention is so strong that it is seen even in films where it makes no sense, such as *Sheena*, in which a jungle-woman who has ruled the savage beasts since infancy is pulled along by a TV anchorman fresh off the plane.

Seeing-Eye Man. Function performed by most men in Hollywood feature films. Involves a series of shots in which (1) the man sees something, (2) he points it out to the woman, (3) she then sees it too, often nodding in agreement, gratitude, amusement, or relief.

Self-Repeating Inevitable Climax (Self-RIC). In the age of the seven-minute attention span, one climax per movie will no longer do. Thus movies like the *Friday the 13th* series are constructed out of several seven-minute segments. At the end of each segment, another teen-ager is dead. When all the teen-agers are dead (or, if you arrived in the middle, when the same dead teen-ager turns up twice), the movie is over.

Semi-Obligatory Lyrical Interlude (Semi-OLI). Scene in which soft focus and slow motion are used while a would-be hit song is performed on the sound track and the lovers run through a pastoral setting. Common from the mid-1960s to the mid-1970s; replaced in 1980s with the Semi-Obligatory Music Video (q.v.).

Semi-Obligatory Music Video. Three-minute sequence within otherwise ordinary narrative structure, in which a song is played at top volume while movie characters experience spasms of hyperkinetic behavior and stick their faces into the camera lens. If a band is seen, the Semi-OMV is inevitably distinguished by the director's inability to find a fresh cinematic approach to the challenge of filming a slack-jawed drummer.

Sequel. A filmed deal.

Still Out There Somewhere. Obligatory phrase in Dead Teen-ager and Mad Slasher Movies, where it is triggered by the words, "The body was never found. They say he/she is . . ."

The Third Hand: Invisible appendage used by Rambo in *Rambo,* in the scene where he hides from the enemy by completely plastering himself inside a mud bank. Since it is impossible to cover yourself with mud without at least one hand free to do the job, Rambo must have had a third, invisible, hand. This explains a lot about the movie.

Thunder Index. Rule of thumb for estimating appeal of children's movies; the movie is working in inverse proportion to the amount of time the little bastards spend thundering up and down the aisles.

Tijuana. In modern Horny Teen-ager Movies, performs the same symbolic function as California did for the Beats and Paris did for the Lost Generation.

Wet. In Hollywood story conferences, suggested alternative to nude, as in: "If she won't take off her clothes, can we wet her down?" Suggested by Harry Cohn's remark about swimming star Esther Williams: "Dry, she ain't much. Wet, she's a star."

The We're Alive! Let's Kiss! Scene. Inevitable conclusion to any scene in which hero and heroine take cover from gunfire by diving side-by-side into a ditch, and find themselves in each other's arms, usually for the first time. See *High Road to China.*

Ukulele picks. What will happen to you if you are a bad movie.

Youngblood Rule. No movie with a hero named "Youngblood" has ever been any good. E.g. *Youngblood Hawke, Youngblood,* etc.

Index